D0087081

DATE DUE

12-09-08			

Demco

MONTEVERDE

DISCARDED

NORMANDALE COMMUNITY COLLEGE
LIBRARY
9700 FRANCE AVENUE SOUTH
BLOOMINGTON MN 55431-4399

MAY 25 2001

MONTEVERDE

Ecology and Conservation
of a Tropical Cloud Forest

Edited by
Nalini M. Nadkarni
Nathaniel T. Wheelwright

New York   Oxford
Oxford University Press
2000

Oxford University Press

Athens   Auckland   Bangkok   Bogotá   Buenos Aires   Calcutta
Cape Town   Chennai   Dar es Salaam   Delhi   Florence   Hong Kong   Istanbul
Karachi   Kuala Lumpur   Madrid   Melbourne   Mexico City   Mumbai
Nairobi   Paris   São Paulo   Singapore   Taipei   Tokyo   Toronto   Warsaw

and associated companies in
Berlin   Ibadan

Copyright © 2000 by Oxford University Press, Inc.

Published by Oxford University Press, Inc.
198 Madison Avenue, New York, New York 10016

Oxford is a registered trademark of Oxford University Press

All rights reserved. No part of this publication may be reproduced,
stored in a retrieval system, or transmitted, in any form or by any means,
electronic, mechanical, photocopying, recording, or otherwise,
without the prior permission of Oxford University Press.

Library of Congress Cataloging-in-Publication Data
Monteverde : ecology and conservation of a tropical cloud forest /
edited by Nalini M. Nadkarni and Nathaniel T. Wheelwright.
p.   cm.
Includes bibliographical references and index.
ISBN 0-19-509560-X; 0-19-513310-2 (pbk.)
1. Natural history—Costa Rica—Reserva del Boaque Nuboso de
Monteverde.   2. Cloud Forest ecology—Costa Rica—Reserva del Bosque
Nuboso de Monteverde.   3. Nature conservation—Costa Rica—Reserva
del Bosque Nuboso de Monteverde.   I. Nadkarni, Nalini M.
II. Wheelwright, Nathaniel T.
QH108.C6M65   1999
578.734'097286'6—dc21   98-26919

9 8 7 6 5 4 3 2 1

Printed in the United States of America
on acid-free paper

39290761

QH
108
.C6
M65
2000

This book is dedicated to John and Doris Campbell,
for their encouragement of research on the ecology and
conservation of Monteverde.

Foreword

Gary S. Hartshorn

While serving as visiting faculty during the Organization for Tropical Studies' Fundamentals of Ecology course in 1968, I had the good fortune to join a small group of naturalists on a day trip to Monteverde. As we departed from La Pacífica, little did I know how rough and wet that day would be. Under the leadership of Jerry James, a resident of Monteverde who was instrumental in discovering the stunning endemic Golden Toad, we drove to his parents' farm and then hiked the horse trail to the Continental Divide, where we explored the gnarled elfin woodland. It was my first, wonderful encounter with the Monteverde cloud forest. Though lowland rain forest became the focus of my own research, Monteverde was our family's favorite escape from San José for some twenty years.

Over the past three decades, Monteverde has become a world-famous destination for nature-loving tourists. The prescient conservation efforts of the Quaker pioneers to protect the upper watershed of the Río Guacimal, the impetus of Harriet and George Powell to protect Golden Toad habitat, and the early involvement of the Tropical Science Center, together with the collaboration of many individuals and organizations, have combined to form a world-class conservation area in the Tilarán Mountains. Less well known is that the Monteverde forests have been the focus of considerable research by field biologists.

Despite the lack of a research-oriented "field station," locally focused scientific library, equipped laboratories, and core funding for research, Monteverde has attracted numerous researchers, many of whom continue to conduct research over the long term. Without a central focus on research such as that of Costa Rica's La Selva Biological Station, Panama's Barro Colorado Island, or Cocha Cashu in the Peruvian Amazon, it is truly remarkable what the editors of and contributors to this book have accomplished with this publication. They have successfully pulled together in one volume virtually all that is known about the habitats and species of Monteverde.

In addition to the standard overviews of the physical setting, fauna and flora, and their ecological interactions, this book is exceptional in its substantive treatment of the role of humans—negative as well as positive—in the Monteverde ecosystems. I can think of no more central theme that characterizes Monteverde than the awareness and involvement of humans in the ecology and conservation of these exceptional forests in the clouds. From the conservative land ethic of the Quaker pioneers to the vibrant involvement of local communities (not just Monteverde) in sustaining their development activities, researchers have always been involved with the communities' interests, concerns, and priorities. The decentralized and individualized focus of researchers at Monteverde has broadened the conservation focus to a larger regional context and integrated local communities and individuals with researchers and their projects.

Those who love Monteverde and have helped to conserve the astoundingly rich and luxuriant cloud forests may think that this special place is unique. Although I regard the Monteverde forests as the most spectacular cloud forest anywhere in the tropics, I hope this book will help to make some aspects of it less unique. Some of the lessons learned in Monteverde can be applied elsewhere. The integration of researchers and local communities has contributed to mutual understanding of common goals while facilitating substantial progress toward conservation objectives. The documentation of migratory movements of flagship bird species such as the Resplendent Quetzal, for example, has broadened the focus of conservation efforts to include land use patterns at the landscape scale. This book not only defines academic questions of interest to other researchers and documents Monteverde ecosystems but also demonstrates that researchers make significant contributions to human communities by helping them understand the importance of ecology and natural history of the natural world.

I congratulate the editors and authors on an outstanding compendium of scientific information on Monteverde that merits its place on the bookshelf with other reviews of tropical research sites. I urge everyone who opens this book, whether researcher or nature aficionado, to visit this special forest in the clouds, to reflect on the importance of community to conservation, and to support the worldwide efforts to save tropical forests.

Foreword

Luis Diego Gómez P.

Canopium is a word from Medieval Latin meaning "a tent," a shelter under which things and people come together. By extension, *canopium*, canopy, has become the term of choice for the crowns of trees, under which blossoms, climbers, epiphytes, birds, and other winged and furried creatures find and make a habitat. I believe it was in this sense that the word was introduced into the nascent ecological lexicon by Eugene Warming at the beginning of the twentieth century.

This insignificant historical factoid suddenly became very meaningful to me when I examined this volume. Its covers are a canopy under which many valuable things come to fruition, the most important of which is the sense of fullness of knowledge harvested from one of the natural jewels of Costa Rica: Monteverde, a proverbial cloud forest, a crown in the Guanacaste-Tilarán Range, itself a canopium for a rich biodiversity and a rich tradition for conservation. In fact, Monteverde was the earliest structured project planned and aimed at the preservation of an ecosystem in this country of ours.

The process of habitat and ecosystem conservation has been a slow and difficult one in the neotropics, but Monteverde was blessed by its isolation, abetted by its early settlers who took only what was needed and respected the rest, a site that was instantly identified as unique in the exuberance of its nature, and beloved by all, scientists and nature gazers alike. The importance of Monteverde as a role model in the environmental movement of Costa Rica cannot be overstated. It is a living example of what could and should be done and what was done at the right time. Some may say that the original idea of the Monteverde Preserve has somewhat deviated over the years, and they may be somewhat right. But change is, precisely, the engine of nature and the very nature of ecological studies.

With the rich documentation that the editors of this volume regale us, the importance of Monteverde increases exponentially because it sets an example of what should be done for many other areas. These chapters reveal the intricate machinery that generates the pulse and forms the characteristics of the cloud forest environments. Even if it were a mere glimpse into the complexity of the cloud forest, this book would amply serve the purpose and compensate the extraordinary effort of the editors.

In a world besieged with the awesome dilemmas that an exploding population and the inherent (and peculiarly human) abuse of its natural resources pose, Monteverde, like other protected areas, takes an added luster of hope. And the emblematic color of hope is the same as that of the canopies: green. Meetings, symposia, and summits seldom result in timely actions. A new era begins for Monteverde and its communities with the production by Nadkarni and Wheelwright, the first a canopiologist extraordinaire observing both the individual organisms as well as the whole, and the second a distinguished population biologist placing the observations into the wider context of conservation and the ecosystem, and in the perspective of the region and the planet.

The stellar cast of scientists united under the canopy of the Monteverdean forest share with us current insights of that complex array of habitats and their creatures, together setting a benchmark from which to record the changes forthcoming, in their beloved fields and forest, in the surrounding landscape and, one hopes, in the attitude of humankind. This volume, however, comes with an implicit caveat for these authors and those they will without doubt inspire: it is just the cornerstone from which an edifice of deeper and better understanding of this magnificent site can grow.

A Manera de Introducción

Luis Diego Gómez P.

Canopium es un vocablo latino del medioevo que significa "tienda, techo," aquello bajo lo que se reúnen y protegen gentes y cosas. Por extensión, *canopium*, se ha convertido en el término para llamar la corona de los árboles, la copa bajo la cual se amparan las flores, las lianas y epífitas, las aves y toda clase de criaturas aladas o de pelo. Y creo que fue con ese mismo sentido que Eugene Warming introdujo *canopium* al incipiente léxico de la ecología descriptiva, al fin de la primera década de este siglo.

Esta minucia histórica, por si insignificante, adquiere hoy para mí una particular importancia al leer el contenido de este volumen, *Monteverde: Ecología y Conservación de un Bosque Nuboso Tropical*, porque sus tapas asemejan una abrigada copa, un *canopium* que encierra un sentido de plenitud, de maduración. De frutos recogidos de una de las más destacadas bellezas naturales de Costa Rica, el bosque nuboso de Monteverde, corona enjoyada de las Cordilleras de Tilarán-Guanacaste. Monteverde, cuna misma del movimiento conservacionista nacional, porque ha sido el primer ejemplo de un proyecto estructurado, planificado, y dirigido a la preservación de un ecosistema discreto.

Si bien la conservación del medio ha sido un proceso lento y penoso en la región neotropical, Monteverde también destaca por lo insólito de su éxito debido, tal vez, a su aislamiento, bendecido por la actitud respetuosa de sus primeros colonizadores que tomaron sólo lo necesario, porque su riqueza natural fue aprehendida desde el primer momento y amada por científicos y simples excursionistas por igual. El valor de la experiencia de Monteverde no se puede soslayar porque así como viven sus bosques y criaturas, es vivo ejemplo de lo que se puede y debe hacer en su debido tiempo. Algunos, tal vez, pueden pensar que de la idea primaria de la conservación del sitio al Monteverde de hoy, se ha divergido un tanto, y están en lo cierto. Pero el cambio es, precisamente, el motor de la naturaleza y es el cambio la misma naturaleza de los estudios ecológicos.

Con la riqueza que nos regalan los editores de esta obra, la importancia de Monteverde crece exponencialmente porque establece, nuevamente un ejemplo, de lo que se puede y debe hacer, a su debido tiempo, con tantas otras áreas rotegidas, comparativamente tan biodiversas y que son el objeto de escrutinio y estudio científico. Estos capítulos nos revelan la intrincada maquinaria que mantiene funcionando al bosque nuboso. Aun si fueran simples esbozos de la complejidad que nutren las neblinas, el propósito y extraordinario esfuerzo de los editores se ve recompensado.

En un mundo nuevo, sitiado por los dilemas que conlleva la explosión demográfica y el inherente (y peculiarmente humano) abuso de los recursos naturales, Monteverde adquiere un brillo especial: el de la esperanza. Y es que el color de la esperanza es el mismo de las copas de sus árboles. Las conferencias, simposios, y cumbres raras veces resultan en acciones tangibles y a tiempo. Monteverde y sus comunidades inician una era con la producción de Nadkarni y Wheelright, la primera, canopióloga extraordinaria que observa tanto el organismo individual como el sistema pleno; el segundo, un destacado biólogo de

la conservación que encauza esas visiones hacia una amplia perspectiva del contexto, del ecosistema, de la región, y del planeta.

El elenco de científicos, estelar, reunidos bajo este singular *canopium* de la foresta monteverdina comparte con nostros su actual y personal comprensión de los hábitats y sus criaturas, establecen un hito para referir, en el futuro, los cambios inexorables de sus disciplinas, de sus bien amados bosques, del paisaje y, hemos de esperar, de actitud de la humanidad hacia el ambiente.

Este volumen también incluye una advertencia para estos autores y aquellos a quienes inspiren: es tan solo la piedra angular con la cual cabe construir un edificio de conocimientos aún mayores sobre este magnífico lugar.

Contents

Contributors

Jon Ågren
Department of Ecological Botany
University of Umea
Umea, S-901 87
Sweden
jon@ekbot.umu.se

John Alcock
Department of Zoology
Arizona State University
Tempe, AZ 85287-1501 USA
j.alcock@asu.edu

Stephen D. Anderson
Pacific Northwest Research
  Foundation
720 Broadway
Seattle, WA 98122 USA
SAnder8643@aol.com

James S. Ashe
Snow Entomology Museum
University of Kansas
Lawrence, KS 66045-2106 USA
ashe@falcon.cc.ukans.edu

John T. Atwood
The Marie Selby Botanical Gardens
811 South Palm Avenue
Sarasota, FL 34236 USA
atwood@virtu.sar.usf.edu

Sergio Barrios
Monteverde
Santa Elena de Monte Verde
Puntarenas 5655, Costa Rica

Seth Bigelow
Institute for Ecosystem Studies
Box AB
Millbrook, NY 12545-0129 USA
bigelows@ecostudies.org

Robin D. Bjork
RARE
Santa Elena de Monte Verde
Puntarenas 5655, Costa Rica
Bjorkr@peak.org

John Boll
Rte. 6, Box 721
Boone, NC 28607 USA

Marlene Brenes
Golden Toad Laboratory for
  Conservation
Monteverde Cloud Forest
  Preserve and Tropical Science
  Center
Apartado 73
Santa Elena de Monte Verde
Puntarenas 5655, Costa Rica

Judith L. Bronstein
Department of Ecology
  and Evolutionary
  Biology
University of Arizona
Tucson, AZ 85721 USA
Judieb@u.arizona.edu

Brian V. Brown
Entomology Section
Natural History Museum of
  Los Angeles
Los Angeles, CA 90007 USA
brianb@mizar.usc.edu

Leslie J. Burlingame
Science, Technology and Society
  Program
Franklin and Marshall College
P.O. Box 3003
Lancaster, PA 17604 USA
L_Burlingame@acad.fandm.edu

William H. Busby
Kansas Biological Survey
2401 Constant Avenue
Lawrence, KS 66047-2906 USA
w-busby@ukans.edu

Stephen P. Bush
Department of Biology
P.O. Box 1954
Conway, SC 29526 USA
bush@coastal.edu

Paul R. Butler
The Evergreen State College
Lab II
Olympia, WA 98505 USA
butlerp@elwha.evergreen.edu

Francisco Chamberlain Gallegos
Apartado 7572-1000
San José, Costa Rica
Fchamber@expeditions.co.cr

Kenneth L. Clark
School of Forestry and Resource
  Conservation
134 Newins-Ziegler Hall
University of Florida
Gainesville, FL 32611 USA
KLCL@gnv.ifas.ufl.edu

Martha L. Crump
Department of Biological Sciences
Northern Arizona University
P.O. Box 5640
Flagstaff, AZ 86011-5640 USA
Peterf@nauvax.ucc.nau.edu

Debra DeRosier
Monteverde
Santa Elena de Monte Verde
Puntarenas 5655, Costa Rica

Gary W. Diller O'Dell
Apartado 20
Santa Elena de Monte Verde
Puntarenas 5655, Costa Rica

Eric Dinerstein
World Wildlife Fund
24th Street NW, Suite 500
Washington, DC 20037 USA
eric.dinerstein@wwfus.org

Vicente Espinoza
Monteverde
Santa Elena de Monte Verde
Puntarenas 5655, Costa Rica

R. Wills Flowers
Agricultural Research Programs
Florida A&M University
Tallahassee, FL 82308 USA
Rflowers@famu.edu

Michael P. L. Fogden
Monteverde
Santa Elena de Monte Verde
Puntarenas 5655, Costa Rica

Ian D. Gauld
Biodiversity Office
The Natural History Museum
London, SW7 5BD
United Kingdom
idg@nhm.ac.uk

Wendy Gibbons
648 E. Pearl Street
Lanark, IL 61046 USA

J. Philip Gibson
Department of Biology
Agnes Scott College
Decatur, GA 30030 USA
pgibson@ness.scottlan.edu

Douglas E. Gill
Department of Zoology
University of Maryland
College Park, MD 20742 USA
dg7@umail.umd.edu

Carolina Godoy
Instituto de Biodiversidad
Apartado 22-3100
Santa Domingo de Heredia
Heredia, Costa Rica
cgodoy@rutela.inbio.ac.cr

Lloyd Goldwasser
Marine Science Institute
University of California,
  Santa Barbara
Santa Barbara, CA 93106 USA
Goldwass@lifesci.lscf.ucsb.edu

S. Robert Gradstein
Institute of Plant Sciences
University of Göttingen
Untere Karspüle 2
37073 Göttingen, Germany
Sgradst@gwdg.de

Dana Griffin III
Bryophyte and Lichen Herbarium
Florida Museum of Natural History
University of Florida
Gainesville, FL 32611 USA
griffin@nervm.nerdc.ufl.edu

Katherine Griffith
Michael Fields Agricultural Institute
955 Ransom Street
Ripon, WI 54971
Kbgriffi@facstaff.wisc.edu

Martha Groom
Department of Zoology
North Carolina State University
Raleigh, NC 27695-7617 USA
mgroom@unity.ncsu.edu

Sam Grosby
3120 Weenonah Place
Minneapolis, MN 55417 USA
Moxie@wavefront.com

Carlos F. Guindon
37 Ernest Avenue, Apt. 9
Exeter, NH 03833 USA
cguindon@prodigy.net

Wilford ("Wolf") Guindon
Monteverde
Santa Elena de Monte Verde
Puntarenas 5655, Costa Rica

William A. Haber
Missouri Botanical Garden
P.O. Box 299
St. Louis, MO 63166-D299 USA
whaber@sol.racsa.co.cr

Paul Hanson
Escuela de Biología
Universidad de Costa Rica
San Pedro, Costa Rica
cgodoy@rutela.inbio.ac.cr

Celia A. Harvey
Agroforesteria Centro Agronómica
Tropical de Investigación y Enseñaza
Aptdo. 7170, Turrialba
Costa Rica
charvey@computo.catie.ac.cr

David Hollis
Entomology
The Natural History Museum
London, SW7 5BD
United Kingdom
dh@nhm.ac.uk

Frank T. Hovore
14734 Sundance Place
Santa Clara, CA 91351-1542
 USA
fthovore@smartlink.net

Stephan W. Ingram
140 Willow Road
Swall Meadows
Bishop, CA 93514 USA
ingram@telis.org

David P. Janos
Department of Biology
University of Miami
Coral Gables, FL 33124 USA
djanos@umiami.ir.miami.edu

Frank Joyce
Monteverde
Apartado 32
Santa Elena de Monte Verde
Puntarenas 5655, Costa Rica
fjoyce@sol.racsa.co.cr

Sharon Kinsman
Department of Biology
Bates College
Lewiston, ME 04240 USA
skinsman@abacus.bates.edu

Lawrence R. Kirkendall
Associate Professor of Zoology
University Bergen Zoological
 Institute
Allegaten 41, N-5007
Norway
lawrence.kirkendall@zoo.uib.no

Suzanne Koptur
Department of Biological Sciences
Florida International University
Miami, FL 33199 USA
kopturs@servax.fiu.edu

Peter Kukle
54 Ontario Street
Dumont, NJ 67628 USA

Catherine A. Langtimm
The Florida Caribbean Science
 Center
Biological Research Division, U.S.
 Geological Survey
7920 NW 71st Street
Gainesville, FL 32653 USA
Cathy_langtimm@usgs.gov

Richard K. LaVal
Monteverde
Apartado 24
Santa Elena de Monte Verde
Puntarenas 5655, Costa Rica
Rlaval@sol.racsa.co.cr

Bob Law
Monteverde
Santa Elena de Monte Verde
Puntarenas 5655, Costa Rica

Marcy F. Lawton
Department of Biological Sciences
University of Alabama
Huntsville, AL 35899 USA
mlawton@ro.com

Robert O. Lawton
Department of Biological Sciences
University of Alabama
Huntsville, AL 35899 USA
lawton@email.uah.edu

Robert W. Lichtwardt
Department of Ecology and
 Evolutionary Biology
University of Kansas
Lawrence, KS 66045-2106 USA
licht@eagle.cc.ukans.edu

Jorge Arturo Lobo
Escuela de Biología
Universidad de Costa Rica
San Pedro
Costa Rica

John T. Longino
The Evergreen State College
Lab I
Olympia, WA 98505 USA
longinoj@elwha.evergreen.edu

Cecile Lumer
P.O. Box 980
Bisbee, AZ 85603 USA
cecile@theriver.com

Harry E. Luther
The Marie Selby Botanical Gardens
811 South Palm Avenue
Sarasota, FL 34236 USA

Blase Maffia
Department of Biology
University of Miami
Coral Gables, FL 33124 USA
Bmaffia882@aol.com

Alan R. Masters
Monteverde
Apartado 26-5655
Santa Elena de Monte Verde
Puntarenas 5655, Costa Rica
amasters@sol.racsa.co.cr

Karen Masters
Monteverde
Apartado 26
Santa Elena de Monte Verde
Puntarenas 5655, Costa Rica
amasters@sol.racsa.co.cr

Teri J. Matelson
75A High Street
San Francisco, CA 94114 USA
tmatelson@aol.com

David B. McDonald
Department of Zoology
University of Wyoming
Laramie, WY USA
dbmcd@uwyo.edu

Juan José Monge
Productores de Monteverde
Apartado 10165
San José 1000, Costa Rica

María I. Morales
Escuela de Biología
Cuidad Universitaria Rodrigo Facio
San José, Costa Rica

K. Greg Murray
Department of Biology
Hope College
Holland, MI 49422-9000 USA
gmurray@hope.edu

Nalini M. Nadkarni
The Evergreen State College
Lab II
Olympia, WA 98505 USA
nadkarnn@elwha.evergreen.edu

Molly Nepokroeff
Laboratory of Molecular Systematics
National Museum of Natural History
MSC, MRC-534
Smithsonian Institution
Washington, DC 20560 USA
Mnepokro@students.wisc.edu

Karen Nielson
Monteverde
Santa Elena de Monte Verde
Puntarenas 5655, Costa Rica

Sean O'Donnell
Department of Psychology
University of Washington
Seattle, WA 98195 USA
sodonnel@u.washington.edu

Gard Otis
Department of Environmental
  Biology
University of Guelph
Guelph, ON N1G 2W1
Canada
Gotis@evbhort.uoguelph.ca

Daniel C. Peck
International Center for Tropical
  Agriculture
AA 6713
Cali, Colombia
dpeck@calima.ciat.cgiar.org

J. Alan Pounds
Golden Toad Laboratory for
  Conservation
Monteverde Cloud Forest Reserve
  and Tropical Science Center
Apartado 5655, Caja 73
Santa Elena de Monteverde
Puntarenas, Costa Rica
goldtoad@sol.racsa.co.cr

George V. N. Powell
Monteverde
Apartado 56
Santa Elena de Monte Verde
Puntarenas 5655, Costa Rica
gpowell@sol.racsa.co.cr

Francis E. Putz
Department of Botany
University of Florida
Gainesville, FL 32611 USA
fep@mailhost.botany.ufl.edu

Alonso Ramírez
Institute of Ecology
University of Georgia
Athens, GA 30602 USA
aramirez@uga.cc.uga.edu

Brett C. Ratcliffe
University of Nebraska State
  Museum
University of Nebraska
P.O. Box 880514
W436 Nebraska Hall
Lincoln, NE 68588-0514 USA
BRATCLIFF@unl.edu

Jacques Rifkind
Entomology Section
Natural History Museum of
  Los Angeles
900 Exposition Boulevard
Los Angeles, CA 90007 USA
clerid@aol.com

Cecilia M. Riley
Director, Gulf Coast Bird
  Observatory
9800 Richmond Avenue, Suite 150
Houston, TX 77042 USA
Criley@nol.net

Sarah Sargent
Department of Biology
Allegheny College
Meadville, PA 16335 USA
antidaphne@aol.com

Jay Savage
Department of Biology, University
  of Miami
P.O. Box 249118
Coral Gables, FL 33124-0421 USA
Savy@miami.edu

Doug Schaefer
Institute for Tropical Ecosystem
  Studies
Box 363682
San Juan, Puerto Rico 00936 USA
Dschaete@upracd.upr.clu.edu

Douglas W. Schemske
Department of Botany KB-15
University of Washington
Seattle, WA 98195 USA
Schemske@botany.washington.edu

Nathaniel Scrimshaw
Monteverde Institute
Apartado 69-5655
Santa Elena de Monte Verde
Puntarenas, Costa Rica
natscrim@sol.racsa.co.cr.

William N. Setzer
Department of Chemistry
University of Alabama
Huntsville, AL 35899 USA
wsetzer@matsci.uah.edu

Jennifer Shopland
Mexico Country Program
The Nature Conservancy
Tucson, AZ 85716 USA

Kimberly G. Smith
Department of Biological Sciences
University of Arkansas
Fayetteville, AR 72701 USA
kgsmith@comp.uark.edu

Monika Springer
Departmento de Biología
Universidad de Costa Rica
San Pedro, Costa Rica

Robert Stevenson
Department of Biology
University of Massachusetts
Boston, MA 02125 USA
rstevenson@umbsky.cc.umb.edu

Joseph Stuckey
Apartado 47
Santa Elena de Monte Verde
Puntarenas 5655, Costa Rica
jstuckey@sol.racsa.co.cr

Kenneth J. Sytsma
Department of Botany
University of Wisconsin
Madison, WI 53706 USA
kjsytsma@facstaff.wisc.edu

Harry M. Tiebout III
Department of Biology
West Chester University
West Chester, PA 19383 USA
Htiebout@wcupa.edu

Robert M. Timm
Natural History Museum—
  Dyche Hall
University of Kansas
Lawrence, KS 66045-2454 USA
btimm@falcon.cc.ukans.edu

Jonathan H. Titus
Oregon Natural Heritage Program
821 SE 14th Avenue
Portland, OR 97214 USA
Jtitus@tnc.org

Jill M. Trainer
Department of Biology
University of Northern Iowa
Cedar Falls, IA 50613 USA
jill.trainer@uni.edu

Robert Unnasch
The Nature Conservancy
1815 North Lynn Street
Arlington, VA 22209 USA
Bunnasch@tnc.org

Lisa K. Valburg
Department of Biology
Pennsylvania State University
Dunmore, PA 18512-1699 USA
LKVI@PSU.EDU

Carlos Valderrama A.
Tulane University
1201 Lake Avenue
New Orleans, LA 70005 USA
Cocampo@mailhost.tcs.tulane.edu

Katy VanDusen Joyce
Apartado 32
Santa Elena de Monte Verde
Puntarenas 5655, Costa Rica
vandusen@sol.racsa.co.cr

Eugenio Vargas
Monteverde Institute
Apartado 69
Santa Elena de Monte Verde
Puntarenas 5655, Costa Rica
Mvipac@sol.racsa.co.cr

Guillermo Vargas
Coupe Santa Elena R.L.
Apartado 10165-1000
San José, Costa Rica
gvargas@sol.racsa.co.cr

José Luis Vargas
Productores de Monteverde
Apartado 10165-1000
San José, Costa Rica

Martha E. Weiss
Department of Botany
University of Maryland USA
College Park, MD 20742

Dan Wenny
Illinois Natural History
   Survey
Savanna Field Station
P.O. Box 241
Savanna, IL 61074 USA
danwenny@internetni.com

Nathaniel T. Wheelwright
Department of Biology
Bowdoin College
Brunswick, ME 04011 USA
bss@polar.bowdoin.edu

Dean A. Williams
Department of Biological
   Sciences
Purdue University
West Lafayette, IN 47907 USA
Dwilliams@bilbo.bio.purdue.edu

Michele Williamson
Department of Entomology
Royal Ontario Museum
100 Queens Park
Toronto, ON M55 2C6
Canada

Kathy Winnett-Murray
Department of Biology
Hope College
Holland, MI 49423-9000 USA
Winnetmurray@hope.edu

Jim Wolfe
Apartado 40
Santa Elena de Monte Verde
Puntarenas 5655, Costa Rica
wolfej@sol.racsa.co.cr

Stephen L. Wood
290 MLBM
P.O. Box 20200
Provo, UT 84602-0200 USA

Bruce E. Young
Latin America and Caribbean
   Region
The Nature Conservancy
4245 N. Fairfax Drive
Arlington, Virginia 22203 USA
Byoung@tnc.org

Manuel A. Zumbado
Instituto Nacional
   de Biodiversidad
Apartado 22-3100
Santo Domingo de Heredia
Heredia, Costa Rica
mzumbado@rutela.inbio.ac.cr

Monteverde

1

Introduction

Nalini M. Nadkarni
Nathaniel T. Wheelwright

Monteverde has been variously described as a virgin tropical cloud forest, a Quaker dairy community, an artists' commune, a haven for those seeking spirituality, a model for tropical rain forest conservation, and a "forest in the clouds" where the sound of the bellbird's call and images of mist-enshrouded trees long linger in visitors' minds. The environment of Monteverde is typical of many tropical montane cloud forest regions, but Monteverde provides a unique setting because of its biogeographic, human, and conservation history.

This book was created to fulfill three objectives: to compile what we know about Monteverde's natural history, ecology, and conservation; to identify areas where information is lacking; and to facilitate communication among those who carry out research, education, and conservation. Contributors include a wide range of people with expertise from many different fields, levels of training, and approaches to understanding the natural world, and they have communicated in many modes, ranging from the objective style of scientific prose, statistics, and tables to the more reflective descriptions of personal experiences. In addition to academic scientists, we have invited the voices of farmers, natural history guides, anthropologists, educators, and homemakers, all of whom have important insights into Monteverde's biology and conservation.

1.1. Historical Overview

In 1951, a band of fewer than fifty North American Quakers bought land and settled in Monteverde (Fig. 1.1; see Guindon, "Monteverde Beginnings," pp. 10–11). (Note that, throughout, when an author refers to another essay in this volume, the essay is cited by author name and a short form of the essay title.) In 1977, visitors to the area were still relatively uncommon. Now, only two decades later, nearly 50,000 visitors walk the trails of Monteverde each year to catch sight of a quetzal or absorb the peaceful outlook of the community. Growth of ecotourism has been phenomenal, eclipsing the small single-family farm as the region's economic mainstay (Fig. 1.2). New agricultural methods, a changing local, regional, and global economy, and the sheer number of visitors have changed Monteverde and surrounding communities.

Figure 1.1. *(top)* Group photograph of the residents of Monteverde at the last Quaker Meeting in 1957 in the old squatter house that they made into a meeting house and school. The expanded dairy plant now covers this site. Photograph by John Campbell. **Figure 1.2.** *(bottom)* Wilford "Wolf" Guindon, one of the original Quaker settlers, describes the biota he has worked to protect as a guard for the Monteverde Cloud Forest Preserve. He practiced dairy farming when the group first arrived in the early 1950s, but later became an ardent advocate and spokesperson for conservation of the preserve. Photograph by Gregory Dimijian.

In the early 1960s, biologists first became aware of Monteverde. Welcomed by the small farming community and working largely independently or in small groups, they overcame the lack of scientific facilities and infrastructure to document the diverse tropical biota. A surprising number of these biologists have taken up residence in Monteverde, weaving their work into the rich tapestry of the human community of Monteverde. Although much of the research from Monteverde has been published as primary scientific literature, it has never before been synthesized. Only one symposium (sponsored by the Association for Tropical Biology, held in 1984) has brought together Monteverde biologists as a group.

A major reason for producing this book is that research from Monteverde has not previously been integrated into forms that can be readily channeled into education and conservation. For two decades, Monteverde has been a mecca for student groups to observe and study tropical montane landscapes (Fig. 1.3). Foremost among these have been the graduate courses offered by the Organization for Tropical Studies (OTS). Many preliminary studies led to dissertation theses and long-term research. Numerous undergraduate groups from North American colleges and universities have also conducted research in Monteverde. Little background material has been available for their research projects, and the scattered

nature of the available information has hampered useful input to the scientific record from these student groups (see Nadkarni, "Scope of Past Work," pp. 11–13).

The mixture of biologists, educators, and ecotourists in Monteverde has produced an opportunity for conservation. Monteverde has been viewed as a model for conservation at the grassroots level. Funds have come from government agencies, foundations, nongovernmental organizations, and individuals to support land acquisition, native tree nurseries, and environmental education. Strong links between conservation and biology are needed to maintain high-quality conservation practices. Compiling and synthesizing existing information is an important first step in forging these connections.

1.2. The Boundaries

The term "monteverde" needs explicit definition because people use it to refer to different areas. Monte Verde, a legal political entity, is District 10 of the County (Canton) of Puntarenas in the Province of Puntarenas. In this book, unless otherwise stated, we use Monteverde to refer to the human community from the creek, Quebrada Maquina, to the Monteverde Cloud Forest Preserve (MCFP). The Monteverde zone,

Figure 1.3. Avian ecologist Carlos Martínez del Río displays a mist-netted Long-tailed Manakin for students on an Organization for Tropical Studies course. Photograph by Nathaniel Wheelwright.

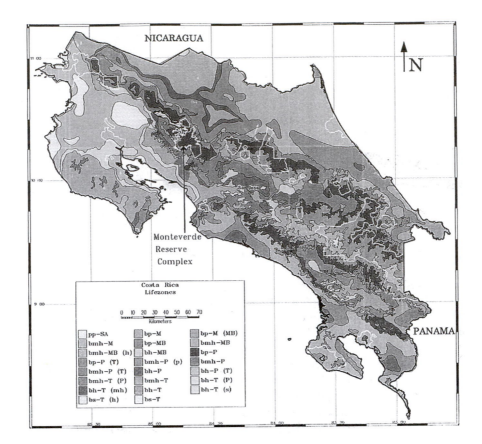

Figure 1.4

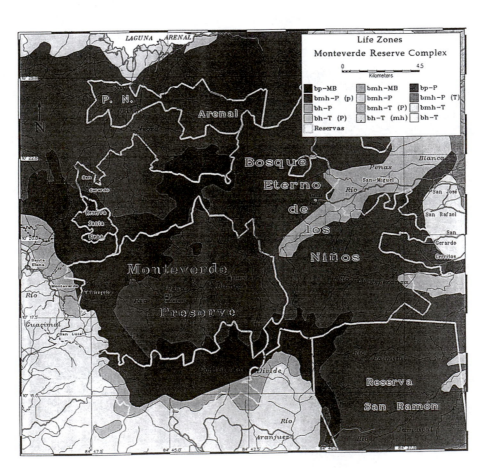

Figure 1.5

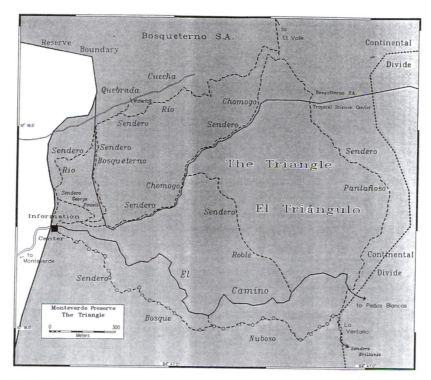

Figure 1.6

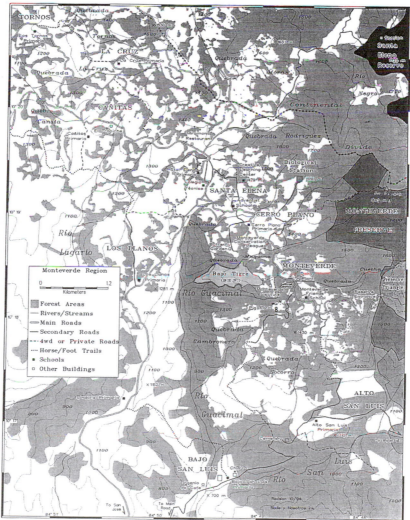

Figure 1.7

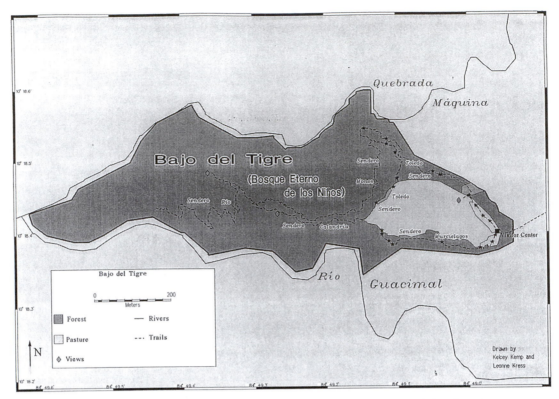

Figures 1.4–1.8 (preceding pages). Maps of the Monteverde area at various spatial scales. Maps are based on figures created by Linda Mather and modified by David King (Monteverde Institute and Monteverde Conservation League). Life zone terminology follows Holdridge (1967).

Holdridge Life Zones Key

Wetness indicators

bp	bosque pluvial	(rain forest)
bh	bosque húmedo	(moist forest)
bmh	bosque muy húmedo	(wet forest)
bs	bosque seco	(dry forest)
h	húmedo	
mh	muy húmedo	
p	pluvial	
s	seco	
pp	páramo pluvial	(rain páramo)

Temperature-altitude indicators

M	montano	(montane)
MB	montano bajo	(lower montane)
P	premontano	(premontane)
SA	sub-alpino	(subalpine)
T	tropical	(basal)

Monteverde region, and Monteverde area (which includes portions of the canton) refer to the larger region including the community, MCFP, the Children's Rainforest, and areas on both sides of the Continental Divide down to about 700 m elevation (Figs. 1.4–1.8).

Much of Monteverde lies within the vegetation type that is loosely termed a tropical montane cloud forest (TMCF), a forest type that has received increas-ing attention from the biological, forestry, and conservation communities (LaBastille and Pool 1978, UNESCO 1981, Stadtmüller 1987, Lugo and Lowe 1995). As defined by Hamilton et al. (1993), TMCF is a relatively narrow altitudinal zone with frequent cloud cover during much of the year. Solar radiation and evapotranspiration are reduced, and precipitation is enhanced by canopy interception of cloud water. Compared to trees in lower altitude tropical moist forests, trees in TMCF tend to be dense and relatively short with gnarled trunks, compact crowns, and small, thick leaves. Epiphytes are common. Soils are frequently wet and highly organic. Biodiversity and endemism are often very high.

The tropical montane cloud forest is one of the world's most threatened ecosystems. In many regions, their rate of loss exceeds that of lowland tropical rain forests that have received far more attention. Annual forest loss in tropical mountains has recently been estimated as 1.1%, versus 0.8% for all tropical forests (Doumenge et al. 1993). The hydrological role of TMCF in water capture of wind-driven mist and fog gives these ecosystems a value in terms of water resources that is distinct from other forests or types of land use (Stadtmüller 1987). Cloud forests protect watersheds by reducing runoff and erosion (Daugherty 1973). Major threats to TMCF include deforestation due to cattle grazing and agriculture, wood harvesting, and exploitation of nonwood forest products. Other potential impacts are hunting, uncontrolled recreation, introduction of alien species, and global climate change and air quality deterioration (Hamilton et al. 1993, Lugo and Lowe 1995). Potential responses to these threats are discussed in this volume (see Chaps. 10–12).

In contrast to established field stations in Costa Rica and elsewhere in the tropics, Monteverde lacks a formal research center. Compared to two neotropical lowland biological stations, La Selva, Costa Rica, and Barro Colorado Island, Panama, Monteverde has offered little in the way of formal laboratory space, library, or equipment. At various times, Monteverde biologists have organized informal seminar series, made resources available to the greater community (e.g., botanist W. A. Haber's herbarium and broad knowledge of plants), loaned equipment, given public lectures, and offered workshops. This self-sufficiency of individual biologists, then, has at least partially compensated for the lack of a central research institution.

Biologists in turn have received a great deal of community support in the form of access to private land, friendship with local residents, outlets for family life, schools, and so forth. At the same time, doing biological research in a community rather than at a field station has required Monteverde biologists to be sensitive to local values. Certain types of research have been discouraged. For example, destructive sampling of animals and vegetation is usually forbidden in the Monteverde Cloud Forest Preserve and frowned upon on private land.

We have organized this book into twelve chapters. At the outset of the project, we invited specialists on a particular taxon or level of community organization in Monteverde to organize a chapter on that subject. Chapter editors were asked to place their work in a conservation context. The book begins with background material on the physical environment and geological history of the region. We then cover the major plant and animal groups, followed by discussions of plant-animal interactions and ecosystem ecology. This is followed by treatments of the human community and its environment, and we conclude with a chapter on conservation biology and areas for future research. Following each chapter are essays written by investigators, which are designed to give a more in-depth look at specific subjects. Species lists and other detailed materials are presented as appendices at the end of the book.

The body of research gathered in this book is a testimony to the good will and energy of biologists, educators, conservationists, farmers, and other residents who, despite the lack of research facilities, libraries, or laboratories at Monteverde, have collectively produced a large body of knowledge on a wide range of subjects concerning the extraordinary landscape of Monteverde and its inhabitants. With additional efforts to ameliorate research coordination and research facilities and more direct circulation of research results to the education, ecotourism, and conservation sectors, the potential for understanding and soundly managing Monteverde's complex ecosystems and human interactions will be even greater.

Acknowledgments   Our greatest thanks and affection go to all the members of the Monteverde community, who opened their homes, schools, and hearts to us and our families, shared information about the history and biology of Monteverde, and encouraged our research on their property, particularly the Campbells, Guindons, Hoges, Rockwells, Stuckeys, and Trostles. More than 140 biologists, artists, photographers, and Monteverde residents made this book possible by writing chapters and short accounts or contributing photographs and figures; we thank them for their professional work. For logistical and other support, we acknowledge the staff of the Tropical Science Center, Monteverde Cloud Forest Preserve, Monteverde Conservation League, Monteverde Institute, Organization for Tropical Studies, The Evergreen State College, and Bowdoin College. The Friends of Monteverde kindly provided a grant for producing color plates for the book. For assistance and ideas, we thank Ana Beatriz Azofeifa (OTS library), Omar Coto, Heladio Cruz, Lindi Guindon, Tomás Guindon, Sue Johansen, David King and Linda Mather (for maps), Bob Law, Ree Scheck, Susan Schick, and Nat Scrimshaw. Students at The Evergreen State College who helped with the book include Alex Cobb, Vizma Schulmeisters, Matt Denton,

Julia Moberg, Andrew Stempel, Danni Kline, Maya Spier, Joselynn Plank, and Josie Heyward. Allison Woodruff contributed greatly in the final stages of manuscript preparation with patience and good humor. Chapters benefited from careful reviews by Bil Alverson, Phil DeVries, Maureen Donnelly, John Eisenberg, Mike Grayum, Craig Guyer, Doug Levey, Bette Loiselle, Robert Marquis, Alan Masters, Gordon Orians, Kent Redford, Dave Roubik, Philip Sollins, F. Gary Stiles, and Harry Tiebout III. Our project was partially supported by a Fulbright Fellowship (to N.T.W.), a grant from the National Science Foundation (to N.M.N.; DEB 96-15341 and Faculty Development funds from The Evergreen State College. Dan Janzen, his keystone book *Costa Rican Natural History* (1983), and his dedication to conservation were a true inspiration. We thank Kirk Jensen and Lisa Stallings, our editors at Oxford University Press. Special thanks and abrazos to Jack Longino and Genie Wheelwright.

MONTEVERDE BEGINNINGS
Wilford "Wolf" Guindon

The founding and development of the Monteverde community were influenced by a number of factors: the diversity of ages of the settlers, their financial and physical abilities, and the importance of day-to-day interactions and interdependence on one another plus Costa Rican friends and neighbors. Being in a frontier setting a long way from a sustaining market and source of supplies, and adjusting to a different culture, language, climate, soils, and season were the challenges to be faced. Each person stretched his or her creative abilities to contribute and fill a niche in the community. The number of "acquired" skills by members was impressive, and whatever the project or emergency, someone would come forward with a solution.

The "research project" that the Green Mountain pioneers set out to develop was a community that sought the good of every one of its members and experimented in ways of living that would naturally lead to peace in the world. To reach solutions through group decision-making, allowing time for all views to be presented and considered, was challenging. The basic belief in the visible and invisible power of creation, and the interrelatedness of all life, and the desire to live simply and close to nature were among the common values that strengthened the community. There was always a concern for the wise use of our natural resources and for the protection of our watershed. Each family practiced sensitive management in the development of its individual homestead. The most concerned people (plus the heavy winds and torrential rains) frequently reminded those less aware of the dangers of destroying our chosen habitat. Saving forested areas, allowing natural windbreaks to regenerate, and planting trees in pastured areas were active demonstrations of this concern.

Among community members with a special interest in biology and natural history were Mary and Walter James. Mary was a graduate of Earlham College with a B.S. in biology. She taught biology classes in her home; many of the class projects were inventive, making use of the materials at hand. One example was the construction of a camera stand to take a photograph of a "nigua" (flea larva, *Pulex irritans*) viewed under a microscope. The enlarged specimen was especially impressive, as many Monteverdeans were host to this pest. Walter James had an interest in natural history and horticulture. His interests led to collecting fern samples for Luis Diego Gómez of the Costa Rica National Museum and later for Dr. Clemens at the University of Pennsylvania. Through his work, three new species were identified.

Charles Palmer, a retired biology professor who visited Monteverde several times, was the first biologist to descend into Peñas Blancas and collect plants. On the excursion, he and I spent three days and reached the last squatter claim (now known as Dos Aces). He was the biologist who taught me the lesson that before sleeping on board planks (as we did for two nights), a person "should always try both sides to determine which side is the softest"—advice that I have often had the opportunity to test. Charles also involved school children in raising fern prothallia for wholesale to labs in the United States, a project that Mary James continued in her biology class. This raised funds for student biology field trips. Carl Rittenmeir, a professor from the University of Kansas, did a research project on army ants. With the help of a chain saw, he was able to capture the entire colony, complete with queen. From Carl, I learned the fascinating ecology of the army ants that periodically invaded our homes to feast on cockroaches, scorpions, and any insect that could not fly away.

In the early 1960s, tropical biologists from the Organization for Tropical Studies arrived. The Golden Toad (*Bufo pereglenes*) was identified not only as a new species but also as endemic to a specific part of the Tilarán mountain range. With this, Monteverde became known to the scientific world. By then, the community boasted a *pensión* (inn), general store, dairy plant, school, community building, and all-weather access road.

Communities of people evolve. Like the flora and fauna that surround us, they must adjust and adapt to the multiple changes in their environment or become extinct. Our desires are for only the best and positive qualities to dominate. Yet negative factors exist and challenge the community in our search for peace and sensitive stewardship of our natural resources. Strolling the trails through the various life zones and tropical tangles, I often reflect on the hundreds of Costa Ricans and the many thousands of internationals who have contributed their *granos de arena* (grains of sand) to create this protected area—a gem, small, but of great value. I feel eternally grateful to each person for his or her part. It has been a privilege to have contributed to the many facets of the preserve and to personally know the impressive list of people contributing their knowledge.

SCOPE OF PAST WORK
Nalini M. Nadkarni

To understand the development and scope of research in Monteverde, I counted the number of journal articles, theses, and dissertations produced by researchers working there (Fig. 1.9). Formal research output began in the late 1960s, steeply increased in the early 1980s, peaked in the early 1990s, and declined sharply thereafter. One explanation for this decline is the recently reduced activity of the Organization for Tropical Studies (OTS), which administers graduate-level courses in tropical ecology and has traditionally taken students to a number of field stations in Costa Rica during their eight-week courses. Until 1989, OTS courses regularly included several weeks in Monteverde, where students carried out group field projects and independent research, many of which led to theses, dissertations, and long-term research. In the early 1990s, however, OTS courses no longer included a visit to Monteverde because of the perception that the MCFP and community had become more oriented toward ecotourism and undergraduate education than research. There was no designated area for student research within the MCFP, and access to private land became increasingly difficult. Although many undergraduate courses have been conducted in Monteverde since the mid-1980s, they have not directly led to the production of research publications.

I also examined the types of studies reported in the scientific record, following McDade et al. (1994). Studies in Monteverde have been dominated by those concerned with general ecology, followed by interspecific ecology, community ecology, ecosystem studies, and systematic work; very few publications have dealt with applied ecology (Table 1.1). Research has concentrated on animals (mainly birds), followed by plants and plant-animal interactions. A small number of studies have reported information on ecosystem ecology, and only about 5% have dealt with human interactions. Fields that are conspicuously absent include aquatic biology, microbial ecology, soils, atmosphere/vegetation interactions, invertebrates (except butterflies, beetles, and social insects), wildlife management, agroecology, large mammals, plant physiology, mycology, and hydrology.

A comparison of the distribution of research with that of the well-established lowland La Selva Biological Station (McDade et al. 1994) shows that propor-

Table 1.1. Distribution of research publications by category based on research in Monteverde (1966–95) and La Selva Biological Station (1951–90).

Category	% of Total	
	Monteverde	La Selva
General ecology	26	29
Community ecology	26	14
Systematic biology	16	26
Interspecific ecology	13	15
Ecosystems ecology	8	6
Conservation and applied ecology	6	7
Physiological ecology	5	3

Total number of publications for Monteverde is 253 and for La Selva is 944. Categories follow McDade et al. (1994).

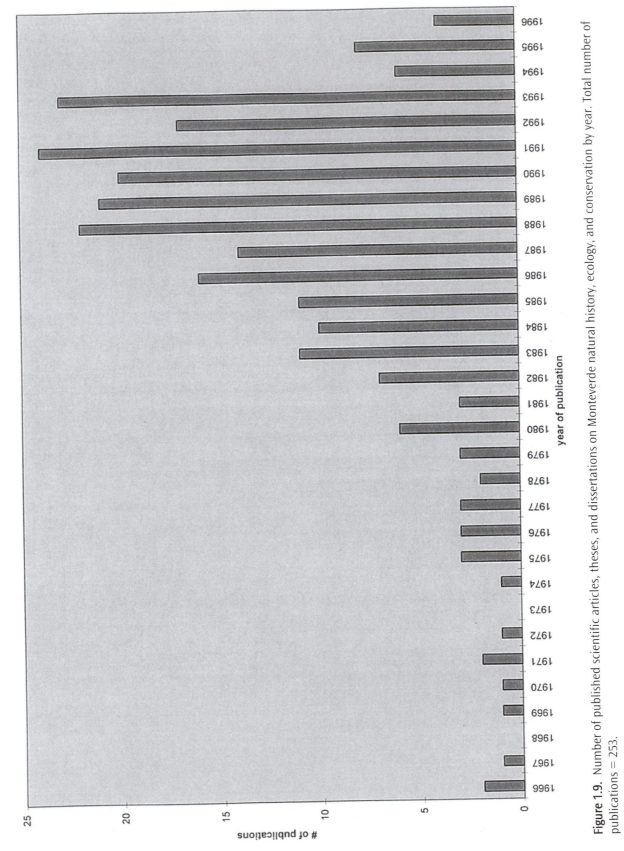

Figure 1.9. Number of published scientific articles, theses, and dissertations on Monteverde natural history, ecology, and conservation by year. Total number of publications = 253.

tionally more studies on community ecology and proportionally fewer systematic studies were carried out in Monteverde than in La Selva (Table 1.1). To date, the number of publications from Monteverde (1966–95) is 253, versus 944 from La Selva (1951–90; McDade et al. 1994). Several patterns emerge from a review of Monteverde publications. Monteverde's biotic and cultural diversity, aesthetic beauty, benign climate, and welcoming human community have attracted dedicated biologists who are strongly motivated to conserve natural resources in the area. Researchers, educators, residents, and conservationists have an extraordinary pool of information at hand, but it is distributed patchily. Certain areas are disproportionately well studied because of the efforts of a single senior scientist (e.g., hummingbird pollination systems), while many areas have never been formally studied (e.g., soil classification). Contribution and access to the existing pool of information are difficult because of the current lack of a central institution that could supply sustained coordination of research, education, and conservation projects, a library or bibliographic system, curation of organismal collections, or a facility for laboratory research or equipment storage in Monteverde. Rather, these functions have been spread thinly and often inefficiently among volunteer resident and sporadically visiting biologists.

Biologists who work in Monteverde have tended to work almost exclusively in Monteverde, so very few cross-site comparisons to other tropical montane forests exist. Opportunities to compare data sets with other sites such as the Luquillo National Forest in Puerto Rico or Los Planados forest in Colombia have not been undertaken. On the other hand, Monteverde has been the site of a great deal of long-term and monitoring-type research, which is often lacking at other tropical field sites. The bulk of the research reported in scientific journals has been carried out by North American biologists. A small number of Costa Rican scientists and field workers have participated in Monteverde research; that number appears to be increasing and needs active encouragement.

The direct and indirect effects of ecotourism have changed many aspects of life in Monteverde over the past decade and the way in which research has been conducted. The advent of telephones, electronic mail, more efficient transportation within the country, and numerous undergraduate courses have facilitated the creation and exchange of scientific information. However, the social setting has altered; understandably, Monteverde residents tend to be less "open" to newcomers using their land to conduct research or interviews. The natural history guides who interpret ecological and natural history research to the over 40,000 ecotourists who visit Monteverde each year are key elements in the transfer of information from biologists to the general public. Mechanisms are needed to enhance the flow of information from biologists to guides by rewarding individuals in both groups for taking the time and energy to share questions and answers. The exchange of information between biologists and the practitioners of conservation is not well facilitated by formal networks. Rather, conservationists have tended to gather information informally, from the few biologists who take the time and have the communication skills (including fluency in Spanish and English) to provide relevant information, with little direct reward.

Literature Cited

Daugherty, H. E. 1973. The Montecristo cloud-forest of El Salvador—a chance for protection. Biological Conservation 59:27–230.

Doumenge, C., D. Gilmour, M. Ruiz Perez, and J. Blockhus. 1993. Tropical montane cloud forests: conservation status and management issues. Pages 18–24 in L. S. Hamilton, J. O. Juvik, and F. N. Scatena, editors, Tropical montane cloud forests. East-West Center, Honolulu.

Hamilton, L. S., J. O. Juvik, and F. N. Scatena, editors. 1993. Tropical montane cloud forests. East-West Center, Honolulu.

Holdridge, L. R. 1967. Life zone ecology. Tropical Science Center, San José, Costa Rica.

LaBastille, A., and D. J. Pool. 1978. On the need for a system of cloud-forest parks in Middle America and the Caribbean. Environmental Conservation 5:183–190.

Lugo, A. E., and C. Lowe, editors. 1995. Tropical forests: management and ecology. Springer, New York.

McDade, L., K. Bawa, H. Hespinheide, and G. Hartshorn. 1994. La Selva: ecology and natural history of a neotropical rain forest. University of Chicago Press, Chicago, Illinois.

Stadtmüller, T. 1987. Cloud forests in the humid tropics. A bibliographic review. United Nations University, Tokyo, and CATIE, Turrialba, Costa Rica.

UNESCO (United Nations Educational, Scientific and Cultural Organization). 1981. Vegetation map of South America. Explanatory notes. UNESCO, Paris.

2

The Physical Environment

Kenneth L. Clark
Robert O. Lawton
Paul R. Butler

Because biological diversity is directly related to diversity of the physical environment, a clear picture of the physical setting of the Cordillera is crucial to understand its ecology and conservation. The physical setting of Monteverde and the Cordillera de Tilarán encompasses a wide range of environmental conditions. The size, position across the trade windflow, geology, erosional dissection, and hydrology of the Cordillera interact to produce extraordinary physical diversity that parallels its great biological diversity. A major difference between tropical montane and lowland regions is the way biological diversity is distributed across the landscape. Montane regions are usually less diverse at the scale of 0.01–0.1 km² but are as rich in species as nearby lowland areas at scales of 10–100 km².

We have two goals in this chapter. First, we review what is known of the climate and weather, geology and geologic history, geomorphology, soils, and hydrology of Monteverde. Our account focuses on higher elevations in Monteverde and wetter areas on the Caribbean slope, with less attention to the drier environments on the lower Pacific slope. Second, we point out areas where our knowledge is incomplete

and suggest promising lines of future research. Although the geology and geomorphology of Monteverde are moderately well known, our knowledge of the rates of many geomorphic processes, particularly erosion, is poor. We also lack information on soils and hydrology, particularly of wind-driven cloud and precipitation inputs, evapotranspiration, and stream outputs from forests and other land-use types in Monteverde. Quantitative information on how variability in the physical environment interacts with biotic processes at the population, community, and ecosystem levels is scant.

2.1. Climate and Weather of Monteverde

Most of the climate and weather data were collected at 1450 m at the Pensión (1956–1971), at 1520 m at John Campbell's residence (1972 to present), and intermittently throughout or near the Monteverde Cloud Forest Preserve (MCFP; Lawton and Dryer 1980, Crump et al. 1992, Clark 1994, Bohlman et al. 1995, W. Calvert and A. Nelson, unpubl. data). The climate of Monteverde is transitional between lowland and montane sites in terms of ambient air temperature, and transitional between the Caribbean and Pacific sides of Costa Rica in terms of incident solar radiation and amounts and seasonality of precipitation (Coen 1983, Herrera 1985, Vargas 1994). Costa Rica is a relatively small landmass between the Caribbean Sea and Pacific Ocean, so continental low pressures are not generated during any season. Rather, the migration of the Intertropical Convergence Zone (ITCZ), a zone of low pressure associated with intense solar radiation and heating that follows the seasonal migration of the sun, largely controls the seasonality of cloud cover and precipitation (Riehl 1979). Weather systems that affect Monteverde are regional to global in scale and include polar cold fronts, tropical storms, and hurricanes. At a smaller scale, topographic position and exposure to trade-wind-driven clouds and precipitation play major roles in controlling microclimate across Monteverde (Lawton and Dryer 1980).

2.1.1. Daylength, Solar Angle, and Solar Radiation

Daylength at Monteverde oscillates seasonally between 11 hr 32 min on 22 December and 12 hr 42 min on 23 June (Fig. 2.1). Solar angle is 90° above

horizontal at noon on 23 April and 23 August and reaches a minimum of 56.6° on 22 December (Fig. 2.2). Calculated clear-sky, instantaneous shortwave radiation at noon varies between 875 and 1085 W/m² (assuming a value of 0.7 for atmospheric transmittance), but reflectance and absorption of solar radiation by clouds strongly affect both daily and seasonal patterns of incident solar radiation. For example, instantaneous noontime incident solar radiation measured at a leeward forest site in the MCFP from October 1991 to September 1992 showed seasonal attenuation by clouds, particularly by cumulus and stratocumulus clouds in July and August, when compared to calculated clear-sky incident solar radiation (Fig. 2.3).

The seasonality of cloud types (Sec. 2.1.3) also has an effect on incident solar radiation, which potentially results in seasonal differences on east- and west-facing slopes (Fig. 2.4). Combined with the seasonal variation in solar angle and daylength, changes in cloud cover and type affect incident radiation, which likely has major effects on ecosystem processes, such as evapotranspiration, primary production, and nutrient cycling, and may also cue phenological changes and other processes in plants and animals. The linkage of this type of abiotic data with information on biotic processes is needed.

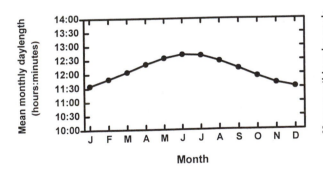

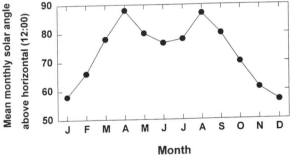

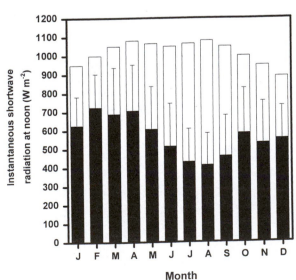

Figure 2.1. *(top left)* Calculated mean monthly daylength (hours:minutes) at the latitude of Monteverde (10° N). **Figure 2.2.** *(top right)* Calculated mean monthly solar angle above horizontal (degrees) at noon at the latitude of Monteverde (10° N). **Figure 2.3.** *(at right)* Mean monthly instantaneous shortwave radiation (W/m²) at noon calculated for clear-sky conditions in Monteverde (▢), and measured at a leeward cloud forest site in the MCFP from October 1991 to September 1992 (■; mean ± 1 S.D.).

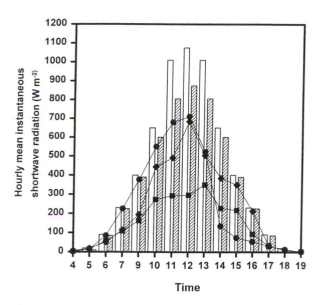

Figure 2.4. Hourly mean instantaneous shortwave radiation (W/m²) calculated for clear-sky conditions during 21 April (□) and 21 December (■), and measured hourly mean instantaneous shortwave radiation at a leeward cloud forest site in the MCFP during days with convective precipitation (●), wind-driven precipitation (■), and mist and cloud (◆). Values for precipitation, mist, and cloud are means of three days each measured during October 1991 to September 1992. See text for a definition of precipitation types.

2.1.2. Temperature

The reduction in ambient air temperature with increasing altitude (adiabatic cooling) causes air temperatures to be lower at Monteverde compared to lowland sites but higher than at montane sites in Costa Rica such as Villa Mills (3000 m) and Volcán Irazú (3400 m; Table 2.1, Fig. 2.5). Mean annual temperature at Monteverde measured at 1460 m from 1956 to 1995 was 18.5°C, with a minimum of 9.0°C and a maximum of 27.0°C (J. Campbell, unpubl. data). Mean monthly minimum and maximum temperatures during the same period had ranges of 14.0-17.6°C in December and 16.5-21.2°C in June, respectively (Fig. 2.5). The coolest air temperatures are associated with outbreaks of polar air, which typically originate in North America (see Sec. 2.1.4). Air temperatures at lower elevations on the Caribbean and Pacific slopes of the Monteverde area are higher, but no long-term records exist.

2.1.3. Cloud Water and Precipitation

Mean annual precipitation depth measured at 1460 m at Monteverde from 1956 to 1995 was 2519 mm. Minimum and maximum annual precipitation during that time were 1715 mm (1959) and 3240 mm (1996), respectively (J. Campbell, unpubl. data; Table 2.1, Fig. 2.6). Reported precipitation depths are minimum estimates for the upper portions of Monteverde because standard rain gauges substantially underestimate wind-driven cloud water and precipitation. For example, at a leeward cloud forest site (20 m higher in elevation and ca. 2.5 km east-southeast from the Monteverde weather station), annual precipitation depth collected in 1991–92 with a standard rain gauge was 3191 mm; an additional 886 mm of wind-driven cloud water and precipitation was collected with a cloud water collector (Clark 1994). Additional wind-driven inputs represented 22% of total hydrologic inputs. In comparison, reported precipitation depth for the Monteverde weather station was 2223 mm for this period.

Precipitation throughout the Cordillera varies spatially with elevation and exposure to the tradewinds.

Table 2.1. Longitude, latitude, elevation in meters, mean annual temperature (in °C), and mean annual precipitation (in mm) for selected locations in Costa Rica.

Location	Longitude	Latitude	Elevation (m)	Mean Annual Temperature (°C)	Mean Annual Precipitation (mm)
Limón	83°02'	10°00'	3	25.3	3531
Villa Mills	83°32'	9°30'	3000	10.9	2679
Volcán Irazu	83°51'	9°59'	3400	7.9	2025
La Selva	83°58'	10°26'	25	25.8	3962
San José	84°04'	9°56'	1172	20.0	1902
Ciudad Quesada	84°25'	10°20'	656	22.6	4543
Monteverde	**84°46'**	**10°15'**	**1460**	**18.8**	**2519**
Caño Negro	84°49'	10°24'	720	(–)	4484
Puntarenas	84°50'	9°58'	4	27.1	1564
Nicoya	85°27'	10°09'	123	26.5	(–)

Source: Data are taken from Herrera (1985), Vargas (1994), and J. Campbell (unpubl. data).

(–) = data unavailable.

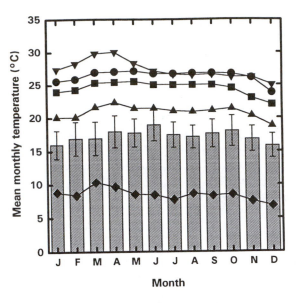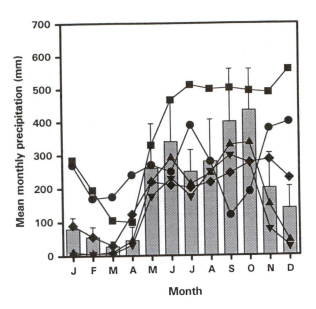

Figure 2.5. *(left)* Mean monthly temperature (°C) at 1460 m at Monteverde (■; mean ± mean monthly minimum and maximum values), Limón (●), Ciudad Quesada (■), Irazú (◆), San José (▲), and Puntarenas (▼). See Table 2.1 for site descriptions. **Figure 2.6.** *(right)* Mean monthly precipitation depth (mm) at 1460 m at Monteverde (■; mean ± 1 S.D.), Limón (●), Ciudad Quesada (■), Irazú (◆), San José (▲), and Puntarenas (▼). See Table 2.1 for site descriptions.

The migration of the ITCZ controls the seasonality of precipitation and the types of clouds and precipitation, particularly on upper slopes and ridges in Monteverde. In areas that are exposed to the trade winds, moisture from clouds and wind-driven precipitation intercepted by the vegetation may represent a major hydrological input; the actual contribution to a forest is difficult to quantify (Stadtmüller 1987, Cavelier and Goldstein 1989, Bruijnzeel and Proctor 1993, Cavelier et al. 1996). Terms for cloud water and mist inputs include "occult precipitation" (Dollard et al. 1983), and "horizontal precipitation" (*sensu* Stadtmüller 1987, Bruijnzeel and Proctor 1993) when wind-driven precipitation is included. We define "convective precipitation" as precipitation that originates from cumulus or cumulonimbus clouds (mean windspeeds < 2 m/s), "wind-driven precipitation" as precipitation that originates from stratus or stratocumulus clouds with minimal cloud immersion (mean windspeeds ≥ 2 m/s), "mist" as precipitation that originates from stratus clouds with cloud immersion, and "cloud water" as nonprecipitating stratus cloud immersion.

Three seasons are recognized in Monteverde on the basis of cloud and precipitation types: (1) wet season (May–October), characterized by clear sky in the morning and cumulus cloud formation and convective precipitation in the afternoon and early evening; (2) transition season (November–January), characterized by strong northeasterly trade winds, stratus and stratocumulus clouds, and wind-driven precipitation

and mist during the day and night; and (3) dry season (February–April), characterized by moderate trade winds, stratus clouds or clear-sky conditions, and wind-driven mist and cloud water, particularly during the night (Fig. 2.6). During the transition and dry seasons, stratus cloud cover and wind-driven precipitation, mist, and cloud water depths typically increase with elevation and exposure to the trade winds.

Maximum monthly precipitation in Monteverde occurs in the wet season in June, September, and October, when the ITCZ is directly over Costa Rica (Fig. 2.6). This occurs during maximum solar heating of land and sea surfaces, which results in high rates of heat (sensible heat) and water vapor release (latent heat) to the atmosphere (referred to as sensible and latent heat exchange, respectively). Absorbance of sensible heat by the atmosphere produces warm, buoyant air masses and generally unstable atmospheric conditions. Adiabatic cooling of these moist, ascending air masses causes water vapor to condense and leads to the formation of cumulus and cumulonimbus clouds by the late morning and early afternoon. Cloud height may reach over 15,000 m. Clouds typically produce convective precipitation by the afternoon or early evening, often associated with intense lightning activity. When the ITCZ is at its northern boundary in late July and August, convective precipitation activity is typically reduced in Monteverde, a period referred to as the "veranillo" (little summer); light to moderate winds with mist and precipitation are interspersed with periods of convective precipitation.

Cloud cover, however, may be greater at this time compared to other times of the year (Fig. 2.3).

Ascending air masses at the ITCZ create a surface low pressure that must be replaced by air masses from regions to the north and south. This produces the surface trade winds associated with global-scale Hadley cell circulation (Riehl 1979). When the ITCZ is located to the south of Costa Rica during the transition and dry seasons, northeasterly trade winds deliver moist air from the Caribbean Sea to the lowlands on the Caribbean side of Costa Rica. Maximum mean wind velocity occurs from sea level up to 2800–3000 m, above which velocities decrease. When these air masses encounter the Cordilleras, they are forced to ascend (orographic uplift), and adiabatic cooling causes condensation and stratus or stratocumulus cloud formation. Cloud base is typically at 1400–1700 m during these two seasons. Cloud immersion on the upper slopes and ridges along the Continental Divide (particularly on the Brillante Ridge and above Río Caño Negro) may approach 20–25% of the time, which is similar to the duration of cloud immersion in some montane forests in northeastern United States (Vong et al. 1991).

Compared to the wet season, cloud immersion and precipitation depths across Monteverde are more variable during the transition and dry seasons and depend strongly on topographic position and exposure to the trade winds. Slopes and ridges on the east-facing (windward) side of the Continental Divide typically receive amounts of precipitation that are more characteristic of the Caribbean side of Costa Rica, primarily due to wind-driven precipitation inputs during the transition season (see Clark and Nadkarni, "Microclimate Variability," pp. 33–34, Fig. 2.6). Cloud immersion and wind-driven precipitation occur with decreasing frequency and duration on east-facing slopes and ridges as the dry season progresses. Slopes and valleys on the west-facing (leeward) side of the Continental Divide have precipitation regimes that are more similar to those on the northern and central Pacific side of Costa Rica (Fig. 2.6). The San Luis valley, for example, experiences relatively small amounts of wind-driven precipitation and minimal cloud immersion during the transition and dry seasons. Wind-driven cloud water and precipitation inputs represented approximately a 20% increase over annual precipitation input for the leeward cloud forest site in the MCFP that was immersed in cloud only about 7% of the time. Intermittent data collected at La Ventana on the Brillante, however, suggest that much higher inputs to windward cloud forests occur (Clark 1994; see Clark and Nadkarni, "Microclimate Variability," pp. 33–34).

A similar pattern for cloud water and precipitation has been documented across a transect in northern Panama (Cavelier et al. 1996). The input of "mist" that augmented precipitation collected with standard rain gauges ranged between <200 mm (500 m elevation) and 2295 mm (on a ridge at 1270 m), which represented 2–60% of total hydrologic inputs. Other estimates of wind-driven cloud water and precipitation in Central American and northern South American montane forests range from 70 to 940 mm/yr (7–48% of total hydrologic inputs; Baynton 1968, Vogelmann 1973, Cavelier and Goldstein 1989, Asbury et al. 1994).

Using a regional hydrologic balance method, Zadroga (1981) estimated cloud water and precipitation inputs for the headwaters of Río Peñas Blancas. He divided the total annual runoff by the total annual rainfall for streams in the San Carlos drainage basin (which includes the Río Peñas Blancas) on the Atlantic slope, and compared these ratios with streams in the Bebedero basin, which flows from the Pacific slope. For the San Carlos basin on the Atlantic slope, the amount of runoff compared to precipitation was 102%, which indicates that more water ran off than fell as direct precipitation. Runoff exceeded monthly precipitation, which was attributed either to an underestimation of rainfall due to an insufficient number of precipitation gauges, or to an underestimation of the total precipitation depth due to inadequate sampling of cloud water and wind-driven precipitation (Zadroga 1981). An average annual cloud water and precipitation depth of up to 9000 mm was calculated for the upper Peñas Blancas watershed. In contrast, runoff was 34.5% of rainfall for the Bebedero basin on the Pacific slope. Runoff exceeded precipitation only in the dry season months (January–April) when the river flows were maintained by water released from bank storage (Zadroga 1981).

Wind-driven hydrologic inputs to tropical cloud forests may be greater than those to temperate montane and coastal forests. Studies in the United States suggest that although cloud water deposition equals approximately 20–30% of total hydrologic inputs, absolute depths are less than in tropical cloud forests (Bruijnzeel and Proctor 1993, Dingman 1994, Cavelier et al. 1996). Tropical cloud forests likely receive greater wind-driven hydrologic inputs due to relatively higher tradewind velocities and "wetter" cloud events, although cloud immersion may be of similar duration (Vong et al. 1991, Bruijnzeel and Proctor 1993, Asbury et al. 1994).

Quantification of wind-driven cloud water and precipitation inputs in Monteverde is a major future challenge. A transect of cloud water and precipitation collectors from the Peñas Blancas valley to the San Luis valley and measurements of other meteorological variables are needed to estimate hydrologic inputs.

A larger network of collectors along the Continental Divide is necessary to estimate maximum amounts of cloud water and precipitation inputs to the region. Micrometeorological techniques to measure cloud water inputs to forests are also promising, but they require complex instrumentation (Gallagher et al. 1992, Vong and Kowalski 1995).

2.1.4. Weather Systems

Weather systems that affect Monteverde are regional to global in scale and can be classified into three categories: (1) temporales del norte, (2) temporales del Pacífico, and (3) hurricanes. Temporales del norte are the result of outbreaks of cold, dry, polar air that originate in the North Pacific, occurring most frequently from December to February. As these strong cold fronts pass over the Gulf of Mexico and the Caribbean Sea, warm, moist air masses are forced to ascend above cooler, denser air. Adiabatic cooling forms stratus and stratocumulus clouds, and the trade winds force these air masses over the Cordilleras. Orographic uplift and further adiabatic cooling result in intense wind-driven precipitation and mist in Monteverde. Temporales del norte typically have the longest duration of the three types of weather systems at Monteverde, lasting up to 14 days with continuous precipitation (J. Campbell, pers. comm.).

Temporales del Pacífico are the result of tropical low-pressure systems in the Caribbean basin, occur frequently from August to October, and correspond with the hurricane season in the Caribbean. They can reverse surface winds such that warm moist air is drawn over Monteverde from the Pacific Ocean. Orographic uplift and adiabatic cooling of these air masses, combined with high rates of sensible and latent heat exchange with land surfaces, produce stratus and stratocumulus clouds that result in cloud immersion and precipitation throughout the day and night. Although temporales del Pacífico are typically shorter in duration than temporales del norte, they may result in high precipitation. The maximum daily precipitation depth recorded during a temporal del Pacífico was 160 mm (J. Campbell, pers. comm.).

Hurricanes are relatively rare in Monteverde. In the last century, only one hurricane hit Costa Rica directly (Hurricane Martha, 21–25 November 1969). However, high rainfall reported for September and October reflects the indirect effects of tropical depressions, some of which form hurricanes as they travel northward. For example, precipitation depth from Hurricane Gilbert (October 1988) totaled 240 mm in 30 hr (J. Campbell, pers. comm.).

2.2. Geology and Geologic History of Monteverde

In recent decades, the earth sciences have been revolutionized by the theory of plate tectonics. The outer layer of the earth is now known to be composed of a series of large rigid plates that move in response to the earth's internal heat flow. Over millions of years, the plates have shifted to create ocean basins, continents, and mountain ranges. The present assemblages of plants and animals in Central America have been strongly influenced by the recent plate movements that connected North and South America.

The geology and geologic history of southern Central America are distinct from those of land masses to the north and south (Dengo 1962, 1985, Escalante 1990). Costa Rica, along with southern Nicaragua, Panama, and a portion of northern Colombia, is part of the Caribbean continental plate (Fig. 2.7). Northern Central America is part of the North American continental plate; the rest of the South American continent is part of the South American plate. As plates move, they can either converge, slide past one another, or separate. Costa Rica is in a zone of plate convergence that occurs along the west coast at the western edge of the Caribbean plate, referred to as the Middle America Trench (Fig. 2.7). At present, two small oceanic plates, the Cocos and Nazca plates, are converging with the continental Caribbean plate. Because the material that makes up oceanic plates (primarily mafic rocks of basaltic composition) is generally denser than the material that makes up continental plates (primarily rocks of intermediate to andesitic composition), the Cocos and Nazca plates are being driven down (subducted) below the Caribbean plate. The present crustal deformation (which includes tectonic uplift), seismic activity, and active vulcanism in southern Central America result from plate motion along this subduction zone (Fig. 2.7). Subduction of oceanic crust beneath the Caribbean plate began in the Cretaceous Period, about 60–70 million years ago (Ma; Minster and Jordan 1978, Lundberg 1982, 1991, DeMets et al. 1990, McIntosh et al. 1993).

The tectonic history of southern Central America over the last 10 million years has been complex. The most important events influencing the modern configuration of Costa Rica and the Central American land bridge were (a) the rotational and translational movement of the Chortis block, a continental fragment associated with rocks currently found in western Mexico, which now composes central and eastern Honduras and Nicaragua; (b) the northeasterly movement of the southern Central American volca-

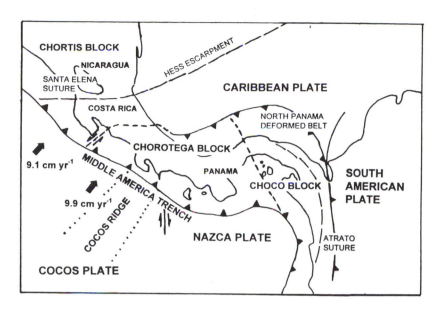

Figure 2.7. Geologic map of the southern Central American Region.

nic arc associated with the subduction of the Cocos plate beneath the Caribbean plate (Burke 1988); (c) the fusion of the southeastern end of the volcanic island arc (now Panama) with northwestern South America at the Atrato suture; and (d) the collision of the submarine Cocos Ridge with the southern Pacific Coast of Costa Rica (Fig. 2.7).

These events had momentous tectonic, biogeographic, and ecologic consequences for southern Central America and the Cordillera de Tilarán. For example, the increased rate of subduction of the Cocos plate along the Middle America Trench further increased island arc volcanic activity, which had been relatively quiescent in the Costa Rican region since the early Tertiary (50–60 Ma; Wadge and Burke 1983, Burbach et al. 1984, Burke 1988). The important biological impact of these events was the creation of the land bridge that allowed intercontinental biotic movement approximately 3.5 Ma (Marshall et al. 1982, Gomez 1986, Coates et al. 1992). The Caribbean Sea was separated from the Pacific Ocean, which limited the movement of marine organisms and floating plant propagules (Coates et al. 1992); warm surface water currents associated with the trade winds were also redirected (Keigwin 1982, Burke 1988).

2.2.1. Recent Volcanic and Tectonic Events in the Cordillera de Tilarán

Both volcanism and tectonic uplift have contributed to the growth of the Cordillera de Tilarán. Renewed and accelerated subduction of the Cocos plate at the Middle America Trench resulted in three major episodes of volcanic activity since the late Miocene.

Compression, fault formation, and tectonic uplift have resulted in the horst block uplift that built the present-day Cordillera.

The Cordillera de Tilarán is composed largely of volcanic rocks of the Aguacate Group (Chaves and Saenz 1974). The oldest of these have radiometric dates of 8.5–10.5 Ma (late Miocene; Chaves and Saenz 1974). They were derived from magma produced at relatively low temperatures and pressures at depths of 80–100 km along the zone of plate contact, early during the renewed subduction (Laguna 1985). The youngest rocks in the Aguacate Group date from 2.6–4.3 Ma (Pliocene). They were derived from magma produced at depths of 150–200 km and at higher temperatures and pressures during later phases of subduction (Laguna 1985). These rocks are conspicuous, forming the dramatic cliffs at 1200–1500 m throughout the Cordillera. The Aguacate Group as a whole has been uplifted as a horst between two large trench-parallel faults: the Las Juntas Fault, which follows the Pan-American Highway on the Pacific side of the Cordillera; and the Arenal Fault, which extends through Volcán Arenal, Cerro los Perdidos, and the Caribbean side of the range (Dengo and Levy 1969). Elevations of the cliffs formed by the Aguacate Group decline to the northwest from a peak on the east flank of Cerro Ojo de Agua. This suggests that the Cordillera de Tilarán horst was uplifted and tilted by the same mechanisms that have produced, and are still producing, similar tilt and rotation of the Nicoya and Osa peninsular blocks (Gardner et al. 1992, Marshall and Anderson 1995).

Subsequent volcanic activity in the Quaternary indicates ongoing maturation of the subduction zone, with a shift in the volcanic axis to the east, farther from the Middle America Trench. Pleistocene (ca. 600,000 years ago) andesitic lavas and tuffs of the Monteverde Formation lie discordantly on the rocks of the Aguacate Group, mantling the upper slopes of the Cordillera to depths of up to several hundred meters. The volcanic foci that produced the Monteverde Formation have not been identified (Alvarado 1989), but several trench-parallel sets of peaks are candidates for relict volcanic structures. For instance, Cerros Chomogo, Amigo, Roble, and Cerro Ojo de Agua lie on a single axis, while Cerro Frio and Cerro la Mesa stand across the Peñas Blancas valley from each other, offset a similar distance (2–3 km) from the prior axis. Seven kilometers farther northeast, Pico 1790, a relict volcanic structure, lies in a line parallel with the peaks at the head of the Río Aranjuez valley. These are all of a scale similar to that of the latest array of Volcán Arenal, Cerro Chato, and Cerro los Perdidos (Borgia et al. 1988).

2.3. Modern Geography of the Cordillera de Tilarán

The present Cordillera de Tilarán consists of a sinuous main ridge, which runs southeast from Cerro Nubes (1020 m) to Cerro Chomogo (1799 m) and Cerro Amigo (1842 m) above Santa Elena and Monteverde, across the Brillante saddle (ca. 1500 m) to Cerro Ojo de Agua (ca. 1800 m; Fig. 2.8; Figs. 1.4, 1.7). The main ridge then turns east over a series of knobs, separating the upper thirds of the Peñas Blancas and Aranjuez watersheds. The higher points on these ridges are likely relict volcanic structures dating from the Quaternary, the age of the Monteverde Formation.

Erosion has dramatically influenced the modern landscape of the Cordillera. The Caribbean slope of the Cordillera is drained by tributaries of the Río San Carlos. Río Peñas Blancas, the largest stream of the range, drains the central Caribbean slope. The Pacific slope of the Cordillera is drained on the northwestern end by the Ríos Cañas and Abangares, both of which flow into the mouth of the Río Tempisque at the head of the Golfo de Nicoya, and the Ríos Lagarto, Guacimal, Aranjuez, and Barranca, which flow directly into the Golfo (Fig. 1.7).

Many of these rivers have parallel, very straight central courses normal to the long axis of the horst. These features suggest they follow faults in the Aguacate Group (Bergoeing and Brenes 1977). Although such fault-directed development of watercourses and drainage patterns is generally obscured by extensive erosional dissection of the landscape, a fault conspicuously redirects the courses of three adjacent streams flowing from the El Valle region into the Río Peñas Blancas on the Atlantic slope (see Fig. 1.5). Faulting of the Aguacate Group core may have dictated much of the erosional pattern and modern configuration of the Cordillera.

Major streams and their tributaries descend rapidly on both sides of the Continental Divide, often through spectacular sets of rapids. The Río Peñas Blancas, for example, descends 500 m in the 10 km between Dos Aces and Poco Sol. Tributary ravines, termed quebradas, descend from the Continental Divide even more dramatically; those in the upper Peñas Blancas valley drop 500–800 m in 2.5 km. These streams carve spectacular gorges and often incise stream channels into the bedrock, particularly as they traverse the upper rocks of the Aguacate Group. Streams 2–5 m wide descend via stepped waterfalls and rapids in the bottom of channels 10–15 m deep in bedrock. The Bajo Tigre trail (Fig. 1.8) offers views of the Río Guacimal cutting through the upper members of the Aguacate Group. The Sendero del Río of the preserve offers views of the upper reaches of the same stream cutting through the breccias of the Monteverde Formation (Fig. 1.5).

Above the cliffs of the Aguacate Group, the landscape is mantled by the less thoroughly dissected lavas and tuffs of the Monteverde Formation (Chaves and Saenz 1974, Castillo-Muñoz 1983, Alvarado 1989). Older relict volcanic structures (e.g., Cerros Chomogo, Amigo, and Frio) are rugged, but younger structures (e.g., Pico 1790 and the peak of Cerro los Perdidos) present broad slopes, which, although steep, are not yet carved into quebradas and ridges. Saddles along the crest of the Cordillera (e.g., the Brillante trail), broad summits (e.g., Cerro la Mesa), and benches (e.g., Monteverde-Cerro Plano-Santa Elena) present areas of conspicuously lower relief, well dissected into small primary watersheds. Watersheds 10 ha in area along the Brillante trail, for example, are drained by permanent streams. The relief within such watersheds, however, is generally less than 50 m, and in some swampy areas much less. These areas of lesser relief have been interpreted as the development of nearly flat, eroded surfaces (peneplains) on the Aguacate formation (Castillo-Muñoz 1983). They are clearly related to the original topography and geological structure of the Pleistocene volcanic terrain of the Monteverde Formation. The Monteverde–Cerro Plano–Santa Elena bench resembles the area at the southwestern foot of Volcán Arenal in terms of geomorphology. Road cuts in the Monteverde–Santa Elena area reveal a heterogeneous mix of tuffs and breccias, similar to those that have accumulated around the base and on the lower slopes of Volcán Arenal (Chaves and Saenz 1974, Alvarado 1989).

Figure 2.8. Atlantic slope of the Continental Divide in the Monteverde Cloud Forest Preserve. Photograph by Stephen Ingram.

Below the cliff outcrops of the uppermost Aguacate Group, the terrain of the Cordillera is highly dissected into a landscape of small, narrow catchments separated by ridges with steep flanks, often scored by landslides. Relief over small watersheds (10–15 ha) is typically >100 m. In some areas, such as the uppermost San Luis and Peñas Blancas valleys, extensive deposits of colluvial debris derived from landslides on both the Aguacate Group and Monteverde Formation have produced areas of less rugged relief.

2.3.1. Geomorphological Processes and Distinctive Terrain Features

Rates of geomorphological activity, particularly denudation due to mass wasting, have influenced landscape development at Monteverde and are central to the concept of site stability (*sensu* Raup 1957). Erosion of the deforested Pacific slope of the Cordillera is of practical importance. The Cordillera itself has not been the subject of quantitative geomorphological study, but research in similar locales provides insight. In volcanic ranges in central and southwestern Japan, which are similar to the Cordillera de Tilarán in elevation, relief, and precipitation depth (although some of the precipitation is in the form of snow), sedimentation rates in small reservoirs have been monitored (Yoshikawa et al. 1981). Sedimentation rates yield average rates of denudation of between 1000 and

10,000 m³/km²·yr (Yoshikawa 1974, Yoshikawa et al. 1981), equivalent to 1–10 mm/yr, which are commensurate with modern rates of uplift on the Osa and Nicoya Peninsulas.

Exposed slopes often produce repeated landslides; they supply debris for fluvial transport for long periods following the initial collapse. Landslides typically occur episodically within an area, with a mean recurrence interval of about 10 years (Yoshikawa et al. 1981). Sediment yield in a northern Californian watershed has also been shown to be strongly episodic; the bulk of long-term sediment yield typically occurs in the few years following widespread mass wasting as a consequence of torrential rains (Dietrich et al. 1982a).

Distinctive terrain features ranging from small permanent pools and swamps to cliffs, waterfalls, quebradas, ridges, and landslides are conspicuous in the Cordillera de Tilarán, although little is known about their formation. These contribute markedly to landscape and microclimate diversity. Geomorphological processes related to stream incision and slope denudation (notably mass wasting) influence local site stability.

Swamps. Small (0.01–1 ha) swampy areas occur along flat ridgetops and summits on the Continental Divide and on the divide between the Peñas Blancas and Caño Negro watersheds. These form because of high wind-driven cloud water and precipitation inputs, low rates of evapotranspiration from the vegetation (Sec. 2.6), and impeded drainage. Permanent puddles 1–4 m in diameter are common within these swampy areas and are filled with up to 0.30–1 m of soft organic material. These swampy areas are often occupied by a distinctive vegetation dominated by *Clusia* sp., *Didymopanax pittieri* in the canopy, and *Ardisia solomonii* in the understory. Larger swampy areas occur on level ground at the windward foot of steep slopes that receive high wind-driven cloud water and precipitation inputs. A large accessible swamp is the Pantano, a 0.75-km² area perched at 1600 m below the peaks of Cerros Frio, Amigo, and Roble and skirted by the Senderos Pantañoso and El Valle of the MCFP (Fig. 1.5). The surface of these swamps is speckled with 2–5-m-diameter pools produced by the uprooting of canopy trees. Because trees are shallowly rooted, a root platform 0.15–0.3 m thick peels free from the saturated underlying soil when uprooting occurs. This leaves a depression filled with water over deep, unconsolidated soil. Although these swamps are forested, some small marshy openings in which water flows as a 10–15-cm-thick sheet also occur, typically dominated by large, tussock-forming sedges.

Forest floor microtopography. The microtopography of the forest floor is sculpted by biotic processes such as treefalls and animal movement, and abiotic processes such as the overland flow of water and erosion of slopes. Small ledges or terraces normal to the direction of maximum slope (terracettes) are conspicuous in steeper areas. These are commonly incorporated into game trails; animal trampling plays a major role in terracette formation (Carson and Kirkby 1972). Debris trapping by tree trunks, surface roots, logs, and tip-up mounds also contributes to the development of these ledges. This microtopographic variation in the forest floor accentuates variation in litter accumulation and likely influences rates of decomposition and nutrient release, with unknown but potentially important consequences for the soil fauna and plant establishment.

Springs and stream incision. Initial stream-channel incision in soils derived from the Monteverde Formation is strongly influenced by soil structure. The A horizon (Sec. 2.5) is typically porous and freely draining, but the underlying B and C horizons are less permeable. As a result, water readily infiltrates the A horizon but moves laterally along the lower horizons. This flow is concentrated in the depressions at the head of primary watersheds and emerges as permanent or intermittent springs at the A–B horizon boundary at the head of incised stream channels ("knickpoints" *sensu* Dietrich et al. 1992), which are 2–3 m deep at the point of origin. The flow at the A–B horizon boundary often erodes a tunnel upslope from the spring ("piping" *sensu* Dietrich et al. 1992). These pipes may serve as part of the den system of pacas (*Agouti paca*). Examples of springhead incision and piping can be seen in the MCFP along portions of the Sendero del Río, Sendero Bosque Nuboso, and Sendero Roble.

Upper ridgecrests in the relatively gentle terrain derived from the Monteverde Formation are often rounded. The size of these catchments varies inversely with cloud water and precipitation inputs throughout the Cordillera. For example, in the very wet region at the head of the Peñas Blancas valley, there may be only a 0.25-ha catchment upstream from the point of stream channel incision; in the much drier La Cruz–Alto Cebadilla region in the lee of Cerro Chomogo, there may be a 1–10-ha catchment above the point of stream incision.

Landslides. Cliffs, waterfalls, quebradas, ridges, and landslides are all ontogenetically related. Feeder creeks typically plummet over valley headwalls via waterfalls into quebradas. As fluvial erosion deepens quebradas, the oversteepened side slopes eventually become unstable and collapse. With continued erosion, adjacent and parallel quebradas become separated by ridges. The oversteepening of slopes due to erosion, combined with buildup of a progressively weaker superficial layer as weathering proceeds and vegetation grows, leads to mass wasting by landslides (Wentworth 1943, White 1949, Day 1980).

Landslides in Monteverde are often triggered by torrential rains, which increase soil water potential and decrease soil strength (Swanston 1970, Day 1980, Crozier 1986, Jibson 1989). Earthquakes can also trigger massive episodic landslides on a regional basis (Simonett 1967, Garwood 1985). Magnitude 6.7 and 7.0 earthquakes off the Darién coast of Panama, for example, triggered landslides covering 12% of a 450-km² area (Garwood et al. 1979). Recent small earthquakes (magnitude < 5) in the Cordillera have not triggered major landslides, but larger earthquakes have occurred in this area, for example, magnitude 7 earthquakes that occur at approximately 25-yr intervals (Marshall and Anderson 1995), so the opportunity for catastrophic landslides in the Cordillera exists.

The spatial patterns of landslides in the physical environment are important to forest structure, particularly on the Caribbean slope where the abundance of landslides can be seen from the Ventana pass in the MCFP. The many small slumps (3–5 m across) that typically involve rotational failure of creek banks do not appear to influence forest structure, although they contribute to the fluvial sediment load. In contrast, the larger slides that are conspicuous on quebrada walls and the flanks of ridges produce one of the major vegetation patterns in the Cordillera, which is a mosaic of forests of various ages. This mosaic indicates that landslides are a natural feature in the Cordillera, much like those on volcanic terrain in Hawaii (Wentworth 1943, White 1949; Fig. 2.9).

Landslides consist of a zone of removal in the upper portions, where more resistant materials are exposed, and a zone of deposition at the bottom, where debris accumulates. In the upper zone, patches of undisturbed or slightly disturbed soil and vegetation may exist on the slide periphery or as islandlike areas within the main body of the slide, amid areas of exposed subsoil and outcrops of bedrock. The lower zone may contain areas where soil and rocks are piled at their angle of repose, or areas where shattered trees are jumbled amid rocks and boulders in giant precarious tangles. Landslides longer than 25–30 m may disintegrate into debris avalanches or, if the water and soil content is high, into debris flows. Many landslides dump debris into stream channels at the bottom of quebradas. Seepage may selectively remove fine-grained soil particles and leave cobbles and boulders. Under these circumstances, stony hummocks comprise the floor of the upper bowl of the valley adjacent to the headwall. In other circumstances, the basal zone is rapidly eroded directly by the stream, and the region of rapid revegetation at the base of the slide is significantly reduced. Large landslides may temporarily dam the stream, until the impounded water breaks the dam and flushes the debris downstream.

Not all portions of the landscape are at equal risk of landslides. In the Cordillera, large slides are most conspicuous on precipitous slopes where rocks of the upper Aguacate Group are exposed. These sites include the headwall of the Peñas Blancas valley, Quebrada Honda, and the gorge of the Río Guacimal. Although landslides are typically more abundant on steeper slopes (Wentworth 1943, White 1949, Swanston 1974, Jibson 1989), geological substrate (Day 1980, Jibson 1989, Gupta and Joshi 1990), soil development

Figure 2.9. A recovering landslide on the slopes of the Monteverde Cloud Forest Preserve. Photograph by Robert O. Lawton.

(Swanston 1974), vegetation structure (Swanston 1969, 1970, 1974), and human activities can also influence their likelihood. These relationships raise numerous questions: Are spatial and temporal variation in landscape dynamics dictated by landslide formation? Is the relatively wetter Caribbean slope more prone to sliding than the Pacific slope? Do deforestation and reforestation influence the likelihood of landslides? Does vegetation mass progressively burden the underlying substrate as succession proceeds on old landslides? Does the recurrence interval of landslides influence vegetation stature by limiting site stability (Raup 1957)?

A landslide chronosequence in the Luquillo Mountains of Puerto Rico suggested that forest basal area requires at least 50 years to recover following landslides (Guariguata 1990). The rate and species composition of revegetation on landslides depend strongly on the nature of the exposed substrates (Garwood 1985, Guariguata 1990, Myster and Fernandez 1995). Revegetation is typically more vigorous in the lower zone of deposition (Garwood 1985, Guariguata 1990), which reflects both greater colonization and more favorable growing conditions. Seed input on landslides may be very patchy in both lower and upper zones (Myster and Fernandez 1995). Although soil nutrient status is also patchy, a gradient of increasing availability may exist from the top to the bottom, and from the center to the periphery in the upper zone of a landslide (Guariguata 1990, Myster and Fernandez 1995). Water availability is typically greater in the lower zone, due to both downslope flow and increased soil volume (Carson and Kirkby 1972, Crozier 1986).

To evaluate the contribution of landslides to landscape patterns, we need information on the size class distribution of slides, their temporal frequency, and their spatial distribution. The distribution of landslides influences the physical structure of vegetation and soil, energy flow (due to the impact on vegetation structure and organic matter export), and biogeochemical cycling (particularly sediment export and rejuvenation of soil profiles). Because landslides are conspicuous on aerial photographs, photogrammetric analysis of aerial photographs of the Cordillera de Tilarán could document the spatiotemporal density of slides (e.g., Gupta and Joshi 1990). Multivariate techniques, including discriminant analysis (e.g., Jibson and Keeper 1989) and logistic multiple regression, can quantify landslide risk.

Vegetation dynamics can also be used in the study of geomorphological processes in Monteverde (Hack and Goodlett 1960, Sigafoos 1964, LaMarche 1968, Veblen et al. 1980). Stand composition can serve as a marker and delimiter of past events of mass wasting and floodplain deposition (Hack and Goodlett 1960, Veblen et al. 1980). Vegetation "markers" (e.g., bent or damaged trees) can determine relative and absolute dating of events of scour and deposition (Sigafoos 1964), and rates of surface creep and erosion (Hack and Goodlett 1960, LaMarche 1968).

2.4. Paleoecology of the Cordillera de Tilarán

Paleoecology is the study of past plant and animal communities and their relationships to environmental conditions. Paleoecological interpretation of pollen in sediments depends on the accuracy of information on species distributions. Oaks, for instance, are characteristic elements of montane forests in Central America and, if present in pollen records, indicate montane conditions (Leyden 1984, Bush et al. 1992). However, the recent discoveries of oaks at 500 m elevation on the ridges of the Osa Peninsula (Soto 1992) and at 800 m on ridges in the Peñas Blancas valley (W. Haber, pers. comm.) illustrate the difficulties of inferring paleoconditions from the presence of pollen.

There have been no formal paleoecological studies in the Cordillera de Tilarán. Lake sediments from other Central American and northern Andean sites record lake geochemistry, sediment character, and pollen composition, allowing paleoecological reconstruction of glacial and postglacial conditions in the area (van der Hammen 1974, Binford 1982, Leyden 1984, Bush et al. 1990, 1992, Islebe et al. 1995). Temperatures in both lowland and montane neotropical regions were about 5°C lower at the last glacial maximum (18,000–20,000 years ago). Palynological evidence (i.e., fossil pollen record) suggests that characteristic elements of the vegetation ranged as much as 1500 m lower in the Andes at the last glacial maximum (van der Hammen 1974, Hooghiemstra 1989, Bush et al. 1990) and 600–900 m lower in Central America (Leyden 1984, Bush et al. 1992, Islebe et al. 1995).

Montane species limited by warmer temperatures at the lower limits of their range would have had much larger ranges in the Cordillera de Tilarán if temperatures were 5°C cooler than at present. The cloud forests of the Cordillera, however, seem influenced as much by exposure to the mechanical stresses and clouds of the trade winds as by temperature (Lawton and Dryer 1980). Knowledge of the paleoecology in the range requires more detail on the paleoclimate, particularly of trade winds, the ITCZ, the impact of cold fronts from continental North America, and empirical studies of lake sediments within the Cordillera.

A remarkably well-distributed set of small lakes exists in the Cordillera. The lake on Cerro Chato

(1050 m), Laguna Poco Sol (760 m) in the lower Peñas Blancas valley, and Laguna Cocoritos (500 m) at the mouth of the same valley are crater lakes covering several hectares (Alvarado 1989). A smaller (1 ha) lake is perched at 1000 m elevation on the north side of the Peñas Blancas valley, and a similar-sized lake lies in the upper Río Palmital valley at 1250 m. Laguna Arancibia lies at 1250 m in the upper Río Aranjuez valley across the Continental Divide. Numerous smaller permanent pools lie hidden under the forest canopy. Pollen records from an altitudinal transect across these lakes would help interpret the paleoecology of the Cordillera de Tilarán.

2.5. Soils of Monteverde

Little quantitative research has been conducted on the soils of Monteverde. We discuss soils in a general manner and rely on data collected from other tropical montane forest sites for characteristics that are undoubtedly similar to soils in Monteverde.

2.5.1. Soil Formation and Classification

Soil formation represents a complex set of interdependent biotic and abiotic factors. For example, geologic factors (primarily rock type and structural features) largely determine the relief and geomorphology of the landscape, which affect microclimate, which in turn strongly influences the flora and fauna. Over time, an unconsolidated mass of rock is altered by physical and chemical processes such that it becomes measurably different from its original parent material. Organic matter derived from vegetation, microbial biomass, and animals is added. The resulting soil develops layers at varying depths below the surface; a vertical section through these layers is referred to as a profile. Soils are classified based on characteristics of their profiles, which result from a unique combination of factors (Jenny 1980, Troeh and Thompson 1993, Ritter et al. 1995).

The upper part of a soil profile is referred to as the A horizon, and it is typically darker in color than the lower horizons, due to the accumulation of organic matter. The middle part of the profile is the B horizon, or subsoil. The lower part of the profile is the C horizon, which extends to unweathered bedrock. Soils that have developed under vegetation typically have accumulations of organic material above the A horizon. Organic matter accumulations are referred to as the O_1 horizon, which is composed of identifiable organic debris, and the O_e horizon, which contains partially decomposed organic debris referred to as humus. These two layers comprise the forest floor. A large accumulation of amorphous organic

matter throughout the O, A, and occasionally the B horizons is referred to as a histic epipedon (zone). Although forests at higher elevations in Monteverde are typically less productive and have lower rates of litterfall compared to those at lower elevations (Vitousek and Sanford 1986, Bruijnzeel and Proctor 1993; see Chap. 9, Ecosystem Ecology), rates of litter decomposition are also lower, which leads to large accumulations of litter and humus in the O horizon and of organic matter in the A and B horizons. This is one of the most striking differences in the soils of tropical montane forests compared to tropical lowland forests (Grubb 1977, Marrs et al. 1988, Grieve et al. 1990, Kitayama 1993, Bruijnzeel et al. 1993).

The majority of soils at Monteverde are formed on slightly to moderately weathered volcanic parent materials of the Aquacate and Monteverde Formations and are classified as Andisols (USDA soil classification system [1992]). Andisols at Monteverde are further classified as Udands because they have formed under udic, or wet, moisture regimes. Inceptisols, which are poorly weathered soils at an early stage of development derived from landslides or alluvium, occur on steeper slopes and along streams. Both Andisols and Inceptisols are characterized by poorly to moderately differentiated soil horizons. Histosols, highly organic "soils" derived primarily from host tree and epiphyte litter on tree stems and branches, occur at higher elevations in forests exposed to high cloud water and precipitation inputs (see Clark and Nadkarni, "Epiphytic Histosols," pp. 34–35).

2.5.2. Physical and Chemical Properties

Volcanic parent materials of the Aguacate and Monteverde Formations were formed by rapid cooling, which resulted in the imperfect crystallization of aluminosilicate minerals. When these and other amorphous minerals are hydrated and the initial weathering reactions occur, the rapid weathering of feldspars and leaching of silica lead to the formation of amorphous clays (e.g., allophane, aluminum, and iron sesquioxides). Organic matter contributes to the weathering process by producing organic acids that exchange hydrogen ions for silica, exchangeable bases (e.g., calcium, magnesium, potassium, sodium), and other ions. Organic matter also interacts with clay particles and promotes their aggregation (flocculation). Because of the relatively young geologic age of the Aguacate and Monteverde Formations, mineral weathering reactions have not occurred to the extent that they have in highly weathered Oxisols and Ultisols in some lowland tropical regions. Those soils have relatively high clay contents and low concentrations of exchangeable bases. Mass wasting and the deposition of ash and other particles from volcanic eruptions periodically contribute to "new," unweathered parent material to the soils of Monteverde.

Undisturbed soils developed on the Aguacate and Monteverde Formations are likely to be similar to udic Andisols at other montane sites in Costa Rica and have low to moderate clay contents. For example, subsoil clay contents along an altitudinal transect on Volcán Barva in the Cordillera Central decreased from 80% at 100 m elevation to less than 10% at 2000 m (Grieve et al. 1990). This pattern is not definitive evidence for decreasing intensity of weathering with altitude; it may also be that younger parent materials occur at higher altitudes on Volcán Barva, a pattern that also occurs in Monteverde.

Soils are typically deep on low-angle slopes and benches of the Monteverde Formation. The upper soil horizons are characterized by high porosity and low bulk density (<0.9 g/cm³), which result in high volumetric moisture contents and hydraulic conductivities when they are saturated. Textures of the A horizon range from silt to sandy loams, with variable amounts of clay. Moist soil is friable, that is, it readily breaks apart when handled. The color of the A horizon is light to dark brown, primarily due to the accumulation of organic matter.

Where it is well differentiated, the B horizon generally has a higher bulk density and lower hydraulic conductivity when compared to the A horizon, reflecting both differences in soil texture and smaller amounts of organic matter. For example, carbon in organic matter decreased from 12% in the A horizon to 5–7% in the B horizon at 1500 m on Volcán Barva (Grieve et al. 1990). In Monteverde, textures of the B horizon range from gravelly to sandy loams. Clay contents typically decrease with depth in the profile, which reflects reduced intensity of weathering reactions. The color of the B horizon is variable, and these differences form the basis for recognizing undifferentiated humic Andisols, and differentiated, or chromic, Andisols. Undifferentiated humic Andisols have no clearly defined soil horizons and are characterized by large amounts of organic matter. For example, studies of leeward cloud forest soils indicated the O and A_1 horizons (ca. 0–20 cm depth) were highly organic. The A_2 and B horizons (ca. 20–180 cm depth) were poorly differentiated, indicating that this soil is a humic Andisol (Vance and Nadkarni 1990). Differentiated or chromic Andisols are characterized by a B horizon that is distinct from the A horizon. In the presence of lesser amounts of acidic organic matter, the relatively slow crystallization of iron oxides produces an ochre color.

The type and amount of electrical charge on soil particles are a function of the clay minerology and the organic matter content. The surface of allophane and iron sequioxides carries a net negative charge and has an affinity for positively charged ions. Organic matter also has a net negative charge and substantially contributes to the overall electrical charge of a soil. The cumulative negative charge per unit mass of a soil is referred to as its cation exchange capacity (CEC). Humic Andisols and Histosols typically have high CECs, but due to weathering reactions and the production of organic acids by organic matter, which results in the leaching of exchangeable bases, a majority of the exchange sites are occupied by hydrogen ions. For example, although the CECs ranged between 590 and 1007 meq/kg in surface soils from 1000 to 2000 m on Volcán Barva, the concentrations of exchangeable bases ranged between 9.5 and 22.1 meq/kg (Grieve et al. 1990). The relatively high concentrations of hydrogen ions on exchange sites also result in moderate to high levels of soil acidity and therefore low pH (see Clark and Nadkarni, "Epiphytic Histosols," pp 34–35). For example, soil pH in the upper soil horizons ranged from 5.4 to 3.0 pH units at other tropical montane sites (Tanner 1977, Zinck 1986, Grieve et al. 1990, Bruijnzeel et al. 1993, Kitayama 1993). Soil pH levels typically increase with depth in the profile.

There is a general increase with altitude in soil organic matter (and therefore soil C and N) in the A and B horizons of tropical montane forests throughout the tropics (e.g., Grubb 1977, Marrs et al. 1988, Grieve et al. 1990, Kitayama 1993). For example, organic matter in soil samples taken at 0–15 cm depth increased from 19% at 100 m to 47% at 2000 m along an altitudinal transect on Volcán Barva (Grieve et al. 1990). At 1500 m and 2000 m, thick amorphous organic material formed a histic horizon to a depth of 50 cm.

On a smaller scale, microclimate also affects soil properties. Physical changes in soils are coincident with exposure to cloud water and precipitation inputs in Monteverde and include persistent waterlogging and increased amounts of organic matter in the A and B horizons.

In many soils, soil organic matter content is positively correlated with clay content, because allophane and other clay particles stabilize organic colloids through physical and chemical interactions (Motavalli et al. 1994, 1995, Ritter et al. 1995). However, the high organic matter content of soils in tropical montane forests is also due to relatively low rates of organic matter decomposition because of lower temperatures and hydric (moist) soil conditions (Jenny 1980), and because of poor litter quality (i.e., high lignin and polyphenol contents, and relatively low N:C and P:C ratios). At the highest elevations in Monteverde, litter from bryophytes (mosses and liverworts) contributes substantially to total litterfall inputs to the forest floor (Nadkarni and Matelson 1992). Due to the high concentrations of polyphenols and aliphatic hydrocarbons in bryophytes, the decomposition rate of bryophyte litter is approximately half that of vascular plant foliage (Clark et al. 1998a). As a result, the large amounts of organic matter in the soils of tropical montane forests typically represent the most significant pools of carbon and nitrogen in the ecosystem (Grieve et al. 1990, Tanner 1977, Marrs et al. 1988, Vance and Nadkarni 1990, Kitayama 1993).

Our understanding of the soils of Monteverde would greatly benefit from a general soil survey. A positive correlation between climate and organic matter exists in soils along altitudinal transects (e.g., Marrs et al. 1988, Grieve et al. 1990, Kitayama 1993). To what extent is this pattern also controlled by parent material and litter quality? How does microclimate, specifically exposure to wind-driven cloudwater and precipitation, interact with other factors in soil formation at Monteverde?

Other questions concern the occurrence of short-statured vegetation, or dwarf forests, in tropical montane sites, which has been attributed to small amounts of available nutrients in soils, particularly nitrogen and phosphorus. To what extent do soil physical properties (e.g., porosity, bulk density, clay content) control soil stability, contribute to mass wasting processes, and control vegetation stature? Although the interaction of factors such as microclimate, soil physical factors, soil nutrient supply, disturbance, and site hydrology is known to influence vegetation stature, explanations for the occurrence of dwarf forests elude ecologists (Grubb 1977, Bruijnzeel and Proctor 1993).

Changes in land use in Monteverde have contributed to changes in carbon and nitrogen storage in soils. The cutting of forests for pastures and other agricultural uses typically involves the removal of the forest floor, but the extent to which organic matter in the A and B horizons is affected has not been studied in Monteverde. How do these practices affect the long-term carbon and nitrogen levels in soil, and how quickly does reforestation restore them?

2.6. Hydrology of Monteverde

The movement and storage of water above, on, and below the earth's surface is called the hydrologic cycle. It forms a key link between the physical environment and living organisms. Given the importance of understanding the movement and storage of water in montane regions, there are astonishingly few data to describe the hydrologic cycle in the Cordillera de Tilarán. Although precipitation records for Monte-

verde extend to 1956, measurements of other elements of the hydrologic cycle are almost entirely lacking. This discussion thus relies on qualitative observations and studies from other areas of the humid tropics.

For a given drainage basin, the hydrologic cycle can be viewed as a system where inputs equal outputs, plus or minus changes in storage. Precipitation and cloud water are the primary inputs; the most significant outputs are evapotranspiration (ET) and streamflow (surface runoff that moves in a definite channel). Evapotranspiration refers to the three major processes that return moisture to the atmosphere in vegetated areas: (1) evaporation of precipitation intercepted by plant surfaces ("interception loss"), (2) transpiration of water through stomata on leaf surfaces, and (3) evaporation of moisture from the soil or open water surfaces. Because it is difficult to separate these pathways, they are commonly treated together as ET (Waring and Schlesinger 1985, Manning 1992).

In the humid tropics, the output from ET and streamflow is nearly continuous. In contrast, precipitation and cloud water events are discrete and may be separated by dry periods of up to several weeks or months. The relationship between precipitation and stream discharge follows a predictable pattern, where discharge is the volume of water moving past a point along a stream over a specific time interval (typically m^3/s; Fig. 2.10). In humid areas such as Monteverde, relatively short periods of higher discharge are associated with precipitation events, followed by longer periods where water is released from storage. Stored

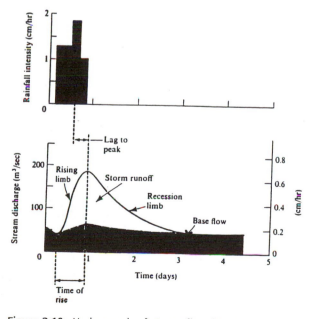

Figure 2.10. Hydrograph of streamflow in response to a rainstorm from a 100-km^2 basin.

water has typically infiltrated into the soil and moves laterally in the shallow subsurface layer.

This relationship between the precipitation event and associated discharge, specifically in the timing and amount of runoff, is affected by climatic conditions, geology, topography, soil characteristics, vegetation type, leaf area, and land use (Dunne and Leopold 1978). The relative importance of these factors varies with precipitation duration and intensity. Because the Monteverde area is within the headwaters of two major drainage basins and contains many primary watersheds, the lag time for peak flows is relatively short compared to areas farther downstream. Even major streams such as the Ríos Peñas Blancas and Guacimal peak and then recede quickly in response to precipitation inputs (Fig. 2.11; Sec. 2.1.3).

2.6.1. Evapotranspiration

Vegetation plays a key role in the hydrology of humid tropical forests (Douglas 1977, Shuttleworth 1989, Grace et al. 1996; Fig. 2.12). Because these forests have relatively high leaf areas and canopies that are essentially closed, virtually all water that reaches the forest floor first comes in contact with the vegetation. This constant contact between precipitation and vegetation also has implications for nutrient cycling (see Chap. 9, Ecosystem Ecology).

Initially, cloud water and precipitation may be stored on plant surfaces ("interception storage"). The volume depends on the form, density, and surface texture of the vegetation and the presence of epiphytes and accumulated organic matter (Dunne and Leopold 1978, Nadkarni 1984, Veneklaas et al. 1990, Ingram and Nadkarni 1993). For example, the canopy of an epiphyte-laden leeward cloud forest stored approximately 8 mm of precipitation, while that of an adjacent second-growth forest (ca. 25 yr old) dominated by *Conostegia* stored <2 mm of precipitation (Clark 1994, K. Clark and N. Nadkarni, unpubl. data). The higher storage capacity of the former site is due to greater leaf area, greater epiphyte mass, and greater water storage on stems. Annual interception loss from the epiphyte-laden leeward cloud forest site was estimated at approximately 1200 mm/yr, representing about 38% of estimated total hydrologic inputs to the canopy (Clark et al. 1998b).

Interception losses of −35% to 35% (negative values represent greater cloud water and mist inputs over precipitation collected with a standard rain gauge) have been reported from a range of tropical montane forests (Bruijnzeel and Proctor 1993). The relatively high interception loss at the leeward cloud forest site

Figure 2.11. The Río Guacimal between the Monteverde Cloud Forest Preserve and the Monteverde dairy plant. Photograph by Stephen Ingram.

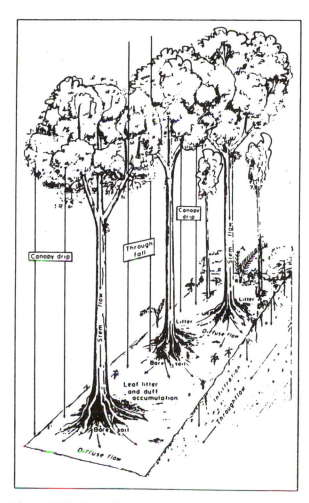

Figure 2.12. Flow of water through the vegetation canopy and the soil in a tropical rain forest.

solar radiation inputs due to cloud cover (Gates 1969, Bruijnzeel and Proctor 1993). Rates of ET of other forests in the MCFP, particularly those on the Pacific slope, are relatively high.

Evapotranspiration from forests alters the microclimate above and within the forest. For example, at a leeward forest 0.5 km northeast of the MCFP, relative humidity was significantly higher within the forest than in a clearing (W. Calvert and A. Nelson, unpubl. data). Estimating annual ET from Monteverde forests is hampered by the lack of data on canopy structure, the unknown role of epiphytes in the ET process, the paucity of meteorological measurements to drive ET models, and the poorly understood environmental and physiological controls over stomatal conductance in montane forest species (e.g., Roberts et al. 1993). Montane forests that receive relatively large wind-driven cloud water and precipitation inputs have calculated ET values of 570–695 mm/yr. Montane forests that receive relatively little wind-driven cloud water and precipitation have ET values of 980–1265 mm/yr (Bruijnzeel and Proctor 1993).

2.6.2. Subsurface Flow and Streamflow

Water that is not evaporated or transpired is stored in the soil, or becomes streamflow or subsurface flow. Monteverde undergoes a pronounced dry season from February through April, yet most streams flow throughout the year. This baseflow is maintained by water seeping out of banks and into streams by means of two pathways. First, it is maintained by throughflow (also termed shallow subsurface flow), defined as water that has infiltrated the soil or parent material and enters the stream channel via subsurface flow paths. Second, streams may intercept the water table. Water entering streams via these pathways typically moves slowly (up to several centimeters per hour or per day) compared to surface water velocities (several meters per second). During periods of high discharge, these two subsurface pathways also contribute significantly to the total volume of runoff. Runoff is also generated from precipitation that flows off the land surface and from precipitation that falls directly on saturated areas adjacent to the channel or onto the surface of the stream (Dunne and Leopold 1978, Ward 1984).

Changes in vegetative cover can affect the timing and peak discharge of flood events and the amount of water that enters the channel as baseflow. In temperate latitudes, tree removal by logging, fire, and wind increases the runoff from the affected area. The magnitude of the increase is roughly proportional to the percentage reduction in tree cover (Dingman 1994) but is also a function of precipitation intensity and

in Monteverde is likely due to intermittent cloud water and precipitation inputs, relatively high windspeeds, high incident solar radiation, and the large water storage capacity of the canopy. Interception loss is likely responsible for a larger proportion of ET for forests exposed to wind-driven cloud water and mist than those lower on the Caribbean and Pacific slopes.

At some precipitation intensity and duration, the storage capacity of the vegetation is exceeded. Increasingly greater amounts of cloud water and precipitation are stored for shorter periods of time on vegetation and then fall to the ground as throughfall or flow down stems as stemflow (Fig. 2.11). Some of the water that falls on the forest infiltrates the litter layer and soil. Roots take up water, which is subsequently transpired through stomata on leaf surfaces. Estimates of ET are lacking for Monteverde, but rates of ET of forest along the Continental Divide are probably relatively lower because of low vapor pressure deficits of the atmosphere, relatively low temperatures, and low duration. The same relationship appears to apply to tropical areas after forests have been logged.

Wind-driven cloud water and precipitation are an important input to the hydrologic cycle of montane forests in the Monteverde area. This source of moisture is significantly reduced when forested lands are cleared, because forests are aerodynamically rough surfaces that catch more of this water (Lovett and Reiners 1986, Monteith and Unsworth 1990). Therefore, the expected increase in runoff may be greater than areas where "occult" precipitation is an important input. More research on this subject in Monteverde is needed.

2.6.3. Erosional Processes

Under undisturbed conditions, the closed canopy and litter layer of forests prevent virtually all rainsplash erosion. When vegetation is removed, however, the cumulative effect of raindrops hitting bare soil can lead to serious erosion problems, especially in areas with steep slopes (Dunne and Leopold 1978). High-speed photography has shown that a raindrop generates a small explosion of soil and water upon impact with the ground; in steep terrain, this material tends to move downslope. When gravelly soils are exposed, rainsplash removes the small particles and leaves the pebbles sitting on top of columns. These are referred to as "capstones" and are common along trails and roads in the Monteverde area. In some cases, especially in pastures, large amounts of soil are removed, leaving behind a surface covered with boulders. As more soil is eroded, each boulder is increasingly exposed. The process is detectable over a period of a few years; local people refer to it as "growing rocks."

If precipitation is of high intensity or long duration, water flows and entrains (transports) soil particles. This process is referred to as sheetwash erosion and may lead to the formation of rills and gullies (Dunne and Leopold 1978). Sheetwash erosion can increase the amount of sediment delivered to a river channel and may have negative impacts. The river channel is formed and maintained by the water and sediment load it carries, but even in undisturbed areas the channel is never large enough to carry all flows without flooding (Dunne and Leopold 1978). Excess sediment can lead to rapid channel adjustments, primarily by causing the river to aggrade (fill in), thus decreasing the cross-sectional area. The river will then flood at lower discharges and/or erode its banks to accommodate the flows delivered to it. These problems are compounded if land-use practices such as deforestation have also increased the volume of runoff.

Because the Monteverde area is located in the headward portions of its drainage basins, the effects of accelerated erosion are primarily on-site, that is, on the scale of a field or a hillslope. In other tropical areas, these effects can be transferred downstream, initiating a cascade of problems (Bruijnzeel 1990). Although erosion problems in the Monteverde area have not reached the point where large volumes of sediment are moved downstream, if serious on-site erosion begins, it may take decades before reductions in surface erosion in upland areas are manifest as a reduction in sedimentation downstream (Bruijnzeel 1990).

Water that infiltrates into the subsurface can also have impacts. Many types of mass wasting are triggered by changes in water pressure generated by the movement of subsurface water. The rate of displacement for slope failures may be slow (e.g., soil creep), on the order of a few centimeters per year, to extremely rapid (e.g., landslides), with speeds in excess of 300 km/hr (Keller 1996). Downslope movement occurs when the gravitational forces acting along the potential failure surface exceed the resistance (or shear strength) of the geologic materials. Subsurface water can increase the pressure in the pore spaces of rock and soil on hillslopes, which in turn reduces their strength or cohesion. Once the downslope force (gravity) exceeds the shear resistance of the material, the hillslope will fail (Dunne and Leopold 1978, Keller 1996; Fig. 2.13). Often, slopes are moved closer to failure by activities such as road-building and removal of vegetation. An increase in water pressure may then become "the straw that breaks the burro's back."

In summary, the forest hydrologic cycle involves complex interactions between the physical environment and the biosphere. The details of many of these interactions, especially in humid tropic forests, are poorly understood. With more land undergoing conversion from forests to other uses, this information is vital to understanding how these systems function and predicting how they will respond to change. In Costa Rica and elsewhere in the humid tropics, forests represent a tremendous resource, but without proper management they will become sources of excess sediment and increased flooding. The cost of reclaiming devastated landscapes can be prohibitive.

Very few hydrologic data are available for the Monteverde area. Many small watersheds in the vicinity could be monitored to determine the relationship between rainfall and runoff for various land uses. The stream that runs near the Estación Biológica is of appropriate size. These studies require that a series of rain gauges be deployed and a discharge-measur-

Figure 2.13. A bulldozer cuts through heavily weathered bedrock to create a road to the San Luis valley below Monteverde. Photograph by Paul Butler.

ing device (e.g., a weir) be installed on the stream at the mouth of the basin. Nonautomated monitoring requires time but is inexpensive in terms of equipment. This type of study can be expanded to quantify other variables of hydrologic significance but would require more funds and expertise. A model is a study of a 10-ha watershed on Barro Colorado Island, which provides insights on the hydrology of the basin based on an evaluation of stream discharge records, precipitation data, and soil analyses (Dietrich et al. 1982b).

MICROCLIMATE VARIABILITY
Kenneth L. Clark & Nalini M. Nadkarni

Microclimate variability across Monteverde is greatest during the transition and dry seasons, primarily because of the high frequency and duration of stratus and stratocumulus cloud immersion along slopes and ridges on the Continental Divide. Cloud water and precipitation depths are substantially greater near the Continental Divide compared to other locations in Monteverde during these seasons (Table 2.2). Cloud immersion at La Ventana typically results in relative humidities of 95–100%, ambient air temperatures of 12–15°C, and low solar radiation inputs compared to clear-sky conditions due to the reflectance and absorption of solar radiation by clouds (K. Clark and N. Nadkarni, unpubl. data).

Table 2.2. Comparison of five precipitation events at two sites in the MCFP.

Weather Conditions	Windspeed[a] (m/s)	Temperature[a] (°C)	Relative Humidity[a] (%)	Precipitation[b] (mm)	Cloud Water + Precipitation[b] (mm)
Stratocumulus cloud, transition season					
Event 1					
Windward	5–10	12.7–17.0	91–97	2.7[c]	74.1
Leeward	2–4	13.0–19.6	78–97	2.7	5.4
Event 2					
Windward	10–15	14.5–17.2	88–97	2.5[c]	108.7
Leeward	2–5	14.9–17.6	74–97	13.3	27.8
Event 3					
Windward	15–20	12.5–17.1	91–97	6.4[c]	114.0
Leeward	4–6	13.6–18.0	79–97	16.1	32.5
Stratus cloud, dry season					
Event 4					
Windward	5–10	15.9–20.0	92–97	trace	4.9
Leeward	2–5	15.9–22.1	78–97	0.7	0.7
Event 5					
Windward	10–15	15.6–17.7	94–97	n.r.	104.7
Leeward	3–6	15.6–21.1	84–97	3.7	9.3

Data are cloud type, season, windspeed, ambient air temperature, relative humidity, and estimated cloud and precipitation deposition for five precipitation events encompassing a range of environmental conditions at two sites in the preserve: a windward cloud forest site located at La Ventana on the Brillante gap (1460 m), and a leeward forest site approximately 1.5 km southwest of the preserve headquarters (1480 m).

[a]Minimum and maximum hourly means.
[b]Total depth for the 24-hr period. Precipitation was sampled with standard rain gauges; cloud water & precipitation was sampled with a cloud water collector (Clark 1994). n.r. = not recorded.
[c]Precipitation depth undersampled due to high windspeeds.

EPIPHYTIC HISTOSOLS
Kenneth L. Clark & Nalini M. Nadkarni

Although of limited distribution, epiphytic Histosol "soils" are one of the most interesting soils in Monteverde. They typically occur on twigs, branches, and stems below epiphytes. The largest accumulations of epiphytic Histosols occur in forests that are exposed to wind-driven cloud water and precipitation in the upper portions of Monteverde. They are derived from epiphytic vegetation, including bryophytes (mosses and liverworts) and vascular epiphytes (foliage, shoots, and roots), and from host trees ("canopy roots" and bark; Nadkarni 1984, Ingram and Nadkarni 1993, Clark et al. 1998a). In contrast to the forest floor, host trees contribute relatively little litterfall to these accumulations (Nadkarni and Matelson 1991). Compared to mineral soils, epiphytic histosols typically have greater carbon and nitrogen contents and lower pH, and are characterized by lower rates of nitrogen mineralization (Vance and Nadkarni 1990; Table 2.3).

Literature Cited

Alvarado, I. G. 1989. Los volcanes de Costa Rica. Editorial Universidad Estatal a Distancia, San José, Costa Rica.

Asbury, C. E., W. H. McDowell, R. Trinidad-Pizarro, and S. Barrios. 1994. Solute deposition from cloud water to the canopy of a Puerto Rican montane forest. Atmospheric Environment 28:1773–1780.

Baynton, H. W. 1968. The ecology of an elfin forest in Puerto Rico. 2. The microclimate of Pico del Oeste. Journal of the Arnold Arboretum 49:419–431.

Bergoeing, J. P., and L. G. Q. Brenes. 1977. Mapa geo-

Table 2.3. Mean percentage of carbon and nitrogen contents, C:N ratios, and pH in arboreal and surface soils from selected montane forest sites.

Location	Sample	% Carbon	% Nitrogen	C:N Ratio	pH
Monteverde, leeward cloud forest[a]	Canopy	37.6	2.4	15.9	3.8
	FF-H	27.0	1.4	18.7	4.6
	A horizon	25.3	1.0	25.8	5.4
Volcán Barva, Costa Rica[b]	0–15 cm (O, A horizons)				
	1000 m	15.7	1.4	11.6	4.4
	1500 m	26.0	1.9	13.7	—
	2000 m	23.0	1.7	13.5	—
Volcán Barva, Costa Rica[c]	0–15 cm (O, A horizons)				
	1000 m	14.6	—	—	4.0
	1500 m	19.0	—	—	3.8
	2000 m	19.6	—	—	3.8
Blue Mountains, Jamaica[d]	0–10 cm				
	West Slope	3.9	0.4	9.8	4.4
	Gap Forest	9.0	0.5	18.0	4.4
	Mull Ridge	29.2	1.7	17.2	3.7
	Mor Ridge	47.4	1.6	29.6	3.0

In Monteverde, canopy samples were from large branches about 20 m above the forest floor, FF-H samples were from the upper 10 cm of the forest floor, and A samples were from 10–20 cm below the forest floor (see Chap. 9 on ecosystem ecology).

[a]N. Nadkarni, unpubl. data.
[b]Marrs et al. 1988.
[c]Grieve et al. 1990.
[d]Tanner 1977. Sample names are those used by Tanner.

morfológico de Costa Rica. Instituto Geográfico Nacional, San José, Costa Rica.

Binford, M. W. 1982. Ecological history of Lake Valencia, Venezuela: interpretation of animal microfossils and some chemical, physical and geological features. Ecological Monographs 52: 307–333.

Bohlman, S. A., T. J. Matelson, and N. M. Nadkarni. 1995. Moisture and temperature patterns of canopy humus and forest floor soil of a montane cloud forest, Costa Rica. Biotropica 27:13–19.

Borgia, A., C. Poore, M. J. Melson, and G. E. Alvarado. 1988. Structural, stratigraphic, and petrologic aspects of the Arenal-Chato volcanic system, Costa Rica: evolution of a young stratovolcanic complex. Bulletin of Volcanology 50:86–105.

Bruijnzeel, L. A. 1990. Hydrology of moist tropical forests and the effects of conversion: a state of knowledge review. Division of Water Sciences, UNESCO, Paris.

Bruijnzeel, L. A., and J. Proctor. 1993. Hydrology and biogeochemistry of tropical montane cloud forests: what do we really know? Pages 25–46 in L. S. Hamilton, J. O. Juvik, and F. N. Scatena, editors. Tropical montane cloud forests: proceedings of an international symposium. East-West Center, Honolulu.

Bruijnzeel, L. A., M. J. Waterloo, J. Proctor, A. T. Kuiters, and B. Kotterink. 1993. Hydrological observations in montane rain forests on Gunung Silam, Sabah, Malaysia, with special reference to the "Massenerhebung" effect. Journal of Ecology 81:145–167.

Burbach, G. V., C. Frohlich, W. D. Pennington, and T. Matumoto. 1984. Seismicity and tectonics of the subducted Cocos Plate. Journal of Geophysical Research 89(B9):7719–7735.

Burke, K. 1988. Tectonic evolution of the Caribbean. Annual Review of Earth and Planetary Science 16:201–230.

Bush, M. B., M. Weinmann, D. R. Piperno, K.-B. Liu, and P. A. Colinvaux. 1990. Pleistocene temperature change and vegetation depression in Ecuadorian Amazonia. Quaternary Research 34:330–345.

Bush, M. B., D. R. Piperno, P. A. Colinvaux, P. E. de Oliveira, L. A. Krissek, M. C. Miller, and W. E. Rowe. 1992. A 14,300-yr paleoecological profile of a lowland tropical lake in Panama. Ecological Monographs 62:251–275.

Carson, M. A., and M. J. Kirkby. 1972. Hillslope form and process. Cambridge University Press, Cambridge.

Castillo-Muñoz, R. 1983. Geology. Pages 47–62 in D. H. Janzen, editor. Costa Rican natural history. University of Chicago Press, Chicago.

Cavelier, J., and G. Goldstein. 1989. Mist and fog interception in elfin cloud forests in Colombia and Venezuela. Journal of Tropical Ecology 5:309–322.

Cavelier, J., D. Solis, and M. A. Jaramillo. 1996. Fog interception in montane forests across the Central Cordillera of Panama. Journal of Tropical Ecology 12:357–369.

Chaves, R., and R. Saenz. 1974. Geología de la Cordillera de Tilarán (Proyecto Aguacate, segunda fase). Informas Tecnicas y Noticias Geológicas 12:1–49. Dirección Geología, Mineralógia, y Petrológia, San José, Costa Rica.

Clark, K. L. 1994. The role of epiphytic bryophytes in the net accumulation and cycling of nitrogen in a tropical montane cloud forest. Ph.D. dissertation, University of Florida, Gainesville.

Clark, K. L., N. M. Nadkarni, and H. L. Gholz. 1998a. Growth, net production, litter decomposition, and net nitrogen accumulation by epiphytic bryophytes in a tropical montane forest. Biotropica 30:12–23.

Clark, K. L., N. M. Nadkarni, D. Schaefer, and H. L. Gholz. 1998b. Atmospheric deposition and net retention of ions by the canopy of a tropical montane forest, Monteverde, Costa Rica. Journal of Tropical Ecology 14:27–45.

Coates, A. G., J. B. C. Jackson, L. S. Collins, T. M. Cronin, H. J. Dowsett, L. M. Bybell, P. Jung, and J. A. Obando.

1992. Closure of the Isthmus of Panama: the near-shore marine record of Costa Rica and western Panama. Geology Society of America Bulletin 104:814–828.

Coen, E. 1983. Climate. Pages 35–46 in D. H. Janzen, editor. Costa Rican natural history. University of Chicago Press, Chicago.

Crozier, M. 1986. Landslides: causes, consequences and environment. Croom Helm, London.

Crump, M. L., F. R. Hensley, and K. L. Clark. 1992. Apparent decline of the golden toad: underground or extinct? Copeia 1992:413–420.

Day, M. J. 1980. Landslides in the Gunung Mulu National Park. Geographical Journal 146:7–13.

DeMets, C., R. G. Gordon, D. F. Argus, and S. Stein. 1990. Current plate motions. Geophysic Journal International 101:425–478.

Dengo, G. 1962. Estudio geológico de la region de Guanacaste, Costa Rica. Instituto Geográfico de Costa Rica, San José, Costa Rica.

———. 1985. Mid America, tectonic setting for the Pacific margin from southern Mexico to northwestern Colombia. Pages 123–180 in A. E. M. Nain and F. G. Stehli, editors. The ocean basins and margins, Vol. 7, The Pacific. Plenum, New York.

Dengo, G., and E. Levy. 1969. Mapa metalogenética de America Central. ICAITI, Guatemala.

Dietrich, W. E., T. Dunne, N. Humphrey, and L. Reid. 1982a. Construction of sediment budgets for drainage basins. General Technical Report PNW-141. U.S. Forest Service, Portland, Oregon.

Dietrich, W. E., D. M. Windsor, and T. Dunne. 1982b. Geology, climate and hydrology of Barro Colorado Island. Pages 21–46 in E. Leigh, A. S. Rand, and D. M. Windsor, editors. The ecology of a tropical forest: seasonal rhythms and long-term changes. Smithsonian Institution, Washington, D.C.

Dietrich, W. E., C. Wilson, D. R. Montgomery, J. M. McKean, and R. Bauer. 1992. Erosion thresholds and land surface morphology. Journal of Geology 20:675–679.

Dingman, S. L. 1994. Physical hydrology. Macmillan, New York.

Dollard, G. J., M. H. Unsworth, and M. J. Harve. 1983. Pollutant transfer in upland regions by occult precipitation. Nature 302:241–243.

Douglas, I. 1977. Humid landforms. Massachusetts Institute of Technology Press, Cambridge, Massachusetts.

Dunne, T., and L. B. Leopold. 1978. Water in environmental planning. Freeman, San Francisco, California.

Escalante, G. 1990. The geology of southern Central America and western Colombia. Pages 201–230 in G. Dengo and J. E. Case, editors. The geology of North America, Vol. H, The Caribbean region. Geological Society of America, Boulder, Colorado.

Gallagher, M. W., K. Beswick, T. W. Choularton, H. Coe, D. Fowler, and K. Hargreaves. 1992. Measurements and modelling of cloudwater deposition to moorland and forests. Environmental Pollution 75:97–107.

Gardner, T. W., D. Verdonck, N. M. Pinter, R. Slingerland, K. P. Furlong, T. F. Bullard, and S. G. Wells. 1992. Quaternary uplift astride the aseismic Cocos Ridge, Pacific coast, Costa Rica. Geological Society of America Bulletin 104:219–232.

Garwood, N. C. 1985. Earthquake-caused landslides in Panama: recovery of the vegetation. National Geographic Society Research Reports 21:181–184.

Garwood, N. C., D. P. Janos, and N. Brokaw. 1979. Earthquake-caused landslides: a major disturbance to tropical forests. Science 205:997–999.

Gates, D. M. 1969. The ecology of an elfin forest in Puerto Rico. 4. Transpiration rates and temperatures of leaves in cool humid environment. Journal of the Arnold Arboretum 50:93–98.

Gomez, L. D. 1986. Vegetación de Costa Rica. Editorial Universidad Estatal a Distancia, San José, Costa Rica.

Grace, J., J. Lloyd, J. McIntyre, A. Miranda, P. Meir, H. Miranda, J. Moncrieff, J. Massheder, I. Wright, and J. Gash. 1996. Fluxes of carbon dioxide and water vapour over an undisturbed tropical forest in south-west Amazonia. Global Change Biology 1:1–12.

Grieve, T. G. A., J. Proctor, and S. A. Cousins. 1990. Soil variation with altitude on Volcán Barva, Costa Rica. Catena 17:525–534.

Grubb, P. J. 1977. Control of forest growth and distribution on wet tropical mountains: with special reference to mineral nutrition. Annual Review of Ecology and Systematics 8:83–107.

Guariguata, M. R. 1990. Landslide disturbance and forest regeneration in the upper Luquillo Mountains of Puerto Rico. Journal of Ecology 78:814–832.

Gupta, R. P., and B. C. Joshi. 1990. Landslide hazard zoning using the GIS approach: a case study from the Ranganga Catchment, Himalayas. Engineering Geology 28:119–131.

Hack, J. T., and J. C. Goodlett. 1960. Geomorphology and forest ecology in the Central Appalachians. Professional Paper 347. U.S. Geological Survey, Washington, D.C.

Herrera, W. 1985. Clima de Costa Rica, Vol. 2, Vegetación y clima de Costa Rica. Editorial Universidad Estatal a Distancia, San José, Costa Rica.

Hooghiemstra, H. 1989. Quaternary and upper-Pliocene glaciations and forest development in the tropical Andes: evidence from a long high-resolution pollen record from the basin of Bogotá. Paleogeography, Paleoclimatology, Paleoecology 72:11–26.

Ingram, S. W., and N. M. Nadkarni. 1993. Composition and distribution of epiphytic organic matter in a neotropical cloud forest, Costa Rica. Biotropica 25:370–383.

Islebe, G. A., H. Hooghiemstra, and K. van der Borg. 1995. A cooling event during the Younger Dryas Chron in Costa Rica. Paleogeography, Paleoclimatology, Paleoecology 117:73–80.

Jenny, H. 1980. The soil resource. Springer, New York.

Jibson, R. W. 1989. Debris flows in Puerto Rico. Pages 29–55 in A. Schultz and R. Jibson, editors. Geological Society of America Special Paper 236. Geological Society of America, Boulder, Colorado.

Jibson, R. W., and D. K. Keeper. 1989. Statistical analysis of factors affecting landslide distribution in the New Madrid seismic zone, Tennessee and Kentucky. Engineering Geology 27:509–542.

Keigwin, L. 1982. Isotopic paleoceanography of the Caribbean and East Pacific: role of Panama uplift in late Neogene time. Science 251:350–353.

Keller, E. A. 1996. Environmental geology (7th ed.). Macmillan, New York.

Kitayama, K. 1993. Biophysical conditions of the montane cloud forests of Mount Kinabalu, Sabah, Malaysia. Pages 115–125 in L. S. Hamilton, J. O. Juvik, and F. N. Scatena, editors. Tropical montane cloud forests: proceedings of an international symposium. East-West Center, Honolulu.

Laguna, J. E. 1985. Posición geotectonica y origen de los magmas productores de las vulcanitas del grupo Aguacate (Costa Rica) por utilización de elementos traza. Brenesia 24:19–29.

LaMarche, V. C. 1968. Rates of slope degradation as determined from botanical evidence, White Mountains, California. Professional Paper 352-I. U.S. Geological Survey, Washington, D.C.

Lawton, R. O., and V. Dryer. 1980. The vegetation of the Monteverde Cloud Forest Preserve. Brenesia 18:101–116.

Leyden, B. W. 1984. Guatemalan forest synthesis after Pleistocene aridity. Proceedings of the National Academy of Sciences USA 81:4856–4859.

Lovett, G. M., and W. A. Reiners. 1986. Canopy structure and cloud water deposition in subalpine coniferous forests. Tellus 38B:319–327.

Lundberg, N. 1982. Evolution of the slope landward of the Middle American Trench, Nicoya Peninsula, Costa Rica. Pages 131–147 in J. K. Legget, editor. Trench-forearc geology. Special Publication 10. Geological Society of London.

———. 1991. Detrital record of the early Central American magmatic arc: petrography of intraoceanic forearc sandstones, Nicoya Peninsula, Costa Rica. Geological Society of America Bulletin 103:905–915.

Manning, J. C. 1992. Applied principles of hydrology (2nd ed.). Macmillan, New York.

Marrs, R. H., J. Proctor, A. Heaney, and M. D. Mountford. 1988. Changes in soil nitrogen-mineralization and nitrification along an altitudinal transect in tropical rain forest in Costa Rica. Journal of Ecology 76:466–482.

Marshall, J. S., and R. S. Anderson. 1995. Quaternary uplift and seismic cycle deformation, Peninsula de Nicoya, Costa Rica. Geological Society of America Bulletin 107:463–473.

Marshall, L. G., S. D. Webb, J. J. Sepkoski, and D. M. Raup. 1982. Mammalian evolution and the great American interchange. Science 251:1351–1357.

McIntosh, K., E. Silver, and T. Shipley. 1993. Evidence and mechanisms for forearc extension at the accretionary Costa Rica convergent margin. Tectonics 12:1380–1392.

Minster, J. B., and T. H. Jordan. 1978. Present day plate motions. Journal of Geophysical Research 81: 5331–5354.

Monteith, J. L., and M. H. Unsworth. 1990. Principles of environmental physics. Arnold Press, London.

Motavalli, P. P., C. A. Palm, W. J. Parton, E. T. Elliot, and S. D. Frey. 1994. Comparison of laboratory and modeling simulation methods for estimating soil carbon pools in tropical forest soils. Soil Biology and Biochemistry 26:935–944.

Motavalli, P. P., W. J. Parton, E. T. Elliot, S. D. Frey, and P. C. Smithson. 1995. Nitrogen mineralization in humid tropical forest soils: minerology, texture, and measured nitrogen fractions. Soil Science Society of America 59:1168–1175.

Myster, R. W., and D. S. Fernandez. 1995. Spatial gradients and patch structure on two Puerto Rican landslides. Biotropica 27:149–159.

Nadkarni, N. M. 1984. Epiphytic biomass and nutrient capital of a neotropical elfin forest. Biotropica 16:249–256.

Nadkarni, N. M., and T. J. Matelson. 1991. Dynamics of fine litterfall within the canopy of a tropical cloud forest, Monteverde. Ecology 72:2071–2082.

———. 1992. Biomass and nutrient dynamics of epiphytic litterfall in a neotropical cloud forest, Monteverde, Costa Rica. Biotropica 24:24–30.

Raup, H. M. 1957. Vegetational adjustment and the instability of the site. Pages 36–48 in Proceedings and papers of the technical meeting, International Union of the Conservation of Nature and Natural Resources, Edinburgh, Scotland.

Riehl, H. 1979. Climate and weather in the tropics. Academic Press, New York.

Ritter, D. F., R. C. Kochel, and J. R. Miller. 1995. Brown, Dubuque, Iowa.

Roberts, J., O. M. R. Cabral, G. Fisch, L. C. B. Molion, C. J. Moore, and W. J. Shuttleworth. 1993. Transpiration from an Amazonian rain forest calculated from stomatal conductance measurements. Agricultural and Forest Meteorology 65:175–196.

Shuttleworth, W. J. 1989. Micrometeorology of temperate and tropical forest. Proceedings of the Royal Society of London B224:299–334.

Sigafoos, R. S. 1964. Botanical evidence of floods and flood plain deposition. Professional Paper 485–A. U.S. Geological Survey, Washington, D.C.

Simonett, D. S. 1967. Landslide distribution and earthquakes in the Bewani and Torricelli Mountains, New Guinea. Pages 64–84 in J. N. Jennings and J. A. Mabbutt, editors. Landform studies from Australia and New Guinea. Cambridge University Press, Cambridge.

Soto, R., coordinador. 1992. Evaluación ecologico rapido. Elaborado por Fundación Neotropica, Programa Boscosa, San José, Costa Rica.

Stadtmüller, T. 1987. Cloud forests in the humid tropics: a bibliographic review. Centro Agronomico Tropical de Investigación y Enseñanza, Turrialba, Costa Rica.

Swanston, D. N. 1969. Mass wasting in coastal Alaska. U.S.D.A. Forest Service Research Paper PNW-83. Pacific Northwest Forest and Range Experiment Station, Portland, Oregon.

———. 1970. Mechanics of debris avalanching in shallow till soils of southeast Alaska. U.S.D.A. Forest Service Research Paper PNW-103. Pacific Northwest Forest and Range Experiment Station, Portland, Oregon.

———. 1974. The forest ecosystem of southeast Alaska: 5. Soil mass movement. U.S.D.A. Forest Service General Technical Report PNW-17. Pacific Northwest Forest and Range Experiment Station, Portland, Oregon.

Tanner, E. V. J. 1977. Four montane rain forests of Jamaica: a quantitative characterization of the floristics, the soils and the foliar mineral levels, and a discussion of the interrelations. Journal of Ecology 65:883–918.

Troeh, F. R., and L. M. Thompson. 1993. Soils and soil fertility (5th ed.). Oxford University Press, New York.

Vance, E. D., and N. M. Nadkarni. 1990. Microbial biomass and activity in canopy organic matter and the forest floor of a tropical cloud forest. Soil Biology and Biochemistry 22:677–684.

van der Hammen, T. 1974. The Pleistocene changes of vegetation and climate in tropical South America. Journal of Biogeography 1:3–26.

Vargas Ulate, G. 1994. El clima de Costa Rica: contraste de dos vertientes. Editorial Guayacan, San José, Costa Rica.

Veblen, T. T., F. M. Schlegel, and B. Escobar. 1980. Structure and dynamics of old-growth Nothofagus forests in the Valdevian Andes, Chile. Journal of Ecology 68:1–31.

Veneklaas, E. J., R. J. Zagt, A. Van Leerdam, R. Van Ek, A. J. Broekhoven, and M. Van Genderen. 1990. Hydrological properties of the epiphyte mass of a montane tropical rain forest. Vegetatio 89:183–192.

Vitousek, P. M., and R. L. Sanford, Jr. 1986. Nutrient cycling in moist tropical forest. Annual Review of Ecology and Systematics 17:137–167.

Vogelmann, H. W. 1973. Fog interception in the cloud forest of eastern Mexico. Bioscience 23:96–100.

Vong, R. J., and A. S. Kowalski. 1995. Eddy correlation measurements of size-dependent cloud droplet turbulent fluxes to complex terrain. Tellus 47B:331–352.

Vong, R. J., J. T. Sigmon, and S. F. Mueller. 1991. Cloud water deposition to Appalachian forests. Environmental Science and Technology 25:1014–1021.

Wadge, G., and K. Burke. 1983. Neogene Caribbean plate rotation and associated Central American tectonic evolution. Tectonics 2:633–643.

Ward, R. C. 1984. On response to precipitation of headwater streams in humid areas. Journal of Hydrology 74:171–189.

Waring, R. A., and W. Schlesinger. 1985. Forest ecosystems: concepts and management. Academic Press, San Diego.

Wentworth, C. K. 1943. Soil avalanches on Oahu. Bulletin of the Geological Society of America 54:53–64.

White, S. E. 1949. Processes of erosion on steep slopes of Oahu, Hawaii. American Journal of Science 247:168–186.

Yoshikawa, T. 1974. Denudation and tectonic movement in contemporary Japan. Bulletin of the Department of Geography of the University of Tokyo 6:1–14.

Yoshikawa, T., S. Kaizuka, and Y. Ota. 1981. The landforms of Japan. University of Tokyo Press, Tokyo.

Zadroga, F. 1981. The hydrological importance of a montane cloud forest area of Costa Rica. Pages 59–73 *in* R. Lal and E. W. Russell, editors. Tropical agricultural hydrology. Wiley, New York.

Zinck, A. 1986. Los suelos. Caracteristicas y fragilidad de los suelos en ambiente de selva nublada: el ejemplo de Rancho Grande. Pages 31–66 *in* O. Huber, editor. La selva nublada de Rancho Grande Parque Nacional "Henri Pittier." Fondo Editorial Acta Cientifica Venezolana, Caracas, Venezuela.

3

Plants and Vegetation

William A. Haber

3.1. Distribution and Diversity

3.1.1. Overview of the Vegetation

The vegetation at Monteverde is characterized by two features that are immediately noted by visitors. The first is the overwhelming abundance of mosses, epiphytes, and tree trunk climbers in the cloud forest (Fig. 3.1). The second is the striking variety of vegetation types, and consequent very high regional plant biodiversity, cramped into a small area by the narrow elevational zonation of habitats along the upper mountain slopes. This luxuriance and diversity have been important factors in the attraction of biologists to Monteverde.

Lawton and Dryer (1980) described the characteristics and distribution of forest types in the upper Monteverde Cloud Forest Preserve (MCFP), emphasizing the effect of the northeast trade winds on forest structure. With exposure to the trade winds and the accompanying heavy mist and clouds, the forest is reduced in height, has a more broken canopy, and supports greater epiphyte loads. Areas in the lee of the winds develop a forest with less abundant epi-

phytes and mosses and much taller, straighter trees, forming a closed canopy and more open understory while the strong winds apparently limit the stature of the forest on the exposed ridges, the mist and rain carried in from the Atlantic side during the dry season maintain the diverse epiphyte community of the upper Pacific slope. In contrast, a short walk down the Pacific slope during the dry season leads to progressively drier vegetation zones where ferns, epiphytes, and climbers nearly disappear. Hartshorn (1983) described vegetation in the zones below the cloud forest, with a description of the Holdridge life zone system (Holdridge 1967) and the life zones in Monteverde.

In this chapter, the focal area of the vegetation is the study area of the Monteverde Flora Project, which is more extensive than the area covered in the references cited above. The aim of the Monteverde Flora, a project of the Missouri Botanical Garden in collaboration with the Manual to the Plants of Costa Rica Project, is to collect and identify the flora of the Monteverde area and produce identification guides. The study area extends from the peaks and ridges on the Continental Divide in Monteverde (1500–1850 m) down to 700 m on both the

Figure 3.1. *Vriesia umbrosa* and other epiphytes crowd the trunk of a tree in the Monteverde Cloud Forest Preserve. Photograph by Stephan Ingram.

Atlantic and Pacific slopes (Fig.1.8). This study area includes the MCFP, the Santa Elena Ecological Reserve, and the Bosque Eterno de los Niños (including Bajo del Tigre), part of Arenal National Park, and private lands in the buffer zone surrounding the Monteverde Reserve Complex. Most of the San Ramón Forest Reserve has been excluded because of the difficulty of access from Monteverde. Nearly all of the study area falls within the premontane and lower montane life zones. A small area of life zones in the tropical belt extends above the 700 m contour in the San Luis valley below Monteverde and in the Peñas Blancas valley on the Atlantic slope. All of this area (ca. 450 km²) is within a day's walk (25 km radius) from Monteverde.

Historically, nearly the entire Monteverde region was covered by closed canopy forest. No natural savannas or grasslands occurred in the area; all current non-forested areas were created by humans through cutting and fire. The dry savanna-like habitat along the road to Monteverde from the Inter-American Highway is maintained by cattle grazing and clearing with machete, chainsaw, and fire. Areas that have not been cut or burned for two years are quickly colonized by shrubs and tree saplings. The extent of forest clearing in this area by indigenous inhabitants is unknown, but it may have been substantial, as suggested by the widespread occurrence of pottery fragments (see Timm, "Prehistoric Cultures," p. 408). No extensive marshes occur in the zone, but a few small lakes lie within the protected area on the Atlantic slope: Laguna Escondida (near Eladio's Refuge), Laguna Poco Sol (near the Poco Sol Field Station) in the Río Peñas Blancas valley, and a small crater lake on top of Cerro Bekom near the source of the Río La Esperanza (south of the Río Peñas Blancas). Before it was dammed and flooded, Laguna de Arenal was a marshy pasture grazed by cattle with only a small area of open water (W. Haber, pers. obs., R. Soto, pers. comm.).

3.1.2. Vegetation Types

The forest habitats in the Monteverde area fall into three general vegetation types: (1) seasonally dry but mostly evergreen forest on the Pacific slope in the rain shadow of the higher peaks and ridges of the Continental Divide below 1500 m, (2) perpetually dripping cloud forest on the mountain top from 1500 to 1850 m on the Pacific slope and down to 1400 m on the Atlantic slope, and (3) nearly aseasonal rain forest on the Atlantic slope below 1400 m. The change in vegetation parallels a gradient in increasing moisture from the Pacific to the Atlantic side. Increase in moisture is partly due to an increase in annual rainfall toward the Continental Divide and Atlantic slope (see Chap. 2, Physical Environment), but cloud condensation and wind-borne mist that occur in the cloud forest during the dry season also form important components of the moisture regime in the Tilarán Mountains. These three forest types are divided into seven life zones (Holdridge 1966, 1967, 1978, Tosi 1969, Bolaños and Watson 1993) and a series of edaphic and atmospheric vegetation types within the life zones.

Pacific slope seasonal forest.   Extending from about 700 m to 1500 m, this area receives an annual rainfall of 2000–2500 mm and experiences a 5–6-month dry season. Except for areas close to the divide (e.g., upper Río San Luis), little moisture comes in from wind-blown mists during the dry season. The forest is mostly evergreen, with a few deciduous species that remain leafless for 1–3 months. Less than 10% of the canopy is leafless during the dry season. With a height of 25–40 m, the forest is composed of tall straight trees forming a closed canopy with a fairly open understory made up of shrubs, treelets, and tree saplings. Herbs are scarce, except in wet spots, and a layer of dry leaf litter accumulates on the ground. Epiphytes are uncommon below 1400 m, but they occur as scattered individuals or in dense mats on large exposed branches. This area includes the premontane moist and premontane wet forest life zones, and small extensions of the tropical moist forest life zone. The communities of Monteverde, Santa Elena, and San Luis, and all of the villages lying northwest as far as Tilarán occur within this zone.

Cloud forest.   Most of the area above 1500 m in elevation on the Pacific slope (above the communities of Monteverde, Santa Elena, La Cruz, and Las Nubes) up to the Continental Divide and extending down to 1300–1400 m on the Atlantic slope supports a luxurious cloud forest. With annual rainfall of 2500–3500 mm and frequent mist and cloud cover in the dry season, this evergreen forest remains wet throughout the year. Leaf litter in the understory rarely dries out for more than a few days, usually near the end of the dry season in March or April. Canopy height varies from 20 to 40 m in sheltered sites to 5–10 m in the elfin forest on ridges and peaks exposed to the trade winds. The forest is characterized by a diverse and abundant epiphyte community, a more broken canopy than on the Pacific slope, and a dense understory of shrubs, treelets, and large herbs (Nadkarni et al. 1995, Matelson et al. 1995). The cloud forest habitat includes the lower montane wet forest and lower montane rain forest life zones. No towns or villages occur in this vegetation zone in the Monteverde region.

Atlantic slope rain forest.   The forest on the Atlantic slope below 1400 m receives annual rainfall ranging between 3500 mm and more than 7000 mm (measured at Eladio's Refuge in the Peñas Blancas valley at 820 m; M. Fogden, pers. comm.). The rain in this area is well distributed through the year, resulting in an almost aseasonal climate. A barely noticeable drier period occurs during March and April. Canopy height (20–40 m) varies with exposure to the trade winds and steepness of the terrain. Forest stands with the largest trees and least broken canopy occur in sheltered valleys and on gentle slopes below 1200 m where huge buttressed trees commonly exceed 50 m in height. On exposed steep ridges, the forest is reduced to 15–20 m in height with a broken canopy, straggly structure, and low diversity. The Atlantic slope ridges appear to receive more precipitation as mist and drizzle; the valleys experience more rain in the form of thundershowers. The life zones in this area include premontane wet forest, premontane rain forest, and tropical wet forest–premontane transition (Tosi 1969, Bolaños and Watson 1993).

3.1.3. Life Zones

Seven of Costa Rica's twelve life zones are represented in the Monteverde area (Tosi 1969, Hartshorn 1983, Bolaños and Watson 1993; Fig. 1.4). Life zones are defined on the basis of mean annual temperature and rainfall data (Table 3.1). Because the life zone system does not incorporate the seasonal distribution of rainfall, variation in vegetation may occur within a life zone in the Monteverde area, depending on exposure of the site to the trade winds in the dry season versus protection from the winds in the rain shadow of the Tilarán Mountain peaks. Although the life zone system provides a useful classification method, life zones do not have sharp boundaries; they blend into one another along the gradients of temperature, moisture, and elevation. In the descriptions of the Monteverde life zones that follow, Spanish language names and

Table 3.1. Characteristics of the Holdridge life zones occurring at Monteverde.

Life Zone	Elevation (m)	Mean Annual Rainfall (mm)	Mean annual Temperature (°C)	Dry Season Duration (months)	Canopy Height (m)
Tropical moist forest (premontane transition)	600–800	1950–3000	21.5–24	0–5	30–40
Premontane moist forest	700–1000	1200–2200	17–24	3.5–5	ca. 25
Premontane wet forest	800–1450	2000–4000	17–24	0–5	30–40
Lower montane wet forest	1450–1600	1850–4000	12–17	0–3	25–35
Lower montane rain forest	1550–1850	3600–8000	12–17	0–3	20–30
Premontane rain forest	700–1400	4000–7000	17–24	0–2	30–40
Tropical wet forest (premontane transition)	0–700	4000–5500	21.5–24	0–3.5	30–50

The life zones are arranged in sequence along a transect across the mountains from the Pacific slope to the Atlantic slope.

Source: Data are from Bolaños and Watson (1993).

codes, as they appear on the life zone maps published in Costa Rica, are shown in parentheses. Tree species that are common or characteristic of each life zone in Monteverde are listed in Table 3.2.

Tropical moist forest–transition to premontane (bosque húmedo–Tropical [bh-T] and bh-TΔ, transición a premontano). This life zone forms a broad band along the Pacific slope of the Tilarán Mountains from near the Inter-American Highway to about 700–800 m. The narrow, northern edge is classified as a transition to premontane. The boundary between the typical tropical moist forest zone and its premontane transition lies halfway between the villages of San Luis and Guacimal. The Chepe Rojas farm, which forms part of the MCFP Corridor system, is within the transition zone 2–4 km downriver from the San Luis bridge; it protects the largest fragment of this forest type in the area. Another small band of this transition zone occurs in the hills at the northwest end of Laguna de Arenal. This life zone experiences a dry season ranging from 0 to 5 months; on the Pacific slope below Monteverde, the dry season lasts almost 6 months (mid-November to mid-May). The natural forest is mostly evergreen, and epiphytes are common. Soils are well suited for agriculture (Bolaños and Watson 1993).

Premontane moist forest (bosque húmedo–Premontano [bh-P]). This life zone occurs on the Pacific slope at 700–1000 m in a band 2 km × 11 km from Los Cerros northwest to the village of San Rafael, and extending into the upper canyon of the Río Guacimal below Monteverde, between 900 and 1100 m in the lower part of Bajo del Tigre. This drier habitat (at the same elevation as the premontane wet forest zone results from a rain shadow caused by the high plateau and peaks above Monteverde (Cerros Amigos, Chomogo, and Sin Nombre). The natural vegetation is evergreen forest with a small component of deciduous species and relatively few epiphytes. Only scattered small

fragments of this forest remain in the area. This life zone, which also covers a large part of the Central Valley around San José, Heredia, and Alajuela, may have the most favorable climate in the country for humans (Bolaños and Watson 1993). The soils support a diversity of agricultural activities, predominantly coffee cultivation.

Premontane wet forest (bosque muy húmedo–Premontano [bmh-P]). This life zone forms a wide band along the Pacific slope from about 800 to 1500 m, encompassing the communities of Monteverde, Santa Elena, and most of the San Luis valley. Straddling both slopes, this life zone spans a range in climate from the highly seasonal San Luis valley to the constantly wet Atlantic slope above Laguna de Arenal. The range of a few tree species spans this life zone, despite its diverse climate regime (Table 3.2). The natural vegetation is an evergreen forest with a few deciduous species, especially on the Pacific slope, with moderate epiphyte diversity and abundance. Primary tracts of this forest type occur within the Monteverde community and downslope into the upper San Luis valley and across the San Luis River into the Buen Amigo area. Most of the towns and villages in the Monteverde region are located within this life zone. The soil and climate are well suited to agriculture (Bolaños and Watson 1993). Most of the locally grown coffee is produced here. Although this life zone is not considered cloud forest, during the wet season the area surrounding the Monteverde community receives an almost daily bath of ground-level clouds from the Pacific side.

The high ridge extending northwest from Las Nubes to La Chirripa (900–1200 m) is classified as a zone of transition between premontane wet and premontane rain forest (bmh-PΔ). An undescribed species of Fabaceae (*Dalbergia tilarana* N. Zamora, ined.) grows on this ridge and has not been been found anywhere else. This forest type also occurs above the town of La Tigra near the villages of San Gerardo and

Los Cerritos, reaching to the Peñas Blancas River at 300–500 m. The classification of this transition zone is based on its annual rainfall being higher (4000–4500 mm) than premontane wet forest (Table 3.1).

Lower montane wet forest (bosque muy húmedo–Montano bajo [bmh-MB]).   This life zone is found in a restricted area of the upper Pacific slope (1450–1600 m), extending from the lower part of the MCFP above Monteverde to Las Nubes, including the upper Río Negro and Río Chiquito drainages. The dry season is ameliorated by the frequent mists that waft over the Continental Divide from the Atlantic side from November to February after the orographic wet season rains have ended. The mist fosters a diverse and abundant epiphyte community and maintains the lush character of this forest through the distinct dry period. This climate supports a tall dense cloud forest (30–40 m). The lower parts of the Nuboso and Río trails in the MCFP fall within this life zone. Although stands of this forest remain in the Monteverde area, the extent of this life zone is small. This life zone provides the main breeding habitat for the Resplendent Quetzal (Wheelwright 1983). The frequent precipitation and cloud cover limit agriculture (primarily milk production) in this life zone.

Lower montane rain forest (bosque pluvial–Montano bajo [bp-MB]).   This life zone occurs above the lower montane wet forest on the high peaks and ridges of the Continental Divide from 1550 to 1850 m in elevation, and along the high ridges that skirt each side of the Río Peñas Blancas valley. The high areas of the MCFP and the Santa Elena Ecological Reserve also lie within this life zone. Wind-blown mist and cloud cover are integral components of the climate. This zone typifies the cloud forest: dense vegetation with a broken canopy 15–30 m high. Epiphytes form dense mats that cover the trunks and branches. The high rainfall, humidity, and cloudy weather restrict agricultural activities in this life zone. Many attempts to use the land for cattle pasture and agriculture have been unsuccessful.

Premontane rain forest (bosque pluvial–Premontano [bp-P]).   This life zone covers most of the Atlantic slope between 700 and 1400 m in the Río Peñas Blancas and Río Caño Negro watersheds. It includes the area of the San Gerardo Field Station, the Alemán Refuge, Eladio's Refuge, and the Poco Sol Field Station. The natural vegetation is dense evergreen forest with the canopy at 30–40 m in height, abundant epiphytes, and high biodiversity. The excessive rainfall and high humidity make agriculture and human habitation difficult and unpleasant. In Monteverde, this life zone is used mainly during the Pacific slope dry season for pasturing dairy cows that are out of milk production.

Tropical wet forest—transition to premontane (bosque muy húmedo–Tropical [bmh-T], transición a premontano [bmh-TΔ]).   Tropical wet forest occurs along the Río Peñas Blancas below 700 m, northwest along the

Figure 3.2. Cloud forest silhouette. Photograph by Tom Blagdon.

Table 3.2. Common or characteristic tree species of the life zones in the Monteverde area.

1. Tropical Moist Forest	2. Premontane Moist Forest	3. Premontane Wet Forest	4. Lower Montane Wet Forest
Anacardium excelsum	*Agonandra macrocarpa*	*Beilschmiedia brenesii*	*Ardisia palmana*
Ardisia revoluta	*Albizia adinocephala*	*Billia colombiana*	*Beilschmiedia*
Astronium graveolens	*Beilschmiedia* sp.	*Cecropia obtusifolia*	*costaricensis*
Beilschmiedia sp.	*Bravaisia integerrima*	*Cedrela tonduzii*	*Casearia tacanensis*
Bombacopsis quinatum	*Bursera simaruba*	*Chionanthus panamensis*	*Chione sylvicola*
Brosimum alicastrum	*Byrsonima crassifolia*	*Cinnamomum*	*Citharexylum caudatum*
Croton draco	*Casimiroa edulis*	*cinnamomifolium*	*Cojoba costaricensis*
Capparis	*Chrysophyllum brenesii*	*Citharexylum*	*Conostegia oerstediana*
cynophallophora	*Cinnamomum brenesii*	*integerrimum*	*Conostegia pittieri*
Cecropia peltata	*Clarisia biflora*	*Conostegia xalapensis*	*Dendropanax querceti*
Cecropia obtusifolia	*Clethra lanata*	*Croton mexicanus*	*Dussia* sp.
Cedrela salvadorensis	*Cordia alliodora*	*Dendropanax arboreus*	*Eugenia guatemalensis*
Ceiba aesculifolia	*Cordia stellifera*	*Eugenia monticola*	*Eugenia octopleura*
Clarisia biflora	*Cupania guatemalensis*	*Exothea paniculata*	*Guarea tonduzii*
Cupania guatemalensis	*Dilodendron costaricense*	*Ficus tuerckheimii*	*Hasseltia floribunda*
Erblichia odorata	*Diphysa americana*	*Gymnosporia haberiana*	*Inga micheliana*
Eugenia salamensis	*Drypetes lateriflora*	*Inga sierrae*	*Matayba* sp.
Ficus citrifolia	*Ficus laterisyce*	*Matayba oppositifolia*	*Maytenus reconditus*
Ficus trachelosyce	*Ilex haberi*	*Meliosma idiopoda*	*Meliosma vernicosa*
Ficus yoponensis	*Licaria triandra*	*Mortoniodendron*	*Mortoniodendron*
Hura crepitans	*Lonchocarpus oliganthus*	*costaricense*	*costaricense*
Lonchocarpus haberi,	*Luehea speciosa*	*Nectandra membranacea*	*Myrcianthes fragrans*
ined.	*Manilkara chicle*	*Ocotea floribunda*	*Ocotea insularis*
Nectandra martinicensis	*Myrcianthes* sp.	*Ocotea monteverdensis*	*Ocotea meziana*
Ochroma pyramidale	*Nectandra salicina*	*Ocotea whitei*	*Persea americana*
Ocotea veraguensis	*Ocotea sinuata*	*Pouteria exfoliata*	*Pleurothyrium*
Picramnia antidesma	*Psidium sartorianum*	*Randia matudae*	*palmanum*
Sideroxylon capiri	*Roupala montana*	*Roupala glaberrima*	*Pouteria fossicola*
Terminalia oblonga	*Sapium macrocarpum*	*Sapium laurifolium*	*Quararibea costaricensis*
Thouinidium decandrum	*Sideroxylon persimile*	*Sideroxylon*	*Sapium glandulosum*
Trichilia glabra	*Styrax argenteus*	*stenospermum*	*Sloanea ampla*
Trichilia martiana	*Zanthoxylum*	*Stauranthus perforatus*	*Symplocos brenesii*
Triplaris	*monophyllum*	*Styphnolobium*	*Weinmannia wercklei*
malaenodendron		*monteviridis*	
		Symplocos limoncillo	

foothills of the San Bosco area to Volcán Arenal above La Fortuna, and around the southeast end of Laguna de Arenal (Bolaños and Watson 1993; Fig.1.5). With the canopy height at 40–50 m and emergents that reach 55–60 m, this forest presents a majestic aspect with the feel of "real rain forest" (Fig. 3.2). It is evergreen, with few deciduous species. Trees with straight trunks and large buttresses are common; epiphytes and lianas are abundant. Vegetable farming and production of ornamentals and beef cattle are successful in this life zone.

3.1.4. Soil, Microclimatic, and Human-Generated Associations within Life Zones

Ridges and canyons. On the Pacific slope, trees characteristic of higher elevation cloud forest tend to grow at lower elevations in steep stream canyons where conditions are moister and cooler than on the sur-

rounding ridges. Some tree species typical of drier habitats on the Pacific slope ascend along exposed, well-drained ridge crests, which are exposed to the desicating trade winds during the dry season. These ridges also sustain "ridge specialists," species that occur almost exclusively on the sharp dry ridges that descend the Pacific slope (Table 3.3). Some of these are endemic to the area and are still undescribed (e.g., *Myrcianthes* sp., *Ilex* sp.). Several species common on the wet Atlantic slope survive in moist canyons and as riparian species (e.g., *Lunania mexicana, Ticodendron incognitum, Trophis mexicana*).

Rock ridges. Dry rocky ridges on the Pacific slope below Monteverde support plants typical of much drier habitats at lower elevations (Table 3.3), some of which are found on limestone ridges behind the field station in Palo Verde National Park at 100 m (e.g., *Euphorbia schlechtendalii, Plumeria rubra*). Most are

5. Lower Montane Rain Forest	6. Premontane Rain Forest	7. Tropical Wet Forest–Transition
Alchornea latifolia	Allophylus psilospermus	Acacia ruddiae
Ardisia solomonii	Bourreria costaricensis	Albizia carbonaria
Billia hippocastanum	Capparis discolor	Alchornea costaricensis
Brunellia costaricensis	Cecropia insignis	Alchornea glandulosa
Calyptranthes monteverdensis, ined.	Cedrela tonduzii	Calatola costaricensis
Cecropia polyphlebia	Chrysophyllum hirsutum	Cespedesia macrophylla
Conostegia rufescens	Citharexylum donnell-smithii	Chimarrhis parviflora
Dendropanax latilobus	Cupania sp.	Chionanthus oblanceolatus
Elaeagia auriculata	Elaeagia uxpanapensis	Chomelia venulosa
Eugenia valerii	Guarea kunthiana	Croton megistocarpus
Ficus crassiuscula	Inga leonis	Dussia sp.
Guarea kunthiana	Lunania mexicana	Ficus crassivenosa
Guettarda poasana	Meliosma glabrata	Hedyosmum bonplandianum
Ilex costaricensis	Meliosma vernicosa	Inga barbourii
Inga longispica	Mortoniodendron anisophyllum	Iriartea deltoidea
Magnolia poasana	Naucleopsis capirensis	Jacaratia spinosa
Ocotea cf. viridiflora	Ocotea tonduzii	Mortoniodendron anisophyllum
Ocotea near insularis	Ocotea meziana	Ocotea dentata
Persea schiedeana	Pleuranthodendron lindenii	Ocotea stenoneura
Podocarpus monteverdeensis	Pleurothyrium palmanum	Oreomunnea pterocarpa
Prestoea acuminata	Pouteria austin-smithii	Otoba novogranatensis
Prunus brachybotrys	Pseudolmedia mollis	Pachira aquatica
Quercus corrugata	Psychotria eurycarpa	Pentagonia costaricensis
Ruagea glabra	Pterocarpus cf. rohrii	Platymiscium sp.
Salacia petenensis	Quararibea costaricensis	Pouteria congestifolia
Sapium rigidifolium	Rauvolfia aphlebia	Sapium rigidifolium
Symplocos povedae	Sapium laurifolium	Sloanea ligulata
Tovomitopsis allenii	Sapium rigidifolium	Terminalia bucidoides
Viburnum venustum	Ticodendron incognitum	Theobroma mammosum
Weinmannia pinnata	Trichilia martiana	Vochysia guatemalensis
Zanthoxylum melanostictum	Trophis mexicana	Zinowiewia costaricensis

leafless during the dry season, including two species of bromeliads (*Pitcairnia heterophylla* and *P. maidifolia*), which grow on bare exposed rocks. Several species of orchids and evergreen succulent lithophytes (plants that grow on rocks) also grow on these ridges (e.g., *Echeveria australis, Furcraea cabuya, Selenicereus wercklei*). A few species of ferns and their relatives are also characteristic of these dry sites (e.g., *Selaginella pallescens, Polypodium* spp.).

Elfin forest. High peaks and ridges exposed to the mist-laden trade winds support a type of forest that is reduced in height and characterized by short, dense, gnarled trees whose trunks are covered in thick mats of bryophytes. This elfin woodland or dwarf forest ("bosque enano") is composed of species more characteristic of higher elevations, some of which grow as epiphytic shrubs in nearby leeward forest (Table 3.3). Examples include *Clusia* spp., *Schefflera rodrigue-*

ziana, and *Cosmibuena valerii*. The canopy of the elfin forest can be extremely uniform, combed smooth by the strong northeast trade winds. In other spots, the canopy is low and broken by occasional straggly emergent trees. The dynamics of this forest have been well studied (Lawton 1980, 1982, 1984, 1990, Lawton and Putz 1988; see Chap. 9, Ecosystem Ecology).

Swamp forest. A swamp forest occurs at 1600 m along the Sendero Pantanoso in the MCFP between the cliff edge above the Peñas Blancas canyon and Cerro Sin Nombre. This poorly drained area has standing pools of water during the wet season and mushy holes where feet sink deep into the mud at any time. The water of one outflowing stream is noticeably tea colored, presumably due to dissolved tannins. This forest has occasional large trees (e.g., *Billia hippocastanum, Magnolia poasana, Ocotea viridifolia, Sapium rigidifolium,*

Table 3.3. Plants characteristic of edaphic and atmospheric associations in Monteverde.

Rock Ridges	Elfin Forest	Swamp Forest
Trees		
Bursera grandifolia (Burseraceae)	*Ardisia solomonii* (Myrsinaceae)	*Billia hippocastanum*
Calyptranthes pallens (Myrtaceae)	*Calyptranthes monteverdensis*, ined.	(Hippocastanaceae)
Chiococca alba (Rubiaceae)	(Myrtaceae)	*Cosmibuena valerii* (Rubiaceae)
Cosmibuena grandiflora (Rubiaceae)	*Clusia* spp. (Clusiaceae)	*Clusia* sp. (Clusiaceae)
Euphorbia hoffmanniana	*Conostegia montana*	*Dendropanax gonatopodus*
(Euphorbiaceae)	(Melastomataceae)	(Araliaceae)
E. schlechtendalii (Euphorbiaceae)	*C. pittieri* (Melastomataceae)	*Hedyosmum goudotianum*
Erythrina berteroana (Fabaceae)	*C. rhodopetala* (Melastomataceae)	(Chloranthaceae)
Ficus obtusifolia (Moraceae)	*Cosmibuena valerii* (Rubiaceae)	*Hyeronima poasana* (Euphorbiaceae)
Garcinia intermedia (Clusiaceae)	*Dendropanax gonatopodus*	*Ladenbergia valerii* (Rubiaceae)
Lonchocarpus acuminatus	(Araliaceae)	*Magnolia poasana* (Magnoliaceae)
(Fabaceae)	*Dendropanax latilobus* (Araliaceae)	*Ocotea* cf. *viridiflora* (Lauraceae)
L. oliganthus (Fabaceae)	*Drimys granadensis* (Winteraceae)	*Ocotea praetermissa* (Lauraceae)
Maytenus segoviarum (Celastraceae)	*Graffenrieda micrantha*	*Podocarpus monteverdeensis*
Montanoa guatemalensis	(Melastomataceae)	(Podocarpaceae)
(Asteraceae)	*Hyeronima poasana* (Euphorbiaceae)	*Psychotria sarapiquensis* (Rubiaceae)
Plumeria rubra (Apocynaceae)	*Miconia amplinodis*	*Quercus* cf. *seemannii* (Fagaceae)
	(Melastomataceae)	*Sapium rigidiflolium*
	M. tonduzii (Melastomataceae)	(Euphorbiaceae)
	Myrsine coriacea (Myrsinaceae)	*Tetrorchidium costaricense*
	Ocotea pittieri (Lauraceae)	(Euphorbiaceae)
	Parathesis glabra (Myrsinaceae)	*Chrysochlamys allenii* (Clusiaceae)
	Rondeletia monteverdensis	*Viburnum venustum* (Caprifoliaceae)
	(Rubiaceae)	*Xylosma oligandra* (Flacourtiaceae)
	Schefflera rodrigueziana (Araliaceae)	
	Chrysochlamys allenii (Clusiaceae)	
	Zanthoxylum melanostictum	
	(Rutaceae)	
Shrubs		
	Hoffmannia leucocarpa (Rubiaceae)	*Palicourea standleyana* (Rubiaceae)
	Macrocarpaea valerii (Gentianaceae)	*Phytolacca rivinoides* (Phytolaccaceae)
	Morella phanerodonta (Myricaceae)	*Psychotria aubletiana* (Rubiaceae)
Climbers		
Ipomoea leucotricha	*Smilax subpubescens* (Smilacaceae)	*Hydrangea peruviana*
(Convolvulaceae)		(Hydrangeaceae)
Pseudogynoxys cummingii		
(Asteraceae)		
Verbesina ovatifolia (Asteraceae)		
Herbs		
Anthurium salvinii (Araceae)	*Gunnera insignis* (Gunneraceae)	*Heliconia monteverdensis*
Echeveria australis (Crassulaceae)	*Heliconia monteverdensis*	(Heliconiaceae)
Epidendrum glumibracteum	(Heliconiaceae)	*Costus wilsonii* (Costaceae)
(Orchidaceae)	*Viola stipularis* (Violaceae)	*Alloplectus tetragonus*
Furcraea cabuya (Agavaceae)		(Gesneriaceae)
Isochilus linearis (Orchidaceae)		
Pitcairnia heterophylla		
(Bromeliaceae)		
P. maidifolia (Bromeliaceae)		
Polypodium plumula		
(Polypodiaceae)		
P. polypodioides (Polypodiaceae)		
P. rhodopleuron (Polypodiaceae)		

Podocarpus monteverdeensis) within a highly broken canopy resulting from frequent wind storms (Table 3.3). The open structure of this forest allows many epiphytes to survive in the well-lit understory.

Secondary vegetation.   "Charral" is the Spanish term used for the early-stage (1–3-year-old) vegetation that takes over cleared land and abandoned pastures. It consists of a dense tangle of 1–5-m-tall herbs, shrubs, vines, and tree saplings. Common plants include Amaranthaceae (*Iresine*), Asteraceae (*Baccharis, Clibadium, Fleischmannia, Mikania, Sinclairia, Vernonia*), Piperaceae (*Piper*), Melastomataceae (*Conostegia, Miconia*), Malvaceae (*Malvaviscus, Sida*), Tiliaceae (*Triumfetta*), Solanaceae (*Cestrum, Solanum, Witheringia*), and Urticaceae (*Boehmeria, Phenax, Pilea, Urera*). Vegetation colonizing naturally disturbed areas is lower in diversity than charral and tends to be composed of local species, in contrast to the widespread roadside weeds that take over large clearings. Charral develops a complete ground cover more quickly than the vegetation colonizing naturally disturbed sites.

While overlapping somewhat with charral, the term "tacotal" usually applies to the older, taller (5–15 m) secondary forest that replaces charral. It consists of a mixture of large herbs (*Calathea, Heliconia*),

shrubs, climbers, and trees (gap-colonizing species and the saplings of primary forest trees; Table 3.4). These secondary forests are often dominated by one or two species, although these vary among sites. Below 1400 m on the Pacific slope, *Conostegia xalapensis, Inga punctata,* and *Psidium guajava* become dominant. Old pastures on the upper Pacific slope above 1500 m are often taken over by *Conostegia oerstediana* (Fig. 3.3). On the upper Atlantic slope, *Neomirandea angularis* and *Piper auritum* can form a distinct monolayer. In the Peñas Blancas valley, monospecific stands of *Heliocarpus appendiculatus* follow in pastures that were colonized by *Miconia smaragdina* and *M. theizans.*

3.1.5. Morphological Patterns

Bark and trunk patterns.   Most trees of the cloud forest have nondescript bark. Tree trunks are so thoroughly covered with bryophytes, epiphytes, and herbaceous climbers that bark patterns cannot readily be seen. Exceptions are the two species of *Calyptranthes* (Myrtaceae) and *Quararibea costaricensis* (Bombacaceae), whose peeling bark effectively sheds trunk epiphytes to expose a smooth naked surface with a dappled pattern of gray, cinnamon, and brown. Spiny trees are largely absent from the cloud forest; for ex-

Figure 3.3. A dense even-aged stand of *Conostegia oerstediana* characterizes secondary succession in abandoned pastures at the edge of the Monteverde Cloud Forest Preserve. Photograph by Nathaniel T. Wheelwright.

Table 3.4. Trees and shrubs characteristic of secondary successional forest in Monteverde.

Pacific Slope	Cloud Forest	Atlantic Slope	Landslides[a]
Acnistus arborescens (Solanaceae)	Baccharis pedunculata (Asteraceae)	Acacia ruddiae (Fabaceae)	Alchornea latifolia (Euphorbiaceae)
Cecropia obtusifolia (Cecropiaceae)	Cecropia polyphlebia (Cecropiaceae)	Albizia carbonaria (Fabaceae)	Baccharis pedunculata (Asteraceae)
Citharexylum costaricensis (Verbenaceae)	Clibadium glomeratum (Asteraceae)	Cecropia insignis (Cecropiaceae)	Bocconia frutescens (Papaveraceae)
Clibadium surinamense (Asteraceae)	C. leiocarpum (Asteraceae)	Conostegia oerstediana (Melastomataceae)	Cecropia polyphlebia (Cecropiaceae)
Conostegia oerstediana (Melastomataceae)	Gonzalagunia rosea (Rubiaceae)	Hampea appendiculata (Malvaceae)	Clethra lanata (Clethraceae)
C. xalapensis (Melastomataceae)	Guettarda poasana (Rubiaceae)	Heliocarpus appendiculatus (Tiliaceae)	Clibadium leiocarpum (Asteraceae)
Croton mexicanus (Euphorbiaceae)	Miconia costaricensis (Melastomataceae)	Inga oerstediana (Fabaceae)	Cyathea caracasana (Cyatheaceae)
Hampea appendiculata (Malvaceae)	M. tonduzii (Melastomataceae)	Miconia smaragdina (Melastomataceae)	Gonzalagunia rosea (Rubiaceae)
Inga punctata (Fabaceae)	Heliocarpus americanus (Tiliaceae)	M. theizans (Melastomataceae)	Guettarda poasana (Rubiaceae)
I. sierrae (Fabaceae)	Koanophyllon pittieri (Asteraceae)	Myriocarpa longipes (Urticaceae)	Gunnera insignis (Gunneraceae)
Myrsine coriacea (Myrsinaceae)	Myriocarpa cordifolia (Urticaceae)	Perrottetia longistylis (Celastraceae)	Miconia tonduzii (Melastomataceae)
Oreopanax xalapensis (Araliaceae)	Myrsine coriacea (Myrsinaceae)	Piper auritum (Piperaceae)	Ocotea pittieri (Lauraceae)
Piper auritum (Piperaceae)	Neomirandea angularis (Asteraceae)	P. lanceifolium (Piperaceae)	Palicourea lasiorrhachis (Rubiaceae)
Podachaenium eminens (Asteraceae)	Piper auritum (Piperaceae)	Saurauia yasicae (Actinidiaceae)	P. standleyana (Rubiaceae)
Psidium guajava (Myrtaceae)	Piper imperiale (Piperaceae)	Solanum aphyodendron (Solanaceae)	Piper lanceifolium (Piperaceae)
Sapium glandulosum (Euphorbiaceae)	Rondeletia monteverdensis (Rubiaceae)	Trema micrantha (Ulmaceae)	Psychotria elata (Rubiaceae)
S. macrocarpum (Euphorbiaceae)	Saurauia pittieri (Actinidiaceae)	Urera elata (Urticaceae)	Saurauia pittieri (Actinidiaceae)
Saurauia montana (Actinidiaceae)	Senecio cooperi (Asteraceae)	Vernonia patens (Asteraceae)	Senecio cooperi (Asteraceae)
Solanum umbellatum (Solanaceae)	S. copeyensis (Asteraceae)	Wercklea insignis (Malvaceae)	S. sp. (Asteraceae)
Trema micrantha (Ulmaceae)	Solanum chrysotrichum (Solanaceae)		Urera elata (Urticaceae)
Urera baccifera (Urticaceae)	Trema micrantha (Ulmaceae)		Wercklea insignis (Malvaceae)
U. caracasana (Urticaceae)	Urera elata (Urticaceae)		
Viburnum costaricanum (Caprifoliaceae)	Wercklea insignis (Malvaceae)		
Xylosma chlorantha (Flacourtiaceae)	Witheringia coccoloboides (Solanaceae)		

[a]See Myster (1993) for data on landslides in the Monteverde cloud forest.

ample, *Zanthoxylum melanostictum* of the cloud forest lacks spines, even though four congeners from the Pacific slope have heavy trunk spines. The best examples of distinctive bark occur in the seasonal habitats on the Pacific slope (Table 3.5).

Buttresses.   Buttresses are less common in the Monteverde forests than in the lowlands and are more common on the Atlantic slope than either the cloud forest or the Pacific slope. Some species that have at least small buttresses include *Cedrela tonduzii, Dussia*

spp., *Ficus tuerckheimii, Ocotea monteverdensis, Ocotea whitei, Pterocarpus rohrii, Pouteria exfoliata, Quercus corrugata,* and *Sloanea* spp. Species of *Ocotea* that occur on both slopes generally develop larger buttresses on the Atlantic side than on the Pacific. Buttresses of a large *Ficus tuerckheimii* can span 10 m; those of the Lauraceae and Sapotaceae are usually less than 2–3 m wide.

Stilt roots.   Stilt roots are found among species of very wet or swampy areas and in a few light gap species.

Table 3.5. Distinctive bark textures and trunk shapes of trees at Monteverde.

Plant Name	Family	Bark and Trunk Characteristics
Allophylus accidentalis	Sapindaceae	Ropy in large individuals
Billia colombiana	Hippocastanaceae	Calico pattern of large chip scars
Bourreria costaricensis	Boraginaceae	Finely textured beige bark with deep fluting
Cecropia spp.	Cecropiaceae	Ringed with regular nodes marked by raised ridges
Cedrela spp.	Meliaceae	Checkered pattern in vertical columns
Chionanthus panamensis	Oleaceae	Fluted
Chomelia venulosa	Rubiaceae	Deeply fluted and peeling in large strips that reveal smooth red-brown bark underneath
Conostegia oerstediana	Melastomataceae	Beige bark, flaking in fine vertical fissures
Crossopetalum tonduzii	Celastraceae	Fluted and ropy
Ficus hartwegii	Moraceae	Ropy and fluted, formed from coalesced aerial roots
F. obtusifolia	Moraceae	Ropy and fluted, formed from coalesced aerial roots
F. tuerckheimii	Moraceae	Ropy and fluted, formed from coalesced aerial roots
F. velutina	Moraceae	Ropy and fluted, formed from coalesced aerial roots
Hampea appendiculata	Malvaceae	Smooth beige, fibrous bark with horizontal cracks, "Frankenstein" scars
Hasseltia floribunda	Flacourtiaceae	Ropy
Myrcianthes fragrans	Myrtaceae	Smooth cinnamon and gray bark (like guava)
Pouteria exfoliata	Sapotaceae	Scalloped pattern formed by small, exfoliating chips
Sideroxylon stenospermum	Sapotaceae	Rough, black bark
Styrax argenteus	Styracaceae	Uniformly cylindrical trunk with red-brown, finely striated bark
Viburnum costaricanum	Caprifoliaceae	Fluted and ropy
Zanthoxylum spp.	Rutaceae	Cone-shaped spines

They are typical of the following species: *Cecropia* spp. (Cecropiaceae), *Chamaedorea tepejilote* (Arecaceae), *Ficus* spp. (Moraceae) (especially *F. hartwegii*, *F. tuerckheimii*, and *F. velutina*), *Iriartea deltoidea* (Arecaceae), and *Tovomitopsis allenii* and *T. psychotrifolia* (Clusiaceae). On the Atlantic slope, *Ocotea monteverdensis* (Lauraceae) often develops masses of stringy stilt roots extending from the buttresses, a feature not seen on the Pacific side.

Crown shapes.   Distinctive crown shapes are less conspicuous in the cloud forest than in the lowlands. Most crowns are hemispherical to conical, cylindrical, or irregular, with branches jutting out opportunistically into light gaps. Monolayer crowns characteristic of some secondary species are found on the Pacific slope (e.g., *Lysiloma divaricata*) and Atlantic slope (e.g., *Acacia ruddiae, Albizia carbonaria*). The leaves of *Sapium rigidifolium*, a canopy tree in the swamp, are uniform in size and arranged in a monolayer with distinct crown shyness (adjacent branches and crowns separated by a clear boundary zone apparently resulting from twigs rubbing together at branch extremities). In the cloud forest, crown shyness is more common where the canopy is exposed to strong trade winds (e.g., east-facing slopes; Rebertus 1988).

Leaf diversity.   Fewer species with compound leaves occur in montane forests than in the lowlands (where the two large compound-leaved families, Fabaceae and Bignoniaceae, dominate). However, the cloud forest supports many species of Meliaceae, Fabaceae (Mimosoideae), and Sapindaceae, whose pinnate leaves have leaflets of the size and texture of an average simple leaf. *Pithecellobium* (Cojoba) *costaricense* is the only example of a tree with finely divided, bipinnate leaves in the cloud forest. Cloud forest lianas also either are simple-leaved (e.g., *Celastrus vulcanicola, Combretum laxum, Passiflora* spp., *Smilax* spp.) or have large leaflets (e.g., *Mucuna urens, Paullinia austin-smithii*).

Leaves in the drier, hotter areas of the Pacific slope generally have thinner leaves that are a light shade of green. Leaves of cloud forest trees are mostly small to medium in size, dark green in color, and often thick and stiff in texture (Kapelle et al. 1990). Trees on the very wet Atlantic slope tend to have large, dark green leaves intermediate in texture. When viewed from a distance, the canopy of secondary forests are usually a lighter shade of green than are primary forests.

Large leaves are common in cloud forest herbs, including gap-colonizing species (e.g., *Calathea crotalifera, C. marantifolia, Costus wilsonii, Gunnera insignis, Heliconia monteverdensis, Renealmia scaposa, Xanthosoma undipes*), tree trunk climbers (e.g., *Monstera, Philodendron, Asplundia, Spaeradenia*), and epiphytes (e.g., *Anthurium caperatum, Pitcairnia atrorubens, Vriesea werckleana, Pleurothallis saccata*). Many epiphytes have thick, leathery, fleshy, or waxy leaves or swollen stems that retain water, such as those in Asteraceae (*Neomirandea* spp.), Cactaceae (*Epiphyllum lepidocarpum*), Ericaceae (*Satyria meiantha*; Fig. 3.4), Loranthaceae (*Psittacanthus ramiflorus*), Orchidaceae (*Epidendrum obesum*), Solanaceae (*Lycianthes synanthera*), and Viscaceae (*Phoradendron* spp.).

Plants often produce larger leaves in the shade than in the sun. A few tree species have leaves with different shapes in the shade than in the canopy. The shade leaves of *Dendropanax arboreus* have three large lobes (shaped like a dinosaur footprint), whereas their canopy leaves are simple. Leaves of both types occur on saplings in light gaps. Saplings of *Roupala glaberrima* and *R. montana* typically have odd-pinnate compound leaves, but adults have simple leaves about the same size as a leaflet of the juvenile leaves.

3.1.6. Species Richness and Diversity

Our knowledge of the Monteverde flora is the product of about 20,000 plant collections made between 1975 and 1995. Valerie Dryer (1979) produced a list of about 850 vascular plant species from the Monteverde area, based on collections made during a Smithsonian Institution/Peace Corps assignment at Monteverde. A tree list for a series of Costa Rican research sites included 272 species known from Monteverde (Hartshorn 1983). In 1990, a list of vascular plants recorded from the Monteverde area above 700 m contained just over 2000 species (Haber 1991). An update of this list contains 3021 species, including a total of 755 species of trees (Appendix 1). New records for the area and undescribed species are being added continually (e.g., Atwood 1995, Hammel 1997, Poveda and Gonzalez 1997).

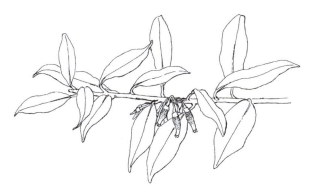

Figure 3.4. *Satyria meiantha* (Ericaceae) branch and flowers. Drawing by Willow Zuchowski.

Species richness. Species richness is defined as the number of species occurring within a designated area. About 9000 vascular plant species are known from Costa Rica (Institute for Biodiversity database for the Manual to the Plants of Costa Rica Project [Manual de las Plantas de Costa Rica], B. Hammel, M. Grayum, and N. Zamora, principal investigators). Thus, about one-third of the Costa Rican flora has been recorded growing outside of cultivation in the Monteverde area (see Bigelow and Kukle, "Ferns," p. 89, and Appendix 1).

Diversity within and between habitats. Forest inventories within life zones and permanent forest plots at Monteverde suggest that species richness of trees is lower within habitats in the mountains than in the wet lowlands (Gentry 1990, Lieberman and Lieberman 1994, Nadkarni et al. 1995; Table 3.6). Overall, species richness tends to be highest in the wettest lowland sites and to decrease in montane habitats and drier habitats with strong seasonality (Gentry 1982, 1990). Even though species richness per unit area (alpha species richness) in Monteverde may be lower than in the Atlantic lowlands, the high diversity of habitats along the steep moisture gradient across the mountains at Monteverde results in high species richness in a small area (beta species richness). The extremely rich epiphyte flora of the cloud forest adds substantially to the total species richness of the Monteverde region compared with the lowlands (Table 3.7, Hammel 1990). Permanent plots in which the trees have been measured, marked, and in some cases mapped have been established at nine sites near Monteverde (Table 3.6; see Haber, "Description," p. 90).

Endemism and new species. Since 1975, 167 species new to science have been collected in Monteverde, equaling 5.5% of the local flora. Of these, 88 species (53%) are thought to be endemic to the Monteverde region. Of the entire Monteverde flora, about 10% of the species are endemic to the Cordillera de Tilarán.

3.1.7. Diversity and Distribution of Growth Forms

The distribution of species among the life zones at Monteverde is poorly known, but the numbers of species recorded from the three major vegetation types have been tabulated (see Sec. 3.2; Fig. 3.5). The montane zone (above 1200 m) supports 1708 species (57% of the total flora). The Atlantic slope (700–1200 m) has 1390 species (46%), and the Pacific slope (700–1200 m) supports only 737 species (25%). The latter area merits special attention because of the presence of rare and undescribed species and the high rate of

Table 3.6. Summary data for tree species in permanent forest plots at Monteverde (see Haber, "Descriptions," p. 90).

Site	Area (ha)	Families	Species	Individuals	Basal Area (m²/ha)	Elevation (m)	Life Zone	Principal Investigator
a. Estación Biológica	0.1	27	41	62	66	1600	Lower montane wet/rain	N. Nadkarni
b. Elfin Forest	2	NA	NA	NA	NA	1550	Lower montane rain	R. Lawton
c. Nadkarni plots								
Plot 1	1	39	76	585	66.3	1450	Lower montane wet	N. Nadkarni
Plot 3	1	NA	41	531	NA	1450	Lower montane wet	N. Nadkarni
All plots	4	47	114	1429	62	1450	Lower montane wet	N. Nadkarni
d. Peñas Blancas	1	39	104	406	37.6	750	Tropical wet (transition)	W. Haber
e. San Gerardo	1	36	115	489	55.2	1150	Premontane rain	M. Kerry and W. Haber
g. Stellar	1	NA	NA	NA	NA	650	Premontane wet	E. Arévalo
h. Los Llanos	1	27	62	644	34.6	1200	Premontane moist	E. Arévalo

NA = information not currently available.

habitat destruction. The dominance of montane species in the region's flora results in large part from the great diversity of orchids and ferns (both epiphytic and terrestrial) in the cloud forest. Epiphytes comprise 29% of the flora and are most conspicuous and abundant in the cloud forest (Table 3.7). The lower species richness of the Atlantic slope may also reflect less intensive collecting there.

Herbs. Herbs are defined here as erect, nonwoody plants to distinguish them from vines (nonerect) and

shrubs (woody). Some plants are intermediate among these three categories; many pasture weeds (e.g., *Ageratina* and *Sida*) develop woody stem bases, and some ferns may grow either as epiphytes or terrestrial herbs. These species were tabulated as their most common growth form. A total of 616 species of terrestrial herbs (including 144 ferns) (21% of the total flora) have been identified in Monteverde (Table 3.7). This includes 245 species of dicotyledons in 44 families (13% of all dicot species) and 227 monocotyledons in 21 families (28% of all monocot species; Appendix 2). Herbaceous species of dicots are most abundant in the families Acanthaceae, Asteraceae, Gesneriaceae, Lamiaceae, and Rubiaceae. The most diverse monocot families are Araceae, Commelinaceae, Cyperaceae, Marantaceae, Orchidaceae, and Poaceae (Fig. 3.6).

Many of the herb species, especially weedy members of the Asteraceae and Poaceae, are more typical of disturbed areas such as roadsides and pastures than natural habitats. Some typical herbs of forest habitats include species of Araceae (*Dieffenbachia, Spathiphyllum*), Cyclanthaceae (*Carludovica, Cyclanthus*), Commelinaceae (*Dichorisandra hexandra, Tradescantia zanonia*), Costaceae (*Costus*), Gesneriaceae (*Alloplectus, Besleria princeps*), Orchidaceae (*Cranichis, Corymborkis*), and Zingiberaceae (*Renealmia*). Compared with wet forests at lower elevations, terrestrial herbs form a smaller percentage of the biomass in undisturbed montane habitats, occurring primarily

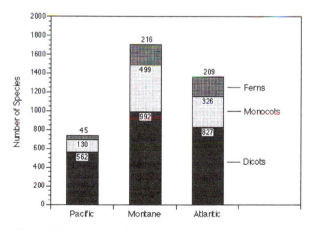

Figure 3.5. Number of species of ferns, monocots, and dicots in the three general vegetation types (Pacific, montane, and Atlantic) of the Monteverde area.

Table 3.7. The distribution of species among the growth forms of native vascular plants at Monteverde.

| Taxa | Growth Form | | | | | | | |
	Herb[a]	Vine	Liana	Shrub	Tree	Epiphyte	Total	% Total
Ferns and Relatives	144	20	2	2	13	177	358	12
Gymnosperms	0	0	0	1	1	0	2	0.1
Monocots	227	46	25	21	11	471	801	27
Dicots	245	81	193	345	730	230	1824	61
Total	616	147	220	369	755	878	2985	
% Total	21	5	7	12	25	29		

[a]The herb category includes only terrestrial species; herbaceous epiphytes are included with epiphytes.

in light gaps and edges (e.g., species of *Calathea*, *Costus*, *Heliconia*).

Shrubs and treelets. Shrubs are defined as woody-stemmed, free-standing plants less than 5 m tall at maturity. The term "treelet" has also been applied to species under 5 m that have a single-stemmed, tree-like growth form. Dicots are represented by 345 species of shrubs (19% of all dicot species) in 46 families (Appendix 2). Dicot shrubs and treelets are well represented in both primary and secondary habitats. Five dicot families dominate the shrub layer of primary forest understory: Acanthaceae, Melastomataceae, Piperaceae, Rubiaceae, and Solanaceae (Fig. 3.7). In disturbed areas, Asteraceae, Euphorbiaceae, Fabaceae, Malvaceae, Solanaceae, and Urticaceae are the most important families. Among monocots, only 21 species (3% of monocots) contain shrublike plants,

all in the families Arecaceae and Poaceae. The Arecaceae (19 species) are prominent in the understory of the wetter life zones, whereas the shrubby Poaceae (e.g., species in the genera *Gynerium*, *Lasiacis*, and *Pennisetum*) form a group of semiwoody shrubs that are common in drier life zones and in disturbed areas.

Trees. Trees are defined as free-standing woody plants reaching at least 5 m tall or 10 cm diameter at breast height (DBH). A total of 755 tree species in 92 families have been identified at Monteverde (Table 3.7; Appendix 2). Tree species make up 25% of all plant species. Of these, 730 species are dicots belonging to 88 families. Eleven species of palms (1.5% of all tree species) commonly grow to tree size. *Podocarpus monteverdeensis* (Podocarpaceae), an endemic and the only native gymnosperm tree at Monteverde, is a canopy tree of the cloud forest and swamp. Thirteen

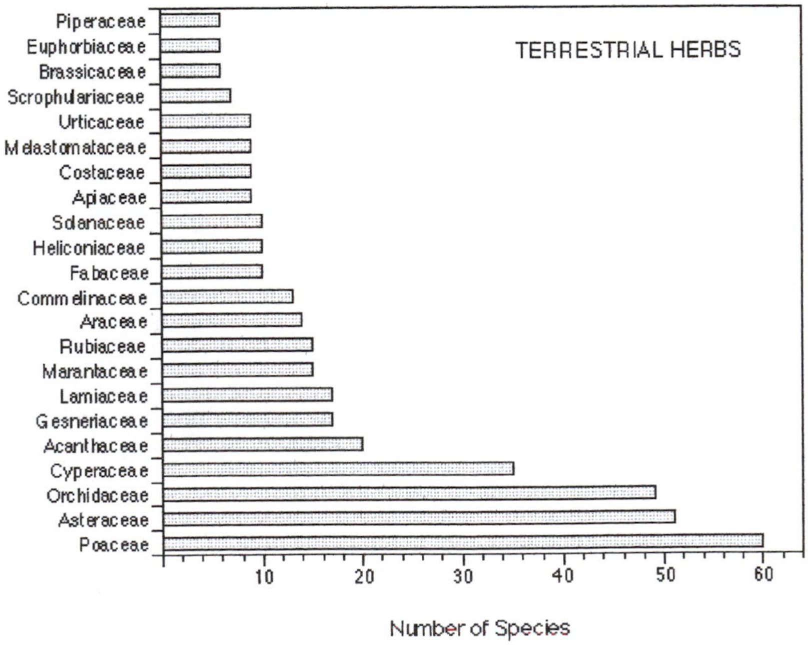

Figure 3.6. Distribution of the number of species of terrestrial herbs by plant family in Monteverde.

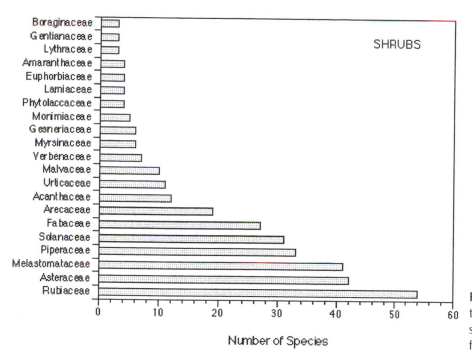

Figure 3.7. Distribution of the number of species of shrubs and treelets by plant family in Monteverde.

species of tree ferns also exceed 5 m in height. Lauraceae is by far the dominant family of trees in species richness (Fig. 3.8) and importance in the canopy. Lauraceae made up 31% of the stem basal area in lower montane wet forest (Nadkarni et al. 1995). At least 228 tree species occur on the Pacific slope (700–1200 m), 410 grow in the montane zone (above 1200 m), and 370 have been recorded from the Atlantic slope (700–1200 m).

Climbers. Climbers are plants that cannot support themselves in an erect position, at maturity. A few lianas (e.g., *Salacia, Paullinia*) can be found as 2 m erect saplings while they are young. Climbers can be divided into three general growth forms: herbaceous tree trunk climbers, vines, and lianas.

Herbaceous tree trunk climbers. These plants are sometimes called tree trunk–climbing epiphytes (Gentry 1993, Hartshorn and Hammel 1994) because their

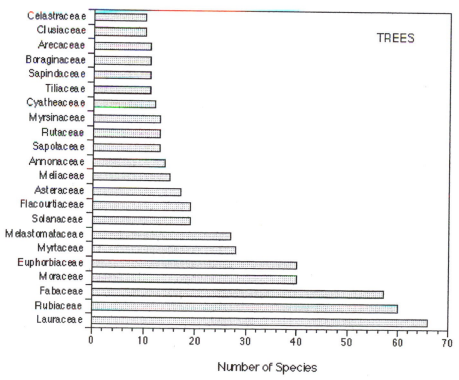

Figure 3.8. Distribution of the number of species of trees by plant family in Monteverde.

lower stems sometimes die back, severing any connection with the ground. Most species are found in the Araceae (32 species of *Philodendron*, *Monstera*, and *Syngonium*), Cyclanthaceae (8 species of *Asplundia* [Fig. 3.9], *Evodianthus*, and *Ludovia*), Gesneriaceae (11 species of *Alloplectus*, *Columnea*, and *Drymonia*), and Scrophulariaceae (4 species of *Schlegelia*; Appendix 2). These plants are prominent in the cloud forest, where they grow on almost every tree; they are least common on the dry Pacific slope. In the cloud forest, bare bark is only rarely visible through the vines and epiphytes. *Quararibea costaricensis* and a few species of Myrtaceae stand out as exceptions because their smooth flaking bark sheds bryophytes and ferns and maintains their trunks largely free of climbers.

Vines. These plants are defined as herbaceous or semiwoody climbers that seldom grow to more than 5 m long. Vines are more abundant in secondary forest, in overgrown pastures, and along roadsides than in primary forest. The Asclepiadaceae, Asteraceae, Convolvulaceae, Cucurbitaceae, Fabaceae, and Malpighiaceae include many species (Appendix 2). A total of 81 species of dicot vines and six species of monocots

(in addition to the aroids and cyclanths) has been identified (Table 3.7). The above-ground stems of some Convolvulaceae species die back annually; in others, the stems are semiwoody and perennial.

Lianas. These plants are perennial woody climbers that reach more than 5 m in length. They may ascend into the canopy (e.g., *Celastrus*, *Mucuna* [Figs. 3.10, 3.11]), *Passiflora*, *Paullinia*; see Diller O'Dell, "Mucuna," p. 72) or form dense tangles in light gaps and edges (*Chusquea* and *Smilax*). Lianas ascend tree trunks using tiny adventitious roots (e.g., *Hydrangea astrolasia*, *Marcgravia brownei*, *Passiflora brevifila*), climb by draping their stems over tree branches (e.g., *Irisine calea*, the bamboos *Arthrostylidium*, *Chusquea*, and *Rhipidocladum*), or spiral up small tree stems (e.g., *Rhynchosia*, *Salacia*). In Monteverde, 43 families contain lianas, the most species-rich being Convolvulaceae, Fabaceae, Malpighiaceae, and Passifloraceae among dicots, and Dioscoreaceae and Smilacaceae among monocots (Fig. 3.12). A total of 220 species of lianas occur at Monteverde (193 dicots, 25 monocots, and at least 2 ferns; Table 3.7, Appendix 2). Lianas are most abundant in secondary forest and drier habitats and least abundant in the cloud forest.

Epiphytes and hemiepiphytes. Epiphytes are plants that grow on other plants. As with lianas, their strategy is to attain a position in the sun without producing supporting stems (Fig. 3.1). With the exception of mistletoes, epiphytes do not parasitize their hosts, but

Figure 3.9. *(above left)* Inflorescence of *Asplundia microphylla* (Cyclanthaceae). Photograph by Stephen Ingram.
Figure 3.10. *(above right)* *Mucuna urens* flowers. Drawing by Willow Zuchowski.

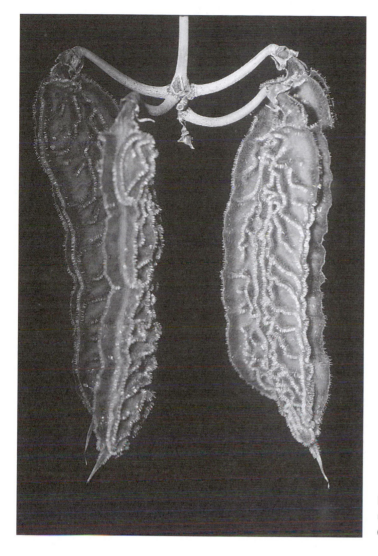

Figure 3.11. *Mucuna urens* seed pods with urticating hairs. Photograph by Barbara L. Clauson.

rather derive all of their moisture and nutrients from the atmosphere, from materials dissolved in mist and rain water flowing down the supporting stems, and from intercepted organic litter accumulated around their roots. The term pertains here to plants whose seeds germinate on other plants (including parasites such as the Loranthaceae). Many normally epiphytic species (especially ferns) can also be found occasionally growing on rocks, fallen logs, or moss mats on soil. In the cloud forest, terrestrial plants, such as palms, occasionally grow as epiphytes, but this is an exception to their normal ground-based growth pattern (but see Putz, "Trees on Trees," p. 70).

Hemiepiphytes ("half epiphytes") begin life as epiphytes; as they grow, they send roots to the ground where they gain access to additional nutrients and water from the soil. Hemiepiphytes may drop long aerial roots directly to the ground (*Ficus, Clusia* [Fig. 3.13]) or send their roots down the trunk of the host tree (*Blakea, Cavendishia, Clusia, Ficus, Markea*). Lianas are distinct from hemiepiphytes in sending up climbing stems from seeds that germinated in the soil (*Marcgravia*), but their functional growth forms can be similar. Many species of Araceae and Cyclanthaceae begin life as tree trunk climbers, but their lower stems do not increase in diameter and may eventually die back, stranding them as apparent epiphytes. Whether a plant grows as a liana or an epiphyte depends on seed germination requirements; seeds of some fig species do not germinate in ground soil, but only in the arboreal soil that accumulates in the crotches of host trees (Titus et al. 1990; see Titus, "Why Strangler Figs," p. 71).

Epiphytes are the most species-rich life form in the Monteverde flora, with 878 species, including 230 dicot species in 25 families, 471 monocot species in 5 families, and 177 ferns and their relatives in 13 families (see Ingram, "Epiphytes, p. 72 and Appendix 2). Orchidaceae is the richest epiphyte family in the Monteverde region, with more than 450 species of epiphytes (see Atwood, "Orchids," p. 74 and Appendix 3), followed by Araceae, Bromeliaceae, Gesneriaceae, and Piperaceae, each with more than 30 spe-

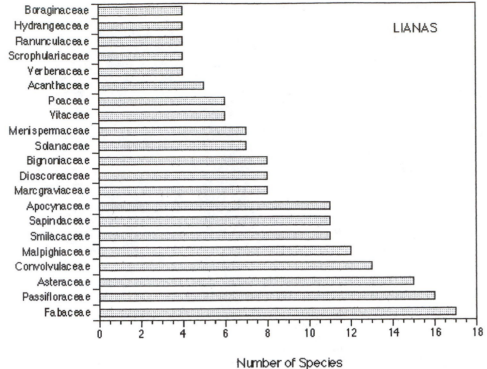

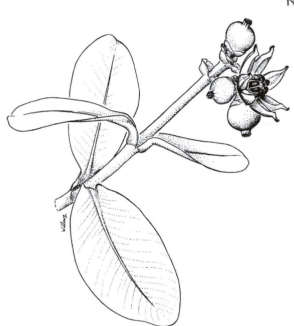

Figure 3.12. *(top)* Distribution of the number of species of lianas by plant family in Monteverde. **Figure 3.13.** *(left)* Leaves and fruit of *Clusia stenophylla* (Clusiaceae). Drawing by Willow Zuchowski.

cies. These families also contain many species that do not grow as epiphytes (Fig. 3.14). For example, 49 species of orchids grow as terrestrial herbs, and one species (*Vanilla planifolia*) is a trunk climber.

The abundance and diversity of epiphytes are greatest in the cloud forest. Epiphyte density is highest on east-facing slopes and ridges where large tree limbs support thick mats of moss, epiphytes, and arboreal soil weighing hundreds of kilograms (Lawton and Dryer 1980, Nadkarni 1984, 1986, 1994). The for-

est of the upper Pacific slope also supports an abundant and diverse epiphyte community (Ingram and Nadkarni 1993). More than 250 epiphyte species were identified from the 4–ha Nadkarni research plots (Ingram 1989, Ingram et al. 1996; see Ingram, "Epiphytes," p. 72, and Appendix 1). Some bromeliads of this forest tract are described in Ingram et al. (1996; see Luther, "Bromeliads," p. 73, and Appendix 4).

Epiphyte biomass is concentrated in the canopy. Low light levels in the understory limit the epiphyte

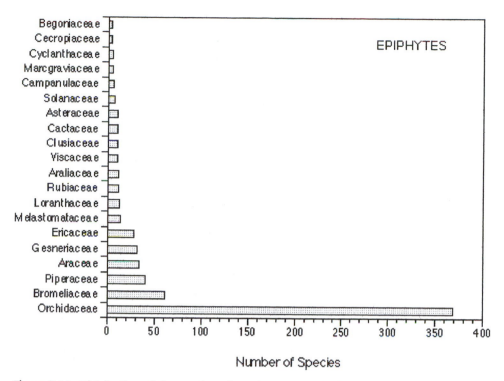

Figure 3.14. Distribution of the number of species of epiphytes by plant family in Monteverde.

species that can grow there, and those that ride down on branchfalls tend to die quickly (Matelson et al. 1993). The abundance and diversity of epiphytes drop dramatically as one descends the Pacific slope, which parallels the decrease in precipitation during the dry season. Bromeliads with tough, narrow leaves (e.g., *Tillandsia* spp.) found in the Río Guacimal valley below Monteverde are adapted to the annual dry season; other species (e.g., *Pitcairnia heterophylla*, *P. maidifolia*) drop their leaves during this time.

The diversity, distribution, and conservation status of Monteverde's orchids are among the best documented for any tropical cloud forest (see Atwood, "Orchids," p. 74). Monteverde is thought to be the site of highest known orchid diversity on earth (J. Atwood and C. Dodson, pers. comm. Atwood essay); the total number of known species exceeds 500 (J. Atwood, G. Barbosa, and R. Dressler, pers. comm.). Thirty-four species of orchids new to science have been found at Monteverde (Atwood 1995, Atwood and Dressler 1995, G. Barbosa, pers. comm.).

It is not unusual to find individuals of typically terrestrial species growing as epiphytes in the crown humus on tree trunks in the cloud forest (e.g., *Chamaedorea tepejilote*, *Pilea* spp., *Solanum americanum*; see Putz, "Trees on Trees," p. 70). In these wet conditions, one can envision an easy transition between understory, light gap, and canopy. Phylogenetic relationships between shrubs

and epiphytes within the genus *Psychotria* (Rubiaceae) have been analyzed, which suggest a possible evolutionary pathway in which epiphytes could evolve from shrubs of the cloud forest understory (see Nepokroeff and Sytsma, "Evolution in *Psychotria*," p. 75).

Epiphylls are tiny plants that grow on the leaves of other plants. Although they have received little attention, they make up another diverse group of epiphytes, especially in the cloud forest and Atlantic slope rain forest (see Morales, "Plant Growing on Living Leaves," p. 80). Some epiphylls fix atmospheric nitrogen that can be taken up by the host leaf. However, when the epiphylls form a dense covering, they may inhibit photosynthesis in the host leaf or increase leaf surface moisture, promoting disease.

Parasites.   Parasitic plants derive at least part of their nutrients from attachments to the tissue of other plants. The Loranthaceae are common parasites of trees at Monteverde (see Sargent, "Mistletoes," pp. 81–82). They are often called *matapalo* (tree killer). Some species are destructive pests of citrus trees and native trees in Monteverde pastures. This group is divided into three families: Eremolepidaceae (*Antidaphne*, one species), Loranthaceae (with 5 genera and 13 species in Monteverde), and Viscaceae (*Dendrophthora* one species, and *Phoradendron*, 9 species; Appendixes 1 and 2). Most species have small and incon-

Figure 3.15. Flower of *Psittacanthus* sp. (Loranthaceae), a parasitic shrub pollinated by humming-birds. Photograph by Stephan Ingram.

spicuous yellow-green flowers, but the species of *Psittacanthus* (Loranthaceae) display red flowers pollinated by hummingbirds (Fig. 3.15). All species are branch parasites of trees or shrubs. *Gaiadendron punctatum* also grows as a small tree, presumably parasitizing tree roots (see Sargent, "An Exceptional Mistletoe," p. 82). Although these parasites remove water and nutrients from their hosts with penetrating, suckerlike adventitious roots called haustoria, their green- or orange-tinted leaves contain chlorophyll and photosynthesize. Field experiments in Monteverde showed how germination and seedling establishment occur in *Phoradendron robustissimum* on its host *Sapium glandulosum* (formerly *S. oligoneurum*; Sargent 1995; see Sargent, "Mistletoes," pp. 81–82).

The Balanophoraceae are parasites with underground stems that attach to tree roots with tubers (modified roots). They lack chlorophyll, have no visible leaves, and appear to be nonspecific in host choice. Their existence becomes conspicuous only when the inflorescences emerge above the soil. The unisexual flowers are among the world's smallest. Although nothing is known of their reproductive biology in Monteverde, some species are fly-pollinated; others have ant-dispersed seeds with elaiosomes (oily bodies affixed to propagules; Cronquist 1981). The distinctly phallic or fungus-like inflorescence of *Helosis cayennensis* is a 10–15-cm stalk with an api-cal red club covered with small geometric scales. These rare plants grow in forest understory at 900–1300 m on the Pacific slope and in the San Gerardo valley (1100 m). The other species of Balanophoraceae in Monteverde, *Langsdorffia hypogaea*, has a pine cone-like inflorescence that is 4–6 cm across and barely protrudes above the soil surface. It is covered with large scales that open to expose a dense column of many tiny, grayish brown flowers. The inflorescences appear in small clusters pushing out of the soil along forested trails from Bajo del Tigre to the cloud forest (Sendero Pantanoso). The colonies may persist in the same locations for several years.

The Ericaceae includes the rare herb *Monotropa uniflora*, Indian Pipe (sometimes segregated into the family Monotropaceae), which produces an unbranched 10–15-cm stalk supporting one or a few large, pinkish white flowers. This mycotrophic (fungus-associated) perennial has reduced scale-like leaves and lacks chlorophyll. The plants depend on an attachment to a fungus for food, water, and minerals. Because the fungus makes a mycorrhizal connection to tree roots, the association is presumed to be indirectly parasitic (Cronquist 1981). This species grows in small colonies under oak trees (*Quercus corrugata*) in the cloud forest (1500–1600 m).

Saprophytes.   Saprophytes are plants that derive their nutrients from dead organic matter, such as decaying plant material. They usually lack chlorophyll and do not photosynthesize. The Burmanniaceae are terrestrial saprophytes related to the Orchidaceae. They lack chlorophyll and have thin stems with spiraled, scale-like leaves. *Gymnosiphon suaveolens* has a weak, 4–8-cm stem with one to several flowers at its tip; both the flower and stem are lavender-white. Usually growing in small groups, it is widespread, though uncommon in Monteverde. *Apteria aphylla* is a similar but much less common herb found in the Peñas Blancas valley (800–900 m). The highly reduced gentian *Voyria flavescens* (Gentianaceae) is a solitary, 7–10-cm herb with a yellow stem and flower. Lacking chlorophyll, with its leaves reduced to scales, this delicate herb superficially resembles *Gymnosiphon*. This rare mycotrophic species has only been collected in the understory of secondary forest in the Monteverde community (1300–1400 m). A similarly shaped monocot, *Triuris* sp. (Triuridaceae), is known from Monteverde from a single individual collected in the elfin forest (Davidse et al. 1994).

Stranglers.   Stranglers begin life as epiphytes. As they increase in size, they send down adventitious roots that coalesce into a network enclosing the trunk of the host tree. The strangler's crown overtops the crown of its host. The combination of shading, competition for nutrients and, possibly, a girdling effect of the fig roots encircling the host's trunk kills the host. Once the host tree is dead, the strangler can persist for decades as a free-standing tree (Fig. 3.16).

Species of *Ficus* are the best-known stranglers, and several species are common at Monteverde (see Burger 1977 for a key to species). Germination experiments with the seeds of *F. pertusa* and *F. tuerckheimii* under simulated epiphytic and terrestrial conditions showed that *Ficus* seeds rarely germinate in soil, but show no autopathic effects (Titus et al. 1990; see Titus, "Why Strangler Figs," p. 71). Evidence for a specific host preference in *F. crassiuscula* was documented by long-term observations (Daniels and Lawton 1991, 1993). The independent evolution of the strangling habit in *F. crassiuscula*, a member of the usually free-standing subgenus *Pharmacosycea*, was discussed by Lawton (1986, 1989) and Ramírez (1988).

Ficus crassiuscula, a common tree in the cloud forest known locally as *chilamate*, is not a true hemi-epiphytic strangler. It begins life as a vine, snaking through the understory in search of an appropriate host tree to climb. The vines show a preference for *Guarea kunthiana*, a canopy tree common in the cloud forest (Lawton 1986, 1989, Daniels and Lawton 1991, 1993). Four species of *Ficus* found on the upper Pacific slope between 1200 m and the Continental Divide are true stranglers of the subgenus *Urostigma*. *Ficus hartwegii* grows to be a huge canopy tree in

Figure 3.16. View upward into the hollow trunk of a strangler fig, *Ficus tuerckheimii* (Moraceae) after the trunk of the host tree has died and rotted away. Photograph by Gregory Dimijian.

Monteverde with a ropey, open trunk. However, on the Atlantic slope it commonly reaches maturity as a hemiepiphytic shrub. *Ficus pertusa* usually achieves reproductive maturity while a hemiepiphyte and less commonly becomes a free-standing tree. *Ficus tuerckheimii* typically becomes a huge canopy tree, the most common strangler in the Monteverde community and lower cloud forest (1300–1550 m). The sympatric *F. velutina* becomes a large canopy tree; it grows in moist canyons and sheltered sites.

Several species in families unrelated to the figs have evolved similar growth forms, including *Alzatea verticillata* (Alzateaceae), a hemiepiphytic shrub that occasionally becomes a large tree with the growth form of a strangler fig. *Ceiba rosea* (Bombacaceae), common at Eladio's Refuge and Poco Sol, is a hemiepiphyte with palmately compound leaves and spiny roots that can become a free-standing tree. *Clusia* spp. often become tree-sized hemiepiphytes in the cloud forest, especially on the highest peaks and ridges. Although some species are described as stranglers elsewhere in the neotropics, the species at Monteverde have not been shown to kill their hosts. *Coussapoa* spp. (Cecropiaceae) commonly grow as large hemiepiphytes on the Atlantic slope from San Gerardo to Poco Sol. They occasionally reach tree size and develop the distinctive growth form of strangler figs.

Ferns. A total of 358 species of ferns and fern allies in 25 families have been identified at Monteverde (see Bigelow and Kukle, "Ferns," p. 89 and Appendixes 1 and 2). The species are divided between terrestrial herbs (144 species, 40%) and epiphytes (177 species, 49%; see Table 3.7). Fifteen species grow as trees and shrubs with distinct erect trunks, and 19 species grow as tree trunk climbers, including several that become semiwoody vines, such as *Lomariopsis* spp. (Lomariopsidaceae), *Polybotrya alfredii* (Dryopteridaceae), *Polypodium ptilorhizon* (Polypodiaceae), *Salpichlaena* spp. (Blechnaceae), and *Sticherus* spp. (Gleicheniaceae).

Ferns are most abundant in the cloud forest, where the tree trunks and canopy support many epiphytic species. The proportion of terrestrial species is much higher in drier forest habitats, where several species commonly grow on rocks (e.g., *Polypodium plumula*, *P. polypodioides*, *P. rhodopleuron*, *Selaginella pallescens*). Only 45 species (13%) of ferns have been collected on the dry Pacific slope below 1200 m; 60% grow in the montane zone above 1200 m; 58% of the species occur on the Atlantic slope, reflecting the extremely wet conditions found there throughout the year (Table 3.5). The largest genera of ferns at Monteverde are *Polypodium* (18 spp.), *Asplenium* (19 spp.),

Thelypteris (24 spp.), and *Elaphoglossum* (38 spp.; Appendix 1).

Tree ferns occur in the families Cyatheaceae (*Alsophila*, *Cyathea*, *Sphaeropteris*), Dicksoniaceae (*Dicksonia gigantea*), and Thelypteridaceae (*Thelypteris decussata*) (Fig. 3.17). Not all members of the Cyatheaceae develop a tree-like growth form (e.g., *Cnemidaria mutica*). Reaching 8 m in height, *Sphaeropteris brunei* is the largest tree fern at Monteverde, with a distinctive trunk covered with dense beige hair-like scales. The distribution of tree ferns along an elevational gradient crossing three life zones was described at Monteverde by Lee et al. (1986). Tree ferns were most abundant and diverse in the lower montane rain forest life zone, where a total of seven species occurred. They found only three species in the lower montane wet forest, and none in the premontane wet forest. However, an *Alsophila* sp. grows in the moist stream canyons down to 1200 m within the premontane zone (W. Haber, pers. obs.).

Some terrestrial ferns form plantlets, which are small plants that grow on fern fronds and that can establish new plants vegetatively. Koptur and Lee (1993) found species capable of producing plantlets to be more common along the Nuboso trail (lower montane rain forest life zone) than in the drier forest of Campbell's woods (6% of species in the 24% of species in the lower montane wet forest life zone).

Bryophytes. Knowledge of Monteverde's bryophytes is rudimentary. However, significant collections have been made by G. Dauphin, S. Ingram, R. Lawton, M. Lyon, and S. R. Gradstein. Floristic studies of the Monteverde bryophytes provide species lists (Reed and Robinson 1971, Gradstein et al. 1994, Sillett et al. 1995). Approximately 190 species of bryophytes in 39 families (133 liverworts, 56 mosses, and 1 hornwort) were collected from the 4-ha Nadkarni tree plots (Gradstein et al. 1994; Gradstein, "Bryophytes," p. 78 and Haber, "Description," p. 90). The bryophyte flora of the canopy and understory are distinct. Liverworts are generally more abundant and diverse than the mosses; liverworts make up the bulk of epiphylls (see Gradstein, "Bryophytes," p. 78; Morales, "Plants Growing on Living Leaves," p. 80).

Fungi and lichens. Fungi and lichens at Monteverde have been studied even less than bryophytes. Lesica and Antibus (1990) examined epiphytes at Monteverde and La Selva Field Station for vesicular-arbuscular mycorrhizal fungi (Maffia et al. 1993; see Maffia, "Mycorrhizae," p. 338). They found mycorrhizae associated with orchids and with most Ericaceae. However, many canopy epiphytes belonging to families that generally support mycorrhizal associations elsewhere

Figure 3.17. Tree ferns (Cyatheaceae). Photograph by Nathaniel T. Wheelwright.

lack them in the canopy. An amazing world of highly specialized relationships between parasitic fungi (Trichomycetes) and insects unfamiliar even to most biologists was studied in Monteverde (see Lichtwardt, "Gut Fungi," pp. 83).

Although there is no mushroom-hunting tradition in Costa Rica, several edible species grow at Monteverde, including the Indigo Milky (*Lactarius indigo*), Chicken of the Woods (*Laetiporus sulphureus*), honey mushrooms (*Armillariella*), meadow mushrooms (*Agaricus*), morels (*Morchella*), and oyster mushrooms (*Pleurotus*) (W. Zuchowski, pers. comm.). The Magic Mushroom (*Psilocybe cubensis*), a toxic hallucinogenic species occasionally eaten for its psychoactive effects, commonly grows in horse dung along with species of *Panaeolus*. Some of the other common macrofungi include species of *Auricularia, Geastrum, Hygrocybe, Marasmius, Mycena,* and *Russula*. Several species of stinkhorns (*Aseroe, Clathrus,* and *Mutinus*) occur in the Monteverde community and lower cloud forest. The orange Slimy-Stalked Puffball (*Calostoma cinnabrina*) and tiny, scarlet waxy caps (*Hygrocybe* spp.) are often seen in the cloud forest.

The general impression among mushroom aficionados is that terrestrial Basidiomycetes are diverse in Monteverde but inconspicuous because they are temporally sporadic, tiny (e.g., *Marasmius* and *Mycena*), or occur as scattered, solitary individuals compared with the large aggregations in temperate forests of certain genera (e.g., *Boletus, Suillus,* and *Tricholoma*) that have mycorrhizal associations with abundant tree species. However, mushrooms that grow on dead wood are sometimes found in large groups in the cloud forest (Fig. 3.18).

3.1.8. Naturalized and Escaped Species

The pastures and roadsides around Monteverde are filled with weedy species of grasses (Poaceae), composites (Asteraceae), mints (Lamiaceae), chickweeds (Caryophyllaceae), and legumes (Fabaceae). Most of these plants do not grow naturally in undisturbed primary forest in the area, although a shade-tolerant subset may invade large tree falls, landslides, roads, and wide trails in the forest. Many of these nonnative species have infiltrated from drier habitats throughout Central America and elsewhere. Most of the grasses either have been introduced from Africa for pasture use or are pantropical weeds. Only half the grasses found countrywide are native species (Pohl 1980, R. Pohl, pers. comm.). With the exception of the bamboo species and some species of *Lasiacis*, no forest grasses occur at Monteverde above 1200 m. A few native species of grasses can be seen along trails in Pacific slope forest (e.g., *Ichnanthus* spp., *Leersia ligularis, Oplismenus burmannii*). Undisturbed stream margins in the Cordillara de Tilarán are generally too

Figure 3.18. Fungi of Monteverde. Photograph by Mitch Valburg.

shady to support grasses. The grasslike *Uncinia hamata* (Cyperaceae) with distinctive hooked seeds commonly grows in forest understory.

In recent years, many weedy species have invaded Monteverde from lower drier habitats on the Pacific slope (e.g., *Aeschynomene fascicularis*, *Hyparrhenia rufa*, *Solanum capsicoides*, and *Zornia reticulata*). This observation matches those of birders who have observed movements up the slope of bird species (M. Fogden and A. Pounds, pers. comm.; see Chap. 6, Birds). These apparent range extensions may be responses to a change in climate (especially a recent series of El Niño years), but many species of weedy plants have probably also been carried in by the large influx of horses brought in for rental to tourists. Several tree species (e.g., *Albizia adinocephala*, *Diphysa americana*, *Zanthoxylum setulosum*) from life zones at lower elevations grow well in the open field conditions of the arboretum at Bajo del Tigre, suggesting that many plants could grow at Monteverde if they are transported there.

One naturalized escapee from cultivation, coffee (*Coffea arabica*), maintains a foothold in forest habitats for many years, either because it was planted or because it germinated from seeds in light gaps and edges. The "China," *Impatiens walleriana* (Balsaminaceae), a roadside herb with explosive fruits and pink or orange flowers pollinated by butterflies, is an escaped ornamental originating in East Africa, which has become established as a self-reproducing weed in disturbed forest edges and stream margins throughout the region (700–1600 m; Fig. 3.19). It even grows along the pristine canyon of the Río Peñas Blancas. The African ornamental *Hypoestes phyllostachya* (Acanthaceae) or Polka-dot Plant (Mabberley 1987, 1997), has become a common weed of shaded yards and pastures around Monteverde. It forms monospecific stands in the crown shadows of pasture trees. In general, introduced species make little headway invading natural habitats because most cannot tolerate the shade of the forest understory. Some of the other conspicuous naturalized

Figure 3.19. The escaped ornamental, *Impatiens walleriana*, in flower with light-tolerant ferns along the road in the Monteverde Preserve. Photograph by Gregory Dimijian.

species include *Conyza canadensis* (Asteraceae), a widespread weed on disturbed soil, and *Eriobotrya japonica* (Rosaceae, Loquat), whose seedlings occasionally establish in pasture and roadside habitats. *Hedychium coronarium* (Zingiberaceae, White Ginger), with large, white, hawk moth–pollinated flowers, grows in marshy pastures and wet ditches. *Psidium guajava* (Myrtaceae, Guayaba, Guava), with seeds dispersed by horses and humans, is a self-sustaining pest in pastures. *Rubus roseifolius* (Rosaceae, Thimbleberry), from East Asia, is a common pasture weed. *Solanum quitoense* (Solanaceae, "Naranjilla"), from Ecuador, has escaped from cultivation. *Taraxacum officinale* (Asteraceae, Dandelion), is now invading. *Youngia japonica* (Asteraceae), which looks like a delicate dandelion, grows in parking lots, lawns, and flower beds.

Some of the common introduced grasses (Poaceae) of the area are *Cynodon dactylon* (Bermuda Grass), *C. nlemfuensis* ("Estrella," African Star Grass), *Digitaria* *abyssinica* (Finger Grass, Crab Grass), *Hyparrhenia rufa* ("Jaraguá"), *Melinis minutiflora* (Molasses Grass), *Pennisetum purpureum* ("Gigante," Elephant Grass), *Sporobolus indicus* ("Pitilla," Smut Grass), and *Stenotaphrum secundatum* ("San Agustín," Lawn Grass; see Chap. 11, Agriculture).

3.1.9. Resources for Plant Identification

An updated plant list for the Monteverde area with authors, voucher collection numbers, and information on distribution, growth form, and pollination is provided in Appendix 1 (Fig. 3.20). *An Introduction to Cloud Forest Trees: Monteverde, Costa Rica* (Haber et al. 1996) provides keys, descriptions, and illustrations of 88 common tree species at Monteverde. The booklet *Common Flowering Plants of the Monteverde Cloud Forest Reserve* (Zuchowski 1996) includes descriptions and illustrations of 50 species that are con-

Figure 3.20. The bright flowers of *Blakea scarlatina* (Melastomataceae), which occurs in Penas Blancas, at the Poco Sol field station, observed by botanist William Haber. Photograph by Nathaniel T. Wheelwright.

spicuous along the main tourist trails in the MCFP. A booklet on common ferns of Monteverde is also available (Bigelow and Kukle 1991; see Bigelow and Kukle, "Ferns," p. 89).

Technical treatments are available for some families in the Fieldiana series *Flora Costaricensis* (e.g., Burger 1977, 1980, Burger and van der Werff 1990, Burger and Taylor 1993). Resources for orchid identification include the *Icones* series from Selby Botanical Gardens (Atwood 1989, 1992, Mora de Retana and Atwood 1993), which includes descriptions and detailed line drawings of many Monteverde species, the country-level species list of Mora de Retana and García (1992), the *Field Guide to the Orchids of Costa Rica and Panama* (Dressler 1993), which offers color plates exemplifying one species for each genus and keys to species, and the treatment of the tribe Maxillariae by Atwood and Mora de Retana (1999). For trees with compound leaves, Holdridge et al. (1997) is useful. *Flora Arborescente de Costa Rica* (Zamora 1989) describes and illustrates selected families of trees with simple leaves. The most useful identification guide for woody plants at the family and genus level is Gentry (1993). Keys and descriptions for the neotropical palms are provided in Henderson et al. (1995), and for the large monocot families (Bromeliaceae, Cyperaceae, Poaceae), keys are in Davidse et al. (1994). The first volume (Monocotyledons) of the *Manual de las*

Plantas de Costa Rica project (B. Hammel, M. Grayum, and N. Zamora, principle investigators) is expected in 1999. Morales (1998) describes 80 species of Costa Rican bromeliads, Rossi (1998) includes descriptions of Costa Rican Cactaceae, and Lellinger (1989) is a useful technical resource for identifying Costa Rican ferns. Several publications useful for the identification of Costa Rican bryophytes are Cole (1983, 1984), Gradstein et al. (1994), Griffin and Morales (1983), Reed and Robinson (1971), and Sillett et al. (1995). A reference collection of laminated, photocopied herbarium sheets is maintained at the Estación Biológica. A reference herbarium at Monteverde is available to botanical specialists. An arboretum at Bajo del Tigre has 70 species of trees with name tags.

3.2. Seasonality

3.2.1. Phenology

The study of the timing of flowering, fruiting, and leaf production is called phenology. Biologists document these patterns to understand the reproductive adaptations of plants in relation to climatic factors and the life cycles of pollinators and seed dispersers. Most plant species in the Monteverde area exhibit a distinct seasonality in the production of flowers and fruits, although the timing and length of flowering and fruiting of a species vary from year to year (as do weather patterns). The altered climate of El Niño years can interrupt or shift normal phenological patterns in some species. Individual species flower on different schedules, responding independently to a variety of environmental cues to initiate flowering, so flowering and fruiting can be observed in at least 10% of the species during any month of the year. Blooming patterns can point to ecological relationships with pollinators. For example, species that produce a few flowers per day over a period of several months (extended flowering or the "trapline" strategy) may favor specialized pollinators such as hummingbirds, hawkmoths, or bats, in contrast to mass flowering species, which bloom for only a week or two (the "big bang" strategy) and often attract large numbers of small unspecialized insects. The timing of fruit production may also be linked with the availability of appropriate seed dispersers (see Chap. 8, Plant-Animal Interactions).

3.2.2. Flowering

Trees. In Monteverde, most phenological observations have been carried out on the upper Pacific slope in the area between the cliff edge and the Continental Divide. In this area, the vast majority of trees flower once per year and the blooming period occurs at about the same time each year (W. Haber, G. Frankie, C. Guindon, and H. Baker, unpubl. data). However, in figs (*Ficus* spp.), individuals often flower out of synchrony with each other and a single tree may flower up to three times per year (Bronstein 1988a, b). The weather at Monteverde varies substantially from year to year (see Chap. 2, Physical Environment), and the flowering phenology of most trees responds to this variation. For example, during the abnormally dry conditions of El Niño years, some species flowered 6 months out of the normal sequence, some flowered twice, and others did not flower at all (W. Haber, pers. obs.). In general, tree species flower at widely different times, so that a minimum of about 60 species of trees are flowering at once in any given month. During months of peak flowering (e.g., March–May), more than 100 species can flower simultaneously. Minimum flowering activity occurs during September–October (the months of heaviest rainfall) and November–December (the windy-misty season).

The apparent avoidance of flowering during the windy-misty season may be due to the difficulty of pollination under these conditions. Flowers become soaked with rain, pollen gets wet, nectar is diluted, and the cold and wind discourage the activity of pollinating insects. Hummingbirds are less deterred by cold rainy weather than insects, but few trees have hum-

mingbird-pollinated flowers. Hummingbird-pollinated plants display a small flowering peak during October–November, the wettest period of the year (Linhart et al. 1987).

Understory plants. Flowering of shrubs and treelets in the understory follows the pattern seen in trees, an increase in flowering in late dry season through the early wet season with a peak in May–June (Koptur et al. 1988). Most species show a pattern of extended flowering, with only 15% exhibiting the mass flowering pattern that is common among trees.

3.2.3. Fruiting

Trees. Fruit production is highest from September through January and lowest from June to August. However, 30–40 species of trees can be found in fruit in any month of the year on the upper Pacific slope. Some tree species (e.g., *Matayba* sp., Sapindaceae, *Beilschmiedia* spp., Lauraceae) fruit heavily only at 2-year intervals and produce few or no fruits in alternate years (Wheelwright 1986; W. Haber, pers. obs.). The timing of fruit maturation can shift substantially within certain species depending on weather conditions.

Understory shrubs and treelets. Although the fruiting of understory shrubs is less seasonal than their flowering and much less concentrated than in trees, most species produce fruit during late wet season and early dry season, as do trees (Koptur et al. 1988).

3.2.4. Leaf Flushing

Trees. A peak in new leaf production in trees occurs during the late dry season (February–April), whereas minimum leaf flushing occurs from August through December, the wettest period of the year. Two major patterns of leaf flushing have been observed at Monteverde: (1) all old leaves drop and are quickly replaced by an entire crown of new leaves, and (2) old leaves are maintained with inconspicuous loss of individual leaves, while the primary addition of new leaves occurs during twig growth, often in April–May, preceding the wet season. The flowering of mass-blooming species is frequently associated with the period of new twig growth and leaf flushing in both patterns (e.g., *Ilex* spp., *Lonchocarpus* spp., *Ocotea* spp., *Xylosma* spp.). A few species of Monteverde trees are deciduous (e.g., *Cedrela tonduzii, Erythrina lanceolata, Meliosma vernicosa, Ormosia cruenta, Persea americana, Sapium glandulosum, Styphnolobium monteviridis, Pouteria fossicola*), dropping all their leaves at once and remaining leafless for a period. In Monteverde pastures, these species remain leafless for a month or two, but in the forest they leaf out within a few weeks. In the San Luis valley, deciduous species are more common and may remain leafless for several months during the dry season.

Understory shrubs. The seasonal pattern of leaf flushing in understory shrubs is less conspicuous than in trees; however, a slight increase in leaf flushing occurs during the dry season (Koptur et al. 1988).

3.2.5. Studies of Guilds

Hummingbird flowers. Shrubs and treelets of the understory with flowers adapted for hummingbird pollination show little seasonal pattern in flowering (Koptur et al. 1988). In a study of all hummingbird-pollinated plants occurring in light gaps and in the understory of the cloud forest, flowering was uniform through the year, with a small increase in the number of species flowering during October through December (Linhart et al. 1987). At a drier site in premontane wet forest below the Monteverde community, more hummingbird flowers bloomed during the dry season, although most species had flowering patterns that extended over several months (Feinsinger 1978).

Inga. Koptur (1983; see Koptur, "Breeding Systems," p. 85) studied the reproductive biology of seven Inga species (Fabaceae) in Monteverde. Flowering was distributed throughout the year, but more species flowered during late wet season to early dry season (September–December) when hawkmoths (Sphingidae) and perching moths (e.g., Geometridae, Noctuidae) were abundant. Few species flowered from late dry season to early wet season. Several species tended to flower twice per year or displayed extended flowering with double peaks. In these cases, the separate flowering episodes resulted mostly from flowering by different individuals i.e., some individuals within populations (e.g., I. longispica) flowered at different times of year from others. The peaks roughly coincided with the two peaks in rainfall (May–June and September–October). For moth-pollinated flowers in general at Monteverde, a peak in flowering occurs in the early wet season (May–June; W. Haber, unpubl. data).

The fruiting phenologies of the Inga species overlapped even more than the flowering periods. Six of the seven species produced mature fruit during the late dry season and early wet season. Because Inga seeds are not protected against desiccation, seed maturation at the beginning of the wet season could be viewed as an adaptation for seedling establishment during favorable growing conditions.

Lauraceae. A phenological study of 23 species of Lauraceae at Monteverde showed that the distribution of the flowering periods through the year was indistinguishable from a random pattern (Wheelwright 1985, 1986, 1988, unpubl. data). Small peaks that occurred during September–October and March–May were not significantly different from a uniform distribution. Because the Lauraceae are pollinated by a wide variety of generalist insects (e.g., Hymenoptera, Diptera, Lepidoptera), the timing of flowering need not conform to the life history of a particular pollinator.

As with the Inga species, fruiting in the Lauraceae is significantly aggregated, with a peak of 13 species in fruit during the early wet season and a low period of three species in fruit during the early dry season. Seeds of Lauraceae cannot withstand desiccation and germinate soon after dispersal (Wheelwright 1985). The fruits are eaten and the seeds dispersed by large birds, such as Emerald Toucanets, Resplendent Quetzals, and Three-wattled Bellbirds (the latter two species are seasonal, intra-tropical migrants). Little evidence exists for the hypothesis that fruiting phenologies are staggered uniformly through the year to avoid competition for seed dispersers (Wheelwright 1985). Rather, the timing of fruiting in the Lauraceae is constrained by the germination requirements of seeds and perhaps also by the life histories of seed dispersers, such as the importance of fruit availability during the nesting period of quetzals (Wheelwright 1983). The timing of flowering, on the other hand, may more likely be influenced by competition for pollinators (see Wheelwright, "Sex Ratios," pp. 87–88).

Hawkmoth flowers. Unlike Inga species, other plants adapted for pollination by hawkmoths show a distinct flowering peak from April through June, at the start of the rainy season. High numbers continue through the rest of the wet season into October. This flowering pattern parallels the changes in seasonal abundance of hawkmoths, whose numbers build up through the wet season and decrease rapidly during the dry season (Haber 1983, 1984, Haber and Frankie 1988, W. Haber, unpubl. data).

3.3. Population Biology

With the exception of the areas of pollination and seed dispersal, little research on the population biology of plants has been done at Monteverde. The detailed demographic studies of Ocotea tenera are an exception (Gibson and Wheelwright 1995, 1996; see Wheelwright, "Sex Ratios," pp. 87–88, and Wheelwright, "A Hypothesis," pp. 281–283. In contrast, demographic studies have been common at La Selva Biological Station (Clark 1994) and Barro Colorado Island (Leigh et al. 1982, D'Arcy and Correa 1985).

Observing that falling branches commonly break up understory plants in the cloud forest and that these broken sticks sometimes take root, Kinsman (1990) tagged broken branches of 28 species of understory cloud forest shrubs and treelets, left them on the forest floor, and censused them annually over a period of five years to record their survival. Fourteen species remained alive for five years and some became reproductive. DNA screening techniques were used to investigate the role of branch fragmentation on the population structure of shrubs in the cloud forest (see Bush, "Clonal Reproduction," p. 88). High genetic relatedness within the colonies of the understory shrub *Poikilacanthus macranthus* indicated that in large part they were clones formed by fragmentation. Adaptations for regeneration by fragmentation in species of Rubiaceae also suggest a possible scenario for these plants to evolve into epiphytes (see Nepokropff and Sytsma, "Evolution in Psychotria," pp. 75–78). In land-

slides in the elfin forest at Monteverde, the standing crop of seeds in the soil was much greater than the number of seeds falling into traps (Myster 1993). The taxa that colonize landslides at Monteverde (Table 3.4) are closely related to those found on landslides in Puerto Rican cloud forests.

3.4. Biogeography

The lower montane zone at Monteverde (the Tilarán Mountain mass above 1200 m) supports 1708 species (57% of the total flora of the study area), which is approximately equal to the native flora of La Selva Biological Station (Hartshorn and Hammel 1994), but much higher than that of Santa Rosa National Park, Barro Colorado Island (Panama), and the lowland Amazonian forest sites in Manú National Park (Peru) and Manaus (Brazil) (Croat 1978, Foster 1990, Gentry 1990, 1993; Table 3.8). Monteverde's high diversity of epiphytes, especially the 419 species of orchids, contributes most to this difference, but the three life zones above 1200 m also support a large number of trees (500 plus species). There are more species

Table 3.8. A comparison of the species richness of floras for several regions and research sites in the neotropics.

Site	All Species	Trees	Ferns	Orchids	Area (km²)	Source
Mexico	ca. 20,000	NA	NA	NA	2,000,000	Rzedowski 1978
America north of Mexico	ca. 20,000[b]	ca. 700	NA	NA	21,461,100	Missouri Botanical Garden (www.mobot.org)
Peru	17,143[a]	NA	NA	1587	283,520	Brako and Zaruchi 1993
Costa Rica	ca. 9000	>2000	1058	ca. 1500	51,100	Mora-Retana and García 1992, Dressler 1993, Atwood, "Orchids," pp. 74–75, INBIO (www.inbio.ac.cr)
Texas	ca. 5000	NA	NA	NA	692,408	Rzedowski 1978, B. Hammel (pers. comm.)
Monteverde area > 700 m	2985[d]	755	358	>500	ca. 350	Haber 1991 (Appendix 1)
Manú National Park, Peru[b]	2874	NA	NA	NA	15,320	Foster 1990
Río Manú, floodplain and upland terrace	1856	NA	NA	NA	100	Foster 1990
Monteverde area > 1200 m	1723[d]	442	175	291	58	Haber 1991 (Appendix 1)
La Selva Biological Station	1678[d]	ca. 312	162	114	16	Atwood 1988, Hartshorn and Hammel 1994
Barro Colorado Island, Panama	1207[c]	ca. 270	80	78	16	Croat 1978, Hartshorn and Hammel 1994
Adolpho Ducke Forest Reserve, Manaus	ca. 1030	NA	37	24	100	Prance 1990
Santa Rosa National Park	603	NA	30	11	103	Janzen and Liesner 1980

[a]Does not include ferns.
[b]Includes ferns and bryophytes.
[c]Native and naturalized species; cultivated species are not included.
[d]Includes pteridophytes.

of epiphytes and ferns in Monteverde and La Selva than at the other sites, although this is in part due to more thorough collecting of these life forms in Costa Rica (Gentry 1985, 1990, 1993). A notable difference among sites is the high proportion of trees and low representation of herbs in the flora of the Manaus site compared with the other sites (Prance 1990). In terms of tree species density (number of species per hectare), the Amazonian sites are much higher than the others (Gentry 1990, Prance 1990). The Altantic slope plots at Monteverde are comparable to lowland sites in species density (Gentry 1990, Nadkarni et al. 1995; see Table 3.6).

The cloud forest at Monteverde is also distinct from the high cloud forest of the Cordillera de Talamanca in southern Costa Rica. Most of the latter forest belongs to a life zone not found in Monteverde, the montane rain forest (which lies mostly above 2400 m) and to the upper elevational limits of lower montane rain forest (extending to 2400 m). Many of the tree species characteristic of the highest peaks at Monteverde are more typical of cloud forests in the Talamancas (e.g., *Alfaroa costaricensis, Billia hippocastanum, Brunellia costaricensis, Ilex vulcanicola, Ocotea pittieri, O. viridiflora, Quercus corrugata, Weinmannia pinnata*) (Kappelle et al. 1990, Kappelle 1995, Kappelle and Leal 1996). In South American cloud forest, most of the genera are the same as those in Costa Rica, but nearly all the species are different (Kelly et al. 1994). The diversity of these montane cloud forests is generally lower than that of the lower montane life zone (Kelly et al. 1994, Kappelle 1995).

Much of the flora of the seasonal moist and dry forest on the Pacific slope extends from northwestern Costa Rica to southern Mexico (Hartshorn 1983, Janzen 1983). Excluding grasses (Poaceae), the flora of Santa Rosa National Park totals 603 species (Janzen and Liesner 1980), or about one-fifth as many species as at Monteverde, which demonstrates the comparatively low diversity of seasonally dry habitats in Costa Rica. In the same study, the whole of lowland Guanacaste Province listed only 992 species, compared with 3021 at Monteverde. The only notable affinity between the floras of Monteverde and Santa Rosa National Park occurs on Pacific slope below 1200 m. A total of 75 species of trees and treelets occur in both Monteverde and Santa Rosa; almost all of these are from the dry Pacific slope. Only 11 species of trees known from Santa Rosa reach the Monteverde community above 1200 m, and of these, only *Trema micrantha* (a weedy light gap colonist) and *Topobea brenesii* (a hemiepiphyte) reach the cloud forest above 1500 m (Janzen and Liesner 1980, Hartshorn and Poveda 1983, Haber 1991; Appendix 1).

Santa Rosa supports 17 species of orchids compared to more than 500 at Monteverde, with only one species (*Polystachya masayensis*) in common between the two sites. The largest family at Santa Rosa, Fabaceae, has 125 species compared to 117 at Monteverde, of which only 10 species reach the cloud forest. Santa Rosa has 30 species of ferns and fern allies compared to 358 at Monteverde. Conspicuous differences in the tree composition of the two sites are the prominence of Fabaceae and Bignoniaceae in the dry lowlands; those families are essentially replaced by Lauraceae, Meliaceae, and Myrtaceae in the cloud forest. *Inga*, with eight species occurring above 1200 m at Monteverde, is the only genus of Fabaceae well represented in the montane flora (see Koptur, "Breeding Systems," pp. 85–87).

In contrast, the flora of the Atlantic slope has a much stronger relationship with the lowland wet forest habitat of La Selva and the similar forests of South America (Croat 1978, Gentry 1983, 1985, 1993, Hartshorn and Hammel 1994). For example, 23% of the 114 species of orchids at La Selva also occur in Monteverde (Atwood 1987; Appendix 3). Both areas are rich in Lauraceae, Rubiaceae, Melastomataceae, and Piperaceae, and both display highly diverse epiphyte communities. La Selva's fern and epiphyte floras appear to be generally more abundant and diverse than at sites in similar life zones in South America (Gentry 1990, Hammel 1990, Hartshorn and Hammel 1994). Epiphytes and ferns of Costa Rica's Atlantic slope are favored by the northeast trade winds, which bring moisture from the ocean during the dry season, and by the cooling influence of cold air drainage down the mountain slope at night at La Selva. In contrast, some tree taxa (e.g., Moraceae and Sapotaceae) are much less prominent in both the premontane and lower montane life zone belts at Monteverde than in the lowland wet forest sites (Gentry 1990, Hartshorn and Hammel 1994).

Several species of Atlantic slope plants (e.g., *Ticodendron incognitum*, Ticodendraceae) indicate a relationship between Monteverde's flora and the Central American flora to the north. A very rare tree on the Atlantic slope of the Tilarán mountains at 700 m, *Deherainia* spec. nov. (Theophrastaceae), has its only known relatives in Mexico, Guatemala, and Cuba. Similarly, *Decazyx macrophyllus* (Rutaceae) was known only from Nicaragua to Mexico previous to the Monteverde Flora Project (Haber 1991). Another rare tree, *Caryodendron angustifolium* (Euphorbiaceae), collected on the Atlantic slope and at La Selva, is the northernmost extension of this South American genus.

The vegetation of the cloud forest in Monteverde has mixed origins, with clear affinities both to the cloud forests of northern Central America (e.g., *Quercus* species extending north to Mexico) and to South America (e.g., *Gymnosporia haberiana*, Celastraceae, an endemic of the Cordilleras de Tilarán and Guanacaste with its only congeners in South America). Several prominent taxa have their origins in the flora of temperate North America and Eurasia, such as *Cornus* (Cornaceae), *Ilex* (Aquifoliaceae), *Oreomunnea* (Juglandaceae), *Magnolia* (Magnoliaceae), *Myrica* (Myricaceae), *Prunus* (Rosaceae), *Quercus* (Fagaceae), some Theaceae, *Ulmus* (Ulmaceae), and *Viburnum* (Caprifoliaceae). A few genera have their origin in the temperate flora of the southern hemisphere, including southern Africa and Australia, such as *Podocarpus* (Podocarpaceae), *Panopsis* and *Roupala* (Proteaceae), and *Weinmannia* (Cunoniaceae; Gentry 1985, 1993).

In contrast to *Podocarpus*, which reaches north to Guatemala, the distribution of the North and Central American conifers (e.g., *Pinus* and *Cupressus* species) stops at or before the Nicaraguan lowlands; thus, no pines occur naturally in Costa Rica. Most of the montane flora that reaches Costa Rica from northern Central America also extends into South America; however, many Andean genera have not extended their ranges north across lowland Panama (Kappelle et al. 1990, Gentry 1993, Kelly et al. 1994, Kappelle 1995). The cloud forest also supports endemic species whose relatives lie either to the north or south, as well as in the lowlands.

3.5. Conservation

Two main conservation issues are of obvious concern for Monteverde's plants: the protection of rare species and the preservation of representative plant communities (i.e., local habitats, life zones, and edaphic associations). An example of a rare species is *Triuris* sp. near *brevistylis* (Triuridaceae). The only known specimen of this possibly undescribed species of saprophyte was collected by R. Lawton in the elfin forest (Davidse et al. 1994, W. Burger, pers. comm.). Another example is *Ocotea* ("tajo"), an undescribed species in the Lauraceae known from three reproductive individuals and a few saplings in the Quebrada Máquina. The entire known distribution of the species covers 10 ha. No part of this range is included within any protected area. Noteworthy new species found at Monteverde are the four species of orchids (then undescribed) in the genus *Stellilabium* found in one pasture near the entry to the MCFP (Atwood 1989). Three of the species were found in flower on a single fallen tree branch on the same day. Subsequently, two more new species have been found in the same area (Atwood and Dressler 1995, G. Barboza, pers. comm.), making Monteverde the worldwide center of diversity and endemism for this genus.

Another example of a rare tree with a limited local distribution is *Dalbergia tilarana* N. Zamora, ined., a new species known only from one hilltop between Monteverde and Tilarán. At this site, which consists of pastures and disturbed forest fragments, the tree is common and appears to reproduce successfully, although almost all of the seeds are killed by weevils. *Dalbergia* is the genus of Rosewood or "Cocobolo," a species of precious tropical hardwood used in making fine furniture and bowls.

The following undescribed or recently published tree species exemplify taxa that occur almost totally outside of officially protected areas: *Amphitecna gentryi* (Bignoniaceae), *Eugenia haberi* P. E. Sánchez, ined. (Myrtaceae), *Eugenia* "monteverdensis" (Myrtaceae), *Gymnosporia haberiana* B. Hammel (Celastraceae), *Ilex* "Cliff Edge" (Aquifoliaceae), *Ilex haberi* (Lundell) W. J. Hahn (Aquifoliaceae), *Mollinedia* "Monteverde" (Monimiaceae), *Myrcianthes* "Black Fruit" (Myrtaceae), *Ocotea* "Los Llanos", and *Pleurothyrium guindonii* van der Werff (Lauraceae). These recently discovered species are known only at Bajo del Tigre (Fig. 1.8), which includes 35 ha of mixed primary and secondary forest, and a few other sites on the upper Pacific slope between Monteverde and Tilarán. Most of this habitat type (a transition from premontane moist to premontane wet forest) has been extirpated from the country. The patches that remain may be too small to maintain viable populations of these species, especially because some of these trees grow only on ridge tops. These species exemplify the common situation in which the main objective should be to protect as much of the remaining habitat as possible. It would be desirable to protect even deforested parts of this habitat adjacent to the remaining fragments as sites for future succession and reforestation (Harris 1984, Alverson et al. 1994).

Conservation priorities for plants of the Monteverde area should focus on the preservation of as much as possible of the rare habitat on the upper Pacific slope within the premontane moist and wet life zones. Forests in these zones have suffered the highest degree of destruction and fragmentation from human impact and occupy a limited area in this region. Specific habitats within these zones, such as hilltops and ridges, merit special attention because of the rare species they support, especially endemics with narrow local distributions.

Acknowledgments I thank John Atwood, Erick Bello, Eladio Cruz, Gordon Frankie, Mike Grayum, Carlos Guindon, Barry Hammel, Chris Ivey, Darin Penneys, and Willow Zuchowski. Many colleagues provided rare specimens and unusual insights. The numerous plant taxonomists who delivered plant identifications over the last 15 years were essential for learning the Monteverde flora. Mike Grayum and Barry Hammel were especially helpful in spotting problem names, weeding out misidentifications and synonyms, finding voucher specimens, and fine-tuning the species lists. I also thank Bil Alverson, Mike Grayum, and Willow Zuchowski for their careful manuscript review.

Financial support was provided by the National Geographic Society, the Missouri Botanical Garden, the Jefferson L. Miller family, the National Science Foundation, C.I.E.E., A. A. Leath, and the Portland Audubon Society. I am grateful to the Monteverde Cloud Forest Preserve (administered by the Tropical Science Center), the Monteverde Conservation League, and many private landowners who gave their permission to carry out collecting and research on their properties. The staff and associates of the Museo Nacional de Costa Rica and the Instituto Nacional de Biodiversidad have always been generous with their time and knowledge about Costa Rica's botany.

TREES ON TREES
Francis E. Putz

In the wind- and mist-enshrouded elfin forest in Monteverde, trees that fall and open canopy gaps might themselves resprout and fill the gaps they create. Our research team measured rates of lateral encroachment by tree crowns bordering canopy gaps to monitor the release of previously suppressed trees in the understory and to compare experimentally the contributions to canopy gap regeneration of freshly dispersed seeds versus buried dormant seeds. Contrary to our expectations, more large seedlings of canopy trees occurred in recently formed gaps than in the adjacent understory.

Disturbed by the seemingly miraculous appearance of seedlings in recently formed treefall gaps, we looked upward and saw the source of the unaccounted-for seedlings: juvenile trees growing as epiphytes on humus-laden branches in the canopy. Seedlings of the most common canopy trees in the elfin forest of Monteverde that frequently grow as epiphytes include representatives of the Araliaceae (*Dendropanax latilobus, Oreopanax nubigenus, Schefflera rodrigueziana*), Melastomataceae (*Blakea chlorantha*), Clusiaceae (*Clusia* spp.), and Rubiaceae (*Cosmibuena valerii*). All were frequently encountered as epiphytes. Even in Monteverde's cloud forest, the canopy is brighter than the understory. The soil that builds up on large tree branches appears similar to the surface soil on the ground. Both are mostly organic, harbor earthworms and other soil invertebrates, and seldom dry out. Growing as an epiphyte in the cloud forest is not much different from growing on the ground, even for seedlings of large canopy trees. By being perched in the canopy, they enjoy the advantage of more light.

After their supporting trees fall, epiphytic tree seedlings reorient to be upright again and send roots down to the ground. The seedling stage is a period of high mortality for forest trees. By first becoming established on the branches of canopy trees, the seedlings circumvent the soil seed bank and avoid the darkness of the understory. The architectural plasticity needed to perform these feats of vegetative acrobatics may seem extraordinary, but these genera (except for *Cosmibuena* and *Dendropanax*, which are normally trees) contain numerous hemiepiphytes (species with a life history that includes both epiphytic and terrestrial phases; Putz and Holbrook 1989). Strangler figs and other hemiepiphytes are known for their protean qualities (Dobzhansky and Murca-Pires 1954). The "terrestrialization" process in hemiepiphytes is normally gradual as roots grow slowly down to the soil. In the elfin forest of Monteverde, however, terrestrialization often involves the trauma of the fallen host tree and startling contortions by the epiphytic tree seedlings carried down to the ground (Lawton and Putz 1988).

WHY STRANGLER FIGS DON'T STRANGLE STRANGLER FIGS
Jonathan H. Titus

Strangler figs (*Ficus* spp.) are trees that germinate in soil cavities on other trees, grow down to the ground, and subsequently "strangle" the tree upon which they grew by completely encircling it (see Fig. 3.16). A question has long puzzled observers: Why are strangler figs almost never observed growing on another strangler fig (Titus et al. 1990)? The rarity of strangler figs on strangler figs may be a case of a plant avoiding competition from its own progeny in a unique way. Although a few observations of fig seedlings and saplings have been described (W. Haber, pers. obs.), their occurrence is far more rare than expected. Mature fig trees produce numerous fleshy fruits that are relished by monkeys, bats, and birds. One would therefore expect an abundant rain of fig propagules on the parent tree. The convoluted growth form of strangler fig trees creates cavities that collect organic debris and seem to provide optimal establishment sites for strangler figs (Putz and Holbrook 1989).

Four hypotheses, not mutually exclusive, have been posed to explain the apparent lack of epiphytic fig seedlings on mature fig trees: (1) strangler figs are autotoxic, that is, produce substances inimical to the establishment of their own seedlings (an example of autopathy, the chemical inhibition of one's own species; Smith 1979, Rice 1984); (2) fig seedlings do not survive on reproductively mature strangler fig trees because soil cavities on strangler figs are not of sufficient volume or depth to support fig seedlings; (3) fig seedlings suffer mortality by pathogens and predators that frequent adult fig trees; and (4) fig seedlings fuse with conspecific hosts and are thus undetectable.

In May–August 1985, my colleagues and I investigated the first two hypotheses. Two strangler fig species, *Ficus pertusa* and *F. tuerckheimii*, common on trees in the pastures and forests of Monteverde, were selected for this study (Titus et al. 1990). To examine potential autotoxic effects at the time of germination, seeds from both fig species were collected and planted in pots and petri plates and subjected to the following six treatments (treatments 4 and 5 were conducted in pots only): (1) watered with conspecific stemflow (water flowing down the trunks of trees was collected); (2) watered with mixed samples of stemflow collected from tree species that frequently host strangler figs (*Inga brenesii*, *Acnistus arborescens*, *Cedrela tonduzii*, and *Ocotea tonduzii*); (3) watered with un-treated spring water; (4) mulched by shredded fresh leaves of *F. pertusa* and *F. tuerckheimii* mixed into the top 2.5 cm of soil and watered with spring water; (5) mulched with shredded fresh leaves of host species mixed into the top 2.5 cm of soil and watered with spring water; or (6) placed into a dark box and watered with spring water.

In another set of trials, seeds were planted into soil-filled branch cavities on 10 *F. pertusa* and 10 *F. tuerckheimii* trees located in pastures and forest fragments. Two large cavities were selected on each tree and 50 seeds were planted in each; one cavity of each pair was watered with conspecific stem flow and the other cavity with spring water. Seeds were also planted in soil-filled branch cavities found on known host trees. To determine if the quantity of soil in fig tree soil cavities was less than that in host tree soil cavities, the volume of soil in cavities was compared between strangler figs and host trees. To determine if *F. pertusa* and *F. tuerckheimii* seedlings can grow on the ground, fig seeds were planted 1 cm deep in areas that receive full sun and in areas under complete (non-*Ficus*) canopy cover. Germination was monitored in all experiments at 2–3-day intervals for 9–12 weeks.

Results showed that neither stemflow nor extracts of macerated *Ficus* leaves affected fig germination; germination levels were similar in all treatments, thereby ruling out autotoxic effects on germination. Germination of fig seeds planted in soil cavities was not correlated with either host species (conspecific *Ficus* or other tree species) or watering; fig seeds germinated in all the soil cavity treatments. No seeds germinated from the ground plots. Seeds have often been observed growing directly out of fruits; however, these seeds quickly succumb to fungal infection. Soil cavity size does not appear to determine germination success since the volume of soil in strangler fig soil cavities was not different from the soil volume of cavities on host trees where epiphytic figs were growing. We observed marginally higher germination in the petri plates than in the soil cavities, suggesting that pathogens on parent or host trees may inhibit *F. pertusa* and *F. tuerckheimii* seed germination and/or survival. Germination was highest in the constantly moist petri plates and lowest on the ground where surface soil dried despite daily watering. This suggests that high humidity levels may improve germination.

The fig enigma remains unsolved. The possibility that pathogens reduce germination and kill seedlings near adult congeners should be tested. Work in Borneo indicated that ants take many fig seeds, particularly from fig trees (Laman 1994). Future studies should include tracking individual fig seedlings planted in conspecific soil cavities for a period of time that would allow observation of possible pathogen attack or fusion with the host. DNA fingerprinting studies would also be of interest.

MUCUNA URENS, A TROPICAL LIANA
Gary W. Diller O'Dell

Lianas, woody perennial vinelike plants, abound in tropical forests. One species, *Mucuna urens* (Fabaceae), is a conspicuous component of secondary forests in Monteverde. Its local name, "ojo de buey" or "bull's eye," derives from its hard black seeds. The seeds contain toxic compounds that defend them against predators such as bruchid beetles, although large rodents such as agoutis ("guatusa," *Dasyprocta puncata*) readily eat and store seeds and serve as the major dispersers of *Mucuna* seeds. Apparently the 2.5-cm seeds can remain dormant in the soil for more than 10 years. Anyone who has handled the seed pods of *Mucuna* will appreciate its other common name, "pica-pica" or "itch-itch." Dangling on long stems from the canopy, the pods are covered by a velvety coat of fine urticating hairs that lodge in the skin (Fig. 3.11). Medicinal uses of the seeds include relief from hemorrhoids. The urticating hairs, mixed with honey, are believed to combat intestinal parasites.

Following germination, *Mucuna* actively grows toward and up small understory trees, ultimately reaching lengths of more than 70 m and heights of more than 20 m in the canopy. Favored hosts include *Conostegia* spp. (Melastomataceae) and hemiepiphytes such as *Clusia* spp. and members of the Araliaceae. Its long tangled vines provide canopy pathways for squirrels (*Sciurus* spp.) and other arboreal mammals and perches for sit-and-wait predators such as forest falcons (*Micraster* spp.) and nightingale thrushes (*Catharus* spp.). Pollination of the greenish yellow flowers is carried out by long-tongued bats such as *Glossophaga* spp., which visit the pendent candelabra-like inflorescence. Among the insects that feed on *Mucuna* leaves are the caterpillars of the iridescent blue morpho butterfly (*Morpho peleides*).

Lianas and vines represent a sizable fraction of all plant species and play an important but underappreciated role in neotropical forests. Besides serving as a food source for rodents, nectar-feeding bats, and butterflies, lianas and vines influence food webs in tropical forests. Some liana species, such as *Mucuna*, enrich tropical soils through their mutualistic interaction with nitrogen-fixing bacteria (*Rhizobium* spp.) that inhabit the plants' root nodules. Their leaves may make up as much as 30% of the dead leaves on the forest floors in the tropics.

Not all of their impacts on other species are positive. Lianas and vines cover nearly half of all canopy trees. In strong winds or heavy rains, they can damage their host plants by breaking branches and providing sites for attack by plant viruses and other pathogens. As a result, they may indirectly create opportunities for shade-intolerant species to colonize light gaps. Because of their impact on the structure and dynamics of tropical forests, lianas and vines should be included in conservation planning.

EPIPHYTES
Stephen W. Ingram

Epiphytes are plants that depend on trees and other plants for mechanical support but not nutrition. Unlike lianas and vines, epiphytes are typically rooted or anchored on a tree and are free of terrestrial connections for at least a portion of their life cycle. In the upper forest canopy, epiphytes are subject to more frequent cycles of wetting and drying, more sunlight, and more air movement than understory plants (Bohlman et al. 1995). Epiphytes differ from forest understory trees and shrubs in their adaptations for water storage, and in their ability to absorb and retain airborne nutrients through rain, mist, and dust. Wet neotropical montane forests, such as the MCFP, harbor more vascular epiphyte species and a greater abundance of epiphytes than any other forest type (Gentry and Dodson 1987; Fig. 3.1). More than 250 vascular epiphyte species were found in 4 ha of Monteverde's lower montane wet forest (Ingram et al. 1996), and many more occur in the Monteverde area (Haber 1991; Appendix 1).

Epiphyte biomass can exceed the foliar biomass of terrestrial herbs and shrubs in Monteverde (Nadkarni 1984). Within trees, epiphytic vegetation is most abundant among the inner canopy branches. Of the total amount (dry weight) of epiphytic matter held by inner canopy branches, 50–60% consists of dead organic matter (Ingram and Nadkarni 1993). The balance of the epiphytic matter is composed of 30–35% living angiosperms and their roots, 5–8% ferns, and 5–20% bryophytes (with bryophytes relatively more abundant on smaller, younger branches of the inner canopy). The living vegetation and associated organic matter are approximately four times more abundant on horizontal than vertical branches, and more abundant (per unit surface area) on larger than smaller branches. Although small epiphytes may grow on large branches and tree trunks, a positive correlation exists between epiphyte size and branch circumference. Large epiphytes on small branches do not persist as long as they would on larger, sturdier branches. Large bromeliads on twigs and small outer branches frequently fall from the canopy.

True or "obligate" epiphytes (sensu Benzing 1990) spend their entire lives perched on trees. Many exhibit adaptations in growth form and habit that enable them to thrive in tree canopies. For example, Anthurium scandens and Encyclia pseudopygmaea, which have creeping growth habits and the ability to root at leaf nodes, are common and widespread epiphytes in Monteverde. Orchids and bromeliads, among the most diverse and abundant epiphyte families, are predominantly obligate epiphytes. Faculta-tive epiphytes, such as many Ericaceae, Araliaceae, Alzatea verticillata (Alzateaceae), and Oerstedella exasperata (Orchidaceae), are more adaptable and typically grow on trees, but they may also grow along roadcuts or in well-drained forest soil. In elfin forest habitats, the distinction between plants growing terrestrially and epiphytically is least clear. Species that grow epiphytically in the lower montane wet forest of the Pacific slope (e.g., Schefflera rodrigueziana) occur as free-standing trees in the elfin forest.

"Accidental" epiphytes are plants that normally grow rooted in terrestrial soil but may occasionally invade the arboreal soil of canopy branches and crotches of tree trunks. In Monteverde, examples of accidental epiphytes include Dioscorea lepida and Weinmannia pinnata (see Putz, "Trees on Trees," p. 70). Hemiepiphytes, or "half" epiphytes, spend part of their life cycle rooted on trees and part rooted in the ground. "Primary" hemiepiphytic trees and shrubs germinate in tree crowns, grow leaves and branches in the canopy, and eventually grow roots down to tap nutrients in the forest soil. Strangler figs (Ficus spp.) have numerous roots that coalesce, eventually forming a "trunk" around the host tree, and finally overgrowing and killing it (see Titus, "Why Strangler Figs," pp. 71–72). "Secondary" hemiepiphytes (e.g., some individuals of some species of Araceae, Cyclanthaceae, Marcgraviaceae) start out rooted in the ground, climb tree trunks, and later lose contact with terrestrial soil (Lawton and Williams-Linera 1996).

The Monteverde epiphyte flora is composed of 27 angiosperm families and 13 pteridophyte (fern) families—as many angiosperm families with epiphyte species as are found in all of Mexico (Aguirre-Leon 1992). Species of Orchidaceae, Pteridophyta, Bromeliaceae, Ericaceae, Araceae, Piperaceae, and Gesneriaceae (in decreasing order of species richness) comprise approximately 80% of the epiphyte flora (Ingram et al. 1996). Families with at least four epiphytic species at Monteverde include (but are not restricted to) Araliaceae, Asteraceae, Begoniaceae, Clusiaceae, Melastomataceae, and Rubiaceae (Appendix 2).

BROMELIADS
Harry E. Luther

The Bromeliaceae is a mostly neotropical, largely epiphytic plant family with about 2750 species (Luther and Sieff 1996). The family was last monographed as part of the Flora Neotropica series (Smith and Downs 1974) and more recently treated for the Central American taxa with keys and descriptions in Spanish by Utley in Flora Meso-americana (Davidse et al. 1994). Nearly 200 species are recorded from Costa Rica (Luther 1995), which includes Mexican, Central American, Andean, and endemic bromeliad species. The family's distribution and ecology in Costa Rica has been presented in Burt-Utley and Utley (1977).

Most bromeliads can be recognized by their rosette of water-impounding leaves, which are covered with scales, and by their conspicuous inflorescence, which often has colorful bracts. Bromeliads are usually notable elements of wet neotropical forests, where they are often the most numerous and massive epiphytes present. They are an important source of shelter and food for a variety of animals (Nadkarni and Matelson 1989, Benzing 1990) and play an important role in forest nutrient cycling (Nadkarni 1986, Benzing 1990).

A total of 72 species have been found in the Monteverde Reserve Complex and immediately outside the MCFP in dry and warmer habitats. Monteverde species belong to the subfamilies Bromelioideae (leaves mostly serrate-margined, ovary inferior, fruit a fleshy berry, seeds unappendaged), Pitcairnioideae (leaves mostly serrate-margined, ovary mostly superior, fruit a dry capsule, seeds caudate or winged), and Tillandsioideae (leaves always entire, ovary superior, fruit a dry capsule, seeds plumose; Appendix 4).

ORCHIDS
John T. Atwood

A project on the Orchidaceae of Monteverde was initiated in 1988. With preliminary estimates ranging from 300 to 350 species (Atwood 1987), the list tallies more than 500, the highest orchid species diversity known from any comparable area of the neotropics (C. H. Dodson, pers. comm.). The orchids of Monteverde represent 39% of the orchids of Costa Rica, with an estimated 1270 species (Dressler 1981). Monteverde's high species diversity is probably due to a variety of life zones providing diverse habitats (Tosi 1969), the high species richness of midelevation tropical sites (Dressler 1981), the diversity of pollinators, and high local collection intensity.

Most orchids of undisturbed forests exhibit narrow elevational distributions. *Maxillaria fulgens*, found from 1600 m to La Selva Biological Station (ca. 50–100 m) is an exception. In Monteverde, the few orchids characteristic of the upper montane regions to the south include species of *Masdevallia* and two rare unidentified species of *Telipogon* (G. Barboza, pers. comm.). Anomalous elevational range extensions from lower sites may be due in part to pastures next to forest fragments, and to locally warmer microclimates. Pastures at 1550 m support *Maxillaria campanulata*, *M. nasuta*, and *Masdevallia nidifica*, also found below 900 m on the Atlantic slope. *Encyclia abbreviata* and *Nidema boothii*, occurring at 1350 m in Monteverde, are also known at La Selva.

Orchids are traditionally viewed as rare plants, and pastures seem an unlikely place for their survival. Yet species counts in two Monteverde pastures exceeded 75. Elevated orchid diversity in fragmented habitats has been documented elsewhere (Williams-Linera et al. 1995), so pastures may be significant for orchid conservation. Threats to orchids include environmental degradation and exploitation of habitat-specific orchids. Examples in Monteverde of exploited species include *Cattleya skinneri* (the national flower of Costa Rica), once locally abundant in rocky semideciduous forests of the Pacific slope (H. Rockwell, pers. comm.). Although the orchids have been exploited for many years, we observed mature plants in the wild (some with capsules) and juveniles within close reach, as well as enormous plants in high canopies out of reach of collectors. The exploitation tolerance of this population is unknown, but remaining plants appear to be reproducing and recolonizing. Removal of the forest would pose the greatest threat to the orchid, as rock-dwelling survivors would be targets for collectors.

Other orchids may be less able to sustain habitat exploitation or collection. *Rossioglossum schlieperianum* is a rare epiphyte in Monteverde, restricted to large tree trunks exploited for lumber. *Oncidium panduriforme* and *Otoglossum chiriquense* occur naturally in low densities and are vulnerable to habitat loss. *Rossioglossum schlieperianum* and *Otoglossum chiriquense* could potentially be further imperiled by commercial exploitation; the latter is virtually impossible to cultivate. Despite its rarity, the relatively unattractive *Oncidium panduriforme* will probably never be threatened by collectors in protected habitats.

One way to minimize collection of orchid species vulnerable to collectors would be to flood markets with plants that have been mass-produced from seed or tissue culture using aesthetically superior clones as parent stock. Monteverde would provide the ideal climate for production of many orchids. Although some species clearly require undisturbed habitats, others are locally weedy on disturbed roadsides, including *Habenaria monorrhiza, H. floribunda, Epidendrum radicans*, and numerous *Elleanthus*. These species, which naturally occur along landslides or areas that are occasionally burned, benefit from patchy human disturbances.

Endemism among orchids of Monteverde appears to be low. Ten species are known only from Monteverde, but these are mostly minute and easily overlooked. Of these minute orchids, five species of *Stellilabium* have been discovered, three of them originating from a single branch fall. One of the five species, *S. barbozae*, was discovered in 1995 growing at the Information Center of the MCFP in public view. The yellow-flowered *Maxillaria haberi* is known only from the lower Peñas Blancas Valley and one site on the Atlantic slope of Volcan Barva.

As at La Selva (Atwood 1988), the largest three orchid genera at Monteverde are *Epidendrum, Maxillaria,* and *Pleurothallis,* comprising 37% of the orchid flora (Appendix 3). No large orchid genus is as well studied as *Maxillaria* in Costa Rica (106 spp.). If the number of *Maxillaria* species is representative of the orchids as a whole, the total number of orchid species in Monteverde could exceed 600. The patchy and lofty distribution of orchids makes documentation a long process.

Acknowledgments   I thank William Haber for his logistic help, access to his continually revised species database, and general encouragement in field efforts, and Robert Dressler for discussions with the species list. I thank Steve Ingram and Karen Ferrell-Ingram for collecting Costa Rican orchids, and Dora Emilia Mora de Retana for identifications of species of Oncidiinae and persistence in obtaining permits. This material is based on work supported by the National Science Foundation and by the Office of Forestry, Environment and Natural Resources, Bureau of Science and Technology, of the U.S. Agency for International Development under NSF Grant DEB-9200812.

EVOLUTION IN CLOUD FOREST *PSYCHOTRIA* SECTION *NOTOPLEURA* VIA GROWTH FORM DIVERSIFICATION

Molly Nepokroeff & Kenneth J. Sytsma

The epiphytic growth form has evolved independently in at least 80 families of vascular plants (Kress 1989; see Ingram, "Epiphytes," pp. 72–73). Their growth form evolution has been little studied in cloud forests. The evolution of epiphytism from terrestrial ancestors has been documented in *Columnea* (Gesneriaceae; Smith and Sytsma 1994) and has been suggested for woody gentians (Sytsma 1987). However, the evolution of epiphytism has most likely occurred via many different evolutionary pathways, even within families and genera (Benzing 1989). The genus *Psychotria* (Rubiaceae) is one of the largest genera of flowering plants, with 1250–1600 species worldwide (Hamilton 1980). Appendix 1 lists three species of epiphytic *Psychotria* (Rubiaceae), a genus of mostly understory shrubs. In growth form, most *Psychotria* are branched understory shrubs. Others are epiphytes, tuberous myrmecophiles (ant-inhabited plants), lianas, and succulent, single-branched forms (Sohmer 1988). In Monteverde, many species of *Psychotria* occur sympatrically. Due to its large number of species, the genus serves as a model system to understand speciation patterns in the tropics.

Phylogenetic systematics provides the historical framework for understanding processes of evolution and adaptive radiation (O'Hara 1988). A promising technique to study the adaptive radiation of a lineage is to superimpose the characters of interest onto a well-supported phylogeny (Harvey and Pagel 1991). A molecular phylogeny derived independently from morphological characters avoids the bias inherent in analyzing evolutionary events based on the characters under examination (Givnish et al. 1994).

One natural group, *Psychotria* section *Notopleura* Bentham, is represented in the MCFP by seven species. Members of section *Notopleura* are characterized by succulent, unbranched, terrestrial habit or branched, epiphytic growth form, a single dorsal median ridge on the seeds, and a single inflorescence in each leaf axil. *Psychotria* section *Notopleura* is well differentiated from other members of the genus *Psychotria,* and molecular evidence suggests that it may hold a basal position in the genus or may be considered a separate genus (Nepokroeff and Sytsma 1996).

A recent phylogeny, based on independent molecular characters (ribosomal DNA sequence data;

Nepokroeff 1992, Nepokroeff et al. 1993), shows that succulent, unbranched, terrestrial forms and branched epiphytes have evolved from shrubby, multibranched ancestors (Fig. 3.21). Succulence and other characteristics in the common ancestors of the epiphytic and the succulent unbranched lineages may have acted as preadaptations (*sensu* Bock 1959) allowing evolutionary radiation into lower understory and canopy level niches.

At least three scenarios for the evolution of epiphytism from the ancestral state of terrestrial branched habit are possible based on this phylogeny. In the first scenario (Fig. 3.22, pathway A), evolution of epiphytism occurred through developmental suppression of the "adult" woody, branched shrub form (found in most *Psychotria*) in the more derived "neotenic" succulent, unbranched, intermediate forms (such as *Psychotria uliginosa*, common in the Monteverde understory; Fig. 3.23), and epiphytes of section *Notopleura*. Neoteny is the evolutionary process that results in an adult organism becoming reproductively mature while maintaining some juvenile characteristics (Futuyma 1986). Because epiphytes are more branched than the succulent, unbranched, terrestrial "intermediates," the branched character could be either regained (Fig. 3.22, pathway A) or retained from ancestral forms (pathway B). Alternatively, the branched habit regained in pathway A in the epiphytic species could be nonhomologous to the ancestral type and evolved separately in the epiphytic lineage. Morphological studies are needed to distinguish among these possibilities. In the case of pathway B, the evolution of a hypothetical intermediate stage (succulent, terrestrial, branched) is implied. Therefore, we suggest that pathway A is the more likely scenario of growth form evolution.

Morphological characteristics shared by both terrestrial and epiphytic members of section *Notopleura* support evolutionary pathway A. Succulence, leaf adaptations, and serial body plan represent innovations developed in the section *Notopleura* lineage. Succulence in the ancestors of section *Notopleura* lineages might be a preadaptation for evolving the epiphytic habit, since epiphytes often are subject to fluctuating levels of available water and nitrogen deficiency (Esau 1977). Specialized leaf adaptations are the most common form of water storage in epiphytes (Madison 1977) with aqueous hypodermis (water storage tissue) found only in epiphytic members of the genus *Psychotria* (Metcalfe and Chalk 1950). Terrestrial members of section *Notopleura* should be examined for presence of this character. Another possible morphological preadaptation in members of *Psychotria* section *Notopleura* is a serial body plan. Members of section *Notopleura* grow clonally from horizontal rhizomes and easily propagate from cuttings. In fluctuating environments such as the canopy, physiologically independent units may have a selective advantage following catastrophic events (Madison 1977).

This proposed evolutionary pathway of growth form suggests one way in which the species-rich genus *Psychotria* has maintained a form of spatial isolation leading to speciation and diversification. Temporal reproductive isolation (e.g., flowering at different times) has been reported for *Psychotria* subgenus *Psychotria* on Barro Colorado Island in Panama (Hamilton 1980). Phenological partitioning in subgenus *Psychotria* exists, but the evolution of distinct growth forms may represent spatial niche partitioning, as species radiate into distinct levels of the forest understory.

Although most species of subgenera *Psychotria* and *Heteropsychotria* are shrubs or small trees reaching

Figure 3.21. Simplified cladogram generated from rDNA sequence data showing evolution of epiphytism from woody branched ancestors through succulent, unbranched subshrub intermediate in *Psychotria* section *Notopleura*. One morphological character involved in the evolutionary pathway from terrestrial to epiphytic habit is branched growth form. Two equally possible scenarios for evolution of this character are shown in Figure 3.22.

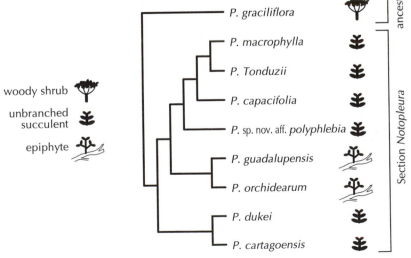

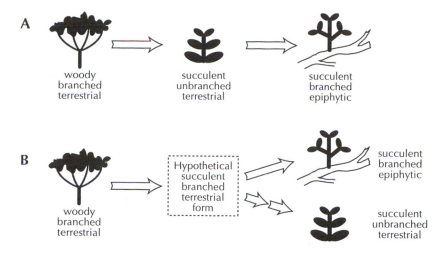

Figure 3.22. *(top)* Evolution of growth form in the genus *Psychotria* may involve one of two possible scenarios regarding the character of branched habit. In pathway A, developmental suppression of "adult" (woody, branched) habit in "neotenic" intermediate species and subsequent release of suppression in epiphytic forms is suggested. An equally likely alternative, shown in pathway B, involves retention of adult branched form in the epiphytic lineage and independent gain of the neotenic unbranched form in two separate lineages of the rest of section *Notopleura*. **Figure 3.23.** *(bottom)* *Psychotria uliginosa* Sw. is the type species for *Psychotria* section *Notopleura* and bears the succulent unbranched growth form that characterizes this group. This species is common in the Monteverde Cloud Forest Preserve and surrounding community.

3 m, members of section *Notopleura* are usually less than 1 m tall. Further stratification occurs by radiation of epiphytic forms into the canopy (Figs. 3.23, 3.24). Such stratification has implications for pollination biology and maintaining reproductive isolation in sympatric taxa. Many congeneric species are sympatrically distributed in the tropics, and spatial isolation as well as temporal partitioning (Grant 1981) may play a role in maintaining reproductive isolation and hence species richness in this genus.

Epiphytism has evolved at least twice in separate lineages in the genus *Psychotria*, once in the neotropics and once in Australasia (Nepokroeff and Sytsma 1996). It is likely that the evolutionary pathway for both lineages is different since the Australasian epiphytes supplement nutrition and moisture intake via ant-inhabited swollen tubers, whereas the neotropical members of section *Notopleura* are not associated with ants and instead dwell on humus mats in the canopy.

Acknowledgments   We are indebted to Kandis Elliot for the illustrations, B. Hammel for field assistance and leaf material, and C. M. Taylor for leaf material.

Figure 3.24. Growth form evolution may be a form of ecological niche partitioning leading to speciation in the genus *Psychotria*. This model predicts evolutionary radiation into distinct levels of the rain forest understory.

BRYOPHYTES
S. Robert Gradstein

Tropical rain forests, including montane cloud forests, harbor a great diversity of bryophytes. Of an estimated 4000 species (2700 mosses, 1300 hepatics) occurring in tropical America, about 80% of the hepatics and 50% of the mosses are confined to these forests (Gradstein and Pócs 1989). Even though they are often small and inconspicuous, bryophytes play significant roles in forest ecosystems. Thick bryophyte mats on trees capture large quantities of rain water and help to keep humidity in the forest high (Pócs 1980). They serve as a substrate for the establishment of vascular epiphytes and offer shelter to many invertebrates and microorganisms.

Most of the bryophytes in cloud forests are epiphytes. Trees, treelets, shrubs, saplings, and woody lianas are colonized by these epiphytes and epiphylls (see Morales, "Plants Growing on Living Leaves," p. 80). Subtle differences in water supply, nutrients, light, and inclination of the substrate affect the ability of bryophytes to establish themselves, so tree bases, trunks, ascending branches, and twigs often support different species (Richards 1984). Some occur exclusively in the moist, shaded understory of the forest ("shade epiphytes"), while others are only found in the forest canopy high above the ground ("canopy epiphytes"). Some species have wide vertical distributions in the forest and occur throughout the understory and the canopy ("generalists").

In forests below 1000 m, bryophyte cover is low and mostly restricted to the canopy. Hepatics of the family Lejeuneaceae are the most important bryophytes of the lowland rain forest; about 30% of the species are members of this family. In montane wet forests, growth of epiphytic bryophytes is much more luxuriant, and the forest floor may be covered with dense bryophyte carpets. The lower temperatures and higher light levels in the montane forests, and the availability of plentiful water due to frequent clouds and fog, favor the accumulation of dead organic material on the ground and the abundant growth of bryophytes. Tree trunks and branches may be covered with a dense fur of bryophytes up to 20 cm thick and made up of different growth forms, including "pendents." Such taxa thrive only in perhumid environments and are entirely absent from the lowland rain forest.

Little work has been done on the bryophytes of Monteverde. Reed and Robinson (1971) published a list of 164 species (90 mosses, 73 hepatics, 1 hornwort) based on random collecting in the forests and in pasture areas. Additional species were reported by Gradstein et al. (1994) and Sillett et al. (1995). The latter study analyzed the epiphytic bryophyte flora in the canopy of six *Ficus tuerckheimii* trees, three in the dense forest and three isolated ones in adjacent pasture land, and demonstrated that the two sets of trees had very different species assemblages.

We conducted an inventory of bryophytes in November 1992 and January 1994 within a 4-ha study site within the MCFP (ca. 1550 m elevation; Nadkarni 1986, Nadkarni and Matelson 1992, Ingram and Nadkarni 1993; see Ingram, "Epiphytes," pp. 72–73). Our inventory yielded 190 bryophyte species: 133 hepatics, 56 mosses, and 1 hornwort (*Megaceros vincentianus*). The mean number of species per hectare was 88. In comparison, a very detailed analysis of the canopy by Sillett et al. (1995) found 109 bryophyte species on three *Ficus tuerckheimii* trees in the MCFP. Species-area curves showed that one plot yielded 45% of total diversity, and two plots yielded 75%. In comparison, when bryophyte diversity on trees only is studied (excluding shrubs, logs, etc.), the 75% level is usually obtained by analysis of only four trees (Wolf 1993).

The absolute dominance of hepatics over mosses at the study site in terms of species number is characteristic of neotropical moist forests. In paleotropical forests, mosses tend to be more abundant (Gradstein and Pócs 1989). *Plagiochila* was by far the most speciose genus (18 spp.), followed by the hepatic genera *Lejeunea* and *Bazzania* (7 spp. each), and *Frullania* and *Radula* (6 spp.). Among the mosses, *Lepidopilum* and *Macromitrium* (4 spp.) were the most speciose genera, the former mainly in the understory, the latter in the canopy.

Thick branches of the lower canopy were by far the richest habitat for bryophytes and yielded about 100 species. Trunk bases, shrubs, lianas, saplings and living leaves were also rich in species, harboring 35–45 species. The lowest number of species (16) was found on rotten logs; however, half of these were exclusive to rotten logs and not found elsewhere. A similar figure was obtained for epiphylls: about half of these species (23) were only found on living leaves; others occurred on other substrates. Species richness in the canopy compared to the understory was 117 versus 121, respectively. Of these, 48 (25%) occurred both in the canopy and the understory, 38% were exclusive to the understory, and 36% to the canopy. From a conservation standpoint, the shade epiphytes of the forest are of particular interest. They are more seriously affected by forest disturbance than are sun epiphytes due to their lower drought tolerance and are the first to disappear when the forest canopy is opened up (Gradstein 1992).

Acknowledgments We thank Rodrigo Solano for logistical support; Riclef Grolle, Andrea Lücking, Jiri Vána, and K. Yamada for help with identifications; and Gregorio Dauphin, who helped with the inventory of the epiphylls. Fieldwork in Costa Rica by the first author was supported by the Netherlands Foundation for Tropical Research (WOTRO) and the National Geographic Society Committee on Research and Exploration.

PLANTS GROWING ON LIVING LEAVES
María I. Morales

Most epiphyllous or foliicolous (leaf-inhabiting) plants in Monteverde are foliose liverworts belonging to the family Lejeuneaceae, a group that comprises about 90 genera and hundreds of species worldwide. Foliicolous mosses are few; most also grow on twigs and spread to leaves. Mosses appear unable to establish themselves on leaves as young plants (Richards 1984). Until recently, foliicolous bryophytes were documented in Central America by a single study from El Salvador, which reported one moss species and 63 epiphyllous liverwort species (Winkler 1967). The epiphyllous bryophyte flora in Braulio Carrillo National Park, Costa Rica, revealed 83 bryophyte species, the highest species number thus far recorded from a single locality (Lücking 1995).

Epiphyllous species are found mostly near the ground, but some colonize the forest canopy if it supports high humidity. Epiphylls colonize many species of higher plants, but "prefer" those with smooth leaf surfaces, which promote the establishment of reproductive devices with adherent cells. Colonized leaves are frequently long-lived, so the epiphyllae are able to complete their life cycles before the leaf falls (Winkler 1967). Epiphyllae have developed means of rapid vegetative reproduction such as plant fragments and gemmae (multicellular structures that are able to develop new plants).

Although many genera of epiphylls can occur on a single leaf and many species within a genus can occur in a small area, the most common colonizers in Monteverde belong to the following genera: (1) *Cyclolejeunea*, which produces rounded gemmae on the leaf border; (2) *Ceratolejeunea*, a brown shiny liverwort with perianths (female structures) that have four small horns at the top; (3) *Odontolejeunea*, with dentate leaves; and (4) *Metzgeria*, a thallose form. There are also very small species, for example, *Drepanolejeunea* and the tiny *Aphanolejeunea*, invisible to the naked eye.

Rhizoids of the epiphyllous liverwort *Radula flaccida* penetrate the leaf cuticle and insert themselves between the cells of the upper epidermis (Berrie and Eze 1975). Water from the host plant may help epiphyllous liverworts survive the dry season. Epiphylls absorb minerals from their hosts and are thus semiparasites (Eze and Berrie 1977).

Is shading of the host leaf by epiphylls sufficient to have an effect on the photosynthetic rate of the host? A coating of epiphyllous *Radula flaccida* intercepts a maximum of 2% of the incident light (Eze and Berrie 1977), a seemingly insignificant amount. Richards (1984) pointed out that the most heavily colonized leaves are the oldest ones, which probably no longer make an important contribution to the energy balance of the plant. On the other hand, colonization by epiphylls may benefit the host plant, because epiphylls provide a suitable environment for nitogen-fixing bacteria and cyanobacteria (Richards 1984). The relationship between some plants and their epiphylls may thus be mutualistic.

There are many unanswered questions about epiphylly. Are foliicolous liverworts obligate epiphyllae? Are they specific to one species of leaf? The latter is unlikely, because epiphylls do not seem to receive organic compounds from the host (Eze and Berrie 1977). Host leaves may exude substances that are needed for growth of some foliicolous species.

Epiphylls only rarely colonize some leaves (e.g., *Costus* and *Dieffenbachia*). An explanation is the irregular surface of the former and the presence of an irritating substance in the latter. Texture or other leaf characteristics and the incidence and distribution of light are considered the most important factors in controlling colonization by epiphyllous plants (Monge-Nájera 1989). Based on a cluster analysis, Lücking (1995) concluded that characteristics of the host plants are responsible for epiphyll composition on different leaves and that microclimate conditions are less important.

MISTLETOES AND WHERE THEY GROW
Sarah Sargent

Mistletoes are unusual flowering plants in several closely related families. The defining characteristic of mistletoes is that they parasitize the aboveground stems of other plants, especially trees (Kuijt 1969). Unlike ordinary epiphytes, mistletoes obtain all of their mineral nutrients and water by forming direct connections with water-conducting xylem inside host branches. Mistletoes are unable to grow normal roots and depend completely on host plants for survival. All mistletoes have photosynthetic pigments and produce their own sugars; they do not parasitize the phloem of their hosts as do other types of parasitic plants. Most people are familiar with mistletoe because of the Christmas mistletoe tradition that originated in Europe, which is based on *Viscum album* (Viscaceae). However, the majority of mistletoes are tropical. Mistletoes are found in four plant families in the order Santalales. The largest of these four are the Viscaceae and the Loranthaceae, with about 370 and 700 species, respectively (Nickrent 1993). Most mistletoes in Monteverde belong to these two large families, but *Antidaphne viscoidea*, in the small family Eremolepidaceae (12 species), is also present (Sargent 1994).

All mistletoes have extremely sticky seeds, which enables them to adhere to the branches of potential hosts rather than falling to the ground where they would be unable to establish the host connections. The stickiness results from a specialized tissue, the viscin, attached to the seeds (Gedalovich-Shedletzky et al. 1989). In all tropical mistletoes, the seeds are dispersed by birds (see Sargent, "Specialized Seed Dispersal," pp. 288–289).

One of the mysteries about mistletoes is why they are so unevenly distributed among trees; some trees are loaded with mistletoes while others have none. What prevents mistletoes from growing on every tree? Within a single host species, why do mistletoes occur on some trees but not on others? One possibility is that mistletoes are limited by seed dispersal; perhaps birds rarely carry seeds to new hosts or to new branches within hosts. Alternatively, perhaps seeds fail to establish the critical connections with the host xylem once they get there.

To address the second possibility, I conducted a seed planting experiment to determine the fate of mistletoe seeds after they become established on a host (Sargent 1995). Working with a common mistletoe species, *Phoradendron robustissimum* (Viscaceae), and its most common host species, *Sapium glandulosum* (Euphorbiaceae), I studied two aspects of the way birds deposit seeds that might influence the ability of seeds to become established: (1) the size of the host stem (i.e., twig or branch) onto which birds deposit seeds, and (2) the number of seeds deposited in one place. I chose 10 trees, in each of which I marked segments of branches in seven diameter classes (< 5 mm to > 80 mm). I stuck seeds at different diameters on the marked twigs by hand. I checked on the seeds over the next 3 years to determine which seeds established as seedlings and which ones died, and to determine why they died.

Few seeds survived: 10% were alive after 1 year, 4% after 2 years, and 3% after 3 years. Seeds in clumps were no more likely to live than single seeds. Twig diameter, however, had a strong impact on a seed's chance of becoming established (Fig. 3.25). Smaller twigs were better for initial establishment, but many of the smallest twigs died (Fig. 3.26). This left the intermediate twig sizes as the best for long-term survival of the mistletoe seedlings.

There was tremendous variation in survival of seeds and seedlings even on twigs in the optimal size range. Many seeds simply disappeared (Fig. 3.26). In another experiment, I placed seeds on branches with three different types of protection: complete protection (inside mesh bags), protection from crawling seed predators (surrounded by Tanglefoot), and protection from dislodgment (roofs of bag material, open on the sides). Control seeds were placed on branches without any protection. As expected, complete protection was best; seeds in bags had the lowest rates of disappearance (near 0%). The Tanglefoot barrier was also effective (22% disappeared), suggesting that many of the seeds that disappeared had been eaten by seed predators that crawl along the host twigs (e.g., ants and arboreal mice; see Timm and LaVal, "Observations," pp. 235–236).

Another cause of variation in establishment success of mistletoe seeds may have been differences in nutrients and water available from the host trees. Formation of new xylem connections between mistletoes and their hosts is a passive process on the part of the mistletoe (Sallé 1983). Newly formed host vessels are tapped by the mistletoe as they form, resulting in xylem-to-xylem connections between host and parasite (Calvin et al.

1991). Such connections cannot form in the absence of host growth at the site of attachment of the mistletoe. Thus, limited host growth may prevent or constrain mistletoe establishment. The nutrient status of the host is also known to influence water-use efficiency of mistletoes, suggesting that nutrient concentration in xylem sap may limit mistletoe growth (Ehleringer et al. 1985). Although water availability may not often be limiting in Monteverde, within- and between-year variation in rainfall may contribute to fluctuations in host water potentials and the ability of mistletoes to become established. A survey of the age structure of a desert mistletoe population showed that mistletoes failed to become established in years of summer drought (Dawson et al. 1990). In Monteverde, trees associated with barnyards or septic systems tend to have much higher levels of mistletoe infections than others, suggesting that both hosts and mistletoes thrive in these rich conditions. Mistletoe seeds thus fare best on intermediate-sized twigs on fast-growing hosts. However, many aspects of the puzzle of mistletoe distribution remain unknown and warrant further research.

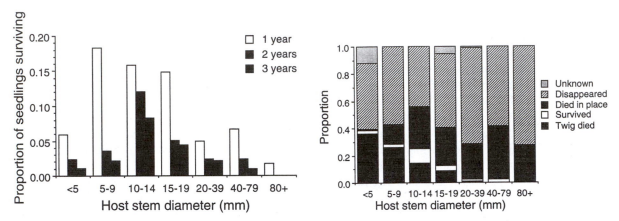

Figure 3.25. *(above left)* Proportion of *Phoradendron robustissimum* seedlings surviving for 1, 2, and 3 years on each size class of host stem diameter, summed over replicate trees. **Figure 3.26.** *(above right)* Fates of *Phoradendron robustissimum* seedlings after 2 years, as a function of initial host stem diameter, reported as proportions of all seeds planted in each size class of host stem, summed over replicate trees.

AN EXCEPTIONAL MISTLETOE, *GAIADENDRON PUNCTATUM*
Sarah Sargent

Monteverde is a site of an unusual species of mistletoe, the terrestrial *Gaiadendron punctatum* (Loranthaceae). A large stand of it grows on the uphill side of the road past "Windy Corner," the sharp turn 200 m before the entrance to the MCFP. *Gaiadendron* is a large shrub or small tree with haustoria that are different from those of other members of the family; they attach to the roots of other plants, often smaller plants including ferns (Kuijt 1963). The seedlings go through a brief free-living period, during which they form a tuber, before they begin to parasitize neighboring plants. *Gaiadendron* can grow on the ground, but it also grows high in trees in epiphyte mats. Their locations are typically places with canopy-like conditions, such as the steep exposed bank near Windy Corner. When it grows off the ground in epiphyte mats, it has never been found to parasitize the supporting tree, only its neighboring epiphytes. It is thus epiphytic with respect to the tree but parasitic with respect to other epiphytes.

There is some debate about the origins of terrestrialism in this species, whether it represents the primitive condition of the Loranthaceae or whether it is a secondary adoption of the habit after its ancestors had been true aerial parasites. A likely scenario is that it is a secondary return to terrestrialism via epiphyte mats (Kuijt 1969).

GUT FUNGI OF INVERTEBRATES
Robert W. Lichtwardt

Our knowledge of tropical fungi is minimal. Fungi associated with insects and other arthropods are just beginning to be studied. In Monteverde, a cryptic but common group of fungi exists whose species live within the digestive tract of certain aquatic insects and other arthropods. These Trichomycetes (Zygomycota) are among the most unusual and specialized fungi known (Lichtwardt 1986, 1997). Gut fungi may live predominantly as commensals in the arthropod, with the fungus taking a neutral role as it obtains its food from substances passing through the intestinal tract. Mosquito larvae, when deprived of certain essential nutrients such as sterols and B vitamins, can benefit from fungal biosynthesis of those nutrients (Horn and Lichtwardt 1981). At the other extreme, *Smittium morbosum* (Harpellales) is lethal to mosquito larvae (Sweeney 1981), and certain Harpellales invade the ovaries of developing adults, forming fungal cysts that repress egg development (Moss and Descals 1986, Lichtwardt 1996). Such cysts are oviposited by the flying adult and serve as a mechanism for fungal dissemination. As a result, gut fungi may reduce populations of aquatic insects, including pests and disease vectors such as mosquitoes and blackflies.

Studies in Monteverde were carried out over four periods from 1984 to 1991 as part of a larger investigation of Costa Rican gut fungi. The emphasis in Monteverde was on Harpellales in aquatic insect larvae, mostly larval Simuliidae (blackflies) and Chironomidae (midges). Collection sites were primarily (a) flowing waters within the MCFP, including Quebrada Cuecha and nearby streams; (b) Quebrada Máquina; and (c) several stretches of the Río Guacimal west of the main road. The streams had a mean temperature of 16.7°C (range = 15.5° –17.4°C), considerably cooler than the lowland streams investigated at La Selva (24.0°–25.8°C; mean 24.4°C) and the lowland portions of streams draining from the Cordilleras in Guanacaste Province (22.5°–28.0°C; mean 25.3°C).

Most trichomycete species reported here are undescribed and are known only from Costa Rica; only their generic identity is given. Lichtwardt (1994) described Trichomycetes inhabiting insects from tank plants and other still-water habitats.

Simuliidae. Blackfly larvae attach to substrates in fast-flowing waters of streams and rivers. In Monteverde, virtually all blackflies are infected with one or more genera of Harpellales (*Harpella, Genistellospora,*

Pennella, or *Smittium*; Figs. 3.27, 3.28) and, more rarely, *Simuliomyces microsporus.* Commonly, two or three species of these fungal genera coinhabit the same blackfly gut. Infected Simuliidae included *Simulium callidium, S. ochraceum,* and *S. metallicum* group, and possibly other species of blackfly larvae.

Species of *Harpella* attach to the midgut's peritrophic membrane. Nearly all blackflies were infected with a new species of *Harpella* (Fig. 3.28A,B), in Monteverde and in all other regions of Costa Rica where blackflies were collected. *H. melusinae* lives in most larval blackfly populations throughout much of the Northern Hemisphere, as well as New Zealand and Australia, but it has never been found in Costa Rica. At least seven species of Harpellales known to occur in Costa Rica have a widespread distribution in temperate zones.

Species of *Genistellospora* and/or *Pennella* (Fig. 3.27A,B,C) were present in most blackfly hindguts, even at the headwaters of small streams where larvae were relatively few. Certain species of these fungal genera were found only in Monteverde or other high-altitude sites sampled in Costa Rica, in contrast to other species of *Genistellospora* and *Pennella*, which appear to infect blackflies only at lower altitudes. A common but new species of *Smittium* was present in Río Guacimal in both blackfly and midge larvae, and was one of several species of *Smittium* isolated in culture.

Chironomidae. Midge larvae were relatively scarce in unpolluted streams in Monteverde, though a number of larvae of *Cricotopus* sp. and *Cardiocladius* sp. were collected in Quebrada Máquina. These were infected with *Smittium* sp., a trichomycete (Harpellales) that can infect both midges and blackflies. Midge larvae (*Lymnophyes* sp., *Metriocnemus* sp.) were collected from water in the leaf bases of several bromeliads and a *Xanthosoma* plant, and some of the larvae were infected with *Smittium* spp. (Lichtwardt 1994).

A remarkably dense insect fauna was found in Río Guacimal below an effluent that consisted mostly of whey discharging through a plastic pipe from the dairy plant (lechería) upstream (see Gill, "Impact of Monteverde Lechería," pp. 446–447). The polluted stretch of Río Guacimal contained abundant populations of the following midges: *Chironomus* sp., *Cryptochironomus* sp., *Cardiocladius* sp., *Cricotopus* sp., *Polypedilum* sp., and an unidentified genus of Orthocladiinae, none of which was collected above the effluent. Río Guacimal midges were hosts to several new species of *Smittium* (Fig. 3.27D,E,F). *Stachylina nana* (Fig. 3.28C) was also present in the midgut of the larvae, and on the anal papillae of bloodworms and blackfly larvae was a new species of *Amoebidium* (Amoebidiales; Fig. 3.28D). *Amoebidium* is the only trichomycete genus whose species live externally on their hosts. Five axenic cultures of four *Smittium* species were obtained in Monteverde. Other genera of Harpellales were unculturable.

Other arthropods. Among other dipterans, mosquitoes were hosts to several species of *Smittium*. A bird bath at Pensión Quetzal contained several kinds of mosquito larvae, including *Culex* sp. Some larvae contained *Sm. culisetae*; others had a new species of *Smittium* in their hindguts (Lichtwardt 1994). Mosquitoes breeding in bromeliads (including *Aedes* [*Howardina*] sp.) were hosts to another undetermined *Smittium* sp., as was a species of cranefly (Tipulidae).

In general, streams in Monteverde did not have the diversity of aquatic insects that occur in high-altitude streams in North America (Lichtwardt and Williams 1988). Among orders of aquatic insects known to host trichomycete fungi, stoneflies (Plecoptera) were noticeably absent in Monteverde studies, as in other parts of Costa Rica, and mayflies were relatively few.

Ten genera and more than 18 species of trichomycete gut fungi have been found in Monteverde. Only four were species that are known to be geographically widespread: *Genistellospora homothallica*, *Simuliomyces microsporus*, *Smittium culisetae*, and *Stachylina nana*. The remainder are currently unnamed species known only from Costa Rican arthropods, and of these a number have been found only in Monteverde.

Acknowledgments   The Costa Rican trichomycete studies were supported by the National Science Foundation (DEB-9220518 and DEB-9521811). I thank the Tropical Science Center for permission to collect in the MCFP. I am grateful to those who identified arthropods: A. J. Shelley and staff of the British Museum (Natural History) (Simuliidae); Leonard C. Ferrington, Jr. (Chironomidae) and Paul Liechti (Ephemeroptera), State Biological Survey of Kansas; Thomas J. Zavortink, University of San Francisco (Culicidae); and Dorothy Lindeman, Carleton University, Canada (Amphipoda).

Figure 3.27. Trichomycete gut fungi from the Monteverde region. A. Small sporulating specimen of *Pennella* sp. detached from the hindgut of a blackfly larva; the holdfast is the bifurcate basal structure. B. Four trichospores (asexual reproductive state) of *Genistellospora homothallica* that serve to disseminate the fungus from one blackfly larva to another. C. Two biconical zygospores (sexual state) of *G. homothallica* as seen within the larval hindgut. D. Sporulating branchlets of a *Smittium*, one of several species present in Río Guacimal midge larvae. E. Posterior hindgut of a midge larva totally packed with *Smittium* sp. F. Released trichospores from a pure culture of the same *Smittium* sp. Scale bars = 50 μm for A and E, 20 μm for B–D and F.

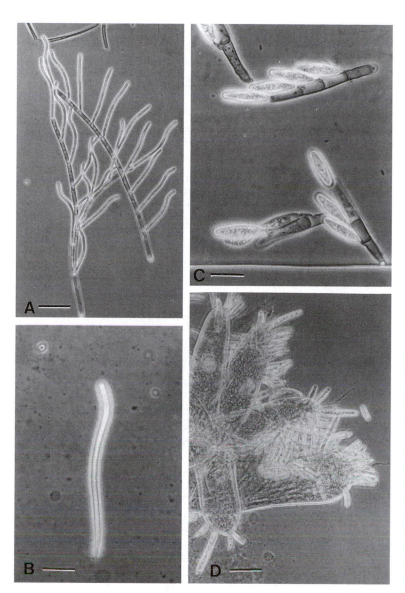

Figure 3.28. Trichomycete gut fungi from the Monteverde region. A. Unbranched *Harpella* sp. bearing cylindrical sigmoid trichospores within the transparent peritrophic membrane of a blackfly larva; this fungal species lives in the midgut of virtually all Monteverde blackfly larvae. B. Released trichospore of *Harpella* sp. with two of four extremely fine appendages barely visible at the basal end. C. Sporulating *Stachylina nana* within the peritrophic membrane of a midge larva. D. Numerous cylindrical bodies of *Amoebidium* sp. attached externally to the anal papillae of a bloodworm living in polluted stretch of Río Guacimal; two released sporangiospores can be seen. Scale bars = 50 μm for A and D, 20 μm for B and C.

BREEDING SYSTEMS OF MONTEVERDE *INGA*
Suzanne Koptur

Inga is the major genus of legume trees in Monteverde. Seven species are canopy or subcanopy trees, occur sympatrically, and have flowers that are similar in structure and appearance (Fig. 3.29). In premontane wet forest (1320–1460 m), *I. brenesii* and *I. punctata* occur in abundance, with occasional *I. mortoniana*, *I. oerstediana*, and *I. quaternata* (*I. hintonii* and *I. longispica* are rare). In the transition forest (1450–1550 m), *I. hintonii* and *I. mortoniana* are common, with occasional *I. quaternata* (*I. brenesii*, *I. longispica*, and *I. punctata* are rare). In the lower montane rain forest (1550–1800 m), *I. hintonii* and *I. longispica* are abundant, with occasional *I. mortonia* [Editor's note: *Inga hintonii* was previously identified as *I. densiflora*.]

Flowers of *Inga* have reduced perianth parts, numerous white stamens that provide the main visual attraction, and nectar in the floral tube, which is accessible to a wide variety of floral visitors. Flower visitors of Monteverde *Inga* include Hemiptera, Coleoptera, Diptera, Hymenoptera, Lepidoptera, hummingbirds, and bats (Koptur 1983). The most effective and common pollinators are hawkmoths and hummingbirds. Hawkmoth species visiting *Inga* flowers include *Aelopos titan*, *Agrius cingulatus*, *Pachygonia subhamata*, *Pachylia ficus*, *Perigonia lusca*, *Xylophanes chiron*, and many others (W. Haber, pers. comm.). Hummingbird visitors include *Amazilia saucerrottei*, *Campylopterus hemileucurus*, *Colibri thalassinus*, *Eupherusa eximia*, *Heliodoxa jacula*, *Panterpe insignis*, and *Calliphlox bryantae* (Feinsinger 1978, Koptur 1983; Appendix 9).

Inga flowering phenologies are not uniformly spaced throughout the year. Most species bloom at the wet/dry season interface, and usually more than one species is in flower in a forest at any time of year. Simultaneously blooming species often attract the same pollinators, regardless of flower size. Differences in seasonal flowering phenology and floral behavior (flower opening times and patterns of flower opening) provide some separation of visitors among co-occurring species, reducing the potential negative consequences of pollinator sharing.

Despite producing multitudes of flowers in many compound inflorescences, most *Inga* trees set very little fruit (Koptur 1984). *Inga* pollen grains are released in polyads (clusters of 16, 24, or 32 pollen grains), which increases the efficiency of compatible pollination. Observations of visitor activity on *Inga brenesii* and *I. punctata* indicate that each flower receives an average of more than two visits per day. Examination of stigmas showed that, in all species, far more flowers had received pollen than normally set fruit. Hand pollination of six species revealed them to be self-incompatible.

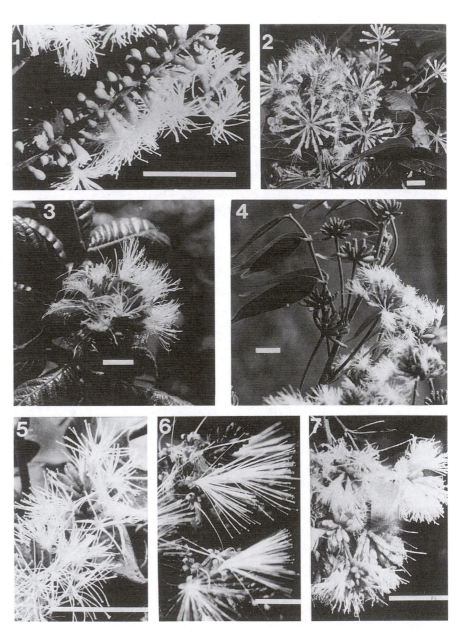

Figures 3.29. Flowers of *Inga* spp. (1) *I. longispica*. (2) *I. quaternata* = *I. nobilis*. (3) *I. brenesii* = *I. sierrae*. (4) *I. mortoniana*. (5) *I. hintonii* = *I. micheliana*. (6) *I. oerstediana*. (7) *I. punctata*. Scale bars = 2 cm.

For three *Inga* species studied in detail, cross-pollinations between individuals of the same species were more successful in setting fruit when the parent trees were at a distance greater than 1 km away from each other than when they were closer than 0.5 km (Koptur 1984), suggesting that near neighbors are likely to be more closely related and therefore less compatible for cross-pollination. A similar distance effect was documented for the hawkmoth-pollinated species *Luehea candida*; distant parents produced more viable seeds (Haber and Frankie 1982). This phenomenon may be widespread among tropical trees, which emphasizes the importance of long-distance pollinators such as hawkmoths and hummingbirds.

SEX RATIOS AND THE DISTRIBUTION OF MALE AND FEMALE TREES
Nathaniel T. Wheelwright

About 20% of tropical plant species are dioecious, that is, have individual plants that fall into one of two distinct sexual types or morphs (Bawa 1980, Renner and Ricklefs 1995). In the simplest cases, the pistillate (female) morph is capable of developing fruits but does not produce pollen whereas the staminate (male) morph produces flowers that have functional stamens but not pistils. Sex expression in plant populations can be more complicated, however. For example, there can be three sexual morphs (male, female, and hermaphrodite). Sometimes the differences between morphs can be extremely subtle; for example, two individual plants of the same species may have flowers that look similar, but functionally one plant acts as a male while the other acts as a female (Haber and Bawa 1984). Alternatively, different plants of the same species may produce morphologically dissimilar flowers that are equally hermaphroditic (Levin 1974). The study of patterns of plant reproduction in sexually polymorphic species addresses several questions. What is the ratio of male, female, and hermaphroditic plants in a plant population, and how is it affected by population age structure? Do males and females tend to occur in different habitats? Is sex expression constant within an individual over the course of its life, or within a population between years?

Ocotea tenera (Lauraceae), an understory tree found in small light gaps and along forest edges, has two sexual morphs, which correspond functionally to male and female. Although male flowers contain pistils as well as stamens, fewer than 0.01% of male flowers produce fruits. (Because some male plants set a small number of fruits, the species could be considered gynodioecious; an uncommon third, hermaphroditic morph also exists [Gibson and Wheelwright 1996]). The species has been the focus of a study of reproduction and growth in Monteverde since 1979 (Wheelwright 1993, Gibson and Wheelwright 1995). The adult sex ratio of natural populations of *O. tenera* in Monteverde is about 1:1, which is typical of the small number of dioecious tropical tree species that have been studied (Melampy and Howe 1977, Opler and Bawa 1978, Ackerly et al. 1990).

Surprisingly, functionally male and female *O. tenera* trees appear to be distributed throughout the forest in a peculiar way. A tree's nearest conspecific neighbor is more likely to be of the opposite sex than one would expect by chance (Wheelwright and Bruneau 1992); the sexes show "negative spatial association" (Bierzychudek and Eckhart 1988). Although one can readily appreciate the selective advantages of being located next to an individual of the opposite sex—greater fruit set or greater success as a pollen donor—it is difficult to imagine how such a spatial pattern could arise under natural conditions.

In 1981 and 1984, I established two experimental populations of *O. tenera* by planting seedlings of known parentage (but unknown sex), arrayed in a Latin square experimental design. When the plants became sexually mature 5 years after germination, males outnumbered females. However, in the experimental populations, the spatial distribution of the sexes proved to be random. During their first 6 years of reproduction, 11% of the young trees altered their functional sex at some point. In a natural population of older trees monitored since 1980, as many as 40% of trees may have changed functional sex at least once in their reproductive lives. In some cases, changes in functional sex could be traced to the production of distinct floral morphs by the same tree in different years. Although sex switching is not common in plants, it occurs in some temperate-zone plant species (Freeman et al. 1980, Lloyd and Bawa 1984). (Some botanists consider changes in sex expression over time as "temporal monoecy" rather than sex switching [M. Grayum, pers. comm.].).

The capability to switch gender in *O. tenera* suggests a mechanism for negative spatial association of the sexes, albeit one that is highly speculative. If a plant improves its reproductive success when it is near a plant of the opposite sex, and if its sex expression is flexible (as this study suggests), natural selection could favor sex switching in response to a plant's social environment. Such a scenario would require that plants be able to determine the sex of their neighbors, perhaps by pheromonal communication, as postulated in plants attacked by herbivores (e.g., Rhoades 1983, Baldwin et al. 1990, but see Fowler and Lawton 1985). Another mechanism might be that plants are able to monitor fruit set and adjust sex expression accordingly. To test whether a plant's nearest neighbors could influence its sex expression, I established a third experimental population in 1991, planting *O. tenera* seedlings near mature, isolated male or female trees. The results of this experiment may bear fruit in the future. Although not designed to determine the mechanism of sex switching, the experiment may suggest hypotheses and stimulate new studies to explain the spatial distribution of tropical trees (Bawa and Opler 1977).

CLONAL REPRODUCTION THROUGH PLANT FRAGMENTS IN *POIKILACANTHUS MACRANTHUS*
Stephen P. Bush

In tropical forests, branches and twigs are routinely broken from understory plants by falling limbs and trees. These fragments may produce roots and, ultimately, mature plants. A majority of shrub species in Monteverde are capable of reproduction through such plant fragments (Kinsman 1990). However, the importance of regeneration through fragmentation in natural populations and its effects on genetic diversity have not been studied. I determined the frequency of regeneration via plant fragments in *Poikilacanthus macranthus* (Acanthaceae), a shrub that persisted throughout the five-year study period of Kinsman (1990). Using DNA fingerprinting, I analyzed the population genetic structure of *P. macranthus*.

To assess the significance of regeneration via plant fragments, I determined the ratio of vegetatively to sexually produced plants in natural populations of *P. macranthus*. Plants derived from fragments and those derived from seed can be distinguished, based on the distinctive pattern of fragment development (Kinsman 1990) and by the presence of a callous ring at the root-stem junction of fragments (Sagers 1993). Six plots (2 × 20 m) were sampled on leeward Pacific slopes (1500–1800 m) below the Continental Divide. Of all the small plants sampled in the transects, 158 were derived from plant fragments and only 2 were derived from seed. Also, the density of these fragmentation-derived plants increased as elevation increased, perhaps because mature populations of *P. macranthus* increased in size and density at higher elevations. Exposure to the intense northeast trade winds is likely to favor regeneration through fragmentation. The increased disturbance at higher elevations likely produces a greater number of fragments, and because fragment survivorship is correlated with increased moisture levels (Kinsman 1990), establishment rates are also likely to be higher in wet, exposed locations.

Excavations to determine possible connections between plants of *P. macranthus* in a mature isolated patch indicated that most plants are physiologically independent. In this plot, DNA fingerprints of unconnected plants indicated that dense patches (more than 10 m across) may be composed of genetically identical individuals, that is, all units of the same clone. Analysis of an entire clump, spanning 30 m across, indicated that more than 50% of the plot (36 of 67 plants) was composed of only two clones; nine smaller clones were intermingled. Thus, preliminary results using DNA fingerprinting to identify clones in populations of *P. macranthus* confirm the significance of regeneration via fragmentation. Repeated cycles of fragment generation through disturbance, followed by growth of fragments into tall shrubs, probably produces large clones. These data suggest that population growth in *P. macranthus* is predominantly through fragmentation.

Asexual reproduction through plant fragments in *P. macranthus* may reduce genetic variability within a population. Genetic differences may be maintained primarily among clones of different populations. For conservation of genetic diversity in *P. macranthus*, the number of clumps conserved, rather than population size, may be critical. Regeneration via fragmentation may also alter community processes. Traditional models of succession, in which disturbance is followed by species replacement, may not hold true for the Monteverde understory. Disturbance may be followed by clonal growth, rather than species turnover (Linhart et al. 1987, Kinsman 1990).

FERNS
Seth Bigelow & Peter Kukle

The cloud forest of Monteverde is graced by an awe-inspiring diversity of ferns, which range in size from minute filmy ferns to towering tree ferns and in habitat from dry roadside to mist-shrouded forest canopy. More than 350 species (Table 3.7) are known from Monteverde and the upper Peñas Blancas valley. The fern flora is decidedly high altitude in character, with over half the species having lower altitude limits above 500 m and a third having lower limits of over 1000 m. More than 60% of the species have ranges extending from southern Mexico down into South America, with 11 species also occurring in the Old-World tropics. Twenty-seven Monteverde fern species are near the northern extent of their ranges in Costa Rica, and seven reach their southernmost extent there. Monteverde itself is not notable as a site of fern endemism, although 29 of its species are endemic to Costa Rica and Nicaragua or Panama.

Ferns constitute a primitive and ancient division of plants, the Polypodiophyta, whose basic features evolved several hundred million years before those of the flowering plants. Their life cycle has two phases, one sexual and one nonsexual, which live independently of each other. The nonsexual, spore-bearing (sporophyte) phase is familiar to most people, but few are aware of the sexual (gametophyte) phase; these forms are tiny and look unfernlike. Features for distinguishing fern sporophytes from other plants are (1) fronds that uncoil as they grow, producing a "fiddlehead" appearance, and (2) spores produced on the underside of fronds.

Though of varied shapes, most ferns have a basic structure of fronds (leaves) attached to a rhizome (stem). Rhizomes may be completely underground and are either massive and woody or trailing and vinelike. Fronds have two main parts, the stipe (leaf stalk or petiole) and the blade (the leafy portion of the frond). The blade may be simple or divided into leaflets (pinae), which may be further subdivided into pinnules. The central axis of a divided leaf is the rachis.

The reproductive features of ferns are used in identifying species. Spores develop in aggregations called sori (singular = sorus), and each group of ferns has a characteristic sorus pattern. Presence or absence of a protective flap of tissue that covers the sorus (indusium) is another useful character. Species that do not bear spores on all fronds are referred to as dimorphic; fertile fronds often look markedly different than sterile ones.

The most common terrestrial ferns of disturbed areas around the MCFP include *Adiantum concinnum* (Dwarf Maidenhair Fern), which coats the banks along the road just above the Pensión FlorMar; *Blechnum occidentale*, small and leathery ferns common along the road 1.5 km before the MCFP; *Odontosoria gymnogrammoides*, a vinelike fern of abandoned fields, steep roadbanks, and landslides; *Pityrogramma tartares* (Silver-back Fern), an open-area fern with a white, flourlike coating on the underside of the fronds; *Pteridium aquilinum* (Bracken Fern), a cosmopolitan species complex that thrives in pastures and along roads throughout the Monteverde area; *Sticherus retroflexus*, a vinelike fern commonly seen dangling down exposed roadbanks in the upper Monteverde area and showing a distinctive architecture in which two pairs of zigzagging secondary rachises emerge from the primary rachis at regular intervals; and *Thelypteris rudis*, one of the most common ferns in Monteverde found lining roadsides and trails through the MCFP.

Common terrestrial ferns of the forest interior include *Bolbitis oligarchica*, found in shady moist spots in the lower elevation of the MCFP; *Diplazium urticifolium*, which is recognized by the combination of chevron-shaped sori and terrestrial growth habit and is common along most trails of the MCFP, in clusters over 1 m tall; and *Pteris altissima*, a large fern found along many trails, especially at lower elevations.

Tree ferns, massive palmlike ferns that may exceed 15 m in height, are mostly in the Dicksoniaceae or Cyatheaceae families (Fig. 3.17). Epiphytic ferns include the genera *Asplenium* (Spleenworts), *Elaphoglossum* (Paddle Ferns), *Grammitis* (Dwarf Polypodies), *Hymenophyllum* and *Trichomanes* (Filmy Ferns), *Oleandra bradei*, *Niphidium nidulare*, *Neurodium lanceolatum*, *Compyloneurum sphenodes*, and *Vittaria* (Shoestring Ferns).

Acknowledgments We are indebted to M. Grayum for discussion, editing, and species identification. We thank N. Nadkarni, J. Longino, K. Clark, N. Barbour, the Monteverde community, and the herbarium of the University of California, Santa Barbara. This was a student project of the University of California Education Abroad Program in Tropical Biology and was published as a field guide pamphlet in 1991 by the Tropical Science Center and The Marie Selby Botanical Gardens.

DESCRIPTION OF PERMANENT FOREST PLOTS IN MONTEVERDE
William A. Haber

Estación Biológica: Lower montane wet forest life zone. A plot of 0.12 ha on a steep, south-facing slope was established by Nalini Nadkarni and a student group in 1993 in primary forest at about 1600 m on the property of the Estación Biológica. Trees in a small area of secondary forest adjoining the primary forest plot were also tagged and identified.

Elfin Forest Plots: Lower montane rain forest life zone (bordering elfin forest). In the later 1970s, Robert Lawton established two 1-ha plots in primary forest near the Continental Divide along the Sendero Brillante (Brillante trail) south of La Ventana in the MCFP. Lawton continues to monitor these plots and identify species as part of a long-term study of elfin forest dynamics (see Chap. 9 on ecosystem ecology).

Nadkarni Plots: Lower montane wet forest life zone. Nadkarni and co-workers tagged and mapped the trees in four adjoining 1-ha plots (1450–1500 m) on a south-facing gentle slope along the Sendero de Investigación (Research Trail) in the MCFP near the Information Center (Nadkarni et al. 1995). The forest at this site is dominated by *Ocotea tonduzil* (= *O. insularis*). All trees more than 10 cm DBH (diameter at breast height) in two of the four plots were identified by Haber. Trees larger than 30 cm DBH were identified in the two remaining plots.

Peñas Blancas Plot: Tropical wet forest life zone. This 1-ha plot lies on flat, poorly drained ground at 750 m in elevation along the Río Peñas Blancas on the Atlantic slope on private property owned by Leyn Rockwell and Thomas Dixon near Eladio's Refuge. The plot was established by Haber and his assistants with the help of Frank Joyce and students of the University of California's Education Abroad Program. A total of 104 species have been identified in this plot. All trees 10 cm DBH and larger have been tagged, measured, and mapped.

San Gerardo Plot: Premontane rain forest life zone. This 1-ha plot is located at 1150 m in elevation on a steep, east-facing slope of 30–40° in the Bosque Eterno de los Niños near the San Gerardo Field Station on land owned by the Monteverde Conservation League. The plot was established by Mara Kerry and Haber. A total of 115 tree species have been identified in this plot.

Los Llanos Plot: Premontane moist forest life zone. A 1-ha tree plot was established in a fragment of disturbed primary forest on the farm of Mariano Arguedas 2 km west of Santa Elena at 1220 m by Edgardo Arévalo and staff of the Monteverde Conservation League.

Stellar Plot: Premontane wet forest life zone. A 1-ha plot was established by Edgardo Arévalo and personnel of the Monteverde Conservation League on the Stellar farm, now part of the Bosque Eterno de los Niños, at 650 m in the hills above La Tigra on the Atlantic slope.

Literature Cited

Ackerly, D. D., J. M. Rankin-de-Merona, and W. A. Rodrigues. 1990. Tree densities and sex ratios in breeding populations of dioecious Central Amazonian Myristicaceae. Journal of Tropical Ecology 6:239–248.

Aguirre-Leon, E. 1992. Vascular epiphytes of Mexico: a preliminary inventory. Selbyana 13:72–76.

Alverson, W. S., W. Kuhlmann, and D. M. Waller. 1994. Wild forests, conservation biology and public policy. Island Press, Washington, D.C.

Atwood, J. T. 1987. The vascular flora of La Selva Biological Station, Costa Rica: Orchidaceae. Selbyana 10:76–145.

———. 1988. An approach to regional orchid floras: The Florula. Pages 46–50 *in* Kamezo Saito, and Ryuso Tanaka, editors. Proceedings of the Twelfth World Orchid Conference. Kokusaibunken Insatsusha Co., Tokyo.

———. 1989. Orchids of Costa Rica 1: plates 1392–1395. Icones Plantarum Tropicarum, Fascicle 14. Selby Botanical Gardens, Sarasota, Florida.

———. 1992. Orchids of Costa Rica 2: plates 1401–1500. Icones Plantarum Tropicarum, Fascicle 15. Selby Botanical Gardens, Sarasota, Florida.

———. 1995. Two overlooked species of *Maxillaria* from Central America. Selbyana 16:242–245.

Atwood, J. T., and R. L. Dressler. 1995. Another new species of *Stellilabium* from Monteverde, Costa Rica. Selbyana 16:239–241.

Atwood, J. T., and D. E. Mora de Retana. 1999. Family #39 orchidaccae: Tribe Maxillariae: Subtribes Maxillariinae and Oncidiinae. *In:* Flora Costancensis. Fieldiana, Botany. New Series. No. 40.

Baldwin, I. T., C. L. Sims, and S. E. Kean. 1990. The reproductive consequences associated with inducible alkaloidal responses in wild tobacco. Ecology 71:252–262.

Bawa, K. S. 1980. Evolution of dioecy in flowering plants. Annual Review of Ecology and Systematics 11:15–39.

Bawa, K. S., and P. A. Opler. 1977. Spatial relationships

between staminate and pistillate plants of dioecious tropical forest trees. Evolution 31:64–68.

Benzing, D. H. 1989. The evolution of epiphytism. Pages 15–41 *in* U. Lüttge, editor. Vascular plants as epiphytes: evolution and ecophysiology. Springer, Berlin.

———. 1990. Vascular epiphytes. General biology and related biota. Cambridge University Press, New York.

Berrie, G. K., and J. M. O. Eze. 1975. The relationship between an epiphyllous liverwort and host leaves. Annals of Botany 39:955–963.

Bierzychudek, P., and V. Eckhart. 1988. Spatial segregation of the sexes of dioecious plants. American Naturalist 132:34–43.

Bigelow, S., and P. Kukle. 1991. The ferns of Monteverde. Tropical Science Center, San José, Costa Rica.

Bock, W. J. 1959. Preadaptation and multiple evolutionary pathways. Evolution 13:194–211.

Bohlman, S., T. Matelson, and N. Nadkarni. 1995. Moisture and temperature patterns of canopy humus and forest floor soil of a montane cloud forest, Costa Rica. Biotropica 27:13–19.

Bolaños, R. A., and V. Watson. 1993. Mapa ecológico de Costa Rica. Centro Científico Tropical, San José, Costa Rica.

Brako, L., and J. L. Zaruchi. 1993. Catalogue of the flowering plants and gymnosperms of Peru. Monographs in Systematic Botany. Vol. 45.

Bronstein, J. 1988a. Limits to fruit production in a monoecious fig: consequences of an obligate mutualism. Ecology 69:207–214.

———. 1988b. Mutualism, antagonism, and the fig-pollinator interaction. Ecology 69:1298–1302.

Burger, W. C. 1977. Flora Costaricensis: Moraceae. Fieldiana, Botany 40:94–215.

———. 1980. Why are there so many kinds of flowering plants in Costa Rica? Brenesia 17:371–388.

Burger, W. C., and C. M. Taylor. 1993. Flora Costaricensis: Rubiaceae. Fieldiana, Botany, New Series 33:1–333.

Burger, W. C., and H. van der Werff. 1990. Flora Costaricensis: Lauraceae. Fieldiana, Botany, New Series 23:1–138.

Burt-Utley, K., and J. T. Utley. 1977. Historia Natural de Costa Rica, Vol. 1, Supplementary notes: phytogeography, physiological ecology and the Costa Rican genera of Bromeliaceae. Departmento de Historia Natural, Museo Nacional de Costa Rica. San José, Costa Rica.

Calvin, C. L., C. A. Wilson, and G. Varughese. 1991. Growth of longitudinal strands of *Phoradendron juniperinum* (Viscaceae) in shoots of *Juniperus occidentalis*. Annals of Botany 67:153–162.

Clark, D. A. 1994. Plant demography. Pages 90–105 *in* L. McDade, K. S. Bawa, H. A. Hespenheide, and G. S. Hartshorn, editors. La Selva: ecology and natural history of a neotropical rain forest. The University of Chicago Press, Chicago.

Cole, M. C. 1983. An illustrated guide to the genera of Costa Rican Hepaticae. 1. Brenesia 21:137–201.

———. 1984. Thallose liverworts and hornworts of Costa Rica. Brenesia 22:319–348.

Croat, T. B. 1978. The flora of Barro Colorado Island. Stanford University Press, Palo Alto, California.

Cronquist, A. 1981. An integrated system of classification of flowering plants. Columbia University Press, New York.

Daniels, J. D., and R. O. Lawton. 1991. Habitat and host preferences of *Ficus crassiuscula*, a neotropical strangling fig of the lower-montane rain forest. Journal of Ecology 79:129–141.

———. 1993. A natural history of strangling by *Ficus crassiuscula* in Costa Rican lower montane rain forest. Selbyana 14:59–63.

D'Arcy, W. G., and M. D. Correa, editors. 1985. The botany and natural history of Panama. Missouri Botanical Garden, St. Louis, Missouri.

Davidse G., M. Sousa, and A. O. Chater, editors. 1994. Flora MesoAmericana, Vol. 6, Alismataceae to Cyperaceae. Missouri Botanical Garden, St. Louis, Missouri.

Dawson, T. E., E. J. King, and J. R. Ehleringer. 1990. Age structure of *Phoradendron juniperinum* (Viscaceae), a xylem-tapping mistletoe: inferences from a nondestructive morphological index of age. American Journal of Botany 77:573–583.

Dobzhansky, T., and B. J. Murca-Pires. 1954. Strangler trees. Scientific American 190:78–80.

Dressler, R. L. 1981. The orchids: natural history and classification. Harvard University Press, Cambridge, Massachusetts.

———. 1993. Field guide to the orchids of Costa Rica and Panama. Comstock Publishing Associates, Ithaca, New York.

Dryer, V. 1979. List of plants collected. Unpublished report, Tropical Science Center, San José, Costa Rica.

Ehleringer, J. R., E. D. Schultz, H. Ziegler, O. L. Lange, G. D. Farquhar, and I. R. Cowan. 1985. Xylem-tapping mistletoes: water or nutrient parasites? Science 227:1479–1481.

Esau, K. 1977. Anatomy of seed plants. Wiley, New York.

Eze, J. M. O., and G. K. Berrie. 1977. Further investigations into the physiological relationship between an epiphyllous liverwort and its host leaves. Annals of Botany 41:351–358.

Feinsinger, P. 1978. Ecological interactions between plants and hummingbirds in a successional tropical community. Ecological Monographs 48:269–287.

Foster, R. B. 1990. The floristic composition of the Río Manú floodplain forest. Pages 99–111 *in* A. H. Gentry, editor. Four neotropical rainforests. Yale University Press, New Haven, Connecticut.

Fowler, S. V., and J. H. Lawton. 1985. Rapidly induced defenses and talking trees: the devil's advocate position. American Naturalist 126:181–195.

Freeman, D. C., K. T. Harper, and E. L. Charnov. 1980. Sex change in plants: old and new observations and new hypotheses. Oecologia 47:222–232.

Futuyma, D. J. 1986. Evolutionary biology. Sinauer, Sunderland, Massachusetts.

Gedalovich-Shedletzky, E., D. P. Delmer, and J. Kuijt. 1989. Chemical composition of viscin mucilage from three mistletoe species: a comparison. Annals of Botany 64:249–252.

Gentry, A. H. 1982. Patterns of neotropical plant species diversity. Evolutionary Biology 15:1–84.

———. 1983. Neotropical floristic diversity: phytogeographical connections between Central and South America, Pleistocene climatic fluctuations, or an accident of the Andean orogeny? Annals of the Missouri Botanical Garden 69:557–593.

———. 1985. Contrasting phytogeographic patterns of upland and lowland Panamanian plants. Pages 147–160 *in* W. G. D'Arcy and M. D. Correa, editors. The botany and natural history of Panama. Missouri Botanical Garden, St. Louis, Missouri.

———, editor. 1990. Four neotropical rainforests. Yale University Press, New Haven, Connecticut.

———. 1993. A field guide to the woody plants of northwest South America. Conservation International, Washington, D.C.

Gentry, A. H., and C. H. Dodson. 1987. Diversity and biogeography of neotropical vascular epiphytes. Annals of the Missouri Botanical Garden 74:205–233.

Gibson, J. P., and N. T. Wheelwright. 1995. Genetic structure in a population of a tropical tree *Ocotea tenera* (Lauraceae): influence of avian seed dispersal. Oecologia 103:49–54.

———. 1996. Mating system dynamics of *Ocotea tenera* (Lauraceae), a gynodioecious tropical tree. American Journal of Botany 83:890–894.

Givnish, T., K. J. Sytsma, J. F. Smith, and W. J. Hahn. 1994. Molecular evolution, adaptive radiation, and geographic speciation in *Cyanea* (Campanulaceae), the largest plant genus endemic to Hawai'i. Pages 000–000 *in* W. L. Wagner and V. A. Funk, editors. Origin and radiation of the Hawai'ian biota. Smithsonian Institution Press, Washington, D.C.

Gradstein, S. R. 1992. Threatened bryophytes of the neotropical rain forest: a status report. Tropical Bryology 6:83–94.

Gradstein, S. R., and T. Pócs. 1989. Bryophytes. Pages 311–325 *in* H. Lieth and M. J. A. Werger, editors. Tropical rainforest ecosystems. Elsevier, Amsterdam.

Gradstein, S. R., A. Lücking, M. I. Morales, and G. Dauphin. 1994. Additions to the hepatic flora of Costa Rica. Lindbergia 19:73–86.

Grant, A. R. 1981. Plant speciation (2nd ed.). Columbia University Press, New York.

Griffin, D., and M. I. Morales. 1983. Key to the genera of mosses from Costa Rica. Brenesia 21:299–323.

Haber, W. A. 1983. Checklist of Sphingidae. Pages 645–650 *in* D. H., Janzen, editor. Costa Rican natural history. University of Chicago Press, Chicago.

———. 1984. Pollination by deceit in a mass-flowering tropical tree, *Plumeria rubra* L. (Apocynaceae). Biotropica 16:269–275.

———. 1991. Lista provisional de las plantas de Monteverde, Costa Rica. Brenesia 34:63–120.

Haber, W. A., and K. S. Bawa. 1984. Evolution of dioecism in *Saurauia* (Dilleniaceae). Annals of the Missouri Botanical Garden 71:289–293.

Haber, W. A., and G. W. Frankie. 1982. Pollination of *Luehea* (Tiliaceae) in Costa Rican deciduous forest. Ecology 63:1740–1750.

Haber, W. A., and G. W. Frankie. 1988. A tropical hawk-moth community: Costa Rican dry forest Sphingidae. Biotropica 21:155–172.

Haber, W. A., W. Zuchowski, and E. Bello. 1996. An introduction to cloud forest trees: Monteverde, Costa Rica. La Nación, San José, Costa Rica.

Hamilton, C. W. 1980. An ecosystematic revision of *Psychotria* L. sect. *Psychotria* in Mesoamerica. Ph.D. dissertation, Washington University, St. Louis, Missouri.

Hammel, B. E. 1990. The distribution and diversity among families, genera, and habitat types in the La Selva flora. Pages 75–84 *in* A. H. Gentry, editor. Four neotropical rainforests. Yale University Press, New Haven, Connecticut.

———. 1997. Three new species of Celastraceae from Costa Rica, one disjunct from Mexico. Novon 7:147–155.

Harris, L. D. 1984. The fragmented forest: island biogeography theory and the preservation of biotic diversity. University of Chicago Press, Chicago.

Hartshorn, G. S. 1983. Plants. Pages 118–157 *in* D. H. Janzen, editor. Costa Rican natural history. University of Chicago Press, Chicago.

Hartshorn, G. S., and B. E. Hammel. 1994. Vegetation types and floristic patterns. Pages 73–89 *in* L. McDade, K. S. Bawa, H. A. Hespenheide, and G. S. Hartshorn, editors. La Selva: ecology and natural history of a neotropical rain forest. University of Chicago Press, Chicago.

Hartshorn, G. S., and L. J. Poveda. 1983. Checklist of trees. Pages 158–183 *in* D. H. Janzen, editor. Costa Rican natural history. University of Chicago Press, Chicago.

Harvey, P. H., and M. D. Pagel. 1991. The comparative method in evolutionary biology. Oxford University Press, New York.

Henderson, A., G. Galeano, and R. Bernal. 1995. Field guide to the palms of the Americas. Princeton University Press, Princeton, New Jersey.

Holdridge, L. R. 1966. The life zone system. Adansonia 6:199–203.

———. 1967. Life zone ecology. Tropical Science Center, San José, Costa Rica.

———. 1978. Ecología basada en zonas de vida. Instituto Inter-Americano de Ciencias Agrícolas, San José, Costa Rica.

Holdridge, L. R., L. J. Poveda, and A. Jiménez. 1997. Árboles de Costa Rica (Vol. 1, 2nd ed.). Centro Científico Tropical, San José, Costa Rica.

Horn, B. W., and R. W. Lichtwardt. 1981. Studies on the nutritional relationship of larval *Aedes aegypti* (Diptera: Culicidae) with *Smittium culisetae* (Trichomycetes). Mycologia 73:724–740.

Ingram, S. W. 1989. The abundance, vegetative composition, and distribution of epiphytes in a Costa Rican lower montane rain forest. Master's thesis, University of California, Santa Barbara.

Ingram, S. W., and N. M. Nadkarni. 1993. Composition and distribution of epiphytic organic matter in a neotropical cloud forest, Costa Rica. Biotropica 25:370–383.

Ingram, S. W., K. Ferrell-Ingram, and N. M. Nadkarni. 1996. Floristic composition of vascular epiphytes in a neotropical cloud forest, Monteverde, Costa Rica. Selbyana 17:88–103.

Janzen, D. H., editor. 1983. Costa Rican natural history. University of Chicago Press, Chicago.

Janzen, D. H., and R. Liesner. 1980. Annotated check-list of plants of lowland Guanacaste Province, Costa Rica, exclusive of grasses and non-vascular cryptogams. Brenesia 18:15–90.

Kappelle, M. 1995. Ecology of mature and recovering Talamancan *Quercus* forests, Costa Rica. Netherlands Foundation for Tropical Research (WOTRO), The Hague.

Kappelle, M., and M. E. Leal. 1996. Changes in leaf morphology and foliar nutrient status along a successional gradient in a Costa Rica upper montane *Quercus* forest. Biotropica 28:331–344.

Kappelle, M., N. Zamora, and T. Flores. 1991. Flora leñosa de la zona alta (2000–3819 m) de la Cordillera de Talamanca, Costa Rica. Brenesia 34:121–144.

Kelly, D. L., E. V. J. Tanner, E. M. NicLughadha, and V. Kapos. 1994. Floristics and biogeography of a rain forest in the Venezuelan Andes. Journal of Biogeography 21:421–440.

Kinsman, S. 1990. Regeneration by fragmentation in tropical montane forest shrubs. American Journal of Botany 77:1626–1633.

Koptur, S. 1983. Flowering phenology and floral biology of *Inga* (Fabaceae: Mimosoideae). Systematic Botany 8:354–368.

———. 1984. Outcrossing and pollinator limitation of fruit set: breeding systems of neotropical *Inga* trees (Fabaceae: Mimosoideae). Evolution 38:1130–1143.

Koptur, S., and M. A. Lee. 1993. Plantlet formation in tropical montane ferns: a preliminary investigation. American Fern Journal 83:60–66.

Koptur, S., W. A. Haber, G. W. Frankie, and H. G. Baker. 1988. Phenological studies of shrub and treelet species in tropical cloud forests of Costa Rica. Journal of Tropical Ecology 4:323–346.

Kress, W. J. 1989. The systematic distribution of vascular epiphytes. Pages 234–261 *in* U. Lüttge, editor. Vascular plants as epiphytes: evolution and ecophysiology. Springer, Berlin.

Kuijt, J. 1963. On the ecology and parasitism of the Costa Rican tree mistletoe, *Gaiadendron punctatum* (Ruiz & Pavon) G. Don. Canadian Journal of Botany 41:927–938.

———. 1969. The biology of parasitic flowering plants. University of California Press, Berkeley.

Laman, T. G. 1994. The ecology of strangler figs (hemi-epiphytic *Ficus* spp.) in the rainforest canopy of

Borneo. Ph.D. dissertation, Harvard University, Cambridge, Massachusetts.

Lawton, R. O. 1980. Wind and the ontogeny of elfin stature in a Costa Rican lower montane rain forest. Ph.D. dissertation, University of Chicago, Chicago.

———. 1982. Wind stress and elfin stature in a montane rain forest tree: an adaptive explanation. American Journal of Botany 69:1224–1240.

———. 1984. Ecological constraints on wood density in a tropical montane rain forest. American Journal of Botany 71:261–267.

———. 1986. The evolution of strangling by *Ficus crassiuscula*. Brenesia 25/26:273–278.

———. 1989. More on strangling by *Ficus crassiuscula* Warb. ex Standley: a reply to Ramírez. Brenesia 32:119–120.

———. 1990. Canopy gaps and light penetration into a wind-exposed tropical lower montane rain forest. Canadian Journal of Forest Research 20:659–667.

Lawton, R. O., and V. Dryer. 1980. The vegetation of the Monteverde Cloud Forest Reserve. Brenesia 18:101–116.

Lawton, R. O., and F. E. Putz. 1988. Natural disturbance and gap-phase regeneration in a wind-exposed tropical cloud forest. Ecology 69:764–777.

Lawton, R. O., and G. Williams-Linera. 1996. Hemiepiphyte-host relationships: research problems and prospects. Selbyana 17:71–74.

Lee, M. A. B., P. A. Burrowes, J. E. Fauth, J. C. Koella, and S. M. Peterson. 1986. The distribution of tree ferns along an altitudinal gradient in Monteverde, Costa Rica. Brenesia 25/26:45–50.

Leigh, E. G., A. S. Rand, and D. M. Windsor, editors. 1982. The ecology of a tropical forest, seasonal rhythms and long-term changes. Smithsonian Institution Press, Washington, D.C.

Lellinger, D. B. 1989. The ferns and fern-allies of Costa Rica, Panama, and the Chocó. I. Psilotaceae through Dicksoniaceae. Pteridologia 2A.

Lesica, P., and R. Antibus. 1990. The occurrence of mycorrhizae in vascular epiphytes of two Costa Rican rain forests. Biotropica 22:250–258.

Levin, D. A. 1974. Spatial segregation of pins and thrums in populations of *Hedyotis nigricans*. Evolution 28:648–655.

Lichtwardt, R. W. 1986. The Trichomycetes, fungal associates of arthropods. Springer, New York.

———. 1994. Trichomycete gut fungi living in the guts of Costa Rican phytotelm larvae and other lentic dipterans. Revista de Biología Tropical 42:31–48.

———. 1996. Trichomycetes and the arthropod gut. Pages 315–330 *in* D. Howard and D. Miller, editors. The Mycota, Vol. 6, Animal and human relations. Springer, Berlin.

———. 1997. Costa Rican gut fungi (Trychomycetes) infecting lotic insect larvae. Revista de Biología Tropical 45:000–000.

Lichtwardt, R. W., and M. C. Williams. 1988. Distribution and species diversity of trichomycete gut fungi in aquatic insect larvae in two Rocky Mountain streams. Canadian Journal of Botany 66:1259–1263.

Lieberman, M., and D. Lieberman. 1994. Patterns of density and dispersion of forest trees. Pages 106–119 *in* L. McDade, K. S. Bawa, H. A. Hespenheide, and G. S. Hartshorn, editors. La Selva: ecology and natural history of a neotropical rain forest. University of Chicago Press, Chicago.

Linhart, Y. B., P. Feinsinger, J. H. Beach, W. H. Busby, K. G. Murray, W. Z. Pounds, S. Kinsman, C. Guindon, and M. Kooiman. 1987. Disturbance and predictability of flowering patterns in bird-pollinated cloud forest plants. Ecology 68:1696–1710.

Lloyd, D. G., and K. S. Bawa. 1984. Modification of the gender of seed plants in varying conditions. Evolutionary Biology 17:253–338.

Lücking, A. 1995. Diversität und Mikrohabitatpräeferenzen epiphyller Moose in einem tropischen Regenwald in Costa Rica. Doctoral dissertation, Universität Ulm.

Luther, H. E. 1995. An annotated checklist of the Bromeliaceae of Costa Rica. Selbyana 16:230–234.

Luther, H. E., and E. Sieff. 1996. An alphabetical list of bromeliad binomials (5th ed.). The Bromeliad Society, Inc., Newberg, Oregon.

Mabberley, D. J. 1987. The plant-book. A portable dictionary of the higher plants. Cambridge University Press, Cambridge.

———. 1997. The plant book. 2nd edition. Cambridge University Press, Cambridge, U.K.

Madison, M. 1977. Vascular epiphytes: Their systematic occurrence and salient features. Selbyana 2:1–13.

Maffia, B., N. M. Nadkarni, and D. Janos. 1993. Vesicular-arbuscular mycorrhizae of epiphytic and terrestrial Piperaceae under field and greenhouse conditions. Mycorrhiza 4:5–9.

Matelson, T. J., N. M. Nadkarni, and J. T. Longino. 1993. Longevity of fallen epiphytes in a neotropical montane forest. Ecology 74:265–269.

Matelson, T. J., N. M. Nadkarni, and R. Solano. 1995. Tree damage and annual mortality in a montane forest in Monteverde, Costa Rica. Biotropica 27:441–447.

Melampy, M. N., and H. F. Howe. 1977. Sex ratio in the tropical tree *Triplaris americana* (Polygonaceae). Evolution 31:867–872.

Metcalfe, C. R., and L. Chalk. 1950. Anatomy of the dicotyledons. Clarendon Press, Oxford.

Monge-Nájera, J. 1989. The relationship of epiphyllous liverworts with leaf characteristics and light in Monte Verde, Costa Rica. Cryptogamie, Bryologie, Lichénologie 10:345–352.

Mora de Retana, D. E., and J. T. Atwood. 1993. Orchids of Costa Rica 3: plates 1501–1600. Icones Plantarum Tropicarum, Fascicle 15. Selby Botanical Gardens, Sarasota, Florida.

Mora de Retana, D. E., and J. B. García. 1992. Lista actualizada de las orquídeas de Costa Rica (Orchidaceae). Brenesia 37:79–124.

Morales, J. R. 1998. Bromelias de Costa Rica. INBIO, Santo Domingo, Costa Rica.

Moss, S. T., and E. Descals. 1986. A previously undescribed stage in the life cycle of Harpellales (Trichomycetes). Mycologia 78:213–222.

Myster, R. W. 1993. Spatial heterogeneity of seedrain, seedpool, and vegetative cover on two Monteverde landslides. Brenesia 39–40:137–145.

Nadkarni, N. M. 1984. Epiphyte biomass and nutrient capital of a neotropical elfin forest. Biotropica 16:249–256.

———. 1986. The nutritional effects of epiphytes on host trees with special reference to alteration of precipitation chemistry. Selbyana 9:44–51.

———. 1994. Diversity of species and interactions in the upper tree canopy of forest ecosystems. American Zoologist 34:321–330.

Nadkarni, N. M., and T. J. Matelson. 1989. Bird use of epiphyte resources in neotropical trees. The Condor 91:891–907.

———. 1992. Biomass and nutrient dynamics of epiphyte litterfall in a neotropical cloud forest, Costa Rica. Biotropica 24:24–30.

Nadkarni, N., T. J. Matelson, and W. A. Haber. 1995. Structural characteristics and floristic composition of a neotropical cloud forest, Monteverde, Costa Rica. Journal of Tropical Ecology 11:481–494.

Nepokroeff, M. 1992. Relationships among *Psychotria* section *Notopleura* and related taxa in the tribe Psychotrieae (Rubiaceae): determining monophyletic groups based on ITS sequence data. Master's thesis, University of Wisconsin, Madison.

Nepokroeff, M., and K. J. Sytsma. 1996. Systematics and patterns of speciation and colonization in Hawaiian *Psychotria* and relatives based on phylogenetic analysis of ITS sequence data. American Journal of Botany 83:181–182.

Nepokroeff, M., C. M. Taylor, and K. J. Sytsma. 1993. Inflorescence morphology, growth form and phylogenetic relationships within *Psychotria* section *Notopleura*, Rubiaceae. American Journal of Botany 80:169.

Nickrent, D. L. 1993. HyperParasite: a Hypercard based data storage system for selected parasitic flowering plants. Golden Bough (Royal Botanic Gardens, Kew) 12:1–6.

O'Hara, R. J. 1988. Homage to Clio, or toward an historical philosophy for evolutionary biology. Systematic Zoology 37:142–155.

Opler, P. A., and K. S. Bawa. 1978. Sex ratios in tropical forest trees. Evolution 32:812–821.

Pócs, T. 1980. The epiphytic biomass and its effect on the water balance of two rain forest types in the Ulugur Mountains (Tanzania, East Africa). Acta Botanica Hungarica Plantarum 26:143–167.

Pohl, R. W. 1980. Graminae. *In* W. Burger, editor. Flora Costaricensis. Fieldiana, Botany. New Series, No. 4.

Poveda, L. J., and J. Gonzalez. 1997. Dos nuevas especies de *Croton* (Euphorbiaceae) para Costa Rica. Novon.

Prance, G. T. 1990. The floristic composition of the forests of central Amazonian Brazil. Pages 112–140 *in* A. H. Gentry, editor. Four neotropical rainforests. Yale University Press, New Haven, Connecticut.

Putz, F. E., and N. M. Holbrook. 1989. Strangler fig rooting habits and nutrient relations in the llanos of Venezuela. American Journal of Botany 76:781–788.

Ramírez, W. 1988. A reply to Lawton's paper on *Ficus crassiuscula* Warb. as a strangler. Brenesia 29:115–116.

Rebertus, A. J. 1988. Crown shyness in a tropical cloud forest. Biotropica 20:338–339.

Reed, C. F., and H. Robinson. 1971. Bryophytes of Monteverde, Costa Rica. Phytologia 21:6–21.

Renner, S. S., and R. E. Ricklefs. 1995. Dioecy and its correlates in the flowering plants. American Journal of Botany 82:596–606.

Rhoades, D. F. 1983. Responses of alder and willow to attack by tent caterpillars and webworms: evidence for pheromonal sensitivity of willows. Pages 55–68 *in* P. A. Hedin, editor. Plant resistance to insects. American Chemical Society, Washington, D.C.

Rice, E. L. 1984. Allelopathy. Academic Press, Orlando, Florida.

Richards, P. 1984. The ecology of tropical forest bryophytes. Pages 1233–1270 *in* R. M. Schuster, editor. New manual of bryology (Vol. 2). The Hattori Botanical Laboratory, Miyazaki, Japan.

Rossi, M. R. 1998. Cactaceas de Costa Rica. EUNED. San José, Costa Rica.

Rzedowski, J. 1978. Vegetación de México. Editorial Limusa, Mexico.

Sagers, C. L. 1993. Reproduction in neotropical shrubs: the occurrence and some mechanisms of asexuality. Ecology 74:615–618.

Sallé, G. 1983. Germination and establishment of *Viscum album* L. Pages 145–159 *in* M. Calder and P. Bernhardt, editors. The biology of mistletoes. Academic Press, Sydney.

Sargent, S. 1994. Seed dispersal of mistletoes by birds in Monteverde, Costa Rica. Ph.D. Dissertation. Cornell University, Ithaca, New York.

———. 1995. Seed fate in a tropical mistletoe: the importance of host twig size. Functional Ecology 9:197–204.

Sillett, S. C., S. R. Gradstein, and D. Griffin III. 1995. Bryophyte diversity of *Ficus* tree crowns from intact cloud forest and pasture in Costa Rica. The Bryologist 98:251–260.

Smith, A. P. 1979. The paradox of autotoxicity in plants. Evolutionary Theory 4:173–180.

Smith, J. F., and K. J. Sytsma. 1994. Evolution of the Andean epiphytic genus *Columnea* (Gesneriaceae). II. Chloroplast DNA restriction site variation. Systematic Botany 19:317–336.

Smith, L. B., and R. J. Downs. 1974. Flora Neotropica Monograph 14, Part 1: Pitcairnioideae. Hafner Press, New York.

Sohmer, S. 1988. The non-climbing species of the genus *Psychotria* (Rubiaceae) in New Guinea and the Bismarck Archipelago. Bishop Museum Bulletin of Botany 1:1339.

Sweeney, A. W. 1981. An undescribed species of *Smittium* (Trichomycetes) pathogenic to mosquito larvae in Australia. Transactions of the British Mycological Society 77:55–60.

Sytsma, K. J. 1987. The shrubby gentian genus *Macrocarpea* in Panama. Annals of the Missouri Botanical Garden 74:310–313.

Titus, J. H., N. M. Holbrook, and F. E. Putz. 1990. Seed germination and seedling distribution of *Ficus pertusa* and *F. tuerckheimii*: are strangler figs autotoxic? Biotropica 22:425–428.

Tosi, J. A. 1969. Mapa ecológico de Costa Rica. Tropical Science Center, San José, Costa Rica.

Wheelwright, N. T. 1983. Fruits and the ecology of the Respendent Quetzals. The Auk 100:286–301.

———. 1985. Competition for dispersers, and the timing of flowering and fruiting in a guild of tropical trees. Oikos 44:465–477.

———. 1986. A seven-year study of individual variation in fruit production in tropical bird-dispersed tree species in the family Lauraceae. Pages 19–35 *in* A. Estrada and T. H. Fleming, editors. Frugivores and seed dispersal. Dr. W. Junk Publishers, Dordrecht.

———. 1988. Four constraints on coevolution between fruit eating birds and fruiting plants: a tropical case history. International Ornithological Congress, Ottawa.

———. 1993. Fruit size in a tropical tree species: variation, preference by birds, and heritability. Vegetatio 107/108:163–174.

Wheelwright, N. T., and A. Bruneau. 1992. Population sex ratios and spatial distribution of *Ocotea tenera* (Lauraceae) trees in a tropical forest. Journal of Ecology 80:425–430.

Williams-Linera, G., V. Sosa, and T. Platas. 1995. The fate of epiphytic orchids after fragmentation of a Mexican cloud forest. Selbyana 16:36–40.

Winkler, S. 1967. Die epiphyllen Moose der Nebelwalder von El Salvador. C.A. Revista de Bryología y Lichénología 35:303–369.

Wolf, J. H. W. 1993. Diversity patterns and biomass of epiphytic bryophytes and lichens along an altitudinal gradient in the northern Andes. Annals of the Missouri Botanical Garden 80:928–960.

Zamora, N. 1989. Flora arborescente de Costa Rica, Vol. 1, Especies de hojas simples. Editorial Tecnológica de Costa Rica, Cartago, Costa Rica.

Zuchowski, W. 1996. Common flowering plants of the Monteverde Cloud Forest. Tropical Science Center, San José, Costa Rica.

4

Insects and Spiders

Edited by Paul Hanson

Arthropods (e.g., insects, spiders, mites, crustaceans) are the most diverse group of organisms in the biosphere. Several families of insects (e.g., staphylinid beetles, ichneumonid wasps) contain more species than all vertebrates combined. Most arthropods do not yet have scientific names. Little is known about the life histories of most species. The insects of Costa Rica and neighboring Panama have received more attention than any other tropical region of comparable size, but it is mainly limited to species descriptions and distribution records. I and colleagues who have contributed subsections throughout this chapter draw upon the published studies from Monteverde, but no attempt has been made to list all insect species reported from Monteverde.

This chapter differs from others in that some contributors focus on tropical cloud forests in general rather than on only Monteverde. The justification is that for most insects, altitude is the single most important factor determining distribution. Most species show widespread geographic distributions but restricted altitudinal distributions. One intensively sampled cloud forest in Costa Rica is Zurquí de Moravia (1600 m), from which considerable informa-

tion is drawn for this chapter. We have included most of the insect groups that have been studied in Monteverde: spittlebugs, treehoppers, rove beetles, scarab beetles, longhorn beetles, butterflies, social wasps, ants, and bees. Major orders of insects not included from this chapter are mayflies, cockroaches, termites, earwigs, barklice, thrips, and lacewings. Termites and other social insects are less prominent in cloud forests than in lowland forests. Spiders are the only noninsect arthropods included; the information is from a cloud forest at a similar elevation in Colombia.

Cloud forests are defined here as forests higher than 1200 m. Our knowledge of cloud forest arthropods is so fragmentary that generalizations are premature. This chapter provides preliminary information on natural history to stimulate entomologists to consider cloud forests as distinct from lowland rain forests. We include practical information on the conservation of cloud forest arthropods, many of which are vital components of the ecosystem. For example, the increase in outdoor lighting in Monteverde may be detrimental to populations of many nocturnal insects (see Sec. 4.4.3). Conservationists must consider the stunning diversity of microhabitats that they occupy (see Sec.

4.4.2). As with certain birds, some insects undergo elevational migrations (see Sec. 4.5.2) and so require the conservation of habitats at different altitudes. Many aquatic insects are sensitive indicators of water quality (see Sec. 4.1), and can be used to monitor the health of cloud forest streams (see Gill, "Impact of Monteverde Lechería," pp. 446–447).

4.1. Aquatic Insects

4.1.1. Introduction
Paul Hanson

Insects that inhabit fresh water include orders that consist almost entirely of aquatic species (Ephemeroptera [mayflies; Fig. 4.1], Odonata [dragonflies and damselflies], Plecoptera [stoneflies], and Trichoptera [caddisflies]) and groups that are predominantly terrestrial (Hemiptera ["true bugs"], Coleoptera [beetles], and Diptera [flies, midges, and mosquitoes]). The largest family of aquatic insects in Costa Rica is Chironomidae (Diptera), with perhaps 2000 species (C. de la Rosa, pers. comm.). In contrast, Plecoptera are less diverse in Costa Rica than in temperate regions, with only one genus, *Anacroneuria* (Perlidae). Of the three entirely aquatic orders, two are discussed below, Odonata (see Sec. 4.1.2) and Trichoptera (see Sec.

4.1.3); the third major order, Ephemeroptera, is described in Flowers (1992).

In most species, the larval stage is aquatic and the adult stage is terrestrial. Exceptions occur in the aquatic bugs and beetles, in which both stages are often aquatic. Species of aquatic insects are often restricted to either running or standing water and sometimes to certain habitat types such as the water contained in tank bromeliads. Rapidly flowing water usually contains more dissolved oxygen than stagnant water but has stronger currents. In many cases, the terrestrial adults fly upstream (Hynes 1970), which prevents the entire population from being washed downstream.

Dragonflies, damselflies, most aquatic bugs, many beetles, and other groups of aquatic insects may be predators, herbivores, or detritivores. Functional groups are based on their feeding mechanisms (Merritt and Cummins 1996): shredders (living or decomposing plant tissue), collectors (fine particulate organic matter), scrapers (attached algae or living plant tissue), piercers (living animal tissue), and engulfers (living animal tissue). One of the few studies of feeding behavior of aquatic insects in Monteverde showed that adult water beetles (*Rhantus guticolis*, Dytiscidae) and dragonfly nymphs (*Sympetrum nigrocreatum*, Libellulidae) preyed more heavily on tadpoles of the treefrog *Hyla pseudopuma* (Hylidae) when the tadpoles were small or in the four-legged stage; intermediate tadpole

Figure 4.1. Predatory mayfly from the Río Guacimal on the Pacific slope below Monteverde. Photograph by David Watson.

stages suffered less predation. However, another species of dragonfly, *Aeshna* sp. (Aeshnidae), was able to capture and kill all stages of tadpoles (Crump 1984). Hunting strategies vary among species: *Sympetrum nigrocreatum* waits in one place whereas *Aeshna* sp. generally stalks its prey (Crump 1984).

Because most aquatic insects are restricted to certain types of water, they are good indicators of water quality and are used in environmental impact studies (Rosenberg and Resh 1993). Such studies require accurate identification, but few keys for the identification of aquatic insects in Costa Rica exist. Keys to North America genera (e.g., Merritt and Cummins 1996) are only marginally useful.

4.1.2. Dragonflies and Damselflies of Costa Rican Cloud Forests
Alonso Ramírez

Dragonflies and damselflies (order Odonata) are the best known of aquatic insects due to their large size, brilliant colors, and conspicuous flight. Dragonflies perch with their wings outstretched; damselflies rest with their wings held together above the body. Adults and nymphs are voracious predators of smaller insects. Nymphs are aquatic and live in standing or running water.

Fourteen families and 280 species of Odonata are recorded from Costa Rica (Paulson 1982), although the actual number is higher. Odonate diversity is greatest in the lowlands and decreases with altitude. Seventy species have been collected from areas above 1200 m, which represents 25% of the species in the country. Of these, only 13 species are restricted to altitudes above 1200 m. However, cloud forests have not been well collected. Biogeography of the cloud forest fauna indicates 41% of the species are of South American origin, 28% are Central American (including endemics), and 7% are North American. The rest are widespread species whose origins are unclear.

Some odonate genera contain discrete lowland and highland species. One highland species, *Sympetrum nigrocreatum*, is probably derived from the widespread mid-elevation species *S. illotum*. *Philogenia peacocki* has only been found in cloud forests, whereas *P. carrillica* is more commonly found at lower altitudes. In the same stream, *P. peacocki* has been found inhabiting the upper parts but is replaced by *P. carrillica* at lower altitudes, with some overlap of the two species around 1200 m. Some cloud forests species occur at intermediate altitudes (800–1500 m). For example, *Heteragrion majus*, a characteristic inhabitant of streams in cloud forests, is also present at lower altitudes (down to 800 m) in streams that share characteristics with cloud forest streams such as high

humidity, steep slopes, and low temperature (17–20°C). Of the species recorded from cloud forests, 60% have nymphs that live in open areas of lakes, marshes, and ponds; 38% inhabit shaded streams; and 2% live in specialized habitats such as bromeliads and tree holes. These proportions depend on the availability of the habitats. In general, open habitats have been better studied than forest streams (Paulson 1982).

Nymphs are adapted to live in specific habitats, for example, accumulations of dead leaves in riffles. The most limiting factor is the availability of habitat suitable for nymph development. Most species tolerate only narrow ranges of conditions such as temperature, oxygen level, forest cover, types of aquatic vegetation, and water pollution. They are good biological indicators and their conservation depends on habitat preservation. Few species are well adapted to highly disturbed habitats.

4.1.3. Caddisflies of Costa Rican Cloud Forests
Monika Springer

Caddisflies (Trichoptera) are a relatively small order of insects that are closely related to the butterflies and moths (Lepidoptera). Adults are not aquatic and are seldom recognized due to their relatively small size and inconspicuous colors. They resemble small moths but lack a coiled proboscis; the wings are covered with hairs rather than scales. Caddisfly larvae construct portable cases from small stones or pieces of vegetation and are common in both standing and running water in all types of microhabitats (MacKay and Wiggins 1979).

The first catalog of Costa Rican caddisflies (Holzenthal 1988) included 174 species in 14 families. Over 450 species are now known from Costa Rica, of which 45% are new to science (R. Holzenthal, pers. comm.). Most of these new species belong to the "microcaddisflies" (family Hydroptilidae).

Cloud forests are characterized by cool running waters, the types of streams believed to be the ancestral habitat of caddisflies (Ross 1956, Wiggins 1977). Cool water has a higher oxygen tension than warmer water and would be better suited for an organism having only the minimum adaptation for aquatic life. Among the typical mountain inhabitants, the holarctic genera *Limnephilus* (Limnephilidae) and *Lepidostoma* (Lepidostomatidae) both reach the southern limit of their distribution in Costa Rica and Panama. Only a few species are known from Costa Rica; both families are diverse and abundant in North America.

Caddisflies are divided into five groups based on their case-building behavior (Wiggins 1977), all of which occur in Costa Rican cloud forests: free-living forms, saddle case makers, purse case makers, net spinning or refuge makers, and tube case makers. Larvae are primarily detritivores, although many feed predominantly on diatoms, other algae, or higher plants, or are carnivores. They secrete silk, which is used in constructing nets and portable cases out of sand grains, small stones, leaf fragments, or tiny twigs cemented together. Caddisfly cases protect the soft-bodied insect from predators and aid in aquatic respiration (Holzenthal 1988). Another group of larvae construct fixed refuges of silk and detritus and spin silken nets that they use to filter food particles from flowing water. Other less well-known caddisfly larvae crawl freely on rocks and prey on other aquatic invertebrates.

Most adult caddisflies are nocturnal and are relatively short-lived. Mating generally takes place on vegetation or on the ground and is often preceded by swarming. Oviposition behavior is varied; eggs may be dropped into the water during flight, deposited below the water surface, or placed on objects above the water after which the newly hatched larvae are washed into the water by rain. The highest diversity of caddisflies is found in unpolluted, cool, well-oxygenated rivers and streams, where they are important in nutrient cycling and secondary production. Because they occupy a wide range of often narrow, well-defined niches, they are useful as biological indicators.

4.2. Orthoptera: Katydids, Crickets, and Grasshoppers
Paul Hanson

Katydids, crickets, and grasshoppers belong to one of the more "primitive" (least specialized) orders of insects, the Orthoptera. Members of this group are notable for their songs, which are typically performed by males as part of their territorial and courtship behavior. Katydids and crickets (Tettigoniidae and Gryllidae) produce sound by rubbing the two front wings together. Grasshoppers (Acrididae) in the subfamily Gomphocerinae produce sound by rubbing the front wing against the hind leg; band-winged grasshoppers (Oedipodinae) snap their hind wings in flight (probably to startle predators); many other grasshoppers are mute. Katydids and crickets are often nocturnal, whereas grasshoppers are usually diurnal. The production of sound implies the existence of hearing organs in both sexes, which are located on the front legs in katydids and crickets and at the base of the abdomen in grasshoppers. Entomologists identify species by their sounds in the same way that birders identify birds by their songs. The songs are also heard by predators, so they are brief to avoid detection.

Once a courting male has "won" a female, he copulates with her, which usually involves the transfer of large packets containing sperm and a substantial amount of protein. After copulation, the female inserts her eggs into plant tissue or in the ground, depending on the species. Juveniles and adults of most species feed primarily on plants, although many katydids and crickets are omnivorous, and some are predatory.

In Costa Rica, there are a dozen families of Orthoptera, of which at least nine are recorded from Monteverde: Suborder Ensifera (antennae usually long)—Stenopelmatidae (Jerusalem crickets), Tettigoniidae (katydids), Gryllidae (crickets); Suborder Caelifera (antennae usually short)—Eumastacidae (monkey grasshoppers), Pyrgomorphidae (grasshoppers), Romaleidae (lubber grasshoppers), Acrididae (grasshoppers), Tetrigidae (pygmy grasshoppers), and Tridactylidae (pygmy mole crickets).

Many visitors to Monteverde encounter a 3-cm-long wingless black "cricket," *Stenoplemater* (Stenoplematidae), along roads (J. Longino, pers. comm.). Although most sightings occur during daylight, members of this family are generally regarded as nocturnal, spending the day hiding in tunnels that they excavate in the ground. They are thought to be predators and/or scavengers. This species appears to be restricted to cloud forests.

A notable katydid (Tettigoniidae) in Monteverde is the lichen-mimicking *Markia hystrix* (Phaneropterina; 1000–1650 m; Fig. 4.2), which is most frequently seen at lights at night (J. Longino, pers. comm.). It is 5 cm long, is whitish green with black mottling, and has two median, laterally compressed horns on the pronotum, with another one on the head. Another Monteverde species, *Melanonotus powellorum* (Pseudophyllinae), is a sluggish, flightless species that emerges at night to forage on the understory vegetation (Rentz 1975). *Sphyrometopa femorata* (Agroeciinae), another flightless species, occurs in the Monteverde Cloud Forest Preserve (MCFP) but is more abundant lower in the community. The green nymphs live on low herbaceous growth in small clearings; the brown and gray adults move to dry leaves in primary forest (Rentz 1976). Keys to the genera and a list of species in Panama are in Nickle (1992b).

Very little information is available on the crickets of Monteverde or of other Central American cloud forests (Nickle 1992a). A checklist of Monteverde grasshopper species is in Rowell (1983a). One of the most impressive species in Monteverde is *Tropidacris cristata* (Romaleidae), the "giant red-winged grasshopper," which measures up to 15 cm in length, making it one of the largest grasshoppers in the world (Rowell 1983d). Some acrid species present in Monteverde also occur in La Selva, for example, *Abacris*

Figure 4.2. *Markia hystrix,* a lichen-mimicking katydid. Photograph by Stephen Ingram.

flavolineata (Rowell 1983c; cited as *Osmilia flavolineata*) and *Microtylopteryx herbardi* (Bracker 1989). *Drymophilacris monteverdensis* and *D. nebulicola* are ecologically almost identical to the lowland species, *D. bimaculata,* so information on the latter (Rowell 1983b) is applicable to the two Monteverde species. Species of *Rachicreagra* have been better studied at lower altitudes (Rowell 1985a,b). Species of *Drymophilacris* and *Rachicreagra* inhabit light gaps and are specialized plant feeders, the former on Solanaceae and Asteraceae, the latter on Asteraceae, Apiaceae, Urticaceae, or Amaranthaceae. Other genera (*Homeomastax* [Eumastacidae], *Hylopedetes,* and *Scirtopaon* [Acrididae]) in Monteverde feed on ferns (Rowell et al. 1983).

More research is needed on the Orthoptera of cloud forests. Their large size (compared with most other insects) makes them good candidates for field investigations, and their interactions with one another via songs, with plants, and with vertebrate predators provide rich possibilities for study.

4.3. Hemiptera: Heteroptera and Homoptera

4.3.1. Introduction
Paul Hanson

The group Hemiptera has often been restricted to the so-called "true bugs" (Fig. 4.3), a name that elicits smirks from the uninitiated (the adjective "true" is used since any insect is called a "bug" by the non-entomologist). Phylogenetic studies (Sorensen et al. 1995) unite the Heteroptera and Homoptera within the Hemiptera. All of these insects are united by their highly modified elongate mouthparts, which function as a syringe; the food substrate is pierced, saliva is injected, and liquid food is sucked up. Metamorphosis is incomplete and the nymphal stages have wing buds rather than fully developed wings.

Heteroptera (true bugs). The front wings of most true bugs are divided into a thickened basal portion and a membranous apex. Many also possess stink glands; the nymphs often display bright or warning colors on the abdomen (Fig. 4.3). The chemical substances liberated by these glands serve as a defense against predators. True bugs include predators and plant feeders. Regardless of diet, saliva is always injected into the food source before being ingested. Of the 75 families of Heteroptera worldwide (Schuh and Slater 1995), about 50 occur in Costa Rica, where they are represented by at least 2000 species. The largest families include the Coreidae (leaf-footed bugs), Lygaeidae (seed bugs), Miridae (plant bugs), Pentatomidae (stink bugs), and Reduviidae (assassin bugs).

Reduviidae are primarily predators; the other families are primarily plant feeders. Most true bugs are terrestrial, but several families are aquatic or semiaquatic. Examples of bugs associated with freshwa-

Figure 4.3. Milkweed bugs (Lygaeidae), order Hemiptera. Photograph by Gregory Dimijian.

ter habitats include backswimmers (Notonectidae), giant water bugs (Belastomatidae), creeping water bugs (Naucoridae), water striders (Gerridae), and ripple bugs (Veliidae). The latter two families are semiaquatic and skate rapidly over the surface of water. In the Monteverde area, intraspecific competition has been studied in *Rhagovelia scabra* (Veliidae) in the Rio Guacímal (Wilson et al. 1978). Adult females predominate in fast-flowing areas of the stream at the head of pools, which contain more food (dead insects floating on the water surface) than the quiet margins of streams, where juveniles are found. The mechanism behind this spatial distribution appears to be interference; ripple bugs spend a lot of time chasing each other.

Homoptera.   Spittlebugs, cicadas, leafhoppers, treehoppers, whiteflies, aphids (Fig. 4.4), scale insects, and their relatives feed almost exclusively on plant sap. These insects are highly specialized for penetrating living tissue and imbibing a liquid diet. Just as mosquitoes transmit animal viruses, homopterans are the most important vectors of viral diseases of plants. Some species feed primarily on plant mesophyll tissue; others tap either xylem or phloem. Xylem carries water up from the roots and is under relatively low pressure; xylem-tapping homopterans (spittlebugs, cicadas, and some leafhoppers) excrete large quantities of water and often have a bulging face that contains well-developed muscles used in pumping.

Phloem carries sugars produced by photosynthesis and is under greater pressure; phloem-tappers excrete a sugary honeydew and usually have a more concave face. The honeydew excreted by phloem feeders attracts ants and other insects that can protect these homopterans from their enemies.

Homoptera is divided into two subgroups: Auchenorrhyncha (planthoppers, spittlebugs, cicadas, leafhoppers, and treehoppers) and Sternorrhyncha (psyllids, whiteflies, aphids, mealybugs, and scale insects). The former are larger, stouter, more active insects, and most adults jump when disturbed, hence the name "hopper." The latter tend to be smaller, more fragile, and less mobile; only psyllids are active jumpers. Scale insects are highly specialized plant parasites that often remain attached to one site for most of their lives. They typically secrete a waxy scalelike covering and are often not recognized as insects.

In Costa Rica, there are at least 40 families of Homoptera. The largest families include the Cixiidae (plant hoppers), Delphacidae (plant hoppers), Derbidae (plant hoppers), Cicadellidae (leafhoppers), Membracidae (treehoppers), Pseudococcidae (mealybugs), and Diaspididae (armored scales). Cixiid nymphs usually feed on roots of plants (especially grasses); nymphs of many derbids feed on fungi associated with rotting wood.

In Costa Rica, Auchenorrhyncha have been better studied than Sternorrhyncha. One of the best-known

Figure 4.4. Stem-sucking aphids. Photograph by Gregory Dimijian.

families is the cicadas (Cicadidae), which is more diverse and abundant in lowland forests than in cloud forests. In Panama, only one species (*Carineta trivittata*) was found in cloud forests (2200 m), and seven species at 1350 m. In contrast, 18 species in nine genera were collected on Barro Colorado Island at 120 m (Wolda and Ramos 1992). In a Costa Rican cloud forest at "Cariblanco" (1500 m), only eight species were reported (Young 1976).

The only group of Sternorrhyncha that has been well-inventoried in Costa Rica is the superfamily Psylloidea (see Sec. 4.3.5.), the tropical equivalents of aphids. The latter are less diverse in the Neotropics than in the north temperate regions. The most frequently encountered aphid in Monteverde is the bright yellow *Aphis nerii*, which feeds on the milkweed, *Asclepias curassavica* (Asclepiadaceae; J. Longino, pers. comm.). Although scale insects (superfamily Coccoidea) are the least studied group of homopterans in Costa Rica, biological information is available

for at least one species occurring in Monteverde (see Sec. 4.3.6).

4.3.2. Biology and Diversity of Monteverde's Spittlebugs and Froghoppers
Daniel C. Peck

The spittlebugs and froghoppers of Monteverde are a diverse group of xylem-sucking insects of the superfamily Cercopoidea. They are among the most conspicuous insects of the area due to their pest status in dairy pastures (see Peck, "Agroecology of *Prosapia*," pp. 409–410). The nymphs (spittlebugs) reside in laboriously constructed masses of spittle; adults (froghoppers) are free-living and commonly show warning colors.

In Monteverde, 30 species of Cercopoidea are known from the areas outside the MCFP: 3 species of Clastopteridae, 3 species of Aphrophoridae, and 24 species of Cercopidae. This represents 5% of the total known New-World cercopid diversity and is remarkably high when compared to the well-known fauna of other regions (Whittaker 1970, Hamilton 1982). Nymphs feed on underground roots, and spittle masses have also been found on epiphytes of the genus *Peperomia* (Piperaceae) 15 m above the forest floor.

The spittle mass partially protects nymphs from desiccation and natural enemies (Whittaker 1970). Spittlebugs construct these shelters from their copious feeding wastes by using abdominal action to add hundreds of tiny bubbles that are stabilized by the presence of mucopolysaccharides (Marshall 1966) and polypeptides (Mello et al. 1987). Nymphs invest in this elaborate defense because they exploit a relatively poor food source (xylem sap) that is energetically expensive to extract (Raven 1983). They require up to seven weeks to mature (Weaver and King 1954, Peck 1996).

Some spittlebugs of the family Aphrophoridae are communal in this defense. As many as 69 individuals of *Cephisus siccifolius* have been observed working together to create voluminous arboreal spittle masses, which cover up to 15 cm of host twigs and drip from the canopy. Sometimes individuals are blown from the branches, but older nymphs can reform spittle masses on plants on the ground and survive to the adult molt. These spittlebugs also abandon their refuge and run along the branches as a potential secondary defense against opportunistic vertebrate predators such as the Yellow-throated Euphonia (*Euphonia hirundinacea*). Once the disturbance has ceased, they quickly return to the shelter of the original spittle mass.

Spittlebugs occur on a wide variety of plants (Appendix 5). Nymphs use a broad range of substrates including stems, leaf axils and twigs, soil surfaces, and epiphytic roots. Although spittlebugs are not host-specific, their diet breadth is constrained by a combination of host and habitat characteristics. For example, the group has an affinity for nitrogen-fixing host plants (Thompson 1994). On a particular host, the suitability of feeding sites is reduced by mechanical barriers such as tissue hardness (Hoffman and McEvoy 1986) and the presence of trichomes (Hoffman and McEvoy 1985, 1986); unavailability of xylem vessels (Hoffman and McEvoy 1986); poor quality of shelter (McEvoy 1986); low amino acid concentration (Horsfield 1977); and unsuitability of growth habit (e.g., lack of secondary roots and poor microclimate; Ferrufino and Lapointe 1989).

Young nymphs of *Prosapia* sp. near *bicincta* (Cercopidae) are largely restricted to the surface roots of forage grasses in the litter layer of pastures. As individuals mature, they move to construct spittle masses on mature stems (Peck 1996). Nymphs of the Piper Froghopper, *Iphirhina quota* (Cercopidae), make their first spittle masses on soil surface roots of *Piper auri-*

tum (Piperaceae). As the nymphs mature, they can emigrate a meter or more above the ground to supportive leaf axils. The Heliconia Spittlebug, *Mahanarva costaricensis* (Cercopidae), produces spittle masses in the cuplike, water-filled bracts of *Heliconia tortuosa*, an aquatic environment in which nymphs resist desiccation (Fish 1977, Thompson 1997).

Nymphs molt to adults within spittle masses of a drier texture that are often constructed *de novo* to provide an airy cave for the new adult's exoskeleton to complete hardening. Upon emergence, froghoppers generally feed on the same host species as nymphs, but they no longer produce spittle. Instead, adults crawl, hop, and fly to evade enemies. *Cephisus siccifolius* adults rely on crypsis to avoid detection. In contrast, most adults of the family Cercopidae have bright warning coloration that advertises their ability to "reflex bleed." The orange and blue warning colors of the Heliconia Froghopper make it one of the most impressive local species. These adults reach 2.1 cm long and are conspicuous diurnal feeders on the flower stalks of *Heliconia tortuosa*. If grabbed by hand from their feeding sites, they exude droplets of amber-colored and distinctive-tasting hemolymph (up to 8.5 µl) from the tips of all legs, probably serving as a general deterrent that startles potential enemies and permits the froghopper to escape by hopping. Reflex bleeding has been observed in 30 cercopid species at Monteverde, most aposematic.

Females lay eggs in or near their host plants. Eggs of some of these species have the ability to enter diapause to survive adverse conditions. The eggs of *Prosapia* sp. near *bicincta* are laid in the soil of pastures at the base of host grasses. These eggs enter diapause to endure the dry season. First-instar nymphs of the new generation are detected just after the arrival of the rains in May (Peck 1996).

4.3.3. Leafhoppers of Costa Rican Cloud Forests
Carolina Godoy

Leafhoppers (Cicadellidae) are the largest family of Hemiptera. Because of their relatively small size (3–30 mm long), leafhoppers are often overlooked even though they are present in nearly all habitats and are sometimes extremely abundant (e.g., in grasses). Leafhoppers vary in color from dull brown (most Agallinae) to green (*Hortensia*, Cicadellinae) to strikingly colored. Among the common cloud forest species, *Barbinolla costaricensis* (Cicadellinae) is bright blue with a yellow-orange collar; *Colladonus decorus* (Deltocephalinae) is mostly black with bright yellow markings.

There are 18 subfamilies of leafhoppers in Costa Rica. The three largest subfamilies are Cicadellinae,

Deltocephalinae, and Typhlocybinae. Most species of the subfamily Agallinae, which in Costa Rica consists of six genera and more than 60 species (Nielson and Godoy 1995), occur in the lowlands. In the largest genus, *Agalliopsis*, 14 of the 35 species (40%) are known from intermediate altitudes, 14 species (40%) are restricted to the lowlands, and 7 (20%) to higher altitudes. Two small subfamilies of leafhoppers (Nioninae and Tinterominae) have never been collected in the lowlands.

Species in most subfamilies feed primarily on phloem, but Cicadellinae feed on xylem sap and Typhlocybinae feed on cell contents of the mesophyll. Nymphal leafhoppers are usually more host-specific than adults, and the host plant on which a species reproduces can be determined only by rearing nymphs to the adult stage. Species identification relies principally on characters in the genitalia of the adult male, so nymphs cannot be readily identified. Unlike many treehoppers, adult leafhoppers rarely show parental care and are not normally found together with nymphs, excluding this as a shortcut to host plant identification. Little is known about the host plants of tropical leafhoppers.

4.3.4. Sex and Social Life of *Umbonia* Treehoppers
Karen Masters

Best known for their bewildering body shapes, treehoppers (Membracidae) are intriguing for ecologists interested in variable sociality and mating strategies. Disparate behaviors can be found even among closely related species, such as *Umbonia ataliba* and *U. crassicornis*, whose biologies reveal how ecological pressures and population genetic histories influence patterns of maternal investment, sex allocation, and mating behavior.

Adults of *Umbonia ataliba* and *U. crassicornis* have thornlike bodies and are noteworthy for their presocial tendencies (Fig. 4.5). In both species, siblings

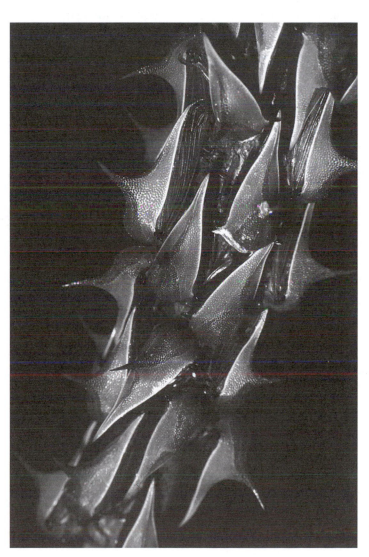

Figure 4.5. *Umbonia* treehoppers on stem. Photograph by Dan Perlman.

are reared together under the care of their mother, who embeds a mass of 50–100 eggs into the branch tip of a host plant (Mimosaceae) and then tends offspring throughout their nymphal development. Maternal investment includes warding off potential predators (reduviid bugs, ants, wasps, and beetle larvae) and parasitoids (e.g., dryinid wasps), and drilling holes into the host branches to facilitate feeding of offspring (Wood 1974, Masters et al. 1994). Nymphs crowd together on their natal branch until they undergo a final molt to adulthood, the sons generally molting before daughters. Males of both species are smaller than females.

Habitat use and population density differ in the two species. *Umbonia ataliba*, which is found on the steep slopes that border the Río Guacímal (1300–1500 m), lives in the understory on young branches of *Pithecellobium* and *Inga* trees. The density of *U. ataliba* in Monteverde is low throughout the year, with family groups widely spaced (ca. 1 per 2000 m²). In contrast, *U. crassicornis*, found along highly disturbed banks on the Río Guacímal (1000 m), is abundant in the rainy season, living on rapidly growing branches of *Acacia*, *Enterolobium*, and *Calliandra* species. In contrast to *U. ataliba*, multiple families of *U. crassicornis* occupy the same tree, often the same branch, and family groups may be dense locally (as many as 25 have been found on a single *Enterolobium* tree). Although individuals of both species may enjoy the benefits of maternal care such as better protection from predators and facilitation of feeding, *U. crassicornis* may have additional advantages associated with a more communal lifestyle, such as increased mating opportunities. Group living also invites interesting maternal care options: mothers may abandon their nymphs to the care of another attending female, since they are capable of producing more than one brood.

Behavior of these two species differs strikingly. Siblings of *U. ataliba* remain on their natal branch well after they reach sexual maturity and mate with each other before females disperse to restart the life cycle. Mating off the natal branch is rare. Close inbreeding is very unusual for animals in nature, due to negative effects on growth and survival (Ralls et al. 1979, Falconer 1981). In *U. ataliba*, sibling matings seem to be promoted by slow dispersal of adults, synchronous sexual maturation of siblings, and a surprising propensity for siblings to copulate, even when non-siblings of similar sizes and ages are offered as possible mates. In contrast, *U. crassicornis* rarely exhibits mating between siblings; instead, they disperse soon after the final molt (Wood and Dowell 1985). Early dispersal may be the principal mechanism for avoiding inbreeding, as suggested by the observation that in the rare cases where mating between siblings occurs, siblings (for unknown reasons) remain together long past the average disappearance day (K. Masters, N. Gerdes, and N. Heller, unpubl. data).

One consequence of mating between siblings in *U. ataliba* is that family sex ratios are significantly biased toward females, with one son produced for every three daughters (Masters et al. 1994). Theory predicts that when brothers compete for mates (such as for sisters under inbreeding conditions), females should be selected to produce only as many sons as necessary to ensure that daughters are fertilized and allocate their remaining resources to daughter production (Hamilton 1967).

The disparate inbreeding/outbreeding behaviors in the two treehoppers may result from ecological and population genetic factors. The more pronounced dry periods of the areas inhabited by *U. crassicornis* likely contribute to seasonal host abundance and variation in host quality and to differences in treehopper densities and aggregation tendencies. With higher population densities, *U. crassicornis* families may find outbreeding a viable, low-cost mating strategy. Another difference is that the habitats used by *U. ataliba* tend to be dominated by one host species, which favors host specialization. Thus, inbreeding, which more faithfully transmits genomes (including genomes adapted to specific ecological conditions) to succeeding generations, may be selected. Inbreeding depression may be low because affected individuals do not reproduce and pass on the harmful genes. Experimental crosses in which sisters of *U. ataliba* mated with either their brothers or nonbrothers revealed that the reproductive success of sibling-mated females was not lower than that of their sisters who mated with non-siblings. In contrast, inbreeding depression is strong in *U. crassicornis* (K. Masters, unpubl. data), which supports the concept that the mating history of the two populations differs, with *U. ataliba* reflecting an inbreeding tradition. Thus, differences in the genetic histories, population densities, aggregation patterns, and possibly host plant relations are likely causes for the diverse behaviors of *Umbonia* species.

4.3.5. Psyllids of Costa Rican Cloud Forests
David Hollis

Adult psyllids (jumping plantlice) resemble minute cicadas and range in length from 1 to 8 mm. They have two pairs of membranous wings that are held rooflike over the body. They differ from other Sternorrhyncha (aphids, whiteflies, and scale insects) in having two-segmented tarsi that end in a pair of claws, normally 10-segmented antennae, and hind legs that are thickened and modified for jumping. They are more active than aphids and jump and fly when disturbed. The immature stages are usually flattened and oval; they often have waxy strands protruding from their bodies and are less active than adults.

Worldwide, there are about 2500 described species of psyllids, in 230 genera and six families. In Costa Rica, there are at least 250 species, with all six families represented. Species diversity peaks in pasture/cloud forest boundary sites at 1600–2400 m. From sites at 1200–2000 m, 123 species are recorded, but the number of species at these sites is undoubtedly greater (Appendix 6). Many psyllids are free-living and are found in clusters around the growing points of the plants on which they live. Others induce gall formation of a variety of shapes. Adults and later immature stages feed by sucking sap from the phloem tissues of their host plants, which are mainly trees and shrubs. Each species of psyllid is highly specific to its host and will usually only complete its life cycle on that host. They can cause severe damage or even kill forest tree seedlings and saplings. One unanswered question is why certain families of plants are heavily used as hosts (e.g., Leguminosae and Myrtaceae) and others hardly at all (e.g., Bignoniaceae and Rubiaceae; Appendix 6).

4.3.6. Small Males and Large Females in a Monteverde Scale Insect
John Alcock

Among mammals, males are often larger on average than females of their species, sometimes to a small degree (e.g., human beings) but sometimes extraordinarily so (e.g., Northern Elephant Seals [*Mirounga leonina*], in which adult males weigh more than twice as much as their mates). In contrast, most female insects are larger than males of their species. Consider the scale insect whose females can be found on the trunks of sapling *Ocotea tenera* (Lauraceae) in Monteverde. Scale insects are known for their extraordinary sexual dimorphism, and this species (an unnamed species in the family Margarodidae) offers an extreme example. The sexes are so different in size and appearance that one would be forgiven for thinking that they belonged to two completely unrelated insect species (Fig. 4.6).

The females are large (for scale insects), thick, squat, camouflaged brown, and wingless. They look more like chunks of bark than an insect and nothing at all like the tiny, delicate, fluorescent pink, winged males. The life styles of the two sexes are correspondingly divergent. Females spend their days pressed tight to their host tree, feeding on the sap of the plant with their piercing mouthparts. They can withdraw their

sucking beaks from the tree and move slowly, but most of the time they are as sessile as barnacles. In contrast, males probably do not feed during their presumably short lives as adults; they are ready to fly whenever nearby females advertise their readiness to mate, which happens between mid-afternoon and early evening (Fig. 4.6). A receptive female announces this by bending the tip of her abdomen upward, away from the substrate. In this distinctive position, the female's genital opening is exposed, which probably allows her to release a sex pheromone (a volatile chemical) that drifts downwind, alerting males who are waiting on neighboring plants. The little pink males respond quickly, zigzagging upwind along the presumptive odor plume in the manner of scent-tracking insects.

Once a male has come close to one or more signaling females, which are often surrounded by non-receptive feeding females, he lands and searches for one with her abdomen raised. The male positions himself on the tip of the female's abdomen to link his genitalia with hers. Mating continues for about 9 min before the male dismounts and searches for other receptive females. The recently mated female slowly lowers her abdomen, eventually adopting the standard resting position with her body flattened against the bark of the sapling. In this position, she is unlikely to mate again, although both males and females are capable of copulating more than once in an afternoon (Fig. 4.7).

Why do these margarodid scale insects (and insects generally) exhibit large females and small males? We recognize fundamental differences between the sexes in their techniques for leaving descendants. Females, whether insects or mammals, rely primarily on themselves in the sense that the number of offspring they will have depends mostly on the number of eggs they can produce. Eggs are relatively big and costly to manufacture; large females can usually make more eggs than small females, which drives evolution toward large body size in this sex.

Males, whether insect or mammal, must find fecund females to bear their offspring, since they typically donate only their small, physiologically inexpensive sperm to their progeny. Because small males can make large quantities of tiny sperm, there is less advantage to being large for males than for females. This pattern breaks down when male reproductive success depends on a male's ability to keep other males away from potential mates. When access to mates depends on fighting, large bodies become advantageous, and so large male size spreads through a species over time. Huge males of the Northern Elephant Seal win vicious fights with other males and are able to acquire harems of females; losers do not mate at all.

Figure 4.6. Winged male of an unidentified species of scale insect (family Margarodidae) copulating with a flightless female on their host plant, *Ocotea tenera*. The wingless female dwarfs the winged male. Photograph by Dan Perlman.

For those insects in which males compete aggressively for partners, the customary big female pattern is sometimes lost. For example, in many rhinoceros beetles (Scarabaeidae-Dynastinae), adult males are larger than their females; males use their horns as weapons in battles over females (see Sec. 4.3). In contrast, the delicate males of the Monteverde scale insect ignore each other in a race to find receptive females. In this insect, the victory goes to the relatively swift male with good pheromone detectors, which has contributed to the evolution of the immense gulf between the sexes in both size and behavior in this scale insect.

4.4. Coleoptera: Beetles

4.4.1. Introduction
Paul Hanson

Beetles (order Coleoptera) comprise more than 400,000 named species, which represent about 25% of all described species of organisms. Adult beetles are characterized by having the front pair of wings hardened and forming protective coverings over the hind pair of wings, the latter used for flying. They display variation in color, shape, and size. In Monteverde, one can find both the world's largest beetle, the Hercules Beetle (*Dynastes hercules*, family Scarabaeidae; Fig. 4.8), which is 160 mm long, including the horn (see Sec. 4.4.3), and the world's smallest beetles, the "feather-winged" beetles (family Ptiliidae), many of which are 0.5 mm long.

Beetles undergo complete metamorphosis, and their larvae usually live in concealed habitats such as leaf litter, rotten wood, bracket fungi, and the rotten cambial layer beneath the bark of logs or standing dead trees (Crowson 1981, Lawrence 1991). Many of the most speciose families of beetles have phytophagous (plant-feeding) larvae. Larvae of many Scarabaeidae (white grubs, which are larval June beetles) and Elateridae (wireworms, which are larval click beetles) feed on roots of plants, while those of many Buprestidae are leaf miners (Fig. 4.9). Larvae of most Chrysomelidae (leaf beetles; see Sec. 4.7) and

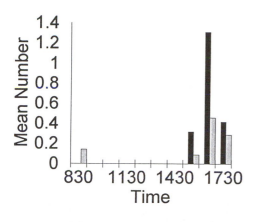

Figure 4.7. *(left)* The mean number of calling females (black bars) and copulating pairs (gray bars) of the Monteverde scale insect. Mean numbers are based on 5–26 censuses of two clusters of females (*N* = ca. 130 and ca. 200, respectively) made around 0830, 1330, 1630, and 1730 hr between 21 February and 3 March 1989.

Figure 4.8. *(below)* One of the world's most massive insects, the Hercules Beetle. Photograph by Robert Timm.

Curculionidae (weevils) feed concealed within plant tissue or on roots in the soil.

Because of the scarce nitrogen in wood, many beetle larvae that feed on dead wood have mutualistic associations with fungi or other microorganisms, as in "ambrosia beetles" (see Sec. 4.4.7). Other beetles associated with wood include many Buprestidae (metallic wood-boring beetles) and Cerambycidae (long-horned beetles; see Sec. 4.4.5). Many groups of beetles have larvae that feed on decomposing organic material, such as leaf litter, dung, and carrion. Dung beetles (Scarabaeidae: Scarabaeinae) can be collected with pitfall traps baited with feces. Such traps yielded 22 species in Panamanian cloud forests (1000–1760 m), with *Ontherus didymus* as the dominant species (Peck and Howden 1984). In Monteverde, some of the more common dung beetles include *Canthidium* sp., *Copris* sp., *Deltochilum mexicanum*, *Dichotomius carolinus colonicus*, and *Uroxys* sp. (B. Ratcliffe, pers. comm.).

Several beetles live in and feed exclusively on fungal fruiting bodies. Examples include a few Staphylinidae (see Sec. 4.4.2), Pselaphidae (short-winged mold beetles), Erotylidae (pleasing fungus beetles), Endomychidae (handsome fungus beetles), and Ciidae (minute tree-fungus beetles). A noticeable fungivorous beetle in Monteverde is an unidentified species of Endomychidae, which forms huge aggregations near streams during the dry season (J. Longino, pers. comm.).

Numerous beetles are predatory, often in both the larval and adult stages. Examples include most Carabidae (ground beetles), Cicindellidae (tiger beetles), most

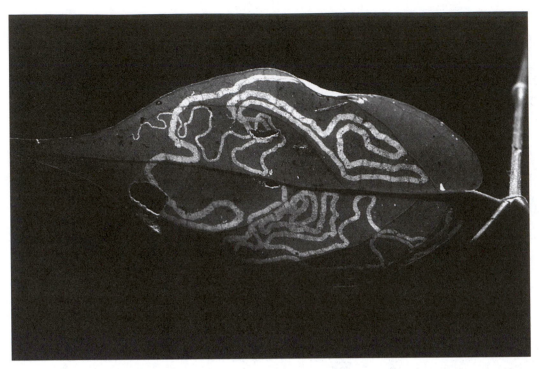

Figure 4.9. Tracks signaling damage from an unidentified leaf-miner. Photograph by Gregory Dimijian.

Staphylinidae (see Sec. 4.4.2), Lampyridae (lightning beetles or fireflies), Cleridae (see Sec. 4.4.4), and Coccinellidae (ladybird beetles). Tiger beetle larvae live in tunnels in the ground where they wait for prey to pass over the opening (Palmer 1976a, 1983a, Pearson 1988). In the Peñas Blancas valley, adults of *Oxycheila polita* run rapidly over rocks near rivers and dive into fast-flowing currents when disturbed, resurfacing from the water downstream (Cummins 1992). The species is more commonly seen at night than day. The larva is unknown (D. Brzoska and R. Huber, pers. comm.). Some lightning beetle larvae are specialized predators on earthworms or snails; others are generalists. Examples from Costa Rican cloud forests include *Lucidota apicalis*, *Lucidota* sp., *Magnoculus* sp., three species of *Photinus*, *Psilocladus scutellaris*, *Psilocladus* sp., and *Vesta* sp. (I. Bohorquez M., pers. comm.).

Of the 178 families of Coleoptera recognized worldwide, nearly 110 occur in Costa Rica (A. Solís, pers. comm.). The largest families, each estimated to have 500 or more species in Costa Rica (R. Anderson and T. Erwin, unpubl. data), include Carabidae, Staphylinidae, Pselaphidae, Scarabaeidae, Buprestidae, Elateridae, Tenebrionidae, Cerambycidae, Chrysomelidae, Curculionidae, and Scolytidae. This list has not incorporated the changes in classification: Pselaphidae is now classified as a subfamily of Staphylinidae; Apioninae has been removed from Curculionidae and

placed in Brentidae; Scolytidae should be a subfamily of Curculionidae.

4.4.2. Rove Beetles (Staphylinidae) of Monteverde
James S. Ashe

Rove beetles (family Staphylinidae) vie with weevils for being the largest family of beetles. Biologists rarely notice these abundant beetles or are aware of their exceptional taxonomic, ecological, and behavioral diversity and their dramatic ecological specialization.

To assess Monteverde staphylinid diversity, R. Brooks, R. Leschen, and I collected in Monteverde in May–June 1989, using flight intercept traps and unbaited pitfall traps on the Pacific side (1240–1800 m) and on the Atlantic side (800–1490 m). We sifted litter from forest floor habitats and extracted the arthropods with Berlese funnels. We also used hand-collecting techniques to collect staphylinids from specialized microhabitats. Specimens were sorted to morphospecies.

Of the 9349 staphylinid specimens examined, we recognized 845 morphospecies, in a minimum of 119 genera; 327 species were not assigned to a genus. The majority of species and specimens are in the subfamily Aleocharinae (356 species, 4109 specimens, 42% of the species), followed by Staphylininae (182 species, 2173 specimens) and Paederinae (101 species,

742 specimens). Three subfamilies, Tachyporinae (66 species), Osoriinae (58 species), and Oxytelinae (35 species), contain a moderate number of species. Relatively few species are found in Megalopinae (13 species), Piestinae (10 species), Steninae (10 species), Proteininae (5 species), and Euaesthetinae (3 species). Four subfamilies (Micropeplinae, Pseudopsinae, Oxyporinae, Omaliinae) contained only one species each.

Distribution of staphylinid species is not uniform within Monteverde. We divided the region into three areas: (1) 1200–1500 m on the Pacific side, (2) 1500–1800 m on the Pacific side, and (3) 800–1400 m on the Atlantic side (Peñas Blancas valley; Fig. 1.4). We collected 270 species from area 1 (118 species exclusive to area 1), 475 species from area 2 (297 species exclusive), and 292 species from area 3 (190 species exclusive). Areas 1 and 2 shared 90 species, and areas 2 and 3 shared 40 species.

The most diverse set of microhabitats were those associated with fungi (134 species total, 68 species found exclusively in this habitat), followed by forest litter (132 species total, 52 exclusively) and subcortical habitats (85 species total, 34 exclusively).

Staphylinids living under bark.   The subcortical (under bark) habitat is complex and dynamic. Its characteristics depend on the kind of tree, the time since the tree has fallen, and local microclimatic conditions. Bark in different parts of a log are often in different stages of decay, so a diversity of staphylinid subcortical communities can occur on the same log, sometimes within a few centimeters of one another.

The most diverse subcortical staphylinid community is found under bark of recently fallen trees on which the cambium has begun to ferment, with slightly loose bark. The staphylinid community is characterized by specialized predatory staphylinids: xantholinines (e.g., *Homalolinus* spp., *Ehomalolinus* spp., *Heterolinus*), a few distinctive species of *Belonuchus* (e.g., *B. dichrous*), and *Holisus*. The community also includes a diverse array of staphylinids that are saprophagous or feed on fungi in the fermenting cambium: *Piestus* (*Zirophorus*), *Hypotelus*; several genera of osoriines (*Eleusis, Renardia, Leptochirus, Priochirus, Lispinus, Nacaeus,* and *Clavilispinus*), several aleocharines (*Placusa*, expected but not yet recorded from Monteverde, and *Homalota*), and the tachyporine *Coproporus*.

The subcortical habitat with fermenting cambium slowly transforms into a less rich habitat as the available carbohydrates are used by bacteria, fungi, and saprophagous arthropods. These communities are usually dominated by saprophagous staphylinids; for example, adult and larval osoriines (especially *Leptochirus, Priochirus, Lispinus, Nacaeus,* and *Thora-*

cophorus) can be abundant in such logs. Species of *Piestus* (sensu stricto), the paederine *Sunius,* and falagriine aleocharines such as *Myrmecocephalus* are found under bark. Bark of very old logs in which the subcortical spaces are filled with dense masses of very decayed frass and mud-frass mixtures have few staphylinids. Some of these logs may contain colonies of the cylindrical osoriine *Osorius.*

The most striking modification among subcortical staphylinids is in body shape, which takes two forms: highly flattened, or slender and cylindrical. Members of the genus *Leptochirus* are common subcortical staphylinids in Monteverde. These are large (2 cm or more in length), usually shining black, with broad and very flattened head, prothorax, and elytra; the abdomen is cylindrical and forms a rigid tube for strength. Species of *Priochirus* have a similar body form. Although these two genera are not closely related, it is difficult to distinguish them. In Monteverde, all *Priochirus* have short cephalic horns, which are absent in *Leptochirus.*

Another frequently encountered and strikingly flattened staphylinid is the xantholinine *Homalolinus.* The most commonly encountered species, *H. canaliculatus,* is more than 2.5 cm long and has a shining black, flattened body, with the tip of the abdomen red. The broad, flattened, arrowhead-shaped head and narrow neck are distinctive. The most flattened staphylinids are osoriines in the genus *Eleusis,* which have paper-thin bodies. Other staphylinids that have strongly flattened bodies include the piestines *Piestus* and *Hypotelus,* the osoriine *Renardia,* and the aleocharines *Placusa, Homalota,* and *Cephalaloxynum.*

Life histories of subcortical staphylinids have not been investigated. The confined spaces of this habitat may place considerable constraint on life history traits; for example, larvae of instars, pupae, and adults of osoriines (particularly *Leptochirus* and *Priochirus*) are found together under bark, suggesting that they may be subsocial. I once encountered colonies of *Osorius* under very decayed bark in which the subcortical space was filled with a soillike mixture of mud and frass. The colony consisted of independent radiating tunnel systems without obvious connections between them. Within each tunnel system were two adults (presumably male and female), an egg at the terminations of most radiating tunnels, and larvae and pupae of all stages, a pattern expected for subsocial insects.

Staphylinids associated with rodents.   One of the most unusual groups of rove beetles is the tribe Amblyopinini. Adults are found in the fur of many rodents and some marsupials in Central and South America. They are relatively large (1 cm or more in length), lightly pigmented, wingless beetles with greatly reduced elytra and eyes. The group is most diverse in South America, where there are five described genera and over 50 described species. Only one genus, *Amblyopinus*, is found in Central America, and two species occur in Monteverde.

Amblyopinines were believed to be obligate, blood-feeding ectoparasites, based on the presence of adults with their heads tightly attached in the fur of their hosts, skin damage occurring when they are removed, large strongly sclerotized mandibles, and the presence of blood in the guts of beetles. Studies in Monteverde have shown that amblyopinines are not parasites (Ashe and Timm 1986, 1987a, 1987b). We live-trapped hundreds of rodents, studied the distribution of the amblyopinines they hosted, kept hosts and beetles together in observation chambers and examined their interactions, and did host choice experiments to determine if the beetles could distinguish among different species of rodents as potential hosts (Ashe and Timm 1986, 1987a,b).

The beetles are host-specific: *Amblyopinus emarginatus* showed a strong preference for the neotropical Rice Rat (*Oryzomys albigularis*); *A. triptoni* was found on two closely related hosts (*Peromyscus nudipes* and *Reithrodontomys creper*; Muridae). Fewer than 1% of the beetles were found on the "wrong" host. This level of host specificity is typical of many parasitic insects and is consistent with the hypothesis of parasitism for these beetles.

We confirmed observations made by P. Hershkovitz in 1952 that the host takes no notice of the beetles, even when they crawl across its face, and no skin damage was found that could be attributed to the beetles. The skin of mice with heavy infestations of beetles appeared healthy. When we transferred beetles to a species of mouse on which the beetles did not normally live, the mouse became irritated by their presence and would scratch at the beetles until it was able to remove and kill them.

The beetles leave the host during the day when the host becomes inactive and roam throughout the nest. They climb back onto the mouse and take up their characteristic position behind or between the ears when the mouse becomes active at nightfall. The mystery of their feeding habits was solved when we observed the beetles eating fleas and other true ectoparasites in the nest during the day. Rather than being ectoparasites, the beetles were actually "ectocommensals," and likely mutualistic, with the hosts. The host primarily provides transport from nest to nest in which the beetles feed on ectoparasites. The blood found in the guts of some beetles probably came from secondary ingestion of blood from the guts of true ectoparasites when the beetles ate them. The hosts appear to actively tolerate the presence of the beetles in their fur, perhaps because their presence is beneficial.

If the beetles are predators only on ectoparasites, why are they so host-specific? Any mouse that tolerates their presence and has ectoparasites would seem to be a suitable host. Where are the immature stages of the beetles? Is this behavior typical of other amblyopines, or have others made the transition to true parasitism? What characteristics of rodents and beetles have driven the evolution of this interaction?

Staphylinids associated with ants. Some staphylinids, especially species in the subfamily Aleocharinae, have been successful at invading the nests of social insects, particularly those of ants (150 staphylinid genera) and termites (over 100 genera). Termites are uncommon in Monteverde, and no termitophilous staphylinids have been reported. Of the staphylinid genera associated with ants ("myrmecophiles"), more than 100 are found in association with army ants in both the Old and New World.

Species of *Tetradonia* and related genera are usually found in association with the edges of raiding columns or swarms of army ants, or in their refuse piles, where they attack injured ants or steal prey from the ants. They avoid contact with the ants and repel the attackers by using defensive chemical secretions from an abdominal gland (Akre and Rettenmeyer 1966, J. Ashe, pers. obs.). Other taxa (e.g., *Ecitodonia* species of which are not myrmecoid) are common in refuse piles of *Eciton* bivouacs; they are found running in the ant columns when the colony moves to a new bivouac. Others (e.g., *Ecitophya, Ecitomorpha, Ecitochara*), which have more myrmecoid bodies, are with *Eciton* army ants in the raiding columns. Species of *Ecitosus*, which have very myrmecoid bodies, have been reported in the columns of *Neivamyrmex* (Akre and Rettenmeyer 1966). The most unusual myrmecophiles in Monteverde are the myrmecoid members of the tribe Leptanillophilini that occur with *Labidus* army ants. Species of *Labidoglobus* and *Mimonilla* are virtually unpigmented, have lost their wings and eyes, have reduced the elytra to a vestigial nub, and are difficult to distinguish from the ants with which they run. Beetles with such highly derived myrmecoid body forms are rarely attacked by the ants.

Staphylinids associated with other substrates. Fungi that produce macroscopic fruiting bodies offer a variety of resources to insects: mycelia (fungal fibers), asexual spores, sexual spores, portions of macroscopic fruiting bodies, and other arthropods. Examples of large, strikingly colored, predaceous staphylinids associated with fungi in Monteverde include all species of *Megalopinus*, *Lordithon*, *Bolitogyrus*, and *Plociopterus*, some species of *Platydracus*, and a few species of *Paederominus* and *Philonthus*. Many smaller Aleocharinae (athetines, bolitocharines, and others) are attracted to mushrooms in the later stages of decay and are primarily predators and specialists on this habitat.

Species of *Oxyporus* are relatively large staphylinids (1 cm or more in length) that are often strikingly colored found primarily on fleshy mushrooms. The only species that occurs in Monteverde, *O. bierigi*, occurs on gilled mushrooms of the genera *Pholiota* and *Gymnopilus* (Cortinariaceae). Little is known about the life history of gyrophaenines and other mushroom-inhabiting staphylinids in Monteverde. Overviews of the biology of mushroom inhabiting staphylinids are in Ashe (1984, 1986, 1987), Leschen and Allen (1988), and Newton (1984).

Species of the aleocharine genus *Tachiona* are found on the inside of webs that cover hepialid (Lepidoptera) burrows on living *Trema* (Ulmaceae) trees. The flattened larvae and black-and-red adults of *Tachiona monteverdensis* are abundant on the insides of these webs and around the hole that contains the moth larva. Virtually every active burrow contains a few beetles, and sometimes 20–25 individuals can be found in a single web. These beetles were considered extremely rare until their association with hepialid burrows was discovered at Monteverde (Ashe 1990).

Members of the aleocharine genus *Charoxus* are small, elongate, subcylindrical beetles that are usually found in the fruits (receptacles) of figs. Little is known about their biology, but they apparently enter the fig through the exit hole chewed by male fig wasps. The adults lay eggs in the fig and larvae mature before the fig drops from the tree. The staphylinids may feed on emerging fig wasps, although all of the larvae that I have examined had their guts filled with fig pollen. Adult *Charoxus* are not found on fig trees before the fig wasps begin to emerge, but adults and larvae may be abundant in figs of the correct age. It is not known how the adult staphylinids arrive at fig trees precisely when fig wasps begin to emerge.

4.4.3. Dynastine Scarab Beetles of Monteverde
Brett C. Ratcliffe

Beetles belonging to the Scarabaeidae are well known because of their beauty, fascinating life histories, often bizarre body forms, and occasional economic significance. There are 13 subfamilies and 400 (over 800 estimated) species of Scarabaeidae in Costa Rica; 62 of these species belong to the subfamily Dynastinae. This subfamily contains species with magnificent

horns, which has given rise to the common names of elephant, unicorn, or rhinoceros beetles for the entire group. Most species of dynastines, however, are smaller June beetle-like insects that lack horns. Adult scarabs are readily distinguished from other families of beetles by the presence of segmented antennae terminating with a lamellate (platelike) club of three to seven leaflike segments that can be expanded fanwise or folded compactly together. Scarabs sense odors with their antennae, and the enlarged "club" increases the surface area of the sensory receptors.

Within the subfamily Dynastinae, there are eight tribes containing about 1400 species worldwide (Endrödi 1985). Six of these tribes occur in Costa Rica, and five are represented at Monteverde. Of the 31 genera of Dynastinae found in Costa Rica, 13 occur at Monteverde. Of the 62 species of Dynastinae found in Costa Rica, I have found 36 at Monteverde. Probably no species of dynastine is endemic to Monteverde, although *Cyclocephala williami* (Fig. 4.10, panel 4) is known only from the Monteverde area (Ratcliffe 1992).

Altitudinal gradients of dynastine species occur in the Monteverde region. Some dynastines (e.g., *Golofa* spp.; Fig. 4.10, panel 9) are found only in the higher wetter areas, whereas some species of *Cyclocephala* are found throughout the area, at all elevations. *Dynastes hercules* (Fig. 4.10, panel 8) is the largest beetle found at Monteverde; males reach a length of 18 cm. Males have smooth, grayish green wing covers mottled with black spots, and a shiny black head and thorax, each of which bears a long, forward-projecting horn. Females have roughened black wing covers and lack horns. In tropical America, this species is generally restricted to lower montane and premontane rain forests above 1000 m.

Adults of nearly all dynastines are active at night and frequently come to lights. During the day, the adults hide beneath leaves and logs, or in the soil. The adults of many Cyclocephalini (Fig. 4.10, panels 2, 3, 5) feed at night on the flowers of plants, including palms and aroids. *Cyclocephala* and *Erioscelis* feed on the small flowers of the club-shaped spadix of *Philodendron* and *Diffenbachia* (Color Plate 2) species (Araceae; Young 1986, 1988, Gottsberger 1989, Gottsberger and Silberbauer-Gottsberger 1991). Adults belonging to the other tribes occasionally feed on rotting fruit or sap flows at night.

Sexual dimorphism is well developed in the horned species. Males are larger and often possess huge, curving horns arising from the head and/or thorax. Horns in scarab beetles occur in a wide array of shapes, forms, and sizes (Arrow 1951). Only males have horns, which suggests that they play a role in sexual selection. The males of some dynastines fight over suitable feeding

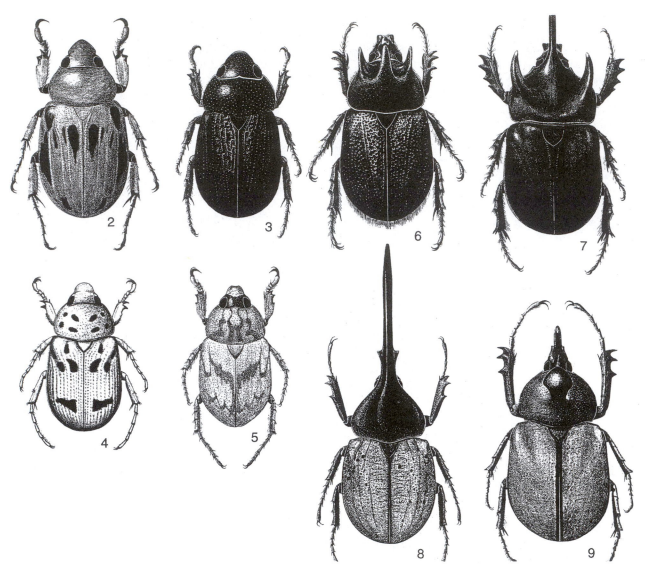

Figure 4.10. Dynastine scarab beetles of Monteverde. 2: *Ancognatha vulgaris*; 3: *Cyclocephala carbonaria*; 4: *Cyclocephala williami*; 5: *Cyclocephala weidneri*; 6: *Heterogomphus mniszechi*; 7: *Strategus jugurtha*; 8: *Dynastes hercules*; 9: *Gologa costaricensis*.

sites that also attract females (Eberhard 1979, 1980). Horns are used in combat to pry a rival male from his perch.

Dynastine females deposit their eggs in humus, litter, soil, or decaying wood. The egg stage lasts from two to three weeks. The larvae of *Dynastes*, *Golofa*, *Heterogomphus* (Fig. 4.10, panel 6), *Strategus* (panel 7), *Xyloryctes*, *Phileurus*, and probably those of *Megaceras*, *Barutus*, and *Ligyrus* are found in rotting logs, compost, or decayed trees where they feed on organic debris, including the spores and hyphae of fungi. Larvae of other dynastines, such as *Cyclocephala*, feed on plant roots. Larval dynastines are C-shaped white grubs (Fig. 4.11). Larvae of most species remain totally unknown.

Species of dynastinae have several natural enemies. Fungi, bacterial diseases, parasitic wasps, and various mammals attack larvae and adults. Individuals attracted to lights are often preyed on by vertebrates, especially the introduced Marine Toad, *Bufo marinus* (Bufonidae). The greatest threats facing nocturnal insects such as dynastines are forest clearing and light pollution. Many nocturnal insects are attracted to lights. Street lights and the floodlights of hotels and other commercial establishments serve as "sinks" where insects are attracted, fail to reproduce, and then die. For the first several years insects are attracted to the lights in abundance, but then they become fewer and fewer. Ultimately, the area becomes a sterile, nearly insect-free desert as local populations of all but

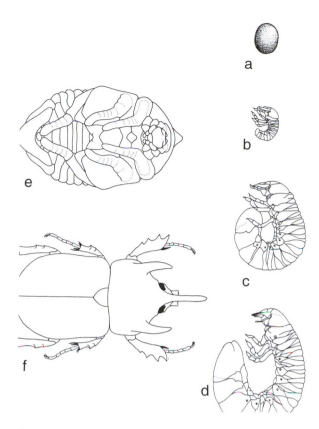

Figure 4.11. Life cycle for *Strategus jugurtha*: (a) egg; (b–d) first-, second-, and third-instar larva; (e) pupa; (f) adult.

the "weedy" species are trapped out and disappear (Janzen 1983, B. Ratcliffe, pers. obs.).

Acknowledgments   I thank Bob Law, John and Doris Campbell, Pedro Belmar, the Monteverde Conservation League, and the Tropical Science Center for logistical support. Mary Liz Jameson (University of Nebraska), Norman Penny (California Academy of Sciences), and Alex Reifschneider (Sierra Madre, Calif.) assisted with collecting and field observations. Fernando Mejia (INBio) assisted with specimen data management for the project. Mark Marcuson (University of Nebraska State Museum) provided artwork (Fig. 4.10). Research was supported by grants from the University of Nebraska Foundation and the National Science Foundation (DEB9200760).

4.4.4. Cleridae of Central American Cloud Forests
Jacques Rifkind

Cleridae is a medium-sized family of predaceous beetles that attains its maximum diversity in the tropics. Sometimes called "checkered beetles," clerids are often colorful and many are mimics of insects that show warning coloration, such as velvet ants (Mutillidae). Members of this family are diverse in body shape and size. There are about 425 described species of Cleridae from Mexico and Central America (Barr 1975), which is an underestimate because Panama and Costa Rica each contain at least as many undescribed as described species. Although clerid diversity is high in lowland rain forests, these beetles become abundant only at 700 m and above.

Some cloud forest clerids have a broad altitudinal tolerance. *Priocera clavipes* and the nocturnal *Cymatodera prolixa* are found in the lowland rain forests of Belize and in the cloud forest of Monteverde. *Colyphus cylindricus* has a more disjunct distribution, but it seems not to be narrowly limited by phytogeographic or climatic factors. It is found in relatively xeric oak and pine forests in Guatemala, in tropical deciduous forests at middle elevations in southern Mexico, and in Honduras in the cloud forest of La Tigra (1800 m). Other clerids occur only in upland rain forests and cloud forests. *Colyphus irazu*, for example, is found in Monteverde and 110 km to the southeast on the high slopes of isolated volcanoes surrounding the central valley of Costa Rica. Some species are restricted to a single isolated cloud forest. Whether these represent relict species, local speciation events, or insufficient collecting is unknown. Some narrowly endemic cloud forest clerids exhibit odd morphologies and apparently lack close living relatives.

Costa Rica, the Central American country with the most extensively studied cloud forests, contains approximately 25 genera of Cleridae. Of these, only *Callotillus*, *Monophylla* and *Lecontella*—genera that appear to be adapted to xeric thorn forests—probably do not contain species that inhabit cloud forests. Although some genera are restricted to higher elevations, none is limited to cloud forests.

Clerid beetles occur on flowers, in dead and dying wood, in fungi, and on vegetation (Clausen 1940). In their larval state, they feed on the larvae of woodboring beetles, although some genera (e.g., *Lecontella*) are predaceous on hymenopteran larvae in their nests, and others specialize on grasshopper eggs or carrion. As adults, clerids will eat most insects that they can overpower, including "distasteful" species such as coccinellid beetles.

In Monteverde, several clerid species are common on the foliage of shrubs and small trees at forest edges and along paths, the rough bark of larger trees, and at blacklight and Malaise traps. *Perilypus* species are very common in shaded areas. With their reddish pronota (upper surface of the first body segment) and bluish black striped or concolorous elytra, they belong to a mimicry complex including similarly colored Cantharidae, Lycidae, Chrysomelidae, and Oede-meridae. Another Monteverde resident is the enopliine *Muisca octonotata*, an obovate flattened species with a distinct pattern of dark elytral spots on a yellowish background. This clerid is remarkably similar to two species of Chrysomelidae: *Neobrotica* sp. and *Malacorhinus* sp. Although it presumably gains protection by mimicking these leaf beetles, *Muisca* also tends to curl itself under when disturbed, which may facilitate its fall from the plant when being pursued by a bird or lizard. Many species of clerids, distributed among several subfamilies, are excellent mimics of Hymenoptera, particularly ants and mutillid wasps. A small, shiny black *Phyllobaenus* common in Monteverde is nearly indistinguishable from the ant *Camponotus canescens*, which runs on the same waxy-leafed vegetation as the beetle.

4.4.5. Long-horned Beetles (Cerambycidae and Disteniidae) of Monteverde
Frank T. Hovore

Members of the families Cerambycidae and Disteniidae are wood-borers. They are known as long-horned beetles because most have relatively long antennae. They have elongate bodies (3–80+ mm in length). Diurnal species are often colorful; nocturnal species tend to be more drab. In the Monteverde area, *Schwarzerion holochlorum* (Tempisque Borer) is bright metallic green with reddish legs and long black antennae and is most active on warm sunny days. However, *Psalidognathus modestus*, which also flies in bright sunlight, is shining black and is recognized by its huge size, spiny head, and enormous, curving mandibles. Examples of nocturnal species include the tan and pale green *Chlorida cincta* and dark brown *Derobrachus longicornis*. The best known long-horned beetle in Monteverde is the ornately patterned Harlequin Beetle, *Acrocinus longimanus*, a species that is distinctive for the extremely long front legs of the male.

The family Cerambycidae is divided into seven New World subfamilies, five of which occur in Costa Rica, plus the closely related family Disteniidae. Parandrinae and Prioninae are medium- to large-sized beetles, brown to black in color. The former is distinguished by their relatively short antennae, with beadlike segments and large curved mandibles in the males. Cerambycinae and Lamiinae, the two most diverse subfamilies, are variable in size and color. Lepturinae are usually brightly colored and diurnal. Disteniidae are nocturnal, often dark metallic colored, and have long hairs laid flat along the inside of the antennae.

There are an estimated 35,000 described species worldwide. Costa Rica has as many as 950 species. Within Monteverde, approximately 260 species, including about 40 undescribed taxa, have been recorded since the 1960s, based on about 4,500 total specimens from the area. As of 1996, 31 species have been found only in the MCFP, 153 have been taken in the greater Monteverde area but not in the MCFP, and 31 occur in both areas.

Adult long-horned beetles may or may not feed. Those that feed generally consume pollen, foliage, bark, plant sap, or fungi. Many species can be found in flowers of *Croton* (Euphorbiaceae). *Cephalodina crassiceps* (Lamiinae-Hemilophini) feeds on leaves of figs (*Ficus*, Moraceae). Captive Harlequin Beetles (*Acrocinus longimanus*, Lamiinae-Acrocinini) have been kept alive for six months on a diet of soft fruits such as mango, cantaloupe, and avocado. Most longhorns are strong fliers, although in several species females are incapable of flying, and both sexes of *Phrynidius echinus* (Lamiinae-Apomecynini) are wingless.

Long-horn beetles exhibit an array of defense mechanisms. Diurnal species often mimic noxious or stinging insects; others are distasteful and exhibit aposematic (warning) coloration. In Monteverde, many flower-inhabiting species of Clytini (Cerambycinae) and Lepturinae appear to mimic wasps and bees, being brightly marked with bands of yellow and black. *Erana fulveola* (Lamiinae-Hemilophini) and species of Rhinotragini (Cerambycinae) resemble ichneumonid wasps when flying; many Tillomorphini (Cerambycinae) and *Acestrilla minima* (Lamiinae-Apomecynini) are ant mimics. The bright red and black *Oedudes bifasciata* (Lamiinae-Hemilophini) chews notches in living stems of urticating plants (e.g., *Urera elata*, Urticaceae), apparently feeding on their sap and acquiring protective chemicals. Most nocturnal longhorns are somber or cryptically colored or have their dorsal surfaces ornately sculptured or clothed with hairs, often closely matching substrates on which they rest. Most long-horned beetles emit an alarming, scraping sound when handled, and some species can inflict a painful bite.

In many Cerambycinae, copulation takes place shortly after the adults emerge from their pupal cells, but in Lamiinae mating usually does not occur until after a period of feeding. Except for flower-visiting species, mating takes place on the host plant. Many long-horned beetles emit a strong-smelling sex pheromone (attractant) that is detectable by human observers. Male beetles with well-developed mandibles often compete violently for females or host resources.

Host plants are located primarily by means of olfactory organs within the elongated antennae. A succession of long-horned beetles appear to arrive at fallen trees; chemical changes in the wood may have a selective influence. In most subfamilies, oviposition consists of little more than using the ovipositor to place eggs in bark crevices or decomposed wood. Species of Lamiinae tend to have more specialized oviposition habits and often use their mandibles to chew an oviposition site. Long-horned beetle larvae usually feed and develop within the stems of woody plants. Most often, they attack dying or dead stems, but some species breed within living stems of larger herbaceous plants (Table 4.1).

Larvae of a few species feed in roots and seeds. Those that attack living or recently dead wood are more host-specific than those that attack wood in later stages of decay. In some long-horned beetles, the female harbors a yeast in intersegmental pouches of her abdomen that aids in the digestion of cellulose. She smears these microbes onto her eggs during oviposition; the larva obtains the yeast by eating the egg shell soon after hatching. Long-horned beetle larvae are cylindrical grubs, often slightly enlarged in the thoracic region. Prior to pupation, the larvae usually construct a cell within the wood or just beneath the bark, and the pupa rests in this "safe area" during its most vulnerable stage. *Lagocheirus* (Lamiinae-Acanthocinini) larvae cut a large elliptical piece from the outer bark prior to entering the sapwood to pupate. Heavily infested logs may have dozens of these "bark cookies" scattered over their surface. Adult emergence is often seasonal and correlated with rainfall patterns. Biology of long-horned beetles is discussed elsewhere (Duffy 1960, Linsley 1961).

4.4.6. High Altitude Leaf Beetles (Chrysomelidae and Megalopodidae) in Costa Rica
R. Wills Flowers

Chrysomelidae is an immense family of over 37,000 described species, which is more than twice the species richness of birds and mammals combined (Klausnitzer 1981). Larvae and adults of most species feed on living plant material. Many larvae are subterranean root-feeders and some are leaf-feeders; stem-boring, leaf-mining, and detritus-feeding are found among few species. The vast majority of adults are aboveground leaf, flower, or pollen feeders. Some are important pests through direct feeding damage and transmission of viruses; others are useful biological control agents of weeds.

Worldwide, 19 subfamilies are recognized, of which 14 are represented in Costa Rica (Seeno and Wilcox 1982, Reid 1995). No formal studies on the altitudinal distribution of tropical chrysomelid faunas exist, although there are scattered references to the altitudes of collecting localities. Leaf beetle diversity in lowland areas is considerably higher than in cloud forests and higher altitudes.

Beetles in the subfamily Megalopodinae resemble aberrant long-horned beetles. In *Megalopus*, which is regularly collected above 1300 m, the males have

Table 4.1. Larval hosts of Cerambycid beetles in the Monteverde area.

Beetle	Host Plant
Cerambycinae	
Anatinomma bispinosum (Hesperophanini)	*Billia colombiana* (Hippocastanaceae); girdling living branches
Pempteurys sericans (Anaglyptini)	On girdled branches; *Persea* (Lauraceae) girdled by *Oncideres fulvostillata*
Ancylocera macrotela (Trachyderini)	*Acacia* girdled by *Oncideres punctatus*
Lamiinae	
Anisopodus costaricensis (Acanthocinini)	Cacao (*Theobroma*, Sterculiaceae)
Acrocinus longimanus (Acrocinini)	*Ficus* spp. (Moraceae) (beneath the bark)
Adetus spp. (Adetini)	Cucurbitaceae
Eulachnesia smaragdina (Hemilophini)	Cacao (*Theobroma*, Sterculiaceae)
Desmiphora hirticollis (Desmiphorini)	*Cordia* spp. (Boraginaceae)
Ischiocentra monteverdensis (Onciderini)	*Mandevilla veraguasensis* (Apocynaceae)
Disteniidae	
Distenia pilatei (Disteniini)	Young coffee (*Coffea*, Rubiaceae)

enlarged hind legs that are used during mating to fend off other males (Eberhard and Marin 1996). Larvae are unknown in most species but some South American species are stem-borers.

Members of the subfamily Criocerinae are recognizable by a constricted pronotum (the dorsal plate of the first thoracic segment) and a shiny body surface. Larvae are free-living, and some construct protective shelters from their own feces. *Lema*, the most abundant genus in this subfamily, exceeds 1300 m elevation only occasionally. In contrast, *Metepoceris* has been regularly collected in Monteverde and other cloud forests; they are large, iridescent green with two pairs of purple patches on the elytra, and feed on Solanaceae (Flowers and Janzen 1997).

Eumolpinae is a large group, most of which have a robust, compact body and shiny or metallic coloration. Larvae are root feeders, and very few have been studied. In Costa Rica, the majority of Eumolpinae live at lower elevations (Flowers 1996), but species have been collected above 1300 m, three of which are true high-altitude species. *Alethaxius* and *Dryadomolpus* are small dark-colored beetles that have been collected in Monteverde and on the peaks of Poas and Barva volcanoes and from the Andes in South America. *Colaspoides batesi* shows an interesting altitudinal separation from its almost identical relative, *Colaspoides unicolor*: *C. batesi*, which is bright metallic green, has only been collected at Monteverde at elevations higher than 1040 m; *C. unicolor*, which is dark shiny blue, is abundant in the Cordillera de Guanacaste from 600 to 1100 m.

Chrysomelinae includes the largest and most colorful of Costa Rica's leaf beetles. Their larvae are free-living. *Plagiodera bistripunctata* and *Stilodes retifera* appear to be restricted to cloud forest elevations, and most specimens of *Doryphora paykulii* (the largest chrysomelid found in Costa Rica) come from above 1300 m in the Talamanca Mountains. Several species of *Calligrapha* are found higher than 1300 m. *Platyphora*, the most diverse chrysomeline genus, only occasionally strays into cloud forest elevations.

The tribe Galerucinae-Galerucini is abundant in tropical regions, and some species of *Diabrotica* and related genera are important crop pests. Larvae of many species are root feeders but some genera (e.g., *Cecropia*-feeding *Monocesta* and *Ceratoma*) have free-living larvae. As in the Eumolpinae, most species occur at low elevations with relatively few species in cloud forests or above. Four species are apparently restricted to higher elevations: *Cochabamba impressipennis*, *Cochabamba* sp., *Diabrotica porracea*, and *Paranapiacaba dorsoplagiata*. *Diabrotica* and *Paranapiacaba* are

very abundant at low elevations; *Cochabamba* appears to be an exclusively high-altitude genus.

Because of their enlarged hind femora and jumping abilities, the tribe Galerucinae-Alticini is called "flea beetles." Adults can be located by finding pinholed leaves caused by their feeding. Many larvae are root feeders, but some are free-living. Alticini is the largest tribe of Chrysomelidae and has been the most successful in colonizing cloud forests. We know of only two cases where all specimens come from above 1300 m (*Acrocyum dorsalis* and *Omophoeta albofasciata*), whereas other cloud forest taxa can also be found at lower elevations. Examples include *Macrohaltica*, which are frequent defoliators of *Gunnera* (Gunneraceae); flightless *Longitarsus*, which occur in forest litter in Atlantic rain forests to páramo; and *Marcapatica* and *Neothona*, which occur in the Talamanca Mountains. The two *Omophoeta* represent another case of altitudinal separation; *O. aequinoctialis* is ubiquitous in the lowlands but is almost absent above 1300 m, whereas *O. albofasciata* has not been collected below this altitude.

Hispinae-Hispini is relatively well-known taxonomically. Larvae of some species of Hispini are leaf miners; species of *Cephaloleia* live in rolled-up emerging leaves of *Heliconia* (Heliconiaceae) and other monocots. This large and abundant tribe decreases in species richness with increasing altitude. *Acentroptera nevermanni* appears to be one of the few exclusively high-altitude species (based on two specimens). More than 60 species of *Cephaloleia* occur in Costa Rica and of these, around 20 are recorded from Monteverde. Their larval host plants are poorly known (Staines 1996). *Alurnus salvini* from the Talamanca Mountains is closely related to the very large and colorful *A. ornata*, which is a palm-feeding beetle limited to lowland rain forests.

Tortoise beetles (tribe Hispinae-Cassidini) have the edges of the pronotum and elytra expanded and flattened, and many are brilliant gold or green, although these colors fade soon after death. Larvae are free-living, some carrying their cast skins on modified projections that they hold over their back to hide. Relatively few tortoise beetles are found in cloud forests: *Stolas costaricensis*, *Stolas* sp., and *Tapinaspis atroannulus* feed on composites (Asteraceae); *Charidotella emarginata* probably feeds on one of the morning glories (Convolvulaceae) (Windsor et al. 1992). Adult females of *Stolas* stay with their young, sheltering them from predators with their greatly expanded elytra.

For 72% of the leaf beetle species, we do not even know the identity of their host plants, and most of the rest are species of the north temperate zone (Jolivet

1988). Understanding how the distribution of cloud forest leaf beetles relates to the distribution of their food plants will help explain how high-altitude leaf beetle fauna evolved. The mosaic of habitats at the edge of reserves—old fields, secondary forest, and patches of primary forest—generates a more diverse leaf beetle fauna than unbroken primary forest. Maintenance of variegated buffer zones around protected wildlands and prevention of high-intensity agriculture from moving to reserve borders benefits both conservation and tropical Chrysomelidae.

4.4.7. The Bark and Ambrosia Beetles (Scolytidae and Platypodidae) of Costa Rican Cloud Forests
Lawrence R. Kirkendall & Stephen L. Wood

Bark and ambrosia beetles (Scolytidae [or Curculionidae-Scolytinae] and Platypodidae) tunnel in woody plants. As with the Cerambycidae, they are primary decomposers of dead woody tissues in forests. A few temperate species have gained notoriety as tree-killers of significant economic importance; in the tropics the most important pest is the Coffee Berry Borer (*Hypothenemus hampei*). The economic impact of other tropical species is greatest from damage to logs by ambrosia beetles; few scolytid or platypodid beetles kill healthy trees.

In Costa Rica, about 500 species of Scolytidae (Wood et al. 1992) and 58 species of Platypodidae (Equihua and Atkinson 1987) are known or expected, which represent two-thirds to three-fourths of the actual number of species in Costa Rica. A total for the two groups of 700–850 species would be at least 10% of the approximately 7,300 species known worldwide (Wood and Bright 1992).

All bark and ambrosia beetles feed and lay eggs in tunnel systems, a habit shared with Bostrichidae, Anobiidae, and a few weevil groups, but otherwise rare in beetles. The term "bark beetles" refers either to scolytids as a whole or to those taxa breeding (tunneling) in inner bark; "ambrosia beetles" encompasses unrelated groups of scolytids and most platypodids, all of which grow fungi on the walls of their tunnel systems. The mutualistic fungi provide the major or sole source of nutrition for adults and larvae (Beaver 1988).

Living in long-lasting defensible tunnel systems has led to the evolution of an unparalleled variety of social behaviors in these cryptic beetles (Kirkendall 1983, 1993, Noguera-Martinez and Atkinson 1990, Kirkendall et al. 1997). Most scolytids and apparently all platypodids are outbreeders, but extreme inbreeding has evolved repeatedly and has proven success-

ful; all xyleborines, for example, reproduce by brother-sister or mother-son mating. In outbreeding species, males stay for most or all of the oviposition period, and in some species (including most platypodids) males die with their mates. Some are monogynous (most platypodids, many scolytids), but simultaneous ("harem") polygyny is common, and some groups are regularly bigynous. Varying degrees of parental care have evolved, ranging from protection from predators by males or females to apparently sterile female "workers" tending the offspring of their mother, as in an Australian platypodid (Kent and Simpson 1992, Kirkendall et al. 1997). Parental behavior is complex in all ambrosia beetles but has been little investigated.

Bark and ambrosia beetles vary in their degree of host plant specificity, and overall are less host specific in the tropics than in temperate regions (Beaver 1979a). Tropical ambrosia beetles and their fungi are thought to be only broadly host specific because differences in biochemical and physical properties of sapwood are minor.

Intensive Malaise trap sampling (P. Hanson and I. Gauld; see Sec. 4.7; Fig. 4.12) has yielded material

Figure 4.12. Paul Hanson with Malaise trap at the Zurquí study area. Photograph by Lawrence Kirkendall.

sufficient to analyze the cloud forest fauna at Zurquí de Moravia, equivalent in habitat and elevation to Monteverde. Although fewer than half as many specimens have been seen from Zurquí as from two lowland sites (La Selva Biological Station and the Osa Peninsula, 0–200 m), Zurquí has produced as many or more species. About one-third of the species collected in Zurquí thus far are new to science. The Zurquí samples were dominated by corthyline and platypodid ambrosia beetles (70% and 25% of ambrosia beetle individuals, respectively). Although many corthyline species were present in the lowlands (21 of 57 species at La Selva, 9 of 59 at the Osa Peninsula), none was common in Malaise samples. Rather, lowland site collections were dominated by ambrosia beetles of the tribe Xyleborini; only a few xyleborines were trapped at Zurquí. The ecological replacement of xyleborines by corthylines at higher altitudes was also documented in Mexico (Noguera-Martinez and Atkinson 1990). The ambrosia beetle communities of Zurquí and other mid- or high-altitude sites in Costa Rica (L. Kirkendall, unpubl. data) are overwhelmingly composed of outbreeding species, whereas the vast majority of ambrosia beetle species at La Selva, less than 50 km away, practice regular mother-son or brother-sister mating.

Specimens from Zurquí were more evenly distributed among species than were those at low-altitude sites. For example, two species of *Monarthrum* and one species of *Tesserocerus* each made up 8–15% of the catch; at La Selva, 48% of all specimens were *Xyleborus affinis*, and 10% were *Xylosandrus morigerus*. Although Zurquí and La Selva share 10 of 14 ambrosia beetle genera, only seven species were common to both sites. The five most frequently trapped Zurquí species have only been found at middle or upper altitudes. Of the five most frequent La Selva species, only *Megaplatypus discicollis* was also common at Zurquí; the other four were common only at low altitudes in Costa Rica and elsewhere. As with many other insects, altitude is a major factor affecting species distributions (Stevens 1992).

Since ambrosia beetles are seldom host specific, the existence of this species-rich community of generalists seems paradoxical. Ambrosia beetle/fungus partnerships may be specializing on environmental factors rather than host plant taxa. "Nonequilibrium" ecological models may explain coexistence of several to many ecologically similar species on the same resource when that resource is patchily distributed and difficult to find. That situation may apply to ambrosia beetles dependent on sporadic branch or tree falls for their sustenance (Beaver 1977, 1979b). Competitive exclusion among ecologically similar species may be prevented by the patchy distribution and ephem-

eral nature of the habitats (Ricklefs and Schluter 1993, Hanski 1994).

4.5. Lepidoptera: Moths and Butterflies

4.5.1. Introduction
Paul Hanson

Moths and butterflies (order Lepidoptera) rank second only to birds in popularity among ecotourists. Their larvae represent the largest group of plant-feeding animals. Caterpillars are one of the most important food resources for insectivorous birds, as are adult moths for bats. Lepidoptera are also ideal organisms as environmental indicators (Holloway 1985).

In Costa Rica, there are at least 80 families and an estimated 13,500 species of Lepidoptera, which is comparable to the fauna of America north of Mexico. The largest families (at least 500 species in the country) are Gelechiidae, Tortricidae, Pyralidae, Geometridae, Notodontidae, Arctiidae, and Noctuidae (J. Corrales and E. Phillips, pers. comm.). Species of Costa Rican butterflies belonging to the families Papilionidae, Pieridae, and Nymphalidae are covered in DeVries (1987) and a checklist of species occurring in Monteverde is in DeVries (1983). Some of the more commonly observed butterflies at Monteverde include morphos (Morphinae), swallowtails (Papilionidae), monarchs (Danainae), *Manataria maculata* (see Sec. 4.5.3), and *Heliconius clysonimus* (Heliconinae). The latter is the only Costa Rican species of *Heliconius* restricted to higher elevations (800–1800 m).

Although the majority of lepidopterans are moths, our knowledge of these families is incomplete, although a checklist of sphinx moths (Sphingidae) in Monteverde exists (Haber 1983). In Costa Rica, studies are being carried out on Limacodidae, Tortricidae, Pyralidae, Geometridae, and Saturniidae. Tortricidae, especially the subfamily Tortricinae, appears to reach its maximal diversity at mid-altitudes in Costa Rica (J. Powell, pers. comm.); research is needed to document similar distribution patterns in other families of moths.

4.5.2. Migration of Butterflies through Monteverde
Rob Stevenson & William A. Haber

More than half of the butterflies recorded in Monteverde are migrants (360 out of 658 species). These butterflies leave the Pacific slopes and lowlands at the end of the wet season when the quality of their larval host plants and other resources in their habitat begin to decline (Haber 1993). About 80% of the Pacific lowland butterfly species migrate. The general pattern is emigration from the Pacific side during October to February; they return with the rains in April or May. The exact timing varies among butterflies. For example, some clearwing butterflies (Nymphalidae-Ithomiinae) fly through in October, pierids in December, and lycaenids even later. A subset of species migrate from the Pacific to the Atlantic side during the short dry period called "veranillo" from late June through early July. This migration consists of the first-generation offspring of Atlantic slope migrants that arrived during April and May. An alternative to migration for a minority of species of the Pacific slope is to pass the dry season in reproductive diapause, a physiological condition in which courtship and egg maturation are inhibited hormonally.

Although migration is not a visually dramatic phenomenon, migrating butterflies are easy to observe in Monteverde. A good place to see migration is at "Windy Corner," located at the entrance to the MCFP, just as the road curves sharply to the left, about 0.5 km before the MCFP headquarters. The road runs east-west, the general direction of the migration. Some of the best days are early in the dry season (November and December), between 1000 and 1300 hr. On the first warm sunny day after a spell of cloudy and rainy weather, hundreds of butterflies fly against the trade winds, headed eastward toward the Continental Divide and the Atlantic slope.

If the wind is brisk, the butterflies fly low, within 2 m of the road surface. Some species, such as *Anartia fatima* (Nymphalinae), fly within 30 cm of the ground. If the wind averages 6 m/s (about 15 miles/h), only the strongest fliers, mainly the skippers (Hesperiidae), can make it through the gap. The majority of nymphalids remain wind-blocked 150 m up the road at the head of the road cut. In brief periods when the wind dies down, some of the stronger nymphalids can ease through. Great swirls of wind produce complex flight tracks; the butterflies sometimes stop in mid-air or suddenly shoot upward, or they get caught in a gust and sail backward. When the wind speed decreases, the butterflies migrate higher above the ground, reaching heights of over 100 m.

In our counts of butterflies migrating through the road cut at Windy Corner during 1994–96, the record observation (16 December 1994) was 6000 butterflies in 5 hours, with a peak intensity of more than 80 individuals/min. The vast majority were skippers. An experienced field worker can identify many of the butterfly species as they fly past, but it is often necessary to see skippers and lycaenids up close to identify them. One can catch 40 species in a few hours. On calmer days, one can also observe dragonflies, flies, beetles, bugs, parasitic wasps, and day-flying

moths migrating along with butterflies (see Williamson and Darling, "La Ventana," p. 438).

The amazing diversity of migrant species in Costa Rica and how they depend on different habitats over a range of elevations have only recently been recognized (Haber 1993, W. Haber and R. Stevenson, unpubl. data). Some migratory species are more vulnerable to population decline than nonmigratory species because migrants depend on at least two different habitats and on the resources along their migratory routes. Thus, preserving habitat at one location is not sufficient to ensure the survival of a migrating species.

4.5.3. *Manataria maculata* (Nymphalidae: Satyrinae)
Rob Stevenson & William A. Haber

Manataria maculata is the largest species of wood nymph in Monteverde. Its dark brown wings with six or seven white spots on both the upper and lower sides of the forewing apex distinguish it from other local butterflies. The scalloped hindwing bears a cryptic pattern of eyespots on the underside. Many people are startled by their first encounter with *Manataria*; dozens of butterflies suddenly explode outward in all directions from a shaded embankment, treehole, or dark hiding place along a forest trail. Clustering together during the day in aggregations ranging from a few individuals to more than four dozen, these satyrines fly into the canopy at dusk, where they spend the night roosting alone. At dawn, they return to their diurnal groups.

Manataria's behaviors mark it as an unusual butterfly. Like a hawkmoth, it vibrates its wings before flying to warm its flight muscles to 7–10°C above the ambient temperature. It flies almost exclusively at dawn and dusk. It is one of few butterfly species in which the same individuals migrate up and down the mountains. It has a potential life span of a year or more but breeds for only one month and does not mate until it is 8–10 months old. As with other satyrines, it feeds on rotting fruit and tree sap instead of nectar, but it seeks food during the day, rather than during its usual crepuscular activity period.

These butterflies are found in Monteverde from the end of June until the following April or May. In Monteverde, all individuals are in reproductive diapause, waiting to return to the Pacific lowlands where they mate and breed on species of bamboo at the beginning of the wet season. The eggs are laid in clusters and the larvae continue to feed in groups until the last instar. Almost immediately on emerging from the plain green chrysalis between the end of June and August, most adults fly eastward, upslope to Monteverde. The migration can be observed if one watches at 1730–1800 hr during the months of July and August. Some butterflies end their migration when they reach the forested areas of the Monteverde community; others continue flying over the mountains to the Atlantic side, ending up in the San Gerardo area. A few travel as far as the lowlands of San Carlos. During the next several months they begin moving westward to higher elevations in the cloud forest. All females dissected during this entire time (July–April) have been virgins in reproductive diapause. No eggs or caterpillars have been found, further suggesting that *Manataria* does not produce a second generation either on the Atlantic slope or in the cloud forest, despite the presence of suitable host plants. Finally, in late April or early May, after nine months as adults, they migrate to lower elevations on the Pacific slope to breed again.

4.5.4. Transparent Butterflies
Alan R. Masters

Butterflies with transparent wings are a common element of the Monteverde forest understory. These "clearwing" or "glasswing" butterflies belong to two subfamilies of the Nymphalidae: Satyrinae and Ithomiinae. A third clear-winged butterfly, *Dismorphia theucharila*, is less common and belongs to a different family (Pieridae). All groups have many species with opaque wings. As with all nymphalids, clear-winged nymphalids have four walking legs, in contrast to the six walking legs in pierids. The two nymphalid subfamilies are also easy to tell apart. Clear-winged satyrines have transparent forewings, but the hindwing is translucent pink with a conspicuous eyespot. Ithomiine clearwings are transparent on both the fore- and hindwing with a definite border of black or brown. Both groups fly near the ground in the understory. Satyrines tend to be on the ground or fly close to it. Ithomiine clearwings rest on leaves and fly higher, usually no more than 2 m above the ground. Pierids in the genus *Dismorphia* are the group on which Bates (1862) developed his theory of mimicry (see Sec. 4.5.5). *Dismorphia* spp. feed as larvae on mimosoid legumes (e.g., *Inga*; DeVries 1987), but host records for the only Central American clear-winged species in the genus, *D. theucharila*, are not reported. In Monteverde, *D. theucharila* is more common in Peñas Blancas and is rarely encountered in the community.

Cithaerias menander is the only clear-winged satyrine in Monteverde; it occurs in Peñas Blancas. The transparent forewing of *C. menander* can appear brown against the forest floor. The closely related satyrine *Pierella helvetica*, also found in Monteverde,

has opaque dark brown forewings. The two species occur together and are often difficult to distinguish. Both satyrines fly quickly along the ground, are difficult to capture, and are probably palatable to a wide range of predators. Larvae probably feed on Marantaceae and Heliconiaceae and adults on sap flows, rotting vegetation, and fruits (DeVries 1987).

Monteverde has 11 clearwing species in several genera (DeVries 1983). Including the Peñas Blancas and San Luis valleys, there are 17 species (W. Haber, pers. comm.). Costa Rican ithomiine clearwings reach their greatest diversity at middle altitudes (Haber 1978). Unlike satyrine clearwings, ithomiines fly so slowly they often can be captured without a net. Unpalatability of clear-winged ithomiines suggests the transparent color, combined with a bold border and some white markings, may be aposematic, though perhaps only at close range. There are species of clear-winged ctenuchid moths and opaque pierids in the genus *Dismorphia* that mimic the clear-winged color pattern using white and black scales. The frequency of such mimics in Monteverde is low.

My research with ithomiine clearwings in Monteverde was to understand their chemical protection (Masters 1990). All Monteverde clearwing species feed as larvae on plants in the Solanaceae, although ithomiines elsewhere feed on Apocynaceae and Gesnereaceae (Haber 1978). These plants are more common along roadsides and open areas, bringing ithomiine clearwings out of the forest to oviposit. Although these plants contain a plethora of secondary compounds, none is sequestered by larvae (Brown 1984), leaving them and recently emerged adults palatable to predators. Adult ithomiines feed on nectar of many flowers, but gain chemical protection against predators by visiting those containing pyrrolizidine alkaloids (Brown 1984, Masters 1990, 1992), which are most commonly found in the Asteraceae, Boraginaceae, caesalpinoid Fabaceae, and some orchids. In Monteverde, it is common to see clear-winged ithomiines feeding on the purple flowers of a low-growing roadside aster, *Ageratum* sp. The majority of visits to these flowers are by males. Pyrrolizidine alkaloids are important to males as mate attractants.

Rarely, clear-winged and opaque ithomiines are found clumped together in the forest, with pockets of abundance that include 20 or more species and thousands of individuals in a space of 10 m² (Drummond 1976). These "hot spots" may be breeding sites or leks created by ithomiine males of many species (Haber 1978). Androconial hairs located between the fore- and hindwing contain pyrrolizidine alkaloid derivatives that are volatilized to attract females. Male aggregations may be necessary to provide a critical threshold of female attractant. Apparently, males pass pyrrolizidine alkaloids to females in the spermato-phore, a packet of sperm and nutrients. Females gain protection and access to pyrrolizidine alkaloids that they place in the shell of their eggs (Brown 1984).

The evolution of transparent wings in Pieridae, Satyrinae, Ithomiinae, and some moths appears to be a classic case of convergence. The groups are not closely allied and almost certainly had opaque common ancestors. The presence of many genera with both transparent and opaque wings also suggests convergence. Among ithomiines, the convergence might be explained by Müllerian mimicry; that is, individuals of all species benefit by mutual resemblance because their unpalatability is more easily recognized and remembered by predators. Convergence between ithomiines and satyrines, and between ithomiines and *Dismorphia,* may be a case of Batesian mimicry, where the palatable satyrine and pierid are mistaken for unpalatable ithomiines and thus avoided by predators. Transparent wings may also be the ultimate cryptic, or camouflage, coloration. Unlike opaque patterns that constrain the organism to match only some of many potential backgrounds, transparency allows perfect crypsis in all situations. In this case, the "linking aspect" favoring convergence in clearwings may be that transparent coloration is the best type of cryptic coloration for organisms that must move freely against a complex background of colors and shapes.

Little is known about the ecology and behavior of these butterflies. The palatability of *D. theucharila* is questionable. Much of the basic natural history of Satyrinae is not known. Feeding experiments with visual predators using the brown satyrine *P. helvetica* and the transparent and pink *C. menander* against many natural backgrounds would provide support for the hypothesis that transparency adds cryptic value over the more normal brown coloration of cryptic butterflies. Comparing palatability of both *D. theucharila* and *C. menander* and ithomiine clearwings will determine their status as Batesian or Müllerian mimicry.

4.5.5. Variable Chemical Defense and Mimicry
Alan R. Masters

Although best known for its clearwing species (see Sec. 4.5.4), the nymphalid subfamily Ithomiinae more commonly displays striking color patterns. Four color patterns are recognized: clear wing, tiger stripe, yellow and black, and tawny (Papageorgis 1975, Drummond 1976, Haber 1978, Masters 1992). Each color pattern is represented in an area by several species in a handful of genera. The color patterns are usually represented in the same geographical area, a puzzling

sympatry. According to classical Müllerian mimicry theory, all unpalatable butterflies in an area should converge on a common color pattern to best educate potential predators and thereby gain greater individual protection.

My research in Monteverde addressed the paradox of sympatric Müllerian mimicry complexes. I chose ithomiines because they (and pierids) were the organisms on which both Bates (1862) and Müller (1879) formulated their concepts of mimicry. Bates examined the mimicry of a *Dismorphia* sp. (Pieridae) and proposed that its resemblance to a sympatric ithomiine was to fool predators into thinking it was also unpalatable. Müller proposed that two unpalatable ithomiines who share a common color pattern both benefit from the resemblance because their predator would make fewer mistakes with just one pattern to associate with unpalatability. Although both naturalists assumed the unpalatability of ithomiines from indirect evidence (tough wings, long life span, beakmarks on their wings, slow flight), no evidence existed for the unpalatability of ithomiines to visual predators, that is, those capable of forming learned aversions to unpalatability that they could associate with the ithomiines' color pattern (though preliminary feeding experiments suggested this; Haber 1978).

I studied butterflies in the tawny complex, which have a brown to orange translucent appearance with white or yellow spots and stripes. *Pteronymia fulvescens* fed to captive Green Fence Lizards (*Sceloperus malachiticus*) and Blue Crowned Motmots (*Momotus momota*) were rejected over palatable *Anartia fatima* (Nymphalinae) (Masters 1992). Further, *P. fulvescens* raised from eggs on *Solanum brenesii* (Solanaceae) were palatable as adults until fed a solution with pyrrolizidine alkaloids, the same chemicals protecting ithomiines from the spider *Nephila clavipes* (Araneae) (Brown 1984, Masters 1990).

Collecting in Monteverde along the Río Guacimal near the dairy plant (ca. 1400 m) for one year (1987–88), I found about 20 tawny ithomiine species. The only similar-looking non-ithomiine, captured twice, was *Lycorea ilione* (Danainae), which flies higher and is almost certainly a Müllerian mimic. Each month, I captured the first 100 ithomiine individuals encountered. In all, 15 species were captured fewer than ten times. Of the remaining five (*Ithomia heraldica, I. xenos, Pteronymia fulvescens, P. notilla,* and *Hypothyris euclea*), all had capture totals of greater than 100 over the year. Of these, I collected at least 20 of each sex for chemical analysis. Mark-release-recapture studies provided population estimates each month. Transects throughout the Monteverde community gave a tally of pyrrolizidine alkaloid–containing flowers.

Butterfly density along the river went from near 0 in January and February to over 2000 in August and September along a strip of river 100 m × 30 m. After individually isolating pyrrolizidine alkaloids from over 1000 butterflies, I found a surprising result: chemical defenses declined as butterfly density increased, perhaps because ithomiines arrive from the lowlands in March filled with pyrrolizidine alkaloids and lay eggs. The next generation emerges without chemical protection and cannot obtain it, since pyrrolizidine alkaloid flowers do not become abundant until August.

Models by Brower et al. (1970) helped assess the effect of variable population size and chemical defense in the five most common tawny ithomiine species. If a bird eats a distasteful butterfly, it stops eating them for a time. If a bird samples a palatable butterfly, it continues to eat. The risk to a single butterfly belonging to a mimicry complex therefore depends on the number of butterflies a bird can eat, the number of butterflies the bird will skip if it eats a bad butterfly, the number of birds, the number of butterflies, and the number of butterflies that taste bad. The number of butterflies increases at the same time chemical defense declines. If the number of birds does not change (and it may), the risk to any one butterfly is nearly identical for any unit of time. Different species varied in both the proportion of chemically defended individuals and their relative abundance throughout the year. The model also showed that the best-protected butterflies belonged to species both of high abundance and with a high proportion of defended individuals. The butterflies most at risk were those of low abundance with no protected individuals. The most common scenario was to be common and poorly protected.

Why do sympatric mimicry complexes exist? If a butterfly species enters an area with a group of similarly colored butterflies of high abundance and low chemical protection, the model suggests they should not evolve to adopt the mimicry pattern. However, they become an excellent model for any species that adopts their pattern. In an evolutionary game of frequency dependence, natural selection favors not just one pattern, as predicted by Müller, but any number of geographically overlapping patterns.

Chemical defense is variable between species, within species, and over time. By incorporating variation, I hypothesized why all unpalatable butterflies do not look the same. That natural selection can create such close color convergence in 20 species in Monteverde, given the ecological sources of variation that affect selection, is remarkable. Another surprising finding was the low incidence of Batesian mimicry. Although there are several likely Batesian mimics in Peñas Blancas, I never saw Batesian mimics of tawny butterflies. A study is needed of the altitudinal abundance of Batesian species and the chemical defense of their models.

4.6. Diptera: Flies

4.6.1. Introduction
Paul Hanson & Brian V. Brown

Adult flies, mosquitoes, and midges (order Diptera) are characterized by having the hind pair of wings reduced to small club-shaped rudiments (halteres) that function as balancing organs during flight. These insects have complete metamorphosis, with legless larval stages that live in a wide variety of habitats (Oldroyd 1964). Larvae of many of the relatively primitive families (suborder Nematocera) are aquatic in still and running water. These include mosquitoes, black flies, biting midges, and chironomids. Of the approximately 140 families of Diptera recognized worldwide, nearly 90 occur in Costa Rica. The largest families in Costa Rica, each estimated to have 500 or more species, include Tipulidae, Cecidomyiidae, Chironomidae, Dolichopodidae, Phoridae, and Tachinidae.

The larvae of relatively more derived families (suborder Brachycera) occur in concealed habitats, such as leaf litter, fungi, live or decomposing plant or animal tissue, and dung. Some scavenging species are common and widespread, often associated with human habitation. One species is *Ornidia obesa* (Syrphidae), a conspicuous metallic green fly often found around latrines. A smaller fly, *Megaselia scalaris* (Phoridae), has been reared from almost every type of decaying organic matter, including remarkably unlikely substances (e.g., paint and boot polish).

Diptera differs from the other large orders of insects in its diversity of parasitic associations with vertebrate animals, notably those in which the adults (usually females) feed on blood. Mosquito populations have increased in Monteverde with the creation of settling ponds at the pig farm. Black flies (Simuliidae), whose larvae occur only in running water, can be annoying to visitors, especially in open habitats such as pastures. Their bites are usually not felt, but the large, itching welts, with a small blood spot in the middle, are impossible to ignore. On some evenings, tiny phlebotomine psychodids and ceratopogonid biting midges can be a nuisance. One of the largest blood-sucking flies in Monteverde is the long-beaked deer fly, *Scione maculipennis* (Tabanidae), which continues to hum (vibrating its wing muscles) even after landing (J. Longino, pers. comm.).

Nycteribiidae and Streblidae are blood-feeding parasites of bats. Larvae are retained within the female fly's body until the end of the third instar, feeding on secretions of a specialized female accessory gland. Adults of both families are highly modified and unusual in appearance; those of Nycteribiidae lack wings. Hippoboscidae show a similar biology but mainly parasitize birds.

The larvae of *Notochaeta bufonivora* (Sarcophagidae) parasitize frogs and toads, and in the Monteverde area, they attack Harlequin Frogs (*Atelopus varius*, Bufonidae). The adult fly deposits 1–10 larvae in the skin of the frog. The maggots first consume the thigh muscles, then the internal organs, and eventually kill the frog (Crump and Pounds 1985). How the maggot contends with the potent neurotoxin present in the skin of this brightly colored frog is unknown.

Flies include species that feed on other insects, usually in the larval stage, although robber flies (Asilidae; Fisher and Hespenheide 1992), dance flies (Empididae), and the small metallic green long-legged flies (Dolichopodidae) are also predatory as adults. Most predatory fly larvae are hidden in the soil, leaf litter, or rotting wood. Among the few exposed on vegetation are species of Syrphidae (see Sec. 4.5.3). Several families of flies include parasitoids, insects whose larvae live in intimate association with their host and eventually kill it. The largest group of parasitoids is the Tachinidae, many of which attack lepidopteran caterpillars. Other parasitoids include many Bombyliidae (bee flies), some Phoridae (see Sec. 4.6.2), and Pipunculidae (big-headed flies).

4.6.2. Phorid Flies of Costa Rican Cloud Forests
Brian V. Brown

Phorids have been called the most biologically diverse family of insects on the planet. The life history of most phorid larvae is unknown, but they can be predators, scavengers, herbivores, parasitoids, parasites, and commensals (Disney 1994). Phorid flies are small (1–7 mm long) flies that occur worldwide; the greatest diversity is found in tropical regions. Tropical phorid diversity is compounded by the numerous species associated with ants and termites. A single lowland site in Costa Rica might contain 150 or more species of a single ant-parasitoid genus (Brown and Feener 1995).

The phorid fauna of cloud forests is distinctive. It is a mixture of lowland elements, middle-elevation elements, and a few northern elements that extend their range from the Nearctic region into the tropics at higher elevations. Of special interest in cloud forests are species that extend their ranges from the

Nearctic region through the Andes of South America at middle to high elevations. In the Phoridae, two such genera, *Phora* and *Lecanocerus*, are represented by species that are the same as those found in North America.

Typical of the lowland elements are the parasitoid species, especially the large genus *Apocephalus*. Most of these flies attack ants, and although they are much less diverse in cloud forests than in the lowlands, they are a large component of the cloud forest fauna. One group of *Apocephalus* attacks leaf-cutter ants, forcing them to carry ant "hitchhikers" that ride on the leaves to protect against phorid attack (Feener and Moss 1990). This can be observed in foraging columns of the ant *Acromyrmex octospinosus*, which is attacked by *Apocephalus luteihalteratus*. Another well-represented group attacks injured or distressed ponerine ants and can be lured by crushing a few ant workers. The flies are quickly attracted by the production of the ants' alarm pheromones (Brown and Feener 1991, Feener et al. 1996). Stingless bees are also heavily used by phorid flies (Fig. 4.13). Species of *Melaloncha* and *Apocephalus* (*Mesophora*) frequently hover or perch near bee nest openings, darting at worker bees to parasitize them. By crushing workers, one can attract flies of the genus *Calamiscus*, which lay their eggs in the injured bees (Brown, in press).

A group of *Apocephalus* in cloud forests in the subgenus *Mesophora* does not attack ants but has divergent hosts such as stingless bees, wasps, and cantharoid beetles (lampyrids and cantharids; Brown 1993, 1996). Species richness of *Mesophora* is much greater in cloud forests than lowlands, with up to 20 species known from a single site (Zurquí), the hosts of which are poorly known. Army ant swarm raids occur in the lower elevation parts of the cloud for-

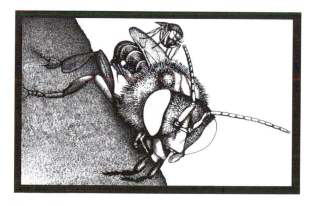

Figure 4.13. A female *Apocephalus* (ant-decapitating fly) has landed on a prospective host, a male stingless bee. Drawing by Jesse Cantley from a photograph by Brian V. Brown.

est, accompanied by phorids of the genera *Acantho-phorides* and *Dacnophora* and the brachypterous (short-winged) females of *Acontistoptera* and *Adelopteromyia*. Unlike army ant swarms at lower elevations, few *Apocephalus* are associated with these raids. These ants occasionally attack millipedes, which produce defensive secretions that attract parasitic females of the genus *Myriophora*.

4.6.3. Syrphid Flies of Costa Rican Cloud Forests
Manual A. Zumbado

Syrphids (family Syrphidae), known as "flower flies" or "hover flies," are often confused with bees and wasps. Mimicry of other insects is much more common in Syrphidae than in any other family of Diptera. In Costa Rica, there are more than 300 species of syrphids in 50 genera. Among specimens collected from the Monteverde cloud forest, about 40 species and 30 genera are represented, but the actual number is certainly greater. Although many of these genera are present in the lowlands, *Eoeristalis* and *Criorhina* are restricted to mid- to high altitudes.

Species in the subfamilies Eristalinae and Syrphinae visit flowers and are sometimes pollinators. Some small species feed exclusively on pollen and have broad mouthparts; species that also ingest nectar have slender, elongate mouthparts. Species of the subfamily Microdontinae do not visit flowers. A striking characteristic of syrphids is their extraordinary maneuverability in flight. In the field, they are frequently encountered hovering, and they can quickly rotate their orientation and dart precisely in any direction. The wing muscles in the thorax, which account for 15% of the total body weight, permit them to move their wings with a frequency of 250 wing-beats/sec.

The larval stages have a variety of habits. Species of Microdontinae live in ant nests. Larvae of Syrphinae are predators of Homoptera and a few other insects. A species of *Allograpta* is a predator on psyllids in San Gerardo de Dota (2300 m), and a species of *Salpingogaster* preys on spittlebugs (Cercopidae) in Monteverde. Larvae of Eristalinae are varied in their habits, depending on the tribe or genus: aquatic filter feeders live in water with high organic content; detritivores live in dung or other organic material; predators of Homoptera live on plants. Aquatic species have an elongated breathing tube extending from the posterior end and are sometimes called "rat-tailed maggots." Larvae of predatory species are often strikingly colored (reddish, bright green); larvae of other species are whitish. Information on syrphid biology is in Gilbert (1986).

4.7. Hymenoptera: Sawflies, Wasps, Ants, and Bees

4.7.1. Introduction
Paul Hanson & Ian D. Gauld

Hymenoptera is one of the largest insect orders. It includes sawflies, wasps, ants, and bees. Although the most familiar species are those that sting, most hymenopteran species are parasitoids (parasitic wasps), which help control populations of other insects. They have been frequently used in biological control projects. Ants are one of the most abundant groups of insect predators, though less so in cloud forests than in lowland tropical forests. Bees are the most important group of animals that pollinate plants. Fig wasps are obligate pollinators of fig trees, whose fruits are a vital resource for numerous frugivorous vertebrates.

There are at least 20,000 species of Hymenoptera in Costa Rica (Hanson and Gauld 1995). Of the 78 families of Hymenoptera (including all bees as one family), 61 have been collected in Costa Rica. The largest families in Costa Rica (those with more than 500 species) are Diapriidae, Platygastridae, Scelionidae, Encyrtidae, Eulophidae, Pteromalidae, Braconidae, Ichneumonidae, Formicidae, and Apidae.

Hymenoptera with carnivorous larvae. Like parasites, parasitoids live in intimate contact with their hosts, but unlike parasites, they always kill their hosts. Hosts are usually immature stages of other insects or spiders. The female wasp searches for a particular type of host, and lays an egg on or in it, and the larva feeds on the host, eventually killing it. Although the distinction is usually made between parasitic and predatory wasps, there is actually a continuous gradation between the two. For example, in Pompilidae (spider wasps) most species build nests in the manner of predatory wasps, but each larva is usually provisioned with just one prey (spider), in the manner of parasitoids. A more useful distinction is that between idiobionts, which permanently paralyze their host, and koinobionts, which allow their host to continue its development after being parasitized. The former usually feed externally and include primitive parasitoids and most predators; the latter feed internally and include physiologically more specialized parasitoids (Hanson and Gauld 1995).

The most primitive type of parasitoid (idiobiont) generally attacks concealed or well-protected hosts such as borers in plant tissue, insect pupae, or egg masses. The female wasp stings the host, injecting a venom that causes paralysis. Examples include some Ichneumonidae and all Scelionidae. In a very few cases, the larva consumes more than one host individual and is a predator, for example, ichneumonids that attack spider egg sacs. Although many idiobionts occur in Costa Rican cloud forests, only one has been documented in detail: the tiphiid, *Pterombrus piceus*, which attacks tiger beetle larvae (*Pseudoxychila tarsalis*) in their burrows (Palmer 1976b, 1983b).

These parasitoids do not generally attack exposed hosts, since such hosts cannot be permanently paralyzed and simply left where they are, lest they be consumed by a scavenger. The problem of attacking exposed hosts has been solved in two ways: (1) by ovipositing on but not incapacitating a host and delaying parasitoid development until after the host has stopped feeding and sought out shelter for pupation (i.e., the koinobiont strategy), or (2) by retaining the primitive (idiobiont) strategy but actively concealing the host in a specially constructed nest. Female koinobionts only rarely paralyze the host to allow oviposition. By avoiding or suppressing the host's immune system, the larva can remain within the host until the latter conceals itself in a pupal retreat, a strategy pursued by all Proctotrupoidea and some Ichneumonidae.

Nest building occurs in Pompilidae, Vespidae (Appendix 7), Formicidae (ants), and Sphecidae. Many cloud forest wasps dig burrows in the ground, for example, pompilids (*Caliadurgus*) and sphecids (Sphecinae, *Pseneo*, *Crossocerus*, Nyssoninae, and Philanthinae). Others construct nests in hollow plant stems or abandoned beetle burrows in wood, for example, pompilids (*Dipogon*), eumenine vespids (*Parancistrocerus*), and sphecids (Pemphredonini, most Crabronini, Miscophini, and many Trypoxylonini). After building the nest, the female wasp hunts, and when prey is encountered she paralyzes it. She then relocates the prey, either by dragging it over the ground (most pompilids) or by carrying it in flight back to the nest (eumenine vespids and most sphecids). After provisioning the cell with paralyzed prey, the female lays an egg, seals it off, and repeats the process (Hanson and Gauld 1995).

Among these nest-building wasps, the only detailed study of a Costa Rican cloud forest species is on *Trypoxylon monteverdae* (Sphecidae) in Monteverde (Brockmann 1992), which constructs exposed mud nests consisting of vertical tubes that open at the bottom, similar to those of other pipe-organ mud daubers. As in other species in the subgenus *Trypargilum*, males guard the nest while the female provisions it, a rare behavior among nest-building hymenopterans. Even more unusual is that *T. monteverdae* males assist in nest construction, which consists of smoothing the wet mud inside walls of the nest. In return for this help, the female allows the male to copulate frequently.

Nest-building wasps are subject to attack by parasitoids and by cleptoparasites. In the latter, the female lays an egg in the nest of another species and the larva that hatches from this egg feeds on the stored food it steals from the other species. Cleptoparasites have evolved either from close relatives (members of the same family) that have abandoned nest building or from parasitoids that have switched from feeding on the host itself to feeding on its stored food (e.g., Gasteruptiidae and Chrysididae).

Polistine vespids and ants have evolved eusocial behavior, living in colonial nests with the occupants showing a division of labor (castes). The queen lays eggs while workers forage and care for the brood. Eusocial hymenopterans are often aggressive toward human intruders; they have more invested in their nest than do solitary nest builders and have evolved effective means of defending their nest, that is, painful stings. Eusocial behavior has evolved more frequently in the order Hymenoptera than any other group of animals.

Hymenoptera with plant-feeding larvae. Whereas members of the suborder Apocrita have larvae that are maggotlike and predominantly carnivorous, members of the more primitive suborder, Symphyta (sawflies), have caterpillarlike larvae that feed on foliage. In the neotropics, sawflies are less conspicuous than those in the suborder Apocrita that have become secondarily phytophagous (e.g., fig wasps, leafcutter ants, and bees; Hanson and Gauld 1995). In Costa Rica, only four families of plant-feeding sawflies are present: Argidae, Pergidae, Tenthredinidae, and Xiphidriidae. Plant host records are available for very few of the 150 species that occur in Costa Rica.

One of the most exciting recent discoveries about the biology of cloud forest Hymenoptera is that the larvae of the two genera of Perryiinae (Pergidae) occurring in Costa Rica appear to be fungivores rather than true phytophages. Little was known about the biology of this subfamily until D. Olson and F. Joyce encountered larvae feeding on a jelly fungus (*Auricularia*) in Monteverde and obtained adults, which were identified as a species of *Decameria*, the first record of a hymenopteran feeding on the fruiting body of a macrofungus. J. Ugalde and E. Quiros reared larvae of *Perreyia* to adults by feeding them on mouldy leaf litter, the former from larvae collected in the San José area (1100 m) and the latter in Las Alturas Biological Station (1500 m). Although the larval diet and identity of this sawfly were previously unknown, the migrating masses of black caterpillars are familiar to Monteverdans. Phytophagous species of the suborder Apocrita consume the most nutritious parts of plants (gall tissue, seeds, and pollen), and are derived from parasitoids (principally Cynipidae and several Chalcidoidea) and predators (a few ants and vespids, and virtually all bees).

In Costa Rica, cynipids (gall wasps) are exclusively associated with oaks (*Quercus*, Fagaceae). All species are undescribed, and their biology has received little attention. Many induce gall formation on leaves, twigs, flowers, fruits, and roots, but others are inquilines, which feed on gall tissue induced by other species of cynipids. Species that form galls have a sexual generation (with both sexes) and an asexual generation (females only). Females from the two generations are morphologically different and induce completely different galls (Askew 1984); an oak tree that has 20 different types of galls probably has only 10 species of gall-forming cynipids. Associating the two generations of each species is an essential first step in life history studies but requires cage experiments or molecular techniques.

Phytophagy has evolved several times in the superfamily Chalcidoidea: Agaonidae (fig wasps), Tanaostigmatidae (associated with galls on legumes), *Megastigmus* (Torymidae), and others (Hanson and Gauld 1995). Most Tanaostigmatidae are gall-formers, although at least one Costa Rican species (*Tanaostigma coursetiae*) is an inquiline in psyllid galls on *Lonchocarpus atropurpureus* (Leguminosae). *Tanaoneura darwini* is known only from Monteverde; although its host there is unknown, other Costa Rican species belonging to this genus induce galls in the aril surrounding the seeds of *Inga* (Leguminosae). Larvae of *Megastigmus* feed in seeds of *Ilex* (Aquifoliaceae) and *Symplocos* (Symplocaceae).

Bees evolved from predatory sphecid wasps. Their biology resembles other sphecids except that the female provisions the nest with pollen, nectar, and other floral resources rather than arthropod prey. Groups that nest in the ground include Colletinae, Diphaglossinae, most Halictinae, Andreninae, Anthophorinae, and Bombinae. Groups that nest in cavities or hollow twigs include Hylaeinae, Xeromelissinae, *Augochlora* (Halictinae), Megachilinae, Xylocopinae, Euglossinae, and Meliponinae. The biology of only few cloud forest species has been studied, including *Crawfordapis luctuosa* (see Sec. 4.7.6), *Ptiloglossa guinnae* (Roberts 1971), *Pseudaugochloropsis graminea*, *P. sordicutis* (Michener and Kerfoot 1967), *Deltoptila* spp. (LaBerge and Michener 1963), *Ceratina ignara* (Michener and Eickwort 1966), *Bombus ephippiatus* (Heithaus 1983), and Meliponinae (see Sec. 4.7.7). As in Sphecidae, cleptoparasitism has evolved in certain groups of bees; in Costa Rican cloud forests, these include at least four genera. Eusocial behavior has evolved in bumblebees (Bombinae), stingless bees (Meliponinae), and the introduced honeybee (Apinae). Keys to the genera of North and Central American bees are in Michener et al. (1994). The biology of tropical bees is described in Roubik (1989).

The color of cloud forest hymenopterans.　High altitude species of cloud forest hymenopterans are generally less brightly patterned than their lowland counterparts. Groups that contain gaudily colored species decrease in species richness with increasing altitude. For example, the speciose chalcidid genus *Conura*, whose members are predominantly patterned with yellow and black, is common in lowland clearings but scarce in cloud forests. In other groups (e.g., Cryptini [Ichneumonidae]), the cloud forest species are darker and more drably colored than their lowland relatives. This trend is particularly strong in nest-building taxa such as sphecids and bees, where there may be a greater need for thermoregulation (see Sec. 4.7.2). Dark color is presumably an adaptation that allows these hymenopterans to absorb radiant energy rapidly when the sun is shining.

Another factor that affects color pattern is mimicry. The color of cloud forest hymenopterans may be partially determined by the availability of models. For example, *Dolichomitus annulicornis* (Ichneumonidae) appears to be a Batesian mimic of species of *Agelaia* (Vespidae). *Apechthis* species (Ichneumonidae), which emit a disagreeable odor when handled, are Müllerian mimics of *Neotheronia* species, ichneumonids that have tarsal claws armed with poison glands. Many conspicuous vespid models in the lowlands, and their mimicry complexes, are absent in cloud forests. There are fewer mimics of predominantly yellow-colored vespids, because these models reach the upper end of their altitudinal distribution in cloud forests (see Sec. 4.7.3).

A common color pattern in the lowlands is black head, reddish orange thorax, and black abdomen. Although the model is not known, this color pattern occurs in diverse taxa, including a few nonhymenopterans. In the lowlands, species belonging to 12 genera of Scelioninae (Scelionidae) show this striking color combination. Only eight of these genera occur in cloud forests, where most of them reach the upper limits of their distribution: *Baryconus*, *Chromoteleia*, *Lapitha*, *Oethococtonus*, *Probaryconus*, *Scelio*, *Sceliomorpha*, and *Triteleia*. More study is needed to document and explain the altitudinal distribution of color patterns in Hymenoptera.

4.7.2. Distribution Patterns of Cloud Forest Hymenoptera in Costa Rica
Ian D. Gauld & Paul Hanson

In Costa Rica, most hymenopterans tend to be restricted to one or sometimes two of three broad altitudinal zones: lowland (0–800 m), intermediate (800–2000 m), and montane (2000+ m). In undisturbed areas, these zones are usually distinct, but deforestation may allow some dry lowland species to become more widespread at higher altitudes. Lowland species occur widely, from the Nicaraguan to the Panamanian border, but no species extends from the lowlands to the summits of the highest mountains. Geographical range generally decreases with increasing altitude; endemism is greatest at high altitudes. Cloud forest hymenopteran faunas reflect their position as intermediate between lowlands and high altitudes. The following discussion is based on six years of Malaise trap samples taken at Zurquí de Moravia (Hanson and Gauld 1995; Fig. 4.12).

Taxa that are less diverse in cloud forests than in lowland forests. Many Hymenoptera either are restricted to lower elevations or are more speciose in the lowlands than in cloud forests (Fig. 4.14). Nest-building species and their associates (parasitoids and cleptoparasites) are one such group. Pompilids, vespids, sphecids, and bees occur at high elevations, although they are represented by few species, but ants are largely absent above 2400 m. The lower diversity of nest-building hymenopterans at higher altitudes may be a consequence of lack of a sustained period of temperature suitable for foraging. In high-altitude sites, sharp diurnal temperature fluctuations, coupled with frequent cloud cover, severely reduce foraging times. Climate unpredictability may have more severe consequences for nest-building species than parasitoids, as the latter can more easily take advantage of short periods of favorable weather while the former must attend to a nest for at least several consecutive days. Although species richness decline occurs with increasing latitude, groups such as ants are present in northern temperate areas where climates are harsher than tropical mountaintops. However, temperate and boreal regions have a predictable short continuous period during which daily temperatures permit foraging and colony growth. An exception to this general pattern of altitudinal and latitudinal decline in species richness are the bumblebees, which overcome temperature restrictions by thermoregulating with their vibrating thoracic muscles (Heinrich 1979).

Parasitoids and cleptoparasites of nest-building hymenopterans also decrease in species richness with increasing altitude. Examples include Trigonalyiidae (parasitoids of social wasps), Gasteruptiidae (cleptoparasites of solitary wasps and bees), diapriids (Proctotrupoidea) associated with ants, Eucharitidae (parasitoids of ants), some ichneumonids, Chrysididae (subfamily Chrysidinae, parasitoids and/or cleptoparasites of solitary wasps and bees), Mutillidae (parasitoids of solitary wasps and bees), and cleptoparasitic genera of pompilids, sphecids, and bees.

Another group that decreases in species richness with altitude are nocturnally active species. Low nighttime temperatures at higher altitudes may severely restrict their activity. Few nocturnal hymenopterans fly later than 2200 hr in the mountains (I. Gauld, unpubl. data). Examples include Ophioninae, *Netelia* (Ichneumonidae), and many Rogadinae (Braconidae). The largest genus of Ophioninae, *Enicospilus*, is represented by about 50 species in Santa Rosa National Park (0–300 m), about 30 species in the greater Monteverde area, and only three species above 2000 m (Gauld 1988).

Parasitoids of wood-boring beetles also decrease in species richness with altitude. Some are completely absent from cloud forests: Orussidae, Stephanidae, Aulacidae, and Phasganophorini (Chalcididae). Other groups, although present in cloud forests, are repre-

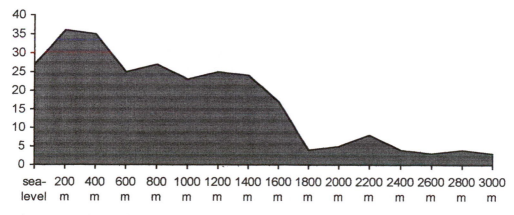

Figure 4.14. The number of species of Anomaloninae occurring at different altitudes in Costa Rica.

sented by fewer species than they are in the low-lands: Liopterini (Ibaliidae), Calosotinae (Eupelmidae), Rhyssinae and Labenini (Ichneumonidae), and certain Doryctinae, Cenocoelinae, and Helconinae (Braconidae). A fourth group of Hymenoptera that is less diverse in cloud forests (and higher altitudes) than in lowland forests are neotropical-centered groups, such as *Conura* (Chalcididae), *Podogaster,* and *Neotheronia* (Ichneumonidae) and diparine pteromalids, which are also poorly represented in North America.

Taxa that are more diverse in cloud forests than in lowland forests.   Some groups are more diverse with increasing altitude, for example, Megaspilidae, Proctotrupidae, two subfamilies of Diapriidae (Ambositrinae and Belytinae), Platygastridae, Cynipidae, Eucoilini (Cynipoidea), some Ichneumonidae (Banchinae, Cylloceriinae, Diplazontinae), phygadeuontine Cryptinae, phaeogenine and platylabine Ichneumoninae, Orthocentrinae and Tryphoninae excluding *Netelia* (Fig. 4.15), and some Braconidae (Aphidiinae and possibly Alysiinae). A few small montane-centered taxa (e.g., Heloridae, charipine Cynipidae, and Ormyridae) are absent from the lowlands below 500 m. A few groups of Hymenoptera are restricted in Costa Rica to cloud forests, such as Monomachidae, thynnine Tiphiidae, and acaenitine Ichneumonidae. Montane- or cloud forest–centered distribution patterns are difficult to explain, although the former clearly include many northern (in the case of Ambositrinae, southern) temperate elements that have barely penetrated tropical habitats. For example, Acaenitinae, Diplazontinae, phygadeuontine Cryptinae, and tryphonine Tryphoninae are more species rich in North America than in tropical South America.

In some cases, this distributional pattern occurs because hymenopteran distribution patterns reflect the species richness of their hosts. For example, Cynipidae are gall-formers on oaks (Fagaceae: *Quercus*), and Ormyridae are parasitoids of the Cynipidae. In Costa Rica, most species of oaks grow at altitudes above 1200 m, and the single species that occurs in the lowland dry forests in the northwestern part of the country (*Q. oleoides*) is depauperate in cynipids (Hanson and Gauld 1995).

Not all of these patterns can be explained by differential host distribution. For example, Diplazontinae parasitize syrphid fly larvae associated with Homoptera (aphids, psyllids, and scale insects). Such syrphid larvae do not appear to be less diverse or abundant in the lowlands and are attacked by other parasitoids (Encyrtidae) in these areas. Two other taxa associated with aphids, Charipini (Cynipoidea) and Aphidiinae (Braconidae), are also more diverse in cloud forests than at lower elevations. No data are available for altitudinal patterns in species richness of aphids, but these hosts are less diverse in Costa Rica than in North America.

Many cloud forest hymenopterans are parasitoids of flies, including some Proctotrupidae, Ambositrinae and Belytinae (Diapriidae), most Platygastridae, Eucoilini, Orthocentrinae (Ichneumonidae), and Alysiinae (Braconidae). Among diapriids, *Entomacis, Idiotypa, Pentapria,* and *Spilomicrus* increase dramatically in numbers of species, as do the platygastrid genera *Amblyaspis, Leptacis, Metaclisis, Synopeas,* and *Trichacis* (L. Masner, pers. comm.). That many fly parasitoids reach their maximum diversity in cloud forests suggests that the dipteran hosts of these parasitoids also reach their maximum diversity there, but this has yet to be documented.

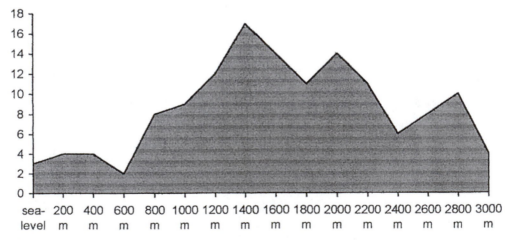

Figure 4.15. The number of species of Tryphoninae (excluding *Netelia*) occurring at different altitudes in Costa Rica.

Further research is needed to explain these patterns. For example, why do the Ophioninae show greatest species richness in lowland Costa Rica whereas in Borneo they are most species rich in montane cloud forests? We should also test the prediction that the hosts of the parasitoids of flies also increase in diversity in cloud forests. In terms of conservation, the leading specialist of the fly parasitoids of the superfamily Prototrupoidea stated: "I am absolutely adamant about one thing, in that the cloud forest proctotrupoid fauna is the richest belt anywhere in the neotropics, much richer than the fabled Amazonia. This observation may be a strong argument in favor of protection of this precious treasure" (L. Masner, pers. comm.). Minute parasitic wasps that attack fly larvae living in leaf litter lack appeal for most biologists and consequently attract few researchers. As a consequence, extinctions may go unnoticed.

4.7.3. Eusocial Wasps (Vespidae: Polistinae)
Sean O'Donnell

In the New World, the family Vespidae comprises four subfamilies: Eumeninae, Masarinae, Polistinae, and Vespinae. The first two are solitary wasps (each female builds and provisions her own nest and lays eggs); the latter two are eusocial (females cooperate in rearing the brood, show a division of labor, and usually only the queen lays eggs). Eusocial wasps often build their colonial nests from masticated wood fibers (hence the name "paper wasps") but are better known for their painful sting, with which they defend the nest. The subfamily Vespinae (the hornets and yellow jackets of North America) does not occur south of Guatemala, whereas the Polistinae are found throughout the New World.

Eusocial wasps exhibit one of two social structures: (1) independent founders, where one or more reproductive females initiate new colonies without the aid of workers (Gadagkar 1991, Reeve 1991), or (2) swarm founders, where colonies are initiated by groups of queens and workers that move in a coordinated manner to new nest sites (Jeanne 1991). Independent founders' nests consist of a single comb of naked cells and are suspended from the substrate by a narrow stalk; their colonies are typically small, comprising up to a few dozen adults. Swarm founders' nests have a more complex architecture, usually enclosed in an envelope (Jeanne 1975), and are populated by hundreds or thousands of adults (Fig. 4.16). In Monteverde, independent founders include *Polistes* and *Mischocyttarus*; swarm founders include *Agelaia, Epipona, Polybia,* and *Synoeca* (Appendix 7).

Figure 4.16. *Polybia occidentalis* wasps guarding their nest. Photograph by Gregory Dimijian.

Eusocial wasp biology in Monteverde is affected by elevation. Many polistine species occur only at particular elevations (Appendix 4.3). However, a number of species exhibit a "cliff edge effect"; that is, they build nests at atypically high or low elevations along steep drop-offs, a pronounced pattern along the eastern end of the San Luis valley. In the course of observations made in different seasons between 1988 and 1996, I have found *Polybia aequatorialis* nests, usually restricted to higher elevations in Monteverde, below the San Luis waterfall down to 1150 m (Fig. 4.16). Conversely, *Mischocyttarus atrocyaneus* and *Synoeca septentrionalis*, which are common in San Luis, have been found nesting along the cliff edge above 1350 m in Monteverde.

Insect elevational migration, which is best studied in butterflies (see Sec. 4.5.2), is exhibited in Monteverde by *Polistes instabilis*. This species does not nest in Monteverde but is common in the seasonally dry lowlands to the west, below 600 m. Nonnesting aggregations of migrant females begin forming on buildings and large forest trees in Monteverde before the onset of the dry season, beginning around late October. Males join the aggregations later. The wasps cluster and are inactive during the evening and on cloudy days but forage on sunny days. Aggregations of this species also occur on Volcán Cacao at similar elevations. There, dissected females did not have developed ovaries during the early aggregation season (J. Hunt, pers. comm.). Changes in female reproductive physiology and the occurrence of copulation (O'Donnell 1994) during the aggregation season warrant further investigation.

Seasonality, particularly in precipitation, can have pronounced effects on tropical wasp life history. For example, in the seasonally dry lowlands, many species of eusocial wasps experience a period of diminishing prey abundance, which leads to reduced colony growth during the dry season (R. Jeanne, pers. comm., S. O'Donnell, pers. obs.). However, little evidence exists for seasonal restriction of nest initiation and colony development in Monteverde. I have found brood of all stages in *Polybia aequatorialis* nests during both wet and dry seasons and collected or reared males (suggesting that colonies are in reproductive mode) from nests in November–January and in May. Some independent founding wasps may be more synchronous in the timing of colony foundation than *Polybia*. For example, the majority of *Mischocyttarus mastigophorous* nests located in October 1995 surveys were abandoned, and many of the colonies located in December and January were recently initiated.

Independent founding wasps frequently nest on human structures in Monteverde, particularly under the eaves of buildings. Possible advantages of nesting in these sites include reduced predation pressure from ants (Jeanne 1979) and more favorable microclimate (Jeanne and Morgan 1992). I have found *Mischocyttarus* species nesting under leaves and on rootlets in roadbanks and landslides. Nests of two swarm founders, *Polybia aequatorialis* and *P. raui*, are also often found on vegetation in road banks, built around a slender vertical support (such as a rootlet) hanging from a rooflike surface. The outer envelopes of *Polybia* nests in Monteverde include many layers of paper and numerous air pockets, presumably as insulation against low temperatures and/or precipitation. Whether envelope thickness varies with elevation within species is unknown. Wasps in the genus *Agelaia* usually nest in cavities in live trees (e.g., *A. yepocapa*) or in fallen logs (e.g., *A. panamensis* and *A. xanthopus*). *Agelaia areata* is unusual in building envelope-covered nests among tree branches.

Nearly all species of Monteverde eusocial wasps have dark brown or black bodies, particularly species occurring at higher altitudes. Pale-colored exceptions (*Agelaia areata* and *A. yepocapa*) include species that nest in open sites. Some Monteverde species that span a wide range of elevations have reduced pale or yellow markings at higher sites (*Polybia diguetana*, *P. raui,* and *Mischocyttarus mastigophorus*). Wasp body coloration may be adapted to life in Monteverde's climate (cool temperatures, limited insolation). Darker coloration may allow wasps' bodies to warm to flying temperatures more quickly.

Parasites and parasitoids (including several families of wasps, flies, and mites) make their homes in nests of eusocial wasps. Parasitoids in the family Trigonalyidae in *Agelaia* and *Polybia* colonies occur in the Monteverde area. Several of these trigonalyids are close Wasmannian mimics (parasites that resemble their hosts) of the vespid wasps with which they were collected.

Surface raiding army ants are important predators of neotropical eusocial wasps (Chadab 1979). Wasps have few defenses against army ants if their nests are discovered (West-Eberhard 1989), although species with costly nests or nest sites (e.g., cavities in trees) may defend against ant raids more vigorously (O'Donnell and Jeanne 1990). *Epipona niger* and *Agelaia areata* nest high up in trees in Monteverde, possibly to avoid army ant predation. *Polybia rejecta* nest almost exclusively in association with *Azteca* ants, often in *Cecropia* trees, thereby gaining protection from army ants (F. Joyce, pers. comm.).

Little is known about vertebrate predators of Monteverde's eusocial wasps. Birds and other visually oriented predators have probably been an important selective factor in the evolution of wasp coloration patterns and mimicry, but avian responses to wasp coloration have been studied surprisingly little. Prey choice by visually hunting insect predators such as dragonflies may also play a role in the evolution of wasp body colors (O'Donnell 1996a). Many Monteverde wasp colonies fall prey to humans, particularly nests on buildings and in road banks. Eusocial wasps are important predators of herbivorous insects in the Monteverde area, and they may also play a role as pollinators (O'Donnell 1996b). Most species that nest near humans are not aggressive and pose little threat if not disturbed. Given their potentially significant role in local ecology, destruction of vespid colonies should be avoided.

Acknowledgments   Thanks to Susan Bulova for helpful comments on the manuscript. Jim Hunt and Frank Joyce generously shared their extensive knowledge and enthusiasm for tropical social wasps and helped with fieldwork in Monteverde. Financial support was provided by the National Science Foundation, and permission for research and collecting, by the Costa Rican Ministry of Natural Resources.

4.7.4. A Dual Mimicry Complex Involving Eusocial Wasps (Hymenoptera: Vespidae)
Sean O'Donnell & Frank Joyce

Batesian mimicry results when nondefended species evolve to resemble noxious models, and Müllerian mimicry results when chemically defended species evolve to resemble each other (Wickler 1968). Several cases of mimicry in the eusocial Vespidae have been described (Richards 1978, West-Eberhard et al. 1995). More aggressive species of neotropical Vespidae, often swarm-founding wasps with large colony sizes (tribe Epiponini), are mimicked by other eusocial wasps. Wasps in the genus *Mischocyttarus* often mimic epiponines. Although capable of stinging, *Mischocyttarus* will not sting humans even in nest defense; some species flee their nests when disturbed.

Mischocyttarus mastigophorus exhibits two color morphs that co-occur in Monteverde. Although other species of *Mischocyttarus* are known to vary in body color over their geographic ranges (J. Carpenter, pers. comm.), this is the first report of a eusocial wasp with two discrete color morphs co-existing within a population. Our research suggests that *M. mastigophorus* exhibits dual mimicry, with two species from the epiponine genus *Agelaia* serving as models for the *M. mastigophorus* color morphs. Furthermore, the relative frequencies of the *M. mastigophorus* color morphs corresponded with the relative abundances of their putative model species at different elevations, as would be expected if the presence of the models affected the fitness of the morphs.

Colonies of *M. mastigophorus* were collected in 1994 and 1996 from the eaves and walls of buildings in Monteverde. Colonies were collected at night to ensure that all adults were present. Adult wasps were frozen for colony population counts. Additional colonies were examined in the field and surveyed for adults during daylight hours. Locations of colonies of putative model species (*Agelaia yepocapa* and *A. xanthopus*) were recorded from July 1988 to January 1996. Presence of foragers of the model species were recorded at meat baits placed at different elevations (O'Donnell 1995).

The color shades and pattern of the *M. mastigophorus* pale morph closely matched those of *Agelaia yepocapa*, and the dark morph closely resembled *A. xanthopus*. *Agelaia yepocapa* and *A. xanthopus* are among the most commonly encountered foraging wasps at Monteverde. Both *Agelaia* species typically have colonies of several thousand adults, which they vigorously defend against intruders (O'Donnell and Jeanne 1990).

Males and females within *M. mastigophorus* morphs are similar in color and in pattern. Males are easily recognized by the possession of elongate, filamentous antennae; no intergradation between the morphs is evident. The pale morph and *A. yepocapa* are extensively yellow laterally, and black with yellow markings on the dorsum. The model and mimic share similar patterns of black markings, particularly on the dorsum of the gaster (distal segments of the abdomen). The greater amount of black on the gaster and the deeper shade of yellow coloration distinguish both model and mimic from sympatric yellow and black congeners (e.g., *M. mexicanus* and *A. areata*). The coloration of the dark morph is almost identical to that of its putative model, *A. xanthopus*. The dark morph's body is deep chocolate brown, with yellow on the legs and yellow mandibles. No other vespids share this color pattern.

Mischocyttarus mastigophorus ranges from 1475 m to at least 1600 m (Table 4.2). The range of *A. yepocapa* appears to include lower elevations than *M. mastigophorus* and may not include the upper elevations of the mimic's range. The range of *A. xanthopus* appears to overlap the elevational range of *M. mastigophorus* completely. The relative frequencies of *M. mastigophorus* morphs change with elevation (Table 4.2), presumably in response to differences in the elevational ranges of the model species. Preferential feeding by predators on one morph, depending on experience with different model species at different elevations, could generate the observed correspondence of mimic and model abundances. Choice tests with visually hunting predators could be used to test this hypothesis.

Table 4.2. Numbers of *Mischocyttarus mastigophorus* colony types and adults of two color morphs at different elevations in Monteverde.

	Elevation (m)			
	1475–1499	1500–1524	1525–1549	1550–higher
Colony type[a]				
All pale	11 (8)	0	3	4 (1)
Mixed	1	0	7 (3)	5
All dark	0	0	1	0
Number of adults[b]				
Pale	69 (8)	0	76 (22)	133 (64)
Dark	2	0	50 (9)	32 (18)

Colony types: all pale, only pale morph adults present; mixed, pale and dark morph adults present; all dark, only dark morph adults present.

Colony types differed in relative abundance at different elevations (likelihood ratio C^2 = 12.90, df = 4, p < .05; Fienberg 1989); colonies containing dark morph adults were more common at higher elevations. The color morphs differed in relative abundance at different elevations (likelihood ratio C^2 = 47.21, df = 2, p < .001); dark morph wasps were more abundant at higher elevations.

[a]Numbers of pre-emergence nests (foundress associations that had not yet produced adult offspring) are given in parentheses.
[b]Numbers of males are given in parentheses.

The fact that pale and dark morph adults can emerge from a nest on the same day suggests that the polymorphism has a genetic basis, but environmental determinants such as temperature or food intake cannot be ruled out. How did two discrete morphs of *M. mastigophorus* evolve? It is possible that the morphs were formerly isolated. Data on differential survivorship of the *M. mastigophorus* morphs with elevation are needed to assess whether there is selection for different morph frequencies, which could maintain the polymorphism at Monteverde.

Dark-bodied insects are likely to warm to flying temperature more readily than pale-bodied conspecifics in cool climates. Body colors of other vespid wasps suggest that selection for efficient thermoregulation could play a role in establishing the elevational patterns of morph frequencies. Some species of Vespidae exhibit reduced pale markings in populations at higher elevations, but this variation is more subtle than the *M. mastigophorus* morph color differences.

The degree to which this *Mischocyttarus/Agelaia* mimicry complex is driven by Batesian versus Müllerian selection is unknown. Since *M. mastigophorus* appears to be rare relative to both model species, its presence is unlikely to select strongly for changes in *Agelaia* spp. color patterns. We hypothesize that *M. mastigophorus*, and other species of *Mischocyttarus*, are effectively Batesian mimics. *Mischocyttarus mastigophorus* nests are often located in sheltered, dark sites. Mimetic protection may accrue mainly to foragers in the field rather than to the nests themselves.

Acknowledgments Eva Chun first noted the existence of two *M. mastigophorus* color morphs and called our attention to this fascinating species. Mary Jane West-Eberhard and Jim Carpenter generously aided in identification of the wasps. We thank the Monteverde Cloud Forest Preserve and the Monteverde community for assistance and permission to collect specimens.

4.7.5. The Ants of Monteverde
John T. Longino

Ants are not a conspicuous feature of the Monteverde landscape. There are occasional marauding army ants, pest ants that inhabit dwellings, and leafcutting ants that plague the garden or even come into the kitchen to steal food. In contrast to lowland sites, ants do not drip from the vegetation, nor do they teem across the ground; in the cold wet cloud forest itself, one could easily conclude that there are no ants. In reality, no place in Monteverde is truly ant-free. Even the wet, windswept elfin forest, which appears to be an inimical habitat for ants, is home to a set of species, albeit relatively few (Longino and Nadkarni 1990). As one descends in any direction, ant species richness increases.

Based largely on my collecting experience in Monteverde from 1983 to 1996, this overview of Monteverde ants highlights common and conspicuous species in six groups: (1) army ants, (2) leafcutting ants, (3) pest ants, (4) large predacious ants, (5) ants of cloud forest leaf litter, and (6) ants of the cloud forest canopy.

Ants are in the family Formicidae. All ants are eusocial (or derived from social ancestors in a few parasitic species), meaning that they exhibit (1) reproductive division of labor, with reproductive queens and sterile or nearly sterile workers; (2) cooperative care of the young; and (3) overlapping generations in the colony. Workers are female and wingless. Queens are differentiated from workers and usually have wings that they discard prior to nest establishment. Males are winged, with small heads and large eyes, and usually do not look like workers or queens. General treatment of ant biology is described in Hölldobler and Wilson (1990), and keys to genera are in Bolton (1994). There are 80 genera of ants in Costa Rica, of which 46 are known in the Monteverde area.

Army ants (including *Simopelta*). The Ecitoninae are the New-World army ants, comprising their own subfamily (Bolton 1990). All Ecitoninae are group hunters, usually taking exclusively live prey in massive raiding parties (Hölldobler and Wilson 1990, Gotwald 1995). Over 15 species of Ecitoninae are known from Monteverde in the genera *Eciton*, *Labidus*, *Nomamyrmex*, and *Neivamyrmex*. Although army ants are a diverse group, almost all behavioral and ecological studies have focused on one lineage, the *Eciton burchelli* complex.

Eciton burchelli subspecies *parvispinum* is the most common army ant in the Monteverde area. Workers hunt in large swarm raids during the day and commonly enter houses during raids. In swarm raids, the ground is blanketed with a dense layer of workers. This layer of ants is up to 4 m wide and 2 m front to back, and slowly moves across the ground, flushing suitable prey that are then captured, dismembered, and moved back to trunk trails that lead rearward from the raid front. Colonies exhibit endogenous activity cycles and synchronized brood development often described for army ants (Hölldobler and Wilson 1990, Gotwald 1995). They alternate between statary phases (remaining in one nest site) and nomadic phases (moving to a new nest site each night). During the statary phase, the queen lays a mass of eggs that hatch at the same time and grow as a cohort of larvae. As food demands of the colony increase due to the growing larval cohort, the colony enters the nomadic phase, moving to fresh hunting grounds each day. When the larvae begin to pupate and food demands decrease, another statary phase begins. During the nomadic phase, the temporary nest sites are often located between tree buttresses, against dead logs, or in other exposed situations. At this time, one can observe prominent bivouacs: globular masses of ants that form the living walls of a nest.

Species of the genus *Labidus* also swarm raid. Swarm raiding species of *Labidus* have generally black workers that are on average smaller than *Eciton* workers, and thus the swarm raids appear more dense. I have seen some spectacularly large *Labidus* swarms crossing the dirt roads of Monteverde—they look like broad bands of black paint. *Labidus coecus* is a species with shiny, dark red, strongly polymorphic workers. It is fairly common even in urban areas and occurs from Texas to Argentina. They are largely subterranean (Perfecto 1992) but will come to the surface to feed at localized food sources; these short forays can take the form of a swarm raid. They are more omnivorous than other army ants and will gather kitchen scraps. Army ants that do not swarm raid, although diverse, are less conspicuous. They hunt exclusively in files and are often nocturnal or subterranean. In Monteverde, they include four additional *Eciton* species, two *Nomamyrmex* species, and at least four species of *Neivamyrmex*.

The genus *Simopelta* is a convergent army ant (Gotwald and Brown 1967) in a different subfamily, the Ponerinae. As with army ants, they have group-raiding workers with reduced eyes, synchronized brood development, and an enlarged, wingless queen that looks remarkably like an army ant queen. They have black, weakly polymorphic workers, and in the field their slow-moving columns look like those of another common cloud forest army ant, *Neivamyrmex sumichrasti*. They are relatively common in primary forest in the 500–1500 m band on the Atlantic slope but appear to be absent from the lowlands. There may be as many as five species in the Monteverde area.

Fungus-growing ants. The fungus-growing ants comprise the tribe Attini. These ants harvest substrates on which they culture fungi, and the fungi provide the food for the colony. Attines vary widely in worker size, colony size, and fungal substrate. The conspicuous leafcutting ant genera are *Atta* and *Acromyrmex*. These ants cut and harvest leaf fragments for their fungal substrate (Fig. 4.17). Other genera of Attini have smaller workers that are not conspicuous leafcutters. Instead, they harvest caterpillar droppings, dead insect parts, or other nutrient-rich substrates for their fungi (Hölldobler and Wilson 1990).

There are two leafcutting ant species in the Monteverde area. *Atta cephalotes* is a big leafcutting ant of open pastures in lower Monteverde. Colonies of *Atta* can be enormous, with over a million workers. Nests are a voluminous system of subterranean galleries, with a superstructure of bare excavated soil that may be meters across. *Acromyrmex coronatus* is a small leafcutting ant and is a major pest in gardens. It will come into houses at night to gather food that has been

Figure 4.17. Leaf-cutter ant (*Acromyrmex* sp.) cutting lily petal. Photograph by Dan Perlman.

left out. Their nests are far smaller than *Atta* nests, often in or under a piece of dead wood and often with a superstructure of loose dead leaf fragments. They do not excavate soil as extensively as *Atta*. They may be subarboreal, nesting in a low branch junction of an epiphyte-laden tree. Unlike *At. cephalotes*, *Ac. coronatus* is more tolerant of cloud forest conditions. Colonies occur in clearings and small gaps up to the ridge crest above Monteverde.

Pest ants. *Monomorium pharaonis* is a tiny yellow species that is a pest ant in some Monteverde houses. This is a classic "tramp" species (Williams 1994), occurring in buildings throughout the world and easily transported by humans. It is not native to the New World and is rarely found outside of buildings. Other Monteverde pest ants are native species that move into houses from surrounding habitats. *Pheidole punctatissima* is a small brown species, the soldiers of which have yellow on the back of the head. This species is common in open disturbed areas and can achieve remarkably high densities in Monteverde houses. *Camponotus albicoxis* is a large brown carpenter ant with contrasting white on the bases of the middle and hind legs and is referred to as "cranny ant" by Monteverde residents (J. Campbell, pers. comm.). They have ephemeral nest sites that they readily abandon. In houses, they may be found in old boxes, behind books on shelves, and beneath unused clothing

in drawers. On discovery by humans or army ants, workers burst into action, grasping brood and running in all directions to establish a new nest site in another dark cavity. They forage nocturnally and are generalized scavengers with a preference for sweets. Nests are also found beneath epiphytes in canopy trees.

Solenopsis geminata is the common tropical fire ant found in frequently disturbed open areas, such as where annual crops are planted and around dwellings. They nest in the soil, forming distinct mounds of excavated soil above their nests. Workers have an inordinately strong sting for their size. They have the habit of stealthily climbing up people's legs in large numbers and then all stinging simultaneously. Fire ants are generalized scavengers with powerful recruitment abilities. They are usually deemed pests because of their general nuisance and their ability to damage small seedlings, but they may also be beneficial as voracious predators on other pest insects. *Solenopsis geminata* is widespread throughout Central America and southern North America. It is native to Costa Rica, where it is the only known fire ant species (Trager 1991).

Large predators. Some of the more conspicuous ants in Monteverde are large black ants in the subfamily Ponerinae. These ants forage solitarily and are predators on live prey. The three most common large ponerines in Monteverde are *Leptogenys imperatrix*,

Pachycondyla aenescens, and *Odontomachus opaciventris*. *Leptogenys imperatrix* is a specialized predator on isopods. Workers scurry across roads or trails, often carrying isopods in their jaws. Their colonies are small, and nests are common and easily spotted in the soil along road cuts in the Monteverde community due to the tell-tale light gray streak of ejected isopod shells below the nest entrance. Foraging workers of *Pachycondyla aenescens* are commonly seen on roads in Monteverde and take a wide range of prey. *Pachycondyla aenescens* is a montane species, occurring above 1000 m in the northern Neotropics (W. L. Brown, pers. comm.). *Odontomachus* is a genus of large ants with long snapping jaws (Brown 1976). *Odontomachus opaciventris*, a primarily montane species, is the most common species in the Monteverde area. Nests are in rotten wood and may be common around dwellings. Winged queens are a common sight. They are generalist predators that actively hunt for prey and have a powerful and rapid sting.

Cloud forest leaf litter ants. Leaf litter in the cold wet cloud forest appears to support no ants, but actually harbors a moderately diverse community (Longino and Nadkarni 1990, Nadkarni and Longino 1990). Cloud forest litter ants are "cryptobiotic": they forage in and under the litter, feign death when disturbed, and are invisible to the casual searcher. However, sifted leaf litter suspended in extraction devices (e.g., Berlese funnels, Winkler bags; Besuchet et al. 1987) can produce a surprising number of ants. Characteristic inhabitants are the well-known and diverse genera *Solenopsis*, *Pheidole*, and *Hypoponera* (but fewer species than in the lowlands), and less well-known groups such as *Stenamma*, *Adelomyrmex*, *Lachnomyrmex*, Dacetonini, Basicerotini, *Cryptopone*, *Gnamptogenys*, *Proceratium*, and *Amblyopone*. The habits of these cryptic leaf litter ants are virtually unknown, but a surprising number of them have been named because of the work of Carlo Menozzi (1927, 1931a, 1931b, 1936).

Canopy ants. An ascent to the canopy in lowland forests reveals ants teeming over the surfaces of trunk, branches, and leaves. In contrast, the Monteverde canopy, with its thick sleeves of epiphytes and canopy soil, appears devoid of ants. Patient searching may reveal the occasional worker of *Procryptocerus* or *Camponotus* on leaf or branch surfaces. There is abundant ant life in the Monteverde canopy, but one must look in and under the epiphytes. Pulling back large contiguous epiphyte mats reveals abundant but very tiny ants living at the interface of branch surface and epiphyte root mat. Colonies of these ants seem to have no bounds. What appear to be continuous columns of ants connect aggregations of workers, dispersed at intervals of a few centimeters to a meter or more. Two common ant species that look similar (a species of *Solenopsis* and of *Myrmelachista*) share this habit. Canopies of individual trees are dominated by one or the other of these two species.

The *Solenopsis* nest almost entirely on branch surfaces, and the aggregations of workers contain larvae, pupae, and one or more colony queens. They appear to be "unicolonial," having multiple queens and no well-defined colony boundaries. The *Myrmelachista* occupy space on the branch surface and extend into cavities inside the branches. The larvae and pupae are concentrated in these branch cavities, rather than on the branch surface. These branch cavities can be extensive, occupying many branches in the crown of a tree. The food of these ants is unknown, but both species tend coccoid Homoptera (mealy bugs and scale insects). Homoptera are abundant along the ant paths on branch surfaces and, in the case of *Myrmelachista*, also inside the stems, on the walls of the branch cavities.

Due to their prevalence across trees and their abundance within trees, these ants must form a large proportion of the animal biomass in these forests. Their presence as major consumers, especially their tending of plant-feeding Homoptera, suggests they may have a major impact on nutrient transfer processes in these forests. Their contribution to forest biomass pools and nutrient transfer processes begs for investigation.

Other Monteverde canopy ants have more discrete nests and more clearly defined colony boundaries. A common and conspicuous species is *Pheidole innupta*. This large ant forms populous colonies in large globose epiphyte mats. They are rarely seen on the surface, and their feeding habits are unknown. They are found by pulling open big epiphyte clumps in the canopy, from which large numbers of black ants emerge. They have weak stings and are no threat to tree climbers.

A species in the *Stenamma schmidti*–complex occurs in the cloud forest canopy. Nests occur under small epiphyte patches, often on narrow branches. The colonies are small, with no more than a few dozen workers and a queen. This canopy species has a complementary distribution with other members of the *S. schmidti* complex, which are common in leaf litter on the cloud forest floor. The *schmidti*–complex species of the cloud forest floor are restricted to montane sites. In contrast, the species from the Monteverde canopy also occurs throughout Costa Rica in lowland wet forests, where it occurs on the forest floor and not in the canopy. This microhabitat shift with elevation could be the result of competitive exclusion from other members of the *schmidti*-complex or the result of adaptation to particular microclimatic conditions. In cloud forests, the canopy is subject to greater extremes of temperature and dryness than the forest floor (Bohlman et al. 1995). Perhaps microclimate variables important to *Stenamma* make cloud forest canopy and lowland forest floor more similar to each other than either is to cloud forest floor.

Biogeography and geographic variation. History has left its mark on the Monteverde ant fauna, with elements derived from both the north and the south. The genera *Stenamma* and *Cryptopone* are Holarctic and are increasingly restricted to the highlands as one moves south in Central America. *Stenamma* fades out in northern South America, and *Cryptopone* occurs no farther south than Costa Rica. These are the ant equivalents of the oaks (*Quercus* spp.), which show a similar pattern. The remaining Monteverde ant genera are widespread in the neotropics.

Species-level patterns in and near Monteverde are complex, and parapatric distributions are common. The lowlands to the west contain a Mesoamerican fauna adapted to seasonal dry forest conditions. The lowlands to the east contain a combination of South American and endemic Central American elements derived from South America and adapted to evergreen rain forest conditions (Gentry 1982). Taxa from the two sides may meet in or near Monteverde, as in the case of the *Eciton burchelli* complex. The cloud forest also harbors montane specialists, for example, *Pachycondyla aenescens*.

Cryptic ants of forest leaf litter often show bands of discrete, parapatric "forms" that segregate by elevation. Two morphologically distinct forms of *Octostruma balzani* occur just east and west of Monteverde, but do not occur in the narrow band of cloud forest that separates them. A large dark form of *Eurhopalothrix* cf. *gravis* occurs throughout the midelevation Atlantic slope, up through the Monteverde cloud forest, and down to the bottom of the evergreen belt on the Pacific side. However, specimens from the narrow cloud forest strip on the ridge crest are subtly distinct from the remainder. *Neostruma brevicornis* and *N. myllorhapha* occur in the lowlands of Costa Rica, and both have distinct forms that are larger and darker in Monteverde and other cloud forest areas in Costa Rica. *Cyphomyrmex salvini* occurs as several distinct sympatric forms in the lowlands, and a distinct, almost black form occurs in the narrow strip of ridge crest cloud forest. *Discothyrea horni* is found from Monteverde cloud forest to sea level on the Atlantic slope, but in the lowlands it co-occurs with a smaller, lighter-colored form. Montane specimens of widespread species are often larger and darker than their lowland counterparts

(Brown 1959). Observations of ants in the Monteverde cloud forest have corroborated this observation and revealed that geographic variation of this kind can be surprisingly discrete and occur over small spatial scales. Monteverde is an ideal location for investigation of the contemporary ecological forces and the historical processes driving character variation. It is an excellent laboratory for the study of ant species and speciation.

4.7.6. *Crawfordapis luctuosa*, a Ground-Nesting Bee of the Central American Highlands
Gard Otis

A popular hiking destination of visitors to Monteverde is La Ventana at the Continental Divide, where walkers encounter numerous holes 1 cm in diameter scattered over the roadway and the cliff edge. A small mound of dirt around them indicates that the inhabitants have been actively digging. One is almost certain to see several large brown and black bees flying slowly near ground level, then landing and entering these holes. These are *Crawfordapis luctuosa* (Colletidae: Diphaglossinae), which is known from the highlands of Central America from Chiriquí, Panama, to Chiapas, Mexico. It was generally considered to be a very rare bee until nesting aggregations were reported along roadcuts in Monteverde (Otis et al. 1982) and Chiriquí (Roubik and Michener 1985). The permanently open nature of these roadcuts has allowed them to remain as active nesting sites for up to 25 years (Roubik and Michener 1985). Large aggregations with several hundred active nests and densities as high as 21 nests/m² can develop, although this may be an artifact of human disturbance. Prior to human occupation, nesting was probably restricted to natural landslides that become overgrown with vegetation within a few years.

A female *Crawfordapis* digs a nearly vertical tunnel into the ground to the surprising depth of 45–120 cm. Along the lower parts of this tunnel, she constructs lateral burrows 3–8 cm in length. At the end of each lateral burrow, the tunnel rises slightly, then turns downward to form a vertically oriented cell 33–38 mm in length. The female works the surface of the cell with fine clay, then secretes material that leaves a shining, whitish, cellophanelike lining to the cell, which is typical of this family. This lining functions to keep water from the surrounding soil from entering the completed cell and to keep the soupy pollen and nectar mixture brought by the female intact. An egg is laid on the surface of the liquid food material, after which the lateral burrow is filled in with soil. The larva floats on the food during its development, but at pupation it spins a floor structure that keeps the pupa above the liquid remaining at the bottom of the cell (Rozen 1984). After completing development, the emerging adult must dig its way out to the main vertical tunnel.

In the cool, windy dry season (late February), most activity of females at La Ventana occurs between 0900 and 1430 hr (Otis et al. 1982). During the wet season (late July) some females forage by 0600 and continue until midafternoon. There are very few observations of *Crawfordapis* foraging at flowers. Some foraging must occur at a considerable distance from the nesting site because bees are absent from their nests for periods of 25–142 min. Detailed analyses of cell contents indicate that 75–99% of the pollen in each cell was from species of Melastomataceae, Solanaceae, and Begoniaceae (Roubik and Michener 1985), families that have nectarless flowers with pollen contained in tubular anthers that open through a small pore. Efficient collection of the pollen from such flowers requires "buzz" pollination by bees. After landing on a flower, a bee vibrates its flight muscles. The vibrations travel through the flower, causing the expulsion of the pollen from the anthers and onto the bee's body (Buchmann 1983). Pollen from other plants in the families Proteaceae, Loranthaceae, Passifloraceae, Polygalaceae, and Sapotaceae can be found in nest cells at low frequency and are probable sources of nectar for female bees.

In one study (Otis et al. 1982), only about one-third of marked bees showed high nest fidelity; most visited more than one nest, although many of these visits lasted less than 1 min and represented either mistakes in orientation or exploratory visits to nests already containing other females. Other bees visited up to five different nests. In some cases, these were young bees initiating nests. However, bees alternate between "floater" and "provisioning" status as they age (Jang et al. 1996). I also observed some nest switching; of the 136 bees marked in late July, 10 were still alive on 3 September. Of these, three had become resident in nests that were previously occupied by other females, and another three were active in the same holes after the intervening period of 36–40 days. Three takeovers were observed in 90 nest holes.

Given the large investment of time and energy to construct and provision cells, one would expect newly emerged females to search for and take over empty nests or nests with partially provisioned cells (Eickwort 1975, Brockmann et al. 1979). Yet the low rates of encounters between females and dual occupancy of nests indicate that direct takeovers of occupied nests occur only rarely. When a bee entered a nest already occupied by a resident female, loud buzzing was heard and the intruding bee left quickly.

There is no evidence of communal nesting or cooperation among females.

Male *Crawfordapis* can be readily observed near the nesting aggregations, especially during sunny weather. They fly over small areas, usually within 1 m of the ground. Although they interact little with other males, they actively pursue females returning to their nests and attempt to mate with them. Once they leave the nest, they may spend the remainder of their lives outside. They must visit flowers to obtain the nectar that fuels their flight. Nothing is known about their foraging.

In excavations of *Crawfordapis* nests in Panama, both larval and adult blister beetles, *Tetraonyx cyanipennis* (Meloidae), were found inhabiting the cells (Roubik and Michener 1985). This species, as with many other blister beetles, is believed to parasitize its bee hosts when the beetle is in the first larval stage. This long-legged larva climbs onto a flower and then attaches to a bee as it forages. Once inside the bee's nest, it attacks the eggs of the bee. Later larval stages probably feed as cleptoparasites on pollen and nectar stored in the cell. It is not known if this or other blister beetles are associated with *Crawfordapis*.

Because *Crawfordapis luctuosa* has discrete nesting aggregations, it offers opportunities for study. Long-term studies of marked females would clarify the ecological basis of nest switching and of multiple nest visitation by some bees. By marking males as they exit nests and observing them over time, male mating strategy could be studied. Migration rates of bees among aggregations, rates of colonization of new nest sites, and seasonal variation in bee activity are rich topics for study.

4.7.7. Stingless Bees of Cloud Forests
Jorge Lobo

Stingless bees (subfamily Meliponinae) are an abundant group of social insects in neotropical forests. Their colonies are organized in societies with castes consisting of a single queen and hundreds or thousands of workers. The majority of species build nests inside hollow trees, but some nest underground, within termite or ant nests, or in exposed constructions. The common name of this group of bees comes from their very reduced sting (functionally stingless), a derived condition with respect to other bees. These bees visit numerous plant species and show wide flexibility in their sources of nectar and pollen. More characteristic is their habit of collecting materials such as resins, gums, mineral salts, excrement, and carrion, which are used to build internal structures of the nest and to provide supplementary food.

In Costa Rica, there are about 50 species of stingless bees in 12 genera. Most species occur exclusively below 1500 m, especially in the lowland rain forests of the Caribbean and on the Osa Peninsula. I have found only seven species at altitudes above 1500 m: *Trigona fulviventris*, *T. corvina*, *Scaptotrigona mexicana*, *Melipona melanopleura*, *Partamona* sp. (near *cupira*), *P. grandipennis*, and *Meliwillea bivea*. Most of these are black to brownish in color, the yellow-colored species being restricted to the lowlands. *Paratrigona ornaticeps* and *Tetragonisca angustula* also occur above 1500 m, although they are rare at this altitude. Some possible factors limiting the diversity of stingless bees in cloud forests include limited ability of individual bees and/or the colony to thermoregulate within the nest in cooler environments, reduced availability of natural cavities suitable for nesting, and the presence of parasite species specific to these altitudes.

Partamona sp., *P. grandipennis*, and *Meliwillea bivea* are common in forests between 1500 and 2000 m and are encountered from the volcanoes in the northwestern part of the country to the Talamanca Mountains in southern Costa Rica and Panama. These are medium-sized stingless bees, nearly uniformly black in color, with a shiny cuticular surface. *Partamona grandipennis* and *M. bivea* are found only above 1500 m. These two species nest in tree trunks, whereas *Partamona* sp. also nests in earthen banks, artificial cavities, and semiexposed mud constructions. *Partamona* sp. has a wide altitudinal distribution (0–2200 m) and is most easily adaptable to mountainous habitats altered by human activity.

Partamona grandipennis is distinguished from *Partamona* sp. by its larger size, darker wings, and wider malar space (area between the eye and mandible). The architecture of its nest is unknown. The nest entrance of the latter species is funnel shaped. In high elevation cloud forests in Costa Rica, these two species are abundant and strongly attracted to sugary substances and campfire ashes. *Partamona* sp. is an especially aggressive species near its nest. Upon disturbance, numerous workers come out of the nest to bite the skin and crawl into the hair of the observer, sometimes even smearing resins carried from the interior of the nest. *Partamona grandipennis* demonstrates the same aggressive habits, which is typical of some stingless bee species.

Among bees of the Costa Rican highlands, *M. bivea* is a genus endemic to Costa Rica and Panama, the only case of endemism at the generic level in the Meliponinae of Central America and Mexico (Roubik et al. 1997). Two nests of this species have been observed in tree cavities, one in *Roupala glaberrima* (Proteaceae) in Cerro Echandi and one in a fig tree in Zurquí de Moravia. The nest entrance is very simple, lacking a tube or other protruding structure con-

structed by the bees, which differs from that of *Partamona* or *Scaptotrigona*. The brood chamber is composed of horizontal combs without connections or pillars extending across the entire brood chamber (unlike *Partamona*). The combs are enveloped by several interconnected sheets of cerumen ("involucrum") having a complex form and a width of 5–6 cm. A difference of up to 10°C between the inside and outside of this covering has been measured. Outside the involucrum are the honey and pollen containers, potlike structures made of fused wax and resin. The pollen is of different colors and forms and is derived from different families of plants, with a single container containing a mixture. This species, together with *Partamona*, *Scaptotrigona mexicana*, and other subfamilies of bees, abound at flowers of secondary growth plants, for example, *Miconia* sp. (Melastomataceae) and *Neomirandea angularis* (Asteraceae).

The existence of a stingless bee genus endemic to the cloud forests of Costa Rica and Panama is of biogeographic interest. *Meliwillea* lacks the derived and distinctive morphological characteristics of other genera and thus appears to be a direct descendent of a primitive branch of stingless bees. Because the subfamily Meliponinae possibly originated from Gondwana (the ancient supercontinent of the southern hemisphere), the origin of an endemic primitive genus in the southern part of Central America suggests pre-Pleistocene migrations. The presence of this bee exclusively in the highlands is puzzling, given that the subfamily is much more diverse in the lowlands. Our ignorance of many aspects of the biology of cloud forest bees, and the discovery of an endemic element in this habitat demonstrate the need to conserve forests.

4.7.8. Africanized Honey Bees, Recent Immigrants to Monteverde
Gard Otis

In 1957, 26 colonies of imported African honey bees escaped from an apiary near Río Claro, São Paulo, Brazil. An uninformed visitor removed the entrance grids from the hives, and some of the experimental colonies escaped. Less publicized was that hundreds of young unmated African queens were distributed to beekeepers in the late 1950s to create more productive hybrid colonies (Spivak et al. 1991). Within a few years, a feral population of "Africanized" honey bees that was very similar in behavior, morphology, and genetics to the bees of the savannah region of east Africa became established.

The Honey Bee (*Apis mellifera*) is native to Europe and Africa. Many different races, or subspecies, have evolved under the widely different environmental conditions. In temperate Europe, bees experience a brief abundance of floral resources in summer followed by a long cold winter, fostering biological traits that are not well suited to conditions in the tropics. Consequently, although the European bees that were shipped to Latin America during colonial times resulted in a beekeeping industry, these races generally did not survive without management and rarely established feral populations.

To obtain larger honey crops, Brazilians imported breeder queens predominantly from South Africa (*A. m. scutellata*) in 1956. Their extreme defensive behavior was a concern and, after their escape, quickly led them to become known as "abejas asesinas," or "killer bees." They reproduced extensively and absconded during periods of low nectar availability. These traits did not endear them to beekeepers, but they thrived in the New World. In 1995, approximately one trillion bees were forecasted to occupy 16,000,000 km² (Roubik 1989). This colonization has been remarkably rapid; within only a few years of their release, they expanded their range at rates of 300–500 km/yr, a rate virtually unchecked until 1994. They frequently attain densities of 10–15 colonies/km² (ca. 90,000–450,000 bees/km²) 2–4 years after arriving to a new area.

Starting in 1976, I followed individual bee colonies in French Guiana over time. By quantifying their birth (swarming) and death rates, I modeled the dynamics of a population in its initial growth period. Beginning with a single established colony, the high swarming rate was estimated to yield an average of 60 "daughter" swarms per year. Colonies lived an average of only seven months, but I estimated that the population grew 16-fold during a single year (Otis 1991). These data support the numerous observations of rapid population growth in many areas of Latin America. The first Africanized bees in Costa Rica were discovered near San Isidro del General on 2 February 1983. Within a month, they were observed foraging in Santa Rosa National Park near the Nicaraguan border. In seasonally dry areas of the Pacific slope, the feral population grew quickly, and by 1986, most beekeepers' colonies had become Africanized. At higher elevations, swarms have been less common and Africanization has proceeded more slowly (Spivak 1991). In Monteverde, the cool, damp, windy weather slows colony growth and reduces swarming rates. Although Africanized bees are probably present in the area, they are uncommon and have caused little disruption to humans or livestock. They are much more common in the warmer, drier region of San Luis.

The invasion of *Apis* into areas previously lacking honey bees has potential consequences for the diverse community of native bee species. In French Guiana the proportion of foragers at a patch of *Mimosa pudica* flowers that were Africanized bees increased from 7% in 1977 (two years after they arrived) to nearly 75% in 1982. This increase in *Apis* was accompanied by a corresponding decrease in the proportion of two stingless bee species (*Melipona*), presumably due to competition with Honey Bees (Roubik 1987).

Such changes in the native bee fauna are likely to affect "buzz-pollinated" plant populations. Africanized bees are not capable of buzz pollination, so as they reduce the populations of other bees through competition, they may indirectly reduce the reproductive success of some plants (Roubik 1989). These long-term processes are poorly understood. Because Africanized bee density is low in highland regions, the impact on Monteverde plant communities is expected to be negligible, but there may be effects on plant species in the Pacific lowlands.

A contentious issue is the significance of hybridization between European and Africanized bees. The two races interbreed (Rinderer et al. 1993), but controversy surrounds the ecological fitness of those hybrids. Some studies suggest that they disappear in tropical regions, perhaps because of genetic incompatibility that is expressed in second- and third-generation hybrids (Harrison and Hall 1993). The establishment of Africanized bees in the New World has provided biologists with an opportunity to study a biological invasion. Surprisingly few studies have been conducted in Costa Rica, given the large database that was assembled on pollination systems prior to the arrival of Africanized bees. Repeat studies under conditions of high densities of Africanized bees will provide insights on the impact of these bees on plant communities.

4.8. Arachnids: Spiders, Scorpions, and Mites

4.8.1. Introduction
Paul Hanson

The other major group of terrestrial arthropods besides insects are the arachnids, which include scorpions (Fig. 4.18), pseudoscorpions, solifugids (sun spiders or wind scorpions), whip scorpions (uropygids), amblypygids, spiders, daddy longlegs, mites, and a few lesser known groups. The largest (most speciose) of these groups are the mites (order Acarina), which occur in almost every type of habitat and include fungivores, predators, ectoparasites of animals (e.g., chiggers and ticks), endoparasites of animals, and plant sap suckers (e.g., spider mites and gall mites). Most other arachnid groups are predatory.

Figure 4.18. Scorpion. Photograph by Barbara Clauson.

Spiders are divided into two major groups: the wandering spiders (e.g., jumping spiders, wolf spiders, and crab spiders) and the sedentary web spiders. All spiders have spinnerets on their abdomen and use silk for making egg sacs, but only web spiders use silk in the building of complex snares to capture prey. Among web-builders, different families build different types of webs (Eberhard 1990). For example, Agelenidae weave a horizontal, slightly concave silk mat with a funnel-shaped retreat at one end; Linyphiidae construct horizontal, slightly convex sheets; Theridiidae and Pholcidae build irregular meshes. The best-known webs are orb webs, which consist of radial threads converging on a central hub, outer frame threads that serve as insertion sites for the radial threads, and a sticky spiral.

Our knowledge of cloud forest arachnids is extremely rudimentary. Four families and 14 species of scorpions are known from Costa Rica, the most common in Monteverde being *Centuroides limbatus* (Buthidae), which occurs in different color morphs (Francke and Stockwell 1987; Fig. 4.18).

4.8.2. Vertical Distribution of Orb-Weaving Spiders in a Colombian Cloud Forest
Carlos Valderrama A. (translated by Bob Law)

I measured the vertical distribution of spiders in a Colombian cloud forest (Reserva Natural La Planada,

1850 m), a site that is similar in elevation and vegetation to Monteverde. Spider communities were compared among three habitats: closed-canopy primary forest (selectively cut in 1981, 15 years before this study), secondary forest (regenerating cattle pastures that had been abandoned more than 10 years before), and natural clearings (formed by recent tree falls within the primary forest; Valderrama 1996). The vertical distribution of flying insects (putative prey) was compared in the three habitats with sticky traps. A total of 1188 adult spiders were collected, representing 46 species and eight families (Anapidae, Araneidae, Deinopidae, Mysmenidae, Symphytognathidae, Tetragnathidae, Theridiosomatidae, and Uloboridae).

Very few spiders were captured in the canopy, most of which were juveniles and small adults. The juveniles belonged to understory species, which may reflect their high capacity for aerial dispersal. In canopy fogging studies, only 2% of the arthropods collected in the canopies were spiders (Erwin 1989). This suggests that spiders may not be more diverse in the canopy than the understory, as are many other arthropod species.

The greater availability of support structures, for example, epiphytes on trunks in the primary forest, apparently allows many species to expand their vertical range. Epiphytes also provide refuges for spiders. For example, *Azilia* normally builds its horizontal

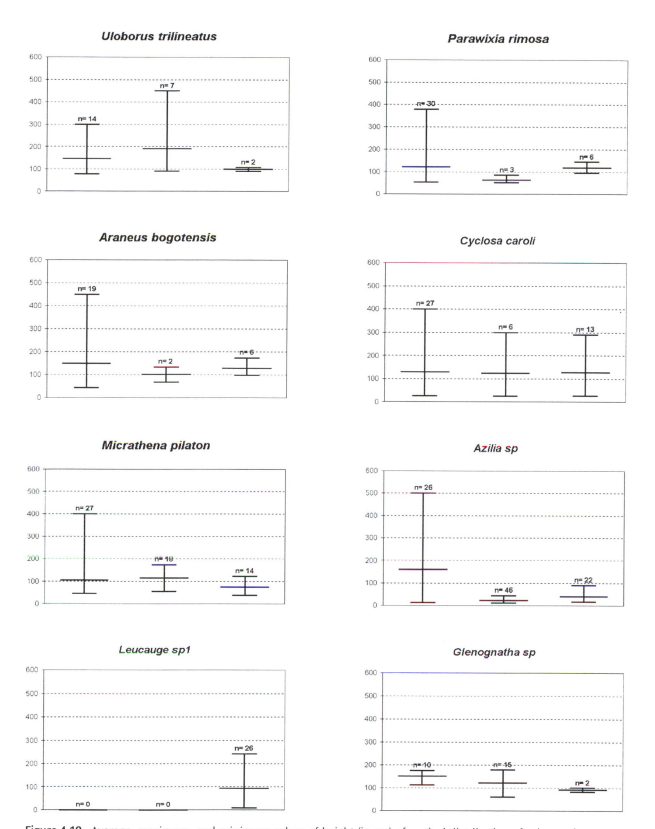

Figure 4.19. Average, maximum, and minimum values of height (in cm) of vertical distribution of orb-weaving spiders in three habitats in the cloud forest. The bars represent, from left to right, closed-canopy primary forest, secondary forest, and natural clearing.

web in leaf litter near trunks or roots, but in primary forest it expands its vertical distribution to epiphytes on vertical trunks. *Cyclosa* constructs its web in relatively protected places such as vertical trunks, small plants, and shrubs. *Micrathena pilaton* and *Chrysometa otavalo* place their webs in open places, such as between two shrubs or small plants; the latter species has a similar vertical distribution in clearings. All of these species except *Azilia* were more abundant in primary forest. *Chrysometa* near *opulenta*, *C.* near *globosa*, and *C.* near *saladito* (Tetragnathidae) occurred mainly in primary forest, perhaps due to the greater abundance of large leaves, as they construct their webs under such leaves. The small spiders Anapidae sp. 1 and Symphytognathidae sp. were also more abundant in primary forest. *Naatlo sutila* (Theridiosomatidae) constructed its webs principally in open spaces, which are more common in secondary than in primary forest. *Uloborus trilineatus* (Uloboridae) and *Epeirotypus* sp. (Theridiosomatidae) constructed webs on vertical trunks, the latter preferring secluded places. *Theridiosoma* sp. (Theridiosomatidae) used shrubs in primary forests and vertical trunks in secondary forest. *Chrysometa* n. sp. (Tetragnathidae) generally constructed its webs beneath branches or large leaves. *Leucauge* sp. 1 (Tetragnathidae) was exceptional in that it was observed only in natural clearings where their webs occur in the upper parts of the vegetation and in abandoned pastures (Fig. 4.19).

Nearly 3000 insects were captured in sticky traps and identified. The largest number of captures was in the secondary forest, followed by natural clearings. In all three habitats, the highest percentage of insects was captured near the ground. In primary forest, the percentage decreased from level 1 (0–0.3 m) to level 2 (1–1.3 m) but showed a slight progressive increase at higher levels. In secondary forest and natural clearings, the proportion of insects captured diminished with increasing height, which contrasts with results reported elsewhere (Sutton 1989). This discrepancy may be because my traps were located below rather than above the top of the canopy.

The most abundant group of insects captured in the sticky traps was Diptera, followed by Hymenoptera and Coleoptera. Diptera constituted a larger proportion in secondary forest, and Hymenoptera in natural clearings and primary forest; Coleoptera (Staphylinidae, Curculionidae, Scolytidae) were similarly distributed in all three habitats. Although numbers of Coleoptera generally decreased with increasing height, in primary forest their numbers increased again at the highest level (15 m). Psocoptera and Homoptera did not follow this general pattern; the greatest number of these were captured in primary forest at level 3

(2.5–2.8 m); the greatest number of Homoptera were taken at the same level in natural clearings.

Although the sticky traps provided comparative evaluations of insect populations in the three forest habitats and at different heights, they may not reflect the types of prey that are captured by spiders (Chacón and Eberhard 1980, Eberhard 1990). In other studies (Uetz and Biere 1980, Uetz and Hartsock 1987), traps of sticky threads captured prey similar to those captured by *Micrathena gracilis*. However, spiders select and consume only a subset of the insects entrapped in the web (Castillo and Eberhard 1983). Presumably both web type and foraging strategy affect prey selection by orb-weaving spiders (Craig 1989).

The greater abundance of insects in the lowest strata of the forest coincided with the greater relative abundance of orb-weaving spiders in these same levels. However, in primary forests, a second peak of insect abundance occurred in the canopy, which was not reflected in a similar increase in spider abundance. More research is needed on all aspects of arachnid biology in Monteverde.

Acknowledgments   I thank William Eberhard for his advisory role during this study, and Prof. Herbert Levi, Jonathan Coddington, and Brend Opell for their help with spider identification. This essay is part of my MSc Thesis at the Universidad de Los Andes (Bogotá, Colombia). This study was made possible by the support of the Fondo FEN-Colombia, the Wildlife Conservation Society (formerly Wildlife Conservation International/New York Zoological Society), and Reserva Natural La Planada; ecological disturbance study funds were provided by Conservation International/John D. and Catherine T. MacArthur Foundation.

Literature Cited

Akre, R. D., and C. W. Rettenmeyer. 1966. Behavior of Staphylinidae associated with army ants (Formicidae: Ecitonini). Journal of the Kansas Entomological Society 35:745–782.

Arrow, G. J. 1951. Horned beetles. A study of the fantastic in nature. Dr. W. Junk Publications, The Hague.

Ashe, J. S. 1984. Generic revision of the subtribe Gyrophaenina (Coleoptera: Staphylinidae: Aleocharinae) with review of the described subgenera and major features of evolution. Quaestiones Entomologicae 20:129–349.

———. 1986. Subsocial behavior among gyrophaenine staphylinids (Coleoptera: Staphylinidae: Aleocharinae). Sociobiology 12:315–320.

———. 1987. Egg chamber production, egg protection and clutch size among fungivorous beetles of the genus *Eumicrota* (Coleoptera: Staphylinidae) and their evolutionary implications. Zoological Journal of the Linnaean Society 90:255–273.

———. 1990. New species, phylogeny and natural history of *Tachiona* Sharp 1883 (Coleoptera: Staphylinidae: Aleocharinae). Tropical Zoology 3:225–235.

Ashe, J. S., and R. M. Timm. 1986. Mammals and beetles in Costa Rica. Field Museum of Natural History Bulletin 57(10):11–18.

———. 1987a. Predation by and activity patterns of "parasitic" beetles of the genus *Amblyopinus* (Coleoptera: Staphylinidae). Journal of Zoology, London 212:429–437.

———. 1987b. Probable mutualistic association between staphylinid beetles (*Amblyopinus*) and their rodent hosts. Journal of Tropical Ecology 3:177–181.

Askew, R. R. 1984. The biology of gall wasps. Pages 223–271 *in* T. N. Ananthakrishnan, editor. The biology of gall insects. Arnold, London.

Barr, W. F. 1975. Family Cleridae, Vol. 4, Family 73. Pages 1–18 *in* R. H. Arnett, editor. Checklist of the beetles of North and Central America and the West Indies. Flora and Fauna Publications, Gainesville, Florida.

Bates, H. L. 1862. Contributions to an insect fauna of the Amazon valley (Lepidoptera: Heliconidae). Transactions of the Linnaean Society of London 23:495–456.

Beaver, R. A. 1977. Bark and ambrosia beetles in tropical forests. Proceedings of the Symposium Forest Pests and Diseases in Southeast Asia, Bogor, Indonesia, April 1976. Biotropica, Special Publication 2:133–149.

———. 1979a. Host specificity of temperate and tropical animals. Nature 281:139–141.

———. 1979b. Non-equilibrium "island" communities; A guild of tropical bark beetles. Journal of Animal Ecology 48:987–1002.

———. 1988. Insect-fungus relationships in the bark and ambrosia beetles. Pages 121–143 *in* N. Wilding, N. M. Collins, P. M. Hammond, and J. F. Webber, editors. Insect-fungus interactions: 14th Symposium of the Royal Entomological Society of London. Academic Press, London.

Besuchet, C., D. H. Burckhardt, and I. Löbl. 1987. The "Winkler/Moczarski" collector as an efficient extractor for fungus and litter Coleoptera. Coleopterists Bulletin 41:392–394.

Bohlman, S., T. Matelson, and N. Nadkarni. 1995. Moisture and temperature patterns of canopy humus and forest floor soil of a montane cloud forest, Costa Rica. Biotropica 27:13–19.

Bolton, B. 1990. Army ants reassessed: the phylogeny and classification of the doryline section (Hymenoptera: Formicidae). Journal of Natural History 24:1339–1364.

———. 1994. Identification guide to the ant genera of the world. Harvard University Press, Cambridge, Massachusetts.

Bracker, H. E. 1989. Oviposition on host plants by a tropical forest grasshopper (*Microtylopteryx herbardi*: Acrididae). Ecological Entomology 14: 141–148.

Brockmann, H. J. 1992. Male behavior, courtship and nesting in *Trypoxylon* (Trypargilum) *monteverdeae* (Hymenoptera: Sphecidae). Journal of the Kansas Entomological Society 65:66–84.

Brockmann, H. J., A. Grafen, and R. Dawkins. 1979. Evolutionarily stable nesting strategy in a digger wasp. Journal of Theoretical Biology 77:473–496.

Brower, L. P., F. H. Pough, and H. R. Meck. 1970. Theoretical investigations of automimicry. I. Single trial learning. Proceedings of the National Academy of Sciences USA 66:1059–1066.

Brown, B. V. 1993. Taxonomy and preliminary phylogeny of the parasitic genus Apocephalus, subgenus Mesophora (Diptera: Phoridae). Systematic Entomology 18:191–230.

———. 1996. Preliminary analysis of a host shift: revision of the neotropical species of *Apocephalus*, subgenus *Mesophora* (Diptera: Phoridae). Contributions in Science 462:1–36.

———. In press. Systematics and fossil evidence of host-parasitoid relationships of Calamiscus Borgmeier (Diptera: Phoridae). Journal of Natural History.

Brown, B. V., and D. H. Feener, Jr. 1991. Behavior and host location cues of *Apocephalus paraponerae* (Diptera:

Phoridae), a parasitoid of the giant tropical ant *Paraponera clavata* (Hymenoptera: Formicidae). Biotropica 23:182–187.

———. 1995. Efficiency of two mass sampling methods for sampling phorid flies (Diptera: Phoridae) in a tropical biodiversity survey. Contributions in Science 459:1–10.

Brown, K. S., Jr. 1984. Adult-obtained pyrrolizidine alkaloids defend ithomiine butterflies against a spider predator. Nature 309:707–709.

Brown, W. L., Jr. 1959. A revision of the Dacetine ant genus *Neostruma*. Breviora 107:1–13.

———. 1976. Contributions toward a reclassification of the Formicidae. Part VI. Ponerinae, tribe Ponerini, subtribe Odontomachiti. Section A. Introduction, subtribal characters. Genus *Odontomachus*. Studia Entomologica 19:67–171.

Buchmann, S. L. 1983. Buzz pollination in angiosperms. Pages 73–113 *in* C. E. Jones and R. J. Little, editors. Handbook of experimental pollination biology. Van Nostrand Reinhold, New York.

Castillo, J. A., and W. G. Eberhard. 1983. Use of artificial webs to determine prey available to orb weaving spiders. Ecology 64:1655–1658.

Chacón, P., and W. G. Eberhard. 1980. Factors affecting numbers and kinds of prey caught in artificial spider webs, with considerations of how orb webs trap prey. Bulletin of the British Arachnological Society 5:29–38.

Chadab, R. 1979. Army-ant predation on social wasps. Ph.D. dissertation, University of Connecticut, Storrs, Connecticut.

Clausen, C. P. 1940. Entomophagous insects. McGraw-Hill, New York.

Craig, C. L. 1989. Alternative foraging modes of orb web weaving spiders. Biotropica 21:257–264.

Crowson, R. A. 1981. The biology of the Coleoptera. Academic Press, New York.

Crump, M. 1984. Ontogenetic changes in vulnerability to predation in tadpoles of *Hyla pseudopuma*. Herpetologica 40:265–271.

Crump, M., and J. A. Pounds. 1985. Lethal parasitism of an aposematic anuran (*Atelopus varius*) by *Notochaeta bufonivora* (Diptera: Sarcophagidae). Journal of Parasitology 71:588–591.

Cummins, M. P. 1992. Amphibious behavior of a tropical, adult tiger beetle, *Oxycheila polita* Bates (Coleoptera: Cicindelidae). Coleopterists Bulletin 46:145–151.

DeVries, P. J. 1983. Checklist of butterflies. Pages 654–678 *in* D. H. Janzen, editor. Costa Rican natural history. University of Chicago Press, Chicago.

———. 1987. The butterflies of Costa Rica and their natural history. Princeton University Press, Princeton, New Jersey.

Disney, R. H. L. 1994. Scuttle flies: the Phoridae. Chapman and Hall, London.

Drummond, B. A. 1976. Comparative ecology and mimetic relationships of ithomiine butterflies in Eastern Equador. Ph.D. dissertation, University of Florida, Gainesville.

Duffy, E. A. J. 1960. A monograph of the immature stages of neotropical timber beetles. British Museum of Natural History, London.

Eberhard, W. G. 1979. The function of horns in *Podischnus agenor* (Dynastinae). Pages 231–258 *in* S. Murray and N. A. Blum, editors. Sexual selection and reproductive competition in insects. Academic Press, New York.

———. 1980. Horned beetles. Scientific American 242:166–182.

———. 1990. Function and phylogeny of spider webs. Annual Review of Ecology and Systematics 21: 341–372.

Eberhard, W. G., and M. C. Marin. 1996. Sexual behavior and the enlarged hind legs of male *Megalopus armatus*

(Coleoptera, Chrysamelidae, Megalopo dinae). Journal of the Kansas Entomological Society 69:1–8.

Eickwort, G. C. 1975. Gregarious nesting of the mason bee *Hoplitis anthocopoides* and the evolution of parasitism and sociality among megachilid bees. Evolution 29:142–150.

Endrödi, S. 1985. The Dynastinae of the world. Dr. W. Junk Publications, Dordrecht.

Equihua, M. A., and T. H. Atkinson. 1987. Catalogo de Platypodidae (Coleoptera) de Norte y Centroamerica. Folia Entomologica Mexicana 72:5–31.

Erwin, T. 1989. Canopy arthropod biodiversity: a chronology of sampling techniques and results. Revista Peruana de Entomología 32:71–77.

Falconer, D. S. 1981. Introduction to quantitative genetics (2nd ed.). Longman, New York.

Feener, D. H., Jr., and K. A. G. Moss. 1990. Defense against parasites by hitchhikers in leaf-cutting ants: a quantitative assessment. Behavioral Ecology and Sociobiology 26:17–29.

Feener, D. H., Jr., L. F. Jacobs, and J. O. Schmidt. 1996. Specialized parasitoid attracted to a pheromone of ants. Animal Behavior 51:61–66.

Ferrufino, A., and S. L. Lapointe. 1989. Host plant resistance in *Brachiaria* grasses to the spittlebug *Zulia colombiana*. Entomología Experimentalis et Applicata 51:155–162.

Fienberg, S. E. 1989. The analysis of cross-classified categorical data. Massachusetts Institute of Technology Press, Cambridge, Massachusetts.

Fish, D. 1977. An aquatic spittlebug (Homoptera: Cercopidae) from a *Heliconia* flower bract in southern Costa Rica. Entomological News 88:10–12.

Fisher, E. M., and H. A. Hespenheide. 1992. Taxonomy and biology of Central American robber flies with an illustrated key to genera (Diptera: Asilidae). Pages 611–632 *in* D. Quintero and A. Aiello, editors. Insects of Panama and Mesoamerica: selected studies. Oxford University Press, Oxford.

Flowers, R. W. 1992. Review of the genera of mayflies of Panama, with a checklist of Panamanian and Costa Rican species (Ephemeroptera). Pages 37–51 *in* D. Quintero and A. Aiello, editors. Insects of Panama and Mesoamerica: selected studies. Oxford University Press, Oxford.

———. 1996. La subfamilia Eumolpinae (Chrysomelidae: Coleoptera) en America Central. Revista de Biología Tropical, Publicación Especial 2:1–60.

Flowers, R. W., and D. H. Janzen. 1997. Feeding records of Costa Rican leaf beetles (Coleoptera: Chrysomelidae). Florida Entomologist 80:334–366.

Francke, O. F., and S. A. Stockwell. 1987. Scorpions (Arachnida) from Costa Rica. Texas Tech University Press, Lubbock.

Gadagkar, R. 1991. *Belonogaster*, *Mischocyttarus*, *Parapolybia*, and independent-founding *Ropalidia*. Pages 149–190 *in* K. G. Ross and R. W. Matthews, editors. The social biology of wasps. Cornell University Press, Ithaca, New York.

Gauld, I. D. 1988. A survey of the Ophioninae (Hymenoptera: Ichneumonidae) of tropical Mesoamerica with special reference to the fauna of Costa Rica. Bulletin of the British Museum (Natural History). Entomology 57:1–309.

Gentry, A. H. 1982. Neotropical floristic diversity: phytogeographical connections between Central and South America, Pleistocene climatic fluctuations, or an accident of the Andean orogeny? Annals of the Missouri Botanical Gardens 69: 557–593.

Gilbert, F. S. 1986. Naturalists' handbooks, Vol. 5, Hoverflies. Cambridge University Press, Cambridge.

Gottsberger, G. 1989. Comments on flower evolution and beetle pollination in the genera *Annona* and *Rollinia* (Annonaceae). Plant Systematics and Evolution 167:189–194.

Gottsberger, G., and I. Silberbauer-Gottsberger. 1991. Olfactory and visual attraction of *Erioscelis emarginata* (Cyclocephalini: Dynastinae) to the inflorescences of *Philodendron selloum* (Araceae). Biotropica 23:23–28.

Gotwald, W. H., Jr. 1995. Army ants, the biology of social predation. Cornell University Press, Ithaca, New York.

Gotwald, W. H., and W. L. Brown, Jr. 1967. The ant genus *Simopelta* (Hymenoptera: Formicidae). Psyche 73: 261–276.

Haber, W. A. 1978. Evolutionary ecology of tropical mimetic butterflies (Lepidoptera: Ithomiidae). Ph.D. dissertation, University of Minnesota, St. Paul.

———. 1983. Checklist of Sphingidae. Pages 645–650 *in* D. H. Janzen, editor. Costa Rican natural history. University of Chicago Press, Chicago.

———. 1993. Seasonal migration of monarchs and other butterflies in Costa Rica. Pages 201–207 *in* S. B. Malcolm and M. P. Zalucki, editors. Biology and conservation of the monarch butterfly. Science Series No. 38. Natural History Museum of Los Angeles County, Los Angeles, California.

Hamilton, K. G. A. 1982. The spittlebugs of Canada (Homoptera: Cercoipidae). The Insects and Arachnids of Canada 10:102.

Hamilton, W. D. 1967. Extraordinary sex ratios. Science 156:477–488.

Hanski, I. 1994. Patch-occupancy dynamics in fragmented landscapes. Trends in Ecology and Evolution 9:131–135.

Hanson, P. E., and I. D. Gauld, editors. 1995. The Hymenoptera of Costa Rica. Oxford University Press, Oxford.

Harrison, J., and H. Hall. 1993. African-European honeybee hybrids have low nonintermediate metabolic capacities. Nature 363:258–260.

Heinrich, B. 1979. Bumble bee economics. Harvard University Press, Cambridge, Massachusetts.

Heithaus, R. 1983. *Bombus ephippiatus* (chiquizá de montaña, bumblebee). Pages 700–701 *in* D. H. Janzen, editor. Costa Rican natural history. University of Chicago Press, Chicago.

Hoffman, G. D., and P. B. McEvoy. 1985. The mechanism of trichome resistance in *Anaphalis margaritacea* to the meadow spittlebug *Philaenus spumarius*. Entomología Experimentalis et Applicata 39:123–129.

———. 1986. Mechanical limitations on feeding by meadow spittlebugs *Philaenus spumarius* (Homoptera: Cercopidae) on wild and cultivated hosts. Ecological Entomology 11:415–426.

Hölldobler, B., and E. O. Wilson. 1990. The ants. Harvard University Press, Cambridge, Massachusetts.

Holloway, J. D. 1985. Moths as indicator organism for categorizing rain-forest and monitoring changes and regeneration processes. Pages 235–242 *in* A. C. Chadwick and S. L. Sutton, editors. Tropical rain-forest: the Leeds symposium. Special publication of the Leeds Philosophical and Literary Society. Blackwell, Oxford.

Holzenthal, R. W. 1988. Catálogo sistemático de los tricópteros de Costa Rica (Insecta: Trichoptera). Brenesia 29:51–82.

Horsfield, D. 1977. Relationship between feeding of *Philaenus spumarius* (L.) and the amino acid concentration in the xylem sap. Ecological Entomology 2:259–266.

Hynes, H. B. N. 1970. The ecology of running waters. University of Toronto Press, Toronto.

Jang, Y., C. T. Wuellner, and C. S. Scott. 1996. Floating and fidelity in nest visitation by *Crawfordapis luctuosa* (Hymenoptera: Colletidae). Journal of Insect Behavior 9:493–504.

Janzen, D. H. 1983. Insects. Introduction. Pages 619–645 *in* D. H. Janzen, editor. Costa Rican natural history. University of Chicago Press, Chicago.

Jeanne, R. L. 1975. The adaptiveness of social wasp nest architecture. Quarterly Review of Biology 50:267–287.

———. 1979. A latitudinal gradient in rates of ant predation. Ecology 60:1211–1224.

———. 1991. The swarm-founding Polistinae. Pages 191–231 *in* K. G. Ross and R. W. Matthews, editors. The social biology of wasps. Cornell University Press, Ithaca, New York.

Jeanne, R. L., and R. C. Morgan. 1992. The influence of temperature on nest site choice and reproductive strategy in a temperate zone wasp. Ecological Entomology 17:135–141.

Jolivet, P. 1988. Food habits and food selection of Chrysomelidae; bionomic and evolutionary perspectives. Pages 1–23 *in* P. Jolivet, E. Petitpierre, and T. H. Hsiao, editors. Biology of Chrysomelidae. Kluwer, Dordrecht.

Kent, D. S., and J. A. Simpson. 1992. Eusociality in the beetle *Austroplatypus incompertus* (Coleoptera: Platypodidae). Naturwissenschaften 79:86–87.

Kirkendall, L. R. 1983. The evolution of mating systems in bark and ambrosia beetles (Coleoptera: Scolytidae and Platypodidae). Zoological Journal of the Linnaean Society 77:293–352.

———. 1993. Ecology and evolution of biased sex ratios in bark and ambrosia beetles (Scolytidae). Pages 235–345 *in* D. L. Wrensch and M. A. Ebbert, editors. Evolution and diversity of sex ratio: insects and mites. Chapman and Hall, New York.

Kirkendall, L. R., D. S. Kent, and K. F. Raffa. 1997. Interactions among males, females and offspring in bark and ambrosia beetles: the significance of living in tunnels for the evolution of social behavior. Pages 181–215 *in* J. C. Choe and B. J. Crespi, editors. The evolution of social behavior in insects and arachnids. Cambridge University Press, Cambridge.

Klausnitzer, B. 1981. Beetles. Exeter, New York.

LaBerge, W. E., and C. D. Michener. 1963. *Deltoptila*, a middle American genus of anthophorine bees (Hymenoptera: Apoidea). Bulletin of the University of Nebraska State Museum 4:211–225.

Lawrence, J. F., coordinator. 1991. Order Coleoptera. Pages 144–658 *in* F. W. Stehr, editor. Immature insects (Vol. 2). Kendall/Hunt, Dubuque, Iowa.

Leschen, R. A. B., and R. T. Allen. 1988. Immature stages, life histories and feeding mechanisms of three *Oxyporus* spp. (Coleoptera: Staphylinidae: Oxyporinae). Coleopterists Bulletin 42:321–333.

Linsley, E. G. 1961. The Cerambycidae of North America, Part 1, Introduction. University of California Publications in Entomology (Vol. 18). University of California Press, Berkeley.

Longino, J. T., and N. M. Nadkarni. 1990. A comparison of ground and canopy leaf litter ants (Hymenoptera: Formicidae) in a neotropical montane forest. Psyche 97:81–93.

MacKay, R. J., and G. B. Wiggins. 1979. Ecological diversity in Trichoptera. Annual Review of Entomology 24:185–208.

Marshall, A. T. 1966. Spittle-production and tube-building by cercopid larvae (Homoptera)—IV. Mucopolysaccharide associated with spittle-production. Journal of Insect Physiology 12:635–644.

Masters, A. R. 1990. Pyrrolizidine alkaloids in artificial nectar protect adult ithomiine butterflies from a spider predator. Biotropica 22:298–304.

———. 1992. Chemical defense in ithomiine butterflies. Ph.D. dissertation, University of Florida, Gainesville.

Masters, K. L., A. R. Masters, and A. Forsyth. 1994. Female-biased sex ratios in the neotropical treehopper *Umbonia ataliba* (Homoptera: Membracidae). Ethology 96:353–366.

McEvoy, P. B. 1986. Niche partitioning in spittlebugs (Homoptera: Cercopidae) sharing shelters on host plants. Ecology 67:465–478.

Mello, M. L. S., E. R. Pimentel, A. T. Yamada, and A. Storopoli-Neto. 1987. Composition and structure of the froth of the spittlebug, *Deois* sp. Insect Biochemistry 17:493–502.

Menozzi, C. 1927. Formiche raccolte dal Sig. H. Schmidt nei dintorni di San José di Costa Rica. Entomologische Mitteilungen 16:266–277, 336–345.

———. 1931a. Contribuzione alla conoscenza del microgenton di Costa Rica. III. Hymenoptera Formicidae. Bollettino del Laboratorio di Zoologia Generale e Agraria della R. Scoula Superiore d'Agricoltura 25:259–274.

———. 1931b. Qualche nuova Formica di Costa Rica (Hym.). Stettiner Entomologische Zeitung 92: 188–202.

———. 1936. Due nuovi Dacetini (Hymenoptera-Formicidae) di Costa Rica e descrizione della larva di uno di essi. Arbeiten über Morphologische und Taxonomische Entomologie aus Berlin-Dahlem 3:81–85.

Merritt, R. W., and K. W. Cummins, editors. 1996. An introduction to the aquatic insects of North America (3rd ed.). Kendall/Hunt, Dubuque, Iowa.

Michener, C. D., and K. R. Eickwort. 1966. Observations on nests of *Ceratina* in Costa Rica (Hymenoptera: Apoidea). Revista de Biología Tropical 14:279–286.

Michener, C. D., and W. B. Kerfoot. 1967. Nests and social behavior of three species of *Pseudaugochloropsis* (Hymenoptera: Halictidae). Journal of the Kansas Entomological Society 40:214–232.

Michener, C. D., R. J. McGinley, and B. N. Danforth. 1994. The bee genera of North and Central America (Hymenoptera: Apoidea). Smithsonian Institution Press, Washington, D.C.

Müller, F. 1879. Ituna and Thyridia: a remarkable case of mimicry in butterflies. Proceedings of the Royal Entomological Society of London May 1879: xx–xxix (trans. by R. Medola from Kosmos, p. 100).

Nadkarni, N. M., and J. T. Longino. 1990. Invertebrates in canopy and ground organic matter in a neotropical montane forest, Costa Rica. Biotropica 22:286–289.

Newton, A. F. 1984. Mycophagy in Staphylinoidea (Coleoptera). Pages 302–353 *in* Q. Wheeler and M. Blackwell, editors. Fungus/insect relationships: perspectives in ecology and evolution. Columbia University Press, New York.

Nickle, D. A. 1992a. The crickets and mole crickets of Panama (Orthoptera: Gryllidae and Gryllotalpidae). Pages 185–197 *in* D. Quintero and A. Aiello, editors. Insects of Panama and Mesoamerica: selected studies. Oxford University Press, Oxford.

———. 1992b. Katydids of Panama (Orthoptera: Tettigoniidae). Pages 142–184 *in* D. Quintero and A. Aiello, editors. Insects of Panama and Mesoamerica: selected studies. Oxford University Press, Oxford.

Nielson, M. W., and C. Godoy. 1995. Studies on the leafhoppers of Central America (Homoptera: Cicadellidae). Contributions on Entomology, International 1:1–236.

Noguera-Martinez, F. A., and T. H. Atkinson. 1990. Biogeography and biology of bark and ambrosia beetles (Coleoptera: Scolytidae and Platypodidae) of a mesic montane forest in Mexico, with an annotated checklist of species. Annals of the Entomological Society of America 83:453–466.

O'Donnell, S. 1994. Nestmate copulation in the neotropical eusocial wasp *Polistes instabilis* de saussure (Hymenoptera: Vespidae). Psyche 101: 33–36.

———. 1995. Necrophagy by neotropical swarm-founding wasps (Hymenoptera: Vespidae, Epiponini). Biotropica 27:133–136.

———. 1996a. Dragonflies (*Gynacantha nervosa* Rambur) avoid wasps (*Polybia aequatorialis* Zavattari and

Mischocyttarus sp.) as prey. Journal of Insect Behavior 9:159–162.

———. 1996b. RAPD markers suggest genotypic effects on forager behavior in a eusocial wasp. Behavioral Ecology and Sociobiology 38:83–88.

O'Donnell, S., and R. L. Jeanne. 1990. Notes on an army ant (*Eciton burchelli*) raid on a social wasp colony (*Agelaia yepocapa*) in Costa Rica. Journal of Tropical Ecology 6:507–509.

Oldroyd, H. 1964. The natural history of flies. Norton, New York.

Otis, G. 1991. Population biology of the Africanized honey bee. Pages 213–234 *in* M. Spivak, D. Fletcher, and M. Breed, editors. The "African" honey bee. Westview Press, Boulder, Colorado.

Otis, G. W., R. J. McGinley, L. Garling, and L. Malaret. 1982. Biology and systematics of the bee genus *Crawfordapis* (Colletidae: Diphaglossinae). Psyche 89:279–296.

Palmer, M. K. 1976a. Natural history and behavior of *Pseudoxychila tarsalis*. Cicindela 8:61–92.

———. 1976b. Notes on the biology of *Pterombrus piceus* Krombein (Hymenoptera: Tiphiidae). Proceedings of the Entomological Society of Washington 78:369–375.

———. 1983a. *Pseudoxychila tarsalis* (abejón tigre, tiger beetle). Pages 765–766 *in* D. H. Janzen, editor. Costa Rican natural history. University of Chicago Press, Chicago.

———. 1983b. *Pterombrus piceus* (avispa escarabajo, tiphiid wasp, beetle wasp). Page 766 *in* D. H. Janzen, editor. Costa Rican natural history. University of Chicago Press, Chicago.

Papageorgis, C. 1975. Mimicry in neotropical butterflies. American Scientist 63:522–532.

Paulson, D. R. 1982. Odonata. Pages 249–277 *in* S. H. Hurlbert and A. Villalobos Figueroa, editors. Aquatic biota of Mexico, Central America and the West Indies. San Diego State University, San Diego.

Pearson, D. L. 1988. Biology of tiger beetles. Annual Review of Entomology 33:123–147.

Peck, D. C. 1996. The association of spittlebugs with grasslands: ecology of *Prosapia* (Homoptera: Cercopidae) in upland dairy pastures of Costa Rica. Ph.D. dissertation, Cornell University, Ithaca, New York.

Peck, S. B., and H. F. Howden. 1984. Response of a dung beetle guild to different sizes of dung bait in a Panamanian rainforest. Biotropica 16:235–238.

Perfecto, I. 1992. Observations of a *Labidus coecus* (Latreille) underground raid in the central highlands of Costa Rica. Psyche 99:214–220.

Ralls, K., K. Brugger, and J. Ballou. 1979. Inbreeding and juvenile mortality in small populations of ungulates. Science 206:1101–1103.

Ratcliffe, B. C. 1992. Nine new species and 11 country records of *Cyclocephala* (Coleoptera: Scarabaeidae: Dynastinae) from Panama and Costa Rica. Coleopterists Bulletin 46:216–235.

Raven, J. A. 1983. Phytophages of xylem and phloem: a comparison of animal and plant sap-feeders. Advances in Ecological Research 13:135–234.

Reeve, H. K. 1991. *Polistes*. Pages 99–148 *in* K. G. Ross and R. W. Matthews, editors. The social biology of wasps. Cornell University Press, Ithaca, New York.

Reid, C. A. M. 1995. A cladistic analysis of subfamilial relationships in the Chrysomelidae *sensu lato* (Chrysomeloidea). Pages 559–631 *in* J. Pakaluk and S. A. Slipinski, editors. Biology, phylogeny, and classification of Coleoptera. Muzeum i Instytut Zoologii PAN, Warszawa, Poland.

Rentz, D. C. 1975. Two new katydids of the genus *Melanonotus* from Costa Rica with comments on their life history strategies (Tettigoniidae: Pseudophyllinae). Entomological News 86:129–140.

———. 1976. Systematics, behavior and bionomics of Costa Rican katydids of the genus *Sphyrometopa* (Orthoptera: Tettigoniidae: Agroeciinae). Entomological News 87:189–202.

Richards, O. W. 1978. The social wasps of the Americas. British Museum (Natural History), London.

Ricklefs, R. E., and D. Schluter, editors. 1993. Species diversity in ecological communities: historical and geographical perspectives. University of Chicago Press, Chicago.

Rinderer, T., B. Oldroyd, and W. Sheppard. 1993. Africanized bees in the U.S. Scientific American 269:84–90.

Roberts, R. B. 1971. Biology of the crepuscular bee *Ptiloglossa guinnae* n. sp. with notes on associated bees, mites, and yeasts. Journal of the Kansas Entomological Society 44:283–294.

Rosenberg, D. M., and V. H. Resh. 1993. Freshwater biomonitoring and benthic macroinvertebrates. Chapman and Hall, New York.

Ross, H. H. 1956. Evolution and classification of the mountain caddisflies. University of Illinois Press, Urbana.

Roubik, D. 1987. Long-term consequences of the Africanized honeybee invasion: implications for the United States. Pages 46–54 *in* Proceedings of the Africanized Honey Bee Symposium. American Farm Bureau, Park Ridge, Illinois.

———. 1989. Ecology and natural history of tropical bees. Cambridge University Press, Cambridge.

Roubik, D. W., and C. D. Michener. 1985. Nesting biology of *Crawfordapis* in Panama. Journal of the Kansas Entomological Society 57:662–671.

Roubik, D. W., J. A. Lobo Segura, and J. M. F. Camargo. 1997. New stingless bee genus endemic to Central American cloudforests: phylogenetic and biogeographic implications (Hymenoptera: Apidae: Meliponini). Systematic Entomology 22:67–80.

Rowell, H. F. 1983a. Checklist of acridoid grasshoppers (chapulines). Pages 651–653 *in* D. H. Janzen, editor. Costa Rican natural history. University of Chicago Press, Chicago.

———. 1983b. *Drymophilacris bimaculata* (saltamonte oroverde, chapulín oroverde, green-and-gold Solanum grasshopper). Pages 714–716 *in* D. H. Janzen, editor. Costa Rican natural history. University of Chicago Press, Chicago.

———. 1983c. *Osmilia flavolineata* (chapulínde raya amarilla, yellow-lined grasshopper. Pages 750–751 *in* D. H. Janzen, editor. Costa Rican natural history. University of Chicago Press, Chicago.

———. 1983d. *Tropidacris cristata* (saltamonte o chapulín gigante, giant red-winged grasshopper). Pages 772–773 *in* D. H. Janzen, editor. Costa Rican natural history. University of Chicago Press, Chicago.

———. 1985a. The feeding biology of a species-rich genus of rainforest grasshoppers (*Rachicreagra*, Orthoptera, Acrididae). I. Foodplant use and foodplant accceptance. Oecologia 68:87–98.

———. 1985b. The feeding biology of a species-rich genus of rainforest grasshoppers (*Rachicreagra*, Orthoptera, Acrididae). II. Foodplant preference and its relation to speciation. Oecologia 68:99–104.

Rowell, H. F., M. Rowell-Rahier, H. E. Bracker, G. Cooper-Driver, and L. D. Gómez P. 1983. The palatability of ferns and the ecology of two tropical forest grasshoppers. Biotropica 15:207–216.

Rozen, J. G., Jr. 1984. Nesting biology of Diphaglossine bees (Hymenoptera: Colletidae). American Museum Novitiates, No. 2786:1–33.

Schuh, R. T., and J. A. Slater. 1995. True bugs of the world (Hemiptera: Heteroptera): classification and natural history. Cornell University Press, Ithaca, New York.

Seeno, T. N., and J. A. Wilcox. 1982. Leaf beetle genera. Entomography 1:1–221.

Sorensen, J. T., B. C. Campbell, R. J. Gill, and J. D. Steffen-Campbell. 1995. Non-monophyly of Auchenorrhyncha ("Homoptera"), based upon 18S rDNA phylogeny: eco-evolutionary and cladistic implications within pre-Heteropterodea Hemiptera (s.l.) and a proposal for new monophyletic suborders. Pan-Pacific Entomologist 71: 31–60.

Spivak, M. 1991. The Africanization process in Costa Rica. Pages 137–155 in M. Spivak, D. Fletcher, and M. Breed, editors. The "African" honey bee. Westview Press, Boulder, Colorado.

Spivak, M., D. Fletcher, and M. Breed. 1991. Introduction. Pages 1–9 in M. Spivak, D. Fletcher, and M. Breed, editors. The "African" honey bee. Westview Press, Boulder, Colorado.

Staines, C. L. 1996. The genus Cephaloleia (Coleoptera: Chrysomelidae) in Central America and the West Indies. Revista de Biología Tropical, Special Publication No. 3:3–87.

Stevens, G. C. 1992. The elevational gradient in altitudinal range and extension of Rappaport's Latitudinal Rule to altitude. American Naturalist 140: 893–911.

Sutton, S. L. 1989. Spatial distribution of flying insects. Pages 427–436 in H. Lieth and M. J. A. Werger, editors. Tropical rain forest ecosystems. Elsevier, Amsterdam.

Thompson, V. 1994. Spittlebug indicators of nitrogen-fixing plants. Ecological Entomology 19:391–398.

———. 1997. Spittlebug nymphs (Homoptera: Cercopidae) in Heliconia flowers (Zingiberales: Heliconiaceae): Preadaptation and evolution of the first aquatic Homoptera. Revista de Biología Tropical 45:905–912.

Trager, J. C. 1991. A revision of the fire ants, Solenopsis geminata group (Hymenoptera: Formicidae: Myrmicinae). Journal of the New York Entomological Society 99:141–198.

Uetz, G. W., and J. M. Biere. 1980. Prey of Microthena gracilis (Waickenaer) in comparison with artificial webs and other trapping devices. Bulletin of the British Arachnological Society 5:101–107.

Uetz, G. W., and S. P. Hartsock. 1987. Prey selection in an orb-weaving spider: Microthena gracilis (Araneae: Araneidae). Psyche 94:103–116.

Valderrama, C. H. 1996. Comparación de la distribución vertical de arañas constructoras de telas orbiculares en tres zonas de un bosque nublado. Master's thesis, Universidad de los Andes, Bogotá, Colombia.

Weaver, C. R., and D. R. King. 1954. Meadow spittlebug. Ohio Agricultural Research Bulletin No. 741:1–99.

West-Eberhard, M. J. 1989. Scent-trail diversion, a novel defense against ants by tropical social wasps. Biotropica 21:280–281.

West-Eberhard, M. J., J. M. Carpenter, and P. E. Hanson. 1995. The vespid wasps (Vespidae). Pages 561–587 in P. E. Hanson and I. D. Gauld, editors. The Hymenoptera of Costa Rica. Oxford Science Publications, New York.

Whittaker, J. B. 1970. Cercopid spittle as a microhabitat. Oikos 21:59–64.

Wickler, W. 1968. Mimicry in plants and animals. McGraw-Hill, New York.

Wiggins, G. B. 1977. Larvae of the North American Caddisfly genera. University of Toronto Press, Toronto.

Williams, D. F., editor. 1994. Exotic ants. biology, impact, and control of introduced species. Westview Press, Boulder, Colorado.

Wilson, D. S., M. Leighton, and D. R. Leighton. 1978. Interference competition in a tropical ripple bug (Hemiptera: Veliidae). Biotropica 10:302–306.

Windsor, D., E. G. Riley, and H. P. Stockwell. 1992. An introduction to the biology and systematics of Panamanian tortoise beetles (Coleoptera: Chrysomelidae: Cassidinae). Pages 372–391 in D. Quintero and A. Aiello, editors. Insects of Panama and Mesoamerica. Oxford University Press, Oxford.

Wolda, H., and J. A. Ramos. 1992. Cicadas in Panama: their distribution, seasonality, and diversity (Homoptera: Cicadoidea). Pages 271–279 in D. Quintero and A. Aiello, editors. Insects of Panama and Mesoamerica: selected studies. Oxford University Press, Oxford.

Wood, S. L., and D. E. Bright. 1992. A Catalog of Scolytidae and Platypodidae (Coleoptera), Part 2: Taxonomic index. Great Basin Naturalist Memoirs 13:1–1553.

Wood, S. L., G. C. Stevens, and H. J. Lezama. 1992. Los Scolytidae (Coleoptera) de Costa Rica: clave de la subfamilia Scolytinae, Tribu Corthylini. Revista de Biología Tropical 40:247–286.

Wood, T. K. 1974. Aggregating behavior of Umbonia crassicornis (Homoptera: Membracidae). Canadian Entomologist 106:169–173.

Wood, T. K., and R. Dowell. 1985. Reproductive behavior and dispersal in Umbonia crassicornis (Homoptera: Membracidae). Florida Entomologist 68:151–158.

Young, A. M. 1976. Notes on the faunistic complexity of cicadas (Homoptera: Cicadidae) in northern Costa Rica. Revista de Biología Tropical 24: 267–279.

———. 1986. Beetle pollination of Dieffenbachia longispatha (Araceae). American Journal of Botany 73:931–944.

———. 1988. Differential importance of beetle species pollinating Dieffenbachia longispatha (Araceae). Ecology 69:832–844.

5

Amphibians and Reptiles

J. Alan Pounds

I like the look of frogs, and their outlook, and especially the way
they get together in wet places on warm nights and sing about sex.
The music frogs make . . . is full of optimism and inner meaning.
                                                    —Archie F. Carr
                                          The Windward Road (1955)

Anyone who stood on the bridge over the Río Guacimal at Monteverde on a wet-season night in the early 1980s would understand Archie Carr's sentiments. Nearly 300 male Fleischmann's Glass Frogs (*Hyalinobatrachium fleischmanni*) defended territories along a 120-m section of the stream, and their loud, incessant "peeps" filled the air (Hayes 1991; Fig. 5.1). In the late 1980s, however, this chorus all but fell silent as the number of glass frogs plummeted. The population has not recovered. In 1998, only a single male could be heard from the bridge.

The dramatic reduction in glass frogs was part of a larger decline of Monteverde's amphibians. A sudden crash of populations in 1987 affected species throughout the area and led to the disappearance of many (Pounds 1990, 1991a, 1997, Crump et al. 1992, Pounds and Crump 1994, Pounds and Fogden 1996, Pounds et al. 1997). The disappearance that has drawn the most attention, however, is that of the Golden Toad (*Bufo periglenes*). This species, known only from elfin cloud forest high on the ridgetops at

Monteverde, is famous for its striking appearance and the colorful spectacle of its breeding congregations (Savage 1966, Jacobson 1983, Fogden and Fogden 1984, Jacobson and Vandenberg 1991; see Savage, "Discovery of the Golden Toad," pp. 171–172; Fig. 5.2). Because the Golden Toad had been locally abundant in seemingly undisturbed habitats for at least 17 consecutive years, its sudden disappearance caused great alarm and dismay (Pounds et al. 1997).

Interest in this case has intensified with the suggestion that it is part of a global pattern (Barinaga 1990, Blaustein and Wake 1990, 1995, Phillips 1990, 1994, Wyman 1990, Wake 1991, Wake and Morowitz 1991, Sarkar 1996; see Pounds, "Monteverde Salamanders," pp. 172–173). Many similar declines and disappearances have been reported for highland areas of other continents (Corn and Fogleman 1984, Heyer et al. 1988, Osborne 1989, Weygoldt 1989, Czechura and Ingram 1990, La Marca and Reinthaler 1991, Carey 1993, Fellers and Drost 1993, Kagarise Sherman and Morton 1993, Drost and Fellers 1996, Laurance et al.

Figure 5.1. *(top)* Fleischmann's Glass Frogs (*Hyalinobatrachium fleischmanni*) in amplexus. Photograph by Michael and Patricia Fogden. **Figure 5.2.** *(above)* Male Golden Toads (*Bufo periglenes*) competing for mates. Photograph by Michael and Patricia Fogden.

1996). The reports, however, have met with some skepticism. Because extreme natural fluctuations could be mistaken for a more significant phenomenon (Pechmann et al. 1991), researchers have been divided over how to interpret the observed patterns (see Pounds, "Monteverde Salamanders," p. 172). The Golden Toad has thus figured prominently in one of the most volatile debates in conservation biology, and Monteverde has provided an important test case (Blaustein 1994, Pechmann and Wilbur 1994, Blaustein et al. 1994a, Sarkar 1996, Pounds et al. 1997). The debate has hinged on standards of scientific proof and the scarcity of long-term data needed to judge whether a population is in decline. Diverse tropical faunas, however, afford an approach that does not rely on these data. A comparison of the number of disappearances at Monteverde to the number that could be expected for an assemblage of demographically unstable populations suggests that the declines go beyond natural fluctuations (Pounds et al. 1997).

It is essential that we identify the causes and explore the implications of these patterns. We could develop a plausible model of how the ecological context has changed if we had sufficient data—from both the past and the present—on levels of resources, interactions with competitors, predators, and parasites and the influences of physical and chemical conditions of the environment. The picture, however, is woefully incomplete. Moreover, some of the potentially most instructive data cannot be obtained because the populations no longer exist. We must therefore rely on the available information on ecology to provide clues that point the way to future research. The present chapter summarizes this information for Monteverde's amphibians and reptiles. Although previous discussion of the declines and disappearances has focused on frogs, toads, and salamanders, I demonstrate that lizards and snakes have also been affected. I provide an overview of the patterns, ask what bearing they may have on our understanding of the declines, and suggest topics for further study.

5.1. The Area and Its Fauna

I focus on amphibians and reptiles in a broad east-west belt that bisects the Cordillera de Tilarán (Fig. 1.5). This belt extends from the 690-m contour in the drainages of the Ríos Lagarto and Guacimal on the Pacific slope, to 1850 m along the continental divide, and to 600 m in the Peñas Blancas valley on the Caribbean slope, following Hayes et al. (1989). Many biologists have contributed to our knowledge of Monteverde's herpetofauna. The first species list (Van Devender 1980) built on the work of Jay Savage and his associates (Savage and Villa 1986, Villa et al. 1988). Subsequent lists (Timmerman and Hayes 1981, Hayes et al. 1989) amplified the study area and added species descriptions, annotations on distribution and natural history, and identification keys. A revised checklist (Appendix 8) includes 161 species, seven of which are additions. The 60 amphibian species include 2 caecilians (elongate limbless animals), 5 salamanders, and 53 anurans (frogs and toads). The 101 reptile species include 29 lizards and 71 snakes. To standardize nomenclature, I follow a 1995 revision of the Costa Rican checklist plus recent changes (J. Savage, unpubl. data). Common names are from Hayes et al. (1989) with some modifications; hereafter I use these rather than the scientific names, which are in Appendix 8. The numbered zones used to describe distribution (Zones 1–6; Appendix 8) also follow Hayes et al. (1989), with one exception: Zone 5 extends down to a point just above the junction of the Peñas Blancas trail and the Río Peñas Blancas (950 m).

Although species composition is well known at Monteverde compared to most tropical localities, the checklist is probably incomplete. Some secretive species—especially snakes, which often occur at low densities in the tropics (Henderson and Hoevers 1977)—are likely to be added for the areas farthest from the Monteverde community (Hayes et al. 1989). Turtles could inhabit the lower elevations (Zones 1 and 6) but are unknown in the region except for an unconfirmed sighting of *Kinosternon scorpiodes* on the Pacific slope. Estimates of diversity (a term I use interchangeably with "species richness" to refer to the number of species) are conservative, because of incomplete sampling, and uncertainties with taxonomy. For example, preliminary data suggest that further study of rain frogs (*Eleutherodactylus*, a large genus rich in species that closely resemble one another; Savage 1975) could reveal the presence of additional representatives.

5.1.1. Recent Changes in the Fauna

Amphibians. Although early studies of disappearances in the Monteverde region focused on the Golden Toad and the Harlequin Frog (Crump et al. 1992, Pounds and Crump 1994; Fig. 5.3), other anuran species have disappeared. To assess the number of disappearances, my co-workers and I surveyed populations in a 15-km east-west belt that averages 2 km in width (Pounds et al. 1997). This belt corresponds to a core area where most earlier sampling had been done and includes habitats in each of the area's climatic and vegetation zones (see Chap. 2, Physical Environment). Before 1987, it contained populations of all anuran species on the Monteverde checklist, although some species were rarely encountered (Hayes

Figure 5.3. A Harlequin Frog (*Atelopus varius*) in the Monteverde cloud forest. Photograph by Michael and Patricia Fogden.

et al. 1986, 1989; Appendix 8). In compiling the list of species we would ordinarily expect to find, we omitted the rare Highland Fringe-limbed Treefrog, Monteverde Rain Frog, and Black Narrow-mouthed Toad. We included the highly arboreal Giant Fringe-limbed Treefrog and Crowned Frog, because their calling sites and distinctive vocalizations were well known (M. P. L. Fogden, unpubl. data). We assessed the number of species missing in 1990 and the number missing throughout 1990–94. Although it is possible to overlook burrowing forms that appear only briefly at temporary pools (e.g., the Golden Toad and the Sheep Frog), this is unlikely during five consecutive years.

To estimate the number of disappearances expected in the context of natural demographic variability, we examined long-term studies of other amphibian assemblages. We chose studies that illustrated how unstable amphibian populations can be (Pechmann and Wilbur 1994) and that were conducted on spatial scales appropriate for comparison with Monteverde. From these studies, we estimated the average probability that a single species would disappear in response to a natural environmental disturbance such as a drought. Substituting this probability in the equation for a binomial distribution, we calculated the likelihood that a particular number of species would disappear simultaneously.

The resultant probability distributions suggest that normal population dynamics cannot easily explain the number of disappearances at Monteverde. Of the 50 species of frogs and toads that we would expect to find, 25 were absent in 1990. Five of the missing species reappeared during 1991–94, so 20 (40%) were absent throughout the study (Appendix 8). Since completion of that study, one species has reappeared (Forrer's Leopard Frog, in 1997). Thus, 11 years after populations crashed, the diversity of frogs and toads is still impoverished. The reappearances were probably due to recolonization from outlying areas. Most of these events took place on the periphery of the study area after several years of absence. Although even limited recolonization might seem encouraging, the species that reappeared (except the Bare-hearted Glass Frog) also inhabited nearby lowlands, where we have seen little evidence of declines. Prospects are dim for high-elevation species such as the Golden Toad and the Green-eyed Frog (see Sec. 5.3).

A comparison of the above patterns with those for breeding birds in the same area puts the loss of anuran diversity in perspective and underscores the importance of further study (Pounds et al. 1997). The relative frequency of absences was much greater for frogs and toads than it was for birds. That for anurans, however, was similar to that for invasive open-country birds whose habitats in the Peñas Blancas valley had largely reverted from farmland to forest after being annexed to the Monteverde Cloud Forest Preserve

(MCFP). The absence of any obvious change in amphibian habitats and the persistence of bird species known to be sensitive to deforestation suggest that subtle but critical changes in the environment have taken place (see Sec. 5.4.3). The extent of these changes is unclear, but recent work suggests that many amphibian populations in the highlands of Costa Rica and western Panama have been affected (Berger et al. 1998, Lips 1998, Bolaños, unpubl. data). Future studies should assess the status of anuran populations in areas surrounding Monteverde. A study of salamander populations is also needed. They declined in the late 1980s (see Pounds, "Monteverde Salamanders," pp. 172–173; Fig. 5.4), but their status is uncertain. Ring-tailed and Monteverde Salamanders were found in small numbers during 1990–94 (Pounds et al. 1997), but not the remaining three species (Appendix 8). The sampling techniques, however, were appropriate only for frogs and toads.

Reptiles. The recognition of an amphibian crisis (Phillips 1994) implies that amphibians have suffered more disappearances than reptiles. A reptile crisis, however, would be harder to recognize. Whereas Monteverde's frogs and toads announce their presence through song, the snakes and lizards are mute. Many are secretive or occur at low densities ordinarily. Nevertheless, there is evidence that reptile diversity has declined (see Sec. 5.4.1). Two species of anoline lizards (the Cloud Forest Anole and Montane Anole; Fig. 5.5) were previously common at a site on the upper Pacific slope (1540 m) but disappeared from there in the 1990s. The Green Frog-Eater, the fourth most common species of diurnal colubrid snake in the Peñas Blancas valley in the mid-1980s, has not been seen since 1987. Likewise, the Green Keelback, previously among the three most common diurnal snakes on the upper Pacific slope, has been missing since 1988. A broad survey of reptile populations is needed.

5.2. Distribution and Diversity

The severity of a faunal collapse may depend in part on how the spatial configuration of the underlying causes is superimposed on local patterns of species distribution and diversity. In this section, I summarize these patterns for the Monteverde region and examine the disappearances of anuran populations in relation to them. Most of the declines and disappearances reported from around the world have taken place in highland areas (Wake 1991); lowland populations seem relatively unaffected (Pechmann et al. 1991, Voris and Inger 1995, F. Bolaños, unpubl. data). Little is known, however, of the geographic patterns of the declines within highland areas, which comprise a variety of climatic and vegetation zones.

Figure 5.4. Endemic Monteverde Salamander (*Bolitoglossa "subpalmata"*). Photograph by Michael and Patricia Fogden.

Figure 5.5. Montane Anole (*Norops altae*) displaying his dewlap in a territorial dispute with another male. This species has declined at Monteverde. Photograph by Michael and Patricia Fogden.

A patch of upland tropical forest ordinarily contains fewer species of amphibians and reptiles than a similar-sized patch of lowland rain forest (Scott 1976, Duellman 1988). The number of leaf-litter species found per plot at Monteverde was similar to that of mid-elevation sites in Costa Rica's Braulio Carillo National Park but was smaller than that of nearby lowland sites such as Tortuguero (Fauth et al. 1989). Seventy-nine species of amphibians and reptiles are known from the highest elevations at Monteverde (Zones 3 and 4; Appendix 8), compared to 135 in lowland rain forest at La Selva (Donnelly 1994, Guyer 1994), despite the smaller sampling area of the latter.

These 79 species, however, are fewer than half of those known from the total Monteverde area (161 species; Appendix 8). Much of the high overall species richness is a consequence of the diverse array of environments. As one travels up the rain-shadowed Pacific slope, over the continental divide, and down the wet Caribbean slope (Fig. 1.5), one encounters different species of amphibians and reptiles in different areas. The maximum number of species known from a single distributional zone is 52% of the overall total (Table 5.1). Differences in species composition between the two slopes contribute strongly to this total; 102 species (64%) are restricted to one slope or the other, extending in some cases to the vicinity of the continental divide (Zones 3 and 4; Table 5.2; Appendix 8). Of these species, 60% of the reptiles inhabit the relatively dry Pacific side, compared to 30% of the amphibians (Fisher exact test, $P = .004$). The pattern is similar when lizards and snakes are compared to anurans (60% vs. 27%; $P = .002$).

The percentage of species inhabiting the highest elevations (Zones 3 and 4) is greater for amphibians than it is for reptiles (63% vs. 41%; $P = .004$; Table 5.2). The same is true when anurans are compared to lizards and snakes (60% vs. 41%; $P = .015$). Few species, however, occur only in these uppermost life zones—13% of the amphibians versus 3% of the reptiles ($P = .015$). The difference is not significant when anurans are compared to lizards and snakes (9% vs. 3%; $P = .094$). Although areas of greatest change in species composition along climatic gradients may correspond to boundaries between vegetation zones (Heyer 1967), the above patterns illustrate that species do not appear and drop out in perfect synchrony at these boundaries. Communities are not discrete but instead intergrade in a complex fashion.

The spatial pattern of the anuran declines at Monteverde helps to explain why so many species disappeared from the area. The 1987 crash affected all climate and vegetation zones in the region (Pounds et al. 1997) and thus all geographic components of species richness. I compared the observed patterns of presence and absence to what they might have been if the declines had affected only the Caribbean slope, only the Pacific slope, or only the highest elevations (Zones

Table 5.1. Numbers of species of amphibians and reptiles by distributional zone in the Monteverde area.

| | Zone | | | | | |
Taxon	1	2	3	4	5	6
Amphibians						
Caecilians ($N = 2$)	1	1	1	0	1	1
Salamanders ($N = 5$)	0	2	3	5	1	1
Anurans ($N = 53$)	18	23	27	28	28	32
Total ($N = 60$)	19	26	31	33	30	34
Percentage of N	31.7	43.3	51.7	55.0	50.0	56.7
Reptiles						
Lizards ($N = 29$)	14	15	10	5	9	16
Snakes ($N = 72$)	31	41	30	21	17	34
Total ($N = 101$)	45	56	40	26	26	50
Percentage of N	44.6	55.4	39.6	25.7	25.7	49.5
Amphibians and reptiles ($N = 161$)	64	82	71	59	56	84
Percentage of N	39.8	50.9	44.1	36.6	34.8	52.2

Values are numbers of species for the decade preceding the 1987 crash of populations (see Appendix 8).

Table 5.2. Numbers of species of amphibians and reptiles by pattern of local distribution in the Monteverde area.

| | Pattern of Distribution | | | | |
Taxon	Pacific Slope only[a] (Zones 1 & 2)	Caribbean Slope only[a] (Zones 5 & 6)	Both Pacific and Caribbean Slopes	Highest Elevations Only (Zones 3 & 4)	Reaching the Highest Elevations (Zones 3 & 4)
Amphibians					
Caecilians ($N = 2$)	1	1	0	0	1
Salamanders ($N = 5$)	1	0	1	3	5
Anurans ($N = 53$)	8	22	18	5	32
Total ($N = 60$)	10	23	19	8	38
Percentage of N	16.7	38.3	31.7	13.3	63.3
Reptiles					
Lizards ($N = 29$)	11	8	9	1	10
Snakes ($N = 72$)	31	20	19	2	31
Total ($N = 101$)	42	28	28	3	41
Percentage of N	41.6	27.7	27.7	3.0	40.6
Amphibians and reptiles ($N = 161$)	52	51	47	11	79
Percentage of N	32.3	31.7	29.2	6.8	49.1

Values are numbers of species for the decade preceding the 1987 population crash (Appendix 8). Only the first four categories of distributional patterns (columns) are mutually exclusive. Some species restricted to one slope in the Monteverde area inhabit both slopes if other regions are taken into account.

[a]Extending in some cases to the highest elevations (Zones 3 & 4).

3 and 4; Fig. 5.6). Of the species missing throughout 1990–94, fewer than half would have disappeared if the declines had affected any one of these areas instead of the entire range of environments.

5.3. Geography and History

A species' susceptibility to extinction in a region depends on its probability of disappearing from there and its likelihood of recolonizing from neighboring regions. Hence, the vulnerability of a fauna depends in part on broad patterns of geographic distribution, which are best understood in the context of evolutionary history. In this section, I summarize ideas concerning the historical biogeography of the Middle American herpetofauna, examine the Monteverde fauna in relation to them, and discuss implications for susceptibility to regional or global extinction.

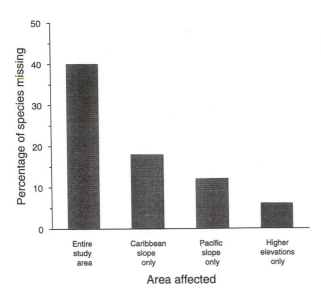

Figure 5.6. Aftermath of the 1987 crash of anuran populations in the Monteverde area in relation to local patterns of distribution and diversity. During 1990–94, 40% of the species were missing (left column) from the study area of Pounds et al. (1997). The remaining columns depict hypothetical percentages of missing species under different assumptions concerning the spatial pattern of the crash. Each percentage was calculated by tallying the number of species missing in the corresponding distributional category (Table 5.2) and dividing by the total number of species (N = 50). Because many of the species restricted to either the Pacific or the Caribbean slope extend to the highest elevations (Zones 3 and 4), these mountaintop areas are affected in each scenario. If the highest elevations alone had been affected, only three species would have disappeared. Since completion of the 1990–94 study, one species has reappeared (Forrer's Leopard Frog on the Pacific Slope in 1997).

The Middle American herpetofauna appears to have evolved into a distinctive assemblage during a long period of isolation (Savage 1982). According to this view, an oceanic barrier isolated the fauna from that of South America, and mountain building and climate change isolated it from the North American fauna. With the uplift of the Middle American highlands and the resultant closure of this oceanic barrier late in the Tertiary, the Middle American and South American assemblages intermixed. About 25% of the genera represented at Monteverde appear to be of South American origin (Savage 1982, J. Savage, unpubl. data).

This uplift of the central axis of volcanic mountains also played a key role in the diversification of amphibians and reptiles within Middle America. The once relatively uniform assemblage of wide-ranging lowland species became fragmented into eastern and western elements. Upland faunas, derived from lineages that rode the uplift or invaded the mountains afterward, became isolated in three principal highland areas—the Sierra Madres of Mexico, the highlands of northern Central America, and the Cordilleras of Costa Rica and Western Panama. These upland assemblages evolved to be strikingly different from one another. As a result, Monteverde's herpetofauna has relatively little in common with the highland faunas of northern Central America. A mix of upland specialists and principally lowland forms, the fauna shares more species with La Selva in the nearby Caribbean lowlands than it does with Sierra de las Minas in the mountains of Guatemala (Fisher exact test comparing the calculated proportions, $P = .00001$; Table 5.3).

The difference between the highland faunas is especially striking for amphibians. The proportion of species in common between Monteverde and Sierra de las Minas is much lower for frogs, toads, and salamanders than it is for lizards and snakes ($P = .00001$). Compared to reptiles, amphibians have undergone greater differentiation into distinctive upland assemblages in the different highland areas. Consistent with this pattern, the proportion of species shared between Monteverde and La Selva is lower for amphibians than it is for reptiles ($P = .001$; Table 5.3). A majority of Monteverde's reptile species are primarily lowland forms that have colonized the mountain slopes; a relatively large fraction of the amphibian species are upland specialists that do not inhabit the lowlands. The difference is also reflected in patterns of endemism. About 40% of Monteverde's amphibian species are restricted to the uplands of Costa Rica and western Panama, compared to about 14% of the reptile species ($P = .0002$; Table 5.4; Appendix 8). The results are similar when anurans are compared to lizards and snakes (36% vs. 14%; $P = .002$). A large core element of Monteverde's amphibians belong to a distinctive upland assemblage rich in endemic species.

Amphibians have apparently experienced stronger geographic isolation than reptiles. During Pleistocene glaciations, climatic and vegetation zones on tropical mountains extended to lower elevations than they do today (Colinvaux et al. 1996). Although these episodes probably facilitated the movement of highland species between massifs (Duellman 1979, Savage 1982), amphibians might have been less likely than reptiles to accomplish this movement, as they are generally poorer dispersers. Also, lowland environments might be stronger barriers to amphibians than to reptiles if the former are more montane in distri-

Table 5.3. Faunal similarity at the species level between the Monteverde area and two other localities, La Selva in the Caribbean lowlands of Costa Rica and Sierra de las Minas in the highlands of Guatemala.

| | Area under Comparison | | | | | |
| | La Selva | | | Sierra de las Minas | | |
Taxon	N'	C	PS	N'	C	PS
Amphibians						
Caecilians ($N = 2$)	1	1	—	1	0	—
Salamanders ($N = 5$)	3	0	—	8	0	—
Anurans ($N = 53$)	44	23	0.474	26	3	0.076
Total ($N = 60$)	48	24	0.444	35	3	0.063
Reptiles						
Lizards ($N = 29$)	25	15	0.555	23	10	0.358
Snakes ($N = 72$)	56	43	0.672	51	23	0.374
Total ($N = 101$)	81	58	0.637	74	33	0.377
Amphibians and reptiles ($N = 161$)	129[a]	82	0.566	109	36	0.267

PS (proportional similarity) = $2C/(N + N')$, where N is the number of species at Monteverde. N' is the number at the locality being compared, and C is the number in common. Data for La Selva are from Donnelly (1994) and Guyer (1994). Those for Sierra de las Minas are from Campbell (1982). For the latter area, only species occurring at or above 550 m elevation are included. PS is not calculated for caecilians and salamanders because of the small sample sizes.

[a]Turtles and crocodilians, present only in the La Selva sample, are omitted from the analysis.

bution. Amphibians might be comparatively tolerant of cool climates and thus apt to colonize highland areas, and may be prone to speciation in these areas because of limited dispersal abilities.

The high proportion of upland endemics among the frogs, toads, and salamanders of Monteverde implies that the area's amphibians are generally more vulnerable to regional or global extinction than are its reptiles. The percentage of anuran species missing during 1990–94 was not significantly greater for upland endemics than it was for nonendemics (53% vs. 33%; $P = .150$; Appendix 8). Of the 20 missing species, however, the nine upland endemics are less

Table 5.4. Numbers of upland endemics among the species of amphibians and reptiles in the Monteverde area.

	Number of Endemics	Percentage of N
Taxon		
Amphibians		
Caecilians ($N = 2$)	0	0
Salamanders ($N = 5$)	5	100.0
Anurans ($N = 53$)	19	35.8
Total ($N = 60$)	24	40.0
Reptiles		
Lizards ($N = 29$)	4	13.8
Snakes ($N = 72$)	10	13.9
Total ($N = 101$)	14	13.9
Amphibians and reptiles ($N = 161$)	38	23.6

"Upland endemics" are species restricted to the uplands of Costa Rica and western Panama (see Appendix 8).

likely to recolonize than are the remaining 11 species. The latter have potential source populations in nearby lowland areas, where there is little evidence of declines beyond those attributable to habitat loss.

Opportunities for recolonization also vary among upland species. At one extreme is the Golden Toad. Because it is known only from ridgetops in the Monteverde area, its prospects are nil, unless unknown populations exist in inaccessible, outlying areas (Pounds and Fogden 1996). The Pin-striped Treefrog and the Green-eyed Frog are likewise restricted to high elevations but have larger geographic ranges. The former is endemic to the Cordillera de Tilarán and Cordillera Central of Costa Rica (Savage and Heyer 1969); the latter ranges to western Panama (Zweifel 1964). The conservation status of these species is unknown. In contrast to the high-elevation forms, some upland endemics have relatively broad altitudinal ranges (Appendix 8). The Tilarán Rain Frog, for example, is restricted to the Cordilleras de Tilarán and Central (Savage 1975) but extends into the foothills on both slopes. The likelihood of recovery for this and similarly distributed species depends in part on their distributional limits relative to the lower altitudinal cutoff of the declines, a subject that needs further study.

5.4. Population Ecology

We know lamentably little about natural rates of reproduction and mortality in Monteverde's amphibians and reptiles and the factors that influence them. We lack sufficient data on growth, maturation, fecundity, and survivorship to develop a life table (schedule of age-specific survivorship and fecundity) for any species in the area. In this section, I outline a potential demographic consequence of living in a cloud forest and discuss patterns of abundance, natural sources of mortality, and possible causes of the declines.

Studies of anoline lizards suggest that slow rates of growth and maturation may be associated with cool, montane environments. Cloud Forest Anoles, which are active at low body temperatures and feed at relatively low rates (see Sec. 5.6.2), grow and mature slowly. A hatchling female (body length of 20 mm) requires 9 months to reach sexual maturity (at 42 mm; Fitch 1973). Gray Lichen Anoles, which inhabit warmer environments and feed more frequently, grow and mature more than twice as quickly. A hatchling female (18 mm) matures in 4 months (at 39 mm). If cloud-forest species commonly grow and mature slowly, their populations may naturally be slow to rebound following declines.

5.4.1. Patterns of Abundance

Amphibians. Ecological studies documented pre-decline abundances of Golden Toads, Meadow Tree-frogs, Fleischmann's and Emerald Glass Frogs, and Harlequin Frogs (Jacobson 1985, Pounds and Crump 1987, 1994, Crump and Pounds 1989, Crump and Townsend 1990, Hayes 1991, Jacobson and Vandenberg 1991, Crump et al. 1992). Hayes (1991) used mark-recapture data to estimate densities of Fleischmann's Glass Frogs. He found that 294 males held territories along a 120-m segment of the Río Guacimal in June 1980, and suggested that inclusion of females, juveniles, and transient males might at times have doubled his estimate. Populations of all these species crashed in 1987 (Crump et al. 1992, Pounds and Crump 1994, Pounds et al. 1997). In April–May 1987, more than 1500 Golden Toads gathered at Brillante, the principal known breeding site of the species. In 1988 and again in 1989, however, only a single male appeared there. Harlequin Frogs in the Monteverde area likewise declined by about 99% between March 1987 and May 1988. Despite intensive searches, neither species has been found in the 1990s.

To test for evidence of recovery among the surviving species, my co-workers and I monitored populations of the Meadow Treefrog, Fleischmann's and Emerald Glass Frogs, the Common Dink Frog, and the Red-eyed Stream Frog during 1990–94 (Pounds et al. 1997). We included the Common Dink Frog, despite the lack of baseline data, because it had been among the most common and widespread species in the area before the 1987 crash. We included the Red-eyed Stream Frog to study recolonization; from field notes, we identified six previously occupied sites, one of which was inhabited in 1990. The species for which baseline data exist remained far less abundant than they were before the 1987 crash and showed no increase during 1990–94. We documented an increase only for the Common Dink Frog—a result that agrees with our impression that several congeners of this species (rain frogs, *Eleutherodactylus*) increased in abundance. We observed two events of recolonization by the Red-eyed Stream Frog, but recovery in this species was limited. Its numbers remained low, and one local extinction took place. Three sites were never recolonized, even though occupied sites occurred within 1 km. Data collected during 1995–98 likewise suggest that anuran populations are not recovering (J. A. Pounds, M. P. L. Fogden, and J. H. Campbell, unpubl. data). The species monitored during 1990–94, including the Common Dink Frog, underwent synchronous downturns in 1998.

Reptiles. Estimates of relative abundance based on sightings recorded in relation to a time line provide evidence of population declines in anoline lizards. In 1983–84, the encounter rate for the Cloud Forest Anole at a site on the upper Pacific slope (1540 m), where it was the most common species (Pounds 1988), averaged 3.01 individuals per hour of daytime search. After the mid-1980s, the population declined and disappeared along with that of the Montane Anole, previously the second most common species at this site (Fig. 5.5). Both species showed a strong downward trend in abundance for 1983–95 (lizards found per hour, vs. year, Kendall's $\tau \leq -.91$, $P < .003$; Fig. 5.7). Neither was observed in 1996–98. In contrast to these high-elevation forms, the wider ranging Gray Lichen Anole, which reaches its greatest abundance at warmer, drier sites farther down the Pacific slope, showed no trend at the 1540 m site ($\tau = -.07$, $P > .70$). This species, previously the third most common anole at the site, is now the most common. Because the Cloud Forest Anole and the Montane Anole still occur at cooler, wetter sites farther upslope, it would be valuable to study the demography of these species at different points along the climatic gradient (see Secs. 5.4.3, 5.5.5, 5.6.1).

A similar decline has affected diurnal frog-eating snakes. In 1986–87 in the Peñas Blancas valley (Zone 6), the average search time required to find a snake was 8.8 hr, based on pooled data for nine species: the Ebony Keelback, Fire-bellied Snake, Pink-bellied Litter Snake, Green Frog-eater, Banded Green Racer, Glossy Litter Snake, Ridge-nosed Snake, Cloud For-

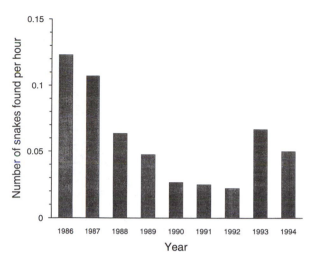

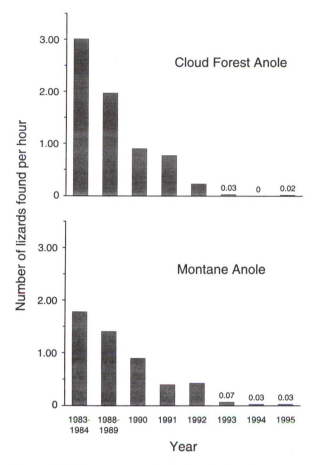

Figure 5.7. Year-to-year variation in the abundance of anoline lizards on the upper Pacific slope at Monteverde. Numbers of lizards found per hour are based on sightings in Zone 3 (just west of the Preserve entrance). Sightings were made along trails, mostly during mornings (0800–1200) in May–October within a 30-ha area. Sampling time per period was a minimum of 60 hr over at least 30 days. Cloud Forest Anoles (*Norops tropidolepis*) inhabit the shaded forest understory, whereas Montane Anoles (*N. altae*) prefer open areas. Sampling effort was divided equally between forest and overgrown pastures. Despite extensive searches in 1996–97, neither species was observed in the area.

Figure 5.8. Year-to-year variation in the abundance of diurnal, frog-eating snakes in the Peñas Blancas valley (Zone 6). Numbers of snakes found per hour are based on pooled sightings of nine species in Zone 6 (see Sec. 5.4.1). Sightings were made along trails, mostly during mornings (0700–1200) in March–June within a 5-km² area. Total sampling time was 1520 hr (304 days; time per year for 1986–94 was, respectively, 195, 280, 440, 105, 150, 40, 135, 75, and 100 hr). Although sampling time in 1991 was comparatively small, results of the correlation analyses (see Sec. 5.4.1) were the same when the data for 1991 and 1992 were combined.

est Racer, and Striped Litter Snake (M. Fogden, unpubl. data). The pattern of change in abundance included a decrease during 1986–92 and a partial recovery in 1993–94 (Fig. 5.8). For the pooled data, there was a strong downward trend for 1986–92 (for snakes found per hour, vs. year, Kendall's $\tau = -1$, $P < .0006$). By 1991–92, the average search time per snake had increased fivefold, to 43.8 hr. In 1993–94, it was 17.5 hr, or about twice what it had been in 1986–87. Although most of the nine species showed this pattern of decline followed by partial recovery, two seemed to disappear from the area. The Green Frog-eater, the

fourth most common species in 1986–87, has been absent since 1988. The Glossy Litter Snake, though never common, was last seen in 1990. Observations in March 1997 suggest that the partial recovery of 1993–94 has not been sustained. Forty-six hours of search during favorable weather failed to yield a single snake (M. P. L. Fogden, unpubl. data). On Monteverde's Pacific slope, many colubrid species, including the Bronze-striped Parrot Snake (see Pounds and Brenes, "The GTLC," p. 174), the Green Keelback (see Sec. 5.1.1), and the Fire-bellied Snake (Fig. 5.9), likewise appear to have declined. Additional sampling is needed to assess the status of snake populations.

5.4.2. Natural Sources of Mortality

Amphibians. Desiccation, parasitism, and predation cause high mortality of anuran embryos and tadpoles. The eggs of Fleischmann's Glass Frogs, laid on the undersurfaces of leaves overhanging streams, are vulnerable to desiccation, infestations of fungi and drosophilid flies, and predation by daddy longlegs (Phalangida) and crickets (Gryllidae; Hayes 1983, 1991). The eggs of leaf-breeding treefrogs (*Agalychnis* and *Phyllomedusa*) often become prey for Cat-eyed

Figure 5.9. The Fire-bellied Snake (*Liophis epinephalus*), a diurnal frog-eater that has declined throughout the Monteverde area. It is eating a Harlequin Frog (*Atelopus varius*). Photograph by Michael and Patricia Fogden.

Snakes and Peppered Tree Snakes (Duellman and Trueb 1986, Donnelly 1994), and the terrestrial eggs of rain frogs are food for Glossy Litter Snakes, Pink-bellied Litter Snakes, and Faded Dwarf Snakes (Hayes 1985, Seib 1985). The aquatic eggs and hatchling tadpoles of Meadow Treefrogs are vulnerable to cannibalism by larger tadpoles (Crump 1983, 1990, 1991b), and all developmental stages are susceptible to predation and drying of pools. Predators of the tadpoles include Fire-bellied Snakes, aquatic insects, and (in Zone 6) tadpoles of the Smoky Jungle Frog, which also eat the eggs (Heyer et al. 1975). In experiments with predaceous diving beetles (Dytiscidae) and dragonfly nymphs (Aeshnidae and Libellulidae), the most vulnerable tadpoles were very small ones and those passing through the four-legged stage (Crump 1984). All stages were equally vulnerable to nymphs of some dragonfly species. In experimental simulations of drying pools, tadpoles developed at enhanced rates and transformed at reduced body sizes (Crump 1989a).

Predators of adult amphibians range from ctenid spiders (Hayes 1983) to snakes, birds, and mammals. Freshwater crabs, which sometimes prey on small anurans (Duellman and Trueb 1986), are common along streams. Larval tiger beetles (Cicendelidae) position their traplike jaws at the entrance to their burrows; twice I have seen a Harlequin Frog with a foot ensnared. Frogs might lose digits or limbs to these predators. Snakes are among the most important predators of frogs and toads. Many colubrids feed primarily or exclusively on anurans, and some eat highly toxic species with apparent impunity. Fire-bellied Snakes, for example, prey on Harlequin Frogs, despite the presence of a potent nerve poison (tetrodotoxin) in the skin of these anurans (Kim et al. 1975; Fig. 5.9). Among the many birds that capture frogs are Sunbitterns and Blue-crowned Motmots. Resplendent Quetzals sometimes feed frogs to nestlings (Wheelwright 1983).

Parasites of adult amphibians include fungi, helminths, leeches, arthropods, protozoans, bacteria, and viruses (Hoff et al. 1984, Duellman and Trueb 1986). The impacts of these organisms on populations are largely unknown. A female sarcophagid fly (*Notochaeta bufonivora*) deposits larvae on the back of a Harlequin Frog's thigh. After making a small opening in the skin, the larvae feed on muscle tissue before entering the body cavity and causing death within a few days (Crump and Pounds 1985, Pounds and Crump 1987). During the dry season of 1982–83, the probability of being attacked by these flies was greatest in waterfall spray zones, where the frogs were most abundant. Experiments in which frog density was manipulated in a series of plots showed that the increased risk in these areas was a hazard associated with habitat choice rather than aggregation (Pounds and Crump 1987).

Reptiles. The most obvious predators of snakes and lizards are birds, although certain snakes and mammals and a host of parasites are also important enemies. Little is known about predation on embryos and juveniles; an unidentified shrew attacked a hatchling Blunt-headed Tree Snake (C. Rojas, pers. comm.). Brown Vine Snakes are important diurnal predators of anoles (Henderson 1974), and Blunt-headed Tree Snakes capture anoles on their nocturnal sleeping perches (Scott 1983d, J. A. Pounds, pers. obs.). Skink-eaters are remarkably skilled predators of lizards; they often subdue and swallow small skinks in less than 10 s (Henderson 1984). Snake-eating snakes include Double-ringed False Corals, Mussuranas, and Montane Mussuranas. Mussuranas are known for their ability to subdue large pit vipers, including Terciopelos (Scott 1983a). Avian predators of snakes and large lizards include raptors such as Swallow-tailed Kites, Black-chested Hawks, and White Hawks. Predators of anoles and other small lizards include Sunbitterns, primarily insect-eating birds such as Blue-crowned Motmots and Streak-breasted Treehunters, and fruit-eaters such as Resplendent Quetzals and Clay-colored Robins. Many kinds of parasites attack reptiles (Hoff et al. 1984), but little is known of their impacts. Malarial protozoans, which are most diverse in the tropics, are chiefly parasites of lizards (Telford 1977, Schall and Vogt 1993).

5.4.3. Possible Causes of Declines

Discussion of possible causes of amphibian declines at Monteverde has focused on ultraviolet (UV) radiation, atmospheric pollution, epidemic disease, and unusual weather (Pounds and Crump 1994). Here I examine these factors in light of recent evidence. I consider both amphibian and reptile declines, which may be components of a single phenomenon. Both began in the late 1980s, have taken place in seemingly undisturbed upland habitats, and have led to disappearances of populations (see Secs. 5.1.1., 5.4.1). Prey scarcity may have reduced the abundance of frog-eating snakes, but it is doubtful that the declines of anoline lizards are a secondary consequence of amphibian declines. The combination of anuran and lizard declines may parallel the case of Australia (Czechura 1991). Although it seems unlikely that a single cause can explain the patterns at Monteverde, there may be a principal underlying factor that has set the stage for proximate causes of mortality.

Ultraviolet radiation, which can damage amphibian embryos and increase their vulnerability to parasitic fungi (Blaustein et al. 1994b, Blaustein and Wake 1995), has probably not played a major role. Many species that have vanished from the area breed under the forest canopy and conceal their eggs. The Tilarán Rain Frog, for example, buries its eggs in a subterranean nest (see Sec. 5.5.3). Moreover, the rapidity of the anuran declines implies high adult mortality, which has not been linked to UV radiation (Pounds and Crump 1994). Even if UV light could affect adults of some species, Golden Toads normally spend most of their time in underground retreats and are rarely exposed to direct sunlight. Lizards that have suffered population extinctions include the Montane Anole, a basking species whose peritoneum (body-cavity lining) contains melanin that shields out UV radiation, and the Cloud Forest Anole, a shade-dwelling species that avoids direct sunlight (see Secs. 5.4.1, 5.6.2).

Although no unusual acidification has been observed at Monteverde (Crump et al. 1992), unexpectedly high concentrations of nitrates and phosphates in cloud water are evidence of atmospheric pollution (see Chap. 2, Physical Environment). The possibility of inputs that are more toxic should be investigated, especially given concern that some widespread chemicals may disrupt endocrine function in many organisms, including amphibians and reptiles (Stebbins and Cohen 1995). The threat of airborne pollution is great in cloud forests, because mist and cloud-water deposition can deliver contaminants at much higher concentrations than heavy rainfall (Glotfelty et al. 1987).

Epidemic disease may have played a role in the declines. The 1987 crash of anuran populations was so unexpected that it went unnoticed at first—nobody searched for afflicted animals. In 1982–83, 40 dead or dying Harlequin Frogs contained larvae of a parasitic fly (*Notochaeta bufonivora*; see Sec. 5.4.2), but the mortality caused no major decline. Reports of dead or dying frogs in the mountains of southern Costa Rica and western Panama (Cordillera de Talamanca) suggest epidemics (Berger et al. 1998, Lips 1998), but there is no evidence that a single outbreak, spreading in a wavelike fashion, has caused all the declines in lower Central America. Sampling has covered too few areas and mostly narrow time windows.

An alternative hypothesis is that an ecological change over a large area (e.g., atmospheric pollution or climate change) may have encouraged epidemics of the same, or different, microparasites at different times and places. Because this underlying factor would only load the dice, not dictate the occurrence of an outbreak, close synchrony in the declines should not be expected. Outbreaks similar to those in Central America have taken place in Australia (Laurance et al.

1996; Berger et al. 1998), where they have spawned a recent debate (Alford and Richards 1997, Hero and Gillespie 1997, Laurance et al. 1997) One point of agreement is that some anuran declines in seemingly undisturbed highlands cannot easily be attributed to pathogen outbreaks. The same applies to the declines of anoline lizards at Monteverde (see Sec. 5.4.1). The implication is that at least one other factor has been important in these and similar cases.

Of the potential changes in ecological context mentioned above, climate change has received the least attention. Unusual weather could exert indirect effects in at least two ways (Pounds and Crump 1994). First, mist and cloud-water deposition punctuating long dry periods might deliver contaminants at critical concentrations (the "climate-linked contaminant pulse hypothesis"). Second, extreme conditions of moisture or temperature could increase the probability of pathogen outbreaks (the "climate-linked epidemic hypothesis"). These conditions might reduce foraging success of host animals (Stewart 1995) or otherwise weaken them and suppress their immune responses, thereby increasing vulnerability to infection (Carey 1993). Also, a lowland microparasite could respond to altered climatic gradients by moving up mountain slopes with its insect vectors (Dobson and Carper 1992). If it encounters host populations that lack innate resistance, it could drive them to extinction even where physical conditions remain within their range of tolerance. Finally, unusual weather might lead to an irruption of lethal microparasites that are ordinarily present in small numbers. An increase in the abundance of vectors or a change in the spatial distribution of hosts might favor rapid population growth in these natural agents of mortality. The 1987 crash of amphibian populations at Monteverde coincided with warm, dry weather associated with the 1986–87 El Niño (a periodic warming of surface waters in the equatorial Pacific; Graham and White 1988). Shortly before the crash, Harlequin Frogs at one site underwent an unprecedented shift in behavior, apparently in response to desiccating conditions (see Sec. 5.6.1). In human populations, recent outbreaks of cholera, malaria, dengue, and hantavirus pulmonary syndrome appear to be associated with climate oscillations related to El Niño (Sprigg 1996).

The hypothesis that unusual weather has played a role in population declines in highland areas is plausible only if there are long-term trends suggestive of climate change. Laurance (1996) discarded this hypothesis for Australia after an analysis of monthly precipitation data. Although rainfall totals were often below average prior to declines, they showed no major trends. Rainfall totals, however, may be less important biologically than temporal patterns in daily precipitation (Stewart 1995). At Monteverde (1540 m), there is a strong 26-year trend toward dry seasons that are more severe (J. A. Pounds, M. P. L. Fogden, and J. H. Campbell, unpubl. data). Variability of daily rainfall has increased, leading to drier extremes without producing detectable trends in monthly or yearly averages. Days with no measurable precipitation have become more frequent and have increasingly coalesced into dry periods. Stream-flow minima have also declined. Fluctuations in sea-surface temperature (i.e., the signal of El Niño) account for much of the interannual variation in these patterns, but there is evidence of long-term drying trends after the effects of El Niño are taken into account.

A model of climate change on tropical mountains. These climate trends suggest a change in the advective processes that account for most precipitation during the dry season (Pounds 1997). As moisture-laden trade winds meet the windward (Caribbean) slope of the Cordillera de Tilarán and flow upward, they cool adiabatically, producing a large orographic cloud bank (see Chap. 2, Physical Environment). I hypothesize that atmospheric warming has raised the mean height at which condensation begins and thereby has increased the average altitude at the base of this cloud bank. Higher clouds should deposit less moisture directly onto vegetation. Because they may pass over the cordillera with reduced turbulence and drag, they are also less likely to produce low-intensity precipitation (mist) before dissipating on the leeward (Pacific) side, and deposit less moisture directly onto vegetation.

Temperature patterns during the dry season are consistent with this lifting-cloud-base model. Despite a nocturnal warming trend, the average daily maximum for dry days has declined, implying that there is an increase in the number of days with cloud cover but no measurable precipitation. Clouds, which reduce radiative heat losses at night and the intensity of solar radiation during the day, are principal modulators of local temperatures in the tropics (Nieuwolt 1977).

Biological patterns also follow the model's predictions (J. A. Pounds, M. P. L. Fogden, and J. H. Campbell, unpubl. data). Many premontane breeding bird species have invaded lower-montane habitats, whereas some lower-montane species have retreated up the mountain slopes. In multiple regression analyses, the number of dry-season days with no measurable precipitation accounts for most of the year-to-year variation in the rate of invasion by premontane bird species. The number of dry days is also strongly correlated with abundance in lizard populations that have declined and disappeared (see Sec. 5.4.1). The driest extremes on record immediately preceded the collapse of amphibian populations and the first major influx of premontane birds into lower-montane habitats. The patterns suggest that climate may have crossed a biologically important threshold during the 1986–87 El Niño.

5.5. Reproductive Ecology

We know little about reproductive cycles, courtship and mating, oviposition, parental care, and life-history traits such as clutch size and frequency for most amphibians and reptiles at Monteverde. Here I summarize breeding modes, review anuran reproductive behavior, and discuss breeding phenology.

5.5.1. Breeding Modes

Amphibians are known for their diverse breeding modes, whereas reptiles are comparatively uniform in this regard. Amphibian breeding modes in the Monteverde area fall into four classes: (1) eggs and larvae aquatic; (2) eggs laid out of water but larvae aquatic; (3) direct development (no larvae) within encapsulated, terrestrial eggs; and (4) live-bearing (viviparous). The caecilians are the only known live-bearing amphibians in the area. The fetuses of these elongate burrowers hatch from eggs retained in their mother's oviduct and feed there on glandular secretions (Wake 1983). Using specialized fetal teeth (lost at birth), they scrape the lining of the oviduct to stimulate food production. The five species of salamanders follow mode 3; the young hatch as miniature replicas of the adults (Wake and Lynch 1976). The same is true for the rain frogs that have been studied and may apply to all 18 species (Hayes 1985, Hayes et al. 1989). Of the remaining 35 anuran species, 24 follow mode 1 and 11 follow mode 2. Treefrogs in the genera *Agalychnis* and *Phyllomedusa* and glass frogs (Centrolenidae) lay eggs on vegetation above water (Duellman 1970, Pyburn 1970, McDiarmid 1983, Hayes 1991). Smoky Jungle Frogs lay eggs in a foam nest built in a hollow that is likely to be flooded (Scott 1983e). Most lizards and snakes at Monteverde are egg-laying (oviparous), although a few are live-bearing. The latter include the Bronze-backed Climbing Skink, the Green Spiny Lizard, the Boa Constrictor, and the four species of pit vipers.

The species of amphibians and reptiles that have declined or disappeared in the Monteverde region represent a wide range of life histories. For frogs and toads, there was no association between the probability of disappearance and breeding mode, although species not dependent on bodies of water were more likely to escape regional extinction than species associated with aquatic habitats (Pounds et al. 1997; see Sec. 5.6.1). The lizards and snakes known to have declined (see Sec. 5.4.1) lay eggs. Hence, the species for which declines have been documented include representatives of all breeding modes except live-bearing.

5.5.2. Courtship and Mating in Frogs and Toads

Much of the variation in anuran mating behavior is best understood in the context of competition among males for access to females. This competition varies in form according to the spatial and temporal distribution of receptive females (Wells 1977). Both "explosive" and "prolonged" breeders have been studied at Monteverde.

Golden Toads and Meadow Treefrogs are examples of explosive breeders. Intense physical competition between male Golden Toads characterizes their 5–10-day mating bouts at temporary pools (Jacobson and Vandenberg 1991; Fig. 5.2). Males ordinarily outnumber females 8-to-1, and unpaired males attempt to dislodge rivals who have achieved amplexus. Balls of up to 10 struggling males sometimes envelope individual females. In the fray, males often clasp one another and sometimes clasp anurans of other species (e.g., Pin-striped Treefrogs) or even tree roots. Single males not engaged in physical interactions with other males may utter a soft "tep-tep-tep" like wooden spoons clicking together, but the most common sound is the release call. Males produce this low-intensity trill along with body vibrations when clasped by other males. When rains fill a seasonal pond, Meadow Treefrogs gather suddenly and breed in a frenzy that may continue night and day (Crump and Townsend 1990). The males, mostly tan and brown at night, often turn bright yellow during the day (Crump 1991b). They greatly outnumber the females, and "mating balls" with up to 16 males have been observed. The principal vocalization is an unmusical "waaank."

Glass Frogs are prolonged breeders. Throughout much of the rainy season, male Fleischmann's Glass Frogs deliver loud, frequent "peeps" from territories along streams, and the females arrive asynchronously (Greer and Wells 1980, Jacobson 1985, Hayes 1991). When a female approaches a calling male, who is usually on the underside of a leaf, he intersperses peeps with "mew" calls. After lengthy preliminaries in which she appears to assess egg-laying sites or other qualities of his territory, she initiates amplexus by backing under him (Fig. 5.1). Mew calls also serve in aggressive interactions between males. A male Emerald Glass Frog sporadically emits two to five loud "beeps," typically from the upper side of a leaf. When a female approaches, he leaps onto her back (Jacobson 1985). In territorial disputes, males of this species often grapple with one another while hanging upside down in the vegetation by their hind limbs; the loser signals his defeat by dropping lower in the vegetation or flattening himself against a leaf. In contrast to male Fleischmann's Glass Frogs, which brood eggs immediately after they are laid (see Sec. 5.5.3), male Emerald Glass Frogs call while in amplexus and shortly afterward.

Mating in Harlequin Frogs, which are also prolonged breeders, is poorly understood. Some pairs stay in amplexus for at least 32 days. Prolonged amplexus may be a result of strong male-male competition due to a relative scarcity of receptive females (Crump 1988). Because oviposition has not been observed, the picture remains unclear. Perhaps males whose territories contain the best oviposition sites mate more times and stay in amplexus for shorter periods than males with poorer territories and "transient" males, who do not hold territories.

Both male and female Harlequin Frogs are territorial (Crump 1986, 1988). "Resident" frogs of both sexes show strong site fidelity; they stay for as long as two years within a small area (recapture radius of a few meters) and usually return within a week if displaced 10 m upstream or down. Transient frogs wander up and down the stream and show no homing tendency. Male aggressive behavior, directed toward other males, includes chasing, pouncing, squashing, wrestling, and calling. Both territory holders and intruders emit a weak call, usually before engaging in any physical contact, and the winner of a fight gives the same call afterward. Males also produce "chirps" during struggles with rival males and when unreceptive females attempt to dislodge them from amplexus. Aggressive behavior of females, which is directed toward both males and other females, is like that of males except for the absence of wrestling and calling. Female aggression toward males seems to function in the avoidance of prolonged amplexus. Females attempt to dislodge males that clasp them prematurely. They also chase them from their territories and may leap onto their backs and pound their heads against the substrate.

Of the two broad strategies—explosive and prolonged breeding—the former is associated with the use of ephemeral pools (Wells 1977). Thus, explosive breeders are often subject to the vagaries of these temporary bodies of water. In 1987, for example, early drying of pools caused high mortality of Golden Toad embryos and larvae (Crump et al. 1992). Harding (1993) interpreted this to mean that "water shortages in temporary pools" had caused this species' decline, and proposed management of pools as a solution to the problem. Nevertheless, many prolonged breeders, which do not depend on these ephemeral habitats, declined along with the Golden Toad (e.g., Fleischmann's and Emerald Glass Frogs, and the Harlequin Frog; see Sec. 5.4.1). Drying of breeding pools due to unusual weather cannot be a general explanation for the declines (Pounds and Fogden 1996; see Sec. 5.4.3).

5.5.3. Oviposition and Parental Care in Frogs and Toads

Anurans are selective about where they lay eggs. Golden Toads, for example, lay small clutches (157–385 eggs) in ephemeral pools, mostly beneath the stilt-like roots of elfin-forest trees (Jacobson and Vandenberg 1991). Meadow Treefrogs deposit large clutches (1800–2500 eggs), divided into masses of several hundred each, in ponds of various sizes (Crump 1991a). Females of the latter species appear to avoid shallow sites that may dry up and pools with conspecific tadpoles that may cannibalize eggs and hatchlings (see Crump, "How Do Meadow Treefrogs Decide," p. 173). Harlequin Frogs lay eggs in fast-flowing streams, probably anchored to rocks; the tadpoles have large ventral sucking discs that help them maintain their position in the current (Starrett 1967, McDiarmid 1971).

Parental care differs among species. Many rain frogs (*Eleutherodactylus*) leave their eggs unattended, often in leaf litter or bromeliads (Taylor 1955, Myers 1969, Scott 1983c), but some species tend their eggs. A nest of the Tilarán Rain Frog containing 77 eggs was buried in soil near a stream (Hayes 1985). For several nights, the female sat on the nest and appeared to defend it by pushing away intruding objects. Likewise, a female Leaf-breeding Rain Frog in Panama laid eggs on the surface of a leaf and stayed closely huddled to them until they hatched (Myers 1969). Fleischmann's Glass Frog exhibits a similar brooding behavior (Hayes 1991). At variable intervals, the male presses his ventral side against the eggs to hydrate them (mean clutch size = 26). Because the eggs are shielded from rain on the undersurfaces of leaves, desiccation causes high mortality of embryos not brooded in this way. Keeping them too wet, however, encourages parasitic fungi and drosophilid fly larvae, which also cause high mortality. Males brood more frequently under dry conditions. Brooding does not guard directly against predation, but hydration thickens the egg jelly, which discourages predaceous arthropods (see Sec. 5.4.2). Brooding is essential immediately after oviposition and is important during early development; it becomes less crucial as development advances. Male Emerald Glass Frogs do not brood eggs (Jacobson 1985). The females brood for variable periods immediately after oviposition (mean clutch size = 20) but do not return to the clutches. The developing embryos, usually on the upper surface of a leaf or other exposed site, depend on moisture from the environment. Male Reticulated Glass Frogs appear to guard eggs against predation (McDiarmid 1983). They attend clutches 24 hr/day, whereas male Bare-hearted Glass Frogs (Fig. 5.10) leave theirs unattended during the daytime. Embryos of the latter species suffer greater mortality due to visually hunting predators, particularly wasps.

The diversity of oviposition sites exhibited by species that have declined or disappeared at Monteverde casts doubt on the hypothesis that UV radiation has caused the declines by reducing hatching success (see Sec. 5.4.3). Eggs of the Golden Toad, typically laid in dark recesses beneath masses of tree roots, are rarely exposed to direct sunlight. Embryos of the Tilarán Rain Frog, which disappeared from the area along with the Golden Toad (Pounds et al. 1997), develop in underground nests where they receive no UV radi-

ation. Although Emerald and Fleischmann's Glass Frogs both declined in the late 1980s (see Sec. 5.4.1), eggs of the former are laid on exposed surfaces, whereas eggs of the latter are shielded on the undersurfaces of leaves (see Sec. 5.5.2).

5.5.4. Tadpole Feeding Ecology

Feeding ecology of anuran larvae at Monteverde needs further study. Tadpoles of the Meadow Treefrog, which develop in temporary pools where food is presumed to be limited, cannibalize eggs and hatchlings (Crump 1983, 1991b). In laboratory experiments, larvae that were fed conspecific tadpoles developed at the same rate as those fed tadpoles of another treefrog species but grew larger before undergoing metamorphosis (Crump 1990). Larger tadpoles generally transform into larger froglets, which presumably have higher survivorship. Another solution to the problem of food scarcity in temporary pools is to forego eating. Golden Toads lay relatively few, large eggs that are well-

Figure 5.10. A male Bare-hearted Glass Frog (*Hyalinobatrachium colymbiphyllum*) attending eggs. Photograph by Michael and Patricia Fogden.

provisioned with yolk (see Sec. 5.5.3). The tadpoles hatch with enough stored energy to develop and transform without eating, but they grow larger before transforming if food is available (Crump 1989b).

5.5.5. Reproductive Phenology

Relationships between reproductive cycles and climate are an important area for future study. Changes in the seasonal breeding cycles of British amphibians are correlated with long-term warming trends (Beebee 1995). In the tropics, many amphibians and reptiles reproduce seasonally (e.g., Fitch 1973, Duellman and Trueb 1986, Guyer 1986, Siegel and Ford 1987), but patterns vary according to seasonality of the environment. The Cloud Forest Anole, for example, inhabits relatively aseasonal areas and normally produces eggs year-round with no apparent reduction in rate (Fitch 1973, J. A. Pounds, pers. obs.). The Gray Lichen Anole inhabits strongly seasonal environments on the Pacific slope and produces few or no eggs during the dry season. The climate trends at Monteverde imply an increase in seasonality manifested as increasingly severe dry seasons (see Sec. 5.4.3). Because the Cloud Forest Anole has disappeared from the more seasonal, western parts of its distribution (see Secs. 5.4.1, 5.6.1), it would be valuable to examine whether the normally aseasonal reproduction of this species has become more seasonal in areas where populations remain. The climate trends may also force pool-breeding frogs and toads to breed later in the year than normal. Increased soil-moisture deficits or an unusual lowering of the water table might delay the formation of temporary pools when the rainy season begins.

5.6. Habitat Use

Habitat complexity is hierarchical. A natural environment is "like a checkerboard of habitats" in which each square has "its own checkerboard . . . of component subhabitats" (MacArthur 1972). This pattern of mosaics-within-mosaics repeated at different spatial scales is especially complex in a tropical forest. Major patches can be defined in relation to bodies of water (well-drained areas vs. streams, pools, and swamps of various sizes) and components of the disturbance mosaic (mature-phase forest and canopy gaps of different sizes and ages). These patches may be subdivided into strata, each containing a mosaic of microhabitats.

5.6.1. Aquatic Habitats

Amphibians. About 60% of the amphibian species at Monteverde, all of them frogs and toads, are ordinarily associated with streams, pools, or swamps during at least part of the year. Although the pattern largely reflects aquatic breeding habits, three terrestrial-breeding species (the Tilarán Rain Frog, Salmon-bellied Rain Frog, and Middle American Stream Frog) frequent stream margins, possibly for reasons of water economy or prey availability. Harlequin Frogs that inhabit the moist cloud forest (Fig. 5.3) are often active far from the watercourses in which they breed, whereas frogs of the same species that inhabit the drier, more seasonal areas of the Pacific slope are typically found within a few meters of stream margins (Crump and Pounds 1989). The difference seems to reflect the constraints of moisture availability, although food availability might also be a factor. Along a gallery-forest stream in the Río Lagarto drainage (1140 m), the abundance of arthropod prey and the predictability of interpatch differences in prey abundance were greater in the dry season than in the wet season (Crump 1988). No data exist to compare prey availability at the stream margins to that in the adjacent forest.

Observations at the same site documented the response of Harlequin Frogs to the El Niño warm episodes of 1982–83 and 1986–87 (Pounds and Crump 1994). The thermal signal of the former event was stronger than any in the preceding century (Graham and White 1988). During the 1983 dry season, as stream flow diminished and moisture availability became increasingly patchy, Harlequin Frogs shifted their home ranges into the remaining wet areas, especially near waterfalls. The pattern of dispersion became highly clumped, and the observed density of frogs decreased as many sought refuge in damp crevices. Because frogs hidden in crevices included a disproportionately large number of females, the operational sex ratio (observed in exposed areas) was strongly male biased. Despite the warm, dry weather, many Harlequin Frogs survived; they were present in large numbers in subsequent years. The population fared worse during the 1986–87 El Niño, which had a greater impact on local weather than the 1982–83 event (Pounds and Crump 1994; see Sec. 5.4.3). In March 1987, when the warm, dry conditions were near their peak, the observed density (1 frog per 0.5 m of stream) was a record high, 4.4 times greater than that predicted from 1982–83 patterns (Fig. 5.11A). The 1987 census was the last before the population disappeared. In May 1988, density was a record low (1 frog per 40 m of stream); by June, it had fallen to zero.

Suspecting that the high density in March 1987 might be a clue to why the population had crashed, Pounds and Crump (1994) considered two hypotheses. First, if recruitment had been high in 1986, the

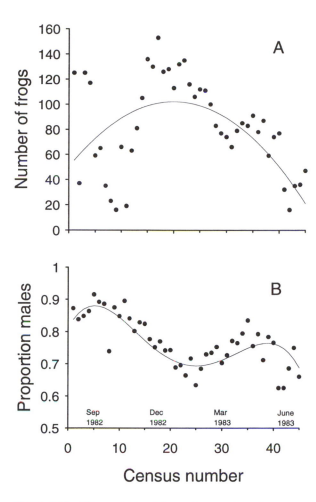

Figure 5.11. Observed densities and operational sex ratios of Harlequin Frogs (*Atelopus varius*) along a gallery-forest stream on Monteverde's Pacific slope during El Niño climate oscillations. The plotted data are from weekly censuses during the 1982–83 event along a 200-m section of the stream. A, Number of frogs per 200 m. The curve is for a quadratic regression. The number of frogs observed in late March 1987, near the peak of the 1986–87 El Niño, was 403, or 4.4 times greater than that predicted by the regression. B, Proportion of frogs that were males. The curve is for a 4° polynomial regression. The proportion in late March 1987 was 0.239, or 60% lower than that predicted by the regression. The bizarre snapshot of frog density and sex ratio in 1987 is from the last census before this population crashed and disappeared (from Pounds and Crump 1994).

population might have been unusually large in 1987. Second, if the warm, dry conditions caused individuals to leave drying crevices and gather in remaining wet areas, observability might have been unusually high. These hypotheses differ in their predictions concerning the sex ratio. Whereas the first predicts a normal (male-biased) operational sex ratio, the sec-

ond predicts a ratio that is less male biased than normal. In accordance with the second hypothesis, the proportion of frogs that were males (0.29) was 60% lower than that predicted from 1982–83 patterns (Fig. 5.11B). The excess of females, a pattern that had not been observed previously, suggested that both sexes had gathered at the stream margins and that males, which are normally more exposed than females, had already begun to decline. The population appeared to be responding to the extreme conditions of moisture and temperature shortly before it crashed.

At the same site, Bransford's Litter Frogs, which survived the 1987 crash, migrate into the stream bed during the dry season. During the wet months of 1993 (May–December), no frogs were found in the stream bed, compared to an average of 2 frogs per 100 m transect in the adjacent gallery forest and overgrown guayaba plantations (J. A. Pounds, unpubl. data). During the dry season, there were 47 frogs per 100 m transect in the stream bed and none in the forest and plantations. Future studies should examine the impacts of climate fluctuations and trends on this and other populations of rain frogs (*Eleutherodactylus*). Climate change may be reducing the numbers of these frogs in the Luquillo Mountains of Puerto Rico (Stewart 1995, R. Joglar, P. Burrowes, and N. Rios, unpubl. data).

Studies of rain frogs may also reveal why some species of anurans persisted in the Monteverde area after the 1987 crash while others vanished. These terrestrial breeders were as likely to disappear as aquatic breeders (see Sec. 5.5.1). Nevertheless, species not dependent on bodies of water (i.e., rain frogs exclusive of stream-dwelling forms) were less likely to disappear than species associated with aquatic habitats (Pounds et al. 1997). Population structure may be a key factor in this pattern. In contrast to the islandlike distribution of many anurans associated with bodies of water, forest-dwelling rain frogs tend to be distributed more continuously over the landscape (Stewart and Woolbright 1996). The comparatively large number of local populations per area may reduce vulnerability to stochastic mechanisms of extinction in the wake of deterministic declines (e.g., the loss of small populations due to random fluctuations; Gilpin and Soulé 1986) and may increase the chances that previously occupied sites will be recolonized (Travis 1994). Tests of these hypotheses should examine both terrestrial-breeding rain frogs and aquatic-breeding species. The latter differ in the number of local populations per area and quantitative characteristics of dispersal. They may differ accordingly in susceptibility to regional extinction.

Reptiles.   In contrast to the pattern for amphibians, only 4% of reptile species are associated with aquatic habitats: the Stream Anole, the Common and Emerald Basilisks, and the Tropical Seep Snake. Frog-eating snakes, however, often hunt in these areas. Reptiles not ordinarily found near bodies of water may be associated with them in some parts of their range. The Cloud Forest Anole, for example, was previously widespread in Zones 3 and 4 and extended into Zone 2 (to 1400 m) along forested watercourses. Because this species has disappeared from the drier, western parts of its distribution (Zone 2 and part of Zone 3; see Sec. 5.4.1), it would be valuable to examine whether surviving populations in Zone 3 have become dependent on streams.

5.6.2. The Disturbance Mosaic

Although many species require undisturbed, closed-canopy forest, others thrive in gaps. Fitzinger's Rain Frog, for example, may be found in undisturbed forest but is most common in open grassy areas (J. A. Pounds, unpubl. data). The chronically disturbed margins of rivers and swamps may be its primary natural habitat in the area. The Terciopelo, the area's largest pit viper, is also most abundant in grassy clearings, possibly because of a high density of rodent prey. Over much of Costa Rica, the Black-tailed Cribo is found below an elevation of 1000 m (Scott 1983b). On Monteverde's Pacific slope, however, it ascends to 1540 m, where it basks in clearings. The availability of open areas for basking also appears to limit the upper altitudinal range of the Green Spiny Lizard.

Thermobiology in relation to canopy cover likewise influences the distribution of anoline lizards (Fitch 1972, 1973, 1975, Pounds 1988). Whereas Cloud Forest Anoles, Ground Anoles, and Blue-eyed Anoles inhabit the shaded understory and allow their body temperatures to track ambient temperatures, Montane Anoles (Fig. 5.5) and Gray Lichen Anoles inhabit gaps and bask to raise their temperatures. Nonbasking anoles in highland forests tend to be relatively inactive. For example, Cloud Forest Anoles averaged 8.9 movements/hr, compared to 14.4 movements/hr by heliophilic Montane Anoles at the same elevation (Pounds 1988, J. A. Pounds and K. Masters, unpubl. data). The former also captured prey less frequently. Sticky traps captured 94% more arthropods in open areas than in the shaded forest understory, so feeding rate appeared to be correlated with prey availability. The low-energy strategy of Cloud Forest Anoles (low gain, low expenditure) is probably important to their ability to exploit a cool environment. Trade-offs include slow growth and maturation (see Sec. 5.4) and reduced running speeds (Van Berkum 1986). Also, because of physiological adaptations that permit these anoles to operate at low

body temperatures, they are extremely heat sensitive; a few minutes in direct sun can be lethal. The potential vulnerability of these and similarly adapted cloud-forest species to unusually warm weather should be studied.

Future research should also examine how climate change affects the spatial pattern of the disturbance mosaic and hence the distribution and abundance of species. Long-term trends in atmospheric pressures—a consequence of warm oceanic conditions in the tropical Pacific in recent decades—suggest a strengthening of the trade winds over Costa Rica (Brenes and Saborio 1994, Graham 1995). If this trend continues, the frequency of tree falls may rise, increasing the prevalence of gaps and altering tree size and age distributions.

5.6.3. Habitat Strata

If tree-fall rates increase, the vertical profile of vegetation structure and microclimate will change, with important consequences for animal communities. Anoline lizards, for example, are behaviorally and morphologically adapted for particular subsets of the available strata (Pounds 1988, 1991b). The vertical distribution of most amphibians and reptiles is poorly known. For a broad comparison, I assigned species to three categories: (1) subterranean, (2) ground and leaf litter, and (3) aboveground vegetation (Miyamoto 1982, Hayes et al. 1989, Guyer 1994; Appendix 8). The caecilians are burrowers. Salamanders are discussed below in relation to epiphyte use. Of the remaining taxa, snakes are most strongly associated with the forest floor and litter, whereas frogs and lizards include greater proportions of climbers (Table 5.5).

5.6.4. Epiphytes

Many species of amphibians and a few species of reptiles are associated with epiphytes. Tropical salamanders are the group of vertebrates most closely associated with these plants (Wake and Lynch 1976, Wake 1987). In the cloud forests of Mexico, Honduras, and Guatemala, salamanders mainly inhabit bromeliads. In the cloud forests of Costa Rica and western Panama, they exhibit a variety of microhabitat specialties and make greater use of moss mats (Wake 1987). The Moss Salamander specializes in the use of moss mats but occasionally inhabits bromeliads. Poelz's and Highland Worm Salamanders are typically found in moss mats covering downed vegetation and soil banks, where they also burrow. The Monteverde Salamander appears to be mostly associated with bromeliads. It thus differs from its close relative, the Mountain Salamander (*Bolitoglossa sub-*

Table 5.5. Distribution of species of anurans, lizards, and snakes among broad habitat strata in the Monteverde area.

Taxon	Habitat Stratum		
	Subterranean	Ground and Leaf Litter	Aboveground Vegetation
Anurans ($N = 53$)	3	15	35
Percentage of N	5.7	28.3	66.0
Lizards ($N = 29$)	0	5	24
Percentage of N	0.0	17.2	82.8
Snakes ($N = 72$)	0.0	40	26
Percentage of N	8.3	55.6	36.1

Each species is assigned to the stratum where observed most often (see Appendix 8).

palmata), which on Costa Rica's Cerro de la Muerte is largely terrestrial (Vial 1968). The Ring-tailed Salamander is most commonly found under debris on the forest floor. Anurans that frequent bromeliads at Monteverde include seven species of rain frogs (*Eleutherodactylus*), plus the Meadow Treefrog, the Drab River Frog, and the Crowned Frog (Hayes et al. 1989). Male Common Dink Frogs often call from within these plants, and the non-aquatic eggs of this and several other species of rain frogs are found there (Taylor 1955, Myers 1969, Scott 1983c). The aquatic eggs and tadpoles of the Crowned Frog develop in water-filled tree cavities and bromeliads (Taylor 1954, Robinson 1961). The possibility that other arboreal anurans (e.g., the Giant Fringe-limbed Treefrog) use bromeliads should be investigated. Eyelash Vipers and Blunt-headed Tree Snakes may take refuge in these epiphytes during the day, but Bromeliad Lizards are the only reptiles in the area thought to use them as their principal microhabitat (Heyer 1967). Secretive forms that are not well studied (e.g., the Green-bellied Caiman Lizard) might also use bromeliads.

Future studies should monitor epiphytes. A long-term study of seed germination and seedling establishment and growth in bromeliads and orchids would be valuable. Monitoring should also examine growth and possible dieback of epiphytic mosses, which may be sensitive indicators of changes in orographic cloud banks and tradewind-conveyed precipitation (see Sec. 5.4.3; see Chap. 2, Physical Environment). The abundance of epiphytes, one of the defining characteristics of cloud forests, may decrease if climate change continues on its current trajectory.

5.7. Conservation

In this section, I discuss action—how policy makers, managers of parks and preserves, and the public in general might respond to the population declines. A large segment of Monteverde's herpetofauna is missing from seemingly undisturbed habitats 11 years after a multispecies population crash that led to a spate of disappearances. Bob Carlson, Director of the MCFP, sees the unexpected erosion of diversity as "the single greatest problem facing the Preserve." He worries about the possible implications for the rest of the area's biota.

Only recently has the scientific community reached a consensus that amphibian declines are a serious conservation threat (Wake 1998). The issue of "standards of proof" has been central to the debate (McCoy 1994). Under the strictest standards, there may be insufficient long-term data to judge how unusual the declines are in the context of natural demographic variability (Pechmann et al. 1991, Pechmann and Wilbur 1994). The same would be true, however, even if there were baseline data demonstrating that species composition had remained constant for, say, 50 years before the 1987 crash. The most extreme fluctuations might occur only once per century or even less frequently. What constitutes an adequate time period for assessing natural variability is unknowable. As conservationists, we cannot wait decades to form an opinion when so much is at stake. The observed patterns, viewed in relation to known variability, warrant concern, which justifies action.

To identify the most appropriate courses of action and avoid the pitfalls of well-meaning but misguided efforts, ongoing research is needed (Beebee 1993). The results obtained so far suggest that climate change and epidemic disease may be key factors in the population declines and disappearances (see Sec. 5.4.3). There is growing evidence that global warming is a real phenomenon with potentially devastating biological consequences (Peters and Lovejoy 1992, Barry et al. 1995, Graham 1995, Diaz and Graham 1996, Houghton et al. 1996, Parmesan 1996, Santer et al. 1996). Ultimately, conservation action geared to this problem must be global in scope. We must educate our elected officials and their constituencies about the costs of complacency. Local action is also important. Without the work of the Tropical Science Center, which manages the MCFP, and the Monteverde Conservation League, which manages the adjacent International Children's Rain Forest (see Chap. 10, Conservation Institutions), the area's forests would be reduced to a small island in a sea of agricultural land. Deforestation would directly ravage biodiversity and, by affecting local hydrology, would exacerbate the effects of greenhouse warming.

We may be granted a reprieve from this global threat. Temperatures have risen over the past century, but in a series of upward and downward swings rather than a steady progression (Houghton et al. 1996). Cooling trends have characterized some decades. Patterns suggest an inherent climate variability on which the greenhouse effect is superimposed. Action taken now may help to determine how much biodiversity survives until a possible reprieve comes. Thus, applied conservation measures such as habitat management, establishment of corridors for dispersal, captive breeding and releases, and reintroduction of species into previously occupied habitats may prove valuable (see Pounds and Brenes, "The GTLC," p. 174). Even if our only accomplishment is to provide another generation of humans with the opportunity to know the "optimism and inner meaning" of a glass frog's song, the effort is worthwhile.

5.8 Summary

A sudden crash of amphibian populations in 1987 led to the disappearance of the endemic Golden Toad and many other species from seemingly undisturbed habitats in the Monteverde region of Costa Rica's Cordillera de Tilarán. This and similar cases in highland areas of other continents have caused alarm and controversy because of the suggestion that subtle agents may be threatening biodiversity on a global scale. Debate has focused on whether the observed patterns differ from those expected from normal population dynamics. Whereas arguments have hinged on standards of scientific proof and the scarcity of long-term demographic data needed to judge whether a population is in decline, diverse tropical faunas afford an approach that does not rely on these data. A comparison of the number of disappearances at Monteverde to the number that could be expected for an assemblage of demographically unstable populations suggests that the declines go beyond natural fluctuations.

Although discussion has focused on amphibian declines, reptiles have also been affected. Prey scarcity may account for a decrease in the abundance of colubrid snakes; the species for which declines have been documented eat anurans (or their eggs or larvae). It is doubtful, however, that declines of anoline lizards are a secondary consequence of amphibian declines. The two may be components of a single phenomenon. Both began in the late 1980s, have taken place in seemingly undisturbed upland habitats, and have led to disappearances of populations. A broad taxonomic focus is needed to identify the causes of the observed patterns and explore the implications.

We must rely on the available information on ecology to guide future research. The spatial configuration of the 1987 crash of anuran populations, viewed in relation to local patterns of distribution and diversity, helps explain why so many species disappeared from the area. Much of the high overall species richness is a consequence of a diverse array of climate and vegetation zones. The crash affected all of these zones and thus all geographic components of diversity. Broad patterns of distribution, examined in the context of evolutionary history, suggest that Monteverde's amphibians are generally more vulnerable to regional or global extinction than its reptiles. The former include a higher proportion of upland species restricted to the cordilleras of Costa Rica and Western Panama. The declines have mostly affected highland areas, and these upland endemics have no potential for recolonizing from nearby lowlands. The anuran species that have disappeared represent a wide range of life histories and reproductive behaviors. The diversity of oviposition sites, including subterranean nests, casts doubt on the hypothesis that UV radiation has caused declines by reducing hatching success. Population structure as a function of habitat use may help to explain why some anuran species have disappeared while others have persisted. Although virtually all anuran populations crashed in 1987, species not dependent on bodies of water were less likely to disappear than species associated with aquatic habitats. In contrast to the island-like population structure of the latter, the former tend to be distributed more continuously over the landscape. The relatively large number of local populations may reduce vulnerability to stochastic mechanisms of extinction in the wake of deterministic declines.

It appears unlikely that a single cause can explain the declines at Monteverde, but there may be a principal underlying factor that has set the stage for proximate causes of mortality. Epidemic disease may have played a role. However, there is no evidence that a single outbreak, spreading in a wavelike fashion, has caused all the declines in Central America. An alternative hypothesis is that a change in the ecological context over a large area may have encouraged epidemics of the same, or different microparasites at different times and places. Airborne pollution may be an important threat in cloud forests, as concentrations in mist and cloud water may greatly exceed those in heavy rainfall. Climate change may increase this threat, because concentrations might reach critical levels when light precipitation punctuates long dry periods. Climate change could also encourage pathogen outbreaks via several possible mechanisms.

At Monteverde, there is a 26-year trend toward increasingly severe dry seasons and concordant biological responses to this trend. Variability of daily precipitation has increased, leading to drier extremes without producing trends in monthly or yearly means. Days with no measurable precipitation have become more frequent and have increasingly coalesced into dry periods. The patterns suggest the hypothesis that global warming has raised the mean height at which condensation of trade-wind-conveyed moisture begins and thereby has increased the average altitude at the base of the orographic cloud bank. As predicted by this lifting-cloud-base model, many premontane breeding-bird species have invaded lower-montane habitats, whereas some lower-montane species have retreated up the mountain slopes. Patterns of daily precipitation during the dry season, which account for most of the interannual variation in the rate of invasion by premontane bird species, are strongly correlated with abundance in the lizard populations that have declined and disappeared. The driest extremes immediately preceded the multispecies crash of amphibian populations and the first major upslope movement of premontane breeding birds. These changes, which suggest that climate may have crossed a biologically important threshold during the 1986–87 El Niño, may foreshadow an uncertain future for natural communities in general, including humankind.

Acknowledgments I thank M. Crump for introducing me to Monteverde. She and many others, especially M. Fogden, M. Hayes, J. Savage, W. Timmerman, and R. Van Devender, have contributed to our knowledge of the herpetofauna. For financial support, I am grateful to the Tropical Science Center, the University of Florida, the Organization for Tropical Studies, the Jessie Smith Noyes Foundation, Stanford's Center for Conservation Biology, the MacArthur Foundation, Chicago's Brookfield Zoo, the University of Miami, and the U.S. National Science Foundation (Grant DEB 9200081 to J. Savage). I thank G. Barboza, G. Bello, F. Bolaños, R. Bolaños, J. Calvo, B. Carlson, G. Gorman, R. Heyer, R. and M. Lawton, D. and M. Lieberman, K. Masters, R. Solórzano, J. Tosi, M. Wainwright, D. Wake, and V. Watson for valuable discussion and assistance; F. Bolaños, J. Campbell, M. Fogden, W. Guindon, N. Rios, C. Rojas, and J. Savage for sharing unpublished data or observations; M. Fogden for providing photographs; and M. Brenes, B. Carlson, M. Donnelly, M. and P. Fogden, C. Guyer, R. Heyer, C. Rojas, and the editors for commenting on the manuscript. I dedicate this chapter to the memory of Archie F. Carr, who was never afraid to admit his attachment to frogs.

Editors' note (added in proof): The study cited as J. A. Pounds, M. P. L. Fogden, and J. H. Campbell, unpubl., was reported in *Nature* (Pounds et al. 1999). This work, widely discussed by the media, was quoted in a speech by U.S. President Clinton (June 3, 1999) as "disturbing new evidence of climate change."

THE DISCOVERY OF THE GOLDEN TOAD
Jay M. Savage

My initial response when I first saw Golden Toads was one of disbelief. Instead of the somber tones of gray, brown, or olive characteristic of most toads in the genus *Bufo*, the males were solid bright orange (Fig. 5.2). I wondered if someone had dipped them in enamel paint, but the color proved to be genuine. The females were equally astonishing. Lacking any hint of orange in their coloration, they were olive to black with large blotches of the brightest scarlet outlined in yellow. This marked difference between the sexes was as unexpected as the brilliant hues. I first learned of this singularly striking toad in October 1963. During a visit to Monteverde, Norman J. Scott, Jr. and I spoke with local resident Jerry James, who brought the species' existence to our attention. Because it was the wrong time of year, however, we were unable to find any examples. When James delivered several specimens to the University of Costa Rica the following May, we returned to the cloud forest at once.

Scott, James, and I hiked up to the ridge above the Monteverde community on 14 May 1964. On reaching the toads' habitat at midafternoon, I was impressed by the eerie atmosphere created by the dark soil, the gnarled, moss-covered trees, and the billowing fog that passed overhead. As we stepped into the forest, everywhere we looked we saw bright blotches of orange standing out against the black soil. Each blotch was a male toad. Within a radius of 5 m, at least 200 males gathered in small pools. There were fewer females, and where pairs were in amplexus, single males struggled to separate them. Late that evening, we returned to this woodland in a driving rain. Few toads were active, yet we saw 10–12 amplectant pairs in the pools. One female had laid 220 relatively large eggs in two strings, and Scott collected a series to raise in the laboratory. The uniformly dark brown tadpoles began to transform on 21 June. The toadlets were brown with pale bluish white spots above and were mottled with black and the same pale color underneath. I coined the scientific name *Bufo periglenes* in reference to the extraordinary coloration of the adults (Savage 1966). "Periglenes" means bright in Greek. Thus a literal translation is "bright toad."

MONTEVERDE SALAMANDERS, GOLDEN TOADS, AND THE EMERGENCE OF THE GLOBAL AMPHIBIAN CRISIS
J. Alan Pounds

The case of Monteverde has played a key role in bringing the plight of amphibians to the world's attention (Phillips 1994). In November 1988, David Wake, a professor at the University of California, Berkeley, visited Monteverde to study salamanders. He was especially interested in the Monteverde Salamander, a brown species of *Bolitoglossa* with rusty blotches (Fig. 5.4). To Wake's surprise, he and his assistants were unable to find a single salamander. Only a year before in precisely the same places he had found several dozen individuals representing four species. "Hard to understand," he wrote in his field notes.

Wake's concern led him to take steps that would bring amphibian declines to the attention of scientists and the popular press. In September 1989, he attended the First World Congress of Herpetology in Canterbury, England. There he learned from Martha Crump that Golden Toads, for the second year in a row, had not gathered at their traditional breeding pools in the Monteverde Preserve. For some time, Wake had been hearing casual reports from colleagues who were having trouble finding amphibians in various places around the world. It was at Canterbury, however, that the reports became disturbingly frequent. A few weeks later, Wake visited the National Academy of Sciences headquarters in Washington, D.C., for a meeting of the National Research Council's Board of Biology. Talking with colleagues there, he mentioned the stories from Canterbury. He spoke of Monteverde's missing salamanders and Golden Toads. Harold Morowitz, a biophysicist at George Mason University, and Oscar Zaborsky, then administrator for the Board of Biology, found the declines especially alarming. They and Wake organized a meeting of scientists to discuss the problem. Morowitz and Zaborsky took charge of raising money to finance the conference; Wake focused on recruiting participants.

It soon became apparent that the patterns that seemed so unusual to Wake were open to more than one interpretation. Amphibian populations naturally undergo strong fluctuations, and the more extreme cases could be mistaken for alarming declines (see Introduction to this chapter and Sec. 5.7). At a luncheon attended by representatives of conservation groups, Morowitz began to tell the story of the Golden Toad's disappearance. One of the attendees, who had worked in Costa Rica, cut him off, insisting there was no evidence that the Golden Toad had declined. Morowitz was stunned and almost derailed by this response, but with Wake's encouragement he continued his efforts as a lobbyist for frogs. As a scientist, Wake recognized that skepticism is healthy, because it forces researchers to adhere to high standards of scientific proof. As a conservationist, however, he felt he could not wait years before expressing his concern.

The efforts of Morowitz and Zaborsky paid off. Funding materialized and the meeting took place. In February 1990, with support from the Smithsonian Institution, Chicago's Brookfield Zoo, and the National Academy of Sciences, 40 scientists gathered at Irvine, California. Thirteen biologists told of declines and disappearances of amphibian populations in many widely scattered parts of the world (Wake and Morowitz 1991). Most of the participants were convinced that the reports were too many and too widespread to be sheer coincidence. Soon after the meeting, however, there were "cautionary tales" about drawing conclusions from "anecdotal observations" (Pechmann et al. 1991), and a heated controversy began (Blaustein 1994, Pechmann and Wilbur 1994, Pounds et al. 1997; see Sec. 5.1.1).

Some of those convinced of the reality of the problem took action. The Species Survival Commission of the World Conservation Union (IUCN) formed the Task Force on Declining Amphibian Populations

(DAPTF). This task force is the central communication point for scientists investigating amphibian declines. It awards seed grants for promising research projects and publishes a newsletter (*Froglog*). Small working groups—some organized by region, others by topic—carry out much of the task force's activities.

For an update of recent meetings and progress, see Wake (1998). Those desiring more information about DAPTF or wishing to receive *Froglog* should contact W. Ron Heyer, Chairman, DAPTF Board of Directors, c/o Biodiversity Programs, NHB 180, Smithsonian Institution, Washington, D.C. 20560 USA.

HOW DO MEADOW TREEFROGS DECIDE WHERE TO LAY EGGS?
Martha L. Crump

Amphibians are choosy about where they lay eggs. As comparisons among species show, aquatic-breeding frogs and toads prefer certain bodies of water over others. Some species breed only in streams; others are pond breeders. Of the latter, some breed in temporary ponds, and others in permanent ones. Within these broad patterns, a female might be choosy about details that can affect her offspring's chances of survival. A pool that is too warm might cause developmental abnormalities. One with the wrong kind of vegetation might be associated with high densities of predators, competitors, or parasites.

To examine how female Meadow Treefrogs (*Hyla pseudopuma*) on Monteverde's upper Pacific slope decide where to lay eggs, I performed experiments along the margins of a seasonal pond shortly after it had filled (Crump 1991a). These frogs lay eggs in temporary pools of various sizes. Although a single female might lay up to 2500 eggs, she typically lays them in several clusters (each with fewer than 500 eggs) at different places within the habitat. My earlier studies had revealed two important sources of mortality: drying of pools before larval development was completed, and cannibalism of eggs and hatchlings by older tadpoles (Crump 1983, 1990, 1991b). I designed experiments to determine whether water depth and the presence or absence of conspecific tadpoles influence a female's choice of sites. I predicted that females would prefer relatively deep water and pools lacking tadpoles.

In four experiments, I used plastic bowls to provide artificial pools in which I manipulated these variables. In experiment I, I asked whether females prefer to lay eggs in pools lacking conspecific tadpoles. I placed 20 bowls, each containing water 3.5 cm deep, in pairs around the edge of the pond. In one bowl of each pair, I put twenty 8-day-old tadpoles (hatched from eggs taken from a nearby pond that had filled earlier). As predicted, the female frogs preferred the bowls without tadpoles. In experiment II, I asked whether females prefer to lay eggs in deep, rather than shallow, water. All bowls lacked tadpoles, but one in each pair contained shallow water (1.0 cm instead of 3.5 cm deep). As predicted, the females preferred bowls with deeper water. In experiment III, I asked whether females choose between two unfavorable options: deep water with tadpoles and shallow water without tadpoles. I found no evidence that females chose one option over the other. Apparently preferring the adjacent pond, they laid few eggs in any of the bowls. In experiment IV, I asked whether females change their preferences over the course of an evening as pools become loaded with eggs. I used a design similar to that of experiment II (deep vs. shallow water), but after putting out the bowls (13 pairs) early in the evening (1900 hr), I checked them late the same evening (2300 hr) and the following morning (0800 hr). During the first part of the evening, females laid eggs preferentially in bowls with deep water. Later, when these containers became crowded with eggs, females preferred shallow water that contained fewer eggs.

These experiments showed that females are choosy about where they lay eggs. Their preferences in experiments I and II were appropriate in light of what we know about natural sources of mortality of embryos and larvae. The avoidance of sites with heavy egg loads (experiment IV) suggests that overcrowding of pools is another source of mortality, but this has not been studied in Meadow Treefrogs. Choice of oviposition sites affects both individual reproductive success and the structure of communities. Future studies should examine interactions between factors such as water depth and vegetation structure and the impact of potential competitors (e.g., Pin-striped Treefrogs at high elevations in the Monteverde area), predators (e.g., aquatic insects), and other possible enemies.

THE GOLDEN TOAD LABORATORY FOR CONSERVATION
J. Alan Pounds & Marlene Brenes

The Golden Toad Laboratory for Conservation (GTLC), established under the auspices of the MCFP and the Tropical Science Center, is devoted to research, applied conservation, and education. Declining populations of amphibians and reptiles are a primary focus. Conservationists founded the MCFP in 1972 to protect the endangered Golden Toad (Pounds and Fogden 1996). This species, which mysteriously vanished following a sudden population crash in 1987 (Pounds 1990, Crump et al. 1992, Pounds and Crump 1994, Pounds et al. 1997), has become a symbol of the global amphibian crisis and the vulnerability of species to rapid extinction (see Pounds, "Monteverde Salamanders," pp. 172–173).

The GTLC is located 0.5 km west of the MCFP entrance. Facilities under construction in a second-growth woodland that adjoins primary forest continuous with the MCFP include a laboratory (ca. 130 m²), three outdoor screen houses (ca. 12 m² each), several outdoor ponds, a research trail, and an amphibian greenhouse rain chamber (12 × 10 × 5.5 m). The rain chamber, which doubles as an educational exhibit, was built for frogs and toads. It includes a central pond, a stream with waterfalls, and a system for producing rain, all operated by electric pumps. A rainfall catchment system, including a 19,000-liter underground cistern, supplies water. A sound system plays music—toad trills, thunderstorms, and the like—to the amphibians that reside within.

The program of research and applied conservation presently focuses on climate change, its effects on natural populations (see Secs. 5.4.3, 5.7), and possible strategies for mitigating these effects. In one project, we are working with Meadow Treefrogs, which still survive in the area but whose populations declined along with those of the Golden Toad. These frogs are important in the food web. They are the mainstay of the Bronze-striped Parrot Snake, a harmless species that was once the most common diurnal snake on the upper Pacific slope but is now rare. We hope that by caring for Meadow Treefrogs during their early life stages, when survivorship is lowest, we can increase their numbers and those of species that depend on them.

During the 1996 wet season, we raised 3121 froglets in the laboratory (from eggs collected at the ponds we had built the preceding year) and released them around the pond margins. On 28 April 1997, after the first heavy rains of the year, we counted 91 adult Meadow Treefrogs at the ponds. The maximum in 1996 was 20 (on 21 May). Encouraged by the increase, we raised and released 12,000 froglets during the 1997 wet season. However, the number of adult frogs returning in 1998 did not differ from that in 1997.

Literature Cited

Alford, R. A., and S. J. Richards. 1997. Lack of evidence for epidemic disease as an agent in the catastrophic decline of Australian rain forest frogs. Conservation Biology 11:1026–1029.

Barinaga, M. 1990. Where have all the froggies gone? Science 247:1033–1034.

Barry, J. P., C. H. Baxter, R. D. Sagarin, and S. E. Gilman. 1995. Climate-related, long-term faunal changes in a California rocky intertidal community. Science 267:672–675.

Beebee, T. 1993. Conservation of the Golden Toad. British Herpetological Society Bulletin No. 46:28.

———. 1995. Amphibian breeding and climate. Nature 374:219–220.

Berger, L., R. Speare, P. Daszak, E. D. Green, A. A. Cunningham, C. L. Goggin, R. Slocombe, M. A. Ragan, A. D. Hyatt, K. R. McDonald, H. B. Hines, K. R. Lips, G. Marantelli, and H. Parkes. 1998. Chytridiomycosis causes amphibian mortality associated with population declines in the rain forests of Australia and Central America. Proceedings of the National Academy of Sciences USA 95:9031–9036.

Blaustein, A. R. 1994. Chicken Little or Nero's fiddle? A perspective on declining amphibian populations. Herpetologica 50:85–97.

Blaustein, A. R., and D. B. Wake. 1990. Declining amphibian populations: a global phenomenon? Trends in Ecology and Evolution 5:203–204.

———. 1995. The puzzle of declining amphibian populations. Scientific American 272:56–61.

Blaustein, A. R., D. B. Wake, and W. P. Sousa. 1994a. Amphibian declines: judging stability, persistence, and susceptibility of populations to local and global extinctions. Conservation Biology 8:60–71.

Blaustein, A. R., P. D. Hoffman, D. G. Hokit, J. M. Kiesecker, S. C. Walls, and J. B. Hays. 1994b. UV repair and resistance to solar UV-B in amphibian eggs: a link to population declines? Proceedings of the National Academy of Sciences USA 91: 1791–1795.

Brenes, A., and V. F. Saborio. 1994. Changes in the general circulation and its influence on precipitation trends in Central America: Costa Rica. Ambio 23:87–90.

Campbell, J. A. 1982. The biogeography of the cloud forest herpetofauna of Middle America, with special reference to the Sierra de las Minas of Guatemala. Ph.D. thesis, University of Kansas, Lawrence.

Carey, C. 1993. Hypothesis concerning the causes of the disappearance of boreal toads from the mountains of Colorado. Conservation Biology 7:355–362.

Colinvaux, P. A., P. E. De Oliviera, J. E. Moreno, M. C. Miller, and M. B. Bush. 1996. A long pollen record from lowland Amazonia: forest and cooling in glacial times. Science 50:85–88.

Corn, P. S., and J. C. Fogleman. 1984. Extinction of montane populations of the northern leopard frog (*Rana pipiens*) in Colorado. Journal of Herpetology 18:147–152.

Crump, M. L. 1983. Opportunistic cannibalism by amphibian larvae in temporary aquatic environments. American Naturalist 121:281–289.

———. 1984. Ontogenetic changes in vulnerability to predation in tadpoles of *Hyla pseudopuma*. Herpetologica 40:265–271.

———. 1986. Homing and site fidelity in a Neotropical frog, *Atelopus varius* (Bufonidae). Copeia 1986: 438–444.

———. 1988. Aggression in Harlequin Frogs: male-male competition and a possible conflict of interests between the sexes. Animal Behavior 36: 1064–1077.

———. 1989a. Effects of habitat drying on developmental time and size at metamorphosis in *Hyla pseudopuma*. Copeia 1989:794–797.

———. 1989b. Life-history consequences of feeding versus non-feeding in a facultatively non-feeding toad larva. Oecologia 78:486–489.

———. 1990. Possible enhancement of growth in tadpoles through cannibalism. Copeia 1990:560–564.

———. 1991a. Choice of oviposition site and egg load assessment by a treefrog. Herpetologica 47:308–315.

———. 1991b. You eat what you are. Natural History 100:46–51.

Crump, M. L., and J. A. Pounds. 1985. Lethal parasitism of an aposematic anuran (*Atelopus varius*) by *Notochaeta bufonivora* (Diptera: Sarcophagidae). Journal of Parasitology 71:588–591.

———. 1989. Temporal variation in the dispersion of a tropical anuran. Copeia 1989:209–211.

Crump, M. L., and D. S. Townsend. 1990. Random mating by size in a Neotropical treefrog, *Hyla pseudopuma*. Herpetologica 46:383–386.

Crump, M. L., F. R. Hensley, and K. L. Clark. 1992. Apparent decline of the golden toad: underground or extinct? Copeia 1992:413–420.

Czechura, G. V. 1991. The twilight zone. Wildlife Australia 28:20–22.

Czechura, G. V., and G. L. Ingram. 1990. *Taudactylus diurnus* and the case of the disappearing frogs. Memoirs of the Queensland Museum 29:361–365.

Diaz, H. F., and N. E. Graham. 1996. Recent changes in tropical freezing heights and the role of sea surface temperature. Nature 383:152–155.

Dobson, A., and R. Carper. 1992. Global warming and potential changes in host-parasite and disease-vector relationships. Pages 201–214 *in* R. L. Peters and T. E. Lovejoy, editors. Global warming and biological diversity. Yale University Press, New Haven, Connecticut.

Donnelly, M. A. 1994. Amphibian diversity and natural history. Pages 199–209 *in* L. A. McDade, K. S. Bawa, H. A. Hespenheide, and G. S. Hartshorn, editors. La Selva: ecology and natural history of a Neotropical rain forest. University of Chicago Press, Chicago.

Drost, C. A., and G. M. Fellers. 1996. Collapse of a regional frog fauna in the Yosemite area of the California Sierra Nevada. Conservation Biology 10:414–425.

Duellman, W. E. 1970. The hylid frogs of Middle America. Monographs, Museum of Natural History, University of Kansas No. 1. University of Kansas, Lawrence.

———. 1979. The herpetofauna of the Andes: patterns of distribution, origin, differentiation and community

structure. Pages 371–459 *in* W. E. Duellman, editor. The South American herpetofauna: its origin, evolution, and dispersal. Monographs, Museum of Natural History, University of Kansas, No. 7. University of Kansas, Lawrence.

———. 1988. Patterns of species diversity in anuran amphibians in the American tropics. Annals of the Missouri Botanical Garden 75:79–104.

Duellman, W. E., and L. Trueb. 1986. Biology of amphibians. McGraw-Hill, New York.

Fauth, J. E., B. I. Crother, and J. B. Slowinski. 1989. Elevational patterns of species richness, evenness, and abundance of the Costa Rican leaf-litter herpetofauna. Biotropica 21:178–185.

Fellers, G. M., and C. A. Drost. 1993. Disappearance of the Cascades frog, *Rana cascadae*, at the southern end of its range. Biological Conservation 65: 177–181.

Fitch, H. S. 1972. Ecology of *Anolis tropidolepis* in Costa Rican cloud forest. Herpetologica 28:10–21.

———. 1973. A field study of Costa Rican lizards. University of Kansas Science Bulletin 50:39–126.

———. 1975. Sympatry and interrelationships in Costa Rican anoles. Occasional Papers of the Museum of Natural History, University of Kansas 40:1–60.

Fogden, M. P. L., and P. M. Fogden. 1984. All that glitters may be toads. Natural History 93:46–50.

Gilpin, M. E., and M. E. Soulé. 1986. Minimum viable populations: processes of extinction. Pages 19–34 in M. Soulé, editor. Conservation biology, the science of scarcity and diversity. Sinauer, Sunderland, Massachusetts.

Glotfelty, D. E., J. N. Seiber, and L. A. Liljedahl. 1987. Pesticides in fog. Nature 325:602–605.

Graham, N. E. 1995. Simulation of recent global temperature trends. Science 267:666–671.

Graham, N. E., and W. B. White. 1988. The El Niño cycle: a natural oscillator of the Pacific Ocean–Atmosphere System. Science 240:1293–1302.

Greer, B. J., and K. D. Wells. 1980. Territorial and reproductive behavior of the tropical American frog *Centrolenella fleischmanni*. Herpetologica 36:318–326.

Guyer, C. 1986. Seasonal patterns of reproduction of *Norops humilis* (Sauria: Iguanidae) in Costa Rica. Revista de Biología Tropical 34:247–251.

———. 1994. The reptile fauna: diversity and ecology. Pages 199–209 *in* L. A. McDade, K. S. Bawa, H. A. Hespenheide, and G. S. Hartshorn, editors. La Selva: ecology and natural history of a Neotropical rain forest. University of Chicago Press, Chicago.

Harding, K. A. 1993. Conservation and the case of the Golden Toad. British Herpetological Society Bulletin No. 44:31–34.

Hayes, M. P. 1983. Predation on the adults and prehatching stages of glass frogs (Centrolenidae). Biotropica 15:74–76.

———. 1985. Nest structure and attendance in the stream-dwelling frog *Eleutherodactylus angelicus*. Journal of Herpetology 19:168–169.

———. 1991. A study of clutch attendance in the neotropical frog *Centrolenella fleischmanni* (Anura: Centrolenidae). Ph.D. thesis, University of Miami, Coral Gables, Florida.

Hayes, M. P., J. A. Pounds, and D. C. Robinson. 1986. The fringe-limbed frog *Hyla fimbrimembra* (Anura: Hylidae): new records from Costa Rica. Florida Scientist 49:193–198.

Hayes, M. P., J. A. Pounds, and W. W. Timmerman. 1989. An annotated list and guide to the amphibians and reptiles of Monteverde, Costa Rica. Herpetological Circulars No. 17:1–67.

Henderson, R. W. 1974. Aspects of the ecology of the Neotropical vine snake, *Oxybelis aeneus* (Wagler). Herpetologica 30:19–24.

———. 1984. *Scaphiodontophis* (Serpentes: Colubridae): natural history and test of a mimicry-related hypothesis. Pages 185–194 *in* R. A. Seigel, L. E. Hunt, J. L. Knight, L. Malaret, and N. L. Zuschlag, editors. Vertebrate ecology and systematics—a tribute to Henry S. Fitch. Museum of Natural History, University of Kansas, Lawrence.

Henderson, R. W., and L. G. Hoevers. 1977. The seasonal incidence of snakes at a locality in northern Belize. Copeia 1977:349–355.

Hero, J., and G. R. Gillespie. 1997. Epidemic disease and amphibian declines in Australia. Conservation Biology 11:1023–1025.

Heyer, W. R. 1967. A herpetofaunal study of an ecological transect through the Cordillera de Tilarán, Costa Rica. Copeia 1967:259–271.

Heyer, W. R., R. W. McDiarmid, and D. L. Weigmann. 1975. Tadpoles, predation, and pond habitats in the tropics. Biotropica 7:100–111.

Heyer, W. R., A. S. Rand, C. A. G. Cruz, and O. L. Peixoto. 1988. Decimations, extinctions, and colonizations of frog populations in southeast Brazil and their evolutionary implications. Biotropica 20:230–235.

Hoff, G. L., F. L. Frye, and E. R. Jacobson, editors. 1984. Diseases of amphibians and reptiles. Plenum, New York.

Houghton, J. T., L. G. Meira Filho, B. A. Callander, N. Harris, A. Kattenberg, and K. Maskell, editors. 1996. Climate change 1995—the science of climate change. Report of the Intergovernmental Panel on Climate Change. Cambridge University Press, Cambridge.

Jacobson, S. K. 1983. Short season of the Golden Toad. International Wildlife 13:25–27.

———. 1985. Reproductive behavior and male mating success in two species of glass frogs (Centrolenidae). Herpetologica 41:396–404.

Jacobson, S. K, and J. J. Vandenberg. 1991. Reproductive ecology of the endangered Golden Toad (*Bufo periglenes*). Journal of Herpetology 25:321–327.

Kagarise Sherman, C., and M. L. Morton. 1993. Population declines of Yosemite toads in the eastern Sierra Nevada of California. Journal of Herpetology 27:186–198.

Kim, Y. H., G. H. Brown, H. S. Mosher, and F. H. Fuhrman. 1975. Tetrodotoxin: occurrence in atelopodid frogs of Costa Rica. Science 189:151–152.

La Marca, E., and H. P. Reinthaler. 1991. Population changes in *Atelopus* species of the Cordillera de Mérida, Venezuela. Herpetological Review 22:125–128.

Laurance, W. F. 1996. Catastrophic declines of Australian rainforest frogs: is unusual weather responsible? Biological Conservation 77:203–212.

Laurance, W. F., K. R. McDonald, and R. Speare. 1996. Epidemic disease and the catastrophic decline of Australian rain forest frogs. Conservation Biology 10:406–413.

———. 1997. In defense of the epidemic disease hypothesis. Conservation Biology 11:1030–1034.

Lips, K. R. 1998. Decline of tropical montane amphibian fauna. Conservation Biology 12:106–117.

MacArthur, R. H. 1972. Geographical ecology: patterns in the distribution of species. Princeton University Press, Princeton, New Jersey.

McCoy, E. D. 1994. "Amphibian decline": a scientific dilemma in more ways than one. Herpetologica 50:98–103.

McDiarmid, R. W. 1971. Comparative morphology and evolution of frogs of the Neotropical genera *Atelopus, Dendrophryniscus, Melanophryniscus,* and *Oreophrynella*. Science Bulletin of the Los Angeles County Museum of Natural History 12:1–66.

———. 1983. *Centrolenella fleischmanni*. Pages 389–390 *in* D. H. Janzen, editor. Costa Rican natural history. University of Chicago Press, Chicago.

Miyamoto, M. M. 1982. Vertical habitat use by *Eleutherodactylus* frogs (Leptodactylidae) at two Costa Rican localities. Biotropica 14:141–144.

Myers, C. W. 1969. The ecological geography of cloud forest in Panama. American Museum Novitiates No. 2396:1–52.

Myers, C. W., and A. S. Rand. 1969. Checklist of amphibians and reptiles of Barro Colorado Island, Panama, with comments on faunal change and sampling. Smithsonian Contributions to Zoology No. 10:1–11.

Nieuwolt, S. 1977. Tropical climatology. Wiley, New York.

Osborne, W. S. 1989. Distribution, relative abundance and conservation status of Corroboree frogs, *Pseudophryne corroboree* More (Anura: Myobatrachidae). Australian Wildlife Research 16:537–547.

Parmesan, C. 1996. Climate and species' range. Nature 382:765–766.

Pechmann, J. H. K., and H. M. Wilbur. 1994. Putting declining amphibian populations in perspective: natural fluctuations and human impacts. Herpetologica 50:65–84.

Pechmann, J. H. K., D. E. Scott, R. D. Semlitsch, J. P. Caldwell, L. J. Vitt, and J. W. Gibson. 1991. Declining amphibian populations: the problem of separating human impacts from natural fluctuations. Science 253:892–895.

Peters, R. L., and T. E. Lovejoy. 1992. Global warming and biological diversity. Yale University Press, New Haven, Connecticut.

Phillips, K. 1990. Where have all the frogs and toads gone? Bioscience 40:422–424.

———. 1994. Tracking the vanishing frogs: an ecological mystery. St. Martin's Press, New York.

Pounds, J. A. 1988. Ecomorphology, locomotion, and microhabitat structure: patterns in a tropical mainland *Anolis* community. Ecological Monographs 58:299–320.

———. 1990. Disappearing gold. BBC Wildlife 8:812–817.

———. 1991a. Amphibian watch: new clues in the case of the disappearing amphibians. Wildlife Conservation 94:16–18.

———. 1991b. Habitat structure and morphological patterns in arboreal vertebrates. Pages 109–119 *in* Susan S. Bell, Earl D. McCoy, and Henry R. Mushinsky, editors. Habitat structure: the physical arrangement of objects in space. Chapman and Hall, London.

———. 1997. Golden Toads, null models, and climate change. Froglog, Newsletter of the Declining Amphibian Populations Task Force of the World Conservation Union's Species Survival Commission No. 23:1–2.

Pounds, J. A., and M. L. Crump. 1987. Harlequin Frogs along a tropical montane stream: aggregation and the risk of predation by frog-eating flies. Biotropica 19:306–309.

———. 1994. Amphibian declines and climate disturbance: the case of the Golden Toad and the Harlequin Frog. Conservation Biology 8:72–85.

Pounds, J. A., and M. P. L. Fogden. 1996. Conservation of the Golden Toad: a brief history. British Herpetological Society Bulletin No. 55:5–7.

Pounds, J. A., M. P. L. Fogden, and J. H. Campbell. 1999. Biological response to climate change on a tropical mountain. Nature 398:611–615.

Pounds, J. A., M. P. L. Fogden, J. M. Savage, and G. C. Gorman. 1997. Tests of null models for amphibian declines on a tropical mountain. Conservation Biology 11:1307–1322.

Pyburn, W. F. 1970. Breeding behavior of the leaf-frogs *Phyllomedusa callidryas* and *Phyllomedusa dacnicolor* in Mexico. Copeia 1970:209–218.

Robinson, D. J. 1961. The identity of the tadpole of *Anotheca coronata*. Copeia 1961:495.

Santer, B. D., K. E. Taylor, T. M. L. Wigley, T. C. Johns, P. D. Jones, D. J. Karoly, J. F. B. Mitchell, A. H. Oort, J. E. Penner, V. Ramaswamy, M. D. Schwarzkopf, R. J.

Stouffer, and S. Tett. 1996. A search for human influences on the thermal structure of the atmosphere. Nature 382:39–46.

Sarkar, S. 1996. Ecological theory and anuran declines. Bioscience 46:199–207.

Savage, J. M. 1966. An extraordinary new toad (*Bufo*) from Costa Rica. Revista de Biología Tropical 14:153–167.

———. 1975. Systematics and distribution of the Mexican and Central American stream frogs related to *Eleutherodactylus rugulosus.* Copeia 1975:254–306.

———. 1982. The enigma of the Central American herpetofauna: dispersals or vicariance. Annals of the Missouri Botanical Garden 69:464–547.

Savage, J. M., and W. R. Heyer. 1969. The tree frogs (family Hylidae) of Costa Rica: diagnosis and distribution. Revista de Biología Tropical 16:1–127.

Savage, J. M., and J. Villa. 1986. Introduction to the Herpetofauna of Costa Rica. Contributions to Herpetology No. 3:1–207.

Schall, J. J., and S. P. Vogt. 1993. Distribution of malaria in *Anolis* lizards of the Luquillo Forest, Puerto Rico: implications for host community ecology. Biotropica 25:229–235.

Scott, N. J. 1976. The abundance and diversity of the herpetofaunas of tropical forest litter. Biotropica 8:41–58.

———. 1983a. *Clelia clelia.* Page 392 *in* D. H. Janzen, editor. Costa Rican natural history. University of Chicago Press, Chicago.

———. 1983b. *Drymarchon corais.* Pages 398–399 *in* D. H. Janzen, editor. Costa Rican natural history. University of Chicago Press, Chicago.

———. 1983c. *Eleutherodactylus diastema.* Page 399 *in* D. H. Janzen, editor. Costa Rican natural history. University of Chicago Press, Chicago.

———. 1983d. *Imantodes cenchoa.* Page 402 *in* D. H. Janzen, editor. Costa Rican natural history. University of Chicago Press, Chicago.

———. 1983e. *Leptodactylus pentadactylus.* Pages 405–406 *in* D. H. Janzen, editor. Costa Rican natural history. University of Chicago Press, Chicago.

Seib, R. L. 1985. Euryphagy in a tropical snake, *Coniophanes fissidens.* Biotropica 17:57–64.

Siegel, R. A., and N. B. Ford. 1987. Reproductive ecology. Pages 210–252 *in* R. A. Siegel, J. T. Collins, and S. S. Novak, editors. Snakes: ecology and evolutionary biology. McGraw-Hill, New York.

Sprigg, W. A. 1996. Doctors watch the forecasts. Nature 379:582–583.

Starrett, P. 1967. Observations on the life history of frogs of the family Atelopodidae. Herpetologica 23:195–204.

Stebbins, R. C., and N. W. Cohen. 1995. A natural history of amphibians. Princeton University Press, Princeton, New Jersey.

Stewart, M. M. 1995. Climate-driven population fluctuations in rain forest frogs. Journal of Herpetology 29:437–446.

Stewart, M. M., and L. L. Woolbright. 1996. Amphibians. Pages 273–320 *in* D. A. Reagan and R. B. Waide, editors. The food web of a tropical rain forest. University of Chicago Press, Chicago.

Taylor, E. H. 1954. Frog-egg-eating tadpoles of *Anotheca coronata* (Stejneger) (Salentia, Hylidae). University of Kansas Science Bulletin 36:589–596.

———. 1955. Additions to the known herpetological fauna of Costa Rica, with comments on other species. No. II. University of Kansas Science Bulletin 37:499–575.

Telford, S. R. 1977. The distribution, incidence, and general ecology of saurian malarias in Middle America. International Journal of Parasitology 7:299–314.

Timmerman, W. W., and M. P. Hayes. 1981. The reptiles and amphibians of Monteverde: an annotated list to the herpetofauna of Monteverde, Costa Rica. Pensión Quetzal and Tropical Science Center, San José, Costa Rica.

Travis, J. 1994. Calibrating our expectations in studying amphibian populations. Herpetologica 50:104–108.

Van Berkum, F. H. 1986. Evolutionary patterns of the thermal sensitivity of sprint speed in *Anolis* lizards. Evolution 40:594–604.

Van Devender, R. W. 1980. Preliminary checklist of the herpetofauna of Monteverde, Puntarenas Province, Costa Rica and vicinity. Brenesia 17:319–325.

Vial, J. L. 1968. The ecology of the tropical salamander *Bolitoglossa subpalmata* in Costa Rica. Revista de Biología Tropical 15:13–115.

Villa, J., L. D. Wilson, and J. D. Johnson. 1988. Middle American herpetology: a bibliographic checklist. University of Missouri Press, Columbia.

Voris, H. K., and R. F. Inger. 1995. Frog abundance along streams in Bornean forests. Conservation Biology 9:679–683.

Wake, D. B. 1987. Adaptive radiation of salamanders in Middle American cloud forests. Annals of the Missouri Botanical Garden 74:242–264.

———. 1991. Declining amphibian populations. Science 253:860.

———. 1998. Action on amphibians. Treads in Ecology and Evolution 13:379–380.

Wake, D. B., and J. F. Lynch. 1976. The distribution, ecology, and evolutionary history of plethodontid salamanders in tropical America. Science Bulletin of the Los Angeles County Museum of Natural History 25:1–65.

Wake, D. B., and H. J. Morowitz. 1991. Declining amphibian populations—a global phenomenon. Report to the Board of Biology, National Research Council, on workshop in Irvine, California, 19–20 February 1990; reprinted in Alytes 9:33–42.

Wake, M. H. 1983. *Gymnopis multiplicata, Dermophis mexicanus,* and *Dermophis parviceps.* Pages 400–401 *in* D. H. Janzen, editor. Costa Rican natural history. University of Chicago Press, Chicago.

Wells, K. 1977. The social behaviour of anuran amphibian. Animal Behaviour 25:666–693.

Weygoldt, P. 1989. Changes in the composition of mountain stream frog communities in the Atlantic Mountains of Brazil: Frogs as indicators of environmental deteriorations? Studies in Neotropical Fauna and Environment 24:249–255.

Wheelwright, N. T. 1983. Fruits and the ecology of Resplendent Quetzals. Auk 100:286–301.

Wyman, R. L. 1990. What's happening to the amphibians? Conservation Biology 4:350–352.

Zweifel, R. G. 1964. Distribution and life history of a Central American frog, *Rana vibicaria.* Copeia 1964:300–308.

6

Birds

Bruce E. Young
David B. McDonald

Why Monteverde?

Birds have been a major focus of study in Monteverde. The first biologists to study in Monteverde were ornithologists William Buskirk and George Powell, who arrived in 1970 on the recommendation of F. Gary Stiles. They were attracted by the low stature of the cloud forest, which made research on mixed-species flocks more tractable than in tall lowland forests. The number of publications since then (110 as of 1996) and the number of different first authors of those publications (31) attest to the extent to which Monteverde birds have been studied. Sixteen Ph.D. students have written dissertations based largely on data collected on the birds of Monteverde (Table 6.1). In comparison, other well-known tropical study sites such as La Selva in Costa Rica or Manú in Peru have supported less graduate work on birds (five and four dissertations, respectively). Two major strengths of the Monteverde bird research are autecological studies and bird-plant interaction studies. Although autecological studies may be declining because of changing scientific fashion (Levey and Stiles 1994), studies on single species or small groups of species have abounded at

Monteverde. We know much about certain species but have little information about the bird community as a whole. Most studies of avian community ecology in Monteverde have been in the context of interactions with plants.

Monteverde's avifauna is attractive to ornithologists for five reasons:

(1) *Unusual behaviors:* From the perspective of temperate ornithologists, many species of birds in Monteverde exhibit bizarre behaviors. For example, dual-male duets and dances by male Long-tailed Manakins are phenomena that are virtually unique in the animal kingdom (McDonald and Potts 1994; Fig. 6.1; see McDonald, "Cooperation Between Male Long-tailed Manakins," pp. 204–205). Similarly, the March–July chorus of Three-wattled Bellbirds, heard for kilometers in every direction, draws attention to this species (Snow 1977; Fig. 6.2). Many who walk into a pasture in the dairy community have been mobbed by Brown Jays and wondered about their communal social behavior (Lawton and Guindon 1981, Lawton and Lawton 1985). These vocal species literally cry out to be studied.

Table 6.1. Doctoral dissertations based on research on Monteverde birds.

Author	Year	Institution	Title
Busby, W. H.	1987	U. Florida	Flowering phenology and density-dependent pollination success in *Cephalis elata*.
Buskirk, W. H.	1972	U. Cal., Davis	Ecology of bird flocks in a tropical forest.
Feinsinger, P.	1974	Cornell	Organization of a tropical guild of nectarivorous birds.
Guindon, C.	1997	Yale	The importance of forest fragments to the maintenance of regional biodiversity surrounding a tropical montane reserve, Costa Rica.
Lawton, M. F.	1982	U. Chicago	Altruism and sociobiology: a critical look and the critical issue.
McDonald, D. B.	1987	U. Arizona	Male-male cooperation in a neotropical lekking bird.
Murray, K. G.	1986	U. Florida	Avian seed dispersal of neotropical gap-dependent plants.
Powell, G.	1977	U. Cal., Davis	Socioecology of mixed species flocks in a neotropical forest.
Sargent, S.	1994	Cornell	Seed dispersal of mistletoes by birds in Monteverde, Costa Rica.
Shopland, J. M.	1985	U. Chicago	Facultative following of mixed-species feeding flocks by two species of neotropical warbler.
Tiebout, H. M., III	1990	U. Florida	Energetics of tropical hummingbirds: effects of foraging mode, competition, and resource availability.
Valburg, L.	1990	Washington State	Flocking, frugivory, and infested fruit consumption: choice in the foraging ecology of the Common Bush-Tanager (*Chlorospingus ophthalmicus*).
Wheelwright, N. T.	1982	U. Washington	Fruit characteristics and the foraging behavior of tropical fruit-eating birds.
Williams, D. A.	1997	Purdue	Multiple pathways to fitness in the cooperatively breeding Brown Jay.
Winnett-Murray, K.	1986	U. Florida	Variation in the behavior and food supply of four neotropical wrens.
Young, B. E.	1993	U. Washington	Geographical variation in avian clutch size: the case of the tropical House Wren, *Troglodytes aedon*.

Figure 6.1. A pair of Long-tailed Manakin males displaying while a female looks on. Photograph by Gregory Dimijian.

Figure 6.2. Male Three-wattled Bellbird calling from a display perch on an emergent tree. Photograph by Gregory Dimijian.

(2) *Abundance and ease of study:* Many species have large populations and occur close to the ground, making them easy to study. In the cloud forest on calm days, the sounds of hummingbird wing beats or call notes are rarely out of earshot, an indication of the ubiquity and research opportunities of species such as the Green Hermit and Purple-throated Mountaingem (Feinsinger et al. 1986, 1991a). Disturbed habitats in the community are alive with the calls of Brown Jays, House Wrens, and Golden-browed Chlorophonias, all of which have inspired in-depth studies (Sargent 1994, Williams et al. 1994, Young 1996).

(3) *Changes in avifauna across small spatial scales:* A striking feature of Monteverde is the turnover of faunas from one life zone (*sensu* Holdridge 1967) to the next, many of which are just a few hundred meters across (Powell 1977a, Young et al. 1998). In a short walk, one can pass through the different avian communities associated with the six life zones in Monteverde (Fig. 1.5). In genera such as nightingale-thrushes (*Catharus*), tropical wood-warblers (*Basileuterus*), and redstarts

(*Myioborus*), species occur in one or two life zones and are replaced by congeners in adjacent life zones, providing the opportunity to study patterns of species replacement (Shopland 1985).

(4) *Dramatic coloration:* The aesthetic appeal of birds such as the Resplendent Quetzal, the Emerald Toucanet, the Blue-hooded Euphonia, and the Golden-browed Chlorophonia has inspired research on these species. The colorful plumages can enliven a seminar or improve the visual appeal of a scientific journal (e.g., McDonald and Potts 1994).

(5) *Alluring setting:* The agreeable climate, spectacular views, and bilingual local populace of Costa Ricans and international expatriates that welcomes biologists draw ornithologists to Monteverde. With the local arts community and fresh dairy products available, Monteverde offers more attractions than other tropical research sites.

These factors have promoted attention to Monteverde's avifauna in the 30 years since its "discovery" by ornithologists. In this chapter, we summarize studies on Monteverde's birds, describing areas that have been well covered and identifying areas for future investigation. We generalize to the bird community as a whole based on (1) published data on a few species, (2) information that was collected elsewhere on species that occur at Monteverde, and (3) our own and colleagues' observations.

Methods

We define Monteverde as an area bounded roughly by the village of Santa Elena to the north, Poco Sol on the east, the southern limit of the Brillante trail of the Monteverde Cloud Forest Preserve (MCFP) to the south, and the village of San Luis to the west (Figs. 1.4, 1.6). Our definition of Monteverde encompasses an area of about 20,000 ha and includes six Holdridge life zones (Table 3.1). We refer to animals' common names; scientific names are listed in Appendixes 9 and 10.

6.1. Distribution, Species Richness, and Diversity

Monteverde's avifauna is derived from three principal regions: (1) the "Guanacaste" fauna on the Pacific slope, which represents the southernmost extent of the Mesoamerican dry forest fauna; (2) the highland fauna, a distinct group of species that occurs in the Costa Rican and Chiriquí, Panama, highlands; and (3) the wet forest fauna of the Caribbean slope. The wet forest fauna is derived primarily from South American groups; the highland and Guanacaste fauna are a mixture of North and South American groups. Although most areas of Costa Rica have either a dry or wet forest fauna plus North American migrants, Monteverde has all three because it straddles the Continental Divide. More extensive reviews of the zoogeography of Costa Rican and Central American avifaunas are available elsewhere (Howell 1969, Stiles 1983).

6.1.1. Life Zone Distribution

Monteverde's geography and climate, with a steep dry season gradient of increasing moisture from Pacific to Caribbean slope, create remarkably distinct vegetation in the different life zones (Table 3.1). Avian species richness also varies across the life zones (Table 6.2). Zone 4 (lower montane rain forest) has the lowest species richness (121 regularly occurring species), perhaps because of its small geographical extent and isolation from the more diverse high elevation faunas of the Central and Talamanca Cordilleras to the south. Zone 4 also has the highest proportion of unique species (9%).

Zones 5 and 6 (premontane rain and tropical wet forests) on the Caribbean slope (315 and 278 species, respectively) are the most species-rich life zones. These middle-elevation zones approach the highest bird species diversity of any site in Costa Rica, rivaling well-studied La Selva Biological Station with 256 breeding species and 155 migrants and rare visitors (Levey and Stiles 1994). Life Zones 5 and 6 are low enough in elevation to include the upper limit of the ranges of many lowland species and support many high-elevation species as seasonal migrants. Zone 6 includes a 2-ha lake and adjacent wetland that attract water birds not seen elsewhere in Monteverde.

Another method to characterize diversity (besides tallying species) is the species accumulation curve. The rate of accumulation of species is plotted as a function of the number of mist-net captures (Karr et al. 1990a). Although canopy species are underrepresented and forests of different statures are not comparable, the data are useful indicators of diversity. Species accumulation curves based on captures in second-growth and old-growth forest indicate that the Caribbean slope site (Zone 6) is much more diverse than the Pacific slope site (Zone 2; Fig. 6.3). The species accumulation curves for Zone 6 are so steep that even after several hundred captures, there is no indi-

Table 6.2. Patterns of bird diversity in the six principal life zones of Monteverde.

	Pacific Slope		Continental Divide		Caribbean Slope	
	Zone 1	Zone 2	Zone 3	Zone 4	Zone 5	Zone 6
Life zone	Premontane moist	Premontane wet	Lower montane wet	Lower montane rain	Premontane rain	Tropical wet
Species richness	165	202	187	121	315	278
Cumulative species	165	219	265	274	394	425
Unique species	—	6	0	11	17	—

Numbers of unique species for Zones 1 and 6 were not calculated due to a lack of information on birds from the adjacent zones downslope. Species listed as accidental or uncertain in Fogden (1993) are not included (see Appendix 9). See Table 3.1 for elevational ranges of zones.

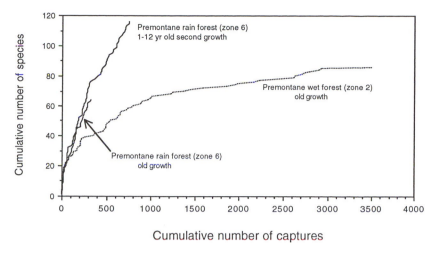

Figure 6.3. Species accumulation curves of birds caught in mist nets for two life zones at Monteverde (B. Young and D. McDonald, unpubl. data).

cation of the level of species richness at which the curves will flatten out. Species accumulation in Zone 6 is similar to that of Manú, Peru, the most diverse of four well-studied lowland neotropical sites (Karr et al. 1990a).

Most research at Monteverde has occurred in the Pacific slope (Zones 2–4) where species richness is intermediate (121–202 species per zone). These zones receive considerably less precipitation than the Caribbean slope zones (2000–2500 mm vs. 5000–6000 mm, respectively) and dry forests generally support fewer bird species than wet forest (Lack and Moreau 1965, Stiles 1983). Also, elevational migration is much less pronounced on the Pacific slope than on the Caribbean slope. Breeding species tend to remain resident year-round on their territories; middle-elevation sites receive fewer elevational migrants than similar sites on the Caribbean slope. Ecological differences between dry forests and the moist highland forests are greater than between wet Caribbean slope forests and the highland forests, which may limit migration. On the lower Pacific slope, seasonal migration is more common locally between adjacent dry and gallery forests, rather than along elevational gradients. Deforestation is most advanced on the Pacific slope, especially at lower elevations, and some species (e.g., the Scarlet Macaw, *Ara macao*) have gone locally extinct.

Most species that occur in Monteverde are restricted to a subset of the six principal life zones. Thirty-four species occur in just a single life zone. The effect of these restricted ranges is that as one travels along a transect up one slope across the Continental Divide and down the other slope, a series of distinct communities of birds is encountered, so the number of species increases throughout the journey. Thus, Monteverde has both high alpha species diversity (many species in one habitat type) and high beta species diversity (a high turnover in species across adjacent habitats).

The pattern of species occurring only in specific life zones is remarkable because habitat specialization occurs on a very small spatial scale. The life zones occur in narrow bands paralleling the ridge top of the Cordillera de Tilarán (Fig. 1.5). One way to appreciate this compression of habitat diversity is to consider the spatial scale of a standard 24-km-diameter Audubon Christmas Count circle. These circles are used by volunteer birdwatchers throughout North and Central America to sample winter bird densities. Count circles typically sample one or at most two life zones; by contrast, the count circle for the Monteverde Christmas Bird Count encompasses all six of Monteverde's life zones. Thus, the Monteverde counters typically record 20–30 more species than the most diverse of the other 1,700 Audubon Christmas Counts conducted annually.

6.1.2. Migration

Monteverde's birds consist of permanent residents, long-distance migrants, and elevational migrants, which is typical for locations on or near mountains in the neotropics (Wetmore 1926, Ridgely 1976, Stiles 1985a, 1988, Hilty and Brown 1986, Loiselle and Blake 1991). Long-distance migrants either breed primarily in the north temperate region during its summer and migrate to the neotropical region during the north temperate winter, or breed in Central America and migrate to South America during the nonbreeding season. Elevational migrants breed at one elevation on mountain slopes and migrate to another elevation during the nonbreeding season. Radio-tracking studies at Monteverde show these "elevational" migrations entail complex patterns of seasonal movement that can span international boundaries (G. Powell, unpubl. data; see Powell et al., "Altitudinal Migrations and Habitat Linkages, pp. 439–442).

Long-distance migration.   Of Monteverde's bird fauna, 91 species (21%) are long-distance migrants (Tramer 1979, Stiles and Smith 1980, Tramer and Kemp 1982, Fogden 1993). The majority breed in North America and pass through Monteverde during migration or overwinter in Monteverde. Four species (Swallow-tailed Kite, Sulphur-bellied Flycatcher, Piratic Flycatcher, and Yellow-green Vireo) breed in Monteverde and migrate to South America during the nonbreeding season. In contrast to elevational migrants, long-distance migrants decrease in abundance with increasing elevation, occurring most commonly in Zones 1–2 and 5–6 (Tramer and Kemp 1982, Fogden 1993, Young et al. 1998). This same pattern occurs throughout Costa Rica (Stiles 1980b). We know little about the ecology of North American migrants in Monteverde other than that they occur in old-growth and secondary forest, some species join mixed-species flocks of resident birds, and some species defend nonbreeding territories (Tramer and Kemp 1980, 1982). Competition between migrant and resident birds may not be very strong because individuals of the two groups rarely fight or interact agonistically (Tramer and Kemp 1980). Key questions such as overwinter survivorship of long-distance migrants in different habitats, population trends, effects of anthropogenic changes on habitat availability, and resource use by different species of migrants need study in Monteverde (Martin and Finch 1995, Rappole 1995).

Elevational migration.   Resplendent Quetzals have long been known to move seasonally from high-elevation nesting sites to lower elevations on both slopes (Wheelwright 1983). In the early 1990s, radio-tracking data provided greater precision concerning the timing and extent of these movements (Powell and Bjork 1995). The broad pattern is a four-stage annual movement. Courtship and nesting occur in cloud forest habitats (1500–1800 m) on both slopes between January and June. After nesting, adults and their offspring move to lower elevations (1100–1300 m) on the Pacific slope. Four months later, the birds move back for a few weeks to the higher elevation sites used for nesting. They then move across the Continental Divide to the Caribbean slope (700–1100 m), until the nesting season approaches. The pronounced variability of movement patterns among years is hypothesized to be due to variation in the availability of their fruit resources, particularly trees in the family Lauraceae (Wheelwright 1983, Powell and Bjork 1995).

An even more complex pattern of movement emerged from radio-tracking studies of Three-wattled

Bellbirds (Fig. 6.2). Bellbird migration begins similar to quetzals with breeding near the Continental Divide from March to July and a postbreeding movement down the Pacific slope to Zone 2 during August and September. They fly to the lowland rainforests of southeastern Nicaragua where they spend October through December. In January, bellbirds travel to the Pacific coast of Costa Rica where they scatter from Nicoya to the Osa Peninsula before returning to Monteverde in March (G. Powell, pers. comm.). Whether bellbirds flew all the way to Nicaragua before most of the northern lowlands of Costa Rica were cleared is unknown.

Smaller birds also make elevational movements, but they are harder to track with radios. For example, Black-faced Solitaires (Fig. 6.4) nearly disappear from Zone 4 during September–December when they migrate down the Caribbean slope (Murray 1986). Juvenile (but not adult) Black-faced Solitaires regularly appear in Zone 2 forests between July and September, suggesting age-related variation in migration (D. McDonald, pers. obs.). Although the migratory patterns of these smaller passerines have not been studied in detail, 68 of Monteverde's bird species are elevational migrants in the Cordillera Central and elsewhere in Costa Rica, and they probably undergo similar seasonal movements in Monteverde (Appendix 8). In general, frugivorous migrants nest at high elevations and descend on the Caribbean slope during the nonbreeding season. Hummingbirds migrate up to breed during the wet season and down in the dry season, although exceptions occur (Stiles 1980a, 1985c, Loiselle and Blake 1991).

6.2. Behavior

The first ornithologists in Monteverde studied the behavior of birds in mixed-species flocks, and several studies have followed up on this theme (Buskirk 1976, Powell 1979, Shopland 1985, Valburg 1992c). Researchers have examined the foraging behavior of individual species in the context of ecological studies of species coexistence, seed dispersal, sexual dimorphism (Winnett-Murray 1986, Riley and Smith 1992, Sargent 1994), and social behavior (Snow 1977, Riley 1986, McDonald and Potts 1994, Williams et al. 1994).

6.2.1. Mixed-Species Foraging Flocks

Many species in Monteverde forage while accompanying a mixed-species flock of birds. These flocks ("flocks" in this section refers to mixed-species assemblages) are one of the most noticeable features of bird-

Figure 6.4. Black-faced Solitaire at its nest on the trunk of a tree in the Monteverde Cloud Forest Preserve. Photograph by Kathy Winnett-Murray.

watching in the nonbreeding season (July–February). One can spend long stretches of time seeing few or no birds and then suddenly be surrounded by a host of flitting shapes and varied calls. These flocks fall into three categories: (1) army ant–following flocks, (2) frugivorous flocks, and (3) insectivorous flocks that do not follow army ants. The first two flock types are drawn by a common resource, either abundant insects flushing in front of a swarm of army ants (see Sec. 4.6.4) or fruits. The insectivorous flocks not associated with army ants form around vocal groups of birds and move through the forest in search of dispersed food.

In Monteverde, army ant–following flocks are generally not as large as in the lowlands, either because ant swarms are smaller or because they are rarer and less dependable food sources. In Zones 1 and 2, Northern Barred-Woodcreepers and Ruddy Woodcreepers (occasionally joined by Collared Forest-Falcons) are the principal army ant followers (Mays 1985, B. Young, unpubl. data). In Zones 3 and 4, army ants are rare and swarms are usually unaccompanied by birds. In Zones 5 and 6, Immaculate, Bicolored, and Ocellated Antbirds, and less frequently Plain-brown Woodcreepers, are the major components of the army ant flocks (B. Young, unpubl. data).

Flocks of frugivorous birds can form around any fruiting tree in any part of Monteverde. Some frugivores (e.g., Silver-throated, Spangle-cheeked, and Common Bush-Tanagers) join or form the nucleus of flocks of mostly insectivorous birds in Zones 3–5. In Zones 5 and 6, large flocks of tanagers (especially the genus *Tangara*), honeycreepers, and other frugivores move in a coordinated fashion through the forest. These frugivorous flocks are restricted to midelevation forests on the Caribbean slope and are virtually unstudied.

The dynamics of flock formation and behavior are better understood in the insectivorous flocks that occur throughout Monteverde. The "nuclear species," around which other species form flocks, are Golden-crowned Warblers and Lesser Greenlets (Zones 1 and 2), Common Bush-Tanagers and Three-striped Warblers (Zones 3–5), and Scarlet-rumped Caciques (Zone 6) (Powell 1979, Tramer and Kemp 1980, Valburg 1992c). In Zone 3, flocks peak in size in the morning and late afternoon and are much larger (by a factor of 3–4) during the nonbreeding season (Powell 1979). Flocks that form without a nuclear species are unstable and disintegrate rapidly. For many of these species, individuals of a given species drop out when the flock reaches their territory boundary and are replaced by individuals from the neighboring territory. Average flock speed is 5.4 (± 2.4) m/min; larger flocks move more slowly than smaller flocks. Physical and social factors influence flock dynamics; increasing wind intensity and precipitation decrease flock size (Powell 1979, Shopland 1985). In Zone 4, flocks con-

185   Birds

tain an average of 4.4 species per flock (range 2–20) and an average of 6.4 individuals per flock (range 2–26; Shopland 1985). Flocks in Monteverde generally have more furnariids (ovenbirds) and fewer antbirds and thamnophilids (antshrikes) than lowland flocks, in which antbirds and thamnophilids are often a major component (Buskirk 1976, Powell 1979, Munn 1985, Shopland 1985). Lowland forests also tend to have a greater variety of flock types than higher elevation forests (Munn and Terborgh 1979, Levey and Stiles 1994).

Common Bush-Tanagers are major components of flocks in Zones 3–5 (Valburg 1992c). In the presence of conspecifics, they eat primarily fruit; in the presence of flocks, they tend to switch to arthropod prey. Flocks may either facilitate access to arthropods that are normally unavailable, or provide assistance in predator vigilance that is unnecessary when feeding on fruit (Valburg 1992c; see Valburg, "Why Join Mixed-Species Flocks?," pp. 205–206). Some birds (Collared and Slate-throated Redstarts) appear to join flocks primarily as a means of territory defense or vigilance against predators; any foraging is simply "making the best of a bad lot" (Shopland 1985; see Shopland, "The Cost of Social Forging," pp. 206–207).

North temperate migrants vary in their propensity to join flocks (Powell 1980, Tramer and Kemp 1980). Black-and-white Warblers and Golden-winged Warblers often join flocks; Philadelphia Vireos and Tennessee Warblers frequently forage with conspecifics (Tramer and Kemp 1979, 1980). Black-and-white and Golden-winged Warblers use foraging methods that prevent them from simultaneously watching for predators (foraging on tree trunks and dead leaf clumps, respectively; Tramer and Kemp 1980), which may make them more dependent on the predator vigilance of flocks than other north temperate migrants with generalized feeding methods.

For many species, the advantage of joining insectivorous flocks appears to be avoidance of predation (Buskirk 1976, 1981, Powell 1985, Munn 1986, Hutto 1994). Flock-joiners tend to be species that are vulnerable to predation, use resources that are difficult to defend, and occur in pairs or small family groups. Species that do not join flocks are less vulnerable to predation (e.g., sentinel foragers that are adept at detecting predators themselves, hummingbirds that feed on the wing and are constantly vigilant when perched, and ground foragers that are protected from direct approaches by winged predators because of low foliage), form single-species flocks, or feed on clumped resources (Buskirk 1976). Observations that species attending flocks do not show positive associations, that flocks move relatively constantly through the forest without slowing at clumps of prey, and that

members forage on a wide variety of prey, support the suggestion that most species join flocks for early detection of predators (Powell 1985, Hutto 1994; see Shopland, "The Cost of Social Foraging," pp. 206–207). Predation avoidance is not the exclusive reason for joining flocks, as the Monteverde redstart study (Shopland 1985) and others in the neotropics have shown (Munn 1986). Some species probably join flocks to enhance foraging efficiency (Krebs 1973, Valburg 1992a; see Valburg, "Why Join Mixed-Species Flocks?," pp. 205–206). Further studies will provide details of how various members of a flock benefit in different ways (Latta and Wunderle 1996).

6.2.2. Foraging Behavior

Birds use similar resources in different ways. Quetzals, toucanets, and bellbirds feed on the fruits of lauraceous trees. Toucanets take fruits while perched, quetzals pluck fruits during sallies, and bellbirds use both techniques. Toucanets and bellbirds tend to forage high in the trees, whereas quetzals feed primarily in lower parts of the crown (Santana and Milligan 1984). Carnivorous birds also vary in their prey capture techniques. When foraging at army ant swarms, for example, Collared Forest-Falcons perch low to capture insects scared up by the ants (Mays 1985). Collared Forest-Falcons also chase lizards by running along the ground with partially opened wings (Mays 1985). Sunbitterns feed frogs, fish, lizards, and insects to their nestlings (Lyon and Fogden 1989). The parents often wash food items before presenting them to nestlings or after nestlings refuse a food item (Lyon and Fogden 1989). House Wrens and Gray-breasted Wood-Wrens (Fig. 6.5) forage faster, attack prey at a higher rate, change their foraging position faster, and use a greater variety of foraging sites (ground level through forest understory, woody tangles, and trees) than the larger Plain Wrens and Rufous-and-white Wrens, which forage in more specialized microhabitats such as aerial leaf clusters (Winnett-Murray 1986; see Winnett-Murray, "Choosiness and Productivity in Wrens," pp. 208–210).

Plants in Monteverde offer a wide variety of fruits as rewards for seed dispersal (Stiles 1985b), and fruits are important in the diets of a wide range of birds. Quetzals feed on the fruits of over 40 species of trees (Wheelwright 1983). Emerald Toucanets feed on the fruits of at least 109 species of plants and the flowers of *Erythrina lanceolata*, *Saurauia* sp., and *Macleania* sp. (Wheelwright et al. 1984, Riley 1986, Riley and Smith 1986; Fig. 6.6). Although they eat mostly fruit as adults, both quetzals and toucanets feed their nestlings a diet of primarily arthropods (Wheelwright 1983, Riley 1986). Yellow-throated Euphonias and

Figure 6.5. Gray-breasted Wood-Wren foraging in the understory of the lower montane wet forest. Photograph by Kathy Winnett-Murray.

Figure 6.6. Emerald Toucanet feeding on *Ficus pertusa* fruits. Photograph by Kathy Winnett-Murray.

Long-tailed Manakins, in contrast, eat primarily fruits as adults and feed their nestlings a fruit-dominated diet (Sargent 1993, D. McDonald, unpubl. data). Even some carnivorous birds, such as vultures, kites, antbirds, and wrens, sometimes eat fruit (Morton 1973, McDiarmid et al. 1977, Buskirk and Lechner 1978, Willis 1980, Keeler-Wolf 1986). Common Bush-Tanagers choose some of the fruits they eat based on the fly larvae infesting the fruits (Valburg 1992a,b,c; Valburg, "Do Fruit-Eating Birds," p. 210). Other species, such as Brown Jays, eat a wide variety of fruit and invertebrate and vertebrate food (Lawton 1983).

The majority of bird species in Monteverde are primarily insectivorous. Slate-throated and Collared Redstarts eat a diet of dipterans, homopterans, coleopterans, orthopterans, odonates, and lepidopterans. Foraging mode and diet vary depending on whether the individuals are in the presence of a mixed-species foraging flock (Shopland 1985; Fig. 6.7). House Wrens have a diet similar to that of redstarts, except that they eat arachnids and some hemipterans but ignore coleopterans (Young 1994a; see Winnett-Murray, "Choosiness and Productivity in Wrens," pp. 208–210).

Epiphytic plants are important resources for both frugivores and insectivores in Monteverde. These plants, which can contribute up to 63% of the plant species richness and 40% of the aboveground foliar biomass, provide habitat for arthropods, small vertebrate prey, fruit, and nectar resources (Nadkarni and Matelson 1989). In Zone 2, 59% of 56 bird species seen in trees foraged in epiphytes (Nadkarni and Matelson 1989, Nadkarni 1994).

Digestive physiology can influence foraging behavior. In Steely-vented Hummingbirds and Canivet's Emeralds (formally "Fork-tailed Emeralds"), the crop empties itself of nectar as fast as the nectar passes through the gut. Gut passage rate may be a time-limiting factor when hummingbirds consume large amounts of nectar during periods of high food demand. Under such conditions, hummingbirds may be forced to perch often to process nectar in their crops. During times of normal demand, however, food is passed rapidly enough that birds need not suspend foraging to process gut contents (Tiebout 1989).

6.2.3. Social Behavior

Two long-term studies of social behavior have been conducted in Monteverde. One is the study of Brown Jays initiated by Marcy and Robert Lawton and continued by Dean Williams (see Williams and Lawton, "Brown Jays," pp. 212–213). The second is the study of Long-tailed Manakins by Dave McDonald (see McDonald, "Cooperation between Male Long-Tailed Manakins," pp. 204–205). Other studies have addressed social behavior in Emerald Toucanets (Riley 1986; see Riley and Smith, "Ecology and Sexual Dimorphism," p. 214) and Three-wattled Bellbirds (Snow 1977).

Figure 6.7. Slate-throated Redstart preparing to hawk for insects. Photograph by Gregory Dimijian.

The major issue addressed by the Brown Jay study is cooperative breeding in the context of rapid population expansion. Cooperative breeding is a social system in which nonbreeding individuals associate with breeders to form social groups that communally occupy and defend a joint territory. In most cases, the nonbreeders are previous offspring of the breeders, but unrelated individuals also join groups. The degree to which these nonbreeders act as helpers at the nest and the root cause of cooperative breeding are controversial (Woolfenden and Fitzpatrick 1984, Brown 1987). A leading hypothesis ("habitat saturation") is that few vacant areas exist within suitable habitat, so young birds have little opportunity to establish their own territories at early ages. They may also benefit from remaining in their natal territories, where they receive help in locating food sources, receive increased vigilance against predators, and increase their inclusive fitness by helping to increase the survivorship of relatives ("kin selection").

The situation of Brown Jays at Monteverde is unusual among cooperative breeders in that the population has expanded rapidly during the past 30 years (see Williams and Lawton, "Brown Jays," pp. 212–213). This species inhabits second growth and disturbed habitats and has spread throughout Central America as a result of deforestation (Stiles and Skutch 1989). The social system of extended family groups has not been altered by widespread breeding vacancies, which challenges the habitat saturation hypothesis. Another unusual feature of the mating system is that unlike Florida Scrub-Jays (*Aphelocoma coerulescens*), in which the pair of behaviorally dominant "breeders" has absolute genetic paternity (J. Quinn, unpubl. data; D. McDonald, W. Potts, J. Fitzpatrick, and G. Woolfenden, unpubl. data), Brown Jay nests often contain eggs of more than one female. The social system more closely resembles that of Acorn Woodpeckers (*Melanerpes formicivorus*; Koenig and Mumme 1987), in which several females also lay in the same nest, than that of other jays.

Long-tailed Manakins are one of approximately 40 species in the neotropical family Pipridae, most of which are frugivorous and have a lek mating system, in which males provide no resources for breeding females (e.g., nest sites, feeding territories, or parental care). Rather, males rely on elaborate displays, often in traditional areas ("lek arenas") to which they attract females for mating. Males compete vigorously for mates either by displaying or by direct male-male combat. In Long-tailed Manakins, male-male cooperation in displays is juxtaposed against fierce competition among males for mates (see McDonald, "Cooperation between Long-Tailed Manakins," pp. 204–205). The most important factor influencing female visits to individual perches is the number of "toledo"

vocalizations given by the male partners. The most successful partnerships call at an average rate of 300 "toledos" per hour, much greater than less successful partnerships (McDonald 1989b). The calling rate, however, is not as closely correlated with copulatory success as it is with visitation success. To succeed in copulations, males engage in protracted portions of the dual-male dance display, particularly the "butterfly" display (Fig. 6.1), in which the partners radiate outward from the perch with labored flights that resemble the erratic flight of Blue Morpho butterflies (*Morpho peleides*; Slud 1957). Mate choice by females is hierarchical. Females visit males that call at high rates and, for copulations, choose among the males they visit on the basis of dance displays.

The large difference in mating success between the most successful and least successful males in Long-tailed Manakins has had profound effects on all aspects of the life history of the species (McDonald 1993b). Males and females differ in many ways: brilliant plumage in males versus cryptic green plumage in the females; intense sociality among males versus an essentially solitary existence for females; one of the most complex vocal repertoires known in male birds (Trainer and McDonald 1993) versus one or two distinct calls given by females. Another dramatic difference between the sexes is in their demographic profiles. Males (17 g) are similar to long-lived Yellow-eyed Penguins (5000 g) and male Northern Elephant Seals (*Mirounga angustirostris*; 3,700,000 g) in that their fitness depends on surviving for a long time. Because females begin reproducing at age 1 or 2 years, long-term survivorship is far less important (McDonald 1993b). The demographic divergence between the sexes within this species is almost as great as that between the extremes found throughout the entire class Aves.

Long-tailed Manakins are unusual in that males take 4 years to attain the definitive male plumage (the full "uniform" of red, black, and blue), in contrast to the 1–2 years it takes for most male passerines to reach definitive plumage. For each of the first 4 years of life, the males have a distinct, age-specific plumage. When they leave the nest, both males and females are green. One year after hatching, the crowns of males become red. Two years after hatching, their faces become black. Three years after hatching, the back begins to show powder blue. Four years after hatching, all traces of green are replaced by black. In an experimental study, males reacted more strongly to taxidermic mounts of males in definitive plumage than they did to males in the predefinitive plumage characteristic of yearling males (McDonald 1993a). This experiment provided evidence that the transitional, predefinitive plumages act as a signal of lower status, which reduces aggression against their bearers. By the time males attain definitive plumage, they probably recognize one another individually by vocalizations and behavior, and the "newcomers' badge" may no longer provide an advantage (McDonald 1993a).

6.2.4. Vocalizations

Vocalizations have been analyzed for three bird species in Monteverde, all of which have lek breeding systems. Long-tailed Manakins have a repertoire of at least 13 functionally and audially distinct vocalizations that serve in signaling between partnered males, in male-male aggression, and in dual-male courtship songs aimed at females. This large repertoire of functionally distinct vocalizations appears to have evolved as an aspect of the long-term cooperative relationships among males (Trainer and McDonald 1993; see Trainer, "Roles of Long-Tailed Manakin Vocalizations," p. 215).

Three-wattled Bellbirds are best known for their loud, ringing "Bong!" song, but males vary considerably in their associated screeching and hissing vocalizations. During the breeding season, males shout their "Bong!" throughout the day from exposed perches in the canopies of tall trees (Fig. 6.2). When a female joins a male on its perch, the male faces the female's ear and continues singing at full volume. Copulation may follow a series of calls if the female does not fly away (Snow 1977).

Male Green Hermits also give monosyllabic songs from their perches 0.75–1.75 m high in the cloud forest. Song rate varies between 34/min when males are alone to 57/min when other males are present. Green Hermits have three or four other calls that they give during male-male chases, male flight displays, and foraging (Snow 1972, M. Harger, unpubl. data).

6.3. Reproductive Biology

6.3.1. Phenology

All of the life zones in Monteverde are seasonal, with a distinct January to mid-May dry season (see Chap. 2, Physical Environment). Nesting in most bird species is also seasonal, with the majority of species nesting between March and July. Most species studied fit this pattern: Emerald Toucanet (Riley 1986), Yellow-throated Euphonia (Sargent 1993), Brown Jay (Lawton and Lawton 1985), Spotted Barbtail (Powell 1983), Resplendent Quetzal (Wheelwright 1983), Long-tailed Manakin (McDonald 1989b), Gray-breasted Wood-Wren (Winnett-Murray 1986), Rufous-and-white Wren (Winnett-Murray 1986), Plain Wren (Winnett-

Murray 1986), and House Wren (Winnett-Murray 1986, Young 1994a). Captures of birds with brood patches and fledgling birds in mist-net studies (D. McDonald, B. Young, G. Powell, unpubl. data) support this trend. The major exceptions to this pattern are the hummingbirds. Most nesting records of hummingbirds (e.g., Steely-vented Hummingbird, Rufous-tailed Hummingbird, Coppery-headed Emerald) are from October through January (Feinsinger 1977). The Green Hermit and Purple-throated Mountain-gem, in contrast, may breed through much of the year (Feinsinger 1977, F. G. Stiles, unpubl. data).

Why do Monteverde's birds breed when they do? Frugivores may nest when fruits are especially abundant. For example, quetzals nest when many trees in the family Lauraceae produce fruits. Lauraceous fruits comprise a large portion of the diet of adults, so quetzals may time their breeding to take advantage of their food resource base (Wheelwright 1983). Similarly, the October–January breeding season for hummingbirds coincides with the period when many hummingbird-pollinated plants (e.g., *Hansteinia, Razisea, Drymonia, Cavendishia, Kohleria, Cuphea, Malvaviscus*, and *Inga*) have their annual flowering peak (Feinsinger 1978, Feinsinger et al. 1986; see Chap. 3, Plants and Vegetation). Insectivores, on the other hand, may not depend on a superabundant resource base to produce eggs or feed young. The breeding season of insectivores spans the latter half of the dry season and the early wet season. In the late dry season, arthropod biomass is typically at its annual low (Feinsinger 1976, Buskirk and Buskirk 1976, Young 1994a), indicating that food is not a crucial resource for nesting insectivores during this period. Instead, birds may time their breeding so that their offspring disperse during the period of increasing food abundance that occurs throughout the first two-thirds of the wet season (Buskirk and Buskirk 1976, Young 1994a).

6.3.2. Nesting

Monteverde has been the site of studies on the nesting biology of 15 bird species. Original nest descriptions of five species are from Monteverde: Three-wattled Bellbird (Snow 1977), Black-and-yellow Silky Flycatcher (Kiff 1979), White-eared Ground-Sparrow (Winnett-Murray 1985), Azure-hooded Jay (Winnett-Murray et al. 1988), and Black-breasted Wood-Quail (McDonald and Winnett-Murray 1989). The first Costa Rican nests of the Sunbittern were described from Monteverde (Lyon and Fogden 1989). Preserved egg sets of Monteverde birds are at the Universidad de Costa Rica, the Burke Museum of the University of Washington, and the Western Foundation for Vertebrate Zoology.

Information on nest location, nest architecture, and construction materials is difficult to generalize. Individual species demonstrate a wide range of adaptations to protect their reproductive investments from the weather and predation. The Brown Jay, which nests in isolated trees to reduce predation by arboreal mammals, must nest in protected microsites to prevent the wind from blowing its nest out of the tree (Lawton and Lawton 1980). Nests in isolated trees produce four times as many fledglings as nests in windbreaks or forest (Williams et al. 1994), but nests in trees with high wind exposure are often blown down in wind storms (Lawton and Lawton 1980).

Many species of birds take advantage of readily available materials for nest construction. Moss grows densely on the bark of most trees in the MCFP (Zones 3–5); birds nesting in these life zones frequently use epiphytic moss in their nests (Table 6.3). Many hummingbirds also use scales from tree ferns (*Cyathea* sp.) in their nests (Stiles and Skutch 1989). Some species use bulky masses of moss to insulate their nests; others weave moss into the exterior of the nest for camouflage. That nests of several common species from these life zones remain undescribed (Stiles and Skutch 1989) suggests that their nests are well camouflaged. On the lower Pacific slope, moss grows much less abundantly on trees and is correspondingly rarer in bird nests. There, twigs, plant fibers, dry leaves, lichen, and fungal rhizomorphs are more typical constituents of forest-bird nests. Pasture and pasture-edge birds use grass in their nests (Table 6.3).

Some bird species build their nests in cavities of trees (Table 6.3). In the MCFP (Zones 3 and 4), 23% of 142 resident birds nest in cavities (Gibbs et al. 1993). Of these, nine species excavate their own cavities and 24 use previously excavated or natural cavities. Monteverde is typical of other tropical sites in having a greater frequency of cavity nesters (1.5–2.0 times as many species) and a higher percentage of its species dependent on existing cavities than in temperate forest sites. The density of standing dead trees (snags), however, is only one-third to one-seventh as great in Monteverde as in temperate sites. This paradox of more cavity-nesting species in habitats with fewer snags may be explained by the lower breeding densities of tropical cavity-nesters, extended breeding periods that permit sequential use of cavities, existence of decay cavities in live trees, and non-tree cavity sources such as termitaria and wasp nests (Gibbs et al. 1993).

6.3.3. Clutch Size

The clutch sizes of Monteverde's birds are small compared to those of temperate birds, as is typical in the humid tropics. The vast majority of forest interior species lay two-egg clutches; pasture and pasture-edge species tend to lay larger clutches (Table 6.4). This pattern of higher clutch sizes in birds of open areas than in related forest birds may be related to the greater seasonality or abundance of food availability in open areas (Lack and Moreau 1965; see Winnett-Murray, "Choosiness and Productivity in Wrens," pp. 208–210).

The question of why tropical birds lay smaller clutches than their temperate relatives was addressed in an experimental study of House Wrens (Young 1996). Tropical House Wrens lay about half as many eggs per clutch as either south- or north-temperate conspecifics (Young 1994b). In Monteverde, House Wrens were able to raise experimentally enlarged broods in two out of three years. Enlarged broods were preyed on at the same rate as smaller broods, contrary to the hypothesis that tropical birds lay smaller clutches to reduce predation risk (Skutch 1949). However, the enlarged broods produced more variance in the number of independent young reared than control broods. Given sufficient environmental variability, a lower-variance strategy (such as that observed in most tropical birds) can yield higher long-term fitness; fewer young are produced during each successful reproductive bout, but the chances of successful reproduction are increased (Gillespie 1977, Boyce and Perrins 1987). Long-term data on yearly variation in conditions for reproduction are needed to support this "bad-years effect" model as the best explanation for the small clutches of tropical birds (Young 1996).

Alternatively, parent birds in the tropics may have small clutches to devote more time to their offspring. Juvenile tropical birds may require more parenting than young temperate birds to learn to distinguish among the greater variety of toxic and nontoxic prey in the tropics (see Chap. 4, Insects and Spiders) and to win social contests for breeding opportunities, which are more competitive due to higher survivorship in the tropics (Fretwell 1969, Garnett 1981, Young 1996). Tropical House Wrens have longer incubation, nestling, and postfledging periods than temperate House Wrens, indicating that tropical House Wrens invest more time in reproduction (Young 1996). Further experimentation on whether offspring of small broods are better foragers and socially dominant to offspring of large broods will clarify whether offspring quality is a factor leading to the small clutch sizes of tropical birds.

One anomalous case is that of the Yellow-throated Euphonia, which lays unusually large clutches in nests built in crevices in earthen banks (modal clutch size of this species in Monteverde is five eggs; Sargent 1993), larger than any other neotropical passerine (Skutch 1985). Larger clutches generally incur higher rates of nest predation because the nesting attempt

Table 6.3. Use of nest material and nest location by birds in Monteverde (based on Stiles and Skutch 1989).

Inhabitants of cloud forest (Zones 3–4) that use moss

Violet Sabrewing	Black-faced Solitaire
Fiery-throated Hummingbird	Slaty-backed Nightingale-Thrush
Stripe-tailed Hummingbird	Black-and-yellow Silky-flycatcher
Purple-throated Mountain-gem	Wrenthrush
Green-crowned Brilliant	Golden-browed Chlorophonia
Red-faced Spinetail	Silver-throated Tanager
Golden-bellied Flycatcher	Spangle-cheeked Tanager
Yellowish Flycatcher	Black-thighed Grosbeak
Gray-breasted Wood-Wren	

Inhabitants of pastures (Zones 1–3) that use grass

Spotted Barbtail	Yellow-faced Grassquit
Tropical Kingbird	White-naped Brush-Finch
Plain Wren	Stripe-headed Sparrow
House Wren	Rufous-collared Sparrow
Gray-crowned Yellowthroat	Eastern Meadowlark
Blue-black Grassquit	

Monteverde species that nest in tree cavities

Barred Forest-Falcon	Hairy Woodpecker
Collared Forest-Falcon	Smoky-brown Woodpecker
Bat Falcon	Rufous-winged Woodpecker
Crimson-fronted Parakeet	Golden-olive Woodpecker
Orange-fronted Parakeet	Lineated Woodpecker
Orange-chinned Parakeet	Pale-billed Woodpecker
Brown-hooded Parrot	Buffy Tuftedcheek
White-crowned Parrot	Plain Xenops
White-fronted Parrot	Plain-brown Woodcreeper
Barn Owl	Ruddy Woodcreeper
Spectacled Owl	Olivaceous Woodcreeper
Mottled Owl	Long-tailed Woodcreeper
Orange-bellied Trogon	Wedge-billed Woodcreeper
Slaty-tailed Trogon	Strong-billed Woodcreeper
Lattice-tailed Trogon	Northern Barred-Woodcreeper
Resplendent Quetzal	Black-banded Woodcreeper
Red-headed Barbet	Spotted Woodcreeper
Prong-billed Barbet	Streak-headed Woodcreeper
Emerald Toucanet	Spot-crowned Woodcreeper
Collared Aracari	Black-headed Antthrush
Keel-billed Toucan	Masked Tityra
Black-cheeked Woodpecker	Blue-and-white Swallow
Hoffman's Woodpecker	House Wren

takes longer, which exposes young to nest predators over a longer period of time (Clark and Wilson 1981). Also, larger broods require more frequent feeding visits by parents, giving predators more opportunity to find the nest by following the movements of the adults. The diet of nestling Yellow-throated Euphonias is mostly fruit, which, due to its lack of protein, can cause nestlings to grow slowly and be exposed to nest predators over a longer period. Paradoxically, data from 52 euphonia nests in Monteverde showed a slightly higher nesting success (35% of all nests fledged at least one young; Sargent 1993) than average for other neotropical passerines that nest outside of holes and cavities (29%; Skutch 1985). Yellow-throated Euphonias visit the nest infrequently and in pairs, with one member of the pair stopping at the nest and the other swooping past the nest, perhaps distracting predators' attention from the nest itself. This behavior, combined with the construction of an "awning" over the nest that hides it from view, may compensate for the longer nesting periods required for this species (Sargent 1993).

Table 6.4. Clutch sizes of birds observed nesting in forest and pastures in Monteverde.

Species	Clutch Size	Species	Clutch Size
Forest interior species			
Black-breasted Wood-Quail (1)	5	White-throated Spadebill (4)	2
Sunbittern (2)	2	Yellowish Flycatcher (3)	2
Ruddy Pigeon (3)	1	Long-tailed Manakin (10)	2
Chiriqui Quail-Dove (4)	1	Rufous-and-white Wren (11)	2–4
Buff-fronted Quail-Dove (5)	2	Gray-breasted Wood-Wren (11)	2
Squirrel Cuckoo (3)	2	Black-faced Solitaire (5)	2–4
Green Hermit (3)	2	Slate-throated Redstart (12)	2–3
Purple-throated Mountain-gem (3)	2	Collared Redstart (12)	2–3
Orange-bellied Trogon (3, 6)	2–3	Three-striped Warbler (5)	2
Resplendent Quetzal (7)	2	Buff-rumped Warbler (3)	2
Emerald Toucanet (8)	3–5	Common Bush-Tanager (3)	2
Spotted Barbtail (9)	2	Olive Tanager (3)	2
Northern Barred-Woodcreeper (4)	2	Slaty Flowerpiercer (3)	2
Eye-ringed Flatbill (3)	2	White-eared Ground-Sparrow (13)	2
Pasture and Edge			
Common Pauraque (14)	2	Plain Wren (12)	3
Stripe-tailed Hummingbird (3)	2	Yellow-throated Euphonia (18)	3–5
Hoffman's Woodpecker (3)	2	Yellow-faced Grassquit (3)	2–3
Brown Jay[b] (15, 16)	2–8	Eastern Meadowlark (3)	3
House Wren (12, 17)	3–5		

[a]*Sources* are as follows: (1) McDonald and Winnett-Murray 1989; (2) Lyon and Fogden 1989; (3) B. Young, pers. obs.; (4) D. McDonald, pers. obs.; (5) D. Wenny, pers. obs.; (6) Wheelwright, pers. obs.; (7) Wheelwright 1983; (8) Riley 1986; (9) Powell 1983; (10) McDonald 1993b; (11) Winnett-Murray 1986; (12) Shopland 1985; (13) Winnett-Murray 1985; (14) C. Howell, pers. comm.; (15) Lawton and Guindon 1981; (16) Lawton and Lawton 1985; (17) Young 1994b; (18) Sargent 1993.

[b]More than one female may lay in a single nest.

6.3.4. Incubation

Because of a lack of study, it is not possible to generalize about incubation in the birds of Monteverde. For all passerines studied in Monteverde, only females incubate (Lawton and Lawton 1985, Shopland 1985, Sargent 1993, Young 1993a), but no data on ancestral passerines such as the furnariids or dendrocolaptids exist. Both sexes incubate in most nonpasserines, except for hummingbirds and wood-quail (Wheelwright 1983, Riley 1986, Lyon and Fogden 1989, McDonald and Winnett-Murray 1989). In quetzals, both sexes incubate but only the female sits on the nest at night (Wheelwright 1983). Each member of a Sunbittern pair incubates for two days during the first portion of the incubation period, and one day during the latter portion (Lyon and Fogden 1989).

Incubating Brown Jays exhibit one of the most puzzling behaviors of any species in Monteverde. Females sit on the nest and "whine" incessantly, beginning before the first egg is laid and lasting throughout the incubation period. This characteristic whine is given only by incubating females and is audible at least 100 m from the nest (Lawton and Guindon 1981). Up to five females may incubate in a nest, and each whines while on the nest (Lawton and Lawton 1985).

This behavior makes Brown Jay nests extraordinarily easy for biologists to find but apparently is not compelling enough to predators to make the behavior maladaptive. The call most likely has a social function, perhaps serving as communication between the lone incubating female and her flock (Skutch 1960). This explanation is supported by the observation that females are four times more likely to whine when other flock members are present within 50 m of the nest (Lawton and Lawton 1985).

6.3.5. Postfledging

Tropical birds are characterized by long postfledging periods in which fledglings remain on their natal territories and receive food and perhaps predator protection from their parents. Monteverde birds are no exception; most fledglings remain with their parents for a considerable time after fledging (Table 6.5). House Wrens, with a postfledging period of 3 weeks to 3 months, are a useful point of comparison because they breed both in the tropics and in the temperate zone. Temperate-zone House Wrens remain in their natal territories for only 12–13 days (Gross 1948).

Table 6.5. Postfledging periods (time during which fledgling birds remain on their natal territories) of some birds of Monteverde.

Species[a]	Postfledging Period (days)	Habitat
Spotted Barbtail (1)	60	Forest
Rufous-and-white Wren (2)	30–60	Forest
Plain Wren (2)	30–180	Edge
House Wren (2)	21–90	Pasture/edge
Gray-breasted Wood-Wren (2)	150–180	Forest
Slate-throated Redstart (3)	28	Forest

[a]*Sources:* (1) Powell 1983, (2) Winnett-Murray 1986, (3) Shopland 1985.

The adaptive significance of long post-fledging periods is poorly understood. Fledglings may remain with their parents to receive more care and better learn how to forage than they would on their own (Young 1996). Parents may also be better at detecting predators and, by alerting them with alarm notes, give their fledglings time to take cover (Karr et al. 1990b). Alternatively, juvenile birds may not disperse because they have nowhere to go; the habitat may be saturated with conspecifics, so the best that juveniles can do is to stay with their parents where they are tolerated but receive no active parental care.

6.4. Responses to Seasonality

Seasonality in abiotic factors drives phenological changes in plants, such as flowering, fruiting, and the production of new leaves (see Chaps. 2 and 3). These seasonal changes in the flora affect the quantities of plant resources available to animals and the capacity of herbivorous insects to exploit their hosts. Although the degree of the seasonal changes in abiotic factors varies among life zones, characteristic patterns of fruit, nectar, and insect abundance occur in each (see Chaps. 3 and 4). Birds respond to some of these seasonal changes by adjusting their reproduction and molt schedules; some species migrate to track the changing abundance of resources (Feinsinger 1977, Wheelwright 1983, Young 1994a, Powell and Bjork 1995).

6.4.1. Migration

Hummingbirds show seasonal movements that are most obviously tied to seasonal resource abundance. Several species occur in Monteverde only when certain plants are flowering. For example, visits of the

Magenta-throated Woodstar and the Blue-throated Goldentail (September–April) coincide with flowering peaks of *Lobelia laxiflora* and *Inga brenesii* (Feinsinger 1977). Similarly, the Plain-capped Starthroat migrates to Monteverde from the Pacific lowlands when the vine *Mandevilla veraguasensis* blooms (May–August; Feinsinger 1977, 1980). On the Caribbean slope, three hummingbird species (White-necked Jacobin, Brown Violetear, and Green Thorntail) are most abundant when *Inga oerstediana* blooms (March–June; Fogden 1993). These flowers also attract Steely-vented Hummingbirds that fly over the divide from Zones 1 and 2 on the Pacific slope where they occur for the remainder of the year (Fogden 1993). Other hummingbird species occur in Monteverde seasonally, but the reasons are more complex than the attraction of one or two species of plants (Feinsinger 1977).

Other species undergo elevational migrations to or from Monteverde. Quetzal movements appear to track geographical differences in the abundance of lauraceous fruits (Wheelwright 1983). At the community level, elevational migration has been studied more intensively on the Caribbean slope of the Cordillera Central where the seasonal occurrence of frugivores in mist nets is positively correlated with fruit abundance (Loiselle and Blake 1991). Seasonal occurrence of migrant nectarivores in other lowland and mid-elevation forest is also correlated with flower availability (Stiles 1978, 1980a, 1985c). Breeding by lowland frugivores, however, is negatively correlated with local fruit abundance. The presence of seasonal migrants may complicate that situation, however, because many residents breed after the migrants have left (Rosselli 1989, Loiselle and Blake 1991). Populations of lowland insectivores generally do not make local seasonal movements (Levey and Stiles 1992). Because the Caribbean slope of the Cordillera de Tilarán in Monteverde shares similar climate, life zones, and fauna with the Caribbean slope of the Cordillera Central, the patterns of migration of Monteverde's frugivores and nectarivores are probably similar; more studies are needed to confirm this pattern.

6.4.2. Physiological Ecology

Fierce winds whip cool horizontal precipitation in the higher elevation areas of Monteverde from December through early March, and presumably birds have physiological adaptations to these conditions. Many species (e.g., House Wrens, Brown Jays) do not begin breeding until these early dry-season winds subside (Lawton and Lawton 1985, Young 1994a). If the wind and mist resume after the onset of nest building, both species stop all nesting activities until the weather improves. The winds calm earlier in some years than others, and House Wrens advance the onset of breeding by as much as one month in response to the fair weather (Young 1994a).

Harsh weather can also affect bird foraging behavior. Stripe-tailed Hummingbirds, which inhabit disturbed habitats, forage at patches of flowering *Hamelia patens*, a plant that produces copious nectar during the wet season (Feinsinger 1976). During sunny weather, many butterflies also visit *Hamelia* plants and take enough nectar to deplete the resource to the extent that the plants do not merit defense by hummingbirds. On rainy days, however, the butterflies are inactive and active defense becomes worthwhile (Thomas et al. 1986).

6.4.3. Timing of Molt

Molt is an energetically costly event in the annual cycle of birds (Walsberg 1983). Whether birds time annual molting periods to coincide with periods of high food abundance or with reproduction is not well studied. House Wrens molt during September and October when their arthropod prey is at its annual peak (Young 1994b). Similarly, frugivores molt during periods of increasing fruit abundance on the Cordillera Central (Loiselle and Blake 1991). Most birds (other than hummingbirds) in Monteverde molt between July and November (Fig. 6.8), when arthropods and nectar are moderately to very abundant (Buskirk and Buskirk 1976, Feinsinger 1976, 1978, Feinsinger et al. 1986, Young 1994b), but fruit abundance is low (W. Haber, unpubl. data). All the hummingbirds that have been studied (Green Hermit, Violet Sabrewing, Green Violetear, Purple-throated Mountain-gem,

Stripe-tailed Hummingbird, Coppery-headed Hummingbird, Green-crowned Brilliant, and Magenta-throated Woodstar) molt between December and April when flower abundance is high (F. G. Stiles, unpubl. data). Although many tropical species exhibit considerable overlap between molt and breeding at the population level (Foster 1974), little is known about molt-breeding overlap at the individual level.

6.5. Population Biology

Although the autecological approach taken by many Monteverde ornithologists makes communitywide comparisons difficult, the focus on individual species has provided good data on the dynamics and demography of certain populations of birds. The focus on three species (Long-tailed Manakins, Brown Jays, and House Wrens) has provided most of the data on the population biology of Monteverde birds.

6.5.1. Density

We do not know the overall density of birds in Monteverde, which prevents comparison with other tropical sites such as Manú, Peru, where the densities of many species are known (Terborgh et al. 1990). However, density estimates of some species that occur in Monteverde exist. An estimated 50 pairs of quetzals bred in or adjacent to the MCFP in 1980 (Wheelwright 1983). The MCFP had an area of 2700 ha at that time, yielding one breeding pair per 54 ha. In 1978, the home range of Brown Jay flocks averaged 20.9 ha, with flocks averaging 10.2 birds/flock (calculated from Williams et al. 1994). Flock size increased to 13.3 birds/flock by 1987, and by 1990, the home range of a flock was 10.8 ha. House Wrens in the upper community (Zone 3) have territories that average 0.77 ha (B. Young, unpubl. data).

Density is difficult to define for species that do not maintain year-round territories. For example, Three-wattled Bellbirds may occur at different densities during the segments of their annual four-part migrations. When they are in Monteverde during the breeding season, males can form aggregations in which each is in acoustical contact with the others (Snow 1977). A 1974 study reported that 2.9 territorial males occurred per 100 ha in Monteverde (Snow 1977); however, calling male bellbirds did not occur for many kilometers in any direction outside of the study area, even though the habitat there appeared to be similar to the habitat within the study area. During the nonbreeding season, the same male bellbirds may be dispersed in forest patches separated by distances of over 100 km (G. Powell, unpubl. data). The density esti-

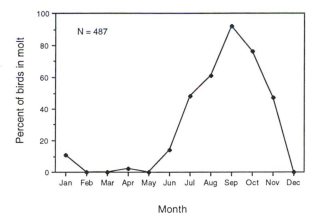

Figure 6.8. Monthly change in the percentage of birds (excluding hummingbirds) molting either flight or body feathers in Monteverde (B. Young, unpubl. data).

mates can differ by several orders of magnitude depending on the scale of measurement and the time that the census occurs relative to the annual cycle of the bird.

6.5.2. Demography

Understanding the demographic parameters of a population requires quantitative knowledge of many life-history parameters, many of which are difficult and time consuming to measure in wild birds. Brown Jays can begin breeding when they are 1–2 years old but rarely do so (Lawton 1983). Older members of a flock usually perform most of the breeding activities (Lawton and Lawton 1985). Flocks made up entirely of 1–2-year-olds occur, but an activity such as nest-building takes three times as long as for more mature flocks (Lawton 1983). In contrast, House Wrens begin breeding at the age of one year; yearling females are just as capable at raising young as older females in terms of clutch size, number of nesting attempts, egg-hatching success, and nestling growth (Young 1993b). In Long-tailed Manakins, as in many lek-mating systems, the sexes differ greatly in their age at first reproduction. Females can breed when they are 1–2 years old, but males rarely copulate before they are at least 8 years old (McDonald 1993b).

Fertility for birds is measured as the average number of eggs, chicks, or fledglings produced per female per year. The fertility term in matrix population models based on postfledging censuses is the number of offspring produced per female per stage (usually one year for models of bird populations) times the probability that these offspring survive to the next stage (usually the first year of age). In Monteverde, fertility has been estimated or calculated directly for three species. Female House Wrens at Monteverde produce on average 4.2 three-day-old nestlings per breeding season (Young 1996). Of these, 3.7 survive to fledge, 2.5 survive the first two weeks post-fledging, and 0.4 survive to the following breeding season (calculated from Young 1996). Female Long-tailed Manakins produce an average of 1.5 offspring each year that survive to the following year (McDonald 1993b). Brown Jay flocks produce an average of 0.7–3.8 fledglings per year (Williams et al. 1994). Other studies have based calculations on the productivity of nests; these do not translate into annual fertility without quantitative information on first-year survival and how many nesting attempts a female, pair, or flock makes per breeding season.

Survivorship has been examined in Long-tailed Manakins and House Wrens in Monteverde. In male manakins, the average annual survival rate for 1–3-year-olds was 0.68, whereas survivorship in older

birds was slightly better (0.78). The survival rate for females was 0.75 (McDonald 1993b). Average survivorship for one-year-old or older House Wrens (assuming age-independent survivorship) was 0.46 for males and 0.47 for females (Young 1996). Direct observations of breeding birds indicate that tropical birds may live longer than related temperate birds (Karr et al. 1990b). No temperate species is directly related to manakins; however, survivorship of temperate House Wrens is 17–49% lower than that of tropical House Wrens (Young 1996).

6.5.3. Sources of Mortality

Predators are probably important sources of mortality for Monteverde's birds, but direct observation of predation events is rare. In a 2-year study of redstart participation in mixed-species flocks, Shopland (1985; Shopland, "The Cost of Social Foraging," pp. 206–207; Fig. 6.7) never witnessed a predation attempt and concluded that redstarts do not join mixed-species flocks to gain protection from predators. Eight attacks (half of which were successful) by either Barred Forest-Falcons or Collared Forest-Falcons on Common Bush-Tanagers were witnessed over a period of 15 months (Valburg 1992c; see Valburg, "Why Join Mixed-Species Flocks?," pp. 205–206). However, an observer's presence can frighten away predators, causing underestimation of their importance (Powell 1985). Also, predation can be a rare but important selection factor (Lima 1987). Anecdotal evidence accumulated over many years in Monteverde supports the importance of predation. Hawks and margays attack quetzals (Wheelwright 1983). An incubating House Wren was killed by a Mouse Opossum. Barred Forest-Falcons attack fledgling and adult House Wrens (Young 1993b) and are frequently seen clutching recently captured birds.

Predation on bird nests is much easier to quantify. Predators leave obvious traces in the form of disheveled nests, egg shells, or blood in nests. Nest predation rates have been calculated for 11 species of birds in Monteverde (Table 6.6). Predation is responsible for variable but substantial losses in bird nests in Monteverde, as is typical for the tropics (Ricklefs 1969). Although cavity nests are considered safer from predators than open nests (Lack 1954), this pattern has exceptions in Monteverde. House Wrens and Emerald Toucanets build cavity nests and lose relatively few nests to predators, but quetzals, which also nest in cavities, have high rates of nest predation (Table 6.6). Some species can defend their nests against predators. Adult quetzals successfully defend nests against Emerald Toucanets and squirrels (Wheelwright 1983). Brown Jay mobs defend their nests from Broad-winged Hawks, Common Black-Hawks, Varie-

Table 6.6. Nest loss rates and predators of bird nests at Monteverde.

Species[a]	Predation rate (%)[b]	N (nests)	Identified Predators
Resplendent Quetzal (1)	67–78%	9	Long-tailed weasel
Emerald Toucanet (2)	20	10	White-faced Capuchin
Long-tailed Manakin (3, 4)	83	12	Emerald Toucanet, Red Squirrel
Brown Jays (5)			Unknown
Isolated trees	4	25	
Nonisolated trees	100	5	
Rufous-and-white Wren (6)	28	11	Unknown
Plain Wren (6)	40	5	Unknown
House Wren (6)	12	38	Unknown
House Wren (7)	27.2	318	Mouse Opossum, Coati
Gray-breasted Wood-Wren (6)	50	6	Unknown
Slate-throated Redstart (8)	66	41	Unknown
Collared Redstart (8)	81	26	Unknown
Yellow-throated Euphonia (9)	66	41	Unknown

[a]Source: (1) Wheelwright 1983; (2) Riley 1986; (3) D. McDonald 1993b; (4) D. McDonald unpubl. data; (5) Lawton and Lawton 1980; (6) Winnett-Murray 1986; (7) Young 1994a; (8) Shopland 1985; (9) Sargent 1993.

[b]Predation rate calculated by dividing the number of nests lost to predators by the total number of nests found or, in the case of House Wrens and Yellow-throated Euphonias, from Mayfield (1975) daily survivorship estimators.

gated Squirrels, White-faced Capuchins, and domestic cats, which may explain the low rate of nest predation in this species (Lawton and Lawton 1980).

The study of tropical bird parasitology is in its infancy, but Monteverde is the site of initial work in this field. Parasites are often invisible to human observers but can cause significant levels of mortality in adult and nestling birds (Brown and Brown 1986, Møller 1990, Toft 1991). In Monteverde, 11% of 479 individuals sampled (representing 60 species) showed evidence of blood parasite infections (Young et al. 1993). Among the parasites, *Haemoproteus* sp. was responsible for 88% of all infections. *Plasmodium* sp., *Leucocytozoon* sp., *Trypanosoma* sp., and microfilarial worms caused the remaining infections. Most birds were free of parasites, with the exception of Emerald Toucanets, tanagers (especially Common Bush-Tanagers), and emberizid finches (especially the brush-finches, White-eared Ground-Sparrows, and Rufous-collared Sparrows). Samples taken during the period when most juveniles were fledging and dispersing (May–November) were 54% more likely to show infections than samples taken during intervening months. This pattern suggests that parasites may time their occurrence in the blood stream to coincide with the time when more susceptible individuals are available in the host population (Young et al. 1993). In a study on the effects of botfly larvae (*Philornis carinatus*) on nestling House Wrens (botflies live just beneath the skin), 8% of nests in Monteverde had at least one nestling infected by botflies but mortality was not higher in these nests (Young 1993a). Rates of infection were much higher in House Wren populations in San Luis (31%; Zone 1) and in La Lucha (27%)

in the Caribbean lowlands below Zone 6. Botfly larvae infestations in Rufous-and-white Wren nestlings did not affect survivorship or fledging weight (Winnett-Murray 1986). Further study of intestinal parasites and the effects of ecto- and endoparasites on host survivorship is needed.

The physical environment can also cause mortality in birds. Long periods of cold wind and rain are conditions in which many insects do not fly and become difficult for insectivores to find. This weather, typical of December through March in Zones 3 and 4, can also increase the metabolic needs of birds. With greater energy needs and fewer resources, some birds, especially insectivores, may die of starvation. Wind also influences bird fitness in Monteverde. During an unusually strong 4-day storm in April, 1978, 10 of 12 Brown Jay nests were destroyed; chicks, eggs, and entire nests were blown out of trees (Lawton and Lawton 1980). Similarly, wind blew a Rufous-and-white Wren nest out of a tree; continuous heavy rain led to chick mortality in other nests of this species (Winnett-Murray 1986). Rain has caused floods that washed out House Wren nests built in road banks (Winnett-Murray 1986) and American Dipper nests along the Peñas Blancas River (F. G. Stiles, unpubl. data).

Human activity in Monteverde also causes mortality in birds. Habitat destruction is the most obvious cause (see Chap. 12, Conservation Biology). Glass windows on houses built in forested areas are responsible for hundreds of window-kills per year. Most of the dozens of specimens from Monteverde in museum collections were prepared from Monteverde birds that died by flying into a pane of glass. Domestic cats and dogs also take their toll on adult and nestling birds. Hunting of birds in most of Monteverde has stopped, but Black and Crested Guans were once sought after for food, and other birds such as Macaws and Cattle Egrets were shot out of curiosity or for sport (M. Leitón, pers. comm.; see Chap. 7, Mammals). Bird capture for the pet trade is not as rampant at Monteverde as in other areas. For example, the Black-faced Solitaire (Fig. 6.4) is common in Zone 4. A singing male is worth $100 in San José, and the species has consequently been driven close to extinction in many unprotected parts of the country. With well-protected private reserves in Monteverde, human-caused mortality of birds will remain minimal (see Young, "How Have Humans Affected Bird Populations?," pp. 433–434).

6.5.4. Among-Year Variation in Fertility and Survivorship

Varying weather patterns cause changes in resource levels, which affect the fertility and survivorship of birds. The annual or stochastic variation that can result in these demographic variables should be incorporated into population models to portray population dynamics accurately (Gillespie 1977, Boyce and Perrins 1987, Caswell 1989, McDonald and Caswell 1993).

For House Wrens, female survivorship varied among years from 0.42 to 0.57; male survivorship varied from 0.40 to 0.66 (Young 1996). Fertility varied little over the course of the three-year study. The ability of parents to raise artificially enlarged broods varied from year to year, suggesting that in years more extreme than the study interval, fertility could decline (Young 1996). In Brown Jays, flocks inhabiting the same territories varied fourfold in the number of fledglings produced over a three-year period (Williams et al. 1994).

6.5.5. Population Dynamics

Population fluctuations may be the norm rather than the exception (Pimm 1991). A dramatic example is the Brown Jay, which first invaded Monteverde in the mid-1950s and has continued to expand in range and increase in population density to the present (Lawton and Lawton 1985, Williams et al. 1994; see Williams and Lawton, "Brown Jays," pp. 212–213). This range extension is not obviously tied to habitat alteration. The disturbed habitats of Monteverde where Brown Jays occur (Zones 1–3) were deforested in the 1940s (10–15 years prior to the arrival of the jays), and the amount of cleared land has probably decreased slightly since then. Similarly, Great-tailed Grackles arrived in Monte-

verde about 1980 and have since invaded most of the farms of the Pacific slope, four decades after deforestation (B. Young and T. Guindon, pers. comm.; see Chap. 12, Conservation Biology). Species such as the Great Kiskadee and Eastern Meadowlark have also expanded their ranges as habitats changed. Other range expansions have been more subtle. Slate-throated Redstarts slowly increased their range upward in Zone 4, and Collared Redstarts retreated to the elfin forest along the Continental Divide, although no obvious habitat change occurred (Shopland 1985, B. Young, pers. obs.; for examples of other apparently climate-driven range changes, see Chap. 5, Amphibians and Reptiles).

These examples of population expansion and contraction result from changes in mortality and/or reproduction. Hummingbird population density at Monteverde also varies dramatically across years depending on flower abundance, but the variation is due to immigration and emigration rather than changes in birth and death rates (Feinsinger 1980). Conversely, population size may remain constant, but only because of constant immigration from other areas where conditions are favorable for reproduction. Such source-sink subsidy is also the case for House Wrens in the upper Monteverde community (see Young, "House Wrens," p. 448).

Changes in habitat via succession and land-clearing also affect population dynamics. The squatters' clearings in the Peñas Blancas valley (Zones 5 and 6) are the sites of the rise and fall of populations of several species of open-country birds (e.g., Groove-billed Ani, Common Pauraque, Tropical Kingbird, House Wren). These species colonized and formed reproductive populations after deforestation in the 1960s and 1970s. After the Peñas Blancas squatters were bought out by the Monteverde Conservation League (MCL) in the late 1980s (see Chap. 10, Conservation Institutions), the clearings began to grow into secondary forest; open-country birds disappeared except in a few small clearings maintained for shelters (Fogden 1993).

The pattern of forest disturbance and regrowth in Peñas Blancas over the last 30 years probably mirrors the prehuman conditions in which these open-country birds evolved. Large-scale disturbances such as those caused by volcanoes, landslides, and river course changes created isolated habitats for which these species were adapted. All of the clearings in the upper Peñas Blancas valley were separated from more extensive clearings on either the Pacific or Caribbean slope by at least 5 km of forest. The observation of a banded juvenile House Wren deep in Peñas Blancas (Zone 5), 12 km distant and 5 weeks after fledging from a nest in Zone 3 in Monteverde (B. Young, pers. obs.), demonstrates their ability to disperse across substantial stretches of unsuitable habitat.

6.6. Community Ecology

Major works on the community ecology of birds in Monteverde include studies on hummingbird population dynamics in relation to flower abundance (Feinsinger 1976, 1977, 1978, 1980), hummingbird pollination guilds and hummingbird-mediated effects of floral neighborhoods on pollination success in plants (Feinsinger et al. 1986, 1987, 1991a, Feinsinger and Tiebout 1991), relationships between large frugivores and fruiting in the Lauraceae (Wheelwright 1983, 1985, 1988, 1991), seed dispersal by small frugivores (Murray 1987, 1988, Murray et al. 1994), and coevolution among euphonias, chlorophonias, and mistletoes (Sargent 1994, 1995). Here we summarize these studies; they are covered in more depth in Chapter 8, Plant-Animal Interactions.

6.6.1. Guilds

The guild (group of species using the same resource) is a useful approach to consider subsets of bird communities (Root 1967). Guilds of hummingbirds were studied in Monteverde for 15 years (Feinsinger 1976, 1980, Feinsinger and Colwell 1978, Feinsinger et al. 1988), particularly in successional habitats along the cliff edge in Zone 2 (Feinsinger 1976). The Steely-vented Hummingbird appears to organize the guild through its aggressive territorial defense of dense clumps of flowers. The Canivet's Emerald traplines dispersed flowers that are not defended by Steely-vented Hummingbirds (see Tiebout, "Do Subordinate Species Have an Advantage?," pp. 216–218). The Magenta-throated Woodstar visits the same flowers defended by Steely-vented Hummingbirds, escaping detection by its bumblebeelike flight and by foraging in the highest portions of *Inga* trees. Whenever detected, the woodstars are easily displaced by the dominant Steely-vented Hummingbird. Another core species, the migratory Green Violetear, which occurs in Monteverde from October to June, uses a mixed strategy of visiting rich clumps of flowers (when attacks from Steely-vented Hummingbirds are infrequent) and traplining dispersed flowers (when Canivet's Emerald populations are low).

Nine other hummingbird species (plus Tennessee Warblers) forage for nectar in these habitats (Feinsinger 1976). These peripheral species arrive for brief periods to take advantage of surplus flowers. The resources available in the cliff-edge habitats in Monteverde are not large enough to support year-round populations of all species of nectarivorous birds. Nectar resources located elsewhere that are available when resources are low in Monteverde maintain the populations of the majority of species that feed on cliff-edge flowers (Feinsinger 1980). Combining observations from Monteverde with other studies in neotropical mainland and island forests, six roles for hummingbirds in nectar-foraging guilds have been proposed: high reward trapliners (e.g., hermits of Zones 3–6 in Monteverde), territorialists (e.g., Steely-vented Hummingbird), low-reward trapliners (e.g., Canivet's Emerald), territory parasite-marauder (no Monteverde example), territory parasite-small filcher (e.g., Magenta-throated Woodstar), and generalists (e.g., Green Violetear; Feinsinger and Colwell 1978).

A series of ingenious experiments examined the physiological ecology of captive Steely-vented Hummingbirds and Canivet's Emeralds (Tiebout 1991a,b, 1992, 1993). Energy consumption was measured with the double-labeled water technique (Tiebout and Nagy 1991). Each species showed metabolic adjustments that allowed it to acclimatize to energetic stresses when placed individually in flight cages with high and low quantities of food at either small or large distances (Tiebout 1991a). The territorialist (Steely-vented Hummingbird), however, was more stressed by flying to a distant food source than was the trapliner (Canivet's Emerald). When one individual of each species was caged with a heterospecific, and nectar "patches" were clumped, territorialist Steely-vented Hummingbirds maintained better energy balances than did the competing trapliners (Tiebout 1992). The trapliners performed better when nectar patches were dispersed than when they were clumped because they could better avoid the aggressive territorialists. In the course of day-long experiments with clumped or dispersed treatments, the two species adjusted their behavior by concentrating on different subsets of feeders. This reduced the rate of aggressive interactions, an adjustment that probably also occurs in the field (Tiebout 1991a, 1992). Emeralds maintained more favorable energy balances when paired with conspecifics than when paired with a heterospecific. In contrast, the aggressive Steely-vented Hummingbirds suffered higher energetic stress when paired with conspecifics than when paired with Emeralds (Tiebout 1993). The "pointer hypothesis" (Tiebout 1996; see Tiebout, "Do Subordinate Species Have an Advantage?," pp. 216–218) suggests that the more aggressive Steely-vented Hummingbirds may benefit from the food-finding ability of the Emeralds.

The forested habitats in Zones 3–6 support two distinct guilds of hummingbirds. One guild has short bills (<25 mm) and exploits flowers with correspondingly short corollas. The second guild has longer, often curved bills (>28 mm) and visits flowers with corollas over 30 mm long (Feinsinger et al. 1986). These guilds are also dominated by few species (the short-billed Purple-throated Mountain-gem and the long-billed Green Hermit), with nine other species appearing for varying periods throughout the year. These two guilds are apparently stable even in habitats that sustain disturbance. Community makeup was similar in forest understory, tree-fall gaps, and experimental cut-over plots that mimicked larger scale disturbances such as landslides (Feinsinger et al. 1986).

Guilds of frugivorous birds in Monteverde have been studied to a lesser degree. A compilation of all feeding records of frugivorous birds in Monteverde (Wheelwright et al. 1984) provides a springboard for biologists who study guilds of birds that feed on specific groups of plants. Large-gaped birds can eat larger fruits than small-gaped birds; however, large-gaped birds can also eat fruits just as small as those eaten by small-gaped birds, which results in less specialized diets for large-gaped birds (Wheelwright 1985). The behavior of individual members of a guild of frugivorous birds may be similar. The four major species that feed on the fruits of trees in the family Lauraceae (Resplendent Quetzal, Emerald Toucanet, Three-wattled Bellbird, and Mountain Robin) spend similar amounts of time (2.9–4.7 min) in a tree and eat about the same number (1–3) of fruits per visit, although their foraging methods and locations may differ (Santana and Milligan 1984, Wheelwright 1991). Members of large- and small-gaped frugivore guilds show greater overlap in both diet and behavior than do guilds of long- and short-billed hummingbirds.

Two guilds of small-gaped frugivores consist of species with unusually narrow diets (Sargent 1994). One guild consists of four tanager species (Golden-browed Chlorophonia, Blue-hooded Euphonia, Yellow-throated Euphonia, Yellow-crowned Euphonia) that feed on five species of mistletoe (family Viscaceae). The sticky seeds of these fruits force the birds to engage in bill or vent-wiping behaviors that glue the seed to the branch where the bird is perched (see Sargent, "Specialized seed dispersal," p. 288). There the seed germinates and infests a new host. Another guild of 10 species includes a diverse group of pigeons, flycatchers, and vireos that feed on six species of mistletoes (families Loranthaceae and Eremolepidaceae). These families have single-seeded fruits whose pulp separates more easily from the seed than does the pulp of fruits in the Viscaceae. The diet of the Blue-hooded Euphonia consists of 81% mistletoes in the Viscaceae; 77% of the diet of the Paltry Tyrannulet is made up of mistletoes in the Loranthaceae and Eremolepidaceae. These diets are unusually restricted compared to frugivores that typically eat dozens of species of fruits (Wheelwright et al. 1984). Having evolved the ability to handle mistletoe fruits more efficiently than other frugivores, Blue-hooded Euphonias and Paltry Tyrannulets may not require very broad diets (Sargent 1994).

Guilds can be defined based on the use of resources other than food. One promising group for future study is the guild of cavity-nesting birds (Table 6.3). Snag density in Monteverde (Zone 4) is less than the snag density of many temperate forests, but 2.5 times more species nest in these cavities (Gibbs et al. 1993). Study of how cavity-nesting birds divide up this resource or compete for suitable nesting sites will help explain the coexistence of species and provide information on how to best manage for these species. Cavity-nesting birds are especially amenable to experimental study because of the ease of manipulating the resource with artificial cavities.

6.6.2. Interactions with Other Taxa

Bird-plant interactions have been the primary focus of bird research at Monteverde. There is strong dependence of Monteverde's plants on birds for seed dispersal (Table 6.7), but Monteverde's flora is much less dependent on birds for pollination. About 9% of the flora is bird-pollinated (Stiles 1981; see Chap. 8, Plant-Animal Interactions). Nevertheless, 29 species of hummingbirds, plus other nectar-feeders (Tennessee Warblers, Bananaquits, Baltimore Orioles, Slaty Flower-Piercers, Scarlet-thighed Dacnis, and three species of honeycreepers) feed on nectar during at least part of the year.

Table 6.7. Dependence of Monteverde's flora on birds for seed dispersal compared to other habitats in Costa Rica (based on Stiles 1985b).

Site (Forest Type)	Percentage of Plant Species That Rely on Birds for Seed Dispersal	
	Shrubs and Small Trees	Canopy Trees
Monteverde (middle elevation cloud forest)	77	63
Palo Verde (lowland dry forest)	45	35
La Selva (lowland rain forest)	63	50
Cerro de la Muerte (highland wet forest)	82	72

The consequences of plant interactions with birds have been investigated repeatedly. For example, fruit phenology, size, shape, color, and abundance on a plant may be influenced by bird foraging patterns (Wheelwright and Orians 1982, Wheelwright and Janson 1985, Bronstein and Hoffman 1987, Murray 1987, Wheelwright 1988, Valburg 1992c, Murray et al. 1994). Flowering biology may also be influenced by foraging in nectarivores (Feinsinger 1978, Feinsinger et al. 1986, 1987, 1988, 1991a, Feinsinger and Busby 1987, Feinsinger and Tiebout 1991, Podolsky 1992, Stiles and Freeman 1993). Plant flowering and fruiting phenologies may be adapted to avoid competition with other bird-pollinated or bird-dispersed plants (see Wheelwright, "A Hypothesis," pp. 281–282). In both pollination and seed-dispersal systems, there is evidence for competition, but not for evolved shifts in phenology to reduce this competition (Feinsinger 1978, Wheelwright 1985, Feinsinger et al. 1986, 1987, 1991b, Busby 1987, Feinsinger and Busby 1987).

Birds are also influenced by how and when plants offer their reproductive rewards. Links between the migrations of hummingbirds and frugivores in and out of Monteverde and seasonal nectar or fruit abundance is one example (Feinsinger 1976, 1980, Wheelwright 1983, Powell and Bjork 1995). Another case is the annual variation in fruit crops of some trees; wide year-to-year variation exists in fruit production of trees in the family Lauraceae, with 10–90% of individuals in a species producing fruit in a given year (Wheelwright 1986b). The amount of fruit production on a tree also varies considerably, resulting in annual fruit resource levels that can vary by over an order of magnitude. Birds dependent on these fruits may respond by migrating, expanding their diets, or delaying reproduction (Wheelwright 1986b). Plants also vary in their annual production of flowers (P. Feinsinger, unpubl. data), and nectarivorous birds may be affected in the same way that frugivores are affected by the variation in fruit production.

6.7. Comparative Ecology

How typical is Monteverde's avifauna compared to the avifauna of cloud forests elsewhere in the tropics? We compared the fauna in Zone 3 (lower montane wet forest) of Monteverde to that of three other sites in Central and South America that occur in the same life zone. Because most species' ranges are smaller than the scale of this comparison, comparing species identity is inappropriate. A comparison of species richness is also biased because the amount of effort needed to identify birds varies among the sites (Remsen 1994). Instead, we compared trophic guilds

at the four sites to examine the structure of communities made up of different species.

We used bird lists from Monteverde (Fogden 1993); Darién, Panama (Robbins et al. 1985); Huila Department, Colombia (Ridgely and Gaulin 1980, Martin 1984); and the Cordillera Vilcabamba, Peru (Terborgh 1977), dividing the avifauna of each site into nectarivores, frugivores, and insectivores (Hilty and Brown 1986, Stiles and Skutch 1989). We ignored carnivores because individuals are scarce (Terborgh 1977). We categorized species based on their primary food, and split true omnivores evenly between the frugivore and insectivore groups. We assumed that where species lists were incomplete, overlooked species belong to the three trophic guilds in the same frequencies as the species that were detected.

The results show a remarkable similarity in the relative abundance of species in the three trophic groups across the four sites (Fig. 6.9). Insectivores account for 53–63% of the faunas; frugivores make up 27–32% of the totals. The importance of nectarivores varies by almost 40% in the four sites, but overall they make up a small proportion of the total species. Monteverde has intermediate numbers of all three trophic groups relative to other sites, so the bird community at Monteverde appears to be typical of cloud forest sites in the neotropics.

Compared to lowland forests, higher elevation forests in the humid tropics tend to support relatively fewer insectivore species and more frugivore species (Terborgh 1977). In Costa Rica, insectivores make up increasingly smaller fractions of the bird communities at higher elevation sites, for example, along a transect including La Selva (35 m), Monteverde (1500 m), and Cerro de la Muerte (2900 m; Stiles 1983). Lowland sites are especially rich in species of the exclusively insectivorous families Dendrocolaptidae (Woodcreepers) and Thamophilidae (antbirds) and

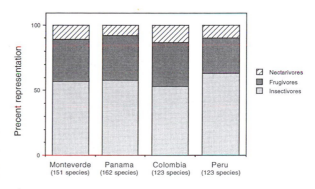

Figure 6.9. Relative abundance of nectarivores, frugivores, and insectivores in lower montane wet forest (Zone 3) at four sites in Central and South America.

large insectivores such as motmots, puffbirds, and small hawks, all of which are less common at higher elevations.

6.8. Conservation Issues

Birds are soft, fuzzy, and photogenic vertebrates. In many parts of the world, birds are the "poster children" of conservation efforts. Spotted Owls (*Strix occidentalis*), cranes, Bald Eagles (*Haliaeetus leucocephalus*), and parrots are the best-known examples. Monteverde is no exception, with its ubiquitous pictures, drawings, and designs of quetzals. As in the case of the Spotted Owl in the Pacific Northwest of the United States, detailed knowledge of quetzal natural history has directed conservation efforts. Radio-tracking data pinpointed areas on the Caribbean slope where Monteverde's quetzals forage from September to December, and the MCL acted quickly to protect those forests (Powell and Bjork 1995). Many of the major conservation issues in Monteverde affect birds (see Chap. 12, Conservation Biology).

6.8.1. Species at Risk

Through strong leadership in conservation efforts, ca. 20,000 ha of forest have been protected in private reserves in Monteverde, concentrated in Zones 3–6. Species that spend their entire life cycle within these life zones and for which ecologically viable populations remain will most likely persist. Species that require forest habitat in Zones 1 and 2 or below Zone 6 for parts of their life cycle are at risk. These life zones have the least remaining forest, and this habitat is fragmented (Guindon 1996; see Guindon, "The Importance of Pacific Slope Forest," pp. 435–437). Both the MCL (working on the Caribbean slope) and the MCFP (on the Pacific slope) have made laudable efforts to protect relict forest, but these are small patches. Large frugivores forage seasonally in these fragments, especially the larger bird species such as quetzals, bellbirds, guans, and toucans (Guindon 1996). Conservation biology theory and research have demonstrated that many species, even competitively dominant ones, inevitably disappear from forest patches after fragmentation (Tilman et al. 1994, Robinson et al. 1995).

On a global scale, the cloud forests (Zones 3–5) of Monteverde are home to 10 species of birds that are considered by Birdlife International as being at risk of extinction due to their restricted worldwide ranges (Collar et al. 1994; Table 6.8). All occur exclusively in the cloud forests of the Cordilleras de Tilarán, Central, and Talamanca. This mountain range is isolated from other mountain ranges in Central America by the lowlands of Nicaragua and central Panama, and these species are endemic to the region.

6.8.2. Effects of Human Activity

Except for one study in progress (A. Pereira, unpubl. data), no quantitative data exist on the effects of current human activity on bird populations in Monteverde. The clearing of forest for agricultural land earlier in the century destroyed habitat for some species and created habitat for others. From the perspective of bird habitat, patterns of land use have changed little in recent decades, and the recent ecotourism boom may be beneficial to bird conservation (see Young, "How Have Humans Affected Bird Populations?," pp. 433–434).

6.8.3. Management

The greatest management challenge in Monteverde is protecting mobile species. Buying a piece of forest and protecting it against squatters and hunters will not guarantee preservation of species that leave during part of the year. In recognition of this management need, Monteverde researchers have championed the need for regionwide conservation efforts. The migration of many species of hummingbirds into and out of Monteverde, for example, signals that habitat alteration elsewhere could affect population levels in Monteverde (Feinsinger 1980). Researchers also pointed out that the protected area in Monteverde during the early 1980s was inadequate to protect quetzals (Wheelwright 1983).

One approach to designing a reserve system is to identify and protect areas used by target species (Powell and Bjork 1995). This strategy was used by

Table 6.8. Monteverde bird species listed by BirdLife International as being vulnerable or nearly threatened with extinction due to their restricted ranges in cloud forests.

Scientific name	Common name
Harpyhaliaetus solitarius	Solitary Eagle
Chamaepetes unicolor	Black Guan
Odontophorus leucolaemus	Black-breasted Wood-Quail
Touit costaricensis	Red-fronted Parrotlet
Calliphlox bryantae	Magenta-throated Woodstar
Pharomachrus mocinno	Resplendent Quetzal
Electron carinatum	Keel-billed Motmot
Micromonacha lanceolata	Lanceolated Monklet
Cephalopterus glabricollis	Bare-necked Umbrellabird
Procnias tricarunculata	Three-wattled Bellbird
Bangsia arcaei	Blue-and gold Tanager
Acanthidops bairdii	Peg-billed Finch

Data are from (Collar et al. 1994). All species occur near the Continental Divide in Zones 3–5.

the MCL for the Children's International Rainforest, in which a major impetus for purchasing land in the San Bosco area was the discovery of nonbreeding quetzals from Monteverde. Using a charismatic symbol such as the quetzal and maps of its migration routes can create a successful fund-raising campaign, but does this method go beyond quetzals to protect the forest and its fauna? The answer depends on the degree to which the movement patterns of other taxa coincide with those of the quetzal. Species such as the Black-faced Solitaire (which breed in the same habitat and migrate to the same areas as the quetzal; Fig. 6.4) will likely survive and benefit. Others, such as the Plain-capped Starthroat (which migrates up and down the Pacific slope) will gain little benefit from a reserve designed to protect quetzals. The target-species approach is not therefore the complete solution for protecting Monteverde's bird community. Conservation efforts must be balanced with human needs and financial limitations; the quetzal-oriented approach in Monteverde has helped to protect a sizable portion of forest that is probably large enough for viable populations of a large number of species, including some that are migratory. Because financial resources available for land acquisition and protection are limited, a better strategy to protect Monteverde's birds may not exist.

6.9. Conclusions

Research in Monteverde has greatly contributed to our understanding of birds in general and neotropical ornithology in particular. We have learned a number of major lessons in 25 years of research:

(1) The fauna of Monteverde is a mix of species of North American, Mesoamerican, and South American origin including both residents and migrants.
(2) Seasonal movements are a regular feature of the biology of many species, especially nectarivores and frugivores.
(3) Species join mixed-species foraging flocks for different reasons, including predator defense, foraging efficiency, and territory defense.
(4) Understanding behaviors of long-lived birds such as manakins and jays requires consideration of the long-term benefits of those behaviors.
(5) The demographic characteristics of montane tropical birds (small clutch size and long adult survivorship) are similar to lowland tropical birds.
(6) Interactions between hummingbirds and the plants they pollinate and between frugivores and the plants they disperse are similar in that seasonal availability of plant resources causes seasonal movements of the birds; they differ in that nectarivores tend to have more specialized diets than frugivores.
(7) Conservation efforts must account for the seasonal movements of threatened species.

By many measures, Monteverde is similar to other montane sites in the neotropics, so these lessons are likely to be valid for bird communities elsewhere in the tropics.

What directions would be fruitful for future research? Communitywide studies of birds are lacking, so our understanding of how birds distribute themselves across the forest landscape is incomplete (Terborgh et al. 1990). Without this information, we cannot estimate bird abundance in Monteverde and cannot assess the importance of birds in the ecosystems they inhabit. We also do not know why congeneric species separate across elevational gradients. Studies similar to Hairston's (1980) studies of salamander distributions in North America would be valuable for understanding the processes causing this widespread pattern.

We have no existing monitoring program to document changes in communities over time. Aside from species-specific studies that show that population sizes and ranges of *Myiobius* Redstarts and Brown Jays are changing (Shopland 1985, Williams et al. 1994), the only communitywide monitoring data available are a 10–16-year series of annual surveys for the presence/absence of breeding species in selected life zones (Pounds et al. 1997). With so much emphasis on the possible decline of North American migrants and the conservation of tropical resident species (e.g., Myers 1988, Terborgh 1990, Martin and Finch 1995, Stotz et al. 1996), more detailed monitoring data will be very useful for identifying population trends. Most research continues to take place in Zones 2 and 3 near the community of Monteverde; the mid-elevation Caribbean slope (Zones 5 and 6) remains among the most poorly studied habitats in Costa Rica.

We emphasize the success of the autecological method in understanding bird biology. The majority of the studies at Monteverde have focused on one or a few species of birds. By focusing attention on individual species, biologists in Monteverde have discovered subtleties about the natural history of tropical birds that broader studies may have missed. Migration patterns in quetzals and bellbirds, causes of cooperation in manakins, costs and benefits of flocking, and demographic patterns in several species would not have come to light without in-depth studies of individual species. Future work in Monteverde should continue in this tradition by building on existing studies or moving to new taxa, as well as providing the communitywide data we currently lack.

Acknowledgments We thank the people of Monteverde, the Monteverde Cloud Forest Preserve, and the MCL for supporting ornithological research on private land. We are grateful to the U.S. National Science Foundation and the Organization for Tropical Studies for financial support. We are indebted to Douglas J. Levey, Bette A. Loiselle, Nalini M. Nadkarni, F. Gary Stiles, Harry M. Tiebout III, and Dan Wenny for providing many useful suggestions for the manuscript. Ana Beatriz Azofeifa of the Organization for Tropical Studies kindly performed bibliographic searches. The Costa Rican Servicio de Vida Silvestre has been courteous and efficient in issuing the necessary permits.

COOPERATION BETWEEN MALE LONG-TAILED MANAKINS
David B. McDonald

The courtship displays of Long-tailed Manakins are elaborate. Their most surprising feature is that they entail coordinated display by a pair of males (Fig. 6.1). The courtship song, which sounds like the word "toledo," is sung in unison and has the resonant quality of a pair of musical instruments (Trainer and McDonald 1993; see Trainer, "Roles of Long-Tailed Manakin Vocalizations," pp. 215–216). If the singers are successful in attracting a female, they move to a low dance perch and begin a dual-male leapfrog dance. One male sidles toward the female, hovering upward as he nears her. Meanwhile, his partner has sidled forward, so that the first male lands behind his partner. The resulting sets of dance hops may continue for many minutes, interspersed with dual-male "butterfly flight," in which the partners flutter, using a labored flight within a hemisphere approximately 30 m in diameter, centered on the dance perch. Eventually, if the female remains, one male drops out of the display, the other continues solo butterfly flight, and if the female is receptive, a copulation occurs on the perch (McDonald 1989b). Males form stable partnerships, with a dominant (alpha) and subordinate (beta) male, and a variable number of lower-ranking males (Foster 1977, 1981, McDonald 1989a, 1993a,b). The partnerships persist for several to many years, but during its course, only the alpha male mates. Why, then, does the nonmating beta partner engage in months or years of vigorous courtship display for no apparent reward?

One possible explanation is that the partners are close relatives. In that case, the beta male would benefit through the copies of his own genes passed through the relative he helped, via kin selection (Hamilton 1964). We tested the kin selection hypothesis in Long-tailed Manakins using a technique called microsatellite DNA (McDonald and Potts 1994). Microsatellites (Queller et al. 1993) are noncoding regions of DNA containing short unit repeats of some combination of the four nucleotides—A, G, C, or T. For example, the microsatellite might consist of CA dinucleotides repeated 10–20 times. Within a population, individuals can vary widely in the number of dinucleotide repeats. One male might inherit a microsatellite with 12 repeats from his father and 14 repeats from his mother; another individual might have 15 repeats on one chromosome and 14 on the other. On each side of the microsatellite is an area of nonrepeating DNA, whose sequence is invariant across the population. These "flanking regions" provide the information for building primers to amplify the microsatellites of sampled individuals by the polymerase chain reaction (PCR). The amplified product can be visualized by ethidium bromide staining. The variants then appear as bands on the gel that can be sized by comparison to a known standard. By developing a sufficient number of highly variable microsatellites, we could address the question of the degree of relatedness among partnered males.

We found that the relatedness of 33 pairs of cooperating males was no greater than that between any two males taken at random from the population. The mean relatedness for the 33 pairs was −0.14 (±0.10), meaning that they were slightly less similar than randomly chosen males. Further, of the 33 pairs, 17 were negatively related, while 16 were positively related. This is what one would expect if partnerships developed without regard to relatedness—some males will pair by chance with males to whom they are dissimilar genetically (negative relatedness) and others with males whom they resemble genetically (positive relatedness). The nonmating male thus does not benefit from the indirect component of inclusive fitness. We therefore looked for direct benefits to the beta male.

I have documented four major direct benefits to the beta male from his cooperation with an alpha male. First, upon the disappearance of an alpha male, it has always been the beta who has succeeded to the alpha role ($n = 11$). Second, although very rare, beta males do sometimes mate (4 of 263 copulations). Third, females tend to return to perches at which they visited or mated in prior seasons. Of 27 banded females seen at perches in two or more seasons, 16 returned to the site at which they had previously been sighted, and 10 mated with the replacement alpha following a turnover. Finally, the success of alpha males was highly correlated with that of their predecessors. While they were betas, the current alpha males played a major role in creating the success that they then "inherited." By expending considerable effort in courtship display as a beta, a male stands to gain considerable, albeit long-delayed, benefits. Because the mean age of mating for males is 10.1 years (McDonald 1993b), young (≤8 years) males have very few options for success anyway, so the deferment of reproduction entailed by being beta seems to be the best strategy. An additional element in the payoff is the age differential between male and female reproduction. Females probably begin nesting by age one, and certainly by age two (McDonald 1993b). Thus, a beta male that helps attract a young female stands to mate with her throughout her prime.

Although the genetic evidence allows rejection of the kin selection hypotheses, and the behavioral data indicate the nature of the direct benefits to beta males, many questions remain. Why, for example, does this form of male-male cooperation occur in this species and its four congeners elsewhere in the neotropics but nowhere else in the animal kingdom? The answer almost certainly lies in the patterns of female choice of mates. The lack of opportunities for mating success by young males arises because over the course of several seasons, virtually all the females in a local population choose one or a few males as mates. A vital component in the difference between female mate choice in this genus and that in all other lekking birds may be a difference in cognitive ability. The hippocampus is a part of the brain that plays a major role in processing spatial information (Krebs et al. 1989). Long-tailed Manakins have a large hippocampal ratio (relative to the rest of the brain), comparable to that of birds that cache their food, such as Clark's Nutcracker (*Nucifraga columbiana*), a jaylike bird of western North America that has been shown to perform amazing feats of spatial memory in laboratory tests (Kamil and Balda 1985). Although Long-tailed Manakins do not cache their food, they may need to remember the time and place at which fruits emerge over very large areas, in order to survive periods of food scarcity. Given a brain capable of acute spatial memory, it may be easy for females to "map" the locations of the best among a large set of pairs of displaying males. Other manakins in wetter habitats may have more easily located food sources and lack the highly developed hippocampus. Females of those species may be relatively incapable of the acute discrimination, spatial mapping, and long-term memory exhibited by Long-tailed Manakins. With more options for present reproductive success, males of other manakin species may not need to cooperate with other males for future opportunities.

WHY JOIN MIXED-SPECIES FLOCKS?: A FRUGIVORE'S PERSPECTIVE
Lisa K. Valburg

Most mixed-species flocks are made up of insect-eaters, with a marked lack of participation from birds that use nectar or fruit resources (Powell 1977b). In Monteverde, however, one of the most prominent species in mixed-species flocks is the Common Bush-Tanager (*Chlorospingus opthalmicus*), a bird known to consume a wide variety of fruits (Wheelwright et al. 1984). Previous work on the flocks of Monteverde demonstrated that Common Bush-Tanagers maintain 0.5-ha home ranges and participate in mixed-species flocks only when they pass through their territories (Powell 1977b). I wished to determine how social group composition and size affected the proportions of fruits and arthropods consumed by Common Bush-Tanagers. I studied this species for four reasons: (1) it is an important member of mixed-species flocks; (2) it feeds alone, in single-species groups, and in mixed-species flocks; (3) it consumes a wide variety of fruits, in contrast to the highly insectivorous diet of most mixed-species flock participants; and (4) these birds are abundant, noisy, and relatively easy to follow on their home ranges.

Differences in behavior between insectivorous and frugivorous birds in flocks have been linked to differences in their diet: insects are cryptic and difficult to find, whereas fruits are often conspicuous (Moermond and Denslow 1985). For insectivores, rates of ingestion do not greatly exceed rates of digestion, so they must forage continuously (Munn and Terborgh 1979). In contrast, frugivores can ingest fruit much more rapidly than they can digest it, which results in episodic searching for food. Exploitation of different resources may therefore favor differences in foraging behavior. For an omnivore, balancing the time constraints of insectivory and the spatial constraints of frugivory requires compromises in both behavior and diet.

Observations on foraging and social behavior of Common Bush-Tanagers suggested that individuals may alter their feeding behavior in the presence of different social groups. For example, the diet of South American primates varies depending on whether individuals forage in single-species or mixed-species groups (Terborgh 1983). When birds join mixed-species flocks in Monteverde, their feeding behavior converges with the nuclear species in that flock (Buskirk 1976, Powell 1977b).

I studied Common Bush-Tanagers in lower montane wet forest (Zone 3 of Holdridge 1967) in Campbell's Woods, adjacent to the MCFP. Common Bush-Tanagers mainly forage in understory and second-growth patches, although many home ranges include primary forest. Bush-tanagers use the heavily fruiting shrubs of second-growth areas and forage mainly within their own territories. They commonly join mixed-species flocks, which include Three-striped Warblers, Slate-throated Redstarts, Spotted Barbtails, Gray-breasted Wood-Wrens (Fig. 6.5), and other species. The only major avian predators of adult birds are Barred and Collared Forest-Falcons. I mist-netted and color-banded 33 Common Bush-Tanagers. Transient birds were not marked but were tallied in single-species flock counts. Each individual's foraging behavior was recorded at 1-min intervals during 45-min observation periods from March 1987 through June 1988. I recorded data on social grouping (flock composition and flock size), and prey type (arthropod or fruit; Valburg 1992c).

The balance of fruits and insect prey consumed by Common Bush-Tanagers changed significantly between mixed-species and single-species groups, with members of single-species groups averaging 66% fruit compared to an average of 28% for individuals in mixed-species groups. Although bush-tanagers only foraged with the mixed-species flocks for 30% of their foraging day, they consumed the bulk of their arthropod diet at that time. As flock size increased, fruit consumption decreased, especially for flock sizes of 5–15 birds. These small flocks were either mixed-species flocks or flocks made up of relatively large numbers of bush-tanagers. The decrease in fruit consumption was truly an increase in insect consumption in small mixed-species flocks only, independent of flock size and composition.

If increased group size alone resulted in decreased risk of predation, as proposed by Powell (1985), there should not have been such a marked difference between single-species and mixed-species flock foraging where flock size was similar. This study supports the hypothesis that foraging behavior of mixed-species flock participants tends to converge regarding food type consumed (Buskirk 1976) and suggests that birds may join mixed-species groups to facilitate the finding and capturing of arthropod prey. Common Bush-Tanagers had access to all insect and fruit prey in both solitary foraging and single-species group foraging modes but selected more insect prey per unit time when in a mixed-species group. This switch to insectivory may enhance foraging technique or copying of insectivorous flock members. For Common Bush-Tanagers participating in mixed species flocks, these results suggest that enhanced foraging for insects may be a primary benefit of mixed-species flocking.

THE COST OF SOCIAL FORAGING IN MIXED-SPECIES BIRD FLOCKS
Jennifer Shopland

Since the time of Henry Bates and Alfred Wallace, naturalists have commented on multi-species flocks around the world, from waterfowl in wetlands to small songbirds in tropical forests. Feeding with a mixed flock may increase the foraging success of its members or protect them from predation (Morse 1977; see Valburg, "Why Join Mixed-Species Flocks?," pp. 205–206). Preliminary observations in Monteverde suggested that the potential predators (primarily hawks) of adult flock members were uncommon. I tested the foraging-success hypothesis for three flocking species.

In lower-elevation woodlands and in the MCFP, mixed flocks form when "nuclear species" travel through their large home ranges, picking up and dropping off members of other species ("facultative joiners") whose smaller territories are nested within the large home ranges (Buskirk 1972, 1976, Powell 1979, Shopland 1985, J. Shopland, unpubl. data). In the MCFP, the nuclear species are the Common Bush-Tanager and the Three-striped Warbler. Nuclear species in lower elevation woodland flocks are the Golden-crowned Warbler and the Lesser Greenlet.

Three questions were central to my studies: (1) does foraging with a flock affect the foraging success of an individual flock member, (2) what are the mechanisms for these changes, and (3) what do they suggest about the evolution of flocking behavior? I studied two facultative joiners, the Slate-throated Redstart (Fig. 6.7) and the Collared Redstart, in MCFP flocks and one nuclear species, the Golden-crowned Warbler, in woodland flocks. I used focal-animal samples (Altmann 1974) of foraging behavior, following one individual and recording how much insect mass was consumed per minute. Intake rate was measured as a composite of the number of foraging maneuvers per minute, the proportion of foraging maneuvers that were successful, and the size of prey caught. I also recorded the bird's rates of social and territorial behaviors, which diminish potential foraging time. I sampled behavior within and outside flocks. To compare success, I pooled events per minute into before-flock, with-flock, and after-flock blocks following Shopland (1985).

Contrary to the predictions of the foraging-success hypothesis, both species of redstarts ate less food per unit time in the company of mixed-species flocks than they could have found on their own. When they joined flocks, their intake rates decreased by one-third (Slate-throated Redstarts) and two-thirds (Collared Redstarts). Neither foraging maneuver rate nor proportion of success could account for these losses; prey size was decisive. Both species caught fewer large insects when they foraged with flocks. Outside flocks, Slate-throats were predominantly aerial hawkers, but in flocks they shifted to striking at and gleaning from leaves and branches. Collareds took up hawking in flocks versus their usual striking-and-gleaning style. Both redstarts' activity levels (perch changes per minute) and rates of social interaction and territorial display ("strutting") increased when they joined

flocks. "Floaters" and neighboring pairs of redstarts often intruded as members of a mixed-species flock, which provoked increased chasing and display. Thus, rather than enjoying greater foraging success in flocks, these facultative joiners suffered two kinds of losses: (1) large insects (which may have been taken by individuals of more specialized flock species), and (2) time and energy spent in chasing invading members of their own species. Nevertheless, redstarts actively joined flocks, making the best of a bad lot.

Golden-crowned Warblers have home ranges that are three times the size of redstart territories (Buskirk 1972) and are found in 97% of woodland flocks. These warblers fared no better in flocks than did the redstarts; their intake rate decreased by 40%. As with redstarts, the loss of large insects was the source of decrease. Unlike the two facultative joiners, however, Golden-crowns did not switch to uncharacteristic foraging methods in the presence of flocks (they continued to glean), nor did they show higher levels of social interactions.

These results challenge the view that multispecies flocking has evolved to improve foraging efficiency. Predation may have been a stronger selective pressure shaping the tendency of these species to flock. Results suggest that feeding with mixed-species flocks can have a large impact on within-species territoriality by increasing the costs of defense. Over evolutionary time, these costs could lead to coincident territories, joint defense, and obligate flocking, as in lowland flocks in South America (Munn and Terborgh 1979, Powell 1985).

These studies raised questions that could be directly explored by focusing on a limited number of gridded territories with color-marked individuals (owners, neighbors, and floaters). Although neotropical migrants' attendance of mixed flocks has been extensively documented, the effects of this sociality on their foraging success (and thus potentially on their nonbreeding season survival) has not been investigated. Mixed-species flocks are a conspicuous part of avifaunas in many regions, but little is known of the effects of habitat degradation and fragmentation on flock formation and the behavioral flexibility of individual flocking species. Monteverde, with its patchwork of pastures, second growth, relict woodlands, and primary cloud forest, is an ideal setting for such research.

CHOOSINESS AND PRODUCTIVITY IN WRENS OF FORESTS, FRAGMENTS, AND FARMS
Kathy Winnett-Murray

Members of the family Troglodytidae (wrens) illustrate an intriguing example of the transition in bird life history strategies along Monteverde's steep elevational gradients. One question is how House Wrens, which thrive in the most disturbed habitats, maintain a reproductive rate that is three to seven times higher than their relatives in less disturbed habitats (Skutch 1960, Alvarez-Lopez et al. 1984, Winnett-Murray 1986, Young 1994a). The answer has to do with differences in the food supply of the wrens, which I compared among House Wrens, Plain Wrens, Rufous-and-white Wrens, and Gray-breasted Wood-Wrens (Fig. 6.5). All four species are opportunists, feeding on a diverse array of invertebrates such as worms, centipedes, slugs, and spiders. Pastures and other early successional habitats frequented by House Wrens support a larger prey biomass than do the gaps, forest edges, and pristine or regenerating forest used by the other three wren species (Winnett-Murray 1986, 1987). The House Wren food supply varies much less (seasonally and by location) than it does in the habitats used by the other species. How do House Wrens exploit their higher food availability and achieve a higher reproductive rate?

I compared the types and sizes of prey that foraging birds ate with those that they fed to nestlings. All wrens captured primarily smaller prey, and successively fewer prey in each of the larger size classes, despite a twofold difference in average wren mass from the smallest (House Wren; Fig. 6.10) to the largest (Rufous-and-white Wren), and a similarly large difference in their beak lengths (Winnett-Murray 1986). All species were highly selective; they brought larger prey items to their nest as compared to what they captured in the field. The most striking difference was in the higher selectivity exercised by House Wrens who were feeding their young. The small House Wrens achieved the largest shift in these two prey size distributions (Fig. 6.11). A similar pattern emerged in the kinds of prey brought to nestlings (Fig. 6.12); House Wrens were much more selective than Plain Wrens in what they brought their nestlings, even though they caught similar prey distributions in the field (Winnett-Murray 1986).

Nearly half of the items that House Wrens delivered to their young were large, soft-bodied insect larvae, which was in far greater proportion to what they captured in the field. House Wrens also fed their nestlings orthopterans (crickets, katydids, and grasshoppers), bees, and wasps, groups that are readily available in the open habitats where they hunt. The other three wren species also fed insect larvae to young but made greater use of adult beetles than did House Wrens. The specialization of House Wrens on larvae was not because more larvae occurred in their habitats; many more larvae occur in cloud forests, where House Wrens seldom foraged (Buskirk and Buskirk 1976). Rather, where food was predictably abundant, House Wrens could be more choosy. The benefit of this may be that nestlings who are fed a higher proportion of large, soft-bodied prey grow faster and/or fledge at higher relative weights (Von Bromssen and Jansson 1980, Biermann and Sealy 1982), which would minimize the length of the nesting cycle, thereby increasing the opportunity for parents to raise subsequent broods. Evidence that tropical House Wrens are generally not food-limited is that experimental food supplementation did not enhance fledging success or weight gain (Freed 1981, Young 1994a).

Nesting in proximity to humans also seems to be a substantial "edge" that House Wrens have over their forest-dwelling relatives, because most (nonintroduced) predators of bird eggs and chicks are less common in the immediate vicinity of dwellings and pastures than they are in forested habitats. Predation at House Wren nests in or on occupied houses and barns was substantially lower (6% of 73 offspring at 21 nests) than predation at House Wren nests in other locations more distant from people (21% of 57 offspring at 17 nests) (Winnett-Murray 1986).

Compared to other wrens, House Wrens are better able to respond to habitat variability and human alteration of habitats by adjusting reproductive parameters, for example, clutch size, timing of breeding, apportionment of parental care, patterns of adult weight changes, and levels of aggression toward their own and other species (Kendeigh 1941, Freed 1986a,b, Kennedy and Power 1990, Kermott et al. 1991, Pribil and Picman 1991, Robinson and Rotenberry 1991, Young 1994a). They exemplify "animal weeds" because they thrive in disturbed areas and are characterized by high reproductive output and rapid dispersal. They also capitalize by selectively foraging on high food levels in early successional environments. In contrast, forest species (e.g., Gray-breasted Wood-Wrens; Fig. 6.5) apparently have greater difficulty finding the fewer less predictable, more cryptic prey. Wood-wrens frequently search leaf undersides, where understory arthropods tend to accumulate in wet

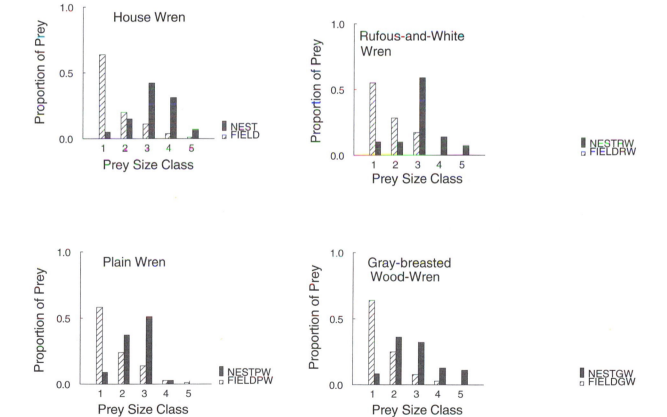

Figure 6.10. *(top)* House Wren feeding insects to young at nest. Photograph by Kathy Winnett-Murray.
Figure 6.11. *(above)* Frequency distribution of prey sizes caught by wrens in the field (Field) and prey sizes brought to nestlings (Nest). Prey size classes are (1) ≤5mm, (2) 6–10 mm, (3) 11–20 mm, (4) 21–35 mm, and (5) 36–55 mm in length. Sample sizes of prey were as follows: House Wrens (159 field, 586 nest), Plain Wrens (170 field, 35 nest), Rufous-and-white Wrens (29 field, 29 nest), Gray-breasted Wood-Wrens (67 field, 47 nest).

habitats (Greenberg and Gradwohl 1980, Remsen and Parker 1984, Winnett-Murray 1986). Their young may depend on longer periods of time spent foraging with their parents more than other wrens, as they learn to recognize and capture highly cryptic prey (Fogden 1972, Morse 1980).

Acknowledgments   Many members of the Monteverde community kindly allowed me to study wrens on their land, and the Tropical Science Center granted permission to study wrens in the MCFP. The University of Florida, Sigma Xi, the Chapman Fund of the American Museum of Natural History, and the Jessie Smith Noyes Foundation of the Organization for Tropical Studies provided financial support. Alexander Villegas and Sarah Sargent assisted with fieldwork, and Bruce Young and Greg Murray provided editorial assistance.

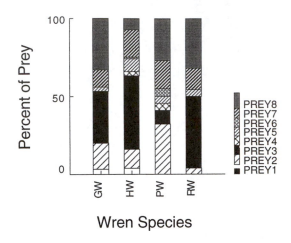

Figure 6.12. Frequency distribution of the types of prey wrens brought to their nestlings. Prey type categories are (1) arachnids, (2) adult lepidopterans, (3) larvae, (4) dipterans, (5) hymenopterans, (6) homopterans and hemipterans, (7) orthopterans, and (8) coleopterans. Sample sizes of prey items were as follows: Gray-breasted Wood-Wrens (GW; 30), House Wrens (HW; 464), Plain Wrens (PW; 22), and Rufous-and-white Wrens (RW; 22).

DO FRUIT-EATING BIRDS ACTIVELY SELECT OR AVOID INSECT-INFESTED FRUITS?
Lisa K. Valburg

Fruit-eating birds in Monteverde have a bountiful smorgasbord of fruits from which to choose (Wheelwright et al. 1984). Much research has been done to discover what makes a fruit desirable or undesirable. Birds can distinguish among fruits of the same species based on sugar content, flavor, ripeness, color, seediness, and other factors (Fleming and Estrada 1993). However, even highly frugivorous birds such as Common Bush-Tanagers may consume insects for as much as 50% of their regular diet (Valburg 1992c).

Tropical plants that bear bird-dispersed fruit are often infested with insect larvae. Some researchers have suggested that infestation should cause rejection by frugivores (Sallabanks and Courtney 1992). However, not all infestation results in the same type or level of damage to seeds, and fruit damage may not always affect palatability (L. Valburg, unpubl. data). I examined whether the presence of insect larvae caused a fruit to be preferentially chosen or avoided by Common Bush-Tanagers. I captured 10 bush-tanagers and, after the birds became accustomed to their aviary cages, offered them simultaneous dichotomous choices between naturally infested and uninfested fruits of a single species. The presence of insect larvae enhanced the rate of fruit removal for three species of fruits, especially *Acnistus arborescens* and *Ardisia palmana* (Valburg 1992b).

I then investigated how different levels of infestation by pulp-mining insect larvae combined with different levels of fruit ripeness might influence fruit choice in four other bird species. Fruits were collected from at least 10 plants per species within Monteverde, Cerro Plano, and Santa Elena. I conducted simultaneous choice trials using four individuals of each of the following species: Clay-colored Robins, Blue-gray Tanagers, Chestnut-capped Brush-Finches, and White-eared Ground-Sparrows. The birds were offered three fruit species: *Citharexylum donnell-smithii*, *Ardisia palmana*, and *Acnistus arborescens*. Fruits were presented in equal masses in pairwise combinations of ripe (uninfested), unripe, and two levels of infestation, light (1–3 pulp-mining larvae) and heavy (>3 larvae, with signs of attack by molds or bacteria).

The birds displayed preferences among the different treatments in all three fruit species, with preferences varying in degree (but not direction) among the bird species (Fig. 6.13). Because individual variation within bird species was not statistically significant, birds were grouped according to species. Frugivores preferred ripe and lightly infested fruits over unripe and heavily infested fruits but did not discriminate between lightly infested and uninfested ripe fruits. Birds avoided both unripe and heavily infested fruits, sampling very small quantities of both, with no significant difference between the two. Unripe fruits were eaten much less often when paired with ripe or lightly infested fruits, and not at all when paired with heavily infested fruits. Chestnut-capped Brush-Finches, Clay-colored Robins, and White-eared Ground-Sparrows ate significantly more lightly infested fruits when these fruits were paired with ripe fruits than when lightly infested fruits were paired with unripe ones.

These responses suggest that fruit-eating birds discriminate between slightly infested fruits and "rotten" fruits, and consume lightly infested fruits as if they were ripe and uninfested. Strong avoidance behavior was elicited only with unripe fruits and heavily infested fruits containing mold, bacteria, fermentation, and a larger number of infesting pulp-mining larvae. Discrimination against infested fruits may be an artifact of microbial infestation rather than of infestation by pulp miners (Travaset 1993), but ingestion of ripe infested fruits may provide nutritional benefits.

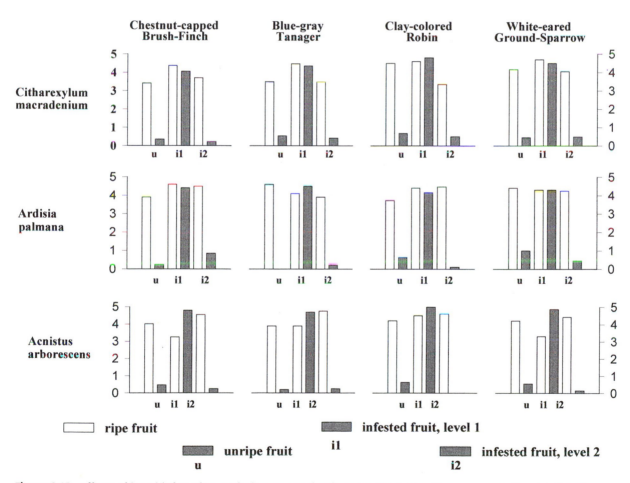

Figure 6.13. Effects of larval infestation on fruit consumption by avian frugivores. Mean consumption (g) of unripe (u) and ripe, lightly infested (i1) and heavily infested (i2) fruits by Chestnut-capped Brush-Finches, Blue-gray Tanagers, Clay-colored Robins, and White-eared Ground-Sparrows in pairwise simultaneous choice trials using ripe (open bars) *Citharexylum macradenium, Ardisia palmana,* and *Acnistus arborescens* fruits. For each bird species; *n* = 6 birds per trial.

BROWN JAYS: COMPLEX SOCIALITY IN A COLONIZING SPECIES
Dean A. Williams & Marcy F. Lawton

Brown Jays were one of the first birds for which cooperative breeding was described (Skutch 1935). Cooperative breeding occurs when members of a social group help raise offspring that are not their own. This behavior occurs in 3% of the 9000 living species of birds (Brown 1987, Stacey and Koenig 1990, Emlen 1991, Solomon and French 1996). In Brown Jays, nonbreeding group members help build nests; feed breeding females, nestlings, and fledglings; and defend the nest and young from predators (Skutch 1935, 1960, Lawton 1983, Lawton and Lawton 1985).

Studies of cooperatively breeding birds have explained these aid-giving behaviors using inclusive fitness theory or "kin selection" (Hamilton 1964, Maynard Smith 1964). Kin selection favors traits that positively affect the survival and reproduction of an individual's kin. This means that an individual can gain fitness benefits either directly (by reproducing) or indirectly (by helping relatives reproduce). The New-World jays are an important group for testing hypotheses about environmental, demographic, and developmental determinants of sociality because they inhabit a wide range of habitats and exhibit the full spectrum of sociality (Brown 1974, Woolfenden and Fitzpatrick 1984, Lawton and Lawton 1986).

The Brown Jay population in Monteverde provides an example of how individuals in complex societies pursue multiple pathways to fitness, and how the behaviors associated with these pathways can change in response to increased population density. This study was started in 1976 by Marcy and Robert Lawton. The original study area covered about 4 km² and extended from the Quebrada Máquina up to the MCFP and out to the cliff edges. As the population grew (in 1990), the main study area was reduced to one-half, including most of Monteverde south of the Río Guacimal and Quebrada Cuecha. Starting in 1988, all nestlings within this area and some surrounding areas were marked (n = 431 by 1996) with a unique combination of colored anodized aluminum bands. All nesting locations were mapped, and data on clutch and brood size were recorded. As part of a genetic study of parentage, previously unmarked adults were captured and banded in 1994–1996 using baited traps and nets, and blood samples have been taken from all captured adults and nestlings (since 1992). By 1996, 157 jays had been banded, of a total of 178 in 15 focal groups.

Brown Jays were absent from the Monteverde plateau prior to the early 1960s (W. Guindon, pers. comm.). After their initial colonization, the number of Brown Jay individuals and social groups increased and the population range expanded from the lower Monteverde community into the MCFP (Williams et al. 1994). Within the study area, the number of individuals and groups has begun to stabilize (Fig. 6.14). Presently, the entire Monteverde plateau is occupied by Brown Jays. This population expansion occurred through a complex process of fissioning of large groups, individual dispersal, and fusion among neighboring groups. Most dispersal (97%, n = 36 individuals between 1994 and 1996) occurred between neighboring groups, although some long-distance dispersal also occurred. A banded jay was found dead in 1992 in La Cruz (~6 km), and banded jays have been reported in San Rafael (~9 km) and La Tigra (>10 km), which has recently been cleared of forest (C. Guindon, pers. comm.).

Brown Jay breeding behavior has changed since 1976. Most striking has been the marked increase in reproductive competition among breeding females residing in the same group (Williams et al. 1994). Groups of Brown Jays in Monteverde may have a single breeding female, a pair of females sharing a single nest, or two or three females, each with her own nest. In recent years, females building individual nests in the same territory have been observed fighting each other on the nest, chasing one another from the vicinity of the nest, and destroying a rival's nest, eggs, and nestlings. These behaviors occur more frequently in large groups (>10 individuals) and when nests are being built or when eggs are being laid. The overt competition among females has not been observed among males, even though more than one male can breed in a group.

Behavioral and preliminary DNA fingerprinting suggests that some females have mated with a single male whereas others mate with multiple males within or between groups. Males have been observed courting several females within a group. At the current jay density, resources critical to a female's reproductive success (e.g., helpers) could be in short supply. When one female disrupts another female's nesting attempt, the female that lost her nest, and other group members that were associated with her, switch and help the "winning" female. This occurs even when a female witnesses the other female destroying her eggs. There is no relationship between the number of helpers and the production of young, or the survival of juveniles (Lawton and Guindon 1981, Williams et al. 1994, D. Williams and M. Lawton, unpubl. data), which suggests that helpers receive few direct fitness benefits from the help they give.

Brown Jays probably receive some indirect benefit from helping. Helping may serve as a way to form social bonds with other group members and become integrated into the group, thereby increasing the probability of obtaining a breeding position. From 1994 to 1996, 21 jays obtained breeding positions; 19 of these had helped for at least one year in the group where they attempted breeding. Dispersal rarely results in filling a breeding vacancy; only 13% of known dispersers between 1994 and 1996 filled breeding positions in the year they immigrated; the rest became helpers. Helping in this population may provide practice in learning how to build nests and take care of young, thereby increasing future potential to reproduce successfully.

Brown Jays apparently must wait a long time before obtaining a breeding position. Of eight individuals of known age that obtained breeding positions between 1994 and 1996 (four females, four males), seven were 5–8 years old and one was 3 years old. Young females (1–2 years old) are frequently observed sitting on their mother's nest for short periods of time,

but whether they are contributing eggs to the clutch is unknown. Young helpers become more efficient nest attendants over the course of a single breeding season (Lawton and Guindon 1981). In 1977–78, there was a strong positive correlation between the number of young fledged and number of experienced (>4 years old) jays in a flock. Groups that contained older, more experienced breeders were also more efficient at building nests and laying eggs (Lawton and Lawton 1985). In 1988–1996, however, these effects were not apparent, possibly due to the increased conflict among breeders, which is usually carried out by the older individuals in a group (Williams et al. 1994).

As deforestation increases throughout Central America, many bird species are threatened by loss of primary forest and food resources. Some, like the Brown Jay, have benefited from human activity. Only with long-term data on marked, genetically sampled individuals can we understand population dynamics of tropical vertebrates and identify key life history characteristics that allow such adaptable species to track changes in habitat availability. Brown Jays respond to a wide variety of social and breeding situations. This behavioral plasticity also typifies other facets of their lives, such as an eclectic diet and the ability to use a variety of human-altered habitats. For a colonizing species such as the Brown Jay, group living potentially lowers predation risks associated with moving into a new area, gives an advantage in interspecific competition for food and nest sites, and allows them to invade human-altered landscapes.

Acknowledgments We thank Benito Guindon, without whose help the study would not have survived, and Laurie Williams, who helped in the field and put up with the disruptions fieldwork brings to family life. Amanda Hale provided invaluable help in the field and laboratory. Norman Pastre provided essential help in the field. Morgan Lewis, Hannah Lowther, Ricardo Guindon, Tino Ramirez, Sue Trostle, and Minor Vargas provided energetic field assistance. Thanks to landowners in Monteverde who gave us access to their property. Kerry Rabenold, Peter Fauth, Carolina Yaber, and Amanda Hale gave us useful comments on the manuscript. Joey Haydock provided advice on DNA fingerprinting and parentage analysis. Kerry Rabenold shared useful discussions, productive ideas, and work in the field. Funding came from the Frank M. Chapman Fund (American Museum of Natural History), American Philosophical Society, Alabama Academy of Sciences, The Ruth Hindman Foundation, a Sigma Xi research grant, a Purdue Research Foundation fellowship, and National Science Foundation Dissertation Improvement Grant DEB 93-11491 to Kerry Rabenold for D. Williams.

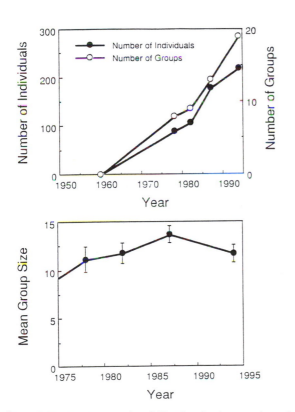

Figure 6.14. Increase and stabilization in the number of Brown Jays and Brown Jay groups in the study area in Monteverde.

ECOLOGY AND SEXUAL DIMORPHISM OF EMERALD TOUCANETS
Cecilia M. Riley & Kimberly G. Smith

Emerald Toucanets are common and conspicuous birds in Monteverde with large, banana-shaped bills. They are medium-sized (31–36 cm long) members of the family Ramphastidae, a group that includes toucans and aracaris. Ramphastids are primarily frugivorous, although they may eat bird eggs, nestlings, and small vertebrates (Skutch 1944, Remsen et al. 1993). Their relatively large size and gape allow consumption of a wide range of fruit sizes (Wheelwright 1985, Moermond and Denslow 1985; Fig. 6.6). Although males and females are identical in color, most species of ramphastids exhibit sexual dimorphism in bill size, with males having bigger bills. A morphological analysis of museum specimens from Costa Rica demonstrated male Emerald Toucanets were larger (in wing and tail length) than females and that male bills were longer and more decurved than those of females (Riley and Smith 1992). The function of larger bills in males and reasons for sexual dimorphism have been debated (Moermond and Denslow 1985, Skutch 1985a). We studied their nesting and foraging behaviors in Monteverde in wet and dry seasons of 1985 to investigate explanations for the dimorphism.

Breeding Biology

Courtship feeding was first observed in mid-March and was followed within a few days by nest excavation by both adults. Thirteen nests, all in pastures or forest edges in old snags, were monitored daily for 1–2 hr, alternating mornings and afternoons (Riley 1986). Nest height varied from 3 to 7.5 m with oval hole openings averaging 7.3 cm wide × 7.7 cm long × 57 cm deep. Females conducted 58% of the excavation and then laid three to five eggs directly on the cavity floor. Both sexes participated in incubation, but females incubated more (66%). The duration of incubation sessions by females and males averaged 11 and 15 min, respectively. Nestling diets consisted primarily of fruits (79%) from 16 species; the remainder of the diet was arthropods. Food items were brought to nestlings at approximately equal rates by adults of each sex; males delivered insects more frequently than did females. Females performed 78% of the nest sanitation, carrying fecal sacs and regurgitated seeds away from nest sites. Overall, nesting success (at least one chick fledged) was 46%. Observed nest losses were the result of tree falls

and predation (Riley 1986). In southern Costa Rica, similar nestling diets and parental division of labor occurred, and nestlings fledged at age 45 days (Skutch 1944, 1967). Because both males and females participated in all aspects of nest construction and brood rearing, sexual bill size differences are apparently not related to roles during the nesting cycle.

Foraging Behavior

Diets of Emerald Toucanets consist of more than 100 species of fruits and flowers (Wheelwright et al. 1984, Riley and Smith 1986; Fig. 6.6). Feeding primarily from twigs on outer branches in mid-canopy, toucanets of both sexes eat the same fruit species, plucking fruits singly and tossing them whole down their throats with a jerk of the head. Although the fruits that were eaten and some foraging behaviors differed between wet and dry seasons, only one aspect of foraging behavior differed between sexes within a season (Riley and Smith 1992): during the dry season (December–March), females spent significantly more time in a single foraging position than did males. We concluded that there were no differences between male and female foraging behaviors or diets that could explain differences in their bill size.

Selective pressures that could lead to sexual dimorphism of bills include different roles in care of offspring, different diets between sexes, and improved mating success (Partridge and Halliday 1984, Jehl and Murray 1986). The first two explanations do not apply to the situation in Emerald Toucanets (Riley and Smith 1992). Because fruits are a patchy and clumped resource, it is unclear how the sexes could partition fruit resources by foraging in different microhabitats, so sexual differences in foraging behaviors and diets should be rare in frugivorous birds (Wheelwright 1986a, 1991, Riley and Smith 1992).

The wide occurrence of sexual dimorphism in bill size among ramphastids remains unresolved. The observed sexual dimorphism in bill size is likely the result of sexual selection or other behavioral interactions. Toucanets and toucans often engage in "dueling," "fencing," or "billing" behaviors, in which two or more individuals interact using their bills (Riley and Smith 1992). Future investigations should focus on intra- and intersexual behavioral interactions.

THE ROLES OF LONG-TAILED MANAKIN VOCALIZATIONS IN COOPERATION AND COURTSHIP
Jill M. Trainer

A familiar sound of Monteverde is the courtship song of the Long-tailed Manakin. The call sounds like one bird singing, but it is actually a well-coordinated duet performed by two males. This vocal duet is part of an elaborate cooperative display and dance (see McDonald, "Cooperation Between Male Long-Tailed Manakins," pp. 204–205). Because males in a lek mating system do not help to rear young, females' choice of mate is thought to be based strictly on the characteristics of males (e.g., song) displayed during courtship (Halliday 1978). The unique social system of the Long-tailed Manakin provides the opportunity to examine the role of vocal behavior in cooperation among males and in the courtship of females. My research, in collaboration with David McDonald, has explored these roles by focusing on the function of Long-tailed Manakin vocalizations, the vocal qualities preferred by females during courtship, and the development of these preferred qualities.

Long-tailed Manakins have diverse vocal repertoires. Males give at least 13 distinct calls, designated with onomatopoeic names (Trainer and McDonald 1993). Some of the most frequently heard include "tee-a-moo," which is given by a male to summon his partner for duet singing. When his partner arrives, they alternate "wit" calls to synchronize before beginning to sing the "toledo" song in unison. The "toledos" attract females to the display arena. Once a female arrives, males begin the dance portion of the cooperative display, which is accompanied by a "nyanyownh" call with each hop as males leapfrog over one another.

When we played tapes of five common calls, we found that male manakins responded differently from territorial birds of other species. They did not behave aggressively or countervocalize with the tape. Instead, males generally responded by soliciting interaction with a cooperative partner. To better understand the impact of cooperation on communication in Long-tailed Manakins, we compared the call repertoire sizes reported in the literature for 13 species of manakins. Manakin species with joint displays that were competitive rather than cooperative did not have a large variety of calls. The presence of obligate, joint displays and the need to mediate long-term cooperative relationships among males may explain why Long-tailed Manakins have such diverse repertoires.

Our studies also demonstrated the importance of these partnerships for the courtship success of males.

The "toledo" song must be sung jointly in order to attract females to the display zone. The duet consists of two nearly identical vocal components sung almost in unison (Fig. 6.15). To the human ear, the songs of some teams sound more coordinated and harmonious than others. Harmonious duets sound like one bird singing but have a noticeably fuller sound, easily distinguished from the rare solo songs. Nonharmonious duets sound dissonant and sometimes poorly synchronized. Sonagrams show that in songs that sound harmonious to human ears, the frequencies of the two male's song components are well matched. To quantify the acoustic differences in song quality, we measured the degree of frequency matching with a sound spectrum analyzer. We found that the degree of frequency matching was correlated with the rate at which females visited the lek arenas (Trainer and McDonald 1995; Fig. 6.16). This suggests that females prefer well-coordinated songs, which could result in higher mating success for alpha males belonging to teams with better singing performance.

In male manakins, singing performance improves with age. In teams including one adult and one immature male, frequency matching increased with the age of the younger partner. The songs of immature males became less variable in acoustic structure with age. The sound frequencies of the contributions of adult males in well-established teams were better

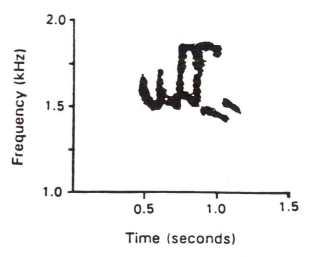

Figure 6.15. *(top)* Sonogram of a Long-tailed Manakin "toledo" song showing the contributions of two male partners.

matched than expected by chance; the mean degree of frequency matching in the songs of established teams was greater than that of artificial teams generated by randomly combining males' song contributions (J. Trainer and D. McDonald, unpubl. data). Because manakin partners are not genetically related (McDonald and Potts 1994), the high degree of matching in such teams may have come about by convergence of the two males' song contributions as the partnerships were forming. Although a major benefit of a cooperative partnership to the younger, nonreproducing males appears to be the eventual assumption of alpha status (McDonald 1993a; see McDonald, "Cooperation Between Male Long-tailed Manakins," pp. 204–205), a corollary benefit may be the opportunity to develop competent performance of well-coordinated songs preferred by females. A next step is to learn how males' songs become coordinated by studying vocal development during partner formation.

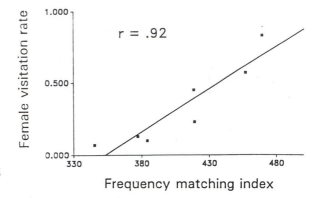

Figure 6.16. *(above)* Rate of female visitation to Long-tailed Manakin display arenas versus frequency matching in the joint "toledo" song.

DO SUBORDINATE SPECIES HAVE AN ADVANTAGE? TESTING THE POINTER HYPOTHESIS WITH TROPICAL HUMMINGBIRDS
Harry M. Tiebout III

The hummingbirds of Monteverde compete for a limited standing crop of floral nectar (Feinsinger 1976, 1978), yet the region supports a high diversity of nectarivores (Feinsinger 1977). A few species have specialized on subsets of flowers by having unusually curved or long bills which enable them to extract nectar from flowers unavailable to the other "generalist" species. Competition is potentially most intense among the numerous generalist hummingbird species with short, straight bills. To determine how these generalist species are able to coexist, I focused on the costs and benefits of different foraging modes (or community roles; *sensu* Feinsinger and Colwell 1978).

One pair of hummingbird species has a marked divergence in their foraging modes and hence a highly asymmetrical competitive relationship. The mid-sized Steely-vented Hummingbird is a behaviorally dominant territorialist which monopolizes rich nectar sources. In contrast, the small Canivet's (Fork-tailed) Emerald is subordinate and forages as a low-reward trapliner. This hummingbird is usually excluded from the high-reward flowers defended by Steely-vented Hummingbirds, and meets its energy demands by visiting flowers that are too widely dispersed to be economically defensible by territorialists (Feinsinger and Colwell 1978). In this competitive diad, the behaviorally dominant foraging mode clearly benefits from unrestricted access to the best feeding sites. The benefits of being a species with a subordinate mode (if any) are not as obvious. One hypothesis is Canivet's Hummingbird, with its relatively long wings, has a lower energetic cost of flight and can profit more from visiting widely dispersed flowers than can the territorialist (Feinsinger et al. 1979), although the experimental evidence is mixed (Tiebout 1991a, 1992, 1993).

Another explanation for the coexistence of this pair is that subordinate species may be better able to discover novel sources of food. This notion has been dubbed the "pointer hypothesis" (Tiebout 1996), in recognition of hunting dogs, whose superior ability to locate prey is taken advantage of by their dominant human companions. Black Vultures exploit Turkey Vultures in a similar fashion. In the case of competing hummingbirds, superior food-finding ability might compensate small trapliners for the usurpation of rich food sources by territorialists. Trapliners might frequently gain first access to new, rich nectar sources (even though they are subsequently excluded by dominant birds), or they may be able to continuously locate and use cryptic or low-reward flowers not likely to be exploited by the larger territorialists.

To test the pointer hypothesis prediction that dominant species exploit the superior food-finding abilities of subordinate species, I conducted two experiments to quantify the abilities of Steely-vented Hummingbirds and Canivet's Hummingbirds to locate novel food sources. Trials were run using naive solitary birds (experiment 1) and naive heterospecific pairs (experiment 2) which were introduced for the first time into an experimental flight cage containing artificial feeders placed at locations unknown to the birds. The cage was constructed from a 20-m tube folded into five segments that were separated from each other by opaque walls (Fig. 6.17). The feeders received regular deliveries of sucrose solution at rates sufficient to keep birds active but unsatiated. For each experiment, I recorded the time at which each bird visited each feeder.

Contrary to the pointer hypothesis, the results demonstrated that birds of both species were equally adept at locating novel feeders in this experimental system. When tested in competing pairs (experiment 2), the subordinate trapliner was not able to discover significantly more new feeders than the territorialist ($\bar{x} = 2.7$ and 2.3 feeders discovered first by Cavinet's Hummingbird and Steely-vented Hummingbird, respectively, of 5 total feeders per trial). However, the dominant Steely-vented Hummingbird was significantly faster at making its first visit to a given feeder once it had already been discovered by its cage-mate ($\bar{x} = 9.8$ vs. 23.0 min elapsed between initial discovery by cagemate and the first visit for Steely-vented Hummingbird and Canivet's Hummingbird, respectively; t-test, $P = .004$). After the trapliner had discovered a feeder first, the territorialist subsequently made its first visit to that same feeder in less than 1 min in more than 60% of the cases (Fig. 6.18). The trapliner was much less effective in exploiting the discoveries of its cagemate, visiting the same feeder within 1 min only 30% of the time.

The territorialist's apparent ability to capitalize on the food-locating efforts of a subordinate are consistent with the pointer hypothesis but inadequate to support it. The combined results offer stronger support for alternative hypotheses formulated for intraspecific competition which propose that dominants can parasitize resources found by subordinates without suggesting any differences in their respec-

Experiment 1:   Solitary Birds

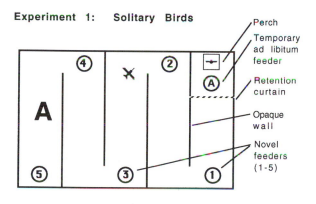

Experiment 2:   Heterospecific pairs

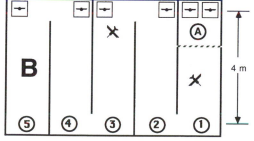

Figure 6.17. Flight cage (top view) to test (top) single individuals of *Amazilia* and *Chlorostilbon* (*n* = 9 birds per species, experiment 1) and (bottom) competing heterospecific pairs (*n* = 14 birds per species, experiment 2).

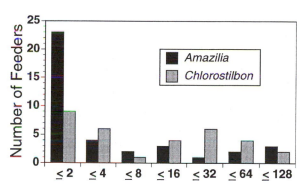

Time (min) to Locate a Feeder After Cage-mate

Figure 6.18. The abilities of *Amazilia* and *Chlorostilbon* to locate novel feeders that had previously been discovered by a cage-mate. The y-axis represents the number of feeders located by each species within a specified time (x-axis categories) after having been first discovered by a heterospecific cage-mate (experiment 2, *n* = 14 birds x 5 feeders = 70 feeders located for both species). Time categories are nonoverlapping and are abbreviated ("≤ 8" represents 4 < *n* ≤ 8, etc.). In the shortest time category (≤ 2), all feeders were located within 1 min (see text for analyses).

tive abilities to locate resources (e.g., the "shepherd's hypothesis" [Rohwer and Ewald 1981], or "producers versus scroungers" [Barnard and Sibly 1981]).

My experiments failed to reveal any potential costs of having a dominant foraging mode, consistent with other experimental work that has unsuccessfully attempted to find the "downside" of territoriality in hummingbirds (Tiebout 1991a, 1992, 1993). These experiments leave open the question of how hummingbirds can benefit from a subordinate rank during interspecific competitive encounters.

More experiments are needed to evaluate food locating and acquiring abilities, especially under competitive conditions with cryptic or low-density food sources. We must also discover whether experiments with free-living birds produce results similar to experiments on captive animals. Such studies should help determine whether there are any advantages of low dominance rank and will contribute to our understanding of the factors that enable a diverse mixture of hummingbird species to coexist in tropical habitats.

Literature Cited

Altmann, J. 1974. Observational study of behaviour: sampling methods. Behaviour 49:227–267.

Alvarez-Lopez, H., M. D. Heredia-Flores, and M. C. Hernandez-Pizarro. 1984. Reproduccíon del cucarachero común (*Troglodytes aedon*, Aves, Troglodytidae) en el Valle del Cauca. Caldasia 14:85–123.

Barnard, C. J., and R. M. Sibly. 1981. Producers and scroungers: a general model and its application to captive flocks of house sparrows. Animal Behaviour 29:543–550.

Biermann, G. C., and S. G. Sealy. 1982. Parental feeding of nestling Yellow Warblers in relation to brood size and prey availability. Auk 99:332–341.

Boyce, M. S., and C. M. Perrins. 1987. Optimizing Great Tit clutch size in a fluctuating environment. Ecology 68:142–153.

Bronstein, J. L., and K. Hoffmann. 1987. Spatial and temporal variation in frugivory at a neotropical fig *Ficus pertusa*. Oikos 49:261–268.

Brown, C. R., and M. B. Brown. 1986. Ectoparasitism as a cost of coloniality in Cliff Swallows. Ecology 67:1206–1218.

Brown, J. L. 1974. Alternative routes to sociality in jays, with a theory for the evolution of altruism and communal breeding. American Zoologist 14: 63–80.

———. 1987. Helping and communal breeding in birds: ecology and evolution. Princeton University Press, Princeton, New Jersey.

Busby, W. H. 1987. Flowering phenology and density-dependent pollination success in *Cephaelis elata* (Rubiaceae). Ph.D. dissertation, University of Florida, Gainesville.

Buskirk, R. E., and W. H. Buskirk. 1976. Changes in arthropod abundance in a highland Costa Rican forest. American Midland Naturalist 95:288–298.

Buskirk, W. H. 1972. Foraging ecology of bird flocks in a tropical forest. Ph.D. dissertation, University of California, Davis.

———. 1976. Social systems in a tropical forest avifauna. American Naturalist 110:293–310.

———. 1981. Ochraceous Wren fails to respond to mobbing calls in an heterospecific flock. Wilson Bulletin 93:278–279.

Buskirk, W. H., and M. Lechner. 1978. Frugivory by Swallow-tailed Kites in Costa Rica. Auk 95:767–768.

Caswell, H. 1989. Matrix population models. Sinauer, Sunderland, Massachusetts.

Clark, A. B., and D. S. Wilson. 1981. Avian breeding adaptations: hatching asynchrony, brood reduction, and nest failure. Quarterly Review of Biology 56:253–277.

Collar, N. J., M. T. Crosby, and A. J. Strattersfield. 1994. Birds to watch 2: The world list of threatened birds. Smithsonian Institution Press, Washington, D.C.

Emlen, S. T. 1991. Cooperative breeding in birds and mammals. Pages 301–335 *in* J. R. Krebs and N. B. Davies, editors. Behavioural ecology: an evolutionary approach (3rd ed.). Blackwell, Oxford.

Feinsinger, P. 1976. Organization of a tropical guild of nectarivorous birds. Ecological Monographs 46:257–291.

———. 1977. Notes on the hummingbirds of Monteverde, Cordillera de Tilarán, Costa Rica. Wilson Bulletin 89:159–164.

———. 1978. Ecological interactions between plants and hummingbirds in a successional tropical community. Ecological Monographs 48:269–287.

———. 1980. Asynchronous migration patterns and the coexistence of tropical hummingbirds. Pages 411–419 *in* A. Keast and E. S. Morton, editors. Migrant birds in the neotropics: ecology, behavior, distribution, and conservation. Smithsonian Institution Press, Washington, D.C.

Feinsinger, P., and W. H. Busby. 1987. Pollen carryover: experimental comparisons between morphs of *Palicourea lasiorrachis* (Rubiaceae), a distylous, bird-pollinated, tropical treelet. Oecologia 73: 231–235.

Feinsinger, P., and R. K. Colwell. 1978. Community organization among neotropical nectar-feeding birds. American Zoologist 18:779–795.

Feinsinger, P., and H. M. Tiebout III. 1991. Competition among plants sharing hummingbird pollinators: laboratory experiments on a mechanism. Ecology 72:1946–1952.

Feinsinger, P., R. K. Colwell, J. Terborgh, and S. B. Chaplin. 1979. Elevation and the morphology, flight energetics and foraging ecology of tropical hummingbirds. American Naturalist 113: 481–497.

Feinsinger, P., K. G. Murray, S. Kinsman, and W. B. Busby. 1986. Floral neighborhood and pollination success in four hummingbird-pollinated forest plant species. Ecology 67:449–464.

Feinsinger, P., J. H. Beach, Y. B. Linhart, W. H. Busby, and K. G. Murray. 1987. Disturbance pollinator predictability and pollination success among Costa Rican cloud forest plants. Ecology 68:1294–1305.

Feinsinger, P., W. H. Busby, K. G. Murray, J. H. Beach, W. Z. Pounds, and Y. B. Linhart. 1988. Mixed support for spatial heterogeneity in species interactions: hummingbirds in a tropical disturbance mosaic. American Naturalist 131:33–57.

Feinsinger, P., H. M. Tiebout III, and B. E. Young. 1991a. Do tropical bird-pollinated plants exhibit density-dependent interactions? Field experiments. Ecology 72:1953–1963.

Feinsinger, P., H. M. Tiebout III, B. E. Young, and K.G. Murray. 1991b. New perspectives on neotropical plant-hummingbird interactions. Acta Congressus Internationalis Ornithologici 20:1605–1610.

Fleming, T. H., and A. Estrada, editors. 1993. Frugivory and seed dispersal: ecological and evolutionary aspects. Kluwer, Dordrecht.

Fogden, M. P. 1972. The seasonality and population dynamics of equatorial forest birds in Sarawak. Ibis 114:307–342.

———. 1993. An annotated checklist of the birds of Monteverde and Peñas Blancas. Published by the author, Monteverde, Costa Rica.

Foster, M. S. 1974. A model to explain molt-breeding overlap and clutch size in some tropical birds. Evolution 28:182–190.

———. 1977. Odd couples in manakins: a study of social organization and cooperative breeding in Chiroxiphia linearis. American Naturalist 111:845–853.

———. 1981. Cooperative behavior and social organization in the Swallow-tailed Manakin (Chiroxiphia caudata). Behavioral Ecology and Sociobiology 9:167–177.

Freed, L. A. 1981. Loss of mass in breeding wrens: stress or adaptation? Ecology 62:1179–1186.

———. 1986a. Territorial takeover and sexually selected infanticide in tropical House Wrens. Behavioural Ecology and Sociobiology 19:197–206.

———. 1986b. Usurpatory and opportunistic bigamy in tropical House Wrens. Animal Behaviour 34: 1894–1896.

Fretwell, S. D. 1969. The adjustment of birth rate to mortality in birds. Ibis 111:624–627.

Garnett, M. C. 1981. Body size, heritability and influence on juvenile survival among Great Tits, Parus major. Ibis 123:31–41.

Gibbs, J. P., M. L. Hunter, and S. M. Melvin. 1993. Snag availability and communities of cavity nesting birds in tropical versus temperate forests. Biotropica 25:236–241.

Gillespie, J. H. 1977. Natural selection for variances in offspring numbers: a new evolutionary principle. American Naturalist 111:1010–1014.

Greenberg, R., and J. Gradwohl. 1980. Leaf surface specializations of birds and arthropods in a Panamanian forest. Oecologia 46:115–124.

Gross, A. O. 1948. Eastern House Wren. Pages 113–141 in A. C. Bent, editor. Life histories of North American nuthatches, wrens, thrashers and their allies. Bulletin No. 195 of the United States National Museum, Washington, D.C.

Guindon, C. F. 1996. The importance of forest fragments to the maintenance of regional biodiversity in Costa Rica. Pages 168–186 in J. Schelhas and R. Greenberg, editors. Forest patches in tropical landscapes. Island Press, Washington, D.C.

Hairston, N. G. 1980. The experimental test of an analysis of field distributions: competition in terrestrial salamanders. Ecology 61:817–826.

Halliday, T. R. 1978. Sexual selection and mate choice. Pages 180–213 in J. R. Krebs and N. B. Davies, editors. Behavioural ecology, an evolutionary approach. Blackwell, Oxford.

Hamilton, W. D. 1964. The genetical evolution of social behavior, I & II. Journal of Theoretical Biology 7:1–52.

Hilty, S. L., and W. L. Brown. 1986. A guide to the birds of Colombia. Princeton University Press, Princeton, New Jersey.

Holdridge, L. R. 1967. Life zone ecology. Tropical Science Center, San José, Costa Rica.

Howell, T. R. 1969. Avian distribution in Central America. Auk 86:293–326.

Hutto, R. L. 1994. The composition and social organization of mixed-species flocks in a tropical deciduous forest in western Mexico. Condor 96: 105–118.

Jehl, J. R., Jr., and B. G. Murray, Jr. 1986. The evolution of normal and reverse sexual size dimorphism in shorebirds and other birds. Current Ornithology 3:1–86.

Kamil, A., and R. Balda. 1985. Cache recovery and spatial memory in Clark's Nutcrackers (Nucifraga columbiana). Journal of Experimental Psychology and Animal Behavioral Processes 11:95–111.

Karr, J. R., S. K. Robinson, J. G. Blake, and R. O. Bierregaard, Jr. 1990a. Birds of four neotropical forests. Pages 237–251 in A. H. Gentry, editor. Four neotropical forests. Yale University Press, New Haven, Connecticut.

Karr, J. R., J. D. Nichols, M. K. Klimkiewicz, and J. D. Brown. 1990b. Survival rates of birds of tropical and temperate forest: will the dogma survive? American Naturalist 136:277–291.

Keeler-Wolf, T. 1986. The Barred Antshrike (Thamnophilis doliatus) on Trinidad and Tobago: habitat niche expansion of a generalist forager. Oecologia 70:309–317.

Kendeigh, S. C. 1941. Territorial and mating behavior of the House Wren. Illinois Biological Monographs 18:1–120.

Kennedy, E. D., and H. W. Power. 1990. Experiments on indeterminate laying in House Wrens and European Starlings. Condor 92:861–865.

Kermott, L. H., L. S. Johnson, and M. S. Merkle. 1991. Experimental evidence for the function of mate replacement and infanticide by males in a north-temperate population of House Wrens. Condor 93:630–636.

Kiff, L. F. 1979. The nest and eggs of the Black-and-yellow Silky Flycatcher. Auk 96:198–199.

Koenig, W. D., and R. L. Mumme. 1987. Population ecology of the cooperatively breeding Acorn Woodpecker. Princeton University Press, Princeton, New Jersey.

Krebs, J. R. 1973. Social learning and the adaptive significance of mixed-species flocks of chickadees. Canadian Journal of Zoology 51:1275–1288.

Krebs, J. R., D. R. Sherry, S. D. Healey, V. H. Perry, and A. L. Vaccarino. 1989. Hippocampal specialization of food-storing birds. Proceedings of the National Academy of Sciences 86:1388–1392.

Lack, D. 1954. The natural regulation of animal numbers. Clarendon Press, Oxford.

Lack, D., and R. E. Moreau. 1965. Clutch-size in tropical passerine birds of forest and savanna. Oiseau 35:76–89.

Latta, S. C., and J. M. Wunderle, Jr. 1996. The composition and foraging ecology of mixed-species flocks in pine forests of Hispaniola. Condor 98: 595–607.

Lawton, M. F. 1983. Cyanocorax morio. Pages 573–574 in D. H. Janzen, editor. Costa Rican natural history. Chicago University Press, Chicago.

Lawton, M. F., and C. F. Guindon. 1981. Flock composition, breeding success, and learning in the Brown Jay. Condor 83:27–33.

Lawton, M. F., and R. O. Lawton. 1980. Nest-site selection in the Brown Jay. Auk 97:631–633.

———. 1985. The breeding biology of the Brown Jay in Monteverde, Costa Rica. Condor 87:192–204.

———. 1986. Heterochrony, deferred breeding, and avian sociality. Current Ornithology 3:187–221.

Levey, D. J., and F. G. Stiles. 1992. Evolutionary precursors of long-distance migration: resource availability and movement patterns in neotropical landbirds. American Naturalist 140: 447–476.

———. 1994. Birds: ecology, behavior, and taxonomic affinities. Pages 217–228 in L. A. McDade, K. S. Bawa, H. A. Hespenheide, and G. S. Hartshorn, editors. La Selva: ecology and natural history of a neotropical rain forest. University of Chicago Press, Chicago.

Lima, S. L. 1987. Clutch size in birds: a predation perspective. Ecology 68:1062–1070.

Loiselle, B. A., and J. G. Blake. 1991. Temporal variation in birds and fruits along an elevational gradient in Costa Rica. Ecology 72:180–193.

Lyon, B. E., and M. P. Fogden. 1989. Breeding biology of the Sunbittern (Europyga helias) in Costa Rica. Auk 106:503–507.

Martin, T. E. 1984. Impact of livestock grazing on birds of a Colombian cloud forest. Journal of Tropical Ecology 25:158–171.

Martin, T. E., and D. M. Finch. 1995. Ecology and management of neotropical migratory birds. Oxford University Press, Oxford.

Mayfield, H. 1975. Suggestions for calculating nest success. Wilson Bulletin 87:456–466.

Maynard Smith, J. 1964. Group selection and kin selection. Nature 201:1145–1147.

Mays, N. 1985. Ants and foraging behavior of the Collared Forest-Falcon. Wilson Bulletin 97:231–232.

McDiarmid, R. W., R. E. Ricklefs, and M. S. Foster. 1977. Dispersal of *Stemmadenia donnell-smithii* (Apocynaceae) by birds. Biotropica 9:9–25.

McDonald, D. B. 1989a. Cooperation under sexual selection: age-graded changes in a lekking bird. American Naturalist 134:709–730.

———. 1989b. Correlates of male mating success in a lekking bird with male-male cooperation. Animal Behaviour 37:1007–1022.

———. 1993a. Delayed plumage maturation and orderly queues for status: a manakin mannequin experiment. Ethology 94:31–45.

———. 1993b. Demographic consequences of sexual selection in the Long-tailed Manakin. Behavioral Ecology 4:297–309.

McDonald, D., and K. Winnett-Murray. 1989. First reported nests of the Black-breasted Wood-Quail (*Odontophorus leucolaemus*). Condor 91:985–986.

McDonald, D. B., and H. Caswell. 1993. Matrix methods for avian demography. Pages 139–185 in D. M. Power, editor. Current ornithology. Plenum Press, New York.

McDonald, D. B., and W. K. Potts. 1994. Cooperative display and relatedness among males in a lek-mating bird. Science 266:1030–1032.

Moermond, T. C., and J. Denslow. 1985. Neotropical avian frugivores: patterns of behavior, morphology, and nutrition, with consequences for fruit selection. Ornithological Monographs 36:865–897.

Møller, A. P. 1990. Effects of parasitism by a haematophagous mite on reproduction in the barn swallow. Ecology 71:2345–2357.

Morse, D. H. 1977. Feeding behavior and predator avoidance in heterospecific groups. BioScience 27:332–339.

———. 1980. Behavioral mechanisms in ecology. Harvard University Press, Cambridge, Massachusetts.

Morton, E. S. 1973. On the evolutionary advantage and disadvantages of fruit eating in tropical birds. American Naturalist 107:8–22.

Munn, C. A. 1985. Permanent canopy and understory flocks in Amazonia: species composition and population density. Ornithological Monographs 36: 683–712.

———. 1986. Birds that "cry wolf!" Nature 319:143–145.

Munn, C. A., and J. W. Terborgh. 1979. Multi-species territoriality in neotropical foraging flocks. Condor 81:338–347.

Murray, K. G. 1986. Avian seed dispersal of neotropical gap-dependent plants. Ph.D. dissertation, University of Florida, Gainesville.

———. 1987. Selection for optimal fruit crop size in bird-dispersed plants. American Naturalist 129: 18–31.

———. 1988. Avian seed dispersal of three neotropical gap-dependent plants. Ecological Monographs 58:271–298.

Murray, K. G., S. Russell, and C. M. Pirone. 1994. Fruit laxatives and seed passage rates in frugivores: consequences for plant reproductive success. Ecology 75:989–994.

Myers, N. 1988. Tropical forests and their species: going, going . . . ? Pages 28–35 in E. O. Wilson, editor. Biodiversity. National Academy Press, Washington, D.C.

Nadkarni, N. M. 1994. Diversity of species and interactions in the upper tree canopy of forest ecosystems. American Zoologist 34:70–78.

Nadkarni, N. M., and T. J. Matelson. 1989. Bird use of epiphyte resources in neotropical trees. Condor 91:891–907.

Partridge, L., and T. Halliday. 1984. Mating patterns and male choice. Pages 222–250 in J. R. Krebs and N. B. Davies, editors. Behavioural ecology: an evolutionary approach. Sinauer, Sunderland, Massachusetts.

Pimm, S. L. 1991. The balance of nature? University of Chicago Press, Chicago.

Podolsky, R. D. 1992. Strange floral attractors: pollinator attraction and the evolution of plant sexual systems. Science 258:791–793.

Pounds, J. A., M. P. L. Fogden, J. M. Savage, and G. C. Gorman. 1997. Tests of null models for amphibian declines on a tropical mountain. Conservation Biology 11:1307–1322.

Powell, G. V. N. 1977a. Monteverde Cloud Forest Preserve, Costa Rica. American Birds 31:119–125.

———. 1977b. Socioecology of mixed species flocks in a neotropical forest. Ph.D. dissertation, University of California, Davis.

———. 1979. Structure and dynamics of interspecific flocks in a neotropical mid-elevation forest. Auk 96:375–390.

———. 1980. Migrant participation in neotropical mixed species flocks. Pages 477–483 in A. Keast and E. S. Morton, editors. Migrant birds in the neotropics: ecology, behavior, distribution, and conservation. Smithsonian Institution Press, Washington, D.C.

———. 1983. *Premnoplex brunnescens*. Page 601 in D. H. Janzen, editor. Costa Rican natural history. University of Chicago Press, Chicago.

———. 1985. Sociobiology and adaptive significance of interspecific foraging flocks in the Neotropics. Ornithological Monographs 36:713–732.

Powell, G. V. N., and R. Bjork. 1995. Implications of intra-tropical migration on reserve design: a case study using *Pharomachrus mocinno*. Conservation Biology 9:354–362.

Pribil, S., and J. Picman. 1991. Why house wrens destroy clutches of other birds: a support for the nest site competition hypothesis. Condor 93:184–185.

Queller, D. C., J. E. Strassman, and C. R. Hughes. 1993. Microsatellites and kinship. Trends in Ecology and Evolution 8:285–288.

Rappole, J. H. 1995. The ecology of migrant birds: a neotropical perspective. Smithsonian Institution Press, Washington, D.C.

Remsen, J. V., Jr. 1994. Use and misuse of bird lists in community ecology and conservation. Auk 111: 225–227.

Remsen, J. V., Jr., and T. A. Parker III. 1984. Arboreal dead-leaf-searching birds of the Neotropics. Condor 86:36–41.

Remsen, J. V., Jr., M. A. Hyde, and A. Chapman. 1993. The diets of neotropical trogons, motmots, barbets and toucans. Condor 95:178–192.

Ricklefs, R. E. 1969. An analysis of nesting mortality in birds. Smithsonian Contributions to Zoology 9:1–48.

Ridgely, R. S. 1976. A guide to the birds of Panama. Princeton University Press, Princeton, New Jersey.

Ridgely, R. S., and S. J. Gaulin. 1980. The birds of Finca Merenberg, Huila Department, Colombia. Condor 82:379–391.

Riley, C. M. 1986. Observations of the breeding biology of Emerald Toucanets in Costa Rica. Wilson Bulletin 98:585–588.

Riley, C. M., and K. G. Smith. 1986. Flower eating by Emerald Toucanets in Costa Rica. Condor 88:396–397.

———. 1992. Sexual dimorphism and foraging behavior of Emerald Toucanets *Aulacorhynchus prasinus* in Costa Rica. Ornis Scandinavica 23:259–266.

Robbins, M. B., T. A. Parker III, and S. Allen. 1985. The avifauna of Cerro Pirre, Darién, eastern Panama. Ornithological Monographs 36:198–232.

Robinson, K. D., and J. T. Rotenberry. 1991. Clutch size and reproductive success of House Wrens rearing natural and manipulated broods. Auk 108: 277–284.

Robinson, S. K., F. R. Thompson III, T. M. Donovan, D. R. Whitehead, and J. Faaborg. 1995. Regional forest fragmentation and the nesting success of migratory birds. Science 267:1987–1990.

Rohwer, S., and P. W. Ewald. 1981. The cost of dominance and the advantage of subordination in a badge signaling system. Evolution 35:441–454.

Root, R. 1967. The niche exploitation pattern of the Blue-gray Gnatcatcher. Ecological Monographs 37:317–350.

Rosselli, L. 1989. El ciclo anual de un ave frugívora migratoria altitudinal, *Corapipo leucorrhoa* (Pipridae) y los frutos que consume. Masters Thesis, Universidad de Costa Rica, San José.

Sallabanks, R., and S. P. Courtney. 1992. Frugivory, seed predation, and insect-vertebrate interactions. Annual Review of Entomology 37:377–400.

Santana, C. E., and B. G. Milligan. 1984. Behavior of toucanets, bellbirds, and quetzals feeding on lauraceous fruits. Biotropica 16:152–154.

Sargent, S. 1993. Nesting biology of the Yellow-throated Euphonia: large clutch size in a neotropical frugivore. Wilson Bulletin 105:285–300.

———. 1994. Seed dispersal of mistletoes by birds in Monteverde, Costa Rica. Ph.D. dissertation, Cornell University, Ithaca, New York.

———. 1995. Seed fate in a tropical mistletoe: the importance of host twig size. Functional Ecology 9:197–204.

Shopland, J. M. 1985. Facultative following of mixed species flocks by two species of neotropical warbler. Ph.D. dissertation, University of Chicago, Chicago.

Skutch, A. F. 1935. Helpers at the nest. Auk 52:257–273.

———. 1944. Life history of the Blue-throated Toucanet. Wilson Bulletin 56:133–151.

———. 1949. Do tropical birds rear as many birds as they can nourish? Ibis 91:430–455.

———. 1960. Life histories of Central American birds, II. Pacific Coast Avifauna 34, Cooper Ornithological Society, Berkeley, California.

———. 1967. Life histories of Central American highland birds. Nuttall Ornithological Club Bulletin 7:59.

———. 1985. Clutch size, nesting success, and predation on nests of neotropical birds, reviewed. Ornithological Monographs 36:575–594.

Slud, P. 1957. The song and dance of the Long-tailed Manakin, *Chiroxiphia linearis*. Auk 74:333–339.

Snow, B. K. 1972. Lek behavior and breeding of Guy's Hermit Hummingbird. Ibis 116:278–297.

———. 1977. Territory behavior and courtship of the male Three-wattled Bellbird. Auk 94:623–645.

Solomon, N. G., and J. A. French, editors. 1996. Cooperative breeding in mammals. Cambridge University Press, Cambridge.

Stacey, P. B., and W. D. Koenig, editors. 1990. Cooperative breeding in birds: long-term studies of ecology and behavior. Cambridge University Press, Cambridge.

Stiles, F. G. 1978. Temporal organization of flowering among the hummingbird food plants of a tropical wet forest. Biotropica 10:194–210.

———. 1980a. The annual cycle in a tropical wet forest hummingbird community. Ibis 122:322–343.

———. 1980b. Evolutionary implications of habitat relations between permanent and winter resident landbirds in Costa Rica. Pages 421–435 *in* A. Keast and E. S. Morton, editors. Migrant birds in the Neotropics: ecology, behavior, distribution, and conservation. Smithsonian Institution Press, Washington, D.C.

———. 1981. Geographical aspects of bird-flower coevolution. Annals of the Missouri Botanical Garden 68:323–351.

———. 1983. Birds. Pages 502–530 *in* D. H. Janzen, editor.

Costa Rican natural history. University of Chicago Press, Chicago.

———. 1985a. Conservation of forest birds in Costa Rica: problems and perspectives. Pages 141–168 *in* A. W. Diamond and T. E. Lovejoy, editors. Conservation of tropical forest birds. International Council for Bird Preservation, Cambridge.

———. 1985b. On the role of birds in the dynamics of neotropical forests. Pages 49–59 *in* A. W. Diamond and T. E. Lovejoy, editors. Conservation of tropical forest birds. International Council for Bird Preservation, Cambridge.

———. 1985c. Seasonal patterns and coevolution in the hummingbird-flower community of a Costa Rican subtropical forest. Ornithological Monographs 36:757–787.

———. 1988. Altitudinal movements of birds on the Caribbean slope of Costa Rica: implications for conservation. Pages 243–258 *in* F. Alameda and C. M. Pringle, editors. Tropical rainforests: diversity and conservation. California Academy of Sciences, San Francisco.

Stiles, F. G., and C. E. Freeman. 1993. Patterns in floral nectar characteristics of some bird-visited plant species from Costa Rica. Biotropica 25: 191–205.

Stiles, F. G., and A. F. Skutch. 1989. A guide to the birds of Costa Rica. Cornell University Press, Ithaca, New York.

Stiles, F. G., and S. M. Smith. 1980. Notes on bird distribution in Costa Rica. Brenesia 17:137–156.

Stotz, D. F., J. W. Fitzpatrick, T. A. Parker III, and D. K. Moskovits. 1996. Neotropical birds: ecology and conservation. University of Chicago Press, Chicago.

Terborgh, J. 1977. Bird species diversity on an Andean elevational gradient. Ecology 58:1007–1019.

———. 1983. Five New World primates. Princeton University Press, Princeton, New Jersey.

———. 1990. Where have all the birds gone? Princeton University Press, Princeton, New Jersey.

Terborgh, J., S. K. Robinson, T. A. Parker III, C. A. Munn, and N. Pierpont. 1990. Structure and organization of an Amazonian forest bird community. Ecological Monographs 60:213–238.

Thomas, C. D., P. M. Lackie, M. J. Biscoe, and D. N. Hepper. 1986. Interactions between hummingbirds and butterflies at a *Hamelia patens* bush. Biotropica 18:161–165.

Tiebout, H. M., III. 1989. Tests of a model of food passage rates in hummingbirds. Auk 106:203–208.

———. 1991a. Daytime energy management by tropical hummingbirds: responses to foraging constraint. Ecology 72:839–851.

———. 1991b. Energetics of competition and guild structure of neotropical hummingbirds. Acta Congressus Internationalis Ornithologici 20:1175–1179.

———. 1992. Comparative energetics of divergent foraging modes: a double-labeled water experiment on hummingbird competition. Animal Behaviour 44:895–906.

———. 1993. Mechanisms of competition in tropical hummingbirds: metabolic cost for winners and losers. Ecology 74:405–418.

———. 1996. Costs and benefits of interspecific dominance rank: are subordinates better at finding novel locations? Animal Behaviour 51:1375–1381.

Tiebout, H. M., III, and K. A. Nagy. 1991. Validation of the double-labeled water method (^{3}HH^{18}O) for measuring water flux and CO_2 production in the tropical hummingbird *Amazilia saucerottei*. Physiological Zoology 64:362–374.

Tilman, D., R. M. May, C. L. Lehman, and M. A. Nowak. 1994. Habitat destruction and the extinction debt. Nature 371:65–66.

Toft, C. A. 1991. Current theory of host-parasite interactions. Pages 3–15 *in* J. E. Loye and M. Zuk, editors. Bird-parasite interactions. Oxford University Press, New York.

Trainer, J. M., and D. B. McDonald. 1993. Vocal repertoire of the Long-tailed Manakin and its relation to male-male cooperation. Condor 95:769–781.

———. 1995. Singing performance, frequency matching and courtship success of long-tailed manakins (*Chiroxiphia linearis*). Behavioral Ecology and Sociobiology 37:249–254.

Tramer, E. J. 1979. First sight records of Lincoln's Sparrow for Costa Rica. Wilson Bulletin 91:469–470.

Tramer, E. J., and T. R. Kemp. 1979. Diet-correlated variations in social behavior of wintering Tennessee Warblers. Auk 96:186–187.

———. 1980. Foraging ecology of migrant and resident warblers and vireos in the highlands of Costa Rica. Pages 285–296 *in* A. Keast and E. S. Morton, editors. Migrant birds in the Neotropics: ecology, behavior, distribution, and conservation. Smithsonian Institution Press, Washington, D.C.

———. 1982. Notes on migrants wintering at Monteverde, Costa Rica. Wilson Bulletin 94:350–354.

Travaset, A. 1993. Weak interactions between avian and insect frugivores: the case of *Pistacia terebinthus*. Vegetatio 107/108:191–203.

Valburg, L. K. 1992a. Eating infested fruits: interactions in a plant-disperser-pest triad. Oikos 65:25–28.

———. 1992b. Feeding preferences of Common Bush-Tanagers for insect-infested fruits: avoidance or attraction? Oikos 65:29–33.

———. 1992c. Flocking and frugivory: the effect of social groupings on resource use in the Common Bush-Tanager. Condor 94:358–363.

Von Bromssen, A., and C. Jansson. 1980. Effects of food addition to Willow Tit *Parus montanus* and Crested Tit *P. cristatus* at the time of breeding. Ornis Scandinavica 11:173–178.

Walsberg, G. E. 1983. Avian ecological energetics. Pages 161–220 *in* D. S. Farner, J. R. King, and K. C. Parkes, editors. Avian biology. Academic Press, New York.

Wetmore, A. 1926. The migration of birds. Harvard University Press, Cambridge, Massachusetts.

Wheelwright, N. T. 1983. Fruits and the ecology of Resplendent Quetzals. Auk 100:286–301.

———. 1985. Fruit size, gape width, and the diets of fruit-eating birds. Ecology 66:808–818.

———. 1986a. The diet of American Robins: an analysis of U.S. Biological Survey Records. Auk 103: 710–725.

———. 1986b. A seven-year study of individual variation in fruit production in tropical bird-dispersed tree species in the family Lauraceae. Pages 19–35 *in* A. Estrada and T. H. Fleming, editors. Frugivores and seed dispersal. Dr. W. Junk Publishers, Amsterdam.

———. 1988. Fruit-eating birds and bird-dispersed plants in the tropics and temperate zone. Trends in Ecology and Evolution 3:270–274.

———. 1991. How long do fruit-eating birds stay in plants where they feed? Biotropica 23:29–40.

Wheelwright, N. T., and C. H. Janson. 1985. Colors of fruit displays of bird-dispersed plants in two tropical forests. American Naturalist 126:777–799.

Wheelwright, N. T., and G. H. Orians. 1982. Seed dispersal by animals: contrasts with pollen dispersal, problems of terminology, and constraints on coevolution. American Naturalist 119:402–413.

Wheelwright, N. T., W. A. Haber, K. G. Murray, and C. F. Guindon. 1984. Tropical fruit-eating birds and their food plants: a survey of a Costa Rican lower montane forest. Biotropica 16:173–192.

Williams, D. A., M. F. Lawton, and R. O. Lawton. 1994. Population growth, range expansion, and competition in the cooperatively breeding Brown Jay, *Cyanocorax morio*. Animal Behavior 48:309–322.

Willis, E. O. 1980. Ecological roles of migratory and resident birds on Barro Colorado Island, Panama. Pages 202–225 *in* A. Keast and E. S. Morton, editors. Migrant birds in the Neotropics: ecology, behavior, distribution, and conservation. Smithsonian Institution Press, Washington, D.C.

Winnett-Murray, K. 1985. First reported nest of the White-eared Ground-Sparrow (*Melozone leucotis*). Condor 87:554.

———. 1986. Variation in the behavior and food supply of four neotropical wrens. Ph.D. dissertation, University of Florida, Gainesville.

———. 1987. Variation in the reproduction, behavior, and food supply of four neotropical wrens. Pages 33–36 *in* H. Alvarez-Lopez, G. Kattan, and C. Murcia, editors. Memorias: III Congreso de Ornitologia Neotropical. Sociedad Vallecaucana de Ornitologia, Cali, Colombia.

Winnett-Murray, K., K. G. Murray, and W. H. Busby. 1988. Two nests of the Azure-hooded Jay with notes on nest attendance. Wilson Bulletin 100: 134–135.

Woolfenden, G. E., and J. W. Fitzpatrick. 1984. The Florida Scrub Jay: demography of a cooperative-breeding bird. Princeton University Press, Princeton, New Jersey.

Young, B. E. 1993a. Effects of the parasitic botfly *Philornis carinatus* on nestling House Wrens, *Troglodytes aedon*, in Costa Rica. Oecologia 93:256–262.

———. 1993b. Geographical variation in avian clutch size: the case of the tropical House Wren, *Troglodytes aedon*. Ph.D. Dissertation. University of Washington, Seattle.

———. 1994a. The effects of food, nest predation and weather on the timing of breeding in tropical House Wrens. Condor 96:341–353.

———. 1994b. Geographic and seasonal patterns of clutch-size variation in House Wrens. Auk 111: 545–555.

———. 1996. An experimental analysis of small clutch size in tropical House Wrens. Ecology 77:472–488.

Young, B. E., M. C. Garvin, and D. B. McDonald. 1993. Blood parasites in birds from Monteverde, Costa Rica. Journal of Wildlife Diseases 29:555–560.

Young, B. E., D. DeRosier, and G. V. N. Powell. 1998. The diversity and conservation of understory birds in the Tilarán Mountains, Costa Rica. Auk 115:998–1016.

7

Mammals

Robert M. Timm
Richard K. LaVal

Costa Rica is one of the most biotically diverse countries on earth, with 4% of known terrestrial plant and animal species in only 0.04% of the world's land surface. The country's mammal fauna is equally diverse, with more than 207 species (4.8% of the world's 4629 species) in an area of 51,022 km². The majority of the world's mammal species and Monteverde's fauna are small (< 0.5 kg), nocturnal, and secretive. We know considerably less about most neotropical mammals and other vertebrates than we do about birds, which are more easily observed and communicate with sounds audible to humans. Although certain species of mammals have been studied in Costa Rica (Janzen 1983a, Timm 1994, Vaughan and Rodríguez 1994), and Monteverde is one of the best-known regions of the country biologically, there has been little work on the ecology, distribution, abundance, altitudinal zonation, systematic relationships, and biogeography of most mammals. Deforestation and other human disturbances have had a significant impact on the native mammals of the region; knowledge of Monteverde's mammals is vital to understand how habitat changes affect tropical montane mammals.

In this chapter, we provide an overview of the mammal fauna of the Monteverde area. We discuss the biology and abundance of some of the area's species, document how these are changing, and explore conservation issues. Most of the research on mammals at Monteverde has centered on bats or rodents, the two most diverse groups. Much of our knowledge of other species consists of isolated observations. We augment published reports with unpublished observations made by ourselves and colleagues. We also examined most of the Monteverde mammal specimens in museum collections to verify species identifications and to understand better their systematics, ecology, and distribution. We integrate this information into a list of the mammals that occur in the region, document their occurrence in each life zone, and estimate their overall abundance (see Appendix 10).

7.1. Methods

Although six major life zones are included in the Monteverde region (Holdridge 1967; see Table 3.1 and

Fig. 1.5), the mammal communities are more appropriately divided into four elevational/vegetational areas: (1) the Monteverde community and San Luis valley (1150–1500 m), premontane moist forest and premontane wet forest (just below the cloud forest) on the Pacific slope (distributional Zones 1 and 2); (2) cloud forest (1500–1800 m), lower montane wet forest and lower montane rain forest (Zones 3 and 4); (3) the Peñas Blancas valley (800–1400 m on the Atlantic slope), premontane rain forest and premontane rain forest/tropical wet forest transition belt (Zone 5 and part of Zone 6); and (4) Poco Sol (800 m), tropical wet forest (Zone 6 only).

In the text, we refer to the first area as the "community," the second as the "preserve," and the third and fourth as the "Peñas Blancas valley" (including Poco Sol). Life zones appear to extend to lower elevations in the upper San Luis valley, so that a site at 1150 m where many mammal observations have been made actually appears to be in premontane wet forest rather than premontane moist forest as predicted by elevational criteria. We use "region" for all four areas combined. We refer to mammals by their common names; scientific names are in Appendix 10.

To assess mammal community structure and population density, a trapping regime for sampling small terrestrial mammals and a netting regime for sampling bats are needed. Research collections that house significant holdings of mammals from the Monteverde region include the Chicago Field Museum, Los Angeles County Museum, University of Kansas Natural History Museum, the University of Michigan Museum of Zoology, the U.S. National Museum of Natural History, and the Universidad de Costa Rica. The majority of specimens from the 1960s and 1970s in collections with the locality "Monteverde" or "Monte Verde" are from the lower and mid-Monteverde community (1200–1450 m). The province is sometimes listed as Guanacaste, but all of these older specimens actually came from Puntarenas Province.

Another Costa Rican locality named Monteverde is in the Atlantic lowlands of Limón Province (10°06'N, 83°26'W). Early specimens of shrews reportedly from Monteverde in Limón Province gave a misleading impression of how widespread these shrews were (Woodman and Timm 1993).

7.2. Distribution, Species Richness, and Diversity

Monteverde's mammals include elements from both North and South America and endemic species. Central America hosts more than 275 species of mammals in 10 orders and 31 families; 18% of the species are endemic. Costa Rica's mammals include more than 207 species in the same 10 orders and 31 families, with 9 species (4%) being endemic to the country. Monteverde's fauna of 121 species includes the same 10 orders and 25 families, with 2 species endemic to the region (2%; see Appendix 10). Both endemic species, a shrew and a harvest mouse, are of North American origin. The mammal fauna of the Monteverde region includes 6 species of marsupials, 3 shrews, at least 58 bats, 3 primates, 7 xenarthrans (edentates), 2 rabbits, 1 pocket gopher, 3 squirrels, 1 spiny pocket mouse, at least 15 long-tailed rats and mice (family Muridae), 1 porcupine, 1 paca, 1 agouti, 2 canids, 5 mustelids, 4 procyonids, 6 cats, 2 peccaries, 2 deer, and 1 tapir (Appendix 10). More species will undoubtedly be found, especially bats. The list includes several additions and corrections to the previous lists of the fauna of the region (Wilson 1983, Hayes et al. 1989), and new distributional information.

Two species that have been locally extirpated, the Giant Anteater and the White-lipped Peccary, were apparently hunted out in the 1940s. Two other species, the Mountain Lion and the Jaguar, are rare. Although Mountain Lions are rare in the region, they may be as abundant now as they have ever been (Fig. 7.1). Mountain Lions are primarily a species of more open areas, especially where White-tailed Deer

Figure 7.1. Mountain Lion (*Felis concolor*). Photograph by Richard K. LaVal.

(Fig. 7.2) are common. Jaguars, however, are exceedingly rare throughout the region but are present in the Peñas Blancas valley.

The majority of small mammals at lower elevations (below 1300 m on the Pacific slope and below 1000 m on the Caribbean slope) are widespread species, typical of neotropical lowland forests. The species of higher elevations (above 1500 m) are also typical of high elevations in other highlands of Costa Rica. In general, lowland species tend to be broadly distributed, whereas high-elevation species often have limited distributions, and many are endemic. Most Costa Rican endemic mammals are species of middle to high elevations. The mammal faunas of Costa Rica's three main mountain ranges (Tilarán, Central, and Talamanca cordilleras) are similar, although all three have some species that are endemic.

7.3. Research on Mammals in Monteverde

Scientific study on the mammals of the region first began in the mid-1960s, conducted by researchers associated with the field courses sponsored by the Organization for Tropical Studies (OTS). The first published accounts of mammals from Monteverde were in 1968. From the 1970s to the mid-1990s, publications and theses on four categories of subjects appeared on mammals in Monteverde: systematics and distribution, community structure and reproductive ecology, mammal-plant interactions, and mammal-insect interactions.

7.3.1. Systematics and Distributions

Studies on systematics, distributions, and natural history are the building blocks for conservation. For ex-

ample, the discovery and description of the Golden Toad helped call attention to and conserve the biologically unique Monteverde Cloud Forest Preserve (MCFP; see Savage, "Discovery of the Golden Toad," p. 171). Papers on systematic relationships among species and geographic distributions are especially important for poorly known regions such as the Monteverde region because they identify the species present in an area, delineate species' distributions, and clarify relationships between closely related species.

Participants in the courses sponsored by the Council on International Educational Exchange and the Education Abroad Program (University of California) have carried out research projects focusing on mammals. These include 22 projects on bats (15 of which dealt with feeding behavior), 9 on rodents, 1 on Two-toed Sloths, and 1 on White-faced Capuchin monkeys. Researchers and residents have made observations which, although anecdotal, add to our knowledge of the mammals of Monteverde (see Timm and LaVal, "Observations on Monteverde's Mammals," p. 235).

Starrett and Casebeer (1968) reported on a single Fringe-lipped Bat caught along the Río Guacimal, which was only the second known specimen of this bat from the country; it is now known as a widely distributed species. Later that year, Hooper (1968) reported a sight record of the Water Mouse, a poorly known animal. Since then, 47 reports have been published on Monteverde's mammals as of 1998.

The order of mammals that has received the most study in Monteverde is Chiroptera (bats), which is unusual, as bats are generally among the least known mammal groups. Early surveys reported 24 species of bats (LaVal and Fitch 1977). LaVal (1973) reported specimens of the bat *Myotis nigricans* from the region in his systematic revision of the genus *Myotis* in Central and South America. Distribution records and in-

Figure 7.2. White-tailed Deer (*Odocoileus virginianus*). Photograph by Barbara L. Clauson.

formation on reproduction for seven other rare species of bats were added: *Hylonycteris underwoodi* (Fig. 7.3) and *Anoura cultrata* (nectar feeders); *Enchisthenes hartii*, *Platyrrhinus vittatus*, and *Sturnira mordax* (frugivores); and *Myotis oxyotus* and *Myotis riparius* (aerial insectivores; LaVal 1977). A checklist of mammals from several OTS sites, including Monteverde, provided the first comprehensive appraisal of mammal distributions in the area. This checklist included 71 species for the Monteverde region, and listed another 11 species as "expected to occur" in the region (Wilson 1983). Dinerstein (1983) reported that he encountered 35 species of bats in Monteverde. The first Costa Rican records of the Doubtful Oak Bat and Tacarcuna Bat were from Monteverde (Dinerstein 1985). Alston's Brown Mouse was studied by E. Hooper and colleagues (Hill and Hooper 1971, Hooper 1972, 1975, Carleton et al. 1975, Hooper and Carleton 1976). This mouse is almost wholly diurnal, with the greatest activity taking place in the morning (0700–1100 hr). It feeds predominantly on insects. Vocalizations contain both sonic and ultrasonic components. Adult mice have a repertoire of squeaks of various intensities and a long (10 sec), sustained call that has been termed a song. The songs carry well in the field and some are audible to the human ear. The Brown Mouse is one of four species of singing mice in Monteverde (see Langtimm, "Singing Mice," p. 236).

Small-eared shrews are extremely abundant but seldom seen in the Monteverde area (Woodman 1992, Woodman and Timm 1993). Blackish Small-eared Shrews occur in a wide array of habitats from 870 to 1800 m. Two other species of small-eared shrews occur at higher elevations in the Monteverde region, and one is being described as a new species by N. Woodman and R. Timm.

In a revision of the pygmy rice mice of the genus *Oligoryzomys*, Carleton and Musser (1995) reported that two species (*O. fulvescens* and *O. vegetus*) occur at Monteverde, which is one of the few localities where the two species are sympatric. The only reported species in this genus in Costa Rica was *O. fulvescens*. However, *O. vegetus* (Fig. 7.4), which was previously known only from Panama, has now been captured in the Monteverde community, in the MCFP, and on adjacent Cerro Amigos. In the Monteverde area, *O. vegetus* ranges in elevation from 1400 to 1760 m. *Oligoryzomys fulvescens* occurs only at lower elevations in the community (1400 m), and in the Guanacaste and Caribbean lowlands.

Other studies that include specimens from Monteverde are concerned with the taxonomy of shrews (Choate 1970) and opossums (Gardner 1973), phylogenetic relationships of rodents (Carleton 1980, Steppan 1995), taxonomy of deer mice (Huckaby 1980), biogeography of rodents (McPherson 1985, 1986), distribution of pocket gophers (Hafner and Hafner 1987), systematics of water mice (Voss 1988), ecology and distribution of bats and rodents (Timm et al. 1989), systematics of spiny pocket mice (Rogers 1989, 1990), and distributions of rodents and bats (Reid and Langtimm 1993).

Reid (1997) provided an extremely useful, beautifully illustrated guide to the mammals of Central America. Much of this work was based on her studies of living and preserved specimens of mammals from Monteverde. Emmons (1997) also provides a well-illustrated field guide to the neotropical mammals; her emphasis, however, is on species found below 1500 m. Another guide (Timm and LaVal 1998), an illustrated key to the Costa Rican bats, is designed for use in the field and has up-to-date diagnostic characters and taxonomy designed for students, wildlife managers, and the lay public.

7.3.2. Community Structure and Reproductive Ecology

Most mammals reproduce seasonally. The ultimate cause is generally seasonal variation in food availability mediated by ambient temperature or rainfall.

Figure 7.3. Underwood's Long-tongued Bat (*Hylonycteris underwoodi*). Photograph by Barbara L. Clauson.

Figure 7.4. Pygmy Rice Mouse (*Oligoryzomys vegetus*). Photograph by Barbara L. Clauson and Robert M. Timm.

Variation in photoperiod (daylength) is often the proximate cue used to trigger or suppress reproduction. Studies on mammal community structure and reproductive ecology in Monteverde, and most other studies of neotropical mammals, are restricted to bats and rodents.

A study of tropical bat faunas compared the structure, movements, and reproductive patterns of the diverse bat communities in Monteverde, La Selva (tropical wet forest), and La Pacífica (tropical dry forest; LaVal and Fitch 1977). The highest species diversity of bats was at La Selva. Much of this diversity is from insectivorous bats, both foliage-gleaners and aerial feeders. The three locations were similar in species diversity of nectar- and pollen-feeding bats, and in frugivorous species, which were common at all three sites. Although most tropical bats breed seasonally, bats in the tropical dry forest, with its clearly defined wet and dry seasons, have the briefest and most distinctly delimited reproductive periods. An extended reproductive season was typical for bats in the lowland tropical wet forest. Bats of the premontane forests of the Monteverde region were intermediate (LaVal and Fitch 1977).

Tropical bats are important in dispersing the seeds of a wide array of tropical shrubs, trees, epiphytes, and vines. Reproductive activity of fruit bats in Monteverde coincides with seasonal peaks in fruit abundance (Dinerstein 1983, 1986). Many of the bat-dispersed plants have two seasonal fruiting peaks per year. The first corresponds to the dry season/wet season transition, the second to late wet season. Fruit-eating bats must consume considerable amounts of fruit; for example, *Artibeus toltecus* eats twice its weight in fruit per night without weight gain (Fig. 7.5). Fruits eaten by Monteverde bats are high in water content (> 80% fresh weight), soluble carbohydrates, and proteins and are higher in nitrogen than many tropical and temperate fruits eaten by birds but are low in lipids. Forty species of plants are consumed by the seven most common species of fruit bats. The diet of fruit-feeding bats is almost exclusively fruits;

Figure 7.5. Leaf tent of the Lowland Fruit-eating Bat (*Artibeus toltecus*) in the Monteverde Cloud Forest Preserve.

they consume very few insects. This contrasts with nectar-feeding bats, which often consume insects, presumably taken in flowers.

An 18-month study of the population dynamics of individually marked Naked-footed Mice (Fig. 7.6) showed that they ate both arthropods and fruits, and that arthropod consumption was highest in the early wet season, especially in breeding females (Anderson 1982; see Anderson, "Reproduction and Dynamics of Deer Mice, p. 238"). Naked-footed Mice readily consumed all animal material presented to them. Reproduction was seasonal, with a peak in the wet season (May–July), when 100% of the females bred. Adult females may have two (rarely three) litters per year, and they seldom breed in the season of their birth. The average litter size for 14 captive-born litters was 2.8 young (see Anderson, "Reproduction and Dynamics of Deer Mice," p. 238). Survivorship can be remarkably high in these high-elevation mice; 75% of the Naked-footed Mice that were individually marked in 1986 were captured in the same area the next year (R. Timm, unpubl. data). Naked-footed Mice reproduce primarily during the rainy season in Monteverde. During the dry season, females ovulate routinely and often mate; how-ever, implantation usually does not occur and no pregnancies proceed beyond mid-gestation (Heideman and Bronson 1992, 1993, Bronson and Heideman 1993). In the laboratory, Naked-footed Mice did not respond to variations in photoperiod, but patterns similar to wild mice could be obtained with mild food restriction. Naked-footed Mice have an opportunistic breeding strategy, which forces them to reproduce seasonally (Heideman and Bronson 1993).

Many Monteverde mammals use both the canopy and the forest floor (see Langtimm, "Arboreal Mammals," p. 239). A variety of high-elevation rodents are behaviorally and morphologically adapted for climbing (Langtimm 1992). Monteverde's arboreal mammal community is more complex than those of both the Caribbean and Guanacaste lowlands.

7.3.3. Mammal-Plant Interactions

Research on mammal-plant interactions has addressed the pollination of a high-elevation flower (*Blakea chlorantha*) by rodents (Lumer 1980, 1983, Lumer and Schoer 1986; see Lumer, "Reproductive Biology of *Blakea* and *Topobea*," p. 273). The pollination system in *B. chlorantha*, a hemiephytic shrub of the cloud forest, is of interest because its odd-shaped flower (it is bell-shaped rather than open as in other species of *Blakea*) opens at night, points downward, and produces a sucrose-rich nectar. Lumer observed two species of rodents covered with pollen and feeding on the flowers of *Blakea* at night. Her initial conclusion was that the rodents were the obligate pollinators of *Blakea*. However, insects (e.g., beetles, hawk moths), hummingbirds, and tanagers have also been observed feeding on the nectar and pollen of *Blakea*, which suggests that the pollination system might be opportunistic or generalized (see Langtimm and Unnasch, "Mice, Birds, and Pollination," p. 241). The photograph Lumer published of a mouse (1980, p. 515) identified as *Oryzomys devius* (=*albigularis*; Tome's Rice Rat) feeding at a flower is more likely the Chiriquí Harvest Mouse, a common species in the habitat where the photograph was taken. Further observations would resolve this question.

The phenomenon of tent-making by bats was previously only known from lowland species. The smaller, high-elevation *Artibeus* of Monteverde also cut leaves to create diurnal roosts (Timm 1987, Timm and Clauson 1990). In the preserve, the fruit-eating bat *Artibeus toltecus* cuts the basal and side veins and interconnected tissues of broad leaves such as philodendrons, causing the sides and tip of the leaf to droop down (Fig. 7.5). The roosting bats hang from the midribs of the leaves and are protected by their tents from predators and the elements (Timm 1987).

Figure 7.6. Naked-footed Mouse (*Peromyscus nudipes*). Photograph by Barbara L. Clauson.

7.3.4. Mammal-Insect and Mammal-Bird Interactions

An insect-vertebrate interaction, that of rove beetles of the tribe Amblyopinini (Coleoptera: Staphylinidae) and their mammal hosts, was discovered in Monteverde (see Sec. 4.3). Amblyopinine beetles have a unique obligate association with mammals. Most of the 40,000 described species of staphylinids are free-living predators (Ashe and Timm 1987a,b), but all known species of amblyopinines are found attached to the fur of mammalian hosts or in the hosts' nests. Until recently, amblyopinines were believed to be obligate, blood-feeding ectoparasites (Fig. 7.7). Central American *Amblyopinus* have a mutualistic relationship with their hosts, not a parasitic one. In Monteverde, Naked-footed Mice (Fig. 7.6) and Chiriquí Harvest Mice (Fig. 7.8) are the primary hosts for *Amblyopinus tiptoni;* Tome's Rice Rat is the primary host for *A. emarginatus* (Figs. 7.9, 7.10). Rather than feeding on blood as was previously supposed, amblyopinine beetles at Monteverde feed on blood-sucking arthropods (fleas, mites, and ticks) and thus have a mutualistic relationship with their rodent hosts. These large, active beetles are host specific; their densities increase with increasing elevations, as do those of fleas. The beetles attach themselves firmly to their rodent hosts by grasping a small cluster of hairs with their mandibles at night while the host is actively moving around (Fig. 7.10). During the day, while the host occupies a nest, the beetles hunt for parasitic arthropods in the nest or on the host's body (Ashe and Timm 1987a,b, 1995, Timm and Ashe 1988).

In Monteverde, flocks of Brown Jays were observed successfully defending nests from Variegated Squirrels, White-faced Capuchins, and domestic cats (Lawton and Lawton 1980). The location of jay nests—high and in isolated trees—and the aggressive defense provided by these large, cooperatively nesting birds may account for low levels of nest predation (see Williams and Lawton, "Brown Jays"). Five jay nests located in trees whose crowns touched other trees were destroyed by nocturnal predators (Lawton and Lawton 1980).

Margays and Long-tailed Weasels have been observed preying on nesting Resplendent Quetzals (*Pharomachrus mocinno*). Quetzals have been observed vigorously defending their nests against squirrels (Wheelwright 1983). Mexican Mouse Opossums are common nest predators of House Wrens (*Troglodytes aedon*) in Monteverde (Young 1996). Artificial wren nest boxes placed along fence rows and along woodlot edges sustained high predation by mouse opossums; those placed on isolated trees or posts had lower predation. Predation on wren nests by all predators was unrelated to brood size. A White-nosed Coati was also observed to prey on wren nests (B. Young, pers. obs.).

7.4. Migration

Many species of birds migrate latitudinally, and as many as half of Costa Rican bird species are likely to be altitudinal migrants (Stiles 1988; see Chap. 6, Birds). Altitudinal migration has also been docu-

Figure 7.7. Steve Ashe (left) and Robert Timm (right) carrying out research on the mouse-beetle relationship in Monteverde. Photograph by Barbara L. Clauson.

Figure 7.8. (*top left*) Chiriquí Harvest Mouse (*Reithrodontomys creper*). Photograph by Barbara L. Clauson and Robert M. Timm. **Figure 7.9.** (*top right*) Tome's Rice Rat (*Oryzomys albigularis*) with mutualistic rove beetles. Photograph by Barbara L. Clauson. **Figure 7.10.** (*above*) Amblyopinine beetle behind ear of Tome's Rice Rat (*Oryzomys albigularis*). Photograph by Barbara L. Clauson.

mented in butterflies (see Sec. 4.4). Only recently has seasonal altitudinal migration been considered significant in tropical mammals. Seasonal migration is well documented for mammals in the north temperate zone but not in the tropics. Long-term studies on bats demonstrate that some species show strong seasonal variation in abundance in Monteverde (LaVal 1977), which we interpret as migrations into and out of the area. Of the 58 species of bats known from the region (based on more than 7500 captures over 15 years), 10 are captured in sufficient numbers that seasonal abundances can be examined, and of these, five species (*Artibeus lituratus*, *A. toltecus*, *Carollia brevicauda*, *Sturnira lilium*—all frugivores—and *Hylonycteris underwoodi* (a nectivore; Fig. 7.3) show a strong seasonal pattern in abundance. Two of the five species (*A. lituratus* and *S. lilium*) are absent from Monteverde for most of the year and common from September through November. *Artibeus lituratus* (Fig. 7.11) and *S. lilium* are primarily lowland species; it is likely they migrate up the Tilarán highlands during part of the year to take advantage of seasonally available fruits. A third species (*H. underwoodi*) is common only from May through October. The remaining two species are present year-round but with strong seasonal peaks in abundance.

The simplest explanation for species with strongly seasonal captures is that they migrate altitudinally to track food resources. Increased capture rates of these species corresponds with the seasonal increases in abundance of preferred foods in Monteverde. Because both adult males and females are captured in high numbers, we do not believe that these data represent seasonal demographic patterns (e.g., a flush of young entering the population) or behavioral changes (e.g., lactating females restricting their movements).

Alternative explanations to seasonal migration exist. It could be that these five species are present in Monteverde year-round in equal numbers but are flying or foraging in spaces where no netting activity was carried out. This explanation could apply to *Artibeus lituratus*, a fig specialist that feeds in the canopy but is frequently captured in ground-level nets. *Hylonycteris underwoodi*, a nectarivore, might be feeding only on flowers in the canopy during part of the year. However, *Sturnira lilium*, *Carollia brevicauda*, and *Artibeus toltecus* feed on the fruits of early successional shrubs and are easily netted, so it is unlikely that they were present but not captured. These species of bats could have moved from the area where netting was carried out without moving any significant elevational distance. However, knowledge of phenological sequences of flowering and fruit ripening (W. Haber, pers. comm.; see Chap. 3, Plants) leads to the prediction that bats moving in search of food would necessarily fly up- or downhill; a short downhill flight from Monteverde can result in an elevational change of 500–1000 m, often in less than 1 km. Future research should include mark-recapture studies, radiotelemetry to follow individuals, and studies of flowering and fruiting of bat-pollinated and bat-dispersed fruits along elevational gradients. We also suspect that Baird's Tapirs and White-lipped Peccaries are seasonal altitudinal migrants, but few data on these species exist (see Lawton, "Baird's Tapir," pp. 242–243).

7.5. Changes in Altitudinal Limits of Life Zones as Suggested by Bats

Many climatologists believe that global warming is taking effect. Widespread deforestation and El Niño events may also affect Costa Rica's climate. In general, short-term impacts on Monteverde's climate are making it drier and less predictable. During an El Niño year, Monteverde experiences dry periods in the rainy season, which could especially affect species that are at or near their climatic or vegetational tolerance lim-

Figure 7.11. Big Fruit-eating Bat (*Artibeus lituratus*). Photograph by Barbara L. Clauson.

its (see Chap. 5, Amphibians and Reptiles). Weather records from Monteverde for the last decade suggest that we are in a period of reduced rainfall and slightly warmer temperatures (although in 1995, 1996, and 1998, rainfall was higher than normal). Changes in mammal altitudinal limits, distributions, and abundance at Monteverde may be correlated with climate changes.

Bats were intensively sampled in Monteverde in 1973 and 1981 (Dinerstein 1983, 1986, R. LaVal, unpubl. data). Subsequently, LaVal has mist-netted bats in Monteverde on 10–20 nights each year. Several lowland species of bats (*Micronycteris hirsuta*, *M. sylvestris*, *Mimon cozumelae*, and *Phyllostomus discolor*, which are gleaners, and *Vampyrodes caraccioli*, a frugivore) were captured in Monteverde for the first time during the last 4 years. *Sturnira lilium*, also a lowland species, was very rare in 1973 (2 captures), more common in 1981 (38 captures), and seasonally abundant in 1995. *Desmodus rotundus*, the Common Vampire Bat (Fig. 7.12), was not encountered in 1973. In 1981, nine were captured, a rate that has continued. Large numbers of cattle were introduced to this dairy farming region in the 1950s, but vampire bats did not arrive for at least 25 years, even though cattle, pigs, dogs, and chickens had existed in nearby areas even in the 1940s. The trend of lowland species moving up into Monteverde has also been observed in birds, reptiles, and amphibians (see Chaps. 5 and 6). These patterns support the climatic change hypothesis for these and other lowland tropical species (see Timm and LaVal, "Observations," p. 235). Long-term weather and population data for a variety of species are needed to assess the climatic factors that affect mammals in Monteverde.

7.6. Historical Use and Change in Abundance of Mammals

The San Luis area (ca. 1100 m) was first settled in 1915 (see Timm, "Prehistoric Cultures and Inhabitants," p. 408); the Monteverde–Cerro Plano area was first settled in 1929. During the 1930s, settlers moved into the San Luis and Santa Elena areas (ca. 1250 m) on the Pacific slope and into San Carlos on the Caribbean slope. Families moved into the Monteverde community area during the 1930s and 1940s (see Chap. 11, Agriculture). The original settlers cleared considerable forest for lumber, pastures, and homesites, creating fragmented patches of forest that exist today as a complex mosaic of primary and secondary habitats, including open pastures. By the late 1940s, appreciable deforestation had taken place at lower and mid-elevations.

Early settlers relied heavily on local wildlife (especially mammals and larger birds) as a source of protein for themselves and their dogs. Overhunting played a role in the decline or extirpation of several species. Guans and chachalacas were so heavily hunted in the 1950s and early 1960s that they became rare in Monteverde, although their populations have increased with protection. Common food items of early Monteverde residents were Black-handed Spider Monkeys, Pacas, Brocket Deer, and Baird's Tapirs. At lower elevations, White-tailed Deer and White-lipped Peccaries were also hunted for meat. Agoutis were generally fed to dogs. Locally obtained animals were many families' primary source of meat. However, many hunters shot everything they saw, and if an animal was not a preferred meat species, they simply left it. At least two species, the Giant Anteater and

Figure 7.12. Common Vampire Bat (*Desmodus rotundus*). Photograph by Barbara L. Clauson.

White-lipped Peccary, were extirpated from the region within a few decades of settlement.

To assess the historical changes in mammal distributions and abundances of the region, we interviewed long-term residents about wildlife species.

Common Vampire Bat Vampire bats have been present in San Luis since at least the 1930s. However, they were absent from Monteverde before the late 1970s. By 1980, they had arrived but were uncommon in the Monteverde community.

Black-handed Spider Monkey The earliest colonists of the region regularly used spider monkeys for meat, for medicinal purposes, and as pets. Spider monkeys, Mantled Howler Monkeys, and White-faced Capuchins were abundant in the San Luis Valley in the 1940s and were hunted for food (M. Leitón, pers. comm.). Spider monkeys were preferred for meat and were still common in what is now the lower Monteverde community, including Bajo del Tigre, in the 1940s (I. Arguedas and M. Vargas, pers. comm.). Spider monkeys were observed by J. and D. Campbell just below the preserve in the 1950s, and they were seen in the lower parts of the Monteverde community in the early 1950s. One troop still exists in El Valle; the Peñas Blancas population is also recovering. R. Lawton saw 20 spider monkeys near the television towers in 1993. R. LaVal saw two individuals above the dairy plant in 1995.

Mantled Howler Monkey Howler monkeys have always been common above 1400 m in the community, but apparently there were few below that elevation in the 1950s.

White-faced Capuchin M. Rockwell remembers the White-faced Capuchin as the only primate found in the Monteverde community, Cerro Plano, and Santa Elena in the 1950s. The yellow fever epidemic that swept through human and primate populations of Costa Rica and much of southern Central America in the early 1950s decimated primate populations in Monteverde (Fishkind and Sussman 1987, Timm et al. 1989, Stoner 1993).

Giant Anteater Giant Anteaters were present in the San Luis region in the 1940s (M. Leitón, pers. comm.). There have been no sightings of Giant Anteaters in the region for several decades; the species is assumed to be extirpated from the region.

Forest Rabbit Rabbits, once common in the area, are now rare.

Cherrie's Pocket Gopher Pocket gophers were common in the community at least into the late 1970s but have since disappeared. Gardeners at higher elevations of the community suffered considerable loss of garden produce to pocket gophers in the 1960s and 1970s.

Variegated Squirrel This large, colorful, and easily identified squirrel was uncommon in the Monteverde area when the Quakers first arrived; they are now locally abundant. Variegated Squirrels are common in edge and disturbed habitats, but they are rarely observed in primary forest.

Coyote Within the past 25 years, Coyotes have expanded their range through Costa Rica and are found in Panama. They are abundant throughout Costa Rica's Pacific lowlands, the high elevations of the Talamanca Mountains, and the Chiriquí Highlands of Panama. The original Costa Rican distribution of the Coyote prior to the Spanish colonial period was northernmost Guanacaste (Vaughan 1983, Monge-Nájera and Morera Brenes 1987). Coyotes are associated with human disturbance; it is unlikely that they occurred in pristine tropical montane forests. Coyotes first appeared in San Luis during the early 1970s. They became common in Monteverde in the 1980s, when there was a pack within 200 m of R. LaVal's house, and they could be heard regularly in the lower parts of the Monteverde community. Coyotes are currently uncommon throughout the region.

Gray Fox Foxes have always been common in the area.

Striped Hog-nosed Skunk Skunks fluctuate in abundance but are much less abundant than they were before the 1980s.

Tayra J. and D. Campbell informed us that tayras were seen in groups in their forest before 1960, whereas now only individuals are observed.

Grison Grisons had never been observed in the community until 1996.

Southern River Otter Otters have always been present but never abundant in the rivers.

White-nosed Coati (Fig. 7.13) Coatis were more abundant in the past, with many large groups. R. LaVal

Figure 7.13. White-nosed Coati (*Nasua narica*). Photograph by Robert M. Timm.

saw a large group in 1995 above the dairy plant and another in 1997 near the Estación Biológica.

Ocelot Ocelots were very common in the 1950s and 1960s, and the population appears stable. In the early years of settlement of the region, ocelots were known to attack chickens.

Jaguar Jaguars were relatively common throughout the region through the late 1950s. They preyed on livestock and were shot whenever possible. Jaguars were common in the San Luis region in the 1940s, but most were shot; the last two killed were in the early 1960s. M. Leitón believes a small population exists in the upper reaches of the San Luis valley, which includes parts of the Children's Rain Forest and the preserve.

Collared Peccary In the 1930s and 1940s, Collared Peccaries were common in the San Luis valley and in Bajo del Tigre. They were uncommon to rare in the community when the Quakers first arrived in the region, and were found only as low as the wetter forests below the preserve. However, since the 1970s, peccaries have become more common and are gradually expanding down the mountain.

White-lipped Peccary White-lipped Peccaries have never been seen in the Monteverde community, according to the older residents interviewed. However, they were common in San Luis in the 1930s and 1940s (M. Leitón, pers. comm.).

White-tailed Deer Deer were not originally present in the Monteverde community. They were common in San Luis until they were hunted out in the 1940s. Since 1990, deer have expanded their range and are now seen throughout the community.

Baird's Tapir Historically, Baird's Tapir was widely distributed throughout all forested habitats in Costa Rica. Tapirs are the largest native terrestrial mammals in the country (150–300 kg), and their meat was highly prized. Populations of tapirs have been greatly reduced throughout the country due to overhunting and habitat destruction. Tapirs were largely eliminated from the higher elevations in the Monteverde area, but they have become relatively common with nearly complete protection from hunting. The distinctive tracks of tapirs can be seen along many of the trails in the preserve (see Lawton, "Baird's Tapir," p. 242).

Tapirs were present in forests above Santa Elena in the 1950s. The population was centered around El Valle, but hunting on the area's margins gradually reduced their numbers (W. Guindon, pers. comm.). Tapirs existed in the San Luis Valley in the 1930s and 1940s, but they disappeared due to overhunting (M. Leitón, pers. comm.). Tapirs were less common in the Monteverde community in the 1940s but were abundant in what is now the preserve. J. and D. Camp-

bell observed tapir tracks below the preserve in the 1950s but have seen none there since then.

With protection, tapir abundance has increased; they are common in the preserve. Areas lacking tapirs for many years are gradually being reoccupied, based on increased sightings of tracks of females with young. Adult tapirs range widely, as do females with older calves. However, females tend to stay in specific areas for parturition and when accompanied by young calves. These are remote from human habitations and activities and are densely vegetated. In the 1960s, 20–30 tapirs were killed per year in the region (W. Guindon, pers. comm.).

Throughout their ranges, all species of tapirs are considered endangered (Terwilliger 1978). The tapir population in Monteverde is small (30–50 individuals; C. Guindon, unpubl. data). The present protected area could support an estimated 115 tapirs. However, a population size of about 185 individuals would be needed to have a high likelihood population viability over even the short term. With 185 individuals, the effective population size would be only 50 because many individuals do not breed in a population of large, widely dispersed herbivores, and selective killing of females with young by hunters may result in a skewed sex ratio (C. Guindon, pers. comm.). For long-term survival, an effective population size of 200 would be needed, requiring a protected area vastly larger than the existing one. Three factors threaten the continued survival of tapirs in the region: (1) the population is isolated, probably permanently, (2) both the present and potential population sizes are low enough to create concern about inbreeding and loss of heterozygosity, and (3) approximately one tapir each year is killed illegally by hunters.

7.7. Conservation of Monteverde Mammals

Families in most rural areas in Costa Rica and the neotropics have traditionally relied heavily on wildlife as a source of protein. In Monteverde, Baird's Tapirs, Pacas, Agoutis, and White-lipped and Collared Peccaries were highly prized meats. Tapirs, White-lipped Peccaries, White-tailed Deer, Pacas, and Black-harded Spider Monkeys are now generally uncommon in Costa Rica, even where adequate habitat remains, except in some national parks. White-lipped Peccaries have been extirpated from much of the country. In the Monteverde region, populations of large mammals were decimated outside of protected areas. Populations of many small and medium-sized mammals have decreased due to widespread habitat fragmentation and hunting. A few generalists (opossums, coyotes, foxes, coatis, raccoons, and some rodents) have adjusted to human disturbances and have even increased in abundance. However, specialists (Giant and Silky Anteaters and bats such as the large predaceous phyllostomatines) have been unable to adapt to human disturbance and habitat fragmentation and are now extremely rare. Elimination of keystone mammal species may have far-reaching impacts on the forest ecosystem. The elimination of White-lipped Peccaries, for example, may alter the structure of Monteverde's forests because peccaries are both major seed dispersers and seed predators.

In terms of mammals, Monteverde is the best-known high-elevation site in Central America, with at least 121 documented species. Mammalogists have worked in the region since the 1960s. As of 1998 nearly 50 publications have been based on Monteverde's mammals, and museum collections hold numerous specimens from the area, but the ecology of its mammals remains poorly documented. Rapid destruction of natural habitats requires expanded conservation efforts to document and conserve the biota.

Deforestation in Costa Rica and elsewhere in Central America began with the earliest human inhabitants (see Timm, "Prehistoric Cultures and Inhabitants," p. 408). Human populations have increased rapidly in the past several decades, resulting in extensive deforestation throughout Central America. Between 70% and 80% of Costa Rica's forests have been cut since the 1960s, among the highest rates in Central America. During the 1980s, the rate of deforestation in Costa Rica averaged 60,000 ha per year; during the early 1990s, forests were disappearing at a mean rate of 20,000 ha per year (Environment Min-

istry, unpubl. data). Costa Rica's current human population growth rate of 2.4% will result in a doubling of its population in less than 30 years. Existing wildlands must be effectively protected, new protected areas be established, and resources be managed for both human use and mammal diversity.

Acknowledgments   We are grateful to the residents in Monteverde who allowed us to work on their property and who saved dead animals for us. We thank Irma Arguedas, John and Doris Campbell, Carlos Guindon, Wilford Guindon, Miguel Leitón, Marvin Rockwell, and Marcos Vargas for sharing historical information on mammals. William Aspinall, former director of the preserve, provided permission to work there. The curators and collection managers of the following collections allowed us to examine specimens: Instituto Nacional de Biodiversidad, Santo Domingo de Heredia; Museo Nacional de Costa Rica, San José; Universidad de Costa Rica, San José; Field Museum, Chicago; Los Angeles County Museum, Los Angeles; Museum of Zoology, University of Michigan, Ann Arbor; and U.S. National Museum of Natural History, Washington, D.C. Portions of this research were supported by the National Geographic Society and the Organization for Tropical Studies. We thank Nalini Nadkarni and Nat Wheelwright for their patience, sound editing, and insightful comments. Cathy Langtimm shared her knowledge of Monteverde's mammals with us over the years, and Neal Woodman's assistance is gratefully acknowledged. Barb Clauson provided constructive suggestions on drafts of the manuscript and many photographs. Meg LaVal's assistance, in the field and with historical and present-day insights, greatly contributed to our understanding of Monteverde.

OBSERVATIONS ON MONTEVERDE'S MAMMALS
Robert M. Timm & Richard K. LaVal

Nests of Mexican Mouse Opossums have been observed on several occasions in Monteverde. N. Nadkarni observed a mouse opossum nest high (20 m) in the canopy, hanging from a liana. The nest was a large ball of moss approximately 0.5 m in diameter. P. Heideman observed a mouse opossum nest approximately 3 m off the ground in a dead *Cecropia* leaf. In both cases, single mouse opossums were in the nest. R. and M. LaVal have observed nests in bunches of ripening bananas. A pair of mouse opossums they kept in captivity for a year would kill and eat large insects and eat a variety of fruits. The captive pair built a nest from plant leaves and stems and slept curled up together within the nest.

Blackish Small-eared Shrews and other shrew species are commonly found dead along trails in habitats where they are common in Monteverde. Mammalian predators such as Gray Foxes, Coyotes, and the smaller cats (including house cats) commonly attack shrews. However, once the shrew is tasted, it is discarded. Most of the specimens of shrews from Monteverde in museum collections were found dead, presumably discarded by predators.

Alfaro's Pygmy Squirrels were observed by R. LaVal, R. Timm, and W. Alverson feeding on the sap of the tree *Quararibea costaricensis* in the preserve. These diminutive squirrels are often seen hanging by all four feet on the trunks of trees, chewing at the bark. The squirrels neatly peel the bark off in large patches with their incisors. The squirrels then feed on the sap exuded by the tree. These feeding patches can be extensive (0.5 × 0.5 m), representing an impressive amount of work for a squirrel whose head and body length is only 125–150 mm. Removal of the bark and cambium likely damages the trees.

White-faced Capuchins have been observed feeding at bromeliads on several occasions. N. Nadkarni described them actively ripping bromeliads apart and apparently consuming insects from the cups at their centers. R. LaVal has observed these monkeys chewing on the base of each bromeliad leaf prior to discarding it. The chewing marks can be seen on the dropped leaves.

Hispid Cotton Rats were first taken by collectors at Monteverde in the 1980s. The distribution and abundance of cotton rats in the region merit further study. In the midwestern United States, cotton rat populations fluctuate (often dramatically) from year to year, with local climatic conditions having a great influence on population sizes. A similar phenomenon may occur in the Monteverde region.

Olingos frequently feed during daylight hours at the hummingbird feeders at the preserve headquarters. They climb down the wire holding the feeders and consume the rich sugar water. Bats also feed on sugar water at these feeders at night.

SINGING MICE
Catherine A. Langtimm

Communication by long-distance vocalizations is common among birds, insects, frogs, and large mammals but relatively rare among mice and rats. In Monteverde, four species of mice make calls that can be heard by humans. Although the functions of these vocalizations are obscure, the calls and songs are loud and appear to communicate information to other individuals that are relatively distant from the mouse making the call.

Alton's Brown Mouse
(*Scotinomys teguina*)

Alston's Brown Mouse (Fig. 7.14). is a small mouse (9–16 g) that trills like a cicada and chirps like a bird. It forages on the ground, eating primarily insects. In contrast to most mice, it is active in the early morning and late afternoon (Hooper and Carleton 1976, Langtimm 1992) instead of at night. Its trill was first described by Hooper and Carleton (1976), who labeled it a "song," which they characterized as similar in duration and complexity to the songs of birds and insects. The mice readily sing in captivity and are especially vocal at dusk. When a mouse sings, it rises on its haunches into a bipedal stance, holds its forefeet before it, throws back its head with the snout pointed upward, and opens its mouth. The sound emanates from the back of the throat; the exact mechanism of sound production is unknown.

The song consists of a series of short loud bursts in rapid succession. At the beginning, the pulses are rapid. As the song progresses, loudness increases and both the pulse and interpulse intervals lengthen into clearly enunciated individual beats. Decreasing cadence and increasing loudness of the pulses give a characteristic signature to the song which distinguishes it from the vocalizations of other species. The songs of individuals in Monteverde were 5.8–8.6 sec long with 72–96 pulses per song (C. Langtimm, unpubl. data). The average duration of a song and the average number of pulses per song vary among populations of *S. teguina* at other sites in Central America (Hooper and Carleton 1976). Sonograms reveal that each pulse consists of a broad range of frequencies starting above 30 kHz to as low as 14 kHz (Hooper and Carleton 1976, C. Langtimm, unpubl. data). The majority of the sound is in the ultrasonic range and only when the pulse sweeps below about 15–20 kHz is it audible to the human ear.

Males sing more frequently than females in captivity, suggesting that the song may function in maintaining territories (Hooper and Carleton 1976). A similar pattern resulted in trials in which a male was held in captivity with a female (Metz 1990, C. Langtimm, unpubl. data). When a pair was separated, singing increased for both sexes, but the female usually sang more frequently, suggesting that mate contact may also be an important function.

Figure 7.14. Alston's Brown Mouse (*Scotinomys teguina*). Photograph by Richard K. LaVal.

Slender Harvest Mouse (*Reithrodontomys gracilis*)

The Slender Harvest Mouse is small (8–14 g) and produces a two-note high-pitched whistle. The call is commonly heard in the forest and pastures at dusk and after dark (Uyehara 1990, C. Langtimm, unpubl. data). The species is extremely arboreal, spending a large portion of its time climbing in plants of pastures and the forest understory and in the crowns of canopy trees (Langtimm 1992). They do not call readily in captivity. Sonograms of calls I recorded from the understory and in the canopy (22 m above the forest floor) show that the dominant frequency of a note ranges between 9 and 10.5 kHz. The second note immediately follows the first and is slightly lower in frequency. Single note calls are also commonly heard. The duration of the entire two-note call ranges from only 0.85 to 0.99 sec (C. Langtimm, unpubl. data). The function of the call is unknown.

Reithrodontomys sp.

This undescribed mouse species makes one-, two-, and three-note calls. It is larger than the Slender Harvest Mouse (ca. 18 g) but similarly appears to be par-tially arboreal, based on the capture of two individuals in traps located 2–3 m above the forest floor onto branches (C. Langtimm and F. Reid, unpubl. data). The call is similar to that of the Slender Harvest Mouse but differs in that the dominant frequency is 1 kHz lower and three-note calls are common; no more than two successive notes have been heard for the Slender Harvest Mouse (C. Langtimm and F. Reid, unpubl. data). The call is similar to that described for *R. fulvescens* in Louisiana by Svihla (1930): "a tiny, clear high-pitched bugling sound." The occurrence of long-distance vocalizations in two other species of *Reithrodontomys* in Monteverde and the similarity in the structure of their calls suggest that long-distance auditory communication may be common in the genus.

Sumichrast's Vesper Rat (*Nyctomys sumichrasti*)

Sumichrast's Vesper Rat is the largest of the vocalizing mice in Monteverde (38–67 g). The species is arboreal (Genoways and Jones 1972, Langtimm 1992). It eats primarily fruits and seeds and is active at night. Calls consisted of single chirps repeated at variable time intervals. The peak frequency of a chirp (near 3.5

kHz) is lower than that of the calls of the other vocalizing species.

Vocalizations of the Vesper Rat during close social interactions in captivity were first noted by Birkenholz and Wirtz (1965). Long-distance vocalizations are an important aspect of their behavior (C. Langtimm, unpubl. data). After sunset on two occasions 1 month apart, I heard loud chirps in the rafters at opposite ends of the house, where I saw two adult Vesper Rats. As they climbed toward each other, they called repeatedly and loudly. On contact, the vocalizations continued but were softer in volume. One individual mounted the other and attempted copulation. Similar vocalizations and behavior (without attempted copulations) have been observed in the wild in Panama (F. Greenwell, pers. comm.), suggesting that Vesper Rats living in the maze of branches and tree trunks of their habitat use vocalizations to locate and navigate toward prospective mates.

REPRODUCTION AND DYNAMICS OF DEER MICE
Stephen D. Anderson

The Naked-footed or Deer Mouse of Monteverde (*Peromyscus nudipes*, family Muridae; see Fig. 7.6) is of ecological interest because it is the most abundant rodent locally and because other species in this well-studied genus are widespread and abundant throughout North America, inviting comparative studies. I carried out mark-recapture and captive studies of *Peromyscus* in Monteverde for 18 months (1978–1980), to describe reproduction and dynamics in this population (Anderson 1982). The study involved three trapping grids at different elevations (1540 m, 1420 m, and 1400 m) and around 13,500 trap-nights.

Population density varied with season and site. It ranged from 8 to 22 individuals per hectare and was lowest in May–July, the beginning of the breeding season. Breeding was correlated with rainfall (and presumably food abundance). The percentage of adult females visibly pregnant or lactating fell to zero during the dry season (January–March), rose to 100% during the early wet season (May–July), fell in August, and had a secondary peak in September–October. Consistent with the breeding pattern, the percentage of immatures in the population was 30–40% in September–December, zero in February–May, and increased in July–August. Survival of field-born juveniles to capturable age was estimated at 55–75%.

"Neutral-arena" encounter experiments and observations in a large outdoor enclosure indicated that overt aggression is low in *P. nudipes*, particularly in adult-juvenile confrontations. Home range size was estimated at 0.2 ha, based on recapture data, and varied little with gender, site, year, or season. Negative dispersion (nonoverlapping home ranges) was observed within "old" (i.e., established adult resident) males and within old females. In contrast, dispersion for old males with respect to old females was positive or random, and that for new animals (with respect to old males, old females, or other new animals) was generally random. These results suggest a system of density regulation based on mutual recognition and avoidance between same-sex adults rather than aggressive adult-juvenile interactions as reported for some temperate mice species.

The average litter size (from 14 captive born litters) was 2.8 ± 0.7 individuals. The average neonate weight was 3.6 ± 0.4 g. Young mice attained 50% of adult weight by 35 days and 90% by 80 days of age. They had pinnae up at 5.6 days and dorsal fur at 10.4 days. Lower incisors erupted at 11.2 days, upper incisors erupted at 13.9 days, ears opened at 16.5 days, and eyes opened at 21 days. Weaning at around 25 days. Later developmental events took longer in field-caught animals than in captives, underscoring the danger of relying solely on data from captive litters. For field animals, molting began at 55 days and ended at 90 days, mature testis size in males was observed at 170 days, vaginal perforation in females at 90 days, and first conception at 175 days or longer. There was high variability in these events. Many juveniles, on first capture in the field, weighed 17–22 g, corresponding to an age of 25–36 days. Adult *P. nudipes* weighed 44–46 g. They ate a variety of plant and animal foods, particularly beetles, orthopterans, and moths. Arthropod consumption (estimated from fecal analysis) was highest in the early wet season and higher for breeding females than for males or immatures.

Most animals in this population probably have life spans between one and two years. Recapture data indicate that individual female *P. nudipes* breed two or three times per season, generally do not breed in the season of their birth, and produce a total of two to six litters in their lifetime, which is far below their reproductive potential (Heideman and Bronson 1993).

In comparison to the widespread and well-studied temperate species *P. maniculatus* and *P. leucopus*, *P. nudipes* in Monteverde exhibits larger body size, slower growth rate, delayed sexual maturity, and lower reproductive effort, four characters that are strongly correlated with each other. *Peromyscus nudipes* also exhibit smaller litter size and less variability in home range size than do temperate species. For these traits, temperate and tropical *Peromyscus* fit the predictions of classic "*r* versus *K* selection" theory.

On the other hand, compared to *P. maniculatus* and *P. leucopus*, Monteverde deer mice exhibit lower breeding frequency, less aggression, and more random dispersion of "new" individuals. These observations are contrary to the predictions of *r/K* theory, which assumes that increased competition leads to increased aggression and territoriality. Finally, according to *r/K* theory, one would expect *P. nudipes* to exhibit higher density, reduced density fluctuation, aseasonal breeding, "type 1" or "type 2" survivorship curve, increased lifespan, reduced habitat vacancy, reduced year-to-year and site-to-site variability in density, higher ratio of neonate weight to adult weight, and greater age at weaning. However, the tropical and temperate species cannot be distinguished in terms of these characters. This may be explained by recognizing that environments (e.g., food availability, precipitation, temperature) in Monteverde are seasonal and/or unpredictable, much like those in temperate habitats.

ARBOREAL MAMMALS
Catherine A. Langtimm

With a pair of binoculars, visitors to the Monteverde Cloud Forest Preserve can scan the treetops and observe differences in the flora and fauna between the forest floor and canopy. The change in species composition in epiphytes and birds among the vertical strata of the forest is dramatic. No less striking is the diversity of climbing mammals that inhabit the forest. Some arboreal species, such as monkeys, spend the majority of their time foraging in the trees, while other semiarboreal species such as coatis spend time foraging on the ground and in the trees.

Larger mammals are the more conspicuous and better known of the climbing species. Mantled Howler Monkeys, White-faced Capuchins, Black-handed Spider Monkeys, Prehensile-tailed Porcupines, Tayras, coatis, Two-toed Sloths, and several species of squirrels (e.g., *Sciurus granatensis*) are often seen by daytime visitors to the forest. If one ventures out at night, eyeshine from kinkajous (Fig. 7.15), olingos, raccoons, coatis, and a diversity of marsupials from Mexican Mouse Opossum (*Marmosa mexicana*) to the Woolly Opossum is often reflected back from the light of a head lamp. The majority of these larger species belong to genera that are primarily tropical in distribution. The same or similar species occur at lowland tropical research stations such as La Selva and Barro Colorado Island.

A diverse community also exists of small mammals (primarily mice and rats) that forage in plants of the

Figure 7.15. Kinkajou (*Potos flavus*) foraging at night. Photograph by Richard K. LaVal.

understory and canopy. Because of their small size (10–250 g), nocturnal habits, and climbing nature, they are rarely seen. Live-trapping at different altitudinal elevations has revealed eight climbing species (Table 7.1). Most of these species belong to genera of the neotomine-peromyscines (family Muridae, subfamily Sigmodontinae), which are primarily temperate and North American in distribution (Carleton 1980). The species that range into Central America are characteristically found in cool high-elevation tropical forests.

How high individuals range within the trees in Monteverde is known for only a few species. The Vesper Rat and the Slender Harvest Mouse apparently forage throughout the vertical strata of leeward cloud forest. I have caught both species in live traps placed at varying heights, including 22 m above the ground in the crowns of canopy trees (Langtimm 1992). The Naked-footed Mouse, on the other hand, is semiarboreal and forages only at lower heights. It was never captured more than 3 m off the ground (Langtimm 1992). The remainder of the species in Table 7.1 have only been captured 2–4 m above the forest floor. Trapping in the higher strata of the forest, particularly in the canopy, has been limited, and more work is needed to define their vertical distribution. Studies thus far have identified two species of harvest mouse new to the area. One species is new to science (R. Timm, pers. comm.); the second (*R. gracilis*) was previously known only from low-elevation, dry, deciduous forests (Reid and Langtimm 1993). Trapping studies have found climbing mice to be diverse and abundant in Monteverde, but their importance in the ecosystem is poorly understood. Undoubtedly, they are important prey to vertebrate predators such as owls, snakes, and large mammals such as White-faced Capuchins or Tayras.

Mice are also important consumers of invertebrates, plants, and fungi. The inclusion of plant parts in their diets has implications for the reproductive success of plants. In January 1984, I observed a Vesper Rat foraging for 20 min in the crown of a fruiting understory shrub, *Psychotria gracilis* (Rubiaceae). Despite a strong northeast trade wind, it hung from its hind feet to reach fruit and then used its tail as a counterweight to maintain its balance on a branch as it sat on its haunches and manipulated fruit with its forefeet. It ate only the fruit pulp, discarding the seeds and the skin. The mouse may have assisted in dispersing seeds to a site away from the parent plant.

Arboreal mice may also act as seed predators, destroying the plant embryo and reducing seedling establishment. One individual of *Reithrodontomys gracilis* in captivity readily consumed mistletoe seeds collected from the feces of birds (Sargent 1995). If the Slender Harvest Mouse routinely feeds in the wild on mistletoe seeds after they have been dispersed, the species could significantly reduce the number of seeds that germinate. Arboreal seed predators such as rodents could be responsible for the 60% loss of dispersed mistletoe seeds documented in a study of *Phoradendron robustissium* in Monteverde (Sargent 1995; see Sargent "Mistletoes," pp. 81–82).

Mice also feed on plant nectar and could be plant pollinators. Lumer (1980) documented flower visitation by mice in a hemiepiphyte, *Blakea chlorantha*, which grows at higher elevations in the preserve. The plant produces nectar only at night; Lumer suggested that the principal pollinators are climbing mice. Although mice were commonly trapped in plants, fluorescent dye experiments indicated pollen transfer occurred only during the day when birds visit the flowers (see Langtimm and Unnasch, "Mice, Birds, and Pollination," p. 241). More research in needed on this pollination system.

Climbing mice may also act as dispersal agents for the spores of mycorrhizal fungi (Johnson 1996). Many tropical plants require a symbiotic association with fungi to increase the mineral uptake of their roots (Janos 1983). Rodents in temperate regions eat sporocarps and pass viable spores in their feces (Maser et al. 1978), and spore dispersal by rodents has been documented in one lowland tropical forest (Janos et al. 1995). This may also be the case in cloud forest and is supported by the results of one Organization for Tropical Studies field project conducted in Monteverde, which found mycorrhizal spores in the feces of four species of mice including the arboreal Slender Harvest Mouse (Bakarr 1990).

Table 7.1. Climbing mice and rats inhabiting the Monteverde cloud forest.

Species	Common name
Nyctomys sumichrasti	Vesper Rat
Tylomys watsoni	Watson's Climbing Rat
Ototylomys phyllotis	Big-eared Climbing Rat
Peromyscus nudipes	Naked-footed Mouse
Reithrodontomys creper	Chiriquí Harvest Mouse
Reithrodontomys gracilis	Slender Harvest Mouse
Reithrodontomys sp.	Harvest Mouse (undescribed species)
Oligoryzomys vegetus	Pygmy Rice Mouse

MICE, BIRDS, AND POLLINATION OF *BLAKEA CHLORANTHA*
Catherine A. Langtimm & Robert Unnasch

In Monteverde, Lumer (1980) documented flower visitation by rodents for the first time in any neotropical plant species. Based on the unusual floral shape and phenology of *Blakea chlorantha*, observations and photographs of rodent visitors, and pollen found in rodent stomachs, she proposed that the plant had evolved specific adaptations for pollination by climbing nocturnal rodents and that rodents were the principal pollinators for this species (see Lumer, "Reproductive Biology of *Blakea* and *Topobea*," pp. 273–276).

Pollination by nonflying mammals is relatively rare in the western hemisphere. Although flower visitation by primates (Janson et al. 1981), marsupials (Janson et al. 1981, Steiner 1981), and procyonids (Janson et al. 1981) has been documented in the neotropics, no study has demonstrated successful pollination. Data on pollen transfer and subsequent seed maturation as a result of exclusive visits by a potential pollinator are needed to document pollination unequivocally. To that end, we extended the research begun by Lumer by examining pollen transfer by nocturnal mice and by birds, another group of visitors we observed at flowers during the day.

To document pollen loads on flower visitors, we captured rodents and birds at the flowers and lightly rubbed cellophane tape across the throat and face of each animal to collect pollen. The pollen was placed on a microscope slide and examined under a compound microscope for the distinctive pollen of *Blakea*. To trap rodents, we tied Sherman live traps (1–2.5 m high) onto the branches of two adjacent *B. chlorantha* that were flowering. To eliminate the possibility that the mice were grooming away the pollen while confined in a trap, we spent one night checking the traps every hour and taking pollen samples. To capture birds, we set up mist nets adjacent to the blooming plants.

We tested for pollen transfer using a fluorescent dye technique. We applied a paste of fluorescent powder and water onto the pollen-producing anthers of open *Blakea* flowers. The paste dries to a fragile crust that is easily broken by flower visitors but not by wind. The powder readily adheres to the visitor and transfers to other flowers if the visitor contacts the sticky stigma. The dye is easily detected on flowers under a dissecting microscope illuminated with ultraviolet light. We looked for nocturnal pollen transfer on eight nights, applying the dye to 12 flowers each night and collecting untreated open flowers at dawn

the following day. To test for diurnal pollen transfer, we did similar trials on four days but applied the dye at dawn and collected flowers at dusk.

During nine nights of trapping within the crowns of *B. chlorantha*, we caught four species of rodents: Watson's Climbing Rat ($n = 1$), Naked-footed Mouse ($n = 1$), Pygmy Rice Mouse ($n = 2$), and Chiriquí Harvest Mouse ($n = 1$). Voucher specimens were deposited in the mammal collection of the U.S. National Museum of Natural History. The five individuals were trapped a total of 15 times in the crowns. No *Blakea* pollen was detected on the samples from any of these individuals, nor was fluorescent powder detected on any flower during the nocturnal dye experiment. However, 13% of the flowers collected during the diurnal dye experiment had powder adhering to the stigmas and the corolla of the flowers, indicating that pollen had been transferred from one flower to another during daylight hours.

During six hours of diurnal observations, we had 12 sightings of four species of birds feeding at *Blakea* flowers. The birds were apparently feeding on nectar remaining from the previous evening. There were two species of tanagers, Sooty-capped Bush-Tanager and Common Bush-Tanager; and two species of hummingbirds, Purple-throated Mountaingem and Violet Sabrewing. We observed one male mountain-gem defending a large *Blakea* in bloom. On two occasions, we captured three of these species in mist nets and found large amounts of *Blakea* pollen on the cellophane tape samples collected from their throats.

The results of our experiments did not confirm pollen transfer by climbing mice, but rather documented that birds visit the flowers of *B. chlorantha* and can transfer pollen between adjacent plants. The definitive experiments to document if these floral visitors succeed in transferring pollen that results in seed maturation are still lacking. The research thus far has focused on plants accessible to biologists from the ground. Many plants, however, inhabit the crowns of mid- to upper canopy trees. Langtimm (1992) documented vertical stratification of the rodent assemblage in the lower elevations of Monteverde, but the assemblage at the elevations where *B. chlorantha* is found is completely different. Information is lacking on the ecology, behavior, and vertical distribution of mice within the high-elevation forest. These interactions will be a rich field of future investigation for botanists and zoologists in Monteverde.

BAIRD'S TAPIR
Robert O. Lawton

The ancestral tapiroids were widespread in the vast broad-leaved forests that covered North America and Eurasia in the early Tertiary. By the mid-Eocene, around 55 million years ago, lineages leading to rhinos and tapirs had diverged, and by the Oligocene, tapirs were well established as a diverse group of forest browsers (Simpson 1945). More recent history has not treated tapirs as well. By the end of the Pliocene, the shrinkage of the mesic broad-leaved forests of the northern hemisphere had restricted tapirs to eastern North America and southeastern Asia. With the opening of the Central American land bridge 3 million years ago, tapirs colonized South America (Marshall et al. 1982), but in the megafaunal extinctions associated with human invasion of the New World about 12,000 years ago, tapirs were eliminated in eastern North America (Martin 1973). They persist in the tropical forests of Central and South America (Martin 1973), although all three neotropical species are threatened by hunting (Janzen 1983b, Bodmer 1988).

Tapirs are large (150–300 kg as adults), shy and secretive where hunted, but accepting of nonthreatening observers in protected areas (Terwilliger 1978). They browse on a broad but selective variety of plants in the forest understory and will stand on their hind legs and grope with their flexible probosces to reach favored forage (Terwilliger 1978, Janzen 1982). Little is known of population densities and patterns of land use. Tapirs live in small loose herds in which individuals forage and sleep alone but meet commonly at creeks, pools, and favored feeding areas. The lowland forest on Barro Colorado Island supported 0.5 individuals per kilometer (Terwilliger 1978).

Baird's Tapir (*Tapirus bairdii*, "danta" locally) undoubtedly roamed both slopes of the Cordillera de Tilarán in the recent past. In the 1930s, men from Guacimal hunted tapirs in what are now the communities of Cerro Plano and Monteverde (F. Arguedas, pers. comm.). Hunting and habitat destruction have now restricted tapirs to the least accessible parts of the Cordillera, the cloud forests of the crest, and the rugged Caribbean slopes. In 1987 and 1988, Wolf Guindon and I established a tapir-monitoring circuit around a high bowl on the crest of the Cordillera in an area of about 3 km². The bowl is bounded to the west by Cerros Amigo and Roble, to the north by Cerro Frio, and to the east by the drop into the Peñas Blancas valley; it is an area of conspicuous tapir presence. Judging from track and trail patterns, it appeared that four to seven tapirs, including a mother and half-grown juvenile, were using the area. Foraging seemed concentrated in areas of lesser relief and away from the worst tangles of the swampy area in the center of the bowl.

What little we know of tapir foraging in the Cordillera de Tilarán comes from interpretation of the signs of browsing along tapir trails. In the presence of fresh tapir tracks and the absence of deer or peccary tracks, we assume that recent browsing was done by tapirs. From this type of evidence, tapirs feed on a broad variety of understory plants, including common herbaceous shrubs of the Acanthaceae (species of *Hansteinia*, *Justicia*, *Razisea*, and *Poikilacanthus*), woody and herbaceous Rubiaceae, palms, bamboos, and tree saplings. This concurs with other reports (Janzen 1982) but gives little perspective on how vegetation structure and composition influence tapirs' food choice and habitat use, or how tapirs influence vegetation.

In the study area, well-worn tapir trails descended from high ridges, crossed creeks, and surrounded a set of pools on Quebrada Danta, apparently used for bathing and defecation. With the first major winter storm in December, tapirs left the area, apparently descending a well-worn trail into the Peñas Blancas valley, and did not return until the end of the dry season. Reconnaisance throughout the Cordillera by Guindon suggests that tapir activity in the mountain range is concentrated in a limited number (10 or so) of favored sites. Such sites lie mostly above 1500 m along the crest of the Cordillera in areas of lesser relief such as the Brillante saddle and below 1200 m on the flanks of major valleys. The precipitous and landslide-scarred slopes in between are crossed by well-worn tapir trails following narrow ridgecrests but do not seem to be used often in foraging.

Conservation of the Cordillera's tapirs must be a priority. As a major forest browser, they may influence forest regeneration and composition (Janzen 1983b). As prey, they may influence the abundance and activity of the few jaguar remaining in the area. Better estimates of population size and a better picture of the patterns of land use are needed. Estimates of the Cordillera's current carrying capacity is about 100 tapirs (C. Guindon, unpubl. data). A herd of at least 200 would be required to avoid potentially deleterious consequences of inbreeding over the next few centuries. On a more optimistic note, tapirs are raising young in the Cordillera and are returning to areas that had been deserted due to earlier hunting.

Given that a small group on Barro Colorado Island has survived for over 60 years, tapirs may persist in Monteverde despite their current limited population size.

Literature Cited

Anderson, S. D. 1982. Comparative population ecology of *Peromyscus mexicanus* in a Costa Rican wet forest. Ph.D. dissertation, University of Southern California, Los Angeles.

Ashe, J. S., and R. M. Timm. 1987a. Predation by and activity patterns of "parasitic" beetles of the genus *Amblyopinus* (Coleoptera: Staphylinidae). Journal of Zoology (London) 212:429–437.

———. 1987b. Probable mutualistic association between staphylinid beetles (*Amblyopinus*) and their rodent hosts. Journal of Tropical Ecology 3:177–181.

———. 1995. Systematics, distribution, and host specificity of *Amblyopinus* Solsky 1875 (Coleoptera: Staphylinidae) in Mexico and Central America. Tropical Zoology 8:373–399.

Bakarr, M. J. 1990. Rodents as dispersers of VA mycorrhizal fungus (VAMF) spores: evidence from a Costa Rican highland forest. Pages 233–237 *in* B. Loiselle, editor. Tropical Biology: an ecological approach. OTS Paper 90-1. Organization for Tropical Studies, Durham, North Carolina.

Birkenholz, D. E., and W. O. Wirtz II. 1965. Laboratory observations on the vesper rat. Journal of Mammalogy 46:181–189.

Bodmer, R. E. 1988. Ungulate management and conservation in the Peruvian Amazon. Biological Conservation 45:303–310.

Bronson, F. H., and P. D. Heideman. 1994. Seasonal regulation of reproduction in mammals. Pages 541–583 *in* E. Knobil and J. D. Neill, editors. The physiology of reproduction (2nd ed.). Raven Press, New York.

Carleton, M. D. 1980. Phylogenetic relationships in neotomine-peromyscine rodents (Muroidea) and a reappraisal of the dichotomy within New World Cricetinae. Miscellaneous Publications Museum of Zoology, University of Michigan 157:1–146.

Carleton, M. D., and G. G. Musser. 1995. Systematic studies of oryzomyine rodents (Muridae: Sigmodontinae): definition and distribution of *Oligoryzomys vegetus* (Bangs, 1902). Proceedings of the Biological Society of Washington 108:338–369.

Carleton, M. D., E. T. Hooper, and J. Honacki. 1975. Karyotypes and accessory reproductive glands in the rodent genus *Scotinomys*. Journal of Mammalogy 56:916–921.

Choate, J. R. 1970. Systematics and zoogeography of Middle American shrews of the genus *Cryptotis*. University of Kansas Publications, Museum of Natural History 19:195–317.

Dinerstein, E. 1983. Reproductive ecology of fruit bats and seasonality of fruit production in a Costa Rican cloud forest. Ph.D. dissertation, University of Washington, Seattle.

———. 1985. First records of *Lasiurus castaneus* and *Antrozous dubiaquercus* from Costa Rica. Journal of Mammalogy 66:411–412.

———. 1986. Reproductive ecology of fruit bats and the seasonality of fruit production in a Costa Rican cloud forest. Biotropica 18:307–318.

Emmons, L. H. 1997. Neotropical rainforest mammals: a field guide. 2nd ed. University of Chicago Press, Chicago, Illinois, USA.

Fishkind, A. S., and R. W. Sussman. 1987. Preliminary survey of the primates of the Zona Protectora and La Selva Biological Station, northeast Costa Rica. Primate Conservation 8:63–66.

Gardner, A. L. 1973. The systematics of the genus Didelphis (Marsupialia: Didelphidae) in North and Middle America. Special Publications, The Museum, Texas Tech University, 4:1–81.

Genoways, H. H., and J. K. Jones, Jr. 1972. Variation and ecology in a local population of the vesper mouse (*Nyctomys sumichrasti*). Occasional Papers, The Museum, Texas Tech University 3:1–22.

Hafner, M. S., and D. J. Hafner. 1987. Geographic distribution of two Costa Rican species of *Orthogeomys*, with comments on dorsal pelage markings in the Geomyidae. The Southwestern Naturalist 32:5–11.

Hayes, M., R. LaVal, C. Langtimm, and F. Reid. 1989. The mammals of Monteverde (mamíferos de Monteverde): an annotated check list of the mammals of Monteverde. Tropical Science Center, Monteverde, Costa Rica.

Heideman, P. D., and F. H. Bronson. 1992. A pseudo-seasonal reproductive strategy in a tropical rodent, *Peromyscus nudipes*. Journal of Reproductive Fertility 95:57–67.

———. 1993. Potential and realized reproduction in a tropical population of *Peromyscus* (Rodentia). Journal of Mammalogy 74:261–269.

Hill, R. W., and E. T. Hooper. 1971. Temperature regulation in mice of the genus *Scotinomys*. Journal of Mammalogy 52:806–816.

Holdridge, L. R. 1967. Life zone ecology. Tropical Science Center, San José, Costa Rica.

Hooper, E. T. 1968. Habitats and food of amphibious mice of the genus *Rheomys*. Journal of Mammalogy 49:550–553.

———. 1972. A synopsis of the rodent genus *Scotinomys*. Occasional Papers of the Museum of Zoology, University of Michigan 665:1–32.

———. 1975. Orbital region and size of eye in species of *Scotinomys* (Rodentia). Journal of Mammalogy 56:667–671.

Hooper, E. T., and M. D. Carleton. 1976. Reproduction, growth and development in two contiguously allopatric rodent species, genus *Scotinomys*. Miscellaneous Publications Museum of Zoology, University of Michigan 151:1–52.

Huckaby, D. G. 1980. Species limits in the *Peromyscus mexicanus* group (Mammalia: Rodentia: Muroidea). Contributions in Science, Natural History Museum of Los Angeles County 326:1–24.

Janos, D. P. 1983. Vesicular-arbuscular mycorrhizal fungi. Pages 340–345 *in* D. H. Janzen, editor. Costa Rican natural history. University of Chicago Press, Chicago.

Janos, D. P., C. T. Sahley, and L. H. Emmons. 1995. Rodent dispersal of vesicular-arbuscular mycorrhizal fungi in Amazonian Peru. Ecology 76:1852–1858.

Janson, C. H., J. Terborgh, and L. H. Emmons. 1981. Non-flying mammals as pollinating agents in the Amazonian forest. Biotropica 13 (Suppl.):1–6.

Janzen, D. H. 1982. Wild plant acceptability to a captive Costa Rican Baird's tapir. Brenesia 19/20:99–128.

———. editor. 1983a. Costa Rican natural history. University of Chicago Press, Chicago.

———. 1983b. *Tapirus bairdii*. Pages 496–497 *in* D. H. Janzen, editor. Costa Rican natural history. University of Chicago Press, Chicago.

Johnson, C. N. 1996. Interactions between mammals and ectomycorrhizal fungi. Trends in Ecology and Evolution 11:503–507.

Langtimm, C. A. 1992. Specialization for vertical habitats within a cloud forest community of mice. Ph.D. dissertation, University of Florida, Gainesville.

LaVal, R. K. 1973. A revision of the Neotropical bats of the genus *Myotis*. Los Angeles County Science Bulletin of the Natural History Museum 15:1–54.

———. 1977. Notes on some Costa Rican bats. Brenesia 10/11:77–83.

LaVal, R. K., and H. S. Fitch. 1977. Structure, movements and reproduction in three Costa Rican bat communities. Occasional Papers, Museum of Natural History, University of Kansas 69:1–28.

Lawton, M. F., and R. O. Lawton. 1980. Nest-site selection in the Brown Jay. Auk 97:631–633.

Lumer, C. 1980. Rodent pollination of *Blakea* (Melastomataceae) in a Costa Rican cloud forest. Brittonia 32:512–517.

———. 1983. *Blakea* (San Miguel). Pages 194–195 *in* D. H. Janzen, editor. Costa Rican natural history. University of Chicago Press, Chicago.

Lumer, C., and R. D. Schoer. 1986. Pollination of *Blakea austin-smithii* and *B. penduliflora* (Melastomataceae) by small rodents in Costa Rica. Biotropica 18:363–364.

Marshall, L. G., S. D. Webb, J. J. Sepkoski, and D. M. Raup. 1982. Mammalian evolution and the Great American Interchange. Science 215:1351–1357.

Martin, P. 1973. The discovery of America. Science 179:969–975.

Maser, C., J. M. Trappe, and R. A. Nussbaum. 1978. Fungal-small mammal interrelationships with emphasis on Oregon coniferous forests. Ecology 59:799–809.

McPherson, A. B. 1985. A biogeographical analysis of factors influencing the distribution of Costa Rican rodents. Brenesia 23:97–273.

———. 1986. The biogeography of Costa Rican rodents: an ecological, geological, and evolutionary approach. Brenesia 25/26:229–244.

Metz, E. 1990. Song communication in the mouse, *Scotinomys teguina*. Pages 256–258 *in* B. Loiselle and G. Mora, editors. Tropical Biology: an ecological approach OTS Paper 90-1. Organization for Tropical Studies, Durham, North Carolina.

Monge-Nájera, J., and B. Morera Brenes. 1987. Why is the coyote (*Canis latrans*) expanding its range? A critique of the deforestation hypothesis. Revista de Biología Tropical 35:169–171.

Reid, F. A. 1997. A field guide to the mammals of Central America and Southeast Mexico. Oxford University Press, New York.

Reid, F. A., and C. A. Langtimm. 1993. Distributional and natural history notes for selected mammals from Costa Rica. Southwestern Naturalist 38:299–302.

Rogers, D. S. 1989. Evolutionary implications of the chromosomal variation among spiny pocket mice, genus *Heteromys* (Order Rodentia). Southwestern Naturalist 34:85–100.

———. 1990. Genic evolution, historical biogeography, and systematic relationships among spiny pocket mice (subfamily Heteromyidae). Journal of Mammalogy 71:668–685.

Sargent, S. 1995. Seed fate in a tropical mistletoe: the importance of host twig size. Functional Ecology 9:197–204.

Simpson, G. G. 1945. Notes on Pleistocene and recent tapirs. Bulletin of the American Museum of Natural History 86:37–81.

Starrett, A., and R. S. Casebeer. 1968. Records of bats from Costa Rica. Contributions in Science, Los Angeles County Museum of Natural History 148: 1–21.

Steiner, K. E. 1981. Nectarivory and potential pollination by a neotropical marsupial. Annals of the Missouri Botanical Garden 68:505–513.

Steppan, S. J. 1995. Revision of the tribe Phyllotini (Rodentia: Sigmodontinae), with a phylogenetic hypothesis for the Sigmodontinae. Fieldiana: Zoology (New Series) 80:1–112.

Stiles, F. G. 1988. Altitudinal movements of birds on the Caribbean slope of Costa Rica: implications for conservation. Pages 243–258 *in* F. Almeda and C. M. Pringle, editors. Tropical rainforests: diversity and conservation. California Academy of Sciences and American Association for the Advancement of Science, San Francisco.

Stoner, K. E. 1993. Habitat preferences, foraging patterns, intestinal parasitic infections, and diseases in mantled howler monkeys, *Alouatta palliata*, in a northeastern Costa Rican rainforest. Ph.D. dissertation, University of Kansas, Lawrence.

Svihla, R. D. 1930. Notes of the golden harvest mouse. Journal of Mammalogy 11:53–54.

Terwilliger, V. J. 1978. Natural history of Baird's tapir on Barro Colorado Island, Panama Canal Zone. Biotropica 10:211–220.

Timm, R. M. 1987. Tent construction by bats of the genera *Artibeus* and *Uroderma*. Pages 187–212 *in* B. D. Patterson and R. M. Timm, editors. Studies in neotropical mammalogy: essays in honor of Philip Hershkovitz. Fieldiana: Zoology (New Series) 39:1–506.

———. 1994. The mammal fauna. Pages 229–237 and 394–398 *in* L. A. McDade, K. S. Bawa, H. A. Hespenheide, and G. S. Hartshorn, editors. La Selva: ecology and natural history of a neotropical rain forest. University of Chicago Press, Chicago.

Timm, R. M., and J. S. Ashe. 1988. The mystery of the gracious hosts. Natural History 9/88:6–10.

Timm, R. M., and B. L. Clauson. 1990. A roof over their feet: tent-making bats of the New World tropics turn leaves into living quarters. Natural History 3/90:54–59.

Timm, R. M., and R. K. LaVal. 1998. A field key to the bats of Costa Rica. Occasional Publication Series, University of Kansas, Center of Latin American Studies, Lawrence 22:1–30.

Timm, R. M., D. E. Wilson, B. L. Clauson, R. K. LaVal, and C. S. Vaughan. 1989. Mammals of the La Selva–Braulio Carrillo complex, Costa Rica. North American Fauna 75:1–162.

Uyehara, J. C. 1990. Acoustic survey of the two-note tooter (*Reithrodontomys gracilis*) at Veracruz. Pages 297–301 *in* B. Loiselle and G. Mora, editors. Tropical Biology: an ecological approach OTS Paper 90-1. Organization for Tropical Studies, Durham, North Carolina.

Vaughan, C. 1983. Coyote range expansion in Costa Rica and Panama. Brenesia 21:27–32.

Vaughan, C., and M. A. Rodríguez, editors. 1994. Ecología y manejo del venado cola blanca en México y Costa Rica. Serie Conservación Biológica y Desarrollo Sostenible, Programa Regional en Manejo de Vida Silvestre, Universidad Nacional, No. 2:1–455.

Voss, R. S. 1988. Systematics and ecology of ichthyomyine rodents (Muroidea): patterns of morphological evolution in a small adaptive radiation. Bulletin of the American Museum of Natural History 188:259–493.

Wheelwright, N. T. 1983. Fruits and the ecology of Resplendent Quetzals. Auk 100:286–301.

Wilson, D. E. 1983. Checklist of mammals. Pages 443–447 *in* D. H. Janzen, editor. Costa Rican natural history. The University of Chicago Press, Chicago.

Woodman, N. 1992. Biogeographical and evolutionary relationships among Central American small-eared shrews of the genus *Cryptotis* (Mammalia: Insectivora: Soricidae). Ph.D. dissertation, University of Kansas, Lawrence.

Woodman, N., and R. M. Timm. 1993. Intraspecific and interspecific variation in the *Cryptotis nigrescens* species complex of small-eared shrews (Insectivora: Soricidae), with the description of a new species from Colombia. Fieldiana: Zoology (New Series) 74:1–30.

Young, B. E. 1996. An experimental analysis of small clutch size in tropical House Wrens. Ecology 77: 472–488.

8

Plant-Animal Interactions

K. Greg Murray
Sharon Kinsman
Judith L. Bronstein

The term "plant-animal interactions" includes a diverse array of biologically important relationships. Plant-herbivore relationships (in which an animal feeds on whole plants or parts of them) are examples of exploitation, because one species benefits from the interaction while the other suffers. Plant-pollinator and plant–seed disperser relationships (in which animals disperse pollen or seeds, usually in return for a food reward) are examples of mutualisms because they are beneficial to both parties. Another class of plant-animal mutualisms involves plants that provide nesting sites and/or food rewards to ants, which often protect the plant from herbivores or competing plants. Plant-pollinator and plant–seed disperser mutualisms probably originated as cases of exploitation of plants by animals (Thompson 1982, Crepet 1983, Tiffney 1986). Many of the distinctive plant structures associated with animal-mediated pollen and seed dispersal (e.g., flowers, nectaries, attractive odors, fleshy fruit pulp, and thickened seed coats) presumably evolved to attract consumers of floral or seed resources while preventing them from digesting the pollen or seeds.

Until the mid-1970s, ecologists paid relatively little attention to the potential roles played by plant-animal mutualisms in structuring ecological communities. Competition and predator-prey interactions were more common subjects. Botanists had described the characteristics of the plant and animal players in pollination and seed dispersal mutualisms (Knuth 1906, 1908, 1909, Ridley 1930, van der Pijl 1969, Faegri and van der Pijl 1979), but these descriptive works did not fully examine plant-animal mutualisms in the context of communities. The opportunity to work in the neotropics, facilitated by the Organization for Tropical Studies (OTS), the Smithsonian Tropical Research Institute (STRI), and other institutions, attracted the attention of temperate-zone ecologists to the mutualisms that are much more conspicuous components of tropical systems than of temperate ones (Wheelwright 1988b).

Plant-pollinator interactions have attracted more attention in Monteverde than plant-frugivore interactions, and plant-herbivore interactions remain conspicuously understudied. This imbalance probably reflects the interests of those who first worked at Monteverde and later returned with their own students, rather than differences in the significance of the interactions at Monteverde or elsewhere. Aside from a few studies of herbivory in particular species (e.g., Peck, "Agroecology of *Prosapia*," pp. 409–410), even basic surveys remain to be done. Monteverde provides an excellent location for comparative studies of plant-animal interactions over an elevational gradient.

In this chapter, we focus on work conducted in Monteverde and make comparisons to other sites. Introductions to plant-animal interactions are in Thompson (1982, 1994), Boucher (1985), Howe and Westley (1988), and Abrahamson (1989). Feinsinger (1983), Real (1983), and Jones and Little (1983) provide introductions to pollination biology, as do Howe and Smallwood (1982). Murray (1986) describes frugivory and seed dispersal, and Gilbert and Raven (1975), Nitecki (1983), and Futuyma and Slatkin (1983) provide a general treatment of coevolution.

8.1. Plant Pollinator Interactions

8.1.1. Who Pollinates What

To reproduce sexually, flowering plants must import and export pollen. Pollen is transported abiotically (by wind or water) or biotically (by invertebrate or vertebrate animals who visit flowers to collect nectar, pollen, or other floral rewards). The vast majority of pollinating animals are insects, including thrips, leafhoppers, flies, beetles, butterflies, moths, bees, and wasps (Proctor et al. 1996). Hummingbirds and other birds pollinate plants as they forage for nectar. Mammals such as bats, rodents, marsupials, and primates also visit flowers, but pollination by mammals other than bats is rare.

Flowers pollinated by animals are remarkably diverse in color, scent, nectar composition and production rate, phenology, shape, symmetry, and design of floral display. Floral traits are thought to reflect coevolution between plants and the animals that pollinate them (Faegri and van der Pijl 1979), because traits of flowers and their pollinator mutualists broadly match. For example, flowers whose pollen is transported on the bills and heads of hummingbirds tend to be red and tubular (matching the visual acuity and bill shape of the birds), whereas moth-visited flowers often have white petals and sweet nocturnal scents (matching the nocturnal habits and visual and olfactory orientation of moths). Naturalists call these patterns "pollination syndromes" (Faegri and van der Pijl 1979) or "pollination systems" (Kress and Beach 1994). Although pollination systems are a useful tool for exploring mechanisms of pollination (Proctor et al. 1996), their assumptions (e.g., that particular plants and their pollinators have coevolved) and predictions (e.g., that the most effective pollinator has had the largest selective impact on floral traits) can limit the questions we pursue (Herrera 1996). The systems approach has not traditionally been linked to studies of plants' mating and population structures (Harder and Barrett 1996), a link that is critical for conservation.

The complementarity between traits of pollen-transporting animals and flowers is one of several plant-pollinator correspondences. Three others are discussed in this section. First is the relationship between floral sexuality (the distribution of male and female structures and functions within and between plants) and pollination systems. For example, many beetle-pollinated plant species have unisexual flowers. Second is the correspondence between pollination systems and plant life-forms (Table 8.1); for example, tropical trees are more likely to be pollinated by bees than by birds or small moths, but pollination by birds is frequent among herbaceous plants. Third, elevation influences the relative frequencies of pollination systems because flight in cool, cloudy conditions is easier for some animals than for others (Cruden 1972). For example, hummingbird pollination is especially conspicuous and frequent in Monteverde, particularly for the rich vascular epiphyte flora.

The 13 pollination systems discussed here are very broad categories (Baker et al. 1983, Wyatt 1983, Bawa 1990) that allow comparison to other tropical sites (Bawa et al. 1985, Kress and Beach 1994). Our information on pollination systems for Monteverde comes primarily from two sources. First, William Haber and colleagues (e.g., Koptur et al. 1988) documented floral characteristics (and flower visitors in many cases) and assigned likely pollination systems to Monteverde's flowering plants. Haber's list (Appendix 1) is the major reference for this section's summary (Table 8.1) of pollination system patterns in the Monteverde flora. The second source was the set of studies that document pollinators or details of pollination for various taxa (Koptur 1984b, Cane 1993). Pollination by hummingbirds has been studied in detail (Feinsinger 1978, Feinsinger et al. 1986, 1987, 1988b). For the majority of plant species at Monteverde, however, few details of reproductive biology are known.

Large flying animals. Flowers adapted for pollination by bats, hummingbirds, and hawkmoths are conspicuous because they are big, bright, or strongly scented. These large fliers pollinate nearly 15% of Monteverde's flowering plants (Table 8.1), and may be especially important to montane plant mutualists because they are strong fliers in cool misty conditions. Because some are able to fly long distances relative to smaller pollinators, they may occasionally effect long-distance pollen movement and gene flow (Janzen 1983).

Table 8.1. Frequencies (% of species) of 13 pollination systems of Monteverde flowering plants, by growth form and sexual system.

Pollination System	Epiphytes	Herbs	Vines and Lianas	Shrubs	All Trees	Canopy Trees[a]	Dioecious Canopy Trees[b]	All Dioecious Species[c]	All Angio-sperms[d]	No. of species
Bat	2.8	0.3	2.8	0.8	1.6	1.6	0	0	1.6	33
Bird	24.8	13.4	6.6	6.7	1.4	1.0	0	0.7	8.8	181
Hawkmoth	10.9	0.6	1.0	1.1	6.7	7.2	2.9	3.9	4.4	91
Other moth	1.5	0.3	1.9	0.8	10.5	9.4	4.3	4.9	4.3	89
Butterfly	2.8	2.7	2.2	5.1	0.6	0	0	1.6	2.4	48
Beetle	2.5	2.4	11.3	0.3	2.3	1.6	0	0.3	3.4	69
Fly	0	0.3	1.0	0	0.1	0	0	0	0.24	5
Large bee	5.3	12.8	18.6	7.2	7.1	6.8	2.9	1.3	9.5	196
Small bee	2.5	14.3	5.0	21.1	15.1	16.2	21.8	16.1	12.5	258
Bee (undesignated)	7.4	15.8	11.6	24.6	12.6	10.6	10.1	9.5	14.4	295
Other insects[e]	37.3	30.3	35.2	26.7	35.8	39.8	45.0	47.6	33.4	687
Wind	1.9	6.8	2.8	5.6	6.2	5.8	13.0	14.1	5.0	103
Other mammals	0.3	0	0	0	0	0	0	0	0.05	1
No. of species	322	336	318	374	706	500	138	305	2056	2056

[a] A subcategory of All Trees.

[b] A subcategory (medium and large trees in Appendix 1) of All Trees.

[c] A subcategory of All Angiosperms.

[d] Includes native plant species for which Appendix 1 identifies or predicts the pollination system, except Orchidaceae (approximately 450 species) and nonforest Cyperaceae and Poaceae (29 and 66 wind-pollinated herbs and grasses, respectively).

[e] "Small diverse insects" in text.

Bats In Monteverde, seven species of bats are primarily nectarivorous (see Chap. 7, Mammals). Bats pollinate 33 Monteverde plant species in 10 families (Table 8.1), particularly Marcgraviaceae, Bombacaceae, Bignoniaceae, and Cactaceae. The plants are primarily epiphytes, vines, and trees whose flowers tend to occur high in the canopy. Research is needed on nectar characteristics, floral and animal structures, how bats locate flowers, the effectiveness of pollen delivery, the identity of pollen on bats, and the degree to which flowers visited by bats depend on them for pollination.

Birds The Monteverde flora conforms to Cruden's (1972) prediction that a relatively high proportion of plant species in tropical montane ecosystems are pollinated by birds; nearly 9% of the Monteverde flora is bird pollinated (Table 8.1), compared to approximately 4% at La Selva (Bawa 1990). Hummingbirds, the predominant bird pollinators in montane Central America, forage diurnally, usually hovering to sip nectar. The flowers they visit tend to be brightly colored, odorless, and tubular (Proctor et al. 1996).

The rich Monteverde hummingbird fauna includes two relatively distinct guilds (groups of functionally similar species that use a common resource in the same way; Feinsinger et al. 1986, 1987; see Busby, "Hummingbird Pollination," pp. 267–268). Members of the long-billed guild (e.g., hermits such as *Phaethornis guy*) have distinctly curved, long bills which fit the curved tubular flowers they visit. They forage in regular routes over large areas, visiting individual plants that often produce only a few flowers daily. In contrast, members of the short-billed guild (e.g., *Lampornis calolaema*) have straight short bills which fit short, straight, tubular flowers. They also forage on regular routes but tend to cover smaller areas and to visit plant species that produce more flowers each day. Some short-billed birds display territorial behavior at dense floral displays (see Busby, "Hummingbird Pollination," pp. 267–268). Hummingbird-pollinated plants also form two guilds, which correspond to the two guilds of birds (Feinsinger et al. 1986).

Nearly half of Monteverde's 181 hummingbird-pollinated plant species (which comprise 60 genera in 28 families) are epiphytes (80 species); the families Bromeliaceae, Gesneriaceae, and Ericaceae are especially well represented (Appendix 1). Bird-pollinated plants are herbs, vines, or shrubs (e.g., Acanthaceae), and a few are small trees. Hummingbird-pollinated canopy trees are rare. In seven monocot genera and three monocot families, every species in Monteverde is hummingbird pollinated. As in lowland forests, many of the herbs and shrubs pollinated by hummingbirds are members of the Acanthaceae, Heliconiaceae, and Costaceae. Monteverde's hummingbird-plant associations have stimulated a diverse body of investigations (Feinsinger 1976, 1978, 1987, Feinsinger et al. 1986, 1987, 1988a,b, 1991, 1992, Lackie et al. 1986, Feinsinger and Busby 1987, Linhart et al. 1987a, b, Murray et al. 1987, Feinsinger and Tiebout 1991, Tiebout 1991, Podolsky 1992).

Hawkmoths (Sphingidae) Hawkmoths are crepuscular and nocturnal, hovering (even in strong winds; Haber 1983a) to sip nectar through their long, unrolled proboscises. Most hawkmoth-pollinated flowers produce copious nectar and strong sweet fragrances at night (Haber and Frankie 1989, Proctor et al. 1996), and deposit their pollen on the moth's proboscis, head, or wings (Haber and Frankie 1983). In some taxa (e.g., *Epiphyllum* sp., Cactaceae), the flowers last only one night. Many of Monteverde's hawkmoth-pollinated plant species bloom during the wet season. In Monteverde, 91 plant species in 12 families appear to be pollinated primarily by hawkmoths (ca. 4% of the flora; Table 8.1). The majority belong to the plant families Rubiaceae, Bromeliaceae, and Fabaceae, and most are trees or epiphytes.

The pollination systems of some of Monteverde's hawkmoth-pollinated plant species have been difficult to infer from their floral traits. Certain *Inga* spp. (Fabaceae) trees, for example, which are pollinated by hawkmoths, appear to be adapted for bird or bat pollination because they lack the potent fragrances generally considered to be characteristic of hawkmoth flowers (Koptur 1983; see Koptur, "Breeding Systems of Monteverde Inga," pp. 85–87). The tree genus *Quararibea* (Bombacaceae) is also pollinated by hawkmoths despite exhibiting characteristics of both moth- and bat-pollination systems and despite visitation by birds and a wide variety of diurnal and nocturnal insects (W. Haber, pers. comm.).

The larvae and adult hawkmoth fauna (88 species; W. Haber, pers. comm.) and plants adapted for hawkmoth pollination of Monteverde have been identified. (Haber and Frankie 1989, W. Haber, unpubl. data, S. Kinsman, W. Haber, and C. Mulder, unpubl. data) Studies of the moths' foraging behavior and foraging ranges (Haber and Frankie 1989) would be helpful to understand their plants' mating structure and the role of increasing forest fragmentation in the persistence of both partners of the mutualism. The increase in streetlights and advertising lights of the Monteverde community may affect hawkmoths' foraging and populations.

Smaller fliers: insects. *Small moths* Small moths, most of them nocturnal, are more likely to settle on flowers than to hover. The pale tubular flowers they visit tend to open and produce sweet scents and nectar through the night, starting at dusk. In the Monteverde flora, adaptation specifically for pollination by small moths is evident in 89 species (ca. 4% of the flora; Table 8.1); nearly half of these species are trees. Plant families richest in moth-pollinated species are the Rubiaceae, Fabaceae, and Meliaceae.

Butterflies Butterflies also settle on flowers to suck nectar but are diurnal. The flowers they visit produce abundant nectar and are colorful, sweet scented, and tubular (or spurred) with a rim. In Monteverde, relatively few plant species (48) are adapted specifically for pollination by butterflies. Possible mimicry for pollination in some species has been studied elsewhere (Endress 1994). One plant family (Asteraceae) accounts for the majority of butterfly-pollinated plants, which are predominantly herbs, shrubs, and epiphytes. Although butterfly mobility and migration have been documented (Haber 1993), little is known about butterfly pollination in neotropical forests (Bawa 1990). Monteverde's butterflies are easily identified (DeVries 1987), and the butterfly-pollinated shrubs in Monteverde are accessible for research. The within- and between-plant patterns of pollen movement associated with pollinator behavior and floral density and phenology are of particular interest.

Beetles Colors, scents, and shapes of flowers pollinated by beetles vary considerably, and pollinating beetles vary substantially in size, morphology, and behavior. Most beetles clamber over flowers as they feed on pollen, and in many beetle-pollinated plants the flowers are open, flat, and produce abundant pollen. Other beetle-pollinated plants have specialized arrangements of flowers (see Goldwasser, "Scarab Beetles," pp. 269–271). In Monteverde, as in other neotropical forests, certain monocot families (e.g., Araceae and Cyclanthaceae) account for most of the 69 beetle-pollinated species. Herbs, vines, and epiphytes are common among beetle-pollinated plants. Many (62% of species) have separate male and female flowers.

Beetle pollination has received little attention but is now considered important in tropical communities (Schatz 1990, Young 1990) and critical for understanding and managing tropical forests (Irvine and Armstrong 1990). One remarkable interaction occurs between scarab beetles and heat-producing flowers in Monteverde (see Goldwasser, "Scarab Beetles," pp. 269–271). Study of the Araceae and Cyclanthaceae in Monteverde could substantially contribute to understanding roles of beetle pollination in tropical montane forests.

Flies Flies are not common pollinators. Fly-pollinated flowers vary in color, odor, and timing of opening, and the nectar tends to be exposed to foragers of diverse morphology and behavior (Proctor et al. 1996). Flowers that appear to be adapted primarily for pollination by flies are not well studied (Bawa 1990) and are infrequent in Monteverde (Table 8.1). The five species in Monteverde are herbs, shrubs, or small trees in the Acanthaceae, Aristolochiaceae, and Rubiaceae.

Large bees Flowers adapted for pollination by large bees (principally Anthophorinae, Apinae, Xylocopinae, Colletidae, and Megachilidae) produce sweet odors but are otherwise very diverse. Some are highly specialized (including bilateral symmetry), corresponding to the traits of particular bees. Nine percent (196 species) of Monteverde's flora is pollinated principally by large bees (Table 8.1). The majority of these plants are vines, lianas, and herbs; some are trees or shrubs (Frankie et al. 1983). Five plant families (Fabaceae, Melastomataceae, Asteraceae, Malpighiaceae, and Convolvulaceae) include most species; 22 families are represented in all.

Small bees Flowers pollinated by small bees (Apidae, especially Apinae and Halictidae) also tend to produce sweet odors and to be diverse in other traits. The flowers are small and not brightly colored and may be visited by other small insects (Bawa 1994). This pollination system is common in Monteverde (Table 8.1); the 258 Monteverde plant species pollinated by small bees are in 31 families, with the majority in the Melastomataceae, Myrtaceae, Fabaceae, Arecaceae, and Asteraceae. In contrast to "large bee plants," the majority of species are trees and shrubs.

Other bees Bee pollination is documented for 295 plant Monteverde species (in 39 families), more than 14% of the flora (Table 8.1). It refers to bee-adapted flowers that have not yet been observed sufficiently to be designated more specifically. The majority of these species are in the Rubiaceae, Solanaceae, or Passifloraceae. Most are shrubs, herbs, and trees.

Small Diverse Insects Many Monteverde plant species have "generalized" flowers; they are visited by a wide variety of small insects, including small bees and wasps, beetles, flies, and butterflies that are able to reach pollen and nectar (Bawa et al. 1985). The small, open, pale-colored flowers are sometimes arranged together to form a flat "landing platform." Interactions among the small visitors may affect their movement patterns and how they function as pollinators (Janzen 1983). This pollination category accounts for over one-third (687) of Monteverde's plant species, including nearly half of the large trees (Table 8.1); *Ocotea tenera* and other Lauraceae are examples (Wheelwright 1985a). The majority of species with such a pollination syndrome are trees, epiphytes, and lianas.

Pollination by small diverse insects is important in tropical montane forests (Bawa 1990), although with further study, many plant species now included in this pollination system may be found to be pollinated by a subset of the animals that visit their flowers. Plants with diverse floral visitors should not be assumed to be buffered from the human-caused depletion of insect populations in tropical forests. The

pollination ecology of such plant species demands attention (Bawa 1994).

Specialized insect-pollination systems.   Extremely specialized plant-pollinator mutualisms are rare but famous (Feinsinger 1983, Bawa 1990, Thompson 1994), and Monteverde offers good opportunities for their study. Euglossine bees (Janzen 1983) and their specialized orchid flowers have been studied elsewhere (Schatz 1990, Proctor et al. 1996), but not in Monteverde, where many of the 450 orchid species are euglossine pollinated (W. Haber, pers. comm.). Buzz pollination, in which pollen is expelled by bees vibrating the anthers, is also associated with highly specialized flowers (Buchmann 1983). In Monteverde, it has been noted in species of Solanaceae (Haber 1983b), Melastomataceae, and Myrsinaceae, among others (W. Haber, pers. comm.). Figs (Moraceae: *Ficus* spp.) and their tiny host-specific pollinating wasps have been the focus of a series of investigations in Monteverde (see Bronstein, "Fig Pollination," pp. 271–273).

Abiotic, rare, and absent pollination systems.   Certain pollination systems are either uncommon or unknown in the neotropics or in Monteverde.

Wind Wind pollination is common in temperate forest trees but uncommon in most tropical wet forests (especially lowland rain forests) because conditions are unsuitable to pollen delivery by wind: low-density plant populations, year-round dense foliage, and high humidity (Whitehead 1983). For Monteverde dicots, wind-pollination is characteristic of only 83 wind pollinated species (in 15 families, half in Urticaceae and Moraceae), which represent less than 5% (103 species) of the dicot flora. Twenty-three of the species are medium-large canopy trees, and 15 are small trees (see sec. 8.1.2). Oak (*Quercus* spp., Fagaceae) is a wind-pollinated genus familiar to temperate biologists, and occurs high in the cloud forest on wind-swept ridges. Another wind-pollinated tree is the single Monteverde representative of the Podocarpaceae. In contrast to the low incidence of wind pollination in the dicot flora, 12% (101 species) of Monteverde's monocot species are wind pollinated. The species richness of two classically wind-pollinated monocot families (Poaceae and Cyperaceae; Faegri and van der Pijl 1979) and some Juncaceae drives this pattern. Most of these species occur in more open habitats.

Nonflying mammals Pollination by mammals, including marsupials, rodents, and primates (Janson et al. 1981, Cunningham 1991, Kress et al. 1994, Proctor et al. 1996), is known from many places in the world. The one apparent Monteverde case occurs when pollen is transferred by mice near the Continental Divide in Monteverde (see Lumer, "Reproductive Biology of *Blakea* and *Topobea*," pp. 273–276).

Systems unknown in Monteverde No Monteverde examples are known for pollination by water, ants, thrips (Thysanoptera), or hoppers (Homoptera: Cicadellidae). All are rare globally (Appanah 1990).

Floral resources. Flowers attract and reward pollinators and other visitors with nectar, pollen, floral oils, and other resources in a variety of ways (Simpson and Neff 1983).

Nectar Nectar composition has evolved in relation to primary pollinators (Baker and Baker 1983, Baker et al. 1983). In Monteverde, constituents of nectar correspond to pollinators and other species that use nectar. Differences exist between the two types of nectar produced by several of Monteverde's *Inga* spp. (Fabaceae): floral nectar (presumably adapted to reward pollinators) and extrafloral nectar (presumably adapted to reward ants and parasitic wasps that protect the tree against certain herbivores; Koptur 1994; Fig. 8.1; see Koptur, "Interactions," pp. 277–278). Nectar in long-lived flowers is vulnerable to contamination by microorganisms carried by pollinators (Lawton et al. 1993). Amounts of nectar also vary considerably, even within a plant species. For example, nectar production by some species may decline with an increase in elevation; cool temperatures may dictate lower activity and metabolic rates of insects that

depend on the nectar (Cruden et al. 1983). Monteverde is ideal for investigating such elevational patterns in nectar variability.

Fine-scale variation in nectar amounts probably influences pollinator movement patterns. For several plant species in Monteverde, substantial within-plant variation exists in nectar availability, which affects patterns of visitation by hummingbirds (Feinsinger 1978). Timing of nectar production can also vary for Monteverde hummingbird-pollinated plants (J. Beach and P. Feinsinger, pers. comm.). These patterns of variability are likely to play a role in pollinator foraging and pollen delivery patterns.

Third parties Many animals feed on (and dwell in) flowers or nectar without transferring pollen. For example, Emerald Toucanets eat hummingbird-pollinated *Erythrina* sp. flowers (Riley and Smith 1986; see Riley and Smith, "Ecology and Sexual Dimorphism," p. 214) and Stripe-tailed Hummingbirds, some bees, ants, and other birds act as "thieves" or "robbers" (Inouye 1983), removing nectar through holes pierced in floral tubes. Insectivorous birds hunting at flowers may affect pollinator movement patterns (Baker et al. 1983) or eat pollinators (Bronstein 1988c). Nectar-feeding mites ride on pollinators to travel from flower to flower, and a variety of insects develop on or in floral structures (see Goldwasser, "Scarab Beetles," pp. 268–271; Weiss "A Fly Larva," pp. 278–279). The impact of these "third parties" can

Figure 8.1. Extrafloral nectaries on compound leaves of *Inga brenesii* tree. Photograph by Nathaniel Wheelwright.

be large. With a few exceptions (Bronstein 1991; Weiss, "A Fly Larva," pp. 278–279), their effects in Monteverde are poorly known. They offer outstanding opportunities for research on constraints on the evolution of defense (Baker et al. 1983), and on the effects of flower-chewing, nectar robbery, and pollen feeding (McDade and Kinsman 1980, Dayanandan et al. 1990). The role of third parties may be particularly important in forest fragments because fragmentation may affect populations of pollinators and third parties in different ways.

8.1.2. Floral Sexuality and Pollinators

Floral sexual systems. Most flowering plants in the world and in Monteverde are hermaphroditic: each flower has functional female and male reproductive organs. In monoecious species, separate female and male flowers occur on each plant; in dioecious species, individual plants have either female flowers or male flowers but not both. There are many variations of these three main sexual systems (Wyatt 1983, Richards 1986).

Correspondences between pollination and sexual systems. In tropical forests, each floral sexual system seems to be associated with particular pollination systems. These patterns were first determined from examination of 276 plant species at La Selva (Kress and Beach 1994), where beetle pollination is associated with monoecy and pollinators of hermaphroditic plants are more diverse. Similar patterns occur in Monteverde. There is no single explanation for correspondences between floral sex and pollinator. Some could be a simple result of phylogeny. For example, beetles could be associated with monoecy simply because over evolutionary time, they have retained associations with the plant families that happen to be monoecious (e.g., Araceae and Cyclanthaceae; Schatz 1990). Alternatively, being associated with beetles might have fostered the evolution of monoecy in these plant families. Another association—one between hummingbirds and understory, self-compatible, hermaphroditic plants—has been explained in terms of outcrossing (Kress and Beach 1994). A comprehensive approach to understanding the pollinator-floral sex correspondences must consider pollen movement patterns and resulting plant mating structures (Bawa 1994; see Wheelwright, "Sex Ratios," pp. 87–88).

Dioecy. The pollination methods of dioecious angiosperms in tropical forests are especially intriguing. Two estimates of the global incidence of dioecy are 6% and 4% of all angiosperm species (but see Bawa 1980a, Richards 1986, Renner and Ricklefs 1995).

Comparatively, dioecy is overrepresented in tropical forests (Bawa 1980a), occurring in around 15% of the Monteverde flora (Table 8.1), 16% of species in a montane forest in Venezuela (Sobrevilla and Arroyo 1982), and 17% of 507 species surveyed at La Selva (Kress and Beach 1994), with a similar frequency in Peninsular Malaysia (Bawa 1992). In two seasonally dry neotropical forests (Jalisco, Mexico, and Guanacaste, Costa Rica), 12% and 22% of angiosperms are dioecious, respectively (Kress and Beach 1994). The frequency of dioecy is even higher when only trees are considered. At two lowland sites, La Selva and Peninsular Malaysia, 23% and 26% of tree species are dioecious (of 334 and 711 tree species, respectively; Bawa 1992). In two montane forests, Monteverde (Table 8.1) and Venezuela (Sobrevilla and Arroyo 1982), 28% and 31% of tree species are dioecious (of 500 medium-large Monteverde trees, and of 36 tree species in the Venezuelan forest). In Monteverde, the frequency of dioecy declines with the forest strata: dioecy occurs in 19% of small trees, 15% of vines, 14% of epiphytes, 9% of shrubs and treelets, and 0.6% of herbs.

Pollination modes of these dioecious species are of interest (Bawa 1994). At La Selva and in a drier forest in Costa Rica, the small, unspecialized, pale or white, open flowers of dioecious species are pollinated predominantly by small bees and small diverse insects (Bawa 1994). Monteverde also reflects this pattern, as dioecy is especially frequent in plants pollinated by small bees (19%) and by small diverse insects (21%); 64% of Monteverde's dioecious species exhibit these pollination systems (Table 8.1). Monteverde differs from La Selva in showing an additional association between dioecy and wind pollination. Dioecy occurs in more than 40% of Monteverde's 103 wind-pollinated species (Table 8.1), but in only 15% of Monteverde's flowering plants overall. Wind pollination occurs in 5% of Monteverde's flowering plants but in 13% of dioecious canopy trees (Table 8.1). In contrast, at La Selva, wind pollination is rarer overall (< 3%) and is not reported for trees (Kress and Beach 1994). Why these particular pollination systems (small bee, small diverse insects, and wind) are especially frequent for dioecious plants is not clear (Bawa 1994).

Pollen delivery. Floral sexual systems, like the composition of nectar and the timing of its availability, can influence pollinator movement and effectiveness. Studies of rare sexual systems provide clues about the ways that evolution can mold floral traits in ways that influence pollinator behavior. Three of these studies are from Monteverde: one a case of intersexual floral mimicry (see Ågren and Schemske, "Deceit Pollination," pp. 279–281), one of andromonoecy, and one of androdioecy.

Bird-pollinated Besleria Besleria triflora (Gesneriaceae), a shrub pollinated by short-billed hummingbirds, is andromonoecious: individual plants bear both hermaphroditic and male flowers. Male flowers in andromonoecious species have been assumed to permit plants to increase the total amount of pollen produced, but this is not the case for *B. triflora*. Male flowers produce nectar but little pollen. In Monteverde, the role of these male flowers is to attract pollinators to the plant (Podolsky 1992). Three factors contribute: (1) the larger the floral display, the more pollinator visits a flower in that display receives; (2) hermaphroditic flowers (which can produce fruit) receive more of the desirable outcrossed pollen if the flowers near them are nectar-supplying male flowers, which help attract the birds; and (3) the structure of these male flowers ensures that they do not remove pollen carried by the visiting birds. Rather, the pollen carried by a bird stays in place while the bird sips nectar from male flowers but can be removed by the stigmas of hermaphroditic flowers when they are visited.

Buzz-pollinated Saurauia A similar pollinator-attracting role seems to explain the unusual androdioecious sexual system of a small tree of *Saurauia* (Actinidiaceae; Cane 1993). In this apparently rare sexual system, individual plants bear only one of two flower types: male flowers or flowers that appear to be hermaphroditic. In this case, the flowers of hermaphroditic plants function only as females because their pollen is sterile. Paradoxically, it is their sterile pollen that ensures these functionally female flowers receive fertile pollen from male plants: bees bearing fertile pollen come to collect the sterile pollen, as all the flowers of this buzz-pollinated species are nectarless (Cane 1993).

8.1.3. Biogeographic and community patterns

Pollinators and forest strata. Monteverde's most common pollination system is pollination by small diverse insects (33% of the flora). It is also the most frequent pollination system for all plant life-forms. However, pollinator frequencies differ among the forest strata (Koptur et al. 1988; Table 8.1). In the understory, the frequencies of pollination by birds, butterflies, small bees, and bees are high compared to the whole flora. Lianas have relatively high incidences of pollination by beetles and large bees. Overall, Monteverde's upper strata (subcanopy and canopy trees) have a high frequency of pollination by small diverse insects, with pollination by hawkmoths, moths, and small bees also relatively high for trees. For large trees (258 species), pollination by small diverse insects

is especially high (48%), beetle pollination is rare (0.8%), and pollination by butterflies and birds is absent. Epiphytes (in the subcanopy and canopy), however, add hummingbird pollination to the upper strata (Table 8.1). La Selva's taller forest shows even more pronounced vertical stratification of pollination systems (Bawa 1992, Kress and Beach 1994, Kato 1996).

Pollinator effectiveness. The flowers of many plant species at Monteverde are visited by a wide variety of animals, and these may vary in their effectiveness as pollinators. Meticulous study is needed to demonstrate which among a variety of potential pollen transport agents is the most effective pollinator (Schemske and Horvitz 1984, Herrera 1987, Murawski 1987, Bawa 1994). Unspecialized flowers that are accessible to a variety of small diverse insects merit particular attention. Monteverde offers opportunities to test the underlying assumptions that (1) fewer pollinators are available at middle elevations, (2) a majority of a plant species' small flower visitors are able to effect pollination, and (3) most small insect flower visitors to such species are essentially interchangeable (Bawa 1994).

Effects of elevation: pollination of trees. Pollination system frequencies among trees apparently shift with elevation (Bawa 1990). Pollination of medium and large trees by small diverse insects and small bees is nearly twice as common in Monteverde (500 tree species examined) than at La Selva (125 tree species examined); (Kress and Beach 1994). Pollination by wind is nearly six times more frequent in Monteverde than in La Selva. Much lower in frequency is pollination by beetles, bats, and large bees. The two other neotropical montane forests studied to date resemble Monteverde in the importance of small diverse insects and small bees as pollinators of trees (Sobrevilla and Arroyo 1982, Tanner 1982). In Jamaica, fewer pollination systems occur, and pollination by wind is more pronounced, as expected for island trees (Tanner 1982).

Three factors could contribute to these elevational differences. First, as physical conditions change with elevation, so should the most effective pollinator type. At high elevations (2750–4000 m), pollination by birds is more frequent and more effective than pollination by bees and hawkmoths, probably because birds can be active in cloudy, rainy, cool conditions (Cruden 1972, Cruden et al. 1976). Monteverde's preponderance of pollination by small bees and small diverse insects that forage as generalists is explained in part by the windy, misty, cool, and unpredictable conditions (Koptur et al. 1988).

Second, floristic and life-form differences between low and mid-elevation sites could drive pollination system differences. For example, the frequencies of Lauraceae (most of which are pollinated by small diverse insects), Fagaceae (some wind pollinated, notably *Quercus* spp.), and Ericaceae (largely bird pollinated) are higher in montane forests, whereas Arecaceae (often beetle pollinated) and Fabaceae (often bee pollinated) decrease in importance in the cloud forest relative to lowland wet forests. Similarly, the incidence of epiphytes increases with elevation, many of which are visited by hummingbirds (Feinsinger et al. 1987; see Busby, "Hummingbird Pollination," pp. 267–268).

Third, elevational shifts in the abundance of different insect groups and in the frequencies of floral sexual systems (hermaphroditism, monoecy, and dioecy) and breeding systems (pollen compatibility; Sobrevilla and Arroyo 1982) could underlie shifts in the frequency of pollination systems. Increases in the frequency of dioecy, for example, might be accompanied by increases in the pollinator types associated with the small open flowers common in neotropical dioecious trees, or vice versa.

Disturbance and pollination interactions.   Natural disturbances occur at a variety of scales; communities are mosaics of patches that differ in age, structure, and species composition. How a forest's natural vegetation heterogeneity affects other components of community structure is poorly understood, particularly with respect to interactions among animals, or among animals and plants. Research in Monteverde directly addressed these questions (Feinsinger et al. 1987, 1988a, b, Linhart et al. 1987a, b). Hummingbird-plant pollination interactions were studied in three "patch" types that reflect the natural scales of disturbance: forest, treefall gaps, and larger gaps cut to mimic natural small landslides (Feinsinger et al. 1987).

Hummingbird-pollinated flowers were visited and pollinated similarly in the three patch types. Although larger gaps had higher densities of a few plant species, and more visits by flower-piercing birds, no evidence for significant disturbance-related variation in bird-plant interactions was found. Pollinators in disturbances were nearly as predictable, carried similar pollen loads, visited flowers of a given species at similar frequencies (with more variability in gaps), and deposited similar pollen loads as pollinators in the forest. The same patches were used to examine patterns of nectar availability and consumption of nectar by birds (Feinsinger et al. 1988b). They documented the availability and diversity of nectar, birds' use of and demand for nectar, and diet breadths and diet overlap. Some characteristics differed among the

patches but in different ways. Overall, responses to the natural disturbance mosaic were subtle, varied, and complex.

These studies of bird-plant interactions suggest a strong distinction between the effects of natural, small-scale disturbance and anthropogenic, large-scale disturbance on interactions, characteristics of populations, and community assemblages. Natural disturbance caused neither the large fluctuations in resource availability nor the shifts in species composition reported for large anthropogenic disturbances in Monteverde (Feinsinger 1976, 1978) or Trinidad and Tobago (Feinsinger et al. 1985). The studies also suggest caution in assuming that large-scale anthropogenic disturbances simply reflect natural disturbances at a larger scale.

8.1.4. Pollinator Sharing: The Plant Guild Perspective

Most plant species share pollinators. They may interact neutrally, compete, or facilitate one another's pollination; the outcome varies with local ecological conditions (Rathcke 1983). Experimental investigations of potential ecological and evolutionary outcomes of pollinator sharing have been based in Monteverde.

Neighborhood effects in bird-pollinated plants.   Building on detailed information about hummingbirds' interactions and guild structure (Feinsinger 1976, 1978), researchers led by Feinsinger examined plant-plant interactions and population and community patterns, providing one of the most comprehensive sets of observations and experiments on plant-plant interactions via pollinator sharing. One focus addressed how neighboring hummingbird-pollinated plant species affect each others' pollination success. Within each of the two bird-pollinated plant guilds, most plant species occur with guildmates and overlap in flowering period. Stigmatic pollen loads of four plant species were examined at several points in the flowering season, in different floral neighborhoods (Feinsinger et al. 1986). If neighbors affect pollination via competition for pollinator service, larger numbers of compatible grains should be delivered to stigmas in neighborhoods with higher densities of flowers of the same species, and lower numbers delivered when neighbors include other species. Pollinator-sharing did not have consistent competitive effects. Neighboring flowers had only sporadic effects on each others' pollination success. In the few instances in which there were effects, some were competitive and others were facilitative.

A mechanism for competition exists (Feinsinger

and Busby 1987, Feinsinger et al. 1988b). In a series of elegant indoor experiments that controlled the sequence in which a bird visited flowers of a single species (no pollinator-sharing) or of two species (pollinator-sharing), pollinator-sharing caused a decline in pollen dispersal and receipt. The mechanism is pollen loss; when a bird visits two species of flowers in a single foraging bout, pollen of one species can be lost to flowers of the other species. The same local effect of neighborhood can occur in the field but differs substantially in degree from one species to another (Feinsinger et al. 1991). Even though some guildmates can negatively affect others' pollination success, they may not exert strong selective pressure (Feinsinger et al. 1986, 1992). Monteverde's bird-pollinated plants do not consistently demonstrate the predicted links among competitive mechanisms, population effects, and community organization (Feinsinger and Tiebout 1991).

Character displacement: predictions and tests.   Plants that share pollinators have been thought to benefit from traits that reduce sharing. For example, plants might be under strong selective pressure to flower at different times, or to place pollen on different parts of their pollinators, especially if counterselection pressures are not strong. Their flowering periods or pollen would then be "displaced" from one another. The idea has come under lively debate (e.g., Poole and Rathcke 1979, Wheelwright 1985a), and research in Monteverde has contributed substantially to it.

Murray et al. (1987) showed that there is potential for competition via pollinator-sharing in the two guilds of shrubs and epiphytes that are pollinated by hummingbirds, because birds move among plant species as they forage, carry more than one species of pollen at a time, and can transfer pollen among species (essentially wasting pollen; Feinsinger et al. 1991). Despite the potential for competition, however, phenological displacement of flowering did not occur in either guild at Monteverde. Using long-term quantitative records of flowering periods and rigorous tests for phenological differences (*sensu* Poole and Ratchke 1979, Fleming and Partridge 1984), Murray et al. (1987) found no evidence of temporal organization. They also found no evidence of the alternative evolutionary divergence in pollen placement: fine-scale measurements of the length and positions of the flowers' female and male reproductive structures did not reveal greater morphological displacement among plant species with similar flowering seasons than among those with very different ones (Murray et al. 1987).

Why don't flowering phenologies and floral morphologies diverge? The reasons do not appear to include seasonal, fruiting, or phylogenetic constraints within these guilds. Although competition for pollination may occur (at the level of the local flower neighborhood), it is limited and sporadic (Feinsinger et al. 1986, 1992). Similar conclusions were drawn for 23 species of lauraceous trees that use the same birds as seed dispersers and may share some of their small insect pollinators (Wheelwright 1985b; see Wheelwright, "A Hypothesis," pp. 281–282). Flowering times are not displaced, and fruiting periods are aggregated rather than separated. These studies illustrate that sharing the services of dispersers does not necessarily result in phenological or morphological character displacement (Feinsinger 1987).

Phenological measurements on a fine scale can also be used to assess the potential for pollinator-sharing. Koptur (1983) documented temporal flowering patterns among individuals, populations, species, and of individual flowers in seven *Inga* (Fabaceae) tree species. Observations suggested significant pollinator-sharing, but fine-scale phenological measurements revealed that it was low. All three studies suggest that for guildmates, plant-plant competition via pollinator sharing cannot be assumed. Neither interactions nor phenological patterns can be studied as isolated phenomena, particularly in species-rich guilds characteristic of Monteverde.

8.1.5. Pollination Patterns

A plant's reproductive success depends in part on how many compatible pollen grains (per ovule) its stigmas accumulate. Inferring the size and purity of pollen loads from information such as frequency of visits by potential pollinators can be misleading. Furthermore, the notion that reproductive success is highly correlated with the size and purity of the pollen load received may be simplistic. Large numbers of compatible pollen grains may not always be optimal for pollination (Young and Young 1992), and some Monteverde species are unaffected by heterospecific grains mixed with compatible grains (S. Kinsman, unpubl. data). Documenting pollination limitation can be difficult and requires experimental techniques (Dafni 1992, Young and Young 1992, Kearns and Inouye 1993). The role of pollination limitation in a plant's reproductive success must be determined to pinpoint whether pollinator-sharing fosters competition or facilitation among plant species (Rathcke 1983, Feinsinger 1987).

Many plants' seed-set or fruit-set may be limited by pollination. If their pollinators delivered more (or more diverse) pollen, the plants could develop more (or genetically superior) seeds (Burd 1994). Pollination limitation of plant reproductive success may be especially common under montane climate conditions, if potential pollinators are less active (or less common) than at lower elevations. Low temperatures and mist may constrain flowering periods or reduce pollinator abundances or may alter the relative proportions of visitor species that differ in their effectiveness as pollinators. Altitudinal migrants or rare visitors may be especially important as pollinators of some plant species. Although related plant species have not been compared over an elevational gradient, some species in Monteverde are not well pollinated (Bronstein 1988a). For 10 species of hummingbird-pollinated plants, stigmatic pollen loads were used to calculate the number of compatible grains delivered per ovule. For only one species did pollinated flowers collect a substantial number of grains per ovule. For the other nine species, the majority of flowers were poorly pollinated (W. Busby and S. Kinsman, unpubl. data).

Even where pollinator activity is high, effective pollination can be rare. For two common mass-flowering self-incompatible *Inga* spp. (Fabaceae) trees at Monteverde, experimental pollinations were combined with detailed observations of pollinators and flowers to determine the frequency of highly effective pollination. Visitors to these trees are strong fliers (hummingbirds, hawkmoths, and skippers) and are able to move pollen over substantial distances, but they do so infrequently. Although visitation is high and half of the flowers receive pollen, relatively few receive the required outcross pollen (Koptur 1984a).

8.1.6. Research and Conservation: Plants' Mates

Population genetic consequences of pollen dispersal. Pollinators and seed dispersers help shape the mating patterns of plants (Hamrick et al. 1993). The potential for a plant's mates to be distant and diverse through pollen exchange is strongly influenced by pollinator populations and movement patterns. For conservation, it is critical to learn how pollinators influence genetic characteristics of plant populations. Flying pollinators that can move pollen relatively long distances are especially important in effecting gene flow (Hamrick and Loveless 1989). Bees, hawkmoths, and bats are strong fliers that can move many kilometers while foraging (Murawski 1995); traplining hummingbirds and Lepidoptera may also effect substantial gene flow. Knowing the role of these pollinators for Monteverde plants will help determine consequences of forest loss and fragmentation, declines in plant and pollinator populations, and changes in resources that support pollinators.

Tropical evidence. Many lowland tree populations appear to outcross frequently (Bawa et al. 1990), to maintain high levels of genetic variation, and to experience substantial gene flow (Hamrick and Loveless 1989, Hall et al. 1994, Murawski 1995, Chase et al. 1996). At La Selva, the great majority of trees require outcrossing (Kress and Beach 1994), and their animal pollen vectors (usually bees) import the required outcross pollen grains (Bawa 1974). On Barro Colorado Island, in Panama, 16 common species of shrubs and trees representing a variety of pollination systems and seed dispersal syndromes show high levels of genetic variation and substantial genetic exchange among populations (Hamrick and Loveless 1989). Less common trees at the same site show less genetic variation (Murawski 1995). Similar variation in Asian tropical forest trees are attributed in part to pollinator behavior (Murawski 1995).

Monteverde questions. We know little about gene flow, genetic variation, and the effectiveness of pollination for most plants in the Monteverde region (Koptur 1984a, Linhart et al. 1987a). The single Monteverde tree species that has been examined (Gibson and Wheelwright 1996; see Gibson, "Seed Dispersal," pp. 289–291) demonstrates gene flow. Effective plant population sizes may be different from those in the lowlands because the steep elevational gradient collapses suitable habitat. Altitudinal migrants (e.g., certain hummingbirds, butterflies, and hawkmoths) may provide occasional long-distance pollen movement, although studying the original patterns may now be impossible because most Pacific slope forest has been eliminated. Mating systems in reforestation windbreaks may not be characteristic if nursery-grown saplings were derived from seeds of one or a few parent trees.

It is critical to maintain the communities and ecosystems that support pollinators' and seed dispersers' travel over both short and long distances (see Williamson and Darling, "La Ventana," p. 438; Nielson and DeRosier, "Windbreaks and Birds," pp. 448–450; and Harvey, "Windbreaks and Trees," pp. 450–451 volume). Demonstration of plant gene flow patterns, especially over an elevational gradient, could provide strong arguments for integrated systems of reserves and corridors to support pollinator and seed disperser populations (see Chap. 12, Conservation Biology). Even individual plant species that occupy a restricted elevational range may have pollinators and seed dispersers that depend on wide-ranging resources (Bronstein 1995). Plant species in forest fragments are especially important to study (Hall et al. 1994, 1996, Boshier et al. 1995a, b, Chase et al. 1995), particularly those on the largely deforested Pacific slope. Their gene flow patterns have probably already been altered by loss of dispersers or mates via extirpation or insularization. Even if plant and pollinator populations persist in fragments for long periods of time, insularization may lead to altered mating and genetic structures, loss of variation, and inbreeding depression (*sensu* Bawa 1990). Studies of plant population structure and gene flow can improve conservation decision-making, help evaluate the need for corridors, and motivate local restoration of plant resources for pollen and seed dispersers (Murawski 1995).

8.2. Plant-Frugivore Interactions

8.2.1. Why Disperse Seeds?

The ubiquity of morphological characteristics associated with seed dispersal begs for an explanation of the advantages of moving seeds away from their source. Howe and Smallwood's (1982) "escape hypothesis" proposes that dispersal, even if directionally random, benefits plants by reducing density-dependent predation on seeds and seedlings and/or competition among seedlings (or between them and their parents) near the parent plant. The "colonization hypothesis" proposes that dispersal benefits plants by increasing the likelihood that some of their offspring will land in patches of suitable habitat, which occur unpredictably in space and time (e.g., treefall gaps). The "directed dispersal" hypothesis suggests that dispersal by certain animals results in nonrandom movement of seeds into particular sites where the probability of germination and establishment is high (e.g., dispersal by ants to refuse piles on rotting logs). These ideas are a useful framework for understanding plant-frugivore coevolution.

8.2.2. Who Eats What, Where, How, and Why

Just as plants can be categorized on the basis of their likely pollinators, ecologists group plants into broad "dispersal syndromes"—suites of characteristics (e.g., color, size, number and sizes of seeds, nutrient content, presence of a surrounding husk) associated with dispersal agents (van der Pijl 1969).

Dispersal syndromes: abiotic. *Wind dispersal* Successful dispersal by wind requires mechanisms to reduce the velocity with which a seed falls, so that lateral air movements will carry it farther from the source. One means is to greatly reduce seed size; the best examples of this reduction in Monteverde are among orchids, bromeliads, and begonias. Highly reduced seeds also occur in families that are typically

associated with animal dispersal, for example, *Centronia phlomoides* and *Monochaetum* spp. and other members of the Melastomataceae, the majority of which are dispersed by birds. Another way to reduce downward velocity is to enlarge some part of the seed coat or fruit to form a wing or plume that increases the surface area of the dispersal unit. In Monteverde, the best examples are herbs or epiphytes in the sunflower family (Asteraceae), for example, *Senecio* and *Neomirandea*. Some Monteverde trees also produce wind-dispersed seeds (e.g., *Roupala glaberrima* [Proteaceae], *Lonchocarpus* sp. [Fabaceae], and *Weinmannia* sp. [Cunoniaceae]).

Water dispersal Water-dispersed seeds generally have the ability to float for an extended period, due either to the high surface area-to-volume ratio of minute seeds or to a flotation device, for example, coconuts and mangroves. The only known native Monteverde example is *Heteranthera reniformis* (Pontederiaceae). Secondary dispersal (the further movement of seeds that have already been dispersed by other means) may occur via water for some species.

Ballistic dispersal Some plants produce fruits (often capsules) that "explode" when mature, throwing the seeds a short distance away. When mature, the fruit wall splits along one or more sutures, allowing part of the fruit wall to change shape rapidly and throw the seeds. Monteverde examples include the vine *Cyclanthera explodens* (Cucurbitaceae), the Pacific-slope tree *Hura crepitans* (Euphorbiaceae), the exotic herb *Impatiens walleriana* (Balsaminaceae), and most members of the family Acanthaceae.

Gravity dispersal or dispersal mechanism unknown In a small number of species, no apparent specialized structures exist for moving seeds away from the parent plant by either physical factors or animals. The seeds seem merely to fall from the plant. Further study of these plants may reveal a more effective means of dispersal, or the dispersal agent with which the plant evolved may be extinct, as with some common trees in Guanacaste Province (Janzen and Martin 1982, but see Howe 1985).

Dispersal syndromes: biotic. *Ants* Seeds adapted for dispersal by ants typically are small, and have an attached lipid-rich (sometimes starch-rich) body ("elaiosome") as a food reward to the ant. Such seeds are usually carried back to the nest where the elaiosome is removed and consumed. The seed itself is usually discarded on a refuse pile near the nest. Refuse piles are often prime seedling establishment sites, being free of other plants and rich in decaying organic material. *Langsdorffia hypogaea* (Balanophoraceae) is a Monteverde species that fits the ant dispersal syndrome. Seed-eating ants may sometimes act as secondary dispersers of seeds dispersed primarily by birds (Byrne and Levey 1993, Levey and Byrne 1993); their importance has not been investigated in Monteverde. Seed-eating ants appear to be considerably less dense in Monteverde than in the lowlands of Costa Rica (see Chap. 4, Insects and Spiders). There is a general paucity of ant-dispersed plant species in Monteverde; predation by ants on seeds in the leaf litter and soil appears to be lower than in other forests (K. G. Murray, unpubl. data).

Vertebrates Vertebrates disperse seeds by three methods: (1) caching and scatterboarding, (2) external adhesion, and (3) consumption. Plants adapted for dispersal by mammals and birds that store seeds for later consumption typically have no specialized structural features other than a thick protective seed coat. Most seeds are consumed later, but those whose locations are forgotten have usually been stored in protected sites where the probability of germination and survival is high. Seeds adapted for this form of dispersal (probably by Variegated Squirrels and Agoutis in Monteverde) include oaks and *Inga* spp.

Seeds adapted for dispersal by adhesion to the exteriors of animals usually have seed coats or other structures modified as hooks or spines that become stuck to a vertebrate's fur or feathers. In Monteverde, as in the temperate zone, the best examples are weedy members of the Fabaceae (e.g., *Desmodium* sp.) and Asteraceae (e.g., *Bidens pilosa*). More conspicuous examples in the MCFP are *Uncinia hamata* (Cyperaceae), which adheres via a bent floral bract, and *Pisonia* sp. (Nyctaginaceae), which has sticky glands.

Among plants adapted for dispersal in vertebrate guts, recognizable syndromes are associated with different animal groups. Fruits adapted for consumption by bats are usually pale yellow, green, or white in color, are often aromatic, and contain a reward rich in carbohydrates or lipids. Fruits eaten by nonflying mammals (primarily monkeys, but also carnivores such as Kinkajous and White-nosed Coatis) are usually a shade of green, brown, white, or yellow, are often aromatic, and often contained within a capsule or pod. Fruits eaten by birds typically are brightly colored, lack any obvious smell, and contain carbohydrates, lipids, and/or proteins as the major reward. Many are contained within capsules that open to reveal seeds with brightly colored arils (fleshy, nutrient-rich appendages that partially or entirely cover the seed). A subset of bird-dispersed plants bears fruits that contain relatively high concentrations of lipids and proteins and a single large seed, and are dispersed primarily by large frugivores such as toucans or Resplendent Quetzals.

Among the plant species that use bright colors to attract visually oriented foragers such as birds, certain fruit colors and combinations of colors are more common than others. Of the 252 species of "bird" fruits surveyed by Wheelwright and Janson (1985) in Monteverde, 41% were classified as "black" (including very dark blue and reddish black), 25% as "red" (including scarlet and pink), 11% as orange, 10% as white, 6% as "blue" (including violet and purple), 4% as "brown" (including dull dark red), 3% as yellow, and 1% as green. These proportions are consistent with those of fruits from forests in Manú National Park, Peru (Wheelwright and Janson 1985), south Florida (Long 1971), Europe (Turček 1963), and New Zealand and Australia (Willson et al. 1989). Many plant species in Monteverde, as elsewhere, combine fruit colors with strongly contrasting colors of unripe fruits, bracts, pedicels, or other accessory structures to produce more conspicuous displays (Fig. 8.2). Among such species, the combination of black and red is most frequent. This pattern occurs in 18% of all species at Monteverde, representing 21 plant families (Wheelwright and Janson 1985).

Elsewhere in the world, plants are adapted for dispersal by reptiles, fish, and land crabs, but we are

Figure 8.2. The showy fruits of *Heisteria acuminata* contain a disproportionately large seed and little pulp. Photograph by Nathaniel Wheelwright.

unaware of any representatives of these in Monteverde. Fruit-eating fish and large herbivorous lizards are absent from the area, probably due to topographic and climatic factors.

The distribution of dispersal syndromes of Monteverde plants. Dispersal syndromes of Monteverde plants are summarized in Figure 8.3 (Wheelwright et al. 1984, Bronstein and Hoffman 1987, Sargent 1994, K. G. Murray, unpubl. data, Appendix 1). In many cases, inferences are based on plant characteristics, rather than on direct observation of dispersal events. Dispersal agents for many species need investigation.

Comparison of the Monteverde flora with those at other neotropical sites is difficult because most studies provide data for only a subset of plants, usually trees (Howe and Smallwood 1982). Dispersal by animals is nearly as common among trees at Monteverde as at other neotropical wet forest sites. More than 81% of the tree species in Figure 8.3 appear to be adapted for consumption and dispersal by vertebrates, compared to 89% at Alto Yunda, Colombia (Hilty 1980), 92% at La Selva, Costa Rica (Frankie et al. 1974), and 92% at Río Palenque, Ecuador (Gentry 1982). As at the other sites, adaptation for dispersal by birds is

especially common, accounting for 80% of the animal-dispersed tree species at Monteverde and distributed widely among plant taxa. Adaptation for dispersal by bats is far less common among Monteverde plants, and is concentrated in a small number of taxa and growth forms, primarily shrubs (Piperaceae and Solanaceae) and vines (Araceae and Cyclanthaceae). We include few species in the "bird/bat" category because most fleshy-fruited plants fit into one or the other of the syndromes; studies focused on both birds and bats are needed (Fig. 8.3). Plants with obvious adaptations for dispersal by ants are uncommon in Monteverde, perhaps because the cool wet conditions are unfavorable for many of the seed-harvesting ant taxa responsible for dispersal at other sites (see Chap. 4, Insects and Spiders). This category does not include species with small seeds that are secondarily dispersed by ants.

Animal-dispersed species do not dominate all growth forms. A majority of epiphytes (66%) and herbs (73%) are adapted for dispersal by abiotic means, especially wind (Appendix 1). The domination of the epiphyte growth form by a single family, the Orchidaceae (>350 epiphytic species, all wind dispersed), however, obscures the importance of bird dispersal among epiphytes. Lianas and shrubs are intermediate between trees and herbs, with approximately 35–45% of species abiotically dispersed. That 35% of terrestrial herbs bear adaptations for wind dispersal is surprising, since wind dispersal is thought to predominate among plants whose fruits occur in the upper strata of the forest (Howe and Smallwood 1982). Most wind-dispersed terrestrial herbs at Monteverde belong to the Asteraceae, and many are weedy plants more characteristic of roadsides and river courses than of closed-canopy forest.

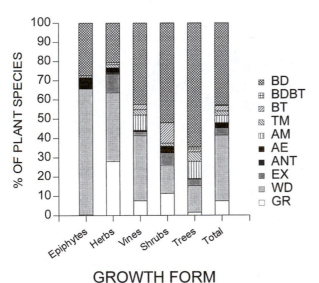

Figure 8.3. Frequencies (% of species) of dispersal systems of Monteverde flowering plants, by growth form. The graph includes native plant species for which Appendix 1 identifies or predicts the dispersal system. Category abbreviations: BD = bird; BDBT = bird/bat; BT = bat; TM = terrestrial mammals; AM = aboreal mammals; AE = animal exteriors; ANT = ant; EX = ballistic (explosive); WD = wind; and GR = gravity.

Fruit-handling techniques of Monteverde frugivores. Guilds of fruit-eating animals obtain and eat fruits in particular ways. Birds and bats may eat fruits while perched in the plant where they are produced, or they may carry the fruit some distance away before eating it. The latter behavior is especially common among bats. In Santa Rosa National Park, for example, *Carollia perspicillata* typically consume fruits at night roosts 30–40 m from their source trees (Heithaus and Fleming 1978). Birds also use different feeding techniques. Flycatchers, cotingas, thrushes, and Resplendent Quetzals typically take fruits on the wing via "sallying," whereas most tanagers and finches pluck fruits while perched. "Mashers" typically crush fruits in the bill after plucking them and then discard the fruit skin and most or all of the seeds before swallowing the remaining pulp; "gulpers" swallow fruits whole, ingesting the skin and all of the seeds (Levey

1986). Analogous spectra of feeding behaviors exist in bats and primates (Jordano 1992).

In Monteverde, the same dichotomy of fruit-handling behaviors occurs among birds that consumed fruits of three species of common "pioneer" plants (Murray 1986b, 1988). Fruits of these species were invariably ingested whole by Black-faced Solitaires, Prong-billed Barbets, and Black-and-yellow Silky-Flycatchers, with the result that seeds were widely dispersed. Common Bush-Tanagers, Spangle-cheeked Tanagers, and Yellow-thighed Finches fed on the same fruit species by mashing and failed to ingest most of the seeds; most were dropped near the parent plant, with little chance of landing in a treefall gap. Seeds ingested by the finch were destroyed in the gut (Murray 1988). Small tanagers are so proficient at separating seeds from pulp that they probably serve as dispersal agents only for plants with minute (<1 mm) seeds (e.g., Ericaceae, Melastomataceae, Gesneriaceae, some Rubiaceae). Visitors to the fig *Ficus pertusa* include small tanagers such as euphonias and Golden-browed Chlorophonias who mash fruits, dropping the seeds beneath the parent. Emerald Toucanets ingest them whole, probably dispersing them more widely (Bronstein and Hoffman 1987).

Diet breadths of animals, "disperser breadths" of plants, and the "specialization-generalization" paradigm. Two seminal papers on plant-frugivore coevolution (Snow 1971, McKey 1975) spawned many studies on plant-frugivore interactions. Most modern students of plant-frugivore interactions (including those at Monteverde) trace their interest to these or related papers (e.g., Howe and Primack 1975, Howe 1977). McKey (1975) proposed that the coevolutionary process led to the development of two groups of fruit-eating birds and fleshy-fruited plants. He defined specialized frugivores as those that derive most or all of their carbohydrates, proteins, and lipids from fruit and that possess the morphological and physiological adaptations that result in "high-quality" dispersal service to their food plants (e.g., reduction in the muscular wall of the stomach, reliability of visitation to fruiting plants, heavy dependence on fruits as a food source). The high-quality dispersal service they render favored the evolution of small crops of fruits with dense, firm flesh rich in proteins and lipids ("high-reward" fruits). Specialized frugivores are large and tend to swallow fruits whole, favoring the evolution of large fruits with single large seeds that cannot be consumed by small birds. Specialized frugivores and high-reward plants should interact intensively, each bird species deriving most of its food from a small set of food plants, and each high-reward plant relying on a small subset of the potential seed dispersers. In Monteverde, Re-

splendent Quetzals, Keel-billed Toucans, and many of their food plants, especially those in the avocado family (Lauraceae), are classic examples of specialized frugivores and their coevolved and specialized food plants under McKey's (1975) scheme.

McKey's "opportunistic" frugivores are those who use fruits primarily as a source of carbohydrates and/or water but rely on other foods as sources of lipids and proteins. Many are primarily insectivorous or are frugivorous as adults but feed insects to their nestlings. The great majority of fruit-eating birds fall into this category. Since they were thought to lack an intimate mutualistic relationship with particular plants, opportunistic frugivores would lack many of the adaptations that ensure the high-quality dispersal service rendered to plants by specialized frugivores. The plants that rely on opportunistic frugivores for seed dispersal must make their fruits available to as wide a variety of birds as possible, so such fruits are small, succulent, and carbohydrate-rich and contain numerous small seeds that can be swallowed even by small birds ("low-reward" fruits). Because they are small, such fruits can be produced in great abundance. Tanagers, finches, and thrushes at Monteverde are opportunistic frugivores, and most members of the Melastomataceae, Solanaceae, and Rubiaceae produce low-reward fruits.

Pollen dispersal and seed dispersal by animals were contrasted by Wheelwright and Orians (1982). They concluded that the expectation of tight coevolution of specialist frugivores and high-reward fruiting plants was largely misguided:

Plants benefit by directing pollen dispersers to a definite, recognizable "target," a conspecific flower, and they can provide incentives at flowers which serve to attract potential pollinators. In effect, there is "payment upon delivery" of the pollen. In contrast, for seeds the target (an appropriate site for germination and establishement) is seldom readily discernible, and dispersal beneath a conspecific plant may actually be undesirable. Another important difference is that frugivores are "paid in advance." (p. 410)

The key requirement for tight coevolution of highly specialized frugivores and high reward plants—consistently higher dispersal quality by dietary specialists than by generalists—is unlikely to occur. Instead, many different birds are likely to provide approximately similar dispersal quality to many plant species. Over time, the net result should not be tight coevolution but "diffuse" coevolution (*sensu* Janzen 1980), whereby many unrelated plants and dispersers converge on the same broad suites of fruit and feeding behavior characteristics. The feeding records for Monteverde (Wheelwright et al. 1984, Bronstein and Hoffman 1987, Wheelwright 1988a, Nadkarni and Matelson 1989) provide an example of how diffuse the interactions among plants and their dispersers are. Very few cases exist in which a plant has only one known disperser, or in which a particular bird species feeds on only one species of fruit (Jordano 1987).

In contrast to the "specialization-generalization" paradigm, Wheelwright (1985b) predicted that diet breadth in Monteverde birds would be proportional to gape width, because all birds could feed on smaller fruits whereas only large birds would have access to larger ones. Larger fruit-eating birds tend to feed on many different fruits (Wheelwright et al. 1984). The "winner" in terms of diet breadth is the Emerald Toucanet (gape 26 mm), with 95 food plants in the Monteverde area. The other large well-studied frugivores, Resplendent Quetzals (21 mm), Three-wattled Bellbirds (25 mm), and Black Guans (31 mm), ate 38, 29, and 26 species, respectively. Several smaller birds, including Long-tailed Manakins (8.5 mm), Mountain Robins (12 mm) and Black-faced Solitaires (11 mm), also have exceedingly broad diets, however (37, 44, and 51 species, respectively), so the positive correlation between bird size and number of fruit species eaten has many exceptions.

Counts of the number of fruit species eaten are inadequate estimators of the relative importance of different bird species in the community because they do not take into account the number of other birds that also provide dispersal service to particular plants. Black-faced Solitaires, for example, which consume many fruits that are also eaten by a wide variety of other species, are usually thought to be less important for maintaining the Monteverde plant community than are Resplendent Quetzals, whose (typically large-seeded) food plants probably support fewer alternative dispersers. However, small frugivores such as solitaires may be more important than some of the larger frugivores, due to their high abundance and broad diet (see Murray, "Importance," pp. 294–295).

Fruit size and shape.   Research on large fruits and their dispersers provides evidence of the effects of disperser morphology and behavior on the shape and upper size limit of seeds (Howe and Richter 1982, Wheelwright 1993). Although they can eat large fruits, quetzals, bellbirds, toucanets, and manakins are often unable to swallow the largest fruits that they pluck from plants (Wheelwright 1985a; Fig. 8.4). Birds often drop the largest fruits from a plant on the ground after trying unsuccessfully to swallow them. Presumably, the negative consequences of large fruit size and seed size

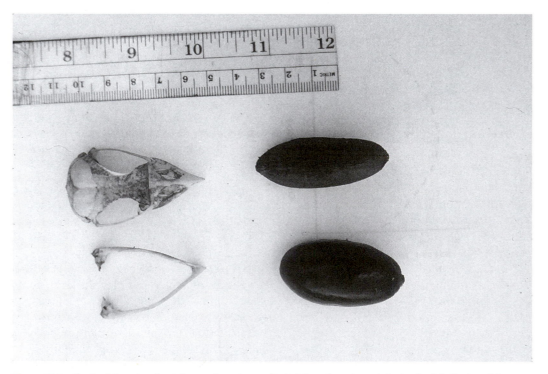

Figure 8.4. Skull of Resplendent Quetzal next to a fruit (above) and seed (below) of *Beilschmeidia brenesii,* one of the large-fruited species of Lauraceae that birds are able to swallow. Photograph by Nathaniel Wheelwright.

have led to allometric relationships (change in fruit shape as a function of size; Mazer and Wheelwright 1993). Both within and among individuals of *Ocotea tenera*, among the species of Lauraceae at Monteverde, and among a sample of 167 bird-dispersed plant species in diverse families, larger fruits are more elongated, whereas smaller ones tend to be more spherical (Fig. 8.5). The same relationship also exists for seeds, suggesting that the evolution of large fruit or seed size is accomplished by constraining diameter to facilitate consumption by birds while allowing length to increase.

Manipulation of disperser behavior and physiology by plants.   Plant-frugivore interactions in Monteverde also concern how plants enhance their reproductive success by influencing the behavior or physiology of fruit-eating animals.

Crop size   The plant characteristic most commonly examined for its effect on disperser behavior has been fruit crop size (Howe and De Steven 1979, Howe and Vande Kerckhove 1979, 1981, Moore and Willson 1982, Stapanian 1982, Davidar and Morton 1986). Large crops of ripe fruits should attract greater numbers of visually oriented dispersers such as birds, which disperse more seeds over a broader area. However, extremely large crops of ripe fruits may enable fruit-eating animals to remain within or near the crown of a fruiting plant for long periods of time and hence disperse the seeds ineffectively. These conflict-

ing selection pressures have led to the prediction that intermediate crop sizes would yield the highest reproductive success (Howe and Estabrook 1977).

Studies in Monteverde lend mixed support to this view. In eight species of Lauraceae, visit frequencies by large frugivorous birds were significantly higher at the four species that produced large crops of small fruits than at the four species producing smaller crops of large fruits (Wheelwright 1991). Because smaller fruits can be swallowed by a greater variety of bird species (Wheelwright 1985b), it is unclear whether the pattern observed derives from crop size, fruit size, or both. Similar comparisons within species, where the range in fruit size is smaller, should allow for a more robust test of the hypothesis. Fruit size can vary considerably even within species: mean fruit diameter in 46 *Ocotea tenera* plants varied from 1.55 to 2.25 cm (Wheelwright 1993). Variation in fruit size within species can also have consequences for reproductive success; in *O. tenera*, the proportion of a plant's fruit crop that was successfully removed by birds (rather than damaged by seed predators or ignored) was positively correlated with its mean fruit diameter (Wheelwright 1993).

Wheelwright (1991) also failed to find a positive relationship between crop size and visit duration predicted by some authors. Instead, birds generally spent only short periods of time (half of all visits were <4 min) in trees of all eight species of Lauraceae, regardless of crop size. Some quetzals remained in trees for

Figure 8.5. Seed size variation in *Ocotea tenera*. Photograph by Nathaniel Wheelwright.

up to an hour, and some toucanets stayed in the same tree for up to 4 hr, but such cases were rare. Visit lengths tended to be longer in large-fruited tree species, perhaps because larger fruits required longer processing times.

Murray (1987) found that the proportion of plants receiving at least some visits from frugivorous birds on a given day increased with increasing crop size in three species of pioneer plants (*Phytolacca rivinoides, Witheringia meiantha* [previously named *W. solanacea*], and *W. coccoloboides*). The absolute number of fruits removed per day increased over the whole range of crop sizes in all three species, but the proportion removed decreased (i.e., removal from plants with large fruit crops did not increase in direct proportion to crop size). There was no indication of a peak in visitation or removal rate at intermediate crop sizes, and because the "waste" of uneaten fruits from individuals with large fruit crops is unlikely to result in lower survival of adult plants in short-lived pioneers, the higher visitation and number of seeds dispersed at high crop sizes implied selection for synchronous fruit ripening (Murray 1987). Studies in Monteverde thus support the general prediction that fruit crop size influences the behavior of dispersers in a manner beneficial to plants although they provide only equivocal support in some particulars.

Chemical control of seed passage rates Plants may enhance their reproductive success by manipulating the treatment that their seeds receive in dispersers' guts. Using artificial fruits made with agar, sugar, and natural seeds and pulp extracts from *Witheringia meiantha* fruits, Murray et al. (1994) showed that some unidentified chemical(s) in the pulp increases the rate at which seeds pass through the gut of its major disperser, the Black-faced Solitaire. This chemical may serve to balance the consequences of seed passage through solitaire guts: rapidly passed seeds emerged in viable condition more frequently than did those spending longer periods of time in the gut, but they were also deposited nearer to the parent plant. Shorter dispersal distances are disadvantageous for pioneer plants because the probability of encountering a gap increases with dispersal distance (Murray 1988). This study was the first empirical evidence of a "laxative" agent in a wild fruit, other than high fiber content. Results might be explained by slight differences in the sugar concentrations of the experimental fruits rather than to laxative chemicals (Witmer 1996), but other data indicate that differences in sugar concentration are too small to produce the observed differences in seed passage rates (K. G. Murray, unpubl. data). Recent work by Wahaj et al. (1998) has shown the existence of a laxative chemical in the fruits of a related species (*Solanum americanum*), but

the chemical itself was not identified. More research is needed to identify the existence of laxative chemicals in *Witheringia* and other species, and to elucidate their roles in dispersal ecology.

Spatial and temporal patterns in plant-frugivore interactions at Monteverde. Plant-frugivore interactions vary in space and time; studies in Monteverde have focused on the causes and consequences of this variation.

Fruiting phenologies Most plant species at Monteverde have distinct fruiting seasons, but in a few cases individual plants are synchronous within crowns but highly asynchronous as a population (Wheelwright 1985a, Murray 1986a; see Bronstein, "Fig Pollination," pp. 271–273). In understory shrubs and treelets, community-level fruiting (the number of species fruiting, not the number of ripe fruits) is less distinctly seasonal than is flowering. Flowering peaks during the dry-wet season interface (April–June) each year, whereas fruiting tends to decrease generally and peak only weakly; small fruiting peaks occur at different times each year. The lower seasonality of fruiting may be because plants differ in the amount of time between flowering and fruit ripening. For example, flowering is highly synchronous in *Meliosma subcordata* (Sabiaceae) and most members of the Araliaceae. *Meliosma* ripens fruits over most of the following year, whereas most Araliaceae do so within a few months of flowering (Koptur et al. 1988). Fruiting at Monteverde is less seasonal than in the dry forests of Guanacaste, but more seasonal than in wet forest at La Selva, which may be related to precipitation. Drier sites tend to have more seasonal flowering and fruiting than wetter ones, and Monteverde is intermediate between Guanacaste and La Selva in annual rainfall (Frankie et al. 1974, Koptur et al. 1988).

Koptur et al. (1988) documented differences in fruiting phenology between the two years of their study. Heavy rains in the second year caused the flowers of many species to rot; fewer species set fruit. Some species of frugivores may have been adversely affected, as were the fruit-eating birds and mammals of Barro Colorado Island, Panama, following a weather-related fruiting failure there (Foster 1982). Many animal seed dispersers migrate altitudinally in response to food abundance, so understanding the periodicity and severity of fruit failures at Monteverde is a high research priority.

Wheelwright (see "A Hypothesis," pp. 281–282) hypothesized that flowering phenologies in lauraceous trees may be affected by competition for pollination, whereas fruiting phenologies may be constrained more by abiotic factors (e.g., rainfall). Similarly, Murray (1986a; see Murray, "Fruiting Phenologies," pp. 283–286) suggested that seasonal patterns of seedling survival in three species of pioneer plants might constrain fruiting phenology in these species more tightly than seasonal patterns of flowering, disperser abundance, or gap formation. Examining temporal constraints on seedling survival is a priority for future work.

Altitudinal migration of fruit-eating birds: causes and consequences Frugivore populations in Monteverde shift spatially. Striking examples are the pronounced seasonal migrations of Resplendent Quetzals and Three-wattled Bellbirds (see Chap. 6, Birds). Censuses of quetzals and their major food plants in the Monteverde area (1350–1550 m), revealed that the birds' movements tracked the ripening seasons of different species of food plants (Wheelwright 1983). Further work confirmed these patterns, but found considerable year-to-year variation in the timing and pattern of quetzal migratory behavior (Powell and Bjork 1995).

Another important Monteverde frugivore that migrates altitudinally is the Black-faced Solitaire (Fig. 6.4, Murray 1986a; see Murray, "Fruiting Phenologies," pp. 283–286). Solitaires leave the upper elevations of Monteverde and return at about the same time as quetzals (Murray 1986a). The details of their movements after they leave Monteverde are unclear; they have been sighted in the Peñas Blancas valley (L. Moreno, pers. comm.). Many solitaires and other species of small frugivorous birds leave the lower montane forest (1000 m) after the breeding season (September) and increase in abundance in the foothills (500 m) (Loiselle and Blake 1991). Solitaires occur down to 50 m at La Selva during the nonbreeding season. The timing of their altitudinal migration does not coincide with the general pattern of fruit availability at that elevation; solitaires move out of lower montane forests despite sharp increases in fruit availability.

Altitudinal migrations of seed dispersers probably have important consequences for the plants that depend on such animals. The predictable absence of such important dispersers as quetzals, bellbirds, and solitaires, even for a few months of the year, implies strong selection pressure on fruiting phenologies, especially in plant species that have few other dispersers.

Reproductive phenology of fruit-eating bats Events in the life histories of fruit-eating bats in Monteverde seem tied to the phenology of their food plants. The peak periods of lactation (the most energetically costly part of the breeding cycle) of two species of fruit-eating bats (*Sturnira ludovici* and *Artibeus toltecus*, Phyllostomidae) coincided with peaks in the abundance of their food plants (see Chap. 7, Mammals), which lends additional support to the idea that their breeding seasons have evolved to coincide with periods of maximum food availability (Dinerstein 1983, 1986).

8.2.3. Consequences of Dispersal for Reproductive Success in Monteverde Plants

Comparing the "quality" of dispersal by different animals necessitates knowing where the seeds go (the "seed shadows") and their fate. The three advantages of seed dispersal identified by Howe and Smallwood (1982)—the "escape," "colonization," and "directed dispersal" hypotheses)—provide a framework for studies of seed movement and its consequences.

Escape from density-dependent mortality: Lauraceae and other large-seeded primary forest species.   As in other neotropical forests, many of the dominant trees of primary forests in Monteverde produce large, single-seeded fruits adapted for consumption by large fruit-eating birds. Because the seeds of such species typically germinate within six weeks of deposition, regardless of the type of habitat in which they are deposited, escape from intense density-dependent predation near the parent is presumed to be the primary advantage of dispersal. Predation rates on large seeds are very high (Janzen 1971, Wheelwright 1988a), and the few detailed studies of distance and density effects demonstrate the positive consequences of dispersal (Clark and Clark 1984, Howe et al. 1985).

In Monteverde, large-seeded fruits adapted for dispersal by birds occur in many families (e.g., Myrtaceae, Sapotaceae, and Simaroubaceae), but the Lauraceae is conspicuous for its large number of species, its numerical importance among canopy and subcanopy trees, its lipid- and protein-rich fruit pulp, and its consequent importance to large fruit-eating birds. Although many species of Lauraceae produce fruit crops in the tens of thousands, fruit-eating birds such as Resplendent Quetzals, Emerald Toucanets, Three-wattled Bellbirds, and Mountain Robins do not merely remain sedentary in tree crowns, dropping seeds directly beneath them. Instead, birds typically leave trees after 3–5 min (Wheelwright 1991), separating the pulp from the seed in the gut and regurgitating the seed elsewhere. Because this internal processing takes an average of 30–40 min, the majority of lauraceous seeds leave the immediate vicinity of the parent tree. However, regurgitated seeds are commonly found beneath these same trees; they may be brought by birds from either conspecific trees nearby or from the same tree visited earlier. In either case, at least some seeds dispersed by birds are deposited in locations just as unfavorable as the area directly beneath their parent.

Seed dispersal by some of these same birds may vary markedly from season to season, sometimes resulting in highly clumped seed distributions away from the parent plant. During the breeding season, male bellbirds spend 80% of the day calling from one or a few display perches, making short foraging trips to nearby fruiting trees (Snow 1977). Most of the seeds they carry are deposited at very high density directly below the display perch, although far from the parent plant. To determine the consequences of such behavior for seed mortality, Wheelwright (1988a) scattered seeds of *Ocotea tonduzii* (ca. 20/m²) at 5-day intervals beneath three bellbird perches and at randomly chosen sites about 20 m from each of the three perches. Removal (and, presumably, mortality) of seeds beneath perches was 100% in every trial, presumably because seed-eating mammals were visiting the areas beneath the perches regularly in anticipation of the seeds dropped by displaying male bellbirds. Seeds only 20 m away went undiscovered by seed predators until the fourth trial, after which 100% were removed by animals who had habituated to the artificially created seed cache. Areas beneath the display perches of male Long-tailed Manakins also collect large numbers of seeds during the breeding season (Wheelwright 1988a, N. Wheelwright and D. McDonald, unpubl. data). The spatial distribution of seeds dispersed by nonbreeding individuals of these bird species has not been measured, but they are probably spread more widely, and thus have a greater chance of escape from predators.

Only two studies have directly measured the predation rates suffered by large seeds at the lower densities typically produced by most dispersers at Monteverde. To understand the benefits of dispersal via both reduced seed density and distance from seed source, seeds of *Nectandra davidsoniana* (Lauraceae) were placed at different densities (clumped vs. dispersed) and at distances from 0 to more than 30 m from conspecific fruiting trees in forested tracts within the Monteverde community. Contrary to expectation, no significant density or distance effects were observed because virtually all of the 520 seeds were removed within 24 hr (chiefly by the Spiny Pocket Mouse), and none survived more than 4 days (Wheelwright 1988a).

A study of rodent predation documented that effects can be severe even on dispersed, low-density seeds in some species (see Wenny, "What Happens," pp. 286–287). Dispersal benefits most large-seeded species by removing them from zones of predictably high predation beneath fruiting trees. However, the effects of consumption by frugivores can vary widely with disperser species, habitat, and season. Research is needed to understand the fitness consequences of dispersal for large-seeded plants.

Colonization of patchily distributed habitats by pioneer plants. Howe and Smallwood's (1982) "colonization hypothesis" provided the framework for studies on three species of pioneer plants in the MCFP (Murray 1986a, b, 1988). *Phytolacca rivinoides* (Phytolaccaceae), *Witheringia meiantha,* and *W. coccoloboides* (Solanaceae; Fig. 8.6) establish only in the high light environment of recently formed canopy gaps. Because such gaps occur at Monteverde at a rate of only 1.5% of land area per year, colonization sites for pioneers are rare and spatially unpredictable. To understand the consequences of dispersal by different species of birds for plant fitness, Murray (1988) compared the seed shadows produced by birds with the spatial and temporal distributions of suitable germination sites. The probability of germination varies as a function of gap size and age in the three plant species. *Phytolacca rivinoides*, for example, requires larger, younger gaps than does *W. meiantha* to stimulate germination.

The three most important dispersers of the plants (Black-faced Solitaires, Black-and-yellow Silky Fly-

Figure 8.6. Fruits of *Witheringia coccoloboides*. Photograph by Nathaniel Wheelwright.

catchers, and Prong-billed Barbets) deposit most seeds within 50–60 m of parent plants, although all are capable of moving seeds several hundreds of meters from their source. Based on a computer model that combines data on seed shadows, germination requirements, and rates of gap formation, dispersal by any of the three bird species results in a 16–36-fold increase in potential lifetime reproductive output (total number of surviving offspring produced by the plants) over the case of no dispersal. Differences in potential reproductive output associated with dispersal by the three bird species were estimated to be minimal (Murray 1988).

Another form of seed "dispersal" is important for these pioneer plants—dispersal in time. Although seeds of the three species normally fail to germinate in the shady forest understory, where most are deposited by birds, they do not die. Their seeds can remain dormant on or in the soil, germinating later if and when a gap forms overhead. The physiological mechanisms that allow such enforced seed dormancy include responses to soil temperature fluctuations and sensitivity to spectral characteristics of light, both of which differ between gap and understory habitats (Vazquez-Yanes and Orozco-Segovia 1984). When dispersal in time via seed dormancy was incorporated into the model, reproductive output of all three plant species was greatly increased. With the ability to remain dormant in the soil for just 2 years, for example, plants could potentially produce 11–16 times as many offspring as those with no capacity for enforced seed dormancy. Plants whose seeds can remain dormant up to 40 years can produce up to 611 times as many offspring (Murray 1988).

These estimates of reproductive output did not include the effects of seed mortality. The rates at which otherwise viable seeds are removed from the soil have important effects on the consequences of dispersal by different birds. This work supports Howe and Smallwood's (1982) "colonization hypothesis," as it demonstrates how seed dispersal enhances plant fitness via colonization of discrete patches of habitat that occur unpredictably in space.

Colonization of host trees by mistletoes. Most mistletoes are obligate parasites that colonize only a narrow range of host plant species. Moreover, their seedlings can establish only on a subset of the branches of host plants (see Sargent, "Specialized Seed Dispersal," pp. 288–289). Mistletoes also provide an opportunity to understand the consequences of dispersal by different animals: species more likely to frequent suitable host plants, and those that use the "correct" deposition behavior (wiping the sticky, viscin-coated seeds onto a branch or twig surface), are more likely to effect successful mistletoe reproduction.

Twelve species of mistletoes were investigated by Sargent (1994; see Sargent, "Mistletoes," pp. 81–82; "An Exceptional Mistletoe," p. 82; and "Specialized Seed Dispersal," pp. 288–289) in Monteverde. They include members of three families (Viscaceae, Loranthaceae, and Eremolepidaceae) that parasitize a variety of host species. One mistletoe, *Phoradendron robustissimum* (Viscaceae), has a narrow host range (nearly obligate on the pioneer tree *Sapium glandulosum*), which made it possible to census all individuals over a broad area (*S. glandulosum* occurs almost exclusively in pastures). The movement patterns of dispersers and the seed deposition patterns they were likely to produce were examined as a function of fruit abundance at three spatial scales (see Sargent, "Mistletoes," pp. 81–82). Although the tanagers that consume *P. robustissimum* fruits moved many seeds over considerable distances, none provided highly efficient, directed dispersal service. They failed to perch preferentially in the appropriate host species, and they spent the greatest proportion of their time perched in mistletoe plants themselves, where the seeds would be unable to grow if deposited. This work suggests that Howe and Smallwood's (1982) "colonization hypothesis" is a better model for understanding the advantages of bird dispersal of mistletoe seeds than is the "directed dispersal hypothesis." As with the pioneer plants studied by Murray (1988), birds transport seeds of mistletoes for considerable distances but do not appear to deposit them preferentially in favorable sites for establishment.

Other potential cases of directed dispersal. Habitat preferences among other fruit-eating animals might form the basis for nonrandom seed dispersal to particular habitats. The clearest demonstration to date is Wenny and Levey's (1998) work on dispersal of *Ocotea endresiana* (Lauraceae) by male Three-wattled Bellbirds at Monteverde. During the breeding season, these birds deposit most of the seeds they carry beneath the courtship display perches where they spend most of their time. Wenny and Levey show that male bellbirds preferentially locate their perches on the edges of canopy gaps, and that survivorship of *O. endresiana* seedlings is higher in gaps (due to lower fungal attack) than at randomly chosen sites in the forest understory. As a result, seedling survival was higher for seeds dispersed by male bellbirds than for those dispersed by other species.

Pioneer plants also might be dispersed preferentially to treefall gaps if their dispersers prefer to feed in such patches (Willson et al. 1982). Evidence for such preferences has been mixed (Schemske and Brokaw 1981, Hoppes 1987, Wunderle et al. 1987, Levey 1988, Loiselle et al. 1996). In Monteverde, no evidence for gap preference among understory fruit-eating birds exists (Murray 1988). The Black-faced Solitaire shows a significant preference for forest understory, not gaps. Even though the solitaire is the primary dispersal agent for many pioneers (based on mist-netting records and analysis of several hundred fecal specimens; Murray 1988 and unpubl. data; see Murray, "Importance," pp. 294–295), its diet is so broad that its most important food sources (subcanopy trees and epiphytes) are most dense outside of gaps. As a result, most of the seeds dispersed by solitaires are probably deposited beneath closed canopy, rather than in gaps. Clearly, the degree to which fine-scale habitat preferences influence seed dispersal patterns remains unresolved.

8.2.4. Population Genetic Consequences of Seed Dispersal

Seed dispersal also accomplishes gene flow. A single seed successfully dispersed several hundreds of meters may result in significant gene flow between semi-isolated subpopulations. The only direct measurements of genetic population structure among plants at Monteverde are for *Ocotea tenera* (Lauraceae; Gibson 1995, Gibson and Wheelwright 1995, 1996; see Gibson, "Seed Dispersal," pp. 289–291). Significant genetic differences exist among subpopulations in remnant and second growth forest patches. Because most saplings within subpopulations were not offspring of trees within the same subpopulation, and because subpopulations always contained more than one sibling group, seed dispersal in this species was considered extensive (Gibson and Wheelwright 1995). These findings are consistent with large fruit-eating birds regurgitating several seeds from plants of one subpopulation while visiting fruiting plants in a different subpopulation. These studies illustrate the potential for linking data on seed dispersal to genetic population structure. Work on *O. tenera* was conducted in a landscape dominated by human-altered habitats. Understanding how animal foraging behavior, seed dispersal, and plant genetic structure are influenced by the patchiness of a pasture-forest matrix awaits comparative studies in the pristine forests of the area.

8.2.5. Insights into Plant-Frugivore Coevolution Gained via Studies at Monteverde: What Next?

Studies in Monteverde have added to our knowledge of plant-frugivore interactions, but much remains to be done. One of the most critical needs is to clarify the nature of the coevolutionary relationships be-

tween plants and frugivorous animals (Howe 1993). Because the fitness consequences to plants of fruit consumption by different animals lie at the heart of those evolutionary relationships, studies that focus on both animal foraging ecology (where seeds go) and plant demography (what happens to them as a result of going there) are needed. Quantitative estimates of vertebrate-generated seed shadows are needed to discern systematic differences among dispersers and to understand the spatial scale on which to conduct studies of the demographic consequences of dispersal. Studies of density- and distance-related effects on seed predation (virtually unstudied at Monteverde for small seeds) and pathogen attack rates (unstudied at Monteverde, but see Augspurger 1983a, b) are also needed.

Research on dispersal consequences should also include the ecophysiology of seedlings, especially in pioneer species and mistletoes with restrictive habitat requirements. For some species, seedling physiology may explain the evolution of fruit ripening phenology (see Wheelwright, "A Hypothesis," pp. 281–283, and Murray, "Fruiting Phenologies," pp. 283–286). Studies on the demographic consequences of different seed dispersal patterns will help develop effective conservation strategies because some dispersers are more effective than others. We are currently restricted to simplistic criteria (e.g., counts of fruit species eaten, proportion of fruits removed) by which to assess the relative importance of different dispersers.

Research on the population biology of important Monteverde frugivores is needed. Detailed studies of Resplendent Quetzals (Wheelwright 1983, Powell and Bjork 1995) have been valuable in documenting how an important frugivore interacts with its food plants and the complexities of preserving it. Many other frugivores are as crucial to the Monteverde ecosystem as quetzals, yet we know virtually nothing of their population biology. No one has even attempted to assess population densities or home range sizes; for some species, we are ignorant about basic breeding biology. For example, the first active nest of the Three-wattled Bellbird—one of Monteverde's most important large frugivorous birds—was found as recently as 1992 (G. Powell, pers. comm.).

Understanding Monteverde's frugivores and their food plants at the community level is also needed. Current data are limited to qualitative feeding records (see Murray, "Importance," pp. 294–295). Quantitative estimates of the proportions of fruit crops dispersed by each frugivore species would provide more informed estimates of the relative importance of each frugivore at the community level, which would enhance conservation efforts. The roles of nonnutritional fruit chemicals and their roles in the plant-disperser interaction need research. Chemical manipulation of seed passage rate is now known from two studies. The possibility that secondary chemicals in fruits might have other pharmacological effects (e.g., antiparasitic) has not been investigated.

There is still a great need for general comparisons of Monteverde plant-frugivore communities to those at other sites to identify similarities or differences between communities derived from their climate, evolutionary history, or anthropogenic manipulations. Studies that integrate the areas of pollination and seed dispersal will be particularly useful. Understanding these interactions is critical for their management in an increasingly fragmented landscape. Of equal importance are plant-animal interactions other than pollination and seed dispersal

mutualisms, areas which are virtually unexplored in Monteverde. One very common type of mutualism in tropical habitats occurs between plants and ants: ants protect the plants from herbivores and receive food and sometimes shelter in return (Schupp and Feener 1991, Rico-Gray 1993, Fonseca and Ganade 1996; see Longino, "Myrmecophytes," pp. 291–293). Little work has been conducted on ant-plant mutualisms in Monteverde or on herbivory, seed predation, and other antagonistic plant-animal interactions (see the following essays by Koptur, Weiss, Wenny, and Longino). These interactions have demographic and genetic consequences for plant and animal populations at the population, community, and regional level.

HUMMINGBIRD POLLINATION OF EPIPHYTIC ERICACEAE IN THE CLOUD FOREST CANOPY
William H. Busby

In Monteverde, members of the Ericaceae (blueberry family) are conspicuous epiphytes, with their shrublike growth form, abundant displays of showy flowers, and fleshy, bird-dispersed fruits. Most of the 15–20 species in Monteverde occur in the wet, upper elevation forests of the MCFP. I studied the pollination ecology of nine species of canopy-dwelling Ericaceae in the preserve to determine floral biology, nectar secretion and sugar ratios, and flower visitors. As part of a larger project (Feinsinger et al. 1987), my colleagues and I examined hummingbirds captured in mist nets to determine which types of pollen were carried by birds.

The floral biology of all but one species indicated adaptations for pollination by hummingbirds (Table 8.2). Most flowers have red, purple, and white tubular corollas oriented at a downward angle. Nectar of moderate concentration (14–22% sugar) is produced during the day. As with most species adapted for hummingbird pollination (Baker and Baker 1979), the dominant sugar in the nectar is sucrose. The exception is *Vaccinium poasanum*, which has greenish white, bell-shaped flowers displayed in pendant clusters that produce nectar composed largely of glucose and fructose. This species was occasionally visited by short-billed hummingbirds, but the most frequent visitors (and presumed pollinators) were bumblebees (*Bombus* spp.).

Seven species of ericads with short tubular corollas were visited by three species of hummingbirds with short bills: Coppery-headed Emerald (very short, slightly decurved bill), Purple-throated Mountain-

gem (short, straight bill), and Fiery-throated Hummingbird (short, straight bill). The Coppery-headed Emerald, a seasonal short-billed visitor that forages in the canopy, visited only the two ericads with the shortest corollas, *Cavendishia complectans* and *C. capitulata*. In contrast, the Purple-throated Mountain-gem, the most conspicuous hummingbird in the MCFP and a year-round resident, was the most frequent visitor to short-corolla flowers and was observed visiting all but one of the short-corolla species. The Fiery-throated Hummingbird is found at higher elevations in the preserve, where it defends rich floral resources (three of the seven species) in the canopy. The Purple-throated Mountain-gem and Fiery-throated Hummingbird are probably able to extract nectar from all short-corolla ericads. However, some species of ericads and hummingbirds occupy narrow elevational and environmental ranges, and not all ericads overlap with all hummingbird species.

The long flowers of *Psammisia ramiflora* were visited by a different set of hummingbirds. The principal flower visitor was the Green-fronted Lancebill, a hummingbird with a long (34.4 mm) straight bill. *Psammisia ramiflora* has long pendent corollas that require pollinators to hover beneath the flowers, probing vertically upward to reach the nectary. Other hummingbirds, particularly the Green Hermit, occasionally visit *Psammisia ramiflora* flowers and may pollinate them, but only the Green-fronted Lancebill appears able to extract nectar efficiently. Analysis of pollen on the bills and heads of five hummingbird species revealed that all frequently carry ericad pollen. Pol-

Table 8.2. Flower measurements, nectar production and sugar ratios [sucrose/(glucose + fructose)], and flower visitors for nine species of Ericaceae in the Monteverde cloud forest.

Species Visitor(s)	Corolla Length in mm (N)	Mean Daily Nectar Production (µl)	S/(G + F)	Principal Flower Visitor(s)
Cavendishia complectans	11.1 ± 0.8 (21)	11.5	1.04	*Elvira, Lampornis*
Cavendishia capitulata	15.8 ± 0.8 (25)	7.0	2.53	*Elvira, Lampornis*
Cavendishia bracteata	19.1 ± 1.6 (52)	28.9	2.19	*Lampornis, Panterpe*
Cavendishia melastomoides	18.6 ± 2.7 (24)	13.7	1.41	*Lampornis*
Cavendishia lactiviscida	25.9 ± 2.0 (18)	—	—	*Lampornis*
Vaccinium poasanum	12.6 ± 0.7 (12)	24.3	0.07	*Bombus*
Satyria warszewiczii	18.6 ± 1.1 (36)	7.5	1.24	*Lampornis, Panterpe*
Gonocalyx pterocarpus	19.5 ± 1.7 (33)	—	—	*Panterpe*
Psammisia ramiflora	32.7 ± 2.3 (40)	21.0	2.64	*Doryfera*

len loads on the Purple-throated Mountain-gem, Fiery-throated Hummingbird, and Green-fronted Lancebill averaged over 800 tetrads (packages of four pollen grains) per bird, whereas the Coppery-headed Emerald and Green Hermit averaged <10 tetrads per bird, suggesting the first three species play more important roles as pollinators of Ericaceae than the Coppery-headed Emerald and Green Hermit.

There are two ecological groups of hummingbirds and bird-pollinated plants (including Ericaceae) in Monteverde: plants with short to medium-length flowers pollinated by several short-billed hummingbirds, and plants with long, straight flowers primarily pollinated by a bird that possesses a correspondingly shaped bill. Among short-flower ericads, the size of a plant's floral display determines to a large extent which hummingbirds visit its flowers. Plants that produce few flowers tend to attract nonterritorial hummingbirds (e.g., female mountain-gems). Large floral displays, such as produced by *Satyria warszewiczii* and *Cavendishia bracteata*, attract territorial hummingbirds (e.g., Fiery-throated Hummingbirds and male mountain-gems). Short-flower ericads are part of a larger plant-pollinator association in the Monteverde cloud forest, comprising at least 20 species of hummingbird-pollinated plants in the canopy and understory that are visited by five species of short-billed hummingbirds (Feinsinger et al. 1986, 1987).

In contrast, the long-flower subcommunity is poorly represented in Monteverde compared to adjoining areas on the Caribbean slope. At a mid-elevation forest site in the Cordillera Central, Stiles (1985) studied other epiphytic species with long flowers visited by the Green-footed Lancebill. This canopy subcommunity appears distinct from the well-documented association between plants with long decurved flowers found mostly in the forest understory that are pollinated by hummingbirds with similarly shaped bills, such as the Green Hermit in the MCFP (Feinsinger et al. 1986, 1987) and other hermit hummingbirds elsewhere in the neotropics (Snow and Snow 1972, Stiles 1975).

This study raises a series of questions: To what extent are canopy plants adapted for pollination by hummingbirds? How are hummingbirds and bird-pollinated ericads affected by the rich nectar resources provided by insect-pollinated plants in the canopy? Such rich nectar resources are highly attractive to hummingbirds. Does this occur at the expense of visitation to bird-pollinated species or does it simply provide a larger pool of potential pollinators? The low height of the cloud forest canopy makes Monteverde a favorable site to address questions about pollination in epiphytes.

SCARAB BEETLES, ELEPHANT EAR (*XANTHOSOMA ROBUSTUM*), AND THEIR ASSOCIATES
Lloyd Goldwasser

The pollination of *Xanthosoma robustum* ("elephant ear" or "pata") by scarab beetles involves a spectacular coordination of intense metabolic heating by the plants with the flights of scarab beetles. Although floral heating in Araceae has been known since the time of Lamarck (1778), Monteverde is one of few places where the connections between the heating and the ecological relationships of these species have been documented. *Xanthosoma robustum* is self-standing, as tall as an adult human, and has up to four leaves, each of which may be 1 m in length and width. It is considered a weed by Monteverde residents, for it grows quickly in damp sunny areas such as pastures. In the early 1980s, the overgrown pastures at the head of the Peñas Blancas valley contained large patches of hundreds of *Xanthosoma*, but trees have now grown over them and only a few remain. The small isolated patches at higher elevations within Monteverde are fairly typical of its original distribution. The inflorescence, a characteristic feature of the family Araceae (aroids), consists of two parts: the spathe, a modified leaf that covers the inflorescence as it develops, and the spadix, a spongy stalk covered by flowers (Fig. 8.7). In *Xanthosoma*, the male flowers on the top of the spadix and the female flowers below these are separated by a ring of sterile flowers. The lower part of the spathe encloses the female flowers, forming a chamber. A flowering individual annually produces 5–15 inflorescences, spaced about 9 days apart. Flowering occurs primarily during the rainy season.

Two species of scarab beetles (Scarabaeidae: Coleoptera) visit *Xanthosoma* in Monteverde; both belong to the genus *Cyclocephela* and are similar in size (ca. 2.5 cm) and behavior. *Cyclocephela nigerrima* is nearly black, and *C. sexpunctata* is light brown with dark spots. In Peñas Blancas, *C. sexpunctata* outnumbers *C. nigerrima* by 2 to 1; within Monteverde, the

relative abundance is reversed and the ratio is about 1 to 20.

On the first day a *Xanthosoma* inflorescence opens, its spadix begins to heat up intensely around 1800 hr (Fig. 8.8). The heat volatilizes a fresh, slightly sweet odor that is easily detected by humans and scarabs from a distance. The temperature peaks at 40–42°C, much hotter than both the air temperature (about 18°C) or human body temperature (37°C); the scarabs then begin to arrive. Their buzz as they hover and land can be loud in the gathering twilight. The scarabs land on the spathe and descend to the chamber, where they remain for 24 hr except for occasional forays up the spadix. The pollen they carry comes off into a sticky orange secretion on the surface of the receptive female flowers. The scarabs eat the ring of sterile flowers. Meanwhile, the spadix cools to the temperature of the night air.

Over the next day, the scarabs mate and consume nectar within the inflorescence. The number of scarabs in an inflorescence of *Xanthosoma robustum* at Monteverde is typically around 7; the most I have seen in one inflorescence was 38. Late during the second afternoon, the inflorescence begins to heat again (Fig. 8.8). This time, the temperature peaks around 34°C; the male flowers release their pollen. The scarabs mill about, crawling up the spadix and becoming covered with pollen, and then fly off to a newly opened inflorescence where the sequence repeats.

During the next few days, the top of the inflorescence (the part with male flowers) rots and falls away. The bottom of the inflorescence (with the lower part of the spathe enclosing the female flowers) remains intact and matures for the next two months. When the fruit is ripe, the spathe splits open and peels back to reveal a ripe "cob" of about 300 soft green fruits with 20–30 seeds each. Bats appear to be their primary consumers and dispersers, biting away fruits as they fly past. Many bats prefer *Xanthosoma* fruit over other foods. Seeds take about half an hour to pass through the bats' guts, which is long enough for dispersal to occur throughout the forest (E. Dinerstein, pers. comm.).

The cue for heating in aroids is light. In *Sauromatum* and *Dracunculus*, a flash of light at a critical time initiates heating as much as several days later (Chen and Meeuse 1972, Meeuse 1975). The chemical mediator is salicylic acid (Raskin et al. 1987), and the sequence, once initiated, runs its course regardless of perturbations. The peak temperature in *Philodendron* is remarkably constant over a 35°C range of ambient temperatures, a feat that at lower temperatures requires metabolic rates in excess of those of hummingbird flight muscles (Nagy et al. 1972). Using a refrigerator as an impromptu cooling chamber, I

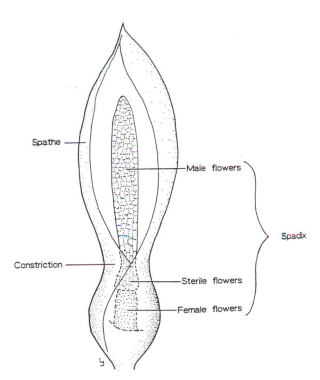

Figure 8.7. An inflorescence of *Xanthosoma robustum*. The upper part of the spathe is white, and the lower part is purple or green. The entire structure is 20–30 cm tall.

Spathe

Male flowers

Spadix

Constriction

Sterile flowers

Female flowers

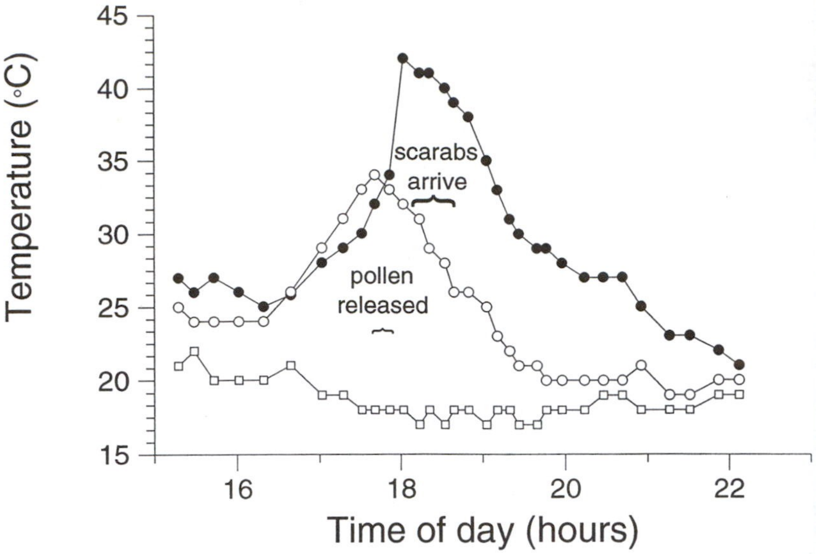

Figure 8.8. Heating of *Xanthosoma robustum* inflorescences (solid circles); open circles show an inflorescence on its second evening; squares show the ambient temperature. Also indicated are the approximate times at which scarabs began arriving at the newly opened inflorescence and at which the second-night inflorescence released its pollen.

found that *Xanthosoma robustum* peaks around 40°C even when the ambient temperature is as low as 8°C. However, after reaching its peak, the inflorescence cooled more rapidly in the refrigerator than at normal air temperatures. These inflorescences had been cut from the plant several hours earlier, but neither the timing of heating nor the temperature reached was affected.

A marking technique that allowed individual identification of each recaptured scarab (Goldwasser et al. 1993) showed that few scarabs move to the nearest available inflorescence; most fly to more distant inflorescences, passing over eligible ones nearby. This tends to maximize outcrossing and enhance gene flow. However, in three years of marking and recapturing scarabs on both sides of the Continental Divide, I never found a scarab on one side that had been marked on the other. These scarabs visit other aroids besides *Xanthosoma robustum*; individuals may switch among it, *Syngonium* sp., and *Philodendron* sp. from one night to the next. This lack of host specificity would reduce the efficiency of pollination.

Three other types of visitors are associated with this pollination system: (1) "interlopers," which exploit the interaction to the detriment of the aroid or scarabs (Goldwasser 1987); (2) predators, which consume other visitors to the inflorescences; and (3) commensal species, which have little effect on the other species. Interlopers include mites of the family Macrochelidae, which are present at any inflorescence that has scarabs. The mites ride from one plant to the next, 20–30 of them on a single scarab. Between rides, the mites drink nectar inside the chamber. Sucking bugs of the family Miridae are consistent visitors to the inflorescences of many aroids and sit on the soft parts

of the spathe, sucking plant juices. The mirids also reproduce on the inflorescences; in Monteverde, about a third of the three dozen individuals typically present are nymphs. Single females of some species of flies arrive at newly opening inflorescences before other visitors arrive, walk around laying eggs, and leave. The larvae grow inside the inflorescence without causing evident damage, but then emerge as adults by tunneling out and leaving holes in the spathe that may increase the vulnerability of the developing fruits to attack by fungus or animals (Madison 1979).

Spiders are the most striking of the predators at aroid inflorescences. They are uncommon visitors to *Xanthosoma robustum*, but deter or remove other visitors so that inflorescences at which a spider is present tend to be bare and free of damage. Other predators include adult and larval staphylinids (rove beetles) and the predatory larvae of syrphids (hover flies). The syrphid larvae remain on the same plant between flowerings and crawl up to each successive inflorescence when it opens, growing larger each time.

Many other species seem to be commensal, including small wasps, drosophilids and other flies, earwigs, thrips, and psocids (lice). Several dozen drosophilids typically sit on the upper part of the spathe; earwigs, thrips, and psocids stay inconspicuously down in the chamber and may feed on detritus. The consistent presence of nonpollinating visitors at aroid inflorescences in Monteverde and elsewhere, and the involvement of several life stages for many of them suggest that some may be specific in their choice of aroids. The pollination interaction between scarabs and aroids provides resources that some species exploit directly and a consistent setting for interacting with other species. The number and variety of visitors reflect the extravagance with which *Xanthosoma robustum* advertises its inflorescences; that extravagance reflects the importance of attracting pollinators among patches that are transient and separated by dense forest.

Acknowledgments I acknowledge with gratitude permission to study aroids on land owned by Bill Calvert, Patricia and Michael Fogden, and the Tropical Science Center, and financial support from the Organization for Tropical Studies, Phi Beta Kappa, the Center for Latin American Studies, and Sigma Xi. I thank Tomás and Lindi Guindon for their hospitality during my field seasons, Peter Feinsinger and other members of SuCoPla for discussions about pollination, Jérôme Casas and Marla Goldwasser for comments on the manuscript, and Bastiaan Meeuse for sparking my interest in aroid inflorescences.

FIG POLLINATION AND SEED-DISPERSAL MUTUALISMS
Judith L. Bronstein

The mutualism between figs (*Ficus* spp., Moraceae) and their obligate pollinator wasps (Hymenoptera: Chalcidoidea: Agaoninae) is one of the best-known plant-animal interactions and one that has become emblematic of the tropics. About 750 species of figs exist, almost all of which have unique pollinators, making this one of the most species-specific and tightly coevolved mutualisms. Figs are also involved in mutualistic interactions with vertebrate seed-dispersers. In contrast to pollination, fig seed dispersal is generalized.

There are five fig species in Monteverde: *Ficus pertusa, F. tuerkheimii, F. velutina, F. crassiuscula*, and *F. yoponensis* (Wiebes 1995). The reproductive biology of only one of these figs (*F. pertusa*) has been studied in depth in Monteverde. *Ficus yoponensis* has been given extensive attention on Barro Colorado Island, Panama (Milton et al. 1982, Herre 1989, Windsor et al. 1989). The others remain unstudied. Here, I focus on *F. pertusa*, which is fairly typical of the roughly 350 species of figs with monoecious breeding systems (Bronstein 1992).

Ficus pertusa trees are common throughout Monteverde and are often left standing as shade trees when forest is cleared for pasture. Individual trees flower unpredictably but usually once to three times each year, initiating up to several hundred thousand inflorescences (figs) in each episode. Nearly all the pollinators (female *Pegoscapus silvestrii*) arrive during a 2–3-day period, apparently in response to species-specific volatiles released when the roughly 200 female florets within each fig are receptive (Bronstein 1987, Anstett et al. 1996). The millimeter-long, pollen-carrying wasps squeeze into the small (1 cm) spherical figs, gaining access to the female florets but becoming fatally trapped in the process. Florets vary greatly in style length and are staggered so that stig-mas form a uniform surface within the fig cavity. Once within the fig, a wasp first actively deposits pollen on the stigmatic surface. She then inserts her ovipositor down the length of a number of styles to lay eggs. If she reaches the ovary at the base of a given style, she deposits one egg. One of her offspring will develop within that ovary, feeding on the seed that starts to develop as a result of the pollen she has lain down. If the style is too long relative to her ovipositor, she does not lay an egg, which allows a seed to develop undisturbed.

Over the next 2 months, seeds and seed-eating fig wasp larvae develop within the figs. Mature males then emerge from the ovaries in which they have developed, search out the still-developing females, and mate with them. Males then chew an exit hole back through the wall of the fig. Females emerge from the ovaries and seek out the handful of newly mature anthers scattered among the female florets in their natal fig. They rip the anthers open and pack pollen into special pockets on their abdomens. Inseminated and pollen laden, they depart their natal figs in search of a receptive fig in which to lay their eggs. In *F. pertusa*, all figs on a single tree develop in tight synchrony, whereas different trees in a population flower out of synchrony with each other (Bronstein 1987, 1988a). The wasps must therefore locate another tree in the correct phenological phase to reproduce. Adult fig wasps live only a day or two in the wild and do not feed; mortality during transit between trees is undoubtedly high.

Major gaps remain in our understanding of *F. pertusa* pollination biology, and of fig-pollinator interactions in general (Janzen 1979, Bronstein 1992, Herre 1996). It is unclear why fig wasps do not leave enough offspring to destroy every seed within figs, that is, why they are mutualists at all. It is believed that figs limit wasp numbers by producing two distinct sets of female florets: short-styled ones, in which the ovaries are accessible to the ovipositing wasps and can receive an egg, and long-styled ones, which have inaccessible ovaries and so are able to produce seeds. Styles are not distributed bimodally in *F. pertusa* (Bronstein 1988b), however, or in any other monoecious fig species (Bronstein 1992, Kathuria et al. 1995). They are unimodal, so that a wasp with a slightly longer ovipositor should have more space in which to lay eggs, resulting in reduced seed production.

Another mystery is how fig wasp populations are able to persist in light of figs' flowering phenology. The likelihood of wasps failing to locate their only host plant seems high, particularly in small fig populations (Fig. 8.9). Simulation models suggest subtle fig phenological traits that should help stabilize dynamics of the interaction (Bronstein et al. 1990, Anstett et al. 1995). We documented one of these traits, prolonged receptivity of female florets, in *F. pertusa*

(Anstett et al. 1996). Another question relates to the large community of nonpollinating wasps that develops alongside pollinators within *F. pertusa* (Bronstein 1991) and other figs. These include gall-formers, parasites, and predators; some are close relatives of the pollinators, and many are as species specific on figs as the pollinators themselves. Their natural history is poorly known, and research on their impact on the ecology and evolution of the pollination mutualism is needed (West and Herre 1994, Machado et al. 1996, West et al. 1996).

Although the pollination biology of *F. pertusa* is broadly representative of monoecious figs, there are many fascinating but poorly understood differences among fig species. *Ficus crassiuscula* has at least five times more florets per fig than *F. pertusa* (although far fewer figs per tree), which may have important consequences for fig-wasp and wasp-wasp interactions (Herre 1987, 1989, 1996). *Ficus tuerckheimii*, the most common Monteverde fig, is unusual in having

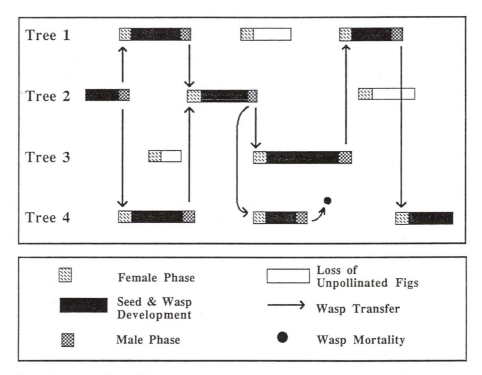

Figure 8.9. Hypothetical flowering sequence of a four-tree population of a fig species such as *Ficus pertusa* in Monteverde. Wasps arrive at the tree during a short interval, pollinate, and lay their eggs (female or pollen-receiving phase); seeds and wasps develop within figs for about two months; the pollinator's offspring mate and depart with pollen during another brief interval (male or pollen-dispersing phase). Because free-living wasps live only a day or two, the male phase of the tree they leave must correspond in time to the female phase of a nearby tree if those wasps are to make the transit successfully. If any one of these trees were absent, then the local pollinator population would go extinct during the time period shown. For example, if tree 1 were absent, then wasps departing tree 3 would go extinct, and no pool of developing or mature wasps would remain.

no obligate agaonine wasps associated with it (Ramirez 1970). Differences also exist among populations of individual species; for example, in northern Mexico, *F. pertusa* lacks the tight within-tree flowering synchrony of Monteverde and Panama (Bronstein 1988a, Smith and Bronstein 1996, A. Herre, pers. comm.). A breakdown in within-tree synchrony is another phenological trait that stabilizes fig wasp population dynamics in models, but it is not found across the species' entire range.

The unusual phenology of figs has important implications for their interactions with seed dispersers. At the population level, fig trees flower year-round. They also fruit year-round, so they are a reliable food source for vertebrates at times of year when little else is available. Nearly all vertebrates in tropical forests are believed to feed on figs at some time in their lives (Janzen 1979). Figs have thus been termed "keystone resources" in tropical forests. Their loss would pose serious threats to maintaining vertebrate populations, even though they make up a relatively small proportion of the biomass of the forest (Terborgh 1986).

Figs can be divided into two widely recognized "fruit syndromes." The first group of species includes those dispersed primarily by mammals, particularly fruit bats. These figs ripen at night and are green, spongy, and fragrant when ripe. Bats feed on four of the five Monteverde fig species: *F. tuerkheimii* (whose fruits are also eaten by large birds), *F. crassiuscula*, *F. velutina*, and *F. yoponensis* (Dinerstein 1983). The second group consists of species whose figs ripen during the day and are red, juicy, and odorless when ripe; they appeal particularly to birds. *Ficus pertusa* is a bird-dispersed species in Monteverde. Twenty-six species of birds from 10 families fed in *F. pertusa*

pasture trees over a 5-month period (Bronstein and Hoffman 1987).

Although figs have community-level importance because of their broad acceptability and availability in times of need, they are not a preferred food. They are nutritionally poor in comparison to other tropical fruits (Dinerstein 1983) and are abandoned when better foods become available. The greatest numbers and diversity of bird visitors (resident and migrant) to *F. pertusa* trees occurred between February and April, when few other Monteverde species were in fruit (Bronstein and Hoffman 1987). This was followed by a dramatic drop in visitation by all species in late April, a time of relatively high fruit abundance in Monteverde (Wheelwright 1983). There is also striking spatial variation in the identities of birds feeding at *F. pertusa* trees, both among different pastures (Bronstein and Hoffman 1987) and between pastures and the upper forested regions of Monteverde 1 km away (Wheelwright et al. 1984). Regional comparisons will provide insights into the ecology and evolution of these interactions. For example, on Barro Colorado Island, *F. pertusa* fruits are green when ripe and are taken by bats (Kalko et al. 1996); in Monteverde, bats consistently reject the red-ripe fruits (J. Rieger and E. Jakob, unpubl. data).

Mutualism is the most poorly understood form of interspecific interaction (Bronstein 1994). Studies comparing different types of mutualism (e.g., *F. pertusa*'s specialized pollination mutualism and generalized seed dispersal mutualism), similar mutualisms involving different species pairs (e.g., the five fig-pollinator combinations in Monteverde), and the same mutualism in different regions (e.g., the *F. pertusa–P. silvestrii* mutualism in Monteverde and Mexico) hold great promise for understanding these fascinating interactions.

THE REPRODUCTIVE BIOLOGY OF *BLAKEA* AND *TOPOBEA* (MELASTOMATACEAE)
Cecile Lumer

Blakea and *Topobea* (Melastomataceae) are two closely related genera of hemiepiphytes (plants germinating on trees but sending roots to the ground as adults). These genera are identical except for the shape of their anthers (Gleason 1945). *Blakea* has squat wedge-shaped anthers (Fig. 8.10); the anthers of *Topobea* are longer and narrower (Fig. 8.11). Five species of *Blakea* occur in Monteverde (*B. anomala*, *B. chlorantha*, *B. gracilis*, *B. grandiflora*, and *B. tuberculata*). *Topobea* is represented by

three species (*T. brenesii*, *T. durandiana*, and *T. pittieri*). *Blakea chlorantha*, *B. grandiflora*, *B. tuberculata*, and *T. pittieri* grow in the MCFP; *B. gracilis* and *T. brenesii* are common in open disturbed areas just below the MCFP. *Blakea anomala* grows at the edge of the MCFP and in the wet montane forest just below it. *Topobea durandiana* occurs only at lower elevations in the Monteverde community. These species are large sun-loving hemiepiphytes that grow at various levels in the canopy. They also grow in open

Figure 8.10. *Blakea gracilis.* Photograph by C. Lumer.

Figure 8.11. *Topobea durandiana.* Photograph by C. Lumer.

areas, on fallen logs, and tree stumps, where I studied their reproductive biology.

In Monteverde, the flowers of *Blakea* and *Topobea* (with the exception of *B. chlorantha*), are pollinated by bees. They have large pink and white flowers that open in the morning, emit a delicate sweet scent during the day, but lack nectar. In all species, the pollen is released through minute pores at the tips of the anthers. Because of the differences in floral size and texture, I expected that each species would be visited and pollinated by a narrow range of bees whose size corresponded to the size of the flower. Instead, these flowers were visited and pollinated by several species of bees (Table 8.3), ranging in size from the very large carpenter bee, *Xylocopa frontalis*, to the medium-sized *Meliponis* spp. The bees collected pollen using the "buzz" or vibratile method of pollination, in which they bend their bodies over the anthers and vibrate their indirect flight muscles. Pollen is ejected from the anther pores directly onto the front of the bee, from where it is easily transferred to the stigma

of the next flower visited. After visiting several flowers, the bee cleans itself, collecting the pollen to feed its young.

These species of *Blakea* and *Topobea* have flexible breeding systems. Because the plants are self-compatible (Fig. 8.12), they can produce fruits with viable seeds without outcrossing. Some plants are quite large, and bees may visit several flowers on one individual. As they move among flowers, pollen remaining on their abdomen is deposited on the stigmas. During two years of experimental manipulations, selfed flowers (flowers in which I placed pollen on the stigma of the same flower from which the pollen came) of *T. brenesii* produced significantly more seeds than outcrossed flowers (C. Lumer, unpubl. data). In addition, *Blakea grandiflora* and *T. brenesii* are autogamous; that is, they are able to produce fruits with viable seeds without a vector to carry the pollen.

The behavior of the bees indicated that outcrossing in these species was primarily performed by the

Table 8.3. Bee visitors to *Blakea* and *Topobea* at Monteverde (1979–1980).

	Blakea anomala	*Blakea gracilis*	*Blakea grandiflora*	*Blakea tuberculata*	*Topobea brenesii*
Large bees					
Bombus ephippiatus Queen	+	+	-	-	+
B. volucelloides Queen	+	+	+	+	+
Epicharis sp.	+	+	-	-	+
Euleama seabrai	+	+	-	+	+
E. polychroma	-	+	-	-	+
E. cingulata	-	+	-	-	-
Xylocopa frontalis	+	+	-	-	+
Medium bees					
B. ephippiatus	+	+	+	+	+
B. volucelloides	-	+	-	-	-
Melipona fasciata	+	+	+	-	+

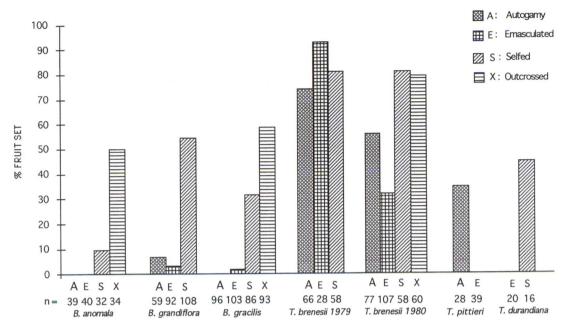

Results of Breeding System Experiments

Legend:
- A: Autogamy
- E: Emasculated
- S: Selfed
- X: Outcrossed

Y-axis: % FRUIT SET

	A E S X	A E S	A E S X	A E S	A E S X	A E	E S
n =	39 40 32 34	59 92 108	96 103 86 93	66 28 58	77 107 58 60	28 39	20 16
	B. anomala	B. grandiflora	B. gracilis	T. brenesii 1979	T. brenesii 1980	T. pittieri	T. durandiana

Figure 8.12. Results of testing for self-compatibility and autogamy in *Blakea* and *Topobea* spp.

larger bees (*Xylocopa frontalis*; two large bumblebee queens, *Bombus ephipiatus* and *B. volulciloides*; *Epicharis* sp. and several large euglossine bees, *Euleama seabrai*, *E. cingulata,* and *E. polychroma*). The bees spent a brief time on one plant, visiting 4–10 flowers before moving to another individual. In contrast, smaller bees, such as the workers of the same *Bombus* species, visited many flowers on a plant (sometimes more than 25) and often returned to the same flowers before moving to another plant.

Blakea anomala, B. gracilis, Topobea brenesii, and *T. pittieri* have individuals in bloom during most of the year, enabling them to use a wide variety of bees as pollinators. In contrast, *Blakea grandiflora* and *B. tuberculata* bloom for relatively short periods (*B. grandiflora,* August–October; *B. tuberculata,* June–July). During my study (1979–1980) fewer bee species visited these flowers than other species. Their most important floral visitor was the medium-size worker bumblebee, *Bombus ephipiatus*. The only exception was an occasional visit by a *B. volucelloides* queen to *Blakea grandiflora* flowers (Table 8.3), which may have been a reflection of the reduced flowering time and/or the unusually long and severe rainy season of 1979. Although *Topobea pittieri* was in flower throughout the year, I never observed an insect visiting the flowers. However, the flowers of *T. pittieri* produced fruits with viable seeds throughout the year, so it is apparently able to reproduce only because it is autogamous.

Blakea chlorantha has a distinctly different mode of pollination, being one of three species of plants in Costa Rica whose flowers are known to be visited and pollinated by rodents (see Langtimm and Anderson, "Mice, Birds, and Pollination," p. 241). All three are hemiepiphytes, occupy similar habitats, and have similar floral syndromes. *Blakea austin-smithii* grows in cloud forest remnants on Volcán Irazu, *B. penduliflora* in cloud forests on Volcán Barba, and *B. chlorantha* along the Continental Divide and elfin forest habitats of the MCFP (Lumer and Schoer 1986). Differences exist between the flowers of the bee-pollinated *Blakea* species and the rodent-pollinated species. Instead of the open, sweet-scented, white and pink flowers of the bee-pollinated species, the flowers of *B. chlorantha* are green and bell-shaped, lack scent, hang down beneath the leaves, and produce nectar from the base of their anthers (Lumer 1980). The anthers are purple and form a circle around the stigma that protrudes from the center (Fig. 8.13). Nectar is produced throughout the night, beginning at dusk. Although the flowers open slowly during the day, it is only at dusk that the anthers open and release their pollen. Thus, the flowers of *B. chlorantha* are well adapted to nocturnal pollinators, which contrasts with the diurnal bee-pollinated *Blakea* flowers.

Mice and rats are pollinators of this species. They visit at night, moving from flower to flower to obtain nectar. The sucrose-rich nectar is similar to the nectar of the rodent-pollinated South African Proteaceae

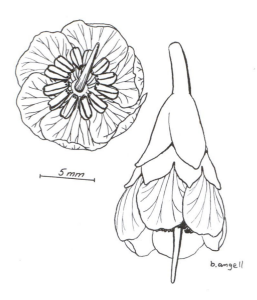

Figure 8.13. *Blakea chlorantha*. Drawing by B. Angel.

Figure 8.14. *Oryzomys fulvescens* (rice rat) feeding at *B. chlorantha* flower (see p. 228). Photograph by R. Schoer.

(Weins and Rourke 1978, Lumer 1980, I. Baker, pers. comm.). The mice and rats do not eat or disturb the flowers and leave little evidence of their visits. They hold a flower between their front paws as they probe for nectar with their tongues (Fig. 8.14). Trapped rodents had *Blakea* pollen on their snouts and in their guts. *Blakea chlorantha* is self-compatible, so mice and rats are responsible for both self- and cross-pollination.

Birds are occasionally seen visiting these flowers. They take nectar remaining from the previous evening, and it is possible that they sometimes effect pollination (see Langtimm and Unnasch, "Mice, Birds, and Pollination," p. 241). However, flowers from which pollen is released at dusk, and in which nectar is produced only during the night, appear better adapted to nocturnal visitors. Several species of ro-

dents (*Oryzomys devius* [or *Reithrodontymys creeper*; see Chap. 7, Mammals] and *Peromyscus nudipes*) visit these flowers for nectar. *Blakea chlorantha* blooms from October through February. Where do the rodents obtain sugar from March through September? Two species that visit *B. chlorantha* also visit flowers of *B. austin-smithii* and *B. penduliflora* in central Costa Rica (Lumer and Schoer 1986; Table 8.4).

The seeds of *Blakea* and *Topobea* are dispersed by several species of birds that eat the fruit, which contain several hundred seeds in a sticky matrix that sticks to the birds' bills. Birds then wipe their beaks on a branch, placing the seeds in position to germinate. In summary, these plant species exhibit great reproductive flexibility and offer resources to their pollinators and seed dispersers throughout most of the year.

Table 8.4. Rodent visitors to *Blakea* flowers in Costa Rica.

	Blakea chlorantha (Monteverde)	*Blakea austin-smithii* (Volcán Irazu)	*Blakea penduliflora* (Volcán Barba)
Oryzomys devius	+	-	-
O. fluvescens	+	+	-
Peromyscus mexicanus nudipes	+	+	-
Reithrodontomys creper	-	+	-
R. rodriguezii	-	+	+
Scotinomys teguina	-	+	-

Suzanne Koptur

Inga is a large genus (ca. 400 spp. in the neotropics) of mimosoid legume trees, many species of which bear extrafloral nectaries (Fig. 8.1), including all of those that occur in Costa Rica (ca. 30 spp.) (León 1966). In Monteverde, 8–10 species occur. In the MCFP (1520–1600 m), *I. densiflora, I. longispica, I. mortoniana,* and infrequently *I. tonduzii* occur. In the middle woods (1460–1520 m), *I. densiflora* and *I. mortoniana* are common, with occasional *I. quaternata* and rarely *I. brenesii, I. longispica,* and *I. punctata.* In the lower woods (1320–1460 m), *I. brenesii* and *I. punctata* are the most abundant, with occasional *I. mortoniana, I. oerstediana,* and *I. quaternata,* and rarely *I. densiflora* and *I. longispica.*

Inga have compound leaves, with foliar nectaries located between each pair of opposite leaflets (Fig. 8.15). These nectaries secrete nectar from the first unfolding of a new leaf until the leaf is fully mature. They provide an incentive for insects to visit the leaves to collect nectar. Two guilds of nectary visitors (ants and parasitic insects) provide protection against herbivores. How do these and other defenses of *Inga* vary over an elevational gradient? *Inga* leaves provide food for many herbivores, including large vertebrates such as Howler Monkeys (*Allouatta palliata*; Milton 1978), sloths (Montgomery and Sunquist 1978), snails, and a variety of insects, including katydids, beetles, sucking insects, leaf-miners, and caterpillars. Individual leaves are long-lived, some surviving three years or more.

Figure 8.15. Ants (*Camponotus substitutus*) visiting foliar nectaries of *Inga densiflora* in Turrialba, Costa Rica. Photo by S. Koptur.

Experiments with saplings of two species (*I. densiflora* and *I. punctata*) in wet forests at elevations lower than Monteverde (600 m, near Turrialba) revealed that ants protect developing leaves against herbivores (Koptur 1984a). Ants collect the nectar and disturb herbivores they encounter on the foliage, attacking and eating some of the slow and soft-bodied ones and generally inciting all insect herbivores to "move along." Extrafloral nectar is produced throughout the day and night, and ants continually visit nectaries at these lower elevations. This benefits the plants because many leaf-feeding herbivores are active at night. The same species of *Inga* occur over a wide elevational range in Costa Rica; for example, *I. densiflora* ranges between 600 and 1500 m. Nectar-feeding ants are less abundant and less active at higher elevations (see Chap. 4, Insects and Spiders), but the nectaries of most *Inga* trees secrete nectar. What is the function of this extrafloral nectar when there are no ants to protect the plants?

This nectar is used by a variety of insects, including adult wasp and fly parasitoids. Parasitoids complete their life cycle within or on the body of one host and ultimately kill it. Female parasitoids lay their eggs in herbivore eggs or larvae, and their own larvae develop inside the egg or body of the host larva. The feeding caterpillar transforms the leaf material into food for the parasitoid larvae living within it. The parasitoid larvae emerge from their host and pupate; new adult parasitoids hatch from the pupae. They leave behind an empty shell of a caterpillar that is a "dead end," even though it might still look alive, for it does not live to reproduce. Some parasitoids are egg parasitoids and emerge as adults without the herbivore egg hatching. In either case, the numbers of herbivores are reduced by parasitoids, which potentially benefits both the *Inga* individual that secretes the nectar and other trees in the area that may have been attacked by those herbivores (Koptur 1991).

Caterpillars of many lepidopteran herbivores of *Inga* are parasitized to a much greater extent at higher elevations, where ants are not abundant (Koptur 1985), than at lower elevations. Chemical analyses of foliage from trees of the same species at different elevations reveal that upland individuals have substantially greater amounts of tannins in their leaves than their lowland counterparts. Tannins bind proteins, and caterpillars eating more tannins in their *Inga* leaves may take longer to develop (also development is slower at cooler temperatures of higher elevations), thus spending more time being vulnerable to parasitoids and predators. Tannins may therefore enhance parasitoid protection of upland *Inga*. Alternative explanations for this increased tannin content, such as greater pressure from fungal pathogens or other environmental factors, have not yet been studied.

Although the antiherbivore properties of higher elevation *Inga* are a fairly effective complex of factultative defenses (parasitoids and tannins) in the absence of ant protection, they are not as effective as ant defense in limiting damage to foliage. Upland *I. densiflora* leaves are damaged substantially more after six months than their lowland, ant-defended counterparts. Nonetheless, the extrafloral nectaries that make *Inga* leaves easy to recognize are also important in antiherbivore defense of *Inga* at all elevations.

A FLY LARVA DIRECTLY ALTERS FLORAL SEX IN *CENTROPOGON SOLANIFOLIUS*
Martha E. Weiss

Some interactions between plants and insects are obvious to the observer (e.g., leaf damage by folivores). Other interactions are more subtle. I studied an interaction in which the larva of a fly, *Zygothrica neolinea* (Drosophilidae), lives inside unopened flowers of *Centropogon solanifolius* (Campanulaceae; Weiss 1996). The larva eats the developing pollen and reduces or eliminates the flower's ability to act as a male without affecting its female function. *Centropogon* is a genus of mostly Andean herbs, shrubs, and vines with brightly colored hummingbird-pollinated flowers (Standley 1938, Stein 1992). The bright orange flowers of *C. solanifolius* grow along the cloud forest trails in Monteverde.

My studies of *C. solanifolius* flowers began in ignorance of the fly. I set out to investigate whether removal of pollen from protandrous flowers shortens the duration of the male phase of the flower. Protandrous flowers have a temporal separation of sexual functions: they are first male and provide pollen; in the subsequent female phase, the stigma becomes receptive. Studies of another protandrous lobelioid, *Lobelia cardinalis*, revealed that pollen removal significantly reduced the length of the male phase and hastened the onset of the female phase relative to that of unmanipulated flowers (Devlin and Stephenson 1984). Two Organization for Tropical Studies field problems have found an effect of pollen removal (Frazee et al. 1990, Koptur et al. 1990). My investigations of *C. solanifolius* flowers demonstrated the same effect; the male phase of bagged (to exclude pollinators), unmanipulated control flowers lasted approximately 3–4 days, while that of treatment flowers from which I removed pollen lasted only 1–2 days.

The discovery of a single small larva inside the anther tubes of many of my test flowers complicated my studies. These larvae seemed to eat only the pollen and did not touch any other part of the flower. Surveys of *C. solanifolius* in Monteverde suggested that larval infestation was intense and widespread. In one population, I found larvae in the flowers and buds in 14 of the 16 plants; in another population, 70% of the flowers contained larvae. The presence of the larvae significantly reduced or eliminated the flowers' male phase. Uninfested flowers remained male for an average of 3.5 days, whereas infested flowers were male for an average of 1.2 days before entering the female phase. Some infested flowers skipped the male phase and opened directly as females.

Larval pollen removal seems to have a profound effect on the sex ratio of flowers in the population. Because larvae were so common in *C. solanifolius* flowers in Monteverde, I could not directly measure the sex ratio of an uninfested population. However, in populations of related species with no evidence of larval infestation, the male phase is longer than the female phase: for *L. cardinalis*, the ratio of days in the male phase to days in the female phase was 2.6:1 (Devlin and Stephenson 1984). In another *Centropogon* species, the ratio was 1.4:1 (Frazee et al. 1990). In contrast, for a population of *C. solanifolius* that included both infested and uninfested flowers, the male phase lasted for 1.8 days, and the female phase for 3.9 days. Larval infestation of the flowers may have shifted the sex ratio of the population toward a female-biased ratio, with potentially important fitness consequences for the plants.

I also documented details of the fly's life history within the flower. The larva is that of *Zygothrica neolinea* (Drosophilidae). Female flies lay single oblong eggs through the corolla onto the surface of the fully developed anther tube when the flower is still a small bud; a tiny droplet of latex on the outside of the bud often reveals the location of a recent oviposition (Fig.

8.16, bottom). The newly hatched larva (ca. 1 mm long) burrows into the anther tube and eats the pollen as the bud grows. After 3 weeks, just prior to anthesis, the larva (now about 5–6 mm long) leaves the anther tube and makes an exit hole (which looks like the work of a nectar robber) in the corolla just above the base of the flower (Fig. 8.16, top). Presumably, the insect pupates in the soil; adult flies emerge from pupae after 14–15 days.

Zygothrica neolinea belongs to a group of drosophilid flies that are known from their massive mixed species aggregations at patches of bracket fungi in the forest (Grimaldi 1987). They gather by the thousands to fight, feed on fungal spores, and mate. Some species oviposit in the fungi; others lay their eggs in flowers. In some cases, the relationship between flower species and fly seems to be very specific, with only one floral host for a given species of fly; in others, the association is more general (Pipkin et al. 1966). The relationship between *C. solanifolius* and *Z. neolinea* does not seem to be species-specific; *Z. neolinea* has been reported from *Passiflora* and *Aphelandra* flowers in Panama (Pipkin et al. 1966, Grimaldi 1987), and larvae of other flies have been found in *Centropogon* species (Pipkin et al. 1966).

Larval infestation may have important reproductive consequences for *C. solanifolius* at the individual and the population levels. Larval pollen removal shortens the duration of the male phase and hastens the onset of the female phase, so relatively fewer flowers are available to donate pollen. Pollen removed by hummingbirds has the potential to reach an appropriate stigma, but pollen consumed by larvae is unavailable for pollination. Larval infestation thus reduces both the time that pollen is available and the total amount of pollen in the system. These studies raise other questions. How does the female-biased floral sex ratio affect patterns of male and female fitness in the population? How patchy is larval infestation across space and time? How does the female fly locate her host flowers, and once there, how does she know if a bud already contains an egg? This phenomenon is an area ripe for future research in Monteverde.

Figure 8.16. *Centropogon solanifolius* bud with latex droplet over site of recent oviposition (bottom); and male-phase flower with larval exit hole above the calyx lobes (top).

DECEIT POLLINATION IN *BEGONIA*
Jon Ågren & Douglas W. Schemske

In many animal-pollinated tropical plants with unisexual flowers (monoecious and dioecious species), female flowers do not provide a reward for pollinators; they are pollinated by deceit (Baker 1976, Renner and Feil 1993). For several of these species, the rewardless female flowers mimic the floral characters of the rewarding male flowers; pollinators may be attracted to the female flowers by intersexual mimicry (Baker 1976, Bawa 1980b, Little 1983, Willson and Ågren 1989).

Begonia is a large tropical genus of predominantly monoecious species in which pollination by deceit is common (Ågren and Schemske 1991, Schemske et al. 1996). In several insect-pollinated *Begonia* species, male and female flowers show a striking similarity. The size and spectral properties of the stigmas in these female flowers closely resemble those of the anthers in the male flowers, and the number and size of petals (or petallike sepals) do not differ between flowers of different genders. The degree of similarity between male and female flowers varies, which may reflect among-species differences in characters that are important for the attraction of pollinators to the rewardless female flowers. For example, in insect-pollinated *B. fisheri* and *B. oaxacana*, petal size and number differ between flowers of different sex, but the visitation rate to female flowers is high enough to result in high levels of fruit set (Schemske et al. 1996, J. Ågren and P. Schemske, unpubl. data).

Similarity between male and female flowers in deceit pollination systems may reflect shared ancestry (unisexual flowers are assumed to be derived from hermaphroditic flowers), selection for similarity, or both. The mimicry hypothesis implies that resemblance is maintained because of selection for similarity (Willson and Ågren 1989) and that the reproductive success of the rewardless female flowers is a function of their degree of resemblance to the reward-producing male flowers (Ågren and Schemske 1991).

Selection for resemblance could potentially take two different forms: the most attractive female flower could resemble either the average male flower in the population, or the male with the highest reward level (Ågren and Schemske 1991, Schemske and Ågren 1995). In the former situation, plants would receive the most pollen and have the highest reproductive success. In the latter, the highest seed production is expected in plants producing female flowers that are most similar to the most rewarding male flowers (Schemske and Ågren 1995). We found a positive correlation between petal size and estimates of pollen production in male flowers of several *Begonia* species, suggesting that flower visitors may use petal size as an indicator of reward level (Schemske et al. 1996, J. Ågren and D. Schemske, unpubl. data).

The perennial herb *B. involucrata* is native to Costa Rica and Panama and is found along roadsides, trails, and pastures in Monteverde (Fig. 8.17). This species flowers during the dry season (January–March), and male and female floral displays are very similar (Ågren and Schemske 1991, Schemske and Ågren 1995). The yellow stigma of the female flower strongly resembles the anthers of the male flower. In ultraviolet light, both the stigma and the anthers appear as dark targets in the center of the flower against the lighter background of the petallike sepals. Both male and female flowers have two petallike sepals of approximately the same size. Similar numbers of male- and female-phase inflorescences open simultaneously; both produce a sweet fragrance.

The main pollinators of *B. involucrata* in Monteverde (bees *Trigona grandipennis* and *Melipona fasciata panamica*) respond to the sexual difference in reward-production by showing a strong preference for male flowers (Fig. 8.18). When pollen was added by hand, seed production was increased by about 40% in the study population at Monteverde in 1990, indicating that pollinator visitation may limit seed production (Ågren and Schemske 1991).

To examine how pollinator preference may shape the evolution of female flower size, we constructed artificial *Begonia involucrata* inflorescences that differed in flower size, and exposed these inflorescences to natural pollinators. Both the number of pollinator approaches and the number of pollinator visits increased monotonically with petal size (Schemske and Ågren 1995; Fig. 8.19). In this species, individuals producing the largest petals were at an advantage. This is consistent with the hypothesis that pollinators use the intensity of visual stimuli to identify flowers with the greatest expected reward, and suggests that female flowers which mimic the most rewarding male flowers will have higher pollinator visitation and reproductive success.

Figure 8.17. Female-phase inflorescence of *Begonia involucrata* in Monteverde. Photograph by J. Ågren.

The pollination system of *B. involucrata* shares several features with those of other bee-pollinated *Begonia* species. A marked discrimination against the rewardless female flowers and a positive relationship between petal size of artificial flowers and attractiveness to pollinators have been documented in *B. oaxacana, B. tonduzii*, and *B. urophylla* (Schemske et al. 1996, J. Ågren and D. Schemske, unpubl. data). Experimental data and field observations of these and other bee-pollinated species indicate that several factors, including the size and orientation of flowers and scent production, may be important for pollinator visitation in *Begonia*. The deceit pollination system of many *Begonia* and the variety of mating systems found within the genus (Ågren and Schemske 1993) make begonias useful for understanding plant reproduction and pollination biology.

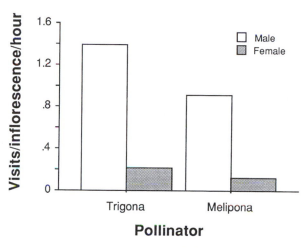
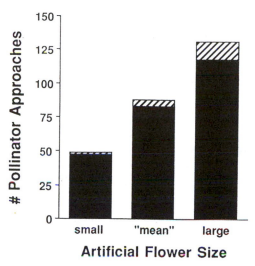

Figure 8.18. *(above left)* Average visitation rate to male- and female-phase inflorescences of *Begonia involucrata* by the bees *Trigona grandipennis* in 1990 (*N* = 220 visits observed) and *Melipona fasciata panamica* in 1992 (*N* = 56). Data from Ågren and Schemske (1991) and Schemske and Ågren (1995). **Figure 8.19.** *(above right)* Pollinator approaches to artificial female flowers in a population of *Begonia involucrata* at Monteverde. The mean flower size is equal to the mean of male flowers, and the small and large flowers are, respectively, 2 S.D. smaller and 2 S.D. larger than the mean male (based on width of the petallike sepal). The sepal areas for the three flower sizes were 86 mm², 139 mm², and 204 mm², respectively. The solid bars indicate the number of approaches followed by a rejection; the hatched bars indicate the number of approaches that were followed by a visit. (From Schemske and Ågren 1995)

A HYPOTHESIS ABOUT THE TIMING OF FLOWERING AND FRUITING IN COMPETING TROPICAL TREES
Nathaniel T. Wheelwright

Seasonal changes in the tropics tend to be more subtle than those of the temperate zone, where annual variation in climate is more extreme. Nonetheless, tropical plants replace senescent leaves, burst into flower, and ripen their fruits at distinct times of the year. The timing of reproduction in tropical plants affects the life histories of animals that feed on nectar, pollen, fruits, and seeds, just as the seasonally changing behaviors and abundance of animal pollinators, seed dispersers, and seed predators influence plant reproductive success. A major challenge in community ecology is to explain the timing (phenology) of major events in the life histories of tropical plants and to understand the relative role of abiotic (physical) factors versus biological factors. For example, abiotic factors such as day length, rainfall, or temperature might constrain plants of different species to reproduce relatively synchronously during a single favorable time of year. On the other hand, biological factors such as competition among plants for a limited number of pollinators or seed dispersers should select for nonoverlapping or staggered phenologies among species (Snow 1965, Levin and Anderson 1970, Stiles 1977).

To understand seasonal rhythms in the forests of Monteverde, I have studied reproduction in 23 small-fruited species of trees whose seeds are dispersed by birds (Wheelwright 1985a, 1986) since 1979. I have focused on a single guild (a group of species that interact strongly because they share ecological requirements; Root 1967). This guild, composed of trees in the family Lauraceae, all provide similar floral and fruit resources and depend upon a similar set of pollinators and seed dispersers. The goals of the study are to quantify the proportion of a given plant population that flowers or fruits in a particular year, the seasonal synchrony of reproduction between in-dividuals within populations and between species, the degree to which flower and fruit production varies from year to year, and community-wide phenological differences between flowering and fruiting.

Almost all of the Lauraceae of Monteverde produce panicles (branched inflorescences) of small, yellowish green flowers that yield small amounts of nectar. Their major insect visitors (and presumed pollinators) are generalist bees, wasps, and flies. Lauraceae fruits also vary little among species in terms of their basic structure—all have a large single seed surrounded by a dense oily pulp. Most fruits turn black when ripe, and in many species, the pedicel (stem) holding the fruit becomes conspicuously swollen and red. Although fruits of different species are structurally similar, the variation in size among species is large; fruits range in diameter from 0.6 to 2.3 cm (Mazer and Wheelwright 1993).

During the first year of my study, I monitored reproduction in 286 trees along a 7-km transect at biweekly intervals. During the second year, I observed trees at monthly intervals. Thereafter, censuses have been conducted once a year at the same time each year (early dry season). Each species is surprisingly predictable and synchronous in its flowering and fruiting phenology. Different species reproduce at characteristic times of the year, with little variation among years despite appreciable annual variation in rainfall. Most individuals of a particular species flower or fruit within several weeks of other members of the population. The proportion of each population that reproduces each year and the magnitude of flower or fruit production, however, vary widely from year to year (20–100% of the individuals of a particular species reproduce). The average number of flowers or fruits produced per tree within species also differs markedly among years. There is also high variation across species in flowering and fruiting patterns, with some species reproducing

annually, biennially, or erratically (Wheelwright 1986).

In terms of community patterns, flowering within the Lauraceae is more evenly distributed throughout the year than fruiting. In every month of the year, at least two species are in flower, with no more than eight species flowering in a given month (Fig. 8.20A). Fruiting is relatively aggregated. In December, it is difficult to find ripe lauraceous fruits, whereas just before the beginning of the rainy season as many as 13 species are in fruit (Fig. 8.20B). Studies of herbaceous and woody plant species from the temperate zone and tropics suggest that staggered or minimally overlapping phenologies may be more likely for flowering than for fruiting (Frankie et al. 1974, Hilty 1980, Wheelwright 1985a).

Natural selection may be greater for temporal divergence among plant species in flowering than it is for fruiting. Plant species that flower simultaneously potentially compete for a limited number of pollinators, just as fruiting plants may compete for seed dispersers. However, different plant species that flower at the same time potentially have another disadvantage: they may suffer reproductive losses to stigma-clogging by foreign pollen, waste of pollen that is transferred to the wrong species, and hybridization, penalties that have no analog in fruiting. Selection against divergence in phenologies may be less for flowering than fruiting. After pollination has occurred, the developing embryo is still nourished and protected by the maternal plant; development associated with flowering can theoretically proceed at any time of the year. In contrast, after fruits have ripened, the dispersed seed and seedling are at the mercy of the environment once they are independent of the parent plant. Unless the seed or seedling can survive desiccation, nutrient scarcity, shade, and predation, the timing of fruiting may be restricted to certain favorable times of year.

I controlled for phylogeny by comparing related plant species, but phylogeny itself may play an important role in determining phenology. It may be that lauraceous species that flower during November in Monteverde do so not because of interspecific competition for pollinators but simply because they originated in the southern hemisphere and have retained an evolutionary legacy of flowering in the spring. The systematics of the Lauraceae is even more uncertain than that of most tropical plant families (Burger and van der Werff 1990). We need to understand evolutionary relationships and the current and historical geographic distributions of tropical tree species in order to explain the timing of flowering and fruiting in tropical forests.

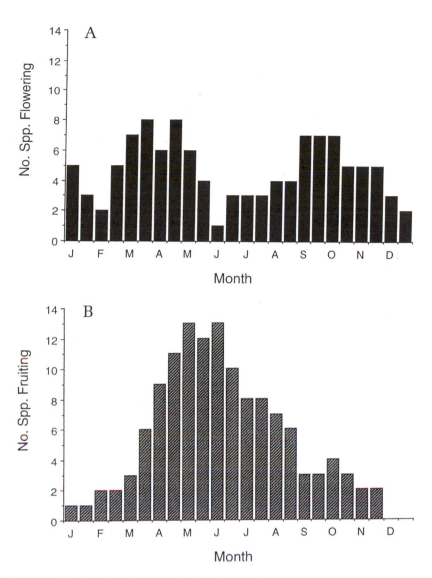

Figure 8.20. Number of species of bird-dispersed trees in the Lauraceae flowering (A) or fruiting (B) in Monteverde. Only species in which at least 20% of the population reproduced are included.

FRUITING PHENOLOGIES OF PIONEER PLANTS: CONSTRAINTS IMPOSED BY FLOWERING PHENOLOGY, DISTURBANCE REGIME, AND DISPERSER MIGRATION PATTERNS

K. Greg Murray

No consensus exists regarding which factors have been important in the evolution of seasonal patterns of flowering and fruiting in the humid tropics. I examined the potential of three factors to act as selective agents in the evolution of fruiting phenology in three species of pioneer plants in Monteverde: seasonal constraints imposed by flowering phenology, seasonal patterns in the availability

of dispersers, and seasonal availability of colonization sites (treefall gaps).

Phenological data were collected on 24 monthly censuses of eight *Phytolacca rivinoides*, 36 *Witheringia meiantha,* and 33 *W. coccoloboides* plants scattered throughout the "Triangle" portion of the MCFP (Murray 1987). Fruit ripening in *P. rivinoides* and *W. coccoloboides* is concentrated in the early rainy

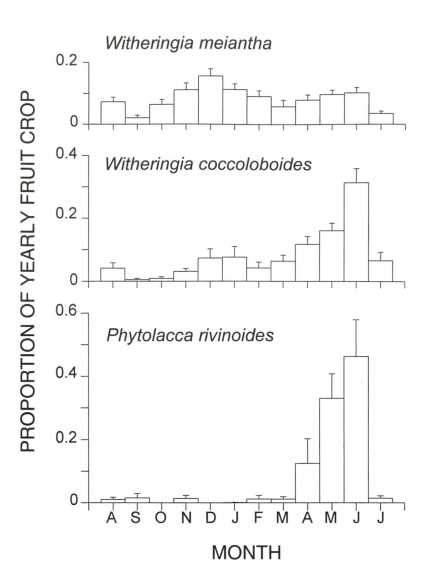

PROPORTION OF YEARLY FRUIT CROP

Witheringia meiantha

Witheringia coccoloboides

Phytolacca rivinoides

A S O N D J F M A M J J

MONTH

Figure 8.21. Fruiting phenology of *Phytolacca rivinoides*, *Witheringia meiantha*, and *W. coccoloboides* at Monteverde. Values given are for the "average" individual of each species, and error bars represent 1 standard error of the mean. (Modified from Murray 1988)

season (June–July), although some fruits can be found in any month (Fig. 8.21). Fruiting of *W. meiantha* is spread more evenly over the year. To determine the extent to which fruiting phenology might be constrained by the timing of flowering, I examined the temporal relationship between peak flowering and fruit ripening within individual plants during the first year. If the timing of fruit ripening is determined wholly by the timing of flowering, then within-plant ripening peaks should always follow flowering peaks by the same amount of time. I determined the dates of flowering and fruiting peaks in each census plant and regressed dates of peak fruiting on dates of peak flowering. Because *W. meiantha* and *W. coccoloboides* usually have two reproductive episodes per year, I computed separate regressions for each of them. In two cases (the early reproductive seasons of *W. meiantha* and *W. coccoloboides*), fruiting phenology followed flowering phenology closely. In *P. rivinoides* and the late reproductive seasons of *W. meiantha* and

W. coccoloboides, plants that flowered later in the season ripened their fruits faster than those that flowered early. It is unlikely that fruiting phenology is tightly constrained by flowering phenology.

To assess disperser abundance, I mist-netted in 14 plots including mature forest, building-phase treefall gaps (*sensu* Whitmore 1975), and large artificial clearings. Although at least 10 bird species are known to take fruits of the three plant species (Wheelwright et al. 1984), Black-faced Solitaires appeared to be the primary dispersers of all three species in the MCFP. They were the most commonly caught understory frugivores and carried the most seeds (assessed from analysis of fecal samples) of the three plant species. However, solitaires migrate down the Caribbean slope following the breeding season (Loiselle and Blake 1991), and are virtually absent from the Monteverde area from late October through December (K. G. Murray, pers. obs.; Fig. 8.22), when *W. meiantha* has a minor fruiting peak.

To understand the relationship between seasonal patterns of solitaire abundance and fruit removal rates, I examined the correlation between solitaire capture rate and daily fruit removal rate from May 1982 to April 1983. Daily fruit removal rate (proportion per day, arcsin-transformed) is correlated with the size of the fruit crop (log-transformed; Murray 1987). I computed partial correlations of removal rate with the monthly solitaire capture rate, controlling for crop size. In *P. rivinoides*, daily fruit removal rate was correlated with solitaire capture rate ($r = 0.635$, 8 df, $p < 0.05$), which suggests the potential for lower reproductive success of individuals ripening their fruits when solitaires were absent. The partial correlations for *W. meiantha* and *W. coccoloboides* indicated the same relationship but were not statistically significant. Thus, disperser seasonality might act as a selective agent on fruiting phenology but not a strong one; removal rates were only slightly depressed during the months when solitaires were entirely absent from the Monteverde area.

Because seeds of the three plant species germinate well only in very young gaps (<8 months), and because gap formation itself is highly seasonal (Murray 1988), there should be a selective advantage for seed germination schedules that coincide with periods of peak gap formation (the "windy-misty" season from October through January; Murray 1988, K. G. Murray, unpubl. data). All three species display "enforced" seed dormancy (*sensu* Harper 1977); seeds remain dormant on or in the soil until a gap forms overhead if they are initially deposited beneath an intact canopy (Murray 1988). This characteristic effectively decouples germination from dispersal, so the exact timing of fruit ripening might be relatively unimportant in these plants.

To estimate the consequences of fruiting phenology for the likelihood of colonizing recent gaps, I used a computer simulation model that combined empirical data on rates of gap formation, germination requirements, seed dormancy, and bird-generated seed shadows (Murray 1986a, b, 1988) to yield an estimate of "lifetime reproductive potential" (number of offspring potentially produced during an individual's lifetime). By shifting the observed phenologies (Fig. 8.21) so that ripening peaked at different times of year, I inferred the consequences of ripening phenology with all other variables held constant. For all runs, I used the estimated seed shadow produced by Black-faced Solitaires (Fig. 8 in Murray 1988), a dormancy capability of 24 months (seeds of all three species can remain viable in the soil for at least 27 months with no loss of viability; Fig. 3 in Murray 1988), and the empirically measured germination response to gaps of different ages. These estimates of reproductive potential were similar for plants fruiting at different times of year, primarily because of the decoupling of seed germination from dispersal.

A confounding factor is seed predation and parasitism. The physiological ability to wait for a gap to occur overhead is irrelevant if seeds are eaten soon after dispersal. Although all three species are taken by predators, removal rates are not so high that the temporal decoupling of dispersal and germination is negated (K. G. Murray, unpubl. data). Rather, it is likely that fruiting seasons that coincide with peak gap formation would carry a greater advantage than implied by the results of the simulations described above.

The fact that none of these factors can explain the seasonal patterns of fruiting in *P. rivinoides*, *W. meiantha*, and *W. coccoloboides* begs other explanations. Strongly seasonal patterns of fruit ripening might

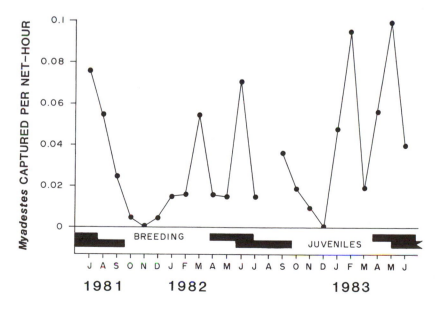

Figure 8.22. Black-faced solitaire capture rates and breeding activity from July 1981 to June 1983. Bars at bottom of figure indicate the presence of breeding adults (i.e., with brood patches) and young of the year on study plots (lower bar).

also result from (1) phylogenetic constraints on phenological plasticity, (2) competition with other plant species for dispersal (Wheelwright 1985a; Wheelwright, "A Hypothesis," pp. 281–283), or (3) seasonal constraints on seed or seedling survival. The latter may be particularly important in Monteverde. Germination of most pioneers on Barro Colorado Island occurs early in the wet season, and older seedlings are better able to survive through the first dry season than younger seedlings, especially at sites where the density of competing seedlings is high (Garwood 1983). The same may be true at Monteverde; surface soils in large gaps dry out during the dry season, and seedlings in gaps commonly die from water stress (K. G. Murray, *unpubl. data*). The evolution of fruiting phenologies of pioneer plants at Monteverde needs more empirical study, especially on seedling demography.

WHAT HAPPENS TO SEEDS OF VERTEBRATE-DISPERSED TREES AFTER DISPERSAL?
Dan Wenny

Postdispersal events, such as seed predation and a second stage of dispersal, may play a key role in plant recruitment. For many species, postdispersal seed predation is a major source of mortality that limits population growth (Crawley 1992). Most data are from temperate zone plants, especially on seed preference by rodents in arid areas, although studies on frugivory and seed dispersal have been conducted in Monteverde (Wheelwright 1983, 1991, Murray 1986a, b, 1988). Seed size may affect predation rates. In general, rodents prefer large seeds over small seeds because larger seeds have more energy than small seeds (Price and Jenkins 1986). Other factors, such as chemical content and handling time, also influence seed choice (Kerley and Erasmus 1991).

I examined rates of cloud forest seed predation as a function of seed characteristics by recording the fate of naturally dispersed seeds. Most studies have used seeds that are "experimentally dispersed" by the researchers (Schupp 1988, Forget 1993). Species were chosen to represent a variety of plant families and seed sizes, but seeds of all species were relatively large compared to other species in the community (Wheelwright et al. 1984; Table 8.5). This study was conducted from May 1993 to August 1994 in a 5-ha area (1600 m) along the Continental Divide near the intersection of the Valley trail (Sendero El Valle) and the Tower trail (Sendero Las Torres).

Dispersed seeds were located by searching the ground for freshly regurgitated, dropped, or defecated seeds. Seeds were marked by glueing 50 cm of unwaxed dental floss to the seed and tying flagging tape to the floss. All sites were censused several times the first week and once each week thereafter for 12 weeks. If a marked seed was removed, the surrounding area was searched until the flagging tape–dental floss assembly was found. If a piece of the seed coat remained, the seed was classified as killed by seed predators. If a seed was partially eaten, tooth or bill marks were used to determine the type of animal that handled the seed.

Table 8.5. Characteristics of seeds in the study of postdispersal survival.

Species	Dispersers[a]	Seed Mass (g)	Seed Coat (mm)	N
Hippocrateaceae				
Salacia petenensis	Birds? bats?	7.35	0.4	42
Lauraceae				
Ocotea endresiana	Birds	0.75	0.3	376
Beilschmiedia pendula	Birds	12.86	1.7	273
Meliaceae				
Guarea glabra	Birds, monkeys	0.76	0.5	401
Myrtaceae				
Eugenia sp.	Bats	2.26	0.3	64
Sabiaceae				
Meliosma sp.	Birds? bats?	1.75	2.2	41

[a]Disperser classification based on Wheelwright et al. (1984), D. Wenny (pers. obs.), and C. Guindon (pers. comm.)

In many cases, the seeds had been taken inside fallen logs, into small burrows, and under trees. I assumed these seeds were eaten by small rodents because the sites were not accessible to Collared Peccaries and larger rodents such as Agoutis. If a marked seed was removed but not eaten, it was left in the new location and included in subsequent censuses.

After 4 weeks, the proportion of seeds remaining varied widely (Fig. 8.23). *Meliosma* and *Beilschmiedia* had very high survival (100% and 90%, respectively); *Salacia* (40%), *Guarea* (30%), and *Ocotea* (5%) had low survival. Survival of *Eugenia* was intermediate (70%). Seed removal continued during the next 8 weeks at a much lower rate for all species. Survival after 12 weeks ranged widely: 2% in *Ocotea*, 20% in *Guarea* and *Salacia*, 50% in *Eugenia*, 80% in *Beilschmiedia*, and 100% in *Meliosma*. The *Ocotea* and *Eugenia* seeds that were removed were always eaten. The main predators were small rodents such as Deer Mice, the most common terrestrial rodent in the study site. *Meliosma* seeds, which remained untouched, germinated several months later. Once the seeds germinated, they lost the protective seed coat and many were eaten. Both small and large rodents were responsible for most of the removal of *Beilschmiedia*. Partially eaten seeds of both *Beilschmiedia* and *Salacia* were able to germinate. Rodents and birds (Black-breasted Wood-Quail) occasionally chewed or pecked the seeds, damaging the cotyledons but leaving the embryo intact. *Salacia* has a thin seed coat and the seeds suffered more damage than *Beilschmiedia*.

Removal of *Guarea* seeds was fairly high, but in contrast to the other species, almost half of the removed seeds were found buried, possibly by scatterhoarding rodents. Scatterhoarding is fairly common for temperate zone species such as oaks (*Quercus*) in which individual seeds are buried in many shallow surface caches by seed predators who later retrieve most of the buried seeds. Scatterhoarding has been reported for only a few tropical trees (Forget and Milleron 1991, Forget 1993). Although peccaries probably ate some seeds, they were not major predators.

The fate of dispersed seeds in this ecosystem depends on a variety of factors. Both seed size and seed coat thickness were correlated with seed survival. Although the smallest seed in this study (*Ocotea*) had the lowest survival, seed size is not sufficient to predict seed survival (D. Wenny, unpubl. data). Regardless of seed size, postdispersal seed predation may play a key role in limiting plant recruitment. Because postdispersal predation can be 90% or more in some species, such mortality is a strong selective force that may be more important than selection on other aspects of the dispersal phase in plants (Wheelwright 1988a).

This study suggests three topics for future research. First, the trade-off between physical and chemical defenses in seeds should be investigated. For example, seeds of most species of Lauraceae are extremely resinous and fragrant when cut and may contain compounds that are toxic to some consumers (Castro 1993). Yet *Beilschmiedia* is the only neotropical Lauraceae genus that has a relatively thick seed coat. In contrast, *Meliosma* has a very thick seed coat but no indication of secondary compounds. Second, long-term studies on the fates of dispersed seeds and survival of seedlings are needed to determine the rates of mortality for each stage between dispersal and recruitment (Herrera et al. 1994). Third, the impact of rodents on recruitment is poorly understood because some species are both dispersers and predators. Scatterhoarding and secondary dispersal by rodents may be important for some tropical tree species that are considered to be bird dispersed (Forget and Milleron 1991). Ascertaining which rodent species are involved in secondary dispersal and measuring their net impact on dispersal will be useful.

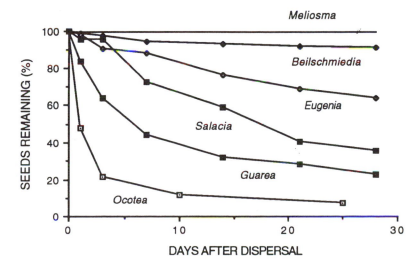

Figure 8.23. Postdispersal survival of seeds of six species of lower montane trees.

SPECIALIZED SEED DISPERSAL:
MISTLETOES AND FRUIT-EATING BIRDS
Sarah Sargent

Small-fruited plants usually have broad, nonspecific mutualistic interactions with the birds who consume their fruits and disperse their seeds. In most cases, fruits of a particular species of plant are eaten by many species of birds, which eat the fruits of other species of plants. Thus, strong specializations between fruiting plants and their avian dispersers are usually absent. In Monteverde, as in many other parts of the world, mistletoe fruits are eaten by only a handful of bird species, and several of the mistletoe-eating birds depend heavily on mistletoe fruits in their diets. This is one of the few examples of interactions between plants and avian seed dispersers that is highly specialized and that may constitute coevolution.

Mistletoes are parasitic plants that have specific requirements for seed dispersal (see Sargent, "Mistletoes," pp. 81–82). Unless their bird-dispersed seeds are deposited on the smaller branches of suitable host trees, the seeds die. Mistletoe seeds can be retained on branches because they are covered with viscin, a thick, gooey mucilage made up of semisoluble and insoluble plant fiber. Birds that eat mistletoe fruits cannot digest the viscin-coated seeds; they must either regurgitate or defecate them and then dispose of them without getting the seeds stuck to their feathers. Usually, the birds wipe the seeds onto the twig where they perch; the viscin dries and glues the seeds in place. Viscin

is thus a key adaptation of mistletoes, one that greatly increases the probability that a seed will be dispersed successfully and be deposited and retained at a suitable site.

The three main families of mistletoes, the Viscaceae, Loranthaceae, and Eremolepidaceae (Table 8.6), have fruits that are substantially different from one another, structurally and nutritionally. These differences dictate which birds eat the fruits and how they handle them. Fruits of all three families at Monteverde are similar in size (4–10 mm long x 2.5–6.5 mm in diameter) and have only one seed per fruit. Viscaceae fruits have small seeds relative to fruit size, a tough skin that separates easily from the pulp layer, a high water content of the pulp, viscin completely surrounding the seed, and energy in the form of sugars in the pulp. In contrast, the Loranthaceae and Eremolepidaceae fruits have large seeds relative to fruit size, thin skins that are firmly attached to the thin layer of pulp, viscin attached at only one end of the seed, pulp that separates easily from the seed, and energy in the form of fats in the pulp (Sargent 1994).

In Monteverde, as in Panama (Davidar 1987) and Colombia (Restrepo 1987), nonoverlapping sets of birds eat the two types of fruits. The Monteverde avifauna includes over 80 species of frugivorous birds (Wheelwright et al. 1984), but only four species of tanagers (Thraupinae) consume fruits of mistletoes in the fam-

Table 8.6. Common species of mistletoes in Monteverde.

Mistletoe Species	Typical Hosts
Viscaceae	
Phoradendron robustissimum	*Sapium* spp. (Euphorbiaceae)
Phoradendron flavens	*Conostegia* spp. (Melastomataceae)
Phoradendron robaloense	*Pouteria* spp. (Sapotaceae), *Ocotea* spp. (Lauraceae)
Phoradendron corynarthron	*Pouteria* spp. (Sapotaceae)
Loranthaceae	
Gaiadendron punctatum	Ferns, herbaceous plants
Struthanthus oerstedii	*Citrus* sp. (Rutaceae), *Hampea* spp. (Malvaceae)
Struthanthus costaricensis	*Citrus* sp. (Rutaceae), *Guarea* spp. (Meliaceae)
Struthanthus quercicola	*Citrus* sp. (Rutaceae), *Solanum* spp. (Solanaceae)
Oryctanthus spicatus	*Eugenia* spp. (Myrtaceae), *Ficus* spp. (Moraceae)
Psittacanthus schiedeanus	*Psidium guayaba* (Meliaceae)
Eremolepidaceae	
Antidaphne viscoidea	*Psidium guayaba* (Meliaceae), *Eugenia* (Myrtaceae)

Other species occur in the area, especially at lower and higher elevations. Mistletoes are most visible in trees in pastures, along forest edges and along roadside edges. Some mistletoes, including *Antidaphne* and *Oryctanthus*, can use other mistletoes as hosts.

ily Viscaceae (Sargent 1994). The four include three species of *Euphonia* and one member of the closely related genus *Chlorophonia*. About 25 species of euphonias and four species of chlorophonias are found in the Neotropics, where they are considered mistletoe specialists (Sutton 1951, Isler and Isler 1987). The degree of mistletoe specialization varies considerably within the two genera. For example, in Monteverde, the Blue-hooded *Euphonia* is a relatively strict mistletoe specialist, with over 80% of its diet consisting of Viscaceae fruits, whereas the Yellow-throated Euphonia has a more generalized fruit diet including figs (*Ficus* spp.) and other sweet juicy fruits, with only about 20% of its diet from Viscaceae. A more diverse set of 10 bird species, including flycatchers, vireos, and pigeons, consume the fruits of the Loranthaceae and Eremolepidaceae in Monteverde (Sargent 1994). The relatively strict specialist in this group of birds is a small tyrannid flycatcher, the Paltry Tyrannulet. Approximately 80% of its diet is composed of Loranthaceae-type mistletoe fruits.

One species of Loranthaceae, *Gaiadendron punctatum*, is exceptional among mistletoes in that it grows on the ground, where it parasitizes the roots of neighboring plants (see Morales "Plants on Leaves," p. 80). Its seeds have very little viscin (not needed to stick onto host twigs), and its fruits differ from those of other species of Loranthaceae. They are juicy and have a high sugar content. They are never eaten by Paltry Tyrannulets or other typical Loranthaceae-feeding bird species. They are eaten by chlorophonias, which handle the fruits in the same way they handle other sweet, juicy fruits such as figs. They squeeze the fruits with their bills, ingesting the juice and some pulp, discarding the skins and seeds.

Why is it that birds that readily consume fruits of mistletoes in the family Viscaceae do not eat those in the Loranthaceae (*Gaiadendron* excepted) and vice versa? Different birds handle and digest fruits in different ways. The euphonias and chlorophonia

squeeze *Phoradendron* fruits by shucking off the tough skins, which separate from the pulp, and swallowing the contents. Anywhere from 8 to 60 min later, they defecate the seeds, often doing a quick wipe-and-sidestep motion to detach them from their cloacas and attach them to the perch. During the short trip through the gut, the sugars in the pulp are rapidly absorbed. Euphonias and chlorophonias have unusually short and unrestricted digestive tracts; they completely lack a gizzard and associated sphincters (Forbes 1880). The euphonias' use of mistletoe fruits might be related to their simplified digestive systems (Wetmore 1914). Other birds may not be able to eat these fruits because of their more complex digestive tracts; they may be unable to handle and process these viscin-laden fruits quickly enough to make them profitable. Alternatively, processing in a gizzard may release toxins from the relatively unprotected seeds. Research is needed to clarify the processes that prevent other birds from eating these fruits.

Loranthaceae-eating birds, such as the Paltry Tyrannulet, swallow *Antidaphne, Struthanthus,* and *Oryctanthus* fruits whole. Five minutes after swallowing a fruit, the bird regurgitates the seed and, with a quick dip of the head, attaches the seed to its perch. The pulp plus skin are separated from the seed in the bird's gizzard. While the seed (with viscin) is sent quickly back out the mouth, the pulp and skin spend a longer time going through the digestive tract where the fats are digested slowly. It takes skill to dispose of the seeds correctly; I have watched young birds struggle to rid themselves of seeds and stringy viscin strands.

The interaction between mistletoes and their avian seed dispersers is an unusually intimate and specialized one in Monteverde as in other parts of the world (Ali 1931, Docters van Leeuwen 1954, Godschalk 1983, Reid 1986, Snow and Snow 1988). Monteverde presents an exciting system to study specific coevolutionary adaptations on the part of plants and avian frugivores that disperse their seeds (Reid 1991).

SEED DISPERSAL AND SEEDLING RECRUITMENT IN A LAURACEOUS TREE SPECIES
J. P. Gibson

Many tropical trees produce fruits that are eaten by foraging birds. Depending on the species, a bird tends either to remain in that tree or to fly to another perch to digest the fruit. The seeds, which birds regurgitate or defecate, are unharmed so birds serve as seed dispersers. Aspects of this rela-

tionship in the Lauraceae (avocado family) have been studied extensively in Monteverde (Wheelwright et al. 1984, Wheelwright, 1988b, 1991, 1993, Wheelwright and Bruneau, 1992). However, little information exists on patterns of seed dispersal and the resulting patterns of seedling recruitment in lauraceous trees.

I investigated the consequences of avian seed dispersal for *Ocotea tenera*, an understory lauraceous tree that colonizes disturbed sites (gaps) in the forest. Dependence on disturbance for establishment leads to a patchy distribution of clusters (subpopulations) of trees in the forest. *Ocotea tenera* fruits are eaten by Emerald Toucanets, Keel-billed Toucans, Resplendent Quetzals, and Three-wattled Bellbirds. Birds typically swallow one to three fruits from a tree and fly to another site to digest the fruits and regurgitate the seeds (Wheelwright 1991). Undoubtedly, birds move many seeds throughout the forest during a fruiting season, but because suitable sites for seedling establishment are uncommon and because seeds may experience postdispersal predation, only a small portion of dispersed seeds successfully germinate. It is impossible to observe seed dispersal in sufficient detail to follow where seeds originate and where they eventually settle. However, because existing subpopulations are the products of previous seed dispersal, genetic data can be collected from these subpopulations for evaluation of seed dispersal and seedling recruitment patterns.

I conducted a genetic analysis of the *Ocotea tenera* population in Monteverde to test two alternative seed dispersal and recruitment hypotheses (Gibson 1995). One hypothesis was that if gaps were colonized with seeds from many maternal trees or if seedlings were recruited from the progeny of many widely distributed trees, there should be low genetic relatedness among trees within subpopulations and low genetic differentiation among subpopulations. Conversely, if gaps were colonized with seeds from few maternal trees or if there were little migration, there should be high genetic relatedness among trees within subpopulations and high genetic differentiation among subpopulations. I surveyed 112 *O. tenera* trees among six subpopulations for 18 allozyme loci (which served as genetic markers) to measure levels and structuring of genetic diversity within and among naturally occurring *O. tenera* subpopulations.

Levels and structure of genetic diversity within and among subpopulations (Table 8.7) were consistent with observations of other tropical trees. However, measures of genetic differentiation among subpopulations were atypically high (mean GST = 0.13), which indicated subpopulations were genetically distinct from one another. Genetic relatedness among trees within subpopulations was estimated by *R*, which can range from 0.00 in groups of unrelated individuals to 0.50 in groups of full siblings (Queller and Goodnight 1989). Relatedness within subpopulations tended to be high and indicated subpopulations contained groups of half-siblings (Table 8.8). Comparisons of sapling and adult genotypes indicated that although

Table 8.7. Estimates of genetic diversity and genetic structure for individual polymorphic loci and means calculated across polymorphic loci for six naturally occurring subpopulations of *Ocotea tenera* in Monteverde (Gibson and Wheelwright 1995).

Locus	HT	HS	GST
Fe1	0.655	0.610	0.082*
Fe2	0.467	0.387	0.135*
Gdh	0.621	0.551	0.134*
Mdh2	0.479	0.405	0.180*
Mnr	0.480	0.357	0.292*
Per1	0.737	0.629	0.167*
Per2	0.457	0.418	0.100*
Per3	0.662	0.604	0.104*
Mean	0.565	0.495	0.128*

*HT, total genetic diversity; HS, genetic diversity within subpopulations; GST, proportion of total diversity due to genetic differentiation among subpopulations.
*X^2 tests comparing genetic differentiation among subpopulations, p < .001.

relatedness within subpopulations was fairly high, most saplings within subpopulations were unquestionably not the progeny of adult trees at that site. Further analyses of relatedness showed that saplings tended to show greater relatedness to one another than adult trees did to one another. I could not determine the number of seeds from different maternal trees that were present within a given subpopulation. However,

Table 8.8. Relatedness coefficient (*R*) estimates for six natural subpopulations (A–F) and two experimental plots (established in 1981 and 1984) of *Ocotea tenera* (Gibson and Wheelwright 1995).

Subpopulation (cohort)	N	R
Natural		
A	26	0.225
B	22	0.091
(sapling)	16	0.060
(adult)	6	0.090
C	27	0.014
(sapling)	21	0.147
(adult)	6	0.145
D	14	0.172
E	12	0.185
F	11	0.265
(sapling)	7	0.213
(adult)	4	0.157
Mean		0.179
Experimental		
1981	28	0.007
1984	25	0.129

When applicable, *R* values for sapling and adult cohorts within subpopulations are also given. N = sample size comparisons of genetic diversity and relatedness values of naturally occurring subpopulations with values from experimental plots (whose establishment history was known; Wheelwright and Bruneau 1992) suggested that naturally occurring subpopulations contain the offspring of five to seven maternal trees (Gibson and Wheelwright 1995).

My data provide three conclusions about avian seed dispersal and seedling recruitment in *O. tenera*. First, genetic relatedness values indicate clumped dispersal of related seeds by birds. Relatedness among groups of seeds dispersed together persists into sapling and adult age classes. Second, saplings underneath adult *O. tenera* trees are not the progeny of the adults; there is relatively long-distance seed dispersal of related seeds. Third, clumped dispersal of related groups of seeds causes high genetic differentiation among subpopulations. The random occurrence in the forest of disturbed sites suitable for germination and the random chance of a bird depositing any given group of seeds at that site cause subpopulations to be genetically distinct from one another. Fruit consumption and seed dispersal behaviors of foraging birds have a profound effect on genetic structure among subpopulations and among age classes of trees within subpopulations. Further genetic analysis of tropical tree populations will provide a foundation for evolutionary and conservation studies in Monteverde.

MYRMECOPHYTES
John T. Longino

In tropical regions throughout the world, one can find myrmecophytes, plants that provide specialized food and housing for ants, and ant species specialized for finding and occupying these plants (Bequaert 1922, Wheeler 1942, Buckley 1982a, b, Beattie 1985, Davidson and McKey 1993a, b). Myrmecophyte-ant interactions are often assumed to be mutualisms; the plants benefit the ants by providing food and nest sites, and the ants benefit the plants by providing a bodyguard service, driving away herbivores and in some cases trimming encroaching vegetation. In a few cases, the assumption has been borne out with field experiments (Janzen 1966, 1967a, b, 1969, Letourneau 1983, Schupp 1986). Now that myrmecophyte-ant interactions are known to be mutualistic, emphasis has shifted to revealing their evolutionary history (McKey 1991, Ward 1991, Davidson and McKey 1993b, Ayala et al. 1996) and explaining temporal and spatial variation in the interactions (Longino 1989a, 1991a, b, 1996, Davidson and Fisher 1991, Davidson et al. 1991). Myrmecophyte-ant interactions that occur in Monteverde are *Cordia alliodora* trees with associated *Azteca* and *Zacryptocerus* ants (Longino 1996), *Triplaris* trees with associated *Azteca* ants (Longino 1996), understory *Ocotea* and *Guarea* trees with associated *Myrmelachista* ants (Stout 1979, Longino and Hanson 1995), and *Cecropia* trees with associated *Azteca* ants. The *Cecropia-Azteca* interaction is the most conspicuous, abundant, and accessible of the myrmecophyte-ant interactions and is the focus of this essay.

Cecropia is a genus of over 100 species of neotropical trees, five of which occur in mainland Costa Rica (Burger 1977). Most species are myrmecophytes, with a suite of traits that facilitate ant habitation (Müller 1876, 1880–1881; Fig. 8.24). The stems are hollow with internal partitions, much like bamboo (Fig. 8.24B), which form ample nesting space for ants. The stem walls produce viscous sap when damaged by chewing, but at regular intervals along the stem there are thin spots through which the ants can safely chew. At the base of each leaf petiole, a dense pad of hairs produces small white beads called Müllerian bodies (Fig. 8.24), which contain glycogen (Rickson 1971) and appear to be the sole food for the ant colonies that inhabit the trees (Fig. 8.24D,E).

Azteca is a genus of ants containing hundreds of neotropical species (Forel 1899, Carroll 1983), of which 13 are known to be obligate *Cecropia* inhabitants (Longino 1991b). New queens fly from their natal nest and find small *Cecropia* saplings. They shed their wings and chew a hole through one of the thin spots. Once inside, they plug the entrance hole with scrapings from the inner stem surface. The hole quickly grows closed, leaving the queen sealed inside. She rears a few small workers which emerge and forage on Müllerian bodies. Many founding queens may inhabit the stacked chambers of a single sapling, but only one ultimately succeeds in establishing the colony that comes to dominate the tree. During this founding phase, multiple species of *Azteca* queens can be found in the same sapling, and multiple queens may occur in the same chamber (Longino 1989a).

Several lineages of *Azteca* are obligate inhabitants of *Cecropia* (Longino 1989b, 1991b, Ayala et al. 1996),

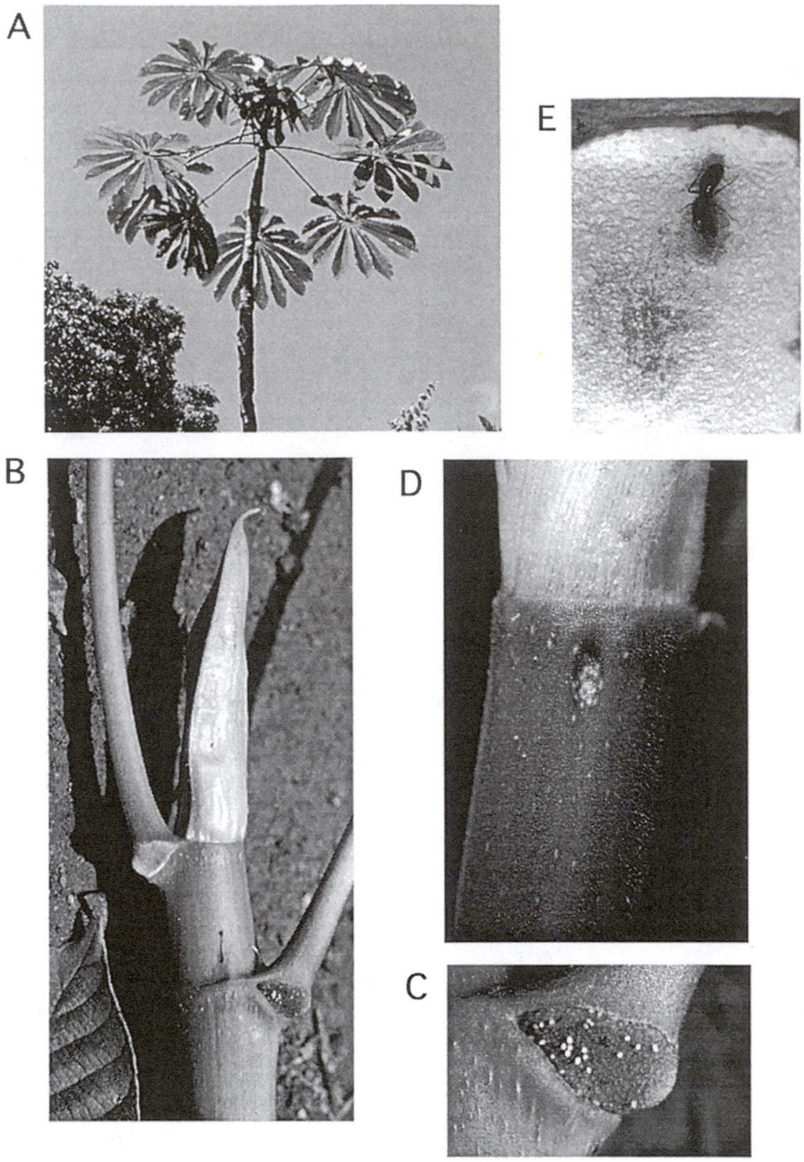

Figure 8.24. Characteristics of myrmecophytic *Cecropia* trees. A, Crown of tree showing radiating long-petioled leaves. B, Apical stem of sapling, showing bamboolike stem segments (internodes) composed of a hollow cylinder and a leaf arising from upper rim of internode. Internode chambers are bounded internally by transverse septa forming floor and ceiling. C, Base of petiole showing velvetlike pad of brown hairs (the trichilium, plural trichilia) from which arise white food bodies (Müllerian bodies). D, Internode wall showing preformed thin spot (prostoma, plural prostomata) through which ants enter. E, Longitudinal section of *Cecropia* sapling stem, showing white internal wall of recently occupied internode, with founding *Azteca constructor* queen at prostomal scar. Note transverse septum forming ceiling of internode about queen. Photographs by John T. Longino.

and they vary in their behavior (Longino 1991a). Members of the *A. muelleri* complex (*A. xanthochroa* and *A. constructor* in Costa Rica) have a central nest in the trunk of the tree where the larvae are concentrated. Internal passageways are kept open between the central nest and all the branch tips, where the Müllerian bodies are produced. The workers are extremely aggressive, and small disturbances cause the workers to rush out onto the branches and trunk. In contrast, members of the *A. alfari* complex (*A. alfari* and *A. ovaticeps* in Costa Rica) have a dispersed nest, with larvae distributed throughout the tree crown in branch tips. Active nest space is only in the branch tips, and internal passageways are not maintained between branches. The workers are relatively passive and often do not emerge when the tree is disturbed. *Azteca coeruleipennis* appears to be a dry forest spe-

cialist. Its nesting behavior is similar to the *A. alfari* complex, but the workers are aggressive and readily emerge when the tree is disturbed.

Myrmecophyte-ant interactions are rarely one-on-one interactions of species pairs. More often, they are multispecies communities of plants and ants (Davidson et al. 1991, Davidson and McKey 1993a, b). Such communities usually contain several species of congeneric myrmecophytes inhabited by several species of congeneric plant-ants. Within these communities, no strict host specificities exist. Each ant species can occur in all the myrmecophyte species. However, associations within the community are not random. Often ant species and myrmecophyte species correlate with habitat and thus with each other (Davidson and Fisher 1991, Longino 1991b). Ant species inhabiting *Cecropia* segregate by high light versus low light, high disturbance versus low disturbance, dry versus wet, and lowland versus upland habitats. The *A. muelleri* complex prefers *Cecropia* trees in low-light, low-disturbance habitats such as small light gaps in mature forest. The *A. alfari* complex prefers *Cecropia* trees in high-light, high-disturbance habitats such as roadsides, abandoned pastures, and river margins. *Azteca coeruleipennis* prefers trees growing in high-light conditions in dry forest. *Cecropia* trees in cloud forests are nonmyrmecophytic (Janzen 1973).

Complex community structure in the *Cecropia-Azteca* system was first described for the Monteverde area (Longino 1989a). A 20-km transect crossing the Continental Divide crosses four distinct assemblages of *Cecropia* and *Azteca*. Populations of *C. peltata* are found on the dry Pacific slope below 1000 m and are inhabited by colonies of *A. coeruleipennis* and *A. alfari* complex. *Cecropia obtusifolia* occurs in a band from 1000 to 1400 m and is inhabited by *A. xanthochroa* and *A. constructor*. *Cecropia polyphlebia* occurs from 1400 m through the cloud forest to 1100 m on the Atlantic slope and is nonmyrmecophytic (Janzen 1973). *Cecropia insignis* occurs at 1100 m and below on the Atlantic slope and is inhabited by *A. xanthochroa* and *A. constructor*.

The nonmyrmecophytic *C. polyphlebia* is possibly derived from myrmecophytic ancestors (Janzen 1973). In Monteverde, it is not sharply differentiated from the *C. obtusifolia* just below it (J. Longino, pers. obs.). Trees in a contact zone between 1400 and 1500 m elevation show a range of phenotypes intermediate between the typical forms of each species. In addition to intermediate forms of foliage and fruit characters, the pads where Müllerian bodies are produced gradually become less distinct and increasingly covered with long hairs. Colonies of *Azteca* in mature trees gradually drop out in this transition zone. Queens of *A. xanthochroa* and *A. constructor* attempt to colonize *C. polyphlebia* at higher elevations (queens can be found in the saplings well up into the cloud forest) but never successfully establish colonies.

When myrmecophytic-ant interactions are considered as spatially variable communities of interacting species, basic ecological questions of distribution and coexistence can be asked. What mechanism drives the habitat segregation between the *A. alfari* and *A. muelleri* complexes? Alternative hypotheses based on light

availability and disturbance regime have been proposed (Davidson and McKey 1993b). The light availability hypothesis (Davidson and Fisher 1991) proposes that *A. alfari* complex species outcompete *A. muelleri* complex species in saplings but also require the high rates of resource input that a high-light environment provides. *Azteca muelleri* complex species may be able to survive with lower resource input rates and can thus occur in habitats where *A. alfari* complex colonies cannot. The disturbance hypothesis (Longino 1991b) proposes that *A. alfari* complex species are more abundant in frequently disturbed habitats because they can reproduce early in small trees. *Azteca muelleri* complex colonies would be at a disadvantage if they required large, long-lived trees to achieve a colony size sufficient for reproduction. In low-disturbance habitats, trees with *A. alfari* complex colonies may soon succumb due to the poor defensive behavior of the ants. In contrast, trees with *A. muelleri* complex colonies may flourish and reach a large size, and the ant colonies produce large numbers of new colonizing queens over a long time span. These hypotheses are not mutually exclusive, and both processes could co-occur.

Monteverde is an excellent site to investigate these hypotheses. Compressed productivity gradients are caused by light availability, temperature (elevation), and water (wet-dry transition). Common garden experiments could be carried out with multiply colonized saplings planted in different habitats to examine predictions of queen survivorship and competitive ability as a function of productivity. The disturbance hypothesis could be examined by demographic studies of tree survivorship, colony growth, and colony reproduction as a function of ant species. Documenting the range of phenotypes between *C. obtusifolia* and *C. polyphlebia* would allow quantification of the myrmecophytic traits (Müllerian body production, reduction of stem pith, development of thin spots in the stem wall) necessary for ant colony survival and how it varies among ant species and along productivity gradients. No hypotheses have been advanced to explain the coexistence of *A. xanthochroa* and *A. constructor*, two relatively similar species that are both common in *C. obtusifolia* trees in Monteverde. These questions await further research on the rich myrmecophyte community of the Monteverde area.

An index that weights the contribution of each bird species relative to that of the alternative dispersers of each of its food plants (Equation 1) is a more useful estimator of "importance" of each bird to the plant community overall than is a simple count of the number of fruit species eaten by each bird. The relative importance of bird species j in the community is

$$I_j = \sum_{i=1}^{s}\left(\frac{C_{i,j} \,/\, T_i}{S}\right), \qquad (1)$$

where T_i is the total number of bird species feeding on plant species i, and S is the total number of plant species included in the community (in this case, the total number of plant species included in the study). $C_{i,j} = 1$ if bird species j consumes fruits of plant species i or 0 if it does not. The index can vary from a minimum of 0 for species that feed on no plants included in the study to a maximum of 1.0 for a bird species that is the only consumer of all plants included. This index ignores the relative intensity of use of each plant species by different animals. It equates all plant species, so a small rare forest floor herb or epiphyte contributes as much to the index as does a dominant canopy tree. Because this index is a function of the total number of plant species included in the diet, intensively studied species tend to have higher importance values than those studied less systematically. Despite these biases, the index provides greater insights than simple counts of fruits consumed.

We computed the importance index for frugivorous birds in the Monteverde area (Wheelwright et al. 1984, Bronstein and Hoffman 1987, Sargent 1994, K. G. Murray, unpubl. data). Data on 75 bird species and 179 plant species were included. Importance values of fruit-eating birds at Monteverde vary over two orders of magnitude. A few species are disproportionately important (Fig. 8.25). The results of the analysis parallel those of the simple counts of food plants reported as marginal totals in Wheelwright et al. (1984): species that feed on many kinds of fruits have high index values. Surprisingly, some small frugivores (e.g., Black-faced Solitaires, Long-tailed Manakins, Prong-billed Barbets, and Common Bush-Tanagers) have values as high as or higher than many of the large species (e.g., Resplendent Quetzals, Three-wattled Bellbirds, and Black Guans) on which large-seeded plants depend. The small frugivores appear to

be disproportionately important to a large number of plants, many of which are less conspicuous. These small birds could be considered "keystone mutualists" (*sensu* Gilbert 1980) just as quetzals, bellbirds, toucanets, and guans; the loss of any of these species could have profound effects on the biodiversity of Monteverde.

We used the same approach to estimate the relative importance of different plant species from the point of view of Monteverde birds. We used the same equation (1), but I_j is the importance of plant species j, T_i is the total number of plants fed on by bird species i, and S is the total number of bird species included in the sample. $C_{i,j} = 1$ if plant species j is included in the diet of bird species i or 0 if it is not. Using the same data matrix, we found that a small

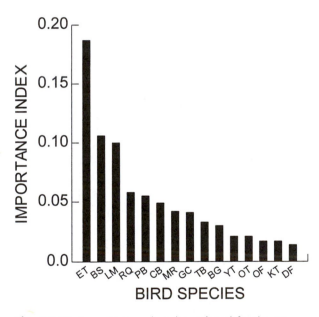

Figure 8.25. Importance values (equation 1) for the 15 frugivorous bird species with the highest indices at Monteverde. Common names of bird species, and numbers of plant species whose fruits are included in the diets of each, are (from left to right) Emerald Toucanet (95), Black-faced Solitaire (51), Long-tailed Manakin (37), Resplendent Quetzal (38), Prong-billed Barbet (30), Common Bush-Tanager (29), Mountain Robin (44), Golden-browed Chlorophonia (14), Three-wattled Bellbird (29), Black Guan (26), Yellow-throated Euphonia (7), Orange-bellied Trogon (14), Olive-striped Flycatcher (9), Keel-billed Toucan (16), and Dusky-capped Flycatcher (8). See text for sources.

number of plant species is disproportionately important to Monteverde frugivores (Fig. 8.26), parallel to the first result. A high correlation exists between the index values for particular plant species and a simple count of the number of bird species known to feed on them. This pattern is difficult to interpret because the seven plant species with the highest importance values (*Acnistis arborescens* [Solanaceae], *Sapium glandulosum* [Euphorbiaceae], *Citharexylum costaricensis* [Verbenaceae], *Hampea appendiculata* [Malvaceae], *Trema micrantha* [Ulmaceae], *Rubus roseafolia* [Rosaceae], and *Conostegia oerstediana* [Melastomataceae]) are pioneers that occur in unnaturally high densities in the pasture–second-growth forest mosaic of the Monteverde community where many of the feeding records were recorded (Wheelwright et al. 1984). Such pioneer species cannot be omitted from the analysis because they occur naturally in small-scale disturbances such as treefalls and are fed on by a large number of forest frugivores. Other species, for example, the mistletoes *Struthanthus oerstedii* (Loranthaceae) and *Phoradendron robaloense* (Viscaceae), have high values because they serve as important food sources for birds (primarily euphonias) that are mistletoe specialists. Our general conclusions are that some plant species are disproportionately important (i.e., are keystone resources) to Monteverde frugivores. We must monitor populations of all keystone mutualists at Monteverde, not just the large frugivores and dominant forest trees that largely determine the physical structure of the forest. The huge variety of epiphytes that make cloud forests unique may depend on smaller, less conspicuous animals such as Black-faced Solitaires, and our conservation efforts and priorities must be directed toward these elements of the community.

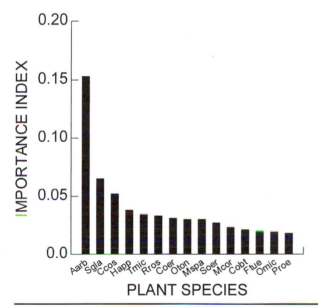

Figure 8.26. Importance values (see equation 1) for the 15 bird-dispersed plant species with the highest indices at Monteverde. Names of plant species, and numbers of bird species known to consume fruits of each are (from left to right) *Acnistus arborescens* (44), *Sapium glandulosum* (formerly *S. oligoneuron*, 23), *Citharexylum costaricensis* (formerly *C. integerrimum*, 23), *Hampea appendiculata* (22), *Trema micrantha* (22), *Rubus roseafolia* (10), *Conostegia oerstediana* (formerly *C. bernouliana*, 17), *Ocotea tonduzii* (18), *Miconia* "species A" (9), *Struthanthus oerstedii* (7), *Myrsine coriacea* (formerly *Rapanea myricoides*, 13), *Cecropia obtusifolia* (11), *Ficus tuerckheimii* (21), *Ossaea micrantha* (6), and *Phoradendron robaloense* (4). See text for sources.

Literature Cited

Abrahamson, W. G. 1989. Plant-animal interactions. McGraw-Hill, New York.

Ågren, J., and D. W. Schemske. 1991. Pollination by deceit in a neotropical monoecious herb, *Begonia involucrata*. Biotropica 23:235–241.

———. 1993. Outcrossing rate and inbreeding depression in two annual monoecious herbs, *Begonia hirsuta* and *B. semiovata*. Evolution 47:125–135.

Ali, S. A. 1931. The role of the sunbirds and the flowerpeckers in the propagation and the distribution of the tree parasite *Loranthus longiflorus* Desr. in the Konkan (W. India). Journal of the Bombay Natural History Society 75:943–945.

Anstett, M. C., G. Michaloud, and F. Kjellberg. 1995. Critical population size for fig/wasp mutualism in a seasonal environment: effect and evolution of the duration of receptivity. Oecologia 103:453–461.

Anstett, M. C., F. Kjellberg, and J. L. Bronstein. 1996. Waiting for wasps: consequences for the pollination dynamics of *Ficus pertusa* L. Journal of Biogeography 23:459–466.

Appanah, S. 1990. Plant-pollinator interactions in Malaysian rain forests. Pages 85–101 *in* K. S. Bawa and M. Hadley, editors. Reproductive ecology of tropical forest plants. Parthenon, Carnforth, UK, and UNESCO, Paris.

Augspurger, C. K. 1983a. Offspring recruitment around tropical trees: changes in cohort distance with time. Oikos 40:189–196.

———. 1983b. Seed dispersal of the tropical tree *Platypodium elegans*, and the escape of its seedlings from fungal pathogens. Journal of Ecology 71: 759–771.

Ayala, F. J., J. K. Wetterer, J. T. Longino, and D. L. Hartl. 1996. Molecular phylogeny of *Azteca* ants (Hymenoptera: Formicidae) and the colonization of *Cecropia* trees. Molecular Phylogenetics and Evolution 5:423–428.

Baker, H. G. 1976. "Mistake" pollination as a reproductive system with special reference to the Caricaceae. Pages 161–169 in J. Burley and B. T. Styles, editors. Tropical trees: variation, breeding and conservation. Academic Press, New York.

Baker, H. G., and I. Baker. 1983. Floral nectar sugar and constituents in relation to pollinator type. Pages 117–141 in C. E. Jones and R. J. Little, editors. Handbook of experimental pollination biology. Van Nostrand Reinhold, New York.

Baker, H. G., K. S. Bawa, G. W. Frankie, and P. A. Opler. 1983. Reproductive biology of plants in tropical forests. Pages 183–215 in F. B. Golley, editor: Tropical rain forest ecosystems structure and function. Elsevier Amsterdam.

Baker, I., and H. G. Baker. 1979. Sugar ratios in nectar. Phytochemical Bulletin 12:43–45.

Bawa, K. S. 1974. Breeding systems of tree species of a lowland tropical community. Evolution 28:85–92.

———. 1980a. Evolution of dioecy in flowering plants. Annual Review of Ecology and Systematics 11:15–39.

———. 1980b. Mimicry of male by female flowers and intrasexual competition for pollinators in Jacaratia dolichaula (D. Smith) Woodson (Caricaceae). Evolution 34:467–474.

———. 1990. Plant-pollinator interactions in tropical rain forests. Annual Review of Ecology and Systematics 21:399–422.

———. 1992. Mating systems, genetic differentiation and speciation in tropical rain forest plants. Biotropica 24:250–255.

———. 1994. Pollinators of tropical dioecious angiosperms: a reassessment? No, not yet. American Journal of Botany 81:456–460.

Bawa, K. S., S. H. Bullock, D. R. Perry, R. E. Coville, and M. H. Grayum. 1985. Reproductive biology of tropical lowland rain forest trees. II. Pollination systems. American Journal of Botany 72:346–356.

Bawa, K. S., P. S. Ashton, and S. Mohd Nor. 1990. Reproductive ecology of tropical forest plants: management issues. Pages 3–13 in K. S. Bawa and M. Hadley, editors. Reproductive ecology of tropical forest plants. Parthenon, Carnforth, UK.

Beattie, A. J. 1985. The evolutionary ecology of ant-plant mutualisms. Cambridge University Press, Cambridge.

Bequaert, J. 1922. Ants of the American Museum Congo expedition. IV. Ants in their diverse relations to the plant world. Bulletin of the American Museum of Natural History 45:333–583.

Boshier, D. H., M. R. Chase, and K. S. Bawa. 1995a. Population genetics of Cordia alliodora (Boraginaceae), a neotropical tree. 2. Mating system. American Journal of Botany 82:476–483.

———. 1995b. Population genetics of Cordia alliodora (Boraginaceae), a neotropical tree. 3. Gene flow, neighborhood, and population substructure. American Journal of Botany 82:484–490.

Boucher, D. H., editor. 1985. The biology of mutualism: ecology and evolution. Oxford University Press, New York.

Bronstein, J. L. 1987. Maintenance of species-specificity in a neotropical fig-pollinator wasp mutualism. Oikos 48:39–46.

———. 1988a. Limits to fruit production in a monoecious fig: consequences of an obligate mutualism. Ecology 69:207–214.

———. 1988b. Mutualism, antagonism, and the fig-pollinator interaction. Ecology 69:1298–1302.

———. 1988c. Predators of fig wasps. Biotropica 20: 215–219.

———. 1991. The nonpollinating wasp fauna of Ficus pertusa: exploitation of a mutualism? Oikos 61: 175–186.

———. 1992. Seed predators as mutualists: ecology and evolution of the fig/pollinator interaction. Pages 1–44 in E. Bernays, editor. Insect-plant interactions (Vol. 4). CRC Press, Boca Raton, Florida.

———. 1994. Our current understanding of mutualism. Quarterly Review of Biology 69:31–51.

———. 1995. The plant-pollinator landscape. Pages 256–288 in L. Hansson, L. Fahrig, and G. Merriam, editors. Mosaic landscapes and ecological processes. Chapman and Hall, London.

Bronstein, J., and K. Hoffman. 1987. Spatial and temporal variation in frugivory at a neotropical fig, Ficus pertusa. Oikos 49:261–268.

Bronstein, J. L., P. H. Gouyon, C. Gliddon, F. Kjellberg, and G. Michaloud. 1990. Ecological consequences of flowering asynchrony on monoecious figs: a simulation study. Ecology 71:2145–2156.

Buchmann, S. L. 1983. Buzz pollination in angiosperms. Pages 73–113 in C. E. Jones and R. J. Little, editors. Handbook of experimental pollination biology. Van Nostrand Reinhold, New York.

Buckley, R. C. 1982a. Ant-plant interactions: a world review. Pages 111–141 in R. C. Buckley, editor. Ant-plant interactions in Australia. Dr. W. Junk Publisher, The Hague.

———. 1982b. A world bibliography of ant-plant interactions. Pages 143–162 in R. C. Buckley, editor. Ant-plant interactions in Australia. Dr. W. Junk Publisher, The Hague.

Burd, M. 1994. Bateman's principle and plant reproduction: the role of pollen limitation in fruit and seed set. The Botanical Review 60:83–139.

Burger, W. 1977. Flora Costaricensis, family #52, Moraceae. Fieldiana, Botany 40:94–215.

Burger, W., and H. van der Werff. 1990. Lauraceae. Flora Costaricensis. Fieldiana, Botany (New Series) 23:12–21.

Byrne, M. M., and D. J. Levey. 1993. Removal of seeds from frugivore defecations by ants in a Costa Rican rain forest. Vegetatio 107/108:363–374.

Cane, J. H. 1993. Reproductive role of sterile pollen in Saurauia (Actinidiaceae), a cryptically dioecious neotropical tree. Biotropica 25:493–495.

Carroll, C. R. 1983. Azteca (hormiga azteca, azteca ants, cecropia ants). Pages 691–693 in D. H. Janzen, editor. Costa Rican natural history. University of Chicago Press, Chicago.

Castro, O. C. 1993. Chemical and biological extractives of Lauraceae species in Costa Rican tropical forests. Recent Advances in Phytochemistry 27:65–87.

Chase, M. R., D. H. Boshier, and K. S. Bawa. 1995. Population genetics of Cordia alliodora (Boraginaceae), a neotropical tree. 1. Genetic variation in natural populations. American Journal of Botany 82:468–475.

Chase, M., R. Kesseli, and K. S. Bawa. 1996. Microsatellite markers for population and conservation genetics of tropical trees. American Journal of Botany 83:51–57.

Chen, J., and B. J. D. Meeuse. 1972. Induction of indole synthesis in the appendix of Sauromatum guttatum Schott. Plant and Cell Physiology 13: 831–841.

Clark, D. B., and D. A. Clark. 1984. Spacing dynamics of a tropical rain forest tree, evaluation of the Janzen-Connell model. American Naturalist 124: 769–788.

Crawley, M. J. 1992. Seed predators and plant population dynamics. Pages 157–191 in M. Fenner, editor. Seeds: the ecology of regeneration in plant communities. CAB International, Wallingford, UK.

Crepet, W. L. 1983. The role of insect pollination in the evolution of the Angiosperms. Pages 31–50 in L. Real, editor. Pollination biology. Academic Press, Orlando, Florida.

Cruden, R. W. 1972. Pollinators in high-elevation ecosystems: relative effectiveness of birds and bees. Science 176:1439–1440.

Cruden, R. W., S. Kinsman, R. E. Stockhouse III, and Y. B. Linhart. 1976. Pollination, fecundity and the distribution of moth-flowered plants. Biotropica 8:204–210.

Cruden, R. W., S. M. Hermann, and S. Peterson. 1983. Patterns of nectar production and plant-pollinator coevolution. Pages 80–125 *in* B. Bentley and T. Elias, editors. The biology of nectaries. Columbia University Press, New York.

Cunningham, S. A. 1991. Experimental evidence for pollination of *Banksia* spp. by non-flying mammals. Oecologia 87:86–90.

Dafni, A. 1992. Pollination ecology: a practical approach. Oxford University Press, New York.

Davidar, P. 1987. Fruit structure in two neotropical mistletoes and its consequences for seed dispersal. Biotropica 19:137–139.

Davidar, P., and E. S. Morton. 1986. The relationship between fruit crop sizes and fruit removal rates by birds. Ecology 67:262–265.

Davidson, D. E., and B. L. Fisher. 1991. Symbiosis of ants with *Cecropia* as a function of light regime. Pages 289–309 *in* C. R. Huxley and D. F. Cutler, editors. Ant-plant interactions. Oxford University Press, Oxford.

Davidson, D. E., and D. McKey. 1993a. Ant-plant symbioses: stalking the Chuyachaqui. Trends in Ecology and Evolution 8:326–332.

———. 1993b. The evolutionary ecology of symbiotic ant-plant relationships. Journal of Hymenoptera Research 2:13–83.

Davidson, D. W., R. B. Foster, R. R. Snelling, and P. W. Lozada. 1991. Variable composition of some tropical ant-plant symbioses. Pages 145–162 *in* P. W. Price, T. M. Lewinsohn, G. W. Fernandes, and W. W. Benson, editors. Plant-animal interactions: evolutionary ecology in tropical and temperate regions. Wiley, New York.

Dayanandan, S., D. N. C. Attygalla, A. W. W. L. Abeygunasekera, I. A. U. N. Gunatilleke, and C. V. S. Gunatilleke. 1990. Phenology and floral morphology in relation to pollination of some Sri Lankan Dipterocarps. Pages 103–134 *in* K. S. Bawa and M. Hadley, editors. Reproductive ecology of tropical forest plants. Parthenon, Carnforth, UK.

Devlin, B., and A. G. Stephenson. 1984. Factors that influence the duration of the staminate and pistillate phases of *Lobelia cardinalis* flowers. Botanical Gazette 145:323–328.

DeVries, P. J. 1987. The butterflies of Costa Rica and their natural history: Papilionidae, Pieridae, Nymphalidae. Princeton University Press, Princeton, New Jersey.

Dinerstein, E. 1983. Reproductive ecology of fruit bats and seasonality of fruit production in a Costa Rican cloud forest. Ph.D. dissertation, University of Washington, Seattle.

———. 1986. Reproductive ecology of fruit bats and the seasonality of fruit production in a Costa Rican cloud forest. Biotropica 18:307–318.

Docters van Leeuwen, W. M. 1954. On the biology of some Javanese Loranthaceae and the role birds play in their life history. Beaufortia 4:105–207.

Endress, P. K. 1994. Diversity and evolutionary biology of tropical flowers. Cambridge University Press, Cambridge.

Faegri, K., and L. van der Pijl. 1979. The principles of pollination ecology (3rd ed., rev.). Pergammon Press, Oxford.

Feinsinger, P. 1976. Organization of a tropical guild of nectarivorous birds. Ecological Monographs 46:257–291.

———. 1978. Ecological interactions between plants and hummingbirds in a successional tropical community. Ecological Monographs 48:269–287.

———. 1983. Coevolution and pollination. Pages 283–310 *in* D. J. Futuyma and M. Slatkin, editors. Coevolution. Sinauer, Sunderland, Massachusetts.

———. 1987. Effects of plant species on each other's pollination: is community structure influenced? Trends in Ecology and Evolution 2:123–126.

Feinsinger, P., and W. H. Busby. 1987. Pollen carryover: experimental comparisons between morphs of *Palicourea lasiorrachis* (Rubiaceae), a distylous, bird-pollinated, tropical treelet. Oecologia 73: 231–235.

Feinsinger, P., and H. M. Tiebout III. 1991. Competition among plants sharing hummingbird pollinators: laboratory experiments on a mechanism. Ecology 72:1946–1952.

Feinsinger, P., L. A. Swarm, and J. A. Wolfe. 1985. Nectar-feeding birds on Trinidad and Tobago: comparison of diverse and depauperate guilds. Ecological Monographs 55:1–28.

Feinsinger, P., K. G. Murray, S. Kinsman, and W. H. Busby. 1986. Floral neighborhoods and pollination success within four hummingbird-pollinated plant species in a Costa Rican cloud forest. Ecology 67:449–464.

Feinsinger, P., J. H. Beach, Y. B. Linhart, W. H. Busby, and K. G. Murray. 1987. Disturbance, pollinator predictability, and pollination success among Costa Rican cloud forest plants. Ecology 68:1294–1305.

Feinsinger, P., W. H. Busby, and H. M. Tiebout III. 1988a. Effects of indiscriminate foraging by tropical hummingbirds on pollination and plant reproductive success: experiments with two tropical treelets (Rubiaceae). Oecologia 76:471–474.

Feinsinger, P., W. H. Busby, K. G. Murray, J. H. Beach, W. Z. Pounds, and Y. B. Linhart. 1988b. Mixed support for spatial heterogeneity in species interactions: hummingbirds in a tropical disturbance mosaic. The American Naturalist 131:33–57.

Feinsinger, P., H. M. Tiebout III, and B. E. Young. 1991. Do tropical bird-pollinated plants exhibit density-dependent interactions? Field experiments. Ecology 72:1953–1963.

Feinsinger, P., H. M. Tiebout III, B. E. Young, and K. G. Murray. 1992. New perspectives on neotropical plant-hummingbird interactions. Acta Congressus Internationalis Ornithologici 20:1605–1610.

Fleming, T. H., and B. L. Partridge. 1984. On the analysis of phenological overlap. Oecologia 62:344–350.

Fonseca, C. R., and G. Ganade. 1996. Asymmetries, compartments and null interactions in an Amazonian ant-plant community. Journal of Animal Ecology 65:339–347.

Forbes, W. A. 1880. Contributions to the anatomy of passerine birds. Part 1. On the structure of the stomach in certain genera of tanagers. Proceedings of the Zoological Society 10:143–147.

Forel, A. 1899. Formicidae. Biologia Centrali-Americana, Hymenoptera 3:1–160.

Forget, P. M. 1993. Post-dispersal predation and scatter-hoarding of *Dipteryx panamensis* (Papilionaceae) seeds by rodents in Panama. Oecologia 94:255–261.

Forget, P. M., and T. Milleron. 1991. Evidence for secondary seed dispersal by rodents in Panama. Oecologia 87:596–599.

Foster, R. B. 1982. Famine on Barro Colorado Island. Pages 201–212 *in* E. G. Leigh, Jr., A. S. Rand, and D. M. Windsor, editors. The ecology of a tropical forest: seasonal rhythms and long-term changes. Smithsonian Institution Press, Washington, D.C.

Frankie, G. W., H. G. Baker, and P. A. Opler. 1974. Comparative phenological studies of trees in tropical wet and dry forests in the lowlands of Costa Rica. Journal of Ecology 62:881–919.

Frankie, G. W., W. A. Haber, P. A. Opler, and K. S. Bawa. 1983. Characteristics and organization of the large bee pollination system in the Costa Rican dry forest. Pages 411–447 *in* C. E. Jones and R. J. Little, editors. Handbook of experimental pollination biology. Van Nostrand Reinhold, New York.

Frazee, J., M. Gargiullo, L. McDade, D. Dearing, E. Macklin, J. Ratsirarson, J. C. Uyehara, and D. Wijesinghe. 1990. Phenology of flower and nectar production in *Cen-*

tropogon. OTS 90–1 coursebook. Organization for Tropical Studies, Durham, North Carolina.

Futuyma, D. J., and M. Slatkin, editors. 1983. Coevolution. Sinauer, Sunderland, Massachusetts.

Garwood, N. 1983. Seed germination in a seasonal tropical forest in Panama: a community study. Ecological Monographs 53:159–181.

Gentry, A. H. 1982. Patterns of neotropical plant species diversity. Evolutionary Biology 15:1–84.

Gibson, J. P. 1995. Evolutionary ecology of reproduction in *Ocotea tenera* (Lauraceae), a gynodioecious tropical tree. Ph.D. dissertation, University of Colorado, Boulder.

Gibson, J. P., and N. T. Wheelwright. 1995. Genetic structure in a population of a tropical tree *Ocotea tenera* (Lauraceae): influence of avian seed dispersal. Oecologia 103:49–54.

———. 1996. Mating system dynamics of *Ocotea tenera* (Lauraceae), a gynodioecious tropical tree. American Journal of Botany 83:890–894.

Gilbert, L. E. 1980. Food web organization and conservation of neotropical diversity. Pages 11–34 *in* M. E. Soulé and B. A. Wilcox, editors. Conservation biology: an evolutionary-ecological perspective. Sinauer, Sunderland, Massachusetts.

Gilbert, L. E., and P. H. Raven, editors. 1975. Coevolution of animals and plants. University of Texas Press, Austin.

Gleason, A. H. 1945. On *Blakea* and *Topobea*. Bulletin of the Torrey Botanical Club 72:385–393.

Godschalk, S. K. B. 1983. Mistletoe dispersal by birds in South Africa. Pages 117–128 *in* M. Calder and P. Bernhardt, editors. The biology of mistletoes. Academic Press, Sydney.

Goldwasser, L. 1987. I. Branching patterns, generating rules, and astogenetic trajectories in *Bugula* (Cheilostomata: Bryozoa); II. Ecological and evolutionary consequences of mutualism. Ph.D. dissertation, University of California, Berkeley.

Goldwasser, L., G. Schatz, and H. Young. 1993. A new method for marking Scarabaeidae and other beetles. Coleopterists Bulletin 47:21–26.

Grimaldi, D. A. 1987. Phylogenetics and taxonomy of *Zygothrica* (Diptera: Drosophilidae). The American Museum of Natural History Bulletin 186:103–268.

Haber, W. A. 1983a. Checklist of Sphingidae. Pages 645–650 *in* D. Janzen, editor. Costa Rican natural history. University of Chicago Press, Chicago.

———. 1983b. *Solanum siparunoides*. Pages 326–328 *in* D. Janzen, editor. Costa Rican natural history. University of Chicago Press, Chicago.

———. 1993. Seasonal migration of monarchs and other butterflies in Costa Rica. Los Angeles County Museum of Natural History, Science Series No. 38:201–207.

Haber, W. A., and G. W. Frankie. 1983. *Luehea candida*. Pages 269–270 *in* D. Janzen, editor. Costa Rican natural history. University of Chicago Press, Chicago.

———. 1989. A tropical hawkmoth community: Costa Rican dry forest Sphingidae. Biotropica 21:155–172.

Hall, P., L. C. Orrell, and K. S. Bawa. 1994. Genetic diversity and mating system in a tropical tree, *Carapa guianensis* (Meliaceae). American Journal of Botany 81:1104–1111.

Hall, P., S. Walker, and K. S. Bawa. 1996. Effect of forest fragmentation on genetic diversity and mating system in a tropical tree, *Pithecellobium elegans*. Conservation Biology 10:757–768.

Hamrick, J. L., and M. D. Loveless. 1989. The genetic structure of tropical tree populations: associations with reproductive biology. Pages 129–146 *in* J. H. Bock and Y. B. Linhart, editors. The evolutionary ecology of plants. Westview Press, Boulder, Colorado.

Hamrick, J. L., D. A. Murawski, and J. D. Nason. 1993. The influence of seed dispersal mechanisms on the genetic structure of tropical tree populations. Vegetatio 107/108:281–297.

Harder, L. D., and S. C. H. Barrett. 1996. Pollen dispersal and mating patterns in animal-pollinated plants. Pages 140–190 *in* D. G. Lloyd and S. C. H. Barrett, editors. Floral biology: Studies on floral evolution in animal-pollinated plants. Chapman and Hall, New York.

Harper, J. L. 1977. Population biology of plants. Academic Press, London.

Heithaus, E. R., and T. H. Fleming, 1978. Foraging movements of a frugivorous bat, *Carollia perspicillata* (Phyllostomatidae). Ecological Monographs 48:127–143.

Herre, E. A. 1987. Optimality, plasticity and selective regime in fig wasp sex ratios. Nature 329:627–629.

———. 1989. Coevolution of reproductive characteristics in 12 species of New World figs and their pollinator wasps. Experientia 45:637–646.

———. 1996. An overview of studies on a community of Panamanian figs. Journal of Biogeography 23: 593–607.

Herrera, C. M. 1987. Components of pollinator "quality": comparative analysis of a diverse insect assemblage. Oikos 50:79–90.

———. 1996. Floral traits and plant adaptation to insect pollinators: a devil's advocate approach. Pages 65–87 *in* D. G. Lloyd and S. C. H. Barrett, editors. Floral biology: studies in floral evolution in animal-pollinated plants. Chapman and Hall, New York.

Herrera, C. M., P. Jordano, L. Lopez-Soria, and J. A. Amat. 1994. Recruitment of a mast-fruiting, bird-dispersed tree: bridging frugivore activity and seedling establishment. Ecological Monographs 64:315–344.

Hilty, S. L. 1980. Flowering and fruiting periodicity in a premontane rain forest in Pacific Colombia. Biotropica 12:292–306.

Hoppes, W. G. 1987. Pre- and post-foraging movements of frugivorous birds in an eastern deciduous forest woodland, USA. Oikos 49:281–290.

Howe, H. F. 1977. Bird activity and seed dispersal of a tropical wet forest tree. Ecology 58:539–550.

———. 1985. Gomphothere fruits: a critique. American Naturalist 125:853–865.

———. 1993. Specialized and generalized dispersal systems: where does "the paradigm" stand? Vegetatio 107/108:3–13.

Howe, H. F., and D. De Steven. 1979. Fruit production, migrant bird visitation, and seed dispersal of *Guarea glabra* in Panama. Oecologia 39:185–196.

Howe, H. F., and G. F. Estabrook. 1977. On intraspecific competition for dispersal agents in tropical trees. American Naturalist 111:817–832.

Howe, H. F., and R. B. Primack. 1975. Differential seed dispersal by birds of the tree *Casearia nitida* (Flacourtiaceae). Biotropica 7:278–283.

Howe, H. F., and W. Richter. 1982. Effect of seed size on seedling size in a neotropical nutmeg (*Virola surinamensis*): a within and between crop analysis. Oecologia 53:347–351.

Howe, H. F., and J. Smallwood. 1982. Ecology of seed dispersal. Annual Review of Ecology and Systematics 13:201–228.

Howe, H. F., and G. A. Vande Kerckhove. 1979. Fecundity and seed dispersal by birds of a tropical tree. Ecology 60:180–189.

———. 1981. Removal of nutmeg (*Virola surinamensis*) crops by birds. Ecology 62:1093–1106.

Howe, H. F., and L. C. Westley. 1988. Ecological relationships of plants and animals. Oxford University Press, New York.

Howe, H. F., E. W. Schupp, and L. C. Westley. 1985. Early consequences of seed dispersal for a neotropical tree (*Virola surinamensis*). Ecology 66: 781–791.

Inouye, D. W. 1983. The ecology of nectar robbing. Pages 153–173 *in* B. Bentley and T. Elias, editors. The biology of nectaries. Columbia University Press, New York.

Irvine, A. K., and J. E. Armstrong. 1990. Beetle pollination in tropical forests of Australia. Pages 135–149 in K. S. Bawa and M. Hadley, editors. Reproductive ecology of tropical forest plants. Parthenon, Carnforth, UK.

Isler, M. L. and P. R. Isler. 1987. The tanagers: natural history, distribution, and identification. Smithsonian Institution Press, Washington, D.C.

Janson, C. H., J. Terborgh, and L. H. Emmons. 1981. Non-flying mammals as pollinating agents in the Amazonian forest. Biotropica 12(Suppl.):1–6.

Janzen, D. H. 1966. Coevolution of mutualism between ants and acacias in Central America. Evolution 20:249–275.

———. 1967a. Fire, vegetation structure, and the ant x acacia interaction in Central America. Ecology 48:26–35.

———. 1967b. Interaction of the Bull's-Horn acacia (Acacia cornigera L.) with an ant inhabitant (Pseudomyrmex ferruginea F. Smith) in eastern Mexico. Kansas University Science Bulletin 47: 315–558.

———. 1969. Allelopathy by myrmecophytes: the ant Azteca as an allelopathic agent of Cecropia. Ecology 50:147–153.

———. 1971. Escape of Cassia grandis L. beans from predators in time and space. Ecology 52:964–979.

———. 1973. Dissolution of mutualism between Cecropia and its Azteca ants. Biotropica 5:15–28.

———. 1979. How to be a fig. Annual Review of Ecology and Systematics 10:3–51.

———. 1980. When is it coevolution? Evolution 34: 611–612.

———. 1983. Insects. Pages 619–645 in D. Janzen, editor. Costa Rican natural history. University of Chicago Press, Chicago.

Janzen, D. H., and P. Martin. 1982. Neotropical anachronisms: what the gomphotheres ate. Science 215: 19–27.

Jones, C. E., and R. J. Little, editors. 1983. Handbook of experimental pollination biology. Van Nostrand Rheinhold, New York.

Jordano, P. 1987. Patterns of mutualistic interactions in pollination and seed dispersal: connectance, dependence asymmetries, and coevolution. American Naturalist 129:657–677.

———. 1992. Fruits and frugivory. Pages 105–156 in M. Fenner, editor. Seeds: the ecology of regeneration in plant communities. CAB International, Wallingford, UK.

Kalko, E. K. V., E. A. Herre, and C. O. Handley, Jr. 1996. Relation of fig fruit characteristics to fruit-eating bats in the New and Old World tropics. Journal of Biogeography 23:565–576.

Kathuria, P., K. N. Ganeshaiah, R. Uma Shaanker, and R. Vasudeva. 1995. Is there dimorphism for style lengths in monoecious figs? Current Science 68: 1047–1049.

Kato, M. 1996. Plant-pollinator interactions in the understory of a lowland mixed Dipterocarp forest in Sarawak. American Journal of Botany 83: 732–743.

Kearns, C. A., and D. W. Inouye. 1993. Techniques for pollination biologists. University Press of Colorado, Niwot.

Kerley, G. I. H., and T. Erasmus. 1991. What do mice select for in seeds? Oecologia 86:261–267.

Knuth, P. 1906. Handbook of flower pollination (Vol. 1). Oxford University Press, Oxford.

———. 1908. Handbook of flower pollination (Vol. 2). Oxford University Press, Oxford.

———. 1909. Handbook of flower pollination (Vol. 3). Oxford University Press, Oxford.

Koptur, S. 1983. Flowering phenology and floral biology of Inga (Fabaceae: Mimosoideae). Systematic Botany 8:354–368.

———. 1984a. Experimental evidence for defense of Inga (Mimosoideae) saplings by ants. Ecology 65: 1787–1793.

———. 1984b. Outcrossing and pollinator limitation of fruit set: breeding systems of neotropical Inga trees (Fabaceae: Mimosoideae). Evolution 38: 1130–1143.

———. 1985. Alternative defenses against herbivores in Inga (Fabaceae: Mimosoideae) over an elevational gradient. Ecology 66:1639–1650.

———. 1991. Extrafloral nectaries of herbs and trees: modelling the interaction with ants and parasitoids. Pages 213–229 in D. Cutler and C. Huxley, editors. Ant-plant interactions. Oxford University Press, Oxford.

———. 1994. Floral and extrafloral nectars of Costa Rican Inga trees: a comparison of their constituents and composition. Biotropica 26:276–284.

Koptur, S., W. A. Haber, G. W. Frankie, and H. G. Baker. 1988. Phenological studies of shrub and treelet species in tropical cloud forests of Costa Rica. Journal of Tropical Ecology 4:323–346.

Koptur, S., E. N. Davila, D. R. Gordon, B. J. D. McPhail, C. G. Murphy, and J. B. Slowinski. 1990. The effect of pollen removal on the duration of the staminate phase of Centropogon talamancensis. Brenesia 33:15–18.

Kress, W. J., and J. H. Beach. 1994. Flowering plant reproductive systems. Pages 161–182 in L. A. McDade, K. S. Bawa, H. A. Hespenheide, and G. S. Hartshorn, editors. La Selva: ecology and natural history of a neotropical rain forest. University of Chicago Press, Chicago.

Kress, W. J., G. E. Schatz, M. Andrianifahanana, and H. S. Morland. 1994. Pollination of Ravenala madagascariensis (Strelitziaceae) by lemurs in Madagascar: evidence for an archaic coevolutionary system? American Journal of Botany 81:542–551.

Lackie, P. M., C. D. Thomas, M. J. Brisco, and D. N. Hepper. 1986. On the pollination ecology of Hamelia patens (Rubiaceae) at Monteverde, Costa Rica. Brenesia 25–26:203–213.

Lamarck, J. B. de. 1778. Flore française, Bd. 3, p. 1150.

Lawton, R. O., L. D. Alexander, W. N. Setzer, and K. G. Byler. 1993. Floral essential oil of Guettarda poasana inhibits yeast growth. Biotropica 25: 483–486.

León, J. 1966. Central American and West Indian species of Inga (Leguminosae). Annals of the Missouri Botanical Garden 53:365–459.

Letourneau, D. K. 1983. Passive aggression: an alternative hypothesis for the Piper-Pheidole association. Oecologia 60:215–217.

Levey, D. J. 1986. Methods of seed processing by birds and seed deposition patterns. Pages 147–158 in A. Estrada and T. H. Fleming, editors. Frugivores and seed dispersal. Dr. W. Junk Publishers, Dordrecht.

———. 1988. Tropical wet forest treefall gaps and distributions of understory birds and plants. Ecology 69:1076–1089.

Levey, D. J., and M. M. Byrne. 1993. Complex ant-plant interactions: rain forest ants as secondary dispersers and post-dispersal seed predators. Ecology 74:1802–1812.

Levin, D. A., and W. W. Anderson. 1970. Competition for pollinators between simultaneously flowering species. American Naturalist 104:455–467.

Linhart, Y. B., P. F. Feinsinger, J. H. Beach, W. H. Busby, K. G. Murray, W. Zuchowski Pounds, S. Kinsman, C. A. Guindon, and M. Kooiman. 1987a. Disturbance and predictability of flowering plants in bird-pollinated cloud forest plants. Ecology 68:1696–1710.

Linhart, Y. B., W. H. Busby, J. H. Beach, and P. Feinsinger. 1987b. Forager behavior, pollen dispersal, and inbreeding in two species of hummingbird-pollinated plants. Evolution 41:679–682.

Little, R. J. 1983. A review of floral food deception mimicries with comments on floral mutualism. Pages 294–309 in C. E. Jones and R. J. Little, editors. Handbook of experimental pollination biology. Van Nostrand Reinhold, New York.

Loiselle, B. A., and J. G. Blake. 1991. Temporal variation in birds and fruits along an elevational gradient in Costa Rica. Ecology 72:180–193.

Loiselle, B. A., E. Ribbens, and O. Vargas. 1996. Spatial and temporal variation of seed rain in a tropical lowland wet forest. Biotropica 28:82–95.

Long, R. W. 1971. A flora of tropical Florida. University of Miami Press, Coral Gables, Florida.

Longino, J. T. 1989a. Geographic variation and community structure in an ant-plant mutualism: *Azteca* and *Cecropia* in Costa Rica. Biotropica 21:126–132.

———. 1989b. Taxonomy of the *Cecropia*-inhabiting ants in the *Azteca alfari* species group: evidence for two broadly sympatric species. Contributions in Science, Natural History Museum of Los Angeles County 412:1–16.

———. 1991a. *Azteca* ants in *Cecropia* trees: taxonomy, colony structure, and behavior. Pages 271–288 *in* C. Huxley and D. Cutler, editors. Ant-plant interactions. Oxford University Press, Oxford.

———. 1991b. Taxonomy of the *Cecropia*-inhabiting *Azteca* ants. Journal of Natural History 25:1571–1602.

———. 1996. Taxonomic characterization of some live-stem inhabiting *Azteca* (Hymenoptera: Formicidae) in Costa Rica, with special reference to the ants of *Cordia* (Boraginaceae) and *Triplaris* (Polygonaceae). Journal of Hymenoptera Research 5:131–156.

Longino, J. T., and P. Hanson. 1995. The ants (Formicidae). Pages 588–620 *in* P. Hanson and I. Gauld, editors. The Hymenoptera of Costa Rica. Oxford University Press, Oxford.

Lumer, C. 1980. Rodent pollination of *Blakea* (Melastomataceae) in a Costa Rican cloud forest. Brittonia 32:512–517.

Lumer, C., and R. Schoer. 1986. Pollination of *Blakea austin-smithii* and *B. penduliflora* (Melastomataceae) by small rodents in Costa Rica. Biotropica 18:363–364.

Machado, C. A., E. A. Herre, S. McCafferty, and E. Bermingham. 1996. Molecular phylogenies of fig pollinating and non-pollinating wasps and the implications for the origin and evolution of the fig-fig wasp mutualism. Journal of Biogeography 23:531–542.

Madison, M. 1979. Protection of developing seeds in neotropical Araceae. Aroideana 2:52–61.

Mazer, S. J., and N. T. Wheelwright. 1993. Fruit size and shape: allometry at different taxonomic levels in bird-dispersed plants. Evolutionary Ecology 7:556–575.

McDade, L. M., and S. Kinsman. 1980. The impact of floral parasitism in two neotropical hummingbird-pollinated plant species. Evolution 34:944–958.

McKey, D. 1975. The ecology of coevolved seed dispersal systems. Pages 159–191 *in* L. E. Gilbert and P. H. Raven, editors. Coevolution of animals and plants. University of Texas Press, Austin.

———. 1991. Phylogenetic analysis of the evolution of a mutualism: *Leonardoxa* (Caesalpiniaceae) and its associated ants. Pages 310–334 *in* C. R. Huxley and D. F. Cutler, editors. Ant-plant interactions. Oxford University Press, Oxford.

Meeuse, B. J. D. 1975. Thermogenic respiration in aroids. Annual Review of Plant Physiology 26: 117–126.

Milton, K. 1978. Behavioral adaptations to leaf-eating by the mantled howler monkey (*Alouatta palliata*). Pages 535–550 *in* G. G. Montgomery, editor. The ecology of arboreal folivores. Smithsonian Institution Press, Washington, D.C.

Milton, K., D. M. Windsor, D. W. Morrison, and M. A. Estribi. 1982. Fruiting phenologies of two neotropical *Ficus* species. Ecology 63:752–762.

Montgomery, G. G., and M. E. Sunquist. 1978. Habitat selection and use by two-toed and three-toed sloths. Pages 329–360 *in* G. G. Montgomery, editor. The ecology of arboreal folivores. Smithsonian Institution Press, Washington, D.C.

Moore, L. A., and M. F. Willson. 1982. The effect of microhabitat, spatial distribution, and display size on dispersal of *Lindera benzoin* by avian frugivores. Canadian Journal of Botany 60:557–560.

Müller, F. 1876. Ueber das Haarkissen am Blattstiel der Imbauba (*Cecropia*), das Gemüsebeet der Imbauba-Ameise. Jenaische Zeitschrift fur Medizin und Naturwissenschaft 10:281–286.

———. 1880–1881. Die Imbauba und ihre Beschützer. Kosmos 8:109–116.

Murawski, D. A. 1987. Floral resource variation, pollinator response, and potential pollen flow in *Psiguria warscewiczii*. Ecology 68:1273–1282.

———. 1995. Reproductive biology and genetics of tropical trees from a canopy perspective. Pages 457–493 *in* M. D. Lowman and N. M. Nadkarni, editors. Forest canopies. Academic Press, San Diego.

Murray, D. R., editor. 1986. Seed dispersal. Academic Press, Sydney.

Murray, K. G. 1986a. Avian seed dispersal of neotropical gap-dependent plants. Ph.D. dissertation, University of Florida, Gainesville.

———. 1986b. Consequences of seed dispersal for gap-dependent plants: relationships between seed shadows, germination requirements, and forest dynamic processes. Pages 187–198 *in* A. Estrada and T. H. Fleming, editors. Frugivores and seed dispersal. Dr. W. Junk Publishers, Dordrecht.

———. 1987. Selection for optimal fruit crop size in bird-dispersed plants. American Naturalist 129: 18–31.

———. 1988. Avian seed dispersal of three neotropical gap-dependent plants. Ecological Monographs 58: 271–298.

Murray, K. G., P. Feinsinger, W. H. Busby, Y. B. Linhart, J. H. Beach, and S. Kinsman. 1987. Evaluation of character displacement among plants in two tropical pollination guilds. Ecology 68:1283–1293.

Murray, K. G., S. Russell, C. M. Picone, K. Winnett-Murray, W. Sherwood, and M. L. Kuhlmann. 1994. Fruit laxatives and seed passage rates in frugivores: consequences for plant reproductive success. Ecology 75:989–994.

Nadkarni, N. M., and T. J. Matelson. 1989. Bird use of epiphyte resources in neotropical trees. Condor 91:891–907.

Nagy, K. A., D. K. Odell, and R. S. Seymour. 1972. Temperature regulation by the inflorescence of *Philodendron*. Science 178:1195–1197.

Nitecki, M. H. 1983. Coevolution. University of Chicago Press, Chicago.

Pipkin, S. B., R. L. Rodriguez, and J. Leon. 1966. Plant host specificity among flower-feeding neotropical *Drosophila* (Diptera: Drosophilidae). American Naturalist 100:135–156.

Podolsky, R. D. 1992. Strange floral attractors: pollinator attraction and the evolution of plant sexual systems. Science 258:791–793.

Poole, R. W., and B. J. Rathcke. 1979. Regularity, randomness and aggregation in flowering phenologies. Science 203:470–471.

Powell, G. V. N., and R. Bjork. 1995. Implications of intratropical migration on reserve design: a case study using *Pharomachrus mocinno*. Conservation Biology 9:354–362.

Price, M. V., and S. H. Jenkins. 1986. Rodents as seed consumers and dispersers. Pages 191–235 *in* D. R. Murray, editor. Seed dispersal. Academic Press, Sydney.

Proctor, M., P. Yeo, and A. Lack. 1996. The natural history of pollination. Timber Press, Portland, Oregon.

Queller, D. C., and K. F. Goodnight. 1989. Estimating relatedness using genetic markers. Evolution 43: 258–275.

Ramírez, W. 1970. Host specificity of fig wasps (Angaonidae). Evolution 24:680–691.

Raskin, I., A. Ehman, W. R. Melander, B. J. D. Meeuse. 1987. Salicylic acid: a natural inducer of heat production in *Arum* lillies. Science 237:1601–1602.

Rathcke, B. 1983. Competition and facilitation among plants for pollination. Pages 305–329 *in* L. Real, editor. Pollination biology. Academic Press, Orlando, Florida.

Real, L., editor. 1983. Pollination biology. Academic Press, Orlando, Florida.

Reid, N. 1986. Pollination and seed dispersal of mistletoes (Loranthaceae) by birds in southern Australia. Pages 64–84 *in* H. A. Ford and D. C. Paton, editors. The dynamic partnership: birds and plants in southern Australia. Government Printer, Carlton, Victoria, Australia.

———. 1991. Coevolution of mistletoes and frugivorous birds? Australian Journal of Ecology 16:457–470.

Renner, S. S., and J. P. Feil. 1993. Pollinators of tropical dioecious angiosperms. American Journal of Botany 80:1100–1107.

Renner, S. S., and R. E. Ricklefs. 1995. Dioecy and its correlates in the flowering plants. American Journal of Botany 82:596–606.

Restrepo, C. 1987. Aspectos ecologicos de la diseminación de cinco especies de muerdagos por aves. Humboldtia 1:1–116.

Richards, A. J. 1986. Plant breeding systems. Allen and Unwin, London.

Rickson, F. R. 1971. Glycogen plastids in Müllerian body cells of *Cecropia peltata*—a higher green plant. Science 173:344–347.

Rico-Gray, V. 1993. Use of plant-derived food resources by ants in the dry tropical lowlands of coastal Veracruz, Mexico. Biotropica 25:301–315.

Ridley, H. N. 1930. The dispersal of plants throughout the world. Reeve, Ashford, Kent, UK.

Riley, C. M., and K. G. Smith. 1986. Flower eating by Emerald Toucanets in Costa Rica. Condor 88:396–397.

Root, R. B. 1967. The niche exploitation pattern of the blue-gray gnatcatcher. Ecological Monographs 37:317–350.

Sargent, S. 1994. Seed dispersal of mistletoes by birds in Monteverde, Costa Rica. Ph.D. Dissertation. Cornell University, Ithaca, New York.

Schatz, G. E. 1990. Some aspects of pollination biology in Central American forests. Pages 69–84 *in* K. S. Bawa and M. Hadley, editors. Reproductive ecology of tropical forest plants. Parthenon, Carnforth, UK.

Schemske, D. W., and J. Ågren. 1995. Deceit pollination and selection on female flower size in *Begonia involucrata*: an experimental approach. Evolution 49:207–214.

Schemske, D. W., and N. Brokaw. 1981. Treefalls and the distribution of understory birds in a tropical forest. Ecology 62:938–945.

Schemske, D. W., and C. C. Horvitz. 1984. Variation among floral visitors in pollination ability: a precondition for mutualism specialization. Science 225:519–521.

Schemske, D. W., J. Ågren, and J. Le Corff. 1996. Deceit pollination in the monoecious, neotropical herb *Begonia oaxacana* (Begoniaceae). Pages 292–318 *in* D. G. Lloyd and S. C. H. Barrett, editors. Floral biology: studies on floral evolution in animal-pollinated plants. Chapman and Hall, New York.

Schupp, E. W. 1986. *Azteca* protection of *Cecropia*: ant occupation benefits juvenile trees. Oecologia 70:379–385.

———. 1988. Seed and early seedling predation in the forest understory and in treefall gaps. Oikos 51:71–78.

Schupp, E. W., and D. H. Feener, Jr. 1991. Phylogeny, lifeform, and habitat dependence of ant-defended plants in a Panamanian forest. Pages 175–197 *in* C. R. Huxley and D. F. Cutler, editors. Ant-plant interactions. Oxford University Press, Oxford.

Simpson, B. B., and J. L. Neff. 1983. Evolution and diversity of floral rewards. Pages 142–159 *in* C. E. Jones and R. J. Little, editors. Handbook of experimental pollination biology. Van Nostrand Reinhold, New York.

Smith, C. M., and J. L. Bronstein. 1996. Site variation in reproductive synchrony in three neotropical figs. Journal of Biogeography 23:477–485.

Snow, B. K. 1977. Territorial behavior and courtship of the male Three-wattled Bellbird. Auk 94:623–645.

———. 1971. Evolutionary aspects of fruit-eating in birds. Ibis 113:194–202.

Snow, B. K., and D. W. Snow. 1972. Feeding niches of hummingbirds in a rinidad valley. Journal of Animal Ecology 41:471–485.

———. 1988. Birds and berries: a study of an ecological interaction. Poyser, Calton, UK.

Snow, D. W. 1965. A possible selective factor in the evolution of fruiting seasons in tropical forest. Oikos 15:274–281.

Sobrevilla, C., and M. T. Kalin Arroyo. 1982. Breeding systems in a montane tropical cloud forest in Venezuela. Plant Systematics and Evolution 140: 19–37.

Standley, P. C. 1938. Flora of Costa Rica. Publication 420, Vol. 18, Part 3, Botanical Series. Field Museum of Natural History, Chicago.

Stapanian, M. A. 1982. A model for fruiting display: seed dispersal by birds for mulberry seeds. Ecology 63:1432–1443.

Stein, B. 1992. Sicklebill hummingbirds, ants, and flowers. Bioscience 42:27–33.

Stiles, F. G. 1975. Ecology, flowering phenology, and hummingbird-pollination of some Costa Rican *Heliconia* species. Ecology 56:285–301.

———. 1977. Coadapted competitors: the flowering seasons of hummingbird-pollinated plants in a tropical forest. Science 198:1177–1178.

———. 1985. Seasonal patterns and coevolution in the hummingbird-flower community of a Costa Rican sub-tropical forest. Ornithological Monographs 36:757–787.

Stout, J. 1979. An association of an ant, a mealy bug, and an understory tree from a Costa Rican rain forest. Biotropica 11:309–311.

Sutton, G. M. 1951. Dispersal of mistletoe by birds. Wilson Bulletin 63:235–237.

Tanner, E. V. J. 1982. Species diversity and reproductive mechanisms in Jamaican trees. Biological Journal of the Linnean Society 18:263–278.

Terborgh, J. 1986. Keystone plant resources in the tropical forest. Pages 330–344 *in* M. E. Soulé, editor. Conservation biology: the science of scarcity and diversity. Sinauer, Sunderland, Massachusetts.

Thompson, J. N. 1982. Interaction and coevolution. Wiley, New York.

———. 1994. The coevolutionary process. University of Chicago Press, Chicago.

Tiebout, H. M., III. 1991. Daytime energy management by tropical hummingbirds: responses to foraging constraint. Ecology 72:839–851.

Tiffney, B. H. 1986. Evolution of seed dispersal syndromes according to the fossil record. Pages 273–305 *in* D. R. Murray, editor. Seed dispersal. Academic Press, Sydney.

van der Pijl, L. 1982. Principles of dispersal in higher plants. Springer, New York.

Turček, F. J. 1963. Color preference in fruit- and seed-eating birds. *In* Proceedings of the XIII International Ornithological Congress, American Ornithologists' Union.

Vazquez-Yanes, C., and A. Orozco-Segovia. 1984. Ecophysiology of seed germination in the tropical humid forests of the world: a review. Pages 37–50 *in* E. Medina, H. A. Mooney, and C. Vazquez-Yanes, editors. Physiological ecology of plants in the wet tropics. Dr. W. Junk Publishers, Dordrecht.

Wahag, S. A., D. J. Levey, A. K. Sanders, and M. L. Cipollini, 1998. Control of gut retention time by secondary metabolites in ripe *Solanum* fruits. Ecology 79:2309–2319.

Ward, P. S. 1991. Phylogenetic analysis of pseudomyrmecine ants associated with domatia-bearing plants. Pages 335–352 *in* C. R. Huxley and D. F. Cutler, editors. Antplant interactions. Oxford University Press, Oxford.

Weins, D., and J. P. Rourke. 1978. Rodent pollination in southern African *Protea* sp. Nature 276:71–73.

Weiss, M. R. 1996. Pollen-feeding fly alters floral phenotypic gender in *Centropogon solanifolius* (Campanulaceae). Biotropica 28:770–773.

Wenny, D. G., and D. J. Levey, 1998. Directed seed dispersal by bellbirds in a tropical cloud forest. Proceedings of the National Academy of Sciences USA 95:6204–6207.

West, S. A., and E. A. Herre. 1994. The ecology of the New World fig-parasitising wasps *Idarnes* and implications for the evolution of the fig-pollinator mutualism. Proceedings of the Royal Society of London, Series B 258:67–72.

West, S. A., E. A. Herre, D. M. Windsor, and P. R. S. Green. 1996. The ecology and evolution of the New World nonpollinating fig wasp communities. Journal of Biogeography 23:447–458.

Wetmore, A. 1914. The development of the stomach in the euphonias. Auk 31:458–461.

Wheeler, W. M. 1942. Studies of neotropical antplants and their ants. Bulletin of the Museum of Comparative Zoology, Harvard 90:1–262.

Wheelwright, N. T. 1983. Fruits and the ecology of Resplendent Quetzals. Auk 100:286–301.

———. 1985a. Competition for dispersers, and the timing of flowering and fruiting in a guild of tropical trees. Oikos 44:465–477.

———. 1985b. Fruit size, gape width, and the diets of fruit-eating birds. Ecology 66:808–818.

———. 1986. A seven-year study of individual variation in fruit production in tropical bird-dispersed tree species in the family Laraceae. Pages 19–35 *in* A. Estrada, and T. H. Fleming, editors. Frugivores and seed dispersal. Dr. W. Junk Publishers, Amsterdam.

———. 1988a. Four constraints on coevolution between plants and their seed dispersers: a tropical case history. Proceedings of the International Ornithological Congress 19:827–845.

———. 1988b. Fruit-eating birds and bird-dispersed plants in the tropics and temperate zone. Trends in Ecology and Evolution 3:270–274.

———. 1991. How long do fruit-eating birds stay in the plants where they feed? Biotropica 23:29–40.

———. 1993. Fruit size in a tropical tree species: variation, preference by birds, and heritability. Vegetatio 107/108:163–174.

Wheelwright, N. T., and A. Bruneau. 1992. Population sex ratios and spatial distribution of *Ocotea tenera* (Lauraceae) trees in a tropical forest. Journal of Ecology 80:425432.

Wheelwright, N. T., and C. H. Janson. 1985. Colors of fruit displays of bird-dispersed plants in two tropical forests. American Naturalist 126:777–799.

Wheelwright, N. T., and G. H. Orians. 1982. Seed dispersal by animals: contrasts with pollen dispersal, problems of terminology, and constraints on coevolution. American Naturalist 119:402–413.

Wheelwright, N. T., W. A. Haber, K. G. Murray, and C. Guindon. 1984. Tropical fruit-eating birds and their food plants: a survey of a Costa Rican lower montane forest. Biotropica 16:173–191.

Whitehead, D. R. 1983. Wind pollination: some ecological and evolutionary perspectives. Pages 97–108 *in* L. Real, editor. Pollination biology. Academic Press, Orlando, Florida.

Whitmore, T. C. 1975. Tropical rain forests of the far east. Clarendon Press, Oxford.

Wiebes, J. T. 1995. The New World Agaoninae (pollinators of figs). North-Holland, Amsterdam.

Willson, M. F., and J. Ågren. 1989. Differential floral rewards and pollination by deceit in unisexual flowers. Oikos 55:23–29.

Willson, M. F., E. A. Porter, and R. S. Condit. 1982. Avian frugivore activity in relation to forest light gaps. Caribbean Journal of Science 18:1–6.

Willson, M. F., A. K. Irvine, and N. G. Walsh. 1989. Vertebrate dispersal syndromes in some Australian and New Zealand plant communities, with geographic comparisons. Biotropica 21:133–147.

Windsor, D. M., D. W. Morrison, M. A. Estribi, and B. de Leon. 1989. Phenology of fruit and leaf production by "strangler" figs on Barro Colorado Island, Panamá. Experientia 45:647–652.

Witmer, M. C. 1996. Do some bird-dispersed fruits contain natural laxatives? Ecology 77:1947–1948.

Wunderle, J. M., A. Diaz, I. Velazquez, and R. Scharrón. 1987. Forest openings and the distribution of understory birds in a Puerto Rican rainforest. Wilson Bulletin 99:22–37.

Wyatt, R. 1983. Pollinator-plant interactions and the evolution of breeding systems. Pages 51–95 *in* L. Real, editor. Pollination biology. Academic Press, Orlando, Florida.

Young, H. J. 1990. Pollination and reproductive biology of an understory neotropical aroid. Pages 151–164 *in* K. S. Bawa and M. Hadley, editors. Reproductive ecology of tropical forest plants. Parthenon, Carnforth, UK.

Young, H. J., and T. P. Young. 1992. Alternative outcomes of natural and experimental high pollen loads. Ecology 73:639–647.

9

Ecosystem Ecology and Forest Dynamics

Nalini M. Nadkarni   Teri J. Matelson
Robert O. Lawton   Doug Schaefer
Kenneth L. Clark

The earth's surface supports living organisms and their environments to form the biosphere, a thin film of life around the planet. Organisms participate in interacting systems or communities, and these communities are coupled to their environments by the transfer of matter and energy and by movements of air, water, and organisms. Human activities in Monteverde and elsewhere can drastically alter forest ecosystems. Textbooks on ecosystem ecology typically include such topics as community structure and composition (including plant growth forms, vertical structure, niche space, species diversity), communities and environments (species distributions along environmental gradients, community classification, succession), production (food chains and webs, decomposition and detritus, photosynthesis), and nutrient cycling (mineral nutrition of organisms, soil development, biogeochemistry).

Our understanding of tropical ecosystem ecology generally falls short of what we know of other aspects of tropical biology. There are far more studies concerning population biology, autecology, and life history of tropical organisms than nutrient cycling, productivity, and landscape ecology. This pattern is true

in Monteverde and in such well-studied tropical forests as La Selva, Barro Colorado Island (BCI), and the Luquillo National Forest (Lugo and Lowe 1995, McDade et al. 1994). Logistical blocks to ecosystem research exist because collaborating teams of scientists are typically needed to tackle the multiple disciplines that ecosystem-level questions require, which demands a large infrastructure and budget. Temporal problems exist because ecosystem-level phenomena (e.g., tree mortality and forest regeneration) may involve time scales longer than the life of a single granting period or lifetime of a researcher. A strong academic base for ecosystem ecology is lacking because the pool of existing studies is too small to draw patterns and extrapolate trends.

These obstacles have not often been overcome in Monteverde. No Monteverde institution has provided the infrastructure to support ecosystem research (e.g., laboratory facilities, meteorological station, technical library). Some community members have negative feelings about experimental manipulations and destructive sampling sometimes needed to answer ecosystem ecology questions. From the 1970s to the 1990s, Organization for Tropical Studies (OTS) courses were the major vehicle for facilitating research, which generally fostered small-scale, low-budget science. Therefore, only those projects that brought their own infrastructure with them and that restricted themselves to largely observational data collection have maintained research projects that produced ecosystem-level research in Monteverde.

Existing information on ecosystem ecology in Monteverde is extremely patchy. Of the areas of ecosystem research, only five are covered in this book: (1) hydrology and soils (Chap. 2, Physical Environment), (2) vegetation classification (Chap. 3, Plants), (3) bird community structure (Chap. 6, Birds), (4) forest structure and dynamics (this chapter), and (5) nutrient cycling (this chapter). Here we report on forest structure, composition, and dynamics of two primary forest types, the windward elfin woodland and the leeward cloud forest; summarize nutrient cycling research that has focused on ecological roles of canopy communities in whole-forest nutrient cycles; compare these patterns with other tropical montane forests; and outline areas for future research.

9.1. Forest Structure, Composition, and Dynamics

Knowledge of structure and floristics is necessary to understand tropical montane forest ecosystem ecology (Grubb et al. 1963, Tanner 1977, Heaney and Proctor 1990, Lugo and Lowe 1995). Forest structure has been investigated in Monteverde to understand forest dynamics, the light environment, nutrient cycling, seed dispersal, and the epiphyte community. Long-term data exist on forest structure and composition from two primary forest types: the windward elfin woodland and the leeward cloud forest (Lawton and Dryer 1980), both located within the Monteverde Cloud Forest Preserve (MCFP).

9.1.1. Windward Cloud Forest Dynamics

The very wet windward cloud forests along the crest of the Cordillera de Tilarán illustrate extreme examples of dynamic forests. The trees that perch on hogback ridges, cling to precipitous slopes, and stand amid the pools on soggy swampland fall with great frequency during the storms of the windy season (see Chap. 2, Physical Environment). The terrain and climate are in some ways favorable to plant growth; water does not appear to be a limiting factor, and mineral nutrients seem to be in good supply. In contrast, conditions may be extraordinarily stressful in a mechanical sense, as severe storms regularly batter the Cordillera. Several times a year, the dwarfed forests

on the peaks, saddles, and ridgecrests most exposed to the trade wind flow are enveloped in howling, hurricane-force winds, and cloud-wrack. The battering of forests by storms has long been of interest to plant ecologists and foresters (Cowles 1899, White 1979, Pickett and White 1985). Hurricanes have provided lessons on the impact of catastrophic storms on tropical forests of the Caribbean region (Beard 1946, 1949, Wadsworth and Englerth 1959, Lugo et al. 1983, Brokaw and Walker 1991, Zimmerman et al. 1994). The patterns of damage and recovery may provide insight into the diversity of forest structures within the Cordillera, and reflect on general ideas about tropical ecosystem stability and the relationship between natural patterns of disturbance and resource partitioning in complex communities.

The ontogeny of dwarf forest stature.   The situation in the Cordillera de Tilarán differs from hurricane-dominated forests of the Caribbean. We focus on the dwarfed, or elfin, forests characteristic of wind-exposed peaks and ridges along the crest of the Cordillera. If one hikes from the Information Center of the MCFP to the Continental Divide at the pass into the Valle de Peñas Blancas, and looks south along the broad saddle of Brillante to the slopes and peak of Cerro Ojo de Agua beyond, one sees an archipelago of smooth-canopied elfin forest on ridgecrests embedded in a sea of taller and rougher canopied cloud forest in the intervening sheltered coves and hollows. Similar dwarfed cloud forests are widespread throughout the tropics, particularly in the trade wind belts (Shreve 1914, Brown 1919, Richards 1952, Beard 1955, Howard 1968, Leigh 1975).

Why are these elfin forests dwarfed? Early botanical explorers were impressed with the inclement climate of such areas. Expedition accounts contain a litany of complaints about the mud, rain, and absence of sun for days, so it is not surprising that they emphasized the impact on trees of the very environmental features that made their own travels difficult (Weberbauer 1911, Seifriz 1923, Lane-Poole 1925, Gleason and Cook 1927, van Steenis 1935, Exell 1944). The ideas in these early accounts can be organized into a set of hypotheses concerning the causes of forest dwarfing (Leigh 1975, Grubb 1977). Elfin forests might be dwarfed because of low productivity (low photosynthetic performance per unit leaf area or mass) due to low temperature, lack of sunlight, or nutrient starvation. The latter could result from soils low in mineral nutrients or from difficulties in acquiring or transporting available mineral ions. Waterlogging and consequent oxygen deprivation might inhibit root metabolism and mineral uptake. Low rates of transpiration in the elfin forest may hinder nutrient transport in the xylem from root to canopy, and result in nutrient-starved leaves (Odum 1970, Leigh 1975). These hypotheses implicate metabolically determined slow growth. Another hypothesis targets the pruning of trees. Vigorously growing plants may be kept small by assiduous pruning by wind (Gleason and Cook 1927, Howard 1968), drought (Shreve 1914, Seifriz 1953), and/or grazing by insects (Howard 1969).

At a larger spatial scale, the stature of a forest is the result of a balance between the growth of its constituent trees and their deaths. Forests recovering from past disturbances change in structure and composition through time, and forests may experience episodes of decline (Jacobi 1983, Stewart and Veblen 1983). They may also achieve a balance at the landscape level in a shifting mosaic steady state (Bormann and Likens 1979) or quasi equilibrium (Shugart and West 1981). Differences in the rates of disturbance across the landscape may influence forest stature by limiting tree lifespans, even if the forest is at quasi equilibrium. Elfin forest trees may simply not live long enough to get very large before they are blown over.

All of the preceding hypotheses are equilibrium based, in which the stresses imposed on trees are viewed as chronic. At the extreme, catastrophic disturbances such as major hurricanes or earthquake-induced landslides may result in nonequilibrium patches of forest that are short simply because they have not had time to grow larger since the last catastrophe (Gómez-Pompa 1973). The "cyclone forests" of Queensland, Australia (Webb 1958), and the palm forests of the lesser Antilles (Beard 1946, 1949) are examples of this phenomenon.

Trees and forests might be short for adaptive reasons. If storms are a regular feature of the environment, the population of trees of the area might be adapted to the mechanical stresses of life there, and acclimate as individuals to their particular circumstances. Increased wood strength is a successful adjustment to mechanically stressful sites, and such responses are widespread among plants (Grace 1977, Wilson and Archer 1977, Jaffe 1980, Niklas 1993). Energy and material invested in strength are diverted from leaf production; investing in strength slows growth.

These conjectures are not mutually exclusive; several or all might act together to determine forest stature. Furthermore, forests may be dwarfed in different places for different reasons. In the most sheltered ravines of the Brillante area, trees can grow to 30–35 m tall; on the adjacent wind-exposed ridgecrests (only about 100 m away), elfin forest thickets with 5-8-m tall canopy trees occur.

To examine this issue, Lawton (1980, 1984, 1990)

established a permanent study area in a 12-ha watershed on the southeastern side of the summit of Cerro de las Centinelas to monitor environmental conditions, natural disturbances, forest regeneration, and vegetation structure (Fig. 9.1). Most of the watershed (10.6 ha) was surveyed with transit and range pole and gridded into contiguous 20 x 20 m plots. The southern and western margins of the study watershed are the Continental Divide. The watershed is drained by a small creek; it runs throughout the wet and windy seasons, becoming intermittent in the driest months. The geomorphology of this watershed is described in Chapter 2, Physical Environment.

Forest structure changes dramatically within the watershed (Figs. 9.2, 9.3). Canopy trees are generally 15–23 m tall on the lower slopes of the watershed bowl; the tallest are 25–27 m tall *Sapium pachystachys* trees growing at the bottom of the ravine on slopes adjacent to the deep incision of the creek channel. On the ridgecrests that bound the watershed, however, the canopy trees are 5–8 m tall and are squat in architecture. The largest are *Clusia* sp., with multiple trunks (each up to 60 cm diameter) rising from dense arrays of rigid prop roots arching down in a manner similar to mangrove trees. Their trunks branch sparingly; massive limbs support dense crowns as broad as the trees are tall. The gradient of forest structure within these Brillante watersheds (ca. 100 horizontal m and ca. 50 vertical m) encompasses Beard's (1955) montane rain forest (cloud forest) through montane thicket almost to elfin woodland. In the schema of Holdridge (1967), the habitat would be considered facies of a wind-exposed atmospheric association of tropical lower montane rain forest. The taller forest is described as windward cloud forest and the shorter as elfin forest by Lawton and Dryer (1980).

The spatial scale at which forest dwarfing occurs is quite clear. But what of the correlates and causes? A year of climate monitoring along this local gradient revealed no differences in light availability or temperature at the forest canopy surface (Lawton 1980). There are no striking differences in soil macronutrient availability. Only extractable calcium is more abundant in the soils lower in the ravine, but the volcanically derived soils throughout the study area are remarkably fertile by agricultural standards (Lawton 1980; see Chap. 2, Physical Environment). Symptoms of nutrient starvation are not conspicuous; chlorotic discolorations are not common in young or mature leaves, and trees flower and fruit prolifically.

The only striking environmental difference between the sheltered Brillante coves with their tall cloud forest and the adjacent elfin-forested ridgecrests is their exposure to wind. This is apparent at the Ventana, the pass across the Continental Divide

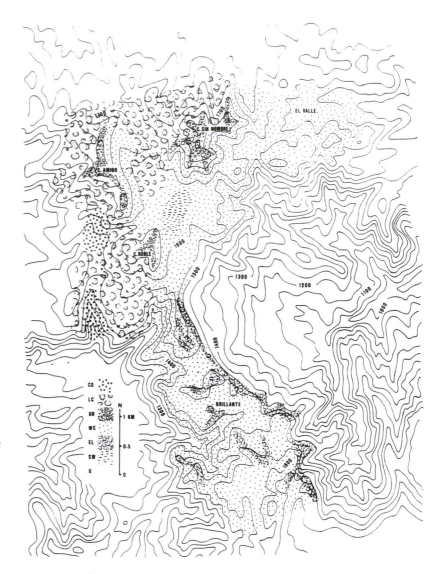

Figure 9.1. The distribution of forest types along the crest of the central Cordillera de Tilarán. CO, leeward cove forest; LC, leeward cloud forest; OR, oak ridge forest; WC, windward cloud forest; EL, elfin forest; SW, swamp forest; U, undetermined. (From Lawton and Dryer 1980)

overlooking the Peñas Blancas valley. Average wind speeds 0.5 m above the forest canopy were twice as high at a ridgecrest weather station than at a station halfway down the windward slope (Lawton 1980, 1982). The drop in windspeed with descent through the canopy is greater on the ridgecrest as well (Lawton 1982). The change in windspeed with a change in height is proportional to the momentum transferred from the airstream to the underlying substrate (i.e., the forest). Thus, the trees of the dwarfed forest are literally shaken more by the wind than those in the taller forest below.

The forest displays a variety of adjustments to wind, ranging from changes in community composition to phenotypically plastic changes of form within the crowns of individual trees. For instance, tree species that have their centers of distribution in the wind-sheltered taller forest tend to have less dense wood (dry weight to wet volume) than those species in more wind-exposed sites (Lawton 1984). Among the tree species characteristic of a site, those that are shade intolerant tend to have less dense wood than those that are shade tolerant. Since denser wood is generally stronger and metabolically more expensive to construct (Kollman and Cote 1968, Panshin and DeZeeuw 1970, Niklas 1993), tree species of wind-stressed sites invest more in mechanical support than those than in more protected places.

The elfin forest is composed of denser woods than the taller forests below. When species wood densities are weighted by the species contribution to the basal area of the stand, the sum gives a stand mean wood density, which is 0.60, 0.47, and 0.56 g/cm^3 for the

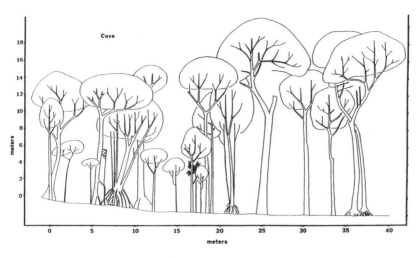

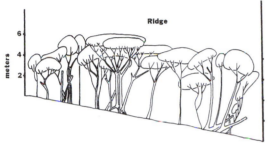

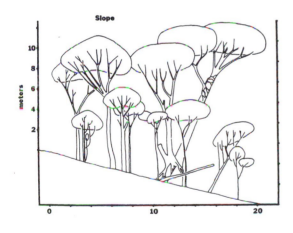

Figure 9.2. *(above)* Profile diagram from a representative 10 × 40 m plot at the foot of the windward slope in the central part of the Cerros Centinelas study watershed.
Figure 9.3. *(left)* Profile diagrams from 5 × 20 m plots on the ridgecrest and middle windward slope of the Cerros Centinelas study watershed.

elfin forest along the ridgecrest, the taller ravine forests, and the windward slope, respectively. The consequences of these contrasts in investment are particularly striking in comparing the dominant shade-intolerant (pioneer) species within the study watershed. *Didymopanax pittieri*, the dominant pioneer of the elfin forest, has a mean wood density of 0.57 g/cm³ (SE) = 0.01, $N = 5$), while *Cecropia polyphlebia*, the pioneer of the tallest forest in the bottom of the watershed bowl, has a mean wood density of 0.28 g/cm³ (SE = 0.012, $N = 5$). Saplings of both species commonly establish together in the well-lit gaps in the forest canopy created by treefalls. In the taller forest

of ravine bottoms, *C. polyphlebia* invests less in wood and grows more rapidly than *D. pittieri*, which eventually dies in the shade of its competitors. In treefall gaps of the windswept elfin forest, however, *D. pittieri*, with its denser wood, is more durable; *C. polyphlebia* saplings are tattered and broken in storms. These mechanically important structural differences vary among individuals and within species. Trees can respond to mechanical stresses by increasing growth of the tissues that deal with such stresses, a widespread form of acclimation in plants, termed thig-momorphogenesis. This produces stouter trunks, branches, and twigs in trees exposed to greater stresses.

The elfin forest pioneer, *Didymopanax pittieri*, has a distinctive growth form (Leeuwenberg's architecture; *sensu* Hallé et al. 1978). Each twig sets a terminal inflorescence bud and sprouts a whorl of twigs below. This simplicity of growth form aids comparisons both within and among trees. In the windward forest study watershed, *D. pittieri* growing on the windy ridgecrests have thicker trunks for a given height than those growing farther downslope (Lawton 1982). Similarly, twigs on trees of the ridgecrest are thicker relative to their length than twigs on trees in less wind-exposed spots.

Twigs might be stouter because they grew more in diameter or because they elongated less. The latter is the case with *D. pittieri*; twigs are thicker on ridgecrest trees, but that is apparently because they start out thicker, since they do not thicken more rapidly during development (Lawton 1982). These mechanically appropriate growth responses and physiognomic trends are at least in part phenotypically plastic; twigs on the windward side of ridgecrest crowns are stouter than those on the lee sides of the same crowns. Decreased stem elongation and increased allocation to trunk thickening will both retard height growth, thus contributing to the ontogeny of elfin stature. Slower growth in height also slows exposure to the higher winds farther above the ground and thus reduces the increase in drag upon the crown.

Natural disturbance in Brillante.   Trees fall, particularly in "nortes" or "temporales," winter storms produced by the impact of polar air masses moving down the Great Plains of North America into the trade wind flows of the Gulf of Mexico and Caribbean (see Chap. 2, Physical Environment). During temporales, sustained winds across elfin forest canopies in Brillante may exceed 100 km/hr[1]. Gusts are even stronger; trees creak and groan. The ground, laced and matted with surface roots, rocks and heaves; the roar of the wind is punctuated with the pop of breaking wood and the crash of falling trees. In most years, 5–10 such storms occur. What impacts does this have on the forest?

In 1982, all 72 existing recent treefall gaps on the windward slope of the 12-ha study area were mapped and measured. We used a modified version of Brokaw's (1982) definition of a gap: an area opened by fallen trees or fallen limbs, or under standing dead trees, where the tallest living plants are less than 3 m tall and less than 50% of the height of the surrounding canopy trees. This clearly delimits canopy disruption, even in the elfin forest thickets. In 1983, the sample was extended to the rest of the watershed, and the area sampled in 1982 was remeasured. In each subsequent year until 1996, the entire watershed

study area has been searched for new gaps (Fig. 9.4). Monthly censuses from June 1986 to June 1987 revealed that 88% of the gaps were opened by treefalls during the windy season temporales (December 1986 and January 1987). Although these storms are locally of hurricane force, catastrophic damage such as that associated with the impact of major hurricanes on the Antilles (Lugo et al. 1983, Brokaw and Walker 1991, Foster and Boose 1995) has not been sustained in the Cordillera de Tilarán.

Demographic analyses of *Didymopanax pittieri*, a facultative hemiepiphyte, suggest that the elfin forest is in quasi equilibrium and not the product of past catastrophes (Lawton 1980). A subpopulation of this elfin forest pioneer occupies the lee boundary ridge of the Brillante study area. Each of the 503 *D. pittieri* stems taller than 50 cm and growing within 3 m of the ground within this subpopulation was mapped, tagged, and measured. Remeasurement a year later revealed size-specific growth and mortality rates. Because establishment of vigorous *D. pittieri* saplings occurs only in treefall gaps or similar canopy openings, the number of saplings entering the study population was calculated from the average number of saplings per treefall gap and the number of new gaps in the census year. If past catastrophic clearing had occurred, *D. pittieri* populations would be dominated by individuals thatons/had become established in their aftermath and grown up together, with a lack of subsequent sapling establishment. The population should exhibit a demographically unstable size (or age) class distribution.

There are, however, abundant saplings and juveniles in the existing population, which suggests no failure of current regeneration. Population projections using a matrix model with the between-size class transition probabilities measured in the census interval yielded a calculated stable size class distribution not significantly different from that observed. Because *D. pittieri*, the dominant pioneer, appears demographically stable, the forest must be in quasi equilibrium; the elfin forest is a stable feature of the vegetation of the Cordillera.

Although treefalls are balanced by regrowth to maintain quasi equilibrium at the scale of small watersheds, the rate of disturbance is both high and variable. In the period between 1981 and 1990, between 13 and 93 gaps formed each year on the 10.6 ha of the Brillante study area (geometric mean = 33; 95% confidence interval [CI] = 23–48 gaps). These opened between 0.6% and 3.8% of the monitored area each year, a sixfold variation. The turnover time (calculated from the geometric mean of the area opened per year) was 77 years (95% CI = 51–116 years).

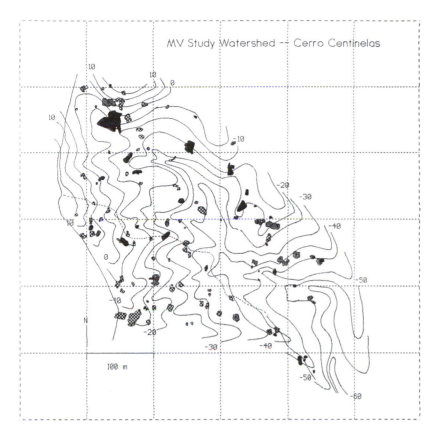

Figure 9.4. Topographic map of the study watershed on Cerros Centinelas. The Peñas Blancas headwall cliff is immediately east of the watershed. Gaps from three years are presented; fine hatching denotes those of July 1987 to June 1988, coarse hatching those of July 1988 to June 1989, solid those of July 1985 to June 1990. Contours are from an arbitrary reference point at an approximate elevation of 1560 m.

Disturbance regimes elsewhere in the Monteverde forests are similar. Gaps covered 1.5% of five 0.5-km line transects through windward and leeward cloud forest each year (Murray 1986, 1988). These Monteverde forest values are similar to values from other neotropical lowland forests (Brokaw 1985, Denslow 1987, Hartshorn 1990). Due to the variation among years, in the Brillante sample, however, turnover times calculated from 3-year periods ranged from 51 to 147 years, which emphasizes the importance of long-term studies.

Variation among gaps Not all gaps in the canopy are created equal. This observation is central to the suggestion that tropical tree species diversity (and the animal diversity dependent upon it) is in part the result of specialization in the "regeneration niche" (Ricklefs 1977, Denslow 1980, Hartshorn 1980, Orians 1982, Brokaw 1985). Gaps vary dramatically in size, ranging from hectares (in areas denuded by landslides or catastrophic storms) to square centimeters (in the spaces between leaves). Within the Cerro de los Centinelas study area in Monteverde, gaps larger than 4 m² in planar projection, the apparent lower limit for shade-intolerant species to become established in elfin forests, were included in gap censuses.

Most gaps are small; on the windward slope of the study area approximately 55% are <15 m² while <5% are >105 m² (Lawton and Putz 1988). The largest 5%,

however, contribute more than one-third of the total area opened by disturbance. These patterns applies elsewhere in Monteverde cloud forests. In the five 0.5-km line transects of Murray (1986, 1988), gaps <5 m² accounted for 57% of the number of gaps formed, but 5% of the gaps were >200 m². These few large gaps accounted for the majority of the area opened.

In a study of 88 gaps in the dwarfed forests of the windward slope of the study area, the following attributes were measured: gap area, gap aperture (the angular opening from the gap center to the sky), the area covered by nurse logs >20 cm diameter, the area of mineral soil disturbed in uprooted pits and mounds, the size and identity of the gap-maker tree, whether the gap-maker snapped or was uprooted, the height above the ground at which the failure occurred, and, for a subset of gaps, the photosynthetically active radiation (PAR, 400–700 nm) 1.5 m above the ground at gap center (Lawton and Putz 1988). Of these gaps, 41% were formed by uprooted trees, 39% by snapped trees, and the remainder by limbfall, the collapse of epiphyte masses, or dead standing trees killed by lightning.

A unique characteristic of the elfin forests is that some trees fall slowly. Snapped trees come down quickly, but uprooting can take months or even years. Many elfin forest trees have strong crowns, so when they topple they do not shatter into a pile of debris on the forest floor but rather remain intact, the trunk suspended well above the ground. This often results in exuberant growth of their woody hemiepiphytes (Lawton and Putz 1988, Williams-Linera and Lawton 1995; see Putz, "Trees on Trees," p. 70).

Many gap attributes are correlated. In the same set of gaps, gap area (logarithmically transformed) was correlated with gap aperture ($r = 0.51$), gap-maker diameter ($r = 0.72$), nurse-log area (log-transformed; $r = 0.83$), and the area of disturbed soil (log-transformed; $r = 0.47$). Bigger gaps are made by bigger trees, which also leave more nurse logs and create bigger pits and mounds if they uproot. Nurse-log area, which is important to a set of shade-intolerant tree species specialized for sapling establishment on logs, is independently related to gap area (log-transformed; partial $r = 0.60$), gap-maker diameter (partial $r = 0.54$), the height of the break (partial $r = -0.23$), and gap aperture (partial $r = 0.22$) (Lawton and Putz 1988).

Because many gap attributes are related to gap size in Monteverde and other forests (Denslow 1980, 1987, Brokaw 1985), there is a temptation to use gap area as a proxy to organize the variation that exists among gaps. Principal components analysis of the variation among gaps in our study area illustrated these hazards (Lawton and Putz 1988). The first principal component, accounting for half of the variation among gaps, is a contrast between measures of gap size and the height at which the gap-maker broke. The second principal component, accounting for about one-sixth of the variation, contrasts gap aperture ("openness") with the position of the gap on the slope, the height of breakage, and gap area. The size of the tree that fell and the amount of nurse log area created are both better correlated with the first principal component than is the area of the gap. Gap area, gap aperture, gap-maker diameter, nurse-log area, and disturbed mineral soil are all important gap characteristics. Although intercorrelations seem intuitively correct, each gap presents its own opportunities and hazards to juveniles and cannot be characterized with a single measure such as gap area.

Gaps and light availability Penetration of light into the understory of Monteverde's forests depends largely on the nature of canopy disruption by limb fall and tree fall (Lawton 1990). The amount of light in the middle of a gap depends logarithmically upon its size. Bigger gaps receive more light than small ones, but this increase tapers off as the effect of adjacent trees shading the gap from oblique light becomes progressively smaller. The aperture of the gap is a better indicator of light availability than is gap area. A small gap surrounded by short trees can be as "open" to light as a larger gap surrounded by taller trees (Figs. 9.5,

9.6). In the Cordillera de Tilarán, where forest stature varies dramatically with exposure to wind, this relationship has important implications. Elfin forest gaps, though small, may be well lit.

Gaps may also contribute to the lighting of the adjacent forest interior, which creates an "extended gap" (Runkle 1982). The impact of canopy disturbance on light availability on the understory in the forest interior is complex (Lawton 1990). In the elfin forest understory, PAR availability decreases with increasing distance from the nearest gap, but the correlation is not strong. In the taller forests of lower elevations, light availability is not correlated with distance from the nearest gap. Light availability in specific gaps suggests that some gaps are walled off from the adjacent forest interior by well-developed edge vegetation (Figs. 9.5, 9.6). Although all regrowth fosters the development of this edge (Williams-Linera 1990), some gaps produce this boundary from the outset, due either to past disturbance history or to the vagaries of understory vegetation structure and gap formation.

Our study demonstrates this pattern (Lawton and Putz 1988). On the southern edge of gap 206, a large *Hieronyma poasana* (57 in Fig. 9.7) had, in an earlier episode of gap creation, snapped its trunk 6 m above the ground. The crown portion of that earlier gap was filled by a large *Urera elata* (62 in Fig. 9.7), whereas the butt end (now the edge of Gap 206) filled in with *Hieronyma* sprouts and hemiepiphytes growing on the broken *Hieronyma* trunk; tree ferns filled the understory. The result was a wall of vegetation that effectively blocked the light that entered this gap from penetrating the understory. Since gaps are aggregated, these local historical effects are common, and generalizations about the influence of gaps on the light environment in the neighboring understory are limited.

Gap colonization and the partitioning of regenerative opportunity. Whether natural disturbances provide sufficient environmental heterogeneity to contribute to the evolution and maintenance of tropical tree diversity is debated (van Steenis 1956, Ashton 1969, Grubb 1977, Ricklefs 1977, Connell 1978, Denslow 1980, 1987, Orians 1982, Hubbell and Foster 1986). In the elfin forests of the Cordillera de Tilarán, two conspicuous guilds of gap colonizing trees exist: species that occupy exposed mineral soil, and those that occupy nurse logs (Lawton and Putz 1988).

In our study area, of the 557 saplings that colonized the eight elfin forest gaps (8–78 months old), 56 saplings (8.3 saplings/m^2) were on the 3% of gap area covered by disturbed soil of tip-up pits and mounds, 168 (6.4/m^2) were on the 10% of the gaps covered by nurse logs, and 333 (1.3/m^2) were on other substrates,

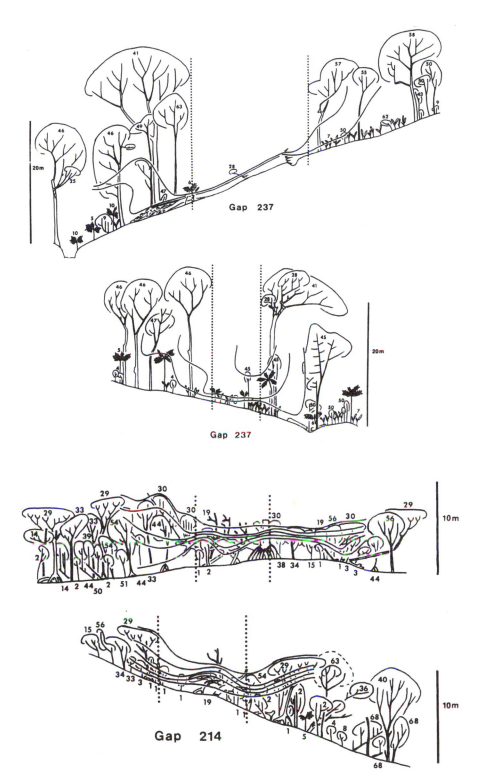

Figure 9.5. *(top)* Gap 237, in the taller forest in the ravine bottom of the Cerros Centinelas study watershed. A 1.5-m-DBH (diameter at breast height) *Ficus crassiuscula* uprooted and in turn uprooted a 40-cm-DBH *Guarea tuisana*. The dotted lines show gap boundaries. Isoclines of photosynthetic photon flux density are (from the bottom) 0.1, 0.25, 0.5 and 0.75 of that above the forest canopy. In the upper profile, the azimuth from left to right is 0°. In the lower profile the azimuth from left to right is 270°. **Figure 9.6.** *(above)* Gap 214, in the elfin forest along the boundary ridgecrest of the Cerros Centinelas study watershed. A *Clusia* sp. (45- and 55-cm-thick trunks) fell apart over a five-year period. The gap indicated by dotted lines is the last episode. In the upper profile, the azimuth from left to right is 90°. In the lower profile the azimuth from left to right is 180°. Isoclines of photosynthetic photon flux density as in Figure 9.5.

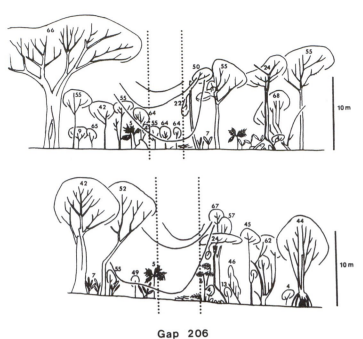

Figure 9.7. Gap 206, in the taller cloud forest in the upper portion of the ravine of the Cerros Centinelas study watershed. A *Dendropanax gonatopodus* (35 cm DBH) snapped 9 m above the ground. The large tree in the upper profile is *Ficus crassiuscula*. In the upper profile, the azimuth from left to right is 270°. In the lower profile the azimuth from left to right is 180°. Isoclines of photosynthetic photon flux density as in Fig. 9.5.

Gap 206

mostly litter-covered soil, which covered 87% of the gaps. The group that colonized the disturbed soil of pits and mounds included *Guettarda poasana*, which has a local center of distribution downslope of the most exposed ridgecrests, and *Cecropia polyphebia* and *Tetrorchidium* sp., which are most abundant in the taller, more sheltered forests of ravine bottoms. All of these species contribute to the soil seed bank; *G. poasana* contributes 220 seeds/m² (SE = 73), which comprises 54% of the elfin forest seed bank. The group of species occupying nurse logs is larger; seven species are more abundant as saplings than expected on nurse logs, including the dominant pioneer of the elfin forest, *Didymopanax pittieri*, and the dominant end member of gap-phase regeneration, *Clusia* sp.

Nurse logs and pits and mounds provide open space, which is a rare commodity in the dense understory of the elfin forest (Putz 1983). Vertical gradients in light availability can be steep in the dense thickets of elfin forest gap-phase regeneration (Lawton 1990), so establishment on nurse logs may offer a head start in competition for light. Saplings of species on nurse logs arrive by two routes. Species of *Conostegia* and *Miconia* (Melastomataceae) commonly establish on nurse logs, but seldom grow on living trees (although "accidental" epiphytism is common in the very wet conditions of Monteverde cloud forests; Williams-Linera and Lawton 1995). This pattern suggests that saplings only become established near the ground, perhaps because of limitations on root growth and water or nutrient acquisition. In contrast, *Didymopanax pittieri*, *Oreopanax nubigenus*, *Cosmibuena*

valerii, *Blakea chlorantha*, and *Clusia* sp. are commonly found both as elfin forest canopy trees established on nurse logs and in taller cloud forest as hemi-epiphytes. Epiphytic seedlings and saplings of the these species often survive host tree collapse; they reorient and become vigorous components of gap-phase regeneration (Lawton and Putz 1988, Williams-Linera and Lawton 1995; see Putz, "Trees on Trees" p. 70).

The rate of gap-phase regeneration. The height and composititon of the vegetation in gaps change quickly during regrowth (Lawton and Putz 1988). Bare ground and wood are covered within 2–3 years as the thicket of regrowth reaches 1–4 m in height. The contribution of canopy tree species to the regrowing canopy increases from around 10% at 8 months to around 50% at 78 months. The rate of height growth is slow compared to lowland forests, which may be due to differences in patterns of biomass allocation. Trees in the elfin forest tend to have dense wood (Lawton 1984) and thick trunks and limbs relative to their height (Shreve 1914, Brown 1919, Lawton 1982). These patterns are presumably adaptive responses to high wind stress. The rate of regrowth relative to mean canopy height and to the height of emergent trees is similar to that in lowland settings. Regrowth of pioneers to 50% of canopy height (3–4 m in the elfin forest, 12–15 m in lowland forest) requires about 6 years in each setting (Brokaw 1985, Lawton and Putz 1988).

Leaf area also recovers rapidly following disturbance. Leaf area increases logarithmically with gap age and with gap area (Lawton and Putz 1988). In 10-m² gaps, leaf area recovers to 50% of the mature phase leaf area index of 5.1 in 3 years. For 120-m² gaps, 75% recovery of leaf area occurs in 3 years and >90% recovery within 6 years. The recovery of leaf area has implications for the recovery of productive capacity, nutrient immobilization, and moderation of the erosive power of rainfall.

Landscape pattern of natural disturbance and regeneration. Natural disturbance imposes a pattern upon vegetation; Hubbell (1979) likened forests to a palimpsest, a parchment written on, erased, and written over. Just as reuse of a particular parchment was not a random matter, the natural disturbances of forests and their recovery are not equally likely everywhere. Gaps in elfin forest of Monteverde are clumped; too many gaps have centers within 20 m of the centers of gaps of similar age for gap formation to be considered a random process (Lawton and Putz 1988). This pattern may be due to the scale of the impact of gusts; nearby trees may fall simultaneously. One mechanism for the latter is that asymmetric crown growth into gaps increases the likelihood of treefall in that direction (Young and Hubbell 1991). The loss of neighbors may also increase exposure to wind in settings such as the Monteverde elfin forests.

Whatever the mechanisms, aggregation of disturbance imposes spatial structure on stands at a scale larger than the individual tree, which should influence the design of ecological studies. In the elfin forest, if there are more gap centers within 20 m of others than expected by chance, then there are disturbed patches of forest 40–50 m (4–5 emergent tree heights) across. This patchiness (0.25 ha) is large relative to the size of elfin forest stands, which are typically 2–10 ha. If the height of the canopy provides a natural metric, and taller forests show similar aggregation of disturbance, then a spatial pattern with a scale of around 1 ha should exist for a 30-m-tall forest. Since intensive sampling for vegetation attributes and ecosystem processes commonly occurs at smaller scales, attention to the disturbance components in ecosystem structure is needed for accurate extrapolation to watershed and landscape scales.

Research in the future. The problem of species diversity remains a critical issue in both theoretical and applied ecological arenas. A montane area such as the Cordillera de Tilarán offers a different perspective on the evolution and ecological maintenance of biological diversity from lowland regions. Environmental gradients are more dramatic in mountains, and offer clearer opportunities to examine partitioning of resources.

Dramatic variation exists in vegetation structure and composition within the Cordillera de Tilarán, but questions of pattern and process have been little explored. The coupling of geomorphic and vegetation processes deserves particular attention. Landslides are dynamic sculptors of steep slopes, and the vegetation patch dynamics they initiate is conpicuous throughout the range. We know little of the temporal scales involved in the patch dynamics, and nothing of the feedbacks between local vegetation structure and slope stability. The coupling of wind exposure, vegetation structure, and vegetation dynamics also deserves quantitative examination at the landscape scale. Exposure to the trade winds establishes conspicuous gradients of water availability and mechanical stress in the Cordillera, but its influence on the tempo and spatial scale of forest dynamics is not documented. Other questions of ecological stability involve the persistence of distinctive vegetation types such as swamps, elfin ridgecrest forests, and xeric cliffsides. Although ambitious programs of long-term monitoring are needed to address these questions, others may be accessible to small, well-designed studies of critical components.

9.1.2. Leeward Cloud Forest

General forest description. A long-term study was initiated in 1987 to characterize the structure, composition, and dynamics of a study area (1480–1550 m) in the leeward cloud forest of the lower montane wet forest (Lawton and Dryer 1980). The 4-ha study area is located in the designated Research Area of the MCFP, about 3 km west of the visitor center (Fig. 9.8). The forest is composed of trees 15–30 m tall, with a well-developed subcanopy. Epiphytes are diverse and abundant (Nadkarni 1986a, Ingram and Nadkarni 1993). In the study area, tree density and size were measured (diameter at breast height, DBH) to 0.1 cm and height estimated to 1 m for all trees >10 cm DBH). Branch surfaces in the crown interior of nearly all trees >30 cm DBH support large hemiepiphytes and bryophytes, herbs, and woody shrubs in interwoven root-humus mats up to 30 cm thick. The climate of the study area follows the description of leeward slope forest described in Chapter 2, Physical Environment.

Forest soils. Four soil pits (1 x 1 x 2 m deep) on the forest floor in the study area were excavated. The continually moist soils of the forest floor are derived from volcanic rhyolites and classified as *typic dystrandept* (Vance and Nadkarni 1990; Table 9.1). These volcanically derived soils are considered to be fairly fertile and recently deposited and to share characteristics with other tropical cloud forests at similar elevations.

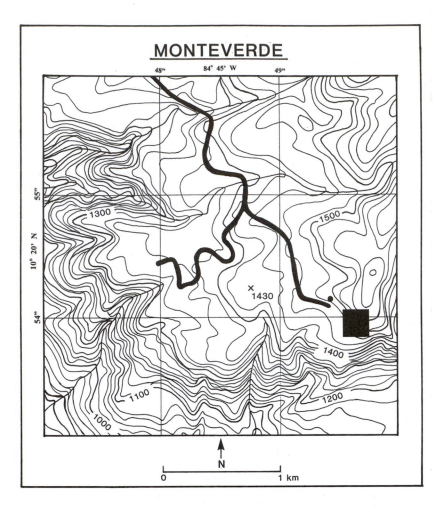

Figure 9.8. Map of study site in Monteverde. Small circle indicates the field station of the Monteverde Cloud Forest Preserve. Black square represents the 4-ha study plot. (From Nadkarni et al. 1995)

Studies of root-soil interactions in tropical montane forests have focused almost exclusively on the forest floor. In Monteverde and many other tropical forests, however, a considerable amount of dead organic matter exists within the crowns of trees (Pócs 1980, Nadkarni 1984). This epiphyte-generated "crown humus" (*sensu* Jenik 1973) is produced from the decomposition of epiphytic plants, the bark of host trees, intercepted canopy detritus, and in organic nutrients impounded from atmospheric sources (Nadkarni and Matelson 1991). Material can accumulate up to 30 cm thick on the surfaces of large branches, in bark crevices, and in the crotches of bifurcating tree trunks and supports a great diversity and biomass of epiphytic plants and associated invertebrates and vertebrates, some which are unique

Table 9.1. Soil description of leeward cloud forest study area in Monteverde (Vance and Nadkarni 1992).

Horizon	Approximate Depth (cm)	pH (H$_2$O)	Color[a]	Texture	Structure	Bulk Density (g/cm^2)
H/root mat	0–15	4.4	Dark reddish brown 5 yr 3/3		Weak to moderate crumb	0.046
A$_1$	15–20	4.7	Dark brown 7.5 yr 3/4	Loam	Weak to moderate crumb	0.31
A$_2$/B$_1$	20–85	5.3	Strong brown 7.5 yr 4/6	Loam to sandy loam	Weak crumb to moderate sub-angular blocky	0.50
B$_2$	85–180	5.5	Strong brown 7.5 yr 4/6	Clay loam	Moderate subangular blocky	0.63

to the canopy microhabitat (Longino and Nadkarni 1990).

This arboreal soil is often permeated by roots and absorptive structures of vascular and nonvascular epiphytes and, in some cases, by the adventitious "canopy roots" of host trees (Nadkarni 1981). It functions as a storage pool for organically bound nutrients and as a "nutrient capaciter" for inorganic nutrients from incoming atmospheric sources and from materials mineralized *in situ* (Nadkarni 1984). This arboreal substrate has never been classified in any standard soil taxonomy system, and its characteristics are poorly understood (Putz and Holbrook 1989, Vance and Nadkarni 1990; Table 9.2; Clark and Nadkarni, "Microclimate Variability," pp. 33–34). As does the forest floor H horizon, epiphytic organic matter hosts an active microbial community, although rates of nitrification are suppressed in the canopy relative to that on the forest floor (Vance and Nadkarni 1990; see Vance and Nadkarni, "Microbial Biomass and Activity," p. 336). The invertebrate community within the arboreal soil is similar in composition to the terrestrial community at the taxonomic level of order, but overall density of invertebrates is much lower in the canopy, which may lead to differences in processing of nutrients (Nadkarni and Longino 1990; see Nadkarni and Longino, "Invertebrates," pp. 336–337).

Particularly important to the distribution of soil-based organisms are soil moisture and temperature. In cloud forests, where cloud cover and wind vary seasonally, differences in the soil moisture and temperature regimes on very small spatial scales may be pronounced. Canopy soils may reflect the higher air temperature (Chacon and Duval 1963), greater wind speed (Lawton 1982), and lower humidity (Longman and Jenik 1987) of the canopy relative to the forest floor.

We measured soil temperature and moisture on the forest floor and in the canopy at the leeward cloud forest site for a 42-month period (Bohlman et al. 1995). Temperatures of the canopy material and forest floor soil fluctuated throughout the year (range 11.5–21.0°C), but remained within an average of 1°C of each other for each measurement interval. Both canopy material and forest floor soils were moist throughout the wet and misty seasons (over 70% water content). However, during the dry season, canopy humus experienced periods of rapid and severe dehydration (20–40% water content), whereas forest floor soils remained at a consistently high water content (60–70%; Fig. 9.9). The more extreme and fluctuating moisture conditions of canopy organic material may affect the distribution and activity of epiphytic plants and associated canopy organisms.

Forest structure.   Stems in the 4-ha study area were categorized as large (>30 cm DBH), medium (10–30 cm DBH), or small (2–10 cm DBH) and identified to species by W. Haber and E. Bello (Nadkarni et al. 1995). Based on a sample of 1850 stems, overall density of live stems in all size classes was 2062 individuals per hectare (large, medium, and small stems were 159, 396, and 1507, respectively). Mean tree DBH was 65.5 cm; canopy height was 18–25 m. A frequency distribution of size classes showed a reversed J-shape, which is typical for a mature stand, with many small stems and a few large ones. Over half of the total basal area was represented by trees >50 cm DBH. The largest trees (>90 cm DBH), which constituted only 1% of the stems, accounted for 30% of the total basal area (Nadkarni et al. 1995).

Forest composition.   Stems represented 47 families, 83 genera, and 114 species and varied among size classes. The distribution of stems among taxa was uneven; more than half of the individuals belonged to members of the three most common families. The stems of 26 plant families accounted for less than 1%

Table 9.2. Comparison of epiphytic and forest floor organic matter.

Location	%C	%N	C:N Ratio	pH
Epiphytic organic matter	37.4	2.36	17.9	3.7
Forest floor				
0–10 cm below	27.0	1.44	18.7	4.6
10–20cm below	25.3	0.98	25.8	5.4

Data are mean percentage C and N, C:N ratios, and pH of epiphytic organic matter and organic matter taken from 0–10 cm below the forest floor and 10–20 cm below the forest floor at the study area in Monteverde, Costa Rica. Samples were taken in May 1987. The epiphytic samples are composites of three to five branches per tree from 13 trees located 1–3 m from the central trunk and 16–23 m above the forest floor. The forest floor samples are from 20 samples taken at random locations and bulked into six composites for each horizon (Vance and Nadkarni 1990).

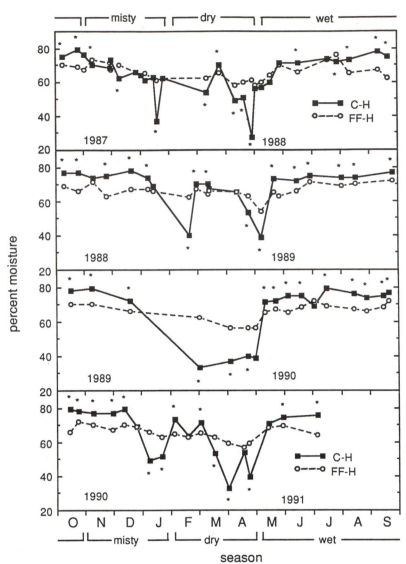

Figure 9.9. Moisture content of canopy organic matter (C-H) and the forest floor H horizon (FF-H) at the study area in Monteverde. Moisture content, determined from 10-gm samples taken from the top 10 cm of soil, is expressed as (water content/ total wet weight). Asterisks (*) represent a significant difference ($P < .05$) between C-H and FF-H. (From Bohlman et al. 1995)

of the relative basal area (Table 9.3). A dominance-diversity curve was computed at the species level by ranking the relative basal area of all stems >10 cm for trees in the subplots for which species were identified. Six species constituted more than 97% of the percent basal area, illustrating the strong dominance by relatively few species. A single dominant species, *Ocotea tonduzii,* made up 23% of the total basal area, and a single dominant family, Lauraceae, made up 31% of the total basal area (Table 9.3).

Comparison of Monteverde forest structure and composition with other forests. Tree densities we report fell in the middle of the range of densities reported elsewhere (Nadkarni et al. 1995; Table 9.4). Only one other study (Edwards 1977) reported a higher total basal area and species richness. Vegetation at the 1500 m site on Volcán Barva, Costa Rica (Heaney and Proctor 1990),

about 40 km from our study area, presents the most interesting comparison to our site due to its proximity and similar elevation and rainfall. Stem density (trees > 10 cm) at the two sites was nearly identical (553/ha[1] at Barva vs. 559/ha[1] at our site). However, basal area at Barva was less than half that at our site (Table 9.4). We identified nearly twice as many species at Monteverde compared to Barva. Our values come from a larger area (3 vs. 1 ha). However, in the one hectare for which identifications were determined for all stems >10 cm at our site, the Monteverde forest was slightly richer in species and families (39 families and 76 species in Monteverde, compared to 34 families and 65 species at Barva). There were 28 families for trees >10 cm DBH in common between the Monteverde and Barva sites; 18 families occurred only at the Monteverede site, and seven families occurred only at the Barva site (Nadkarni et al. 1995).

Table 9.3. Tree families with percentage of mean total basal area (BA) and mean density (numbers of individual trees per hectare).

| | Stem Size Class | | | | | | | | |
| | 2–10 cm | | 10–30 cm | | >30 cm | | All Stems | |
Family	% BA	N	% BA	N	% BA	N	% BA	N
Annonaceae	1.9	14	1.1	4	1.5	3	1.5	21
Apocynaceae	1.2	21	0.4	2			0.1	23
Aquifoliaceae			0.5	2	1.3	2	1.2	4
Araliaceae	0.5	7	0.4	1			0.1	8
Arecaceae	2.3	86	0.1	3			0.1	89
Asteraceae	_10.6_	_161_	4.4	27			0.6	_188_
Bombacaceae	0.5	11	4.8	13	1.6	6	1.9	30
Boraginaceae	1.7	18	0.4	1	2.4	7	2.2	26
Cecropiaceae	0.9	18	_10.9_	_32_	3.3	_10_	_3.9_	60
Celastraceae			0.2	1	0.4	1	0.4	2
Clusiaceae	t	4	3.7	17	0.2	1	0.5	22
Cunoniaceae	t	4	0.2	1	2.2	2	2.0	7
Cyatheaceae	_28.7_	_164_	1.2	13			0.7	_177_
Ebenaceae	0.1	4					t	4
Elaeocarpaceae					1.6	1	1.4	1
Euphorbiaceae	2.4	25	0.6	3			0.1	28
Fabaceae	5.4	71	6.0	27	3.2	3	3.6	101
Flacourtiaceae	1.1	25	3.2	11	4.1	8	_3.9_	44
Hippocrateaceae	0.1	4					t	4
Icacinaceae	2.4	50	0.9	3	t	1	0.2	54
Juglandaceae					0.3	1	0.2	1
Lauraceae	6.2	121	6.3	18	_33.9_	_37_	_30.9_	176
Malpighiaceae	1.2	18					0.1	18
Malvaceae	0.9	25	3.3	13	2.1	6	2.1	44
Melastomataceae	1.9	50	9.5	27	1.4	7	2.2	84
Meliaceae	6.0	89	_9.6_	_36_	4.2	9	4.7	134
Moraceae	2.5	54	1.4	5	_15.2_	4	_13.7_	63
Myrsinaceae	2.0	18	_10.5_	30	0.9	5	1.9	53
Myrtaceae	1.7	36	0.5	3	2.6	5	2.3	44
Nyctaginaceae	0.2	11					t	11
Piperaceae	t	4					t	4
Proteaceae			0.4	1	0.3	1	0.3	2
Rhizophoraceae			0.1	1			t	1
Rubiaceae	_10.5_	_196_	7.5	_37_	0.7	3	1.6	_236_
Rutaceae	0.5	4	0.2	2	1.0	3	0.8	9
Sabiaceae	0.8	18	1.1	3	4.0	7	3.7	28
Sapindaceae	0.7	21	0.4	1	0.5	1	0.5	23
Sapotaceae	0.7	14	1.5	3	3.4	3	3.1	20
Simaroubaceae	t	4					t	4
Solanaceae	3.4	121					0.1	121
Staphyleaceae			0.3	1			t	1
Symplocaceae	0.2	4	0.9	2	0.2	1	0.3	7
Thymelaeaceae	0.1	4	0.3	1	0.5	1	0.3	6
Tiliaceae			0.4	3	_6.3_	_10_	5.6	13
Urticaceae	0.3	7	4.6	18	0.2	1	0.6	26
Verbenaceae	0.4	4	1.8	3	0.5	1	0.6	8

Underlining indicates the dominant three families for each category. t = trace (less than 1% of the basal area; Nadkarni et al. 1995).

Dominance was imposed by different taxa at the two sites. At Barva, the dominant family was Euphorbiaceae (14.5% of basal area), whereas this taxon comprised only 1.1% of the total basal area at our site. The dominant family at Monteverde, Lauraceae (31% of total basal area), comprised only 5.8% of the basal area at the Barva site. These differences may be due to different forest disturbance regimes. The dominant trees at Barva tend to be early gap colonizers, in contrast to the primarily long-lived primary forest trees that dominate in Monteverde. The much higher basal area (2.5 times greater) in Monteverde versus Barva

Table 9.4. Structural and floristic characteristics of seven tropical montane cloud forests.

Location	Forest Type	Elevation (m)	Annual Rainfall (mm)	Plot Size (m²)	Tree Density (ha^{-1})	Basal Area (m²/ha)	Tree Species Richness (sp./ha)	Source
Luquillo Mountains, Puerto Rico	"Colorado" Lower montane wet	725	3725	4000	185[a]	40	40	Weaver and Murphy 1990
Volcán Barva, Costa Rica	Lower montane rain	1500	3426	10,000	553[b]	29.2	65	Heaney and Proctor 1990
Blue Mountains, Jamaica	Mull ridge	1550	3000	1000[c]	52[b]	nr	35	Tanner 1977
Papua New Guinea	Lower montane rain	2500	3960	600[d]	19[e]	98	119	Edwards 1977, Edwards and Grubb, 1977
Ecuador, Eastern Andes	Lower montane rain	1710	nr	465[f]	28[e]	nr	59[e]	Grubb et al. 1983
Monteverde, Costa Rica	Lower montane wet	1480	2500	40,000	1507[g] 396[h] 159[i] 2062[j]	11,8[g] 9.6[h] 52.4[i] 73.8[j]	111	This chapter

[a]Stems > 4 cm DBH.
[b]Stems > 10 cm DBH.
[c]Ten 10 x 10 m plots.
[d]Three 20 x 10 m plots.
[e]Stems > 20 cm DBH.
[f]One 61 x 7.6 m plot.
[g]Stems 2–10 cm DBH.

also suggests disturbance is more frequent at Barva. Thus, similar elevation and environmental conditions do not necessarily dictate similar structure and floristics in montane forests.

Forest dynamics.   The frequency and types of loss of tree crowns and the death of whole trees affect forest regeneration, nutrient cycling, and species richness. Relatively few studies exist for tropical lower montane forests. The rates and frequency of tree damage might be expected to be greater in higher elevation forests because of steeper slopes, less stable soil, and exposure to more wind. Small-scale forest disturbances such as loss of crowns (herein "tree damage") and treefalls are determined by local climatic forces, physical characteristics of the substrate, and biological attributes of the trees (Putz and Brokaw 1989). When whole trees and their associated epiphytes fall to the forest floor, they (1) present pulses of organic material and nutrients that can subsequently become available to terrestrially rooted plants (Denslow 1987); (2) increase the biomass of the forest floor, which creates additional habitats for terrestrial organisms; 3) reduce resources used by arboreal animals and epi-

phytes and create snags for nesting by key bird seed dispersers (Wheelwright et al. 1984); (4) crush seedlings, saplings, and understory plants (Aide 1987); and (5) affect microclimate of the ensuing gap, which may subsequently deter or facilitate the germination of seeds of some species (Putz and Milton 1982).

Although many damaged trees die, some continue to live by producing new shoots from above- or belowground parts. Regeneration from broken plant segments ("resprouting") has been noted in some forest trees (Clark and Clark 1989, R. Lawton, pers. comm.) and shrubs (Kinsman 1990). Resprouting of damaged individuals might replace lost substrate in the same location and affect the form and duration of gap regeneration faster than regeneration from seedlings.

Three censuses of marked trees in the leeward forest study area were made in September 1990, 1991, and 1992 (Matelson et al. 1995). Tree damage and mortality were divided into five categories: (1) standing broken stems, classified by the relative height of the break (high, middle, low); (2) uproots (fallen trees with exposed root wads); (3) knockdowns (trees falling as a result of a neighboring tree hitting them); (4) standing dead trees (stems not broken or uprooted);

or (5) missing (trees not found again). During the final census, standing broken stems were checked for sprouting of foliage. Longevity of standing broken stems was calculated by counting the number of months between the time of damage and when we noted the stem fallen to the ground.

A total of 1403 trees were tagged. The number of standing broken was 77 (19.3/ha), or 5%. The number of trees that were damaged or died during the study period was 147. The mean number of damaged and dead trees was 15.9 trees/ha (2.8% of the tagged trees). Tree damage was highest during the 6-month wet season (47%), intermediate months in the dry season (31%), and lowest in the windy-misty season (22%) (Matelson et al. 1995).

Of the damaged trees, 61% were standing broken stems, 22% were uproots, 7% were knockdowns, 4% were standing dead trees, and 10% were missing. Larger trees were more likely to be damaged or die (Fig. 9.10). Trees that were damaged or died during the study were in 19 plant families, 20 genera, and 21 species (Matelson *et al.* 1995). Trees in most of the plant families died at similar proportions to that expected from their distribution in the live population. However, trees in three plant genera (*Cecropia, Hampea, Heliocarpus*) died at strikingly higher rates than expected, more than twice their proportion in the total marked population. These are gap-colonizing, rapidly growing, short-lived trees.

Of the 91 standing broken stems that were created during the study, 30 (34%) had resprouted by the final census. The identified damaged trees that resprouted were in 10 plant families; those that did not resprout were in 18 families. Two of the most common genera

in the sample (*Ocotea* and *Guarea*) accounted for 50% of the damaged trees that resprouted (Matelson et al. 1995).

A total of 116 of the 147 damaged trees died during the study period. Most of this mortality was due to standing broken stems that did not resprout (53%), followed by uproots (28%), knockdowns (7%), standing dead (3%), and 9% due to missing trees. The mean annual mortality was 12.7 trees/ha[1], equivalent to an annual mortality of 2.2% for all size classes. The expectation of further life (calculated as the inverse of the average proportion of trees dying per year; Putz and Milton 1982) was 43.8 yr overall. Turnover time, calculated as the number of years necessary for all of the originally inventoried trees to die (number of originally tagged trees/[number of dead and snapped trees/ time observed]; Uhl 1982), was 55.5 yr for 10–30 cm DBH, and 42.4 yr for trees > 30 cm DBH.

Annual mortality rate in this study is similar to other tropical forests (1–3%; Putz and Milton 1982, Hartshorn 1990, Lieberman et al. 1990, Swaine et al. 1990), most of which are from lowland tropical regions. The length of expectation of further life, turnover rates, and seasonality of tree damage and death were also within the range of other forests even though the wet steep slopes of montane sites, coupled with strong seasonal winds and high epiphyte loads, might be expected to increase the incidence of tree damage and tree falls.

The mode of damage and death in our site was also similar to other forests. Our study area experienced 65% of tree damage and mortality due to snaps and 22% to uprooting of whole trees. On Barro Colorado Island (BCI), Panama, 52% of the mortality was due to snapping and 17% to uprooting (Putz and Milton 1982). In La Selva, Costa Rica, fallen dead trees (uproots and snaps combined) accounted for 31% of total mortality (Lieberman and Lieberman 1987). The major difference between our montane site and lowland sites was that tree mortality that occurs as standing dead stems was rare in the Monteverde forest (3% of total mortality) compared to lowland tropical sites. La Selva had 26% of mortality as standing dead trees (Lieberman and Lieberman 1987); BCI, 15% (Putz and Milton 1982); and tierre firme forest in Venezuela, 10% (Uhl 1982).

One-third of the standing broken stems that formed during our study resprouted. Few studies have measured this phenomenon or incorporated it into their calculations of tree mortality; the rates of annual "mortality" reported in some studies may thus be overestimates. Resprouting would be expected to be more common where wind and/or forceful storms are frequent, such as in lower montane forests. In the forest on BCI, chronic disturbance is thought to lead to

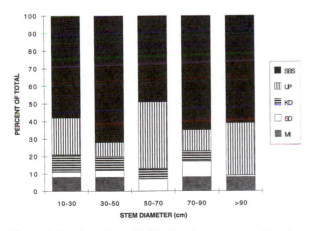

Figure 9.10. Size class distribution (percentage of total stems) of the 147 trees that were damaged or died during the study divided into five categories (MI, missing; SD, standing dead; KD, knockdown; UP, uproot; SBS, standing broken stem). (From Matelson et al. 1995)

local dominance by species that recover quickly from injury (Knight 1975, Putz and Brokaw 1989). As predicted, the common canopy species in Monteverde were those that sprout readily (Matelson et al. 1995).

In mature forests, gap-colonizing taxa have a higher incidence of mortality than their proportion in the forest. Pioneer species that grow fast and have weak wood might be prone to breaking and therefore have a propensity for resprouting (Putz and Brokaw 1989). More long-term data are needed to record such phenomena as standing broken stem regeneration and attrition of dead standing stems, which operate on a time scale of several years to several decades.

9.2. Forest Biogeochemistry and Nutrient Cycling

In all ecosystems, materials circulate in characteristic paths from the environment through living organisms and back to the environment in biogeochemical cycles. The movement of elements that are essential to life is designated nutrient cycling. "Nutrient" applies to any substance taken into an organism that is metabolized or becomes part of ionic balances (excluding toxins and substances used only as behavioral signals). Most often, the emphasis in biogeochemical studies is on inorganic elements and ions that are present in water and soil and may be taken up to become part of community function. The processes of transfer and concentration of materials have increasingly urgent significance to humans.

In contrast to the storage and movement of energy, which cannot be recycled, chemical nutrients, the building blocks of biomass, can change the form of the molecule of which they are a part (e.g., organically bound nitrogen can shift to ammonium nitrate). They can be converted and recycled among different components of the forest, and the process of locking some up in living biomass reduces the supply remaining to the community. The categories of supply and loss of nutrients in terrestrial ecosystems are similar for all forest ecosystems (Table 9.5), but the magnitude of different components varies among forest types.

Some early studies of nutrient cycling in tropical forests described productive forests rich in nutrients, but others described tropical soils as acid, infertile clays. In fact, patterns of nutrient cycling in tropical forests are diverse (Vitousek and Sanford 1986). Montane tropical forests in general appear to be lower in nitrogen and phosphorus than fertile lowland forests, even though the former are located on what would be classified as fertile soils (Grubb and Edwards 1982). Decomposition rates in montane forests are lower than in lowland forests (Proctor 1983), probably due to lower temperatures.

Typically, the first step in building an ecosystem nutrient budget is to estimate the amount of biomass and nutrient capital in the standing stocks of vegetation. Ideally, subsamples of each component of interest (e.g., foliage, stems, fine roots) are taken in a manner and at a sampling intensity that encompasses the natural variability of the material. Subsamples of each component are then analyzed for nutrient content, and this amount is used to extrapolate the total amount of nutrients from the estimates of biomass of that component.

We carried out a study of ecosystem nutrient cycling from 1987 to 1997 in the leeward cloud forest study area. Our objective was to quantify and characterize epiphyte communities and their accompanying organic matter and nutrients in an ecosystem context. Canopy components form a forest subsystem thatons/has received increasing attention from ecosystem ecologists (Coxson and Nadkarni 1995). Drawing on botanists, soil scientists, a microbial ecologist, an atmospheric chemist, and an ecological modeller, we generated estimates of the major pools and fluxes of terrestrially rooted and canopy components in this forest.

Epiphytic organic matter (EM) is composed of roots and shoots of vascular and nonvascular plants, abscised leaves and stems of host trees and epiphytes thatons/have been intercepted by branches, invertebrates, fungi, and microorganisms associated with

Table 9.5. Major routes of import, export, and circulation of nutrients in terrestrial communities.

Import	Export	Circulation
Precipitation (rain, mist)	Runoff and stream outflow	Litterfall
Particulate fallout	Particulate loss by wind	Crownwash (throughfall and stemflow)
Biotic immigration	Biotic emigration	Decomposition
Fixation from the atmosphere (e.g., nitrogen fixation)	Release to the atmosphere (e.g,. denitrification)	Plant uptake
Weathering of substrate	Loss by leaching	Defecation of animals
Fertilizer application	Human harvest	Plant retranslocation
Pollution deposition		

canopy foliage (see sec. 9.1). It influences nutrient cycles by altering ecosystem nutrient pools and pathways and rates of nutrient fluxes (Pike 1978, Coxson and Nadkarni 1995). This material reaches its greatest abundance and diversity in tropical montane cloud forests (Madison 1977). Trunk cover is highly variable and is dominated by climbers, scramblers, and bryophytes, with little associated organic matter. Outer branches support a low biomass of herbaceaous plants and very little accumulated humus. Inner branch surfaces and branch junctions are where most of the EM occurs. Understory vegetation and herbaceous plants support mainly bryophytes and very little dead EM. The live components of EM determine the overall structure of canopy communities and contribute to nutrient exchange by exudation and uptake by epiphyte roots, mycorrhizae, and host tree canopy roots (Nadkarni 1981). Humus and other dead EM components are important in nutrient cycling because they represent a large pool of carbon and nutrients that is microbially active (Vance and Nadkarni 1990).

In the leeward forest study area, all trees >10 cm DBH were stratified to a quartile EM cover class. There were 78 trees/ha with an epiphyte cover class of 3 or 4 (>50% cover). A random subsample of trees >50 cm DBH were selected for intensive sampling of inner branch surface and branch junction EM. Trees were rigged with mountain-climbing ropes following Nadkarni (1988). We stratified EM into seven types, based on its substrate: (1) surfaces of trunks, (2) surfaces of outer branches, (3) surfaces of inner branches, (4) junctions of branch major branches and trunks, (5) branch tips, (6) understory vegetation (2–10 cm DBH), and (7) groundcover (plants <3 m in height).

Destructive sampling of other trees (six 10–30 cm DBH, six >30 cm) involved rigging and climbing to the top of the trunk. To assess trunk EM, all EM within a 20-cm cylindrat encircling the trunk was taken every 3 m. For branch and branch tip EM samples, a professional arborist climbed into the crown and cut and lowered three randomly chosen branches to the ground. The branch was measured and divided into thirds. A 20–cm swatch of EM was collected from each third and taken to the lab for processing. The remaining EM was removed and weighed in the field. Subsamples of the branch, including branch tips, were collected for dry weight determination and analyzed for nutrients. To extrapolate to a larger spatial scale, we counted the number of branches and estimated their lengths on each sample tree, and all the surrounding trees. For the understory and groundcover biomass components, we established subplots (9 and 1 m², respectively) from which all the plant material was taken and separated into epiphytes, leaves, and stems. To assess EM composition, branch samples

were separated into seven constituents: higher vascular plant leaves, stems, ferns, roots, reproductive parts, cryptogams (bryophytes and lichens), and dead organic matter, which consisted of crown humus and detritus.

9.2.1. Biomass and Characteristics of Forest Components

Biomass and composition of terrestrially rooted material. Estimates of aboveground biomass of trees were made by multiplying tree-level estimates of component biomass by the density of trees of each size class. Sapling and forest biomass was calculated by multiplying sample plots to a per-hectare basis. Total aboveground terrestrially rooted biomass was 490.1 tons/ha, of which 85% was trunk wood and 12% was branch wood; other constituents made up only 3% (Table 9.6). The nonwoody constituents (foliage, reproductive parts, and parasites) contain the most labile (readily decomposed) portions, and constituted 9.3 tons/ha (2%) of the terrestrially rooted aboveground biomass. Nutrients followed the same trends as biomass; the component with the greatest pool of nutrients was trunk wood, followed by branch wood, tree foliage, groundcover, understory wood, reproductive parts, and parasites (Table 9.6).

Biomass and composition of canopy EM. The biomass of EM on inner branch surfaces was 2450 g/m² (branch surface area basis). The mean volume of EM at branch junctions in the sample trees was 115.8 dm³/junction (SE = 40.1). The biomass of EM in branch junctions varied considerably, ranging between 125.1 g/dm³ and 6.3 g.dm³ (mean = 56.2 g/dm³). The greatest proportion of EM was located in the branch junctions (68%). Branch tips and ground cover vegetation had very small amounts (0.34 g/tip and 0.02 ton/ha, respectively), equivalent to less than 0.004% and 0.0001% of the total EM biomass (Table 9.6). Estimates of whole system EM biomass were extrapolated by multiplying single-tree estimates by the mean density of trees in the same epiphyte cover and size classes. Total EM ecosystem biomass was 33.1 tons/ha (Table 9.6)

In general, the amounts of nutrients contained in EM components followed the pattern of biomass. However, disproportionately larger amounts of calcium were found in trunk epiphytes. The majority of nutrients were found in branch junctions, followed by branch mats and on trunks, with smaller amounts on branch tips, the understory, and ground cover (Table 9.6).

The overwhelming majority of biomass was in dead organic matter (DOM). Roots and bryophytes

Table 9.6. Aboveground biomass (tons/ha) and nutrient capital (kg/ha) contained in terrestrially rooted and epiphytic material in the Monteverde Cloud Forest Preserve leeward cloud forest study area.

	Biomass	N	P	Ca	K	Mg
Terrestrially rooted material						
Trunk wood	418.8	2847.8	167.5	2931.6	3476.0	879.5
Branch wood	60.0	624.0	42.0	702.0	372.0	84.0
Sapling wood	2.0	37.8	2.2	17.0	21.0	4.2
Groundcover	2.4	68.9	2.9	30.9	55.3	8.7
Tree foliage	6.5	149.5	7.1	63.1	69.6	19.5
Reproductive Parts	0.2	4.1	0.5	1.2	2.9	0.4
Parasites	0.2	2.3	0.2	1.4	1.1	0.3
Total	490.1	3734.1	222.4	3747.2	3997.9	996.6
Nonwoody	9.3	224.8	10.7	96.6	128.9	28.9
Epiphytic material						
On trunks	3.0	41.9	2.2	35.9	23.0	3.9
Branch junctions	22.4	305.0	13.5	112.0	76.9	25.8
Branch mats	6.2	72.1	4.4	36.7	44.3	11.2
Inner branches	1.1	13.8	0.7	6.2	5.2	1.6
Branch tips	0.2	2.6	0.2	0.9	1.4	0.3
Sapling cover	0.1	2.7	0.1	1.6	0.7	0.2
Ground cover	0.02	0.5	0.05	0.4	0.5	0.1
Total	33.1	438.7	21.1	193.7	152.0	43.1
Total ecosystem	523.2	4172.8	243.5	3940.9	4149.9	1039.4
% Epiphytic/total	6.3	10.5	8.7	4.9	3.7	4.2
% Epiphytic/nonwoody terrestrial	360	190	200	200	120	150

Total for each category indicates all components; nonwoody terrestrial material is foliage, reproductive parts, herbaceous vegetation, and parasitic plants. Percentages of epiphytic material as part of the forest are calculated as (1) the proportion of epiphytic material to the total aboveground ecosystem (terrestrially rooted + epiphytic totals) and (2) the proportion of epiphytic material to nonwoody terrestrially rooted components.

had similar amounts (12% and 15%, respectively); reproductive parts, stems, ferns, and epiphytic foliage made up a very small proportion (Table 9.7). Inner branch mats of EM were dominated by organic matter, which occurred in four forms: DOM, foliage, roots, and bryophytes. Roots made up approximately 15% of the inner branch mats; around 30% of them were fine roots (<2 mm). Branch junction EM contained primarily humus and roots. Fine roots comprised a larger proportion of the total root biomass in the branch junctions (45%) than on the mats on branch surfaces (Vance and Nadkarni 1992). Bryophytes predominated on branch tips, understory vegetation, and on groundcover (Table 9.7).

Comparison of canopy and forest floor organic matter. The pH of dead organic matter in the canopy and at two levels of the forest floor differed strikingly. There was a significant difference in percentages of carbon and nitrogen between canopy EM and forest floor humus horizon (0–10 cm deep; Table 9.2). Canopy EM was higher in nitrogen. All types of organic matter had a similar C:N ratio. Our results are comparable to the few published values of nutrient content and characteristics from other studies in tropical forests (Edwards 1977, Tanner 1980b, Putz and Holbrook 1989). They are slightly lower in nitrogen, carbon, and exchangeable bases than those reported for organic soils of Colombia (Lopez and Cortes 1978).

Roots. Biomass and nutrient pools of roots are two of the great unknowns in the study of forest productivity and nutrient cycling, due to the difficulty in excavating root samples at depth (Vitousek and Sanford 1986). In the leeward cloud forest study area, we studied soil characteristics and fine and coarse root biomass in the soil and in the canopy (Vance and Nadkarni 1992). The canopy provides a second habitat for roots as functional absorptive organs that could be potentially important in ecosystem functioning. Canopy roots can be derived from vascular epiphytes growing in the canopy, from the host tree themselves

Table 9.7. Biomass (kg/ha) of epiphytic material (EM) components on seven substrates in the Monteverde leeward cloud forest study area.

Substrate	EM Component							
	Bryo	DOM	Stems	Ferns	Fol	Roots	Rep	Total
Trunk	482	498	1590	43	155	222	3	2993
	[16]	[17]	[53]	[1]	[5]	[8]	t	
Branch crotches	0	18,600	0	0	0	3800	0	22400
		[83]				[17]		
Inner branches	86	698	0	0	140	150	0	1074
	[8]	[65]			[13]	[14]		
Branch mats	3149	948	465	198	366	1072	0	6198
	[51]	[15]	[8]	[3]	[6]	[17]		
Branch tips	200	0	0	0	0	0	0	200
	[100]							
Understory	120	0	0	0	0	0	0	120
	[100]							
Groundcover	21	1	0	0	1	0	0	23
	[92]	[4]			[4]			
Total	4058	20,745	2055	241	662	5244	3	33,008
	[12]	[63]	[6]	[1]	[2]	[16]	[t]	

Data are based on destructive sampling in 17 trees, understory, and groundcover plots. Proportion (%) of each EM component for a given substrate is in brackets. Bryo = bryophytes and lichens; DOM = dead organic matter (crown humus, dead leaves and stems); Fol = foliage; Rep = reproductive parts (flowers and fruits). t = trace (<0.01%).

(Nadkarni 1981), or from neighboring plants with roots that grow apogeotropically (Sanford 1987).

We excavated four 1-m² pits. Living roots were sieved, sorted, dried, and weighed. To encompass horizontal variation in the upper horizon in the forest floor, we sampled 15 randomly located points within the study area to a depth of 20 cm. Biomass estimates were comparable between pit and core samples. Total belowground root biomass ranged between 1500 g/m² and 7220 g/m², which is similar to root biomass for other tropical montane forests (Vitousek and Stanford 1986). Fine root biomass (<2 mm) ranged from 300 g/m² to 1300 g/m²; it made up 20–40% of total belowground root biomass. Although we noted the presence of a thick root mat in the highly organic H and A₁ horizons, more than 30% of the fine root biomass occurred below this depth (ca. 0–20 cm). The substantial biomass of fine roots at lower soil depths suggests a potential mode of nutrient conservation thatons/has not been widely documented (Vance and Nadkarni 1992).

Mycorrhizae, a fungal-root relationship that appear to enhance water and nutrient uptake for the host plants, have been little investigated at this site. One survey was carried out in the canopy and forest floor of the Monteverde leeward cloud forest study area (Maffia et al. 1993; Maffia et al., "Vesicular-Arbuscular Mychorrhizae," pp. 338–339).

Root biomass in the canopy was assessed as described above. On inner branch surfaces, total root biomass averaged 150 g/m² of branch area. The deep humus pockets located at branch junctions of mature trees contained around 80% of the total root biomass and five times more fine root biomass than inner branch surfaces.

The substantial biomass of fine roots at lower soil depths suggests a potential avenue for nutrient conservation. Although the biomass of canopy roots is smaller than that of their belowground counterparts, they appear to occupy an important niche in this forest due to their access to potentially large fluxes of nutrients passing through the canopy in mist and rain and mineralized from canopy humus. High concentrations of roots at branch junctions could be particularly effective in exploiting nutrients in stemflow. Canopy roots could thus act as an important nutrient-conserving mechanism in the montane rain forest ecosystem by trapping nutrients before they reach the forest floor, and trees capable of creating them may be favored in cloud forest environments (see Nadkarni, "Factors Affecting Initiation and Growth," pp. 339–341).

9.2.2. Nutrient Inputs

Nutrient inputs can take many forms and are difficult to quantify. Potential sources of nutrients include an array of "autochthonous" (originating within the system) and "allochthonous sources" (originating from outside the system; see Nadkarni and Matelson, "Fine Litter Dynamics," pp. 341–343, and Table 9.24). The relative contribution of each of these sources to tropical forest communities is unknown. From an ecosystem standpoint, it is important to distinguish between them in order to assess the vulnerability of a forest to disruptions in external and internal nutrient cycles.

Precipitation inputs.   A major pathway of nutrient input to forest ecosystems is via precipitation; nutrients derived from atmospheric sources (aerosols, dissolved chemicals and gases, dust, and particulates) as well as pollutants can arrive as wet or dry fallout as allochthonous sources. These can be intercepted, retained, modified, and conducted within the ecosystem as authochthonous sources before being stored in or exiting the forest.

Precipitation and cloud water chemistry, and atmospheric deposition and retention at tropical montane forest sites have been an increasing focus of research (Veneklaas 1990, Asbury et al. 1994). The precipitation pathway is especially important for tropical montane forests. Cloud water accounts for a significant portion of the total ion deposition in montane forests because (a) ion concentrations in cloud water are 3–10 times greater than those in precipitation (Weathers et al. 1988), (b) montane areas are frequently immersed in cloud (Bruijnzeel and Proctor 1995), and (c) foliage, branches, and epiphytic vegetation are aerodynamically rough surfaces. Ion deposition is typically greater in montane cloud forests when compared to lower elevation forests, which receive only wet and dry deposition (Fowler et al. 1988, Johnson and Lindberg 1992).

Increased combustion of biomass and fossil fuels, and changes in land use practices have led to an increase in the emissions of nitric oxide and ammonia at tropical latitudes (Keller et al. 1991). Reports from lowland sites have indicated regional effects of biomass burning and conversion of forests to pasture on precipitation and air chemistry (Lewis 1981, Andreae et al. 1988, Keller et al. 1993). These activities potentially lead to greater concentrations of NO_3^- and NH_4^+ in cloud water and precipitation in tropical montane forests.

At the leeward cloud forest study site, cloud water and precipitation depth were estimated using an artificial surface of plastic "foliage" mounted above a funnel connected to a tipping bucket rain gauge. The gauge was mounted on a boom on a 27-m meteorological tower in a small gap in the forest. Bulk cloud water and precipitation (BCWP) samples for ion analyses were collected with a passive cloud collector (Falconer and Falconer 1980). Bulk precipitation (BP) was collected with a polypropylene funnel and bottle. Windspeed (u) was measured with a 3-cup anemometer. Events were categorized as $u < 2$ m/s or $u > 2$ m/s. All instruments were connected to an automated datalogger.

Average weighted mean concentrations of H, NO_3^-, and NH_4^+ in cloud water were 7, 14, and 17 times greater (respectively) than those in precipitation with windspeeds >2 m/s and 10, 30, and 45 times greater for precipitation where wind was <2 m/s (Table 9.8). The molar ratio of sodium and magnesium in cloud water was similar to that in seawater, indicating that these ions originated primarily from wind-driven marine aerosols (Blanchard 1983).

Cloud water samples collected toward the end of the dry season (late February to early May) had greater concentrations of NO_3^-, NH_4^+, K, and Ca than those collected at the end of the transition season and in the early dry season (December and January). Sampling periods toward the end of the dry season coincided with noticeable haze layers, presumably due to burning of agricultural and forest biomass. It is likely that ion enrichment in cloud water samples collected toward the end of the dry season resulted from the incorporation of gases and particles derived from burning (Andreae et al. 1988, Lobert et al. 1990).

Concentrations of inorganic nitrogen in cloud water and mist measured in Monteverde were high

Table 9.8. Ion concentrations of canopy water sources.

Sample Type	Ion Concentration (µmol/liter)						
	H+	NO₃⁻	NH₄⁺	Na⁺	Mg⁺²	Ca⁺²	K⁺
Cloud water	132.1	102.8	148.9	365.0	63.4	35.2	30.7
	(2.5–489.8)	(32.1–382.9)	(47.2–739.4)	(144.4–713.4)	(18.1–121.8)	(8.7–70.1)	(7.7–76.5)
Mist	30.8	37.3	45.3	183.0	21.9	16.8	13.5
	(0.2–251.2)	(10.8–106.1)	(2.8–131.1)	(45.7–839.5)	(4.9–137.4)	(6.0–78.6)	(2.3–71.4)
Precipitation $u > 2$ m/s	19.0	7.5	8.9	75.4	8.8	6.6	4.1
	(3.7–91.2)	(1.3–47.1)	(0.6–87.2)	(7.4–765.6)	(0.8–104.9)	(3.0–49.4)	(1.3–94.6)
Precipitation $u < 2$ m/s	13.8	3.4	3.3	7.8	1.2	3.4	2.1
	(2.8–55.0)	(bdl–46.8)	(bdl–127.8)	(2.6–107.0)	(bdl–8.2)	(bdl–11.7)	(bdl–27.6)

Data are volume-weighted mean ion concentrations (µmol/liter) in cloud water ($n = 15$), mist ($n = 32$), precipitation where mean $u > 2$ m/s ($N = 54$), and precipitation where mean $u < 2$ m/s ($N = 47$). Ranges are in parentheses; bdl = below detection limits.

relative to other tropical and temperate sites (Table 9.9), suggesting that emissions of NO_x, NH_3, and particles are high downwind from the sites. Because no major urban areas exist, emissions likely originate from forest and agricultural ecosystems. The burning of vegetation typically results in considerable loss of nitrogen and other ions from the site (Ewel et al. 1981, Crutzen and Andreae 1990). Emissions of NO from soils may also be stimulated following burning (Anderson et al. 1988). Other sources of NO include lightning discharges and downward transport of NO_x from the stratosphere (Logan 1983). Regional emission inventories for the tropics are limited and still uncertain (Crutzen and Andreae 1990). Because they are projected to increase in the future, it is important to understand the potential effects of increased nitrogen deposition to tropical cloud forests such as Monteverde.

Nutrient retention by the forest canopy.   Net retention of ions by the canopy is typically estimated by comparing measured or modeled estimates of total deposition to fluxes in throughfall (TF) and stemflow (ST). Canopy-atmosphere interactions are complex, but clear patterns have emerged for individual ions. For example, many canopies retain H+ and inorganic nitrogen from atmospheric deposition, and net retention rates are positively correlated with deposition rates, whereas potassium is leached from most canopies (Parker 1983).

Fewer estimates exist for atmospheric deposition and retention of ions by the canopy in tropical montane forests (Steinhardt and Fassbender 1979, Veneklaas 1990). Their canopies are aerodynamically rough due to high leaf areas and abundant epiphytes, and therefore intercept wind-driven cloud water and precipitation. Because many epiphytes are closely linked to atmospheric sources of nutrients (Nadkarni and Matelson 1991), estimates of atmospheric deposition and net retention of ions by the canopy are necessary to evaluate the potential effects of increased H+ and nitrogen deposition on the canopy and the ecosystem.

Our studies estimated net retention of deposited ions by the canopy at the Monteverde leeward cloud forest site (Clark et al. 1998). Throughfall was collected in 20 plots distributed at random over 1 ha of the primary forest study site adjacent to the meteoro-

Table 9.9. Cloud water chemistry (mean µmol/liter) at montane forest sites in northern South, Central, and North America.

Location	Ion Concentration (µmol/liter)						
	H+	NO_3^-	NH_4^+	Na+	Mg^{2+}	Ca^{2+}	K+
Tropical Sites							
Caracas, Venezuela[a]	23	94	177	64	9	29	9
	9	31	80	62	8	10	5
Pico del Oeste, Puerto Rico[b]	20	60	32	650	85	63	25
	28	64	32	397	44	31	13
Monteverde, Costa Rica[c]	132	103	149	365	63	35	31
Temperate Sites							
Whiteface Mountain, New York[d]	122	62	74	3	3	11	3
	274	115	124	—	—	—	—
Shaver Hollow, Virginia[f]	171	94	93	—	—	—	—
	205	155	84	13	2	5	3
Mt. Moosilauke, New Hampshire[e,g]	263	132	107	—	—	—	—
	270	180	102	32	19	10	11
	288	195	108	30	—	—	10
Mt. Mitchell, North Carolina[e,h]	335	130	175	—	—	—	—
	398	174	184	—	—	—	—

[a]Gordon et al. 1994 (dry season samples collected at Pico del Avila and Altos de Pipe).
[b]Weathers et al. 1988, Ashbury et al. 1994.
[c]This chapter.
[d]Mohnen and Kadkecek, 1989 (5-year mean of summer values).
[e]Mohnen and Vong 1993 (3-year mean of warm clouds).
[f]Sigmon et al. 1989.
[g]Schaefer and Reiners 1990, Lovett et al. 1982.
[h]Aneja et al., 1992.

Table 9.10. Precipitation event data by event category.

Event Category and number of Collections	Mean Length (hr/event)	Mean Intensity (mm/hr)		Total Hours	Total Depth (mm/yr)		
		BCWP	BP		BCWP	BP	TF
Windspeed > 2 m/s (N = 65)	33.2 ± 3.4	1.24 ± 0.18	0.83 ± 0.13	1990	2678	1792	1054 ± 83
Windspeed < 2 m/s (N = 37)	6.6 ± 1.2	2.79 ± 0.58[a]	2.79 ± 0.58	442	1399[a]	1399	1014 ± 63
All events (N = 102)				2432	4077	3191	2068 ± 132

Data are mean event length (mean ± 1 SE), mean bulk cloud water and precipitation (BCWP) or bulk precipitation (BP) intensity, total wet hours, and total depths of BCWP, BP, and throughfall (TF; mean ± 1 SE, n = 20) by event category. (a) = precipitation depth estimated from BP.

logical tower. Ion fluxes in stemflow were assumed to be 10% of those in TF, and these values were added to mean ion fluxes in TF (Ulrich 1983).

Annual BCWP and BP depths were 408 cm and 319 cm, respectively; annual TF depth was 207 cm (Table 9.10). Free acidity and NO_3^- concentrations in TF were less than those in BCWP and BP for all events; NH_4^+ concentrations were intermediate between those in BCWP and BP, and PO_4^- and cation concentrations were greatest in TF. Free acidity and inorganic nitrogen fluxes in TF were 0.004 ± 0.001 kg H^+/ha/yr and 1.9 ± 0.3 kg N/ha/yr (Table 9.11). Based on a calculated mass balance flux of Na, total deposition of the ions were calculated (Clark 1994). Calculated net retention of H^+ and inorganic nitrogen by the canopy represented 92% and 70% of total deposition, respectively. Net leaching of PO_4^- and cations occurred from the canopy (Table 9.12).

Comparison of precipitation with other forests. Volume-weighted mean pH in both BCWP and BP was intermediate compared to values from other tropical sites in Central and South America (Table 9.13). The proportion of wind-driven cloud water and precipitation depth to precipitation depth at Monteverde is within the range reported from other tropical montane forests (Table 9.14). Rates of ion deposition in both BCWP and BP in Monteverde were generally within the range of deposition rates in BP reported from other tropical premontane and montane forest sites (Table 9.15). Concentrations of NH_4^+ in BCWP and BP in Monteverde were at the low end of the range of the concentrations from other sites (Table 9.15). Cation concentrations in BCWP and BP in Monteverde were intermediate; deposition of H^+ was at the low end of estimates. Few estimates exist for the net retention of ions by the canopy in tropical montane forests. The canopy in Monteverde retained a greater proportion of NO_3^- in atmospheric deposition and a greater proportion of the deposited NH_4^+ retained by the canopy compared to others. Greater proportions of PO_4^- and Ca were removed from the canopy in Monteverde.

Concentrations of inorganic nitrogen, calcium, and potassium in precipitation declined rapidly through

Table 9.11. Precipitation ionic activity by event category.

Event Category	Collector	Ion Deposition or Flux (kg/ha/yr)							
		H^+	NO_3^--N	NH_4^+-N	PO_4^{3-}-P	K^+	Ca^{2+}	Mg^{2+}	Na^+
Windspeed >2 m/s (N = 65)	BCWP	0.37	3.1	3.2	0.05	4.5	7.2	6.0	45.6
	BP	0.16	1.1	1.1	0.03	2.0	3.9	2.0	17.9
	TF	0.02	0.2	0.7	0.25	38.4	15.0	4.8	27.9
		(0.01)	(0.1)	(0.1)	(0.05)	(4.5)	(1.3)	(0.5)	(3.5)
Windspeed < 2 m/s (N = 37)	BP	0.16	0.6	0.6	0.02	1.0	1.9	0.4	2.6
	TF	0.02	0.4	0.6	0.23	25.2	8.7	2.9	13.4
		(0.01)	(0.1)	(0.1)	(0.06)	(4.7)	(1.2)	(0.5)	(1.7)
All events (N = 102)	BCWP	0.53	3.7	3.8	0.07	5.5	9.1	6.4	48.2
	BP	0.32	1.7	1.7	0.05	3.0	5.8	2.4	20.5
	TF	0.04	0.6	1.3	0.48	63.6	23.7	7.8	41.3
		(0.01)	(0.2)	(0.2)	(0.10)	(8.8)	(2.3)	(1.0)	(5.1)

Data are ion deposition (kg/ha/yr) in bulk cloud water and precipitation (BCWP) and bulk precipitation (BP), and ion fluxes in throughfall (TF). Standard errors for ion fluxes in TF are shown in parentheses (N = 20).

Table 9.12. Ion deposition in bulk precipitation (BP).

Ion	Deposition (kg/ha/yr) BP	CW	BP + CW	TF + ST (kg/ha/yr)	Percentage Net Retention
H^+	0.32	0.17	0.49	0.04	92 ± 2
NO_3^--N	1.7	1.7	3.4	0.6	82 ± 6
NH_4^+-N	1.7	1.7	3.4	1.4	61 ± 6
PO_4^{3-}-P	0.05	0.02	0.07	0.50	-614 ± 149
K^+	3.0	2.2	5.2	66.8	-1185 ± 69
Ca^{2+}	5.8	2.4	8.7	26.1	-200 ± 26
Mg^{2+}	2.4	3.2	5.6	8.6	-54 ± 18
Na^+	20.9	22.9	43.8	43.8	0 ± 12

Data were estimated ion deposition in cloud water and mist (CW) using Na^+ mass balance to calculate ion deposition to the canopy, the sum of BP and CW, ion fluxes in throughfall and stemflow (TF + ST), and percentage net retention of ions by the canopy (mean ± 1 SE).

Table 9.13. Volume weighted mean pH and ion concentrations in bulk precipitation (BP) at tropical premontane and tropical montane forest sites in Central and northern South America.

Location	Ion Concentration (mg/liter) pH	NO_3^--N	NH_4^+-N	PO_4^{3-}-P	K^+	Ca^{2+}	Mg^{2+}	Na^+
Santa Rosa de Cabal, Colombia[a]	4.40	n.d.	0.86	0.034	0.38	0.48	0.15	1.14
	4.39	n.d.	0.77	0.033	0.48	0.51	0.17	1.10
San Eusebio, Venezuela[b]	4.55	n.d.	n.d.	n.d.	0.17	0.36	0.33	0.21
Monteverde, Costa Rica[c]	4.88	0.09	0.09	0.002	0.14	0.22	0.16	1.23
	5.00	0.05	0.05	0.002	0.09	0.18	0.07	0.63
El Verde, Puerto Rico[d]	5.14	0.04	0.02	0.001	0.09	0.34	0.22	1.63
Turrialba, Costa Rica[e]	5.34	0.02	0.05	0.004	0.11	0.06	0.04	0.25

[a]Veneklaas 1990 (sites at 2550 m and 3370 m elevation).
[b]Steinhardt and Fassbender 1979 (2300 m elevation).
[c]This chapter (1480 m elevation, values for BCWP and BP).
[d]McDowell et al. 1990 (400 m elevation, NO_3^--N and NH_4^+-N for wet-only deposition).
[e]Hendry et al. 1984 (650 m elevation).

Table 9.14. Comparison of precepitation at selected tropical montane forest sites.

Location	Precipitation Depth (mm)	Cloud water and Precipitation Depth (mm)	%
Pu'u La'au, Hawaii[a]	257	98	38
Jalapa, Mexico[b]	597	125	21
Altotonga, Mexico[b]	746	166	22
Serranía de Macuira, Colombia[c]	853	796	93
Teziutlan, Mexico[b]	942	159	17
Tortutla, Mexico[b]	1082	339	31
Cordillera Central, Panama[d]	1495	2295	154
Santa Ana, Venezuela[c]	1630	522	32
Monteverde, Costa Rica[e]	3191	886	28
Cordillera Central, Panama[d]	3630	1130	31
Cerro Copey, Venezuela[c]	4461	458	10
Cordillera Central, Panama[d]	5696	448	8

Precipitation depth data were collected with standard rain gauges; additional cloud water and precipitation depth data were collected with ASRC or Nageltype collectors. Cloud water and precipitation data are expressed as percentage of precipitation at selected tropical montane forest sites.

[a]Juvik and Nullet 1995.
[b]Vogelmann 1973.
[c]Cavelier and Goldstein 1989.
[d]Cavelier et al. 1996 (three separate locations).
[e]This chapter.

Table 9.15. Ion deposition in bulk precipitation (BP) at tropical premontane and montane forest sites in Central and northern South America.

Location	Ion Deposition (kg/ha/yr)							
	H+	NO$_3^-$-N	NH$_4^+$-N	PO$_4^{3}$-P	K+	Ca^{2+}	Mg^{2+}	Na+
Siguartepeque, Honduras[a]	n.d.	0.4	n.d.	0.10	3.0	18.3	18.5	4.4
Turrialba, Costa Rica[b]	0.090	0.5	1.2	0.09	2.5	1.4	1.1	5.9
El Verde, Puerto Rico[c]	0.25	2.0	1.5	n.d.	3.3	11.4	7.7	55.4
Pico del Este, Puerto Rico[d]	0.32	5.3	6.9	n.d.	27	47	30	247
Monteverde, Costa Rica[e]	0.49	3.4	3.4	0.06	5.2	8.7	5.6	43.8
	0.32	1.6	1.6	0.04	3.0	5.8	2.4	19.5
San Eusebio Venezuela[f]	0.81	n.d.	n.d.	n.d.	2.6	5.6	5.2	3.3
Santa Rosa de Cabal, Colombia[g]	0.84	n.d.	11.2	0.72	7.9	10.1	3.2	24.1
	0.59	n.d.	18.3	0.48	6.9	7.3	2.5	15.9

n.d. = not determined.
[a]Kellman et al. 1982.
[b]Hendry et al. 1984.
[c]McDowell et al. 1990 (NO$_3^-$-N and NH$_4^+$-N for wet-only deposition).
[d]Asbury et al. 1994.
[e]This chapter (estimates for deposition to the canopy and BP).
[f]Steinhardt and Fassbender 1979.
[g]Veneklaas 1990 (sites at 3370 m and 2550 m elevation).

the three wet seasons monitored, as reported for other tropical sites (Lewis 1981, Kellman et al. 1982). Decreases in ion concentrations are presumably due to the washout of haze layers and reduced agricultural burning as the wet season progresses (Crutzen and Andreae 1990).

Compared to sites in North America (Johnson and Lindberg 1992), Monteverde experienced relatively low H+ and inorganic nitrogen deposition. This pattern can be explained because no major urban areas or point sources of H+, NO$_x$, or NH$_3^+$ exist in the vicinity, and because dry deposition of HNO$_3^-$ and NH$_3^+$ was likely underestimated in Monteverde. Although relatively long dry periods occurred infrequently, they were concentrated toward the end of the dry season, when regional biomass burning activities were greatest. Because NO$_3^-$ and NH$_4^+$ concentrations were highest in cloud water and precipitation during this period (Clark 1994), it follows that atmospheric concentrations of HNO$_3^-$, NH$_3^+$ and other gases and particles containing inorganic nitrogen were also relatively high during the end of the dry season.

Net retention of H+ and inorganic nitrogen by the canopy at Monteverde was within the range reported from the 12 sites in the Integrated Forest Study (IFS; Johnson and Lindberg 1992). Percentage net canopy retention of inorganic nitrogen was greater at Monteverde compared with most IFS sites, but was closer to the values reported from the four sites where canopies had a substantial coverage of nonvascular epiphytes. Net retention of NO$_3^-$ by the canopy was greater than that of NH$_4^+$ at this site (80% vs. 61%), and NO$_3^-$ flux in TF was only 47% of that of NH$_4^+$.

The lower net retention rate of NH$_4^+$ may be partially due to the leaching of NH$_4^+$ mineralized from litter and humus in the canopy (Vance and Nadkarni 1990, Coxson 1991, Clark 1994). Net retention of NO$_3^-$ averaged 57% of inorganic nitrogen deposition for the four canopies in the IFS that had a substantial coverage of epiphytic vegetation (Clark 1994).

Deposition of inorganic nitrogen was low compared to estimates from other sites. The majority of H+ and inorganic nitrogen was retained by the canopy. Results from other work suggest that epiphytic bryophytes and assemblages of epiphytic bryophytes, vascular epiphytes, litter, and humus retained roughly 80% of the inorganic nitrogen retained by the canopy (Clark 1994). These abundant epiphytes may initially retain inorganic nitrogen as a function of nitrogen deposition from the atmosphere, and apparently buffer "pulses" of inorganic nitrogen before they reach the forest floor. Epiphytic bryophytes are only moderately productive, but bryophyte-derived litter decomposes very slowly (Clark 1994). Retained nitrogen is added to the relatively large pools of nitrogen in litter and humus in the canopy, and eventually to the very large pool of nitrogen in soil organic matter (Edwards and Grubb 1977, Bruijnzeel and Proctor 1995).

There is little information on leaching of NO$_3^-$ from tropical montane forests. They may be more resistant to increases in nitrogen deposition than many temperate montane forests, because increased nitrogen inputs may stimulate the production of both epiphytes and their host trees and then get stored in soil organic matter. However, the effects of chronic increase nitrogen deposition are unknown.

Plate 1 *(top left)*. *Pleurothallis crescentilabia*, an epiphytic orchid found in the Monteverde Cloud Forest Preserve. Photograph by Stephen Ingram.

Plate 2 *(top right)*. Clearwing butterfly feeding on a composite flower. Photograph by Dan Perlman.

Plate 3 *(bottom left)*. Golden Toads (*Bufo periglenes*) in amplexus. Photograph by Michael and Patricia Fogden.

Plate 4 *(middle right)*. Cat-eyed Snake eating eggs of a Red-eyed Leaf Frog. Photograph by Michael and Patricia Fogden.

Plate 5 *(bottom right)*. Male Resplendent Quetzal entering nest cavity. Photograph by Michael and Patricia Fogden.

Plate 6. *(top left)* Young Two-toed Sloths. Photograph by Gregory Dimijian.

Plate 7. *(top right)* Lower montane wet forest in the Monteverde Cloud Forest Preserve. Photograph by Nathaniel Wheelwright.

Plate 8. *(bottom)* Life zones of the Monteverde region.

9.2.3. Litterfall Fluxes

The deposition and subsequent decomposition of fine litter represents a major pathway for transferring carbon and most nutrients from vegetation to soils, and is the most frequently measured nutrient flux in forest ecosystems (Bray and Gorham 1964, Brown and Lugo 1982, Proctor 1983, Vitousek 1984, Vitousek and Sanford 1986). Litter dynamics may be especially important in tropical montane forests because litterfall is the major path of flux for limiting nutrients such as nitrogen and phosphorus (Vitousek and Sanford 1986).

Terrestrially rooted vegetation.   We studied litter dynamics for a 36-month period in the leeward cove forest study area to describe the dynamics of fine litter, which includes abscised leaves, small stems, and reproductive parts of trees and understory plants rooted in the forest floor and soil. We measured (1) forest floor standing litter mass, composition, and nutrient content; (2) biomass and nutrients of litter components deposited to the forest floor; (3) biomass and nutrient turnover of litter, assuming a forest in steady state; and (4) calculations of nutrient use efficiency and retranslocation (removal of nutrients from foliage prior to abscission, which conserves nutrients within the plant; Nadkarni and Matelson 1992a).

Forest floor standing litter was sampled at six intervals and sorted into four components: leaves, small stems (<3 cm diameter), bryophytes, and miscellaneous. Litterfall collections were made twice monthly. A random subset of 14 climbable trees in the largest size class in the study plot was chosen for biweekly sampling live foliage of trees. These included species in seven genera (*Ficus, Ocotea, Beilschmedia, Meliosma, Dussia, Pouteria,* and *Matayba*) that are among the six most common families of trees (Moraceae, Lauraceae, Sabiaceae, Fabaceae, Sapotaceae, and Sapindaceae; Lawton and Dryer 1980).

The mean total mass of the forest floor standing litter was 10.1 tons/ha, and varied considerably among seasons (range 0.7–13.0 tons/ha). Standing litter composition differed significantly between sampling dates (Fig. 9.11). There was an effect of year, with greater amounts of litter on the forest floor in 1988–1989, which coincided with the aftermath of high winds in the 1987–1988 misty-windy and dry seasons (Nadkarni and Matelson 1992a). The mean nutrient pool (kg/ha) was N, 159; P, 6.7; Ca, 213; Mg, 17; and K, 16.

The mean biomass of fine litterfall was 7.0 tons/ha[1]/yr. There appeared to be seasonal distribution in litterfall (Fig. 9.12). Time series analysis revealed that there was one primary peak at a low frequency that

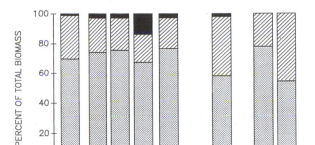

Figure 9.11. Composition of forest floor standing litter as a percentage of total litter biomass between 1988 and 1990 at the leeward cloud forest study area. (From Nadkarni and Matelson 1992b)

closely matched the seasonal trend. Litterfall was greatest in the misty-windy season (18.1 g/m²/wk[1]); lowest in the wet season (9.3 g/m²/wk), and intermediate in the dry season (14.4 g/m²/wk). Mean nutrient concentrations of litterfall (Table 9.17) were generally comparable to those in the forest floor standing litter. The concentration of nitrogen in litterfall was slightly lower than in leaves and stems on the floor, probably due to microbial immobilization in the forest floor litter. The slightly lower concentrations of magnesium in leaves and stems and of potassium in stems and miscellaneous material in the standing litter were probably due to leaching of these materials after they had been deposited on the forest floor. The mean annual nutrient input (kg/ha/yr) for fine litter was N, 93; P, 6; Ca, 115; Mg, 15; and K, 12.

Mean concentrations of live foliage (mg/g) were N, 19.7; P, 1.4; Ca, 8.5; Mg, 2.0; and K, 7.4. The concentration of all elements except magnesium was higher in live leaves (Table 9.18) than in the leaf component of litterfall (Table 9.17). Retranslocation of nitrogen and phosphorus was calculated following Veneklaas (1991), by dividing the difference between elemental concentrations of live foliage and litterfall by the concentration of that element in live foliage. The percentage retranslocation of nitrogen and phosphorus was calculated as 25% and 42%, respectively, which is comparable to other montane forests (Tanner 1980a; Table 9.19).

In Monteverde, the values for the mass and nutrient concentrations in the forest floor standing litter and litterfall are similar to those of tropical montane forests (Table 9.20). As with other tropical forests, there were seasonal differences in the rates of litterfall, with the greatest amounts falling in the windy-misty

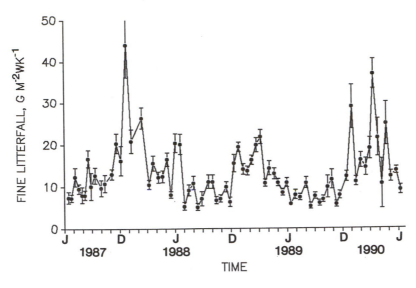

Figure 9.12. Biomass of litterfall (g/m2/wk) of terrestrially rooted material collected from study plots between 1987 and 1990. Error bars represent one standard error of the mean. (From Nadkarni and Matelson 1992b)

Table 9.16. Estimated ion deposition to the canopy (D), ion fluxes in throughfall (TF), and percentage net retention (% NR) of ions by the canopy.

Location	Ion Deposition or Flux (kg/ha/yr)							
	H+	NO₃⁻-N	NH₄⁺-N	PO₄³⁻P	K+	Ca²⁺	Mg²⁺	Na+
San Eusebio, Venezuela[a]								
D	n.d.	n.d.	n.d.	1.96	3.5	7.5	6.9	4.4
TF	n.d.	n.d.	n.d.	1.38	69.7	6.9	3.3	4.4
% NR	—	—	—	30	-1891	8	52	0
Santa Rosa de Cabal, Colombia[b]								
D	n.d.	n.d.	22.8	0.80	8.8	11.3	3.6	26.9
TF	n.d.	n.d.	21.5	1.67	95.2	27.1	10.7	26.9
% NR	—	—	6	-109	-982	-140	-197	0
Santa Rosa de Cabal, Colombia[b]								
D	n.d.	n.d.	11.2	0.48	6.9	7.3	2.5	15.9
TF	n.d.	n.d.	11.6	0.40	33.0	18.8	7.0	14.4
% NR	—	—	-3	17	-378	-158	-180	9
Monteverde, Costa Rica[c]								
D	0.49	3.4	3.4	0.06	5.2	8.7	5.6	43.8
TF	0.04	0.6	1.4	0.50	66.8	26.1	8.6	43.8
% NR	92	82	61	-614	-1185	-200	-54	0

n.d. = not determined.

[a]Steinhardt and Fassbender 1979.

[b]Veneklaas 1990 (sites at 2550 m and 3370 m elevation).

[c]This chapter.

Table 9.17. Mean nutrient concentration (mg/g) (± SEM) of components of litterfall from the leeward cloud forest study area, Monteverde (Nadkarni and Matelson 1992a).

Component	Nutrient				
	N	P	Ca	Mg	K
Leaves	14.7	0.8	19.1	2.7	1.2
	(0.5)	(0.02)	(0.5)	(0.1)	(0.2)
Stems	10.9	0.6	16.8	1.7	2.2
	(0.5)	(0.04)	(0.6)	(0.1)	(0.4)
Reproductive	12.5	1.1	12.3	1.8	3.8
	(0.5)	(0.1)	(0.6)	(0.1)	(0.3)
Miscellaneous	19.3	1.2	14.4	1.7	2.8
	(0.5)	(0.04)	(0.3)	(0.1)	(0.2)

Table 9.18. Mean nutrient concentrations (mg/g ± SEM) of live foliage collected from trees between 24 April 1988 and 14 January 1989, pooled for all species and sampling intervals.

Nutrient	Season			
	Misty	Dry	Wet	p
N	18.4 (1.2)	26.7 (3.4)	21.9 (2.7)	.007
P	1.4 (0.2)	2.3 (0.5)	1.3 (0.7)	.002
Ca	11.9 (2.3)	5.7 (1.3)	7.8 (0.6)	.024
Mg	2.4 (0.3)	2.0 (0.1)	1.9 (0.1)	.265
K	2.3 (0.5)	11.7 (1.1)	8.5 (0.8)	.001

Values represent means from 14 trees in six plant families. N = 44 sampling intervals overall, with three to six replicates per tree; p values indicate the results of a one-way ANOVA testing the effects of season on nutrient concentration. See Section 9.1.3 for mean annual values.

Table 9.19. Elemental concentration, nitrogen to phosphorus ratios, and nitrogen and phosphorus retranslocation of live foliage and leaf litter in tropical montane forests (Nadkarni and Matelson 1992a).

Site	Elements (%) N	Elements (%) P	N:P Ratio	Retranslocation[a] N (%)	Retranslocation[a] P (%)
Venezuela[b]					
Live foliage	1.74	0.08	22		
Leaf litter	1.2	0.06	20	31	25
Papua New Guinea[c]					
Live foliage	1.32	0.09	15		
Leaf litter	1.3	0.07	19	2	22
Colombia[d]					
Live foliage	1.8	0.1	18		
Leaf litter	1.1	0.06	18	38	40
Costa Rica[e]					
Live foliage	1.97	0.14			
Leaf litter	1.47	0.08	18	25	42

[a]Calculated as % retranslocation = (element concentration in live foliage - litterfall)/ (concentration in live foliage).
[b]Fassbender and Grimm 1981.
[c]Grubb and Edwards 1982.
[d]Veneklaas 1991.
[e]This chapter.

season. The relationship of litterfall to weather patterns, which has been documented for other montane forests (Tanner 1980a), awaits quantified measurements of weather, especially windspeed and mist. The amounts of nitrogen, phosphorus, calcium, and potassium transferred in litter to the forest floor at Monteverde are high compared to those reported from other tropical montane forests (Table 9.20). In Monteverde, the large quantity of nutrient return in litterfall (despite moderate retranslocation rates) is due to comparatively high concentrations of nutrients (except Mg) in live tree foliage (Grubb and Edwards 1982, Tanner 1985). The foliar nutrient levels we measured in Monteverde (Table 9.17) fall more closely within the range reported for forests growing on alfisols and other moderately fertile tropical soils (Vitousek and Sanford 1986).

Table 9.20. Forest litter data from various tropical locations.

	Litter Fall (tons/ha/yr)	Nutrient Transfer (kg/ha/yr) N	P	Ca	Mg	K	Forest Floor Standing Crop (tons/ha)	Annual Decay Constant (K_a)[a]	Biomas Element Ratio N	P	Source
Costa Rica	7.0	93	6	115	15	12	10.1	0.69	75	1270	This chapter
Venezuela	7.0	69	4	43	*	*	*	*	101	1750	Fassbender and Grimm 1981
Jamaica											Tanner 1977
Mor ridge	6.6	39	1.3	34	*	*	*	*	169	5076	
Mull ridge	5.5	94	1.5	50	*	*	*	*	112	3666	
Wet slope	5.5	34	2.1	53	*	*	*	*	162	2620	
Puerto Rico	*	*	*	*	*	*	5.1	0.94	*	*	Wiegert and Murphey 1970
Colombia	11.6	*	*	*	*	*	16.5	0.61	*	*	Jenny et al. 1949
New Guinea	7.6	90	5	95	*	*	6.4	1.17	84	1520	Edwards 1982

Data are fine litter production, nutrient transfer in litter, forest floor standing litter mass, annual decay constant (K_a), and biomass:element ratio of fine litter in tropical montane forests, based on steady state assumptions. * = not reported.

[a]K_a = annual litterfall/forest floor standing crop (Olson 1963).

Why might trees in this forest support foliage with high nutrient concentrations? One reason is that large amounts of nutrients come into the system via interception of precipitation, especially wind-blown mist, which may be facilitated by the interceptive capacity of the abundant epiphytes (Nadkarni 1986b). Other montane and lowland forests may not receive as much direct atmospheric input in this form (Vitousek and Sanford 1986). Second, the soils on which the forest grows may be relatively fertile, in at least some macronutrients, as they are of recent volcanic origin (see Chap. 2, Physical Environment). Mineralization rates of nitrogen and phosphorus in the field on the forest floor are also fairly high (Vance and Nadkarni 1990).

Nitrogen and phosphorus availability in our study area, as indicated by high foliar concentrations and only moderate retranslocation, appears comparable or even higher than in other tropical montane forests. Nutrient use efficiency (calculated as biomass/nutrient return) is low relative to other tropical forest and other montane forests (Table 9.20). The Monteverde forest may be less limited by nutrients than in other cloud forests. Cloud forests as a vegetation type are diverse with respect to their nutrient cycling regimes.

Epiphytic litter.   In many tropical moist forests, live epiphytes and their associated dead organic matter on branches and trunks constitute up to 45% of the foliar mineral capital (Pócs 1980, Nadkarni 1983). Nutrients from live and dead ephiphytic organic matter (EM) are released into the nutrient cycles of terrestrially rooted vegetation by three pathways: (1) epiphyte mats on host tree branches and trunks are permeated by host tree canopy roots (Nadkarni 1981), (2) epiphyte mats are leached by precipitation and the nutrients are transferred to the forest floor via stemflow and throughfall, and (c) EM falls to the forest floor and decomposes. Processes that cause EM to fall to the forest floor include senescence, wind, disruption by birds and mammals, and the falling of supporting branches and whole trees. The contribution of the epiphyte community to nutrient transfer in tropical forests is poorly understood. The few reports in which epiphyte litterfall has been reported in tropical forests have been anecdotal or based on small collectors designed to trap tree fine litter (Tanner 1980a, Songwe et al. 1988), rendering estimates of the total input of nutrients to the forest floor inaccurate in forests where epiphytes are a substantial canopy component.

We quantified the dynamics of fallen EM in our study area, specifically (1) EM standing crop biomass, composition, and nutrient pools on the forest floor; (2) input of EM biomass, composition, and nutrients to the forest floor; (3) rates of EM biomass and nutrient turnover (Nadkarni and Matelson 1992b); we

also made preliminary estimates of short-term decomposition. Samples of fallen EM were separated to vascular plants, bryophytes, and dead organic matter. To collect the large discrete pieces of EM litterfall that would not fit into standard litterfall traps, we collected newly fallen EM from twenty 5 x 5 m cleared plots twice per month. To measure EM that fell in the form of smaller pieces, we used the tree fine litterfall collectors on the forest floor (Nadkarni and Matelson 1992b).

In 1988, the mean biomass of EM standing crop was 50 g/m^2; in 1990, the mean was 27 g/m^2. There was a great deal of spatial variation in the amount of standing crop (range 330–8190 kg/ha). Composition of standing crop was dominated by dead organic matter (58%), followed by bryophytes (22%), and vascular plants (20%). The nutrient pool of standing crop on the forest floor (Table 9.21) was calculated by multiplying the biomass of each component by the nutrient concentration of that component.

The biomass of EM input from plots during the study period was 350 kg/ha/yr. Input was highly variable spatially, with biomass from individual plots ranging between 0 and 232 g/m^2 per collection period. Standard deviations for a given collection interval were between 6% and 360% of the mean. EM input measured with the fine litter collectors was 140 kg/ha/yr, which is equivalent to 2% of the total terrestrially rooted fine litter (Nadkarni and Matelson 1992a). This bryophyte component was added to plot collection input, for a mean total annual EM input of 0.5 tons/ha.

Input of EM was temporally sporadic; greater amounts fell in 1988–1989 than in 1989–1990 (Fig. 9.13). The highest values of EM litterfall occurred during 1988 windstorms, which were the most severe recorded in the past 15 years (J. Campbell, pers. comm.). Of 1234 collections of individual plots, 99% contained bryophytes, 62% contained vascular plants, and 56% contained dead organic matter. Composition of EM input to the forest floor on a dry weight basis was bryophytes, 76%; dead organic matter, 13%; and vascular plants, 11%. Individual collections of extremely large samples were infrequent; only 26 (2%) of all collections exceeded 10 g/m^2 per collection. These sporadic pulses of large EM comprised 53% of the total EM input. A continual but unpredictable input of small amounts of material fell throughout the year (Fig. 9.13). Nutrient input via EM litter (Table 9.21) was calculated by multiplying the nutrient concentration (Table 9.22) for each component at each collection period by the mean biomass of that component for that collection period.

In our study site, the biomass of EM litterfall (0.5 tons/ha/yr) is equivalent to 5–10% of the total fine

Table 9.21. Summary of biomass and nutrient pools and transfers in fine litter during the study period.

	Biomass	N	P	Ca	Mg	K
			Nutrient			
Standing crop						
EM	0.4	46	3	29	5	15
TM	10.1	159	7	213	17	16
Total standing crop	10.5	205	9	242	22	31
% EM of total standing crop	4	22	33	12	23	48
Litterfall						
EM	0.5	7.5	0.5	4.2	0.8	0.1
TM	7.0	93	6	115	15	12
Total litterfall	7.5	100.5	6.5	119.2	15.8	12.1
% EM of total litterfall	7	7	8	4	5	1
Annual decay constant and turnover time						
Annual decay constant (yr^{-1})						
EM K_a	1.3	0.16	0.17	0.14	0.16	10
TM K_a	0.7	0.6	0.9	0.5	0.9	0.8
Turnover time (yr)						
EM	0.8	6.3	5.9	7.1	6.3	0.1
TM	1.4	1.7	1.1	2.0	1.1	1.3

Data are biomass (tons/ha) and nutrient pools (kg/ha/yr) in standing crop of epiphytic matter (EM) and terrestrial rooted material (TM); biomass (tons/ha) and nutrient transfer (kg/ha/yr) via litterfall in EM and TM; and calculated annual decay constants (yr^{-1}) and turnover time (yr) based on a steady state assumption (K_a = annual litter input/forest floor standing crop, turnover time = $1/K_a$). TM measurements were made at the same study area at the same time and are reported in Nadkarni and Matelson (1992a).

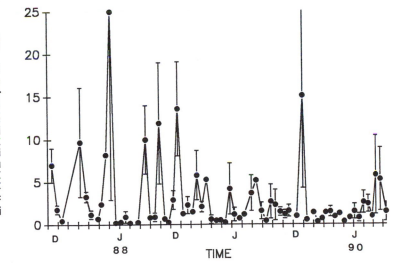

Figure 9.13. Epiphyte litter (g/m^2/month) collected from 5×5 m plots and fine litter collectors between December 1987 and September 1990. Error bars represent one standard error of the mean. (From Nadkarni and Matelson 1992a)

Table 9.22. Mean nutrient concentration (mg/g ± SEM) of standing crop and litterfall of epiphytic components for 29 collection intervals between 16 May 1988 and 10 January 1989.

	Nutrient				
Component	N	P	Ca	Mg	K
Standing crop, Total	18.4	1.3	11.9	1.9	6.0
	(0.7)	(0.003)	(1.2)	(0.1)	(0.4)
Litterfall					
Vascular plants	10.7	0.8	58.6	2.5	0.7
	(0.7)	(0.5)	(0.9)	(0.3)	(0.1)
Bryophytes	15.8	1.1	8.4	1.7	0.3
	(0.8)	(0.04)	(0.5)	(0.06)	(0.02)
Dead organic matter	15.5	0.7	10.8	1.2	0.2
	(1.3)	(0.02)	(1.3)	(0.1)	(0.03)

litter biomass (7.5 tons/ha/yr; Nadkarni and Matelson 1992b). The nutrient transfer via EM litterfall is up to 8% of the annual nutrient transfer in total fine litterfall (Table 9.21). If we assume that this primary forest is in a steady state, then over an annual cycle, litter decomposition equals litter deposition (Olson 1963). The annual decay rate (K_a) of this material is the annual litter input divided by the forest floor pool, and was calculated as 1.3 for EM biomass (Table 9.21). The fractional turnover time ($1/K_a$) for EM biomass would be 0.8, or approximately 10 months. We found a more rapid decay rate and shorter turnover time for EM than measured for terrestrially rooted material at the same time and place ($K_a = 0.7$, $1/K_a = 1.4$; Nadkarni and Matelson 1991). However, we found a much slower decay rate for nutrients in EM litter (except potassium) than for nutrients in terrestrially rooted fine litter. Turnover time for all nutrients except potassium were four to six times longer for EM than terrestrially rooted material. The turnover time for potassium was 10-fold faster in EM than terrestrially rooted material (Table 9.21).

These results indicate that at least a portion of EM is recalcitrant and highly resistant to decomposition and mineralization. However, certain components of EM decompose very rapidly. Input of bryophytes was 76% of fallen EM, but only 22% of the EM standing crop, which suggests that this component decomposes quickly. The calculated decay rate for bryophytes is 4.3, with a turnover time of only 0.23 yr. Conversely, dead organic matter appears to have a much slower decay rate, comprising only 13% of input, but 58% of the EM standing crop; K_a for this material is 0.28, and the turnover time is 3.6 yr. Vascular plants are intermediate; K_a is 0.68 and turnover time is 1.5 yr. Further studies of particular components are needed to determine the timing of nutrient mineralization and release from this material.

The deposition of EM is patchy; over half of the EM fell in less than 2% of the collections. One implication

for plants rooted in the forest floor is that nutrient deposition from EM concentrates input in unpredictable locations. This contrasts to TM litter, which is distributed fairly evenly across the forest floor. Second, nutrients deposited in EM that ride down treefalls and large branch falls co-occur with higher levels of light associated with resulting gaps. This pulse of nutrients released from EM may alter nutrient availability in the immediate vicinity of regenerating gap species. Another factor is that there may be delays in the death of epiphytes and subsequent release of their nutrients after they fall to the forest floor (see Matelson et al., "Longevity of Fallen Epiphytes," pp. 344–345).

Fallen EM has been either overlooked or inaccurately measured in nearly all nutrient cycling studies. In a tropical evergreen lowland forest in Cameroon, Songwe et al. (1988) found 105 kg/ha/yr from epiphytic mosses and ferns (0.8% of total fine litter). In a Jamaican montane forest, Tanner (1980a) reported 4–180 kg/m²/yr (0–3% of total fine litter) as EM (mainly bromeliads). In a lower montane rain forest, Veneklaas (1991) documented 220 kg/ha/yr of fallen vascular and nonvascular EM (3% of total fine litter) using 0.5 x 0.5 m wire frames. If we had collected only the epiphytic material identified in our TM litterfall collectors, we would have underestimated EM by 72%, as only 14 g/m²/yr in the bryophyte category fell into our collectors. It is thus critical to use collecting areas of the appropriate sizes for fallen EM.

9.2.4. Decomposition Fluxes

Terrestrially rooted material.   The slower rate of litter decomposition in tropical montane forests, compared to tropical lowland forests, has been attributed to the high frequency of misty conditions, low air and soil temperatures, lack of drying-rewetting cycles, a high degree of sclerophylly, and waterlogged soils (Leigh 1975, Tanner 1981, Vitousek 1984). Nutrients and carbon in montane forests may be bound in organic forms for long periods of time (Edwards and Grubb 1977, Tanner 1985) before they are released by invertebrate, fungal, and microbial decomposers.

Only preliminary work on leaf decomposition in Monteverde has been published (Nadkarni and Matelson 1991). One study involved the incubation of fallen litter in tethered litterbags in the canopy of the leeward forest site to quantify the amount of input of intercepted host tree litterfall into epiphyte communities. Litterbags ($N = 140$) were tethered to randomized locations on the upper surface of large interior branches of four trees; subsets were retrieved at trimonthly intervals for 15 months. A linear regression was performed using the natural logarithm of the mean dry mass remaining over time to calculate k, the fractional loss rate for the entire 15-month study period, following the formula

$$\ln (X_t/X_o) = -kt$$

where X_t and X_o are the mass remaining at time t and time 0, respectively (Olson 1963).

Biomass loss from the beginning to the end of the study was approximately 69% of the original biomass. The k_d value was 0.36, with 64% of the variance explained by an exponential model. The regression of percentage biomass loss with time was significant (linear regression, p < .03). Calculated leaf litter turnover is 2.8 yr, which is considerably slower than decomposition rates in other tropical montane forests (Wiegert and Murphy 1970, Edwards 1977). Further work is needed to quantify long-term litter decomposition rates of other abscised materials (stems, reproductive parts, branches, whole trunks) and the processes that regulate the immobilization and release of energy and nutrients from dead organic matter in this forest.

A second study monitored short-term rates of EM decomposition. We carried out a six-month field study to measure changes of biomass and nutrient concentration from EM (N. Nadkarni and T. Matelson, unpubl. data). In April 1988, we collected epiphyte mats from the upper canopy (17–22 m) of three *Ficus tuerckheimii* (Moraceae) trees in the study area. These were cut into small pieces (10 x 10 x 3 cm) of humus/dead organic matter (65%), vascular plant roots (15%), vascular plant shoots (5%), and bryophytes (15%). Each of a further 20 replicates was placed on top of the leaf litter layer at random locations on the forest floor, 10 in recent treefall gaps, and 10 randomly located in the forest interior. All samples were tethered to the ground and collected after six months.

Decomposition of individual pieces of EM was visually apparent during the study period. Tethered epiphyte mats on the ground had a significantly lower biomass at the end of the six-month field incubation

than their original biomass (mean percentage loss = 16.4). Nutrient concentration and total amount of nutrients for all macronutrients except potassium were significantly higher, and potassium was significantly lower, than the original concentration and amounts at the end of the incubation, suggesting that epiphyte mats are net immobilizers of all of the measured macronutrients except potassium in the short term (N. Nadkarni and T. Matelson, unpubl. data). Extrapolation of net immobilization and flux by fallen EM to longer-term time scales is an important measurement to make in the future.

9.3. Future Research Directions

Assembling the jigsaw puzzle of the ecology of Monteverde ecosystems has only just begun. Existing data are fragmentary and undoubtedly specific to the sites where research was carried out. Nonetheless, some of the primary precursors for understanding the Monteverde landscape at the ecosystem level are in place. Several protected permanent study plots have been established where trees have been identified and mapped; baseline data on some of the fundamental descriptors of forest structure, composition, biomass, and nutrient capital have been described; and we have the capacity to carry out basic laboratory studies. A small cadre of trained local field assistants exists. We lack sophisticated laboratory equipment and highly trained technical assistance of field stations such as at La Selva or BCI. Knowledge of basic abiotic factors that influence the biota (e.g., soil physical properties, hydrological attributes such as canopy interception, groundwater fluxes, micrometeorological conditions) is incomplete, and an interdisciplinary group of scientists with whom to collaborate on the complex ecosystem-level interactions that occur in Monteverde needs to be assembled.

Acknowledgments We thank Rodrigo Solano for his help with field and managerial aspects of this project. We also thank Eric Vance, Frank Setaro, William Haber, Eric Bello, John Campbell, Jim Crisp, John T. Longino, the Monteverde community, Doug Schaefer, and Steve and Karen Ingram. Support was provided from research grants and Research Experience for Undergraduate Grant Supplements from the National Science Foundation (BSR 87–14935, BSR 90–18006, BIR 93–07771, and BSR 96–15341), the Whitehall Foundation, the National Geographic Society Committee on Research and Exploration, the University of California Santa Barbara Academic Senate, The Marie Selby Botanical Gardens, and The Evergreen State College.

MICROBIAL BIOMASS AND ACTIVITY IN CANOPY ORGANIC MATTER AND THE FOREST FLOOR
Eric Vance & Nalini M. Nadkarni

The environment of tropical cloud forests results in large accumulations of organic matter and nutrients on the forest floor relative to most lowland tropical forests due to slower rates of decomposition (Grubb 1977). Although soils under montane forests may have a high nutrient capital, the availability of nutrients, especially nitrogen, is often low and limiting to forest productivity (Vitousek and Sanford 1986). Another characteristic of these cloud forests is their high biomass of epiphytes (Nadkarni 1984). As epiphytes die and decompose, they form mats of organic matter on tree branches that are permeated by epiphyte and host tree roots (Jenik 1973, Nadkarni 1981). This organic matter may be an important component of the nutrient cycling characteristics of this forest by trapping and transforming nutrients that are deposited in rain, mist, and intercepted litter. To understand the significance of epiphytic organic matter (EM), we determined whether EM is microbially active, and what role microorganisms might play in conserving and transforming nitrogen and carbon. Our study took place in the leeward cloud forest of the MCFP.

Our study revealed that EM has high microbial activity and that levels of biomass carbon and nitrogen were similar to those on the forest floor H (FF-H) and A_1 (FF-A) horizons (Table 9.23). Carbon dioxide evolution in the laboratory (an indicator of overall microbial activity) and laboratory nitrogen mineralization were also higher or similar for EM relative to the forest floor. In contrast to the H and A_1 horizons of the forest floor, however, nitrification was not detectable or was only very low in EM during laboratory and field incubations. The potential for denitrification was higher in the forest floor than in the canopy (Vance and Nadkarni 1990). Because of their high biomass and acivity, microorganisms in the canopy should be considered when studying the regulation of nitrogen availability in this forest type.

Table 9.23. Microbial biomass composition at various forest levels.

| Sample | Biomass | |
	Carbon	Nitrogen
EM	2650[a] ± 330	340[a] ± 70
FF-H	2670[a] ± 170	320[a] ± 20
FF-A	1950[a] ± 30	220[a] ± 20

Data are microbial biomass concentrations (µg/g soil mean ± SD) in epiphytic organic matter (EM), forest floor soil, H horizon (FF-H), and forest floor A_1 horizon (FF-A). Values designated by different letters are significantly different at the $P = .05$ level (Vance and Nadkarni 1990).

INVERTEBRATES IN CANOPY AND GROUND ORGANIC MATTER
Nalini M. Nadkarni & John T. Longino

An important functional aspect of dead organic matter in forest ecosystems is the composition and abundance of the detritivore fauna. These invertebrates participate in the regulation of nutrient transfer and contain a pool of nutrients and energy. They are the main agents of litter fragmentation and mixing of leaf litter with mineral soil, exposing a greater surface area for microbial colonization (Seastedt 1984). In many tropical cloud forests, considerable amounts of intercepted litter and crown humus accumulate on branches and trunks of mature trees (Nadkarni 1984). We compared the composition and abundance of invertebrates that inhabit canopy and forest floor litter and humus in a leeward cloud forest in Monteverde (Nadkarni and Longino 1990).

Field research was conducted in and around the MCFP. Trees from which samples were taken included those in the largest size class of the most common tree species (*Clusia alata, Didimopanax pittieri, Quercus* sp., *Pouteria viride,* and *Ficus* sp.). We climbed with single-rope techniques (Perry 1978), which provided access to the inner crowns of the middle canopy. Litter invertebrates were sampled by sifting bulk litter and humus through a mesh sieve. Approximately 17 liters of this bulk dead organic matter produced one liter of sifted litter; each sample consisted of 2–8 liters of sifted litter. For each canopy sample, a paired ground sample was obtained. Invertebrates from sifted litter were extracted using a Winkler extractor (Ward 1987). Data were tabulated in terms of number of individuals per liter of sifted litter. For each category, ground versus canopy differences in density were tested with a paired t test ($P < .05$).

The numerically dominant taxa in both canopy and ground samples were mites, beetles, holometabolous insect larvae, ants, Collembola, and Crustacea (amphipods and isopods). Members of these taxa are the major agents of fragmentation of organic matter (Leakey and Proctor 1987). Relative proportions of these major taxa were the same in the canopy and ground samples, showing that the canopy shares a fundamentally similar invertebrate community (Fig. 9.14). Total invertebrate abundance was higher on the ground than in the canopy for all sample pairs, with a mean density 2.6 times greater on the forest floor than in the canopy. Canopy organic matter was clearly depauperate in beetles and larvae. Ants were the only exception to this pattern. Our results differ from another study at a similar site in Costa Rica (Atkin and Proctor 1988) in that we found very few oligochaetes (earthworms). The difference may be due to sampling techniques; the hand-sorting methods of the latter study underestimated meso- and microarthropods, and our sifting techniques underestimated soft-bodied annelids.

What factors might explain the lower invertebrate densities in the canopy? Differences in microclimate could affect their composition and abundance. Tree crowns are subject to greater amounts of insolation and wind and more severe "dry-downs" than the forest floor (Bohlman et al. 1995). Invertebrates are sensitive to microclimate regimes, particularly moisture and temperature. Difficulties of dispersal to the canopy and/or within crowns of trees may exist for particular invertebrate groups, especially many of the sedentary groups and those living in nest structures (Moran and Southwood 1982). Elucidation of which factors depress invertebrate density in the canopy, and which canopy organic matter characteristics may be caused by depressed invertebrate density await further investigation. We showed that canopy-held organic matter, an ecosystem component of lower montane forests, differs from forest floor organic matter. This implies that organic matter in the canopy should be treated as a separate component in ecosystem studies and cannot be subsumed under studies of organic matter on the forest floor.

Acknowledgments We thank the MCFP and the Monteverde community. John Campbell and William Calvert provided access to study sites. Work was supported by a Faculty Career Development Grant from the University of California, Santa Barbara, grants from the National Geographic Society Committee on Research and Exploration, the Whitehall Foundation, and the National Science Foundation (BSR 86-14935).

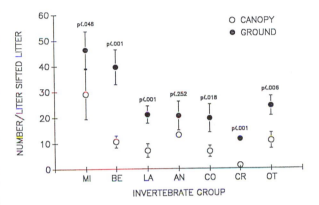

Figure 9.14. Invertebrate density (number of individuals/liter of sifted litter) by invertebrate group for ground and canopy samples. MI = mites, BE = adult beetles, LA = holometabolous insect larvae, AN = adult ants, CO = collembola, CR = amphipods and isopods, OT = other (Hemiptera, Homoptera, Orthoptera, Dictyoptera, Dermaptera, adult Diptera, Thysanoptera, parasitic Hymenoptera, Apterygota, Symphyla, millipedes, centipedes, spiders, other Arachnida, Gastropoda, Annelida). Significance values above categories are results of paired sample t tests. Error bars represent two standard errors of the means. (From Nadkarni and Longino 1990)

VESICULAR-ARBUSCULAR MYCORRHIZAE OF EPIPHYTIC AND TERRESTRIAL PIPERACEAE

Blase Maffia, Nalini M. Nadkarni, & David P. Janos

In order to survive the oligotrophic (nutrient-poor) conditions in forest canopies (Benzing 1981, 1990), epiphytes have developed morphological and physiological adaptations for garnering and retaining nutrients. Epiphytes derive nearly all of their nutrients from atmospheric sources (Nadkarni and Matelson 1991), which are generally dilute, especially in phosphorus (Vitousek and Sanford 1986). Vesicular-arbuscular mycorrhizal fungi (VAM) are one means by which epiphytes might increase nutrient uptake. The ability of VAM to reach the canopy is uncertain, however, because the large spores of these fungi are not normally dispersed by wind (Janos 1993). Several studies have documented VAM in the Piperaceae (St. John 1980, Garcia Yazquez-Yanes 1985, Bermudes and Benzing 1987, Mohankumar and Mahadevan 1987), a common tropical plant family with epiphytic and terrestrial species. However, nine species of this family collected in montane forests of Costa Rica did notons/have VAM (Lesica and Antibus 1990).

We surveyed the occurrence of VAM among 27 species of Piperaceae in the field in Monteverde (Maffia et al. 1993). We focused on this family because it is species-rich (Burger 1971) and includes many epiphytes. Some of these are facultative (found in both terrestrial and arboreal habitats), which allows for comparison of VAM between the canopy and the ground. Preliminary work documented low levels of VAM of terrestrial *Pothomorphe umbellatum* L. (Piperaceae) and revealed VAM structures (e.g., internal and external hyphae, vesicles, and spores) in root sections collected from random locations in canopy root mats (Maffia 1990).

We collected roots of epiphytic and terrestrial Piperaceae in and adjacent to the leeward cloud forest study site and secondary vegetation (pasture trees, secondary forest, and along roadside), including 17 species of *Peperomia*, 8 species of *Piper*, and 1 species each of *Pothomorphe* and *Sarcorachis* (Maffia et al. 1993). Epiphytic samples were taken from bare branches, tree trunks, and interwoven "mats" of live roots and humus on horizontal branches. We separated apparently living roots following St. John and Uhl (1983), preserving them in formalin-propanol-acetic acid within 3 hr of collection, and cleared and stained samples following Phillips and Hayman (1970). The amount of mycorrhizal colonization was determined by recording the presence or absence of VAM in 1–cm sections of root. We also noted extra-matrical spores and auxiliary cells associated with root segments.

Of the 27 species examined, two terrestrial *Peperomia* species, two terrestrial *Piper* species, and *Pothomorphe umbellatum* contained internal vesicles and/or arbuscules. Overall, colonization was extremely low, with only 21 cm of 4867 cm of fine roots examined having internal colonization (<1%). The terrestrial *Po. umbellatum* accounted for half of all internal colonization. In contrast, we found moderate amounts of typical coarse VAM external hyphae associated with both epiphytic and terrestrial root segments, which included 15% of all epiphytic and 13% of all terrestrial Piperaceae root segments. *Glomus* and *Acaulospora* spores and *Gigaspora* auxiliary cells occurred in both terrestrial and epiphytic habitats, although fewer than 1% of root segments had associated spores (Maffia et al. 1993).

The low colonization of roots of Piperaceae suggests no consistent pattern of usage of VAM by terrestrial or epiphytic plants. A greenhouse study carried out on *Peperomia costaricensis* produced significantly higher amounts of internal colonization (up to 28%) with native and commercial inoculum when the plants were raised on an infertile substrate (Maffia 1990, Maffia et al. 1993). Two non-exclusive hypotheses may explain the paucity of VAM on Piperaceae in the field. First, low colonization levels could be a consequence of relatively high site fertility. High atmospheric inputs of dissolved inorganic nutrients, characteristic of tropical cloud forests (Kellman et al. 1982, Clark 1994), may make VAM unnecessary to meet nutrient requirements. Second, VAM formation in the canopy might be limited by a lack of inoculum (Benzing 1983, Lesica and Antibus 1990).

We hypothesize that the canopy comprises a "habitat mosaic" (Janos 1993). Developing canopy mats accruing vegetation might progressively accumulate VAM inocula dispersed by any of several potential vectors (e.g., birds, ants, small mammals). The greatest inoculum potentials in the canopy should occur in old-growth forest with low tree and branch turnover. Chance deposition of large numbers of VAM propagules, however, would cause a "young" canopy mat to have a high inoculum potential, but we predict that this occurs less often than gradual accretion of inoculum.

Although spatially patchy, canopy mats with abundant VAM might serve as inoculum sources through one-way, downward transfer by stemflow and through-fall. Spores or hyphae might be dislodged during rain events and swept down branches and trunks in stem-flow, inoculating mats or epiphytes below. The trapping of even one spore (Daft and Nicolson 1969) on the moist underside of a root might be sufficient to form mycorrhizae and to begin the inoculum accretion process. That some epiphytes have moderate to high numbers of VAM suggests that the inoculum potential of some canopy mats is adequate for mycorrhizal formation. In ecosystems with stable canopy mats, epiphyte species that specialize on such mats could be obligately mycotrophic (Janos 1980). Consequently, a canopy inoculum mosaic could influence the distribution of epiphytic species in a way similar to that suggested for terrestrial habitats by Janos (1980).

Acknowledgments We thank Erin Addison, Norman Dill, Wayne Ferren, Anne Gripp, Ian Ross, and Carolyn Stange for their support. This work was completed as a partial requirement of the Master of Arts degree of University of California, Santa Barbara. We acknowledge National Science Foundation Grants BSR 87-14935 and BSR 90-18006 for support.

FACTORS AFFECTING THE INITIATION AND GROWTH OF ABOVEGROUND ADVENTITIOUS ROOTS IN A TROPICAL CLOUD FOREST TREE: AN EXPERIMENTAL APPROACH

Nalini M. Nadkarni

Aboveground adventitious roots (AAR) characterize many species of tropical and temperate wet forest trees (Lanner 1966, Jenik 1973, Moore 1989) and have been termed "canopy roots" (Nadkarni 1981), "aboveground adventitious roots" (Herwitz 1991), and "apogeotropic roots" (Sanford 1987). They are structured much like their below-ground counterparts and possess similar capacities to absorb nutrients and water (Nadkarni and Primack 1989). These organs are often directly associated with and/or penetrate accumulations of epiphytes and accompanying humus suspended in host tree crowns.

Aboveground adventitious roots may enhance nutrient use efficiency by retrieving leached nutrients from stemflow (Herwitz 1991) or function as a "short-cut" in nutrient cycles by allowing host trees to exploit the abundant nutrients contained in organic matter suspended within their own crowns (Nadkarni 1981). Little is known about the anatomy of AAR, their absorptive capacities of water and/or nutrients under natural conditions, or the physiology of their initiation and growth. Epiphytes and crown humus–produced or related factors possibly responsible for inducing AAR include darkness, moisture, inorganic nutrients, hormones, or other organic exudates. I carried out an experiment to identify stimuli that may promote the growth of AAR in the crown of *Senecio cooperi* (Compositae), a tropical cloud forest tree (Nadkarni 1994).

Experiments were performed between May and September 1982 in the MCFP. The 2-ha study area was located on the windward side of the area known as "La Ventana," which straddles the Continental Divide.

The area experienced a landslide 12–15 yr previous to the study (W. Guindon, pers. comm.). Soils in the area are derived from volcanic rhyolites (Vance and Nadkarni 1990), contain very small amounts of organic matter, and are extremely clayey. Local vegetation consists of a thick cover of arborescent shrubs with a uniform 3–5 m canopy dominated by *S. cooperi*. These shrubs are multibranched, with all of the foliage on the ends of branches, leaving the crown interiors unobstructed and easily accessible. Other common landslide-following plants such as *Gunnera insignis* (Gunneraceae) and *Bocconia frutescens* (Papaveraceae) ringed the study area.

Senecio cooperi was used because of its uniform height, low stature, and propensity for forming AAR under natural conditions (pers. obs.). An aggressive pioneer following major disturbances, this tree can reach 6 m in height. Thirty-nine *S. cooperi* trees of uniform height and structure were chosen. Sixty stem segments adjacent to accessible branch nodes were marked on the experimental trees. Each designated stem segment was subjected to one of the following six treatments and the number of roots initiated and their rates of growth were recorded. Factors tested were the presence of (1) wet epiphytes (live moist mosses, liverworts, filmy ferns, and crown humus collected from three *Didymopanax pittieri* trees collected from the adjacent primary elfin woodland), (2) dry epiphytes (air-dried epiphytes and crown humus), (3) wet sponges (foam sponges saturated with distilled water), (4) inorganic nutrient solution sponges (foam sponges, water, and dissolved commercial nutrient solution, equivalent to a Hoagland's solution), (5) dry sponges (air-dried foam sponges), and (6) control (nothing applied to stem).

Modified techniques of air-layering (Hartmann and Kester 1975) were used to stimulate shoot segments to root. A clump of epiphytes (wet or dry) or a sponge (dry, or saturated with distilled water or nutrient solution) was wrapped securely around each stem section with a 50 x 50 cm gas-permeable polyethylene sheet and tied off at each end with nylon cord to exclude crownwash. Every two weeks, 10 ml of distilled water or nutrient solutions was applied with a syringe to maintain desired conditions. The polyethylene sheet was removed carefully to count and measure roots with minimal disturbance every two weeks. The number of roots per treatment was tallied, and the total length of the roots was summed for each sample. Each stem segment was treated as an independent sample.

The adventitious roots that appeared on stems appeared to be derived from hypertrophied lenticels and aerenchyma tissue and were observed as early as 8 days after the experiment began. As early as 4 days after root initiation, thick white roots with no obvious rootons/hairs had grown into the media or between the sponges and the bark. Three days later, many of the roots had branched and possessed rootons/hairs just above the root cap. After 4 weeks, the larger roots developed a light purple color, which darkened as they thickened. This sequence of AAR formation is similar to the sequence described for flooded individuals of *Fraxinus pennsylvanica* (Sena Gomes and Kozlowski 1980) and *Tamarix* (Ginzburg 1967). Hypertrophied lenticels preceded the presence of white and then colored roots.

The roots appeared to differentiate from the lenticels themselves, with subsequent connection of procambial strands to those of the parent stem.

Treatments differed in their effects on root initiation (ANOVA, $p < .01$). Wet epiphytes and nutrient solutions were most effective. Several of the others, including the control treatment, induced roots, but these appendages disappeared within days, probably through desiccation. Root growth responded similarly; those stimulated by epiphytes were longest (mean root length per segment = 114.0 cm), followed by those growing from stems subjected to the nutrient solution treatment (mean root length per segment = 54.7 cm; Fig. 9.15). Distilled water affected root initiation and elongation only slightly (mean root length per segment = 6.2 cm).

The inducement of AAR by the wet epiphyte and nutrient solution treatments indicates that stimuli involving more than simply moisture or darkness trigger the growth of AAR (Gill 1969). Further studies are needed to determine the ultimate factors that induce the formation of these roots and to determine their functional capacities. A positive feedback mechanism between the growth of epiphytes and the nutrition of their host trees may exist. A variety of inorganic nutrients (Nadkarni 1986b) and organic nutrients (Coxson et al. 1992) are leached from epiphyte communities (especially those dominated by bryophytes) to which trees gain access via these root systems (Nadkarni and Primack 1989). As epiphyte communities colonize, grow, and accumulate dead organic matter, more AAR initiate and elongate. The presence of root systems appears to provide better substrate for epi-

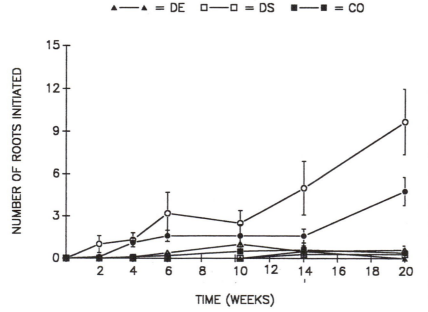

Figure 9.15. Mean (and standard error) number of aboveground adventitious roots initiated by *Senecio cooperi* trees over the 20-week study period for each of six experimental treatments. Treatments are as follows: WE = wet epiphytes, including crown humus; DE = air-dried epiphytes; NS = nutrient solutions with foam sponges; DW = distilled water with foam sponges; DS = dry foam sponges; CO = control. (From Nadkarni 1994)

phyte colonization than does bare bark by "roughening" the surface of the stem and providing more locations for colonization by epiphyte propagules and retention of water and nutrient. As the epiphyte community develops, the host tree may derive more leachates from the epiphytes and put forth more AAR, which would in turn create a better substrate for further epiphyte colonization.

Acknowledgments I thank Israel Mendez for his help in the field. I acknowledge the Tropical Science Center and the MCFP. Fieldwork was completed while I was a graduate student at the College of Forest Resources, University of Washington, and received support from the Minority Affairs Office and the Bloedel Fellowship. I thank Charles Grier, members of my graduate committee, and David Benzing. This was funded by a Man and the Biosphere research grant to C. Grier. Data analysis was partially supported with a grant from the National Science Foundation (DEB 90-18006), administered through The Evergreen State College.

FINE LITTER DYNAMICS WITHIN THE TREE CANOPY OF A TROPICAL CLOUD FOREST
Nalini M. Nadkarni & Teri J. Matelson

Potential sources of nutrients for epiphytes include an array of both autochthonous (within-ecosystem) and allochthonous (outside of ecosystem) sources (Table 9.24). It is important to distinguish between these two source types in forests where nutrient availability may limit productivity of the ecosystem (Grubb 1977, Vitousek 1984). If epiphytes were to obtain all of their nutrients from autochthonous sources, they would simply be diverting nutrients from the tree-ground flux pathway; they would not increase the total pool but merely change the form or compartment in which nutrients were stored. Alternatively, if they were to obtain nutrients from allochthonous sources, they would potentially increase the total nutrient input to the ecosystem in addition to altering the form and location of these nutrients.

Because epiphytic plants have no direct vascular connection to the bank of nutrients in the forest floor, they must rely on morphological and physiological attributes such as litter-impounding pools, foliar trichomes, insectivory, myrmecochory, and poikilohydric foliage to acquire and conserve nutrients in an environment that may deliver nutrients only sporadically and in dilute concentrations (Benzing and Seeman 1978, Nadkarni 1981). Some specialized epiphytes gain nutrients exclusively from precipitation and dry deposition (Benzing 1983), but many epiphytes are unable to obtain nutrients from atmospheric sources. These epiphytes, such as woody shrubs in the Ericaceae, have well-developed root systems that penetrate the dead organic matter and "crown humus" (Jenik 1973) that accumulates as mats on upper branch surfaces. We quantified the nutrient dynamics of one potential autochthonous source of nutrients to the epiphyte community, the abscised plant litter that is intercepted within the upper tree canopy by inner branches and their epiphytes, in the leeward cloud forest area of the MCFP (Nadkarni and Matelson 1991).

Fine litter dynamics within the canopy may be critical for epiphyte productivity and may differ from litter dynamics on the forest floor for three reasons. First, canopy litter may be ephemeral, as it can be removed from branches by within-canopy disturbances such as wind, rain, and arboreal animal activities. In contrast to fallen leaves on the forest floor, which can shift their position on the ground with only minor consequences for plants rooted in soil (Orndorff and Lang 1981), leaf movement in the canopy may remove a potentially substantial contribution to epiphyte nutrition. Second, leaf litter in the canopy may be deposited in smaller amounts than is leaf litter in the forest floor due to lack of input from subcanopy and understory vegetation. Third, decomposition rates of litter deposited and retained within the canopy may differ from litter on the forest floor due to microclimate and substrate differences between the canopy and forest floor, as well as differences in community structure and density of macroinvertebrate detritivores and microbial decomposers (Nadkarni and Longino 1990).

Table 9.24. Potential sources of nutrient input to epiphyte communities in forest ecosystems.

Autochthonous sources	Allochthonous sources
Soil-rooted phytomass	Atmospheric
Intercepted litterfall	wet deposition
Bark decomposition	dry deposition
Leachate of live foliage	gaseous input (including
Animal defecation and death	nitrogen-fixation)

We measured fine litter deposition and decomposition within the upper tree canopy and on the forest floor with standard litterfall collectors and litterbags (Nadkarni and Matelson 1991). A comparable amount of fine litter passed through the canopy ($752 g/m^2/yr$) as arrived on the forest floor ($820 g/m^2/yr$), but less than 1% of the biomass and nutrients of this gross litterfall was retained within the canopy. Canopy standing litter (ca. $170 g/m^2$ branch surface area, $8.8 g/m^2$ ground area) is equivalent to only 1% of standing crop of litter on the forest floor. Measurements of marked leaves documented that 70% of leaves deposited on branches are lost within a 2-week period, and nearly all are gone in 16 weeks. Branch characteristics such as branch angle and number of epiphyte stems and clumps appear to affect the amount of litter retained at particular microsites. Leaf litter decomposition of tethered leaves within the canopy over a 12-month period was half that of leaves on the forest floor (canopy turnover time = 2.8 yr; Nadkarni and Matelson 1991).

Assuming that litter accumulation within the canopy is at steady state, the biomass of fine litter retained and decomposed within the canopy was calculated as only $2.0 g/m^2/yr$ and less than $0.02 g/m^2/yr$ for all nutrients (Fig. 9.16). Nutrient replenishment of epiphyte communities appears to be decoupled from the litterfall pathway, as input from litterfall retained within the canopy is small relative to epiphyte productivity and nutrient requirements reported in other studies.

In most terrestrial systems, the major portion of the nutrients required for net primary production is replenished via the litterfall pathway, especially for nitrogen, phosphorus, and calcium. Within mature tree crowns in tropical cloud forests, where vascular plants, bryophytes, root mats, and humus occur, nutrients are bound in organic matter as they are in the forest floor below. However, the amount of intercepted tree litterfall on inner branches is extremely small (<1% in this study) relative to gross litterfall. The reasons for low litter interception and high litter attrition include disturbances such as wind, falling branches and rain and animal activities such as monkeys and rodents moving along branches and birds foraging in leaf litter. These disturbances cause substantial leaf litter displacement before the nutrients contained in the intercepted litter can be mineralized and thus made available for epiphyte uptake. The few leaves that do remain in the canopy decompose very slowly, which may at least be due in part to dry environmental conditions and low densities of canopy macroinvertebrates (Nadkarni and Longino 1990).

Because the replenishment of nutrients to many cloud forest epiphytes appears to be only partially derived from litterfall decomposition, the balance must be derived from the other sources outlined in Table 9.24. Two sources, foliar leachate (autochthonous) and atmospheric deposition (allochthonous), seem the most likely candidates for most of the balance. Nutrients derived from foliar leachates (especially mobile nutrients K^+ and NO_3^-) may be important, as throughfall concentrations collected at the forest floor are occasionally lower than in bulk precipitation (Clark 1994), indicating that at least some of the canopy components are "scavenging" nutrients from bulk precipitation. The majority of host tree foliage, however, is sclerophyllous, with waxy cuticles, and many cloud forest trees retranslocate high proportions of nitrogen and phosphorus, which presumably minimizes water and nutrient transfer through foliage (Grubb 1977, Tanner 1977).

Atmospheric deposition is an allochthonous source that is likely to contribute nutrients to all epiphytes. On outer branches, poikilohydric epiphytes such as bryophytes and filmy ferns capture atmospheric nutrients and incorporate them into their biomass. When they die, their detritus contributes to the development of humus buildup, which no doubt increases nutrient retention. The epiphytes that occupy inner branch areas and lack morphological adaptations for direct atmospheric uptake must acquire nutrients by root uptake from nutrients sequestered in the accumulated mats. These plants may obtain at least some of their nutrients by physically intercepting precipitation (especially wind-blown mist) with their shoots and channeling it to the humus mats that are permeated with their root systems. Understanding the ultimate nutrient sources of canopy solutions and sinks of nutrients by quantifying the uptake and release of specific canopy components is needed to differentiate these two sources.

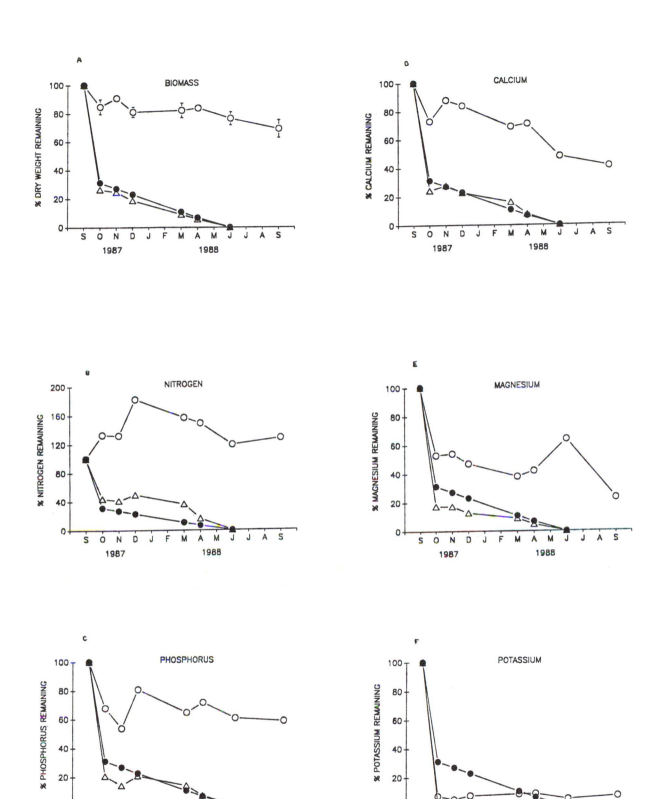

Figure 9.16. Measured and calculated rates of biomass and nutrient change of intercepted litterfall of litter material in tethered bags in the canopy, as a percentage of orginal mass or amount of nutrients from September 1987 to September 1988. Open circles shows the percentage of the original biomass (mean ± 1 SE) and nutrient content of the original material contained in tethered litterbags. Filled circles show calculated amounts of leaves remaining after leaf attrition (loss of whole leaves from the canopy, L_a). Open triangles are amounts of material remaining as a function of the integration of leaf attrition and leaf decomposition (L_d). (From Nadkarni and Matelson 1991)

LONGEVITY OF FALLEN EPIPHYTES
Teri J. Matelson, Nalini M. Nadkarni, & John T. Longino

Although the vertical distance between canopy and forest floor may be small, the differences between canopy and forest floor microhabitats can be great. Canopy environments are generally characterized by more extreme fluctuations in moisture supply and temperature, stronger insolation, higher windspeeds, and more severe and variable vapor pressure deficits (Chacon and Duval 1963, Chazdon and Fetcher 1984). Other differences may include the invertebrate fauna (Nadkarni and Longino 1990) and microbial activities (Vance and Nadkarni 1990). Canopy habitats, in contrast forest floor habitats, presumably have more limited storage capacity for available nutrients and water, more sporadic and dilute nutrient inputs, less physical stability, and more patchy "safe sites" for establishment (Ackerman and Montalvo 1990, Benzing 1990).

The movement of live epiphytes from the canopy to the forest floor is a frequent event in epiphyte communities. Live epiphytes fall to the forest floor because they are dislodged by wind or animals or because branches and trees break and fall (Strong 1977). Some epiphytes (e.g., tank bromeliads) tend to fall as individuals. Others, connected by interwoven root systems and a layer of crown humus (Jenik 1973), often fall intact, as "clumps." Anecdotal observations of fallen epiphytes include a range of responses; some epiphytes vanish within weeks, while others persist and even thrive for months or years. If we could understand why certain epiphytes live or die on the ground, we might better understand the nature of epiphytism, the factors that contribute to the widespread occurrence of epiphytic plants (10% of all vascular plants are epiphytic; Kress 1986), and the relatively low incidence of facultative epiphytism (see Atwood, "Orchids"). The longevity of fallen epiphytes also has implications for nutrient cycling since epiphytes derive all or nearly all of their nutrients from atmospheric sources (Benzing 1990, Nadkarni and Matelson 1991). The nutrients in live epiphytes that fall to the ground will ultimately be mineralized and absorbed by terrestrial vegetation. However, their prolonged survival on the ground would delay mineralization with consequent effects on storage, cycling, and potential loss of nutrients from the ecosystem.

We documented the longevity of a variety of fallen epiphytes relative to light regime (intact forest understory, hereafter "shade," vs. gap), attachment to fallen branch, physical dimensions of the "clump" (defined as a contiguous epiphyte mat that falls from the canopy), and the number of epiphytes in the clump (Matelson et al. 1993).

We conducted fieldwork in the leeward cove forest study area in the MCFP (Nadkarni et al. 1995). In May 1989, we collected 49 newly fallen epiphyte clumps from the forest floor within the study plot. Each clump consisted of live and robust-appearing epiphytes with associated dead organic matter and roots intact. All clumps had fallen within the previous two weeks. Each clump was placed in one of four plots; two of the plots were in gaps with little or no understory cover. The other two plots were in the shaded understory. Individual plants were identified to one of the following plant categories: Piperaceae ($N = 15$ plants), Araceae (12), Orchidaceae (26), Bromeliaceae (31), Ericaceae (24), other angiosperms (26), Pteridophyta (40), and nonvascular plants (49). Nonvascular plants, mainly mosses and liverworts, were not monitored individually but were considered a single entity on a clump. Each of the 223 plants was examined and scored as live or dead at monthly intervals during the first year and again near the end of the second year (day 637). Longevity was defined as the time between day 1 and the last sampling day a plant was recorded alive after placement on the forest floor, with the time interval being an integer from 1 to 12, representing the day of placement and the 11 subsequent censuses. Individual plant longevity, which was not normally distributed, was analyzed with nonparametric tests (Systat 1988).

By the end of the first year, only 27% of the plants remained alive, and by the end of the study (21 months), only 7% had survived (Fig. 9.17). All plant categories exhibited similar rates of mortality. Discounting spatial association, there were no significant differences in longevity among the eight plant categories. In contrast, there was a significant plot effect on longevity. Gap plots had higher mean ranks than the two shade plots. There was no effect of epiphyte attachment to branches on clump longevity, and no significant regressions of clump longevity on clump volume or number of plants per clump (Matelson et al. 1993).

A variety of factors might cause live epiphytes to die after falling to the ground. First, epiphytes may die due to diminished photosynthesis caused by environmental differences between canopy and forest floor, especially light and moisture regimes and air movement. Water and nutrient inputs may differ because fallen epiphytes receive primarily throughfall, which is deposited in larger drops than in mist or fog; throughfall chemistry is often altered by contact with the canopy (Vitousek and Sanford 1986, Veneklaas and Van Ek 1990). Extremes of temperature, substrate moisture content, wetting/drying cycles, and relative humidity are greater in the canopy than on the forest floor (Bohlman et al. 1995). The most striking microenvironmental difference is the lack of extremely dry periods on the forest floor during the dry and windy-misty seasons.

Second, biotic factors may distinguish the canopy from the forest floor, including differences in pathogens, herbivores, and symbionts. Overall density of invertebrates is lower in the Monteverde canopy than on the forest floor, and certain taxa are virtually absent in the canopy (Nadkarni and Longino 1990; see Nadkarni and Longino, "Invertebrates," pp. 336–337). Third, accumulation of leaf litter on top of fallen epiphytes may encourage their death on the forest floor. Leaf litter accumulation blocks insolation, changes the moisture regime, and may influence herbivores and pathogens. Rates of litter accumulation differ between canopy and forest floor, due to higher wind in the canopy and the noncontiguous surface area of canopy substrates (Nadkarni and Matelson 1991).

Although little is known about the spatial distribution of fallen epiphytes, much fallen epiphytic material is deposited in gaps, as it "rides down" large branch- and treefalls (Nadkarni and Matelson 1992b). Epiphytes also fall in a continual manner in smaller amounts, reaching the forest floor on smaller branches or as individual epiphytes. The latter encounter closed-canopy conditions overhead and are then subject to conditions that might cause them to die rapidly, relative to the rates of those deposited in gaps. Environmental conditions (especially light and temperature regimes) in gaps are more "canopylike" than on closed-canopy forest floor, thus allowing fallen epiphytes in gaps to survive longer than in deeper shade.

Other studies have shown that epiphytes can contribute appreciably to biomass and nutrient inputs to the forest floor (Veneklaas 1991); up to 10% of total deposition in fine litter at our site; Nadkarni and

Matelson 1992a). Before nutrients in epiphytes can be released through decomposition, however, the live plants must die. Thus, fallen epiphytic material probably affects nutrient cycles differently than does litterfall from terrestrially rooted plants, whose nutrients can be mineralized faster because that material is already dead. For fallen live epiphytes, then, there is a potential lag time in nutrient release via mineralization. In forests with well-developed canopy communities, epiphytes can profoundly affect both the amounts of nutrient storage and the timing of nutrient release. Further investigations should pursue the spatial and temporal distribution of fallen epiphytes at the species level in relation to microhabitat characteristics in order to determine the role of epiphytes at an ecosystem and to gain insights into mechanisms that foster epiphytism.

Acknowledgments We thank the MCFP and the Tropical Science Center. Research was supported by NSF Grant BSR 86-14935 and BSR 89-18006, the Whitehall Foundation, and the National Geographic Society.

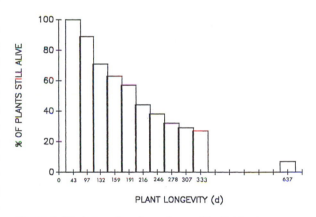

Figure 9.17. Longevity of a cohort of individual epiphytes after falling to the forest floor. Longevity is defined as time (d) between day 1 and the last sampling day a plant was recorded alive after placement on the forest floor. *N* = 223 plants (including nonvascular plants). (From Matelson et al. 1993)

Literature Cited

Ackerman, J. D., and J. C. Montalvo. 1990. Short and long term limitations to fruit production in a tropical orchid. Ecology 71:263–272.

Aide, T. M. 1987. Limbfalls: a major cause of sapling mortality for tropical forest plants. Biotropica 19:284–285.

Anderson, I., J. Levine, M. Poth, and P. Riggan. 1988. Enhanced biogenic emissions of nitric oxide and nitrous

oxide following surface biomass burning. Journal of Geophysical Research 93:3893–3898.

Andreae, M., E. Browell, M. Garstang, G. Gregory, R. Harriss, G. Hill, D. Jacob, M. Pereira, G. Sachse, A. Setzer, P. Silva Dias, T. Talbot, A. Torres, and S. Wofsy. 1988. Biomass-burning emissions and associated haze layers over Amazonia. Journal of Geophysical Research 93:1509–1527.

Aneja V. P., Robarge W. P., Claiborn C. S., Murthy A., Soo-

Kim D., and Li Z. 1992. Chemical climatology of high elevation spruce-fir forests in the southern Appalachian mountains. Environmental Pollution 75:89–96.

Asbury, C., W. McDowell, R. Trinidad-Pizarro, and S. Berrios. 1994. Solute deposition from cloud water to the canopy of a Puerto Rican montane forest. Atmospheric Environment 28:1773–1780.

Ashton, P. S. 1969. Speciation among tropical forest trees: some deductions in the light of recent evidence. Biological Journal of the Linnean Society 1:155–196.

Atkin, L., and J. Proctor. 1988. Invertebrates in the litter and soil on Volcán Barva, Costa Rica. Journal of Tropical Ecology 4:307–310.

Bates, J. 1992. Mineral nutrient acquisition and retention by bryophytes. Journal of Bryology 17:223–240.

Baylis, G. 1975. The magnolioid mycorrhiza and myotrophy in root systems derived from it. Pages 373–390 in F. Sanders, B. Mosse, and P. Tinker, editors. Endomycorrhizas. Academic Press, London.

Beard, J. S. 1946. The natural vegetation of Trinidad. Oxford Forestry Memoirs 20. Clarendon Press, Oxford.

———. 1949. The natural vegetation of the Windward and Leeward Islands. Oxford Forestry Memoirs 21. Clarendon Press, Oxford.

———. 1955. The classification of tropical American vegetation types. Ecology 36:89–100.

Bentley, B. 1987. Nitrogen fixation by epiphylls in a tropical rainforest. Annals of the Missouri Botanical Garden 74:234–241.

Benzing, D. 1981. Mineral nutrition of epiphytes: an appraisal of adaptive features. Selbyana 5:219–223.

———. 1983. Vascular epiphytes: a survey with special reference to their interactions with other organisms. Pages 11–24 in S. Sutton, T. Whitmore, and A. Chadwick, editors. Tropical rain forest: ecology and management. British Ecological Society and Blackwell Scientific Publications, Oxford.

———. 1990. Vascular epiphytes. Cambridge University Press, Cambridge.

Benzing, D., and J. Seeman. 1978. Nutritional piracy and host decline: a new perspective on the epiphyte-host relationship. Selbyana 2:133–148.

Bermudes, D., and D. Benzing. 1987. Fungi in neotropical epiphyte roots. BioSystems 23:65–73.

Blanchard, D. 1983. The production, distribution, and bacterial enrichment of the sea-salt aerosol. Pages 407–454 in P. Liss and W. Slinn, editors. Air-sea exchange of gases and particles. Reidel, Dordrecht.

Bohlman, S., T. Matelson, and N. Nadkarni. 1995. Moisture and temperature patterns of canopy humus and forest floor soil of a montane cloud forest, Costa Rica. Biotropica 27:13–19.

Bormann, F. H., and G. E. Likens. 1979. Pattern and process in a forested ecosystem. Springer, New York.

Bowden, R. 1991. Inputs, outputs, and accumulation of nitrogen in an early successional moss (Polytrichum) ecosystem. Ecological Monographs 61: 207–223.

Bray, J., and E. Gorham. 1964. Litter production in forests of the world. Advances in Ecological Research 2:101–157.

Brokaw, N. V. L. 1982. The definition of treefall gap and its effect on measures of forest dynamics. Biotropica 14:158–160.

———. 1985. Treefalls, regrowth, and community structure in tropical forests. Pages 53–69 in S. T. A. Pickett and P. S. White, editors. The ecology of natural disturbance and patch dynamics. Academic Press, New York.

Brokaw, N. V. L., and L. R. Walker. 1991. Summary of the effects of Caribbean hurricanes on vegetation. Biotropica 23:442–447.

Brown, S., and A. Lugo. 1982. The storage and production of organic matter in tropical forests and their role in the global carbon cycle. Biotropica 14:161–187.

Brown, W. H. 1919. Vegetation of Phillipine mountains. Bureau of Science Pub. 13. Department of Agriculture and Natural Resources, Manila.

Bruijnzeel, L., and J. Proctor. 1995. Hydrology and biogeochemistry of tropical montane cloud forests: what do we really know? Pages 25–46 in L. Hamilton, J. Juvik, and F. Scatena, editors. Tropical montane cloud forests. East-West Center, Honolulu.

Burger, W. 1971. Flora Costaricensis. Fieldiana, Vol. 35. Field Museum of Natural History, Chicago.

Cavelier, J., and G. Goldstein. 1989. Mist and fog interception in elfin cloud forest in Colombia and Venezuela. Journal of Tropical Ecology 5:309–322.

Cavelier, J., D. Solis, and M. A. Jaramillo. 1996. Fog interception in montane forests across the Central Cordillera of Panamá. Journal of Tropical Ecology 12:357–369.

Chacon, P., and J. Duval. 1963. Variations microclimatiques verticales et saisonnieres dans la forêt sempervirente de Basse Côte d'Ivoire. Annales Faculté Sciences, Dakar 8:89–155.

Chazdon, R. L., and N. Fetcher. 1984. Photosynthetic light environments in a lowland tropical rain forest in Costa Rica. Journal of Ecology 72:553–564.

Clark, D. B., and D. A. Clark. 1989. The role of physical damage in the seedling mortality regime of a neotropical rainforest. Oikos 55:225–230.

Clark, K. 1994. The role of epiphytic bryophytes in the net accumulation and cycling of nitrogen in a tropical montane cloud forest. Ph.D. dissertation, University of Florida, Gainesville.

Clark, K., and N. Nadkarni. 1990. Nitrate and ammonium ions in precipitation and throughfall of a neotropical cloud forest: implications for epiphyte mineral nutrition. Ecological Bulletin 71:59.

Clark, K L.., N. M. Nadkarni, D. Schaefer, and H. L. Gholz. 1988. Atmospheric deposition and net retention by the canopy in a tropical montane forest, Monteverde, Costa Rica. Journal of Tropical Ecology 14:27–45.

Connell, J. H. 1978. Diversity in tropical rain forests and coral reefs. Science 199:1302–1310.

Cowles, H. C. 1899. The ecological relations of the vegetation on the sand dunes of Lake Michigan. Botanical Gazette 27:95–117, 167–202, 281–308, 361–391.

Coxson, D. 1991. Nutrient release from epiphytic bryophytes in tropical montane rain forest (Guadeloupe). Canadian Journal of Botany 69:2122–2129.

Coxson, D., and N. Nadkarni. 1995. Ecological roles of epiphytes in nutrient cycles of forest ecosystems. Pages 495–543 in M. Lowman and N. Nadkarni, editors. Forest canopies. Academic Press, San Diego.

Coxson, D. S., D. D. McIntyre, and H. J. Vogel. 1992. Pulsed release of sugars and polyols from canopy bryophytes in tropical montane rain forest (Guadeloupe, French West Indies). Biotropica 24:121–133.

Crutzen, P., and M. Andreae. 1990. Biomasss burning in the tropics: impacts on atmospheric chemistry and biogeochemical cycles. Science 250: 1669–1678.

Daft, M., and T. Nicolson. 1969. Effect of Endogone mycorrhiza on plant growth. III. Influence of inoculum concentration on growth and infection in tomato. New Phytologist 68:953–963.

Denslow, J. 1980. Gap partitioning among tropical rainforest trees. Biotropica 12(Suppl.):2–7.

———. 1987. Tropical rainforest gaps and tree species diversity. Annual Review of Ecology and Systematics 18:431–451.

Edwards, P. J. 1977. Studies in a montane rain forest in New Guinea. II. The production and disappearance of litter. Journal of Ecology 65:971–992.

———. 1982. Studies of mineral cycling in a montane rain forest in New Guinea. Journal of Ecology 65: 971–992.

Edwards, P. J., and P. J. Grubb. 1977. Studies of mineral cycling in a montane rain forest in New Guinea. I. The distribution of organic matter in the vegetation and soil. Journal of Ecology 65: 943–969.

Ewel, J., C. Barish, B. Brown, N. Price, and J. Raich. 1981. Slash and burn impacts on a Costa Rica wet forest site. Ecology 62:816–829.

Exell, A. W. 1944. Catalogue of the vascular plants of San Tome. British Museum, London.

Falconer, R., and P. Falconer. 1980. Determination of cloud water acidity at a mountain obervatory in the Adirondack Mountains of New York State. Journal of Geophysical Research. 85:7465–7470.

Fassbender, H.W., and V. Grimm. 1981. Ciclos bioquímicos en un ecosistema forestal de los Andes Occidentales de Venezuela. II. Producción y descompsición de los residuos vegetales. Turrialba 31:39–47.

Foster, D. R., and E. R. Boose. 1995. Hurricane disturbance regimes in temperate and tropical forest ecosystems. Pages 305–339 in M. P. Coutts and J. Grace, editors. Wind and trees. Cambridge University Press, Cambridge.

Fowler, D., J. Cape, I. Leith, T. Choularton, M. Gay, and A. Jones. 1988. The influence of altitude on rainfall composition at Great Dun Fell. Atmospheric Environment 22:1355–1362.

Garcia Yazquez-Yanes, C. 1985. Presencia de micorrizas vesiculo-arbusculares en especies de *Piper* de Los Tuxtlas, Veracruz, México. Biotica 10: 223–228.

Gill, A. M. 1969. The ecology of an elfin forest in Puerto Rico, 6. Aerial roots. Journal of the Arnold Arboretum 50:197–209.

Ginzburg, C. 1967. Origin of the adventitious root apex in *Tamarix aphylla*. American Journal of Botany 54:4–8.

Gleason, H. A., and M. T. Cook. 1927. Plant ecology of Porto Rico. I and II. Scientific Survey of Porto Rico and the Virgin Islands 7:1–173.

Gómez-Pompa, A. 1973. Ecology of the vegetation of Veracruz. Pages 37–52 in A. Graham, editor. Vegetation and vegetational history of northern Latin America. Elsevier, New York.

Gordon, C. A., R. Herrera, and T. Hutchinson. 1994. Studies of fog events at two cloud forests near Caracas, Venezuela—I. Frequency and duration of fog. Atmospheric Environment 28:317–322.

Grace, J. 1977. Plant response to wind. Academic Press, New York.

Grubb, P. J. 1977. Control of forest growth and distribution on wet tropical mountains: with special reference to mineral nutrition. Annual Review of Ecology and Systematics 8:83–107.

Grubb, P. J., and P. J. Edwards. 1982. Studies of mineral cycling in a montane rain forest in New Guinea. III. The distribution of mineral elements in the aboveground material. Journal of Ecology 70:623–648.

Grubb, P. J., Lloyd, J. R., Pennington, T. D. A., and Whitmore, T. C. 1963. A comparison of montane and lowland rain forest in Ecuador. I. The forest structure, physiognomy, and floristics. Journal of Ecology 51:567–601.

Hallé, F., R. A. A. Oldeman, and P. B. Tomlinson. 1978. Tropical trees and forests: an architectural analysis. Springer, New York.

Hartmann, H. T., and D. E. Kester. 1975. Plant propagation: principles and practices (3rd ed.) Prentice-Hall, Englewood Cliffs, New Jersey.

Hartshorn, G. 1990. An overview of neotropical forest dynamics. Pages 585–599 in A. H. Gentry, editor. Four neotropical rainforests. Yale University Press, New Haven, Connecticut.

———. 1980. Neotropical forest dynamics. Biotropica 12(Suppl.):23–30.

Heaney, A., and Proctor, J. 1990. Preliminary studies on forest structure and floristics on Volcán Barva, Costa Rica. Journal of Tropical Ecology 6:307–320.

Hendry, C. D., C. Barrish, and E. Edgerton. 1984. Precipitation chemistry at Turrialba, Costa Rica. Water Resources Research 20:1677–1684.

Herwitz, S. 1991. Above-ground adventitious roots and stemflow chemistry of *Ceratopetalum virchowii* in an Australian montane tropical rain forest. Biotropica 23:210–218.

Hofstede, R., J. Wolf, and D. Benzing. 1993. Epiphytic biomass and nutrient status of a Colombian upper montane rain forest. Selbyana 14:37–45.

Holdridge, L. R. 1967. Life zone ecology. Tropical Science Center, San José, Costa Rica.

Howard, R. A. 1968. The ecology of an elfin forest in Puerto Rico, 1. Introduction and composition studies. Journal of the Arnold Arboretum 49:381–418.

———. 1969. The ecology of an elfin forest in Puerto Rico. 8. Studies of stem growth and form and of leaf structure. Journal of the Arnold Arboretum 50:225–262.

Hubbell, S. J. 1979. Tree dispersion, abundance, and diversity in a tropical dry forest. Science 203: 1299–1309.

Hubbell, S. P., and R. B. Foster. 1986. Biology, chance, and history and structure of tropical rain forest tree communities. Pages 313–329 in J. Diamond and T. J. Case, editors. Community ecology. Harper and Row, New York.

Ingram, S., and N. Nadkarni. 1993. Composition and distribution of epiphytic organic matter in a neotropical cloud forest, Costa Rica. Biotropica 25: 370–383.

Jacobi, J. D. 1983. *Metrosideros* dieback in Hawaii: a comparison of adjacent dieback and non-dieback rain forest stands. New Zealand Journal of Ecology 6:79–97.

Jaffe, M. J. 1980. Morphogenetic responses of plants to mechanical stimuli or stress. Bioscience 30: 239–243.

Janos, D. 1980. Vesicular-arbuscular mycorrhizae influence tropical succession. Biotropica 12(Suppl.): 56–64.

———. 1993. Vesicular-arbuscular mycorrhizae of epiphytes. Mycorrhiza 4:1–4.

Jenik, J. 1973. Root systems of tropical trees. 8. Stilt-roots and allied adaptations. Preslia 45:250–264.

Jenny, H., S. P. Gessel and F. T. Bingham. 1949. Comparative study of decomposition rates of organic matter in temperate and tropical regions. Soil Science 68:419–432.

Johnson, D., and S. Lindberg. 1992. Atmospheric deposition and nutrient cycling in forest ecosystems. Springer, New York.

Juvik, J. O., and D. Nullet. 1995. Relationships between rainfall, cloud-water interception, and canopy throughfall in a Hawaiian montane forest. Pages 102–114 in L. S. Hamilton, J. Juvik, and F. Scatena, editors. Tropical montane cloud forests. Springer, New York.

Keeney, D., and Nelson, D. 1982. Nitrogen-inorganic forms. Pages 643–698 in A. L. Page, editor. Methods of soil analysis, Part 2 (2nd ed.). American Society of Agronomy, Madison, Wisconsin.

Keller, M., D. Jacob, S. Wofsy, and R. Harriss. 1991. Effects of tropical deforestation on global and regional atmospheric chemistry. Climatic Change 19:139–158.

Keller, M., E. Veldkamp, A. Weitz, and W. Reiners. 1993. Pasture age effects on soil-atmosphere trace gas exchange in a deforested area of Costa Rica. Nature 365:244–246.

Kellman, M., J. Hudson, and K. Sanmugadas. 1982. Temporal variability in atmospheric nutrient influx to a tropical ecosystem. Biotropica 14:1–9.

Kinsman, S. 1990. Regeneration by fragmentation in tropical montane forest shrubs. American Journal of Botany 77:1626–1633.

Knight, D. H. 1975. A phytosociological analysis of species-rich tropical forest on Barro Colorado Island, Panama. Ecological Monographs 45:259–284.

Kollman, F., and W. A. Cote. 1968. Principles of wood science technology. I. Solid wood. Springer, New York.

Kress, W. J. 1986. The systematic distribution of vascular epiphytes: an update. Selbyana 9:2–22.

Lane-Poole, C. E. 1925. The forests of Papua and New Guinea. Empire Forestry Journal 4:206–234.

Lanner, R. 1966. Adventitious roots of *Eucalyptus robusta* in Hawaii. Pacific Science 220:379–381.

Lawton, R. O. 1980. Wind and the ontogeny of elfin stature in a Costa Rican lower montane rain forest. Ph.D. dissertation, University of Chicago, Chicago.

———. 1982. Wind stress and elfin stature in a montane forest tree: an adaptive explanation. American Journal of Botany 69:1224–1230.

———. 1984. Ecological constraints on wood density in a tropical montane rain forest. American Journal of Botany 71:261–267.

———. 1990. Canopy gaps and light penetration into a wind-exposed tropical lower montane rain forest. Canadian Journal of Forest Research 20:659–667.

Lawton, R. O., and V. J. Dryer. 1980. The vegetation of the Monteverde Cloud Forest Reserve. Brenesia 18:101–116.

Lawton, R. O., and F. E. Putz. 1988. Natural disturbance and gap-phase regeneration in a wind-exposed tropical cloud forest. Ecology 69:764–777.

Leakey, R., and J. Proctor. 1987. Invertebrates in the litter and soil at a range of altitudes in Gunung Silam, a small ultrabasic mountain in Sabah. Journal of Tropical Ecology 3:119–128.

Leigh, E. G. 1975. Structure and climate in tropical rain forest. Annual Review of Ecology and Systematics 6:67–86.

Lesica, P., and R. Antibus. 1990. The occurrence of mycorrhizal in vascular epiphytes of two Costa Rican forests. Biotropica 22:250–258.

Lewis, W., Jr. 1981. Precipitation chemistry and nutrient loading by precipitation in a tropical watershed. Water Resources Research 17:169–181.

Lieberman, D., and M. Lieberman. 1987. Forest tree growth and dynamics at La Selva (1969–1982). Journal of Tropical Ecology 3:347–358.

Lieberman, D., G. S. Hartshorn, M. Lieberman, and R. Peralta. 1990. Forest dynamics at La Selva Biological Station 1969–1985. Pages 509–521 in A. H. Gentry, editor. Four neotropical rainforests. Yale University Press, New Haven, Connecticut.

Lobert, J., D. Scharffe, W. Hao, and P. Crutzen. 1990. Importance of biomass burning in the atmospheric budgets of nitrogen-containing gases. Nature 346:552–554.

Logan, J. 1983. Nitrogen oxides in the troposphere: global and regional budgets. Journal of Geophysical Research 88:10785–10807.

Longino, J., and N. Nadkarni. 1990. A comparison of ground and canopy leaf litter ants (Hymenoptera: Formicidae) in a neotropical montane forest. Psyche 97:81–94.

Longman, K., and J. Jenik. 1987. Tropical forest and its environment. Longman, Essex, UK.

Lopez, A. H., and A. L. Cortes. 1978. Los suelos orgánicos de Colombia: su origen, constitución, y clasificación. Instituto geográfico "Agustin Codazzi," Vol. 14, No. 2, Colombia.

Lovett, G. M., W. A. Reiners, and R. K. Olsen. 1982. Cloud droplet deposition in subalpine balsam fir forests: hydrological and chemical inputs. Science 218:1303–1304.

Lugo, A., and C. Lowe. 1995. Tropical forests: management and ecology. Springer, New York.

Lugo, A., and F. Scatena. 1992. Epiphytes and climate change research in the Caribbean: a proposal. Selbyana 13:123–130.

Lugo, A. E., M. Applefield, D. J. Pool, and R. B. McDonald. 1983. The impact of Hurricane David on the forests of Dominica. Canadian Journal of Forest Research 13:201–211.

Madison, M. 1977. Vascular epiphytes: their systematic occurrence and salient features. Selbyana 2:1–13.

Maffia, B. 1990. Endomycorrhizal status of selected plants in a neotropical cloud forest with special emphasis on *Peperomia costaricensis* C.DC. (Piperaceae). Master's thesis, University of California, Santa Barbara.

Maffia, B., N. Nadkarni, and D. Janos. 1993. Vesicular-arbuscular mycorrhizae of epiphytic and terrestrial Piperaceae under field and greenhouse conditions. Mycorrhiza 4:5–9.

Matelson, T. J., N. M. Nadkarni, and J. T. Longino. 1993. Survivorship of fallen epiphytes in a neotropical cloud forest, Monteverde, Costa Rica. Ecology 74:265–269.

Matelson, T. J., N. M. Nadkarni, and R. Solano. 1995. Tree damage and annual mortality in a montane forest in Monteverde, Costa Rica. Biotropica 27: 441–447.

McDade, L., K. Bawa, H. Hespenheide, and G. Hartshorn. 1994. La Selva: ecology and natural history of a neotropical rain forest. University of Chicago Press, Chicago.

McDowell, W. H., C. Sanchez, C. Asbury, and C. Ramos Perez. 1990. Influence of sea salt aerosols and long range transport on precipitation chemistry at El Verde, Puerto Rico. Atmospheric Environment 24A:2813–2821.

Mohankumar, V., and A. Mahadevan, 1987. Vesicular-arbuscular mycorrhizae associations in plants of Kalakud Reserve Forest, India. Agnewissenschaft Botanisch 61:255–274.

Mohnen, V. A., and J. A. Kadkecek. 1989. Cloud chemistry research at Whiteface Mountain. Tellus 41B: 79–91.

Mohnen V. A., and R. J. Vong. 1993. A climatology of cloud chemistry for the eastern United States derived from the mountain cloud chemistry project. Environmental Review 1:38–54.

Moore, P. D. 1989. Upwardly mobile roots. Nature 341:188.

Moran, V., and T. R. E. Southwood. 1982. The guild composition of arthropod communities in trees. Journal of Animal Ecology 51:289–306.

Murray, K. G. 1986. Consequences of seed dispersal for gap-dependent plants: relationships between seed shadows, germination requirements, and forest dynamic processes. Pages 187–198 in A. Estrada and T. H. Fleming, editors. Frugivores and seed dispersal. Dr. W. Junk Publishers, Dordrecht.

———. 1988. Avian seed dispersal of three neotropical gap-dependent plants. Ecological Monographs 58:271–298.

Nadkarni, N. M. 1981. Canopy roots: convergent evolution in rainforest nutrient cycles. Science 214: 1023–1024.

———. 1983. The effects of epiphytes on nutrient cycles within temperate and tropical rainforest tree canopies. Ph.D. dissertation, University of Washington, Seattle.

———. 1984. Epiphyte biomass and nutrient capital of a neotropical elfin forest. Biotropica 16:249–256.

———. 1986a. An ecological overview and checklist of the epiphytes in the Monteverde Cloud Forest Reserve. Brenesia 10:35–39.

———. 1986b. The nutritional effects of epiphytes on host trees with special reference to alteration of precipitation chemistry. Selbyana 9:44–51.

———. 1988. Tropical rainforest ecology from a canopy perspective. Memoirs of the California Academy of Sciences 12:57–67.

———. 1994. Factors affecting the initiation and elongation of above-ground adventitious roots in a tropical cloud forest tree: an experimental approach. Oecologia 100:94–97.

Nadkarni, N., and J. T. Longino. 1990. Invertebrates in canopy and ground organic matter in a neotropical montane forest, Costa Rica. Biotropica 22:286–289.

Nadkarni, N., and T. Matelson. 1991. Dynamics of fine litterfall within the canopy of a tropical cloud forest, Monteverde. Ecology 72:2071–2082.

———. 1992a. Biomass and nutrient dynamics of epiphyte litterfall in a neotropical cloud forest, Costa Rica. Biotropica 24:24–30.

———. 1992b. Biomass and nutrient dynamics of fine litter of terrestrially rooted material in a neotropical montane forest, Costa Rica. Biotropica 24:113–120.

Nadkarni, N., and R. Primack. 1989. A comparison of mineral uptake by above- and below-ground roots of *Salix syringiana* using gamma spectrometry. Plant and Soil 113:39–45.

Nadkarni, N., T. Matelson, and W. A. Haber. 1995. Structural characteristics and floristic composition of a neotropical cloud forest, Monteverde, Costa Rica. Journal of Tropical Ecology 11:481–495.

Nelson, D., and L. Sommers. 1980. Total nitrogen analysis of soil and plant tissues. Journal of the Association of Analytical Chemistry 63:770–778.

Niklas, K. 1993. Plant biomechanics. University of Chicago Press, Chicago.

Odum, H. T. 1970. Rain forest structure and mineral cycling homeostasis. Pages H-7–H-14 *in* H. T. Odum, editor. A tropical rain forest. U.S. AEC Division of Technical Information, Springfield, Virginia.

Olson, J. 1963. Energy storage and the balance of producers and decomposers in ecological systems. Ecology 44:322–331.

Orians, G. H. 1982. The influence of tree-falls in tropical forest on tree species richness. Tropical Ecology 23:255–279.

Orndorff, K., and G. Lang. 1981. Leaf litter redistribution in a West Virginia hardwood forest. Journal of Ecology 69:225–235.

Panshin, A. J., and C. DeZeeuw. 1970. Textbook of wood technology, Vol. 1, Structure, identification, uses and properties of the commercial woods of the United States and Canada. McGraw-Hill, New York.

Parker, G. 1983. Throughfall and stemflow in the forest nutrient cycle. Advances in Ecological Research 13:57–133.

Parkinson, J., and S. Allen. 1975. A wet oxidation procedure suitable for the determination of nitrogen and mineral nutrients in biological material. Communications in Soil Science and Plant Analysis 6:1–11.

Perry, D. 1978. A method of access into the crowns of emergent and canopy trees. Biotropica 10:155–157.

Phillips, J., and D. Hayman. 1970. Improved procedures for clearing roots and staining parasitic and vesicular-arbuscular mycorrhizal fungi for rapid assessment of infection. Transactions of the British Mycological Society 55:158–161.

Pickett, S. T. A., and P. S. White, editors. 1985. The ecology of natural disturbance and patch dynamics. Academic Press, New York.

Pike, L. 1978. The importance of lichens in mineral cycling. The Bryologist 81:247–157.

Pócs, T. 1980. The epiphytic biomass and its effect on the water balance of two rainforest types in the Uluguru Mountains. Acta Botanica Academiae Scientiarum Hungaricae 26:143–167.

Proctor, J. 1983. Tropical forest litterfall. I. Problems of data comparison. Pages 267–285 *in* S. Sutton, T. Whitmore, and A. Chadwick, editors. Tropical rain forest: ecology and management. Blackwell, Oxford.

———. 1984. Tropical forest litterfall. II. The data set. Pages 83–115 *in* S. Sutton, T. Whitmore, and A. Chadwick, editors. Tropical rain forest: The Leeds Symposium. Blackwell, Oxford.

Proctor, J., M. Anderson, and H. Vallack. 1983. Comparative studies on forests, soils and litterfall at four altitudes on Gunung Mulu, Sarawak. Malaysian Forester 46:60–76.

Putz, F. E. 1983. Treefall pits and mounds, buried seeds, and the importance of soil disturbance to pioneer tree species on Barro Colorado Island. Ecology 64:1069–1074.

Putz, F. E., and N. V. L. Brokaw. 1989. Sprouting and of broken trees on Barro Colorado Island, Panama. Ecology 70:508–512.

Putz, F. E., and N. M. Holbrook. 1989. Strangler fig rooting habits and nutrient relations in the llano of Venezuela. American Journal of Botany 51: 264–274.

Putz, F., and K. Milton. 1982. Tree mortality rates on Barro Colorado Island. Pages 95–100 *in* E. G. Leigh, Jr., A. S. Rand, and D. M. Windsor, editors. The ecology of a tropical forest: seasonal rhythms and longterm changes, Smithsonian Institution Press, Washington, D.C.

Richards, P. W. 1952. The tropical rainforest: an ecological study. Cambridge University Press, Cambridge.

Ricklefs, R. E. 1977. Environmental heterogeneity and plant species diversity: a hypothesis. American Naturalist 111:376–381.

Rieley, J., P. Richards, and A. Bebbington. 1979. The ecological role of bryophytes in a North Wales woodland. Journal of Ecology 67:497–527.

Runkle, J. 1982. Patterns of disturbance in some old-growth mesic forests of eastern North America. Ecology 63:1533–1546.

Sanford, R. L., Jr. 1987. Apogeotropic roots in an Amazon rain forest. Science 235:1062–1064.

Schaefer, D. A., and W. A Reiners. 1990. Throughfall chemistry and canopy processing mechanisms. Pages 241–284 *in* S. E. Lindberg, L. Page, and S. Norton, editors. Acid precipitation, vol. 3, Sources, deposition and canopy interactions. Springer, New York.

Seastedt, T. R. 1984. The role of microarthropods in decomposition and mineralization processes. Annual Review of Entomology 29:25–46.

Seifriz, W. 1923. The altitudinal distribution of plants on Mt. Gedeh, Java. Bulletin of the Torrey Botanical Club 50:283–305.

———. 1953. The oecology of thicket formation. Vegetatio 4:155–164.

Sena Gomes, A. R., and T. T. Kozlowski. 1980. Growth responses and adaptations of *Fraxinus pennsylvanica* seedlings to flooding. Plant Physiology 66:267–271.

Shreve, F. 1914. A montane rain-forest. A contribution to the physiological plant geography of Jamaica. Publication No. 109. Carnegie Institution, Washington, D.C.

Shugart, H. H., and D. C. West. 1981. Long-term dynamics of forest ecosystems. American Scientist 69:647–652.

Sigmon, J. T., F. S. Gilliam, and M. E. Partin. 1989. Precipitation and throughfall chemistry for a montane hardwood forest ecosystem: potential contributions from cloud water. Canadian Journal of Forest Research 19:1240–1247.

Songwe, N. C., F. E. Fasehun, and D. U. Okali. 1988. Litterfall and productivity in a tropical rain forest, Southern Bakundu Forest Reserve, Cameroon. Journal of Tropical Ecology 4:25–37.

Sousa, S. M. 1968. Ecología de las leguminosas de Los Tuxtlas. Anales del Instituto de Biología, Universidad Nacional de México, Serie Botánica 39: 121–166.

Steinhardt, U., and H. Fassbender. 1979. Características y composición química de las lluvias de los Andes occidentales de Venezuela. Turrialba 29: 175–182.

Stewart, G. H., and T. T. Veblen. 1983. Forest instability and canopy tree mortality in Westland, New Zealand. Pacific Science 37:427–431.

St. John, T. 1980. Uma lista de especies de plantas tropicais brasileiras naturalmente infectadas com micorriza vesicular-arbuscular. Acta Amazonica 10:229–234.

St. John, T., and C. Uhl. 1983. Mycorrhiza at San Carlos de Rio Negro, Venezuela. Acta Cientifica Venezuelano 34:233–237.

Strong, D. R. 1977. Epiphyte loads, tree falls, and perennial forest disruption: a mechanism for maintaining higher tree species richness in the tropics without animals. Journal of Biogeography 4:215–218.

Swaine, M. D., D. Lieberman, and J. B. Hall. 1990. Structure and dynamics of a tropical dry forest in Ghana. Journal of Tropical Ecology 88:31–51.

Systat. Ver. 4.0. 1988. The system for statistics. Systat, Inc., Evanston, Illinois.

Tanner, E. 1977. Four montane rain forests of Jamaica: a quantitative characterization of the floristics, the soils and the foliar mineral levels, and a discussion of the interrelations. Journal of Ecology 65:883–918.

———. 1980a. Litterfall in montane rain forests of Jamaica and its relation to climate. Journal of Ecology 68:833–848.

———. 1980b. Studies on the biomass and productivity in a series of montane rain forests in Jamaica. Journal of Ecology 68:573–588.

———. 1981. The decomposition of leaf litter in Jamaican montane rain forests. Journal of Ecology 69:263–273.

———. 1985. Jamaican montane forests: nutrient capital and cost of growth. Journal of Ecology 73:553–568.

Uhl, C. 1982. Tree dynamics in a species rich tierra firme forest in Amazonia, Venezuela. Acta Cientifica Venezuelana 33:72–77.

Ulrich, B. 1983. Interaction of forest canopies with atmospheric constituents: SO_2, alkali, and earth alkali cations and chloride. Pages 33–45 in B. Ulrich and J. Pankrath, editors. Effects of accumulation of air pollutants in forest ecosystems. Reidel, Dordrecht.

van Steenis, C. G. 1935. On the origin of the Malaysian mountain flora. Part 2. Altitudinal zones, general considerations, and renewed statement of the problem. Bulletin Jardin Botanique Buitenzorg 13:389–417.

———. 1956. Rejuvenation as a factor in judging the status of vegetation types: the biological nomad theory. Pages 212–215 in Proceedings of the Kandy Symposium on Tropical Vegetation. UNESCO, Paris.

Vance, E., and N. Nadkarni. 1990. Microbial biomass and activity in canopy organic matter and the forest floor of a tropical cloud forest. Soil Biology and Biochemistry 22:677–684.

———. 1992. Root biomass distribution in a moist tropical montane forest. Plant and Soil 142:31–39.

Veneklaas, E. 1990. Rainfall interception and above-ground nutrient fluxes in Colombian montane tropical rain forest. Ph.D. thesis, University of Utrecht, Utrecht.

———. 1991. Litterfall and nutrient fluxes in two montane tropical rain forests, Colombia. Journal of Tropical Ecology 7:319–335.

Veneklaas, E., and R. Van Ek. 1990. Rainfall interception in two tropical montane rain forests, Colombia. Hydrological Processes 4:311–326.

Vitousek, P. 1984. Litterfall, nutrient cycling and nutrient limitation in tropical forest. Ecology 65: 285–298.

Vitousek, P., and R. Sanford, Jr. 1986. Nutrient cycling in moist tropical forest. Annual Review of Ecology and Systematics 17:137–167.

Vogelmann, H. W. 1973. Fog interception in the cloud forest of eastern Mexico. Bioscience 23:96–100.

Wadsworth, F. H., and G. H. Englerth. 1959. Effects of the 1956 hurricane on forests in Puerto Rico. Caribbean Forester 20:38–51.

Ward, P. 1987. Distribution of the introduced Argentine ant (Iridomyrmex humilis) in natural habitats of the lower Sacramento valley and its effects on the indigenous ant fauna. Hilgardia 55:1–16.

Weathers, K., G. Likens, F. Bormann, S. Bicknell, H. Bormann, B. Daube, J. Eaton, J. Galloway, W. Keene, K. Kimball, W. McDowell, T. Siccama, D. Smiley, and R. Tarrant. 1988. Cloud water chemistry from ten sites in North America. Environmental Science and Technology 22: 1018–1026.

Weaver, P. L., and P. G. Murphy. 1990. Forest structure and productivity in Puerto Rico's Luguillo Mountains. Biotropica 22:69–82.

Webb, L. J. 1958. Cyclones as an ecological factor in tropical lowland rainforest, North Queensland. Australian Journal of Botany 6:220–228.

Weberbauer, A. 1911. Die Pflanzenweld der peruanischen Anden. Vegetation der Erde 12.

Wheelwright, N. T., W. A. Haber, K. G. Murray, and C. Guindon. 1984. Tropical fruit-eating birds and their food plants. A survey of a Costa Rican lower montane forest. Biotropica 16:173–192.

White, P. S. 1979. Pattern, process, and natural disturbance in vegetation. Botanical Review 45:229–299.

Wiegert, R., and P. Murphy. 1970. Effect of season, species, and location on the disappearance rate of leaf litter in a Puerto Rican rain forest. Pages H-101–H-104 in H. T. Odum and R. F. Pigeon, editors. A tropical rain forest. Division of Technical Information U.S. Atomic Energy Commission, Oak Ridge, Tennessee.

Williams-Linera, G. 1990. Vegetation structure and environmental conditions of forest edges in Panama. Journal of Ecology 78:356–373.

Williams-Linera, G., and R. O. Lawton. 1995. The ecology of hemiephiphyte in forest canopies. Pages 255–283 in M. Lowman and N. Nadkarni, editors. Forest canopies. Academic Press, San Diego.

Wilson, B. F., and R. R. Archer. 1977. Reaction wood: induction and mechanical action. Annual Review of Plant Physiology 28:23–43.

Young, T. P., and S. P. Hubbell. 1991. Crown asymmetry, treefalls, and repeat disturbance in a broadleaved forest. Ecology 72:1464–1471.

Zimmerman, J. K., E. M. Everham, R. B. Waide, D. J. Lodge, C. M. Taylor, and N. V. L. Brokaw. 1994. Responses of tree species to hurricane winds in subtropical wet forest in Puerto Rico: implications for tropical tree life histories. Journal of Ecology 82:911–922.

10

Conservation in the Monteverde Zone

Contributions of Conservation Organizations

Leslie J. Burlingame

Monteverde is renowned among tropical biologists, conservationists, and ecotourists for its cloud forests, quetzals, and Golden Toads. These forest ecosystems have been preserved while many other rain forests in Latin America have been destroyed for agriculture, wood products, and development. Initially, the area was preserved because it was nearly inaccessible; it remains protected because of dedicated efforts by local inhabitants, the development of effective grassroots organizations, and funds and expertise from the international scientific and conservation communities.

In this chapter I document the development and contributions of grassroots conservation organizations that promote conservation practices and thinking. Four organizations preserved forested areas that now constitute the Monteverde Reserve Complex (see Fig. 1.7): (a) Bosqueterno, a reserve and organization formed by the Quaker settlers to protect their watershed; (b) the Monteverde Cloud Forest Preserve (MCFP) managed by the San José–based Tropical Science Center (TSC); (c) Bosque Eterno de los Niños (Children's Eternal Forest; BEN), whose land was acquired by the Monteverde Conservation League

(MCL); and (d) the Santa Elena High School Cloud Forest Reserve (SER) established by the local high school (*colegio*).

Other activities discussed in this chapter are efforts to (1) protect reserve areas, (2) protect forest fragments outside the reserves and create corridors to link forested areas, (3) reforest and rehabilitate damaged land, (4) develop environmental education at all levels, (5) develop complementarity and cooperation among organizations, and (6) establish projects in sustainable development. These topics are linked with the growth of scientific knowledge and the development of ecotourism in the zone.

The thesis of this chapter is that conservation organizations emerged as a series of responses to newly perceived environmental needs and opportunities. I identify successes and failures of conservation efforts by organizations in the Monteverde Zone and the factors responsible for them, analyze problems that have been or need to be resolved, and determine the extent to which institutional developments in the Monteverde Zone may serve as models in conservation and sustainable development for other areas.

Little has been published on the history and current practices of conservation organizations in the Monteverde Zone (Caufield 1984, Wallace 1992). Tourist guidebooks for Costa Rica have brief discussions of conservation organizations in the Monteverde Zone because it is a prime tourist destination (Sheck 1996). Newsletters, booklets, and brochures published by Monteverde Zone conservation organizations are locally available. Most other sources for this chapter are in the "gray literature": annual reports, position papers, grant applications and reports, newsletters, letters, theses, and printouts of data. These sources are available only from the organizations or individuals that produced them. This chapter is complemented by a thesis (Stuckey 1988) and a dissertation (Vivanco 1999). Names and acronyms of organizations are listed in the Key to Abbreviations.

Another information source is a set of interviews that I conducted during 11 two-week visits to the Monteverde Zone between 1992 and 1998. Different sources provide different views and interpretations of the same event, action (or motivation for an action), or institution, reflecting the different standpoints, assumptions, or selective memories of the individuals or organizations. Two approaches used to allow individuals to "speak with their own voices" are essays written by individuals and direct quotations in the text from documents and interviews.

10.1. The Context

Conservation in the Monteverde Zone has been influenced by conservation and broader social, economic, political, and cultural developments at the global level, in Costa Rica, and in the Monteverde Zone.

10.1.1. International Level

The meaning of the term "conservation" changes over time and in different contexts. Through the 1960s, it was applied to soil and water conservation and to efficient and supposedly sustainable management of natural resources such as national forests in the United States. "Preservation" was applied to the protection of pristine wilderness areas. The environmental movement of the 1960s and 1970s was primarily concerned with pollution and the protection of individual endangered species. In the 1980s, conservationists identified a global "biodiversity crisis" and a related crisis in tropical deforestation; the focus of conservation shifted to the ecosystem level. Conservationists concluded that to preserve biodiversity, degraded habitats and watersheds must be restored and isolated patches of surviving forests must be linked (Wilson 1988, McCormick 1989, Grumbine 1992, Worster 1994, Takacs 1996).

In the 1980s and 1990s, park managers realized that the concept of a "wall around a park" was not viable, especially in developing countries. Environmental education for those who live near protected areas and the creation of alternatives to deforestation (e.g., ecotourism) became crucial. Conservation leaders realized that long-term protection of natural areas required more efficient and equitable use of natural resources, or people would move to pristine areas and repeat the process of degradation (McNeely and Miller 1982, Miller and Tangley 1991). Thus, sustainable development ("development that meets the needs of the present without compromising the ability of future generations to meet their own needs") became a goal for modern conservationists (World Commission on Environment and Development 1987, p. 43).

10.1.2. National Level (Costa Rica)

Costa Rica has a long-standing stable democracy, high literacy rate, large middle class, relative prosperity, and a small population. After a brief civil war in 1948, it abolished its army and placed resources into social programs and education. The country has a tradition of welcoming foreigners, including scientists who founded two organizations that had major impacts in the Monteverde Zone (Gómez and Savage 1983).

The TSC, established in San José in 1962 as a private nonprofit association, is a scientific consulting organization that conducts research in ecology, forestry, land-use and watershed planning, environmental impact assessments, and economic evaluations of environmental issues (Hartshorn et al. 1982). One of TSC's founding members, Leslie Holdridge, developed a broadly used life zone classification system (Holdridge 1967). The TSC owns and manages the MCFP. The OTS, founded in 1963, is an educational consortium based in the United States. With more than 50 North American and Costa Rican member institutions in 1998, its primary mission is training graduate and undergraduate students in tropical biology and operating three field stations in Costa Rica (Stone 1988, Tangley 1988). Students taking OTS courses began visiting Monteverde in 1971; most of the biologists who have done research in the zone have been OTS graduates, the students of OTS graduates, or resource scientists for OTS courses. Their publications have enhanced the Monteverde Zone's reputation among scientists and contributed to the growth of research and conservation.

Costa Rica has received international acclaim for its national park system, which underwent great expansion in the 1970s and 1980s. Following standards of the International Union for the Conservation of Nature (IUCN), Costa Rica created management categories for protected lands under government control. Biological reserves and national parks received the highest level of protection, followed by wildlife reserves and forest reserves. In the case of privately held land, the government may mandate conservation restrictions if the area is declared a "protected zone."

In the late 1980s, the government under President Oscar Arias grouped management categories into regional administrative units surrounded by buffer zones. These units ("conservation areas") were administered by the Ministry of Natural Resources, Energy, and Mines (MIRENEM) with the goal of promoting sustainable development around the areas that received strict protection (12% of the country). In 1996, all forms of management were consolidated under the Ministry of the Environment and Energy (MINAE) in the National System of Conservation Areas (SINAC). Administration was decentralized to the directors of each of the ten conservation areas (McNeely et al. 1990, MIRENEM 1992, 1993b, Umaña and Brandon 1992, Wallace 1992, Boza 1993, MINAE 1996a, b).

Much of the Monteverde Zone has been affected by the Arenal Hydroelectric Project, the country's largest generator of electricity, which was inaugurated in 1979 (Hartshorn et al. 1982). Two years earlier, the Costa Rican government had established the Arenal Forest Reserve to protect the watershed and to keep the artificial lake of Arenal (Fig. 1.4) from silting due to runoff. A large reliable supply of water was also important for the Arenal-Tempisque Irrigation Project, which used water that passed through the generators to irrigate dry areas of Guanacaste. Declaration of the Arenal Forest Reserve meant that people living in the reserve area (which includes much of the Monteverde Zone) were not allowed to cut their trees or change land use. The government promised to buy them out but did not have the funds to do so (Lober 1990).

The Arenal Conservation Area (ACA), created in 1991, includes much of the Monteverde Zone; the privately owned MCFP and BEN are part of ACA's Zona Protectora Arenal-Monteverde, which confers a higher level of protection than they previously had as forest reserves. The ACA receives major financial assistance from the Canadian International Development Agency (CIDA) and World Wildlife Fund–Canada (WWF-Canada) for programs in environmental education, government land purchases from private owners, extension, protection, research, and ecotourism (MIRENEM 1993a, b, MINAE 1996a).

Costa Rica's successes in establishing its park system and its special political, economic, and social features attracted large foreign contributions from international government aid programs and conservation organizations when Costa Rica was struck by a debt crisis in the early 1980s. Many nonprofit conservation organizations developed in Monteverde and elsewhere to tap into these funding sources and debt-for-nature swaps (Abramovitz 1989, The Nature Conservancy 1993, Boza et al. 1995).

In the 1980s, Costa Rica became a prime destination for ecotourists. Ecotourism involves traveling to relatively undisturbed natural areas (generally in developing countries) to observe "exotic" plants and animals. It can provide financial benefits to the people living around the protected area and is thus an incentive to continue to protect it. Ecotourism provided economic benefits at the national level; by 1994, tourism replaced bananas as the primary source of foreign exchange for Costa Rica. Ecotourism can also have negative effects. For example, too many tourists in an area can destroy the environment, economic benefits may not go to local people, and negative cultural influences may occur (see Chamberlain, "Pros and Cons of Ecotourism," p. 376).

Costa Rica's success in attracting ecotourists was due to many factors: (1) the country has a high biodiversity (an estimated 5% of the world's species) in a wide range of ecosystem types contained in a small area; (2) a worldwide interest in rain forests was growing; (3) Costa Rica was viewed as a safe, peaceful, democratic, and welcoming place to visit ("the Switzerland of Central America"); and (4) travel logistics from North America and Europe were easy. Costa Rica's park system and its protection of natural attractions were internationally famous and held as a model for other Latin American countries. The Costa Rican government actively promoted tourism, and ecotourism companies emerged in San José to provide guided tours (Boo 1990, Rovinski 1991).

10.1.3. Regional and Local Level

Settlement and development of the area.   The earliest settlers in the Monteverde Zone (Figs. 1.2, 1.4) were indigenous people about whom relatively little is known; their artifacts have been found in the zone (see Timm, "Prehistoric Cultures," pp. 408–409). Specific knowledge of people coming into the area dates to the early 1900s. The Guacimal Land Company had a gold mine where the current town of Guacimal is located, and miners hiked up to the Monteverde area to hunt. Around 1915, a family moved to San Luis and began farming; other settlers arrived in Santa Elena in 1922. In 1929, the first settler families arrived in Monteverde and Cerro Plano; they sold corn, potatoes, sugarcane, guaro (local alcohol), and pigs to miners in Guacimal and in Las Juntas (L. Vivanco, pers. comm.). By 1940, there were 12 farms in Monteverde and more in Santa Elena. About 175 subsistence farmers lived in the zone by 1950 (Gallup 1987). These early settlers practiced some conservation measures, such as reforesting, farming without agrochemicals, and leaving trees to protect water sources and act as windbreaks.

When Quakers from the United States settled in Monteverde in 1951, the land above Cerro Plano and the plateau of Monteverde still had considerable forest cover. Most of the Quakers bought out the "improvements" made by the Costa Rican settlers; land that was cleared of forest and planted with crops was considered more valuable (F. Joyce, pers. comm.). Other Quakers partially cleared forested land, leaving some trees for windbreaks. Some settlers were familiar with U.S. government–sponsored soil and water conservation practices for agriculture (W. Guindon, pers. comm.). Quaker values also encouraged conservation of natural resources (see Guindon, "Monteverde Beginnings," pp. 10–11).

Agriculture, particularly dairy farming, initially built economic prosperity in the area without extremes of wealth or poverty (Fig. 10.1). Organizations such as Productores de Monteverde (dairy plant) and the CoopeSanta Elena (Coope) helped farmers in-

crease production on land that had already been cleared and "helped stabilize the economic situation of many households. This benefited the 'conservation organizations' by leaving them free to preserve, protect, educate and restore, rather than side-tracking them in confrontational clashes over economic issues" (J. Stuckey, pers. comm.; see Chap. 11, Agriculture). The remoteness of the Monteverde Zone from markets and provincial and national governments created a tradition of forming local organizations and committees to deal with issues that would ordinarily be handled by government. By 1995, there were more than 40 local organizations working in conservation, education, production, commercial services, and community infrastructure. These organizations try to resolve problems through consensus and are connected through interlocking memberships (Stuckey 1992, Stuckey et al. 1995; see Burlingame, "Monteverde 2020," pp. 378–379).

The Coope is an example of an organization that although not primarily focused on conservation, has

Figure 10.1. Holstein and Guernsey cows grazing in a Monteverde pasture overlooking the Pacific lowlands. Photograph by Dan Perlman.

played a major role in interinstitutional environmental cooperation. It has sponsored annual school contests and week-long ecological-cultural festivals. The Coope started the school contest in 1985 to encourage children to work together to learn more about environmental problems in the area (e.g., garbage, water sources, birds and their habitats, reforestation, organic gardening). Expenses are underwritten by the Coope, the dairy plant, MCFP, MCL, Monteverde Institute (MVI), and donations. The festival, supported by the same organizations and by hotels and ecotourism businesses, promotes community interaction and awareness of environmental issues and problems of the zone through educational, cultural, and sporting events (C. Vargas and G. Vargas, pers. comm.).

The development of ecotourism. Rapid ecotourism development from the mid-1980s onward created a second economic base for the zone and greatly affected conservation organizations. Those involved in conservation organizations acknowledge that "ecotourism is embedded in conservation here" (F. Joyce, pers. comm.). The types of ecotourists attracted to the area have changed over the years (see Grosby, "Changing Face of Tourism," p. 376).

The development of a tourism infrastructure began with the first pensión, which was built in the early 1950s. Most of the early scientists who came to Monteverde stayed there (M. Moss, pers. comm.). By the late 1980s, hotels and pensións had multiplied; almost all of these were locally owned. By 1998, there were at least 15 medium to large hotels and more than 20 pensións and small hotels in the zone for a total of about 450 rooms and 1000 beds. Individuals also rent rooms in their homes to tourists and students. In 1991, the larger hotels created a chamber of tourism (la camarata); the smaller pensións later formed their own association (G. Arguedas and P. Smith, Jr., pers. comm.).

Large hotels have their own restaurants; restaurants and snack bars ("sodas") have also sprung up. Souvenirs, gifts, local crafts, books, postcards, slides, and artworks featuring local natural history themes are available in shops (see Burlingame, "Comité de Artesanías," pp. 383–384 and "La Campesinita," p. 384). Other tourism businesses include horseback-riding stables and tree canopy tours. The establishment of limits on the number of visitors in the MCFP created an incentive to open nature walks and natural history slide shows on private property. Tourists can observe local animals at the Monteverde Butterfly Garden (see Wolfe, "Monteverde Butterfly Garden," pp. 382–383), the Serpentarium, and the Hummingbird Gallery. These ecotourism businesses serve an educational function and promote conservation and sustainable development (Baker 1994, Rachowiecki 1994, Sheck 1996, Blake and Becher 1997).

Another source of ecotourism employment has been natural history guiding. The first guides had only a familiarity with the area; they showed trails and likely spots for quetzals to bird watchers and scientists. By 1996, guiding provided full-time jobs in the high season for 30 local people. Guides explain complex interactions of the cloud forest to thousands of tourists a year. Although the MCFP, MCL, and MVI have occasionally sponsored classes for local guides to improve their English and guiding skills, most guides learn on their own from bird books (e.g., Stiles and Skutch 1989) and resident biologists, and then pick up group management techniques from more experienced guides (S. Grosby, pers. comm.).

For most tourists, the guide is the local person with whom they may have the most contact. During the tour, the focus is on education and entertainment, with explanations of what exists in the cloud forest, how it works, and the way it affects tourists' lives at home. Most guides finish the tour by pointing out to visitors ways in which they can contribute to conservation in the zone (G. Diller, pers. comm.). Although scientists generate the information about the biota, it is the guide who makes that information accessible to tourists, and tourists who make future conservation an economic reality (S. Grosby, pers. comm.). Guiding can have a strong conservation impact on the guided and on the guide. For example, one Monteverde-born resident killed birds with a slingshot when he was young and later hunted for meat. He repaired chain saws and cut trees for neighbors. As he moved into dairy farming, he developed a claim in the Peñas Blancas valley and resented conservationists' efforts to buy land there because he saw the land as being suited to farming. When he later worked for the dairy plant and MVI, his attitudes changed. In 1990, he started guiding and initiated a night walk program at the MCFP and realized he could make a living because forests had been preserved. In 1996, he launched his own conservation project and foundation to create a new private reserve bordering Rincón de la Vieja National Park (T. Guindon, pers. comm.).

Why did Monteverde become such a popular tourist destination in Costa Rica? In the early 1970s, George Powell published a site report on quetzals in the journal *American Birds* (Fig. 10.2). Other scientists who studied in Monteverde published articles on rare and interesting birds in scholarly journals that were read by serious bird-watchers (Snow 1977, Wheelwright 1983). Larger audiences were reached by BBC's 1978 televised film *Forest in the Clouds* (Tosi 1992). The widely read magazine *International Wildlife* published an illustrated article, "Is this the

Figure 10.2. George Powell, who was among the first biologists to carry out field studies in Monteverde and who was instrumental in the founding of the Monteverde Cloud Forest Preserve. Photograph by John Campbell.

Garden of Eden?" featuring Monteverde and La Selva (Shaw 1978). The popular book *In the Rainforest* (Caufield 1984) contained a favorable chapter on Monteverde and highlighted the connections among politics, biology, and conservation. The National Geographic Society featured Monteverde in a book on "mountain worlds" (D. Robinson 1988); numerous publications and films reached a wide audience by the late 1980s. The reputation of Costa Rica as peaceful democratic country was exemplified in Monteverde; the Quaker community was seen to have a mystique. It was an easy place for people to go who did not speak Spanish, and the MCFP was more accessible than most Costa Rican parks. Guide books for tourists featured Monteverde as a "must visit" location.

Tourism leveled off in the Monteverde Zone between 1992 and 1997 due to four factors: (1) many other places with good tourist facilities developed in Costa Rica; (2) the national parks improved their infrastructure; (3) some tour companies found the Monteverde Zone too expensive, and some individual tourists disliked the high level of tourism; and (4) national tourism slowed since its high point in 1992.

Since late 1997, tourism has again increased in Costa Rica, including the Monteverde Zone, partly due to an international advertising campaign by the Costa Rican government's Tourist Institute (Escofet 1998a, G. Arguedas, pers. comm.). Studies of ecotourism in the Monteverde Zone stress its benefits for conservation and sustainable development but have also documented negative impacts (Tobias 1988, Boo 1990, Rovinski 1991, Tobias and Mendelsohn 1991, Rojas 1992, Solórzano and Echeverría 1993, Wearing 1993, Morrison 1994, Echeverría et al. 1995, Aylward et al. 1996; see Chamberlain, "Pros and Cons of Ecotourism," p. 376).

10.2. The Quakers and Bosqueterno, S.A.

Most of the Quakers who settled in Monteverde came from a Quaker community in Fairhope, Alabama. Several members had refused to register for the peacetime draft after World War II and went to jail. In 1950, Hubert and Mildred Mendenhall, members of the Fairhope meeting, visited Costa Rica and were impressed that Costa Rica had abolished its army. They convinced some Quakers in Fairhope to move there, and an advance team looked for affordable land in April 1951. Shortly afterward, 41 Quakers settled there (Mendenhall 1995, Lucky and W. Guindon, pers. comm.; see Guindon, "Monteverde Beginnings," pp. 10–11).

Most of the land (1400 ha), purchased in a single block from the Guacimal Land Company, was divided among the Quaker families according to the amount of land each family estimated it needed. A parcel in the community center was used for a meeting house and school. The community set aside about one-third of the original purchase to protect their watershed, the headwaters for the Río Guacimal. This portion, the highest steepest land, was forested, wet, and unsuitable for farming but was crucial for their water supply, hydroelectric plant, and community sawmill (Wolinsky 1989, W. Guindon, pers. comm.).

In 1974, the Quakers established an ownership group, Bosqueterno, S.A. (The Eternal Forest), and signed a contract leasing the 554 ha of land they had originally set aside to the TSC for 90 years for one colón per year to be protected and administered as part of the MCFP. The lease was to be renewed automatically every five years unless either party objected in writing three months before the five-year term ended (W. Guindon, B. Law, and J. and S. Trostle, pers. comm.). The mission of Bosqueterno is to serve as the owner of the land and to "preserve, protect, and administer the land of its shareholders" (Stuckey 1992, p. 19). Part of the parcel forms the "Triangle" area, which includes the most heavily used trails in the MCFP. Another portion, Cerro Amigos (1842 m), has several television towers on land leased to the government and private firms (Figs. 1.5, 1.7). As visitation at the MCFP grew, some Bosqueterno stockholders became concerned that TSC was not fulfilling the original terms of the contract. The TSC agreed to give the corporation money from the tower lease on Cerro Amigo to support community projects. In 1998, a Bosqueterno commission established a conservation easement with TSC on Bosqueterno land to restrict development both by Bosqueterno stockholders or their heirs and by TSC.

10.3. The Monteverde Cloud Forest Preserve

The MCFP, founded in 1972, was the first biological reserve in the Monteverde Zone. It initially attracted scientific researchers and later became a magnet for huge numbers of ecotourists. The MCFP has grown from an original 328 ha and two volunteer administrators to about 10,500 ha and a professional staff of 30 (see Figs. 10.3, 10.4).

10.3.1. Origins and Development

The discovery of the Golden Toad or sapo dorado (*Bufo periglenes*) made Monteverde known to the

scientific world. The brilliant orange color of the males and the toads' very limited range were known to some of the Quakers. Publication of a scientific description of the toad caught the attention of the herpetological community (Savage 1966; see Savage, "Discovery of the Golden Toad," pp. 171–172).

In 1970, George Powell (Fig. 10.2) came to Monteverde from the University of California to study mixed-species feeding flocks of birds and used the partially forested farm of John and Doris Campbell, two of the original Quaker settlers (J. Campbell, pers. comm.; Fig. 10.5). Powell became concerned about the rapid disappearance of the forest and focused on two areas to conserve. The first area, east of Bosqueterno on the Atlantic side of the Continental Divide, belonged to the government and people were homesteading on it. If they made "improvements" (e.g., cut trees, planted crops, built a cabin), they obtained rights to the land after one year and would get title to the land after ten years. Powell used his savings to buy out the homesteaders and improvised a bill of sale to provide a legal claim. The second area, the Brillante Tract, the only known breeding area of the Golden Toad, was on the Pacific side of the Continental Divide and belonged to the Guacimal Land Company. The company offered to donate the land if Powell could find a nonprofit organization that was legally recognized in Costa Rica to take it over (G. Powell, pers. comm.).

Figure 10.3. Multilingual entrance sign to the Monteverde Cloud Forest Preserve. Photograph by Leslie Burlingame.

Figure 10.4. Main building of the Monteverde Cloud Forest Preserve. Photograph by Leslie Burlingame.

In 1972, Powell approached the TSC, the eventual owner (Tosi 1992). Powell raised funds from the Explorers Club in New York, The Nature Conservancy (TNC; their first international effort), the German Herpetological Society, and individuals and organizations concerned with bird conservation. The World Wildlife Fund-U.S. (WWF-US) focused on protecting individual endangered species, so Powell's proposal stressed protection of the Golden Toad, Resplendent Quetzal, Bare-necked Umbrella Bird, tapir, and wild cats (G. Powell, pers. comm.).

The MCFP grew as adjoining parcels were purchased with additional funds from WWF and others. In the late 1970s, TSC dealt with three threats: (1) attempts to build a road through the MCFP to develop the Peñas Blancas valley, (2) an attempted government takeover of Bosqueterno land to build a television repeating tower, and (3) government-issued mining concessions in the Peñas Blancas valley (J. Tosi, pers. comm.). By 1986, the MCFP was 4000 ha in size. When MCL started a campaign to purchase additional land in the Peñas Blancas valley in 1986, the plan was

Figure 10.5. John and Doris Campbell, North American Quakers who settled in Monteverde and encouraged biological research on their farm and forest. Photograph by Dan Perlman.

to buy 6000 ha and then turn it over to TSC. By 1998, the deeds to the land had not been given to TSC because of lack of agreement over transfer terms; the dispute is now limited to 4000–5000 ha that are included in the 10,500 ha MCFP cites for its current size (E. Arévalo and B. Carlson, pers. comm.).

The first available figure for annual visitorship to the MCFP is 471 (1973–1974). For the first few years, most visitors were scientists. As they published accounts on the rare and interesting birds in the area, amateur bird-watchers began to visit there. The annual number of visitors climbed to about 50,000 in the 1990s (Fig. 10.6). The number of visitors fluctuated seasonally, with fewest in September and October and the most between January and April, with a second peak in July. A three-year WWF grant provided salary for an administrator and a forest guard. As the size of the MCFP and the number of visitors increased, professional staff grew. By 1993, 53 employees worked in seven departments; the number of employees was reduced to 35 in 1994 because of the leveling off of tourism (Chamberlain 1993, Tropical Science Center 1992–1994). Forest guards (all local Costa Ricans) were added as the MCFP expanded. The guards, who are unarmed, patrol in pairs, communicate by radio telephone, and meet regularly with guards and Directors of the MCFP, MCL, and ACA (Lober 1990, W. Guindon, pers. comm.).

Infrastructure at the MCFP evolved gradually. The main building, which houses the field station, dining room, kitchen, administration offices, library, snack bar, and gift shop, was completed in 1979 with funds from TNC and TSC and construction assistance from Monteverde residents. It was used primarily for OTS graduate courses and MVI courses. In 1991, TSC restricted the living quarters to students on short stays and volunteers working for the MCFP.

A 1982 report for the U.S. Agency for International Development (USAID) published by TSC pointed out that the MCFP had no master plan (Hartshorn et al. 1982). This inspired the management and development plan produced by consultants at the Centro Agronómico Tropical de Investigación y Enseñanza (CATIE 1985). This plan was written before visitation at the MCFP had increased exponentially. Later, TSC obtained a planning grant from the MacArthur Foundation and assembled a team of architects, biologists who had worked at the MCFP, and the MCFP director. They released their "Master Plan for Monteverde Cloud Forest Preserve" in 1991, which proposed a large new visitor center, interpretative trail system, housing complex, and scientific laboratory. The authors extrapolated from rates of increase in visitation and planned for facilities costing $2.5 million with an annual capacity of 135,000 visitors by the late 1990s (Aspinall et al. 1991).

Reaction to the plan by Monteverde residents was negative; they were appalled at the prospect of so many visitors, objected that the community had not been consulted, and wished to consider alternatives, for example, setting limits on the number of visitors. The controversy succeeded in catalyzing community planning for the future and led to improved relations between TSC and the Monteverde community and to TSC's decision to limit the number of visitors. The projected increase in annual visitation proved to be too high; it reached a plateau of about 50,000 starting in 1992, a partial result of limits to visitation imposed at the MCFP. The TSC developed a more modest building plan. By 1998, new construction included a visitor's center with interpretive displays, a bath-

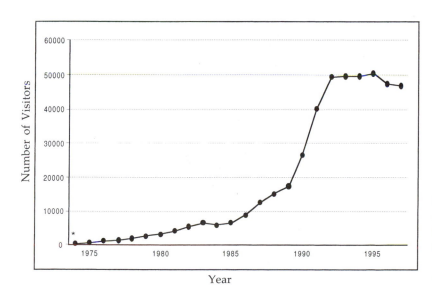

Figure 10.6. Total annual number of visitors to the Monteverde Cloud Forest Preserve (* = May 1973–74). Source: Tropical Science Center (1992–1994), R. Bolaños and B. Carlson (pers. comm.)

room building, a kiosk, ticket booth, workshop and storage building, and a parking lot. The TSC also improved relations with the Monteverde community by contributing money, labor, and equipment to community projects and local schools (R. Bolaños, pers. comm.).

The trail system near the main building (the "Triangle") has expanded, and trails have been developed in the Peñas Blancas valley (Fig. 1.7). Most visitors walk in the Triangle area, which represents only 2% of the total MCFP. About half of the 90 km of trails are used only by guards (B. Carlson, pers. comm.). As tourist usage increased, trails became eroded; in 1990, the MCFP began "hardening" the most frequently used trails (at a cost of $15/m), funded with entrance fees and a grant from USAID (Chamberlain 1993). By 1998, more than 12 km of trails were hardened, mainly with volunteer labor. Three shelters at distant locations are maintained for hikers, researchers, and guards.

Consideration of the master plan also led to the imposition of visitor limits in 1992. Initial proposals for 100 visitors a day met strong protests from hotel owners, and a compromise was worked out. As of 1998, 120 visitors at a time are admitted; they are spread among the trails in the Triangle by MCFP employees (R. Bolaños, pers. comm.). In 1992, the MCFP formalized land-use zoning, designating high use in the Triangle, research use in an area outside the Triangle, and no use in sensitive ecological areas (F. Chamberlain, pers. comm.). A variable fee structure exists; residents of the area are admitted free (Aylward et al. 1996).

10.3.2. Environmental Education

The MCFP established its own environmental education program (EEP) in 1992. The mission of the MCFP's EEP is "to create awareness in local, regional and national populations regarding the importance of natural resource conservation and the critical role of protected areas in preserving wildlife as the heritage of Costa Rica and the biosphere" (Tropical Science Center 1995, Annex 3, p. 19). Ecological concepts and human impacts on the environment are stressed for grades 4–6, which concur with those of the Ministry of Education (Ministerio de Educación Pública, MEP). By 1998, the MCFP's staff was visiting 23 schools each month and providing MCFP-based workshops for teachers. About 300 local students come to the MCFP annually for programs in the EEP classroom and for guided walks. In 1999, the EEP changed the focus to adults, working with the parents of children in six Monteverde Zone schools to increase awareness of the importance of biodiversity conservation and biological corridors (M. Díaz, pers. comm.).

Students from elsewhere in Costa Rica (primary grades through university level) attend workshops and go on hikes. Staff work with communities on local events such as the Ecological-Cultural Festival in Santa Elena. In 1996, the EEP started recycling projects in the zone (Fig. 10.7) and established demonstration projects on organic farming. About 7000 people per year are involved in some aspect of the preserve's EEP, which is funded with proceeds from natural history walks and entry fees (M. Díaz, L. Matarrita, and O. Quirós, pers. comm.).

Educational materials are distributed and sold at the MCFP. A trail map and information brochure are given to all visitors. Illustrated pocket natural history guides can be purchased in the MCFP's gift shop. Resident and visiting scientists convinced TSC they were needed; the scientists wrote and illustrated the guides *pro bono* so that proceeds would provide a fund at TSC to cover the costs of printing guides. Guides contain a short introduction followed by an annotated species list and illustrations (Zuchowski 1987, 1995, Hayes and LaVal 1989, Hayes et al. 1989, Law 1991, Law and Timmerman 1992, Fogden 1993, Nadkarni 1993, Haber et al. 1996, Ingram et al. 1996). The MCFP shop sells photographic slides of animals and plants. In 1992, the Cornell Laboratory of Ornithology made an audio tape of the sounds of the MCFP (Ross 1992); in 1994, TSC produced a videotape, *Life in the Cloud Forest* (Tropical Science Center 1994).

The MCFP established a formal visitors' program and started guided natural history walks in 1989 (Fig. 10.8). Between 1992 and 1995, an annual average of 10,000 people went on the MCFP's natural history walks, which included a slide show (R. Bolaños, pers. comm.). By 1997, the number of people on these walks had declined to 6336 (Tropical Science Center 1998) because more visitors arrived at the MCFP with private guides arranged by their hotels. Guide training courses in 1990 and 1991 were cosponsored by the MCFP and MCL. The 1991 course lasted four months, and participants were paid a stipend. Local biologists gave talks on their specialty areas; daily instruction in English was provided, but it did not provide fluency for the participants. All graduates were immediately employed (Paaby and Clark 1995). A longer guide training program in 1994 that put more emphasis on achieving fluency in English was funded by the RARE Center for Tropical Conservation, Guanacaste Conservation Area, and Horizontes Nature Travel (G. Powell, pers. comm.).

10.3.3. Scientific Research and Its Applications

Although much scientific research has been carried out at the MCFP, many biologists have felt that TSC

Figure 10.7. One of the three recycling stations established by the Monteverde Cloud Forest Preserve in the Monteverde Zone. Photograph by Leslie Burlingame.

could do more to promote research. Some feel that tourism has been promoted at the cost of facilitating research; the number of researchers has declined as tourism has increased (see Chap. 1, Introduction). The MCFP has limited and primitive laboratory facilities with equipment supplied mainly by researchers (N. Nadkarni and N. Wheelwright, pers. comm.). The TSC has sought to rectify this; the master plan of 1991 called for the construction of laboratory facilities and housing for long-term researchers. The MCFP director affirmed in 1996 TSC's commitment to encourage more research; TSC approved plans for a new laboratory building in 1998 and expects to complete construction by 1999 (B. Carlson, pers. comm.). The TSC offers annual specialized scientific courses at the MCFP, including courses on life zone ecology taught in Spanish.

The MCFP is thus emerging as a functioning conservation entity. Biologists have documented the importance of altitudinal migrations in many animal species. They recognize that the land protected in the

Monteverde Reserve Complex is not sufficient to protect altitudinal migrants. A collaborative proposal to establish corridors running from the MCFP to the Inter-American Highway and the Gulf of Nicoya has been made (Musinsky 1991, Tropical Science Center 1995). As a first step to establish this corridor, TSC purchased the largest remaining forest patch on the Pacific side, a 240-ha farm, called the San Luis Biological Station. A fund-raising group established as the Friends of the Monteverde Cloud Forest was formed in 1990 as a U.S.-based tax-exempt organization.

10.4. The Monteverde Conservation League and Bosque Eterno de los Niños

The MCL, founded in 1986, initially focused on land purchase for conservation. Its BEN included more than about 18,000 ha by 1998. The MCL emphasizes long-term protection through environmental education, forest protection, reforestation and restoration of degraded land, sustainable development, and scientific research. Its mission is "to conserve, preserve, and rehabilitate tropical ecosystems and their biodiversity" (MCL *Tapir Tracks*, vol. 7, no. 1, 1992. p. 3; Fig. 10.9).

10.4.1. Origins and Development

By 1985, agricultural development in the Monteverde Zone was threatening much of the remaining Pacific slope forest. A group of community members recognized the urgent need for a locally administered conservation organization. The TSC administered the MCFP from San José and did not manifest concern about activities outside preserve borders. Conversations at town meetings and informal settings led to the formation of the MCL (A. Pounds, pers. comm.). The main organizers at these meetings were Monteverde residents and visitors, many with science backgrounds. The statutes of the MCL laid out its main conservation objectives, which reflect general conservation priorities of the 1980s: "a) the conservation, protection, and recovery of the country's natural resources, including its land, water, air, flora, and fauna; b) the improvement and protection of the physical, biotic, and cultural environment; and c) the search for an adequate balance and a healthy relationship between the inhabitants and nature" (Monteverde Conservation League 1986, p. 1).

The MCL's attention shifted from the Pacific to the Atlantic side of the Continental Divide because of a deforestation crisis threatening the Peñas Blancas valley (Fig. 1.5). Government promises to buy out

Figure 10.8. Natural history guide Gary Diller O'Dell explaining the pollination biology of *Xanthosoma* to tourists in the Monteverde Cloud Forest Preserve. Photograph by Dan Perlman.

claims of valley residents and squatters had not materialized since 1977, when the valley was included in a forest reserve to protect the Arenal Hydroelectric Project. Residents and squatters wanted TSC either to buy them out or open the road through the MCFP into the valley to permit development. Several Monteverde residents and Canadian researchers started a fund-raising campaign to purchase claims and protect the valley. The Portland Audubon Society donated funds, and slide shows at Monteverde Zone hotels raised more than $1000 in 10 days (M. and P. Fogden, pers. comm.). The first land purchase was a farm belonging to Eladio Cruz, who had worked for the MCFP since 1972, marking boundaries, clearing trails, and watching for squatters; his farm house later became a shelter for scientists and guards (E. Cruz and F. Joyce, pers. comm.). The MCL and TSC agreed that MCL would mount a fund-raising campaign, purchase land in the valley up to a certain boundary, and then turn over this land to TSC.

Fund-raising was enormously successful. The WWF-Canada and a widely read Canadian nature magazine helped publicize the campaign and WWF-Canada channeled tax-deductible contributions to MCL. Donors received certificates from MCL showing how many acres they purchased for $25 an acre (Forsyth et al. 1988, B. Robinson 1988, J. Crisp, pers. comm.). William Haber, the first director of the MCL, obtained a $25,000 challenge grant from WWF-US that was matched by funds raised locally and in the United States.

International funding had a profound effect on the MCL. A debt-for-nature swap (see Burlingame, "Debt-for-Nature-Swaps," pp. 377) transformed the MCL from a small organization made up primarily of foreign-born volunteers to a large organization with a paid staff composed primarily of Costa Ricans (C. Echeverría, pers. comm.). In 1987, W. Haber negotiated with the Minister of MIRENEM to include MCL in Costa Rica's first debt-for-nature swap. The WWF-Canada agreed that MCL could use $50,000 raised for

Figure 10.9. Entrance sign to the Monteverde Conservation League office and information center in Cerro Plano. Photograph by Leslie Burlingame.

the Peñas Blancas Campaign as its contribution to the swap (W. Haber, pers. comm.). This swap provided MCL with $200,000 plus interest over five years (1988–1993) to be used for land purchase, administration, and environmental and protection programs (MCL *Tapir Tracks*, vol. 3, no. 1, 1988).

Another debt swap in 1991 funded MCL's purchase of land in the San Gerardo area (see Boll, "San Gerardo," pp. 380–381) and salaries for guards to protect MCL's land. Most of the money for this swap came from the U.S.-based Rainforest Alliance, which organized a radiothon that raised $292,000; TNC contributed $15,000, and MCL put up $53,000. These funds were used to buy $600,000 of discounted debt from the Central American Bank for Economic Integration (CABEI), yielding $540,000 in Costa Rican bonds and interest. This was Costa Rica's sixth debt swap and was the first with a private Central American development bank rather than a public national central bank (Rainforest Alliance 1991; see Burlingame, "Debt-for-Nature Swaps," p. 377).

When settlers and squatters in Peñas Blancas learned that MCL was buying land and claims, they lined up outside the Pensión Quetzal, whose co-owner handled MCL's financial records. Problems surfaced immediately; few people had legal papers for their claims, and some claims overlapped others (B. Law, pers. comm.). Once people had been paid for their claims, MCL had to work through the Costa Rican bureaucracy to get legal title to untitled land. Land also had to be protected from new squatters who, under Costa Rican law, could easily establish claims to it. The MCL and the MCFP hired forest guards to make regular patrols in the Peñas Blancas valley. The guards were unarmed, which was perceived as a "good neighbor" approach. When they intercepted hunters or squatters, their primary goal was to inform and educate. A verbal warning would be given, and with repeat offenses, violators would be subjected to a legal claim ("denuncia") in the local courts (J. Crisp, pers. comm.).

The BEN has become MCL's central focus (Fig. 1.5). In 1987, Sharon Kinsman, a U.S. biologist who had lived in Monteverde during research visits, traveled to Sweden. A Swedish teacher, Eha Kern, invited Kinsman to give a slide presentation at her school. The students came up with the idea of raising money to save rain forests, and Kinsman put them in touch with MCL. The children raised money to purchase 6 ha of cloud forest near the MCFP (Kinsman 1991). Kern and her husband Bernd formed the Swedish nonprofit Barnens Regnskog (Children's Rainforest) to raise and channel funds for MCL's Peñas Blancas Campaign (B. Kern and S. Kinsman, pers. comm.). When the targeted land was purchased, MCL bought additional land that they called Bosque Eterno de los Niños to honor the Quaker settlers who had established Bosqueterno and the children who contributed (Patent 1996).

Barnens Regnskog expanded its support for BEN. Between 1988 and 1992, they raised $2 million for land purchases and obtained grants from the Swedish International Development Agency (SIDA) (B. Kern, pers. comm.). In 1988, SIDA made an $80,000 grant to support reforestation, environmental education, and guards (MCL *Tapir Tracks*, vol. 4, no. 1, 1989). They also purchased equipment for guards and funded construction of a hydroelectric project for the El Buen Amigo project in San Luis (see Vargas, "El Buen Amigo," p. 379). By 1992, SIDA had provided $350,000 in grants to Monteverde Zone projects (B. Kern, pers. comm.).

In 1988, Kinsman established a nonprofit organization, The Children's Rainforest U.S., to formalize fund-raising for BEN. As of 1997, the group had raised almost $500,000 for BEN, contributing to land purchase and later to protection (MCL *Tapir Tracks*, vol. 7, no. 1, 1992, S. Kinsman, pers. comm.). They also prepared educational resources for teachers (Children's Rainforest U.S. 1994, 1996). Other groups raised funds for BEN: Save the Rainforest (Dodgeville, Wisc.), the Chico Friends in Unity with Nature (Chico, Calif.), the Children's Tropical Forests U.K., Kinderregenwald Deutschland, and Nippon Kodomo no Jungle in Japan (MCL *Tapir Tracks*, vol. 6, no. 1, 1991; vol. 8, no. 1, 1993; vol. 9, no. 1, 1994). These seven groups met in Monteverde in 1991 and founded the International Children's Rainforest Network, coordinated by Bernd Kern. They started similar conservation groups in Costa Rica, Belize, Ecuador, Guatemala, and Thailand (Children's Rainforest U.S. 1996). Support for the MCL and BEN has come from schools, individuals (children and adults), and foundations from more than 40 countries (F. Joyce, pers. comm.).

In 1992, MCL's board of directors consolidated all land holdings under BEN, adding 3934 ha purchased with other funds to the 9351 ha in BEN for a total of 13,285 ha (MCL *Tapir Tracks*, vol. 7, no. 1, 1992). By 1998, BEN included about 18,000 ha in three provinces (Puntarenas, Guanacaste, and Alajuela), making BEN the largest private reserve in Central America (F. Joyce, pers. comm.). To aid in the administration of the eastern section of BEN, MCL established a second office in La Tigra (Fig. 1.5). The MCFP assumed guard and maintenance functions in the Peñas Blancas valley. In 1992, MCL launched its "Rain Forest Partners" program (MCL *Tapir Tracks*, vol. 7, no. 2, 1992). Until then, most contributions from individuals to BEN had been earmarked for land purchase. As money from the debt-for-nature swap and other grants was spent, the MCL urged donors to earmark contributions for purposes other than land purchase (R. Sheck, pers. comm.). By 1995, additional land purchase became a low priority for MCL, which had begun formal long-range planning and developed a mission statement in 1991 (MCL *Tapir Tracks*, vol. 7, no. 1, 1992c). The MCL obtained grants in 1993 to hire consultants to draft part of a master plan for BEN (O. Coto, pers. comm.). By 1996, MCL had created several educational centers in BEN (field stations at Poco Sol and San Gerardo and a center at Bajo del Tigre); in 1997, donations funded construction of an educational center and planning for a children's nature center near La Tigra (R. Sheck, pers. comm; MCL Annual Report 1998).

The 30-ha Bajo del Tigre sector in Monteverde (Fig. 1.8) was acquired primarily by donations. The parcel (1020–1380 m on the Pacific slope) contains primary and secondary forest, regenerating pasture, and an arboretum. Three kilometers of trails are maintained with help from volunteers; an interpretative trail guide is available (Law et al. 1998). The trails are used heavily

by bird-watchers, because sighting birds in the open habitat is easy and because lower elevations support birds not found in higher elevation reserves (Law 1993). In 1996, MCL constructed a visitors' center and a children's nature center near the entrance to the trails. The MCL provides facilities and activities especially for children (F. Joyce, pers. comm.). Funds are raised at Bajo del Tigre through entrance fees and the sale of merchandise, such as a BEN video (MCL 1994a) and gifts (S. Sprague, pers. comm.).

10.4.2. Environmental Education

The importance of environmental education was stressed in MCL's statutes. MCL launched its EEP in 1986 by working in local schools and focusing on problems of garbage and pesticide misuse. At that time, the Costa Rican government had not yet included environmental education in the public school curriculum. Money from the first debt-for-nature swap and SIDA supported the expansion of the EEP. Guillermo Vargas, a local teacher, directed and designed environmental education activities in communities around BEN. The EEP staff used a broad definition of environmental education linked to social needs and cultural values (see G. Vargas, "Community Process," pp. 377–378). The goals were to improve the quality of people's lives, to ensure the long-term survival of BEN by helping people make better use of adjacent land, and to understand the importance of protecting BEN.

Efforts of the EEP have focused on children. Staff worked with teachers in local schools to develop programs that related to their curriculum. Emphasizing topics as recycling, composting, water pollution, pesticides, organic gardening, reforestation, and natural history, EEP staff worked in classrooms and led field trips to farms and forests. They established voluntary youth groups that increased environmental awareness through theater presentations to communities (G. Vargas, pers. comm.). Environmental education was linked to MCL's reforestation program; children were taken to MCL's tree nurseries, talked with farmers involved in reforestation, and planted trees on their own farms. The EEP also ran environmental workshops for adults, including teachers, parents, groups of farmers, and women in the craft cooperative, CASEM (G. Vargas, pers. comm.; see Burlingame, "Comité de Artesanías," pp. 383–384).

In 1991, EEP's staff became involved in a controversy with members of MCL's board, who thought environmental education should focus more on the natural history of the forests. The conflict was resolved by recognizing that environmental education should do both. Additional staff were hired to develop pilot programs in natural history in schools (G. Vargas and W. Zuchowski, pers. comm.). The EEP also co-operated with other organizations, including the Coope-sponsored annual school contests, the Santa Elena Ecological-Cultural Festival, and the EEP of the MCFP. In 1994, MCL's EEP worked with ten schools in the Monteverde Zone and five in the La Tigra area and reached other children and adults. The MCL's economic difficulties ended the EEP in 1995, except for projects supported by outside grants. However, many programs and efforts that MCL's EEP initiated continue through other conservation organizations.

10.4.3. Reforestation and Rehabilitation of Degraded Land

MCL's reforestation program has been successful because it improved production on farms, decreased pressure on remaining forest, and created more habitat for wildlife (F. Joyce, pers. comm.). More than half a million trees have been planted in MCL's windbreak project; thousands more have been planted under special projects. Forest fragments are being preserved on farms, and corridors that connect forest fragments with reserves are being established (see Nelson and DeRosier, "Windbreaks and Birds," pp. 448–450 and Harvey, "Windbreaks and Trees," pp. 450–451).

Even before large-scale funding was available, MCL volunteers launched a reforestation program, using

a tree nursery that the Coope had in Cerro Plano (C. Vargas, pers. comm.; Fig. 10.10). The MCL set up a second nursery with different species in lower, warmer, and drier San Luis. Adrian Forsyth, a Canadian naturalist and author, played a key role in the establishment of MCL's reforestation program; in 1988, he obtained a three-year $500,000 grant for MCL from the CIDA and WWF-Canada (MCL *Tapir Tracks*, vol. 4, no. 2, 1989). Other reforestation funds came from a grant the Kerns obtained from SIDA.

The windbreak project meshed MCL's push for reforestation with the stated needs of farmers. Most of the farms in the zone are small; farmers could not afford to use a large portion of their farms for reforestation or natural forest regeneration. The negative effects of strong winds during the dry season in the zone (soil erosion, stress on pasture and crops, and resulting decreases in milk and crop production) created intense interest among farmers to plant windbreaks (F. Joyce, pers. comm.). Farmers also needed trees for fenceposts, lumber, fuel wood, food for cattle, and soil enrichment. Windbreaks that included leguminous trees were the solution. Tree seedlings were produced with help from the U.S. Peace Corps and other volunteers and delivered to farms by MCL personnel, who also provided technical assistance. The farmers had to invest their own labor, which tied them to the project. They received financial incentives provided by The Netherlands through the Costa Rican

Figure 10.10. Seedling nursery administered by the Monteverde Conservation League. Photograph by Dan Perlman.

Forest Service (Dirección General Forestal, DGF) to cover expenses of planting and fencing in the form of a loan that was forgiven if the farmer cared for the trees for three years. Windbreaks are usually mixed species of trees planted in strips four trees wide, with fencing to keep out cattle (Fig. 12.4). Wooden fence posts were used until 1991, when they were replaced in part by living fence posts to reduce tree-cutting (MCL *Tapir Tracks*, vol. 6, no. 1, 1991, vol. 7, no. 1, 1992, vol. 7, no. 2, 1992). By 1994, more than 500,000 trees produced in the nurseries had been planted by 263 farmers in 320 windbreak projects (MCL Annual Report 1994; *Monteverde Journal*, vol. 2, no. 2, 1995). Farmers perceived that windbreaks increased milk and crop production and contributed to their wood needs and to wildlife habitat (M. V. Zamora and O. Varela, pers. comm.).

At first, exotic species such as casuarina (*Casuarina equisetifolia*) and cypress (*Cupressus lusitanica*) were planted because they were known to farmers and foresters and were on the DGF list of species approved for incentives. The MCL investigated the use of native species in its nurseries, asking farmers about promising trees and then collecting seeds by hand from local trees. Some species worked well for windbreaks; they were resistant to diseases and pests that affected exotic species. The DGF eventually added some native species to their list of approved trees. Demonstration plots led farmers in the zone to use native species and naturalized exotics such as Colpachi (*Croton niveus*). Another windbreak species, Tubú (*Montanoa guatemalensis*), is native to Pacific slope elevations between 700 and 1200 m but grows well above that elevation. It is the most widely used "native" species in windbreaks because it grows very quickly and its high leaf volume creates an effec-

tive barrier to wind (MCL 1994b, c, d, F. Joyce, pers. comm.).

The MCL promoted success in reforestation by recognizing the achievements of reforesters through the Day of the Reforester, which honored the best windbreak projects of the year. The reforesters wanted more of a voice in MCL, and in 1992 they staged a demonstration at MCL's office, demanding to be made full members of the general assembly. If this were granted, reforesters would have had the majority vote in determining MCL policies since the general assembly elects the board. The MCL instead set up a separate Foresters' General Assembly, which created some resentment among reforesters (W. Guindon, pers. comm.). In 1995, MCL's grants for windbreaks ran out and government restructuring ended DGF's incentive program, so the reforestation program ended. The windbreaks are likely to remain since they benefit the farmers (G. Vargas, pers. comm.).

The MCL developed two forest preservation projects with local communities. In 1989, MCL signed an agreement with El Buen Amigo cooperative in San Luis (Fig. 1.7) to lease their forest for ten years and help them with sustainable development (Fig. 10.11). The cooperative used lease money to buy an adjoining dairy farm to expand their milk production (see E. Vargas, "El Buen Amigo," p. 379). In 1990, community members of La Cruz asked MCL to raise funds to purchase 7.9 ha of primary and secondary forest containing springs, their sole source of water. The community established a legally recognized association to manage and protect the La Cruz Reserve when MCL turned it over to them (MCL Annual Report 1997).

The Forests on Farms and Corridors Project, an extension of the reforestation program (1993–1997), was funded by international conservation organiza-

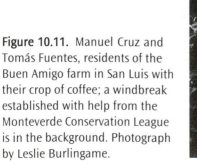

Figure 10.11. Manuel Cruz and Tomás Fuentes, residents of the Buen Amigo farm in San Luis with their crop of coffee; a windbreak established with help from the Monteverde Conservation League is in the background. Photograph by Leslie Burlingame.

tions. It focused on buffer zone management around the Monteverde Reserve Complex, particularly the protection of forest fragments on farms that researchers had deemed important for altitudinal migrations of birds and butterflies. Researchers, environmental educators, and extensionists worked with 42 farmers to protect fragments with fences, encourage reforestation with native species to create corridors that linked the fragments with larger protected areas, and protect water caption locations and the banks of water courses. New government incentives, consisting of forest certificates that provide $50/ha yearly, were available to farmers who protected forests with fencing and agreed not to cut or use that forest (F. Joyce, pers. comm.). In 1995 and 1996, 260 ha of forest fragments were protected. The project promoted sustainable use of forests in buffer zones by stressing the economic and ecosystem benefits forests provide (MCL *Tapir Tracks*, vol. 9, no. 1, 1994, Guindon 1996, MCL Annual Report 1998, E. Arévalo and C. Guindon, pers. comm.). This reflected a larger scale shift among conservationists in the general approach of restoration and rehabilitation of watersheds.

The MCL, ACA, and the Ministerio de Agricultura y Ganadería (MAG) cooperated on a grant from the Dutch government in 1995 for sustainable development and watershed rehabilitation in the La Tigra area. The project supported research on water pollution, land-use capacity, and biodiversity conservation. It also worked on reforestation, soil improvement with emphasis on organic fertilizers, involvement of women in tree nurseries and organic gardening, and environmental education in local schools (MCL *Tapir Tracks*, vol. 10, no. 1, 1995; Y. Morales, pers. comm.). A three-year project (funded by WWF-Holland) synthesizing elements of the Forests on Farms and the La Tigra projects began on the Atlantic side of BEN in 1996 (MCL Annual Report 1997, E. Arévalo, pers. comm.).

10.4.4. Recent Directions

In 1994, MCL created a biological research program for BEN at the urging of biologists. They hired a research coordinator to promote and facilitate research and information flow in BEN and nearby areas (F. Joyce, pers. comm.). Previous research in BEN included a 1991 rapid biological assessment of the Poco Sol area (MCL *Tapir Tracks*, vol. 6, no. 1, 1991) and a few individual studies. The MCL operates two field stations in BEN, San Gerardo (see Boll, "San Gerardo," pp. 380–381) and Poco Sol (MCL *Tapir Tracks*, vol. 10, no. 1, 1995). In 1994, the MCL sponsored its first scientific symposium, "Altitudinal Migrations in Tropical Forests," in cooperation with TSC and ACA at the San Gerardo station (E. Arévalo, pers. comm.). Biologists from the MCL car-

ried out ecological studies on Bare-necked Umbrella birds in 1997–1998, with a grant from the British Embassy (MCL Annual Report 1997, 1998).

By 1994, MCL developed economic problems because the original debt-for-nature swap and several major grants ran out of funds and contributions were still earmarked for land purchase. "The League was forced to cut back its operations because its income was not keeping up with costs. This predicament occurred in part because MCL's board and staff had not developed the ability to obtain the financial resources needed to continue operating at the same level" (F. Joyce, pers. comm.). The MCL was reorganized and personnel cut sharply (MC Annual Report, 1995; R. Sheck, pers. comm.). In 1995, publication of *Tapir Tracks* ceased. New statutes for the MCL were adopted (MCL 1996), and a building in Cerro Plano was purchased for its offices in 1996. Since then, it has been successful in obtaining grants to support projects. Since 1997, MCL has taken a leadership role in the new Costa Rican Network of Private Reserves and in the Costa Rican Federation of Environmental Organizations, which are lobbying the government for changes in environmental laws and policies. In 1997, MCL began to get Costa Rican government Forest Protection Certificates and funds for a small portion of BEN. The MCL signed a landmark agreement in 1998 with a private hydroelectric company to receive up to $30,000 per year for 99 years for watershed protection by BEN (MCL Annual Report, 1997, 1998; E. Arévalo, F. Joyce, and S. Murillo, pers. comm.). The MCL requires at least $250,000 a year to cover basic operations, and much more to include environmental education and reforestation (F. Joyce pers. comm.).

10.5. Santa Elena High School Cloud Forest Reserve

The highest elevation reserve (1700 m) in the Monteverde Reserve Complex is the SER. It opened in 1992 and is located off an unpaved road 6 km north of the town of Santa Elena (Fig. 1.7). The SER's 310 ha consist of 80% primary and 20% secondary forest. It borders BEN and is part of the Arenal-Monteverde Protected Zone in ACA. The SER has become a popular tourist destination and is involved in environmental education. It was the first Costa Rican reserve in which the government leased property to a high school for an ecotourism project.

Originally, SER was part of government-owned land available for homesteading, and a private farm was established there. The farm became part of the Arenal Forest Reserve in 1977. Legal irregularities led to government expropriation, and in 1982 DGF gave a long-term lease on this farm to the Santa Elena high school. The school, which focused on vocational training in agriculture and home economics (Stuckey 1992), tried to develop the farm, but the wet conditions and bad road hampered farming. By 1988, the high school's declining enrollments and economic problems led to a search for new uses for the farm.

This search coincided with the growth of ecotourism. Some Santa Elena residents resented the MCFP because they perceived that the money was going to TSC in San José instead of providing local benefits (L. Vivanco, pers. comm.). The high school proposed to MIRENEM that the farm be developed as an ecotourism reserve to provide local financial benefits. Funds from entrance fees would provide money for school programs, facilities, and supplies. The SER would also provide employment for local people, including high school students. Tourism in Santa Elena would increase the need for local housing, food, and taxis. Several of the hotels in the Monteverde area, concerned over the impact of visitor limitations at the MCFP, were willing to offer support for the development of an alternate tourist destination (Wearing 1993, F. Valverde, pers. comm.).

In 1991, the high school signed a five-year lease with MIRENEM to develop the farm as an ecotourism project. A Canadian volunteer group, Youth Challenge International (YCI), brought volunteers from Canada, Australia, and Costa Rica to join volunteers from the high school and build the infrastructure of SER. They constructed the visitor's center and its displays, cafeteria, guard station, and dormitory. They built trails and an Arenal volcano viewing platform, conducted community impact surveys of tourism, established a biological garden, and obtained support for SER from WWF-Canada (Wearing 1993, Youth Challenge International 1994). Other volunteers have extended the trail system; four trails covered 12 km by 1998. Improved signage, better road access, and bathroom facilities also have been constructed (F. Valverde, pers. comm.). Several local hotels, alarmed by the increasingly long lines of disgruntled tourists waiting to get into the MCFP, donated construction materials, and MIRENEM gave funds for the dormitory (L. Sáenz, pers. comm.).

The visitor's center at SER has an extensive interpretative display. The walls are covered with bilingual posters and murals that educate visitors on general cloud forest ecology and the history and mission of the SER. Students from the zone and other areas of Costa Rica are given educational tours. The high school's applied ecology program uses SER for study and research, training students for jobs with biologists, and preparing students to become natural history guides (L. Vivanco, pers. comm.).

When SER opened, there were relatively few visitors; visitation increased from 3100 in the first year of operation (March–December 1992) to more than 13,000 in 1994 and 1995 (Fig. 10.12). Increase in visitorship was due to five factors: (1) local hotels recommended SER because there were waiting lines at the MCFP; (2) lower entrance fees ($5 for foreign tourists versus $8 for the MCFP); (3) SER was more rustic, providing a greater sense of adventure and opportunities to see more birds; (4) SER directly aided the local community, which appealed to many tourists; and (5) travel guides included it beginning in 1994 (L. Sáenz, pers. comm.). Decreases in visitorship in 1996 and 1997 (Fig. 10.12) were primarily due to declining numbers of tourists coming to Costa Rica, but some of the decline in 1997 was due to the opening of the "Skywalk" on the road leading to the SER, which siphoned off some potential visitors.

The SER was originally managed by the high school's administrative board. In 1994, a nonprofit foundation, Fundación Centro Ecológico Bosque

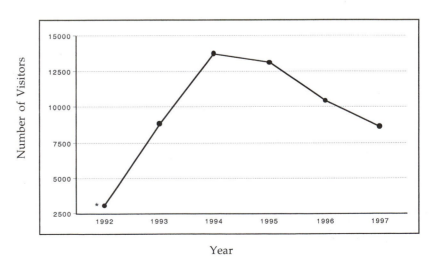

Figure 10.12. Total annual number of visitors to the Santa Elena Reserve (* = March-December 1992). Source: L. Sáenz and F. Valverde (pers. comm.).

Nuboso de Monteverde, was established by community leaders to operate SER and use its profits to improve local education and encourage the development of local ecotourism services (F. Valverde, pers. comm.). Management of SER was returned in 1995 to the high school, which negotiated a five-year lease that began in 1997 with MINAE, the successor to MIRENEM (L. Sáenz, pers. comm.).

10.6. The Monteverde Institute

The MVI complements other conservation organizations in the Monteverde Zone. Founded in 1986, MVI provides courses in tropical ecology, conservation, agroecology, and Spanish language instruction for high school and undergraduate college students and teachers and other adults from the United States. The proceeds from those courses fund culturally enriching activities for the Monteverde community and focus on education and sustainable development (MVI 1996b).

10.6.1. Origins and Development

According to John Trostle, one of MVI's founders, its roots lie in biology classes at the Monteverde Friend's School from the 1960s, a growing "love of nature" among Quaker families who welcomed the presence of biological researchers, and the visits of graduate tropical biology courses run by OTS (Trostle 1990). Several Monteverde researchers wished to bring undergraduate courses to the cloud forest. Twenty-eight residents of Monteverde, almost all of whom were originally from North America, served as founders of the nonprofit "Asociación Instituto de Monteverde." The original aims of MVI were to "a) promote education, culture, and scientific investigation in the areas of biology and agriculture; and b) organize musical and dramatic presentations, as well as congresses, symposia, conferences, courses, and talks, on cultural, educational, or scientific themes" (MVI 1986, p. 2). In 1990, MVI broadened its focus to highlight sustainable development and developed a mission statement:

> The Monteverde Institute is a non-profit association dedicated to peace, justice, knowledge, and the vision of a sustainable future. It provides and coordinates programs that promote the appreciation of diversity and community, spirituality and the well-being of living things. These opportunities are designed for people from abroad and Costa Rica, and for residents of the Monteverde community and surrounding areas (MVI 1993a, p. 1).

The first University of California Education Abroad Program (UCEAP) in Monteverde in 1987 developed a format that is used for courses of 8–10 weeks that receive college credit in the United States. The central focus of the program is tropical biology, which introduces students to tropical diversity and ecology through lectures by faculty and resident or visiting researchers, and field projects. Conservation issues are essential components of the courses (F. Joyce, pers. comm.). These programs also include components on agroecology, taught by local biologists and farmers. Students are introduced to farming, land-use practices, sustainable agriculture, conservation practices, and ecotourism (Council on International Educational Exchange 1993). Spanish language and local culture are taught by local native Spanish-speaking instructors, and homestays are provided by local Costa Rican families. An independent study project is based on fieldwork; each student makes an oral presentation in a session open to the community and leaves a copy of his or her paper at MVI.

The "long courses" are modified to an abbreviated form for "short courses" (10–14 days) that MVI arranges for North American colleges, universities, high schools, and conservation organizations. These courses, which generally enroll about twice as many students as the long courses, provide over half of MVI's income (MVI Annual Report 1995). In keeping with MVI's focus on sustainable development, a long course, "Sustainable Futures," was launched in 1995 for students in landscape architecture and planning. They planned and designed projects for institutions in the area, including MCL, MVI, the dairy plant, and the Monteverde Greenways Project (Enlace Verde; L. Schneekloth and B. Shibley, pers. comm; see Scrimshaw et al., "Conservation Easements," pp. 381–382). In 1997, MVI started an international development seminar, Sustainability: Social and Environmental Consciousness in Costa Rica (MVI Annual Report 1997). By 1998, MVI had run 45 long and 113 short courses (MVI Annual Report 1996, 1997; L. Wirtanen, pers. comm.). Student enrollments show a generally increasing trend (Table 10.1). All courses directly and indirectly provide employment for local people, including biologists, teachers, MVI staff, taxi drivers, cooks, and guides. In 1998, MVI employed a staff of fifteen local residents (L. Wirtanen, pers. comm.).

As MVI expanded, a house near the dairy plant was purchased for offices and a library. The latter was named to honor Quaker residents John and Doris Campbell. The new (in 1997) headquarters of the MVI was designed, built, and landscaped to embody principles of sustainable development through "maximum use of passive solar lighting, cisterning water, storm drainage systems, and materials choice" (MVI Annual

Table 10.1. Number of students in Monteverde Institute courses by fiscal year (October–September).

Fiscal Year	Long Courses	Short Courses	Total
1986–87	18	0	18
1987–88	23	41	64
1988–89	37	126	163
1989–90	36	230	266
1990–91	32	249	281
1991–92	50	217	267
1992–93	99	284	383
1993–94	98	303	401
1994–95	89	153	242
1995–96	110	116	226
1996–97	121	181	302
1997–98	166	101	267
Total	879	2001	2880

Source: L. Wirtanen, J. Longino (pers. comm.).

Report 1997, p. 2). Located adjacent to the dairy plant in the center of Monteverde, the facility houses offices, computers, the library, classroom space, and community meeting areas. Establishing model conservation easements for this and other property and linking easements with the Guacimal River Greenway Project were a high priority (MVI Annual Report 1997).

Students in MVI courses lived and had classes in MCFP's main building and in local pensións and hotels until 1991, when the TSC limited housing to short-term groups. The long-term courses moved to the Biological Station (Estación Biológica), which had been built by Canadian entomologist Monty Woods. The building contains sleeping and dining facilities and laboratory and computer space and offers access to primary and secondary forest (Q. Newcomer, pers. comm.). MVI produces brochures and annual reports and published a newsletter (*Monteverde Journal*) in 1994–1995. The Alliance for the Monteverde Institute, a U.S. tax-exempt organization, was established in Massachusetts in 1993.

10.6.2. Community Development Programs

The MVI uses funds from contributions and courses to support programs that benefit the community, such as biological field trips for teachers and students, ecology classes at the SER, bird identification walks, environmental education in schools, and a children's ecology group. They cooperate with other organizations in the annual Ecological Festival (MVI Annual Reports 1987–1997). In 1996, MVI cooperated with MCL to give a short course for natural history guides at the San Gerardo field station (R. Kropp, pers. comm.).

In 1992, MVI developed support groups for women.

They helped local women's groups (e.g., La Campesinita; see Burlingame, "La Campesinita," p. 384) to develop administrative skills and to link women's groups in the Monteverde Zone with other organizations in Costa Rica. They developed the Family Life Program for women, which dealt with economic autonomy, self-esteem, leadership, nutrition and health, literacy, and domestic violence, recognizing that women's concerns and activities are crucial for sustainable development (A. Marin, pers. comm.). Although women in the region have had little public role in decision-making, they make many daily decisions about using natural resources such as water, firewood, and electricity. They also decide what the family eats, produce some of that food, and determine what to do with wastes (*Monteverde Journal*, vol. 1, no. 2, 1994). In 1997, MVI launched a Gender and Women's Studies Program, with faculty seminars and undergraduate programs that focus on women and development (MVI Annual Report 1997; I. Leitinger, pers. comm.).

In another approach to fundraising, the MVI produced a 1996 "Monteverde Artists Postcard-Calendar." Local artists donated their work; proceeds from sales supported the Family Life Program and the scholarship fund for local schools (MVI Annual Report 1995). A ceramics center was built in 1995 as a cooperative project among MVI, resident potters, and the Comité de Artesanías Santa Elena–Monteverde (CASEM; *Monteverde Journal*, vol. 2, no. 2, 1995; see Burlingame, "Comité de Artesanías," pp. 383–384). The MVI Volunteer Center was established jointly with the MCL in 1990 to place the many volunteers attracted to the Monteverde Zone. By 1997, the center had placed 386 volunteers with nonprofit groups in the area. Volunteers have contributed to local schools, helped the MCL with tree nurseries and reforestation, maintained trails, and staffed visitor's centers in the MCFP, SER, and MCL's Bajo del Tigre section of BEN (MVI Annual Reports 1987–1997, L. Wirtanen, pers. comm.).

10.7. Environmental Education in Public and Private Schools

Costa Rica has compulsory free public education for grades 1–8. All communities in the Monteverde Zone with at least 18 potential students have government-supported primary schools. These schools lack adequate resources, and they have difficulty attracting and retaining qualified teachers (Stuckey 1992). Schools are controlled by the centralized Ministry of Public Education (Ministerio de Educación Pública, MEP), which has developed curriculum plans that incorporate environmental education. However, to implement the curriculum plans, local rural teachers need training and materials, which have come primarily from the environmental education programs at the MCFP and MCL (M. Díaz, pers. comm.).

There are three private schools in the area. The oldest school, the Monteverde Friends School (MFS), was established when the Quakers settled in Monteverde to provide an education based on Quaker values. The school shares facilities with the meeting house (Mendenhall 1995). The MFS has a kindergarten and grades 1–12, with instruction primarily in English and a high teacher-to-student ratio (Stuckey 1992). In 1998, the MFS had 67 students, many of whom were on scholarships (T. Curtis, pers. comm.). The school works toward being accredited in Costa Rica, which involves developing a more formal curriculum, including an environmental component that fits with the Quaker values of living in harmony with nature (K. VanDusen, pers. comm.). Environmental awareness has been important since the MFS began, when students were affected by the example of their parents' protection of their watershed. Many helped clear its boundaries (L. Guindon, pers. comm.). By the mid-1990s, most science presented was ecologically or environmentally oriented. For example, classes have visited reforestation projects and tree nurseries, been involved in organic gardening projects, and created interpretative nature trails. Resident and visiting biological researchers give school presentations. MFS students regularly visit the MCFP and participate in its EEP (T. Curtis, pers. comm.).

The bilingual Seventh Day Adventist School was founded in 1991. The Adventist founders of the school felt that there was a need for another Christian bilingual school since the growth of ecotourism was creating job opportunities. They used the skeleton of MEP's curriculum and adapted it to bilingual and Adventist religious instruction. In 1998, the school had 38 students in kindergarten through ninth grade. The school is interested in teaching conservation awareness and participates in the MCFP's EEP. Teachers emphasize the importance of vegetarianism from the perspectives of ecology and world hunger, ethics and religion, and health. Reflecting local Adventist values, the school stresses responsibility for the stewardship of the earth and the necessity of sustainable living (L. Guindon, pers. comm.).

The Centro de Educación Creativa (CEC) represents two firsts for conservation in Costa Rica: it is the first school with a curriculum focused around environmental education, and the land for the school has been protected by one of the country's first conservation easements (CEC Bulletin, Aug. 1991, Apr. 1992; M. Wallace, pers. comm.). By 1992, the group established legal status as a non-profit association in Costa Rica and developed a fund-raising document (CEC 1992b).

The CEC was founded to respond to the special educational needs of Monteverde, Costa Rica. This community is surrounded by rare and endangered Cloud Forest. We believe the survival of our forest requires a new generation of ecologically aware, bilingual residents to respond to increasing pressures of tourism and development. The CEC promises its students academic excellence from Kindergarten through High School in an interdisciplinary curriculum centered around environmental education. (CEC Bulletin, Mar. 1994)

The CEC participated in a loan fund established by TNC. Their Latin American Program worked with the Costa Rican environmental law group, Centro de Derecho Ambiental y de los Recursos Naturales (CEDARENA), to protect privately owned forests in Costa Rica (R. Wells, pers. comm.). Costa Rican law has recognized one type of deed restriction on private property: rights-of-way (easements) for certain purposes. Lawyers at CEDARENA argued that endangered species could be given rights-of-way for critical food and breeding sites between protected areas (parks, biological reserves) and residual forest patches on private property. These rights would be similar to those traditionally granted for cattle that require access to water, thus justifying conservation corridors and the conservation of forest fragments on private property in the vicinity of protected areas (Atmetlla 1995).

The Nature Conservancy purchased a 42-ha farm that was partially forested. George Powell wrote an ecological justification for its purchase based on his radiotelemetry studies of Resplendent Quetzals. He concluded that the "wide strips of forest . . . provide a bridge for migrating quetzals and a critical source of food in this altitudinal zone" (G. Powell, pers. comm.). The CEC negotiated an option to buy the property with TNC. A conservation easement, held by MCFP's owner TSC, was added to the deed. In 1993, CEC established a U.S.-based non-profit organization, Cloud Forest School Foundation, which raises funds, recruits staff, and organizes the transport of supplies from the U.S. (CEC Bulletin, Mar. 1994).

Volunteers assist teachers in the classrooms, organize the library, work in an organic garden at the school, and develop curriculum. Staff, board members, consultants, and parents developed a curriculum that makes bilingual environmental education a unifying theme across all academic subjects and school activities. Students visit the MCFP, the Bajo del Tigre sector of BEN, and SER. The CEC is working toward being accredited in Costa Rica and having its curriculum recognized as a model for environmental education. By 1998, the school went through the eighth grade and matriculated 130 students, more than half of whom were on scholarships (Cloud Forest School Foundation 1998, R. LaVal, pers. comm.).

The Monteverde Zone has inspired six books and materials that provide environmental education for children. Biologist Adrian Forsyth's book for children, *Journey through a Tropical Jungle* (1988), describes a trip from the Pan American Highway to the MCFP and into the Peñas Blancas valley; he emphasizes ecology and conservation. Martha Moss, a long-time resident of Monteverde and owner of the original pensión, created an audio tape in which she tells *Animal Stories from the Cloud Forest for Children of All Ages* (1988). Her stories are based on real events involving animals, their human caregivers, and their rehabilitation and release into the wild. A story from this tape (translated into Spanish) is included in the illustrated *Cuentos del Bosque Nuboso* (Stories from the Cloud Forest; Gorini et al. 1996). Stories deal with forest ecology, impacts of deforestation, and the importance of protected areas. *Children Save the Rain Forest* (Patent 1996) focuses on the ecology of BEN, the way children helped buy it, and MCL's programs in forest protection and environmental education. Another children's book describes Monteverde forests through the eyes of scientists working there and emphasizes interactions between researchers and conservation activities (Collard 1997). *Flute's Journey* (Cherry 1997) portrays the migration of a wood thrush between Maryland and the MCL's BEN, and explains how both of its "homes" have been preserved.

10.8. Conclusion: Lessons from Monteverde and Topics for Future Research

The Monteverde Zone has produced a rich set of case studies in conservation and sustainable development, including promotion of community cooperation (Monteverde 2020; see Burlingame, "2020," pp. 378–379), community projects in sustainable development (El Buen Amigo, San Gerardo, Enlace Verde), and ecotourism projects (Monteverde Butterfly Garden, CASEM, and La Campesinita). Most of these case studies are success stories, but some illustrate good ideas that have not worked out in practice.

Success and failure in conservation are relative terms. Quantitative data on the amount of forest that has been preserved are available, but whether that is enough to sustain the biodiversity of the Monteverde Zone and whether the Monteverde Reserve Complex is in danger of becoming an isolated island are unknown. Data on the number of trees that have been planted for windbreaks and in watershed restoration projects exist, but determining the success of these trees in countering environmental degradation is problematic. We tally how many children have been exposed to environmental education programs in the area, but how this education affects their behavior as adults is unknown. Data on the number of visitors to the reserves and estimates of the amount of money ecotourists spend in Monteverde exist, but we do not know whether ecotourism will create more harm than good. Further research should evaluate progress in these areas and those discussed below over short- and long-term time scales.

10.8.1. Successes of Conservation Organizations

(1) One aspect of conservation success is the amount of forest that has been acquired. By 1998, MCL's BEN included about 18,000 ha (excluding Peñas Blancas), the MCFP included about 10,500 ha (including Bosqueterno and Peñas Blancas), and SER included 310 ha, making a total of about 29,000 ha in the Monteverde Reserve Complex (Fig. 1.7). These are all part of the larger Arenal Conservation Area, including the new Arenal National Park, which gives a measure of protection to 800,000 ha. Wolf Guindon (Fig. 1.2), a Quaker settler who played a role in land acquisition for BEN and MCFP, recounted:

> I emerged onto a ridge with a super view of Arenal volcano some 8 km away as those with wings travel, or 14 km, as those without wings travel. The volcano looked its majestic self, but it was those dozens of forested wrinkles between us that impressed me. At that moment, the realization hit me that this scene, with all of the forest I could see as I turned full circle, was now owned and managed by organizations that have as their number one commitment the preservation of this area. (MCL *Tapir Tracks*, vol. 9, no. 2, 1994)

(2) The use of local residents as unarmed guards to patrol and explain the importance of protected areas to local people has been successful in curbing squatting, poaching, and tree-cutting (Lober 1990, 1991). Reserve administrators realize they cannot build walls around protected areas, so it is crucial to develop constructive relationships with people living around them.

(3) MCL's "Forests in Farms" project initiated the idea of linking forest fragments on private property to create corridors for altitudinally migrating fauna. Two other corridor projects are under development,

Enlace Verde (see Scrimshaw et al., "Conservation Easements," pp. 381–382), and TSC's proposed biological corridor from the MCFP to the Inter-American Highway. Both projects are developing conservation easements along the corridors, following the precedent set by the CEC. In 1998, Bosqueterno, S.A. established conservation easements on its land.

(4) Large scale reforestation began with MCL's reforestation program, which planted more than 500,000 trees as windbreaks on farms in the area. Both exotic and native species have been planted. Windbreaks benefit farmers by increasing agricultural productivity and providing habitat for wildlife; windbreaks that link forest patches are used as biological corridors (see Nielsen and DeRosier, "Windbreaks and Birds," pp. 448–450 and Harvey, "Windbreaks and Trees," pp. 450–451). The MCL has also pioneered watershed rehabilitation projects.

(5) Environmental education is offered in the Monteverde Friends School and the Adventist School and is the focus of the curriculum in the CEC. Local public schools, aided by MCL and MCFP, include environmental education due to national curricular reform by MEP. The MVI includes environmental education in its program for foreign university students. Ecotourists receive environmental education in the MCFP's natural history walks, from private guides, and through interpretative trails and visitors' centers in the Monteverde Reserve Complex. These environmental education programs demonstrate how conservation organizations have moved beyond the "wall around the park" concept.

(6) A key to the success of conservation in the Monteverde Zone has been the emergence of organizations to meet new needs. Each organization has focused on certain aspects of conservation or in a certain geographical location; there is surprisingly little duplication of efforts. Organizations are often linked by members of one serving on the board or a committee of another. Tensions among organizations have forced them to resolve their difference and to recognize the importance of planning for the longer term (J. Stuckey, pers. comm.). Monteverde 2020 helped motivate local organizations to work together. Successful examples of cooperation among organizations are the forest guards, the environmental education programs, and the demonstration farm and tree nurseries.

The successes of conservation organizations in these six areas have been possible because of four developments, which are the main lessons of conservation success in the zone:

(1) Resident and visiting scientists have provided knowledge on the natural history and ecology of this area, which has served as an underlying basis for programs of conservation organizations. Some scientists have also applied their knowledge to local problems of conservation and restoration ecology, agroecology, sustainable development, and environmental education. Biologists have also served as mentors for Costa Rican field assistants and colleagues.

(2) The prosperity of the Monteverde Zone was first based on agriculture. Ecotourism has diversified the economic base and added to the relative prosperity of the area, freeing the conservation organizations to focus on conservation rather than situations of mass poverty as is the case in many other places (J. Stuckey, pers. comm.). The growth of ecotourism has helped support forest protection and education, providing jobs for many local people and businesses and functioning as a form of sustainable development for the zone. Conservation organizations themselves have provided jobs and tremendous inflows of cash for land purchases, which have circulated in the economy.

(3) Initially, Costa Rican settlers established farms in the area by clearing portions of forests, but they frequently left patches of forests for windbreaks and protection of water sources. They were able to farm without using agrochemicals and they planted trees. When the Quakers arrived in the early 1950s, they left windbreaks and protected their water sources. The Quakers brought with them knowledge of soil and water conservation from the United States, and Quaker values. As more people, including biologists, arrived from outside the area, they contributed new ideas and practices, expanding the base for conservation.

(4) The establishment of the MCFP in 1972 reflected the environmentalist focus on protecting endangered species. By the mid-1980s, when MCL and MVI were established, the global biodiversity crisis had been identified, and the MCL and MVI realized that action was needed on threatened rain forest ecosystems and the promotion of sustainable ecosystems. Monteverde's conservation organizations included people who could tap into the debt-for-nature swaps and obtain funding from North American and European foreign aid and private conservation organizations. They were able to attract large numbers of volunteers. As ecotourism boomed in the late 1980s, the Monteverde Zone became a prime destination in Costa Rica, and some of the zone's ecotourism money was channeled to conservation and sustainable development efforts. Skilled and dedicated residents and visitors, including many biologists, have devoted enormous amounts of time and energy to conservation organizations. Whether this "subsidy" can lead to sustainability and whether the endeavors of local organizations can function without the subsidy are unknown (J. Stuckey, pers. comm.).

10.8.2. Failures or Problems of Conservation Organizations

Disputes or tensions exist among some conservation groups that are related to specific issues, different visions, and different management styles. Conservation organizations share common goals and would achieve more if they could communicate and work together better. One resource that the area lacks is a central library that would serve as a repository for scientific and other publications based on research in the zone, and for the extensive local "gray literature." A commitment from local organizations to maintain information storage and dissemination is needed.

Some organizations have angered members of local communities by actions that resulted from a failure to understand the concerns of people with different goals and lifestyles. For example, small farmers from San Luis feel resentment toward two of the conservation organizations (see E. Vargas, "Human Voices," p. 385). Conservation organizations in the Monteverde Zone stress the need to deal with this issue: "[I]f the people who make their living from the land are not included in the process of discovering how to conserve biodiversity, then the struggle to preserve becomes prohibitively expensive and, in the long run, may be lost" (*Monteverde Journal*, vol. 2, no. 1, 1995).

There are tensions related to economic development that are more than a simple conflict between conservation organizations and local communities. The divisions are voiced in debates over whether to pave the road from the Inter-American Highway to Santa Elena and Monteverde (L. Vivanco, pers. comm.), plans to expand the operations of the dairy plant (see Chap. 11, Agriculture), and the relative merits of ecotourism. Concerted efforts to deal with negative impacts of ecotourism are needed. The Santa Elena Development Association has organized garbage collection, and the MCFP has instituted recycling. More studies are needed on the impact of tourism on the quality of life and the socioeconomic problems caused by seasonal and annual fluctuations in tourism; if tourism decreases, what effects will this have on the communities and protected areas?

All of the conservation organizations in Monteverde must develop solid funding bases, especially endowments. Getting nonprofit status in the United States is one step; the MCFP, MVI, and CEC have done this. But the organizations need to develop more creative financing mechanisms as competition for grants from international conservation funding sources grows. They must also combat the sense that Costa Rica has received a disproportionate share of foreign conservation money (Abramovitz 1989).

10.8.3. The Monteverde Zone and Its Conservation Organizations as Models

To what extent can the Monteverde Zone serve as a model for others in conservation and sustainable development? Costa Rica is atypical among developing countries. Its unique political, economic, demographic, social, and cultural factors have led to impressive conservation achievements. Within Costa Rica, the Monteverde Zone is atypical, with its multicultural population, the large number of people with high educational levels, sharp awareness of conservation and sustainable development, relative prosperity based on dairy farming and ecotourism, and ability to create grassroots organizations to deal with local issues. All of the successes have the potential to be models for other areas. However, the zone's successful conservation organizations and their programs cannot simply be copied without adaptations.

The MCFP, SER, BEN, and Bosqueterno offer four different models for the creation and management of protected areas by nongovernmental organizations. Reserves similar to the MCFP and SER can be established in areas where ecotourism can be developed to attract tourists who will both support the reserve and provide local people with financial benefits. The "technical aspects" of the MCFP can serve as a model for other private and public reserves in areas where ecotourism is growing (Aylward et al. 1996). The SER offers a novel approach for the management of government-owned land by a local organization, and it has been adopted by at least one other school in Costa Rica. The BEN began with the ideas and efforts of children that were channeled to an existing conservation organization (MCL) that was open to new ideas and was able to react quickly to purchase forested land and build on rapidly growing worldwide support. The model of an international children's rain forest has spread to other locations in Costa Rica, Belize, Ecuador, Guatemala, and Thailand (B. Kern, pers. comm.). Bosqueterno, S.A. can be a model wherein a group holds land or other resources in common; the common property can be managed by an organization for the group.

The zone's successes with ecotourism offer additional exemplars. CASEM is an excellent model for involving women in conservation and economic development. Monteverde's experience of beginning with small locally owned pensións for lodging is also applicable elsewhere. If sufficient ecotourism develops, other ecotourism businesses such as the Monteverde Butterfly Garden can be developed.

The Monteverde Zone's conservation organizations may also be models. The CEC specifically aims to serve as a model in environmental education for Costa

Rica and other tropical countries. The MVI is probably the most difficult organization to use as a model because it requires a pool of highly trained people to give courses and a recognized way to grant U.S. academic credit for courses. However, accredited programs for U.S. college students are spreading rapidly in the neotropics. For example, the Organization for Tropical Studies (OTS) has started a program in Costa Rica that resembles MVI's long courses. Local people can be trained as natural history guides. The reserve's guard programs using local unarmed people and educating them about conservation can be adapted to areas that do not have high levels of violence (Lober 1990, 1991). The potential for using the zone's conservation organizations as models is being amplified as they establish electronic communication links; this trend was led by MVI and CEC in 1996. The Monteverde Zone can also serve as a model through its ex-ample of how much can be accomplished by cooperative private efforts of dedicated people and grassroots organizations.

Acknowledgments I am grateful to individuals who generously supplied oral and written information. I thank those who reviewed drafts: Edgardo Arévalo, Bruce Aylward, Rafael Bolaños, Jan Drake-Lowther, Lucky and Wolf Guindon, Bill Haber, Frank Joyce, Sharon Kinsman, Richard LaVal, Bob Law, Marcy Lawton, Martha Moss, Nalini Nadkarni, Quint Newcomer, Alan Pounds, Ree Sheck, Susan Sprague, Joe Stuckey, Joseph Tosi, John and Sue Trostle, Eugenio Vargas, Guillermo Vargas, Luis Vivanco, Meg Wallace, Nat Wheelwright, Lisa Wirtanen, and Willow Zuchowski. The people mentioned in this chapter provided valuable feedback. I am also grateful to Franklin and Marshall College for grants that supported my research.

Editors note: Two of Monteverde's original North American settlers, John Campbell (Fig. 10.5) and Eston Rockwell, died shortly before publication of this book.

KEY TO ABBREVIATIONS USED IN THIS CHAPTER

ACA: Arenal Conservation Area (Area de Conservación Arenal)

BEN: Bosque Eterno de los Niños (Children's Eternal Forest)

CABEI: Central American Bank for Economic Integration

CASEM: Comité de Artesanías Santa Elena–Monteverde (crafts cooperative)

CATIE: Centro Agronómico Tropical de Investigación y Enseñanza (Tropical Agronomy Center for Research and Teaching)

CEC: Centro de Educación Creativa (CLC: Creative Learning Center)

CEDARENA: Centro de Derecho Ambiental y de los Recursos Naturales (environmental and natural resources law center)

CI: Conservation International

CIDA: Canadian International Development Agency

Coope: CoopeSanta Elena (Santa Elena Cooperative)

DGF: Dirección General Forestal (Costa Rican Forestry Service)

EEP: environmental education program

IUCN: International Union for the Conservation of Nature

LDCs: less developed countries

MAG: Ministerio de Agricultura y Ganadería (Ministry of Agriculture and Livestock)

MBG: Monteverde Butterfly Garden

MCFP: Monteverde Cloud Forest Preserve

MCL: Monteverde Conservation League

MDCs: more developed countries

MEP: Ministerio de Educación Pública (Ministry of Public Education)

MFS: Monteverde Friends School

MINAE: Ministerio del Ambiente y Energía (Ministry of the Environment and Energy)

MIRENEM: Ministerio de Recursos Naturales, Energía y Minas (Ministry of Natural Resources, Energy, and Mines)

MVI: Monteverde Institute

OTS: Organization for Tropical Studies

SER: Santa Elena High School Cloud Forest Reserve

SIDA: Swedish International Development Agency

SINAC: Sistema Nacional de Areas de Conservación (National System of Conservation Areas)

TNC: The Nature Conservancy

TSC: Tropical Science Center (CCT: Centro Científico Tropical)

UCEAP: University of California Education Abroad Program

USAID: U.S. Agency for International Development

WWF: World Wildlife Fund

THE CHANGING FACE OF TOURISM
Sam Grosby

1974

A tourist arrives in Monteverde after long bus trips from San José to Puntarenas and from there to Santa Elena, prepared to spend a week or more bird watching and walking in the rain forest. He finds the town's only pensión and hopes there will be space in one of its four rooms for him. The biologists staying there give him tips on the best places to find the Resplendent Quetzal, and in the morning he sets out alone with his notebook and binoculars.

1996

A tourist arrives in Monteverde by tour bus with 15 other tourists. They will spend one day and two nights in Monteverde, at one of the zone's more than 35 hotels and pensións. In the morning, they have reservations for a guided natural history walk in the MCFP (Fig. 10.8); they are among the 50,000 tourists to visit it each year.

Although ecotourists constitute a diverse group, the majority of tourists in the mid-1990s arrive with package tours. According to guides, one of the main differences they encounter between present-day tourists and those of two decades ago is the amount and kind of information they have and want. Early tourists were largely bird-watchers, scientists, or naturalists who came with information about the area and specific interest in the Resplendent Quetzal or other species. Recent tourists have less information about what to expect from Monteverde itself but a greater consciousness of the need to conserve rain forests due to the subject's popularity in the media.

PROS AND CONS OF ECOTOURISM
Francisco Chamberlain

Tourism in the Monteverde Zone has had major positive and negative effects on the communities and the environment. Positive economic growth of the area is strongly related to the MCFP, as most of the establishments (e.g., hotels, restaurants) that generate economic activities depend on it to attract tourists. The economic impact of this industry on a community of 4000 inhabitants was estimated at $5 million in 1992, of which only 13% was spent in the MCFP (Solórzano and Echeverría 1993). The remainder was dispersed in the Monteverde economy. The MCFP has also contributed to economic development by creating work opportunities. In 1992, it employed 48 workers and paid 39 million colones ($283,500) in wages and benefits; in 1993, it employed 53 workers with a budget for wages and benefits of 55 million colones ($400,000).

The tourism industry employs an increasing number of residents. It generally offers better pay than farm jobs and provides more status, which siphons workers out of agriculture. There is a high demand in tourism businesses for workers who speak English and operate a computer, which results in competition for workers. Tourism provides higher salaries at mid-level educational positions than the Costa Rican average. As new hotels developed, the demand for personnel increased, which produced unprecedented immigration to Monteverde.

Social, economic, and infrastructure problems accompany increased immigration and tourism. The demand for basic public services (water, electricity, telephone) grew faster than the supply, and roads have deteriorated due to increased traffic. The price of land in the community of Monteverde has increased to an average of $15–$20/m², which is comparable to San José. Another impact is waste management; no community waste collection system existed until local institutions started one in 1993.

DEBT-FOR-NATURE SWAPS
Leslie J. Burlingame

Thomas Lovejoy (WWF-US) proposed the innovative idea of debt-for-nature swaps in 1984 as a way to generate funds for conservation in less developed countries (LDCs). By the mid-1980s, LDCs had borrowed enormous amounts from private banks of more developed countries (MDCs). One of the easiest ways for LDCs to repay interest and loans was to convert their natural resources (e.g., rain forests) into cash. Thus, debt burden was indirectly a cause of deforestation. Private MDC banks realized there was little chance of getting their money back and traded discounted debt in a secondary market. The debt-for-nature swaps began when conservation groups (e.g., WWF, TNC, and Conservation International, CI) bought discounted debt with tax-free contributions. Some of the Costa Rican debt purchases were also funded by foundations (e.g., the John D. and Catherine T. MacArthur Foundation) and by foreign aid programs of Sweden and The Netherlands. They could buy discounted debt from an MDC bank and then multiply that money for conservation. The interest-bearing bonds issued in local currency by the central bank of the indebted country, although not equal to the face value of the debt, were worth more than the discounted amount for which they had been purchased (The Nature Conservancy N.d., Umaña and Brandon 1992, World Resources Institute et al. 1992).

Bolivia and Ecuador were the first countries to participate in debt-for-nature swaps (1987). Costa Rica has carried out the greatest number of swaps and has retired 5% of its foreign debt in this manner (Klinger 1994). The first of these swaps, arranged in 1988 by Alvaro Umaña, Costa Rica's Minister of MIRENEM, retired $5.4 million of debt. At that time, one dollar of Costa Rican debt could be purchased for 15–17 cents (Fuller and Williamson 1988). By 1991, six Costa Rican debt swaps had generated about $43 million plus interest for conservation through contributions of $12.5 million, which purchased almost $80 million of Costa Rica's debt (Umaña and Brandon 1992, World Resources Institute et al. 1992). The Fundación de Parques Nacionales, a nongovernmental organization, was established to receive these funds and other contributions, exchange debt swap money for bonds issued by the Central Bank of Costa Rica, disburse interest and principal to Costa Rican conservation organizations such as MCL, and monitor accounting and management of funds (MCL *Tapir Tracks*, vol. 3, no. 1, 1988, Larrea and Umaña N.d., Umaña and Brandon 1992).

THE COMMUNITY PROCESS OF ENVIRONMENTAL EDUCATION
Guillermo Vargas (translated by Leslie J. Burlingame)

Some consider that environmental education began in the zone with the creation of the MCFP and the formation of local conservation organizations. Others trace the birth of a conservation culture in Monteverde and the roots of a culture that evolved toward harmony between human communities and their natural surroundings to the arrival of the Quakers, or to the distant past of the colonists from the first half of this century. What motivated many *campesinos* (peasants) to leave strips of forest next to springs and rivers? How could our forebears grow corn, beans, vegetables, sugarcane, coffee, and other crops with a minimal use of agrochemicals? Why are there still farms that retain patches of forest on land suitable for agriculture? How did the local community learn to limit the use of fire in the preparation of the soil and to obtain economic benefit from the forest without cutting it? Through the process of living, the campesino families of yesterday and today developed systems of production that satisfy their needs by relying on their knowledge and skills and on the available resources. These systems are based on concepts that they learned in school, from their families, in their community, through the media, and in religious beliefs.

Some of their actions are now considered environmentally damaging and not ecologically sustainable. They have cut the forest on steep slopes and replaced it with pastures and crops, used fire to control weeds and to eliminate the residue from forest cutting, left watersheds unprotected, eliminated natural wind-breaks, and imported exotic crops. They sold their "improved" farms to cattle ranchers in the lower areas of Monteverde. Many farmers have given up farming and devote themselves to business and activities related to tourism. The population has become concentrated in semiurban nuclei with inadequate waste management. They are rapidly advancing toward the establishment of a standard of living that consumes nonrenewable resources and generates little biodegradable waste.

Programs and processes of environmental education exist in Monteverde. The former developed through the initiative of nongovernmental organizations and public institutions. These programs elucidate the causes of environmental problems and elaborate educational processes that contribute to their resolution. The community processes of environmental education have evolved in the daily life of the population and are nourished by life experiences in their successes and failures.

The community of Monteverde educates itself environmentally in its daily practice, transforming the forest into cultivated areas; hunting; extracting products from the forest; producing milk, coffee, and crafts; seeking recreation in the forests and rivers; and practicing its religious faiths. The conservation institutions seek to identify their roles in this process of living, a process that is also environmental education: how do they succeed in making conservation an essential element of the culture? The communities have gradually passed from being people who lived in the midst of the mountains to people located in buffer zones of natural forest reserves. On the upper part of the mountain, forest protection is the center of attraction for researchers and tourists. Lower elevations are home to the people and to agricultural and craft production, business, services for tourism, and habitat restoration projects.

The conservation movement has grown; campesinos maintain sustainable production practices, immigrant Quakers practice a culture of respect and love for their fellow humans and for their natural surroundings, immigrant researchers bring their knowledge and environmental ethics, business people make a reality of ecotourism's promise, and artisans give visible shape to elements of natural history in their materials and forms.

The process of environmental education in Monteverde faces many challenges. It is certain that more people earn their living thanks to the conservation of the cloud forest. It is also certain that many people value the forest for its potential to attract visitors with dollars. Ecotourism is seen by many residents more in economic rather than in ecological terms. Monteverde is an important center of research on the cloud forest. However, most research results are not readily available to the local population. Environmental educators and researchers must unite their efforts toward the formulation of programs that allow residents to discover, value, and use the biological knowledge that is generated in our forests.

Monteverde is not an isolated community; it is more open to the influence of external factors than most in Costa Rica. Conditions are favorable for being a tourism zone, mixing nationalities and cultures that live together, developing communication pathways, and fostering visits of students and biologists. Good and bad customs mold lifestyles and develop a quality of life different from that which has governed local development for five decades. Environmental educators must facilitate processes that promote the capacity of the community to select habits, develop forms of sustainable production, and resist the objects that the promoters of the consumer system make us believe are necessary. In the long term, the protection of natural ecosystems and their biodiversity will be favored to the extent that the local population develops attitudes, knowledge, and skills to sustain development in Monteverde. The community will develop its potential to form a concept of life that is fuller and more sustainable to the extent that environmental education is a conscious process of the people and reaches beyond programs of conservation institutions.

MONTEVERDE 2020
Leslie J. Burlingame

Monteverde 2020 was an "organization of organizations" established to promote democratic dialogue to develop a shared vision for sustainable development and to facilitate cooperation among organizations to plan actions to achieve this vision. It grew out of the Monteverde Zone's long tradition of forming committees to deal with local problems and issues. By 1991, there were more than 40 committees and 12 membership organizations in the zone (Stuckey 1992).

Originally, TSC formed a "Monteverde Committee" to foster positive relations with the community.

In 1988, they articulated 12 ideals, including "harmony between production and the environment" and "broad participation in decision making" (J. Stuckey, pers. comm.). Monteverde 2020 was established as an umbrella organization to foster coordination among the areas' many organizations with a three-year grant from the Interamerican Foundation. In 1990, they developed a mission statement and set up 10 commissions to work on issues including conservation, tourism, and roads. When funding ran out, they became dormant for several reasons: no one had experience running such an organization, some institutions held their own priorities over the group's, political power and a solid economic base were lacking, and insufficient benefits were provided to member organizations. Monteverde 2020 had some successes: it awoke awareness of the need for long-term planning, started a garbage collection program, helped improve education in the zone, and trained participants to plan in the long term (J. Stuckey and T. Ewing, pers. comm.).

EL BUEN AMIGO
Eugenio Vargas
(reprinted with permission from MCL *Tapir Tracks*, vol. 5, no. 3, 1991)

Asociacíon El Buen Amigo, "The Good Friend Association," consists of a group of families who farm in Los Altos de San Luis, 4 km from Monteverde (Fig. 1.7). The group formed in 1984, when two brothers of the Leitón family donated a 131-ha farm and families worked the land as a cooperative. This farm includes a forest reserve, which has about 75% of its area in virgin forest. Because of its elevation and location near the MCFP, many birds and other animals live there year-round. Other species migrate: Brocket Deer, quetzals, Three-wattled Bellbirds, oropendolas, toucans, Swallow-tailed Kites, Lineated Woodpeckers, and manakins. It is common to come upon groups of Coatis, White-faced Capuchins, Howler Monkeys, and Collared Peccaries.

Our first plan was to build a sugar mill to make *dulce* (brown sugar) from sugarcane. We had only the help and determination of friends and organizations that gave us moral and material support to buy the first cows and build a milking shed. With more economic help, we built houses and a bridge over the San Luis River. Five houses, the sugar mill, and two milking sheds were made with our own hands. The group started with 20 members. Some dropped out because of economic difficulties or due to misunderstandings in the group. In 1991, seven families were in the group. The salary distributed among the members came from milk production, based on the number of hours each person worked. We also planted cane, coffee, and vegetables (Fig. 10.11).

El Buen Amigo could perhaps be called the San Luis Conservation Association because we have not destroyed the forest by working here. Little by little, we have produced without using much modern technology, without going into debt with banks, and above all, with the help from others and our own efforts. Our goal is to produce the things necessary for our families, to make use of the resources of this farm without destroying them, and to discover ways to help maintain a balance between conservation of this beautiful place and our needs for production.

One result of meetings with MCL was our proposal to find financing for a hydroelectric plant. We have no electricity. This plant will make use of water sources and the steep topography of the land. Our hope is to produce energy for light in our houses and to install a woodworking shop. We could make use of wood from fallen trees in the forest and offer our children a place to learn how to make useful and beautiful things with their hands. Another important step in our relation with the MCL was an agreement to give El Buen Amigo economic support to increase milk production without clearing more forest for pasture. Instead, we purchased pasture land below our farm. In exchange, El Buen Amigo members committed themselves to preserve about half of our forests.

Chapter Editor's Update: An assessment of El Buen Amigo in 1998 indicated changes from the original vision; members found it hard to survive financially through subsistence farming. By 1998, only five families still lived on the farm. One person from the farm has become a parataxonomist for the Institute of Biodiversity. The cooperative aspects of farming have ended; members divide the pasture and crop area and pursue farming as individuals. In 1994, the community began obtaining money from ecotourism by building a 16-bed hostel for Costa Rican and foreign students studying agroecology and forest conservation. El Buen Amigo still acts as a cooperative to run the hostel. Members are interested in preserving their forest after the MCL lease runs out in 1999 but need a new lease from MCL or another conservation group (*Monteverde Journal*, vol. 1, no. 2, 1994, M. Cruz, T. and Z. Fuentes and E. Vargas, pers. comm.).

LA BELLA FARM
Leslie J. Burlingame

The La Bella Farm (Finca La Bella) Project in San Luis (Fig. 1.7) is similar to the Buen Amigo project. Ann Kriebel was a Quaker resident of Monteverde in the early 1980s who developed programs in San Luis in education, health, and nutrition. The North American Quaker group Friends Committee on Unity with Nature established the Ann Kriebel/San Luis Project in 1992 and worked with the Coope to raise money to purchase the 49-ha La Bella farm. The project is establishing a land trust to promote conservation and sustainable develop-

ment with landless farmers. By 1998, 18 families had been located on the farm and were producing coffee, milk, and vegetables, tending an organic farming demonstration plot (established by the MCFP's EEP), conserving the soil, improving yields with help from the Coope, and reforesting with native species. A preschool and community health center operate on the farm as joint efforts of the Coope, the San Luis Development Association, and the community (Balderston 1993, W. Howenstine and C. Vargas, pers. comm.).

SAN GERARDO: AN EXPERIMENT IN SUSTAINABLE DEVELOPMENT
John Boll

San Gerardo Arriba encompasses portions of the Caño Negro and San Gerardo River watersheds. The area (800–1300 m), which lies between Monteverde and Lake Arenal, receives 5000 mm of annual precipitation and is classified as Atlantic slope premontane rain forest (Holdridge 1967). Subsistence Costa Rican farmers have lived in the area for at least 45 years; the majority of land clearing has been done in the last 25 years. The original settlers raised beans, corn, bananas, sugarcane, pigs, and cattle. Cattle have always been an important source of milk, cheese, and meat for consumption and market. Hunting of deer, monkeys, pacas, and other mammals and birds provided food supplements.

In 1977, the Costa Rican government established what is now called the Arenal-Monteverde Protected Zone in a territory that includes San Gerardo. It stretched from the San Ramón Protected Zone in the south (now the Alberto Brenes Biological Reserve) to the shore of what would become the greatly enlarged Lake Arenal. This was established to protect natural resources and the watershed of the Lake Arenal hydroelectric and irrigation project. Although the government did not have funds to purchase land in this area, the rules of the zone were restrictive for the inhabitants, limiting their hunting activities and forbidding them to cut trees. Government assistance for infrastructure was curtailed and banks would not issue credit.

In 1991, the MCL bought most of the land in the San Gerardo area for inclusion in the BEN. They used funds from a debt-for-nature swap; the initial purchase was 1102 ha. Some landowners did not wish to sell or leave their land. The MCL entered into an agreement with community members to provide for the sustainable development of the area, to improve the people's livelihoods, and to serve as an example for other communities. A master plan for the community was drawn up by graduate students from the University of Costa Rica, working with MCL support (Montero and Zarate 1991). The Alex C. Walker Educational and Charitable Foundation provided a three-year grant toward the construction of housing and laboratory space, a visitor center, an access road, technical coordination, and administration. The Barnens Regnskog and WWF-Costa Rica also provided funds. A group of biologists located a site with access to primary and secondary forest, regenerating pasture, and a spectacular view of Lake Arenal and the Arenal volcano.

The station opened in 1994. It consists of a large (350 m²) two-story building with laboratory space, dining room, kitchen, office, and bunks for 24. The station has provided jobs for people from the community. Trail systems (10 km) are being improved, supported by a grant from the Tina Joliffe Memorial Fund in England. A hydroelectric facility that provides electricity for the station is supported by a grant from

SIDA through Barnens Regnskog. A program in organic gardening was started by volunteers with funds from the Monteverde Brand coffee conservation rebate program with Montana Coffee Traders. Housing, schools, and stable employment are being sought to bring back former community members who left to find better jobs or to educate their children.

Chapter Editor's Update: An assessment of San Gerardo in 1998 indicated that San Gerardo has not been the successful sustainable development experiment that was envisioned; the only functioning element is the field station operated by MCL. By 1995, only one of the original families was still living in San Gerardo, with no school or means to make a living. The MCL has promised cash and land as compensation for the contributions and labor of families involved in the project. The deeds will contain a conservation easement, restricting land use to activities that have low impacts on the environment (F. Joyce, pers. comm.).

The groups and individuals involved in this experiment have strongly differing views on the reasons for its failure to meet expectations (L. Vivanco, pers. comm.). Such experiments are very difficult in remote areas. Participants need to be less idealistic about outcomes and more aware of limitations imposed by the environment. Although organic produce was harvested, the organic gardening project was not continued because of too much rain and a lack of labor. The rain also hampered construction of an all-weather road, making transport difficult (J. Boll, pers. comm.).

Participants also need better planning and training to ensure coordination. The grants MCL obtained were primarily for the construction of the station, road, and hydroelectric plant. The original vision was that construction and operation of the station would provide community jobs, but there was not enough income to support all the community members and there was no school, so most of them left San Gerardo. Participants need to have written agreements open for revision as circumstances change; this is particularly important when there are personnel shifts in the grassroots organization and changing community membership configurations (J. Boll, pers. comm.). Grassroots organizations depend heavily on volunteers and others from outside the organizations; they must ensure that these people have the necessary training and technical expertise, logistical support, and abilities to interact productively with a local community in flux.

CONSERVATION EASEMENTS IN MONTEVERDE: THE ENLACE VERDE PROJECT
Nathaniel Scrimshaw, Wendy Gibbons, and Leslie J. Burlingame

Monteverde is undergoing rapid change. Originally, dairying was the most important source of income for permanent residents. Farms have been subdivided, construction of buildings proceeds apace, the population is growing, and land values have shot up, all of which places pressure on land resources. It has also meant anguish for residents who want to keep the Monteverde environment rural. People do not agree on precisely what it is they want to protect. Some wish to preserve the community's agricultural character, others its rural residential feel, and others its remaining natural forests. There is wide agreement, however, that something must be done to prevent uncontrolled development.

There is a general distrust of large organizations among Monteverde residents. Zoning has historically put control in the hands of distant bureaucrats. In the early 1990s, a group of residents formulated a commission to explore ways that maintain control inside the community within Costa Rican law. The commission initiated a project that encourages and supports landowners to voluntarily restrict development through conservation easements (termed "servidumbres ecológicas" in Costa Rican law).

Easements appeal to property owners because they place limits on land development only. Each property owner designs the restrictions he/she believes works best. Activities permitted by an easement might include timber management, agriculture, recreation, education, and research. Parcels of land can be set aside for future construction or subdivision. Easements serve as an alternative to zoning, in which an agency such as a city or state government limits development and has the burden of enforcing these restrictions. In this system, the rights that usually define private property (e.g., the right to be on the land, use its resources, and develop it) are divided into separate rights. The landowner may retain the right to use the land but not to cut the remaining forest. He or she may give up the right to construct further buildings on the land.

In 1994, the Enlace Verde (Green Network) project was formally proposed within the Monteverde town meeting and is a continuing community project supported by MVI. The first proposed easements create a network of protected forest along a wedge of land bordering the river between the Bosque Eterno portion of the MCFP and the Bajo del Tigre sector of BEN and buffer the river below the MCFP (see Fig. 1.8). Enlace Verde passes through the heart of Monteverde and encompasses a community walking path and MVI's education center. Enlace Verde is working with over fifty properties and six neighborhood clusters. In 1998, the first easements were written into three deeds and registered.

One innovation in the Enlace Verde project is the use of mutual easements (easements written into two or more deeds between neighbors). This contrasts with the traditional conservation easement in which a conservation organization "holds" the development rights in trust and is responsible for monitoring and enforcing the terms of the easement. In a mutual easement, a group of neighbors as a whole develops a set of reciprocal land use restrictions that preserves important aspects of the land. Neighbors are also responsible for enforcement and for future changes in the agreements. The first easements within Enlace Verde include a clear community-based conflict resolution process written into the deed.

The greatest challenge with developing mutual easements is defining property clusters of optimal size, both from a landscape and a social perspective. Large groups are likely to be too heterogeneous and unwieldy; small groups may provide weaker protection in the long run, as it is easier to achieve consensus to change the restrictions. In many cases, biologists must be consulted about which restrictions are most environmentally valuable and which land should be included. The economic impacts of the easements must also be considered.

Since 1995, the MVI, in partnership with the University of New York in Buffalo and the University of Maryland, has fostered Enlace Verde through the Sustainable Futures program. Students in urban planning, architecture, and landscape architecture have helped develop Enlace Verde by bringing neighbors together in focus group discussions and by integrating biological knowledge into the community dialogue. In late 1996, CEDARENA received a one-year grant to work on conservation easements in Costa Rica and Central America. Monteverde was selected as one of three focal communities for the country.

THE MONTEVERDE BUTTERFLY GARDEN
Jim Wolfe

The growth of ecotourism in Monteverde has provided opportunities for local natural-resource-based enterprises. The Monteverde Butterfly Garden (MBG) is an example of sustainable use of the area's natural resources. The MBG is a family-owned business dedicated to the conservation of butterflies through education. It operates under permission from the Costa Rican Wildlife Department (Vida Silvestre).

The facility includes a reception area and nature center that houses displays on butterfly biology and ecology. Three greenhouses and a 465-m^2 screened botanical garden contain hundreds of adult butterflies representing more than 40 local species. Butterfly and plant species correspond to different habitats in each enclosure. A gift shop contains displays on butterfly conservation and items for sale. Trained multilingual guides cover themes such as diversity, relationships with plants and animals, life cycles, migration, caterpillar defenses, chrysalis formation, and butterfly emergence. Written material in several languages and a botanical guide that corresponds to tagged plants in the gardens are provided.

The MBG plays an educational role for tourists, MBG employees (many are volunteer overseas students), and the local community. It offers free tours to local schools. University students and local biologists also use the MBG for research (e.g., color preferences by butterflies, pollination, and sugar preferences of emerging butterflies). The MBG creates employment for 6–10 people (guiding, gardening, butterfly egg collection, rearing of caterpillars, and gift shop attendance).

These benefits have been achieved on a very small piece of land and without damaging local butterfly populations. The garden's butterflies are hand-raised from eggs collected at MBG with only occasional wild-caught individuals to provide genetic mixing.

Although only 2–5% of butterfly eggs in the wild survive to the adult stage, careful hand-raising allows for a 70–80% success rate. Thus, the quantity of butterflies can sometimes surpass MBG's capacity; surplus butterflies are released to the wild. Unlike other butterfly gardens and butterfly farms in Costa Rica, which raise butterflies to sell to collectors, the MBG raises butterflies only for educational purposes. Most people care about and protect what they see and what they know; environmental education provided by the MBG thus contributes to conservation and serves as a model for other areas with ecotourism.

COMITÉ DE ARTESANÍAS SANTA ELENA–MONTEVERDE
Leslie J. Burlingame

The Comité de Artesanías Santa Elena–Monteverde (CASEM) is an example of sustainable ecotourism involving local people. In 1998, the cooperative included about 140 people, nearly all women, who produce high-quality handmade crafts featuring designs based on local biota (Fig. 10.13). Most of the items for sale to tourists in Monteverde are clothes with designs of birds, frogs, butterflies, orchids, and other plants and animals of the cloud forest. Together CASEM and MVI established a Monteverde ceramics studio in 1995. Eight local women founded CASEM in 1982; they recognized in the mid-1970s that the Monteverde Zone must diversify its economic base beyond dairy farming. Rural women needed economic opportunities that could be combined with taking care of their children at home (K. VanDusen, pers. comm.). The founders obtained a loan from the Interamerican Foundation to train women in marketing. They received substantial training and materials from Jean Andrews (J. Andrews and P. Jiménez, pers. comm.).

By 1983, the 80 women involved in the project established a formal cooperative. In 1985, they became a division of the Coope Santa Elena (Coope). With a gift from Andrews, Monteverde fund-raising activities, and a bank loan backed by the Coope, CASEM's building was completed in 1987 (C. Vargas, pers. comm., Fig. 10.14). It has an elected board and a paid staff. Members set their own prices; 65% of the money from the sale of articles returns directly to the artisan; 10% goes into a savings account for the artisan; the remaining 25% covers salaries, expenses, and training classes and materials.

A major key to CASEM's success lies in dedicated women who established training workshops in Monteverde and neighboring communities. The artisans benefit because they receive fair wages for their work, work at home and stay with their children, and have learned skills in business, leadership, and social interactions. Their self-confidence and independence have increased, and with economic success they have improved their status in their families and communities (*Monteverde Journal*, vol. 1, no. 2, 1994, Leitinger 1997, P. Jiménez, pers. comm.).

Figure 10.13. One of the "members" at the women's artisan cooperative center (CASEM) in Monteverde, displaying handmade crafts and artwork, many of which depict nature themes. Photograph by Leslie Burlingame.

Many members of CASEM have also increased their understanding of the natural environment and have become more aware of the need to protect it. They realize their income depends on the preservation of the forests that attract tourists. They educate other family members, especially their children, about the importance of caring for nature (*Monteverde Journal*, vol. 1, no. 2, Sept. 1994, M. I. Salazar and P. Jiménez, pers. comm.). In 1994, CASEM's annual contest focused on the theme of "Protection of the Environment" (C. Castro, pers. comm.). Representatives from CASEM attended a 1994 national conference on Women and the Environment in San José. Many see CASEM as a model for sustainable development in locations with substantial ecotourism. Members of CASEM have shared their experiences with groups in Latin America (P. Jiménez and I. Leitinger, pers. comm.).

Figure 10.14. The women's artisan cooperative center (CASEM), located in the middle of Monteverde, which sells crafts and artwork to tourists and residents. Photograph by Leslie Burlingame.

LA CAMPESINITA
Leslie J. Burlingame

La Campesinita, founded by 14 women in 1988, offered an alternative for women living in the community of La Cruz. They formed a legal entity to produce and sell natural preserves. Their jars of fruit cocktails, marmalades, and pickles are sold to tourists in the dairy plant and the Coope. Aided by MVI, La Campesinita helped members develop confidence, self-esteem, an income of their own, and new financial skills tied to environmental concerns. The MCL helped them obtain a grant, and its reforestation program planted fruit trees, which supply some of their fruit (MCL *Tapir Tracks*, vol. 6, no. 2, 1991, *Monteverde Journal*, vol. 1, no. 2, 1994, P. Jiménez, pers. comm.).

HUMAN VOICES AROUND THE FOREST
Eugenio Vargas
(reprinted with permission from *Monteverde Journal*, vol. 2, no. 2, 1995)

I share thoughts on the separate proposals presented by TSC and MCL for biological corridors that encompass the San Luis and Guacimal rivers. These thoughts arose from having grown up in the San Luis community and from being a descendent of parents and grandparents who supported their families from the fruits of their work on this land since 1915. Also, I helped my father plant hundreds of trees for timber and fruit long before the reforestation program of the MCL. A few years later, we picked the fruit of these trees, and the first money I ever earned was selling oranges in Monteverde. For years, the subsistence of the people of San Luis was based on the production of beans, corn, coffee, plantain, milk, beef, and fruit and on hunting. More recently, the history of San Luis has been marked by the monopoly of the best agricultural lands in few hands. Much of the destruction of the forests and the soils was caused by the abuse by cattle and by the fires set on these big farms. For over 25 years, the people of San Luis have looked for help to achieve a better distribution of the cultivable land, with an eye to the growing population.

It is known only too well that the TSC and MCL have carried out international campaigns to obtain donations for buying land. The contributors to these campaigns feel proud to save a piece of wilderness for future generations. But in the case of San Luis, the recent purchases by the TSC (the José Rojas farm) and other ecotourism ventures have helped inflate land prices to a level out of reach of any small farmer. As a result, some feel resentful toward the conservation groups, especially when rangers arrive at their farms to tell them they cannot cut a tree to build a house or for firewood and that hunting is forbidden even on their own land.

On the other side of the coin, how can the reserves grow so that the jaguar, tapir, and quetzal have more space to move around? To create a biological corridor, one needs control over the land, which is best achieved by buying it. Although members of the MCL and TSC have said the proposals do not require the purchase of farms, it is hard to see how the organizations will avoid the temptation if they can afford to do so and the owners are willing. Clearly, any farmer would feel attracted to the idea of selling land, especially when he has passed many years working hard under storms and droughts, without having a good road or paid vacations, without a bonus or pension. But is the message that farmers themselves cannot conserve the land and its natural resources?

One can easily see how the fashionable slogans of sustainable development and better quality of life are used to attract more donations and more visitors and to further expand the reserves, especially when President Figueres's government is applying this policy with fireworks. What is left for the peasant farmer? To convert from one day to the next into a tourism impresario? Or perhaps to become a pawn of more powerful business interests? Perhaps he can make a living from the very air his forests produce. Don't we still need the farmer who is proud to grow the food that feeds his family and to sell the rest to the administrator, the professional, or the office worker who does not plant the earth?

There should be more openness to the idea that the communities near big reserves have the opportunity to organize associations to manage small areas of forest communally with the help of the conservation groups. These associations should have the power to establish mechanisms so that income generated by ecotourism stays in the community and is invested in health, education, and agricultural credit associations. Several examples of such ventures already exist here (El Buen Amigo, La Bella Farm), and they should receive support. Information must be communicated clearly and sincerely to the neighbors of protected areas because their support is as critical as the support of foreign donors.

Literature Cited

Abramovitz, J. 1989. A survey of U.S.-based efforts to research and conserve biological diversity in developing countries. World Resources Institute, Washington, D.C.

Aspinall, W., G. Powell, A. Pounds, J. Gradwohl, N. Nadkarni, M. Carr, E. Miles, C. Williams, and R. Villamil. 1991. Master plan for Monteverde Cloud Forest Preserve. Tropical Science Center, San José, Costa Rica.

Atmetlla, A. 1995. Manual de instrumentos jurídicos privados para la protección de los recursos naturales. Fundación Neotrópica/Editorial Heliconia, San José, Costa Rica.

Aylward, B., K. Allen, J. Echeverría, and J. Tosi. 1996. Sustainable ecotourism in Costa Rica: the Monteverde

Cloud Forest Preserve. Biodiversity and Conservation 5:315–343.

Baker, C. 1994. Costa Rica handbook. Moon Publications, Chico, California.

Balderston, J. 1993. Gracias a la vida: the Ann Kriebel/San Luis story. Friends Committee on Unity with Nature, Burlington, Vermont.

Blake, B., and A. Becher. 1997. The new key to Costa Rica (13th ed.) Ulysses Press, Berkeley, California.

Boo, E. 1990. Ecotourism: the potentials and pitfalls (2 vols.). World Wildlife Fund, Washington, D.C.

Boza, M. 1993. Conservation in action: past, present, and future of the national park system in Costa Rica. Conservation Biology 7:239–247.

Boza, M., D. Jukofsky, and C. Wille. 1995. Costa Rica is a laboratory, not ecotopia. Conservation Biology 9:684–685.

CATIE (Centro Agronomico Tropical de Investigacíon y Enseñanza). 1985. Plan de manejo y desarrollo: Reserva Biológica Monteverde. CATIE, Turrialba, Costa Rica, and Tropical Science Center, San José, Costa Rica.

Caufield, C. 1984. In the rainforest. Knopf, New York.

CEC (Centro de Educación Creativa). Bulletin. 1991–1996. Centro de Educación Creativa, Monteverde, Costa Rica.

———. 1992b. Creative Learning Center/Centro de Educatión Creativa. Centro de Educatión Creativa, Monteverde, Costa Rica.

Chamberlain, F. 1993. The Monteverde Cloud Forest Preserve. Tropical Science Center, San José, Costa Rica.

Cherry, L. 1997. Flute's journey: the life of a wood thrush. Harcourt, Brace, San Diego.

Children's Rainforest U.S. 1994. The Children's Rainforest U.S. Lewiston, Maine.

———. 1996. Rainforest routes: an occasional newsletter for teachers and others. Lewiston, Maine.

Cloud Forest School Foundation. 1998. Rainbow Fall. Cloud Forest School Foundation, Sewanee Tennessee.

Collard, S. B., III. 1997. Monteverde: science and scientists in a Costa Rican cloud forest. Grolier, Danbury, Connecticut.

Council on International Educational Exchange. 1993. Cooperative study centers: Monteverde Institute, Costa Rica. Ecology of the rainforest: tropical biology and conservation. CIEE, New York.

Echeverría, J., M. Hanrahan, and R. Solórzano. 1995. Valuation on non-priced amenities provided by the biological resources within the Monteverde Cloud Forest Preserve, Costa Rica. Ecological Economics 13:43–52.

Escofet, G. 1998a. One million visitors by 1999? The Tico Times, San José, Costa Rica, 2 October.

———. 1998b. Tourism boom shows slump over. The Tico Times, San José, Costa Rica, 19 June.

Fogden, M. 1993. An annotated checklist of the birds of Monteverde and Peñas Blancas. Litografía e Imprenta, San José, Costa Rica.

Forsyth, A. 1988. Journey through a tropical jungle. Simon and Schuster, New York.

Forsyth, A., M. Fogden, and P. Fogden. 1988. The lessons of Monteverde. Equinox, Mar./Apr., 56–61.

Friends Committee on Unity with Nature. 1993. Ann Kriebel/San Luis project. Annual Report. N.p.

Fuller, K., and D. Williamson. 1988. Debt-for-nature-swaps. International Environmental Reporter, May, 301–303.

Gallup, C. 1987. The relationship between the Monteverde Cloud Reserve and the neighboring communities of: Cerro Plano, La Cruz, Santa Elena and Monteverde. TRI Working Paper No. 34, Vol. 2. Tropical Resources Institute, New Haven, Connecticut.

Gómez, L. D., and J. M. Savage. 1983. Searchers on that rich coast: Costa Rican field biology, 1400–1980. Pages 1–11 in D. H. Janzen, editor. Costa Rican natural history. University of Chicago Press, Chicago.

Gorini, P., M. Adelman, M. Moss, and A. Mata. 1996. Cuentos del bosque nuboso. Tropical Science Center, San José, Costa Rica.

Grumbine, R. E. 1992. Ghost bears: exploring the biodiversity crisis. Island Press, Washington, D.C.

Guindon, C. 1996. The importance of forest fragments to the maintenance of regional biodiversity in Costa Rica. Pages 168–186 in J. Schelhas and R. Greenberg, editors. Forest patches in tropical landscapes. Island Press, Washington, D.C.

Haber, W., W. Zuchowski, and E. Bello. 1996. An introduction to cloud forest trees: Monteverde, Costa Rica. La Nación, San José, Costa Rica.

Hartshorn, G., L. Hartshorn, A. Atmetlla, L. D. Gómez, A. Mata, L. Mata, R. Morales, R. Ocampo, D. Pool, C. Quesada, C. Solera, R. Solórzano, G. Stiles, J. Tosi, A. Umaña, C. Villalobos, and R. Wells. 1982. Costa Rica: country environmental profile. Tropical Science Center, San José, Costa Rica.

Hayes, M., and R. LaVal. 1989. The mammals of Monteverde (2d ed.) Tropical Science Center, San José, Costa Rica.

Hayes, M., J. A. Pounds, and W. Timmerman. 1989. An annotated list and guide to the amphibians and reptiles of Monteverde, Costa Rica. University of Texas, Tyler.

Holdridge, L. 1967. Life zone ecology. Tropical Science Center, San José, Costa Rica.

Ingram, S., K. Ferrell-Ingram, and N. Nadkarni. 1996. Epiphytes of the Monteverde Cloud Forest Reserve. The Marie Selby Botanical Gardens, Sarasota, Florida.

Kinsman, S. 1991. Education and empowerment: conservation lessons from children. Conservation Biology 5:9–10.

Klinger, J. 1994. Debt-for-nature swaps and the limits to international cooperation on behalf of the environment. Environmental Politics 3:229–246.

Larrea, R. S., and A. Umaña. N.d. Por qué canjear deuda por naturaleza? MIRENEM, San José, Costa Rica.

Law, B. 1991. The birds of Monteverde (7th ed.). Tropical Science Center, San José, Costa Rica.

———. 1993. Birds of Bajo del Tigre/Aves del Bajo del Tigre. Monteverde Conservation League, Monteverde, Costa Rica.

Law, B., and W. Timmerman. 1992. Nature trail guide: an interpretative guide to the Sendero Nuboso of the Monteverde Cloud Forest Preserve. Tropical Science Center, San José, Costa Rica.

Law, B., R. LaVal, and W. Zuchowski. 1998. Bajo del Tigre guide. Monteverde Conservation League, Monteverde, Costa Rica.

Leitinger, I. A. 1997. Long-term survival of a Costa Rican Women's Crafts Cooperative. Pages 210–233 in I. A. Leitinger, editor. The Costa Rican women's movement: a reader. University of Pittsburgh Press, Pittsburgh, Pennsylvania.

Lober, D. 1990. Protecting a Costa Rican biological reserve: forest guards of Monteverde. TRI Working Paper No. 46. Tropical Resources Institute, New Haven, Connecticut.

———. 1991. Protecting the Costa Rican Biological Reserve: forest guards of Monteverde. TRI, Spring, 4–6.

McCormick, J. 1989. Reclaiming paradise: the global environmental movement. Indiana University Press, Bloomington.

MCL (Monteverde Conservation League. 1986. Statutes of the Monteverde Conservation League. Monteverde, Costa Rica.

———. 1994a. Bosque Eterno de los Niños. Videocassette. MCL, Monteverde, Costa Rica.

———. 1994b. Colpachi (Croton niveus Jacq.). MCL, Monteverde, Costa Rica.

———. 1994c. Guachipelin (Diphysa robinioides Benth.). MCL, Monteverde, Costa Rica.

———. 1994d. Tubú (Montanoa guatemalensis Klatt). MCL, Monteverde, Costa Rica.

MCL Annual Report. 1987–1998. MCL, Monteverde, Costa Rica.

MCL *Tapir Tracks*. 1986–1995. Vols. 1(1) (July–Aug.) through 10(1) (Aug.). MCL, Monteverde, Costa Rica.

McNeely, J., and K. Miller. 1982. National parks, conservation, and development. Smithsonian Institution Press, Washington, D.C.

McNeely, J., K. Miller, W. Reid, R. Mittermeier, and T. Werner. 1990. Conserving the world's biological diversity. International Union for Conservation of Nature and Natural Resources, Gland, Switzerland; World Resources Institute, Conservation International, World Wildlife Fund-US, and the World Bank, Washington, D.C.

Mendenhall, M. 1995. Monteverde. Argenta Friends Press, Argenta, British Columbia.

Miller, K., and L. Tangley. 1991. Trees of life: saving tropical forests and their biological wealth. Beacon Press, Boston, Massachusetts.

MINAE (Ministerio de Ambiente y Energía). 1996a. Area de Conservación Arenal. MINAE, San José, Costa Rica.

———. 1996b. Sistema Nacional de Areas de Conservación. MINAE, San José, Costa Rica.

MIRENEM (Ministerio de Recursos Naturales Energía y Minas). 1992. Sistema Nacional de Areas de Conservación. MIRENEM, San José, Costa Rica.

———. 1993a. Conozcamos Arenal—Area de Conservación Arenal. MIRENEM, San José, Costa Rica.

———. 1993b. Parques Nacionales de Costa Rica. MIRENEM, San José, Costa Rica.

Montero, V., and Z. Zarate. 1991. Comunidades socio-bióticas: un modelo operativo de sostenibilidad. M.A. thesis, Universidad de Costa Rica.

———. 1996. Estatutos Asociación Conservacionista de Monteverde. MCL, Monteverde, Costa Rica.

Monteverde Journal. 1994–1997. Newsletter. Vols. 1(1) (June) through 2(2) (Dec.). MVI, Monteverde, Costa Rica.

Morrison, P. 1994. The Monteverde area of Costa Rica: a case study of ecotourism development. M.A./M.S. thesis, The University of Texas, Austin.

Moss, M. 1988. Animal stories from the cloud forest. Audiocassette. Monteverde Institute, Monteverde, Costa Rica.

Musinsky, J. 1991. The design of conservation corridors in Monteverde, Costa Rica. TRI Working Paper No. 60. Tropical Resources Institute, New Haven, Connecticut.

MVI (Monteverde Institute). 1986. Constitution of the Monteverde Institute. Monteverde, Costa Rica.

———. 1993a. Bylaws of the Monteverde Institute Association. MVI, Monteverde, Costa Rica.

———. 1996b. Monteverde Institute. MVI, Monteverde, Costa Rica.

MVI Annual Report (Informe Anual). 1987–1996. MVI, Monteverde, Costa Rica.

Nadkarni, N. 1993. Canopy plants of the Monteverde Cloud Forest (4th ed.). Tropical Science Center, San José, Costa Rica.

Paaby, P., and D. B. Clark. 1995. Conservation and local naturalist guide training programs in Costa Rica. Pages 261–275 *in* S. K. Jacobson, editor. Wildlife conservation: international case studies of education and communication programs. Columbia University Press, New York.

Patent, D. M. 1996. Children save the rain forest. Cobblehill/Dutton, New York.

Rachowiecki, R. 1994. Costa Rica, a travel survival kit (2nd ed.). Lonely Planet, Berkeley, California.

Rainforest Alliance. 1991. Unique debt swap to protect forest. The Canopy, Spring, 1–2.

Robinson, B. 1988. The Costa Rican connection. Equinox, Mar.-Apr., 8–10.

Robinson, D. 1988. In the clouds of Costa Rica. Pages 98–113 *in* M. Sedeen, editor. Mountain worlds. National Geographic Society, Washington, D.C.

Rojas, C. 1992. Monteverde: estudio inicial de los nexos entre la Reserva, el turismo, y la communidad local. Tropical Science Center, San José, Costa Rica.

Ross, D. L., Jr. 1992. Voices of the cloud forest. Cornell Laboratory of Ornithology, Ithaca, New York.

Rovinski, Y. 1991. Private reserves, parks, and ecotourism in Costa Rica. Pages 39–57 *in* T. Whelan, editor. Nature tourism. Island Press, Washington, D.C.

Savage, J. M. 1966. An extraordinary new toad (*Bufo periglenes*) from Costa Rica. Revista de Biología Tropical 14:153–167.

Shaw, S. 1978. Is this the Garden of Eden? International Wildlife 8:50–54.

Sheck, R. S. 1996. Costa Rica, a natural destination (4th ed.). John Muir Publications, Santa Fe, New Mexico.

Snow, B. K. 1977. Territory behavior and courtship of the male Three-wattled Bellbird. Auk 94:623–645.

Solórzano, R., and J. Echeverría. 1993. Impacto económico de la Reserva Biológica Bosque Nuboso Monteverde. Tropical Science Center, San José, Costa Rica.

Stiles, F. G., and A. Skutch. 1989. A guide to the birds of Costa Rica. Cornell University Press, Ithaca, New York.

Stone, D. 1988. The Organization for Tropical Studies (OTS): a success story in graduate training and research. Pages 143–187 *in* F. Almeda and C. Pringle, editors. Tropical rainforest diversity and conservation. California Academy of Sciences, San Francisco.

Stuckey, J. 1988. Kicking the subsidized habit: viewing rural development as a function of local savings mobilization—the Santa Elena case: modifications for the 1990's. MBA Thesis, National University, San José, Costa Rica.

———. 1992. Organizaciones de Monteverde. Monteverde Institute, Monteverde, Costa Rica.

Stuckey, J., P. Salgado and participants at CARE Regional Partnering Workshop, Costa Rica. 1995. New perspectives: partnering profiles from outside CARE. CARE USA, Atlanta, Georgia.

Takacs, D. 1996. The idea of biodiversity. Johns Hopkins University Press, Baltimore, Maryland.

Tangley, L. 1988. Studying (and saving) the tropics. Bioscience 38:375–385.

The Nature Conservancy N.d. Swapping debt for nature. The Nature Conservancy, Arlington, Virginia.

———. 1993 Fuentes de información en Centro América: Costa Rica: un directorio institucional de información sobre recursos naturales y medio ambiente. The Nature Conservancy, Arlington, Virginia.

Tobias, D. 1988. Biological and social aspects of ecotourism: the Monteverde case. TRI Working Paper No. 34, Vol. I. Tropical Resources Institute, New Haven, Connecticut.

Tobias, D., and R. R. Mendelsohn. 1991. Valuing ecotourism in a tropical rain-forest reserve. Ambio 20:91–93.

Tosi, J. 1992. A brief history of the Tropical Science Center's Monteverde Cloud Forest Preserve, 1972 to 1992. Tropical Science Center, San José, Costa Rica.

Tropical Science Center (TSC). 1992–1994. Reserva Biológica Bosque Nuboso Monteverde: Informe del Director. TSC, San José, Costa Rica.

———. 1994. Life in the cloud forest. Videotape. TSC, San José, Costa Rica.

———. 1995. USIJI project proposal. Monteverde–Gulf of Nicoya biological corridor. Costa Rica. Tropical Science Center, San José, Costa Rica.

———. 1998. Estadisticas de visitantes al 31 diciembre de 1997. Reserva biológica bosque nubose Monteverde Tropical Science Center, San José, Costa Rica.

Trostle, J. 1990. The origins of the Monteverde Institute. Monteverde Institute, Monteverde, Costa Rica.

Umaña, A., and K. Brandon. 1992. Inventing institutions for conservation: lessons from Costa Rica. Pages 85–107 *in*

S. Annis, editor. Poverty, natural resources, and public policy in Central America. Transaction, New Brunswick, New Jersey.

Vivanco, L. 1999. Green mountains, greening people: negotiating environmentalism in Monte Verde, Costa Rica. Ph.D. dissertation, Princeton University, Princeton, New Jersey.

Wallace, D. R. 1992. The quetzal and the macaw: the story of Costa Rica's National Parks. Sierra Club Books, San Francisco, California.

Wearing, S. 1993. Ecotourism: the Santa Elena Rainforest project. The Environmentalist 13:125–135.

Wheelwright, N. T. 1983. Fruits and the ecology of Resplendent Quetzals. Auk 100:286–301.

Wilson, E. O., editor. 1988. Biodiversity. National Academy Press, Washington, D.C.

Wolinsky, G. 1989. Water scarcity in the humid tropics: community water resources in Monteverde, Costa Rica.

TRI Working Paper No. 40. Tropical Resources Institute, New Haven, Connecticut.

World Commission on Environment and Development. 1987. Our common future. Oxford University Press, Oxford.

World Resources Institute, United Nations Environment Programme, and United Nations Development Programme. 1992. World resources 1992–1993. Oxford University Press, New York.

Worster, D. 1994. Nature's economy: a history of ecological ideas (2nd ed.). Cambridge University Press, New York.

Youth Challenge International. 1994. Santa Elena Forest Reserve. Self-guided trail. Centro Ecológico Bosque Nuboso de Monteverde, San José, Costa Rica.

Zuchowski, W. 1987. Common flowering plants of the Monteverde Cloud Forest Preserve (3rd ed.). Tropical Science Center, San José, Costa Rica.

———. 1995. Guide to the cloud forest of Monteverde, Costa Rica. Massachusetts Audubon Society, Lincoln.

11

Agriculture in Monteverde

Moving Toward Sustainability

Katherine Griffith
Daniel C. Peck
Joseph Stuckey

This chapter is an overview of how Monteverde settlers transformed their environment into a diversity of agricultural systems. We first discuss "people living in nature," how Monteverdans have viewed natural resources and defined sustainability. We describe the environmental and social conditions that determined agronomic options in the area, and outline the area's major agricultural activities (dairy, coffee, and beef), other crops, and efforts at agricultural diversification. Where possible, we cite published studies, but few exist for some issues. We rely heavily on local experts, including long-term community members, local agronomists, veterinarians, and farmers (Table 11.1). We also draw on agricultural production data collected by local organizations.

People Living with Nature

From the earliest indigenous settlers to today's commercial farmers, biologists, and artists, Monteverde's inhabitants have exhibited a wide spectrum of approaches to natural resource use. The community's ongoing debate over the meaning and practice of "sustainability" throws into sharp relief residents' differing worldviews, kinds of knowledge, and perceptions of constraints and opportunities. People's decisions on how to use natural resources depend on three factors: their attitudes and beliefs, their knowledge, and the opportunities, constraints, and conditions that they confront. For example, beliefs may demand that people be "stewards" of the land, that they use resources to maximize economic returns during their lifetime, or that they use resources as sparingly as possible. Their knowledge may prepare them to be organic vegetable farmers, traditional dairy farmers, business people, or biologists. The social, environmental, and economic context in which they make decisions further defines which options are available or attractive. As one local farmer stated, "We do the best we can with what we have, based on what we know, and what the circumstances permit or encourage us to do."

Defining Sustainable Agriculture

Monteverdans generally agree that "sustainable agriculture" is a good thing, but there is less agreement on what it means. Following the taxonomy of Gillespie

Table 11.1. Monteverde area residents cited in Chapter 11.

Resident	Community Activities
John Campbell	Quaker settler, dairy farmer
Ovidio Leitón	Dairy farmer
Jaime Lopez	Coffee technician, CoopeSanta Elena, R.L. (Coope)
Juan José Monge	Veterinarian, Productores de Monteverde
Daniel Peck	Insect ecologist
Marvin Rockwell	Quaker settler, tour guide, hotel owner
Joseph Stuckey	Dairy farmer, economic and community development specialist
Katy VanDusen	Horticulturist, homemaker
Carlos Vargas	Manager, Coope
José Luis Vargas	Manager, dairy plant
Christina Villalobos	Homemaker, farmer
Marco Vinicio	Forester, Monteverde Conservation League
Jim Wolfe	Farmer, biologist, Butterfly Farm owner

(1998), three sustainable agriculture "schools of thought" exist in Monteverde. The first group is the "Ecocentric Agriculture" school, whose approach focuses on what is sustainable in a biological/ecological sense. Many local biologists and organic producers espouse this view. They maintain that agriculture should mimic natural systems as much as possible, maintain species diversity within a cropping system, and rely on biological, cultural, and mechanical control of pests. Methods of biological pest control include breeding resistant crops, augmenting natural enemies, introducing new parasites, and controlling the behavior of pests (e.g., with pheromones). Cultural control includes plant spacing, tillage, intercropping, and crop rotations. Mechanical control includes physical removal of insects and weeds, or physical barriers such as fences or protective mesh (National Research Council 1989).

The second group is the "Green Productionist" school, who wish to improve the ecological sustainability of agriculture while maintaining financial soundness. If the system can function physically and economically over the long term, it is "sustainable." In Monteverde, this group comprises the more business-oriented farmers and those who work for agricultural enterprises such as the dairy plant.

The third group, the "Agrarian Sociocentric" school, includes ecological and economic considerations, human communities, and social justice. A system is sustainable if it does not degrade the environment, if it is economically feasible, and if it promotes social justice and healthy human communities.

In practice, achieving all these goals simultaneously is rare and may require some modification of standards. This group includes many small farmers and nonfarmers who are sympathetic to farming.

Each view has inspired attempts to improve the sustainability of Monteverde agriculture. The ecocentric agriculture view has increased the demand for organic produce and led to the local agricultural cooperative's (Coope's) efforts to encourage organic coffee and vegetable production. The green productionist view has inspired the dairy plant's efforts to raise dairy productivity and reduce environmental impacts of dairying. The agrarian sociocentric view has given life to the Buen Amigo project of San Luis and the Coope's coffee project. Although their emphases differ, these approaches ultimately converge, since an agrarian society requires healthy land and adequate incomes for farmers. Sustainability thus includes economic, social, and agronomic factors. No practice is sustainable under all circumstances.

In this chapter, our goals are to define current parameters, identify obstacles, and suggest research to overcome nonsustainable agriculture in Monteverde. A completely sustainable system must be able to function indefinitely as a closed system, cycling products without generating wastes or requiring outside inputs. Except in rare cases, a completely closed system cannot be maintained. This analysis focuses on farm-level systems in Monteverde. For example, we examine how feeding grain concentrates to cows affects the sustainability of a dairy farm, but we do not attempt to analyze whether Costa Rican feed grain production is sustainable, a question that is beyond the scope of this chapter.

The Agricultural Environment in Monteverde

We define the Monteverde area as the dairy plant's "milkshed," that is, the area that produces milk received by Productores de Monteverde. This area, about 100 km across at its widest point, spans several life zones and includes the communities of: Monteverde, San Luis, Cerro Plano, Santa Elena, La Lindora, La Guaría, Guacimal, and Los Llanos (Puntarenas Province); Cañitas, La Cruz, Las Nubes, San Rafael, Los Tornos, Cebadilla, Campos de Oro, San Bosco, Cabeceras, San Ramón del Dos, La Florida, La Chiripa, El Dos Arriba, El Dos Abajo, Monte de los Olivos, Río Negro, Turín, and La Esperanza (Guanacaste Province). We separate the milkshed into two parts: upland (above 900 m) and lowland (below 900 m). Specialized dairy farms generally occur in the upland area, and beef and dual-purpose (combined milk and beef) operations occur in the lowland area.

Pronounced seasonality is a major factor that determines agricultural options in the area. The upland areas receive an annual average of about 2500 mm of rain, about 85% of which falls during the wet season (May–November; CATIE 1983). Rains are frequently heavy (several cm/h), so uncovered soil is vulnerable to erosion. The prolonged rains—as well as the mist in the early part of dry season—favor the growth of fungi, which local farmers cite as a significant impediment to crop production during much of the year. Seasonality also affects the behavior and impacts of pasture pests (e.g., spittlebug outbreaks in pastures between June and August).

The dry season presents other agricultural challenges. From January to March, strong trade winds stress vegetation and livestock, which slows growth rates and reduces productivity (CATIE 1983, J. J. Monge, pers. comm.). High winds cause mechanical damage to fruits and vegetables and foster damage from viruses and bacteria. Wind also limits arable plot size because of the need for windbreaks at close intervals (J. Wolfe, pers. comm.). Later in the dry season, some crops may be stressed by heat and need irrigation. Grass production slows, which reduces milk production by 15–20% (Productores de Monteverde, S.A., pers. comm.). Irrigation is a challenge because of the cost of installing systems, the scarcity of water during the dry season, and the steep slopes of much of the land. Only 21% of the land is flat; the rest has slopes of 16–26% (CATIE 1983, Vasquez 1988). Building terraces on slopes is viable agronomically but not economically.

Most of Monteverde's agricultural soil is well-drained sandy loam, high in organic matter, though this varies with soil management practices (J. Stuckey, pers. comm.; see Chap. 2, Physical Environment). The pH is typically between 5.6 and 6.8. As in many tropical soils, phosphorus appears to be the limiting nutrient. Potassium, magnesium, zinc, and manganese are also generally low (CATIE 1983, Vasquez 1988). The region's heat and moisture regimes mean that organic matter breaks down rapidly and must be replenished often (J. Wolfe, pers. comm.).

Factors Influencing Early Agricultural Development

Prior to the early Creole and Quaker settlers, an indigenous population engaged in hunting, gathering, and some agriculture (see Timm, "Prehistoric Cultures," pp. 408–409). Older residents of the community of San Luis have corn-grinding stones left by the Native American inhabitants. One elderly resident stated, "When my father-in-law got here in the 1930s, he found buried pots and containers and some grind-ing stones" (C. Villalobos, pers. comm.). One neighbor recalled that the land cleared by the original inhabitants was largely grown up, and that it must have been several decades since they had left. "We found 'platano cuadrado' [a variety of small banana], wheat, and sugarcane. There were just a few plants, but we figured the Indians must have grown those crops" (O. Leitón, pers. comm.)

The first upland Creole settlers arrived in the 1920s and 1930s. Most were poor, and many had previously worked as farm hands in the San Ramón area or the gold mines in Guacimal and La Sierra de Abangares (J. L. Vargas, pers. comm.). Roads were primitive. The first motorized vehicles to use the dirt road up from the Panamerican highway belonged to the Quaker settlers who came in 1950. They were accompanied by men with shovels, who widened the road as they went along (J. Campbell, pers. comm.). During the early years, vehicular travel depended on winches. One resident recalls, "We had a sort of a tree-thinning program along the road. We'd winch our way up the mountain . . . and the little trees that couldn't take it would just come out" (M. Rockwell, pers. comm.; Fig. 11.1).

Poor road conditions had implications for agriculture. For most settlers in the first half of the century, it necessitated subsistence agriculture, as transport of products to outside markets and transport of inputs such as fertilizer were not feasible. In the upland area, most farmers produced corn, beans, vegetables, fruits, herbs, and livestock for family consumption. The few commercial upland farms produced garlic, flax, beef, and homestead cheese. One settler recalls the existence of a "still" for making cane alcohol (J. Campbell, pers. comm.). In the lowland area, commercial beef and grain production predominated (J. L. Vargas, pers. comm.). Early settlers also hunted. "When we first got here, there was more than enough meat!" said an older Costa Rican resident of the San Luis valley (C. Villalobos, pers. comm.). In the 1930s, families hunted tapirs, deer, monkeys, pacas, and birds. By the 1940s, the wild animal population had diminished, so some families raised pigs for meat.

During the late 1950s and the 1960s, the roads gradually improved and "export agriculture" (outside the area, not outside the country) became an option. Whatever was shipped out had to withstand a long, pounding trip. This ruled out most fruits, vegetables, and anything requiring refrigeration. Two options were attractive: cheese and beef. Cheese had advantages over fresh milk; milk was heavy, bulky, and liable to spoil over the long trip to outside markets (Fig. 11.2). Cheese was also more profitable as a "value-added" product. Another factor favoring dairy production was farm size; most upland farms were too

Figure 11.1. Quaker settlers en route to Monteverde on the Pan American Highway in 1951. Photograph by John Campbell.

small to generate sufficient income through beef. However, on larger farms beef production was attractive. The cows could graze slopes that were too steep to cultivate, and walk to market regardless of road conditions. Where management skills, infrastructure, flat land, and investment capital were minimal, beef was one of the few options.

11.1. The Monteverde Dairy Industry

11.1.1. History of the Monteverde Upland Dairy Industry

The background and education of the Quaker settlers who arrived in 1950 were key influences on agricul-

Figure 11.2. Transportation of milk and other fresh commodities was difficult in the early days of Monteverde's establishment, which led to the establishment of the dairy plant. Photograph by John Campbell.

tural development. Many were originally from Iowa and Alabama and were raised on dairy farms. They were familiar with high-production European dairy breeds and management techniques. Monteverde's dairy industry, which began in the early 1950s, quickly became the primary engine of economic development and a significant factor in the alteration of the natural environment in the upland area. In 1953, John Campbell, a Monteverde farmer with surplus milk and a U.S. Department of Agriculture brochure on farmstead cheese production, made the first batch of aged cheese. Later that year, the dairy plant was established, and the community brought in its first Guernsey heifers to replace the traditional Criollo cows, "the best fence jumpers in the world" according to one disgruntled owner. The dairy plant, incorporated in 1954 as Productores de Monteverde, S.A., produced cheese commercially.

Limited cash and the ready availability of virgin forest and recently cleared land led to a form of dairy farm capitalization in Monteverde termed an "ecological subsidy" (Stuckey 1989). The communities of Monteverde, Cerro Plano, Santa Elena, La Cruz, Cañitas, and La Lindora had been substantially deforested between 1920 and 1950. In other communities (Río Negro, San Bosco, Las Nubes, San Gerardo), new land was cleared for dairying between 1950 and 1980 (J. L. Vargas, pers. comm.). The flush of nutrients left by the organic matter that was burned or left to decompose after deforestation were "free" (albeit temporary) inputs that spurred early production in the upland area. They functioned as a major source of "capital" for developing the local dairy industry (Stuckey 1989). During the 1960s, the milkshed expanded beyond Monteverde and adjacent communities. Over the next two decades, milk came from communities as far as 40 km away, and the dairy plant expanded to process the additional milk (Table 11.2, Fig. 11.3).

In the early 1960s, farmers encountered problems with pasture pests such as spittlebugs and froghoppers that attacked Kikuyu Grass (*Pennisetum clandestinum*; see Peck, "Agroecology of Prosapia," pp. 409–

410). Kikuyu is a highly productive East African grass well suited to the Monteverde environment; it was widely planted as the primary forage for dairy cattle. By the late 1950s, there were scattered pockets of pasture blighted by froghoppers. By the late 1960s, entire pastures were severely damaged (J. Campbell, pers. comm.). These native pests may have finally reached injurious levels after a slow buildup following the widespread establishment of Kikuyu pastures. Producers speculate that declining soil fertility may have weakened Kikuyu Grass, which increased its susceptibility to insect pests. Chemical fertilizers were not widely used on pastures at the time, since dairying was profitable without them.

By the early 1970s, milk production had declined significantly, particularly in older pastures. Faced with declining milk production, farmers adopted four new herd and pasture management practices. First, they switched from Kikuyu to East African Star Grass ("estrella"). Although less nutritious and less palatable to livestock than Kikuyu, Star Grass was more resistent to spittlebug attack. Second, farmers adopted intensive rotational grazing. In this system, cows were moved (typically once a day) to a new paddock, the size of which depended on the herd size and length of grazing time (Voisin and Lecomte 1962). This system resulted in more complete consumption of the grass, facilitated consumption at its optimal nutrient value, reduced weed growth, produced more even manure deposition, and reduced soil compaction and damage to the grass (Mott 1974, Russell et al. 1974). Third, farmers regularly fed their cows grain and applied chemical fertilizers to their pastures. Although this raised production costs, the increased productivity compensated for the inputs. Fourth, farmers improved the genetic quality and the health of their herds with artificial insemination and better veterinary care. Holstein cows became widely preferred due to their high productivity.

Another event that reshaped the Monteverde dairy industry was the national financial crisis of the early 1980s. In 1982, Costa Rica's Central Bank ran out of dollars to buy imported goods. The Ministry of Agriculture and Ranching (Ministerio de Agricultura y Ganadería, MAG) discouraged dairy farmers from using outside inputs such as fertilizer, which resulted in lower milk production. On many older farms where land had been deforested prior to the 1960s, milk production fell by nearly one-half, to 4–8 kg per cow per day. Milk production remained at 8–10 kg per cow per day in more recently deforested areas and on the few farms in which fertilizer and grain concentrates were still used (Stuckey 1989). These anecdotal data suggest that the "ecological subsidy" that sustained dairy farms in the early years had been largely used up.

Table 11.2. Dairy plant building expansion and processing capacity from 1954 to 1995.

Year	Total Space (m²)	Milk Processing Capacity (kg/day)
1954–73	370	2,700
1974	740	8,000
1979–84	900	11,000
1987–88	1700	27,000
1994–95	2000	36–38,000

Source: Productores de Monteverde, S.A. (unpubl. data).

Figure 11.3. The deforested slopes of the Pacific foothills below Monteverde are due to burning, cattle grazing, and other agricultural activities. Photograph by Nathaniel Wheelwright.

It was not until the 1990s that Monteverde dairy farms returned to the production levels of the 1970s, which was accomplished through genetic improvements, improved veterinary care, better pasture management, and greater use of feed concentrates (Table 11.3). In the mid-1990s, dairy farming was by far the most important agricultural activity in the area, with 210 families contributing 9.7 million kg of milk to the dairy plant during 1993–94. These farmers collectively received gross earnings of 426 million colones (ca. $2.7 million). Gross revenue at the dairy plant was about 838 million colones ($5.2 million; Productores de Monteverde, S.A., pers. comm.). However, the profitability of dairy farming remained stagnant or declined for most farmers. Production expenses consumed a greater portion of earnings. Increasingly, farmers have turned to other economic activities.

11.1.2. Sustainability of Monteverde Upland Dairy Production

Monteverde dairy farmers perform a juggling act. For most, earning an adequate income is their primary consideration, which involves integrating production levels, availability and cost of labor and other inputs, management abilities, the quantity and quality of land required, capital needs, and the environment. Dairying is not lucrative and many farmers are challenged to practice environmentally sustainable farm manage-

ment. We discuss five major environmental impacts of Monteverde dairy production and management options for improved sustainability.

Deforestation. Conversion of forest to pasture is associated with loss of habitat, reduced biodiversity, changes in hydrology and microclimate, and increased soil erosion. Although much of the land currently devoted to dairy was deforested prior to 1950 for other purposes, dairy pasture establishment was a major cause of deforestation in several upland communities. Approximately 40 upland farms (ca. 560 ha of pasture) were established for dairy after 1950 (J. L. Vargas, pers. comm.). In lowland areas, dairying enhanced the profitability of existing beef farms but was not the initial impetus for deforestation. Dairying no longer stimulates the clearing of additional land in Monteverde or elsewhere in Costa Rica (Janzen 1988, D. Kaimowitz, pers. comm.).

Erosion. Although pastures occupy only 37% of Costa Rica's territory and over half the land in use, 84% of the country's erosion occurs in pastures (Hartshorn et al. 1982). In the Arenal watershed, erosion on improved (planted) pastures was estimated at 109 metric tons/ha (compared to 1.4 for primary forest and 18.8 for perennial crops). These statistics are based on the Universal Soil Loss Equation (USLE), rather than field data. The USLE may underestimate erosion

Table 11.3. Portrait of a typical upland dairy farm in the 1990s.

Herd size	16 cows, 67% of herd in production
Cow breeds	In order of importance: Holstein, Jersey, Brown Swiss, Guernsey
Feed	Rotational grazing on Star Grass pasture; 0.5–2.5 kg/day grain; Elephant or King Grass; salt, minerals, urea, molasses
Stocking rate	1.8 cows/ha
Milking	Twice per day
Farm size	18 ha total, 14 ha in pasture (CATIE 1983)
Milk production	10 kg per cow per day
Pasture management	Manual fertilization and liming, herbicides (CATIE 1983, Stuckey 1989)
Fertility	Artificial insemination; birth rate 58%; calf mortality 8% (CATIE 1983)
Mechanization	In 1995, 60% of farmers used milking machines (up from less than 5% in 1979). Some farms had electric fencing and/or a tractor. No farms had refrigeration (cold water was used to cool milk).
Labor	Mostly family labor supplemented by part-time hired help
Family size	4.5 dependents per farm

Data compiled by Juan José Monge, José Luis Vargas, Joseph Stuckey, and Katherine Griffith.

by ignoring mechanical factors such as cattle hooves, but may overestimate erosion by failing to integrate the effects of rotational grazing and fertilization, which reduce erosion. Erosion on upland dairy farms, even those on steep hillsides in high rainfall areas, is less than that for lower elevation beef and crop production (Hartshorn et al. 1982). Research is needed to determine true erosion rates under pasture management systems in the Monteverde milkshed.

Loss of biodiversity. Establishing pastures reduces the diversity of fauna in the area, although several species are favored (e.g., Cattle Egrets, Brown Jays). Pastures that retain some overstory trees attract more wildlife species than those that have been cleared completely. Monocultures (single species systems) are more vulnerable to pests, diseases, and changing environmental conditions than are polycultures (multiple species systems; National Research Council 1989, 1993). Diversifying forage crops may check pest outbreaks.

Manure management. Improperly handled manure can be a source of pollution. In the Monteverde upland area, most farmers use rotational grazing, which limits contamination from manure by spreading it around the fields. Manure may concentrate around barns where cows spend several hours a day, but many farmers channel this runoff into pastures.

Pesticide management. Three types of pesticides are used in dairying: herbicides, pasture insecticides, and external parasite control substances on cows. Herbicide use on pastures has increased since the 1980s. Traditionally, weeds were controlled by machete. Spot spraying of herbicides reduces labor costs while providing effective control of pasture weeds. Pasture insecticides are used to combat localized eruptions of minor pest species and to control infestations of spittlebugs, primarily in Kikuyu Grass pastures (Table 11.4; see Peck, "Agroecology of *Prosapia*," pp. 409–410). The localized use and spot spraying typical of dairy farms means that most problems concern human and domestic animal safety. Nevertheless, any pesticide can affect nontarget species (e.g., spittlebug predators or parasitoids) that might have a role in naturally controlling these pests. Further study is needed to determine the environmental consequences of pesticide use on Monteverde dairy farms. Major external parasites are ticks and botfly larvae; these are managed with external chemical controls, which may be harmful not only to cows and farmers

Table 11.4. Pasture pests of Monteverde.

English Common Name	Spanish Common Name	Order: Family	Scientific Name
Chinch bug	Chinche	Hemiptera: Lygaeidae	*Blissus leucopterus*
Spittlebug/froghopper	Salivazo/baba de culebra	Homoptera: Cercopidae	*Aeneolamia postica/ Prosapia* spp.
Aphid	Pulgón del pasto, afido	Homoptera: Aphididae	*Aphis* spp., *Sipha* spp.
White grub	Joboto	Coleoptera: Scarabaeidae	*Phyllophaga* spp.
Wire worm	Gusano alambre	Coleoptera: Elateridae	*Agriotes* spp.
Army worm	Gusano cogollero	Lepidoptera: Noctuidae	*Spodoptera frugiperda*
Cutworm	Gusano cortador	Lepidoptera: Noctuidae	*Spodoptera* spp.
Looper	Falso medidor	Lepidoptera: Noctuidae	*Mocis latipes*
Nematode	Nematodo	—	*Meloidogyne* spp.

Source: D. Peck (pers. obs.).

but also to Cattle Egrets, which can be poisoned by consuming ticks on recently treated cows (J. J. Monge, pers. comm.).

11.1.3. Opportunities for Improved Sustainability

Policies that are critical to farm operations are those that control prices, allocate credit and technical assistance, set research agendas and interest rates, regulate environmental quality, establish minimum wages, and subsidize or tax agricultural inputs. Such policies can encourage environmentally destructive or benign practices and can affect the availability of production technologies. The management practices described below are amenable in varying degrees to policy interventions on the part of national or local agencies.

Manure management.   The beneficial effects of manure on soil are well documented (Mott 1974, Vicente-Chandler 1974, National Research Council 1989). Proper manure application increases organic matter content and releases nutrients slowly so that they are more likely to be taken up by plants rather than being lost to leaching and becoming an environmental problem. Many obstacles to mechanical manure spreading exist in Monteverde. A manure spreader and tractor are not affordable for most farmers and cannot be used on steep slopes. Slurry system installation is costly and is feasible only if pastures are downhill from the barn. Manure composting prior to spreading requires careful management to prevent nutrient loss and contamination problems. Manure management systems reduce but do not eliminate the need for chemical fertilizers.

Fertilizer management.   Leaching and weathering in the tropics reduce fertility of soils in most high-rainfall areas (Ter and Kang 1986). Soil tests on limed and fertilized Monteverde pastures have revealed the following: organic matter 10–12%; pH 5.6–6.0; phosphorus deficiency 70–90 kg/ha/yr; magnesium deficiency, 45 kg/ha/yr; and potassium deficiency, 20–25 kg/ha/yr (Stuckey 1989). Fertilizer use is labor-intensive; it is generally broadcast by hand. It requires reliable local suppliers, affordable transport, and management skills to avoid waste and optimize timing of applications, and is expensive. Alternatives to fertilizing are generally inadequate for Monteverde dairies. For example, grass-legume mixtures are difficult to establish and require nonnitrogen fertilizers to flourish.

Many temperate zone proponents of sustainable and organic agriculture argue that use of chemical fertilizers is unsustainable, as nonrenewable re-sources such as fossil fuel will be depleted and poorly managed fertilizers can contaminate groundwater. However, properly applied chemical fertilizers can increase the vigor of pasture plants and reduce compaction and erosion (Vicente-Chandler 1974). Healthier pastures are less susceptible to diseases and pests, which reduces or eliminates the need for pesticides. Fertilizers increase yields, which potentially reduces the amount of land needed for agriculture. The U.S. National Research Council (1993) concluded that fertilizer use is a sustainable management practice in the tropics.

Feed and mineral supplements.   Most Monteverde farmers feed their cows combinations of grain, mineral supplements, molasses, and urea. Use of supplementary feeds is environmentally positive. A large proportion of the minerals is recovered in manure and urine. When these wastes are deposited on pastures (as they are in a rotational grazing regime), a significant source of nutrients is added (Mott 1974, De Geus 1977, Humphreys 1987), which reduces the need for purchased fertilizers. Supplementary feeds and minerals can also reduce pressure on the land base (McDowell et al. 1986). The major disadvantage of feed supplements is cost; they represent half the milk production cost in the Monteverde uplands (McDowell et al. 1986, Guzman Zamorra 1989). The need for local suppliers and affordable transport are other obstacles. Research should identify alternative feed supplements that could reduce production costs.

Cut feeds.   Cut feeds (tall grasses cut with a machete and carried to cows) have been widely promoted for dairy farmers in Costa Rica. They are used primarily to increase forage availability during the dry season. The two main types used in Monteverde are King Grass (*Pennisetum* spp.) and Imperial (*Axonopus* spp.; CATIE 1983). Some species provide excellent erosion control. They can also be effective windbreaks for row crops. Cut feeds can substantially reduce the amount of land needed for pasture; 0.1 ha of cut feed can supply all the dry matter and nearly all the protein for a producing dairy cow (CATIE 1983). In contrast, a typical upland pasture requires about 0.5 ha per cow.

An environmental disadvantage to cut feeds is that some types are difficult to eradicate once they become established. Management can also be problematic. Correct harvesting intervals are key; if harvested when maximum volume is achieved, crude protein is reduced. Cut feeds are also labor intensive; farmers spend several hours a day cutting, hauling, chopping, and distributing forage. A growing number of Monteverde farmers allow cows to graze the forage directly, which reduces stem consumption (the stems must later be cut down with a machete) but greatly reduces labor.

Alternative forages.   Since 1985, the dairy plant, the Coope, and farmers have tried alternative forages (sugarcane, alfalfa, sorghum, and oats), but none has been adopted (Madrigal Chavarria 1988b). Although experimental farm results were moderately promising (Madrigal Chavarria 1988a), most farmers found the crops demanding and risky. During the 1980s, the dairy plant promoted silos to increase dry season production. Most have been abandoned due to marginal feed quality and high labor demands. One farmer has planted oats, clovers, and brassicas as forage with good results. A significant positive contribution of the brassicas is their "soil plowing" effect. Their roots infiltrate the soil as they grow, aerate it, and bring up nutrients from lower soil horizons (see Wolfe, "Brassicas as Biological Plows," p. 411). Research is needed to investigate this legume and other alternative forage and cover crops for Monteverde.

Pest management.   Most upland dairy farmers plant grasses that tolerate spittlebugs. Even so, pest populations increasingly overwhelm them. Researchers are developing forage grass cultivars that are resistant to spittlebug attack (Ferrufino and Lapointe 1989, Lapointe et al. 1992). Maintaining healthy soil and a vigorous sward reduces invasions of weeds and damage from some insect pests. Cutting weeds by hand is labor intensive, less effective than herbicides in controlling some weeds, and can facilitate the broadcast of weed seeds (Mendoza et al. 1986).

Windbreaks.   The trade winds that buffet the area between December and March are a major limitation to dairy production. Windbreaks reduce pasture desiccation, mechanical damage, and energy loss in cows. They increase milk production and provide other benefits: reduced soil erosion, watershed protection, habitat for wildlife and beneficial insects, fodder for cows, nitrogen for the soil, and fruit and wood for farmers.

In the Monteverde upland area, well over a million trees (many native species) have been planted for pasture windbreaks. About 70% of the farms have participated in windbreak projects (J. L. Vargas, pers. comm.). The first of these was started by the Dairy Plant in 1981 using exotic, fast-growing species (mostly cypress, eucalyptus, pine, and casuarina). This project provided nursery-grown trees and technical assistance to producers. The Monteverde Conservation League (MCL) project focused on native species trees (see Chap. 10, Conservation Institutions).

Obstacles to widespread planting of windbreaks, particularly of native species trees, are high. In 1990, windbreaks were estimated to cost $800 per farm including the trees themselves, fencing to protect them from cows, herbicides to prepare the ground, fertilizers, and labor. Because it takes several years to realize any benefits from windbreaks, most farmers have needed subsidies.

Alternatives to wooden fenceposts.   The hardwoods that provide long-lasting posts have already been cut. Farmers have cut progressively softer trees, the posts of which decompose faster (some in less than five years), which accelerates the need to cut more trees. The advantage of wooden posts is that farmers can usually obtain them from their farms; labor and the tree-cutting permit process are the only costs. In recent years, the MCL has made a trunk borer available to farmers to help them determine whether a tree is sound and will make good posts, thus preventing unnecessary cutting of unsuitable trees.

There are three alternatives to cut wooden fenceposts: living trees, cement fenceposts, and metal fenceposts. Living fenceposts are obtained by cutting branches from trees that coppice (sprout roots and regrow from sticks, or grow new branches from stumps). In the lowlands, living fenceposts are used extensively (Fig. 11.4). Their main disadvantages are that they grow over barbed wire, they cannot be used for electric fencing, and no known species coppice well in upland Monteverde.

Cement posts are long-lasting and may be used with electric or barbed wire fencing. They are expensive, costing several times more than wooden posts (J. Wolfe, pers. comm.). It is unlikely they will be widely adopted in the uplands. Metal fenceposts are gaining popularity in Monteverde because of their durability and cost, which is comparable to purchased wooden posts. They must be used with electric fencing, as they cannot withstand the weight of leaning cows. Operating costs of electric fencing are low because animals quickly learn to avoid the fence. They are also easy to move to adjust paddock size for rotational grazing.

Genetic improvement.   The dairy plant has played an active role in genetic improvement of the area's herds. The original goal of their artificial insemination program was to increase production efficiency. However, their goal has shifted toward producing higher quality milk rather than greater quantity. Since the mid-1980s, Jersey cows (which produce a lower volume of higher fat milk) have replaced Holsteins on many farms. Jerseys are also hardier and cause less soil compaction and erosion because they are smaller.

Figure 11.4. *Bursera simarouba* trees planted as "living fenceposts" along the road to Monteverde. Photograph by Dan Perlman.

11.1.4. Directions for Future Research

The most important research area for sustainability is pasture management. Alternative forages, particularly legumes and grass-legume mixes, could make a significant contribution toward environmental sustainability and reduce production costs. Successful species must be hardy, low cost, low risk, and able to survive spittlebugs.

11.2. Lowland Dual-Purpose and Beef Production

11.2.1. History and Development

With the exception of a few degraded farms that cannot produce milk economically, there are few specialized beef farms in the Monteverde upland area. Most beef within the Monteverde milkshed is produced by culling dairy herds or employing the lowland dual-purpose system. Dairy breeds are crossed with beef breeds and the farmer produces both milk and beef. The most common beef breed is Zebu (*Bos indicus*), originally from India. Dairy breeds (*Bos taurus*) include Holstein, Jersey, and Brown Swiss. The average dual-purpose herd in the Monteverde milkshed is 18 cows. Typically the farmer will produce five or six calves per year (J. J. Monge, pers. comm.). Animals reach slaughter weight or have their first calf in four years, and typically calve in alternate years (McDowell 1976). The animals are sold by live weight after being trucked to public auction or slaughterhouses for export.

Dual-purpose and beef farms in the Monteverde milkshed occur below 900 m in premontane wet forest and lower montane wet forest (Pacific slope), and lower montane rain forest and premontane rain forest (Atlantic slope and transitional Atlantic-Pacific). Most are in the lowland communities of La Lindora, La Guaria, Guacimal, Los Tornos, Cebadilla, San

Rafael, Campos de Oro, El Dos de Abangares (Pacific slope), and La Chiripa and Cabeceras (Atlantic slope). Many of these farms started as beef farms and added dairying after 1985 to increase their income. Milk production in dual-purpose herds is low (4.5 kg/day in the rainy season, 3 kg/day in the dry season). Low productivity increases the minimum economically viable farm size, so dual-purpose farms are typically larger than specialized dairy farms (20–150 ha, average ca. 40 ha), of which around 75% is in pasture (J. J. Monge, pers. comm.). Dual-purpose farms are a growing source of milk for the dairy plant; in 1996, 80 of the plant's 210 producers were dual-purpose operations (J. L. Vargas, pers. comm.).

The cattle graze on deforested slopes that have either native grasses (pitilla, kalinguero, San Augustín, and Guinea, in order of importance) or improved grasses (jeragua and Star Grass). About 85% of the farms use improved grasses for their producing cows. For many years, annual pasture burning was the only form of pasture fertilization and weed control (see Griffith, "Pasture Burning," pp. 411–412). Since the mid-1980s, burning has been outlawed; it is no longer practiced on area farms (J. J. Monge, pers. comm.). Dual-purpose farm stocking rates are low (<1 cow/ha). Pasture rotations are common; paddocks are larger and grazed longer (5–10 days) than on the upland farms. Cows are usually fed mineral salts with molasses. Reproductive health is fair (J. J. Monge, pers. comm.). Only 5% of the farmers use programmed veterinary visits; the majority wait until a problem arises.

Despite its environmental costs, farmers have adopted the dual-purpose system for compelling reasons. First, it requires minimal financial investment. The main inputs are the land, fencing, and the animals. Production costs are low. The cows receive only minerals and molasses, pastures are not fertilized, and labor inputs are low. The system requires little infrastructure, farm management skills, or education. Land and forage can be of marginal quality (Cipaguata 1993). This semidiversified production system partially insulates farmers from milk and beef price fluctuations. Milk provides a steady dependable income; cow and calf sales provide seasonal sporadic income. The system limits risks, which is an important consideration for families on the economic margin (Hartshorn et al. 1982, Jarvis 1986, Cipaguata 1993). This system is also attractive from a macroeconomic perspective. It is practiced mostly on small and medium-sized farms, which has positive implications for land tenure and social equity. It does not require high-quality land and absorbs more rural labor than specialized beef production. It relies on minimal credit and extension services compared to specialized dairying. In contrast to specialized dairy and beef opera-

tions, dual-purpose cows do not compete with humans for grain, which reduces prices of grains, meat, and milk. The dual-purpose system is both biologically and economically more efficient than specialized milk or beef production (Preston 1976, Jarvis 1986, McDowell 1993).

11.2.2. Sustainability of Lowlands Dual-Purpose and Beef Production

Although the relationship between beef cattle and deforestation has been discussed (Myers 1981, Hartshorn et al. 1982, Williams 1986, Leonard 1987, Annis 1990, Rifkin 1992), how sustainable beef/dual purpose production is and how sustainability can be increased in the Monteverde milkshed are not known. Regional data suggest unsustainably high erosion rates on beef operations in the same life zones as the Monteverde dairy producers. Erosion from cattle operations in the very moist forest life zone is estimated to be 400–800 tons/ha/yr (Hartshorn et al. 1982).

The same study classified almost 30% of the Pacific slope as "severely" or "extremely" eroded, and another 30% as "lightly" or "moderately" eroded. In contrast, the Atlantic slope was classified as only 5% extremely or severely eroded, and 18% lightly or moderately eroded. The greater erosion on the Pacific slope is a result of (1) widespread deforestation for cattle-raising, (2) the more erosive pattern of rainfall (almost all precipitation occurs during a few months), (3) pasture burning during the dry season, and (4) clayey, relatively shallow soils that resist water absorption (Hartshorn et al. 1982). Water infiltration rates on forested land in Guanacaste province (which includes part of the Monteverde lowland milkshed) were 49 times higher than in adjacent pasture land that had been subjected to a decade of overgrazing and periodic burning (C. Quesada, pers. comm.).

National beef production declined during the 1970s and 1980s (Saborío 1981, Leonard 1987, D. Kaimowitz, pers. comm.). Pasture area and stocking rates have declined in Puntarenas province (of which the Monteverde milkshed is a part), which may reflect, at least in part, pasture degradation caused by erosion, overgrazing, and soil compaction (D. Kaimowitz, pers. comm.). Data on productivity, soil, and economic factors are needed to determine the sustainability of Monteverde's dual-purpose farms.

11.2.3. Opportunities for Improving Sustainability

Practices that could improve the sustainability of the dual-purpose and beef operations center on intensification of production, which would reduce pressure on remaining forest and improve soil and forage management (Hartshorn et al. 1982, McDowell 1993, Parsons 1983).

Forage management.   The greatest limitation to productivity is the seasonal variation in forage availability (Preston 1976, Stobbs 1976, McDowell 1993), which is more acute in the Monteverde lowlands than uplands. Low stocking rates are necessary to ensure minimally adequate nutrition during the dry season, but this creates a problem in the rainy season because forage matures faster than the animals can consume it, and it rapidly loses nutritional value. Weedy and less palatable species are left untouched and can gradually take over the pasture. Optimal stocking densities during the rainy season usually mean overgrazing during the dry season, which causes erosion and damage to the grass.

Other forage management practices include fertilization, rotational grazing, improved grasses, grass-legume mixes, and weed control. Challenges in this system are similar but greater in magnitude than in the upland systems. The low productivity of the dual-purpose system puts constraints on increasing inputs. For example, fertilization is an economic necessity in the upland farms, but its value is uncertain in the dual-purpose setting (Stobbs 1976, Bunderson and Frye 1986, P. Sanchez and M. Ara, unpubl. data). Research is needed on the agronomic and economic aspects of pasture fertilization, rotational grazing, forage species, and weed control in the Monteverde lowlands.

Animal nutrition.   Cattle in the tropics frequently suffer from mineral deficiencies, which reduce productivity, increase illness, and cause reproductive problems (McDowell 1976, Warnick 1976). These deficiencies become more acute as production rises through improved forage management; tropical forages alone are usually inadequate sources of minerals. The economic return on mineral supplements is generally high (McDowell et al. 1986); almost all Monteverde farms use them. The primary challenge for farmers is to feed their cows adequately during the dry season. Dry season forage maintains body weight, but not growth or milk production. Improved forage management can only partially ameliorate this. Farmers may also supplement pasture forage with other feeds (grain, agroindustrial wastes such as cottonseed or rice polishings, sugarcane, molasses, banana plants, and cassava; Donefer 1976, Preston 1976). If the supplemental feed is produced on the farm, it must coincide with seasonal labor availability, and the farmer's land and capital constraints. Research is needed on promising feeds for the Monteverde lowlands.

Animal genetics.   Most of the lowland producers have Zebu cows or crosses of Zebu with dairy breeds. Zebu cows are hardy and well adapted to the hot climate and to low-quality forages. Crossed with specialized dairy breeds, milk production can increase considerably but only with adequate nutrition. Genetic improvement has been a major focus of research and extension with mixed results (Plasse 1976). The best policy is to create a range of genetic mixes available to farmers through artificial insemination programs (McDowell 1993). Aggressive culling of heifers that do not conceive in a 3–4-month breeding season or that produce inferior calves can give excellent results (Plasse 1976).

Herd health.   Increasing the proportion of European dairy breeds in a herd, intensifying production, and increasing stocking rates can increase the incidence of disease. Maintaining substantial Zebu blood in the crosses helps, as they are more resistant to ticks and many diseases than are European breeds. Very intensive grazing, frequent paddock changes, and preventive veterinary care can dramatically reduce parasite problems (Ellis and Hugh Jones 1976).

Reforestation.   Reforestation is undoubtedly a good environmental practice on the steep slopes of the lowland farms. However, establishing forest on degraded pasture is costly and difficult due to the depleted soils, the harsh dry season, and the need to reestablish rhizobia for many tree species. Reforestation costs around $2000/ha (J. Segleau, unpubl. data), an immense investment for most farmers. Reforestation is also labor intensive and produces no immediate income.

11.3. Coffee Production

11.3.1. History and Development

Many farms in the Monteverde uplands produce coffee for personal and commercial use. Several hectares of coffee can provide enough income to support a family. It produces an unusually high return and is attractive for farmers with limited land. In the upland area, coffee establishment grew out of an economic diversification strategy sparked by the financial troubles of the late 1970s. Most of the land committed to coffee in the early years was marginal, steeply sloping dairy pasture. Under coffee production, these soils became better stabilized and milk production was minimally affected. Coffee is typically one of several farm activities. Seventy percent of the coffee producers regard dairying as their main activity, 10%

raise beef, 8% raise crops, and 12% generate income through some other activity (CoopeSanta Elena, R.L., unpubl. data).

Since 1989, coffee production has received stimulus from the efforts of the Coope, a 500–member cooperative involved with five community enterprises: (a) grocery outlets, (b) an agricultural inputs store, (c) coffee processing and roasting facilities, (d) an artesans' workshop and retail outlet, and (e) a farm in San Luis for local landless farmers. The Coope is also involved in organic vegetable production and marketing, technical assistance and financing for coffee production, and environmental education. It finances 50% of the cost of establishing a coffee patch, provides technical assistance to producers, and processes and markets the coffee. In 1988, there were about 60 ha of coffee on as many farms. In 1996, about 90 ha were planted by 75 producers (CoopeSanta Elena, R.L., unpubl. data).

Marketing has been a key element of the cooperative's success. Monteverde producers receive among the highest prices in the world for their coffee because of its high quality and favorable marketing outlets. The Coope roasts and attractively packages the coffee locally, thereby serving the substantial local tourist trade. Local sales represent 10% of the total coffee sales and generate 20% of the coffee revenue. Of the coffee sold on the national and international markets, 40% is sold through a specialty coffee trader in the United States. Advertised as "coffee grown in har-

mony with the cloud forest," it fetches a premium price. As the owner of the outfit explains, "It's not just good coffee—it has 'mistica' (mystique). There are other places that can produce good coffee, but not every place is Monteverde" (R. C. Beall, pers. comm.).

Although coffee production is increasingly attractive compared to dairying, labor is an impediment. The coffee harvest requires three full-time workers per hectare during the relatively brief harvest season. These coincide with the peak tourist months; the higher wages in the tourism sector reduce labor available for harvesting coffee. Over three-fourths of the labor on coffee farms in Monteverde is family labor. Much of the growth in coffee production has occurred in the San Luis valley, a community where tourism has had minimal impact. The Coope expects aggregate production in the area to increase by about 150% by the year 2000 but for labor constraints to limit growth beyond that.

11.3.2. Agroecology of Coffee

The seasonal labor requirements of the coffee harvest is a product of the plant's phenology. During the dry season, flower buds enter dormancy until the wet season, which prompts a synchronous bloom in April and May. The fruit ripens during the rainy season, and the harvest is concentrated during the beginning of the following dry season in December and January (Boucher 1983, Wrigley 1988; Fig. 11.5). Not coinci-

Figure 11.5. Ripening coffee beans ready for harvest. Photograph by Leslie Burlingame.

dentally, Costa Rican school vacation begins at this time.

Producers grow their coffee bushes in nurseries with seed supplied by the Coope. The bushes are transplanted to the field the following year, in rows 2 m apart (ca. 5000 coffee plants/ha). Coffee patches are small (<2 ha). The first harvest occurs the third year, and the bushes are replaced after five years of production. The major varieties of *Coffea arabica* planted in the area include Arabigo (38%), Caturra, and Catuai (40% together). The latter two are improved varieties that thrive without shade trees. Minor varieties include Hibrido Tico, Extranjero, Katimor, and Villa Sarchi. Coffee is traditionally grown under a canopy of shade trees, which create the understory environment to which the species is adapted. Shaded coffee agroecosystems offer multiple benefits: the trees provide fruit (banana and plantain), fuelwood and lumber, nitrogen fixation, soil stabilization, water retention, pest and disease control, and habitat for wildlife and beneficial insects (Smithsonian Migratory Bird Center 1994).

The productivity of coffee patches varies widely in Monteverde, but it has generally risen with involvement of the Coope. The producers with newer or renovated plantations typically obtain yields of about 1800 kg/ha of dry coffee. Top yields nationally and in Monteverde reach 3200–3700 kg/ha (CoopeSanta Elena, R.L., unpubl. data), making Costa Rica's productivity among the highest in the world.

Coffee is vulnerable to pests and weeds, mainly fungi: *Hemileia vastatrix, Mycena citricolor, Cercospora coffeicola,* and *Rosellinea* spp. Leaf-cutter ants (*Acromyrmex* and *Atta*) are significant pests of young bushes. Their principal combatant, the insecticide Mirex (a chlorinated hydrocarbon; Hill 1983), was banned in 1991. One of the most damaging insect pests of coffee, the coffee berry borer ("broca del cafe," Coleoptera: Scolytidae, *Hypothenemus hampei*), has not yet appeared in Costa Rica. The control of weeds is labor intensive. Although some removal is done by hand, many producers use herbicides such as Roundup (glyphosate).

11.3.3. Sustainability of Coffee Production

Historically, the intensification of coffee production has coincided with the elimination of shade trees (London 1994). With the development of sun-tolerant dwarf varieties, shade trees are removed and bushes are planted in dense formations. This trend has contributed to Costa Rica's rise as a world leader in productivity. However, the high yields of sun-tolerant varieties require heavy use of nitrogen fertilizer and pesticides. Erosion rates may also rise with the removal of the overstory trees.

Environmentally beneficial management practices include the use of pest-resistant coffee varieties, wide spacing among bushes to control disease, pruning shade trees and infected bushes, and use of organic and/or chemical fertilizers to strengthen plant resistance to diseases and pests. Groundcovers can improve sustainability by suppressing weeds, reducing spread of diseases, limiting erosion, providing nutrients and organic matter, and reducing evaporation from the soil. In San Luis, some producers have used perennial groundnut (*Arachis pintoi*) as a cover crop. This plant does not thrive in Monteverde's higher elevations, so other options are needed (J. Lopez, pers. comm.). Terracing is another beneficial practice. Erosion can be severe on coffee plantations, partly due to aggressive weed control efforts that expose the soil. Some farmers use terraces to reduce erosion, but they are labor intensive. The Coope promotes use of bench terraces for slopes of 10% or more.

Waste pulp from processing is a pressing environmental issue in coffee production. The Tropical Science Center (TSC) cites it as one of the worst causes of surface water contamination in the country (Hartshorn et al. 1982). It is acidic and generates a substantial biological oxygen demand in the rivers into which it is dumped. Alternatives are limited, as it is heavy, bulky, and centrally generated. It is also wet, requiring at least some drying for most uses. Although the pulp is high in organic matter, it contributes only 10–20% of the nutrients of chemical fertilizers and it must be composted. Alternative pulp treatments that do not work well include caffeine and pectin extraction, commercial-scale animal feeding, and biogas production. The best alternatives are to use dried pulp for fuel and composted pulp as a soil amendment. The Coope processes 100% of the coffee pulp generated from processing into organic fertilizer, which is sold for use on coffee, sugarcane, and vegetable plots.

11.3.4. Organic Coffee Production

As of 1995, several organic coffee plots that meet the guidelines established by the International Organic Crop Improvement Association (OCIA) have been maintained. There is little organic premium-quality coffee available on the international market, so this is an attractive market opportunity. In organic production, varietal selection is one of the principal techniques used to combat pests and diseases. Organic producers prefer Katimor and other older varieties of coffee for their resistance, particularly to coffee leaf rust (*Hemileia vastatrix*). They also use the traditional shade system. OCIA-certified plots are permitted the use of Bordeaux Mix (lime with 5% copper) as a fungicide; otherwise they use no agrichemicals. They use organic fertilizers and composted coffee pulp in lieu of chemical fertilizers and rely on organic foliar feedings, which improve productivity and resistance to disease. They do this by soaking organic fertilizer in a barrel of water and spraying the resultant brew directly onto the bushes.

11.4. Other Crops

Other crops are grown in Monteverde for family consumption and diversification, including sugarcane, citrus, bananas, vegetables, and medicinal and other herbs. Many farms also raise poultry and hogs. Some crops are used for a combination of livestock feed and human consumption. In general, these crops are only marginally suited to the Monteverde environment because of low productivity, pests, the limited local market, and difficulties of gaining access to larger markets. However, they may use resources that would otherwise remain underused. Many households have a "kitchen garden" (see VanDusen, "Monteverde's Kitchen Gardens," pp. 412–413).

11.4.1. Commercial Vegetables, Fruits, and Herbs

Truck farming has been attempted several times in the Monteverde area with mixed results. Some farmers have produced vegetables in quantities that they were not able to market effectively. Those who tried marketing outside the area faced high transportation costs, the loss of perishable products, and competition from better situated producers. The local area has traditionally relied on imports of small amounts of produce from other parts of Costa Rica. However, the growth of tourism in the 1990s considerably enlarged the local market. Local producers produce a greater share of the fruits and vegetables consumed in the area (Tables 11.5, 11.6). More farmers are experimenting with organic production to meet a growing local demand.

11.4.2. Sustainability of Other Crops

Vegetable and fruit production in the Monteverde area is generally carried out on such a small scale that environmental impacts are minimal. However, a study by local high school students on pesticide use in the area identified deficiencies in pesticide handling that could result in negative environmental impacts (see Griffith, "Pesticide Use," p. 414). Other studies in Costa Rica confirm the results of the Santa Elena study (Hartshorn et al. 1982, Hilje et al. 1987, Thrupp 1988). Since the late 1980s, the Coope, the Dairy Plant, and

Table 11.5. Monthly demand for produce, eggs, and chicken in the Monteverde–Santa Elena area during the low season.

Product	Quantity
Cauliflower	472 units
Bell pepper	3040 units
Onion	680 kg
Potato	1883 kg
Beet	550 units
Cabbage	957 kg
Tomato	140 crates
Green bean	580 kg
Carrot	688 kg
Cilantro	1290 bunches
Cucumber	520 kg
Lettuce	900 units
Chayote	1580 units
Ayote	230 units
Celery	178 units
Eggs	1074 kg
Chicken	2295 kg

Demand roughly triples during the tourist season, November–April.

Source: CoopeSanta Elena, R.L., "Estimación de la Demanda de Productos Horticolas en la Zona de Santa Elena de Monteverde," 1992.

the MCL have improved on-farm management of pesticides. Safety equipment is now sold locally, safety information is available, and some training and public education efforts with environmental and safety messages have been undertaken.

11.4.3. Organic Vegetable Production

In 1992, 12–15 producers from Monteverde, Cabeceras, and La Cruz joined the Small Organic Producers Association of Costa Rica (Asociación de Pequeños Productores Orgánicos de Costa Rica). They have taken field trips to organic farms, experimented on their own farms, and sought technical assistance. They produce commercially, but quantities are small. Irrigation is a problem for which they receive technical assistance. They have learned to make organic fertilizer and have found that powdered charcoal provides potassium, helps aerate the soil, and improves moisture retention. They have found that rabbit manure, *Impatiens*, and the liquid produced in the process of making charcoal are effective fungicides and/ or nematocides. Madero negro (*Gilricidia sepium*) is an effective insecticidal tree, and intercropping (planting several crops in the same bed) and crop rotations help reduce pest and disease problems. Colostrum (milk produced in the first days after the birth of a calf) is an effective fertilizer for foliar feedings. Some farmers plant windbreaks to reduce mechanical damage to the crops. This reduces disease since

Table 11.6. Other crops grown in the Monteverde uplands.

English Name	Spanish Name	Scientific Name
Vegetables		
Beet	Remolacha	*Beta vulgaris*
Broccoli	Broccoli	*Brassica oleracea*
Cabbage[a]	Repollo	*Brassica campestris*
Carrot	Zanahoria	*Daucus carota*
Cauliflower	Coliflor	*Brassica oleracea*
Celery	Apio	*Apium graveolens*
Chyote	Chayote	*Sechium edule*
Cucumber	Pepino	*Cucumis sativus*
Eggplant	Berenjena	*Solanum melongena*
Green bean	Vainica	*Phaseolus vulgaris*
Lettuce	Lechuga	*Lactuca sativa*
New Zealand spinach	Espinaca	*Tetragonia tetragonioides*
Onion[a]	Cebolla	*Allium cepa*
Potato[a]	Papa	*Solanum tuberosum*
Radish	Rábano	*Raphanus sativus*
Sweet pepper	Chile dulce	*Capsicum annuum*
Sweet potato	Camote	*Ipomoea batatas*
Swiss chard	Acelga	*Beta vulgaris*
Spinach	Espinaca	*Spinacia oleracea*
Tiquisque	Tiquisque	*Xanthosoma violaceum*
Zucchini	Zapallo	*Cucurbita pepo*
Fruits		
Apple	Manzana	*Malus pumila*
Banana	Banano	*Musa acuminata*
Blackberry	Mora	*Rubus* spp.
Grapefruit	Toronja	*Citrus paradisi*
Lemon	Limón	*Citrus limon*
Orange	Naranja	*Citrus cinensis*
Papaya	Papaya	*Carica papaya*
Peach	Durazno	*Prunus persica*
Pineapple	Piña	*Ananus comosus*
Tomato	Tomate	*Lycopersicon esculentum*
Tree tomato	Tomate de palo	*Cyphomandra betacca*
Herbs		
Basil	Albahaca	*Ocimum basilicum*
Cilantro	Culantro	*Coriandrum sativum*
Dill	—	*Anethum graveolens*
Lemon grass	Zacate limón	*Cymbopogon citratus*
Mint	Menta	*Mentha* spp.
Other		
Black bean	Frijol negro	*Phaseolus vulgaris*
Buckwheat	Trigo	*Fagopyrum polygonaceae*
Coffee[a]	Café	*Coffea arabica*
Corn (dry)	Maíz	*Zea mays*
Sugarcane	Caña	*Saccharum officinarum*

[a]Crops that have been grown at a commercial scale for sale within or outside the Monteverde area. Others are sold locally in small quantities (a few kilograms per week per farmer).

pathogens are more likely to enter damaged crops (J. Wolfe, pers. comm.). The greatest successes for the organic producers have been cabbage, celery, carrots, radishes, cilantro, and beets. They have also successfully produced broccoli, "aracache," covered beans ("frijol tapado"; see Griffith and Wolfe, "Frijol Tapado, p. 414), and sweet peppers. Tomatoes have been unsuccessful. Research is needed to further adapt organic production techniques to the Monteverde environment.

11.5. Livestock and Fowl

11.5.1. Commercial Poultry

Although some families sell homestead eggs and chickens, the area has only one commercial poultry operation (Union VARSAN, S.A.), which began egg production in 1991 and chicken production in 1992. The company is owned by six local shareholders. Varsan's operation has 2500 layers out of a total chicken inventory of 4200. They produce 54,000 eggs and 1750 chickens of 1.6 kg per month. Chicks become layers at 5 months and lay for 16 months. All the feed (240 tons/yr) is purchased from outside the area. All the manure from the operation (10 tons/yr) is used as fertilizer on coffee and pasture. The operation has had minimal disease problems (J. L. Vargas, pers. comm.).

11.5.2. Commercial Hog Raising

As of 1996, there were three commercial hog operations in the Monteverde area. The largest one (2000 hogs), belongs to the dairy plant as its waste treatment facility and an agricultural enterprise. The controversy it has generated illustrates the different coexisting conceptions of sustainable agriculture in Monteverde (see Griffith, "The Pig Farm," p. 415).

The hog farm was conceived as a solution to a problem generated by the dairy plant, whose wastewater and whey from cheese-making had been polluting the Río Guacimal for many years (See Gill, "Impact of Lechería," pp. 446–447), to the increasing objections of community members. The dairy plant had taken some steps to reduce the problem (e.g., dripping the whey into the river slowly, in small quantities, rather than sporadically in large amounts). They also sold whey to a nearby hog producer but recognized that his farm polluted another river with hog wastes. More drastic measures were economically unattractive; the dairy plant averred that it would be at an economic disadvantage if it undertook pollution control measures and its competitors did not. As one factory employee stated, "As long as there's no law [which

applies to everyone], whatever we do has to pay for itself" (J. J. Monge, pers. comm.).

Two developments spurred the dairy plant to action. One was the growing threat that environmental regulations would be imposed at a national level. The other was the size of the problem. After many years of growing at about 10% per year, by 1993 the dairy plant was producing 24,000 liters of whey and 80,000 liters of other wastewater per day. These large volumes made other treatment alternatives economically viable. The dairy plant elected to install a commercial hog facility that would solve the waste problem and pay for itself (and possibly generate a profit) by using the whey to fatten hogs. With an initial investment of $275,000, they built a confinement facility for 1800 hogs, with separate buildings for breeding and gestation, birth and early development, fattening, and cattle, which would be partially fattened on treated hog wastes. They also constructed two lagoons of 1800 and 2200 m^2 to treat the water and chemical wastes from the dairy plant and the water and manure wastes from the hog operation. The smaller, deeper lagoon is anaerobic, with water hyacinths. The larger, shallower, aerobic lagoon receives the treated wastes from the first lagoon.

The first step is to mix, dilute, and neutralize wastewater (excluding whey) in a 40,000-liter tank. This mix is then filtered before going to either the 42,000-liter biodigestor or directly to the anaerobic lagoon (Fig. 11.6). The solids (mostly undigested protein and fiber) from the filtering process are fed to cattle; whey goes to the hogs. The hog waste is diluted and filtered. Some is fed to cows, some goes to the biodigestor, which produces gas and organic compost, and some goes directly to the first lagoon. The waste that finally leaves the system is 96% pure water, well above the Ministry of Health's standard of 85% (J. J. Monge, pers. comm.). Measurements of biological oxygen demand (BOD), a statistic indicating the amount of oxygen needed to break down organic pollutants, indicate a healthy system. A heavy biological oxygen demand implies greater stress on the body of water that receives the pollutants. As of 1996, the operation achieved a 98.5% reduction in the BOD of the factory's wastes (Table 11.7).

11.6. Future Directions and Conclusions

11.6.1. How Sustainable Is Monteverde Agriculture?

Dairy production.   Specialized dairying in Monteverde has made significant environmental progress in recent years. Farmers have intensified production by

Figure 11.6. Settling ponds used to process waste from the Productores de Monteverde's dairy plant and the hog farm. Photograph by Dan Perlman.

environmentally sound measures such as cut feeds, use of grain concentrates, moderate pasture fertilization, rotational grazing, and genetic improvements. Because productivity is increasing without heavy use of agrichemicals, the system is probably not unsustainably "mining" the environment. However, most of the intensification measures increase the cost of production, and some farmers question the long-term economic viability of intensive dairying in Monteverde. The dairy plant's hog farm has nearly eliminated waste whey. Although some residents debate the overall sustainability of this operation, its efflu-

ents are more benign than those that came directly from the dairy plant.

Dual-purpose farms. Low and declining productivity in dual-purpose operations suggests that environmental deterioration will continue under current practices. Without management changes, these systems will probably not survive agroecologically or economically.

Coffee production. Commercial coffee production started in Monteverde when the principles of sustainable agriculture were being widely discussed. Since the institutions responsible for the growth in local coffee production are committed to sustainability, environmentally benign production practices have been encouraged. Many (but not all) of the farmers are producing successfully with apparently minimal adverse impacts on the environment. The Coope's processing practices eliminate some of the most serious environmental impacts of coffee production. The high prices farmers receive for their coffee expands the management possibilities to include those that might otherwise be too costly (e.g., terracing).

Vegetable production. Commercial vegetable production is generally sustainable. Many farmers produce

Table 11.7. Characteristics of daily effluents before and after treatment at the Monteverde Hog Farm, 1995 (including the wastes from the swine operation).

Waste Volume (liters)	Concentration of BOD (mg/liter)	Total BOD (kg)
Before treatment		
Whey: 24,000	38,000	912
Other liquid waste:		
80,000	2250	180
After treatment		
Mixed: 140,000	120	16.8

organically with small amounts of output, which minimizes some sources of environmental damage. Localized problems with pesticide management or erosion occur with some vegetable operations.

Poultry production. Commercial poultry production occurs at a relatively small scale, and chicken manure, its primary waste product, is a valuable fertilizer. Few environmental problems are associated with chicken or egg production. VARSAN, S.A., produces Styrofoam and plastic packaging waste, however, and intense competition from national producers limits alternatives to this packaging system.

Hog production. Swine production as practiced by the dairy plant is considered by many to be environmentally sustainable. Most sustainability questions concern animal welfare, quality of life for neighbors, and aesthetic and moral considerations. The low profits generated by the hog farm may limit the opportunities to address these problems.

11.6.2. Directions for Future Research

The primary obstacles to achieving greater agricultural sustainability in Monteverde are low profitability (which limits management options to those that are most profitable, not necessarily most environmentally sound) and a lack of proven production alternatives. Agronomic, economic, and policy research will help reduce barriers to sustainability by demonstrating which practices are most promising, helping to fine-tune management to local conditions, and expanding the range of production alternatives. In some cases, national policies (e.g., price controls, input taxation, pesticide regulation) can limit or expand the opportunities for farmers to become more sustainable.

Dairy. A key area for future research is alternative forages, which are underused in Monteverde. Grass-legume mixtures could reduce the need for chemical fertilizers and improve cow nutrition. Oats and brassicas need research to evaluate their potential, fine-tune management, and achieve greater adoption. Resistance to spittlebugs and other pasture pests will be a key characteristic of successful alternative forages. Breeding resistance into Kikuyu Grass would be a valuable project. Research on the relative costs and effectiveness of herbicides, "weed-eater," and machete use will identify the most promising directions for weed control efforts. Economic analysis of windbreaks will provide insight into whether they should receive continued support and subsidies.

Dual-purpose production. Data on pasture erosion rates, soil compaction, and degree of over- or under-grazing are needed to evaluate this system's sustainability. Research should determine the extent of rotational grazing and how to optimize this system for lowland farm conditions and sharp seasonal fluctuations in forage availability. One of the highest priorities for dual-purpose farms is research on silvipastoral systems. Live fenceposts are widely used on lowland farms; biological and ecological studies on their agroecological and economic benefits are needed.

Coffee production. A key area for research is organic and low chemical input production. Farmers need effective strategies for combating common diseases, fungi, and leaf-cutter ants. Further research is needed on *Arachis pintoi* and other cover crops for upland farms.

Vegetable crops. Research is needed on organic production methods that are adapted to the Monteverde environment. Fungi pose a particular problem for producers. Inexpensive, preferably "homemade" organic fungicides are needed.

Pesticide management. Informal surveys have revealed serious deficiencies in pesticide management. Research is needed on successful educational and outreach programs elsewhere that could be adapted to Monteverde.

Swine production. The agroecological sustainability of Monteverde's swine production, particularly waste management, must be studied. Although the dairy plant has a sophisticated waste management system, other producers do not. Research is needed on inexpensive ways to mitigate noise and odors.

11.6.3. Summary and Conclusions

The lessons and experiences from Monteverde provide insights that may help other communities meet the challenge of agricultural sustainability. One of the primary lessons of the Monteverde experience is that sustainability is a moving target, requiring reevaluation as political, economic, and cultural realities evolve, and as new agroecological information becomes available. To ensure continued progress, a social context is needed that encourages honest discussion and evaluation, commits sufficient resources to sustainability research, and creates a climate of shared commitment to sustainability. Monteverde's robust, activist social structure has been a powerful force for progress toward sustainability, and may serve as an inspiration to other communities.

Acknowledgments We thank the many people we interviewed for this chapter. Special thanks to José Luis Vargas and Juan José Monge, who answered questions about dairy, swine, and poultry production and corrected drafts of the manuscript. John Campbell helped with the history of the Quaker settlers. Carlos Vargas and Jaime Lopez provided information on coffee and vegetable production. Jim Wolfe provided insights on dairy and vegetable production from his personal experience as a farmer and biologist.

PREHISTORIC CULTURES AND INHABITANTS
Robert M. Timm

Recent archaeological, linguistic, and genetic information document that the modern Amerindian groups of Costa Rica are descendants of pre-Columbian groups that occupied the area for thousands of years, rather than transition cultures between the major groups of northern Central America and Mexico or of South America. Indigenous peoples inhabited the Monteverde region for millennia as documented by pottery shards found in the vicinity of Santa Elena, but we know little of their population density and impact on the local environment.

The first human inhabitants of Costa Rica were bands of hunters and gatherers who arrived in the area roughly between 12,000 and 8000 B.C. Archaeological evidence of workshops and artifacts have been recorded in the Turrialba valley, in Guanacaste, and from Lake Arenal. One of the earliest artifacts known, a Clovis-style point made from local quartz (chalcedony), is from Lake Arenal, dated at 10,000 B.C. The cultures inhabiting the mountains from Volcán Orosi to Monteverde were similar and distinct from those to the west in Guanacaste and to the east in the Atlantic lowlands. The region has been termed the Cordilleran cultural subarea (Sheets et al. 1991, Sheets 1994).

The combination of deposits of volcanic ash associated with the eruptions of Volcán Arenal (Melson 1984, 1994), radiocarbon dates from charcoal, and stratigraphic relationships from pottery and stone implements has allowed investigators to document much about the lives of people living in the vicinity of Lake Arenal during the past 6000 years (Sheets et al. 1991, Sheets and McKee 1994). Around the second or third millennium B.C., early agriculture was practiced, the staple crops being tubers, fruit trees, berries, and palms. Expanding agriculture changed the indigenous societies, which led to the establishment of permanent settlements, the development of ceramics, and social changes. During the Archaic Period (3300–2000 B.C.), subsistence shifted from primarily hunting and gathering to agriculture. Villages were established, although population densities were low. The Early and Late Tronadora phases (2000–500 B.C.) are characterized by well-built houses and extensive use of ceramics and by many small villages scattered throughout the region.

The period from 500 B.C. to A.D. 300 in Costa Rica marked a transition from small tribal societies to chiefdom societies associated with the cultivation of seeds, primarily maize. A mixed system of horticulture involving tubers, berries, and fruit trees and seed agriculture (primarily corn, beans, and squash) was present throughout much of the country. Main villages contained constructions such as stone foundations, house mounds, paved causeways, ovens, storage wells, and statuary. Many of the carved jade objects and ceremonial metates now exhibited in museums are funerary offerings during this period.

The major occupancy of the Arenal area occurred during the Early and Late Arenal phases (500 B.C.–A.D. 600). There is evidence of large-scale land clearing during this time, which was related to an increase in the human populations living along the lake and an expansion beyond the lakeshores (Piperno 1994). Some of the early volcanic eruptions of Arenal could have weathered by this time to form relatively fertile soils. The general pattern throughout Costa Rica is a rapid population increase until about A.D. 500. Deforestation increased rapidly after 500 B.C., as a result of increased cultivation. The population density in the Arenal region and throughout the mountains reached its peak during these phases (Sheets 1994).

During the period from A.D. 300–800, the organization of societies in Costa Rica evolved from simple chiefdoms to complex chiefdoms with structures such as foundations, paved causeways, mounds, and burial sites. From A.D. 800 until the arrival of the Spaniards in the sixteenth century, large villages with intricate infrastructure were formed. Some of the elements of Costa Rican societies at the time of the Conquest included multiple, simple, and complex cemeteries; elaborate structures in main villages (house mounds, aqueducts, public squares, paved causeways, and supporting walls); a diversity of domestic property; regional exchange of goods; the introduction of goldwork; and the rivalry of chiefdoms.

At Lake Arenal during the Silencio Phase (A.D. 600–1300), the Río Piedra valley was heavily populated. Settlements were large but widely separated. Population may have shifted to the west away from the lake in response to increased volcanic activity from adjacent Volcán Arenal (Mueller 1994). The Silencio and Tilarán phases were periods of general population decline and abandonment of long-used sites. Population declines during these phases were not directly correlated with volcanism and are thought to be a regional phenomenon (Mueller 1994). Based on analysis of the carbon isotopes $^{13}C/^{12}C$ from human bone recovered from burial sites, less than 12% of the diet was maize, which is a far lower percentage than was consumed by most historical populations in Mesoamerica (Friedman and Gleason 1984, Bradley 1994).

The arrival of the Spaniards in A.D. 1502 began a painful transition period for the indigenous societies of Costa Rica, with marked population declines of the indigenous peoples, the decimation of cultures, and the extinction of some tribal groups. The cultures that the Spanish found in Costa Rica fiercely resisted them for two generations. Costa Rica was the last of the Central American countries to be conquered by the Spanish. The most recent estimate of the peak pre-Columbian population of indigenous peoples is about 400,000 people (Denevan 1992). The population was reduced to 80,000 by 1563 (MacLoed 1973, J. W. Hoopes, pers. comm.).

The combination of wild-gathered and garden-cultivated plants along with protein provided by wild game was probably the characteristic diet of most indigenous people in Costa Rica (Hoopes and Chenault 1994, Sheets and McKee 1994). People seemed to prefer living in the drier life zones present on Arenal, the tropical moist forest/premontane transition, and humid premontane forest. Highland areas above 1500 m in the Cordillera de Tilarán generally were not inhabited.

Throughout much of the period of occupancy, the cultures of the Arenal region appear to have been self-sufficient and relatively independent of outside groups, compared to other Mesoamerican villages. Maize was cultivated by 2000 B.C., but did not become the mainstay of the diet. The cultures living around the lake instead based their subsistence on the exploitation of the rich and diverse indigenous flora and fauna. Population densities fluctuated considerably but in general were relatively low compared with densities farther north in Mesoamerica or in the Andes of South America. However, the peoples of the Arenal region had an impact on their environment and were responsible for considerable deforestation (Sheets et al. 1991).

THE AGROECOLOGY OF *PROSAPIA*: SPITTLEBUGS, FROGHOPPERS, AND PASTURE PESTS
Daniel C. Peck

Pasture pests known as spittlebugs and froghoppers pose a major obstacle to dairying in Monteverde. These insects nearly brought an end to the dairy industry in the 1960s, and forced a conversion from the principal forage, Kikuyu Grass (*Pennisetum clandestinum*), to a more tolerant but less productive species, East African Star Grass (*Cynodon nlemfuensis*).

Insects in the family Cercopidae are known as spittlebugs when they are nymphs and froghoppers when they are adults. They are relatives of other economically important insects in the order Homoptera, including leafhoppers, planthoppers, and aphids. They are commonly known as "la Prosapia" after the generic name of the principal species. Grassland cercopids are sap-feeders that specialize on forage grasses and sugarcane. In grazing lands of the New World, their rise in pest status has paralleled the spread of improved pastures and the establishment of more productive African grasses (Guagliumi 1954, Enkerlin and Morales 1979). *Prosapia* and seven other native genera of cercopids are the most damaging pasture pests in the neotropics (Lapointe et al. 1992).

Spittlebugs and froghoppers cause stress in plants and reduce pasture productivity by usurping resources that would otherwise be channeled into growth. Susceptible grasses also suffer "froghopper burn" when they are attacked by adults (Byers and Wells 1966). Their saliva induces a phytotoxemia that causes the blade and stem to yellow and die. Heavy infestations of adults can "burn" entire pastures, stunting growth and lowering nutritive value and palatability (Fagan and Picado 1971, Valerio and Nakano 1988). Infestations may also reduce the persistence of improved pastures by promoting the invasion of undesirable weeds and grasses (Taliafero et al. 1967, Valerio and Nakano 1987). In Monteverde, conversion to a more pest-tolerant pasture species (Star Grass) was an adequate short-term control. However, in recent years, Star Grass pastures have later suffered high pest densities and increased froghopper burn. Declining soil fertility and drier wet seasons may reduce pest tolerance of this grass.

Dairy farmers in Monteverde rely largely on cultural controls to reduce the incidence of outbreaks. The dairy plant and the Ministry of Agriculture and Ranching (Ministerio de Agricultura y Ganadería, MAG) promote heavy grazing and regular use of fertilizer to reduce habitat favorability to spittlebugs and to promote vigorous regrowth of the sward. The ministry also promotes biological control with *Fusarium*, a fungus that attacks adult *Prosapia*. Poor insect scouting and application techniques, however, limit the fungus's effectiveness. If these preventive measures fail, farmers can opt to do nothing and absorb the damage or to use remedial measures such as Malathion (an organophosphate) and Vidate (a systemic nematocide). Pesticide use is heaviest in pastures where farmers persist in managing Kikuyu Grass.

The persistence of outbreaks in Monteverde is partly due to the lack of information on this pest's ecology. I studied the agroecology of spittlebugs and froghoppers in Monteverde during the wet seasons of 1991–94, focusing on factors that influence their abundance and distribution, including their behavior, population dynamics, and natural enemies. Four species are pests in local pastures: *Aeneolamia postica, Prosapia simulans, P. plagiata*, and a undetermined species related to *P. bicincta*. The most abundant species, *P.* nr. *bicincta*, feeds on all the local forage grasses, including East African Star Grass, Kikuyu Grass, Pitilla (*Sporobolus* spp.), and King Grass (*Pennisetum purpureum*). The nymphs construct masses of protective spittle at their feeding sites on host grasses low in the pasture sward. The adult froghoppers are black and crimson with three transverse red stripes across the back. They are approximately 10.7 mm long and 4.8 mm wide. At peak times, more than 250 nymphs/m² and 500 adults per 100 sweeps of an insect net can be captured (Peck 1996).

Adult *P.* nr. *bicincta* lay eggs in the top layer of the soil at the base of the host plants. Eggs hatch at the beginning of the wet season (April–May). Nymphs pass through five instars before they molt to adults; they require six weeks to mature. Eggs enter a period of diapause that lasts throughout the dry season. Unlike other grassland cercopids, this species achieves only one relatively synchronous generation per year (Peck 1996).

A key step for cercopid management is prediction of outbreaks. Early season rainfall may determine the timing and synchrony of the egg hatch, which may allow prediction of when nymphs and adults will appear and when pressure on pastures will peak. Scouting fine-tunes those predictions and identifies problem areas, which guides the timing and location of chemical application. If the time of hatching can be accurately predicted, the feeding of first-instar nymphs on roots can be predicted, and heavy grazing of pastures at that point may reduce pest populations.

Local population surveys revealed that froghoppers migrate; colonists arrive in Monteverde from areas where nymphs have already matured (Peck 1996). Thus, pest management must be considered on a regional scale. A paddock treated on one day may be swamped with new colonists the following day. Research should address how cercopids damage their hosts to predict how colonizing adults affect grasses that are already stressed by local nymph populations. Nymphs and adults are attacked by natural enemies. Maggots of the syrphid fly *Salpingogaster nigra* (Diptera: Syrphidae) crawl into spittle masses to feed on the nymphs. Two entomopathogens, *Fusarium* and *Baktoa*, also attack adults in the zone. Further research is needed on the factors that influence the abundance of these enemies and their potential as agents of biological control. An expanded knowledge base will equip farmers to consider pest management alongside pasture management. Effective management requires an integrated approach that addresses (1) vulnerable windows in the pest's life cycle, (2) pest life span and capacity for reproduction, (3) the impact of local natural enemies, and (4) the role of grazing and forage management.

BRASSICAS AS BIOLOGICAL PLOWS
Jim Wolfe

A major threat to the sustainability of Monteverde farms is soil compaction. Decades of intensive dairying have created a hard soil pan. Precipitation and fertilizer run off this pan rather than percolating into the soil, which wastes fertilizer, diminishes grass production, and causes erosion. Traditional methods of loosening the soil are plowing with a moldboard plow pulled by oxen or tractor, or shoveling by hand. These methods improve forage growth but also cause substantial soil erosion. Many farmers plow just before the wet season to ensure moisture for grass growth; freshly loosened soil is most vulnerable to erosion. A modern alternative that avoids erosion is the use of plows that break up the subsoil without disturbing the surface horizon. Subsoil plowing requires a powerful tractor and cannot be used on steep slopes, so it has limited application in Monteverde.

A successful alternative is to plant brassicas (Brassicaceae). A cross between Chinese cabbage and mustard (known commercially as Tyfon) and forage rape have produced the best results. First, existing pasture grasses are chemically "burned" back but not killed with an herbicide. A complete fertilizer (NPK 10–30–10) is applied to the field. Seed is broadcast during a wet period (usually in June and October). Seeding rates are 20% higher than recommended for a commercial harvest. After spreading the seed, cows are herded over the entire area; their hooves push the seeds into the soil.

The brassicas are quick to germinate and grow rapidly enough to shade out most weeds and retard the growth of grasses. Their wide leaves protect soil from rain-induced erosion. Their thick roots reach down to about 80 cm and effectively loosen the soil. As they die and decompose, the root channels allow water and nutrients to infiltrate the soil. Although pasture does not produce grass when it is planted in brassicas, the brassicas themselves are a high-protein forage. After 2–3 months, they reach a height of nearly 1 m and are ready for harvest. Tyfon may be fed directly to lactating cows; rape is cut into smaller pieces. Both offer 20% protein and are more digestible than alfalfa. Two cuttings are possible before grasses take over. Within several months, the field returns to maximum grass production.

Using brassicas as biological plows has many advantages. Expensive machinery and intensive manual labor are unnecessary. The high-quality forage compensates for the time the land is removed from grass production. Soil compaction is reversed and erosion is prevented, which helps farmers maintain long-term pasture productivity.

PASTURE BURNING
Katherine Griffith

Pasture burning can be an agronomically sound practice (Sanchez 1982, 1987), providing phosphorus, reducing acidity and aluminum toxicity, and returning unpalatable, overly mature forage to the soil in the form of ash. Fires cost nothing, in contrast to fertilizers. They require little managerial skill or labor, no infrastructure, and little institutional support. In many environments, however, burning is a largely destructive practice. In hilly areas, it exposes the soil to the highly erosive rains at the beginning of the wet season. Wind carries away much of the ash, and a potentially large portion of the nutrients are volatilized. Fires frequently burn out of control. A continuous smoky haze covers much of Costa Rica's Pacific coastal plain during the last month of dry season as fires burn for days at a time.

During the 1970s, burning became illegal, in recognition of air pollution, safety hazards, and the soil degradation that it caused over the long run. When oil prices rose sharply in 1979, fertilizers were too costly for many farmers, so government policy changed; agronomists recommended burning as a way to maintain pasture fertility. This practice is used in beef and dual-purpose enterprises in the Monteverde milkshed but is much less frequently used on dairy farms. The current legality of burning is ambiguous.

Deliberate fires are regulated by the Ley Forestal (Forestry Law), which prohibits burning forests or areas adjacent to forests without a permit. Permits are granted after a site inspection, and upon evidence of containment measures (Law 7575, Article 35, published in the Costa Rica Gazeta Vol. 21, No. 72, 16 April 1996).

In the Monteverde milkshed, burning is probably environmentally unsustainable in the long term. In the short term, it may be the most profitable system in the lowland areas and on the more economically and agronomically marginal farms. The profitability of this pasture management system will probably decline over time.

MONTEVERDE'S KITCHEN GARDENS
Katy VanDusen

If you ask Costa Ricans in the Monteverde area if they have a "huerta" or vegetable garden, usually the answer will be no. If you ask what they produce in their yard near their house, they might list fifteen or twenty products. Traditional home gardens in the Monteverde region, as in most of the tropics, are a seemingly disorganized array of trees, shrubs, herbs, root crops, and animals. They are agroforestry systems; about half the crops may be tree crops. Kitchen gardens supplement the family diet and provide medicinal plants, firewood, live fenceposts, and other materials and a pleasant environment around the house, protecting it from sun and wind (Table 11.8).

Traditional gardens require less labor and other inputs than temperate-zone row gardens. Work in the garden is often shared among all family members and may be done sporadically. Because many of the crops are perennial, they do not need replanting or frequent weeding. Seeds are purchased for only a few crops (e.g., cabbage, carrots, radishes, lettuce, onions). Seeds are exchanged or saved; vegetative material is used for propagation. These home gardens do not require fences to protect them from animals. Rather, animals are an integral part of the system, roaming freely in the garden. Chickens are the most common animals and help to control insects, recycle kitchen scraps without the need for a compost pile, and fertilize plants directly. Commercial fertilizers are used selectively in traditional home gardens; manures and ashes are more frequently applied.

Although these gardens can have considerable outputs for the minimal inputs they require, they are often considered marginal or insignificant by those who promote temperate-style row vegetable gardens. Traditional gardens may not maximize production of widely recognized fruit and vegetable crops, but they efficiently fill an important niche in the household economy. One study concluded that this understudied form of agriculture was one of the few agroforestry systems that could simultaneously meet household, economic, and conservation goals in the humid tropics.

Table 11.8. Common plants and animals in traditional kitchen gardens (for scientific names, see Table 11.6, Appendix 1).

English Name	Spanish Name	Use
Trees		
Avocado	Aguacate	Fruit
—	Guaba	Fruit
Guava	Guayaba	Fruit, firewood, tree climbing, shade
Grapefruit	Toronja	Fruit
—	Guitite	Live fenceposts, host to orchids, edible berries
—	Itavo	Live fenceposts, edible flowers
Jocote	Jocote	Fruit
Lemon	Limón	Fruit
Orange	Naranja	Fruit
Sour orange	Naranja agria, naranja ácida	Fruit (for juice)
Sweet lemon	Limón dulce	Fruit

(continued)

English Name	Spanish Name	Use
Shrubs		
Blackberry	Mora	Fruit
Hot pepper	Chile picante	Fruit
Thimbleberry	Frambuesa	Fruit
Vines		
Chayote	Chayote	Vegetable (squash)
Passion fruit	Granadilla	Fruit
Squash	Ayote	Vegetable
Vegetables		
Cabbage	Repollo	Vegetable
Green bean	Vainica	Vegetable
Sweet pepper	Chile dulce	Vegetable
Tomato	Tomate	Fruit
—	Tomatillo	Fruit
Root crops		
carrot	Zanahoria	Vegetable
—	Chamol	Vegetable
Onion	Cebolla	Vegetable
Potato	Papa	Vegetable
Radish	Rábano	Vegetable
Sweet potato	Camote	Vegetable
—	Tiquisque	Vegetable
Yam	—	Vegetable
Herbs		
Cilantro	Culantro	Cooking herb
Lemon grass	Zacate limón	Herb tea
Mint	Menta	Herb tea
Oregano	Oregano	Cooking and tea herb
Parsley	Perejil	Cooking herb
Thyme	Tomillo	Cooking herb
—	Yerba buena	Herb tea
Other Plants		
Bamboo	Bambú	Poles
Banana	Banano	Fruit, stems for cow forage
—	Cuadrado	Fruit
—	Guineo	Fruit, vinegar production
Animals		
Chicken	Gallina	Meat, eggs, pest control
Duck	Pato	Meat
Goat	Cabra	Meat, milk
Goose	Ganso	Meat
Pig	Chancho	Meat
Rabbit	Conejo	Meat
Turkey	Pavo, chompipe	Meat

PESTICIDE USE IN THE SANTA ELENA AREA
Katherine Griffith

A survey of pesticide use, management practices, and poisonings was administered to 32 farmers in 1990. The findings signaled that greater concern for personal and environmental safety is warranted. Results included the following (K. Griffith and N. Trejos, unpubl. data):

(1) The major local pesticide supplier carried pesticides that had been banned for safety and environmental reasons in the United States and Europe.

(2) No safety equipment was for sale locally, and almost no farmers had ever used safety equipment.

(3) Many farmers purchased the herbicide Paraquat at bulk prices by bringing their own containers, so they had no label information after leaving the shop.

(4) Most farmers had no standard way of measuring pesticides for mixing with water. Quite a few used cough syrup cups or made rough estimates of quantities ("one trickle per backpack sprayer"). They had little idea of appropriate application rates and were routinely confused by the instructions and safety information on the labels.

(5) Storage practices were unsafe and inadequate; for example, farmers stored pesticides in bedrooms, in bathrooms, and in unmarked containers in their barns.

(6) Cases of accidental poisoning of cows, pets, and humans were common; nearly every farmer interviewed had suffered at least a mild poisoning or lost an animal or knew someone who had.

(7) The concept of environmental persistence was poorly understood; for example, one herbicide recommended for use only on areas in which permanent plant eradication was desired (such as train track beds) had been used locally for ground preparation prior to seeding crops.

(8) A high percentage of the respondents had begun to use pesticides during the previous 2–3 years, which suggests that use was increasing rapidly.

FRIJOL TAPADO OR "COVERED BEANS"
Katherine Griffith & Jim Wolfe

Beans are a staple food in Costa Rica. Although they are not a highly profitable crop (due in part to government price controls), beans provide dietary security for many families with a limited or uncertain cash income. A traditional but poorly documented agricultural system in the Monteverde area is the *frijol tapado*, or "covered bean" system in which farmers plant black beans on unplowed fallow land. The farmer lets land grow up in scrub for 2–3 years until the vegetation (which must not include much grass) is 1–3 m high. The farmer broadcasts seed between September and November. The brush is cut down with a machete and left in place as mulch. About 70 days later, the beans are harvested. The producer uproots and dries the plants, and then spreads them out on a tarpaulin to thresh and winnow them.

Although this is a low-productivity system, it has many advantages. As a form of "no-till" agriculture, it allows steep hillsides to be planted with minimal risk of erosion. It maintains or increases organic matter and available phosphorus in the soil. As nitrogen-fixers, beans improve the soil, although their contribution should not be overstated because much of the nitrogen is removed when the beans are harvested (National Research Council 1993). The system is a relatively biologically diverse one that minimizes pests and diseases; agricultural chemicals are not used in this system. Finally, it requires relatively little labor compared to tilling the soil. This and similar slash/mulch systems have been described in favorable terms by several researchers (Rosenmeyer 1990, National Research Council 1993), who have found the system to minimize erosion, increase soil organic matter, provide nutrient cycling benefits, and reduce labor, herbicide, and fungicide needs. In warm wet conditions, relatively rapid decomposition of the mulch provides nutrient recycling benefits unavailable through burning while protecting the soil surface and increasing the amount of organic matter (National Research Council 1993).

THE PIG FARM: "SUSTAINABLE AGRICULTURE" OR "AN ABOMINATION"?
Katherine Griffith

The pig farm conflict in Monteverde in the early 1990s had several underlying causes. During the first year, improper mixing of wastes in the lagoons resulted in an overwhelming stench emanating from the operation (Fig. 11.6). Although most people agreed that this problem was largely solved when the lagoons functioned properly, this initial mistake cost the dairy plant support and trust. Another problem was the noise of pigs squealing. When a swine disease dramatically reduced pork sales nationwide, the dairy plant's facility, built for 1800 animals, was crammed with as many as 2300 pigs, increasing animal stress and noise levels. The dairy plant, in its efforts to "sell" the idea to the community, had claimed that the farm would be noise- and odor-free. Some residents felt deceived and thought the measures the dairy plant took (reforestation, enclosing the buildings, and changing some management practices) did not constitute a good faith effort to solve the problem. The dairy plant felt that many of the farm's opponents did not appreciate the environmental significance of the whey and wastewater treatment or the financial constraints under which the operation must function.

A fundamental question concerns the place of agriculture in human activities in general, and a large commercial hog operation in Monteverde in particular. This conflict involves a vision of appropriate local land use: what constitutes a "good" way to make a living, and what is an acceptable price to pay for agricultural development? Asked in 1995 whether the pig farm was sustainable agriculture, community residents gave the following answers:

"Definitely. As a treatment system, it gives us 96% purification (of wastes), and the income guarantees that it can continue to function." (dairy plant employee)

"Steady permanent cacophonic scream of 2000 stressed pigs in captivity is an abomination in the soundscape of Monteverde." (Artist)

"It was started because of the whey problem. It was a response to a necessity. They've worked hard to make it work better. . . . As long as the animals are well and healthy, it's okay." (dairy farmer/artisan)

"The pig farm's great. It's a pretty closed system; they've done a good job." (farmer/biologist)

"I see they use standard procedure [for raising pigs], but I question the standard procedure. It's cruel to put animals in such a small place. That's what you have to do to be competitive. Is it worth it?" (teacher)

"I like the pig farm because it identifies that end of the community as agricultural. Maybe it'll keep tourist development out!" (dairy farmer)

"It's so inappropriate. It's a residential community and they put this huge commercial pig farm in it. It just doesn't belong." (artist)

"Feeding whey and other kitchen wastes to pigs is something that has been done in this zone since before the Quakers arrived. . . . The problem with the pig farm is scale. . . . I think that the dairy plant is really trying to be ecologically and socially responsible. . . . The difficulty is that the dairy plant is competing against Borden, and Borden is not responsible to any local community because it does not have a local community. Sustainability will only be realized when companies like Borden have to be socially and ecologically responsible. People who are living off outside [U.S.] investments rather than farming are not any less damaging to the environment, even though they don't directly see and feel the damage done by their economic activities." (homemaker)

"It'll drive tourists away." (hotel owner)

"We're proud of our pig farm and we're offering a tour because we think tourists will be interested." (dairy plant employee)

Thus, people view the issue of sustainability through different lenses. Some see the farm from a biological systems standpoint or the financial bottom line and describe it as sustainable. Others look at animal welfare, farm size and social justice, compatibility with tourism (for some, a preferred form of economic development), and lifestyle issues; they have minor doubts or major objections.

Literature Cited

Annis, S. 1990. Debt and wrong-way resource flows in Costa Rica. Ethics and International Affairs 4:107–121.

Boucher, D. H. 1983. Coffee. Pages 86–88 in D. H. Janzen, editor. Costa Rican natural history. University of Chicago Press, Chicago.

Bradley, J. E. 1994. The Silencio site: an Early to Middle Polychrome Period cemetery in the Arenal region. Pages 106–121 in P. D. Sheets and B. R. McKee, editors. Archaeology, volcanism, and remote sensing in the Arenal Region, Costa Rica. University of Texas Press, Austin.

Bunderson, W. T., and D. Frye. 1986. Adaptive strategies for successful pastoral development. Pages 37–45 in Proceedings of the 1986 International Rangeland Development Symposium. International Affairs Committee of the Society for Range Management and Winrock International Institute for Agricultural Development, Orlando, Florida.

Byers, R. A., and H. D. Wells. 1966. Phytotoxemia of coastal bermudagrass caused by the two lined spittlebug, Prosapia bicincta (Homoptera: Cercopidae). Annals of the Entomological Society of America 59:1067–1071.

CATIE (Centro Agronómico Tropical de Investigación y Enseñanza). 1983. Investigación aplicada en sistemas de producción de leche: informe técnico final del proyector CATIE-BID 1979–1983. CATIE, Turrialba, Costa Rica.

Cipaguata, H. M. 1993. Producción de ganado bovino de doble propósito. Pages 36–44 in Informe de la Mesa Redonda Sobre Investigación, Capacitación y Transferencia de Tecnología en Producción Bovina de Doble Proposito en el Trópico. Food and Agriculture Organization, United Nations, Santiago, Chile.

De Geus, J. G. 1977. Production potentialities of pastures in the tropics and subtropics. Centre d'Étude de L'Azote, Zurich, Switzerland.

Denevan, W. M. 1992. The native population of the Americas in 1492. The University of Wisconsin Press, Madison.

Donefer, E. 1976. Beef cattle production from processed sugar cane. Pages 258–264 in A. J. Smith, editor. Beef cattle production in developing countries. University of Edinburgh, Edinburgh.

Ellis, P. R., and M. E. Hugh Jones. 1976. Disease as a limiting factor to beef production in developing countries. Pages 105–116 in A. J. Smith, editor. Beef cattle production in developing countries. University of Edinburgh, Edinburgh.

Enkerlin, D., and J. A. S. Morales. 1979. The grass spittlebug complex Aeneolamia albofasciata and Prosapia simulans in northeastern Mexico and its possible control by resistant buffelgrass hybrids. Miscellaneous Publication No. 1451. Texas Agricultural Experiment Station. Lubbock.

Fagan, E. B., and O. V. Picado. 1971. The influence of adult Prosapia distanti feeding on the forage quality of Kikuyu Grass in Costa Rica. Turrialba 21:181–183.

Ferrufino, A., and S. L. Lapointe. 1989. Host plant resistance in Brachiaria grasses to the spittlebug Zulia colombiana. Entomologia Experimentalis et Applicata 51:155–162.

Friedman, I., and J. Gleason. 1984. C13 analysis of bone samples from site G-150, El Silencio. Vínculos 10:113–114.

Gillespie, G. W., Jr. 1998. Sustainable agriculture and prospects for rural community development in the U.S. Research in rural sociology and development 6. Cornell University, Ithaca, New York.

Guagliumi, P. 1954. Contribuciones al estudio de la candelilla de las gramineas en Venezuela. I. Historia de la plaga en el país. Separata de Agronomía Tropical 4:151–161.

Guzman Zamorra, J. F. 1989. Evaluación técnico-económica en una muestra de quince fincas lecheras ubicadas en la zona de Monteverde de Puntarenas. Practicum report for B.S. in Farm Administration, Instituto Technológico de Costa Rica, San José.

Hartshorn, G. L. Hartshorn, A. Atmetlla, L. D. Gómez, A. Mata, L. Mata, R. Morales, R. Ocampo, D. Pool, C. Quesada, C. Solera, R. Solórzano, G. Stiles, J. Tosi, Jr., A. Umaña, C. Villalobos, and R. Wells. 1982. Costa Rica country environmental profile: a field study. Agency for International Development Contract No. 000–C-00–1004–00. Centro Cientifico Tropical, San José, Costa Rica.

Hilje, L., L. Castillo, L. A. Thrupp, and I. Wesseling. 1987. El uso de los plaguicidas en Costa Rica. Editorial Universidad Estatal a Distancia, San José, Costa Rica.

Hill, D. S. 1983. Agricultural insect pests of the tropics and their control. Cambridge University Press, Cambridge.

Hoopes, J. W., and M. L. Chenault. 1994. Excavations at Sitio Bolívar: a late Formative village in the Arenal Basin. Pages 87–105 in P. D. Sheets and B. R. McKee. Archaeology, volcanism, and remote sensing in the Arenal Region, Costa Rica. University of Texas Press, Austin, Texas.

Humphreys, L. R. 1987. Tropical pastures and fodder crops. Longman and Wiley, New York.

Janzen, D. 1988. Buy Costa Rican beef. Oikos 51:257–258.

Jarvis, L. S. 1986. Livestock development in Latin America. The World Bank, Washington, D.C.

Lapointe, S. L., M. S. Serrano, G. L. Arango, G. Sotelo, and F. Cordoba. 1992. Antibiosis to spittlebugs (Homoptera: Cercopidae) in accessions of Brachiaria spp. Journal of Economic Entomology 85: 1485–1490.

Leonard, J. K. 1987. Natural resources and economic development in Central America: a regional environmental profile. Transaction Books, New Brunswick, UK.

London, C. E. 1994. The cultural politics of technical change in Colombian coffee production. Masters thesis, Cornell University, Ithaca, New York.

MacLoed, M. J. 1973. Spanish Central America: a socioeconomic history, 1520–1720. University of California Press, Berkeley.

Madrigal Chavarria, G. 1988a. Informe final sobre la investigación los forrajes gramineos. CoopeSanta Elena, R.L., Proyecto DISE, Monteverde, Puntarenas, Costa Rica.

———. 1988b. Informe final sobre la investigación en los forrajes leguminosos: la alfalfa, Medicago sativa. CoopeSanta Elena, R.L., Proyecto DISE, Monteverde, Puntarenas, Costa Rica.

McDowell, L. R. 1976. Mineral deficiencies and toxicities and their effect on beef production in developing countries. Pages 217–241 in A. J. Smith, editor. Beef cattle production in developing countries. University of Edinburgh, Edinburgh.

McDowell, L. R., J. H. Conrad, and G. L. Ellis. 1986. Mineral deficiencies and toxicities of tropical forages for grazing livestock. Pages 139–146 in Proceedings of the 1986 International Rangeland Development Symposium. International Affairs Committee of the Society for Range Management and Winrock International Institute for Agricultural Development, Orlando, Florida.

McDowell, R. E. 1993. Dual purpose cattle production in sustainable agriculture systems. Pages 113–132 in Informe de la Mesa Redonda Sobre Investigación, Capacitación y Transferencia de Tecnología en Producción Bovina de Doble Propósito en el Trópico. Food and Agriculture Organization, United Nations, Santiago, Chile.

Melson, W. G. 1984. Prehistoric eruptions of Arenal Volcano, Costa Rica. Vínculos 10:35–59.

———. 1994. The eruption of 1968 and tephra stratigraphy of Arenal Volcano. Pages 24–47 in P. D. Sheets and

B. R. McKee. Archaeology, volcanism, and remote sensing in the Arenal region, Costa Rica. University of Texas Press, Austin.

Mendoza, P. E., L. Torres, and H. Llanos. 1986. Evaluation of two different weed control systems under grazing conditions for beef production in the tropics. Pages 111–114 in Proceedings of the 1986 International Rangeland Development Symposium. International Affairs Committee of the Society for Range Management and Winrock International Institute for Agricultural Development, Orlando, Florida.

Mueller, M. 1994. Archaeological survey in the Arenal Basin. Pages 48–72 in P. D. Sheets and B. R. McKee. Archaeology, volcanism, and remote sensing in the Arenal region, Costa Rica. University of Texas Press, Austin.

Myers, N. 1981. The hamburger connection: how Central America's forests become North America's hamburgers. Ambio 10:2–8.

Mott, G. O. 1974. Nutrient recycling in pastures. Pages 323–340 in D. A. Mays, editor. Forage fertilization. American Society of Agronomy, Crop Science Society of America, and Soil Science Society of America, Madison, Wisconsin.

National Research Council. 1989. Alternative agriculture. National Academy Press, Washington, D.C.

———. 1993. Sustainable agriculture and the environment in the humid tropics. National Academy Press, Washington, D.C.

Parsons, J. J. 1983. Beef cattle (Ganado). Pages 77–79 in D. Janzen, editor. Costa Rican natural history. University of Chicago Press, Chicago.

Peck, D. C. 1996. The association of spittlebugs with grasslands: ecology of Prosapia in upland dairy pastures of Costa Rica. Ph.D. dissertation, Cornell University, Ithaca, New York.

Piperno, D. R. 1994. Phytolith records from the Proyecto Prehistórico Arenal. Pages 286–292 in P. D. Sheets and B. R. McKee. Archaeology, volcanism, and remote sensing in the Arenal Region, Costa Rica. University of Texas Press, Austin.

Plasse, D. N. 1976. The possibility of genetic improvement of beef cattle in developing countries with particular reference to Latin America. Pages 308–331 in A. J. Smith, editor. Beef cattle production in developing countries, University of Edinburgh, Edinburgh.

Preston, T. R. 1976. Prospects for the intensification of cattle production in developing countries. Pages 242–257 in A. J. Smith, editor. Beef cattle production in developing countries. University of Edinburgh, Edinburgh.

Rifkin, J. 1992. Beyond beef: the rise and fall of the cattle culture. Dutton, New York.

Rosemeyer, M. E. 1990. The effect of different management strategies on the tripartite symbiosis of bean (Phaseolus Vulgaris L.) with Rhizobium and vesicular-arbuscular mycorrhizal fungi in two agroecosystems in Costa Rica. Ph.D. thesis, University of California, Santa Cruz.

Russell, D., A. W. Joe Free, and D. L. McCune. 1974. Potential for fertilizer use on tropical forages. Pages 39–65 in D. A. Mays, editor. Forage fertilization. American Society of Agronomy, Crop Science Society of America, and Soil Science Society of America, Madison, Wisconsin.

Saborío, R. 1981. Programa de reactivación de ganaderia bovina de carne en Costa Rica. IICA (Instituto Interamericano de Cooperación para la Agricultura) and SEPSA (Secretaría Ejecutiva de Planificación Sectorial de Desarrollo Agropecuario y de Recursos Naturales), San José, Costa Rica.

Sanchez, P. 1982. Legume-based pasture production strategy for acid infertile soils in tropical America. Pages 97–120 in D. M. Kral, editor. Soil erosion and conservation in the tropics. American Society of Agronomy and the Soil Science Society of America, Madison, Wisconsin.

———. 1987. Management of acid soils in the humid tropics of Latin America. Pages 63–107 in P. A. Sanchez, E. R. Stoner, and E. Pushparajah, editors. Management of acid tropical soils for sustainable agriculture: proceedings of the International Board for Soil Research and Management (IBSRAM) inaugural workshop held in Yurimaguas, Peru, Brasilia, Brazil, and Bangkok, Thailand.

Sheets, P. D. 1994. Summary and conclusions. Pages 312–325 in P. D. Sheets and B. R. McKee. Archaeology, volcanism, and remote sensing in the Arenal region, Costa Rica. University of Texas Press, Austin.

Sheets, P. D., and B. R. McKee, editors. 1994. Archaeology, volcanism, and remote sensing in the Arenal region, Costa Rica. University of Texas Press, Austin.

Sheets, P., J. Hoopes, W. Melson, B. McKee, T. Sever, M. Mueller, M. Chenault, and J. Bradley. 1991. Prehistory and volcanism in the Arenal area, Costa Rica. Journal of Field Archaeology 18:445–465.

Smithsonian Migratory Bird Center. 1994. Why migratory birds are crazy for coffee. SMBC Fact Sheet No. 1, Smithsonian Institution, Washington, D.C.

Stobbs, T. H. 1976. Beef production from sown and planted pastures in the tropics. Pages 164–183 in A. J. Smith, editor. Beef cattle production in developing countries. University of Edinburgh, Edinburgh.

Stuckey, J. 1989. Kicking the subsidized habit: viewing rural development as a function of local savings mobilization—the Santa Elena case: modifications for the 1990s. MBA thesis, National University, San José, Costa Rica.

Taliafero, C. M., R. A. Byers, and G. W. Burton. 1967. Effects of spittlebug on root production and sod reserves of coastal bermudagrass. Agronomy Journal 50:530–532.

Ter, K., and B. T. Kang. 1986. Farming systems principles for improved food production and the control of soil degradation in the arid, semi-arid and humid tropics. ICRISAT (International Crops Research Institute for the Semi-Arid Tropics) and UNEP (United Nations Environment Program), ICRISAT Center, India.

Thrupp, L. A. 1988. Pesticides and policies: approaches to pest-control dilemmas in Nicaragua and Costa Rica. Latin American Perspectives 15: 37–70.

Valerio, J. R., and O. Nakano. 1987. Daño causado por adultos da cigarrinha Zulia entreriana (Berg, 1879) (Homoptera, Cercopidae) na producao de raízes de Brachiaria decumbens Stapf. Anais da Sociedade Entomologica do Brasil 16:205–221.

———. 1988. Daños causados pelo adulto da cigarrinha Zulia entreriana na producao de Brachiaria decumbens. Pesquisa Agropecuaria Brasileira 23:447–453.

Vasquez, J. D. 1988. Estudio de prefactibilidad para el establecimiento de un beneficio de café en la zona de Monteverde. CoopeSanta Elena, R.L., Proyecto DISE, Santa Elena, Costa Rica.

Vicente-Chandler, J. 1974. Fertilization of humid tropical grasslands. Pages 277–301 in D. A. Mays, editor. Forage fertilization. American Society of Agronomy, Crop Science Society of America, and Soil Science Society of America, Madison, Wisconsin.

Voisin, A., and A. Lecomte. 1962. Rotational grazing: the meeting of cow and grass. A manual of grass productivity. Crosby Lockwood, London.

Warnick, A. C. 1976. Management factors affecting reproductive efficiency of beef cattle in developing countries. Pages 132–137 in A. J. Smith, editor. Beef cattle production in developing countries. University of Edinburgh, Edinburgh.

Williams, R. C. 1986. Export agriculture and the crisis in Central America. University of North Carolina Press, Chapel Hill.

Wrigley, G. 1988. Coffee. Longman, Essex, UK.

12

Conservation Biology

Nathaniel T. Wheelwright

Each February, when I return to Monteverde to study the reproductive ecology of lauraceous trees, I stay with friends in their farmhouse tucked on the edge of the lower montane moist forest. On my first morning back, I am always eager to listen to the dawn bird chorus. During my most recent visit, I awoke to hear a cacophony of Great-tailed Grackles, a noisy flock of Brown Jays, an exuberant House Wren, and a gang of Bronzed Cowbirds squabbling over spilled grain by the cow barn. Back in 1978, during my first visit, there were no Great-tailed Grackles in Monteverde. Brown Jays had colonized the area, but their flocks were relatively small and restricted to the lower parts of the community. House Wrens, always familiar denizens of Monteverde's yards and farms, are more abundant today than ever. Once a rarity in Monteverde, Bronzed Cowbirds are now common. Monteverde has changed, and more changes are coming.

The rest of Monteverde's avifauna has undoubtedly felt an impact from the explosive population growth of these bird species. Grackles and jays prey on the eggs, nestlings, and fledglings of other birds; wrens also occasionally destroy other birds' eggs. Cowbirds

are brood parasites. All four species potentially compete with other species for food. Without censuses from earlier years, it is impossible to know how newly colonizing species have affected the fauna and flora of Monteverde. Contributors to this book have provided evidence that various species of animals and plants, especially widespread species of Costa Rica's lowlands and foothills, have expanded their ranges and increased their population sizes in Monteverde. At the same time, other species are rarer than they used to be only a few decades ago. I used to marvel at the frenzied breeding aggregations of Golden Toads, hold multicolored Harlequin Frogs, and listen to nightly serenades of glass frogs along the Río Guacimal. Most of them no longer exist in Monteverde.

In this chapter my goals are to (1) highlight aspects of the biodiversity of Monteverde that are relevant to conservation, (2) give a brief overview of general concepts in conservation biology, (3) discuss conservation problems that are specific to Monteverde and neotropical highland forests, and (4) consider how principles of conservation biology might provide solutions to those problems.

12.1. Richness, Endemism, and Biodiversity

Monteverde's diverse habitats—forest canopies dense with epiphytes, deeply shaded understories and bright tangled light gaps, networks of streams, diverse soil types—support a vast number of species of animals, plants, fungi, and microbes, far more than one would find in virtually any temperate zone site of comparable area. Nowhere on earth are there as many species of orchids as in Monteverde (see Atwood, "Orchids," pp. 74–75). Beta species richness, the accumulation of new species as one moves between adjacent habitats, is extremely high, particularly on the Pacific slope (see Chap. 3, Plants).

Biodiversity is more than just a species tally, however. The concept incorporates the ways that species interact with one another as predators, prey, parasites, hosts, mutualists, or competitors. Monteverde is also rich in species interactions and ecosystem processes. The vast majority of plant species depend on animals for pollinators or seed dispersal (see Chap. 8, Plant-Animal Interactions). The interception of wind-driven cloud moisture along the Continental Divide is one of several distinctive ecosystem processes that occur in Monteverde and in other high-elevation habitats, but not in the lowland tropics. (Doumenge et al. 1994; see Chap. 9, Ecosystem Ecology). Even habitats that have been extensively modified by humans, such as pastures and gardens, are biologically diverse in Monteverde. Biodiversity in the broadest sense is a characteristic feature of Monteverde.

Another distinctive feature of Monteverde's biodiversity is that most of its species and interactions occur only in the highlands of Central America, and many are restricted to the Cordillera de Tilarán. Endemism is particularly high, and the local extinction of endemic species has a far greater impact on global biodiversity than the local extinction of widespread species. Monteverde also safeguards a disproportionately high percentage of Central America's remaining forests. Extensive deforestation in the lowlands from Mexico to Panama has isolated or eliminated most highland forests in the region (Fig. 12.1; see also Fig. 1.4). These aspects of the biology of Monteverde—the region's great richness of species, habitats, interactions, and ecosystem functions; its high degree of endemism; its preservation of Costa Rica's shrinking forest cover; and its accelerating extinction pressures—are the critical background for understanding the conservation biology of the region.

Why should we be concerned with protecting biodiversity? Biologically rich, intact ecosystems provide services such as nutrient cycling and the maintenance of clean water and air (Daily et al. 1997). Ecosystem processes in Monteverde help sustain ecological communities over a wide area of Costa Rica. Preserving the genetic diversity of populations and species and the complexity of interactions among species can also yield direct economic benefits, many of them still unrecognized. Less easily measured but equally important are the aesthetic, cultural, and spiritual values we gain by exploring and protecting our natural heritage (Wilson 1984, Wilson and Peter 1986). The Resplendent Quetzal exemplifies both the tangible and intangible values of preserving wildlife, and the challenges we face in arguing convincingly that we must preserve biodiversity (see Wheelwright, "Enduring Reasons," pp. 432–433).

12.2. An Overview of Key Concepts in Conservation Biology

Conservation biology is dedicated to protecting genetic diversity, species and ecosystems by drawing insights and techniques from a variety of disciplines, particularly the biological sciences—population biology, behavior, ecosystem ecology, molecular biology, genetics, and evolutionary biology—as well as atmospheric chemistry, geology, and other physical sciences; economics, political science, and sociology; and history, philosophy, and related fields. Conservation biologists deal with such problems as the evaluation and maintenance of biodiversity, endangered species management, the design of nature reserves, restoration of degraded habitats, environmental ethics, and ecological economics. Specific references in conservation biology are available in several excellent recent books (Soulé 1986, Primack 1993, Hunter 1996, Meffe and Carroll 1997, Fiedler and Kareiva 1998) and in such journals as *Conservation Biology, Biological Conservation*, and *Ecological Applications*.

The fundamental threats to biodiversity can be classified into four general concerns: (1) the scarcity or loss of certain species; (2) the proliferation of other species, including pests; (3) the impoverishment of ecological interactions because of declines or changes in populations of interacting species; and (4) the disruption of ecosystem functions such as nutrient cycling or energy flow. Conservation biology is particularly concerned with understanding the factors that make species rare. In some cases, such as the North American Passenger Pigeon (*Ectopistes migratorius*), populations may fall from staggeringly large numbers to extinction in a decade or less. Most threatened species become rare more gradually, however. A species can be considered rare by any combination of a variety of criteria: if its population size is very small, if it has a restricted geographical range, or if it can exist or reproduce only in a limited subset of habi-

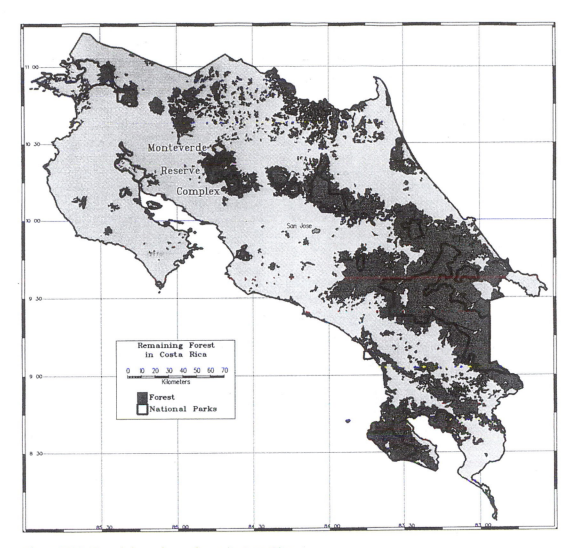

Figure 12.1. Remaining primary forest in Costa Rica.

tats (Rabinowitz 1981). Each type of rarity has different causes and implications for conservation management. Some species have always been rare in one or more of these respects. For example, they may be represented solely as a small population that only recently became isolated and diverged from a more widespread species. The loss of such species has less of an impact on global biodiversity than, for example, the extinction of an ancient, evolutionary distinctive lineage. Alternatively, some aspect of a species' biology may make it constitutionally uncommon—its position as a top carnivore in a food web, or its geographical restriction to a mountaintop or small island. To the extent that rarity is a fundamental feature of the biology of such species, they may be less prone to extinction than they appear. By studying the dynamics of naturally rare species, conservation biologists may be able to draw lessons about populations that have been driven to rarity by human activities.

Of particular concern are once-abundant species that have experienced sudden population declines. These species may have been driven to rarity due to predators (including excessive harvesting by humans), disease organisms and other parasites, competitors for limited resources, or amensals (species that have a negative impact on other species but are not themselves harmed by the interaction). For species that depend on other species (e.g., plants that have obligate mycorrhizal associations or plants that rely on specialized insects for pollination), the loss of their mutualists can cause their own rarity. Short-term physical perturbations such as fire, storms, or drought can lead to rarity, as can longer term disturbances such as climate change (for specific examples, see references in Soulé and Wilcox 1980, Meffe and Carroll 1997). Alone, each of these factors can negatively affect population growth; in combination, agonistic species interactions plus physical perturbations can jeopardize local populations. The effects of interactions and disturbance can also be indirect. For example, an introduced species can reduce the availability of food or nest sites for resident species, making it more difficult for them to reproduce or survive environmental stresses.

Habitat fragmentation (the isolation of habitats into islandlike "fragments," remnants, or patches separated by physical barriers to dispersal) plays a major role in rarity and extinction (Saunders et al. 1991). If the habitat patch in which a population occurs is separated from other populations by inhospitable habitat (e.g., large agricultural areas for forest-dwelling species, or lowland areas for highland endemics), the exchange of individuals and genes among populations will be reduced. Even if isolation acts as a filter rather than a strict barrier, allowing only certain species or genotypes to disperse, the composition of isolated communities and the structure of individual populations (e.g., age distribution, sex ratio, genetic diversity) may be altered. Moreover, isolation reduces the probability that a patch in which a population has gone locally extinct will be recolonized. Edge effects can also arise from habitat fragmentation (Angelstam 1992, Murcia 1995). For example, forests that are penetrated by roads, reduced in size by logging, or surrounded by fields experience an altered microclimate along their edges; conditions may be hotter, more desiccating, and windier at the edge and as much as 100 m into the forest. Brood parasites and predators, many of which prefer open habitats, are more likely to penetrate core areas within forests by entering along newly created edges, water lines, or roads. Although habitat fragmentation and edge effects are usually thought of on the scale of forest patches, they also occur at the scale of vast geographical regions (Edwards et al. 1994). Changes in the landscape can disrupt gene flow among populations, prevent recolonization following local extinctions, alter regional climates, and facilitate the spread of predators and parasites (Dunning et al. 1992).

As populations decline, the probability of their going extinct increases for several reasons. Individuals in small populations are more likely to be related than individuals in large populations, which means the risk of inbreeding rises (Soulé 1987). Inbreeding leads to greater homozygosity (the state of having two copies of the same allele, or variant of a particular gene) and, consequently, the increased expression of deleterious recessive alleles (harmful traits whose effects are not ordinarily apparent except when homozygous). The results of excessive inbreeding include reduced fecundity, developmental defects, lowered life expectancy, and loss of genetic variability within individuals and populations (Pusey and Wolf

1996). Over the long term, populations that are genetically homogeneous may be more susceptible to disease or physical stresses, and they may not be able to evolve adaptations that could enable them to survive in a dynamic or hostile environment. We do not know how large populations must be before they are safe over the long term from the effects of inbreeding or the random loss of genes through genetic drift in small populations. Effective population sizes (N_e) might have to be as large as 500 for species prone to inbreeding depression, or far less for species that have passed through population "bottlenecks" and eliminated most deleterious alleles (Lande and Barrowclough 1987).

In small populations, the risk of random demographic events such as skewed population sex ratios or unbalanced age distributions quickly becomes a major factor in population declines. Small localized populations no longer have a margin of safety in the face of random population fluctuations and environmental disturbances. Below a certain population size, such "demographic stochasticity" becomes increasingly perilous. Rarity begets rarity until small populations are drawn into "extinction vortices" in a positive feedback cycle (Soulé and Wilcox 1980). For example, small populations can by chance become dominated by older age classes or pre-reproductive individuals, by a single sex, or by relatives, which makes it more likely that the populations will continue to shrink (Soulé and Wilcox 1980, Nunney and Campbell 1993).

The conservation of biodiversity must be considered not only at the scale of populations but also in the context of landscapes (Dunning et al. 1992). The assemblage of plants and animals can be viewed as the net outcome of a dynamic process of colonizations, local extinctions, and recolonizations (MacArthur and Wilson 1967). Under natural conditions, habitats are heterogeneous or patchy at every scale, broken up by landscape features (e.g., rivers, valleys) and disturbances (e.g., landslides, fires, treefalls). A habitat such as a swamp forest may be effectively disconnected from other habitats of the same type, and become an ecological "island" in a matrix of an unlike habitat. To the degree that the surrounding habitat matrix is inhospitable or that patches are isolated from one another, the matrix acts as a barrier. The forest fragmentation that results from clearing for agriculture is the most familiar example of the creation of ecological islands by humans. The model of "island biogeography" and the concept of habitat heterogeneity can be applied at scales from individual plants (or parts of plants) to ecosystems and broad geographical regions (MacArthur and Wilson 1967, Williamson 1989). As deforestation moves up Costa Rica's mountain slopes, the Monteverde Reserve Complex becomes increasingly isolated from the country's other lower montane forests (Fig. 12.1). Costa Rica's highland forests are already separated from highland forests elsewhere in Central America and Mexico (LaBastille and Pool 1978, Hamilton et al. 1994).

Climate change, ozone depletion, acid rain, and the alteration of hydrological cycles are examples of disruptions of biogeochemical cycles and atmospheric chemistry that can affect biodiversity. Many species, particularly in the tropics, exist within a relatively narrow range of physical conditions. If temperatures rise, ultraviolet radiation increases, or droughts become more frequent, prolonged, or severe, certain species may no longer be able to survive or reproduce, as appears to be the case with Monteverde's amphibian fauna (see Chap. 5, Amphibians and Reptiles). Such perturbations are often caused by human activities far from the area they impact, which emphasizes that conservation biologists must think and work globally as well as locally (Orians and Wheelwright 1997). Another example of a major conservation problem whose solution must be found outside the local area is the introduction of pest species and disease organisms (Mooney and Drake 1986).

12.3. The Status of Biodiversity in Monteverde: What Is at Stake?

Conservation begins with an assessment of biodiversity and a clear set of values and objectives. What is the current status of populations, communities, and ecosystems? What will be lost if conditions remain as they are, or if they change? How will the disappearance of species, interactions, or ecosystems affect humans and other species? Nowhere in the tropics do we have a complete inventory of all species, let alone their population sizes, dynamics, or genetic structure. The demography of populations and the spatial relationships of populations to one another within a "metapopulation" (a group of populations; Levins 1969, Hanski and Gilpin 1996) are virtually unknown. This section briefly reviews what we currently know about the number of species in Monteverde.

For a few taxa in Monteverde, particularly terrestrial vertebrates, species inventories are nearly complete (see Chaps. 5–7). Thirty years of observations by residents of Monteverde and by visiting ornithologists, students, and bird-watchers have produced an accurate list of the area's bird species, their habitat preferences, their basic life histories, and their seasonal movements (Young et al. 1998). When a new bird species is spotted in Monteverde, we can be confident that it only recently arrived; when a species can

no longer be found, we can be reasonably certain that it has become locally extinct. As a result, we know that the Atlantic slope of Monteverde supports the greatest bird diversity in Costa Rica. The area's high species richness is caused by the intersection of three biogeographically distinct avifaunas (South American, Mesoamerican, and North American) in Monteverde, and six distinct life zones occurring within an area the size of a standard 24-km radius Christmas Bird Count (see Chaps. 3 and 6). Ten of Monteverde's bird species are listed as "at risk" by the International Union for the Conservation of Nature (see Table 6.8). Mammals in Monteverde have also been well inventoried (see Chap. 7, Mammals), and like birds they are exceedingly diverse. More than 40% of all of Central America's mammal species are found in Monteverde.

Reptiles and amphibians are also diverse in Monteverde. Amphibians, perhaps because of their limited dispersal abilities, show greater endemism than reptiles: 40% of Monteverde's amphibians are restricted to the highlands of Costa Rica, compared to only 15% of the area's reptiles. For both groups, there is high beta diversity. Unfortunately, the opportunity to understand Monteverde's complete fauna of amphibians and reptiles has passed. The stupefying declines and disappearances of many amphibian and several reptile species in Monteverde may be the most alarming conservation problem in the region (see Chap. 5, Amphibians and Reptiles).

It will be many decades before we have a detailed inventory of insects in Monteverde comparable to that of birds, mammals, amphibians, and reptiles (see Chap. 4, Insects and Spiders). Butterflies may be an exception, because their biology is well known for many of the same reasons as birds: they are diurnal, distinctly colored, and identifiable with available field guides. So far, 250 species of butterflies have been listed for Monteverde. Approximately 50% of Monteverde's butterfly species are elevational migrants, which makes them vulnerable to local extinction if their lowland habitats are disrupted. Monteverde is rich in other insect taxa. For example, Monteverde has as many species of cercopoid hoppers (order Homoptera) as all of Canada, and three times as many species as Great Britain. As with other taxa, endemism in insects is much greater in highland regions such as Monteverde than in lowland regions. Dragonflies and damselflies (order Odonata) and bees, wasps, and ants (order Hymenoptera) are examples of taxa whose geographical ranges are more restricted at higher elevations. For most insects, however, we know little more than their names, if that. For example, the host plants of nearly three-quarters of Monteverde's leaf beetle species (family Chrysomelidae) have not been determined. The population status and interactions of other invertebrates and virtually all bacteria and protists are likely to remain a mystery for a long time. K. Master's work on spittlebugs in the genus *Umbonia* (see Sec. 4.2.3) is one of the few studies of invertebrates in Monteverde to provide detailed information on demography, sex ratio, and dispersal. Insects comprise the vast majority of species in the region (Mawdsley and Stork 1995), and they play crucial roles as pollinators, seed dispersers, herbivores, predators, and prey (Wilson 1987). Even as this book was in press, new invertebrate species were being discovered at Monteverde, including an undescribed species of army ant in a subfamily (Leptanilloidinae) previously known only from four scattered sites in South America (J. Longino, pers. comm.).

The number of people able to identify plant species is smaller than those who can identify vertebrates or butterflies, so until recently we have known little about the ecology and distribution of plants in Monteverde. In 1979, 850 plant species were listed for the area. By 1990, the list had grown to 2000 species. The total was more than 3000 species in 1998, including 166 species new to science (see Appendix 1). As with other montane and lower montane forests in the neotropics (Hamilton et al. 1994, Churchill et al. 1995), Monteverde is especially rich in plant species. More than 350 species of ferns and fern allies have been identified in Monteverde, 10 times as many as are found at Santa Rosa, Costa Rica. As for orchids, over 500 species are listed for the area; species-rich lowland rain forest sites such as La Selva have fewer than one-third as many orchid species as Monteverde, and Santa Rosa has only 17 orchid species. Overall, plant species richness in Monteverde is three times as great as the entire lowland area of Guanacaste Province. For elevations higher than 1200 m in Monteverde, there are as many plant species as at La Selva. In fact, one-third of Costa Rica's plant species occur in Monteverde, and the region has as many families of epiphytic plants (40) as all of Mexico. Special conservation concerns are that many tree species are represented by only one or a few individuals confined to small areas, particularly dry ridgetops on the Pacific slope, and that many species are endemic to the area. Ten percent of the plant species of Monteverde are not found outside of the Cordillera de Tilarán. Fungi have hardly been studied in Monteverde, but more than 18 undescribed species have been found in the guts of midges and blackflies alone (see Lichtwardt, "Gut Fungi," pp. 83–85), implying that many more new species will be discovered.

Not surprisingly, we know most about biology at eye level, and about big organisms. Ecosystem-level work has begun to bring the canopy down to earth (see Chap. 9, Ecosystem Ecology). Far less is understood about what happens underground, and almost nothing is known about the biology of microbes in Monteverde. The vast majority of species, interactions, and ecosystem processes in Monteverde are so poorly understood that we can only estimate their current status and imagine the conservation threats they face. By the time we have gathered enough information to be able to consider more sophisticated conservation biology techniques such as population viability analysis or metapopulation models (Wooton and Bell 1992, Haig et al. 1993, Harrison 1994), it may be too late for some species or unique associations. The description of conservation biology as a "crisis discipline" (Soulé 1985) seems especially apt for Monteverde, where so much remains to be understood and so much is changing in a short time (see Chap. 10 on conservation institutions).

12.4. Conservation Problems in Monteverde

For bird populations, many local conservation problems have largely abated in Monteverde. Direct threats to populations, such as hunting and poaching, and indirect threats, such as habitat alteration and fragmentation, are of much less concern than they were prior to the 1980s (see Young, "How Have Humans Affected Bird Populations?", p. 433). Anyone who searched fruitlessly for Black Guans or Baird's Tapirs in the 1970s can testify that their populations rebounded tremendously after hunting in and around the Monteverde Cloud Forest Preserve (MCFP) was stopped. Since 1978, when I first stood at La Ventana, looking out from the Continental Divide toward the vast expanse of Peñas Blancas and beyond, the vista has been utterly transformed. Deforestation has been halted and the abandoned pastures of the Atlantic slope have rapidly reverted to secondary forest. Ecotourism may introduce new problems—the construction and use of recreational trails, near which nesting success by birds may be reduced (Miller et al. 1998), and the overuse of song playbacks to attract birds—but such effects will remain local and insubstantial compared to the conservation benefits of ecotourism (Honey 1994; see Young, "How Have Humans Affected Bird Populations?", p. 433).

The habitat changes on the Atlantic slope of Monteverde that favored the recovery of forest birds may have had the opposite impact on open-habitat birds and on reptiles that thrive along the edges of forest clearings (see Chap. 5, Amphibians and Reptiles). A consequence of residential expansion and rural electrification is the proliferation of streetlights and houselights, which causes two problems: concentrations of insects around lights may make them vulnerable to predation, and lights may interfere with the orientation and navigation of insects that migrate altitudinally in Monteverde.

Earlier hunting pressure and habitat modification virtually eliminated large raptorial birds such as hawk-eagles and large carnivorous mammals in Monteverde. Their populations are unlikely to rebound in the future because pressures on them are even more severe elsewhere in their ranges. After the loss of carnivorous mammals on Barro Colorado Island (BCI), Panama, for example, there was a rapid increase in the abundance of their prey (rodents such as Agoutis). Because Agoutis are major seed predators, the decline in top carnivores resulted in a change in the structure of the plant community on BCI (Leigh et al. 1982). In similar fashion, the disappearance of top carnivores may have affected animals and plants in Monteverde. Redford (1992) evoked the image of an "empty forest," one that still has towering trees but has lost much of its fauna, including many of the animals on which plants depend for seed dispersal. Fruit-eating bats, which are less affected by forest fragmentation than less mobile animals, may continue to serve as seed dispersers even in isolated forest remnants, although the composition of plant communities is likely to change because of bats' preference for particular fruits (see Dinerstein, "Influence of Fruit-Eating Bats," p. 434).

Straddling the Continental Divide, Monteverde's forest must have always been home to species that are chronically rare because of the restriction of their habitats to mountain peaks. The Golden Toad and the Ruddy-capped Nightingale-Thrush exemplify obligate highland species that probably never had large population sizes. In theory, populations that have been rare and isolated in the past are less prone to inbreeding depression because most deleterious alleles have been exposed by inbreeding and eliminated by natural selection. The risk to these historically small populations is not genetic but demographic; minor population fluctuations can cause them to crash (Soulé 1986).

At the scale of landscapes, the distribution of Costa Rica's remaining forests illustrates some of the threats to biodiversity that are peculiar to Monteverde and other highland habitats. Not only is the area of suitable habitat on mountaintops restricted, but also habitats are isolated on two fronts. Deforested or climatically inhospitable lowlands act as dispersal filters or barriers between peaks (Fig. 12.2). At the other altitudinal extreme, there is nowhere to go, so high-elevation species become stranded on mountain peaks. If global warming continues to the point where local climates change appreciably (Kerr 1997) or plant communities are altered, conditions may become unsuitable for lower montane forest species (Abrahamson 1989, Peters and Lovejoy 1992, Tosi et al. 1992). In fact, models predict that even a slightly warmer climate will increase the altitude at which clouds form in tropical mountains, drastically diminishing the cloud-born precipitation vital to cloud forest ecosystems (Still et al. 1999). Long-term precipitation,

Figure 12.2. Soil erosion on the deforested and heavily grazed Pacific slopes below Monteverde. Photograph by Robert Timm.

stream flow, and vertebrate population data show that warming effects are already being felt abiotically and biotically in Monteverde (Pounds et al. 1999).

Deforestation has broken what was once an interconnected chain of highland forests in Costa Rica into isolated habitats (Fig. 12.3). The Monteverde Reserve Complex remains one of the country's largest intact highland forests, but it is still isolated from other highland forests (Fig. 12.1; see also Fig. 1.4). As genetic diversity in many species diminishes in Monteverde, other unconnected forests can no longer replenish it or provide colonists to reinforce small populations or reestablish locally extinct species. The same factors play out on a smaller spatial scale within Monteverde, where the landscape has become increasingly transformed into unconnected woodlots surrounded by pastures, roads, gardens, and houses (Fig. 12.4; see also Fig. 1.7). Each forest patch can support fewer individuals and species than it would have if it were part of a continuous forest, so diversity over the entire area diminishes (Saunders et al. 1991). Forest fragmentation is also likely to change the ecological dynamics of mixed-species flocks of birds and the evolutionary dynamics of guilds of competing species.

The relatively small amount of research directed specifically toward conservation biology in Monteverde has mainly addressed questions at the level of landscapes. Deforestation has been much more severe on the Pacific slope below Monteverde than on the Atlantic side, and it has created a patchwork of for-

est fragments (Fig. 12.4). Neighboring forest patches turn out to be unexpectedly distinctive in terms of plant species composition (see Guindon, "Importance of Pacific Slope Forest," p. 435). Because animal species differ in the way that they respond to discontinuities in habitat structure, the forest fragments also have distinctive animal communities. Two habitat patches that are connected from the perspective of one species may be isolated for another species. Emerald Toucanets and Resplendent Quetzals are similar in size and diet, yet the former easily cross open areas and are found in most forest fragments, regardless of their isolation; the latter occur only in patches near extant forest. Alarmingly, more than half of the tree species found in certain Pacific slope forest fragments do not occur within protected areas such as the MCFP. A substantial proportion of the individual trees and tree species in forest remnants are members of the Lauraceae, and they depend mainly on five bird species for dispersal of their seeds (Wheelwright 1991; see Guindon, "Importance of Pacific Slope Forest," pp. 435–437). The elimination of either set of "keystone species" would have disproportionate effects on plant and animal communities of lower montane forests (Guindon 1996).

The potential asymmetry in dispersal ability of different animal mutualists raises an unexplored but potentially important set of questions. An overwhelming proportion of plant species in Monteverde (and in tropical forests generally) depend on animals for pollination and seed dispersal (see Chap. 8, Plant-Animal Interac-

Figure 12.3. Logging trucks transport primary forest logs from forest to market. Photograph by Robert Timm.

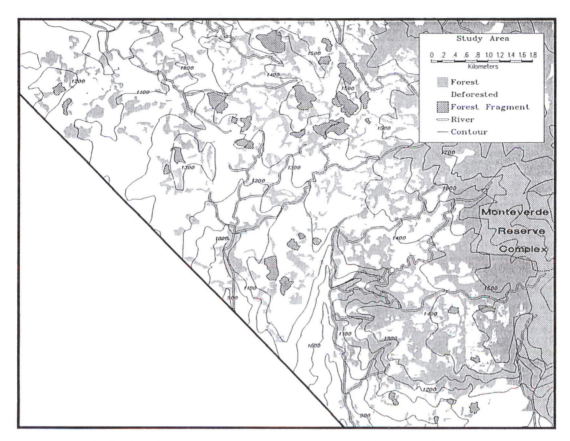

Figure 12.4. Distribution of the 30 forest remnants with respect to altitude and the continuous forest of the Monteverde Reserve Complex.

tions, and Guindon, "Importance of Pacific Slope Forest," p. 435). What happens to plants isolated in pastures, windbreaks, or small forest patches when their avian seed dispersers can easily cross open habitats but their insect pollinators cannot? What are the implications of long-distance seed dispersal but short-distance pollination for plant population genetic structure and for sexual or natural selection on plant reproductive traits?

The isolation of spatially separated habitat patches can be mitigated, at least in part, if the patches are connected by habitat corridors. Research on insect migrations over the Continental Divide emphasizes the importance of maintaining contiguous forest (see Williamson and Darling, "La Ventana," p. 438). Without adequate cover, weakly flying insects cannot make headway against Monteverde's powerful prevailing northeast trade winds during the insects' dry season migration from the leafless Pacific slope forests to the moister Atlantic slope forests. Just as Black Guans may be reluctant to cross open areas to reach isolated forest patches, flying insects may be deterred by exposed windy areas. Many flying insects are parasitic wasps and flies, which control populations of insect pests and contribute to biodiversity. The loss of parasitoids or pollinators due to disruption of mi-

gration corridors could have a substantial impact on the nature of insect and plant communities in Monteverde. Paradoxically, roads may make it easier for some insects to migrate, although an unexplored question is whether they also increase the insects' conspicuousness to predators or facilitate migration of their parasitoids. The matrix of cleared land in which Monteverde's forest fragments are embedded can take on the attributes of a habitat corridor for taxa that are effective dispersers, and even for ineffective dispersers if pasture trees are not too distantly spaced.

Habitat linkages and migration corridors are also important on a regional scale. Many species of fruit- and nectar-feeding birds migrate altitudinally in rhythm with seasonal changes in rainfall and food availability (see Chap. 6, Birds). Radio-tracking studies provide crucial details about how Resplendent Quetzals move in complex sequences between Pacific and Atlantic slope habitats (see Powell et al., "Altitudinal Migrations," pp. 439–442). Among vertebrates, Three-wattled Bellbirds, hummingbirds, and fruit bats also migrate altitudinally, but the details of their movements are poorly known (see Chaps. 6 and 7).

Adequate linkages and migration corridors appropriate for different taxa must be maintained among regions on a broad scale. That 25% of Costa Rica is now protected in the form of national parks and forest reserves tells only part of the conservation story. If reserves are isolated from one another, the value of setting aside a large percentage of the country is diminished. A high conservation priority is to connect Monteverde to a regional system of parks that encompasses a broad elevational gradient similar to Braulio Carrillo National Park on Costa Rica's Atlantic slope (LaBastille and Pool 1978; see Fig. 1.4). Migratory animals pay no attention to international borders, which greatly complicates conservation solutions (Young et al. 1998, Powell and Bjork, in press). Three-wattled Bellbirds and possibly other species of Monteverde animals spend part of their lives in Nicaragua or Panama. Simply setting aside more park land in Monteverde will not assure their protection.

Land-use patterns in Monteverde are constantly changing. As ecotourism becomes increasingly important in the economy of the region and as some farmers reduce the scale of their dairy operations, pastures revert to forest (see Chaps. 10 and 11), and it is important to understand processes such as the regeneration of abandoned pastures. The role that shade trees play in promoting seed dispersal and facilitating secondary succession in pastures is such a process (see Groom, "Regeneration in Abandoned Pastures," pp. 442–444).

Many of the conservation problems that plague other forests in Costa Rica are less serious in Monteverde (see Young, "How Have Humans Affected Bird Populations?", p. 433). Compared to animals and plants of the lowland tropics, species of highland forests appear not to be as specialized ecologically (see Chap. 6, Birds). No animal or plant studied in Monteverde is absolutely dependent on a single type of food, nest site, microhabitat, pollinator, or seed disperser, although orchids and other cloud forest epiphytes may reveal themselves to be an exception to this generalization. Wenny and Levey (1998) provide an example of an advantage to a plant species of seed dispersal by a particular bird species. The importance of the interaction between the species would have been overlooked in a study that failed to examine the fate of seeds following dispersal. Monteverde's flora and fauna are not generally characterized by the kinds of life history features that predispose species to extinction (other than the need to migrate altitudinally). For example, the sizes of seed crops of plants and the clutch sizes of animals do not seem to be distinctively small (and some are distinctively large; Sargent 1993). The ages at first reproduction are not particularly delayed in Monteverde's flora and fauna, compared to other tropical sites (but see McDonald, "Cooperation," p. 204).

The character and history of the Monteverde human community have reduced some conservation problems, through private ownership of the land by conservation-minded residents, protection of watersheds, a tradition of collaborative solutions to community problems, and the early and effective establishment of controls on hunting, tree-cutting, and excessive scientific collecting (see Chap. 10, Conservation Institutions). Monteverde's efforts to reduce pollution in the Río Guacimal caused by wastes from the dairy plant are an example of community conservation action (see Chap. 11, Agriculture, and Gill, "Impact of Lechería," p. 446).

The focus of conservation concerns in Monteverde may have already shifted from local problems to regional and global influences. Climate change has been implicated in the decline of numerous species worldwide (Peters and Lovejoy 1992, Barry et al. 1995). Of all conservation problems in Monteverde, the most alarming one is the local extinction of 40% of amphibian species in the last decade (see Chap. 5, Amphibians and Reptiles). Once common, Fleischmann's Glass Frogs, Golden Toads, Harlequin Frogs, Cloud Forest Anoles, and other amphibians and reptiles are extremely scarce or absent. The vast number of species lost over an area as large as the Monteverde region implicates climate change, pollution, introduced pathogens, or some combination of all of these factors. The last 25 years of temperature records in Monteverde mirror global warming trends; temperatures have risen, the length of dry spells has increased, and the hydrology of watersheds has been altered (Crump and Pounds 1989; see Chap. 5). Anecdotal evidence suggests that the distributions of various species of birds and plants have gradually shifted to higher elevations on the Pacific slope, presumably in response to climatic changes (see Chaps. 5 and 6, Birds). During the last four years, four species of lowland bats appeared in Monteverde for the first time (see Chap. 7, Mammals). Although ultraviolet radiation has not been measured in Monteverde, it has probably risen there as it has elsewhere in the world (Herman et al. 1996, Yan et al. 1996). UV-B radiation can harm amphibians directly or indirectly by making them more vulnerable to parasites or predators (Blaustein et al. 1996). The growing scarcity of frog-eating snakes in Monteverde, attributed to the decline in their prey (see Chap. 5), may be an example of an indirect effect of climate changes on animal populations.

12.5. Can Conservation Biology Offer Solutions to Monteverde's Conservation Problems?

Monteverde has an aura of a Shangri-la, a pristine and distant mountain forest in the clouds, removed from the rest of the world's environmental problems. However, the very nature of tropical lower montane forests—their great biodiversity, high degree of endemism, and insularity—makes them especially susceptible to the impoverishment of genetic diversity, demographic stochasticity, and other problems that plague small isolated populations and increase their risk of extinction (Harrison 1994, Meffe and Carroll 1997).

The first step in conservation management is an accurate species inventory of the area. Without baseline data on the species present, it is impossible to predict the risk of extinction or to recognize extinctions when they occur. An inventory of the flora and fauna of Monteverde is nearly complete for the more familiar taxa, such as amphibians, reptiles, birds, mammals, and plants (see Appendices). For many other taxa, it has hardly begun (see Chap. 4, Insects and Spiders). The MCFP and the Tropical Sciences Center (TSC) may be the appropriate institutions for facilitating and coordinating systematic species inventories in the area.

The next step is to determine the current status of populations and ecosystems—their sizes, structure, and functions—and to implement a monitoring system to detect changes in populations or ecosystems, and to forecast future trends. At present, there is no long-term system for monitoring populations and ecosystems in Monteverde. The cost of a long-term monitoring system is an immediate constraint. Beyond that, there is the problem of which species to follow and what data to collect. No one questions that an understanding of reproductive biology, nutritional needs, demography, population age structure and genetic structure, and population size is essential for managing cultivated crops, domesticated animals, game species, or endangered species (Lande and Barrowclough 1987, Ruggiero et al. 1994). How can we protect plant and animal species in Monteverde over the long term in the absence of such information? Young's study of House Wrens illustrates the potential pitfalls of simply recording the occurrence of a species rather than understanding its population dynamics. A species may be present in a particular habitat and appear as if it is thriving, but conditions in the habitat may be unsuitable because of insufficient food availability or quality, or excessive predator or parasite pressure. Populations can persist in such "sink" habitats only if immigrants continuously arrive from "source" habitats (Pulliam 1988; see Young, "House Wrens," p. 448).

There are some shortcuts for conservation managers that may provide reasonable interim protection while we gather the information required for effective long-term management. The concepts of indicator species, keystone species, umbrella species, island biogeography, metapopulation dynamics, and ecosys-

tem management have been particularly useful in conservation biology, all the more so because in conservation decisions must often be made quickly with insufficient data.

Changes in the behavior, population size, structure, or function of a carefully selected subset of species (or habitats) can serve as an early warning of threats to other species or habitats. By focusing monitoring efforts on a few indicator species, we may be able to identify and mitigate environmental problems at an early stage, before they become irreversible (Noss 1990). Of the hundreds of bird species in Monteverde, thousands of plant species, tens of thousands of invertebrate species, how do we select the most useful indicator species? Indicator species should be chosen after analyzing the species' natural history and population dynamics, which should be sensitive to environmental changes and representative of a broader group of species. Dense, stable populations of aquatic insects such as caddisflies indicate clean water, whereas an abundance of sludge midges indicates eutrophication or other types of stream pollution (see Chap. 4, Insects and Spiders, and Gill, "Impact of Lechería," p. 446). Monitoring caddisflies and midges and measuring stream water levels would provide a relatively low-investment means of assessing water quality, hydrological conditions, and aquatic biodiversity.

Although rare species should be monitored when possible, they are unsuitable as indicator species. Their biology is seldom representative of many other species, and they are impractical to study because they are difficult to find or because studying them exacerbates their rarity. Instead, we should pick easily observable organisms as indicator species. They should be common enough to provide adequate sample sizes for statistical analyses and to allow experimental manipulations (transplants, removals, introductions, exclosures). Other key elements of sound experimental design include randomization of treatments and study plots, replication, controls, baseline data, and continuity and longevity of the study. The esthetics of doing field biology are also a consideration, for how else can researchers be expected to dedicate themselves to long-term, often tedious studies unless they enjoy the process (Wheelwright and Smith 1994)?

Conservation biologists often have to resort to exploiting whatever data sets are available. Few long-term monitoring programs exist in Monteverde; most studies began as short-term undergraduate or graduate research projects designed to answer specific questions unrelated to conservation. Nonetheless, a preliminary sense of the impact of recent climate changes on reproduction in forest trees in Monteverde can be obtained by examining the timing of flowering and fruiting in one plant family, Lauraceae, over the last 17 years (N. Wheelwright, unpubl. data). One advantage of studying plant reproductive phenologies is that fruit set and development reflect environmental conditions integrated over periods as long as two years. So far, there is no indication that reproduction in the Lauraceae has changed over the last decade and a half. Whether lauraceous trees indicate anything about other plant species in Monteverde is unknown, but the responses of trees to environmental changes is likely to be quite different than that of animals. For animals, the most useful—and alarming—data on population trends in Monteverde come from the field notes and casual observations of resident and visiting herpetologists, ornithologists, and mammalogists.

Another important concept in conservation biology is that of the "umbrella species" (Launer and Murphy 1994). If we protect species that have expansive and sensitive habitat requirements, we automatically confer protection on species occupying the same habitats. The Bare-necked Umbrellabird is a large fruit-eating bird found on Monteverde's Atlantic slope. The bird's common name was inspired by the parasol of ebony feathers adorning its head, but it is an umbrella in more than one way. Umbrellabirds occupy large home ranges and exist at low population densities. They migrate altitudinally in response to seasonally changing fruit availability. If enough forest along an elevational gradient were set aside to ensure the survival of umbrellabirds, it would safeguard many other Atlantic slope animals and plants. Even though some of the most basic aspects of the biology of tapirs and Three-wattled Bellbirds are unknown, protecting sufficient habitat to ensure their persistence will protect thousands of species of plants, invertebrates, fungi, and microbes whose biology will remain unknown for decades.

In ecosystems throughout Central America, top carnivores have been eliminated, populations have become inbred, and ecosystem functions have been disrupted. Although Monteverde remains pristine by comparison, more aggressive population-centered management may someday be necessary, including transplants of individuals between populations to increase local genetic diversity, supplementation of food resources, addition or protection of nesting sites, culling of excess individuals or of pest species, and habitat manipulations such as prescribed burning. The effort has begun, with the provision of nest boxes for quetzals (M. Fogden, pers. comm.), devices to guard quetzal nests from predators (G. Powell, pers. comm.), captive breeding of amphibians at the Golden Toad Research Laboratory (A. Pounds, pers. comm.; see Pounds and Brenes, "Golden Toad Laboratory," pp. 171–172), and the Monteverde Conservation League's reforestation projects (see the essays by Harvey, p. 450, and Nielsen and DeRosier, p. 448). Understanding subtle aspects of animal behavior will be important in the management of critical species (Curio 1996).

Increasingly, conservation practice favors ecosystem management over critical species- or population-centered management (Grumbine 1994; see Chap. 10, Conservation Institutions). It is widely accepted that ecosystem management is effective for many of the reasons that make the protection of umbrella species attractive. Ecosystem management relies less on labor-intensive and costly species-specific data collection and intervention. By preserving intact ecosystems of sufficient size, normal ecological processes can take place. Numerous species depend on disturbances to reduce populations of competitors or predators, or to provide opportunities for reproduction or open new sites for colonization. For example, in Monteverde landslides and wind storms are essential perturbations. Unless ecosystems are large enough, such processes may not take place or may produce different effects, and disturbance-dependent species may be lost.

Monteverde's protected areas should apply landscape principles and reflect a design that has become standard in conservation biology. First, core zones should be established, centered on unique natural features or imperiled populations and expansive enough to support sufficiently large populations to avoid excessive inbreeding or demographic stochasticity. Within core zones, ecotourism, hunting, harvesting, and other potentially disruptive activities should be prohibited or tightly regulated. Second, buffer zones, where tourism, forestry, and wildlife management are concentrated, should surround core areas. Third, transition zones, where more intensive activities such as agriculture and residences occur, should be located outside of buffer areas (Meffe and Carroll 1997). Land-use practices such as leaving isolated fruiting trees in pastures, which serve as "stepping stones" for dispersing forest inhabitants, or retaining or planting corridors and windbreaks to facilitate dispersal by animals between habitat patches can be effective for conservation. Birds (including avian seed dispersers) use agricultural windbreaks as corridors in Monteverde (see Nielsen and DeRosier, "Windbreaks," p. 448), and as a consequence, windbreaks that are connected to forest or that have remnant forest trees harbor more species and higher densities of trees, (Harvey 1999; see Harvey, "Windbreaks and Trees," pp. 450–451). Ironically, windbreaks were planted in Monteverde to improve milk production and crop yields and to sustain the agricultural activities that fragmented the forest in the first place. In the future, windbreaks should be situated more intentionally in a landscape context, using appropriate native plant species, to provide more effective habitat corridors.

12.6. Conclusions

Restoration ecology, which deals with efforts to reclaim or rehabilitate degraded habitats (Hobbs and Norton 1996), is in its infancy in the tropics. We need tools to evaluate the vulnerability of species and habitats at local, regional, and global scales, so that management efforts can be prioritized (Dinerstein et al. 1995). For example, ridgetops in Monteverde harbor plant species found nowhere else in Monteverde, often with perilously low population sizes; such habitats deserve special protection (see Chap. 3, Plants). Increasingly, molecular techniques must be applied to evaluate the genetic structure and distinctiveness of populations, an approach that is just beginning at Monteverde (Gibson and Wheelwright 1995).

Tropical biological field stations such as Costa Rica's La Selva Biological Station, which is operated by the Organization for Tropical Studies, or Panama's BCI, operated by the Smithsonian Tropical Research Institute, have a legacy of multicollaborator projects supported by major grants. The productivity of those field stations, as reflected in the scientific literature, is in a different league than Monteverde's: a new publication about the biology of La Selva currently appears on average every 84 hr (B. Young, pers. comm.). A crucial difference is that Monteverde has never had funding support or an institutional infrastructure for research comparable to La Selva or BCI. Investigations in Monteverde have traditionally been led by graduate students or small teams of researchers pursuing their own research and educational objectives. How can Monteverde provide future opportunities for scientists to ask questions that are theoretically challenging and intellectually broadening, while encouraging them to generate information useful for conservation? In the 1970s and 1980s, the residents of Monteverde generously opened up their homes and farms for visiting biologists. In the face of the explosion of tourism in the area, however, such support for research is no longer realistic. One of the most crucial challenges for conservation in Monteverde will be to develop physical facilities, institutions, and financial resources for biological research to take the place of old informal Monteverde traditions. Encouragingly, the MCFP began plans in 1997 to construct a research facility and completed a new laboratory in 1999 (B. Carlson, pers. comm.).

Human-altered landscapes are here to stay (Orians 1994, Janzen 1998). How do we manage them to maintain the maximum number of species, especially those that are endemic or endangered? Research in Monteverde should widen its focus to include biological processes at habitat "boundaries" and on altered habitats such as plantations, and we should ask a broader set of questions. How do populations of different species respond to edge effects? How do their interactions with other species such as brood parasites, predators, herbivores, competitors, or mutualists change in human-modified landscapes? More research is needed on the restoration of degraded landscapes, especially as Monteverde's traditional dairy economy shifts. Which native tree species are most effective in enriching soils, reducing soil erosion, supporting a diversity of wildlife, and providing products that are useful to humans?

Only with planning and the development of conservation policies based on the strongest possible science will habitats such as the lower montane forests of Monteverde be protected over the long term (Eisner et al. 1995). The Tropical Rainforest Programme of the International Union for the Conservation of Nature (IUCN) is a promising monitoring campaign that is designed to collect and exchange information on tropical montane cloud forests. If such international programs serve to coordinate studies in the tropics using methods that are similar enough to allow meaningful comparisons among sites, they will achieve the important objective of replication. Chemical prospecting (Eisner 1991) is an exciting approach which highlights economic incentives for conserving tropical forests and which can complement other arguments for saving tropical species (see Wheelwright, "Enduring Reasons," p. 432). The search for medical compounds in the plants of Monteverde has begun, with some promising results (see Setzer, "Search for Medicines," p. 452).

In the rush toward research that is "relevant" to conservation, we must remember that conceptual breakthroughs in conservation have typically been born out of simple curiosity about the natural world. Research driven by basic theoretical questions must continue to play an important role in providing baseline data and exposing subtle threats to biodiversity that may be hidden from the narrower view of strict applied science (Wheelwright and Smith 1994). Systematics is an example of a seemingly arcane field that is playing a growing role in conservation biology by clarifying taxonomic relationships and distinguishing cryptic species (Avise and Nelson 1989), and drawing attention to lineages that are unique or whose life history features predispose them to extinction. Likewise, delimiting the geographical distributions and demography of species will allow us to determine whether a particular species in Monteverde is endemic to the area, or whether it serves as an important source for colonists that help sustain other populations. Other populations in Monteverde may act as sinks, persisting tenuously on the periphery of the species' range or occupying unsuitable habitat (Pulliam 1988), in which case working to save them may be a poor conservation investment.

The rationale for protecting Monteverde's flora and fauna must be widened beyond the simple appeal to economic self-interest. Conservationists must frame the argument so that it endures in the face of economic and social pressures (see Wheelwright, "Enduring Reasons," below). This is where the Monteverde traditions of political engagement, artistry, philosophy, industry, ingenuity, and practicality can join with the scientific research of conservation biologists to preserve the region's rich natural heritage.

ENDURING REASONS TO PRESERVE SPECIES
Nathaniel T. Wheelwright

Glittering golden-green and ruby, Resplendent Quetzals look like giant hummingbirds. When a male quetzal soars in a courtship display over Monteverde's tangled forest canopy, iridescent plumes extend more than half a meter beyond his tail and wave like a shining green banner. Roger Tory Peterson (1973), renowned author of field guides to birds, called the quetzal "the most beautiful bird in the New World." These magnificent birds are in trouble throughout much of their range. The reason is simple: many of the Central American highland forests in which they live and that provide their diet of fruit are being cut down. Despite the protection quetzals receive in the MCFP and the International Children's Rainforest, their future is not secure. The story is the same for thousands of "resplendent species" throughout the tropics, such as jaguars, orchids, and birds of paradise. For other species, such as the Golden Toad (see Chap. 5, Amphibians and Reptiles), it is already too late.

Everyone agrees that we must forestall the accelerating loss of species. But who takes responsibility for making the arguments to persuade a reluctant public to make the sacrifices necessary to preserve biodiversity? The conventional thinking is that the only successful arguments are those that appeal to people's self-interest. Such is the premise of news articles heralding rain forest plants that might contain the cure for AIDS. The rationale for protecting tropical forests rests on the notion that it is in human beings' best interest to preserve them. It is economists and ecologists who are charged with marshaling supporting evidence. Unfortunately, in many cases, none exists.

Economic arguments follow these lines: if we do not save Resplendent Quetzals or the montane forests that house them, we may have unwittingly bid goodbye to the cure for AIDS (or other diseases), which awaits discovery in the bark of a plant that depends on quetzals to disperse their seeds. The vanishing tropical forest may hold the key to solving global food shortages. Even more attractive is the thought that the tropics may yield some product—a lubricant, a fiber, a pharmaceutical, a gene, a lure for ecotourists—that could make someone rich.

However, once we agree to play the "profit-motive" game, we implicitly accept as our guiding principle the assumption that a species' right to exist depends on its usefulness to humans. Yet what happens when we justify the existence of a particular species because it provides us with some valuable natural product, and then discover a synthetic equivalent that is cheaper to produce? Who will care about *Ancistrocladus korupensis*, a nondescript vine of Cameroon that contains an anti-AIDS compound, when we can manufacture it in the laboratory? How safe are whales, mahogany trees, or any commercially exploitable species if it can be demonstrated that more money could be made by harvesting the last one and investing the profits in cattle futures?

Ecologists have added their voices, warning that the loss of keystone species could ripple through food webs, shaking the structure until the whole system collapses. Some have predicted an acceleration of extinctions following the disappearance of a single species. The implicit threat is that dying species foreshadow a dying planet, and that humans may be the next to go. This argument is undermined because it exaggerates the consequences of the disappearance of a single species. If a surgeon were to remove one of your vital organs, you would die. But if habitat disruption removes Resplendent Quetzals, Monteverde's remaining forest will not die. It will surely be a different forest—quieter, far less dazzling—but it will not unravel. Species are not equivalent to vital organs, and ecosystems are not comparable to organisms. They couldn't be, or life on our planet already would have been destroyed by the effects of the countless extinctions that have occurred throughout evolutionary history.

Traditional economic or ecological arguments are insufficient to protect most species over the long term.

Species are disappearing at a far more rapid rate than did the dinosaurs at the end of the Cretaceous Period. It is poor conservation strategy to bank on the arguments of ecologists or economists alone, because the most convincing case for tropical forests is simply that the loss of species, like the destruction of a Renoir painting or the Taj Mahal, would be a loss of resplendence. Michelangelo's magnificent fresco "The Creation of Adam," which adorns the ceiling of the Sistine Chapel, was recently restored at huge expense by patrons of the arts, not because it is economically valuable, but because it is inspired, intricate, irreplaceable, historical, resplendent—the same qualities that Monteverde's plants and animals possess.

Who can make the argument for preserving resplendence? To begin with, musicians, artists, and writers can, for they can translate aesthetic value into new images. They can also show us a different way to see objects that may appear at first to be commonplace, ugly, or disturbing. Artists can illuminate the resplendence of a flaming orange slime mold as it creeps along a rotting log, or the power of a strangler fig as it silently wrestles its host tree. Religious leaders and philosophers have the training to raise the moral and philosophical values of preserving species. Traditionally, they have had the courage to explore life's most difficult issues. But so far their voices have hardly been heard in the debate over biodiversity. Political leaders have more direct power to protect species. International conferences such as the 1992 Earth Summit in Río de Janeiro have heightened public awareness of the magnitude of environmental problems.

The most important roles in conservation can be played by ordinary people. School teachers must instill curiosity and wonder, educating the next generation to understand and value the diversity of life. They can begin by introducing their students to the plants and animals in their local communities. Students can learn the same biological principles in those places that govern tropical forests and can witness, albeit on a smaller scale, the same resplendence. Office workers, garage mechanics, computer programmers —everyone whose life is made richer and more interesting by knowing tropical forests exist—can speak up in support of spending the money and making the sacrifices needed to preserve disappearing species. We must develop persuasive arguments that endure, not rely on short-term economic rationales or warnings of ecological disasters. If tropical forests contain a cure for AIDS, so much the better. If not, let us be content with resplendence.

Note: This essay first appeared in the June 1, 1994 issue of the Chronicle of Higher Education.

HOW HAVE HUMANS AFFECTED BIRD POPULATIONS?
Bruce E. Young

The major effects of human activity on bird populations in Monteverde have already passed. Deforestation is not a current problem locally. Hunting pressure has diminished, at least in the core protected areas, a situation in marked contrast to the recent past. As recently as 1987, hunters on horseback with three or four hunting dogs would boldly ride through the MCFP entrance on their way to hunt tapir and Paca in the then-unprotected Peñas Blancas valley. A bagged Black or Crested Guan en route would serve as dinner. Squatters and legitimate land owners in Peñas Blancas enlarged their clearings whenever they had money to buy gas for their chainsaws. Farmers on the Poco Sol side of Peñas Blancas also felled old-growth forest, pushing their settlements closer to those higher up in the valley.

This activity ceased precipitously with the Monteverde Conservation League's land-purchase campaign in the Peñas Blancas valley, San Gerardo, which gained momentum in the late 1980s and early 1990s (see Chap. 10, Conservation Institutions). As cleared forest regenerates and populations of large vertebrates recover, discussion turns to the effects of the vastly increased numbers of ecotourists on the very species these people have traveled so far to see. What are the effects of a continual stream of people walking on the popular trails in the MCFP? Does use of tape recordings of bird calls by tour guides cause territory abandonment or otherwise disrupt social systems? In broad spatial and temporal scales, the answer may not be very important. Ecotourists directly influence just a few hundred of the 20,000 ha preserved in Monteverde. Even if humans caused complete breeding failure in their areas of influence, their effects on bird populations at the scale of the whole reserve system would be minor. The international recognition and fund-raising opportunities brought by the tourists helped create the reserves and protect the land. No matter what the local negative effects are, the ecotourism boom in Monteverde has had an overall positive influence on bird conservation. If the boom continues, it may help create the funding and political will to protect and restore Pacific slope habitats.

THE INFLUENCE OF FRUIT-EATING BATS ON THE DYNAMICS AND COMPOSITION OF NEOTROPICAL PREMONTANE CLOUD FORESTS
Eric Dinerstein

Neotropical lower montane forests are rich in bat species (Dinerstein 1983). The Phyllostomidae, the family of bats that include specialized fruit-eaters, are particularly diverse in Monteverde (see Appendix 10). Fruit bats are abundant, second only to insectivorous bats among mammals recorded in the MCFP and surrounding forested habitats. In an 18–month study of the feeding ecology of frugivorous bats, I found that (1) fruit-eating bats consume almost exclusively fruit, (2) the most common fruits eaten by bats are early to mid-successional shrub and tree species, (3) fruits of strangler figs (*Ficus* spp.) are much less important for montane bats than low-elevation bats, and (4) frugivorous bats play an important role in the natural regeneration of lower montane forests, removing fruits from at least 52 species of plants (Dinerstein 1983, 1986). Studies of transects along trails and roads in Monteverde and in naturally or anthropogenically disturbed habitats, revealed an abundance of bat-visited species with remarkably long fruiting seasons (e.g., *Solanum aphyodendron*, *S. umbellatum*, *Cecropia obtusifolia*) and relatively large fruit crops (e.g., *Conostegia oerstediana*, *Piper amalago*, *P. auritum*, *P. lancifolium*). Bat-visited plants of lowland neotropical moist forests, such as La Selva, typically have much shorter fruiting seasons and smaller fruit crops (Dinerstein 1983).

The abundance of fruit bats and other frugivores raises two questions related to forest conservation. First, how much does fruit removal and seed dispersal by frugivores affect the structure and distribution of plants? Second, how will the selective defaunation of tropical forests (Redford 1992) affect their future composition? Data to answer the first question have come from field investigations in Monteverde and elsewhere. Transects in successional areas affirmed that the most abundant shrub species were largely dispersed by bats (Dinerstein 1983). Studies in lowland habitats in Venezuela and Brazil demonstrate that the first shrub and successional tree species to colonize abandoned human settlements tend to be bat-visited plants. As shrubs and successional trees create roosting perches and cover for other frugivores, the seed rain increases in volume and diversity.

The second question is posed in response to the provocative essay by Redford (1992) titled "The Empty Forest," defined as a tropical forest with its impressive trees seemingly intact but its fauna eliminated. Redford hypothesized that the structure and composition of neotropical forests will be affected by the extirpation of large mammalian frugivores, fruit-eating birds, predators, and herbivores, whose absence may greatly influence plant recruitment. Typically, large fruit-eating birds and mammals are among the first species to disappear in heavily hunted forests. The meat of large fruit-eaters is highly prized. Most large frugivores reproduce at low rates and are slow to recolonize hunted areas. Throughout the neotropics, sites containing intact large frugivore, herbivore, and predator assemblages are increasingly rare. Redford (1992) used the term "minimum ecologically operational population size" to describe situations where tropical frugivores may still exist at very low densities, but their numbers are so low that the ecological processes in which they take part are reduced to the point of having no significance.

However, "empty forests" are hardly empty of frugivores; unlike their Asian counterparts, the Pteropidae, neotropical fruit bats are not heavily hunted. As long as adequate roost sites remain, it is difficult to imagine a neotropical forest without an ecologically viable population of fruit-eating bats. Future research on bats in Monteverde should determine the role phyllostomid bats play in the regeneration of abandoned pastures. On a larger spatial scale, several questions emerge. (1) How will the structure of forests that have lost frugivores other than bats be different from similar habitats that maintain the full frugivore assemblage? To what extent will Redford's "empty forests" become fruit bat–influenced forests? To what extent do bat-visited plant species overlap with species dispersed by other frugivores?

In tropical forests used as extractive reserves, the experiment is underway. Many of these sites have lost an important component of the larger avian and mammalian disperser pool. Unfortunately, in highly threatened tropical forests, it is likely that the time lag between the loss of large frugivores and the loss of mature individuals of large-fruited trees is so great that habitat loss will occur before we are able to document the erosion of dispersal processes.

THE IMPORTANCE OF PACIFIC SLOPE FOREST FOR MAINTAINING REGIONAL BIODIVERSITY
Carlos F. Guindon

As recently as 1935, most of the upper slopes of the Cardillera de Tilarán range were forested. In the 1990s, forest occurs as remnants varying in size and isolation, especially below 1500 m (see Fig. 12.4). How important are Pacific slope forest remnants for maintaining the biological diversity of the region? In my study of conservation biology of forest fragments, I asked (1) how great is tree species richness in forest fragments, (2) how is this diversity distributed, (3) what proportion of tree species depend on vertebrates for seed-dispersal, and (4) what aspects of forest fragmentation influence the use of fragments by large frugivorous birds?

I selected 30 forest fragments (1000–1500 m in elevation) that varied in size and isolation (see Fig. 12.4). Tree species richness was determined from a systematic 10% sample of each fragment. Transects were established along parallel lines running the length of each fragment. All trees located within 2.5 m of the transect line were measured and identified to species. The same transects were used to census bird and Lauraceae fruit abundance. Bird censuses were conducted by walking the transects at a pace of 10 m/min and recording all individuals seen or heard within 25 m on each side of the transect.

Tree species richness was high in the fragments. The sample included 5800 stems representing 59 plant families, 130 genera, and 225 species. Many of these tree species occur only within narrow climatic bands along the sharp altitudinal moisture gradient of the Pacific slope and are not represented within the protected forest. This shift in species along the altitudinal gradient is evident by comparing the 10 most common species within three elevational ranges (Table 12.1). The long-term survival of many of these tree species, now restricted to forest remnants, windbreaks, or pastures, will depend on the ability of pollinators and seed dispersers to locate them. Of the 225 tree species identified in the fragments, 88% depend on vertebrates for seed dispersal, with most (63%) primarily dispersed by birds. The long-term survival of many of the seed dispersers and pollinators may depend on the continued existence of the trees distributed along the Pacific slope. The Lauraceae, with 26 species, was the most species-rich tree family within the 30 forest remnants. All of these are dispersed by vertebrates, and all but two species by birds. The Lauraceae also contributed the most to overall stem density and basal area within many of the remnants.

Sixteen of the 24 bird-dispersed species in the forest remnants produce large fruit (>1.7 cm diameter). Their seeds are dispersed almost exclusively by Black Guans, Keel-billed Toucans, Emerald Toucanets, Resplendent Quetzals, and Three-wattled Bellbirds. All of these species spend at least part of the year within forest remnants on the Pacific slope (Table 12.2), where they feed on the fruits of Lauraceae and other plant species. Only toucanets were found in all remnants and during every month of the year. Bellbirds and toucans were most abundant in the forest remnants with the most Lauraceae fruit, even when these remnants were isolated and small. Guans and quetzals were not observed in the more isolated remnants. They were most abundant in the larger remnants closer to the extensive forest and at higher elevations. They were also observed (but not censused) in large remnants located along the cliff-edge that drops down into the Guacimal and San Luis river valleys at 1200 m. This suggests that isolation, rather than elevation itself, limits the use of lower forest remnants by guans and quetzals (Table 12.3).

Data from captive birds suggest that they may disperse considerable numbers of seeds while using forest remnants along the Pacific slope. A bellbird may consume more than 30 large Lauraceae fruits (e.g., *Beilschmiedia brenesii* or *Ocotea monteverdensis*) in one day. Assuming that an individual consumes only large fruits and is present in the remnants for four months of the year, it may disperse more than 3600 seeds. Many of these seeds are dispersed within the same remnant as the parent tree, but some are dispersed to other remnants. In the case of the bellbirds and toucans, seeds may be dispersed several kilometers. Within a fragmented landscape, occasional long-distance dispersal may be critical for the maintenance of isolated plant populations.

These results suggest that continuous forest should extend down from the cloud forest to at least 1000 m to maintain the dynamics and heterogeneous climatic and topographic conditions that have produced Monteverde's rich biological diversity. Increased forest cover and connectivity along the altitudinal gra-dient will help maintain plants that are limited to narrow microclimates along the gradient. Habitat corridors could facilitate the seasonal movements of species such as quetzals and guans, thus increasing the number of potential seed dispersers for large-seeded bird-dispersed plant species, as well as movements of vertebrates and invertebrates that adjust to seasonal changes in resources or environments by moving up and down altitudinal gradients.

Table 12.1. Ten most common tree species occurring within forest fragments grouped by altitudinal range.

Species	Frequency of Occurrence (stems/ha)		
	Lower (1000–1200m)	Middle (1200–1400m)	Upper (1400–1535m)
Inga punctata	160	57	
Nectandra salicina	93	32	
Sorocea trophoides	50	28	
Dendropanax arboreus	34	31	
Pseudolmedia mollis	34		
Beilschmiedia sp.	24		
Zanthoxylum fagara	22		
Capparis pringlei	18		
Styrax argentea	16		
Cecropia obtusifolia	16		
Matayba oppositifolia		47	
Croton monteverdensis		34	
Ocotea sp.		30	
Ocotea floribunda		28	
Beilschmiedia brenesii		21	
Viburnum costaricanum		21	26
Pouteria exfoliata			40
Mortoniodendron cf. guatemalense			37
Meliosma idiopoda			26
Stauranthus perforatus			25
Hasseltia floribunda			25
Eugenia guatemalensis			20
Ocotea whitei			19
Chione sylvicola			19
Cecropia polyphlebia			18

The sample area within each altitudinal range was 0.7 ha in 6 lower fragments, 2.6 ha in 12 middle remnants, and 4.0 ha in 12 upper fragments.

Table 12.2. Use of 30 forest remnants on the Pacific slope of the Cordillera de Tilarán, Costa Rica, by five species of frugivorous birds.

Remnant	Emerald Toucanet	Three-wattled Bellbird	Keel-billed Toucan	Black Guan	Resplendent Quetzal	Total
JW	167	13	3	40	17	240
AC2	181	10	1	34	10	236
MA	77	114	28	0	0	219
RLC	138	0	4	42	25	209
AC1	147	23	9	0	4	183
FA4	38	42	37	0	0	117
RA2	92	8	8	0	0	108
AF2	49	0	2	34	0	85
VP	27	34	22	0	0	83
CM	51	6	21	0	0	78
AB	62	6	6	0	3	77
AF1	27	0	4	25	10	66
RC	20	11	25	0	1	57
TS	37	14	5	0	0	56
FA3	16	26	1	0	0	43
FV2	23	0	3	10	5	41
JH	38	1	0	0	0	39
RA1	29	4	5	0	1	39
RB1	34	0	4	0	0	38
FA1	5	21	11	0	0	37
FA2	5	19	11	0	0	35
RB2	32	0	0	0	0	33
TG	26	0	1	3	0	30
FV1	15	0	2	12	0	29
FC	23	0	3	0	0	26
ER	18	0	0	0	2	20
WG	17	0	1	0	1	19
RB3	17	0	0	0	0	17
TH	8	0	0	2	0	10
BM	2	1	2	0	0	5
Total	1421	353	219	202	79	2274

Numbers are based on an average of 24 censuses conducted in each remnant between June 1991 and January 1993. Remnants are listed in order of decreasing total number of frugivores observed.

Table 12.3. Relationships between frugivore abundance and forest fragmentation.

No. of Individuals	Fruit Abundance	Fragment Size	Total Distance	Open Distance	Percentage Forest	Altitude
All species	0.68***	0.78***	0.38*	0.22	0.17	0.26
Three-wattled Bellbird	0.63***	0.24	0.58***	0.74***	-0.09	-0.24
Black Guan	-0.08	0.46**	-0.26	-0.49**	0.38*	0.77***
Keel-billed Toucan	0.74***	0.32*	0.72***	0.66***	-0.20	-0.31*
Emerald Toucanet	0.58***	0.75***	0.14	-0.04	0.17	0.25
Resplendent Quetzal	0.26	0.42*	-0.05	-0.28	0.31*	0.54**
No. of Species	0.71***	0.80***	0.36*	0.15	0.25	0.41*

Data are Spearman rank correlation coefficients between frugivore abundance, expressed as mean number of birds or species observed per census (20–25 censuses), and Lauraceae fruit abundance, fragment size, total distance and open distance to extensive forest (which reflects isolation), percentage forest within a 200-m radius, and altitude for 30 forest fragments (June 1991 to January 1993; Guindon 1996).

*, $P < 0.05$; **, $P < 0.01$; ***, $P < 0.001$.

LA VENTANA IN MONTEVERDE: A MIGRATION CORRIDOR FOR INSECTS
Michelle Williamson & Chris Darling

In the tropics, insects cross major barriers during migration. Movements across mountains have been recorded for members of 15 orders of insects in Venezuela (Beebe and Fleming 1951) and for butterflies and moths in Costa Rica (Janzen 1987, Haber and Frankie 1989, Haber 1993), Mexico (Young 1982, Powell and Brown 1990), Panama (Robbins and Small 1981), and Venezuela (Beebe 1949a, b, 1950a, b, 1951a, b; see also Johnson 1978). Migrating insects must cross the Continental Divide as they move between Atlantic and Pacific habitats in Costa Rica (Janzen 1987, Haber and Frankie 1989). Migrants could cross the MCFP along routes such as La Ventana, an abandoned road traversing the divide, which can be easily traveled by crawling insects because it contains low, meadowlike vegetation. Haber (1993) observed numerous butterflies traversing the divide via two flyways including La Ventana; they move east to the wet Atlantic forest in the dry season and then return to the dry Pacific forest in the wet season (see Chap. 4, Insects and Spiders).

Eastward Migration

In February 1988, during the dry season, we observed insects moving across La Ventana from the Pacific to the Atlantic side of the Cordillera. Most abundant were beetles (Coleoptera), wasps (Hymenoptera), and flies (Diptera). Although little is known about migration in these insects (Johnson 1978), many insects traverse Venezuelan cloud forest passes: 198 species in 17 families of beetles, 126 species in 20 families of moths, 170 species in 7 families of butterflies, 34 species in 17 families of flies, and 70 species in 15 families of wasps (Beebe 1949a, b, 1950a, b, 1951a, b, Beebe and Fleming 1951). In Costa Rica, insects may migrate to avoid the dry Pacific forest during the dry season (Janzen 1987, Haber 1993), when many plants lose their leaves or deteriorate in quality. Some hymenopterans and dipterans are pollinators and may migrate to exploit pollen in the Atlantic forest. Other wasps and flies are parasitoids and may migrate with their hosts. Tachinid flies, which parasitize Lepidoptera, may migrate east over the Costa Rican divide during the dry season (Janzen 1987).

Westward Migration

In July and August 1988, during the wet season, we confirmed that insects migrate west across La Ventana to Pacific habitats based on 13 samples collected in a trap placed at 0, 0.5, and 1.5 m above ground, which simultaneously trapped insects moving in opposite directions. The trap was rotated between samples to ensure that both sides collected equally. Representatives of numerous species were collected with 20–30 insects trapped per hour. The most abundant migrants were beetles (e.g., Blue Scarab), wasps (e.g., velvet ants and parasitoids such as ichneumonoids and proctotrupoids), and flies (e.g., muscids and parasitoids such as tachinids).

La Ventana: A Migration Corridor?

Strong winds at La Ventana force insects to travel close to the ground. However, westbound butterflies in Monteverde fly in relatively calm weather 1–2 m above the surface and over trees and buildings (Haber 1993). Butterflies are better fliers and less susceptible to wind than the small insects observed or trapped in this study as they crawled westward along the ground. Much of the migration of the insects across mountains occurs along old roads or through passes at elevations below the peaks surrounding Monteverde. Westbound butterflies are not restricted to these corridors since they can migrate through forest (Haber 1993). La Ventana in Monteverde is an ideal migration corridor for insects crossing the divide between Atlantic and Pacific habitats. Corridors between Pacific and Atlantic forests in Costa Rica (e.g., Harris and Gallagher 1990) may be crucial for connecting habitats occupied by migrating animals.

ELEVATIONAL MIGRATIONS AND HABITAT LINKAGES: USING THE RESPLENDENT QUETZAL AS AN INDICATOR FOR EVALUATING THE DESIGN OF THE MONTEVERDE RESERVE COMPLEX

George V. N. Powell, Robin D. Bjork, Sergio Barrios, & Vicente Espinoza

The migration of songbirds between their breeding areas in the temperate zone and wintering grounds in the neotropics illustrates the seasonal dependencies of birds on ecosystems far removed from each other. Many bird species also migrate even though they never leave the tropics (Wheelwright 1983, Stiles 1985, 1988, Levey 1988, Stiles and Clark 1989, Loiselle and Blake 1991, 1992, Levey and Stiles 1992). These migrations complicate the task of protecting biodiversity because they create complex ecological linkages and interdependencies among tropical habitats. Unless all habitats in the linkages are maintained, species that depend on them are likely to be extirpated from their entire range, even though representative samples of all the habitats may be protected in scattered locations (Noss 1990).

Intratropical migrations in the Tilarán mountain range must be a primary consideration in the design of the Monteverde Reserve Complex (hereafter, the preserve), the MCFP, and the International Children's Rainforest. We monitored the seasonal movements of the Resplendent Quetzal (Powell and Bjork, in press), which was a principal symbol used to justify the preserve's establishment. Our objective was to use the quetzal as an indicator to evaluate the preserve's capacity to protect regional biodiversity. Quetzals had been identified as elevational migrants (Wheelwright 1983, Loiselle et al. 1989), but the details of their migrations were unknown.

We used radiotelemetry to track individuals of the Monteverde quetzal population to elucidate their annual life cycle. The birds were captured during the breeding season at their nests or in feeding trees, and tiny radio-transmitters weighing less than 6 g (3% of a bird's body mass) were placed on them with harnesses in the form of a backpack. With the radio-tagged birds, we were able to record individuals' movements and habitat use precisely. Over a three-year study period (1989–1991), we radio-tagged 21 individuals; four birds were recaptured once and two were captured all three years, for a total of 29 transmitters placed on birds. We documented a two-parted seasonal migratory pattern that linked the quetzals to habitats on both sides of the Continental Divide, from 1000 m on the Pacific slope to as low as 500 m on the Atlantic slope (Powell and Bjork, in press).

In the Monteverde area, quetzals breed between 1500 and 1800 m primarily on the Pacific slopes and within the preserve (Fig. 12.5). Their breeding season lasts from mid-February until the end of July. With the completion of breeding, the radio-tagged quetzals move down the Pacific slope to elevations between 1000 and 1400 m. At this elevation, the birds occur outside the protected area (Fig. 12.5), in small remnants of forest on farms in Monteverde and nine other rural communities. The landscape in this area is dominated by cattle pastures, agriculture, and other human development. The quetzals remain 3–4 months (August–October) in the small forest fragments. In October or November, they move back up the slopes, across the Continental Divide and down the Atlantic slope (Fig. 12.5) into forests between 500 and 1100 m. They remain in these Atlantic slope locations for 2–3 months (November into January) before returning to their breeding areas.

The greatest surprise of this study was the discovery that most individuals migrated to both sides of the mountains during the annual cycle. More than 80% of the radio-tagged birds undertook the first phase of the migration (down the Pacific slope) and more than 90% of the birds undertook the second phase (down the Atlantic slope). Documenting this complex pattern of movements in each of three years allowed us to conclude that it was a consistent pattern.

To provide an index of habitat diversity in the areas used by quetzals, we classified the middle elevation communities in terms of the Holdridge life zone system (Holdridge 1967, Bolaños and Watson 1993). We identified which life zones were used by quetzals and used a geographic information system (GIS) to analyze the extent of each life zone in the preserve.

There are five life zones (including one transitional belt) in the Tilarán Mountains above the 500 m elevation that marks the lower limit of quetzal migrations. The quetzal population breeds primarily in the lower montane rain forest life zone, which is well represented within the preserve with more than 6100 ha of habitat protected (Fig. 12.6). The premontane rain forest life zone on the Atlantic slopes, used by quetzals during the second part of their annual migration, is also well represented in the preserve (Fig. 12.6). Recent expansion of the preserve (the International Children's Rain Forest) and creation of Arenal National Park in the northern part of the Tilarán Mountains protect much of the premontane rain forest habitat in that area. However, the

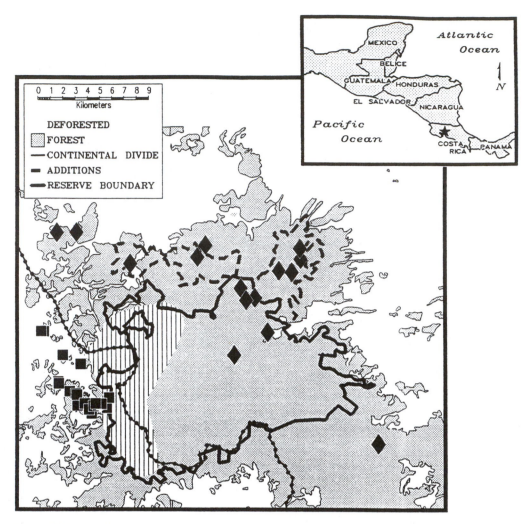

Figure 12.5. Distribution of individual radio-tagged Resplendent Quetzals in the Tilarán Mountains, in west-central Costa Rica during their two-parted migration from the breeding area (vertical lines) to the Pacific slope (squares) and about three months later to the Atlantic slope (diamonds). From Powell and Bjork (in press).

life zones used by quetzals on the Pacific slope during their first migration (lower montane wet and premontane wet forest) are poorly represented, with 600 ha and 300 ha protected, respectively (Wheelwright 1983; Fig. 12.7).

This study demonstrates biological linkages among the major habitats that typify montane areas of Mesoamerica. Quetzals are only one of dozens of seasonal migrant species in Monteverde (Stiles 1985). The full array of migratory species (including mammals and insects; see Lawton, "Baird's Tapir") creates a complex web of linkages among a greater range of habitats than have been identified by this species. As the migratory pathways of other elevational migrants are elucidated, it will be necessary to expand the altitudinal range of protection. A likely example of a montane species that requires continuity between middle-elevation and lowland Atlantic habitats is the Bare-necked Umbrellabird. This rare species is believed to migrate between its breeding range in premontane rain forest to lowland Atlantic tropical west forests (Stiles and Skutch 1989).

The lack of adequate protection for Pacific slope habitats makes it likely that quetzals and other altitudinal migrants will decline in numbers and eventually be extirpated if remaining natural habitat in this area is destroyed. The two linked Pacific slope life zones that are lacking from the preserve are poorly represented in Costa Rica except in Guanacaste National Park. However, protection of these zones affords little habitat value to quetzals because the habitats are not sufficiently high to include breeding habitat to support a local quetzal population. Consideration must be given to habitat linkages.

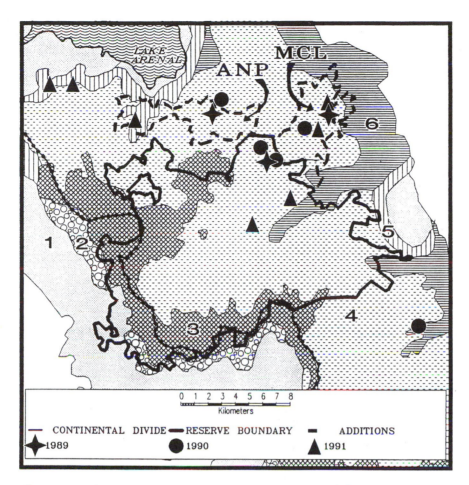

Figure 12.6. Distribution of radio-tagged Resplendent Quetzals in 1989 (stars), 1990 (circles), and 1991 (triangles) on the Atlantic slope during the second part of their migration. The quetzals' locations, which were determined from a combination of aerial reconnaisance and ground verification, represent areas that they used for about three months. Life zones (Holdridge 1967), or habitats occurring in altitudinal bands, are numbered and represented by different hatching patterns: (1) premontane wet, (2) lower montane wet, (3) lower montane rain, (4) premontane rain, (5) premontane moist transition to rain, and (6) tropical wet forest transition. Arenal National Park (ANP) and the International Children's Rainforest administered by the Monteverde Conservation League (MCL) were recent expansions. From Powell and Bjork (in press).

To maintain populations of elevational migrants in the preserve, efforts must be taken to expand the protection of Pacific slope habitats either through their inclusion in the preserve or through cooperative forest conservation programs with land owners (Powell and Bjork 1994). Because most of the forest that remains on the Pacific slopes adjacent to the preserve is in the form of remnant forest patches (see Guindon, "Importance of Pacific Slope Forests," p. 435), it is unlikely that extensive tracts will be incorporated into it. The most viable option for protecting sufficient habitat within these life zones may be to work with land owners in collaborative agreements to conserve existing forest fragments. That action, which is being successfully pursued by the Monteverde Conservation League (see Chap. 10, Conservation Institutions), coupled with selective purchase of the most critical fragments and selective habitat restoration, may provide a model for protecting critical tropical habitats in fragmented landscapes.

The future conservation of biodiversity, particularly in tropical environments, will soon depend largely on well-designed protected natural areas. The complexity of seasonal movements by Resplendent Quetzals is one demonstration of the challenge to ensure that protected areas are well designed. Our findings call for prompt concentrated efforts to identify conservation priorities before remaining unprotected habitats are eliminated.

Acknowledgments The success of our work depended on the generosity of residents of Monteverde and surrounding towns for allowing us free access to their farms to monitor the quetzals' movements. Benito Guindon provided invaluable assistance with project management and aspects of the fieldwork. The study benefited from discussions with resident biologists Carlos Guindon, William Haber, and Willow Zuchowski. This work was supported by grants from Pew Charitable Trusts, W. Alton Jones Foundation, and Homeland Foundation.

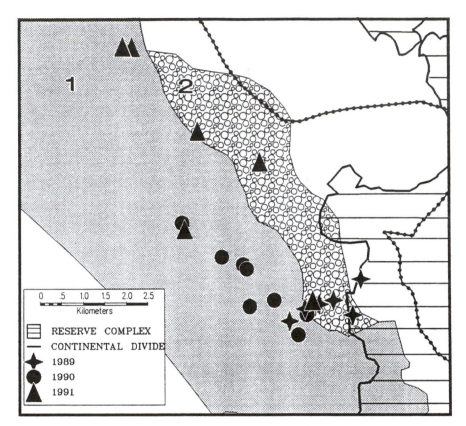

Figure 12.7. Distribution of radio-tagged Resplendent Quetzals in 1989 (stars), 1990 (circles), and 1991 (triangles) on the Pacific slope during the first part of their migration. Life zones are numbered as in Figure 12.6. The quetzals' locations, which represent centers of their home ranges that they used for about three months, illustrate their dependency on habitats outside the preserve.

PATTERNS IN THE REGENERATION OF LAURACEOUS TREES IN ABANDONED PASTURES
Martha Groom

The regeneration of abandoned pastures is limited by the survival of seeds in the soil, the arrival of new seeds, the germination of seeds, and the survival of seedlings and mature shrubs and trees. By the time pastures are abandoned, most of the seeds present at the time the forest was cleared have died or germinated and been eaten or trampled by cows (Nepstad et al. 1990). New seeds may be brought in by wind or by bats, but bird-dispersed species are not as likely to be dispersed into large clearings due to the avoidance of open areas by birds. Soils in abandoned agricultural land are often depleted of nutrients, and in pastures their structure is compacted by cows (Nepstad et al. 1990). Thus, recruitment of many plants into abandoned agricultural lands could be limited, and succession of these areas might differ from that of treefall gaps. In landscapes that are highly fragmented, some plant species may decline in abundance, perhaps to the point that they no longer support fruit-eating animal populations (Howe 1984).

Some plant species are more heavily used by birds than others. Particularly important are fruits of the avocado family (the Lauraceae), which are rich in lipids and amino acids and which provide critical components of the diet of two of the most threatened species in the area, the Resplendent Quetzal and the Three-wattled Bellbird (Wheelwright 1983, Wheelwright et al. 1984). Although the Lauraceae are often found in regenerating pastures, it is not known which factors influence the successful recruitment of these species.

Monteverde pastures vary in size and shape, and the number and identity of tree species that farmers leave in the pasture to serve as shade for cows. My research focused on whether these differences influence the pace or pattern of forest regeneration. I had observed that shade trees were used as perches by many bird species, presumably because they provided fruits and protection from predators. I also investigated the potential for these shade trees to attract fruit-eating birds, and thereby increase the frequency with which birds disperse seeds into the pasture near the shade tree. The shade trees I observed were mostly fruiting trees (usually a species of fig [*Ficus* sp.] or Lauraceae), but a few were wind-dispersed species (e.g., *Heliocarpus appendiculatus*) that do not offer fruit that birds would find suitable. I asked if the species of shade tree influenced the species of plants that were dispersed into the pasture, and the overall rate of pasture growth.

In spring of 1988, I documented regeneration of lauraceous trees and other species in abandoned pastures. I asked whether (1) lauraceous trees colonize abandoned pastures and (2) shade trees influence the number and species identity of recruiting plants in pastures. I counted the number of individuals in the Lauraceae, and the total numbers of all species of plants in 5 x 5 m sampling quadrats placed randomly at the pasture edge, in the open, or under shade trees (a total of 12 quadrats/site). I examined three pastures in each of three successional age groups, defined by the length of time since the last cows were removed from the pasture: 2–5 years, 11–15 years, and >25 years. For comparison, I censused the numbers of lauraceous plants and other juvenile shrubs and trees under tree canopies and in more open areas in the primary forest of the MCFP and in forest fragments near each of the pastures where I worked.

Lauraceous trees recruit to abandoned pastures, although they are rare in early successional pastures (Fig. 12.8). The total number of stems of all species reached peak density in the mid-successional pastures, but juvenile lauraceous trees reached densities typical of primary forest only in later successional

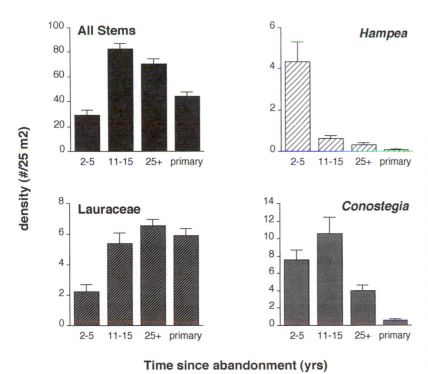

density (#/25 m2)

Time since abandonment (yrs)

Figure 12.8. Density of stems as a function of time since pasture abandonment, and compared with densities in primary forest, for all species combined and for Lauraceae, the early-successional species *Hampea* and the mid-successional species *Conostegia*. In all cases, there is a significant relationship between time since abandonment and the number of stems (seedlings + saplings) of each species group. (Kruskal-Wallis ANOVA, N = 144, *p* < .001 in all cases). Error bars in this and all other figures represent ±1 standard error.

pastures. I report the occurrence of two other species for contrast, *Hampea*, a bird-dispersed species, and *Conostegia* spp., which are bat- and bird-dispersed species. *Hampea* reached peak density in early successional pastures, whereas *Conostegia* was most common in mid-successional pastures. Rapid growth of these two fleshy-fruited species may play a critical role in pasture regeneration. *Conostegia* provided an almost continuous canopy cover after 10 years, providing shelter for many species that do not eat its fruit, but which perch in its branches.

Lauraceous plants were restricted to forest edge or beneath shade trees until later successional stages. In contrast, the total number of stems (seedlings, saplings, and adults of all species) were evenly distributed throughout the pasture after 10 years (Fig. 12.9). Because *Conostegia* grows up quickly in abandoned pastures, its distribution may influence the subsequent distribution of other plant species. Birds are attracted to *Conostegia* for cover and for fruit and, while perched, may regurgitate and spread lauraceous seeds.

The species of tree that was left as a shade tree influenced the recruitment of Lauraceae to pastures (Fig. 12.10). The largest number of lauraceous seedlings were found beneath lauraceous trees. Most lauraceous seedlings and saplings were the same species as the shade tree, but other species of Lauraceae were also found beneath these trees. Only fig trees had close to as many lauraceous seedlings growing beneath their canopies. To ensure the recruitment of lauraceous trees into abandoned pastures, one or more lauraceous shade trees should be left. Both figs and Lauraceae had many more young plants beneath their canopies than did wind-dispersed species, suggesting that for overall recruitment, a tree with edible fruit attracts more dispersers.

My study was a "snapshot" census of pastures at different ages. The ideal study would document how each pasture changes over time. Understanding which individuals grow to maturity will provide guidance for adopting management practices that accelerate pasture regeneration. My data suggest that planting of particular species or setting up artificial perches may increase the influx of seeds into more open areas. In some temperate areas, the position of trees, snags, and other perching areas is correlated with enhanced deposition of seeds (McDonnell and Stiles 1983, McClanahan and Wolfe 1993, Robinson and Handel 1993). As primary habitats dwindle, how we influence regeneration of fallow lands to enhance conservation and management objectives become increasingly important. Analysis of pasture regeneration gives insight into variables that influence recruitment into fallow pastures. Accelerating the dispersal of targeted plant species by birds or other animal dispersers may be a key component of directed regeneration projects.

Acknowledgments This work was supported by an OTS 88–1 postcourse research grant. I am grateful to Bob Lawton, Peter Feinsinger, Doug Levey, Bob Podolsky, and Nat Wheelwright for inspirational discussions and to William Haber and Willow Zuchowski for help with plant identification.

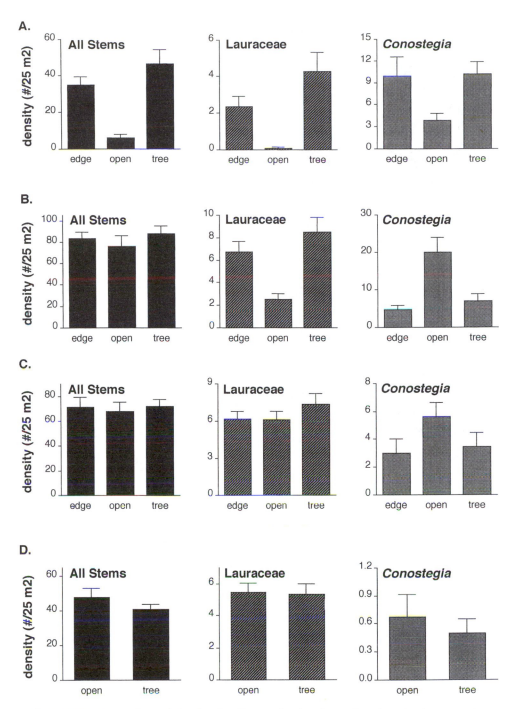

Figure 12.9. Comparison of the density of stems in plots located at the edge between the pasture and adjacent forest, in the open areas of the pasture, or under the shade tree. Numbers of all species combined and for Lauraceae and *Conostegia* are shown separately. A. Early-successional pastures (2–5 years since abandonment, *N* = 36); B. mid-successional pastures (11–15 years since abandonment, *N* = 36); C. late-successional pastures (>25 years since abandonment, *N* = 36); D. primary forest (*N* = 36). Kruskal-Wallis ANOVA showed significant (*p* < .05) differences in the density of stems found between plot locations in all panels of A, and only for the Lauraeae in B. There were no significant differences among any of the panels in C or D.

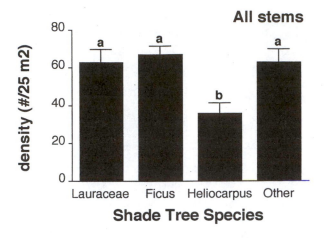

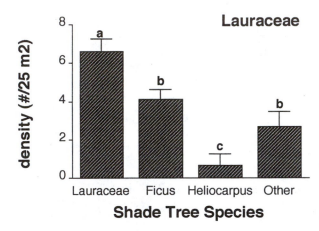

Figure 12.10. Density of stems as a function of the species identity of the shade tree left in the pasture for all species combined and for the Lauraceae. Kruskal-Wallis ANOVA showed significant differences in both cases ($H = 9.54$, $p = .02$ and $H = 20.9$, $p < .001$, respectively). Significant differences among means are signified by lowercase letters.

THE IMPACT OF THE MONTEVERDE LECHERÍA ON THE QUEBRADA GUACIMAL
Douglas E. Gill

Dairy farming and cheese-making have been economically important activities in Monteverde since its founding in the 1950s. Sequential pulses of acidic and caustic soda washes and whey from the cheese-making were discharged into the stream every day for 30 years. Beginning in 1983, the washes and whey were mixed in a holding tank and dripped continuously into the stream. What impact has the discharge from the lechería (dairy plant) had on the Quebrada Guacimal?

The rocks below the bridge have always been coated with slime, but mats of choking filamentous algae were never seen downstream. An unpleasant pungence usually hung in the air below the bridge. A succession of Organization for Tropical Studies (OTS) field problems compared the stream insect fauna in sections of the stream above and below the discharge at the lechería.

Below the outfall, there was a sharp reduction in diversity and an enormous increase in the number of larval chironomids (sludge midges). Groups of high oxygen-demanding insects, including mayflies, stoneflies, and caddisflies, declined in sections of the stream that received the discharge (Table 12.4).

These results did not fit standard patterns of eutrophication, which were derived from the study of temperate lakes. The absence of mats of green or blue-green algae downstream indicated that the discharge was not enriching the primary producers with phosphate or nitrate. Chemical analyses of the stream water and the contents of the holding tank confirmed that pattern. The slime, elevated carbon dioxide levels, and elevated respiration in downstream waters (Table 12.5) compared to upstream indicated that lac+ bacteria, most likely *Lactophilus* spp., responded

Table 12.4. Comparison of stream fauna in the Quebrada Guacimal during 10 years when invertebrates were collected from upstream (Up) and downstream (Down) sites, relative to a point of discharge from the lechería.

| | 1980 | | 1982 | | 1984 | | 1985 | | 1990 | |
	Up	Down	Up	Down	Up	Down	Up	Down	Up	Down
Odonata	4	0.9	2	1	5	0.2	2	0	0.3	0
Ephemeroptera	30	23	49	8	24	0.2	10	1	15	0
Plecoptera	nr	nr	nr	nr	7	0	6	0	2	0
Trichoptera	30	6	7	3	12	0	8	1	8	0
Coleoptera	nr	nr	nr	nr	4	0	0	0	9	0
Diptera										
Chironomidae	19	63	0	80	0	100	1	98	1	nr
Others	nr	nr	nr	nr	nr	nr	0	0	64	nr
Planaria	2	2	nr	nr	nr	nr	0	0	0.6	nr
Amphipoda	9	6	42	8	2	0	70	0.1	0.3	0

Numbers are the percentage of total invertebrates based on morphospecies counts. nr = not reported.

positively to the 3–4% lactose in the discarded whey. As a consequence, bacterial populations flourished downstream as a result of the constant supply of their limiting resource. The bacterial slimes that coated the downstream rocks used up oxygen, created anoxic conditions on those surfaces, and accounted for the absence of high oxygen-demanding insects. Chironomid larvae filter feed on the bacteria and thrive.

Studies by OTS highlighted an important environmental problem in the Monteverde community and helped redirect the management of the lechería (see Chap. 10 on conservation institutions). This research also revealed that microbial components of freshwater ecosystems respond to direct organic carbon enrichment, which contributes to our understanding of ecosystem processes in tropical streams.

Table 12.5. Measures of water quality and results of light bottle–dark bottle measures of primary productivity and respiration in the Quebrada Guacimal during 5–7 August 1990.

	Upstream	Downstream
Ammonia (mg/l)	0.35	0.35
CO_2 (mg/liter)	8.0	19.6
Chloride (mg/liter)	3.3	5.3
Dissolved O_2 (mg/liter)	9.1	7.8
Hardness (Ca^2 and Mg^2) (mg/liter)	110	850
Nitrite	0	0
pH	7.0	7.0
Temperature (ºC)	14	14
Discharge (m^3/s)	0.16	0.22
Oxygen light–dark bottle experiment		
Rock–light	9.8	1.6
Rock–dark	8.3	1.8
Water–light	8.7	6.6
Water–dark	8.6	6.6
Gross primary production	1.5	-0.2
Net primary production	0.7	-6.2
Respiration	0.8	6.0

HOUSE WRENS IN MONTEVERDE: A POPULATION SINK?
Bruce E. Young

Some habitats provide better conditions for survival and reproduction than others. Individuals that live in "source" habitats generally survive and reproduce well, with births outnumbering deaths. In "sink" habitats, deaths outnumber births and the local population is maintained by the immigration of surplus individuals from source habitats (Pulliam 1988). House Wrens living in pastures and gardens in the upper Monteverde community appear to be a species that occurs in a sink habitat maintained by immigration.

In Monteverde, I individually marked all adult House Wrens and their young in an area encompassing 60 territories. During three years, I monitored the survivorship of all individuals and the success of all nesting attempts. I calculated λ, the population multiplication rate (B. Young, unpubl. data); λ is less than 1 in declining populations, equal to 1 in stable populations, and greater than 1 in expanding populations. I found that λ varied from 0.79 ± 0.18 (95% confidence interval) to 0.81 ± 0.19 in different years (B. Young, unpubl. data), indicating that the population should be declining. However, the number of occupied territories on the study area never fluctuated by more than one or two during the study. Instead, the population was maintained by immigration from outside the study area.

At the onset of each breeding season, I found that about 60% of the marked adults from the previous season had disappeared and been replaced primarily by unbanded birds not born on the study site.

What caused the study area to be a sink? Based on my observations of attacks, I suspect that Barred Forest-Falcons in the woodlots surrounding pastures took a heavy toll on fledgling and adult House Wrens. Forest-falcons were common near my study area, which was confirmed by Valburg's (1992) observations of their attacks on Common Bush-Tanagers. The source habitat may be lower down on the Pacific slope, where woodlots are smaller and forest-falcons are less common (D. McDonald, pers. comm.). Two female House Wrens that I banded as nestlings at a lower site turned up as breeders in Monteverde, showing that dispersal upslope occurs.

In the triage of conservation efforts, we should be certain that the habitat we are protecting supports source populations of the species we wish to protect (Pulliam 1988). If the Bare-necked Umbrellabird occurs across 40,000 ha of forest and we can only protect 15,000 ha, we need to choose the portions that contain source populations. Unfortunately, we seldom have time for the in-depth studies that pinpoint where the source populations are.

WINDBREAKS AS CORRIDORS FOR BIRDS
Karen Nielsen & Debra DeRosier

Fragmentation of habitats can negatively affect animal and plant populations by restricting gene flow, immigration, emigration, or foraging (Saunders and de Rebeira 1991). Deforested areas between remnant forest habitats may impose barriers that hinder movements of many forest-dwelling species. The landscape surrounding the protected forests of Monteverde has been fragmented into a patchwork of large forest tracts, small remnant forest patches, and open agricultural land. Farmers have planted windbreaks or maintained existing natural windbreaks to protect their cattle and forage from the detrimental effects of strong winds (Fig. 12.11). The planting of

these windbreaks has been aided by the Monteverde Conservation League, which has planted more than 1000 windbreaks on farms throughout the Monteverde zone in a program that has both economic and ecological benefits (see Chap. 10, Conservation Institutions). We asked whether animals use these windbreaks as passageways, or "corridors," to move among forest patches.

The idea of constructing a corridor between isolated forest fragments makes intuitive sense. However, since the inception of the corridor concept, there has been much debate about the actual use and biological importance of corridors (Noss 1987, Simberloff and Cox 1987, Hobbs 1992, Simberloff et al. 1992). Since June 1993, we have spent over 1000 hours on local farms investigating whether birds use planted and natural remnant windbreaks as corridors. We mist-netted birds in windbreaks, pastures, and forest fragments, recorded the net in which each bird was captured and the direction from which it entered the net, and marked and released them. The sampled windbreaks were short and narrow (50 x 5 m) and were connected on both ends to a forest fragment, connected on one end only, or totally unconnected. Forest fragments of various degrees of isolation and pastures were also sampled.

Natural remnant windbreaks were used by at least 68 species of birds; 52 species were found in planted windbreaks composed of only two introduced tree species: cypress (*Cupressus lusitanical,* Cupressaceae) and tubú (*Montanoa dumicola,* Asteraceae), neither of which produce resources such as fruit. Five neotropical migrants occurred in planted windbreaks, as well as 14 others in natural windbreaks and forest fragments. Insect-eating birds comprised almost one-half of the species captured. The large amount of edge of windbreaks may make the areas good places to forage. Birds that feed on fruit and insects, and hummingbirds (which eat nectar and insects) were the next two largest guilds of birds captured, followed by fruit- and seed-eaters, despite the fact that trees in planted

windbreaks did not have fruit, nectar, or seeds at the time of sampling. In unconnected windbreaks, frugivores and seed-eaters comprised a much smaller percentage of the total number of birds captured than in the connected windbreaks.

However, there were more forest edge species using connected windbreaks than unconnected windbreaks. Moreover, we found more forest-dwelling species in connected windbreaks than in unconnected windbreaks. The total number of species captured and the hourly capture rate were significantly higher in windbreaks connected to forest fragments than in those without connections. There was also a positive correlation between hourly capture rate and distance to the nearest forest fragments.

Windbreaks appeared to serve as corridors for many bird species. The daily capture rates should have dropped to nearly zero after 4–5 consecutive days of mist-netting if only birds residing in the area were using the windbreaks (Karr 1981). However, in connected windbreaks, the daily capture rate increased after 3 consecutive days of mist-netting, whereas the daily capture rate in unconnected windbreaks declined monotonically. Many birds were captured while using windbreaks to return to forest fragments, rather than crossing open ground. Several forest-dwelling species were also captured in windbreaks other than the one in which they

Figure 12.11. Windbreaks planted in the San Luis valley below Monteverde. Photograph by Paul Butler.

were originally captured, showing that birds use windbreaks to move from one area to another. Furthermore, there were large differences in species diversity between isolated and connected fragments; isolated forest fragments had approximately one-half as many species as connected forest fragments.

Thus, connected windbreaks are used as corridors between forest fragments by many bird species in Monteverde. Linking habitats with windbreaks may help maintain biodiversity by enabling birds to use forest fragments that would otherwise have been left as isolated remnants.

WINDBREAKS AS HABITATS FOR TREES
Celia A. Harvey

Windbreaks are common features in temperate and tropical agroecosystems (Caborn 1965, Forman and Baudry 1984, Budowski 1987). Their primary function is to protect farms from wind damage or soil erosion, but they also increase the amount of forest in the landscape and provide habitat for forest species (Caborn 1965). In temperate regions, windbreaks and hedges serve as important habitats or corridors for a variety of species (birds: Yahner 1982, Haas 1995; see Nielsen and DeRosier, "Windbreaks"; mammals: Yahner 1983, Bennett 1980; insects: Lewis 1970, Pasek 1988; see Williamson and Darling, "La Ventana"; plants: Corbit 1995), especially in areas where forest habitat is scarce (Forman and Baudry 1984, Forman 1995). Species composition, structure, age, width, and proximity of windbreaks to the forest can influence the abundance and diversity of forest species that use them (Forman and Baudry 1984, Johnson and Beck 1988; Bennett 1990). Little is known about the value of windbreaks as habitat for tropical forest species. If agricultural windbreaks provide essential habitat, the planting of windbreaks could offer a pragmatic approach to the conservation of forest species within agroecosystems.

In the Monteverde region, more than 180 km of windbreaks have been planted on dairy farms as part of the Monteverde Conservation League's reforestation program (see Chap. 10, Conservation Institutions). These windbreaks are excellent study systems because the majority of windbreaks are of known age and similar in species composition and design. The objectives of my study were to determine whether windbreaks in Monteverde provided habitat for forest trees and to examine how the location of windbreaks influences the abundance and species richness of trees within them. I compared tree abundance and species richness in windbreaks connected to forests to those of windbreaks that were not connected, and between windbreaks with or without remnant trees.

In 1995, I surveyed understory vegetation in 51 windbreaks on 20 farms in Monteverde and the nearby communities of Cerro Plano, Santa Elena, Los Llanos, La Cruz, and Cañitas. All the windbreaks had been planted in pastures 5–6 years earlier and contained 2–4 rows of trees (primarily *Montonoa guatemalensis*, *Croton niveus*, *Cupressus lucitanica*, and *Casuarina equisetifolia*). They were all fenced to protect them from cattle grazing. Eight pairs of windbreaks were established; one windbreak of each pair was connected to forest and the other was not connected. There were also 10 pairs in which one windbreak contained a remnant tree and the other did not. The remainder of the windbreaks were chosen randomly. To survey tree seedlings, I divided windbreaks into 20 m segments and randomly placed 10 plots (1.5 x 1 m) within each segment. Within each plot, I counted and identified all woody plants greater than 4 cm in height. Identifications were verified by W. Haber.

My survey indicated that Monteverde windbreaks provided habitat for at least 83 forest tree species. Although the most common species (*Viburnum costaricanum* and *Trichilia havenensis*) were pioneer species, 50 of the 83 species were primary forest species. Most of the forest tree species occurred infrequently within the windbreaks; 12% of the species were represented by only a single individual. Such low frequencies may reflect the relatively short time for seed dispersal and colonization to occur. Alternatively, the low frequencies could indicate that the physical conditions of windbreaks (higher temperatures, higher light levels, and lower humidity compared to forests) are unfavorable for forest tree species.

Windbreaks that were connected to forests had significantly more forest tree species than windbreaks that were not connected (paired rank sign test, $P = .016$). Connected windbreaks also had significantly higher forest tree seedling densities than isolated windbreaks ($P = .008$; Fig. 12.12). These differences are most likely due to the preferential use of connected windbreaks and greater levels of seed dispersal by fruit-eating birds (see the essays by Nielsen and DeRosier and by Groom). A seed-trapping study is underway to examine whether the seed rain is higher in connected windbreaks.

Although the presence of remnant trees did not increase the number of forest tree species within windbreaks, windbreaks with remnant trees had significantly greater densities of forest trees than windbreaks lacking remnant trees ($P = .004$; Fig. 12.13). In windbreaks with remnant trees, the majority of the forest tree seedlings were concentrated directly be-

neath the remnant tree crowns. Other studies have shown that forest regeneration may be enhanced under remnant trees, which serve as perch sites for avian seed-dispersers (McDonnell and Stiles 1983, Guevara et al. 1986, Guevara and Laborde 1993).

This study suggests that windbreaks can enhance conservation efforts by serving as habitat for many forest tree species. As the trees mature, windbreaks will more closely resemble forest edge habitat and foster a greater variety of forest plant and animal species. Because the location of windbreaks influences the rate of forest regeneration within windbreaks, they should be connected to forest fragments and include remnant trees whenever possible (Harvey 1999).

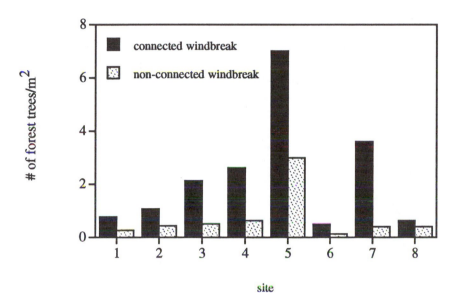

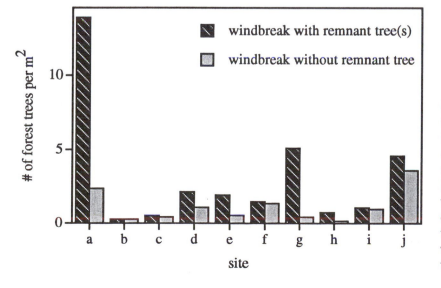

Figure 12.12. *(top)* Windbreaks connected to forest fragments had a significantly higher density of forest tree seedlings than nonconnected windbreaks.
Figure 12.13. *(left)* Windbreaks with remnant trees had significantly higher densities of forest trees regenerating in them than windbreaks lacking remnant trees.

THE SEARCH FOR MEDICINES FROM THE PLANTS OF MONTEVERDE
William N. Setzer

More than 3000 species of flowering plants in 185 families are known from the Monteverde region (see Appendix 1). This biological diversity and selective pressure by herbivores and parasites have led to the development of diverse chemical defenses. Up to 10% of the dry weight of plants can be made up of chemicals designed for defense against infection or herbivory, including novel substances that may be used as medicines or as starting materials for the development of new drugs. Despite considerable research on natural products, the medicinal potential of tropical plants has not been exploited. Many species of tropical plants have never been described, much less surveyed for biologically active constituents.

Our research in Monteverde has focused on the isolation, biological testing, and identification of potentially useful natural products from the MCFP. We pose three questions: (1) what potential new pharmacopeia from natural sources might we uncover? (2) How different is the chemistry of lower montane plants from that of lowland tropical rain forest plants? (3) Can we identify new potential alternative (and ecologically less damaging) "cash crops" for critical tropical habitats?

A starting point for these endeavors is local traditional medicine or ethnobotany of the aboriginal population. Monteverde has little ethnobotanical tradition to draw from; the aboriginal people apparently did not live or farm in the cloud forests of this area (see Timm, "Prehistoric Cultures"). The search for tropical medicinal agents from Monteverde must involve either a hit-or-miss approach or concentrate on plant families that have active members from other areas. We used both approaches.

Initially, we concentrated on the Araliaceae (Setzer et al. 1992). Some members of this family (the "ginseng" family) have been used in traditional Oriental medicine, notably members of the genera *Panax* (Hou 1978), *Schefflera* (Adam et al. 1982), and *Acanthopanax* (Xie et al. 1989, Wang et al. 1991). We obtained crude extracts from leaves of *Dendropanax arboreus*, *D. gonatopodus*, *D. latilobus*, *D. querceti*, *Schefflera rodrigueziana*, *S. robusta*, *Oreopanax capitatus*, *O. liebmanii*, *O. nubigenus*, *O. oerstedianus*, *O. standleyi*, and *O. xalapensis* and screened them for antimicrobial activity (fungicidal and bacteriocidal activity) and for *in vitro* anticancer activity (cytotoxic activity against a number of cancer cell lines in culture).

Chloroform extracts from three species (*Oreopanax standleyi*, *O. xalapensis*, and especially *Dendropanax latilobus*) showed antifungal activity. Crude ethanol extracts of *D. latilobus*, *D. arboreus*, *D. querceti*, *D. gonatopodus*, *O. liebmanii*, and *O. xalapensis* showed remarkable cytotoxic activity against Hep G2 human hepatocellular carcinoma cells, A-431 human epidermoid carcinoma cells, H-4IIE rat liver hepatoma cells, and L-1210 murine lymphocytic cells. These extracts were not toxic to normal, nonproliferating cultures of adult rat hepatocytes. The extract of *D. arboreus* was non-toxic to normal liver cells.

The active component from *D. arboreus* was isolated by activity-directed separation (Setzer et al. 1995b) using liquid chromatography (0.011% yield based on weight of fresh leaves). The structure of the cytotoxic material was determined by spectroscopic techniques to be the acetylenic compound *cis*-1,9,16–heptadecatrien-4,6–diyn-3,8–diol. This compound is very toxic to tumor cells in culture (IC_{50} values are in the µg/ml range) but nontoxic to normal hepatocytes. Similarly, bioactivity-guided isolation and structure determination of the cytotoxic component of *D. querceti* revealed the active substance to be the relatively common triterpenoid lupeol (W. Setzer, unpubl. data)

$$H_2C=CH\text{-}CH\text{-}C\equiv C\text{-}C\equiv C\text{-}CH\text{-}CH=CH\text{-}(CH_2)_5\text{-}CH=CH_2$$

$$\underset{OH}{\phantom{H_2C=CH\text{-}CH\text{-}}}\underset{OH}{\phantom{C\equiv C\text{-}C\equiv C\text{-}CH\text{-}}}$$

cis-1,9,16–Heptadecatrien-4,6–diyn-3,8–diol

Lupeol

The plant family Clusiaceae is also a rich source of antibacterial substances. Sap from various *Clusia* species showed bacteriocidal activity (W. Setzer, unpubl.data). The crude ethanol extract from the leaves of *Tovomitopsis psychotriifolia* exhibited antibacterial activity against *Bacillus cereus*, *Staphylococcus aureus*, and *Pseudomonas aeruginosa*. The biologically active agent in the extract has been isolated by chromatographic techniques and identified by nuclear magnetic resonance spectroscopy as the vitamin E derivative *trans-d*-tocotrienoloic acid (Setzer et al. 1995a).

trans-d-Tocotrienoloic acid

The MCFP is a unique study area for our search for medicinal agents from tropical plants. We continue to discover new biological activity and interesting chemical structures. Our future research efforts will include other plant families known to contain medicinally important substances (e.g., Euphorbiaceae, Rutaceae).

We will also screen for antiviral activity and peptide receptor blocking activity.

Acknowledgments This work would not be possible without our collaborators, most notably Bob Lawton and Debbie Moriarity from the Department of Biological Sciences, the University of Alabama in Huntsville. The efforts of William Haber with plant identification, Bob Bates (University of Arizona) with structure determination, and numerous student researchers are gratefully acknowledged. I am indebted to the Monteverde Cloud Forest Preserve and the Tropical Science Center for granting permission to collect leaves. I thank the National Institutes of Health and the University of Alabama in Huntsville for financial support for our research.

Literature Cited

Abrahamson, D. 1989. The challenge of global warming. Island Press, Washington, D.C.

Adam, G., M. Lischewski, H. V. Phiet, A. Preiss, J. Schmidt, and T. V. Sung. 1982. 3a-Hydroxy-lup 20(29)-ene-23,28-dioic acid from *Schefflera octophylla*. Phytochemistry 21:1385–1387.

Angelstam, P. K. 1992. Conservation of communities—the importance of edges, surroundings and landscape mosaic structure. Pages 9–70 *in* L. Hansson, editor. Ecological principles of nature conservation. Elsevier, London.

Avise, J. G., and W. S. Nelson. 1989. Molecular genetic relationships of the extinct dusky seaside sparrow. Science 243:646–648.

Barry, J. P., C. H. Baxter, R. D. Sagarin, and S. E. Gilman. 1995. Climate-related, long-term faunal changes in a California rocky intertidal community. Science 267:672–675.

Beebe, W. 1949a. Insect migration at Rancho Grande in north-central Venezuela. Zoologica NY 34: 107–110.

———. 1949b. Migration of Papilionidae at Rancho Grande, north-central Venezuela. Zoologica NY 34:119–126.

———. 1950a. Migration of Danaidae, Ithomiidae, Acraeidae and Heliconidae (butterflies) at Rancho Grande, north-central Venezuela. Zoologica NY 35:57–68.

———. 1950b. Migration of Pieridae (butterflies) through Portachuelo Pass, Rancho Grande, north-central Venezuela. Zoologica NY 35:189–196.

———. 1951a. Migration of insects (other than Lepidoptera) through Portachuelo Pass, Rancho Grande, north-central Venezuela. Zoologica NY 36:255–266.

———. 1951b. Migration of Nymphalidae (Nymphalinae), Brassolidae, Morphidae, Libytheidae, Satyridae, Riodiinadae, Lycaenidae and Hespiriidae (butterflies) through Portachuelo Pass, Rancho Grande, north-central Venezuela. Zoologica NY 36:255–266.

Beebe, W., and H. Fleming. 1951. Migration of day-flying moths through Portachuelo Pass, Rancho Grande, north-central Venezuela. Zoologica NY 36:243–254.

Bennett, A. F. 1990. Habitat corridors and the conservation of small mammals in a fragmented forest environment. Landscape Ecology 4:109–122.

Blaustein, A. R., J. M. Kiesecker, S. C. Walls, and D. C. Hokit. 1996. Field experiments, amphibian mortality, and UV radiation. BioScience 46:386–388.

Bolaños, R. A., and V. Watson. 1993. Mapa ecológico de Costa Rica. Tropical Science Center, San José, Costa Rica.

Budowski, G. 1987. The development of agroforestry in Central America. Pages 69–88 *in* H. A. Steppler and P. K. R. Nair, editors. Agroforestry: a decade of development. ICRAF, Nairobi.

Caborn, J. M. 1965. Shelterbelts and windbreaks. Faber and Faber, London.

Churchill, S. P., H. Balslev, E. Forero, and J. L. Luteyn. 1995. Biodiversity and conservation of neotropical montane forests. New York Botanical Garden, New York.

Corbit, M. D. 1995. Hedgerows as habitat corridors for forest herbs in Central New York (USA). Masters thesis, Cornell University, Ithaca, New York.

Crump, M. L., and J. A. Pounds. 1989. Temporal variation in the dispersion of a tropical anuran. Copeia 1989:209–211.

Curio, E. 1996. Conservation needs ethology. Trends in Ecology and Evolution 11:260–263.

Daily, G. C., et al. 1997. Ecosystem services: benefits supplied to human societies by natural ecosystems. Issues in Ecology, No. 2.

Dinerstein, E. 1983. Reproductive ecology of fruit bats and the seasonality of fruit production in a Costa Rican cloud forest. Ph.D. dissertation, University of Washington, Seattle.

———. 1986. Reproductive ecology of fruit bats and the seasonality of fruit production in a Costa Rican cloud forest. Biotropica 18:307–318.

Dinerstein, E., D. M. Olson, D. J. Graham, A. L. Webster, S. A. Primm, M. P. Bookbinder, and G. Ledec. 1995. A conservation assessment of the terrestrial ecoregions of Latin America and the Caribbean. The World Bank, Washington, D.C.

Doumenge, C., D. Gilmour, M. Ruíz Pérez, and J. Blockhus. 1994. Pages 17–24 *in* L. S. Hamilton, J. O. Juvik, and F. N. Scatena. Tropical montane cloud forests. Ecological Series 110. Springer, New York.

Dunning, J. B., B. J. Danielson, and H. R. Pulliam. 1992. Ecological processes that affect populations in complex landscapes. Oikos 65:169–175.

Edwards, P. J., R. M. May, and N. R. Webb, editors. 1994. Large scale ecology and conservation biology. Blackwell Press, Oxford.

Eisner, T. 1991. Chemical prospecting: a proposal for action. Pages 196–202 *in* F. H. Bormann and S. R. Kellert, editors. Ecology, economics, ethics: the broken circle. Yale University Press, New Haven, Connecticut.

Eisner, T., J. Lubchenco, E. O. Wilson, D. S. Wilcove, and M. J. Bean. 1995. Building a scientifically sound policy for protecting endangered species. Science 269:1231–1232.

Fiedler, P. L., and P. M. Kareiva. 1998. Conservation biology for the coming decade. Chapman and Hall, New York.

Forman, R. T. T. 1995. Land mosaics: the ecology of landscapes and regions. Cambridge University Press, Cambridge.

Forman, R. T. T., and J. Baudry. 1984. Hedgerows and hedgerow networks in landscape ecology. Environmental Management 8:495–510.

Gibson, J. P., and N. T. Wheelwright. 1995. Influence of avian seed dispersal on genetic structure in a population of a tropical tree, *Ocotea tenera* (Lauraceae). Oecologia 103:49–54.

Grumbine, R. E. 1994. What is ecosystem management? Conservation Biology 8:27–38.

Guevara, S., and J. Laborde. 1993. Monitoring seed dispersal at isolated standing trees in tropical pastures: consequences for local species availability. Vegetatio 107/108:319–338.

Guevara, S., S. E. Purata, and E. Van der Maarel. 1986. The role of remnant forest trees in tropical secondary succession. Vegetatio 66:77–84.

Guindon, C. F. 1996. The importance of forest fragments to the maintenance of regional biodiversity in Costa Rica. Pages 168–186 *in* J. Schelhas and R. Greenberg, editors. Forest patches in tropical landscapes. Island Press, Washington, D.C.

Haas, C. 1995. Dispersal and use of corridors by birds in wooded patches on an agricultural landscape. Conservation Biology 9:845–854.

Haber, W. A. 1993. Seasonal migration of monarchs and other butterflies in Costa Rica. Natural History Museum of Los Angeles County Science Series No. 38:201–207.

Haber, W. A., and G. W. Frankie. 1989. A tropical hawkmoth community: Costa Rican dry forest Sphingidae. Biotropica 21:155–172.

Haig, S. M., J. R. Belthoff, and D. H. Allen. 1993. Population viability analysis for a small population of Red-cockaded Woodpeckers and an evaluation of enhancement strategies. Conservation Biology 7:289–301.

Hamilton, L. S., J. O. Juvik, and F. N. Scatena. 1994. Tropical montane cloud forests. Ecological Series 110. Springer, New York.

Hanski, I., and M. Gilpin, editors. 1996. Metapopulation dynamics: ecology, genetics, and evolution. Academic Press, New York.

Harris, L. D., and P. B. Gallagher. 1990. The need for movement corridors. New initiatives for wildlife conservation. Florida Agricultural Experimental Station, Journal Series No. 9668.

Harrison, S. 1994. Metapopulations and conservation. Pages 111–128 *in* P. J. Edwards, R. M. May, and N. R. Webb, editors. Large scale ecology and conservation biology. Blackwell Press, Oxford.

Harvey, C. A. 1999. Seed dispersal into windbreaks and pastures in Monteverde, Costa Rica: Do windbreaks enhance the dispersal of tree seeds into agricultural landscapes? Ecological Applications.

Herman, J. R., P. K. Bhartia, J. Ziemke, Z. Ahmad, and D. Larko. 1996. UV-B increases (1979–1992) from decreases in total ozone. Geophysical Research Letters 23:2117–2120.

Hobbs, R. J. 1992. The role of corridors in conservation: solution or bandwagon? Trends in Ecology and Evolution 7:389–392.

Hobbs, R. J., and D. A. Norton. 1996. Toward a conceptual framework for restoration ecology. Restoration Ecology 4:93–110.

Holdridge, L. R. 1967. Life zone ecology. Tropical Science Center, San José, Costa Rica.

Honey, M. 1994. Paying the price of ecotourism. America 46:6.

Hou, J. P. 1978. The myth and truth about ginseng, Barnes, New York.

Howe, H. F. 1984. Implications of seed dispersal by animals for tropical reserve management. Biological Conservation 30:261–280.

Hunter, M. L., Jr. 1996. Fundamentals of conservation biology. Blackwell, Cambridge, Massachusetts.

Janzen, D. H. 1987. When, and when not to leave. Oikos 49:241–243.

———. 1998. Gardenification of wildland nature and the human footprint. Science 279:1312–1313.

Johnson, C. G. 1978. Migration and dispersal of insects by flight. Methuen, London.

Johnson, R. J., and M. M. Beck. 1988. Influences of shelterbelts on wildlife management and biology. Agriculture, Ecosystems and Environment 22/23:301–335.

Karr, J. R. 1981. Surveying birds with mist nets. Studies in Avian Biology 6:62–67.

Kerr, R. 1997. Greenhouse forecasting still cloudy. Science 276:1040–1042.

LaBastille, A., and D. J. Pool. 1978. On the need for a system of cloud-forest parks in Middle America and the Caribbean. Environmental Conservation 5:183–190.

Lande, R., and G. F. Barrowclough. 1987. Effective population size, genetic variation, and their use in population management. Pages 87–125 *in* M. Soulé, editor. Viable populations for conservation. Cambridge University Press, New York.

Launer, A., and D. D. Murphy. 1994. Umbrella species and the conservation of habitat fragments: a case of a threatened butterfly and a vanishing grassland ecosystem. Biological Conservation 69: 145–153.

Leigh, E. G., Jr., A. S. Rand, and D. M. Windsor, editors. 1982. The ecology of a tropical forest: seasonal rhythms and long-term changes. Smithsonian Institution Press, Washington, D.C.

Levey, D. J. 1988. Spatial and temporal variation in Costa Rican fruit and fruit-eating bird abundance. Ecological Monographs 58:251–269.

Levey, D. J., and F. G. Stiles. 1992. Evolutionary precursors of long-distance migration: resource availability and movement patterns in neotropical landbirds. American Naturalist 140:447–476.

Levins, R. 1969. Some demographic and genetic consequences of environmental heterogeneity for biological control. Bulletin of the Entomological Society of America 15:237–240.

Lewis, T. 1970. Patterns of distribution of insects near a windbreak of tall trees. Annals of Applied Biology 65:213–230.

Loiselle, B. A., and J. G. Blake. 1991. Temporal variation in birds and fruits along an elevational gradient in Costa Rica. Ecology 72:180–193.

———. 1992. Population variation in a tropical bird community: implications for conservation. Bioscience 42:838–845.

Loiselle, B., T. C. Moermond, and D. J. Mason. 1989. Low elevation record for Resplendent Quetzals in Costa Rica. Journal of Field Ornithology 60:86–88.

MacArthur, R. H., and E. O. Wilson. 1967. The theory of island biogeography. Princeton University Press, Princeton, New Jersey.

Mawdsley, N. S., and N. E. Stork. 1995. Species extinctions in insects: ecological and biogeographical considerations. Pages 322–371 *in* R. Harrington and N. E. Stork, editors. Insects in a changing environment. Academic Press, London.

McClanahan, M. J., and R. W. Wolfe. 1993. Accelerating forest succession in a fragmented landscape; the role of birds and perches. Conservation Biology 7:279–288.

McDonnell, M. J., and E. W. Stiles. 1983. The structural complexity of old field vegetation and the recruitment of bird-dispersed plant species. Oecologia 56:109–116.

Meffe, G. K., and C. R. Carroll. 1997. Principles of conservation biology. Sinauer, Sunderland, Massachusetts.

Miller, S. G., R. L. Knight, and C. K. Miller. In press. Influence of recreational trails on breeding bird communities. Ecological Applications.

Mooney, H. A., and J. A. Drake, editors. 1986. Ecology of biological invasions of North America and Hawaii. Springer, New York.

Murcia, C. 1995. Edge effects in fragmented forests: implications for conservation. Trends in Ecology and Evolution 10:58–62.

Nepstad, D., C. Uhl, and E. A. Serrão. 1990. Surmounting barriers to forest regeneration in abandoned, highly degraded pastures: a case study from Paragominas, Pará, Brazil. Pages 215–229 in A. B. Anderson, editor. Alternatives to deforestation: steps toward sustainable use of the Amazon rain forest. Columbia University Press, New York.

Noss, R. F. 1987. Corridors in real landscapes: a reply to Simberloff and Cox. Conservation Biology 1: 159–163.

———. 1990. Indicators for monitoring biodiversity: a hierarchical approach. Conservation Biology 4:355–364.

Nunney, L., and K. A. Campbell. 1993. Assessing minimum viable population size: demography meets population genetics. Trends in Ecology and Evolution 8:224–229.

Orians, C. M., and N. T. Wheelwright. 1997. Thinking globally, team-working globally. Trends in Ecology and Evolution 12:1–3.

Orians, G. H. 1994. Prospects for a comparative tropical ecology. Pages 329–338 in L. A. McDade, K. S. Bawa, H. A. Hespenheide, and G. S. Hartshorn, editors. La Selva: ecology and natural history of a neotropical rain forest. University of Chicago Press, Chicago.

Pasek, J. E. 1988. Influence of wind and windbreaks on local dispersal of insects. Agriculture, Ecosystems, and Environment 22/23:539–554.

Peters, R. L., and T. E. Lovejoy. 1992. Global warming and biological diversity. Yale University Press, New Haven, Connecticut.

Peterson, R. T., and E. L. Chalif. 1973. A field guide to Mexican birds. Houghton Mifflin, Boston, Massachusetts.

Pounds, J. A., M. P. L. Fogden, and J. H. Campbell. 1999. Biological response to climate change on a tropical mountain. Nature 398:611–614.

Powell, G. V. N., and R. Bjork. 1994. Implications of altitudinal migration for conservation strategies to protect tropical biodiversity: a case study of the Resplendent Quetzal Pharomachrus mocinno at Monteverde, Costa Rica. Bird Conservation International 4:161–174.

———. In press. Implications of intratropical migration on the design of protected natural areas: a case study using Pharomachrus mocinno. Conservation Biology.

Powell, J. A., and J. W. Brown. 1990. Concentrations of lowland sphingid and noctuid moths at high mountain passes in eastern Mexico. Biotropica 22:316–319.

Primack, R. B. 1993. Essentials of conservation biology. Sinauer, Sunderland, Massachusetts.

Pulliam, H. R. 1988. Sources, sinks, and population regulation. American Naturalist 132:652–661.

Pusey, A., and M. Wolf. 1996. Inbreeding avoidance in animals. Trends in Ecology and Evolution 11:201–206.

Rabinowitz, D. 1981. Seven forms of rarity. Pages 205–217 in H. Synge, editor. The biological aspects of rare plant conservation. Wiley, Chichester.

Redford, K. H. 1992. The empty forest. Bioscience 42:412–422.

Robbins, R. K., and G. B. Small, Jr. 1981. Wind dispersal of Panamanian hairstreak butterflies (Lepidoptera: Lycaenidae) and its evolutionary significance. Biotropica 13:308–315.

Robinson, G. R., and S. N. Handel. 1993. Forest restoration on a closed landfill: rapid addition of new species by bird dispersal. Conservation Biology 7:271–278.

Ruggiero, L. F., G. D. Hayward, and J. R. Squires. 1994. Viability analysis in biological evaluations: concepts of population viability analysis, biological population and ecological scale. Conservation Biology 8:362–372.

Sargent, S. 1993. Nestling biology of the Yellow-throated Euphonia: large clutch size in a neotropical frugivore. Wilson Bulletin 105:285–300.

Saunders, D. A., and C. P. de Rebeira. 1991. Values of corridors to avian populations in a fragmented landscape. Pages 221–240 in B. M. Hussey, R. J. Hobbs and D. A. Saunders, editors. Guidelines for bush corridors. State Mutual Book and Periodical Service, New York.

Saunders, D. A., R. J. Hobbs, and C. R. Margules. 1991. Biological consequences of ecosystem fragmentation: a review. Conservation Biology 5:18–32.

Setzer, W. N., M. N. Flair, K. G. Byler, J. Huang, M. A. Thompson, A. F. Setzer, D. M. Moriarity, R. O. Lawton, and D. B. Windham-Carswell. 1992. Antimicrobial and cytotoxic activity of crude extracts of Araliaceae from Monteverde, Costa Rica. Brenesia 38:123–130.

Setzer, W. N., T. J. Green, R. O. Lawton, D. M. Moriarity, R. B. Bates, S. Caldera, and W. A. Haber. 1995a. An antibacterial vitamin E derivative from Tovomitopsis psychotriifolia. Planta Medica 61:275–276.

Setzer, W. N., T. J. Green, K. W. Whitaker, D. M. Moriarity, C. A. Yancey, R. O. Lawton, and R. B. Bates. 1995b. A cytotoxic diacetylene from Dendropanax arboreus. Planta Medica 61:470–471.

Simberloff, D., and J. Cox. 1987. Consequences and costs of conservation corridors. Conservation Biology 1:63–69.

Simberloff, D., J. A. Farr, J. Cox, and D. Mehlman. 1992. Movement corridors: conservation bargains or poor investments? Conservation Biology 6:493–501.

Soulé, M. E. 1985. What is conservation biology? Bioscience 35:727–734.

———. 1986. Conservation biology: the science of scarcity and diversity. Sinauer, Sunderland, Massachusetts.

———. editor. 1987. Viable populations for conservation. Sinauer, Sunderland, Massachusetts.

Soulé, M. E., and B. A. Wilcox. 1980. Conservation biology: an evolutionary-ecological perspective. Sinauer, Sunderland, Massachusetts.

Stiles, F. G. 1985. Conservation of forest birds in Costa Rica: problems and perspectives. ICBP Technical Publication No. 4:141–168.

———. 1988. Altitudinal movements of birds on the Caribbean slope of Costa Rica: implications for conservation. Pages 243–258 in F. Almeda and C. M. Pringle, editors. Tropical rainforests: diversity and conservation. California Academy of Sciences, San Francisco.

Stiles, F. G., and D. A. Clark. 1989. Conservation of tropical rain forest birds: a case study from Costa Rica. American Birds 43:420–428.

Stiles, F. G., and A. F. Skutch. 1989. A guide to the birds of Costa Rica. Cornell University Press, Ithaca, New York.

Still, C. J., P. N. Foster, and S. H. Schneider. 1999. Simulating the effects of climate change on tropical montane cloud forests. Nature 398:608–610.

Tosi, J. A., Jr., V. Watson, and J. Echeverría. 1992. Potential impacts of climate change on the productive capacity of Costa Rican forests. Tropical Science Center, San José, Costa Rica.

Valburg, L. K. 1992. Flocking and frugivory: the effect of social groupings on resource use in the Common Bush-Tanager. Condor 94:358–363.

Wang, J. Z., X. J. Mao, H. Ito, and K. Shimyra. 1991. Immunomodulatory activity of a polysaccharide from Acanthopanax obovatus roots. Planta Medica 57:335–336.

Wenny, D. G., and D. J. Levey. 1998. Directed seed dispersal by bellbirds in a tropical cloud forest. Proceedings of the National Academy of Science USA 95:6204–6207.

Wheelwright, N. T. 1983. Fruits and the ecology of Resplendent Quetzals. Auk 100:286–301.

———. 1991. How long do fruit-eating birds stay in the trees where they feed? Biotropica 23:29–40.

Wheelwright, N. T., and J. N. M. Smith. 1994. Contributing to conservation biology: how to get started? Bulletin of the Ecological Society of America 75:286.

Wheelwright, N. T., W. A. Haber, K. G. Murray, and C. Guindon. 1984. Tropical fruit-eating birds and their food plants: a survey of a Costa Rican lower montane forest. Biotropica 16:173–192.

Williamson, M. 1989. The MacArthur and Wilson theory today: true but trivial. Journal of Biogeography 16:3–4.

Wilson, E. O. 1984. Biophilia. Harvard University Press, Cambridge, Massachusetts.

———. 1987. The little things that run the world. Conservation Biology 1:344–346.

Wilson, E. O., and F. M. Peter, editors. 1986. Biodiversity. National Academy Press, Washington, D.C.

Wooton, T. J., and D. A. Bell. 1992. A metapopulation model of the Peregrine Falcon in California: viability and management strategies. Ecological Applications 2:307–321.

Xie, S., Z. Long, and F. Qin. 1989. Primary study on the mechanism of immunoregulatory effect of the polysaccharide from *Acanthopanax senticosus*. Zhong hua Weishengwuxue He Mianyixue Zazhi 9:153–155.

Yahner, R. H. 1982. Avian use of vertical strata and plantings in farmstead shelterbelts. Journal of Wildlife Management. 46:50–60.

———. 1983. Small mammals in farmstead shelterbelts: habitat correlates of seasonal abundance and community structure. Journal of Wildlife Management 47:74–84.

Yan, N. D., W. Keller, N. M. Scully, D. R. S. Lean, and P. J. Dillon. 1996. Increased UV-B penetration in a lake owing to drought-induced acidification. Nature 381: 141–143.

Young, A. M. 1982. An evolutionary-ecological model of the evolution of migratory behavior in the Monarch Butterfly and its absence in the Queen Butterfly. Acta Biotheoretica 31:219–237.

Young, B. E., D. DeRosier, and G. V. N. Powell. 1998. Diversity and conservation of understory birds in the Tilarán Mountains, Costa Rica. Auk 115:998–1016.

Appendix 1

Vascular Plants of Monteverde

William A. Haber

This list includes plants of the Monteverde area occurring above 700 m elevation on both slopes. Groups are listed in the order Dicotyledons, Monocotyledons, Gymnosperms, Ferns and fern allies. Column codes are defined at the end of the list. Representative collection numbers listed in parentheses are Haber collections except where the collector's last name is noted. The designation of pollinators, seed dispersers, and sexual system is based on observations of the author and colleagues over many years, supplemented by inferences from morphology and specific citations in the literature, including *Flora of Costa Rica*, (Standley 1937) *Flora of Panama* (Woodson and Schery 1943–1980), Croat (1978), Cronquist (1981), Dinerstein (1986), Haber and Bawa (1984), Kress and Beach (1994), and Mabberley (1987).

The nomenclature follows recent treatments in the *Manual of Costa Rican Plants* project (see Chap. 3, p. 39).

Dicotyledons	Zone[a]	Poll[b]	Seed[c]	Sex[d]	Habit[e]
Acanthaceae					
Aphelandra					
aurantiaca (Scheidw.) Lindl. (2737)	MA	BD	EX	HE	H
dolichantha Donn. Sm. (Dryer 1490)	P	Fly	EX	HE	H
scabra (Vahl) Sm. (950)	P	BD	EX	HE	S
tridentata Hemsl. (662)	M	BD	EX	HE	H
Barleria					
micans Nees (Bello 4370)	P	BD?	EX	HE	H
Blechum					
pyramidatum (Lam.) Urb. (9676)	P	SB	EX	HE	H
Bravaisia					
integerrima (Spreng.) Stand. (438)	P	LB	EX	HE	Tm
Dicliptera					
iopus Lindau (Dryer 844)	M	BD	EX	HE	H
unguiculata Ness (10463)	PM	LB	EX	HE	H
Dyschoriste					
valeriana Leonard (9673)	P	SB	EX	HE	H
Habracanthus					
blepharorhachis (Lindau) Gómez-Laur., ined. (7610)	M	BD	EX	HE	S
silvaticus Nees (8382)	A	BD	EX	HE	S
Hansteinia					
sessilifolia (Oerst.) (7119)	P	BD	EX	HE	S
stricta (Leonard) D. N. Gibson (5996)	A	BD	EX	HE	S
Hypoestes					
*phyllostachya Baker (9607)	M				H
Justicia					
arborescens Durkee & McDade (893)	P	BD	EX	HE	S
aurea Schltdl. (875)	PMA	BD	EX	HE	S
brenesii (Leonard) D. N. Gibson (10392)	A		EX	HE	H
costaricana Leonard (Dryer 1109)	M	LB	EX	HE	H
crenata (Leonard) Durkee (9195)	A	BD	EX	HE	S
macrantha Benth. (430)	PM	BD	EX	HE	S
oerstedii Leonard (1366)	M	BD	EX	HE	H-S
sarapiquensis McDade (1687)	A	BD	EX	HE	L
valerii Leonard (9125)	M	LB	EX	HE	H
Louteridium					
costaricense Radlk. & Donn. Sm. (8681)	A	BD	EX	HE	H
Mendoncia					
brenesii Standl. & Leonard (7332)	A	BD	BD?	HE	L
retusa Turrill (8255)	A	BD	BD?	HE	L
tonduzii Turrill (4768)	A	BD	BD?	HE	L
Odontonema					
tubiforme (Bertol.) Kuntze (8003)	A	BD	EX	HE	S
Poikilacanthus					
macranthus Lindau (707)	M	BD	EX	HE	S
Pseuderanthemum					
cuspidatum (Nees) Radlk. (2670)	M	BF	EX	HE	H
Razisea					
spicata Oerst. (785)	PMA	BD	EX	HE	S
Ruellia					
inundata Kunth (8962)	P	BD	EX	HE	H
Spathacanthus					
hoffmannii Lindau (Bello 2747)	PA	HM?	EX?	HE	Ts
Tetramerium					
nervosum Nees (10339)	P	IN	EX?	HE	H
Thunbergia					
*alata Bojer ex Sims (9917)	M				V
*erecta (Benth.) T. Anderson (10698)	M				S
*fragrans Roxb. (8654)	PM				V
*grandiflora Roxb. (5648)	A				V

Dicotyledons	Zone[a]	Poll[b]	Seed[c]	Sex[d]	Habit[e]
Actinidiaceae					
Saurauia					
montana Seem. (9818)	MA	LB	BD,AM	DI	Tm
pittieri Donn. Sm. (9963)	M				
rubiformis Vatke (10009)	M		LB	BD,AM	DITs
yasicae Loes. (11226)	A	LB	BD,AM	DI	Tm
sp. A (9304)	M	LB	BD,AM	DI	Ts
Alzateaceae					
Alzatea					
verticillata Ruiz & Pav. (7660)	MA	IN	WD	HE?	E
Amaranthaceae					
Achyranthes					
aspera L. (9683)	P	WD	GR	HE	S
Alternanthera					
costaricensis Kuntze (10846)	A	WD	GR	HE	H
laguroides (Standl.) Standl. (9768)	P	WD	GR	HE	V
sessilis (L.) R. Br. (9674)	P	WD	GR	HE	H
Amaranthus					
hybridus L. (10453)	P	WD	GR	MO	H
altissima (Jacq.) Kunth (9682)	P	WD	BD	HE	L
Gomphrena					
serrata L. (9179)	P	WD	GR	HE	H
Iresine					
angustifolia Euphrasén (Bello 685)	P	WD	GR	HE	S
calea (Ibáñez) Standl. (10586)	M	WD	GR	HE	L
diffusa Humb. & Bonpl. ex Willd. (836)	MA	WD	GR	HE	H
Pleuropetalum					
pleiogynum (Kuntze) Standl. (11332)	A	IN	BD	HE	S-L
sprucei (Hook. f.) Standl. (9397)	PMA	IN	BD	HE	S
Anacardiaceae					
Anacardium					
excelsum (Bertero & Balbis ex Kunth) Skeels (6817)	P	IN	AM	HE	Tl
Astronium					
graveolens Jacq. (9924)	P	SB	WD	DI	Tl
Mauria					
heterophylla Kunth (269)	PM	WA	BD	DI	Tm
Mosquitoxylum					
jamaicense Krug & Urb. (6362)	A	SB	BD	DI	Tl
Tapirira					
mexicana Marchand (8726)	MA	SB	BD	DI	Tl
Annonaceae					
Annona					
pruinosa G. E. Schatz (10110)	P	CO	AM	HE	Ts
Cymbopetalum					
costaricense (Donn. Sm.) Saff. (6947)	A	CO	BD	HE	Ts
Desmopsis					
bibracteata (Rob.) Saff. (9765)	M	CO	BD	HE	Ts
microcarpa R. E. Fr. (4917)	MA	CO	BD	HE	Ts
schippii Standl. (Bello 1060)	A	CO	BD	HE	Ts
Guatteria					
diospyroides Baill. (Bello 558)	A	CO	BD	HE	Ts
oliviformis Donn. Sm. (Bello 4153)	M	CO	BD	HE	Tm
costaricensis R. E. Fr., cf. (5089)	A	CO	BD	HE	Tm
Rollinia					
membranacea Triana & Planch. (11067)	PA	CO	BD	HE	Tm
Sapranthus					
viridiflorus G. E. Schatz, ined. (Bello 1385)	A	CO	AM	HE	Tm
Unonopsis					
costaricensis R. E. Fr. (Bello 2229)	A	CO	BD	HE	Ts
Xylopia					
bocatorena Schery (8401)	A	CO	BD	HE	Ts

Dicotyledons	Zone[a]	Poll[b]	Seed[c]	Sex[d]	Habit[e]
Apiaceae					
Centella					
erecta (L. f.) Fernald (Bello 4948)	M	IN	GR	HE	H
Ciclospermum					
leptophyllum (Pers.) Sprague (10372)	PM	IN	GR	HE	H
Hydrocotyle					
bowlezioides Mathias & Constance (Grayum 7918)	M	IN	GR	HE	H
leucocephala Cham. & Schltdl. (9650)	M	IN	GR	HE	H
mexicana Schltdl. & Cham. (10399)	A	IN	GR	HE	H
torresiana Rose & Standl. (5794)	MA	IN	GR	HE	H
umbellata L. (10594)	M	IN	GR	HE	H
Sanicula					
liberta Cham. & Schltdl. (2891)	M	IN	TM	HE	H
Spananthe					
paniculata L. (10315)	PM	IN	GR	HE	H
Apocynaceae					
Allomarkgrafia					
brenesiana Woodson (9858)	A	LB	WD	HE	L
plumeriiflora Woodson (7061)	A	HM	WD	HE	L
Alstonia					
pittieri (Donn. Sm.) A. H. Gentry (10006)	P	MO	WD	HE	Tm
Echites					
woodsoniana Monach. (Bello 5278)	P	IN	WD	HE	L
Forsteronia					
monteverdensis J. F. Morales (127)	M	IN	WD	HE	L
Mandevilla					
hirsuta (A. Rich.) K. Schum. (1779)	PA	BD	WD	HE	L
pittieri Woodson (8334)	A		WD	HE	L
subsagittata (Ruiz & Pav.) Woodson (6855)	PMA		WD	HE	L
veraguasensis (Seem.) Hemsl. (864)	MA	BD	WD	HE	L
Peltastes					
isthmicus Woodson (10755)	P	IN	WD	HE	L
Plumeria					
rubra L. (6891)	P	HM	WD	HE	Tm
Prestonia					
longifolia (Sessé & Moc.) J. F. Morales (10715)	MA	LB	WD	HE	L
portobellensis (Beurling) Woodson (7513)	PA	LB	WD	HE	L
Rauvolfia					
aphlebia (Standl.) A. H. Gentry (1780)	PA	MO	BD	HE	Tm
Stemmadenia					
alfari (Donn. Sm.) Woodson (11061)	A	LB	BD	HE	Ts
donnell-smithii (Rose) Woodson (9995)	P	LB	BD	HE	Tm
litoralis (Kunth) L. Allorge (7114)	PM	HM	BD	HE	Tm
Tabernaemontana					
amygdalifolia Jacq. (9448)	A	MO	BD	HE	Tm
longipes Donn. Sm. cf. (7104)	PM	MO	BD	HE	Ts
Aquifoliaceae					
Ilex					
chiriquensis Standl. (3223)	M	SB	BD	DI	Ts
costaricensis Donn. Sm. (7384)	M	SB	BD	DI	Tl
hemiepiphytica W. J. Hahn (7773)	M	SB	BD	DI	Tm
lamprophylla Standl. (258)	M	SB	BD	DI	Tl
pallida Standl. (Bello 1125)	A	SB	BD	DI	Tl
haberi (Lundell) W. J. Hahn (9939)	PM	SB	BD	DI	Tl
skutchii Edwin ex W. J. Hahn (Bello 2076)	A	SB	BD	DI	Tl
vulcanicola Standl. (4344)	M	SB	BD	DI	Ts
sp. A. (10539)	M	SB	BD	DI	Tl
Araliaceae					
Dendropanax					
arboreus (L.) Decne. & Planch. (1637)	MA	IN	BD	DI	Tl
caucanus (Harms) Harms (7593)	A	IN	BD	DI	Tm
gonatopodus (Donn. Sm.) A. C. Sm. (6785)	MA	IN	BD	DI	Tl

Dicotyledons	Zone[a]	Poll[b]	Seed[c]	Sex[d]	Habit[e]
latilobus M. J. Cannon & Cannon (6611)	M	IN	BD	DI	Tm
querceti Donn. Sm. (Bello 594)	MA	IN	BD	DI	Ts
Oreopanax					
anomalus M. J. Cannon & Cannon (Bello 1341)	M	IN	BD	DI	E
capitatus (Jacq.) Decne. & Planch. (10040)	M	IN	BD	DE	E
nicaraguensis M. J. Cannon & Cannon (9839)	A	IN	BD	DI	E
nubigenus Standl. (6244)	M	IN	BD	DI	E
obtusifolius L. O. Williams (8790)	M	IN	BD	DI	E
oerstedianus Marchal (4944)	M	IN	BD	DI	E
pycnocarpus Donn. Sm. (Bello 4576)	M	IN	BD	DI	E
standleyi A. C. Sm. (11078)	M	IN	BD	DI	E
vestitus A. C. Sm. (8366)	MA	IN	BD	DI	E
xalapensis (Kunth) Decne. & Planch. (4288)	MA	IN	BD	DI	Tm
Schefflera					
brenesii A. C. Sm. (783)	A	IN	BD	HE?	L
robusta (A. C. Sm.) A. C. Sm. (9328)	MA	IN	BD	HE?	E
rodrigueziana Frodin ex M. J. Cannon & Cannon (6707)	M	IN	BD	HE?	E
Aristolochiaceae					
Aristolochia					
grandiflora Sw. (1823)	A	FLY	WD	HE	L
maxima Jacq. (7849)	A	FLY	WD	HE	L
tonduzii O. C. Schmidt (4862)	A	FLY	WD	HE	L
Asclepiadaceae					
Asclepias					
curassavica l. (8876)	PMA	BF	WD	HE	H
Blepharodon					
mucronatum (Schltdl.) Decne. (Koptur 118)	M	IN	WD	HE	V
Cynanchum					
filisepalum (Standl.) L. O. Williams (9474)	M	IN	WD	HE	V
glaberrimum (Woodson) L. O. Williams (11674)	A	IN	WN	HE	V
schlectendalii (Deche.) Standl. and Steyerm. (10771)	P	IN	WD	HE	V
Fischeria					
blepharopetala S. F. Blake (Penneys 287)	M	IN	WD	HE	V
panamensis Spellman (Fuentes 4)	PM	IN	WD	HE	V
Gonolobus					
denticulatus (Vahl) W. D. Stevens (10830)	A	IN	WD	HE	V
edulis Hemsl. (10001)	PM	IN	WD	HE	V
heterophyllus (Hemsl.) W. D. Stevens (7186)	MA	IN	WD	HE	V
Marsdenia					
engleriana Rothe (10767)	P	IN	WD	HE	L
Matelea					
brasiliensis (Schltr.) Spellman (Bello 749)	A	IN	WD	HE	V
magnifolia (Pittier) Woodson (7457)	A	IN	WD	HE	V
mediocris Woodson (7041)	A	IN	WD	HE	V
pseudobarbata (Pittier) Woodson, cf. (650)	M	IN	WD	HE	V
Tassadia					
obovata Decne. (6648)	A	IN	WD	HE	V
Asteraceae					
Acmella					
oppositifolia (Lam.) R. K. Jansen (10038)	M	SB	WD	HE	H
radicans (Jacq.) R. K. Jansen (10203)	M	SB	WD	HE	H
Ageratina					
anisochroma (Klatt) R. M. King & H. Rob. (1438)	M	IN	WD	HE	S
pichinchensis (Kunth) R. M. King & H. Rob. 10572)	M	IN	WD	HE	S
Ageratum					
conyzoides L. (Fuente 5)	PMA	BF	WD	HE	H
microcarpum (Benth. ex Oerst.) Hemsl. (906)	P	BF	WD	HE	H
petiolatum (Hook. & Arn.) Hemsl. (593)	M	BF	WD	HE	H
rugosum J. M. Coult. (10164)	PM	BF	WD	HE	H
Archibaccharis					
panamensis S. F. Blake (10419)	M	IN	WD	DI	L
schiedeana (Benth.) J. Jacks. (10415)	M	IN	WD	DI	L

Dicotyledons	Zone[a]	Poll[b]	Seed[c]	Sex[d]	Habit[e]
Baccharis					
pedunculata (Miller) Cabrera (2518)	M	IN	WD	DI	S
trinervis (Lam.) Pers. (9977)	PM	IN	WD	DI	L
Bidens					
pilosa L. (601)	M	LB	TM	HE	H
reptans (L.) G. Don (843)	PMA	LB	BD,AM	HE	L
squarrosa Kunth (10458)	P	LB	BD,AM	HE	L
sp. A (3555)	P	LB	TM	HE	H
Calea					
prunifolia Kunth (10951)	P	SB	WD	HE	S
ternifolia Kunth (10167)	P	SB	WD	HE	S
Calyptocarpus					
wendlandii Sch. Bip. (10366)	PM	IN	WD,GR	HE	H
Chaptalia					
nutans (L.) Pol. (10522)	MA	IN	WD	HE	H
Chromalaena					
collina (DC.) R. M. King & H. Rob. (10369)	PM	IN	WD	HE	S
Cirsium					
mexicanum DC. (10371)	M	BF	WD	HE	H
Clibadium					
anceps Greenm. (5362)	M	BF,SB	BD	HE	S
asperum (Aubl.) DC., cf. (Kotur 177)	M?	BF,SB	BD	HE	S
erosum DC., cf. (7394)	A	BF,SB	BD	HE	S
glomeratum Greenm., cf. (Dryer 521)	M	BF,SB	BD	HE	S
leiocarpum Steetz (Dryer 1227)	M	BF,SB	BD	HE	S
microcephalum, aff. (5479)	A	BF,SB	BD	HE	S
surinamense L. (10247)	M	BF,SB	BD	HE	S
Conyza					
apurensis Kunth (10436)	PM	IN	WD	HE	H
bonariensis (L.) Cronquist (10221)	M	IN	WD	HE	H
canadensis (L.) Cronquist (10307)	M	IN	WD	HE	H
chilensis Spreng. (10429)	M	IN	WD	HE	H
Critonia					
billbergiana (Beurl.) R. M. King & H. Rob. (9196)	M	IN	WD	HE	L
daleoides DC. (10973)	P	IN	WD	HE	T
hebebotrya DC. (Burger 9617)	M	IN	WD	HE	T
morifolia (Mill.) R. M. King & H. Rob. (10589)	PA	IN	WD	HE	T
sexangularis (Klatt) R. M. King & H. Rob (Hammel 15101)	PA	IN	WD	HE	S
Decachaeta					
thieleana (Klatt) R. M. King & H. Rob. (10480)	P	IN	WD	HE	S
Delilia					
biflora (L.) Kuntze (10344)	PM	SB	WD	HE	H
Dyssodea					
montana (Benth.) A. Gray (10354)	P	BE	WD	HE	H
Elephantopus					
mollis Kunth (10191)	PM	IN	WD	HE	H
Emilia					
fosbergii Nicolson (10363)	PM	LB	WD	HE	H
Erato					
vulcanica (Klatt) H. Rob. (586)	M	LB	WD	HE	S
Erechtites					
hieracifolia (L.) Raf. ex DC. (3488)	P	IN	WD	HE	H
valerianifolia (Wolf) DC. (2754)	M	IN	WD	HE	H
Erigeron					
karvinskianus DC. (10881)	P	LB	WD	HE	H
Fleischmannia					
capillipes (Benth. ex Oerst.) R. M. King & H. Rob. (8856)	P	BF	WD	HE	S
gentryi R. M. King & H. Rob (Burger 8637)	M	BF	WD	HE	S
hymenophylla (Klatt) R. King & H. Rob. (4078)	M	BF	WD	HE	S
plectranthifolia (Benth.) R. M. King & H. Rob. (10568)	PM	BF	WD	HE	S
pratensis (Klatt) R. M. King & H. Rob. (3731)	P	BF	WD	HE	S
pycnocephala (Less.) R. M. King & H. Rob. (10447)	M	BF	WD	HE	S

Dicotyledons	Zone[a]	Poll[b]	Seed[c]	Sex[d]	Habit[e]
sideritides (Benth. ex Oerst.) R. M. King & H. Rob. (8247)	A	BF	WD	HE	S
sinclairii (Benth. ex Oerst.) R. M. King & H. Rob. (8963)	P	BF	WD	HE	S
Galinsoga					
parviflora Cav. (10277)	MA	SB	WD,GR	HE	H
quadriradiata Ruiz & Pav. (10217)	PM	SB	WD,GR	HE	H
Gamochaeta					
americana (Mill.) Wedd. (10249)	M	IN	WD	HE	H
Gnaphalium					
roseum Kunth (10386)	PM	IN	WD	HE	H
sp. A (10387)	M	IN	WD	HE	H
Gongrostylus					
costaricensis (Kuntze) R. M. King & H. Rob. (6847)	A	IN	WD	HE	V
Heterocondylus					
vitalbae (DC.) R. M. King & H. Rob. (1227)	A	IN	WD	HE	V
Hidalgoa					
ternata La Llave Lex. (714)	MA	BF	GR,WD?	HE	L
Jaegeria					
hirta (Lag.) Less. (3774)	P	SB	GR	HE	H
Koanophyllon					
hylonomum (B. L. Rob.) R. M. King & H. Rob. (10997)	M	BF	WD	HE	Ts
pittieri (Klatt) R. M. King & H. Rob. (698)	M	MO	WD	HE	Ts
solidaginoides (Kunth) R. M. King & H. Rob. (Bello 574)	PM	IN	WD	HE	S
Lasianthaea					
fruiticosa (L.) K. M. Becker (2497)	M	LB	WD	HE	Ts
Liabum					
bourgeaui Hieron. (1504)	M	LB,BF	WD	HE	H
Melampodium					
divaricatum (Rich.) DC. (10431)	M	IN	GR	HE	H
Melanthera					
aspera (Jacq.) Small (9167)	M	BF	GR	HE	S
nivea (L.) Small (10207)	MA	BF	GR	HE	S
Mikania					
banisteria DC. (1230)	A	IN	WD	HE	V
castroi R. M. King & H. Rob. (2637)	M	IN	WD	HE	V
cristata B. L. Rob. (3071)	M	IN	WD	HE	V
hookeriana DC. (Bello 739)	A	IN	WD	HE	V
miconioides B. L. Rob. (2346)	M	IN	WD	HE	V
micrantha Kunth (3720)	P	IN	WD	HE	V
tonduzii B. L. Rob. (4374)	MA	IN	WD	HE	L
Milleria					
quinqueflora L. (10763)	P	SB	GR	HE	H
Montanoa					
guatemalensis B. L. Rob. & Greenm. (425)	PM	BE	GR	HE	Tm
hibiscifolia Benth. (Bello 673)	A	BE	GR	HE	S
tomentosa Cerv. (10288)	P	BE	GR	HE	Ts
Munnozia					
wilburii H. Rob. (10420)	M	BE,BF	WD	HE	H
Neomirandea					
angularis (B. L. Rob.) R. M. King & H. Rob. (9325)	MA	BF	WD	HE	Ts
araliifolia (Less.) R. M. King & H. Rob. (9758)	M	BF	WD	HE	E
arthodes (B. L. Rob.) R. M. King & H. Rob. (10015)	MA	BF	WD	HE	E
biflora R. M. King & H. Rob. (Koptur 175)	M?	BF	WD	HE	E
carnosa (Kuntze) R. M. King & H. Rob. (Bello 269)	A	BF	WD	HE	E
eximia (B. L. Rob.) R. M. King & H. Rob. (Gentry 48746)	M	BF	WD	HE	E
guevarae R. M. King & H. Rob. (Zuchowski 231A)	M	BF	WD	HE	E
parasitica (Klatt) R. M. King & H. Rob. (720)	M	BF	WD	HE	E
psoralea (B. L. Rob.) R. M. King & H. Rob. (694)	M	BF	WD	HE	E
standleyi (B. L. Rob.) R. M. King & H. Rob. (10569)	A	BF	WD	HE	E
Neurolaena					
cobanensis Greenm. (4273)	M	LB	WD	HE	S
lobata (L.) R. Br. (796)	MA	LB	WD	HE	Ts

Dicotyledons	Zone[a]	Poll[b]	Seed[c]	Sex[d]	Habit[e]
Onoseris					
onoseroides (Kunth) B. L. Rob. (10493)	P	BD,BF?	WD	DI	S
Otopappus					
verbesinoides Benth. (10200)	M	LB	WD	HE	L
Pluchea					
carolinensis (Jacq.) G. Don (11016)	MA	IN	WD	HE	S
Podachaenium					
eminens (Lag.) Sch. Bip. (10527)	M	BE	WD,GR	HE	Ts
Polyanthina					
nemorosa (Klatt) R. M. King & H. Rob. (2744)	A	IN	WD	HE	H
Pseudelephantopus					
spicatus (Juss.) C. F. Baker (10192)	PM	IN	GR	HE	H
Pseudogynoxys					
cummingii (Benth.) H. Rob. & Cuatrec.	P	BE	WD	HE	V
Schistocarpha					
eupatorioides (Fenzl) Kuntze (10794)	M	LB	WD	HE	S
Senecio					
arborescens Steetz (Dryer 1371)	M	LB	WD	HE	Ts
calyculatus Greenm. cf. (10384)	M	LB	WD	HE	L
candelariae Benth. (11029)	M	LB	WD	HE	L
chenopodioides Kunth (10494)	P	BF	WD	HE	L
copeyensis Greenm. (Obando 18)	M	LB	WD	HE	Ts
cooperi Greenm. (10578)	M	LB,BF	WD	HE	Ts
multivenius Benth. (10853)	M	BF	WD	HE	Ts
parasiticus Sch. Bip. ex Hemsl. (10517)	M	LB	WD	HE	L
streptothamnus Greenm. (3047)	M	LB	WD	HE	L
Sinclairia					
polyantha (Klatt) Rydb. (587)	PMA	LB,BF	WD	HE	E
Smallanthus					
maculatus (Cav.) H. Rob. (10414)	M	BE	GR	HE	H
uvedalius (L.) Mack. Ex Small (10417)	M	BE	GR	HE	H
Sonchus					
asper (L.) Hill (2688)	M	BE	WD	HE	H
oleraceus L. (10208)	M	BE	WD	HE	H
Spiracantha					
cornifolia Kunth (10303)	P	SB	GR	HE	H
Synedrella					
nodiflora (L.) Gaertn. (10335)	PM	SB	TM	HE	H
Tagetes					
erecta L. (10345)	P	SB	GR,WD	HE	H
filifolia Lag. (8878)	PM	SB	GR,WD	HE	H
Taraxicum					
**officinale* L. (10424)	M				H
Tithonia					
rotundifolia (Mill.) S. F. Blake (8837)	P	LB	GR	HE	S
Tridax					
procumbens L. (10331)	P	LB	WD	HE	S
Trixis					
inula Crantz (10495)	P	LB	WD	HE	S
Verbesina					
oerstediana Benth. (10248)	M	IN	WD	HE	Ts
ovatifolia A. Gray (10443)	P	IN	WD	HE	V
punctata Robinson & Greenm. (3740)	P	IN	WD	HE	S
ricacosta B. L. Turner ined. (10336)	P	BE	WD	HE	S
turbacensis Kunth (603)	PM	SB	WD	HE	S
sp. A (11374)	MA	BE	WD	HE	H
sp. B (10410)	P	BE	WD	HE	H
Vernonia					
arborescens (L.) Sw. (10411)	PMA	IN	WD	HE	L
brachiata Benth. (10536)	PA	IN	WD	HE	S
patens Kunth (9787)	PMA	IN	WD	HE	Ts
salzmannii DC. (10564)	M	IN	WD	HE	S

Dicotyledons	Zone[a]	Poll[b]	Seed[c]	Sex[d]	Habit[e]
scorpioides PERS. (11005)	M	IN	WD	HE	V
triflosculosa Kunth (Bello 824)	PM	IN	WD	HE	S
Viguiera					
cordata (Hook & Arn.) D'Arcy (Bello 571)	PM	LB	GR	HE	S
strigosa Klatt (10476)	P	LB	GR	HE	H
sylvatica Klatt (10434)	P	LB	GR	HE	H
Wamalchitamia					
aurantiaca (Klatt) Strother (8836)	P	BE	WD,GR	HE	H
Wedelia					
acapulcensis Kunth (10350)	P	BE	WD,GR	HE	H
fruticosa Jacq. (8854)	P	BE	WD,GR	HE	H
iners (S. F. Blake) Strother (10747)	P	BE	WD,GR	HE	H
Youngia					
japonica (L.) DC. (10516)	M	SB	WD	HE	H
Zexmenia					
virgulta Klatt (10472)	PA	BE	WD,GR	HE	L
Balanophoraceae					
Helosis					
cayennensis (Sw.) Spreng. (10079)	P	IN	Ants?	MO	H-Sap
Langsdorffia					
hypogaea Mart. (7984)	M	IN	Ants?	MO	H-Sap
Balsaminaceae					
Impatiens					
*walleriana Hook. F. (10043)	PMA				H
Begoniaceae					
Begonia					
broussonetiifolia A. DC. (1268)	A	BE	WD	MO	H
conchifolia A. Dietr. (9008)	PM	BE	WD	MO	E
cooperi C. DC. (1288)	MA	BE	WD	MO	S
estrellensis C. DC. (Zuchowski 22)	M	BE	WD	MO	V
glabra Aubl. (3902)	M	BE	WD	MO	E
heydei C. DC. (7645)	MA	BE	WD	MO	E
hirsuta Aubl. (8860)	P	BE	WD	MO	H
involucrata Liebm. (Zuchowski 167)	M	BE	WD	MO	H
oaxacana A. DC. (10259)	M	BE	WD	MO	V
plebeja Liebm. (8859)	P	BE	WD	MO	H
strigillosa A. Dietr. (6030)	M	BE	WD	MO	E
ureophylla Hook. (9773)	P	BE	WD	MO	H
Betulaceae					
Alnus					
acuminata Kunth (9848)	MA	WD	WD	MO	Tm
Bignoniaceae					
Amphilophium					
paniculatum (L.) Kunth (630)	P	LB	WD	HE	L
Amphitecna					
haberi A. H. Gentry, ined. (492)	P	BT	TM	HE'	Tm
donnell-smithii (Spr.) L. O. Williams, aff. (5841)	A	BT	TM	HE	Ts
gentryi W. C. Berger ined. (9272)	PMA	BT	TM	HE	Tm
Arrabidaea					
patellifera (Schltdl.) Sandwith (7211)	P	LB	WD	HE	L
verrucosa (Standl.) A. H. Gentry (5649)	A	LB	WD	HE	L
Callichlamys					
latifolia (Rich.) K. Schum. (7410)	A	LB	WD	HE	L
Crescentia					
*cujete L. (1008)	P				Ts
Godmania					
aesculifolia (Kunth) Standl. (10649)	P	LB	WD	HE	Ts
Mansoa					
hymenaea (DC.) A. H. Gentry (Bello 680)	P	LB	WD	HE	L
Martinella					
obovata (Kunth) Bureau & K. Schum. (2211)	PM	LB	WD	HE	L
Melloa					
quadrivalvis (Jacq.) A. H. Gentry (Bello 206)	P	LB	WD	HE	L

Dicotyledons	Zone[a]	Poll[b]	Seed[c]	Sex[d]	Habit[e]
Pithecoctenium					
crucigerum (L.) A. H. Gentry (555)	P	LB	WD	HE	L
Tabebuia					
rosea (Bertol.) DC. (9996)	P	LB	WD	HE	Tl
Tecoma					
stans (L.) C. Juss. ex Kunth (423)	P	LB	WD	HE	Tm
Tourrettia					
lappacea (L'Hér.) Willd. (1034)	MA	IN	WD	HE	V
Bombacaceae					
Bombacopsis					
quinata (Jacq.) Dugand (9991)	P	HM,BT	WD	HE	Tl
Ceiba					
aesculifolia (Kunth) Britt. & Baker (9582)	P	BT	WD	HE	Tl
pentandra (L.) Gaertn. (Bello 2886)	A	BT	WD	HE	Tl
Ochroma					
pyramidale (Cav. ex Lam.) Urb. (Bello 650)	PA	BT	WD	HE	TI
Pachira					
aquatica Aubl. (1891)	A	BT	TM	HE	TI
Quararibea					
costaricensis W. S. Alverson (251)	MA	HM	AM	HE	Tl
funebris (La Llave) Vischer (558)	P	HM	AM	HE	Tl
pterocalyx Hemsl. (6596)	A	HM	AM	HE	Tm
Spirotheca					
rosea (Seem.) P. E. Gibbs (1933)	A	BT	WD	HE	E
Boraginaceae					
Bourreria					
costaricensis (Standl.) A. H. Gentry (759)	MA	HM	AM	HE	Tl
Cordia					
alliodora (Ruiz & Pav.) Oken (10004)	P	MO	WD	HE	Tm
croatii James S. Mill. (7138)	M	SB	BD	DI?	Tm
cymosa (Donn. Sm.) Standl. (460)	M	SB	BD	DI	Tl
eriostigma Pittier (2610)	PA	SB	BD	DI?	Tl
lucidula I. M. Johnst. (Bello 321)	PA	SB	BD	HE	Ts
megalantha S. F. Blake (Bello 787)	A	LB	WD	HE	Tl
panamensis Riley (10709)	P	SB	BD	DI	Tm
spinescens L. (2809)	MA	SB	BD	HE	L
Ehretia					
latifolia DC. (6907)	PM	SB	BD	HE	Tm
Heliotropium					
indicum L. (9997)	P	BF	GR	HE	H
transalpinum Vell. (9688)	P	BF	GR	HE	H
Tournefortia					
angustiflora Ruiz & Pav. (9954)	M	IN	BD	HE	L
brenesii Standl. (Zuchowski 458)	M	IN	BD	HE	Ts
glabra L. (7112)	PMA	BF	BD	HE	L
hirsutissima L. (6632)	PMA	IN	BD	HE	L
maculata Jacq. (10048)	M	IN	BD	HE	S
poasana Cufod. (4524)	M	IN	BD	HE	S
ramonensis Standl. (Dryer 518)	M	IN	BD	HE	S
Brassicaceae					
Brassica					
juncea (L.) Czerniak. (685)	M	LB	GR	HE	H
Cardamine					
africana L. (9142)	M	IN	GR	HE	H
bonariensis Pers. (Mill's)	M	IN	GR	HE	H
flexuosa With. (9026)	M	IN	GR	HE	H
fulcrata Greene (3658)	M	IN	GR	HE	H
Lepidium					
virginicum L. (Bello 1135)	PM	IN	GR	HE	H
Rorippa					
nasturtium-aquaticum (L.) Hayek (12530)	MA				H

Dicotyledons	Zone[a]	Poll[b]	Seed[c]	Sex[d]	Habit[e]
Brunelliaceae					
Brunellia					
costaricensis Standl. (532)	M	IN	GR	DI	Tm
darienensis Cuatrec. & D. Porter (8050)	A	IN	GR	DI	Tm
standleana Cuatrec. (Bello 1527)	A	IN	GR	DI	Tm
Burseraceae					
Bursera					
grandifolia (Schlec.) Engl. (11322)	P	SB	BD	DI	Tm
simaruba (L.) Sarg. (9988)	P	SB	BD	DI	Tl
Protium					
costaricense (Rose) Engl. (Bello 473)	A	IN	BD	DI?	Tm
schippii Lundell (6979)	A	IN	BD	DI?	Tm
sp. A (7508)	A	IN	BD	DI?	Tm
Cactaceae					
Disocactus					
himantocladus (Rol.-Goss.) Kimnach, cf. (8467)	A	BE?	BD	HE	E
ramulosus (Salm-Dyck) Kimnach, cf. (Bello 11)	A	BE?	BD	HE	E
Epiphyllum					
lepidocarpum (F.A.C. Weber) Britton & Rose, cf. (9842)	M	HM	BD	HE	E
phyllanthus (L.) Haw. (8512)	PM	HM	BD	HE	E
thomasiana (K. Schum.) Kimnach (Hammel 14214)	A	HM	BD	HE	E
Hylocereus					
costaricensis (F. A. C. Weber) Britton & Rose (9893)	P	HM	BD	HE	E
Rhipsalis					
baccifera (Mill.) Stearn, cf. (7840)	PMA	BE	BD	HE	E
Selenicereus					
wercklei (F. A. C. Weber) Britton & Rose (507)	PM	HM	BD	HE	E
Stenocereus					
aragonii (F. A. C. Weber) F. Buxb.	P	BT	BD	HE	Ts
Weberocereus					
biolleyi (F. A. C. Weber) Britton & Rose (147)	MA	BT?	BD	HE	E
tonduzii (F. A. C. Weber) G. D. Rowley (10088)	M	BT	AM	HE	E
Campanulaceae					
Burmeistera					
chiriquiensis Wilbur (Bello 1827)	A	BD?	BD	HE	E
cyclostigmata Donn. Sm. (1684)	MA	BT	BD	HE	E
microphylla Donn. Sm. (722)	MA	BD	BD	HE	E
parviflora E. Wimm. ex Standl. (1669)	M	BD	BD	HE	E
tenuiflora Donn. Sm. (9124)	M	BD	BD	HE	E
vulgaris E. Wimm. (2426)	M	BD	BD	HE	E
Calcaratolobelia					
cordifolia (Hook & Arn.) Wilbur (10330)	P	IN	GR,WD	HE	H
Centropogon					
costaricae (Vatke) McVaugh (1991)	M	BD	BD	HE	H
granulosus C. Presl (734)	A	BD	BD	HE	S
solanifolius Benth (3302)	M	BD	BD	HE	H
Diastatea					
micrantha (Kunth) McVaugh (10293)	P	IN	GR,WD	HE	H
Hippobroma					
longiflora (L.) G. Don (1483)	A	HM	GR,WD	HE	H
Lobelia					
laxiflora Kunth (3122)	PM	BD	GR,WD	HE	S
xalapensis Kunth (8326)	M	IN	GR,WD	HE	H
Capparidaceae					
Capparis					
amplissima Lam. (Bello 399)	P	HM	BD	HE	Ts
cynophallophora L. (9248)	P	HM	BD	HE	Tm
discolor Donn. Sm. (543)	PMA	HM	AM	HE	Tm
frondosa Jacq. (475)	P	HM	BD	HE	S
mollicella Standl. (478)	P	HM	BD	HE	Tm
pringlei Briq. (6806)	P	HM	BD	HE	Tm

Dicotyledons	Zone[a]	Poll[b]	Seed[c]	Sex[d]	Habit[e]
Cleome					
hassleriana Chodat (9696)	M				H
pilosa Benth. (8863)	P	MO	GR	HE	H
Forchhammeria					
trifoliata Radlk. (9774)	P	SB	BD	HE	Tm
Podandrogyne					
decipiens (Triana & Planch.) Woodson (8677)	MA	BD	BD	HE	Ts
Caprifoliaceae					
Sambucus					
mexicana K. Presl ex DC. (Penneys 953)	M				Ts
Viburnum					
costaricanum (Oerst.) Hemsl. (302)	M	IN	BD	HE	Tm
stellatotomentosum (Oerst.) Hemsl. (10510)	M	IN	BD	HE?	Tm
vernustum C. V. Morton (9797)	PM	IN	BD	DI	Tm
Caricaceae					
Carica					
cauliflora Jacq. (9245)	P	HM	AM	DI	S
papaya L. (Herrera 937)	PM	Ts			
Jacaratia					
dolichaula (Donn. Sm.) Woodson (7589)	A	HM	Am	DI	Tm
spinosa (Aubl.; DC. (7589)	A	MO?	AM	DI	Tl
Caryophyllaceae					
Arenaria					
lanuginosa (Michx.) Rohrb. (10271)	M	IN	GR	HE	H
Cerastium					
glomeratum Thuill. (10273)	M	IN	GR	HE	H
guatemalense Standl. (10133)					
Drymaria					
cordata (L.) Willd. ex Roem. & Schult. (10134)					
villosa Cham. & Schltdl. (10296)	M	IN	GR	HE	H
Stellaria					
ovata Willd. ex Schltdl. (Zuchowski 134B)	M	IN	GR	HE	H
Cecropiaceae					
Cecropia					
insignis Liebm.	A	WD	BD,AM	DI	Tm
obtusifolia Bertol. (6117)	PMA	WD	BD,BT	DI	Tl
peltata L. (9970)	P	WD	BD,BT	DI	Tl
polyphlebia Donn. Sm. (455)	M	WD	BD,BT	DI	Tl
Coussapoa					
contorta Cuatrec. (Bello 4018)	A	WD	BD	DI	E
nymphaeifolia Standl. (Bello 890)	A	WD	BD	DI	E
parviceps Standl. (11174)	A	WD	BD	DI	E
villosa Poepp. & Endl. (4826)	A	WD	BD	DI	E
Celastraceae					
Celastrus					
liebmannii Standl. (Bello 2778)	M	IN	BD	HE?	L
vulcanicola Donn. Sm. (11121)	MA	IN	BD	HE?	L
Crossopetalum					
enervium Hammel. (Obando 15)	MA	IN	BD	DI	S
tonduzii (Loes.) Lundell (9788)	M	IN	BD	DI	Tm
Euonymus					
costaricensis Standl. (10811)	PM	IN	BD	DI	Ts
Gymnosporia					
haberiana Hammel. (6728)	M	IN	BD	DI	Tl
Maytenus					
reconditus Hammel. (446)	MA	IN	BD	DI	Tm
segoviarum Standl. & Steyerm. (9882)	P	IN	BD	DI	Tl
Perrottetia					
longistylis Rose (9509)	PMA	IN	BD	DI	Tm
multiflora Lundell (6675)	A	IN	BD	DI	Tm
sessiliflora Lundell (Bello 1561)	A	IN	BD	DI	Tm
Quetzalia					
occidentalis (Loes.) Lundell (11003)	M	IN	BD	DI	Tm

Dicotyledons	Zone[a]	Poll[b]	Seed[c]	Sex[d]	Habit[e]
Zinowiewia					
costaricensis Lundell (495)	M	IN	WD	DI	Tl
Chenopodiaceae					
Chenopodium					
ambrosioides L. (11373)	PM	WD?	GR	HE?	S
Chloranthaceae					
Hedyosmum					
bonplandianum Kunth (5111)	A	IN	BD	DI	Ts
brenesii Standl. (1699)	A	IN	BD	DI	S
costaricense C. E. Wood (Bello 1486)	MA	IN	BD	DI	Ts
goudotianum Solms-Laub. (7651)	M	IN	BD	DI	Ts
Chrysobalanaceae					
Hirtella					
racemosa Lam. (10756)	P	IN	BD	HE	Ts
triandra Sw. (6497)	A	IN	BD	HE	Tm
Licania					
belloi Prance (Bello 783)	A	SB	AM	HE?	Tl
jefensis Prance (Bello 1081)	A	SB	AM	HE?	Tl
kallunkii Prance (Bello 1629)	A	SB	AM	HE?	Tl
platypus (Hemsl.) Fritsch (Bello 1321)	A	SB	AM	HE?	Tl
Clethraceae					
Clethra					
lanata M. Martens & Galeotti (Bello 514)	PM	SB	WD	HE	Tm
mexicana A. DC. (9853)	M	SB	WD	HE	Tm
pyrogena Sleumer (10929)	M	SB	WD	HE	Tm
Clusiaceae					
Calophyllum					
brasiliense Cambess. (Bello 517)	A	IN	BD	DE	Tl
Chrysochlamys					
allenii (Maguire) Hammel (10031)	M	SB	BD	DI	Tm
glauca (Oerst., Planch. & Triana) Hemsl. (11363)	MA	SB	BD	DI	Ts
psychotriifolia (Oerst., Planch. & Triana) Hemsl. (11626)	MA	SB	BD	DI	Tm
Clusia					
cylindrica Hammel (1743)	A	CO	BD	DI	E
gracilis Standl. (8051)	A	CO	BD	DI	E
minor L. (9229)	M	BE	BD	DI	E
modesta Standl. & L. O. Williams ex Hammel, ined. (9068)	P	BE	BD	DI	E
multiflora Kunth (11409)	M	MO	BD	DI	Ts
palmana Standl. (7128)	M	BE	BD	DI	E
stenophylla Standl. (9445)	MA	MO	BD	DI	E
torresii Standl. (9220)	M	CO	BD	DI	E
uvitana Pittier (7994)	A	BE	BD	DI	E
valerii Standl. (7149)	A	BE	BD	DI	E
Garcinia					
intermedia (Pittier) Hammel (9744)	PA	SB	AM	DI	Tm
Hypericum					
pratense Cham. & Schldtl. (10276)	M	BE	WD,GR	HE	H
Marila					
laxiflora Rusby (8466)	A	BE	WD	HE	Tm
Symphonia					
globulifera L. f. (4442)	PMA	BD	AM	HE	Tm
Vismia					
baccifera (L.) Triana & Planch. (11201)	P	SB	BD,BT	HE	Ts
billbergiana Beurl. (8405)	A	SB	BD,BT	HE	Tm
sp. A. (9828)	M	SB	BD,BT	HE	Tm
Cochlospermaceae					
Cochlospermum					
vitifolium (Willd.) Spreng.	P	LB	WD	HE	Tm
Combretaceae					
Combretum					
laxum Jacq. (3905)	MA	SB	WD	HE	L

Dicotyledons	Zone[a]	Poll[b]	Seed[c]	Sex[d]	Habit[e]
Terminalia					
bucidoides Standl. & L. O. Williams (8345)	A	IN	WD	HE	Tl
oblonga (Ruiz & Pav.) Steud. (Bello 688)	PA	IN	WD	HE	Tl
Connaraceae					
Connarus					
costaricensis Schellenb., cf. (9065)	A	LB	BD	HE	L
Rourea					
schippii Standl. (Bello 1458)	A	LB	BD	HE	L
suerrensis Donn. Sm. (7989)	MA	LB	BD	HE	L
Convolvulaceae					
Convolvulus					
nodiflorus Desv. (410)	P	SB	GR	HE	L
Dichondra					
sericea Sw. (10376)	M	IN	GR	HE	V
Ipomoea					
alba L. (3629)	P	HM	GR	HE	V
aurantiaca L. O. Williams (7965)	P	LB	GR	HE	L
batatas (L.) Lam (1188)	PMA				V
batatoides Choisy (6823)	PA	LB	GR	HE	L
**indica* (Burm. f.) Merr. (684)	M				V
leucotricha Donn. Sm. (9712)	PM	LB	GR	HE	L
lindenii M. Martens & Galeotti (8861)	P	LB	GR	HE	L
nil (L.) Roth (8875)	P	LB	GR	HE	L
parasitica (Kunth) G. Don (8889)	P	LB	GR	HE	L
reticulata O'Donell (2937)	P	LB	GR	HE	L
santillanii O'Donell (2937)	P	LB	GR	HE	V
setosa Ker Gawl. (8862)	P	LB	GR	HE	V
trifida (Kunth) G. Don (8894)	P	LB	GR	HE	L
umbraticola House (8874)	P	LB	GR	HE	L
Maripa					
nicaraguensis Hemsl. (1741)	A	LB	AM	HE	L
Merremia					
discoidesperma (Donn. Sm.) O'Donell (7718)	A	LB	GR	HE	L
tuberosa (L.) Rendle (9153)	A	LB	GR	HE	V
Operculina					
pteripes (Don) O'Donell (8891)	P	LB	GR	HE	L
Cornaceae					
Cornus					
disciflora DC. (8027)	M	IN	BD	HE	Tl
Crassulaceae					
Echeveria					
australis Rose (9714)	P	BD?	WD,GR	HE	H
Cucurbitaceae					
Cayaponia					
buraeavii Cogn. (10817)	M	IN	AM?	MO	V
glandulosa (Poepp. & Endl.) Cogn. (1522)	MA	IN	BD	MO	V
macrocalyx Harms (Bello 719)	A	IN	AM	MO	V
racemosa (Mill.) Cogn. (6112)	PM	IN	BD	MO	V
Cyclanthera					
explodens Naudin (8660)	P	IN	EX	MO	V
langaei Cogn. (Bello 658)	A	IN	EX	MO	V
Elateriopsis					
oerstedii (Cogn.) Pittier (Dryer 461)	M	BT?	EX	MO	V
Fevillea					
cordifolia L. (Bello 442)	A	IN	AM	DI	L
Gurania					
coccinea Cogn. (6914)	MA	BF,BD	AM	DI	V
costaricensis Cogn. (9476)	A	BF,BD	AM	DI	L
eriantha (Poepp. & Endl.) Cogn. (9183)	A	BF	BD	AM	DIL
makoyana (Lem.) Cogn. (11295)	MA	BF,BD	AM	DI	V
megistantha Donn. Sm. (1551)	A	BF,BD	Am	DI	V

Dicotyledons	Zone[a]	Poll[b]	Seed[c]	Sex[d]	Habit[e]
Melothria					
dulcis Wunderlin (Bello 484)	A	IN	BD	MO	V
pendula L. (11173)	MA	IN	BD	MO	V
scabra Naudin (3700)	M	IN	BD	MO	V
Momordica					
charantia L. (Bello 2303)	A	BE	BD	MO	V
Polyclathra					
cucumerina Bertol. (4303)	P	IN,BT?	GR	MO	V
Psiguria					
bignoniacea (Poepp. & Endl.) Wunderlin (Dryer 597)	M	BF	AM	DI	L
warscewiczii (Hook. f.) Wunderlin (11151)	A	BF	AM	DI	V
Rytidostylis					
carthaginensis (Jacq.) Kuntze (10761)	P	MO	EX	MO	V
gracilis Hooker & Arnott (Bello 33)	P	MO	EX	MO	V
Sechium					
pittieri (Cogn.) C. Jeffrey (11825)	M	IN	AM	MO	V
*edule (Jacq.) Sw. ("Chayote")	M				V
Selysia					
prunifera (Poepp. & Endl.) Cogn.	A	BT?	AM	MO	V
Sicydium					
tamnifolium (Kunth) Cogn. (429)	M	IN	BD	DI	V
Tecunumania					
quetzalteca Standl. & Steyerm. (6145)	A	IN?	BD?	MO?	V
Cunoniaceae					
Weinmannia					
pinnata L. (190)	MA	SB	WD	HE	Tl
wercklei Standl. (6610)	M	SB	WD	HE	Tm
sp. A (Bello 1338)	A	SB	WD	HE	Tl
Dichapetalaceae					
Dichapetalum					
axillare Woodson (72277)	MA	SB	AM,BD	HE	Ts
brenesii Standl. (11461)	M	IN	AM,BD	HE	Ts
donnell-smithii Engl. (5920)	A	SB	AM,BD	HE	Ts
pedunculatum (DC.) Baill. (4558)	M	IN	AM,BD	HE	Ts
Dilleniaceae					
Doliocarpus					
dentatus (Aubl.) Standl. (10750)	P	IN	BD	HE	L
Ebenaceae					
Diospyros					
blancoi A. DC.	P	MO?	AM	DI	Tl
digyna Jacq. (Bello 116)	P	MO?	AM	DI	Tm
hartmanniana S. Knapp & Whitef. (Gentry 71605)	M	MO	BD	DI	Tm
salicifolia (Willd.) (11326)	P	MO	BD	DI	Ts
sp. C (6087)	A	MO?	BD	DI	Tl
Elaeocarpaceae					
Sloanea					
ampla I. M. Johnst. (9308)	MA	IN	BD	HE	Tl
brenesii Standl. (549)	MA	IN	BD	HE	Tm
faginea Standl. (7091)	MA	IN	BD	HE	Tl
ligulata D. A. Sm., ined. (Bello 873)	A	IN	BD	HE	Tl
Eremolepidaceae					
Antidaphne					
viscoidea Poepp. & Endl. (Grayum 5409)	M	IN	BD	DI	E-P
Ericaceae					
Cavendishia					
axillaris A. C. Sm. (9382)	A	BD	BD	HE	E
bracteata (Ruiz & Pav. ex J. St.-Hil.) Hoerold (7571)	M	BD	BD	HE	E
callista Donn. Sm. (7437)	A	BD	BD	HE	E
capitulata Donn. Sm. (1099)	MA	BD	BD	HE	E
chiriquensis A. C. Sm. (7376)	M	BD	BD	HE	E
complectens Hemsl. (986)	MA	BD	BD	HE	E
endresii Hemsl. (Dryer 259)	M	BD	BD	HE	E
lactiviscida Luteyn (7016)	M	BD	BD	HE	E

Dicotyledons	Zone[a]	Poll[b]	Seed[c]	Sex[d]	Habit[e]
melastomoides (Klotzsch) Hemsl. (2010)	M	BD	BD	HE	E
quercina A. C. Sm. (8024)	M	BD	BD	HE	E
quereme (Kunth) Benth. & Hook. (1284)	A	BD	BD	HE	E
Disterigma					
humboldtii (Klotzsch) Nied. (3174)	M	IN	BD	HE	E
Gaultheria					
erecta Vent. (Bello 225)	MA	IN	BD	HE	E
gracilis Small (10251)	MA	IN	BD	HE	E
Gonocalyx					
costaricensis Luteyn (6638)	M	BD	BD	HE	E
pterocarpus (Donn. Sm.) Luteyn (Bello 1764)	M	BD	BD	HE	E
Marcleania					
insignis M. Martens & Galeotti (1541)	M	BD	BD	HE	E
Monotropa					
uniflora L. (10135)	M	IN	GR,WD	HE	H-Sap
Psammisia					
ramiflora Klotzsch (848)	A	BD	BD	HE	E
Satyria					
meiantha Donn. Sm. (Penneys 23)	A	BD	BD	HE	E
panurensis (Benth.) Benth. & Hook. (9462)	A	BD	BD	HE	E
Sphyrospermum					
buxifolium Poepp. & Endl. (2898)	M	IN	BD	HE	E
cordifolium Benth. (706)	M	IN	BD	HE	E
Themistoclesia					
costaricensis Luteyn & Wilbur (Bello 898)	A	IN	BD	HE	E
pentandra Sleumer (Bello 983)	A	IN	BD	HE	E
smithiana (Standl.) Sleumer (7810)	M	IN	BD	HE	E
Thibaudia					
costaricensis Hoerold (6876)	MA	IN	BD	HE	E
Vaccinium					
monteverdense Wilbur, ined. (6639)	M	BD	BD	HE	E
poasanum Donn. Sm. (2814)	M	SB	BD	HE	E
Erythroxylaceae					
Erythroxylum					
macrophyllum Cav. (1067)	M	BE	BD	HE	Ts
Euphorbiaceae					
Acalypha					
apodanthes Standl. & L. O. Williams (8310)	AM	WD?	GR	MO	Ts
diversifolia Jacq. (4756)	A	WD?	GR	MO	Ts
leptopoda Müll. Arg. (10497)	P	WD?	GR	MO	Ts
macrostachya Jacq. (4837)	PMA	WD?	GR	MO	Ts
mortoniana Lundell (Bello 317)	A	WD?	GR	MO	H
schiedeana Schltdl. (9912)	P	WD?	GR	MO	Ts
Adelia					
triloba (Müll. Arg.) Hemsl. (6581)	A	IN	EX	DI	Tm
Alchornea					
costaricensis Pax & K. Hoffm. (1762)	A	IN	BD	DI	Tm
glandulosa Poepp. (7654)	A	IN	BD	DI	Tm
guatemalensis Lundell (551)	M	IN	BD	DI	Tm
latifolia Sw. (453)	MA	IN	BD	DI	Tl
Bernardia					
nicaraguensis Standl. (10483)	P	SB	GR	DI	S
Chamaesyce					
hirta (L.) Millsp. (8868)	P	IN	GR	MO	H
hypericifolia (L.) Millsp. (11244)	PM	IN	GR	MO	H
hyssopifolia (L.) Small (11204)	M	IN	GR	MO	H
Croton					
billbergianus Müll Arg. (1688)	A	SB	EX	MO	Ts
draco Cham. & Schltdl. (Bello 1113)	PM	SB	EX	MO	Tl
megistocarpus Poveda & Gonz. Ram. (11172)	A	SB	EX	MO	Tl
mexicanus Muell. Arg. (10724)	M	SB	EX	DI	Tm
*niveus Jacq. (9918)	M				Ts
pachypodus G. L. Webster (Bello 293)	A	IN	EX	DI	Tm

Dicotyledons	Zone[a]	Poll[b]	Seed[c]	Sex[d]	Habit[e]
schiedeanus Schltdl. (11239)	A	IN	EX	DI	Tm
watsonii Standl. (9944)	P	SB	EX	DI	Tm
xalapensis Kunth (9993)	PM	IN	EX	MO	Ts
Dalechampia					
cissifolia Poepp. (Bello 4902)	A	BE	GR	MO	V
Drypetes					
brownei Standl. (5730)	A	IN	BD	DI	Tm
lateriflora (Sw.) Krug & Urb. (9856)	PM	IN	BD	DI	Tm
standleyi G. L. Webster (11431)	A	IN	BD	DI	Tm
sp. A (Bello 35)	P	IN	BD	DI	Tm
Euphorbia					
elata Brandegee (1122)	M	IN	EX	MO	Ts
graminea Jacq. (10535)	P	IN	EX	MO	H
heterophylla L. (9721)	P	IN	EX	MO	H
hoffmanniana (Klotzsch & Garcke) Boiss. (10501)	P	IN	EX	MO	Ts
schlechtendalii Boiss. (10500)	P	IN	EX	MO	Ts
Gymnanthes					
riparia (Schltdl.) Klotzsch (6788)	PMA	IN	EX	DI?	Ts
Hura					
crepitans L. (1617)	P	BT	EX	MO	Tl
Hyeronima					
alchornioides Allemao (5579)	A	IN	BD	DI	Tm
oblonga (Tul.) Müll. Arg. (9330)	MA	IN	BD	DI	Tl
Margaritaria					
nobilis L. F. (5656)	PA	SB	BD	DI	Tm
Phyllanthus					
acuminatus Vahl (7460)	MA	IN	EX	MO	S
amarus Schumach. & Thonn. (6209)	M	IN	EX	MO	S
anisolobus Müll. Arg. (6015)	P	IN	EX	MO	Ts
niruri L. (10838)	MA	IN	EX	MO	S
valerii Standl. (Bello 789)	M	IN	EX	MO	Ts
Plukenetia					
stipellata L. J. Gillespie (11543)	A	IN	EX	MO	L
Ricinus					
communis L.	M				Ts
Sapium					
glandulosum (L.) Morong (449)	M	IN	BD	MO	Tl
laurifolium (Rich.) Griseb. (Bello 1205)	PMA	IN	BD	MO	Tl
macrocarpum Müll. Arg. (9366)	PM	IN	BD	MO	Tl
pachystachys K. Schum. & Pittier (9332)	A	IN	BD	MO	Tl
rigidifolium Huft (7225)	MA	IN	BD	MO	Tl
Tetrorchidium					
costaricense Huft (7607)	M	IN	BD	DI	Tm
euryphyllum Standl. (7874)	A	IN	BD	DI	Tm
Tragia					
bailloniana Muell. Arg. (8072)	A	IN	EX	MO	V
Fabaceae					
(Caesalpiniodeae)					
Chamaecrista					
nictitans (L.) Moench (10320)	PM	LB	GR	HE	S
Senna					
cobanensis (Britton & Rose) H. S. Irwin & Barneby (11709)	P	LB	GR	HE	S
hayesiana (Britton & Rose) H. S. Irwin & Barneby	A	LB	GR	HE	S
nicaraguensis (Benth.) H. S. Irwin & Barneby (916)	P	LB	GR	HE	S
obtusifolia (L.) H. S. Irwin & Barneby (934)	P	LB	GR	HE	S
pallida (Vahl) Irwin & Barneby (10534)	P	LB	GR	HE	S
papillosa (Britton & Rose) H. S. Irwin & Barneby	P	LB	GR	HE	S
skinneri (Benth.) H. S. Irwin & Barnaby (12436)	P	LB	GR	HE	Ts
spectabilis (DC.) H. S. Irwin & Barnaby (7963)	P	LB	GR	HE	Tm
(Mimosoideae)					
Acacia					
angustissima (Mill.) Kuntze (7966)	P	SB	WD	HE	Ts
centralis (Britton & Rose) Lundell (1628)	P	SB	WD	HE	Tm

Dicotyledons	Zone[a]	Poll[b]	Seed[c]	Sex[d]	Habit[e]
ruddiae D. H. Janzen (Bello 5099)	A	SB	BD	HE	Tl
tenuifolia (L.) Willd. (Bello 90)	PA	SB	WD	HE	L
Albizia					
adinocephala (Donn. Sm.) Britton & Rose (10198)	P	MO	WD	HE	Tl
carbonaria Britton ex Britton & P. Wilson (4838)	A	MO	WD	HE	Tm
Calliandra					
bijuga Rose (8430)	P	HM	EX	HE	Ts
brenesii Standl. (11550)	A	BD	EX	HE	Ts
calothyrsus Meissn. (Bello 1387)	A	BD	EX'	HE	Tm
Cojoba					
catenata (Donn. Sm.) Britton & Rose (5069)	PMA	MO	BD	HE	Ts
costaricensis Britton & Rose (454)	MA	MO	BD	HE	Tm
valerioi (Britton & Rose) Standl. (9450)	A	MO	BD	HE	Ts
Enterolobium					
cyclocarpum (Jacq.) Griseb. (9582 A)	P	MO	TM	HE	Tl
Hymenaea					
courbaril L. (11328)	P	BT	GR	HE	Tl
Inga					
barbourii Standl. (Bello 2585)	A	MO	TM	HE	Tl
brenesii Standl. (641) (= *sierrae* Britton & Killip)	M	HM	TM	HE	Tl
exalata T. S. Elias (11528)	A	HM	TM	HE	Tl
herrerae N. Zamora	A	HM	TM	HE	Tl
hintonii Sandwith (3871) (= *micheliana* Harms)	M	MO	TM	HE	Tl
latipes Pittier (Bello 1128)	P	MO	TM	HE	Tl
leonis N. Zamora (6097)	A	HM	TM	HE	Tl
longispica Standl. (Koptur 217)	M	MO	TM	HE	Tl
marginata Willd. (408)	P	MO	TM	HE	Tl
mortoniana Jorge León (3022)	MA	MO	TM	HE	Tl
oerstediana Benth. ex Seem. (9914)	PMA	HM	TM	HE	Tl
punctata Willd. (1115)	PMA	MO	TM	HE	Tm
quaternata Poepp. (181) (= *nobilis* Harms)	M	HM	TM	HE	Tm
sapindoides Willd. (7621)	A	HM	TM	HE	Tl
stenophylla Standl. (Bello 2585)	A	MO	TM	HE	Tm
tonduzii Donn. Sm. (Bello 132)	MA	HM	TM	HE	Tl
venusta Standl. (5577)	A	MO	TM	HE	Tl
Lysiloma					
divaricatum (Jacq.) J. F. Macbr. (Bello 678)	PA	MO	WD	HE	Tl
Mimosa					
albida Humb. & Bompl. ex Willd. (617)	P	SB	TM?	HE	L
pudica L. (598)	PMA	SB	TM?	HE	S
Samanea					
saman (Jacq.) Merrill (9927)	P	HM	TM	HE	Tl
Zapoteca					
costaricensis (Britton & Rose) H. M. Hern. (7217)	P	HM	EX	HE	Ts
formosa (Kunth) H. M. Hern. (Bello 1112)	P	HM	EX	HE	Ts
tetragona (Willd.) H. M. Hern. (11055)	P	HM	EX	HE	Ts
Zygia					
latifolia (L.) Benth. (Bello 2178)	A	MO	TM	HE	Ts
longifolia (L.) (Humb. & Bonpl. ex Willd.) Britton & Rose (Bello 2178)	A	MO	TM	HE	Tm
palmana (Standl.) L. Rico (7450)	MA	MO	TM	HE	Ts
(Papilionoideae)					
Aeschynomene					
fascicularis Cham. & Schltdl.	PM	SB	TM?	HE	S
compacta Rose (8886)	P	SB	TM?	HE	V
Cajanus					
*cajan (L.) Millsp. (1153)	P				S
Calopogonium					
caeruleum (Benth.) Sauv. (9595)	M	LB	EX	HE	V
galactioides (Kunth) Benth. ex Hemsl. (Bello 4205)	P	BE	EX	HE	H
mucunoides Desv. (11386)	P	LB	EX	HE	V
Canavalia					
oxyphylla Standl. & L. O. Williams (Bello 747)	A	LB	EX	HE	L
villosa Benth. (10311)	P	LB	EX	HE	L

Dicotyledons	Zone[a]	Poll[b]	Seed[c]	Sex[d]	Habit[e]
Coursetia					
caribaea (Jacq.) Lavin (6122)	PM	BE	EX?	HE	S
Crotalaria					
maypurensis Kunth (9667)	PM	LB	EX?	HE	H
pilosa Mill. (10319)	P	LB	EX?	HE	H
retusa L. (Fuentes 550)	P	LB	EX?	HE	H
sagittalis L. (Bello 4013)	PM	LB	EX?	HE	H
vitellina Ker Gawl. (2534)	P	LB	EX?	HE	H
Dalbergia					
melanocardium Pittier (8410)	PA	LB	WD	HE	L
tilarana N. Zamora, ined. (11050)	M	LB	WD	HE	Tl
Desmodium					
adscendens (Sw.) DC. (8678)	MA	SB	TM	HE	S
angustifolium (Kunth) DC. (9947)	P	SB	TM	HE	S
axillare (Sw.) DC. (9947)	P	SB	TM	HE	S
barbatum (L.) Benth. & Oerst. (8849)	PA	SB	TM	HE	S
distortum (Aubl.) J. F. Macbr. (10976)	P	SB	TM	HE	S
incanum DC. (Bello 4206)	P	SB	TM	HE	S
intorium (Mill.) Urb. (10374)	P	SB	TM	HE	S
purpusii Brandegee (Bello 1219)	A	SB	TM	HE	V
sericophyllum Schltdl. (10427)	M	SB	TM	HE	S
triflorum (L.) DC. (10340)	P	SB	TM	HE	S
Dioclea					
malacocarpa Ducke (1769)	A	LB	TM	HE	L
reflexa Hook. f. (7649)	A	LB	TM	HE	L
Diphysa					
americana (Mill.) M. Sousa (6818)	P	LB	WD	HE	Tm
humilis Oerst. (9767)	P	LB	WD	HE	S
Dussia					
macroprophyllata (Donn. Sm.) Harms, cf. (3813)	A	LB	BD	HE	Tl
sp. A	M	LB	BD	HE	Tl
Eriosema					
crinitum (Kunth) G. Don (Bello 2910)	P	BE	EX?	HE	H
diffusum (Kunth) G. Don (9946)	P	BE	EX?	HE	S
Erythrina					
berteroana Urb. (10636)	P	BD	BD	HE	Tm
gibbosa Cufod. (802)	A	BD	BD	HE	Tm
lanceolata Standl. (Bello 311)	PMA	BD	BD	HE	Tm
Indigofera					
suffruticosa Mill. (Fuentes 548)	P	SB	EX?	HE'	S
thibaudiana DC. (10905)	PM	SB	EX?	HE	S
trita L. F. (Fuentes 105)	P	SB	EX?	HE	S
Lonchocarpus					
acuminatus (Schltdl.) M. Sousa (10655)	P	LB	WD	HE	Tm
calcaratus F. J. Herm. (6873)	A	LB	WD	HE	Tl
guatemalensis Benth. (Bello 205)	P	LB	WD	HE	Tl
haberi N. Zamor, ined. (9581)	M	LB	WD	HE	Tl
macrophyllus Kunth (8229)	A	LB	WD	HE	Tm
minimiflorus Donn. Sm., aff. (Bello 98)	P	LB	WD	HE	Tm
oliganthus F. J. Herm. (8519)	PMA	SB	WD	HE	Tm
sericeus (Poir.) DC. (6575)	A	LB	WD	HE	Tm
sp. A (11102)	M	LB	WD	HE	Tl
sp. B (9987)	P	LB	WD	HE	Tl
Machaerium					
biovulatum Micheli (7198)	P	LB	WD	HE	Tm
cobanense Donn. Sm. (5247)	A	LB	WD	HE	L
floribundum Benth. (Bello 893)	A	LB	WD	HE	L
seemannii Benth. (7669)	A	LB	WD	HE	L
Macroptilium					
atropurpureum (DC.) Urb. (11667)	M	LB	GR	HE	V
Mucuna					
mutisiana (Kunth) DC. (Bello 2015)	A	BT	TM	HE	L
urens (L.) DC. (9231)	M	BT	TM	HE	L

Dicotyledons	Zone[a]	Poll[b]	Seed[c]	Sex[d]	Habit[e]
Nissolia					
fruticosa Jacq. (8881)	P	LB	GR	HE	L
Ormosia					
cruenta Rudd (471)	M	LB	BD	HE	L
Pachyrhizus					
erosus (L.) URB. (11553)	P	LB	EX	HE	V
Phaseolus					
*vulgaris L. (3046)	M				V
Platymiscium					
sp. A (8302)	A	LB	WD	HE	L
Pterocarpus					
rohrii Vahl., cf. (8515)	PMA	LB	WD	HE	Tl
Pueraria					
*phaseoloides (Roxb.) Benth. (4882) (Kudzu)	A				L
Rhynchosia					
edulis Griseb. (8724)	M	SB	BD	HE	L
erythrinoides Schltdl. & Cham. (10604)	PM	SB	BD	HE	L
longeracemosa M. Martens & Galeotti (Bello 4226)	P	SB	BD	HE	L
quercetorum Standl. (3674)	M	SB	BD	HE	L
reticulata (Sw.) DC. (16353)	P	SB	BD	HE	L
Styphnolobium					
monteviridis M. Sousa & Rudd (9118)	PM	LB	AM	HE	Tl
Stylosanthes					
guyanensis (Aubl.) Sw. (10352)	P	SB	GR,TM?	HE	H
Swartzia					
simplex (Sw.) Spreng. (5887)	A	LB	BD	HE	Ts
Teramnus					
uncinatus (L.) Sw. (8883)	PM	SB	GR	HE	S
Trifolium					
*repens L.	M	BE	GR	HE	H
Vigna					
adenantha (G. Mey.) Merechal, Mascherpa & Stainer (8842)	P	SB	GR	HE	V
caracalla (L.) Verdc. (4055)	P	SB	GR	HE	V
speciosa (Kunth) Verd. (9874)	P	LB	EX	HE	L
Zornia					
reticulata Sm. (8884)	PM	SB	GR	HE	S
Fagaceae					
Quercus					
brenesii Trel. (= *cortesii*) (7274)	M	WD	AM,TM	MO	Tm
corrugata Hook. (= *lancifolia*) (Dryer 1173)	MA	WD	AM,TM	MO	Tl
insignis M. Martens & Galeotti (9264)	M	WD	AM,TM	MO	Tl
seemannii Liebm. (= *solicifolia*) (Dryer 593)	M	WD	AM,TM	MO	Tm
Flacourtiaceae					
Casearia					
aculeata Jacq. (9979)	P	IN	BD	HE	Tm
arguta Kunth (7046)	A	IN	BD	HE	Tm
coronata Standl. & L. O. Williams (6598)	A	IN	BD	HE	Tm
corymbosa Kunth (10639)	PA	IN	BD	HE	Ts
sylvestris Sw. (285)	PM	IN	BD	HE	Tm
tacanensis Lundell (1611)	M	IN	AM	HE	Tm
Hasseltia					
floribunda Kunth (6992	MA	BE	BD	HE	Tm
Hasseltiopsis					
dioica (Benth.) Sleumer (6509)	M	BE	BD	DI	Ts
Lacistema					
aggregatum (Bergius) Rusby (Bello 1410)	M	IN	BD	HE	Tm
Lozania					
mutisiana Roem. & Schult. (316)	MA	IN	BD	HE	Tm
pittieri (S. F. Blake) L. B. Sm. (Bello 1079)	A	IN	BD	HE	Tm
Lunania					
mexicana Brandegee (778)	MA	SB	BD	DI	Tm

Dicotyledons	Zone[a]	Poll[b]	Seed[c]	Sex[d]	Habit[e]
Macrohasseltia					
macroterantha (Standl. & L. O. Williams) L. O. Williams (305)	MA	SB	WD	HE	Tl
Pleuranthodendron					
lindenii (Turcz.) Sleumer (Bello 1168)	A	SB	BD	HE	Tl
Prockia					
crucis P. Browne ex L. (1619)	P	IN	BD	HE	S
Xylosma					
chlorantha Donn. Sm. (10598)	M	SB	BD	HE	Ts
flexuosa (Kunth) Hemsl. (11755)	P	SB	BD	HE	Ts
hispidula Standl. (10021)	MA	SB	BD	HE	Ts
intermedia (Seem.) Triana & Planch. (7959)	M	SB	BD	DI	Tm
oligandra Donn. Sm. (9779)	M	SB	BD	HE	Tm
quichensis Donn. Sm. (9283)	M	SB	BD	HE	S
Gentianaceae					
Centaurium					
quitense (Kunth) B. L. Rob. (Fuentes 540)	A	SB	WD,GR	HE	H
Lisianthius					
seemannii (Griseb.) Kuntze (8656)	P	BD	WD/GR	HE	S
skinneri (Hemsl.) Kuntze (Bello 940)	A	BD	WD/GR	HE	S
Macrocarpaea					
valerii Standl. (336)	M	BT	WD/GR	HE	S
Schultesia					
lisianthoides (Griseb.) Benth. & Hook. ex Hemsl. (10294)	P	IN?	WD/GR	HE	H
Symbolanthus					
calygonus (Ruiz & Pav.) Griseb. (7389)	M	BD	WD/GR	HE	H
Voyria					
flavescens Griseb. (858)	M	IN	GR	HE	H-Sap
Gesneriaceae					
Achimenes					
longiflora DC. (8627)	P	BD	WD	HE	H
pedunculata Benth (10083)	P	BD	WD	HE	H
Alloplectus					
panamensis C. V. Morton (10554)	A	BD	BD	HE	H
tetragonus (Oerst.) Hanst. (3050)	M	BD	BD	HE	S
trichocalyx Wiehler (9403)	A	BD	BD	HE	V
Besleria					
formosa C. V. Morton (1565)	M	BD	BD	HE	S
laxiflora Benth. (1465)	A	BD	BD	HE	S
macropoda Donn. Sm. (7672)	A	BE?	BD	HE	H
notabilis C. V. Morton (972)	MA	BD	BD	DI	S
princeps Hanst. (2643)	M	BD	BD	HE	H
solanoides Kunth (1026)	MA	BD	BD	HE	S
triflora (Oerst.) Hanst. (Koptur 116)	MA	BD	BD	HE	S
Capanea					
grandiflora (Kunth) Decne. ex Planch. (3167)	M	BT	BD	HE	E
Columnea					
angustata (Wiehler) L. E. Skog (Bello 248)	A	IN	BD	HE	V
anisophylla DC. (6248)	M	BD	BD	HE	E
consanguinea Hanst. (9131)	MA	BD	BD	HE	E
glabra Oerst. (6718)	M	BD	BD	HE	E
gloriosa Sprague (Bello 475)	MA	BD	BD	HE	E
hirta Klotzsch & Hanst. (Bello 418)	A	BD	BD	HE	E
kalbreyeriana Mast. (9189)	A	BD	BD	HE	E
lepidocaulis Hanst. (8567)	M	BD	BD	HE	E
linearis Oerst. (7998)	A	BD	BD	HE	E
magnifica Klotzsch ex Oerst. (4002)	M	BD	BD	HE	E
microcalyx Hanst. (7548)	M	BD	BD	HE	E
microphylla Klotzsch & Hanst. ex Oerst. (7055)	A	BD	BD	HE	E
oerstediana Klotzsch ex Oerst. (1403)	PA	BD	BD	HE	E
purpurata Hanst. (1247)	A	BD	BD	HE	E
querceti Oerst. (9016)	MA	BD	BD	HE	E
sanguinolenta (Klotzsch ex Oerst.) Hanst. (8320)	A	BD	BD	HE	V
verecunda C. V. Morton (1401)	PMA	BD	BD	HE	E

Dicotyledons	Zone[a]	Poll[b]	Seed[c]	Sex[d]	Habit[e]
Cremosperma					
maculatum L. E. Skog, cf. (10866)	A	BE	BD	HE	H
Diastema					
affine Fritsch (10400)	A	IN	WD,GR	HE	H
racemiferum Benth. (10782)	P	IN	WD,GR	HE	H
Drymonia					
alloplectoides Hanst. (1706)	A	BD?	BD	HE	E
conchocalyx Hanst. (727)	MA	BD	BD	HE	E
coriacea (Oerst. ex Hanst.) Weihler (9381)	A	BD	BD	HE	E
lanceolata (Hanst.) C. V. Morton (9826)	MA	IN	BD	HE	H
macrophylla (Oerst.) H. E. Moore (7603)	A	IN?	BD	HE	E
multiflora (Oerst. ex Hanst.) Wiehler (8422)	A	IN	BD	HE	E
rubra C. V. Morton (2802)	MA	BD	BD,BT	HE	E
serrulata (Jacq.) Mart. (7860)	A	BD?	BD	HE	E
stenophylla (Donn. Sm.) H. E. Moore (10837)	A	IN?	BD	HE	E
turrialvae Hanst. (788)	A	BD	BD	HE	H
warscewicziana Hanst. (6750)	A	BD?	BD	HE	E
Gasteranthus					
wendlandianus (Hanst.) Wiehler (4562)	MA	BD	BD?	HE	H
Koellikeria					
erinoides (DC.) Mansf. (2576)	P	IN	WD,GR	HE	H
Kohleria					
spicata (Kunth) Oerst. (740)	PMA	BD	WD,GR	HE	H
tubiflora (Cav.) Hanst. (8628)	P	BD	WD,GR	HE	H
Monopyle					
macrocarpa Benth. (9414)	A	LB	GR	HE	H
maxonii C. V. Morton (9869)	MA	LB	GR	HE	H
Moussonia					
strigosa (C. V. Morton) Wiehler (3660)	M	BD	WD,GR	HE	H
Napeanthus					
apodemus Donn. Sm. (9394)	A	IN	GR	HE	H
Neomortonia					
rosea Wiehler (6105)	A	IN	BD	HE	E
Oerstedina					
cerricola Wiehler (7554)	M	IN	BD	HE	E
Paradrymonia					
lineata (C. V. Morton) Wiehler (8692)	MA	IN?	WD	HE	E
metamorphophylla (Donn. Sm.) Wiehler (4679)	MA	IN?	WD	HE	E
Rhynchoglossum					
azureum (Schltdl.) Burtt (7357)	MA	LB	BD?	HE	H
Rufodorsia					
congestiflora (Donn. Sm.) Wiehler (Bello 546)	A	IN	BD	HE	E
major Wiehler (Bello 299)	A	IN	BD	HE	E
minor Wiehler (Bello 465)	A	IN	BD	HE	E
Solenophora					
calycosa Donn. Sm. (730)	MA	BD	WD?	HE	H
Grossulariaceae					
Phyllonoma					
ruscifolia Willd. ex Schult. (4540)	MA	IN	BD	HE	E
tenuidens Pittier (3159)	M	IN	BD	HE	S
Gunneraceae					
Gunnera					
insignis (Oerst.) A. DC. (6870)	M	WD	BD?	MO	H
Hernandiaceae					
Gyrocarpus					
jatrophifolius Domin (9992)	P	IN?	WD	MO	Tl
Hernandia					
stenura Standl. (1567)	A	IN	BD?	MO	Tl
Hippocastanaceae					
Billia					
colombiana Planch. & Lindl. (451)	PMA	LB	TM	HE	Tl
hippocastanum Peyr. (367)	M	LB	TM	HE	Tl

Dicotyledons	Zone[a]	Poll[b]	Seed[c]	Sex[d]	Habit[e]
Hippocrateaceae					
Pristimera					
austin-smithii (Lundell) A. C. Sm. (9687)	P	IN	WD	HE	L
celastroides (Kunth) A. C. Sm. (8262)	P	IN	WD	HE	L
Salacia					
petenensis Lundell (319)	MA	IN	AM	HE	Tm
sp. A (8297)	M	IN	AM	HE	L
Hydrangeaceae					
Hydrangea					
asterolasia Diels (7725)	M	SB	WD	HE	L
peruviana Moric. (6654)	MA	SB	WD	HE	L
preslii Briq. (Bello 632)	A	SB	WD	HE	L
steyermarkii Standl. (Bello 4286)	MA	SB	WD	HE	L
Hydrophyllaceae					
Wigandia					
urens (Ruiz & Pav.) Kunth (Bello 207)	PM	LB	WD	HE	Ts
Icacinaceae					
Calatola					
costaricensis Standl. (528)	MA	WD	AM	DI	Tm
Citronella					
costaricensis (Donn. Sm.) R. A. Howard (6964)	M	IN	BD	DI?	Tl
Juglandaceae					
Alfaroa					
costaricensis Standl. (528)	MA	IN	TM	MO	Tl
guanacastensis D. Stone (7092)	A	IN	TM	MO	Tl
williamsii A. Molina (Bello 1358)	M	IN	TM	MO	Tl
Juglans					
*olanchana Standl. & L. O. Williams (11044)	M				Tl
Oreomunnea					
pterocarpa Oerst. (8351)	A	IN	WD	MO?	Tl
Lamiaceae					
Hyptis					
brachiata Briq. (10168A)	P	SB	GR	HE	H
capitata Jacq. (10349)	P	SB	GR	HE	H
mutabilis (L. Rich.) Briq. (10368)	PM	SB	GR	HE	H
obtusiflora C. Presl ex Benth. (11284)	A	SB	GR	HE	H
pectinata Poit. (10196)	PM	SB	GR	HE	H
suaveolens (L.) Poit. (10162)	PM	SB	GR	HE	H
urticoides Kunth (10409)	M	SB	GR	HE	H
vilis Kunth & Bouché (11303)	MA	SB	GR	HE	H
Marsypianthes					
chamaedrys (Vahl) Kuntze (2592)	P	SB	GR	HE	H
Salvia					
comayaguana Standl. (10408)	PM	LB	GR	HE	S
costaricensis Oerst. (10095)	PM	LB	GR	HE	H
lasiocephala Hook. & Arn. (10326)	PM	LB	GR	HE	S
longimarginata Briq. (Feinsinger 620)	M	LB	GR	HE	S
occidentalis Sw. (10194)	P	LB	GR	HE	H
pteroura Briq. (10508)	P	LB	GR	HE	S
Scutellaria					
costaricana H. Wendl. (9859)	M	BD	GR	HE	H
isocheila Donn. Sm. (7015)	M	BE	GR	HE	H
purpurascens Sw. (8317)	A	BE	GR	HE	H
Solenostemon					
scutellarioides (L.) Codd (2286)	A	BE	GR	HE	H
Stachys					
costaricensis Briq. (Dryer 1485)	A	BE	GR	HE	H
guatemalensis Epling (7623)	A	BE	GR	HE	H
Lauraceae					
Beilschmiedia					
brenesii C. K. Allen (266)	PM	IN	BD	HE	Tm
costaricensis Mez & Pittier (9838)	MA	IN	BD	HE	Tl
immersinervis Sa. Nashida, ined. (6967)	M	IN	BD	HE	Tl

Dicotyledons	Zone[a]	Poll[b]	Seed[c]	Sex[d]	Habit[e]
ovalis (S. F. Blake) C. K. Allen (8502)	MA	IN	BD	HE	Tl
tilaranensis Sa. Nashida, ined. (Bello 4017)	A	IN	BD	HE	Tl
sp. A. Lindora near *brenesii* (10749)	P	IN	BD	HE	Tl
Cinnamomum					
brenesii (Standl.) Kosterm. (9945)	P	IN	BD	HE	Tl
cinnamomifolium (Kunth) Kosterm. (9309)	M	IN	BD	HE	Tl
neurophyllum (Mez & Pittier) Kosterm. (10367)	M	IN	BD	HE	Tl
paratriplinerve Lorea-Hern., ined. (Bello 589)	M	IN	BD	HE	Tl
Licaria					
brenesii W. C. Burger (11265)	A	IN	BD	HE	Ts
excelsa Kosterm. (3032)	MA	IN	BD	HE	Tl
misantlae (Brandegee) Kosterm. (4396)	A	IN	BD	HE	Tl
triandra (Sw.) Kosterm. (7199)	PM	IN	BD	HE	Tl
Nectandra					
cissiflora Nees, cf. (Bello 505)	A	IN	BD	HE	Tl
cuspidata Nees (Bello 1126)	PM	IN	BD	HE	Tl
lineata (HBK) Rohwer (262)	P	IN	BD	HE	Tl
martinicensis Mez (Bello 119)	P	IN	BD	HE	Tl
membranacea (Sw.) Griseb. (10583)	MA	IN	BD	HE	Tl
purpurea (Ruiz & Pav.) Mez (Bello 1002)	A	IN	BD	HE	Tm
reticulata (Ruiz & Pav.) Mez (7838)	A	IN	BD	HE	Tl
salicina C. K. Allen (385)	M	IN	BD	HE	Tl
smithii Allen (9831)	M	IN	BD	HE	Tl
umbrosa (Kunth) Mez (6831)	P	IN	BD	HE	Tl
Ocotea					
atirrensis Mez & Donn. Sm. (5917)	A	IN	BD	HE	Ts
austinii C. K. Allen (1115)	M	IN	BD	HE	Tm
brenesii Standl. (6988)	A	IN	BD	HE	Tm
cernua (Nees) Mez (Bello 2047)	A	IN	BD	DI	Tl
dentata van der Werf (5557)	A	IN	BD	HE	Tl
dendrodaphne Mez (11145)	A	IN	BD	HE	Ts
endresiana Mez (Dryer 862)	MA	IN	BD	HE	Tl
floribunda (Sw.) Mez (198)	M	IN	BD	DI	Tl
gomezii W. C. Burger (10633)	MA	IN	BD	HE	Tm
holdridgeiana W. Burger, Aff. (11093)	MA	IN	BD	DI?	Tm
insularis (Meisn.) Mez, aff. (11515)	M	IN	BD	HE	Tl
laetevirens Standl. & Steyerm., aff. (Bello 746)	A	IN	BD	HE	Tl
leucoxylon (Sw.) Laness. (9539)	PM	IN	BD	HE	Tl
meziana C. K. Allen (238)	MA	IN	BD	HE	Tl
mollifolia Mez & Pittier (Bello 2213)	A	IN	BD	HE	Tl
monteverdensis W. C. Burger (7136)	M	IN	BD	HE	Tl
nicaraguensis Mez (8239)	MA	IN	BD	HE	Ts
paulii C. K. Allen (9004)	MA	IN	BD	HE	Ts
pittieri (Mez) van der Werff (346)	M	IN	BD	HE	Tm
praetermissa van der Werff (10668)	M	IN	BD	HE	Ts
sinuata (Mez) Rohwer (7201)	PM	IN	BD	HE	Tm
stenoneura Mez & Pittier (11456)	A	IN	BD	HE	Tl
tenera Mez. & Donn. Sm. ex Mez (160)	MA	IN	BD	DI	Ts
tonduzii Standl. (10041)	M	IN	BD	HE	Tl
valeriana (Standl.) W. Burger (6643)	MA	IN	BD	HE	Tl
veraguensis (Meissn.) Mez (10647)	P	IN	BD	HE	Tl
viridiflora Lundell, aff. (9791)	M	IN	BD	DI	Tl
whitei Woodson (525)	PM	IN	BD	HE	Tl
sp. A (8388)	A	IN	BD	HE	Tl
sp. B (10808)	M	IN	BD	HE	Tm
sp. C (11063)	PM	IN	BD	HE	Tl
Persea					
americana Mill. (9850)	PM	IN	AM	HE	Tl
caerulea (Ruiz & Pav.) Mez (9783)	PM	IN	BD	HE	Tl
povedae W. C. Burger (Bello 121)	A	IN	BD	HE	Tl
rigens C. K. Allen (S. Berrios, s.n.)	A	IN	BD	HE	Tl

Dicotyledons	Zone[a]	Poll[b]	Seed[c]	Sex[d]	Habit[e]
schiedeana Nees (8185)	MA	IN	AM	HE	Tl
silvatica van der Weff	A	IN	BD	HE	Tl
veraguasensis Seem. (8282)	PM	IN	BD	HE	Tl
sp. A (8499)	MA	IN	AM	HE	Tl
Pleurothyrium					
palmanum (Mez & Donn. Sm.) Rohwer (9526)	M	IN	BD	HE	Tl
guindonii van der Werff (11089)	M	IN	BD	HE	Tl
Rhodostemonodaphne					
kunthiana (Nees) Rohwer (6791)	A	IN	BD	HE	Tl
Lentibulariaceae					
Utricularia					
jamesoniana Oliv. (7486)	MA	LB	WD	HE	E
praetermissa P. Taylor (3266)	M	LB	WD	HE	E
Loasaceae					
Klaprothia					
fasciculata (C. Presl) Poston (10212)	M	IN	GR,WD	HE	S
Loasa					
grandis Standl. (Bello 646)	A	IN	GR,WD	HE	S
triphylla Juss. (3091) (Bello 1230)	M	LB	GR,WD	HE	H
Loganiaceae					
Buddleja					
americana L. (6514)	P	IN	WD	HE	S
Mitreola					
petiolata (J. F. Gmel.) Torr. & A. Gray (8844)	P	IN	GR,WD	HE	S
Spigelia					
palmeri Rose (10682)	MA	SB	GR	HE	H
Strychnos					
chlorantha Progel (7065)	A	IN	TM	HE	L
Loranthaceae					
Gaiadendron					
punctatum (Ruiz & Pav.) G. Don (10256)	M	BD	BD	HE	E-P
Oryctanthus					
occidentalis (L.) Eichler (Bellow 532)	A	IN	BD	HE	E-P
spicatus (Jacq.) Eichler (634)	M	IN	BD	HE	E-P
Phthirusa					
stelis (L.) Kuijt. (9972)	P	IN	BD	DI	E-P
Psittacanthus					
krameri Kuijt (9431)	A	BD	BD	HE	E-P
ramiflorus (DC.) G. Don (8019)	PM	BD	BD	HE	E-P
rhynchanthus (Benth.) Kuijt (10082)	P	BD	BD	HE	E-P
sp. A	P	BD	BD	HE	E-P
Struthanthus					
consjerifolius (Oliv.) Eichler (5219)	M	IN	BD	DI	E-P
costaricensis Standl. (Sargent 15)	M	IN	BD	DI	E-P
oerstedii (Oliv.) Standl. (2256)	M	IN	BD	DI	E-P
quercicola (Schltdl. & Cham.) Blume (3114)	PM	IN	BD	DI	E-P
subtilis Kuijt (Bello 197)	M	IN	BD	DI	E-P
Lythraceae					
Cuphea					
appendiculata Benth. (1330)	PM	BD	GR	HE	S
carthagenensis (Jacq.) J. F. Macbr. (Zuchowski 10)	MA	SB	GR	HE	S
epilobiifolia Koehne (9865)	A	SB	GR	HE	S
Magnoliaceae					
Magnolia					
poasana (Pittier) Dandy (9808)	M	CO	BD	HE	Tl
Talauma					
gloriensis Pittier (574)	M	CO	BD	HE	Tl
Malpighiaceae					
Banisteriopsis					
muricata (Cav.) Cuatrec. (10165)	P	LB	WD	HE	L
Bunchosia					
costaricensis Rose (10074)	M	LB	BD	HE	Ts
ocellata Lundell (7210)	P	LB	BD	HE	Tm

Dicotyledons	Zone[a]	Poll[b]	Seed[c]	Sex[d]	Habit[e]
ternata Dobson (4152)	M	LB	BD	HE	S
veluticarpa W. R. Anderson (303)	MA	LB	BD	HE	Tl
Byrsonima					
crassifolia (L.) Kunth (9942)	P	LB	BD	HE	Tm
Gaudichaudia					
hexandra Nied. (8853)	P	LB	WD	HE	V
Heteropterys					
brachiata (L.) DC. (Bello 2926)	P	LB	WD	HE	L
macrostachya A. Juss. (8406)	A	LB	WD	HE	L
panamensis Cuatrec. & Croat (Bello 1307)	A	LB	WD	HE	L
Hiraea					
haberi W. R. Anderson (7247)	A	LB	WD	HE	L
smilacina Standl. (9898)	PMA	LB	WD	HE	L
Malpighia					
albiflora (Cuatrec.) Cuatrec. (1648)	MA	SB	BD	HE	Ts
glabra L. (7263)	PM	SB	BD	HE	Ts
Mascagnia					
divaricata (Kunth) Nied. (6828)	PA	LB	WD	HE	L
Stigmaphyllon					
ellipticum (Kunth) A. Juss. (3722)	PM	LB	WD	HE	V
lindenianum A. Juss. (Bello 467)	A	LB	WD	HE	L
Tetrapteris					
discolor G. Mey. (Bello 1210)	A	LB	WD	HE	L
donnell-smithii Small (Bello 308)	MA	LB	WD	HE	L
monteverdensis W. R. Anderson (5217)	M	LB	WD	HE	L
schiedeana Schltdl. & Cham. (2036)	MA	LB	WD	HE	L
Malvaceae					
Abutilon					
divaricatum Turcz. (10533)	P	IN	GR,WD	HE	S
Hampea					
appendiculata (Donn. Sm.) Standl. (350)	PMA	IN	BD	DI	Tl
Hibiscus					
acetosella Welw. ex Hiern, cf. (621)	P	LB	GR?	HE	S
Malachra					
fasciata Jacq. (Bello 520)	A	IN	GR	HE	S
Malvaviscus					
arboreus Cav. (9771)	PMA	BD	BD	HE	L
concinnus Kunth (9373)	A	BD	BD	HE	L
palmanus Pittier & Donn. Sm. (Feinsinger 413)	MA	BD	BD	HE	Ts
Pavonia					
penduliflora (Standl.) Standl. (Dryer 968)	M	SB	TM	HE	H
rosea Schltdl. (680)	M	SB,BD	TM	HE	S
schiedeana Steud. (10151)	A	SB	TM	HE	S
Sida					
collina Schlect. (10338)	P	SB	GR	HE	S
rhombifolia L. (10333)	PM	SB	GR	HE	S
urens L. (10505)	P	SB	GR	HE	S
Urena					
lobata L. (10910)	MA	LB	GR	HE	S
Wercklea					
cocleana (Robyns) Fryx. (877)	P	BD	WD	HE	S
insignis Pittier & Standl. ex Standl. (733)	PMA	BD	WD	HE	Tm
Marcgraviaceae					
Marcgravia					
brownei (Triana & Planch.) Krug & Urb. (Dryer 594)	MA	BT	BD	HE	L
caudata Triana & Planch. (7048)	A	BT	BD	HE	L
mexicana Gilg (6931)	A	BT	BD	HE	L
nepenthoides Seem. (6765)	A	BT	BD	HE	L
pittieri Gilg (6534)	A	BT	BD	HE	L
serrae de Roon (8080)	A	BT	BD	HE	L
Norantia					
brenesii Standl. (7453)	PMA	BT	BD	HE	E
costaricensis Gilg (10071)	PM	BT	BD	HE	E
jimenezii (Standl.) de Roon (Bello 2777)	MA	BT	BD	HE	E

Dicotyledons	Zone[a]	Poll[b]	Seed[c]	Sex[d]	Habit[e]
Ruyschia					
phylladenia Sandwith (2921)	PMA	IN	BD	HE	L
valerii Standl. (Bello 4020)	A	IN	BD	HE	L
Sarcopera					
sessiliflora (Triana & Planch.) Bedell (Bello 2879)	A	BT	BD	HE	E
Souroubea					
loczyi (V. A. Richt.) de Roon (Fuentes 303)	A	IN	BD	HE	E
Melastomataceae					
Adelobotrys					
adscendens (Sw.) Triana (6424)	A	LB	WD	HE	V
Arthrostemma					
ciliatum Pav. ex D. Don (10125)	PM	LB	GR,WD	HE	H
Blakea					
anomala Donn. Sm. (725)	M	LB	BD	HE	E
chlorantha Almeda (1197)	M	AM	BD	HE	E
gracilis Hemsl. (3236)	M	LB	BD	HE	E
grandiflora Hemsl. (5356)	M	LB	BD	HE	E
litoralis L. O. Williams (Bello 2443)	A	LB	BD	HE	E
scarlatina Almeda (1873)	A	LB	BD	HE	E
tuberculata Donn. Sm. (723)	A	LB	BD	HE	E
Centradenia					
inaequilateralis (Schltdl. & Cham.) G. Don (672)	M	SB	GR,WD	HE	S
Clidemia					
biolleyana Cogn. (10395)	A	SB	BD	HE	S
costaricensis Cogn. & Gleason (1010)	A	SB	BD	HE	S
dentata D. Don (9418)	A	SB	BD	HE	S
epiphytica (Triana) Cogn. (7717)	A	SB	BD	HE	E
evanescens Almeda (Bello 1540)	A	SB	BD	HE	S
fraterna Gleason (4808)	A	SB	BD	HE	S
globuliflora (Cogn.) L. O. Williams (10688)	M	SB	BD	HE	S
mortoniana Standl. (10925)	M	SB	BD	HE	S
ombrophila Gleason (Bello 1084)	A	SB	BD	HE	S
radicans Cogn. (6077)	A	SB	BD	HE	S
reitziana Cogn. & Gleason ex Gleason (4787)	A	SB	BD	HE	S
sericea D. Don (9925)	P	SB	BD	HE	S
sessiliflora (Naudin) Cogn. (Bello 1633)	A	SB	BD	HE	S
setosa (Triana) Gleason (10394)	A	SB	BD	HE	S
spectabilis Gleason (4468)	M	SB	BD	HE	H
Conostegia					
brenesii Standl. (179)	M	LB	BD	HE	Ts
lasiopoda Benth. (11225)	A	LB	BD	HE	Ts
micrantha Standl. (11507)	A	LB	BD	HE	S
montana (Sw.) D. Don ex DC. (Bello 981)	MA	LB	BD	HE	Ts
monteleagreana Cogn. (7590)	A	LB	BD	HE	Ts
oerstediana O. Berg ex Triana (9967)	MA	LB	BT,BD	HE	Tm
pittieri Cogn. (9817)	M	LB	BD	HE	Ts
rhodopetala Donn. Sm. (Dryer 1076)	M	LB	BD	HE	Ts
rufescens Naudin (178)	MA	LB	BD	HE	Tm
setifera Standl. (6745)	A	LB	BD	HE	Ts
subcrustulata (Beurl.) Triana (7647)	PA	LB	BD	HE	S
tenuifolia Donn. Sm. (4458)	A	LB	BD	HE	S
vulcanicola Donn. Sm. (Dryer 532)	M	LB	BD	HE	S
xalapensis (Bonpl.) D. Don (512)	PM	LB	BD	HE	Tm
Graffenrieda					
micrantha (Gleason) L. O. Williams (358)	M	SB	WD	HE	Ts
Henriettea					
tuberculosa (Donn. Sm.) L. O. Williams (Bello 250)	A	SB	BD	HE	S
Leandra					
grandifolia Cogn. (5507)	A	SB	BD	HE	S
subseriata (Naudin) Cogn. (10282)	M	SB	BD	HE	S
subulata Gleason (3168)	M	SB	BD	HE	S
Meriania					
phlomoides (Triana) Almeda (10019)	M	IN?	GR,WD	HE	Ts

Dicotyledons	Zone[a]	Poll[b]	Seed[c]	Sex[d]	Habit[e]
Miconia					
albicans (Sw.) Triana (10770)	P	SB	BD	HE	S
amplinodis Umaña & Almeda (10014)	M	SB	BD	HE	Ts
argentea (Sw.) DC. (10540)	P	SB	BD	HE	Tm
astroplocama Donn. Sm. (6526)	A	SB	BD	HE	S
brenesii Standl. (4371)	MA	SB	BD	HE	S
carnea Cogn. (9123)	M	SB	BD	HE	S
confertiflora Almeda (10674)	MA	SB	BD	HE	E
costaricensis Cogn. (10685)	M	SB	BD	HE	S
cuspidatissima Pittier (5338)	M	SB	BD	HE	Ts
desmantha Benth. (6977)	M	SB	BD	HE	S
dodecandra (Desr.) Cogn. (Bello 5366)	A	SB	BD	HE	Ts
dolichopoda Naudin (Haber 11107)	M	SB	BD	HE	Ts
doniana Naudin (288)	MA	LB	BD	HE	Tm
friedmaniorum Almeda & Umaña (3242)	M	SB	BD	HE	S
globuliflora (Rich.) Cogn. (7379)	M	SB	BD	HE	Ts
gracilis Triana (774)	MA	SB	BD	HE	Ts
grandidentata Almeda (10379)	M	SB	BD	HE	E
incurva Gleason (828)	A	SB	BD	HE	Ts
ligulata Almeda (9374)	A	SB	BD	HE	Ts
livida Triana (Bello 1661)	M	SB	BD	HE	S
lonchophylla Naudin (10571)	M	SB	BD	HE	Ts
longibracteata Almeda (6620)	M	SB	BD	HE	E
loreyoides Triana (5463)	A	SB	BD	HE	S
melanotricha (Triana) Gleason (7305)	A	SB	BD	HE	H
oraria Wurdock (Bello 957)	A	SB	BD	HE	Ts
smaragdina Naudin (971)	A	SB	BD	HE	Ts
theizans (Bonpl.) Cogn. (812)	MA	SB	BD	HE	Ts
tonduzii Cogn. (Bello 713)	M	SB	BD	HE	Ts
valeriana (Standl.) Wurd. (9376)	A	SB	BD	HE	S
sp. A (10283)	M	SB	BD	HE	S
Monochaetum					
floribundum (Schltdl.) Naudin (1169)	MA	SB	GR,WD	HE	S
linearifolium Almeda (Zuchowski 53)	M	SB	Gr,WD	HE	S
Mouriri					
exilis Gleason (11009)	MA	LB	BD	HE	Tl
Ossaea					
brenesii Standl. (1013)	A	SB	BD	HE	S
laxivenula Wurdack (Bello 253)	A	SB	BD	HE	S
macrophylla (Benth.) Cogn. (5900)	A	SB	BD	HE	S
micrantha (Sw.) Macfad. (7620)	MA	SB	BD	HE	Ts
quinquenervia (Mill.) Cogn. (4835)	A	SB	BD	HE	S
robusta (Triana) Cogn. (Bello 2892)	A	SB	BD	HE	S
Pilocosta					
erythrophylla (Gleason) Almeda & Whiffin (1787A)	M	IN	GR?	HE	H
nubicola Almeda (6757)	A	IN	GR?	HE	H
Pterolepis					
trichotoma (Rottb.) Cogn. (10290)	P	SB	GR,WD	HE	H
Schwackaea					
cupheoides (Benth.) Cogn. ex Durand (10153)	PMA	SB	GR,WD	HE	H
Tibouchina					
longifolia (Vahl) Baill. ex Cogn. (842)	A	SB	GR,WD	HE	S
Tococa					
platyphylla Benth. (7285)	A	IN	BD	HE	H
Topobea					
brenesii Standl. (7737)	M	LB	BD	HE	E
dimorphophylla Almeda (8469)	A	LB	BD	HE	V
maurofernandeziana Cogn. (966)	MA	LB	BD	HE	E
Triolena					
hirsuta (Benth.) Triana (4788)	A	SB	GR,WD	HE	H

Dicotyledons	Zone[a]	Poll[b]	Seed[c]	Sex[d]	Habit[e]
Meliaceae					
Cedrela					
odorata L. (10645)	PA	MO	WD	MO,DI	Tl
salvadorensis Standl. (Bello 702)	P	MO	WD	He?	Tl
tonduzii C. DC. (465)	MA	MO	WD	HE?	Tl
Guarea					
glabra Vahl (10670)	MA	MO	BD	DI	Tm
grandifolia DC. (4825)	A	MO	BD	DI	Ts
kunthiana A. Juss. (3799)	MA	MO	BD	DI	Tl
pterorhachis Harms (Bello 1631)	A	MO	BD	DI	Tl
rhopalocarpa Radlk. (908)	PMA	MO	BD	DI	Tl
tonduzii C. DC. (10791)	M	MO	BD	DI	Tm
sp. A (7102)	A	MO	BD	DI	Ts
sp. B (Mariano)	PM	MO	BD	DI	Ts
Ruagea					
glabra Triana & Planch. (6769)	MA	SB	BD	DI	Tl
Trichilia					
adolfi Harms (6987)	A	SB	BD	DI	Tl
glabra L. (9928)	P	SB	BD	DI	Tl
havanensis Jacq. (286)	PMA	SB	BD	DI	Tl
martiana C. DC. (1623)	PA	SB	BD	DI	Tl
Menispermaceae					
Abuta					
panamensis (Standl.) Krukoff & Barneby (10620)	PMA	IN	BD	DI	L
Anomospermum					
reticulatum (Mart.) Eichler (8407)	A	IN	BD	DI	L
Cissampelos					
andromorpha DC. (7902)	A	IN	BD?	DI	L
grandifolia Triana & Planch. (5223)	M	IN	BD?	DI	L
pareira L. (5983)	PMA	IN	BD?	DI	L
tropaeolifolia DC. (4869)	A	IN	BD?	DI	L
Disciphania					
calocarpa Standl. (4453)	A	IN	BD	DI	L
Monimiaceae					
Mollinedia					
costaricensis Donn. Sm. (7220)	A	IN	BD	DI	Ts
pinchotiana Perkins (7126)	M	IN	BD	DI	Ts
sp. A (10573)	M	IN	BD	DI	S
Siparuna					
gesnerioides (Kunth) A. DC. (9511)	A	IN	BD	DI	S
grandiflora (Kunth) Perkins (11213)	M	IN	BD	DI	S
guianensis Aub. (Dryer 600)	M	IN	BD	DI	S
macra Standl. (Zuchowski 240)	M	IN	BD	DI	S
pauciflora (Beurl.) A. DC. (11148)	A	IN	BD	DI	Ts
tonduziana Janet Perkins (4800)	MA	IN	BD	DI	S
Moraceae					
Brosimum					
alicastrum Sw. (Bello 18)	P	WD,IN?	BD,AM, TM	DI	Tl
Clarisia					
biflora Ruiz & Pav. (Bello 435)	P	WD	AM	DI	Tl
mexicana (Liebm.) Lanj. (7429)	A	WD	BD	DI	Tl
Dorstenia					
choconiana S. Watson (9236)	PMA	WD	EX	MO	H
contrajerva L. (9941)	PA	WD	EX	MO	H
Ficus					
americana Aubl. (Bello 1915)	A	IN	BD	MO	Tm
aurea Nutt. (8228)	A	IN	BD	MO	Tl
brevibracteata W. C. Burger (7187)	A	IN	BD	MO	Tl
cervantesiana Standl. & L. O. Williams (8316)	A	IN	BD	MO	Tl
citrifolia Mill. (7982)	PA	IN	AM,BD	MO	Tl
colubrinae Standl. (7495)	A	IN	BD	MO	E

Dicotyledons	Zone[a]	Poll[b]	Seed[c]	Sex[d]	Habit[e]
costaricana (Liebm.) Miq. (9910)	PA	IN	BD	MO	Tl
cotinifolia Kunth (9981)	P	IN	BD	MO	Tl
crassiuscula Warb. ex Standl. (530)	MA	IN	AM,BT	MO	Tl
crassivenosa W. C. Burger (1737)	A	IN	AM,BD	MO	Tl
cuatrecasana Dugand (7945)	A	IN	BD	MO	Tm
davidsoniae Standl. (Bello 1315)	A	IN	BD	MO	Tl
glaucescens (Liebm.) Miq. (Bello 2217)	A	IN	BD	MO	Tl
goldmanii Standl.	P	IN	BD	MO	Tl
hartwegii (Miq.) Miq. (8565)	MA	IN	BD	MO	Tl
jimenezii Standl. (8228)	A	IN	BD	MO	Tl
laterisyce W. C. Burger (5267)	PA?	IN	BD	MO	Tl
macbridei Standl. (8665)	MA	IN	AM	MO	Ts
maxima Mill. (810)	A	IN	AM,BD	MO	Tl
obtusifolia Kunth (1624)	P	IN	AM,BD	MO	Tl
schippii Standl. (8316)	A	IN	BD	MO	Tl
pertusa L. f. (771)	MA	IN	BD	MO	Tm
tonduzii Standl. (7850)	A	IN	AM	MO	Tl
trachelosyce Dugand (Bello 686)	P	IN	BD	MO	Tl
tuerckheimii Standl. (643)	M	IN	BD,AM, BT	MO	T
velutina Humb. & Bonpl. ex Willd. (9902)	MA	IN	AM,BT	MO	Tl
yoponensis Desv. (9911)	PM	IN	BT,AM, BD	MO	Tl
Helicostylis					
tovarensis (Klotzsch & H. Karst.) C. C. Berg (Bello 1229)	A	WD	BD	DI	Tm
Maclura					
tinctoria (L.) G. Don (Bello 412)	P	WD	BT,AM	DI	Tl
Maquira					
costaricana (Standl.) C. C. Berg (11231)	A	WD	BD	DI	Ts
Naucleopsis					
capirensis C. C. Berg. (7507)	A	WD	AM	DI	Tm
Poulsenia					
armata (Miq.) Standl. (Bello 875)	A	WD	AM	MO	Tl
Pseudolmedia					
mollis Standl. (Bello 4540)	MA	WD	AM	DI	Tm
oxyphyllaria Donn. Sm. (11065)	P	WD	BD	DI	Tm
Sorocea					
pubivena Hemsl. (11511 cf)	A	WD	BD	DI	Ts
trophoides W. C. Burger (773)	MA	WD	BD	DI	Tm
Trophis					
mexicana (Liebm.) Bureau (364)	MA	WD	BD	DI	Tm
racemosa (L.) Urb. (Bello 400)	PA	WD	BD	DI	Tl
Myricaceae					
Morella					
cerifera (L.) Small (7813)	PM	WD	BD	DI	S
phanerodonta (Standl.) Wilbur (Bello 846)	M	WD	BD	DI	S
Myristicaceae					
Otoba					
novogranatensis Moldenke (7723)	A	IN	BD	DI	Tl
Virola					
guatemalensis (Hemsl.) Warb. (Bello 470)	A	IN	BD	DI	Tl
koschnyi Warb. (Bello 553)	A	IN	BD	DI	Tl
sebifera Aubl. (Bello 1402)	A	IN	BD	DI	Tl
Myrsinaceae					
Ardisia					
auriculata Donn. Sm. (7655)	A	SB	BD	HE	S
brenesii Standl. (6997)	A	BE	BD	HE	Ts
calycosa Hemsl. (4431)	A	BE	BD	HE	S
compressa Kunth (Haber 7373)	PMA	BE	BD	HE	Ts
costaricensis Lundell (Pipoly 7101)	M	BE	BD	HE	S
crassiramea Standl. (Pipoly 7094)	M	BE	BD	HE	Ts
nigropunctata Oerst. (1671)	A	SB	BD	HE	Ts
opegrapha Oerst. (2276)	MA	BE	BD	HE	S

Dicotyledons	Zone[a]	Poll[b]	Seed[c]	Sex[d]	Habit[e]
palmana Donn. Sm. (712)	MA	BE	BD	HE	Tm
paschalis Donn. Sm. (3626)	P	BE	BD	HE	S
revoluta Kunth (3530)	P	BE	BD	HE	Ts
solomonii (Lundell) Pipoly (2428)	M	BE	BD	HE	Tm
tilaranensis Standl. (Haber 9358)	A	BE	BD	HE	S
Cybianthus					
costaricanus Hemsl. (3171)	M	IN	BD	HE	E
Gentlea					
costariceusis Lundell (11111)	M	SB	BD	HE	Ts
Myrsine					
coriacea (Sw.) R. Br. ex Roem. & Schult. (312)	M	IN	BD	DI	Tm
pellucido–punctata Oerst. (11212A)	MA	IN	BD	DI	Tm
Parathesis					
crassiramea Lundell (Bello 1757)	M	BE	BD	HE	Tm
glabra Donn. Sm. (10860)	M	BE	BD	HE	Ts
obovalifolia Lundell, ined. (2444)	M	BE	BD	HE	Tm
Myrtaceae					
Calyptranthes					
chytraculia (L.) Sw. (10869)	A	SB	BD	HE	Tm
monteverdensis P. E. Sánchez, ined. (10665)	M	SB	BD	HE	Tm
pallens Griseb. (11321)	PA	SB	BD	HE	Tm
pittieri Standl. (513)	M	SB	BD	HE	Tl
Eugenia					
acapulcensis Steud. (Bello 61)	P	SB	BD	HE	Tm
austin-smithii Standl. (11651)	M	SB	BD	HE	Tm
cartagenensis O. Berg (Bello 4110)	M	SB	BD	HE	Tm
costaricensis O. Berg (Bello 821)	M	SB	BD	HE	Tm
glandulosopunctata P. E. Sánchez & Poveda, ined. (Bello 4028)	A	SB	BD	HE	Tm
guatemalensis Donn. Sm. (224)	M	SB	BT,BD	HE	Tl
haberii P. E. Sánchez, ined. (Bello 2120)	M	SB	BD	HE	Tl
matagalpensis P. E. Sánchez (9613)	M	SB	BD	HE	Tm
monticola (Sw.) DC. (10175)	PM	SB	BD	HE	Tm
octopleura Krug & Urb. ex Urb. (10036)	M	SB	BD	HE	Tl
oerstediana O. Berg (499)	M	SB	BD	IIE	Tm
salamensis Donn. Sm. (7268)	P	SB	BD	HE	Tl
*uniflora L. (10072)	M				Tm
valerii Standl. (2434)	MA	SB	AM	HE	Tm
Marlierea					
mesoamericana P. E. Sánchez (Bello 4265)	A	BE	BD	HE	Tl
Myrcia					
fallax (Rich.) DC. (207)	M	SB	BD	HE	Tl
splendens (Sw.) DC. (2240)	PM	SB	BD	HE	Tm
sp. A. (9897)	M	SB	BD	HE	Tm
Myrcianthes					
fragrans (Sw.) McVaugh (9276)	M	SB	BD	HE	Tl
sp. A. (297)	PM	SB	BD	HE	Tl
Pimenta					
*dioica (L.) Merr. (6861)	A				Tm
guatemalensis (Lundell) Lundell (11222)	A	SB	BD	HE	Tm
Plinia					
salticola McVaugh (7047)	A	SB	AM	HE	Tm
Psidium					
guaiava L. (10046)	PMA	BE	TM,BT	HE	Ts
guineense Sw. (Bello 2904)	M				S
salutare (Kunth) O. Berg (Bello 2927)	P	BE	TM	HE	S
sartorianum (O. Berg) Nied. (9922)	P	BE	TM	HE	Tm
Nyctaginaceae					
Guapira					
costaricana (Standl.) Woodson (6822)	P	IN	BD	He	Tm
Mirabilis					
*jalapa L. (Fuentes 455)	PM				H
violacea (L.) Heimerl. (10475)	P	BE	TM?	HE?	H

Dicotyledons	Zone[a]	Poll[b]	Seed[c]	Sex[d]	Habit[e]
Neea					
amplifolia Donn. Sm. (7498)	MA	IN	BD	DI	S
psychotrioides Donn. Sm. (468)	PM	IN	BD	DI	Ts
sp. A (1008)	MA	IN	BD	DI	Ts
sp. B (Bello 37)	P	IN	BD	DI	Tm
Pisonia					
aculeata L. (9786)	PM	MO	BD,AM	DI	L
sylvatica Standl. (7705)	M	MO	BD,AM	DI	Ts
Ochnaceae					
Cespedesia					
macrophylla Seem. (Bello 775)	A	BE	WD	HE	Tl
Ouratea					
lucens (Kunth) Engl. (5544)	PA	BE	BD	HE	Ts
prominens Dwyer (7667)	A	BE	BD	HE	Ts
Sauvagesia					
erecta L. (9406)	A	IN	GR	HE	H
Olacaceae					
Heisteria					
acuminata (Humb. & Bonpl.) Engl. (1077)	M	BE	BD	HE	S
Oleaceae					
Chionanthus					
oblanceolatus (B. L. Rob.) P. S. Green (6746)	A	IN	BD	HE	Tm
panamensis (Standl.) Stearn (7272)	M	MO?	BD	HE	Tl
Forestiera					
cartaginense Donn. Sm. (Bello 2097)	M	WD	BD	DI	Ts
Fraxinus					
*uhdei (Wenz.) Lingelsh. (11181)	M				Tm
Opiliaceae					
Agonandra					
macrocarpa L. O. Williams	P	IN	BD	DI	Tl
Onagraceae					
Fuchsia					
jimenezii Breedlove, P. E. Berry & P. H. Raven (434)	M	BD	BD	HE	S
Hauya					
lucida Donn. Sm. & Rose (588)	P	HM	WD	HE	Tm
Ludwigia					
foliobracteolata (Munz) H. Hara (9420)	A	BE	GR	HE	H
octovalvis (Jacq.) P. H. Raven (1170)	M	BE	GR	HE	H
peruviana (L.) H. Hara (2988)	M	BE	GR	HE	H
Oxalidaceae					
Oxalis					
corniculata L. (10270)	M	BE	EX	HE	H
debilis Kunth (Dryer 1448)	M	BE	EX	HE	H
frutescens L. (Bello 99)	P	BE	EX	HE	H
latifolia Kunth (10728)	M	BE	EX	HE	H
spiralis (Ruiz & Pav.) G. Don (Bello 5247)	M	BE	EX	HE	H
Papaveraceae					
Bocconia					
frutescens L. (819)	MA	WD	BD	MO	Ts
Passifloraceae					
Passiflora					
adenopoda DC. (1061)	M	BE	AM	HE	L
ambigua Hemsl. (11052)	A	BE	AM?	HE	L
apetala Killip (4930)	PM	BE	BD	HE	V
biflora Lam. (4783)	PMA	BE	BD	HE	L
brevifila Killip (2075)	M	BE	AM	HE	L
capsularis L. (3884)	M	BE	BD	HE	L
coriacea Juss.	PM	LB	AM	HE	L
costaricensis Killip (8224)	A	BE	AM?	HE	L
dioscoreifolia Killip (2227)	M	BE	BD?	HE	L
*edulis Sims (4601)	M				V
guatemalensis S. Watson (Bello 721)	A	BE	AM?	HE	L
helleri Peyr. (9165)	M	BE	BD	HE	L

Dicotyledons	Zone[a]	Poll[b]	Seed[c]	Sex[d]	Habit[e]
lancearia Mast. (3396)	M	BE	BD	HE	L
ligularis Juss. (3201)	M	BE	AM	HE	L
lobata (Killip) Hutch. ex J. M. MacDougal (5083)	A	BE	BD	HE	L
membranacea Benth. (7077)	M	BE	AM	HE	L
nubicola J. M. MacDougal (MacDougal 220)	M	BE	BD	HE	V
obovata Killip (640: trunk climber)	M	BE	AM	HE	L
oerstedii Mast. (5644)	A	BE	AM	HE	L
sexflora Juss. (9536)	M	BE	BD	HE	V
tica Gómez-Laur. & L. D. Gómez (Bello 1531)	A	BE	AM?	HE	Ts
vitifolia Kunth (6590)	A	BD	AM	HE	L
Phytolaccaceae					
Petiveria					
alliacea L. (7971)	P	IN	TM	HE	H
Phytolacca					
icosandra L. (10440)	PM	BE	BD	HE	S
rivinoides Kunth & Bouché (1820)	MA	BE	BD	HE	S
rugosa A. Braun & Bouché (Dryer 583)	M	BE	BD	HE	S
Rivina					
humilis L. (962)	M	BE	BD	HE	S
Trichostigma					
octandrum (L.) H. Walter (8002)	PA	IN	BD	HE	L
polyandrum (Loes.) H. Walter (7484)	A	IN	BD	HE	L
Piperaceae					
Peperomia					
alata Ruiz & Pav. (Bello 859)	A	IN?	BD,AM	MO	E
alpina (Sw.) A. Dietr. (Haber 6624)	M	IN?	BD,AM	MO	E
angularis C. DC. (8801)	M	IN?	BD,AM	MO	E
carlosiana C. DC. (5977)	P	IN?	BD,AM	MO	E
claytonioides Kunth (8537)	M	IN?	BD,AM	MO	E
deppeana Schltdl. & Cham. (8288)	M	IN?	BD,AM	MO	E
distachya (L.) A. Dietr. (9193)	A	IN?	BD,AM	MO	E
dotana Trel. (Dryer 57)	M	IN?	BD,AM	MO	E
flexinervia Yunck. (8091)	A	IN?	BD,AM	MO	E
glabella (Sw.) A. Dietr. (9162)	PM	IN?	BD,AM	MO	E
hernandiifolia (Vahl) A. Dietr. (8335)	MA	IN?	BD,AM	MO	H
hoffmannii C. DC. (Dryer 1183)	M	IN?	BD,AM	MO	E
hylophila C. DC. (8571)	M	IN?	BD,AM	MO	E
lancifolia Hook. (Zuchowski 388)	M	IN?	BD,AM	MO	E
lignescens C. DC. (5981)	P	IN?	BD,AM	MO	E
maculosa (L.) Hook. (7120)	M	IN?	BD,AM	MO	E
magnoliifolia A. Dietr. (6338)	A	IN?	BD,AM	MO	E
martiana Miq. (8623)	M	IN?	BD,AM	MO	E
matlalucaensis C. DC. (9208)	A	IN?	BD,AM	MO	E
montium C. DC. (9161)	M	IN?	BD,AM	MO	E
obtusifolia (L.) A. Dietr. (7857)	A	IN?	BD,AM	MO	E
olivacea C. DC. (7343)	MA	IN?	BD,AM	MO	E
omnicola C. DC. (Zuchowski 465)	M	IN?	BD,AM	MO	E
palmana C. DC. (Dryer 54)	M	IN?	BD,AM	MO	E
panamensis C. DC. (7876)	MA	IN?	BD,AM	MO	E
peltilimba C. DC. ex Trel. (Dryer 58)	M	IN?	BD,AM	MO	E
pernambucensis Miq. (8426)	A	IN?	BD,AM	MO	E
pittieri C. DC. (9081)	M	IN?	BD,AM	MO	E
poasana C. DC. (Dryer 249)	M	IN?	BD,AM	MO	E
pseudoalpina Trel. (8800)	M	IN?	BD,AM	MO	E
pseudopererkiifolia C. DC.	P	IN?	BD,AM	MO	E
pseudorhynchophora C. DC. (8091)	A	IN?	BD,AM	MO	E
quadrifolia (L.) Kunth (8919)	M	IN?	BD,AM	MO	E
rotundifolia (L.) Kunth (9208)	A	IN?	BD,AM	MO	E
seemanniana Miq. (6697)	M	IN?	BD,AM	MO	E
serpens (Sw.) Loudon (Bello 129)	A	IN?	BD,AM	MO	E
syringifolia C. DC. (7943)	A	IN?	BD,AM	MO	E

Dicotyledons	Zone[a]	Poll[b]	Seed[c]	Sex[d]	Habit[e]
tenella (Sw.) A. Dietr. (7236)	M	IN?	BD,AM	MO	E
tenelliformis Trel. (Dryer 471)	M	IN?	BD,AM	MO	E
ternata C. DC. (7928)	A	IN?	BD,AM	MO	E
tetraphylla (G. Forst.) Hook. & Arn. (9160)	M	IN?	BD,AM	MO	E
urocarpoides C. DC. (1422)	P	IN?	BD,AM	MO	E
vulcanicola C. DC., cf. (8747)	M	IN?	BD,AM	MO	E
Piper					
aequale Vahl (1126)	M	IN?	BT	MO	S
amalago L. (1381)	M	IN?	BT	MO	S
arboreum Aubl. (4907)	A	IN?	BT?	MO	S
artanthopse C. Dc. (9633)	P	IN?	BT?	MO	S
augustum Rudge (11547)	A	IN?	BT?	MO	S
auritum Kunth (Dryer 87)	M	IN?	BT	MO	Ts
biauritum C. DC. (9127)	M	IN?	BT?	MO	S
biseriatum C. DC. (4401)	A	IN?	BT?	MO	Ts
bredemeyeri Jacq. (9845)	M	IN?	BT?	MO	S
carpinteranum C. DC. (Dryer 767)	M	IN?	BT?	MO	S
chrysostachyum C. DC. (1487)	A	IN?	BT?	MO	S
concepcionis Trel. (Bello 4541)	A	IN?	BT?	MO	S
crassinervium Kunth (6130)	A	IN?	BT?	MO	S
cuspidispicum Trel. (Dryer 1199)	M	IN?	BT?	MO	S
decurrens C. DC. (4402)	MA	IN?	BT?	MO	S
dotanum Trel. (4042)	P	IN?	BT	MO	S
epigynium C. DC. (Koptur 128)	M	IN?	BT	MO	S
friedrichsthalii C. DC. (Fuentes 495)	P	IN?	BT?	MO	S
garagaranum C. DC. (Bello 601)	A	IN?	BT?	MO	S
gibbosum C. DC. (4956)	M	IN?	BT	MO	S
glabrescens (Miq.) DC. (4237)	M	IN?	BT	MO	S
hispidum Sw. (1718)	A	IN?	BT?	MO	S
imperiale (Miq.) C. DC. (8330)	MA	IN?	BT?	MO	Ts
jacquemontianum Kunth (Grayum 5387)	M	IN?	BT?	MO	S
lanceifolium Kunth (833)	A	IN?	BT?	MO	S
marginatum Jacq. (Bello 5277)	P	IN?	BT?	MO	S
nemorense C. DC. (Zuchowski 207)	MA	IN?	BT?	MO	S
nudifolium C. DC. (4799)	PA	IN?	BT?	MO	S
oblanceolatum Trel. (12308)	M	IN?	BT?	MO	S
obliquum Ruiz & Pav. (Bello 623)	MA	IN?	BT	MO	S
phytolaccifolium Opiz (Dryer 1030)	MA	IN?	BT	MO	S
polytrichum C. DC. (1690)	A	IN?	BT?	MO	S
pseudofuligineum C. DC. (5618)	M	IN?	BT?	MO	S
pseudolindenii C. DC. (1621)	P	IN?	BT?	MO	S
sanctum (Miq.) Schltdl. (5253)	A	IN?	BT?	MO	S
schiedeanum Steud. (4793)	A	IN?	BT?	MO	S
subsessilifolium C. DC. (Zuchowski 160)	MA	IN?	BT?	MO	V
trigonum C. DC. (2294)	A	IN?	BT?	MO	S
umbellatum L. (Penneys 32)	PMA	IN?	BT?	MO	S
wagneri C. DC., (Pennys 172)	PM	IN?	BT?	MO	S
yucatanense C. DC. (7204)	P	IN?	BD?	MO	S
yzabalanum C. DC. (1057)	P	IN?	BT?	MO	S
Sarcorhachis					
naranjoana (C. DC.) Trel. (3910)	M	IN	BT	MO	L
Plantaginaceae					
Plantago					
australis Lam. (Zuchowski 457)	M	WD	GR,BD?	HE	H
major L. (10037)	M	WD	GR,BD?	HE	H
Podostemaceae					
Tristicha					
trifaria (Bory ex Willd.) Spreng. (9675)	P	IN?	WD	HE	H
Polemoniaceae					
Cobaea					
gracilis (Oerst.) Hemsl. (8252)	A	BT	BD	HE	V
panamensis Standl. (Bello 2152)	A	BT	BD	HE	V
Loeselia					
ciliata L. (10343)	P	IN	WD	HE	S
glandulosa (Cav.) G. Don (10295)	PM	IN	WD	HE	S

Dicotyledons	Zone[a]	Poll[b]	Seed[c]	Sex[d]	Habit[e]
Polygalaceae					
Monnina					
saprogena Donn. Sm. (Dryer 582)	M	BE	BD	HE	S
sylvatica Schltdl. & Cham. (Dryer 1033B)	M	BE	BD	HE	S
Polygala					
fendleri Chodat (10185)	P	BE	GR	HE	H
paniculata L. (8867)	PM	BE	GR	HE	H
Securidaca					
diversifolia Pol. (9852)	PMA	BE	WD	HE	L
micheliana Chodat (8453)	M	BE	WD	HE	L
Polygonaceae					
Coccoloba					
liportizii Gómez-Laur. & N. Zamora (9504)	MA	BE	BD	DI	Ts
obovata Kunth (11604)	A	BE	BD	DI	Ts
porphyrostachys Gómez-Laur. (7489)	A	BE	BD	DI	Ts
tuerckheimii Donn. Sm. (Bello 1301)	A	BE	BD	DI	Tm
Muehlenbeckia					
tamnifolia (Kunth) Meisn. (7567)	M	IN	GR	MO	L
Rumex					
nepalensis Spreng. (3531)	PM	WD?	GR?	HE?	H
obtusifolius L. (Bello 4434)	M	WD?	GR?	HE?	H
Triplaris					
melaenodendron (Bertol.) Standl. & Steyerm. (Bello 675)	P	BE	WD	DI	Tm
Proteaceae					
Panopsis					
suaveolens (Klotzsch & H. Karst.) Pittier (6705)	M	MO	AM,TM	HE	Tl
Roupala					
glaberrima Pittier (472)	M	MO	WD	HE	Tl
montana Aubl. (10738)	P	MO	WD	HE	Tm
sp. A (Bello 1075)	A	MO	WD	HE	Tl
Ranunculaceae					
Clematis					
dioica L. (1349)	PMA	IN?	WD	DI	L
guadelupae Pers (5582)	MA	IN?	WD	DI	L
haenkeana Presl (Bello 1928)	M	IN?	WD	DI	L
polygama Jacq. (6562)	A	IN?	WD	DI	L
Rhamnaceae					
Colubrina					
spinosa Donn. Sm. (7999)	A	SB,IN	BD	HE	Tm
Gouania					
polygama (Jacq.) Urb. (11382)	PA	IN	WD	HE	L
Rhamnus					
sphaerosperma SW. (8721)	M	IN	BD	HE	Tm
Rhizophoraceae					
Cassipourea					
elliptica (Sw.) Poit. (583)	MA	SB	BD	HE	Tm
Rosaceae					
Alchemilla					
aphanoides L. f. (10285)	M	IN?	GR?	HE?	H
Prunus					
brachybotrys Zucc. (10971)	M	BE	BD	HE	Tm
cornifolia Koehne (Bello 4440)	MA	BE	BD	HE	Tm
skutchii I. M. Johnst. (10971)	MA	BE	BD	HE	Tl
fortunensis McPherson (10623)	A	BE	BD	HE	Tm
sp. A (2687)	A	BE	BD	HE	Tm
Rubus					
costaricensis Liebm. (Bello 5079)	M	LB	BD,AM	HE	L
glaucus Benth. (10284)	A	BE	BD	HE	L
*nivenus Thunb. (10267)	M				L
pittieri Rydb. (10269)	M	LB	BD,AM	HE	L
*roseifolius Sm. (Zuchowski 222)	M				S
urticifolius Poir. (10268)	M	BE	BD	HE	L

Dicotyledons	Zone[a]	Poll[b]	Seed[c]	Sex[d]	Habit[e]
Rubiaceae					
Borojoa					
panamensis Dwyer (10630)	A	HM	AM,BD	DI	Tm
Chimarrhis					
parviflora Standl. (6837)	A	IN	WD	HE	Tl
Chiococca					
alba (L.) Hitchc. (10753)	PM	MO	BD	HE	Ts
pachyphylla Wernham (10754)	P	MO	BD	HE	L
phaenostemon Schltdl. (10609)	MA	MO	BD	HE	L
Chione					
sylvicola Standl. (6837)	A	IN	WD	HE	Tl
Chomelia					
recordii (Standl.) W. C. Burger (330)	A	MO	BD	HE	Ts
venulosa W. C. Burger & C. M. Taylor (7631)	MA	MO	BD	HE	Tm
Cinchona					
pubescens Vahl (Bello 315)	A	MO	WD	HE	Tm
Coccocypselum					
cordifolium Nees & Mart. (522)	M	BE	BD	HE	H
herbaceum P. Browne (6770)	A	BE	BD	HE	H
hirsutum Bartling ex DC. (2333)	PMA	BE	BD	HE	H
Coffea					
*arabica L.					
Cosmibuena					
grandiflora (Ruiz & Pav.) Rusby (409)	P	HM	WD	HE	Tm
macrocarpa Benth (5863)	A	HM	WD	HE	Ts
valerii (Standl.) C. M. Taylor (548)	M	HM	WD	HE	Tm
Coussarea					
austin-smithii Standl. (3474)	M	MO	BD	HE	Ts
caroliana Standl. (1406)	PA	MO	BD	HE	Ts
chiriquiensis (Dwyer) C. M. Taylor (8271)	M	MO	BD	HE	Ts
impetiolaris Donn. Sm. (5449)	A	MO	BD	HE	Ts
Didymaea					
alsinoides (Schltdl. & Cham.) Standl. (Dryer 881)	M	IN	BD	HE	H
Elaeagia					
auriculata Hemsl. (232)	MA	BE	WD	HE	Tm
uxpanapensis D. Lorence (7088)	A	BE	WD	HE	Tl
Exostema					
mexicanum A. Gray (Bello 93)	P	HM	WD	HE	Tm
Faramea					
capulifolia Dwyer (6235)	M	IN	BD	HE	Ts
multiflora A. Rich. (3574)	MA	BF	BD	HE	S
occidentalis (L.) A. Rich. (3033)	MA	MO	BD	HE	Tm
ovalis Standl. (Bello 1755)	M	MO	BD	HE	Tm
suerrensis (Donn. Sm.) Donn. Sm. (6651)	A	BF	BD	HE	Ts
Gonzalagunia					
bracteosa (Donn. Sm.) B. L. Rob. (11149)	A	BE	BD	HE	S
ovatifolia (Donn. Sm.) B. L. Rob. (9408)	A	IN	BD	HE	S
panamensis (Cav.) K. Schum. (11334)	P	IN	BD	HE	S
rosea Standl. (754)	PMA	IN	BD	HE	S
stenostachya (Standl.) W. C. Burger (10822)	A	IN	BD	HE	S
Guettarda					
crispiflora Vahl (7338)	A	MO	BD	HE	Tm
foliacea Standl. (Bello 946)	A	MO	BD	HE	Tm
macrosperma Donn. Sm. (1632)	PA	MO	BD	HE	Tm
poasana Standl. (353)	MA	HM	BD	HE	Tm
tournefortiopsis Standl. (4392)	M	MO	BD	HE	Tm
turrialbana N. Zamora & Poveda (11245)	A	HM	BD	HE	Tl
Hamelia					
axillaris Sw. (11331)	PA	BD	BD	HE	S
patens Jacq. (9999)	PM	BD	BD	HE	Ts
Hillia					
allenii C. M. Taylor (2081)	PM	HM	WD	HE	E
loranthoides Standl. (8393)	PA	HM	WD	HE	E

Dicotyledons	Zone[a]	Poll[b]	Seed[c]	Sex[d]	Habit[e]
macrophylla Standl. (8464)	A	HM	WD	HE	E
maxonii Standl. (7083)	M	HM	WD	HE	E
palmana Standl. (10145)	PMA	HM	WD	HE	E
panamensis Standl. (Bello 2782)	M	HM	WD	HE	E
triflora (Oerst.) C. M. Taylor (1158)	MA	HM	WD	HE	E
Hoffmannia					
arborescens Donn. Sm. (Bello 1620)	A	BE	BD	HE	S
areolata Standl. (7130)	M	BE	BD	HE	S
bullata L. O. Williams (8417)	PA	BE	BD	HE	S
congesta (Oerst.) Dwyer (851)	MA	BE	BD	HE	S
dotae Standl. (9298)	MA	BE	BD	HE	S
hamelioides Standl. (Bello 1099)	A	BE	BD	HE	S
inamoena Standl. (4748)	A	BE	BD	HE	S
laxa Standl. (681)	M	BE	BD	HE	S
leucocarpa Standl. (10545)	MA	BE	BD	HE	S
liesneriana L. O. Williams (Bello 153)	A	IN	BD	HE	H
longipetiolata Pol. (10908)	MA	BE	BD	HE	S
pallidiflora Standl. (8049)	A	BE	BD	HE	S
psychotriifolia (Benth.) Griseb. (6833)	MA	BE	BD	HE	S
subauriculata Standl. (985)	MA	BE	BD	HE	S
valerii Standl. (10833)	A	BE	BD	HE	S
Ladenbergia					
brenesii Standl. (Bello 2144)	MA	HM	WD	HE	Tm
valerii Standl. (501)	MA	HM	WD	HE	Tm
Manettia					
flexilis Brandegee (Bello 548)	M	IN	WD	HE	V
reclinata L. (6000)	PA	BD,BF	WD	HE	V
Mitracarpus					
hirtus (L.) DC. (10323)	P	IN	WD,GR	HE	H
Nertera					
granadensis (Mutis ex L. f.) Druce (483)	M	IN	BD	HE	H
Palicourea					
adusta Standl. (4598)	M	BE	BD	HE	S
albocaerulea C. M. Taylor (7372)	M	BE	BD	HE	Ts
garciae Standl. (Bello 184)	M	BE	BD	HE	Ts
gomezii C. M. Taylor (10552)	A	IN	BD	HE	S
lasiorrhachis Oerst. (3329)	M	BE	BD	HE	S
macrocalyx Standl. (9795)	M	BE	BD	HE	S
montivaga Standl. (485)	M	BE	BD	HE	Ts
padifolia (Roem. & Schult.) C. M. Taylor & Lorence (5229)	M	BD,BF	BD	HE	Ts
standleyana C. M. Taylor (484)	M	BE	BD	HE	S
tilaranensis C. M. Taylor (9821)	M	BE	BD	HE	Ts
Pentagonia					
costaricensis (Standl.) W. C. Burger & C. M. Taylor (7659)	A	HM,BD?	AM	HE	Tm
donnell-smithii (Standl.) Standl. (7659)	A	BD	AM	HE	Tm
Posoqueria					
coriacea M. Martens & Galeotti (7037)	A	HM	AM	HE	Tm
latifolia (Rudge) Roem. & Schult. (197)	MA	HM	AM	HE	Tm
Psychotria					
aggregata Standl. (481)	M	BE	BD	HE	S
alfaroana Standl. (3233)	A	BE	BD	HE	S
angustiflora K. Krause (Bello 602)	A	BE	BD	HE	S
aubletiana Steyerm. (1665)	M	BE	BD	HE	S
burgeri C. M. Taylor (9778)	M	BE	BD	HE	S
capacifolia Dwyer (2839)	MA	BE	BD	HE	H
chiriquiensis (Standl.) C. M. Taylor (4614)	MA	BE	BD	HE	S
correae (Dwyer & M. V. Hayden) & C. M. Taylor (7664)	A	BE	BD	HE	S
deflexa DC. (11333)	P	BE	BD	HE	S
dukei Dwyer (2230)	M	BE	BD	HE	S
elata (Sw.) Hammel (726)	MA	BE	BD	HE	Ts
eurycarpa Standl. (333)	MA	MO,HM	BD	HE	Ts

Dicotyledons	Zone[a]	Poll[b]	Seed[c]	Sex[d]	Habit[e]
goldmanii Standl. (9138)	MA	BE	BD	HE	S
graciliflora Benth. (3240)	MA	SB	BD	HE	S
grandis Sw. (7574)	MA	BE	BD	HE	S
guadalupensis R. A. Howard (1964)	MA	BE	BD	HE	E
guapilensis (Standl.) Hammel (Bello 486)	A	BE	BD	HE	S
hazenii (Standl.) (9804)	MA	BE	BD	HE	S
horizontalis Sw. (8855)	M	BE	BD	HE	S
jimenezii Standl. (4658)	M	BE	BD	HE	S
macrophylla Ruiz & Pav. (798)	PMA	BE	BD	HE	H
maxonii Standl. (10010)	M	BE	BD	HE	E
monteverdensis Dwyer & C. W. Ham. (470)	M	BE	BD	HE	Ts
neillii C. W. Ham & Dwyer (Bello 2171)	A	IN	BD	HE	S
orosiana Standl. (10550)	MA	BE	BD	HE	S
panamensis Standl. (6672)	A	BE	BD	HE	Ts
aff. *panamensis* (10590)	M	BE	BD	HE	S
parvifolia Benth. (2273)	M	BE	BD	HE	S
pilosa Ruiz & Pav. (1907)	M	BE	BD	HE	S
pithecobia Standl. ((10389)	M	BE	BD	HE	E
pittieri Standl. 6774)	A	IN	BD	HE	S
polyphlebia Donn. Sm. (6475)	A	BE	BD	HE	H
pubescens Sw. (2254)	MA	BE	BD	HE	S
quinqueradiata Pol. (8446)	MA	BE	BD	HE	S
sarapiquensis Standl. (9401)	MA	BE	BD	HE	Ts
solitudinum Standl. (5901)	A	BE	BD	HE	S
steyermarkii Standl. (664)	M	BE	BD	HE	S
stockwellii C. W. Ham. (6622)	M	BE	BD	HE	S
sylvivaga Standl. (5192)	M	BE	BD	HE	S
uliginosa Sw. (1093)	M	BE	BD	HE	H
valeriana Standl. (156)	MA	BE	BD	HE	S
Randia					
aculeata L. (Bello 2240)	A	HM	AM,BD	DI	S
armata (Sw.) DC. (5262)	A	HM	AM,BD	DI	Ts
brenesii Standl. (565)	MA	HM	AM,BD	DI	Ts
calycosa Standl. (590)	P	HM	AM,BD	DI	S
grandifolia (Donn. Sm.) Standl. (11257)	A	HM	AM,BD	DI	Ts
matudae Lorence & Dwyer (6704)	MA	HM	AM,BD	DI	Tl
monantha Benth.	PM	HM	AM,BD	DI	Ts
retroflexa Lorence & M. Nee, cf. (4823)	A	HM	AM,BD	DI	L
sp. A (9753)	M	HM	AM,BD	DI	Tm
Raritebe					
palicoureoides Wernham (Bello 1025)	A	IN	BD	HE	S
Richardia					
scabra L. (10279)	PM	BE	GR	HE	H
Rondeletia					
amonea (Planch.) Hemsl. (8489)	M	FLY	WD	HE	Ts
aspera Standl. (6513)	PM	MO	WD	HE	Ts
brenesii Standl. (6798)	PMA	MO	WD	HE	Ts
buddleioides Benth. (2348)	MA	MO	WD	HE	Ts
chaconii Lorence (Bello 1080)	A	MO	WD	HE	S
monteverdensis Lorence (523)	M	MO	WD	HE	Ts
tayloriae Lorence (10549)	A	MO	WD	HE	Ts
torresii Standl. (7030)	MA	MO	WD	HE	Ts
Rudgea					
monofructus Gómez-Laur. & Dwyer (7415)	A	IN	BD	HE	Ts
reducticalyx Dwyer (7837)	A	IN	BD	HE	Ts
Sabicea					
panamensis Wernham (7466)	A	IN	BD	HE	V
villosa Roem. & Schult. (11169)	A	IN	BD	HE	V
Schradera					
costaricensis Dwyer (8077)	A	IN	BD	HE	E
Sommera					
donnell-smithii Standl. (329)	PMA	BE	BD	HE	Ts

Dicotyledons	Zone[a]	Poll[b]	Seed[c]	Sex[d]	Habit[e]
Spermacoce					
assurgens Ruiz & Pav. (375)	PMA	IN	GR	HE	H
latifolia Aubl. (10195)	P	IN	GR	HE	H
ovalifolia (M. Martens & Galeotti) Hemsl. (10895)	PM	IN	GR	HE	H
Rutaceae					
Amyris					
balsamifera L. (2979)	P	IN	BD	HE?	Ts
brenesii Standl. (Bello 5120)	A	IN	BD	HE?	Ts
Casimiroa					
edulis La Lalave & Lex. (508)	M	BE	AM	DI	Tl
Decazyx					
macrophyllus Pittier & S. F. Blake (7449)	A	BE	EX?	DI	Tm
Galipea					
dasysperma Gómez-Laur. & Q. Jiménez (11244)	A	HM	EX?	HE	Ts
Peltostigma					
guatemalense (Standl. & Steyerm.) Gereau (9227)	MA	IN	EX?	HE?	Ts
Pilocarpus					
racemosus Vahl (7431)	A	IN	EX	HE?	Ts
Stauranthus					
perforatus Liebm. (10421)	M	BE	BD	DI	Tm
Taxosiphon					
lindenii Baill. (Bello 1044)	A	IN	EX?	HE	S
Zanthoxylum					
fagara (L.) Sarg. (11488) (ex *insulare*)	PM	IN	BD	DI	Tm
juniperinum Poepp. (10934) (ex *procerum*)	PMA	IN	BD	DI	Tm
melanostictum Schltdl. (11189)	M	IN	BD	DI	Tm
monophyllum (Lam.) P. Wilson (10729)	PM	IN	BD	DI	Tm
rhoifolium Lam. (Bello 4197)	P	IN	BD	DI	Tm
setulosum P. Wilson (9982)	P	IN	BD	DI	Tl
Sabiaceae					
Meliosma					
brenesii Standl. (6367)	A	IN	AM	HE	Tm
donnell-smithii Urb. (Bello 1053)	A	BE	AM	HE	Tm
glabrata (Liebm.) Urb. (1886)	MA	IN	AM	HE	Tm
idiopoda S. F. Blake (267)	PMA	IN	BD	HE	Tm
subcordata Standl. (8496)	M	IN	AM	HE	Tm
vernicosa (Liebm.) Griseb. (8949)	MA	IN	AM	HE	Tl
Sapindaceae					
Allophylus					
occidentalis (Sw.) Radlk. (Bello 1503)	P	IN	BD	DI	Tm
psilospermus Radlk. (9763)	A	IN	BD	DI	Tm
Cardiospermum					
grandiflorum Sw. (1219)	P	IN	WD	HE	L
microcarpum Kunth (10448)	P	IN	WD	HE	L
Cupania					
glabra Sw. (7094)	M	IN	BD	DI	Tm
guatemalensis (Turcz.) Radlk. (1221)	PA	SB	BD	DI	Tm
latifolia Kunth (9873)	M	IN	BD	DI	Tl
macrophylla A. Rich. (9066)	MA	IN	BD	DI	Tm
sp. A (6980)	A	IN	BD	DI	Tm
Dilodendron					
costaricense (Radlk.) A. H. Gentry & Steyerm. (10187)	P	IN	WD?	DI?	Tl
Exothea					
paniculata (Juss.) Radlk. (3706)	PM	BE	BD	DI	Tl
Matayba					
oppositifolia (A. Rich.) Britton (Bello 694)	M	BE	BD	DI	Tl
Paullinia					
austin-smithii Standl. (10619)	M	IN	BD	HE	L
brenesii Croat (Bello 1106)	P	IN	BD	HE	L
costaricensis Radlk. (2208)	M	IN	BD	HE	L
cururu L. (7264)	P	IN	BD	HE	L
faginea (Triana & Planch.) Radlk. (9302)	M	IN	BD	HE	L
fuscescens Kunth (8026)	M	IN	BD	HE	L

Dicotyledons	Zone[a]	Poll[b]	Seed[c]	Sex[d]	Habit[e]
grandifolia Benth. ex Radlk. (Bello 142)	A	IN	BD	HE	L
macrocarpa Radlk. (10141)	MA	IN	BD	HE	L
pterocarpa Triana & Planch. (854)	A	IN	BD	HE	L
trisulca Radlk. (Bello 307)	A	IN	BD	HE	L
Serjania					
paniculata Kunth (7893)	MA	IN	WD	HE	L
racemosa K. Schum. (6767)	MA	IN	WD	HE	L
rufisepala Radlk. (11066)	PM	IN	WI	HE	L
Thouinidium					
decandrum (Humb. & Bonpl.) Radlk. (7215)	P	IN	WD	DI?	Tl
Sapotaceae					
Chrysophyllum					
brenesii Cronquist (2902)	P	IN	BD	HE	Tl
hirsutum Cronquist (4394)	A	IN	BD	HE	Tm
Manilkara					
chicle (Pittier) Gilly (9936)	P	BT	BD	HE	Tl
Pouteria					
austin-smithii (Standl.) Cronq. (Bello 160)	A	IN	BD?	HE	Tl
caimito (Ruiz & Pav.) Radlk., aff. (4428)	A	IN	AM?	HE	Tl
congestifolia Pilz (Bello 1300)	A	IN	AM	HE	Tl
exfoliata T. D. Penn. (7278)	M	IN	AM	HE	Tl
fossicola Cronquist, cf. (7497)	MA	MO	AM	HE	Tl
glomerata (Miq.) Radlk. (7427)	A	IN	AM	HE	Tl
juruana K. Krause (11164)	A	IN	AM	HE	Tl
reticulata (Engl.) Eyma (9961)	MA	IN	BD	HE	Tl
Sideroxylon					
capiri (A. DC.) Pittier (6820)	P	IN	BD	HE	Tl
persimile (Hemsl.) T. D. Penn. (Bello 698)	P	IN	BD	HE	Tm
stenospermum Standl.) T. D. Penn. (9277)	M	BE	BD	HE	Tl
Scrophulariaceae					
Asarina (= *Lophospermum*)					
erubescens (D. Don.) Penn. (Kaptur 181)	M				V
Bacopa					
salzmannii (Benth.) Wettst. ex Edwall (9429)	A	IN	WD,WT	HE	H
Buchnera					
pusilla Kunth (10186)	PM	IN	GR	HE	H
Castilleja					
arvensis Schltdl. & Cham. (1041)	PM	IN	GR	HE	H
Gibsoniothamnus					
alatus A. H. Gentry (7657)	A	BD	BD	HE	E
epiphyticus (Standl.) L. O. Williams (9881)	PA	BD	BD	HE	E
pterocalyx A. H. Gentry (4789)	A	BD	BD	HE	E
Lamourouxia					
viscosa Kunth (9580)	P	BD	WD,GR	HE	S
Leucocarpus					
perfoliatus (Kunth) Benth. (6525)	A	IN	BD	HE	H
Russelia					
sarmentosa Jacq. (1213)	PM	BF,BD	WD,GR	HE	S
Schlegelia					
brachyantha Griseb. (4025)	M	BE	BD	HE	L
fuscata A. H. Gentry (859)	MA	BE	BD	HE	L
nicaraguensis Standl. (5710)	A	BE	AM?	HE	L
parviflora (Oerst.) Monach. (4139)	M	BE	BD	HE	L
Scoparia					
dulcis L. (10297)	PM	IN	WD,GR	HE	H
Stemodia					
peduncularis Benth. (9015)	M	IN	WD,GR	HE	H
Veronica					
polita R. E. Fr. (8541)	M	IN	WD,GR	HE	H
Simaroubaceae					
Picramnia					
antidesma Sw. (941)	P	IN	BD	DI	Ts
teapensis Tul. (6832)	M	IN	BD	DI	Ts

Dicotyledons	Zone[a]	Poll[b]	Seed[c]	Sex[d]	Habit[e]
sp. A (9242)	M	IN	BD	DI	Ts
sp. B (246)	M	IN	BD	DI	Ts
sp. C (2713)	P	IN	BD	DI	Ts
Picrasma					
excelsa (Sw.) Planch. (9001)	M	IN	BD	DI	Tl
Solanaceae					
Acnistus					
arborescens (L.) Schltdl. (462)	PM	IN	BD,BT	HE	Tm
Brachistus					
stramoniifolius (Kunth) Miers (10575)	M	BE	BD	HE	S
Browallia					
americana L. (8730)	M	IN	GR,WD	HE	H
Brugmansia					
*candida Pers. (Grayum 9852)	M				Ts
Capsicum					
annuum L. (7977)	PM	BE	BD	HE	S
rhomboidea (Dunal) Kuntze (2260)	M	BE	BD	HE	S
Cestrum					
fragile Francey (1045)	M	MO	BD	HE	Ts
irazuense Kuntze (11468)	M	MO	BD	HE	Ts
lanatum M. Martens & Galeotti (Bello 825)	PM	MO	BD	HE	Ts
megalophyllum Dunal (974)	MA	MO	BD	HE	Ts
racemosum Ruiz & Pav. (1151)	MA	MO	BD	HE	Ts
rugulosum Francey, cf. (8504)	MA	MO	BD	HE	Ts
sp. A (11086)	MA	MO	BD	HE	S
sp. B (589)	P	MO	BD	HE	S
sp. C (10584)	PMA	MO	BD	HE	Ts
Cuatresia					
exiguiflora (D'Arcy) Hunz. (9300)	M	BE	BT	HE	Ts
riparia (Kunth) Hunz. (Zuchowski 346)	PMA	BE	BT	HE	Ts
Cyphomandra					
hartwegii (Miers) Dunal (9233)	A	LB	AM	HE	Ts
Jaltomata					
procumbens (Cav.) J. L. Gentry (1317)	PMA	BE	BD	HE	H
sp. A	M	BE	BD	HE	E
Juanulloa					
mexicana (Schltdl.) Miers (Bello 17)	P	BD?	BD?	HE	E
Lycianthes					
amatitlanensis (J. M. Coult. & Donn. Sm.) Bitter (1068)	MA	BE	BD	HE	S
escuintlensis (J. M. Coult.) D'Arcy (841)	PA	BE	BD	HE	S
furcatistellata Bitter (11035)	M	BE	BD	HE	S
heteroclita (Sendtn.) Bitter (7585)	A	BE	BD	HE	S
multiflora Bitter (705)	PMA	BE	BD	HE	L
sanctaeclarae (Greenm.) D'Arcy (1883)	A	LB	BD	HE	E
synanthera (Sendtn.) Bitter (136)	M	BE	BD	HE	E
Lycopersicon					
*esculentum Mill. (10121)	M				H
Merinthopodium					
neuranthum (Hemsl.) Donn. Sm. (9533)	MA	BT	AM	HE	E
Nicandra					
physalodes (L.) Gaertn. (9079)	M	HM,BT?	AM	HE	E
Physalis					
cordata Mill. (420)	M	BE	BD,TM	HE	H
nicandroides Schltdl. (Dryer 863)	M	BE	BD,TM	HE	H
pubescens L. (10433)	P	BE	BD,TM	HE	H
Schultesianthus					
leucanthus (Donn. Sm.) Hunz. (11053)	M	HM	AM	HE	E
megalandrus (Dunal) Hunz. (6722)	MA	BE	BD	HE	E
venosus (Standl. C. V. Morton) S. Knapp (9544)	M	HM	BT,BD	HE	E
Solandra					
grandiflora Sw. (Bello 429)	PM	HM	AM	HE	L
Solanum					
accrescens Standl. & C. V. Morton (653)	M	BE	BT,BD	HE	S
acerifolium Dunal (9307)	MA	BE	BT?	HE	H

Dicotyledons	Zone[a]	Poll[b]	Seed[c]	Sex[d]	Habit[e]
americanum Mill. (11198)	MA	BE	BD	HE	S
aphyodendran S. Knapp (652)	PMA	BE	BT	HE	Ts
arboreum Humb. & Bonpl. ex Dunal (3928)	MA	BE	BT	HE	S
argenteum Dunal ex Poir. (5834)	MA	BE	BD,BT	HE	Ts
brenesii Standl. (10694)	PM	BE	BT	HE	Ts
canense Rydb. (9672)	PM	BE	BD	HE	S
*capsicoides All. (1162)	M				S
caripense Humb. & Bonpl. ex Dunal (9697)	M	BE	TM	HE	S
chrysotrichum Schltdl. (10253)	MA	BE	BT,BD	HE	Ts
cordovense Sessé & Mociño (1080)	M	BE	BD	HE	Ts
evolvulifolium Greenm. (8087)	A	BE	BD	HE	V
granelianum D'Arcy (1644)	PA	BE	BD?	HE	L
hartwegii Benth. (12573)	P	BE	BD	HE	S
jamaicense Mill. (Bello 1638)	A	BE	BD	HE	S
lanceifolium Jacq. (904)	PM	BE	BD	HE	L
lepidotum Humb. & Bompl. ex Dunal (Bello 1824)	A	BE	BD	HE	S
macrotonum Pittier (10051)	MA	BE	BD	HE	S
nigrescens M. Martens & Galeotti (Zuchowski 136)	M	BE	BD	HE	S
oxycarpum Schiede (8029) (=*longicarpum* Schiede)	M	BE	TM	HE	H
pastillum S. Knapp (9260)	M	BE	BT	HE	S
pensile Ruiz & Pav. (7479)	M	BE	BD	HE	L
pertenue Standl. & C. V. Morton (9301)	M	BE	BT	HE	S
phaseoloides Pol. (7300)	M	BE	TM	HE	S
*quitoense Lam. (10404)	MA				S
ramonense C. V. Morton & Standl. (11884)	M	BE	BT	HE	S
rovirosanum Donn. Sm. (744)	PMA	BE	BT	HE	Ts
rudepannum Dunal (821)	PMA	BE	BT,BD	HE	Ts
rugosum Dunal (10834)	A	BE	BT	HE	Ts
siparunoides Ewan (1760)	MA	BE	BD	HE	L
trizygum Bitter (5138)	MA	BE	TM,BT	HE	H
tuerckheimii Greenm. (9263)	M	BE	BT	HE	S
umbellatum Mill. (4252)	M	BE	BT	HE	Ts
wendlandii Hook. f. (7234)	MA	BE	AM	DI	L
Witheringia					
asterotrichia (Standl.) Hunz., aff. (Bello 865)	A	BE	BD	HE	S
coccoloboides (Dammer) Hunz. (3413)	M	BE	BD	HE	S
correana D'Arcy (7358)	A	BE	BD	HE	S
cuneata (Standl.) Hunz. (6896)	PM	BE	BD	HE	S
macrantha (Standl. & Morton) Hunz. (Bello 2010)	A	LB	BD	HE	H
maculata (C. V. Morton & Standl.) Hunz. (7280)	MA	BE	BD	HE	H
meiantha (Donn. Sm.) Hunz. (Bello 4607)	MA	BE	BD	HE	S
solanacea L'Hér. (Fuentes 28)	PMA	BE	BD	HE	S
Staphyleaceae					
Turpinia					
occidentalis (Sw.) G. Don (4475)	MA	BE	BD	DI	Tl
sp. A	M	BE	BD	DI	Tm
Sterculiaceae					
Guazuma					
ulmifolia Lam. (9662)	P	IN	TM	HE	Tm
Melochia					
lupulina Sw. (10511)	P	IN	GR	HE	S
Theobroma					
mammosum Cuatrec. & Jorge León (Bello 1290)	A	IN	AM	HE	Tm
simiarum Donn. Sm. (Bello 2802)	A	IN	AM	HE	Tm
Styracaceae					
Styrax					
argenteus C. Presl (11381)	PM	BE	BD	HE	Tl
conterminus Donn. Sm. (3173)	M	BE	BD	HE	Tm
glabrescens Benth. (7353)	PM	BE	BD	HE	Tm
Symplocaceae					
Symplocos					
bradei Brandegee (Fuentes 581)	PM	BE	BD	HE	Tm
brenesii Standl. (8918)	M	BE	BD	HE	Tl

Dicotyledons	Zone[a]	Poll[b]	Seed[c]	Sex[d]	Habit[e]
chiriquensis Pittier (Bello 570)	M	BE	BD	HE	Tl
costaricana Hemsl. (9278)	MA	BE	BD	HE	Tl
limoncillo Humb. & Bonpl. (8722)	M	BE	BD	HE	Tl
povedae Almeda (10032)	M	BD	BD	HE	Ts
tribracteolata Almeda (1117)	M	BE	BD	HE	Tl
sp A. (Bello 1874)	A	BE	BD	HE	Tl
Theaceae					
Cleyera					
theioides (Sw.) Choisy (345)	M	IN	BD	HE	Ts
Freziera					
candicans Tul. (9812)	M	BE	BD	DI	Tm
friedrichsthaliana (Szyszyl.) Kobuski (11074)	M	BE	BD	DI	Tm
Gordonia					
brandegeei H. Keng (7116)	M	BE	WD	HE	Tl
Symplococarpon					
purpusii (Brandegee) Kobuski (9285)	M	BE	BD	DI	Tl
Ternstroemia					
tepezapote Schltdl. & Cham. (9752)	M	BE	BD	HE	Tm
Theophrastaceae					
Clavija					
costaricana Pittier (Bello 1537)	A	IN	TM	DI	S
Deherainia					
sp. A (11453)	A	BT?	TM	DI?	Ts
Thymeliaceae					
Daphnopsis					
americana (Mill.) J. R. Johnst. (7414)	PM	IN	BD	DI	Tm
Ticodendraceae					
Ticodendron					
incognitum Gómez-Laur. & L. D. Gómez (Bello 447)	MA	WD	AM	DI	Tm
Tiliaceae					
Apeiba					
membranacea Spruce ex Benth. (Bello 786)	A	LB	AM	HE	Tl
tibourbou Aubl. (10744)	P	BE	AM	HE	Tm
Heliocarpus					
americanus L. (10877)	MA	IN	WD	DI	Tl
appendiculatus Turcz. (9747)	PM	IN	WD	DI	Tm
Luehea					
candida (DC.) Mart. (10300)	P	HM	WD	HE	Tm
speciosa Willd. (Bello 2953)	P	HM	WD	HE	Tm
Mortoniodendron					
anisophyllum (Standl.) Standl. & Steyerm. (8383)	A	BE	BD	HE	Tl
costaricense Standl. & L. O. Williams (7704)	PM	BE	BD	HE	Tm
guatemalense Standl. & Steyerm. (1598)	M	BE	BD	HE	Tm
Trichospermum					
grewiifolium (A. Rich.) Kosterm. (Bello 555)	A	BE	WD	DI	Tm
Triumfetta					
calderonii Standl. (8846)	P	BE	AM,BD	DI	Ts
semitriloba (Zuchowski 390)	M	BE	TM,BD	HE	S
Tovariaceae					
Toivaria					
pendula Ruiz & Pav. (794)	PMA	IN	BD	HE	S
Tropaeolaceae					
Tropaeolum					
emarginatum Turcz. (1239)	A	BD	WD?	HE	V
moritizianum Klotzsch (7142)	MA	BD	WD?	HE	V
Turneraceae					
Erblichia					
odorata Seem. (11329)	P	LB	WD	HE	Tm
Ulmaceae					
Ampelocera					
macrocarpa Forero & A. H. Gentry (Bello 891)	A	WD	BD	MO	Tm
Celtis					
iguanaea (Jacq.) Sarg. (1731)	PA	WD	BD	MO	L

Dicotyledons	Zone[a]	Poll[b]	Seed[c]	Sex[d]	Habit[e]
Trema					
micrantha (L.) Blume (170)	PMA	WD,IN?	BD	MO	Tm
Ulmus					
mexicana (Liebm.) Planch. (8259)	PM	WD	WD	MO	Tl
Urticaceae					
Boehmeria					
aspera Wedd. (11168)	A	WD	GR	MO	S
caudata Sw. (8461)	A	WD	GR	DI	S
ulmifolia Wedd. (Hammel 15171)	P	WD	GR	MO	S
Discocnide					
mexicana (Liebm.) Chew (Bello 828)	P	WD	GR?	DI?	Ts
Myriocarpa					
bifurca Liebm. (9750)	PM	WD	GR,WD	DI	Ts
cordifolia Liebm. (9805)	M	WD	GR,WD	DI	Ts
longipes Liebm. (1340)	PA	WD	GR,WD	MO	Ts
Phenax					
angustifolius (Kunth) Wedd. (Dryer 1631)	P	WD	GR	MO	S
hirtus (Sw.) Wedd. (Zuchowski 58)	M	WD	GR	MO	S
mexicanus Wedd. (9919)	PM	WD	GR	MO	S
rugosus (Poir.) Wedd. (Zuchowski 184)	M	WD	GR	MO	S
senneratii (Poir.) Wedd. (11176)	A	WD	GR	MO	S
Pilea					
acuminata Liebm. (Hammel 15165)	PMA	WD?	GR?	DI	H
angustifolia Killip (Hammel 15169)	PM	WD?	GR?	MO	H
auriculata Liebm. (Dryer 35)	M	WD?	GR?	DI	H
dauciodora (Ruiz & Pav.) Wedd. (Hammel 15118)	M	WD?	GR?	MO	H
gracilipes Killip (Hammel 15119)	M	WD?	GR?	MO	H
hyalina Frenzl (11293)	A	WD?	GR?	MO	H
imparifolia Wedd. (8427)	PA	WD?	GR?	DI	E
microphylla (L.) Liebm. (10892)	P	WD?	GR?	MO	H
parietaria (L.) Blume (10730)	PM	WD?	GR?	MO	H
pittieri Killip (Hammel 15167)	PM	WD?	GR?	MO	E
ptericlada Donn. Sm. (Dryer 90)	M	WD?	GR?	MO	E
pubescens Liebm. (11306)	A	WD?	GR?	MO	H
Urera					
baccifera (L.) Gaudich. (8447)	PA	WD	BD	DI	Ts
caracasana (Jacq.) Griseb. (Hammel 15173)	PMA	WD	BD	DI	Ts
corallina (Liebm.) Webb. (10889)	M	WD	BD	DI	S
eggersii Hieron. (9377)	A	WD	BD	DI	L
elata (Sw.) Griseb. (Hammel 15174)	MA	WD	BD	DI	Ts
sp. A (11279)	MA	WD	BD	MO	S
Valerianaceae					
Valeriana					
palmeri A. Gray (8841)	P	IN	WD	HE	H
scandens L. (9014)	M	IN	WD	HE	V
Verbenaceae					
Aegiphila					
anomala Pittier (11483)	P	IN	BD	HE?	Tm
cephalophora Standl. (Bello 1020)	A	IN	BD	HE?	L
costaricensis Moldenke (6958)	A	IN	BD	HE?	Ts
elata Sw. (Bello 743)	A	IN	BD	HE?	L
odontophylla Donn. Sm. (7304)	M	IN	BD	HE?	Ts
quararibeana Rueda (Bello 4880)	A	IN	BD	HE?	L
valerii Standl. (11215)	M	IN	BD	DI	Tm
Citharexylum					
caudatum L. (702)	M	IN	BD	DI	Tl
costaricensis Moldenke (6958)	A	IN	BD	DI	Tm
donnell-smithii Greenm. (11101)	MA	IN	BD	DI	Tl
Cornutia					
pyramidata L. (11479)	M	BE	BD	HE	Tm
Duranta					
*erecta L. (Dryer 1445)	M				Ts

Dicotyledons	Zone[a]	Poll[b]	Seed[c]	Sex[d]	Habit[e]
Lantana					
camara L. (10007)	PM	IN	BD	HE	S
costaricensis Hayek (1208)	PM	IN	BD	HE	S
hirta Graham (9916)	PM	IN	BD	HE	S
trifolia L. (11523)	P	IN	BD	HE	S
Lippia					
cardiostegia Benth. (9311)	M	IN	GR	HE	S
Petrea					
volubilis L. (6824)	P	IN	WD	HE	L
Stachytarpheta					
frantzii Pol. (9976)	P	IN,BD	WD,GR?	HE	S
Verbena					
litoralis Kunth (1137)	M	IN	GR,WD	HE	H
Vitex					
cooperi Standl. (Bello 1302)	A	BE	BD	HE	Tl
Violaceae					
Hybanthus					
costaricensis Melch. (Bello 47)	P	IN	EX	HE	S
guanacastensis Standl. (9234)	MA	IN	EX	HE	S
Viola					
stipularis Sw. (9140)	MA	BE	EX	HE	H
Viscaceae					
Dendrophthora					
haberi Kuijt (9956)	M	IN	BD	DI?	E-P
Phoradendron					
chrysocladon A. Gray (Bello 963)	MA	IN	BD	DI	E-P
corynarthron Eichler (Sargent 24)	M	IN	BD	DI	E-P
quadrangulare (Kunth) Krug & Urb. (9663)	P	IN	BD	DI	E-P
robaloense Rizzini (Sargent 26)	M	IN	BD	DI	E-P
robustissimum Eichler (9983)	PM	IN	BD	DI	E-P
tonduzii Ttrel. (9720)	P	IN	BD	DI	E-P
undulatum Eichler (9949)	M	IN	BD	DI	E-P
vernicosum Greenm. (9973)	P	IN	BD	DI	E-P
Vitaceae					
Cissus					
biformifolia Standl. (10136)	MA	IN	BD	HE	L
martiniana Woodson & Seibert (Bello 5213)	M	IN	BD	HE	L
microcarpa Vahl (10137)	A	IN	BD	HE	L
pseudosicyoides Croat? (4792)	A	IN	BD	HE	L
rhombifolia Vahl (8655)	PM	IN	BD	HE	L
verticillata (L.) Nicolson & C. E. Jarvis (11120)	PMA	IN	BD	HE	L
Vitis					
tiliifolia Humb. & Bonpl. (383)	M	IN	BD	HE	L
Vochysiaceae					
Vochysia					
guatemalensis Donn. Sm. (Bello 1095)	A	BE	WD	HE	Tl
Winteraceae					
Drimys					
granadensis L. f. (7382)	M	BE	BD	HE	Tm

Monocotyledons

Agavaceae					
Furcraea					
cabuya Trel. (9892)	PM	BT	GR	HE	H
Alstroemeriaceae					
Bomarea					
caldasii (Kunth) Asch. & Graebn. (9872)	MA	BD	BD	HE	V
edulis (Tussac) Herb. (9312)	P	BD	BD	HE	V
hirsuta (Kunth) Herb. (9871)	MA	BD	BD	HE	V
obovata Herb. (Bello 365)	A	BD	BD	HE	V

Monocotyledons	Zone[a]	Poll[b]	Seed[c]	Sex[d]	Habit[e]
Anthericaceae					
Echeandia					
leucantha Klotzsch (Bello 70)	P	BE	GR	HE	H
Hagenbachia					
panamensis (Standl.) Cruden (8372)	A	BE	GR	HE	H
Araceae					
Anthurium					
acutangulum Engl. (8303)	A	IN	BD	HE	E
austin-smithii Croat & R. A. Baker (8589)	PM	IN	BD	HE	E
bakeri Hook. f. (10868)	AM	IN	BD	HE	E
bradeanum Croat & Grayum (11154)	A	IN	BD	HE	E
brenesii Croat & R. A. Baker (8996)	M	IN	BD	HE	E
caperatum Croat & R. A. Baker (1751)	MA	IN	BD	HE	H
cubense Engl. (9661)	P	IN	BD	HE	E
cuspidatum Mast. (9463)	A	IN	BD	HE	E
davidsoniae Standl. (2228)	M	IN	BD	HE	H
durandii Engl. (9218)	A	IN	BD	HE	E
flexile Schott (10884)	MA	IN	BD	HE	V
friedrichsthalii Schott (8794)	M	IN	BD	HE	E
hoffmannii Schott (9344)	M	IN	BD	HE	E
interruptum Sodiro (7173)	A	IN	BD	HE	V
michelii Guillaumin (9186)	A	IN	BD	HE	E
microspadix Schott (9861)	MA	IN	BD	HE	E
monteverdense Croat & R. A. Baker (8617)	M	LB	BD	HE	E
obtusilobum Schott (9184)	MA	LB	BD	HE	E
obtusum (Engl.) Grayum (9494)	M	IN	BD	HE	E
panduriforme Schott (6650)	A	IN	BD	HE	E
pentaphyllum (Aubl.) Don (1885)	A	IN	BD	HE	V
pittieri Engl. (8588)	M	IN	BD	HE	E
protensum Schott (9043)	M	IN	BD	HE	E
ramonense Engl. ex K. Krause (10144)	PMA	IN	BD	HE	E
ranchoanum Engl. (10487)	PM	IN	BD	HE	E
salvinii Hemsl. (9217)	PMA	IN	BD	HE	E
scandens (Aubl.) Engl. (7683)	PMA	IN	BD	HE	E
tenerum Engl. (Bello 1040)	A	IN	BD	HE	E
testaceum Croat & R. A. Baker (7563)	MA	IN	BD	HE	E
tilaranense Standl. (7345)	MA	IN	BD	HE	E
upalaense Croat & R. A. Baker (4819)	A	IN	BD	HE	E
utleyorum Croat & R. A. Baker (9042)	M	IN	BD	HE	E
watermaliense hort. ex L. H. Bailey & Nash (9306)	M	IN	BD	HE	H
Chlorospatha					
croatiana Grayum (10403)	A	IN	BD?	MO	H
Dieffenbachia					
longivaginata Croat & Grayum, ined. (11175)	A	CO	BD	MO	H
oerstedii Schott (7191)	PA	CO	BD	MO	H
Monstera					
adansonii Schott (Bello 21)	P	CO	BD	HE	V
buseyi Croat & Grayum (9494)	A	CO	BD,AM	HE	V
dissecta (Schott) Croat & Grayum (6685)	M	CO	BD,AM	HE	V
luteynii Madison (Bello 1468)	A	CO	BD,AM	HE	V
molinae Grayum, ined. (4446)	A	CO	BD,AM	HE	V
oreophila Madison (8948)	M	CO	BD,AM	HE	V
standleyana G. S. Bunting (7955)	A	CO	BD,AM	HE	V
tenuis K. Koch (Bello 413)	M	CO	BD,AM	HE	V
Philodendron					
anisotomum Schott (9518)	MA	CO	BD,AM	MO	V
aurantiifolium Schott (Bello 2849)	MA	CO	BD,AM	MO	V
bakeri Croat & Grayum (6932)	A	CO	BD,AM	MO	V
brenesii Standl. (9827)	M	CO	BD,AM	MO	V
brunneicaule Croat & Grayum (Bello 369)	A	CO	BD,AM	MO	V
crassispathum Croat & Grayum (4584)	M	CO	BD,AM	MO	E

Monocotyledons	Zone[a]	Poll[b]	Seed[c]	Sex[d]	Habit[e]
cretosum Croat & Grayum (Bello 1070)	A	CO	BD,AM	MO	V
findens Croat & Grayum (Bello 2667)	A	CO	BD,AM	MO	V
jacquinii Schott (Bello 20)	P	CO	BD	MO	V
rhodoaxis G. S. Bunting (Bello 2398)	A	CO	BD,AM	MO	V
rothschuhianum (Engl.) Croat & Grayum (8409)	A	CO	BD,AM	MO	E
standleyi Grayum (7905)	A	CO	BD,AM	MO	V
sulcatum K. Krause (Bello 125)	PA	CO	BD,AM	MO	V
tenue K. Koch & Augustin (8241)	A	CO	BD,AM	MO	V
tripartitum (Jacq.) Schott (Bello 362)	A	CO	BD,AM	MO	V
verrucosum L. Mathieu ex Schott (8458)	A	CO	BD,AM	MO	V
wendlandii Scott (Grayum 8712)	A	CO	BD,AM	MO	E
wilburii Croat & Grayum (10069)	M	CO	BD,AM	MO	V
Pistia					
stratiotes L.	A	IN	BD	MO	H
Spathiphyllum					
atrovirens Schott (Bello 147)	PA	BE	BD	HE	H
laeve Engl. (9439)	A	BE	BD	HE	H
montanum (R. A. Baker) Grayum (11088)	PM	BE	BD	HE	H
Stenospermation					
angustifolium Hemsl. (9214)	PA	IN	BT?	HE	E
majus Grayum (11153)	A	IN	BT?	HE	E
marantifolium Hemsl. (8053)	A	IN	BT?	HE	E
robustum Engl. (7067)	A	IN	BT?	HE	E
sessile Engl. (7246)	M	IN	BT?	HE	E
spruceanum Schott (7168)	A	IN	BT?	HE	E
Syngonium					
hoffmannii Schott (8997)	M	CO	BT?	MO	V
podophyllum Schott (4587)	M	CO	BT?	MO	V
schottianum H. Wendl. ex Schott (6957)	A	CO	BT?	MO	V
standleyanum G. S. Busting (9472)	A	CO	BT?	MO	V
triphyllum Birdsey ex Croat (8349)	A	CO	BT?	MO	V
Xanthosoma					
mexicanum Liebm. (8527)	P	CO	BT	MO	H
wendlandii (Schott) Schott (9975)	PM	CO	BT	MO	H
undipes (K. Koch & C. D. Bouché) K. Koch (Dryer 1475)	MA	CO	BT	MO	H
Arecaceae					
Astrocaryum					
alatum H. F. Loomis (Ivey 254)	A	CO	TM	MO	Ts
Bactris					
dianeura Burret (Ivey 36)	M	CO	BD	MO	Ts
hondurensis Standl. (7344)	A	CO	BD	MO	Ts
Calyptrogyne					
brachystachys H. Wendl. ex Burret (Ivey 18)	M	BT?	BD	MO	S
ghiesbreghtiana (Linden & H. Wendl.) H. Wendl. (9814)	M	BT?	BD	MO	S
trichostachys Burret (Bello 141)	A	BT?	BD	MO	S
Chamaedorea					
allenii L. H. Bailey, cf. (6455)	A	WD	BD	DI	S
costaricana Oersted (5966)	PM	WD	BD	DI	S
dammeriana Burret (6688)	A	WD	BD	DI	S
deckeriana (Klotzsch) Hemsl. (Bello 1289)	A	WD	BD	DI	S
lucidifrons L. H. Bailey (5113)	A	WD	BD	DI	S
macrospadix Oerst. (9813)	M	WD	BD	DI	S
parvifolia Burret (9289)	M	WD	BD	DI	S
pinnatifrons (Jacq.) Oerst. (10017)	M	WD	BD	DI	S
pumila H. Wendl. ex Dammer (9341)	A	WD	BD	DI	S
robertii Hodel & N. W. Uhl (5456)	A	WD	BD	DI	S
scheryi L. H. Bailey (Bello 263)	A	WD	BD	DI	S
tepejilote Liebm. (8253)	M	WD	BD	DI	Ts
undulatifolia Hodel & N. H. Uhl (Bello 910)	M	WD	BD	DI	S
Cryosophila					
grayumii R. Evans (11199)	P	CO	BD	HE	Ts

Monocotyledons	Zone[a]	Poll[b]	Seed[c]	Sex[d]	Habit[e]
Euterpe					
precatoria Mart. (Ivey 24)	M	SB	BD	MO	Tm
Geonoma					
cuneata H. Wendl. ex Spruce (2396)	MA	Fly	BD	MO	S
edulis H. Wendl. ex Spruce (4097)	MA	SB	BD	MO	Ts
ferruginea H. Wendl. ex Spruce (7661)	A	SB	BD	MO	S
procumbens H. Wendl. ex Spruce (Bello 1565)	A	IN	BD	MO	S
Iriartea					
deltoidea Ruiz & Pav. (Ivey 242)	A	SB	TM	MO	Tl
Neonicholsonia					
watsonii Dammer (11452)	A	IN	BD	MO	S
Prestoea					
acuminata (Willd.) H. E. Moore (Ivey 265)	M	SB	BD	MO	Tm
decurrens (H. Wendl. ex Burret) H. E. Moore (9392)	A	SB	BD	MO	Tm
longepetiolata (Oerst.) H. E. Moore (Bello 2161)	MA	SB	BD	MO	S
Reinhardtia					
gracilis (H. Wendl.) Drude ex Dammer (Bello 2066)	A	IN	BD	MO	S
Synechanthus					
warscewiczianus H. Wendl. (10851)	A	IN	BD	MO	Ts
Bromeliaceae					
Aechmea					
mariae-reginae H. Wendl. (Fuentes 316)	MA	IN	BD	HE	E
pubescens Baker (Bello 654)	A	IN	BD	HE	E
Androlepis					
skinneri Brongn. ex Houllet (9169)	M	IN	BD	HE	E
Catopsis					
nitida (Hook.) Griseb. (9003)	MA	MO?	WD	DI	E
nutans (Sw.) Griseb. (9611)	PM	MO?	WD	DI	E
paniculata E. Morren (Grant 1862)	M	MO?	WD	DI	E
wangerinii Mez & Wercklé ex Mez (3145)	P	IN	BD	HE	E
Greigia					
sylvicola Standl. (10691)	M	IN	BD?	HE	H
Guzmania					
angustifolia (Baker) Wittm. (Bello 5214)	M	BD	WD	HE	E
blassii Rauh (9466)	A	BD	WD	HE	E
compacta Mez (Obando 227)	M	BD	WD	HE	E
coriostachya (Griseb.) Mez (8683)	MA	BD	WD	HE	E
desautelsii Read & L. B. Sm. (Bello 420)	A	BD	WD	HE	E
dissitiflora (André) L. B. Sm. (Bello 245)	A	BD	WD	HE	E
donnellsmithii Mez ex Donn. Sm. (Tisna 32)	MA	BD	WD	HE	E
glomerata Mez & Wercklé (9465)	A	BD	WD	HE	E
monostachia (L.) Rusby ex Mez (5008)	P	BD	WD	HE	E
nicaraguensis Mez & C. Baker (8993)	M	BD	WD	HE	E
obtusiloba L. B. Sm. (Bello 1154)	MA	BD	WD	HE	E
plicatifolia L. B. Sm. (Zuchowski 692)	MA	BD	WD	HE	E
polycephala Mez & Wercklé ex Mez (Bello 209)	A	BD	WD	HE	E
scandens H. Luther & W. J. Kress (10542)	A	BD	WD	HE	E
scherzeriana Mez (9470)	A	BD	WD	HE	E
sprucei (Andre) L. B. Sm. (Bello 1258)	A	BD	WD	HE	E
stenostachya L. B. Sm. (2270)	M	BD	WD	HE	E
subcorymbosa L. B. Sm. (9460)	A	BD	WD	HE	E
Racinaea					
adpressa (Andre) J. R. Grant (8990)	M	BD	WD	HE	E
Pitcairnia					
atrorubens (Beer) Baker (Bello 4066)	MA	BD	WD	HE	E
brittoniana Mez (8528)	M	BD	WD	HE	E
heterophylla (Lindl.) Beer (10482)	P	BD	WD	HE	H
kalbreyeri Baker (9807)	M	BD	WD	HE	E
maidifolia (C. Morren) Decne. (10484)	P	BD	WD	HE	H
valerii Standl. (8346)	A	BD	WD	HE	E
wendlandii Baker (Bello 2794)	A	BD	WD	HE	E
Tillandsia					
anceps Lodd. (9467)	A	BD	WD	HE	E
brachycaulos Schltdl. (Tisna 25)	P	BD	WD	HE	E

Monocotyledons	Zone[a]	Poll[b]	Seed[c]	Sex[d]	Habit[e]
bulbosa Hook. (10143)	A	BD	WD	HE	E
butzii Mez (10984)	M	BD	WD	HE	E
excelsa Griseb. (9007)	M	BD	WD	HE	E
fasciculata Sw. (Fuentes 663)	P	BD	WD	HE	E
insignis (Mez) L. B. Sm. & Pittendr. (9046)	MA	BD	WD	HE	E
juncea (Ruiz & Pav.) Poir. (9889)	PM	BD	WD	HE	E
leiboldiana Schltdl. (Bello 5391)	A	BD	WD	HE	E
monadelpha (E. Morren) Baker (Bello 1291)	A	BD	WD	HE	E
multicaulis Steud. (Dryer 1317)	M	BD	WD	HE	E
punctulata Schltdl. & Cham. (Lepiz 164)	M?	BD	WD	HE	E
schumanniana (Wittm.) Mez (Grant 1875)	M	BD	WD	HE	E
singularis Mez & Wercklé (Bello 2017)	A	BD	WD	HE	E
spiculosa Griseb. (Grant 1867)	M	BD	WD	HE	E
venusta Mez & Wercklé (6585)	A	BD	WD	HE	E
Vriesea					
apiculata L. B. Sm. (Bello 1255)	A	HM,BT?	WD	HE	E
bracteosa (Mez & Wercklé) L. B. Sm. & Pittendr.	M?	HM,BT?	WD	HE	E
burgeri L. B. Sm., cf. (8947)	M	HM,BT?	WD	HE	E
capitata (Mez & Wercklé) L. B. Sm. & Pittendr.	M?	HM,BT?	WD	HE	E
comata (Mez & Wercklé) L. B. Sm. (9017)	M	HM,BT?	WD	HE	E
gladioliflora (H. Wendl.) Antoine (Bello 5398)	A	BT	WD	HE	E
graminifolia Mez & Wercklé (10235)	A	HM,BT?	WD	HE	E
greenbergii Utley (Bello 5405)	MA	HM,BT?	WD	HE	E
hygrometrica (André) L. B. Sm. & Pittendr. (Dryer 318)	M	HM,BT?	WD	HE	E
incurva (Griseb.) Read (Tisna 4)	M	HM,BT?	WD	HE	E
latissima (Mez & Wercklé) L. B. Sm. & Pittendr. (Dryer 1324B)	MA	HM,BT?	WD	HE	E
monstrum (Mez) L. B. Sm. (Dryer 1495)	MA	HM,BT?	WD	HE	E
nephrolepis L. B. Sm. & Pittendr. (Dryer 1339)	M?	HM,BT?	WD	HE	E
notata L. B. Sm. & Pittendr. (Grant 1870)	MA	HM,BT?	WD	HE	E
pedicellata (Mez & Wercklé) L. B. Sm. & Pittendr. (Bello 185)	M	HM,BT?	WD	HE	E
stenophylla (Mez & Wercklé) L. B. Sm. & Pittendr. (Selby?)	M?	HM,BT?	WD	HE	E
subsecunda Wittm. (Grant 92–1869)	M	HM,BT?	WD	HE	E
tonduziana L. B. Sm. (Morales 2465)	M?	HM,BT?	WD	HE	E
umbrosa L. B. Sm. (Dryer 1389)	M?	HM,BT?	WD	HE	E
viridiflora (Regel) Wittm. ex Mez (Morales 2464)	M?	HM,BT?	WD	HE	E
vittata (Mez & Wercklé) L. B. Sm. & Pittendr. (Ingram)	M	HM,BT?	WD	HE	E
werckleana Mez (Grant 92–1865)	M	HM,BT?	WD	HE	E
Burmanniaceae					
Apteria					
aphylla (Nutt.) Barnhart (9378)	A	IN	GR?	HE	H
Burmannia					
kalbreyeri Oliv. (Dryer 1364A)	M	IN	WD?	HE	H
Gymnosiphon					
suaveolens (H. Karst.) Urb. (1092)	M	IN	WD,GR?	HE	H
Cannaceae					
Canna					
*glauca L. (10075)	P				H
*tuerckheimii Kränzl. (2734)	P				H
Commelinaceae					
Callisia					
monandra (Sw.) Schult. & Schult. f. (10432)	M	SB	GR?	HE	H
Commelina					
diffusa Burm. f. (10128)	PMA	SB	GR	HE	H
erecta L. (10348)	P	SB	GR	HE	H
texcocana Matuda (10903)	PM	SB	GR	HE	H
Dichorisandra					
amabilis J. R. Grant (10759)	M	SB	BD	HE	H
hexandra (Aubl.) Standl. (11675)	A	SB	BD	HE	V
Tinantia					
erecta (Jacq.) Schltdl. (7980)	PM	LB	BD?	HE	H
standleyi Steyerm. (Bello 1323)	M	LB	BD?	HE	H

Monocotyledons	Zone[a]	Poll[b]	Seed[c]	Sex[d]	Habit[e]
Tradescantia					
gracillima Standl. (10129)	M	SB	GR	HE	H
grantii D. Hunt, ined. (11291)	A	SB	GR	HE	H
poelliae D. Hunt (10115)	M	SB	GR	HE	H
zanonia (L.) Sw. (1088)	M	SB	GR	HE	H
*zebrina hort ex Bosse (10199)	M	H			
Tripogandra					
purpurascens (Schauer) Handlos (8797)	M	SB	GR	HE	H
serrulata (Vahl) Handlos (8796)	M	SB	GR	HE	H
Convallariaceae					
Maianthemum					
monteverdense LaFrankie (8792)	M	SB	BD	HE	E
Costaceae					
Costus					
barbatus Suess. (1383)	M	BD	BD	HE	H
curvibracteatus Maas (7110)	A	BD	BD	HE	H
glaucus Maas (Bello 366)	A	BD	BD	HE	H
malortieanus H. Wendl. (8223)	A	BD,LB	BD	HE	H
montanus Maas (10581)	M	BD	BD	HE	H
nitidus Maas (9458)	A	BD	BD	HE	H
pulverulentus C. Presl (3269)	A	BD	BD	HE	H
scaber Ruiz & Pav. (1697)	A	BD	BD	HE	H
wilsonii Maas (10798)	M	BD	BD	HE	H
Cyclanthaceae					
Asplundia					
euryspatha Harling (5120)	A	CO	BD	MO	E
microphylla (Oerst.) Harling (9020)	M	CO	BD	MO	V
sanctae-ritae Galeano & Bernal (4508)	M	CO	BD	MO	V
sanluisana Hammel, ined. (Hammel 13964)	P	CO	BD	MO	V
stenophylloides Hammel, ined. (Hammel 13870)	M?	CO	BD	MO	V
utilis (Oerst.) Harling (4863)	A	CO	BD	MO	V
vagans Harling (7496)	M	CO	BD,BT	MO	V
Carludovica					
drudei Mast. (Hammel 15067)	A	CO?	BD	MO	H
rotundifolia H. Wendl. ex Hook. f. (Dryer 1705)	A	CO?	BD	MO	H
Chorigyne					
ensiformis (Hook. f.) R. Erikss. (2411)	M	CO?	BD?	MO	E
Cyclanthus					
bipartitus Poit. (Bello 252)	PA	CO	ANT?	MO	H
Evodianthus					
funifer (Poit.) Lindm. (7420)	A	CO?	BD?	MO	V
Ludovia					
integrifolia (Woodson) Harling (Bello 2862)	A	CO?	BD	MO	V
Sphaeradenia					
acutitepala Harling (9346)	A	CO?	BD	MO	E
laucheana (Mast.) Harling (7086)	M	CO?	BD	MO	E
occidentalis R. Erikss (Bello 2163)	MA	CO?	BD	MO	E
Cyperaceae					
Carex					
donnell-smithii L. H. Bailey (9135)	PM	WD	GR	MO	H
jamesonii W. Boott (Bello 2187)	A	WD	GR	MO	H
polystachya Sw. ex Wahlenb. (9746)	PM	WD	GR	MO	H
standleyana Steyerm. (10888)	PM	WD	GR	MO	H
Cyperus					
hermaphroditus (Jacq.) Standl. (9606)	PM	WD	GR	HE	H
luzulae (L.) Retz. (10171)	PA	WD	GR	HE	H
simplex Kunth (Bello 1220)	A	WD	GR	HE	H
surinamensis Rottb. (9641)	M	WD	GR	HE	H
tenuis Sw. (9689)	P	WD	GR	HE	H
Eleocharis					
elegans (Kunth) Roem. & Schult. (10213)	A	WD	GR	HE	H
montana (Kunth) Roem. & Schult. (Bello 4571)	MA	WD	GR	HE	H

Monocotyledons	Zone[a]	Poll[b]	Seed[c]	Sex[d]	Habit[e]
retroflexa (Poir.) Urb. (9698)	MA	WD	GR	HE	H
schaffneri Boeck. (Bello 5113)	M	WD	GR	HE	H
sellowiana Kunth (11042)	M	WD	GR	HE	H
Fimbristylis					
dichotoma (L.) M. Vahl (10170)	PM	WD	GR	HE	H
littoralis Gaudich. (9643)	P	WD	GR	HE	H
Kyllinga					
brevifolia Rottb. (9706)	PM	WD	GR	MO	H
pumila Michx. (9645)	P	WD	GR	MO	H
Pycreus					
bipartitus (Torr.) C. B. Clarke (8596)	M	WD	GR	HE?	H
lanceolatus (Poir.) C. B. Clarke (9427)	A	WD	GR	HE?	H
niger (Ruiz & Pav.) Cufod. (9709)	M	WD	GR	HE?	H
Rhynchospora					
andresii Gómez-Laur. (Bello 2193)	A	WD	GR	MO	H
nervosa (Vahl) Boeck. (9592)	M	WD	GR	MO	H
polyphylla Vahl (5828)	A	WD	GR	MO	H
radicans (Schltdl. & Cham.) Pfeiff. (9384)	A	WD	GR	MO	H
ruiziana Boeck. (Bello 791)	M	WD	GR	MO	H
tuerckheimii C. B. Clarke ex Kük. (3073)	M	WD	GR	MO	H
vulcani Boeck. (Bello 792)	M	WD	GR	MO	H
watsonii (Britton) Davidse (9736)	M	WD	GR	MO	H
Scleria					
latifolia Sw. (Bello 1844)	A	WD	GR	MO	H
melaleuca Rchb. f. ex Schltdl. & Cham. (10840)	A	WD	GR	MO	H
secans (L.) Urb. (11157)	A	WD	GR	MO	H
Torulinium					
odoratum (L.) Hooper (9679)	PA	WD	GR	MO	H
Uncinia					
hamata (Sw.) Urb. (8738)	M	WD	TM	MO	H
Dioscoreaceae					
Dioscorea					
convolvulacea Schltdl. & Cham. (965)	MA	IN	WD	DI	L
cyanisticta Donn. Sm. (Bello 2169)	M	IN	WD	DI	L
matagalpensis Uline (10896)	P	IN	WD	DI	L
natalia Hammel, ined. (8675)	M	IN	WD	DI	L
polygonoides Humb. & Bonpl. ex Willd. (6511)	P	IN	WD	DI	L
racemosa (Klotzsch) Uline (7936)	A	IN	WD	DI	L
spiculiflora Hemsl. (Bello 1054)	A	IN	WD	DI	L
standleyi C. V. Morton (10257)	MA	IN	WD	DI	L
Haemodoraceae					
Xiphidium					
coeruleum Aubl. (801)	PA	SB	BD	HE	H
Heliconiaceae					
Heliconia					
atropurpurea G. S. Daniels & F. G. Stiles (Bello 1216)	A	BD	BD	HE	H
aurantiaca Ghiesbr. ex Lem. (8243)	A	BD	BD	HE	H
irrasa R. R. Sm. (11546)	A	BD	BD	HE	H
latispatha Benth. (809)	A	BD	BD	HE	H
mathiasiae G. S. Daniels & F. G. Stiles (9438)	PA	BD	BD	HE	H
monteverdensis G. S. Daniels & F. G. Stiles (4114)	MA	BD	BD	HE	H
reticulata (Griggs) H. J. P. Winkl. (9216)	A	BD	BD	HE	H
tortuosa Griggs (8520)	M	BD	BD	HE	H
trichocarpa G. S. Daniels & F. G. Stiles (5896A)	A	BD	BD	HE	H
vaginalis Benth. (1402)	P	BD	BD	HE	H
Hypoxidaceae					
Hypoxis					
decumbens L. (9576)	PM	BE	WD,GR?	HE	H
Iridaceae					
Sisyrinchium					
micranthum Cav. (8915)	MA	SB	GR?	HE	H

Monocotyledons	Zone[a]	Poll[b]	Seed[c]	Sex[d]	Habit[e]
Juncaceae					
Juncus					
effusus L. (3418)	M	WD	WD,GR	HE	H
Marantaceae					
Calathea					
brenesii Standl. (7786)	MA	LB	BD	HE	H
cleistantha Standl. (8369)	A	LB	BD	HE	H
crotalifera S. Watson (Zuchowski 433)	M	LB	BD	HE	H
foliosa Rowlee ex Woodson (5420)	A	LB	BD	HE	H
guzmanioides L. B. Sm. & Idrobo (Bello 1190)	A	LB	BD	HE	H
indecora Woodson (7932)	A	LB	BD	HE	H
lasiostachya Donn. Sm. (10823)	A	LB	BD	HE	H
leucostachys Hook. f. (Bello 1217)	A	LB	BD	HE	H
macrosepala K. Schum. (8631)	P	LB	BD	HE	H
marantifolia Standl. (9491)	M	LB	BD	HE	H
micans (L. Mathieu) Koern. (8423)	A	LB	BD	HE	H
Hylaeanthe					
hoffmannii (K. Schum.) A. M. E. Jonker & Jonker (7615)	A	LB	GR?	HE	H
Pleiostachya					
leiostachya (Donn. Sm.) Hammel (Hammel 15393)	M	LB	GR?	HE	H
Stromanthe					
guapilesensis (Donn. Sm.) H. A. Kenn. & Nicolson (7184)	A	LB	GR	HE	H
tonckat (Aubl.) Eichler (11272)	PMA	LB	GR	HE	H
Orchidaceae: See Appendix 3					
Poaceae					
Andropogon					
bicornis L. (9584)	M	WD	WD	HE	H
glomeratus (Walter) Britton, Stearns, & Poggenb. (9739)	M	WD	WD	HE	H
Arthraxon					
hispidus (Thunb.) Makino (9596)	M	WD	GR,WD	HE	H
Arthrostylidium					
merostachyoides R. W. Pohl (10026)	M	WD	GR,WD	HE	H
Arundinella					
berteroniana (Schult.) Hitchc. & Chase (11288)	A	WD	GR,WD	HE	H
deppeana Nees ex Steud. (9622)	P	WD	GR,WD	HE	H
Axonopus					
compressus (Sw.) P. Beauv. (9628)	P	WD	GR,WD	HE	H
fissifolius (Raddi) Kuhlm. (9708)	M	WD	GR,WD	HE	H
Chusquea					
liebmannii Fourn. (10780)	P	WD	GR,WD	HE	L
longifolia Swallen (10029)	MA	WD	GR,WD	HE	L
patens L. G. Clark (Pohl 13248)	M	WD	GR,WD	HE	L
pohlii L. G. Clark (10027)	M	WD	GR,WD	HE	L
scabra Soderstr. & Calderón (10008)	MA	WD	GR,WD	HE	L
Coix					
lacryma-jobi L. (9635)	PM	WD	GR,WD	HE	H
Cynodon					
dactylon (L.) Pers. (9175)	M	WD	GR,WD	HE	H
nlemfuensis Vanderyst (9586)	M	WD	GR,WD	HE	H
Digitaria					
abyssinica (Hochst. ex A. Rich.) Stapf (9598)	M	WD	GR,WD	HE	H
ciliaris (Retz.) Koeler (9678)	P	WD	GR,WD	HE	H
Eleusine					
indica (L.) Gaertn. (9657)	PM	WD	GR,WD	HE	H
Eragrostis					
ciliaris (L.) R. Br. (9690)	P	WD	GR,WD	HE	H
tenuifolia (A. Rich.) Hochst. ex Steudel (9724)	M	WD	GR,WD	HE	H
Gynerium					
sagittatum (Aubl.) P. Beauv. (Bello 314)	A	WD	GR,WD	HE	H
Hyparrhenia					
rufa (Nees) Stapf (9630)	PM	WD	GR,WD	HE	H

Monocotyledons	Zone[a]	Poll[b]	Seed[c]	Sex[d]	Habit[e]
Ichnanthus					
nemorosus (Sw.) Doell (9717)	M	WD	GR,WD	HE	H
pallens (Sw.) Munro ex Benth. (Bello 495)	M	WD	GR,WD	HE	H
tenuis (J. Presl) Hitchc. & Chase (10157)	P	WD	GR,WD	HE	H
Isachne					
arundinacea (Sw.) Griseb. (9695)	MA	WD	GR,WD	HE	H
Ischaemum					
rugosum Salisb. (9646)	P	WD	GR,WD	HE	H
timorense Kunth (10239)	A	WD	GR,WD	HE	H
Lasiacis					
nigra Davidse (9631)	PMA	WD	BD	HE	S
oaxacensis (Steud.) Hitchc. (9659)	PM	WD	BD	HE	H
procerrima (Hack.) Hitchc. (9654)	MA	WD	BD	HE	S
rhizophora (Fourn.) Hitchc. (9589)	M	WD	BD	HE	H
ruscifolia (Kunth) Hitchc. (9617)	M	WD	BD	HE	H
standleyi Hitchc. (9727)	M	WD	BD	HE	H
Leersia					
ligularis Trin. (10099)	PM	WD	GR,WD	HE	H
Lithachne					
pauciflora (Sw.) P. Beauv. (7637)	A	WD	GR,WD	HE	H
Melinis					
minutiflora P. Beauv. (8882)	PM	WD	GR,WD	HE	H
Muhlenbergia					
ciliata (Kunth) Trin. (10891)	M	WD	GR,WD	HE	H
lehmanniana Henrard (9660)	P	WD	GR,WD	HE	H
tenella (Kunth) Trin. (10893)	PM	WD	GR,WD	HE	H
Oplismenus					
burmannii (Retz.) P. Beauv. (9602)	PM	WD	GR,WD	HE	H
hirtellus (L.) P. Beauv. (9715)	PM	WD	GR,WD	HE	H
Panicum					
laxum Sw. (9640)	P	WD	GR,WD	HE	H
maximum Jacq. (9636)	P	WD	GR,WD	HE	H
polygonatum Schrad. (9729)	M	WD	GR,WD	HE	H
trichoides Sw. (9637)	P	WD	GR,WD	HE	H
Paspalum					
botterii (E. Fourn.) Chase, cf. (9600)	M	WD	GR,WD	HE	H
candidum (Humb. & Bonpl. ex Floeggé) Kunth (9725)	M	WD	GR,WD	HEH	
conjugatum Bergius (9604)	PM	WD	GR,WD	HE	H
convexum Humb. & Bonpl. ex Floeggé (9626)	PM	WD	GR,WD	HE	H
decumbens Sw. (2719)	A	WD	GR,WD	HE	H
nutans Lam. (Bello 4941)	M	WD	GR,WD	HE	H
paniculatum L. (9620)	P	WD	GR,WD	HE	H
saccharoides Nees ex Trin. (8206)	MA	WD	WD	HE	H
squamulatum E. Fourn. (9732)	M	WD	GR,WD	HE	H
Pennisetum					
clandestinum Hochst. ex Chiov. (Grayum 10192)	M	WD	GR,WD	HE	H
purpureum Schumach. (9595)	M	WD	GR,WD	HE	H
setosum (Sw.) Rich. (9658)	PA	WD	GR,WD	HE	H
Pereilema					
diandrum R. W. Pohl (10305)	P	WD	GR,WD	HE	H
Pharus					
lappulaceus Aubl. (11422)	P	WD	GR,WD	HE	H
parvifolius Nash (10883)	P	WD	GR,WD	HE	H
Poa					
annua L. (9704)	M	WD	GR,WD	HE	H
Pseudechinolaena					
polystachya (Kunth) Stapf (8679)	MA	WD	TM	HE	H
Rhipidocladum					
pittieri (Hack.) McClure (8279)	P	WD	GR,WD	HE	L
Setaria					
paniculifera (Steud.) E. Fourn. ex Hemsl. (6172)	A	WD	GR,WD	HE	H
parviflora (Poir.) Kerguélen (9623)	M	WD	GR,WD	HE	H
sphacelata (Schumach.) Stapf & C. E. Hubb. ex Chipp (10214)	MA	WD	GR,WD	HE	H

Monocotyledons	Zone[a]	Poll[b]	Seed[c]	Sex[d]	Habit[e]
Sporobolus					
indicus (L.) R. Br. (9587)	PM	WD	GR,WD	HE	H
Stenotaphrum					
secundatum (Walter) Kuntze (9614)	M	WD	GR	HE	H
Pontederiaceae					
*Eichornia					
crassipes (Mart.) Solms	MA	H			
Heteranthera					
reniformis Ruiz & Pav. (9649)	PA	BE	Water	HE	H
Smilacaceae					
Smilax					
chiriquensis C. V. Morton (9009)	M	IN	BD	DI	L
dominguensis Willd. (10804)	A	IN	BD	DI	L
engleriana F. W. Apt (5670)	A	IN	BD	DI	L
kunthii Killip & C. V. Morton (5578)	MA	IN	BD	DI	L
mollis Humb. & Bonpl. ex Willd. (10805)	M	IN	BD	DI	L
panamensis Morong (9067)	A	IN	BD	DI	L
spinosa Mill. (10797)	M	IN	BD	DI	L
standleyi Killip & C. V. Morton (1949)	A	IN	BD	DI	L
subpubescens A. DC. (11202)	M	IN	BD	DI	L
vanilliodora F. W. Apt (10806)	M	IN	BD	DI	L
velutina Killip & C. V. Morton (Grayum 5422)	M	IN	BD	DI	L
Triuridaceae					
Triuris					
sp. A (Lawton 1317)	M	IN?	BD?	HE?	H-Sap
Typhaceae					
Typha					
domingensis Pers., cf. (6579)	MA	WD	WD	HE	H
Zingiberaceae					
Hedychium					
*coronarium J. Konig (2885)	M	HM	BD	HE	H
Renealmia					
cernua (Sw.) J. F. Macbr. (8994)	M	BD	BD	HE	H
congesta Maas (Bello 1266)	A	BD	TM	HE	H
scaposa Maas (7609)	MA	BD	TM	HE	H

Gymnosperms

	Zone[a]	Poll[b]	Seed[c]	Sex[d]	Habit[e]
Cycadaceae					
Zamia					
skinneri Warsz. ex A. Dietr. (7817)	A	CO?	TM?	D	S
Podocarpaceae					
Podocarpus					
macrostachyus Parl. (8525)	M	WD	BD?	D	Tl
monteverdeensis de Laub. (9796)	M	WD	BD?	D	Tl

Polypodiophyta (ferns and fern allies)

	Zone[a]	Poll[b]	Seed[c]	Sex[d]	Habit[e]
Aspleniaceae					
Asplenium					
aethiopicum (Burm. f.) Bech. (Grayum 5424)	M				E?
auriculatum Sw. (Ivey 168)	A				E
auritum Sw. (8572)	M				E
cirrhatum Rich. ex Willd. (Ivey 208)	A				E
cristatum Lam. (Bigelow 23)	M				H
cuspidatum Lam. (7731)	MA				E
dissectum Sw. (Hennipman 6663)	M				E
formosum Willd. (9934)	P				E
gomezianum Lellinger (Obando 162)	MA				E
harpeodes Kunze (Bello 5195)	M				E,H
holophlebium Baker (Bello 5377)	A				E,V
laetum Sw. (Ivey 138)	A				H,R
maxonii Lellinger (Martinez 405)	M				E,V

Polypodiophyta	Zone[a]	Poll[b]	Seed[c]	Sex[d]	Habit[e]
pteropus Kaulf. (Bello 4101)	A				E
pululahuae Sodiro (9353)	A				E
riparium Liebm. (Moran 5832)	MA				H,R
rosenstockianum Brade (Rojas 1856)	MA				H
serra Langsd. & Fisch. (Bello 4500)	A				E
volubile N. Murak & R. C. Moran (Ivey 240)	A				E?
Blechnaceae					
Blechnum					
chiriquanum (Broadh.) C. Chr. (Grayum 10170)	M				H
divergens (Kunze) Mett. (10381)	M				H
ensiforme (Liebm.) C. Chr. (Martínez 475)	A				H,V
falciforme (Liebm.) C. Chr. (Bello 793)	M				H,E
fragile (Liebm.) C. V. Morton & Lellinger (Ingram 358)	MA				E,H
glandulosum Kaulf. ex Link (Azofeifa 116)	A				H
lherminieri (Bory) C. Chr. (Koptur 148)	MA				H
occidentale L. (8872)	PA				H
polypodioides Raddi (Azofeifa 118)	A				H
proliferum Rosenst. (Moran 5860)	MA				H
werckleanum (H. Christ) C. Chr. (Grayum 10177)	MA				E,H
Salpichlaena					
thalassica Grayum & R. C. Moran (5383)	M				L
volubilis (Kaulf.) J. Sm. (9395)	A				L
Cyatheaceae					
Alsophila					
cuspidata (Kunze) D. S. Conant (Bello 5013)	A				T
firma (Baker) D. S. Conant (Bello 5019)	A				T
amrayanum (Hook) D. S. Conant (Coto 14)	MA				T
polystichoides H. Christ (Bello 5066)	MA				T
Cnemidaria					
mutica (H. Christ) R. M. Tryon (10263)	M				H
Cyathea					
bicrenata Liebm. (Moran 5868)	MA				T
caracasana (Klotzsch) Domin (Grayum 10190)	MA				T
delgadii Sternb. (Coto 11)	A				T
divergens Kunze (Burger 9716)	M				T
fulva (M. Martens & Galeotti) Fée (Bello 4137)	M				T
gracilis Griseb. (Moran 5874)	M				S
nigripes (C. Chr.) Domin (Moran 5870)	MA				T
schiedeana (C. Presl) Domin (Fuentes 150)	PM				T
Spaeropteris					
brunei (H. Christ) R. M. Tryon (Moran 5846)	M				T
Dennstaedtiaceae					
Dennstaedtia					
arborescens (Willd.) E. Ekman ex Maxon (Hennipman 6674A)	M				H
bipinnata (Cav.) Maxon (Ivey 140)	A				H
globulifera (Poir.) Hieron. (Bello 4457)	MA				H
wercklei (H. Christ) R. M. Tryon (Bello 4603)	A				H
Histiopteris					
incisa (Thunb.) J. Sm. (Bello 4506)	A				H
Lonchitis					
hirsuta L. (Bigelow 38)	M				H,E
Odontosoria					
gymnogrammoides H. Christ (Bigelow 118)	M				V
Ormoloma					
imrayanum (Hook.) Maxon (Bigelow 115)	M				E,H
Pteridium					
arachnoideum (Kaulf.) Maxon (Bigelow 131)	M				H
Saccoloma					
inaequale (Kunze) Mett. (Bello 4410)	A				H
Dicksoniaceae					
Dicksonia					
gigantea H. Karst. (Bello 5152)	M				T
karsteniana (Klotzsch) T. Moore (Rojas 1854)	M				H

Polypodiophyta	Zone[a]	Poll[b]	Seed[c]	Sex[d]	Habit[e]
Dryopteridaceae					
Arachniodes					
denticulata (Sw.) Ching (Bigelow 32)	M				H,E
Didymochlaena					
truncatula (Sw.) J. Sm. (Bello 4497)	A				H
Dryopteris					
patula (Sw.) Underw. (Bigelow 120)	M				E,H
Olfersia					
cervina (L.) Kunze (Moran 5848)	M				E
Polybotrya					
alfredii Brade (Moran 5838)	M				V
gomezii R. C. Moran (Grayum 5378)	M				V
Stigmatopteris					
contracta (H. Christ) C. Chr. (Grayum 5374)	M				H
heterophlebia (Baker) R. C. Moran (Bigelow 82)	A				H
longicaudata (Liebm.) C. Chr. (Moran 5872)	M				H
Equisetaceae					
Equisetum					
bogotense Kunth (9151)	A				H
giganteum L. (6577)	A				H
Gleicheniaceae					
Sticherus					
bifidus (Willd.) Ching (8943)	M				H
brevipubis (H. Christ) A. R. Sm. (Grayum 10185)	M				H
hypoleucus (Sodiro) Copel. (10557)	A				H
pteridellus (H. Christ) Copel. (Rojas 1894)	M				H,V
retroflexus (J. Bommer & H. Christ) Copel. (9730)	M				H
Grammitidaceae					
Ceradenia					
knightii (Copel.) L. E. Bishop (Penneys 307)	A				E
Cochlidium					
rostratum (Hook.) Maxon ex C. Chr. (9516)	MA				E
serrulatum (Sw.) L. E. Bishop (8544)	MA				E
Enterosora					
campbellii Baker (Grayum 10176)	M				E
trifurcata (L.) L. E. Bishop (Ivey 295)	M				E
Lellingeria					
isidrensis (Maxon ex Copel.) A. R. Sm. & R. C. Moran (Grayum 10174)	M				E
limula (H. Christ) A. R. Sm. & R. C. Moran (5516)	M				E
melanotrichia (Baker) A. R. Sm. & R. C. Moran (Bello 4335)	M				E
subsessilis (Baker) A. R. Sm. & R. C. Moran (Bello 2822)	M				E
Melpomene					
anfractuosa (Kunze ex Klotzsch) A. R. Sm. & R. C. Moran (Bello 1795)	MA				E
pilosissima (M. Martens & Galeotti) A. R. Sm. & R. C. Moran (Jiménez 1225)	M				E
xiphopteroides (Liebm.) A. R. Sm. & R. C. Moran (5243)	M				E
Micropolypodium					
cookii (Underw. & Maxon) A. R. Sm. (6154)	A				E
taenifolium (Jenman) A. R. Sm. (9515)	MA				E
truncicola (Klotzsch) A. R. Sm. (Bigelow 109)	M				E
Terpsichore					
alfarii (Donn. Sm.) A. R. Sm. (Grayum 10175)	M				E
alsopteris (C. V. Morton) A. R. Sm. (Bello 2676)	A				E
aspleniifolia (L.) A. R. Sm. (Bello 4439)	M				E
atroviridis (Copel.) A. R. Sm. (Ivey 156)	A				E
cultrata (Bory ex Willd.) A. R. Sm. (Bello 4564)	A				E
lanigera (Desv.) A. R. Sm. (Bello 2648)	MA				E
lehmanniana (Hieron.) A. R. Sm. (Bello 5101)	A				E
mollissima (Fée) A. R. Sm. (Moran 5861)	M				E
semihirsuta (Klotzsch) A. R. Sm. (Hahn 6288)	M				E

Polypodiophyta	Zone[a]	Poll[b]	Seed[c]	Sex[d]	Habit[e]
senilis (Fée) A. R. Sm. (Moran 5871)	M				E
taxifolia (L.) A. R. Sm. (9146)	M				E
turrialbae (H. Christ) A. R. Sm. (Bello 5158)	M				E
Zygophlebia					
sectifrons (Kunze ex Mett.) L. E. Bishop (9075)	M				E
Hymenophyllaceae					
Hymenophyllum					
asplenioides (Sw.) Sw. (Bello 4407)	A				E
consanguineum C. V. Morton (9134)	M				E
crispum Kunth (Zogg 12116)	M				E
ectocarpon Fée (Ivey 153)	MA				E,R
fendlerianum J. W. Sturm (6389)	M				E
fragile (Hedw.) C. V. Morton (Moran 5834)	MA				E
fucoides (Sw.) Sw. (5528)	MA				E
hemipteron Rosenst. (Grayum 10181)	M				E
hirsutum (L.) Sw. (Gómez 1289)	M				E
microcarpum Desv. (Ivey 235)	A				E
polyanthos (Sw.) Sw. (5371)	MA				E
saenzianum L. D. Gomez, cf. (Grayum 10209)	A				E
sieberi (C. Presl) Bosch (Rojas 1877)	M				E
subrigidum H. Christ (Grayum 10183)	M				E
tunbrigense (L.) Sm. (Rojas 1880)	M				E
Trichomanes					
capillaceum L. (Ivey 278)	MA				E
collariatum Bosch (9205)	MA				V,E
crinitum Sw. (Rojas 1869)	M				E
crispum L. (8939)	MA				E
diaphanum Kunth (Ivey 212)	A				E
diversifrons (Bory) Mett. ex Sadeb. (Azofeifa 134)	P				E
hymenophylloides Bosch (Rojas 1879)	M				E
krausii Hook. & Grev. (Bello 2806)	A				E
lucens Sw. (Grayum 10184)	M				E
ludovicinum Rosenst. (Ingram 1755)	M				E
membranaceum L. (Bello 4558)	A				E
polypodioides L. (Bigelow 122)	M				V
radicans Sw. (Hammel 13806)	MA				V
reptans Sw. (Bello 2805)	M				E
rigidum Sw. (10558)	MA				E
Lomariopsidaceae					
Bolbitis					
nicotianifolia (Sw.) Alston (Bello 4556)	A				E,V
oligarchica (Baker) Hennipman (6190)	PMA				H
pergamentacea (Maxon) Ching (Bello 4556)	A				E
portoricensis (Spreng.) Hennipman (Bello 4388)	P				H
Elaphoglossum					
amygdalifolium (Mett. ex Kuhn) H. Christ (Penneys 453)	MA				E,V
auripilum H. Christ (8585)	MA				E
biolleyi H. Christ (8582)	M				E
brenesii Mickel (5158)	M				E
caricifolium Mickel (Bello 979)	A				E
caroliae Mickel (Rojas 1881)	MA				E
ciliatum (C. Presl) T. Moore (Bello 2712)	M				E
conspersum H. Christ (8580)	M				E
coto-brusense A. Rojas, ined. (Ivey 131)	A				E
crinitum (L.) H. Christ (9239)	MA				E
croatii Mickel (Martínez 439)	MA				E
cuspidatum (Willd.) T. Moore (9239)	MA				E
decoratum (Kunze) T. Moore (10013)	MA				E
decursivum Mickel (Grayum 5376)	MA				E
doanense L. D. Gómez (9459)	A				E
erinaceum (Fée) T. Moore (Moran 5858)	M				E,H
eximium (Mett.) H. Christ (9144)	M				E

Polypodiophyta	Zone[a]	Poll[b]	Seed[c]	Sex[d]	Habit[e]
furfuraceum (Mett. ex Kuhn) H. Christ (8741)	M				E
gloeorrhizum Mickel (Rojas 1888)	M				E
hammelianum A. Rojas, ined. (9239)	M				E
heterochroum Mickel (9347)	A				E
killipianum Mickel (Fuentes 39)	P				E
lanceiforme Mickel (Bello 4503)	A				E
latifolium (Sw.) J. Sm. (8743)	M				E
lingua (Raddi) Brack. (8583)	M				E
micropogon Mickel (Bello 134)	A				E
mitorrhizum Mickel (8580)	M				E
moranii Mickel Haber (8584)	MA				E
muscosum (Sw.) T. Moore (8548)	M				E
paleaceum (Hook. & Grev.) Sledge, cf. (9347)	A				E
pallidum (Baker ex Jenman) C. Chr. (Rojas 1865)	MA				E
palmense H. Christ (9145)	M				E
peltatum (Sw.) Urb. (Bello 969)	MA				E
pseudoboryanum Mickel (9148)	M				E
siliquoides (Jenman) C. Chr. (Bello 135)	A				E
smithii (Baker) H. Christ (Rojas 1901)	M				E
standleyi Mickel (Grayum 3840)	M				E
tenuiculum (Fée) T. Moore (Ivey 324)	PA				E
Lomariopsis					
fendleri D. C. Eaton (Bello 1953)	A				V
maxonii (Underw.) Holttum (Bello 4555)	MA				V
vestita E. Fourn. (Grayum 10199)	A				V
Lophosoriaceae					
Lophosoria					
quadripinnata (J. F. Gmel.) C. Chr. (Bello 4428)	MA				H
Lycopodiaceae					
Huperzia					
acerosa (Sw.) Holub (9543)	MA				E
bradeorum (H. Christ) Holub (11034)	M				E
capillaris (Sodiro) Holub (10234)	A				E
chamaeleon (Herter) B. Ollg. (Bello 1654)	M				E
dichaeoides (Maxon) Holub (11282)	A				E
dichotoma (Jacq.) Trevis. (Bello 4589)	A				E
filiformis (Sw.) Holub (5683)	A				E
funiformis (Spring) Trevis. (9185)	A				E
lancifolia (Maxon) Holub (Bello 4563)	A				E
myrsinites (Lam.) Trevis. (8917)	M				E
polycarpos (Kunze) B. Ollg. (10234)	A				E
reflexa (Lam.) Trevis. (9074)	MA				H
taxifolia (Sw.) Trevis. (8663)	M				E
tubulosa (Maxon) B. Ollg. (Bello 1794)	M				E
wilsonii (Underw. & F. E. Lloyd) B. Ollg. (Bello 4590)	A				E
Lycopodiella					
cernua (L.) Pic. Serm. (9583)	M				H
Lycopodium					
clavatum L. (9541)	M				V
Marattiaceae					
Danaea					
elliptica Sm. (Ivey 124)	A				H
moritiziana Presl (Rojas 1849)	M				H
nodosa (L.) Sm. (Bigelow 92)	A				H
Marattia					
excavata Underw. (Moran 5829)	M				H
interposita H. Christ (Martínez 459)	MA				H
laxa Kunze (Burger 10848)	M				H
Oleandraceae					
Nephrolepis					
biserrata (Sw.) Schott (9415)	A				H
multiflora (Roxb.) F. M. Jarrett ex C. V. Morton (10841)	A				H,E
pectinata (Willd.) Schott (Bello 137)	MA				E

Polypodiophyta	Zone[a]	Poll[b]	Seed[c]	Sex[d]	Habit[e]
pendula (Raddi) J. Sm. (8787)	PMA				E,H
rivularis (Vahl) Mett. ex Krug (Ivey 255)	A				E,H
Oleandra					
bradei H. Christ (Ivey 312)	M				E
costaricensis Maxon (10236)	MA				E
Ophioglossaceae					
Cheiroglossa					
palmata (L.) C. Presl (7298)	MA				E
Ophioglossum					
reticulatum L. (10373)	M				H
Polypodiaceae					
Campyloneurum					
angustifolium (Sw.) Fée (9513)	MA				E
brevifolium (Lodd. ex Link) Link, *sensu* Leon (Bello 4473)	A				E
fasciale (Humb. & Bonpl. ex Willd.) C. Presl (9238)	PMA				V
falcoideum (Kuhn ex Hieron.) M. Mey. ex Lellinger (10119)	M				E
irregulare Lellinger (Bello 2715)	M				H
phyllitidis (L.) C. Presl (6436)	A				E
repens (Aubl.) C. Presl (Bello 2678)	A				V
sphenodes (Kunze ex Klotzsch) Fée (6199)	MA				E,V
Dicranoglossum					
panamense (C. Chr.) L. D. Gómez (Azofeifa 132)	P				E
Microgramma					
lycopodioides (L.) Copel. (8545)	MA				E
percussa (Cav.) de la Sota (Ivey 130)	A				E,R
Neurodium					
lanceolatum (L.) Fée (2219)	M				V,E
Niphidium					
crassifolium (L.) Lellinger (4947)	PMA				E
nidulare (Rosenst.) Lellinger (8669)	M				E
Pecluma					
alfredii (Rosenst.) M. G. Price (Ivey 127)	P				E
camptophyllaria (Fée) M. G. Price (Bello 2676)	A				E
divaricata (E. Fourn.) Mickel & Beitel (Moran 5931)	MA				E
plumula (Humb. & Bonpl. ex Willd.) M. G. Price (11315)	P				E,H,R
Phlebodium					
pseudoaureum (Cav.) Lellinger (Bello 2941)	MA				E
Pleopeltis					
angusta Humb. & Bonpl. ex Willd. (7764)	M				E
astrolepis (Liebm.) E. Fourn. (Azofeifa 77)	PM				E
fructuosa (Maxon & Weath. ex Weath.) Lellinger (8546)	MA				E
complanata (Weath.) E. A. Hooper (8546)	MA				E
wiesbaurii (Sodiro) Lellinger (Obando 188)	A				E
Polypodium					
dulce Poir. (Hammel 14209)	MA				E,H,R
echinolepis Fée (A. Jiménez 1275)	M				E
fraxinifolium Jacq. (7731)	MA				V,E
friedrichsthalianum Kunze (6758)	A				E
furfuraceum Schltdl. & Cham. (Palmer 142)	PMA				E
fuscopetiolatum A. R. Sm. (10177)	P				V,E
giganteum Desv. (Ivey 284)	PA				E
lindenianum Kunze (Ivey 142)	A				E
loriceum L. (Zogg 12188)	M				V
loriciforme Rosenst. (Bello 2396)	A				E
myriolepis H. Christ (Bigelow 59)	M				E
plectolepidioides Rosenst. (Ivey 129)	A				E
plesiosorum Kunze (Burger 9624)	M				H
polypodioides (L.) Watt (Ivey 132)	PMA				E
ptilorhizon H. Christ (8744)	PMA				V,E
remotum Desv. (Bigelow 16)	MA				V

Polypodiophyta	Zone[a]	Poll[b]	Seed[c]	Sex[d]	Habit[e]
rhodopleuron Kunze (11316)	P				V,E,R
triseriale Sw. (Obando 137)	PMA				E,H
Pteridaceae					
Acrostichum					
danaeifolium Langsd. & Fisch. (Bello 2902) (aquatic)	A				H
Adiantopsis					
chlorophylla (Sw.) Fée (10113)	P				H
Adiantum					
andicola Liebm. (A. Jiménez 1205)	M				H
concinnum Humb. & Bonpl. ex Willd. (8871)	PM				H
macrophyllum Sw. (9632)	PA				H
patens Willd. (Obando 146)	A				H
princeps T. Moore (9685)	P				H
tetraphyllum Humb. & Bonpl. ex Willd (9241)	MA				H
trapeziforme L. (9686)	P				H
urophyllum Hook. (9241A)	MA				H
Eriosorus					
flexuosus (Kunth) Copel. (Palmer 118)	M				H
glaberrimus (Maxon) Scamman (Bello 2845)	M				V
Mildella					
intramarginalis (Kaulf. ex Link) Trevis. (10799)	PM				H,R
Neurocallis					
praestantissima Bory ex Fée (Hammel 15090)	M				H
Pityrogramma					
calomelanos (L.) Link (8873)	PMA				H
dealbata (C. Presl) R. M. Tryon (9769)	PM				H
ebenea (L.) Proctor (Azofeifa 123)	PM				H
ferruginea (Kunze) Maxon (Ivey 170)	PA				H
trifoliata (L.) R. M. Tryon (9680)	PA				H
Pteris					
altissima Poir. (Bello 4566)	M				H
muricata Hook. (Grayum 10180)	M				H
navarrensis H. Christ (Grayum 10193)	A				H
paucinervata Fée (A. Jiménez 1183)	M				H
podophylla Sw. (Grayum 10208)	A				H
quadriaurita Retz. (Grayum 10186)	MA				H
speciosa Mett. ex Kuhn (Bello 5386)	A				H
Schizaeaceae					
Anemia					
hirsuta (L.) Sw. (8632)	P				H
oblongifolia (Cav.) Sw. (Bello 2919)	P				H
phyllitidis (L.) Sw. (9713)	PM				H
Selaginellaceae					
Selaginella					
anceps (C. Presl) C. Presl (Bello 4413)	PA				H
atirrensis Hieron. (Grayum 10196)	A				H
diffusa (C. Presl) Spring (Bello 4417)	A				H
geniculata (C. Presl) Spring (Moran 5841)	M				H
oaxacana Spring (9005)	MA				H
pallescens (C. Presl) Spring (9652)	P				H
silvestris Aspl. (6230)	M				E
tarapotensis Baker (Grayum 7593)	M				E
viticulosa Klotzsch (11220)	A				H,R
Tectariaceae					
Ctenitis					
excelsa (Desv.) Proctor (Bello 4450)	M				H
hemsleyana (Baker ex Hemsl.) Copel. (A. Jiménez 1182a)	M				H
Lasteopsis					
effusa (Sw.) Tindale (Bello 4606)	MA				H
exculta (Mett.) Tindale (Grayum 10203)	PA				H,R

Polypodiophyta	Zone[a]	Poll[b]	Seed[c]	Sex[d]	Habit[e]
Megalastrum					
acrosorum (Hieron.) A. R. Sm. & R. C. Moran (Martínez 452)	MA				H
atrogriseum (C. Chr.) A. R. Sm. & R. C. Moran (9499)	MA				H
lunense (H. Christ) A. R. Sm. & R. C. Moran (Burger 10774)	M				H
subincisum (Willd.) A. R. Sm. & R. C. Moran (9354)	A				H
Tectaria					
antioquiana (Baker) C. Chr. (Grayum 10202)	A				H
athyrioides (Baker) C. Chr. (Bello 4451)	MA				H
heracleifolia (Willd.) Underw. (Fuentes 180)	P				H,R
nicaraguensis (E. Fourn.) C. Chr. (Bello 4102)	A				H
nicotianifolia (Baker) C. Chr. (9198)	A				H
plantaginea (Jacq.) Maxon (Ivey 160)	A				H,R
subebenea (H. Christ) C. Chr. (Bittner 1265)	A				H
Thelypteridaceae					
Thelypteris					
atrovirens (C. Chr.) C. F. Reed (Zogg 12119)	MA				H
biolleyi (H. Christ) Proctor (Ivey 125)	A				H
blanda (Fée) C. F. Reed (Grayum 5416)	M				H
cheilanthoides (Kunze) Proctor (Ivey 197)	A				H
curta (H. Christ) C. F. Reed (Grayum 10210)	A				H
decussata (L.) Proctor (Bigelow 53)	M				S
delasotae A. R. Sm. & Lellinger (Bello 4395)	MA				H
equitans (H. Christ) C. F. Reed (Moran 5842)	A				H
falcata (Liebm.) R. M. Tryon (9803)	MA				H
francoana (E. Fourn.) C. F. Reed (4909)	A				H,R
funckii (Mett.) Alston (Ivey 296)	A				H
gigantea (Mett.) R. M. Tryon (5844)	A				H
glandulosa (Desv.) Proctor (Bello 4382)	PM				H
gomeziana A. R. Sm. & Lellinger (Bello 4508)	A				H
grayumii A. R. Sm. (4542)	M				H
nicaraguensis (E. Fourn.) C. V. Morton (Ivey 145)	A				H
obliterata (Sw.) Proctor (Bello 4562)	A				H
patens (Sw.) Small (Bello 4618)	A				H
pilosula (Klotzsch & H. Karst. ex Mett.) R. M. Tryon (Martínez 448)	A				H
resinifera (Desv.) Proctor (10172)	P				H
rudis (Kunze) Proctor (Bigelow 1)	M				H
torresiana (Gaudich.) Alston (Bello 4505)	A				H
turrialbae (Rosenst.) C. V. Morton (Grayum 10207)	A				H
urbanii (Sodiro) A. R. Sm. (Grayum 10211)	A				H
Vittariaceae					
Antrophyum					
cajenense (Desv.) Spreng. (Bello 1069)	A				E
ensiforme Hook. (9774a)	MA				E
lanceolatum (L.) Kaulf. (Fuentes 470)	P				E
lineatum (Sw.) Kaulf. (Bello 2647)	MA				E
Vittaria					
gardneriana Fée (Bello 4565)	A				E
graminifolia Kaulf. (8742)	M				E
lineata (L.) Sm. (8804)	M				E
remota Fée (Bigelow 87)	A				E
stipitata Kunze (9452)	MA				E
Woodsiaceae					
Diplazium					
atirrense (Donn. Sm.) Lellinger (Obando 219)	A				H
ceratolepis (H. Christ) H. Christ (9355)	A				H
cristatum (Desr.) Alston (Obando 168)	PA				H
diplazioides (Klotzsch & H. Karst.) Alston (Martínez 463)	A				H
hians Kunze ex Klotzsch (Grayum 10194)	A				H
lindbergii (Mett.) H. Christ (Bello 4054)	A				H
myriomerum (H. Christ) Lellinger (Grayum 10201)	A				H

Polypodiophyta	Zone[a]	Poll[b]	Seed[c]	Sex[d]	Habit[e]
negectum (H. Karst.) C. Chr. (9352)	A				H
obscurum H. Christ (Martínez 477)	MA				H
plantaginifolium (L.) Urb. (9240)	MA				H
prominulum Maxon (Grayum 10182)	MA				H
seemannii T. Moore (Ivey 207)	MA				H
solutum (H. Christ) Lellinger (Bello 4411)	A				H,E
striatastrum Lellinger (Grayum 10197)	A				H
striatum (L.) C. Presl (Bello 4560)	PA				H
subsilvaticum H. Christ (Penneys 452)	A				H
tablazianum H. Christ (Burger 8582)	M				H
urticifolium H. Christ (Bello 5265)	M				H
wilsonii (Baker) Diels (Rojas 1892)	M				H
Hemidictyum					
marginatum (L.) C. Presl (9404)	A				H

Species of Asteraceae are listed as HE if male and female florets occur in the same head. Technically, some of these are monoecious, but most have female and hermaphroditic florets mixed together.

GR includes seeds and fruits that do not have obvious adaptations for removal from the plant other than by dropping such as species that are eaten by seed-eating birds or carried away by ants and rodents after they reach the ground.

Because of late additions and subtractions of species names from the checklist, species numbers will not exactly match those of Table 3.7 and Appendix 2.

*Species introduced or escaped from cultivation. Pollinator and dispersal data are not included for these species.

[a]Zones of distribution (Zone)
P = Pacific slope 700—1200 m in elevation
M = montane area above 1200 m on both slopes
A = Atlantic slope 700—1200m

[b]Pollination (Poll)
BD = bird (hummingbird)
BE = bee
BF = butterfly
BT = bat
cleist. = cleistogamous
CO = Coleoptera
HM = hawkmoth
IN = insect (insects of several orders or insect types not known specifically)
LB = large bee
MO = moth (non-hawkmoth)
SB = small bee
WA = wasp
WD = wind

[c]Seed dispersal (Seed)
AM = arboreal mammal
BD = bird
BT = bat
EX = explosive
GR = gravity, unspecialized
TM = terrestrial mammal
WD = wind

[d]Sexual system (Sex)
DI = dioecious
HE = hemaphroditic (includes andromonoecious and polygamo-dioecious species)
MO = monoecious

[e]Growth form (Habit)
E = epiphyte
H = herb—erect terrestrial herbaceous plants
L = liana—large woody climbers reaching more than 5 m
P = parasite
S = shrub, woody plants less than 5 m
Sap = saprophyte
Ts = small tree, understory, 5–9 m
Tm = medium tree, subcanopy, 10–20 m
Tl = large tree, canopy, 20–50 m
V = vine, small nonwoody climbers less than 5 m

Appendix 2

Number of Species with Different Plant Growth Forms

William A. Haber

Family	Herb	Vine	Liana	Shrub	Tree	Epiphyte	Total
Dicotyledons							
Acanthaceae	20		5	12	2		39
Actinidiaceae					5		5
Alzateaceae						1	1
Amaranthaceae	5	1	2	4			12
Anacardiaceae					5		5
Annonaceae					14		14
Apiaceae	9						9
Apocynaceae			11		8		19
Aquifoliaceae					9		9
Araliaceae			1		6	11	18
Aristolochiaceae			3				3
Asclepiadaceae	1	13	3				17
Asteraceae	51	9	15	42	17	10	144
Balanophoraceae	2						2
Begoniaceae	4	2		1		4	11
Betulaceae					1		1
Bignoniaceae		1	8		7		16
Bombacaceae					8	1	9
Boraginaceae	2		4	3	11		20
Brassicaceae	6						6
Brunelliaceae					3		3
Burseraceae					4		4
Cactaceae					1	10	11
Campanulaceae	5			2		6	13
Capparidaceae	1			1	7		9

Family	Herb	Vine	Liana	Shrub	Tree	Epiphyte	Total
Dicotyledons (*continued*)							
Caprifoliaceae					3		3
Caricaceae				1	2		3
Caryophyllaceae	4						4
Cecropiaceae					4	4	8
Celastraceae			2	1	10		13
Chenopodiaceae				1			1
Chloranthaceae				1	3		4
Chrysobalanaceae					6		6
Clethraceae					2		2
Clusiaceae	2				10	10	22
Cochlospermaceae					1		1
Combretaceae			1		2		3
Connaraceae			2				2
Convolvulaceae		5	13				18
Cornaceae					1		1
Crassulaceae	1						1
Cucurbitaceae		22	3				25
Cunoniaceae					3		3
Dichapetalaceae					5		5
Dilleniaceae			1				1
Ebenaceae					6		6
Elaeocarpaceae					4		4
Eremolepidaceae						1	1
Ericaceae	1					28	29
Erythroxylaceae					1		1
Euphorbiaceae	5	1		4	40		50
Fabaceae/Caesalpinoideae				7	1		8
Fabaceae/Mimosoideae			2	1	36		39
Fabaceae/Papilionoideae	10	6	15	19	20		70
Fagaceae					4		4
Flacourtiaceae				2	19		21
Gentianaceae	4			3			7
Gesneriaceae	17	3		6		32	58
Grossulariaceae				1		1	2
Gunneraceae	1						1
Hernandiaceae					2		2
Hippocastanaceae					2		2
Hippocrateaceae			2		1		3
Hydrangeaceae			4				4
Hydrophyllaceae					1		1
Icacinaceae					2		2
Juglandaceae					4		4
Lamiaceae	17			4			21
Lauraceae					66		66
Lentibulariaceae						2	2
Loasaceae	1			1			2
Loganiaceae	1		1	2			4
Loranthaceae						13	13
Lythraceae				3			3
Magnoliaceae					2		2
Malpighiaceae		2	12	1	6		21
Malvaceae	1		2	10	3		16
Marcgraviaceae			8			5	13
Melastomataceae	9	2		41	27	14	93
Meliaceae					15		15
Menispermaceae			7				7
Monimiaceae				5	2		7
Moraceae	2				40	1	43
Myricaceae				2			2
Myristicaceae					4		4
Myrsinaceae				6	13	1	20
Myrtaceae				2	28		30
Nyctaginaceae	1		1	1	4		7

Family	Herb	Vine	Liana	Shrub	Tree	Epiphyte	Total
Dicotyledons (*continued*)							
Ochnaceae	1				3		4
Olacaceae				1			1
Oleaceae					4		4
Onagraceae	3			1	1		5
Opiliaceae					1		1
Oxalidaceae	5						5
Papaveraceae					1		1
Passifloraceae		3	16		1		20
Phytolaccaceae	1		2	4			7
Piperaceae	1	1	1	33	3	40	79
Plantaginaceae	2						2
Podostemaceae	1						1
Polemoniaceae		1		2			3
Polygalaceae	1		2	2			5
Polygonaceae	2	1			5		8
Proteaceae					4		4
Ranunculaceae			4				4
Rhamnaceae			1		2		3
Rhizophoraceae					1		1
Rosaceae	1		2		5		8
Rubiaceae	15	4	3	54	60	12	148
Rutaceae				1	13		14
Sabiaceae					6		6
Sapindaceae			11		11		22
Sapotaceae					13		13
Scrophulariaceae	7		4	2		3	16
Simaroubaceae					6		6
Solanaceae	10	1	7	31	19	7	75
Staphyleaceae					2		2
Sterculiaceae				1	3		4
Styracaceae					3		3
Symplocaceae					8		8
Theaceae					6		6
Theophrastaceae				1	1		2
Thymelaeaceae					1		1
Ticodendraceae					1		1
Tiliaceae				1	11		12
Tovariaceae				1			1
Tropaeolaceae		2					2
Turneraceae					1		1
Ulmaceae			1		3		4
Urticaceae	9		1	11	7	3	31
Valerianaceae	1	1					2
Verbenaceae	1		4	7	9		21
Violaceae	1			2			3
Viscaceae						10	10
Vitaceae			6				6
Vochysiaceae					1		1
Winteraceae					1		1
Totals	245	81	193	345	730	230	1824
Monocotyledons							
Agavaceae	1						1
Alstroemeriaceae		4					4
Anthericaceae	2						2
Araceae	14	32				34	80
Arecaceae				19	11		30
Bromeliaceae	3					62	65
Burmanniaceae	3						3
Commelinaceae	13	1					14
Convallariaceae						1	1
Costaceae	9						9

Family	Herb	Vine	Liana	Shrub	Tree	Epiphyte	Total
Monocotyledons (*continued*)							
Cyclanthaceae	3	8				5	16
Cyperaceae	35						35
Dioscoreaceae			8				8
Haemodoraceae	1						1
Heliconiaceae	10						10
Hypoxidaceae	1						1
Iridaceae	1						1
Juncaceae	1						1
Marantaceae	15						15
Orchidaceae	49	1				369	419
Poaceae	60		6	2			68
Pontederiaceae	1						1
Smilacaceae			11				11
Triuridaceae	1						1
Typhaceae	1						1
Zingiberaceae	3						3
Totals	227	46	25	21	11	471	801
Gymnosperms							
Podocarpaceae					1		1
Zamiaceae					1		1
Polypodiophyta							
Aspleniaceae	4					15	19
Blechnaceae	9		2			2	13
Cyatheaceae	1			1	12		14
Dennstaedtiaceae	8	1				1	10
Dicksoniaceae	1				1		2
Dryopteridaceae	5	2				2	9
Equisetaceae	2						2
Gleicheniaceae	5						5
Grammitidaceae						28	28
Hymenophyllaceae	1	2				27	30
Lomariopsidaceae	2	3				40	45
Lophosoriaceae	1						1
Lycopodiaceae	2	1				14	17
Marattiaceae	6						6
Oleandraceae	2					5	7
Ophioglossaceae	1					1	2
Polypodiaceae	2	9				31	42
Pteridaceae	25	1					26
Schizaeaceae	3						3
Selaginellaceae	7					2	9
Tectariaceae	15						15
Thelypteridaceae	23			1			24
Vittariaceae						9	9
Woodsiaceae	20						20
Totals	145	19	2	2	13	177	358
Dicotyledons	245	81	193	345	730	230	1824
Monocotyledons	227	46	25	21	11	471	801
Gymnosperms					1	1	2
Polypodiophyta	145	19	2	2	13	177	358
Totals	617	146	220	369	755	878	2985

Appendix 3

Orchids of Monteverde

John T. Atwood

The following annotated list is based on the database at Selby Botanical Gardens (AMOData), augmented with a list published by Haber (1991) and notes provided by R. L. Dressler. Species marked with an asterisk (*) are known only in Monteverde and are possibly endemic. Species marked with a plus (+) are members of subtribe Oncidiinae. Representative collection numbers are included in parentheses after the species names (A = Atwood, B = Bello, H = Haber, I = Ingram, M = Morris).

Acostaea costaricensis Schltr.   (H8772)
Acrorchis roseola Dressler   (H10242)
+*Ada chlorops* (Endres & Rchb. f.) N. H. Williams   (H3024)
Arpophyllum giganteum Hartweg ex Lindl.   (H8005)
Barbosella geminata Luer, cf.   (A89-303)
B. prorepens (Rchb. f.) Schltr.   (I254)
Barkeria lindleyana Bateman ex Lindl.   (H411)
B. obovata (C. Presl) Christenson   (H9692)
*Baskervilla leptantha Dressler
B. nicaraguensis Hamer and Garay   (B538)
Beloglottis costaricensis (Rchb. f.) Schltr.   (H11898)
B. hameri Garay   (H10529)
Bletia purpurea (Lam.) DC. (plant normally of lower elevations; appeared in garden in Monteverde community)
*Brachionidium haberi Luer   (H7027)
B. pusillum Ames & C. Schweinf.   (H10625)
+*Brassia arcuigera* Rchb. f.   (A89-289)
+*B. verrucosa* Lindl.   (H6970)
Campylocentrum longicalcaratum Ames & C. Schweinf.   (B929)

C. sp.   (H10114)
Cattleya skinneri Bateman   (A89-95A)
Chaubardiella pacuarensis Jenny
Chondrorhyncha reichenbachiana Schltr.   (H11286)
Cochleanthes aromatica (Rchb. f.) R. E. Schult. & Garay   (B536)
C. discolor (Lindl.) R. E. Schult. & Garay   (A89-22)
C. picta (Rchb. f.) Garay   (I225)
Corymborkis flava (Sw.) Kuntze   (H11277)
C. forcipigera (Rchb. f. & Warsz.) L. O. Williams   (H9570)
Cranichis lankesteri Ames & C. Schweinf.   (H9569)
C. reticulata Rchb. f.   (H6208)
C. sylvatica A. Rich. & Galeotti, aff.   (A4107)
C. wageneri Rchb. f.   (M4011)
Crossoglossa blephariglottis (Schltr.) Dressler & Dodson   (A89-280)
C. eustachys (Schltr.) Dressler & Dodson, cf.   (A89-65)
C. fratra (Schltr.) Dressler & Dodson   (H5345)
C. tenuis Dressler & Dodson   (H5344)
Cryptocentrum calcaratum (Schltr.) Schltr.   (A89-294)

C. lehmanii (Rchb. f.) Garay (syn.: *C. gracilis* Schltr.) (B629)

C. latifolium Schltr. (A89-334)

C. standleyi Ames (H5464)

Cyclopogon olivaceus (Rolfe) Garay (H8000)

C. prasophyllum (Rchb. f.) Schltr. (H9022)

C. sp. A

Dichaea ciliolata Rolfe (I739)

D. cryptarrhena Kraenzl. (H8620)

D. glauca (Sw.) Lindl.

D. lankesteri Ames (previously identified as *D.* aff. *brachypoda* Rchb. f.) (A89-182)

D. morrisii Fawc. & Rendle (H9368)

D. oxyglossa Schltr., cf. (I1592)

D. poicillantha Schltr. (H8620)

D. trichocarpa (Sw.) Lindl. (A89-258)

Dracula erythrochaete (Rchb. f.) Luer (A89-243)

Dryadella pusiola (Rchb. f.) Luer, cf. (Palmer s.n., CR-36883)

Elleanthus aurantiacus (Lindl.) Rchb. f. (H10022)

E. conifer (Rchb. f. & Warsz.) Rchb. f., aff. (H7668)

E. glaucophyllus Schltr. (H4492)

E. hymenophorus (Rchb. f.) Rchb. f. (B904)

E. jimenezii (Schltr.) C. Schweinf. (H8601)

E. lancifolius C. Presl (syn.: *E. laxus* Schltr.) (A88-61)

E. lentii Barringer (H1936)

E. muscicola Schltr. (B1024)

E. poiformis Schltr. (H8835)

E. scopula Schltr. (H7560)

E. stolonifer Barringer (H8925)

E. tonduzii Schltr. (flowers orange-red) (H10022)

E. tonduzii Schltr. aff. (flowers purple) (B997)

E. wercklei Schltr. (yellow bracts) (H4733)

Encyclia abbreviata (Schltr.) Dressler (H10659)

E. brassavolae (Rchb. f.) Dressler (H8563)

E. campylostalix (Rchb. f.) Schltr. (B808)

E. ceratistes (Lindl.) Schltr. (A89-113)

E. chacaoensis (Rchb. f.) Dressler & G. Pollard (H10660)

E. cochleata (Lindl.) Lemée (H9890)

E. fragrans (Sw.) Lemée (H7185)

E. ionocentra (Rchb. f.) Mora-Retana & J. García (H5779)

E. livida (Lindl.) Dressler (A89-309)

E. pseudopygmaea (Finet) Dressler & G. E. Pollard (H9087)

E. pygmaea (Hook.) Dressler (H8700)

E. vespa (Vell.) Dressler (H5546)

Epidendrum anoglossum Schltr. (H9388)

E. atwoodchlamys Hágsater (89-238)

E. barbae Rchb. f., cf. (= *E. polychlamys* Schltr., aff.) (H10690)

E. bilobatum Ames (H8001)

E. candelabrum Hágsater (H7363)

E. carolii Schltr. (previously included as synonym of *E. laucheanum*; occurs in the lower community)

E. ciliare L. (H7842)

E. congestoides Ames & C. Schweinf. (*E. schlechterianum* Ames and others) (A89-4)

E. criniferum Rchb. f. (H6584)

E. firmum Rchb. f. (H1608)

E. flexicaule Schltr. (H8935)

E. glumibracteum Rchb. f. (syn.: *E. purpurascens* Focke?) (H9877)

E. lacustre Lindl. (H5342)

E. lankesteri Ames, cf. (H9136)

E. laucheanum Rolfe ex Bonhof (H8693)

E. miserrimum Rchb. f. (H5470)

E. mora-retanae Hágsater (H7245)

E. muscicola Schltr. (syn.: *Epidanthus muscicola* [Schltr.] L. O. Williams) (H8600)

E. myodes Rchb. f. (H8514)

E. oerstedii Rchb. f. (B2915)

E. oxyglossum Schltr.

E. palmense Ames (A89-46)

E. parkinsonianum Hook. (H7017)

E. peperomia Rchb. f. (syn.: *E. porpax* Rchb. f.) (H8909)

E. phragmites L. O. Williams & A. H. Heller, cf. (I1593)

E. pseudoramosum Schltr. (A4054)

E. radicans Pavon ex Lindl. (H1101)

E. ramonianum Schltr. (H8593)

E. ramosum Jacq. (A4101)

E. raniferum Lindl.

E. resectum Rchb. f. (H7249)

E. rugosum Ames, aff. (H8814)

E. sanchoi Ames (H8931)

E. sanctiramoni Kraenzl. (Syn.: *Epidanthus paranthicus* [Rchb. f.] L. O. Williams, *sensu lato*) (H8933)

E. santaclarense Ames, cf. (H7245)

E. scriptum A. Rich. & Galeotti (H2083)

E. selaginella Schltr. (A89-121)

E. subnutans Ames & C. Schweinf. (A89–76)

E. summerhayesii Hégsater (A88-76)

E. trachythece Schltr. (A4102)

E. turialvae Rchb. f. (H8327)

E. vincentinum Lindl., cf. (B2042)

E. wercklei Schltr. (syn.: *Neowilliamsia wercklei* [Schitr.] Dressler) (H9738)

Erythrodes bimentata Dressler (H9577)

E. calophylla (Rchb. f.) Ames (B367)

E. killipii Ames (H11026)

E. roseoalba Dressler (B5242)

E. vaginata (Hook.) Ames (H9573)

E. vesicifera (Rchb. f.) Ames (H6682)

Eurystyles auriculata Schltr. (H5379)

E. standleyi Ames (A89-79)

Gongora amparoana Schltr. (B342)

+*Goniochilus leochilinus* (Rchb. f.) M. W. Chase (H8834)

Goodyera major Ames & Correll (H7535)

Govenia liliacea (La Llave & Lex.) Lindl. (possibly this is actually two species) (H10076)

Habenaria floribunda Lindl. (A89-6)

H. monorrhiza (Sw.) Rchb. f. (A89-335)

H. sp. (seen in open swamp at about 1700 m)

Hexisea imbricata (Lindl.) Rchb. f. (H9423)

Huntleya burtii (Endres & Rchb. f.) Pfitz. (H8428)

I. chiriquensis Schltr. (earlier determined as *major* Cham. & Schltdl., cf.) (A89-212)

Isochilus linearis (Jacq.) R. Br., cf. (A89-310)

Jacquiniella equitantifolia (Ames) Dressler (A4004)

J. globosa (Jacq.) Schltr. (B1173)

J. teretifolia (Sw.) Britton & Wilson (including *J. teres* [Rchb. f.] Hamer & Garay) (A4000)

Lepanthes acostae Schltr. (A89-23a)

L. ciliosepala Schltr. (I586)

L. comet-hallii Luer (A89-122a)

L. confusa Ames & C. Schweinf. (I1529)

L. elata Rchb., cf.   (A88-6)

L. eximia Ames   (A89-194)

L. horrida Rchb. f.   (A89-112)

L. infundibulum Luer   (A89-250)

L. jimenezii Schltr.   (A89-194)

L. johnsonii Ames

L. macalpinii Luer   (A89-194a)

L. mentosa Luer   (A89-114)

L. minutilabia Ames & C. Schweinf.   (A245)

L. monteverdensis Luer & Escobar   (A89-115)

L. pygmaea Luer   (A89-185)

L. ramonensis Schltr.

L. standleyi Ames, cf.   (H7781)

L. turialvae Rchb. f., aff.   (A89-158)

Liparis nervosa (Thunb.) Lindl.   (A4010)

+*Lockhartia amoena* Endres & Rchb. f. (syn.:
   L. dipleura Schltr.)   (H8526)

+*L. hercodonta* Rchb. f. ex Kraenzl.   (H9552)

+*L. micrantha* Rchb. f.   (B880)

+*L. oerstedii* Rchb. f.   (H5705)

Lycaste brevispatha (Klatt) lindl.   (MSBG89-610)

L. leucantha Lindl.   (H7511)

L. powellii Schltr.   (H7155)

+*Macroclinium lineare* (Ames & C. Schweinf.)
   Dodson   (I819)

+*M. ramonense* (Schltr.) Dodson   (H5533)

Malaxis brachyrrhynchos (Rchb. f.) Ames   (H7257)

M. hastilabia (Rchb. f.) Kuntze (vegetative and ecological
   differences suggest that there are at least 2, perhaps 3
   species in this complex in Monteverde)   (H10795)

M. histionantha (Link, Klotzsch, & Otto) Garay &
   Dunsterville   (A4114)

M. monsviridis Dressler   (H9315)

M. simillima (Rchb. f.) Kuntze   (H9314)

Masdevallia calura Rchb. f.   (A89-119)

M. chasei Luer   (H8942)

M. chontalensis Rchb. f.   (H9091)

M. erinacea Rchb. f.   (H10624)

M. molossoides Kraenzl.   (A4052)

M. nidifica Rchb. f.   (H10555)

M. pygmaea Kraenzl.   (Morales 4425)

M. rolfeana Kraenzl.   (H9063)

M. schizopetala Kraenzl.   (I1543)

M. striatella Rchb. f.   (8942)

M. zahlbruckneri Kraenzl.   (B857)

Maxillaria acervata Rchb. f. (Syn.: *M. foliosa* Ames & C.
   Schweinf.)   (H8936)

M. acutifolia Lindl.   (H8468)

M. adendrobium (Rchb. f.) Dressler   (H8055)

M. alba (Hook.) Lindl.   (H9457)

M. ampliflora C. Schweinf.   (Dryer 1602)

M. anceps Ames & C. Schweinf.   (H3851)

M. angustisegmenta Ames & C. Schweinf.   (H8815)

M. angustissima Ames, Hubbard, & C. Schweinf.
   (Boyle 89-79)

M. appendiculoides C. Schweinf.   (B460)

M. attenuata Ames & C. Schweinf.   (H6464)

M. bicallosa (Rchb. f.) Garay   (B1488)

M. bracteata (Schltr.) Ames & Correll   (H9033)

M. bradeorum (Schltr.) L. O. Willianis (syn.:
   M. semiorbicularis Ames & C. Schweinf.)   (H5561)

M. brunnea Linden & Rchb. f. (syn. *M. brenesii*
   Schltr.)   (H9053)

M. campanulata C. Schweinf.   (A4085)

M. chartacifolia Alues & C. Schweinf.   (B1312)

M. confusa Ames & C. Schweinf.   (B2634)

M. costaricensis Schltr.   (Boyle 89-60)

M. crassifolia (Lindl.) Rchb. f.   (A89-344)

M. cryptobulbon Carnevali & J. T. Atwood
   (H6104)

M. ctenostachya Rchb. f. (Mora 19)

M. dendrobioides (Schltr.) L. O. Williams   (H8937)

M. dichotoma (Schltr.) L. O. Williams   (H5713)

M. diuturna Ames & C. Schweinf.   (Boyle 89-86)

M. endresii Rchb. f. (record needs to be
   confirmed)   (H3987)

M. exaltata Kraenzl.   (H7869)

M. flava Ames, Hubbard & C. Schweinf.   (A89-818)

M. fulgens (Rchb. f.) L. O. Williams   (H9498)

**M. haberi* J. T. Atwood   (Haber & Cruz 7474)
   (yellow-flowered)

M. inaudita Rchb. f.   (H9082)

M. lankesteri Ames (close to *M. wercklei* [Schltr.]
   L. O. Williams but flowers twice as large)   (H8701)

M. linearifolia Ames & C. Schweinf.   (I236)

M. longiloba (Ames & C. Schweinf.) J. T. Atwood
   (M&A4083)

M. lueri Dodson   (B510)

M. microphyton Schltr.   (H8695)

M. minor (Schltr.) L. O. Williams   (H8602)

M. monteverdensis J. T. Atwood & G. Barboza (previously
   misdetermined as *M. biolleyi* [Schltr.] L. O.
   Williams)   (H10425)

M. nasuta Rchb. f.   (H7469)

M. neglecta (Schltr.) L. O. Williams   (H8697)

M. nicaraguensis (Ames & Garay) J. T. Atwood
   (B614)

M. pachyacron Schltr.   (H8927)

M. parvilabia Ames & C. Schweinf.   (A89-32)

M. pittieri (Ames) L. O. Williams   (Penneys 88)

M. ponerantha Rchb. f., aff.   (M4041)

M. pseudoneglecta J. T. Atwood   (H7601)

M. punctostriata Rchb. f.   (M&A4006)

M. ramonensis Schltr.   (B1469)

M. reichenheimiana Endres & Rchb. f.   (H8698)

M. ringens Rchb. f., cf.   (H10230)

M. sanguinea Rolfe   (H6752)

M. schlechteriana J. T. Atwood   (H8945)

M. sigmoidea (C. Schweinf.) Ames & Correll
   (H8827)

M. tonduzii (Schltr.) Ames & Correll   (H7541)

M. trilobata Ames & C. Schweinf.   (M4021)

M. umbratilis L. O. Williams   (H9084)

M. uncata Lindl.   (A89-174)

M. valerioi Ames & C. Schweinf.   (H8055)

M. variabilis Bateman ex Lindl.   (A89-27)

M. wercklei (Schltr.) L. O. Williams   (H8701)

+*Mesospinidium horichii* I. Bock (*M. endresii* of various
   authors, but not (Kraenzl.) Garay ex H. R. Sweet;
   determination based on photo in R. Laval collection)

+*M. warscewiczii* Rchb. f.   (H7926)

+*Miltoniopsis warscewiczii* (Rchb. f.) Garay &
   Dunst.   (A4017)

Myoxanthus schroederianum (Luer) Luer   (Grayum
   6652)

Nidema boothii (Lindl.) Schltr.   (H9389)

Oerstedella centradenia Rchb. f.   (H8913)

O. centropetala (Rchb. f.) Rchb. f.   (H6543)

O. endresii (Rchb. f.) Hágsater   (H9050)

O. exasperata (Rchb. f.) Hágsater   (H8813)

O. pansamalae (Schltr.) Hágsater   (H7650)

O. wallisii (Rchb. f.) Hágsater (including *O. pseudo-
   wallisii* (Schltr.) Hágsater)   (H1482)

+*Oncidium ansiferum* Rchb. f. (live plant at Selby)   (SEL
   1990-803)

+*O. bracteatum* Warsz. & Rchb. f.   (H9224)

+*O. bryolophotum* Rchb. f. (previously as *Oncidium
   heteranthum* Poepp. & Endl.)   (H8908)

+*O. cheirophorum* Rchb. f.   (H9021)

+*O. dichromaticum* Rchb. f. (syn.: *O. cabagrae*
   Schltr.)   (H4886)

+*O. globuliferum* Kunth   (H6872)

O. klotschianum Rchb. f.   (H9051)

+*O. luteum* Rolfe   (M&A4066)

+*O. obryzatoides* Kraenzl.   (H9223)

+*O. panduriforme* Ames & C. Schweinf.   (A88-22)

+*O. parviflorum* L. O. Williams   (H8413)

+*O. schroederianum* (O'Brian) Garay & Stacy   (H7577)

Ornithocephalus cf. *gladiatus* Hook.   (A89-323)

+*Osmoglossum egertonii* (Lindl.) Schltr.

+*Otoglossum chiriquense* (Rchb. f.) Garay &
   Dunst.   (H8538)

Palmorchis trilobulata L. O. Williams, cf.
   (H10547)

Pescatorea cerina (Lindl. & Paxton) Rchb. f.   (H11497)

Phragmipedium longifolium (Warsz. & Rchb. f.)
   Rolfe   (H7886)

Platystele caudatisepala (C. Schweinf.) Garay

P. lancilabris (Rchb. f.) Schltr.   (A89-151)

P. microtatantha (Schltr.) Garay   (H9558)

P. ovalifolia (Focke) Garay & Dunst.   (H6496)

P. oxyglossa (Schltr.) Garay   (H7808)

Pleurothallis abjecta Ames, aff.   (Boyle 89-31)

P. amparoana Schltr.   (A89-126)

P. bothros Luer   (I1252-B)

P. calyptrostele Schltr.   (H6796)

P. cardiothallis Rchb. f.   (H7792)

P. carpinterae Schltr.   (H7799)

P. cogniauxiana Schltr.   (H4628)

P. convallaria Schltr.   (B383)

P. costaricensis Rolfe   (H9096)

P. crescentilabia Ames   (H8095)

P. crocodiliceps Rchb. f. (syn.: *P. arietina* Ames)
   (H9098)

P. cuspidata Luer   (I1341)

P. dentipetala Rolfe ex Ames   (H7700)

P. deregularis (Barb. Rodr.) Luer   (M4002)

P. dolichopus Schltr.   (A4114)

P. eumecocaulon Schltr.   (H8770)

P. excavata Schltr.   (H9031)

P. floribunda Poepp. & Endl.   (H7804)

P. grandis Rolfe   (H9083)

P. homalantha Schltr. (including *P. nemorum*
   Schltr.)   (H8816)

P. immersa Linden & Rchb. f.   (H8975)

P. imraei Lindl.   (B1736)

P. janetiae Luer   (B382)

P. palliolata Ames   (H8611)

P. papillifera Rolfe   (A89-132)

P. phyllocardia Rchb. f.   (B3405)

P. pompalis Ames   (A89-325)

P. racemiflora Lindl. ex Lodd.   (B4209)

P. rowleei Ames   (H8934)

P. ruscifolia (Jacq.) R. Br.   (H8805)

P. saccata Ames   (H3228)

P. sanchoi Ames   (H8706)

P. segoviensis Rchb. f. (there may be as many as four
   different entities in Monteverde lumped as
   P. segoviensis)   (H9557)

P. segregatifolia Ames & C. Schweinf.   (H8606)

P. sempergemmatus Luer (identified previously as *P.
   uncinata* (Fawc.) Luer)   (A89-269)

P. sicaria Lindl.   (A89-169)

P. simmleriana Rendle   (A89-40)

P. strumosa Ames   (M&A4028)

P. thymochila Luer   (B181)

P. tonduzii Schltr.   (H7541)

P. tribuloides (Sw.) Lindl.   (H9883)

P. tuerckheimii Schltr.   (A4117)

Polystachya foliosa (Hook.) Rchb. f.   (H2934)

P. masayensis Rchb. f., cf.   (H10154)

Ponthieva maculata Lindl., cf. (possibly-*P. brenesii*
   Schltr.)   (H8219)

P. racemosa (Walter) C. Mohr   (M&A4007)

P. tuerckheimii Schltr.   (M&AA4117)

Prescottia cordifolia Rchb. f.   (B1088)

P. stachyodes (Sw.) Lindl., cf.   (A4063)

Psilochilus macrophyllus (Lindl.) Ames, cf.
   (A89-68)

Restrepia subserrata Schltr.   (H6678)

Restrepiopsis ujarensis (Rchb. f.) Luer   (A89-9)

+*Rossioglossum schlieperianum* (Rchb. f.) Garay & G. C.
   Kenn.   (A89-226)

Sarcoglottis hunteriana (Rchb. f.) Schltr.   (H10528)

Scaphosepalum anchoriferum (Rchb. f.) Rolfe
   (B795)

Scaphyglottis acostae (Schltr.) C. Schweinf.
   (A89-5)

S. amparoana (Schltr.) Dressler   (H3685)

S. bifida (Rchb. f.) C. Schweinf.   (A4059)

S. densa (Schltr.) B. R. Adams   (H7992)

S. jimenezii Schltr.   (H9047)

S. lindeniana (A. Rich & Galeotti) L. O. Williams (this
   probably includes two different species)
   (H6691)

S. mesocopis (Endres & Rchb. f.) Benth. & Hook. f. ex
   Hemsl.   (H6693)

S. micrantha (Lindl.) Ames & Correll   (H10657)

S. prolifera Cogn.   (H7855)

S. pulchella (Schltr.) L. O. Williams   (B1440)

S. sessiliflora B. R. Adams   (I1709)

+*Sigmatostalix hymenantha* Schltr.   (B2079)

+*S. macrobulbon* Kraenzl.   (B878)

S. picta Rchb. f., *sensu lato*   (H6060)

+*S. racemifera* L. O. Williams   (Boyle 89-84)

Sobralia amabilis (Rchb. f.) L. O. Williams
   (H7011)

S. atropubescens Ames & C. Schweinf.

S. bradeorum Schltr.   (H6779)

S. dissimilis Dressler   (A89-343)

S. helleri A. D. Hawkes   (H7252)

S. macra Schltr.   (H8662)

S. mucronata Ames & C. Schweinf.   (H10152)

S. powellii Schltr.   (H9182)

S. warscewiczii Rchb. f., cf.   (A89-322)

Solenocentrum costaricense Schltr.   (H9574)

Stanhopea wardii Lodd. ex Lindl.

Stelis aprica Lindl., aff.   (A89-354)

S. argentata Lindl., cf.   (H8414)

S. crescentiicola Schltr., aff.   (M4003)

S. gracilis Ames (A4074)

S. longipetiolata Ames, aff. (A4003)

S. microchila Schltr. (A89-145)

S. pardipes Rchb. f. (A89-203)

S. parvula Lindl., cf. (A89-134)

*Stellilabium barbozae J. T. Atwood (Atwood et al. 5051)

*S. boylei J. T. Atwood (A89-28)

*S. bullpenense J. T. Atwood (A89-100)

*S. campbellorum J. T. Atwood (A89-101)

*S. monteverdense J. T. Atwood (A89-99)

Stenorrhynchos (*Coccineorchis*) *bracteosum* Ames & C. Schweinf. (H9743)

S. (*Coccineorchis*) *navarrense* Ames (H4007)

S. speciosum (Jacq.) Rich. (A4106)

S. (*Coccineorchis*) *standleyi* Ames (H11672)

+*Systelloglossum acuminatum* Ames & C. Schweinf. (H10684)

+*S. costaricense* Schltr. (H7100)

Telipogon spp. (*fide* W. Haber and G. Barboza)

Teuscheria sp. (B1443)

+*Ticoglossum krameri* (Rchb. f.) Lucas Rodr. ex Halb. (B1645)

Trevoria glumacea Garay (Atwood s.n.)

+*Trichopilia suavis* Lindl. & Paxton (B1921)

+*T. turialbae* Rchb. f. (B760)

Trichosalpinx blaisdellii (S. Watson) Luer (H8824)

T. cedralensis (Ames) Luer (H9027)

T. foliata (Griseb.) Luer (A89-297)

T. memor (Rchb. f.) Luer (H8824)

T. rotundata (C. Schweinf.) Luer

Trigonidium lankesteri Ames (H8085)

Trisetella triaristella (Rchb. f.) Luer, cf. (H5474)

Vanilla planifolia Andrews (H8471)

Warrea costaricensis Schltr. (Ivey 230)

Warreopsis parviflora (L. O. Williams) Garay (H4484)

Xylobium elongatum (Lindl. & Paxton) Hemsl. (H9090)

X. powellii Schltr. (A88-56)

Zootrophion endresianum (Kraenzl.) Luer (H7351)

Appendix 4

Bromeliads of Monteverde

Harry E. Luther

The following annotated list of 28 species of Bromeliaceae is based largely on the collections of S. Ingram and K. Ferrell-Ingram from the preserve Triangle area deposited at the herbarium of the Marie Selby Botanical Gardens and the files maintained at the Mulford B. Foster Bromeliad Idontification Center. A total of 65 species have been found in the larger area of the Monteverde reserve (Appendix 1). The species are arranged first by subfamilies, then alphabetically by genus and species. Taxa proposed to be reclassified in the newly erected genera *Racinaea* and *Werauhia* are noted in parentheses.

Subfamily Bromelioideae

Leaves mostly serrate-margined, ovary inferior, fruit a fleshy berry, seeds unappendaged. No taxa from this subfamily are known from the preserve Triangle; they are mostly from lower elevations in Costa Rica.

Subfamily Pitcairnioideae

Leaves mostly serrate-margined, ovary mostly superior, fruit a dry capsule, seeds caudate or winged.

Pitcairnia atrorubens (Beer) Baker. Inflorescence dense and cylindrical; plant stemless, terrestrial or epiphytic.
Pitcairnia brittoniana Mez. Inflorescence laxly secund-flowered; plant a hemiepiphytic vine.

Subfamily Tillandsioideae

Leaves always entire, ovary superior, fruit a dry capsule, seeds plumose.

Catopsis nitida (Hook.) Griseb. Completely green, tubular epiphytes.
Guzmania angustifolia (Baker) Wittm. An epiphyte with an elongate, leafy stem, red bracts and yellow petals.
G. compacta Mez. Red-striate, soft foliage with a capitate, yellow or red and yellow inflorescence.
G. coriostachya (Griseb.) Mez. Inflorescence conelike, tan with nocturnal, cream flowers.
G. nicaraguensis Mez & C. F. Baker ex Mez. Red-striate leaves and a short, cylindrical inflorescence of red bracts and yellow petals; the rosette is leafy and compact.
G. plicatifolia L. B. Sm. The only Costa Rican *Guzmania* with conspicuously plicate leaf blades and a compound inflorescence; the inflorescence has red bracts and yellow flowers.

G. scandens H. Luther & W. J. Kress. This rhizomatous epiphyte can be distinguished by a combination of narrow plicate leaves and a simple inflorescence with purplish bracts and yellow-green flowers.

G. stenostachya L. B. Sm. Usually a rather lax and untidy rosette of leaves; the inflorescence is slenderly cylindrical with red bracts and yellow petals.

Tillandsia adpressa André var. tonduziana (Mez) L. B. Smith. A pseudobulbous canopy epiphyte with soft leaves and a drab, small-flowered, compound inflorescence (*Racinaea schumanniana* [Wittmack] J. R. Grant).

T. excelsa Griseb. A variable rosette-forming epiphyte with soft, straplike green or reddish leaves and a showy, branched inflorescence of red bracts and lavender-purple petals.

T. insignis (Mez) L. B. Sm. & Pittendr. A small, erect, caulescent epiphyte with a simple inflorescence of red bracts and very dark blue-violet petals. Clusters of sterile plants may not be recognized as a bromeliad, appearing more like a gigantic moss.

T. punctulata Schltdl. & Chamisso. A bulbous rosette with green leaf blades and nearly black leaf sheaths; the inflorescence is simple or compound with red and green bracts and violet petals tipped with white.

Vriesea bracteosa (Mez & Wercklé) L. B. Sm. & Pittendr. The green, capitate inflorescence with two-flowered, nearly aborted branches is similar to other members of the "Thecophylloid" complex of *Vriesea* (Utley 1983). The leaves are usually erect and unmarked.

(With the exception of *V. incurva*, the following members of the genus *Vriesa* have earlier been classified in the genus *Werauhia* [J. R. Grant].)

V. capitata (Mez & Wercklé) L. B. Sm. & Pittendr. Very similar to V. bracteosa but leaves are usually narrower and somewhat silver beneath.

V. comata (Mez & Wercklé) L. B. Sm. & Pittendr. This species is very similar to *V. bracteosa*, but usually somewhat smaller and more compact.

V. graminifolia Mez & Wercklé. Usually densely clustering with narrow triangular leaf blades and a short secund-flowered inflorescence.

V. hygrometrica (André) L. B. Sm. & Pittendr. Another "Thecophylloid" but with colorfully tesselated leaf blades.

V. incurva (Griseb.) Read. A gray or silver, pseudobulbous canopy epiphyte with a pendent inflorescence of pink bracts and yellow-green petals.

V. notata L. B. Sm. & Pittendr. A rather small "Thecophylloid" usually with reddish suffused or tesselated leaf blades. To accurately determine any of these related *Vrieseas* species, one should refer to Utley (1983).

V. pedicellata (Mez & Wercklé) L. B. Sm. & Pittendr. Leaves often suffused with red, and the lateral branches may have up to five flowers instead of the usual two of most "Thecophylloids."

V. stenophylla (Mez & Wercklé) L. B. Sm. & Pittendr. This "Thecophylloid" is usually somewhat caulescent (*Werauhia stenophylla* [Mez & Wercklé] J. R. Grant).

V. tonduziana L. B. Sm. From a rosette of spreading, dark green leaves is produced a stout, swordlike inflorescence; the nocturnal flowers are exerted from the underside of the bracts.

V. umbrosa L. B. Sm. Similar to *V. pedicellata* but usually with plain green leaves and a denser cylindrical inflorescence.

V. viridiflora (Regel) Wittm. ex Mez. Rather like a smaller, more delicate version of *V. tonduziana*; the scape is relatively much longer.

V. vittata (Mez & Wercklé) L. B. Sm. & Pittendr. The brown-banded leaf blades and the simple, few-flowered inflorescence distinguish this species.

V. werckleana Mez. The largest epiphyte in the preserve, with a rosette of dark green leaves to over 1 m in diameter; the compound inflorescence produces pale green, nocturnal flowers visited by bats.

Appendix 5

Host Plants of Selected Cercopoidea from Monteverde

Daniel C. Peck

Plant determinations were made by William A. Haber.

Species	Nymph	Adult	Host Family	Host Species
Clastopteridae				
Clastoptera sp.	x		Rubiaceae	*Spermacoce assurgens*
		x	Verbenaceae	*Verbena litoralis*
Aphrophoridae				
Cephisus siccifolius	x	x	Euphorbiaceae	*Croton* sp.
	x	x	Rutaceae	*Zanthoxylum insulare*
	x		Solanaceae	*Acnistus arborescens*
Cercopidae				
Mahanarva costaricensi	x	x	Heliconiaceae	*Heliconia tortuosa*
		x	Marantaceae	*Calathea* sp.
Iphirhina quota	x	x	Acanthaceae	*Justicia oerstedii*
		x	Boraginaceae	*Bourreria costaricensis*
	x		Piperaceae	*Piper amalago*
	x	x	Piperaceae	*Piper auritum*
	x	x	Piperaceae	*Piper* sp.
	x	x	Piperaceae	*Pothomorphe umbellata*
Prosapia sp. near *bicincta*		x	Aquifoliaceae	*Ilex haberi*
	x		Cyperaceae	*Kyllinga brevifolia*
	x		Cyperaceae	*Kyllinga* sp.
	x	x	Poaceae	*Cynodon nlemfuensis*
	x	x	Poaceae	*Digitaria abyssinica*
		x	Poaceae	*Ichnathus nemorosus*
		x	Poaceae	*Lasiacis* sp.
	x		Poaceae	*Paspalum conjugatum*
	x	x	Poaceae	*Pennisetum clandestinum*
	x	x	Poaceae	*Pennisetum purpureum*
	x	x	Poaceae	*Sporobolus* spp.

Appendix 6

Preliminary List of Psylloidea Known from Costa Rican Cloud Forests (1200–2000 m).

David Hollis

Species	Host Species
Carsidaridae	
Paracarsidara sp.	*Quararibea* sp. (Bombacaceae)
Homotomidae	
Synoza cornutiventris	*Ficus hartwegii* (Moraceae)
Synoza (2 spp.)	*Ficus mcbrideii*
	Ficus tuerckheimii
Phacopteronidae	
Pseudophacopteron sp.	Unknown
Calophyidae	
*Calophya monticola	*Mauria heterophylla* (Anacardiaceae)
*Calophya (4 spp.)	Loranthaceae and Rutaceae
Mastigimas schwarzi	*Cedrela tonduzii* (Meliaceae)
Psyllidae: Togepsyllinae	
Syncoptozus bifurcatus	Unknown
Psyllidae: Aphalarinae	
Burckhardtia montana	Unknown
*Gyropsylla clypeata	*Ilex lamprophyla* (Aquifoliaceae)
*Gyropsylla (2 spp.)	Aquifoliaceae
*Neaphalara fortunae	Araliaceae
Genus and species unknown	*Nectandra membranacea* (Lauraceae)
Psyllidae: Paurocephalinae	
Haplaphalara (6 spp.)	Melastomataceae, also Clusiaceae
Paurocephala (2 spp.)	*Roupala montana* (Proteaceae)
Psyllidae: Euphalerinae	
*Euphalerus certus	*Lonchocarpus atropurpureus* (Leguminosae)
Euphalerus (2 spp.)	*Gaiadendron punctatum* (Loranthaceae)
	Oryctanthes spicatus (Loranthaceae)

Species	Host Species
Psyllidae: Diaphorininae	
Caradocia delongi	*Tapirira brenesii* (Anacardiaceae)
Caradocia sp.	*Billia hippocastanum* (Hippocastanaceae)
Katacephala (4 spp.)	*Eugenia* spp., *Calyptranthes pittierii* and other Myrtaceae
Tuthillia latipennis	*Myrcianthes fragrans* (Myrtaceae)
Tuthillia sp.	Unknown
Psyllidae: Ciriacreminae	
Auchmerina hirsuta	*Inga skutchii, I. paterno* (Leguminosae)
Euceropsylla breviforceps	*Inga* spp.
Euceropsylla martorelli	*Inga oerstediana*
Euceropsylla stylicauda	*Inga oerstediana*
Euceropsylla rotundi- *forceps*	*Inga oerstediana*
Euceropsylla russoi	*Inga skutchii*
Euceropsylla orizabensis	*Cojoba sophorocarpum* (Leguminosae)
Euceropsylla torus	*Cojoba costaricensis*
Euceropsylla (8 spp.)	Leguminosae: Mimosoideae
Limbopsylla nigrivenis	*Guatteria tonduzii* (Annonaceae)
Limbopsylla sp.	*Guatteria oliviformis*
Manapa tumida	*Inga* sp.
Manapa sp.	Unknown
Mitrapsylla (2 spp.)	Leguminosae
Platycorypha princeps	*Myroxylon balsamum* (Leguminosae)
Triozidae	
Hemitrioza (2 spp.)	Unknown
Izpania acona	*Citharexylum donnell-smithii* (Verbenaceae)
Izpania sp.	Unknown
Leuronota inusitata	*Clusia* spp. (Clusiaceae)
Leuronota (3 spp.)	*Clusia* spp.
Leuronota flexinota	Unknown
Leuronota flavipennis	*Weinmannia pinnata* (Cunoniaceae)
Leuronota tumida	*Weinmannia pinnata, W. wercklei*
Leuronota forcipata	*Alfaroa costaricense* (Juglandaceae)
Leuronota robusta	*Alfaroa costaricense*
Leuronota (2 spp.)	*Oreamunnea mexicana* (Juglandaceae)
Leuronota longigena	Unknown
Leuronota (5 spp.)	*Sapium oligneuron* (Euphorbiaceae), *Zanthoxylum insulare* (Rutaceae)
Neolithus sp.	*Sapium oligoneurum* (Euphorbiaceae)
Rhegmoza tinctoria	*Myrcianthes fragrans* (Myrtaceae)
Rhegmoza sp.	*Calyptranthes pittierii* (Myrtaceae)
Rhinopsylla antennata	Unknown
Schedoneolithus sp.	Lauraceae
Trichochermes magna	*Pseudolmedia* sp. (Moraceae)
Trichochermes sp.	Unknown
Trioza arribensis	*Nectandra membrancea* (Lauraceae)
Trioza dentata	Unknown
Trioza longigenae	*Quercus costaricensis* (Fagaceae)
Trioza nomei	*Dendropanax* sp. (Araliaceae)
Trioza panamensis	*Pentacalia andicola* (Compositae)
Trioza psyllihabitus	*Arctostaphylos arbutoides* (Ericaceae)
Trioza sp.	*Diospyros digyna* (Ebenaceae)
Trioza sp.	*Cinnamomum hammelianum* (Lauraceae)
Trioza sp.	*Nectandra salicina* (Lauraceae)
Trioza sp.	Myrtaceae
Trioza sp.	*Solanum storkii* (Solanaceae)
Trioza (2 spp.)	*Pseudobaccharis trinervis* (Compositae)
Trioza (20 spp.)	Lauraceae, Clethraceae, Clusiaceae, Ebenaceae, Styracaceae, Loranthaceae, Moraceae, Juglandaceae, Betulaceae, Cunoniaceae
Triozoida ingens	Myrtaceae

* = species known to induce gall formation.

Appendix 7

Eusocial Wasps (Hymenoptera: Vespidae: Polistinae) Collected from Monteverde

Sean O'Donnell

Taxon	Elevational Distribution (m)
Polistini	
Polistes aterrimus	Above 1540
P. instabilis	Elevational migrant (does not nest in Monteverde)
Mischocyttarini	
Mischocyttarus atrocyaneus	Up to 1350
M. basimacula	Up to 1400
M. labiatus	Up to 1500
M. mastigophorus	Above 1450
M. mixtus	1400–1500
M. pallidipectus	1350–1540
Epiponini	
Agelaia areata	Up to 1400
A. panamensis	Up to 1500
A. xanthopus	1400–1550
A. yepocapa	1300–1450
Epipona niger	Up to 1540
Polybia aequatorialis	1300–1700
P. diguetana	Up to 1450
P. raui	1480–1700
P. rejecta	Up to 1400
P. simillima	1100
Synoeca septentrionalis	Up to 1350

Appendix 8

Amphibians and Reptiles of Monteverde

J. Alan Pounds
M. P. Fogden

Scientific Name[a]	Common Name	Distribution[b]		Habitat Stratum[c]
		CLASS AMPHIBIA		
Order Gymnophiona				
Family Caeciliidae				
Demophis mexicanus	Gray Caecilian	<u>5</u> <u>6</u>		S
Gymnopis multiplicata	Purple Caecilian	<u>1</u> <u>2</u> <u>3</u>		S
Order Caudata				
Family Plethodontidae[d]				
Bolitoglossa robusta	Ring-tailed Salamander	2 3 4 <u>5</u> 6	E	T
Bolitoglossa "subpalmata"[e]	Monteverde Salamander	3 4	E	C
Nototriton picadoi (1)	Moss Salamander	4	E	C
Oedipina poelzi	Poelz's Worm Salamander	4	E	S,T
O. uniformis[g]	Highland Worm Salamander	2 3 4	E	S,T
Order Anura				
Family Bufonidae				
Atelopus varius	Harlequin Frog	1 2 3 4 5 6	E	M	T
Bufo coccifer	Dry Forest Toad	1 2 <u>3</u>		T
B. coniferus	Green Climbing Toad	<u>2</u> <u>3</u> <u>4</u> 5 6		C
B. haematiticus	Leaf Litter Toad	6	M	T
B. marinus	Giant Toad	1 2 3		T
B. melanochloris	Foothill Stream Toad	6	A	T
B. periglenes	Golden Toad	4	E	M	S
Family Centrolenidae				
Centrolenella prosoblepon	Emerald Glass Frog	1 2 3 4 5 <u>6</u>		C
Cochranella euknemos (2)	Cascade Glass Frog	1	M	C
C. granulosa (2)	Granular Glass Frog	1 6	M	C

Scientific Name[a]	Common Name	Distribution[b]		Habitat Stratum[c]	

CLASS AMPHIBIA

Scientific Name[a]	Common Name	Distribution[b]		Habitat Stratum[c]	
Hyalinobatrachium colymbiphyllum (2)	Bare-hearted Glass Frog	2 3 4		A	C
H. fleischmanni (2)	Fleischmann's Glass Frog	1 2 3 4			C
H. valerioi (2)	Reticulated Glass Frog	5 6			C
H. vireovittatum (2)	Green-striped Glass Frog	5 6	E		C
Family Hylidae					
Agalychnis annae	Golden-eyed Leaf Frog	2 3 4 5	E	M	C
A. callidryas	Red-eyed Leaf Frog	6		M	C
Anotheca spinosa	Crowned Frog	5		M	C
Hyla angustillineata	Pin-striped Treefrog	3 4	E	M	C
H. fimbrimembra	Highland Fringe-limbed Treefrog	4	E		C
H. loquax	Orange-and-Yellow Swamp Frog	6			C
H. miliaria	Giant Fringe-limbed Treefrog	6		M	C
H. pseudopuma	Meadow Treefrog	2 3 4 5 6	E		C
H. rivularis	Mountain Stream Frog	2 3 4 5	E	M	C
H. ruficoculis	Rufous-eyed Stream Frog	1 2 5 6	E		C
H. tica	Lichen Stream Frog	2 3 4	E	M	C
H. uranochroa	Red-eyed Stream Frog	2 3 4 5	E		C
Phyllomedusa lemur	Lemur Frog	3 4 5 6		M	C
Smilisca phaeota	Masked Treefrog	5 6			C
S. sordida	Drab River Frog	1 6			C
Family Leptodactylidae					
Eleutherodactylus altae	Coral-spotted Rain Frog	5 6			C
E. andi	Salmon-bellied Rain Frog	4 5 6	E	M	C
E. angelicus	Tilarán Rain Frog	1 2 3 4 5 6	E	M	T
E. biporcatus	Broad-headed Rain Frog	6		A	T
E. bransfordii	Bransford's Litter Frog	1 2 3 4 5 6			T
E. caryophyllaceus	Leaf-breeding Rain Frog	6		M	C
E. cerasinus[h]	Clay-colored Rain Frog	6		M	C
E. crassidigitus	Spot-shouldered Rain Frog	1 2 3 4 5 6			C
E. cruentus	Golden-groined Rain Frog	3 4 5 6			C
E. cuaquero	Monteverde Rain Frog	4	E		C
E. diastema	Common Dink Frog	1 2 3 4 5 6			C
E. fitzingeri	Fitzinger's Rain Frog	2 3 5 6			C
E. hylaeformis	Montane Dink Frog	3 4 5	E		C
E. melanostictus	Quark Frog	3 4 5	E		C
E. podiciferus	Piglet Litter Frog	1 2 3 4 5	E		T
E. ridens	Pygmy Rain Frog	4 5 6			C
E. rugulosus	Middle American Stream Frog	6		M	T
E. underwoodi[h]	Underwood's Litter Frog	1 2 3 4 5	E		T
Leptodactylus pentadactylus	Smoky Jungle Frog	6			T
Family Microhylidae					
Hypopachus variolosus	Sheep Frog	1 2 3		A	S
Nelsonophryne aterimma	Black Narrow-mouthed Toad	5 6			S
Family Ranidae					
Rana forreri[i]	Forrer's Leopard Frog	1 2		M	T
R. vibicaria	Green-eyed Frog	3 4	E	M	T
R. warszewitschii	Spot-thighed Frog	1 2 3 4 5 6		A	T

CLASS REPTILIA

Scientific Name[a]	Common Name	Distribution[b]		Habitat Stratum[c]	
Order Squamata, Suborder Sauria					
Family Anguidae					
Celestus cynaochloris	Green-bellied Caiman Lizard	1 2 3	E		C
C. hylaius[h]	Rain Forest Caiman Lizard	6			C
Diploglossus bilobatus	Galliwasp	1 2 5 6			T
Family Corytophanidae					
Basiliscus plumifrons	Emerald Basilisk	6			C
B. basiliscus	Common Basilisk	1			C
Corytophanes cristatus	Casque-headed Lizard	6			C
Family Gekkonidae					
Phyllodactylus tuberculosus[h]	Tuberculate Leaf-toed Gecko	1			C

Scientific Name[a]	Common Name	Distribution[b]		Habitat Stratum[c]
		CLASS REPTILIA		
Family Gymnothalmidae				
Anadia ocellata	Bromeliad Lizard	6		C
Family Iguanidae				
Ctenosaura similis	Ctenosaur	1		C
Family Phrynosomatidae				
Sceloporus malachiticus	Green Spiny Lizard	1 2 3		C
Family Polychrotidae				
Dactyloa insignis (3)	Giant Banded Anole	2 3 4 5 6		C
Norops altae (3)	Montane Anole	3 4	E	C
N. biporcatus (3)	Green Tree Anole	1 5 6		C
N. capito (3)	Short-snouted Anole	2 6		C
N. cupreus (3)	Dry Forest Anole	1		C
N. humilis (3)	Ground Anole	1 2 3 4 5 6		C
N. intermedius	Gray Lichen Anole	2 3		C
N. lemurinus (3)[h]	Red-throated Trunk Anole	2 6		C
N. limifrons (3)	Slender Forest Anole	5 6		C
N. oxylophus (3)	Stream Anole	1 2 5 6		C
N. sericeus (3)	Indigo-throated Anole	1 2		C
N. tropidolepis (3)	Cloud Forest Anole	2 3 4	E	C
N. woodi (3)	Blue-eyed Anole	1 2 3 4 5	E	C
Polychrus gutturosus	Green Canopy Lizard	6		C
Family Scincidae				
Mabuya unimarginata	Bronze-backed Climbing Skink	1 2 3		C
Sphenomorphus cherriei	Cherrie's Litter Skink	2 3 5 6		T
Family Teiidae				
Ameiva festiva	Central American Whiptail	5 6		T
A. undulata	Barred Whiptail	1 2		T
Family Xantusiidae				
Lepidophyma flavimaculatum	Tropical Night Lizard	6		T
Suborder Serpentes				
Family Boidae				
Boa constrictor	Boa Constrictor	1 2		C
Family Colubridae				
Amastridium veliferum	Ridge-nosed Snake	6		T
Chironius exoletus	Green Keelback	1 2 3 4 5		C
C. grandisquamis	Ebony Keelback	1 2 5 6		C
Clelia clelia	Mussurana	6		T
C. scytalina	Montane Mussurana	3 4 5		T
Coluber mentovarius (4)	Dry Forest Racer	1		T
Coniophanes fissidens	Glossy Litter Snake	1 6		T
C. piceivittis	Twin-striped Litter Snake	1 2		T
Dendrophidion nuchalis	Pink-tailed Forest Racer	1		T
D. paucicarinatum	Cloud Forest Racer	2 3 4 5 6	E	C
D. percarinatum	Brown Forest Racer	1		C
D. vinitor	Banded Green Racer	6		C
Drymarchon corais	Black-tailed Cribo	1 2 3		T
Drymobius margaritiferus	Speckled Racer	1 2 3		T
D. melanotropis	Green Frog-eater	6		T
Elaphe triaspis (5)	Olivaceaous Rat Snake	1 2 3		C
Enulius sclateri	Collared Snake	5 6		T
Erythrolamprus bizonus	Double-ringed False Coral	1 2 3		T
E. mimus[h]	Split-ringed False Coral	6		T
Geophis brachycephalus	Gray Earth Snake	2 3 4 5 6		S
G. godmani	Yellow-bellied Earth Snake	3 4		E
G. hoffmani	Hoffman's Earth Snake	2		S
G. ruthveni	Ruthven's Earth Snake	6		S
Hydromorphus concolor	Tropical Seep Snake	1 6		S
Imantodes cenchoa	Blunt-headed Tree Snake	1 2 3 4 5 6		C
I. gemmistratus	Many-banded Tree Snake	1		C
I. inornatus	Peppered Tree Snake	3 5 6		C
Lampropeltis triangulum	Tropical Kingsnake	2 3 4		T
Leptodeira septentrionalis	Cat-eyed Snake	2 6		C

539   Appendix 8

Scientific Name[a]	Common Name	Distribution[b]	Habitat Stratum[c]
CLASS REPTILIA			

CLASS REPTILIA

Scientific Name[a]	Common Name	Distribution[b]	Habitat Stratum[c]
Leptodrymus pulcherrimus	Green-headed Racer	1	T
Leptophis ahaetulla	Green Parrot Snake	1	C
L. mexicanus	Mexican Parrot Snake	1 <u>2</u>	C
L. nebulosus	Bronze-striped Parrot Snake	2 3 4 <u>6</u>	C
Liophis epinephalus	Fire-bellied Snake	1 2 3 4 5 6	T
Mastigodryas melanolomus	Salmon-bellied Racer	1 2 3	T
Ninia maculata	Spotted Wood Snake	6	T
N. psephota	Upland Wood Snake	2 3 4 E	T
Oxybelis aeneus	Brown Vine Snake	1 <u>2</u>	C
O. brevirostris	Short-snouted Vine Snake	6	C
O. fulgidus	Green Vine Snake	1 2 <u>3</u> <u>4</u> <u>5</u> 6	C
Pseustes poecilonotus	Bird-eating Snake	6	C
Rhadinaea calligaster	Green Litter Snake	3 4 <u>5</u> E	T
R. decorata	Pink-bellied Litter Snake	6	T
R. serperaster	Striped Litter Snake	<u>2</u> 3 4 <u>5</u> 6 E	T
Scaphiodontophis annulatus (6)	Skink-eater	6	T
Scolecophis atrocinctus	Harlequin Snake	1 2	C
Sibon annulatus	Caribbean Banded Snail-eater	<u>2</u> 3 5 6	C
S. dimidiatus	Pacific Banded Snail-eater	<u>2</u> <u>3</u> 4	C
S. longifrens	Licheny Snail-eater	6	C
Spilotes pullatus	Mica	2	C
Stenorrhina freminvillii	Scorpion-eater	1 2	T
Tantilla armillata	Striped Crowned Snake	1 2	T
T. ruficeps (7)	Orange-bellied Crowned Snake	1 2 3	T
T. schistosa	Red-tailed Crowned Snake	2 <u>6</u>	T
T. supracincta (8)	Tricolored Crowned Snake	6	T
T. reticulata[h]	Reticulate Crowned Snake	6	T
Trimetopon gracile	Slender Dwarf Snake	2 <u>3</u> <u>4</u> E	T
T. pliolepis	Faded Dwarf Snake	2 3 4	T
T. simile	White-bellied Dwarf Snake	4 E	T
T. slevini	Slevin's Dwarf Snake	<u>2</u> E	T
Urotheca decipiens (9)	Long-tailed Litter Snake	3 4 5	T
U. euryzona (10)	Halloween Snake	<u>2</u> 6	T
U. guentheri (9)	Orange-bellied Litter Snake	2 3 4 <u>5</u>	T
Xenodon rhabdocephalus	False Fer-de-lance	1 <u>2</u>	T
Family Elapidae			
Micrurus alleni	Allen's Coral Snake	6	T
M. nigrocinctus	Central American Coral Snake	1 2 3	T
Family Typhlopidae			
Typhlops costaricensis	Costa Rican Blind Snake	2 3	S
Family Viperidae			
Bothrops asper	Terciopelo	1 5 6	T
Bothriechis lateralis	Green Palm Viper	1 2 3 4 <u>5</u> 6 E	C
B. nigroviridis	Green-and-black Palm Viper	<u>2</u> 3 4 E	C
B. schegelii	Eyelash Viper	1 <u>2</u> 6	C

[a]Species with numbered superscripts are listed in previous checklists under the following names: 1, *Chiroptriton picadoi*; 2, *Centrolenella*; 3, *Anolis*; 4, *Masticophis*; 5, *Senticolis*; 6, *Scaphiodontophis venustissimus*; 7, *Tantilla melanocephala*; 8, *Tantilla annulata*; 9, *Rhadinaea*; 10, *Pilocercus*.
[b]Numbers correspond to altitudinal zones: (1) Pacific slope (690–1300 m); (2) Pacific slope (1300–1450 m); (3) upper Pacific slope to the vicinity of the Continental Divide (1450–1600 m); (4) Continental Divide, including the highest peaks (to about 1850 m), down to 1450 m on the upper Caribbean slope; (5) Caribbean slope (950–1450 m); (6) Caribbean slope (600–950 m). Underlining of a zone number indicates that a species was rare in that zone (or there were no recent records) prior to the declines (see sec. 5.1.1, p. 151). E = endemic species = restricted to the uplands of Costa Rica and western Panama (west of the Canal Zone). Scorings are conservative (underestimating the number of endemics) inasmuch as further study may show extralimital populations of some upland forms to be separate species (e.g., *Phyllomedusa lemur* in eastern Panama; J. Savage, pers. comm). For these scorings I have relied on numerous works (Myers and Rand 1969, Savage and Heyer 1969, Duellman 1970, 1990, Savage 1972, 1975, Starrett and Savage 1973, Wake and Lynch 1976, Savage and Talbot 1978, Lynch 1979, Scott et al., 1983, Peters et al. 1986, Savage and Villa 1986, Wake 1987, Villa et al. 1988, Campbell and Lamar 1989, Donnelly 1994, Guyer 1994). Presence-absence patterns are given for anurans only (for the study area of Pounds et al. 1997; see text). A = absent in 1990 but reappeared in 1991–94; M = missing throughout 1990–94.
[c]S = subterranean; T = terrestrial; and C = climbing on aboveground vegetation (i.e., semiarboreal or arboreal).
[d]All tropical salamanders are bolitoglossine plethodontids (supergenus *Bolitoglossa*; Wake 1987).
[e]*Bolitoglossa "subpalmata"* is probably a separate species from the nominal form (D. Wake, pers. comm.).
[f]Currently being described as a new species of *Nototriton* by D. Wake.
[g]*Oedipina uniformis* is a separate species from the lowland forms of *O. "uniformis"* such as that listed for La Selva by Donnelly (1994).
[h]New (not included on previous checklists).
[i]This is the only species that has reappeared in the study area of Pounds et al. since 1990–94. It reappeared in 1997.

Appendix 9

Birds of the Monteverde Area

M. P. Fogden

Modified from Fogden (1993) to conform to American Ornithologists' Union (AOU) order and nomenclature (through the 7th ed., AOU 1998) and to reflect the six Holdridge Life Zones in the Monteverde region (see Table 3.1, Fig. 1.4).

Scientific Name[a]	Common Name	Life Zone[b]					
		Zone 1 Prmtn Moist	Zone 2 Prmtn Wet	Zone 3 L Mntn Wet	Zone 4 L Mntn Rain	Zone 5 Prmtn Rain	Zone 6 Wet, Prmtn T
Tinamidae (tinamous)							
Tinamus major	Great Tinamou						U
Nothocercus bonapartei	Highland Tinamou			F	F	F	
Crypturellus soui	Little Tinamou						U
Podicipedidae (grebes)							
Tachybaptus dominicus	Least Grebe		*			C	C
Podilymbus podiceps	Pied-billed Grebe						U
Phalacrocoracidae (cormorants)							
Phalacrocorax brasilianus	Neotropic Cormorant					R	U
Anhigidae (darters)							
Anhinga anhinga	Anhinga						R
Fregatidae (frigatebirds)							
Fregata magnificens	Magnificent Frigatebird		*		*	*	

Scientific Name[a]	Common name	Zone 1 Prmtn Moist	Zone 2 Prmtn Wet	Zone 3 L Mntn Wet	Zone 4 L Mntn Rain	Zone 5 Prmtn Rain	Zone 6 Wet, Prmtn T
Ardeidae (herons and allies)							
Tigrisoma fasciatum	Fasciated Tiger-Heron					U	?
Ardea herodias(l)	Great Blue Heron						R
Ardea alba(l)	Great Egret					R	U
Egretta caerulea(l)	Little Blue Heron					*	R
Bubulcus ibis	Cattle Egret	C	C	U		?	C
Butorides virescens	Green Heron					R	U
Nycticorax nycticorax	Black-crowned Night-Heron						U
Ciconiidae (storks)							
Mycteria americana	Wood Stork				*	*	
Cathartidae (New World vultures)							
Coragyps atratus	Black Vulture	C	C	U	U	U	C
Cathartes aura(l)	Turkey Vulture	C	C	F	F	F	C
Sarcoramphus papa	King Vulture			*		R	R
Accipitridae (kites, hawks, and eagles)							
Pandion haliaetus(l)	Osprey			*			R
Chondrohierax uncinatus	Hook-billed Kite	R	R	R		R	R
Elanoides forficatus(l, e)	Swallow-tailed Kite	U	F	C	C	C	C
Elanus leucurus	White-tailed Kite					*	
Harpagus bidentatus	Double-toothed Kite	R	R	*		F	F
Ictinia plumbea(l)	Plumbeous Kite					*	*
Circus cyaneus	Northern Harrier					*	
Accipiter superciliosus	Tiny Hawk					U	U
Accipiter striatus(l)	Sharp-shinned Hawk	R	R	R	R	U	U
Accipiter cooperii(l)	Cooper's Hawk			R	R	R	
Accipiter bicolor	Bicolored Hawk		?	R	R	R	R
Leucopternis princeps(e)	Barred Hawk		R	U	F	F	F
Leucopternis albicollis	White Hawk					F	F
Asturina nitida	Gray Hawk	F	U	R			U
Buteogallus anthracinus	Common Black-Hawk	R	R	R		R	?
Buteogallus urubitinga	Great Black-Hawk			R	R	U	U
Harpyhaliaetus solitarius	Solitary Eagle					R	
Buteo platypterus(l)	Broad-winged Hawk	F	F	F	F	F	F
Buteo brachyurus(l)	Short-tailed Hawk	R	R	R	U	F	F
Buteo swainsoni(l)	Swainson's Hawk					R	R
Buteo albicaudatus	White-tailed Hawk					*	
Buteo albonotatus	Zone-tailed Hawk	U	R				
Buteo jamaicensis	Red-tailed Hawk			*		*	
Spizaetus tyrannus(e)	Black Hawk-Eagle			R	R	U	U
Spizaetus ornatus	Ornate Hawk-Eagle		R	R	R	U	U
Falconidae (falcons)							
Micrastur ruficollis	Barred Forest-Falcon	U	F	F	F	F	F
Micrastur semitorquatus	Collared Forest-Falcon	?	R	R	R	R	R
Herpetotheres cachinnans	Laughing Falcon	U	R				
Falco sparverius(l)	American Kestrel	U	R				R
Falco rufigularis	Bat Falcon	U	U	R	R	F	F
Falco peregrinus(l)	Perigrine Falcon		*				

Scientific Name[a]	Common name	Zone 1 Prmtn Moist	Zone 2 Prmtn Wet	Zone 3 L Mntn Wet	Zone 4 L Mntn Rain	Zone 5 Prmtn Rain	Zone 6 Wet, Prmtn T
Cracidae (curassows and guans)							
Ortalis cinereiceps	Gray-headed Chachalaca	U					U
Penelope purpurascens	Crested Guan					F	F
Chamaepetes unicolor	Black Guan		R	F	F	F	
Crax rubra	Great Curassow						R
Odontophoridae (New World quail)							
Colinus cristatus	Crested Bobwhite	F	R				
Odontophorus leucolaemus	Black-breasted Wood-Quail		F	F	F	F	F
Rhynchortyx cinctus	Tawny-faced Quail						R
Rallidae (rails and gallinules)							
Laterallus albigularis	White-throated Crake					F	C
Laterallus exilis	Gray-breasted Crake						U
Aramides cajanea	Gray-necked Wood-Rail			*			U
Amaurolimnas concolor	Uniform Crake					R	?
Porzana carolina(l)	Sora			*			
Porphyrula martinica	Purple Gallinule			*			U
Gallinula chloropus	Common Moorhen						R
Eurypygidae (sunbitterns)							
Eurypyga helias	Sunbittern	U	R	R	R	U	U
Jacanidae (jacanas)							
Jacana spinosa	Northern Jacana						U
Scolopacidae (sandpipers and allies)							
Tringa solitaria(l)	Solitary Sandpiper	R	R			*	R
Actitis macularia(l)	Spotted Sandpiper	U				F	F
Bartramia longicauda(l)	Upland Sandpiper		*				
Numenius phaeopus(l)	Whimbrel					*	
Laridae (terns)							
Sterna fuscata(l)	Sooty Tern				*		
Columbidae (pigeons and doves)							
Columba flavirostris	Red-billed Pigeon	C	C			F	C
Columba fasciata(e)	Band-tailed Pigeon	U	C	C	C	C	?
Columba subvinacea(e)	Ruddy Pigeon		F	C	C	C	
Columba nigrirostris(e)	Short-billed Pigeon					F	F
Columbina inca	Inca Dove	U					
Columbina passerina	Common Ground-Dove	U					
Leptotila verreauxi	White-tipped Dove	C	C	*		*	
Leptotila cassini	Gray-chested Dove					R	F
Geotrygon chiriquensis	Chiriqui Quail-Dove	F	F	R		R	
Geotrygon lawrencii	Purplish-backed Quail-Dove					U	U
Geotrygon costaricensis	Buff-fronted Quail-Dove			U	F	U	

Life Zone[b]

Scientific Name[a]	Common name	Zone 1 Prmtn Moist	Zone 2 Prmtn Wet	Zone 3 L Mntn Wet	Zone 4 L Mntn Rain	Zone 5 Prmtn Rain	Zone 6 Wet, Prmtn T
Psittacidae (parakeets, macaws, and parrots)							
Aratinga finschi	Crimson-fronted Parakeet	R	R	R	R	F	C
Aratinga canicularis	Orange-fronted Parakeet	C	R	R			
Ara ambigua(e)	Great Green Macaw					R	?
Bolborhynchus lineola(e)	Barred Parakeet			R	R	R	
Brotogeris jugularis	Orange-chinned Parakeet	C	R				C
Touit costaricensis(e)	Red-fronted Parrotlet			U	U	U	U
Pionopsitta haematotis	Brown-hooded Parrot	F	F	C	C	C	C
Pionus senilis(e)	White-crowned Parrot					F	F
Amazona albifrons	White-fronted Parrot	C	F				
Amazona autumnalis	Red-lored Parrot	?	R				
Cuculidae (cuckoos and anis)							
Coccyzus erythropthalmus(l)	Black-billed Cuckoo			R			R
Coccyzus americanus(l)	Yellow-billed Cuckoo			R		R	
Coccyzus minor(l)	Mangrove Cuckoo	*					
Piaya cayana	Squirrel Cuckoo	F	F	F		F	F
Morococcyx erythropygus	Lesser Ground-Cuckoo	F	R				
Crotophaga sulcirostris	Groove-billed Ani	C	C	*		R	C
Tytonidae (barn owls)							
Tyto alba	Barn Owl	U					
Strigidae (typical owls)							
Otus choliba	Tropical Screech Owl	?	R				
Otus clarkii	Bare-shanked Screech-Owl			F	F	F	
Lophostrix cristata	Crested Owl		?				
Pulsatrix perspicillata	Spectacled Owl	U	U	U		U	U
Glaucidium griseiceps	Central American Pygmy-Owl					F	F
Ciccaba virgata	Mottled Owl	F	F	F	F	F	?
Caprimulgidae (goatsuckers)							
Lurocalis semitorquatus	Short-tailed Nighthawk					U	U
Chordeiles minor(l)	Common Nighthawk					R	?
Nyctidromus albicollis	Common Pauraque	C	C			F	C
Caprimulgus carolinensis(l)	Chuck-will's-widow	?	R			R	?
Caprimulgus saturatus	Dusky Nightjar				U		
Apodidae (swifts)							
Cypseloides niger(l)	Black Swift	R	R	?	?	?	?
Cypseloides cryptus	White-chinned Swift					F	F
Cypseloides cherriei	Spot-fronted Swift					R	?
Streptoprocne rutila	Chestnut-collared Swift	U	U	R	R	U	U
Streptoprocne zonaris	White-collared Swift	C	C	C	C	C	C
Chaetura pelagica(l)	Chimney Swift				R		
Chaetura vauxi	Vaux's Swift	C	C	C	C	C	C
Chaetura cinereiventris	Gray-rumped Swift					R	U
Panyptila cayennensis	Lesser Swallow-tailed Swift						U
Trochilidae (hummingbirds)							
Threnetes ruckeri	Band-tailed Barbthroat					R	F
Phaethornis guy(e)	Green Hermit		F	C	C	C	C

Scientific Name[a]	Common name	Zone 1 Prmtn Moist	Zone 2 Prmtn Wet	Zone 3 L Mntn Wet	Zone 4 L Mntn Rain	Zone 5 Prmtn Rain	Zone 6 Wet, Prmtn T
Phaethornis longuemareus	Little Hermit	?	R	R		C	C
Eutoxeres aquila(e)	White-tipped Sicklebill				*	U	F
Doryfera ludovicae(e)	Green-fronted Lancebill			U	U	U	U
Campylopterus hemileucurus(e)	Violet Sabrewing		C	C	C	U	R
Florisuga mellivora(e)	White-necked Jacobin			*		U	U
Colibri delphinae(e)	Brown Violetear		R	U		F	F
Colibri thalassinus(e)	Green Violetear	C	C	C		R	
Anthracothorax prevostii(e)	Green-breasted Mango					*	
Klais guimeti	Violet-headed Hummingbird					C	C
Lophornis helenae	Black-crested Coquette					U	U
Discosura conversii	Green Thorntail			*		U	U
Chlorostilbon canivetii	Canivet's Emerald	C	C	*		R	
Thalurania colombica(e)	Violet-crowned Woodnymph					C	C
Panterpe insignis(e)	Fiery-throated Hummingbird			R	F		
Hylocharis eliciae(e)	Blue-throated Goldentail	U	U	*		U	U
Amazilia saucerrottei	Steely-vented Hummingbird	C	C	R		F	U
Amazilia tzacatl	Rufous-tailed Hummingbird	F	F	*		F	F
Eupherusa eximia(e)	Stripe-tailed Hummingbird	U	F	C	C	C	
Elvira cupreiceps(e)	Coppery-headed Emerald	F	F	C	C	C	
Microchera albocoronata(e)	Snowcap				R	?	
Lampornis hemileucus	White-bellied Mountain-gem				F		
Lampornis calolaema	Purple-throated Mountain-gem		F	C	C	F	
Heliodoxa jacula	Green-crowned Brilliant			C	C	C	U
Heliothryx barroti	Purple-crowned Fairy					F	F
Heliomaster constantii	Plain-capped Starthroat	U	U				
Calliphlox bryantae	Magenta-throated Woodstar		F	C		R	
Archilochus colubris(l)	Ruby-throated Hummingbird	U	U	R	*		
Selasphorus scintilla(e)	Scintillant Hummingbird			F	R	R	

Trogonidae (trogons)

Trogon violaceus	Violaceous Trogon					U	F
Trogon aurantiiventris	Orange-bellied Trogon		C	C	C	C	C
Trogon massena	Slaty-tailed Trogon					F	C
Trogon clathratus	Lattice-tailed Trogon					F	R
Pharomachrus mocinno(e)	Resplendent Quetzal		C	C	C	R	?

Momotidae (motmots)

Momotus momota	Blue-crowned Motmot	F	C	F			
Baryphthengus martii	Rufous Motmot					C	F
Electron carinatum	Keel-billed Motmot					R	R
Electron platyrhynchum	Broad-billed Motmot			?		F	C

Alcedinidae (kingfishers)

Ceryle torquata	Ringed Kingfisher						U
Chloroceryle amazona	Amazon Kingfisher						U
Chloroceryle americana	Green Kingfisher		*			R	F

Scientific Name[a]	Common name	Zone 1 Prmtn Moist	Zone 2 Prmtn Wet	Zone 3 L Mntn Wet	Zone 4 L Mntn Rain	Zone 5 Prmtn Rain	Zone 6 Wet, Prmtn T
Bucconidae (puffbirds)							
Micromonacha lanceolata	Lanceolated Monklet					R	U
Monasa morphoeus	White-fronted Nunbird						U
Galbulidae (jacamars)							
Galbula ruficauda	Rufous-tailed Jacamar			*		C	C
Ramphastidae (New World barbets and toucans)							
Eubucco bourcierii(e)	Red-headed Barbet			R		F	
Semnornis frantzii(e)	Prong-billed Barbet			C	C	F	
Aulacorhynchus prasinus(e)	Emerald Toucanet	C	C	C	C	C	U
Pteroglossus torquatus	Collared Aracari	*		*		?	C
Selenidera spectabilis(e)	Yellow-eared Toucanet					F	?
Ramphastos sulfuratus	Keel-billed Toucan	F	C	R		R	C
Picidae (woodpeckers and allies)							
Melanerpes pucherani	Black-cheeked Woodpecker					F	C
Melanerpes hoffmannii	Hoffman's Woodpecker	C	C	*			
Sphyrapicus varius(l)	Yellow-bellied Sapsucker		R	R			
Picoides villosus	Hairy Woodpecker			R	U		
Veniliornis fumigatus	Smoky-brown Woodpecker			F	R	F	F
Piculus simplex	Rufous-winged Woodpecker					U	U
Piculus chrysochloros	Golden-olive Woodpecker		F	F		F	F
Dryocopus lineatus	Lineated Woodpecker	U	R	*		R	F
Campephilus guatemalensis	Pale-billed Woodpecker	U	R				
Furnariidae (ovenbirds)							
Synallaxis brachyura	Slaty Spinetail					F	F
Cranioleuca erythrops	Red-faced Spinetail			C	C	C	
Premnoplex brunnescens	Spotted Barbtail		*	C	C	C	F
Margarornis rubiginosus(e)	Ruddy Treerunner			*	F		
Pseudocolaptes lawrencii	Buffy Tuftedcheek				U		
Hyloctistes subulatus	Striped Woodhaunter					F	F
Syndactyla subalaris	Lineated Foliage-gleaner			F	F	F	
Anabacerthia variegaticeps	Scaly-throated Foliage-gleaner					U	
Phylidor rufus	Buff-fronted Foliage-gleaner					R	
Automolus ochrolaemus	Buff-throated Foliage-gleaner					F	F
Thripadectes rufobrunneus	Streak-breasted Treehunter			C	F	F	
Xenops minutus	Plain Xenops					U	U
Sclerurus mexicanus	Tawny-throated Leaftosser			U	?	U	U
Sclerurus albigularis	Gray-throated Leaftosser			F	?	U	?
Dendrocolaptidae (woodcreepers)							
Dendrocincla fuliginosa	Plain-brown Woodcreeper					R	R
Dendrocincla homochroa	Ruddy Woodcreeper	F	U	R			
Sittasomus griseicapillus	Olivaceous Woodcreeper	F	C	C			
Deconychura longicauda	Long-tailed Woodcreeper						R
Glyphorynchus spirurus(e)	Wedge-billed Woodcreeper			*		F	F
Xiphocolaptes promeropirhynchus	Strong-billed Woodcreeper					U	
Dendrocolaptes sanctithomae	Northern Barred-Woodcreeper	U	U			U	U
Dendrocolaptes picumnus	Black-banded Woodcreeper			R	R		
Xiphorhynchus erythropygius	Spotted Woodcreeper			C	C	C	C

Scientific Name[a]	Common name	Life Zone[b]					
		Zone 1 Prmtn Moist	Zone 2 Prmtn Wet	Zone 3 L Mntn Wet	Zone 4 L Mntn Rain	Zone 5 Prmtn Rain	Zone 6 Wet, Prmtn T
Lepidocolaptes souleyetii	Streak-headed Woodcreeper	F	F	*			
Lepidocolaptes affinis	Spot-crowned Woodcreeper				R		
Campylorhamphus pusillus(e)	Brown-billed Scythebill			R		U	?
Thamnophilidae (antbirds)							
Thamnophilus doliatus	Barred Antshrike						U
Thamnophilus atrinucha	Western Slaty-Antshrike						R
Thamnistes anabatinus(e)	Russet Antshrike					C	C
Dysithamnus mentalis	Plain Antvireo		F	C		C	
Dysithamnus striaticeps	Streak-crowned Antvireo					U	F
Myrmotherula fulviventris	Checker-throated Antwren					R	R
Myrmotherula schisticolor	Slaty Antwren		U	C		C	C
Cercomacra tyrannina	Dusky Antbird					C	C
Myrmeciza exsul	Chestnut-backed Antbird					R	U
Myrmeciza laemosticta	Dull-mantled Antbird					R	R
Myrmeciza immaculata(e)	Immaculate Antbird			U	U	C	C
Gymnopithys leucaspis	Bicolored Antbird					U	F
Phaenostictus mcleannani	Ocellated Antbird					R	F
Formicariidae (antthrushes and antpittas)							
Formicarius nigricapillus	Black-headed Antthrush					F	F
Formicarius rufipectus	Rufous-breasted Antthrush					U	
Pittasoma michleri	Black-crowned Antpitta					U	?
Grallaria guatimalensis	Scaled Antpitta		R	R	R	R	R
Hylopezus dives	Thicket Antpitta						U
Grallaricula flavirostris	Ochre-breasted Antpitta					U	U
Rhinocryptidae (tapaculos)							
Scytalopus argentifrons	Silvery-fronted Tapaculo			C	C	F	
Tyrannidae (tyrant flycatchers)							
Ornithion brunneicapillum	Brown-capped Tyrannulet					*	
Elaenia flavogaster	Yellow-bellied Elaenia	F	F	R		U	F
Elaenia frantzii(e)	Mountain Elaenia		C	C	C	C	U
Serpophaga cinerea	Torrent Tyrannulet	U	R			C	C
Mionectes olivaceus(e)	Olive-striped Flycatcher		R	C	C	C	F
Mionectes oleagineus	Ochre-bellied Flycatcher	U					
Leptopogon superciliaris	Slaty-capped Flycatcher					F	U
Phylloscartes superciliaris	Rufous-browed Tyrannulet					C	
Phyllomyias burmeisteri	Rough-legged Tyrannulet					R	
Zimmerius vilissimus(e)	Paltry Tyrannulet	C	C	C	C	C	C
Lophotriccus pileatus	Scale-crested Pygmy-Tyrant		F	R		C	C
Todirostrum sylvia	Slate-headed Tody-Flycatcher	?				R	?
Todirostrum cinereum	Common Tody-Flycatcher	U	U			C	C
Todirostrum nigriceps	Black-headed Tody-Flycatcher					R	R
Rhynchocyclus brevirostris	Eye-ringed Flatbill		F	F	F	F	
Tolmomyias sulphurescens	Yellow-olive Flycatcher	U	*			F	F
Platyrinchus mystaceus	White-throated Spadebill		C	C	C	C	C
Platyrinchus coronatus	Golden-crowned Spadebill					R	?
Terenotriccus erythrurus	Ruddy-tailed Flycatcher					R	U
Myiobius sulphureipygius	Sulphur-rumped Flycatcher					F	F
Mitrephanes phaeocercus	Tufted Flycatcher		R	U	U	C	U

Scientific Name[a]	Common name	Life Zone[b]					
		Zone 1 Prmtn Moist	Zone 2 Prmtn Wet	Zone 3 L Mntn Wet	Zone 4 L Mntn Rain	Zone 5 Prmtn Rain	Zone 6 Wet, Prmtn T
Contopus cooperi(l)	Olive-sided Flycatcher	F	F	F	F	F	F
Contopus lugubris(e)	Dark Pewee				R	R	
Contopus sordidulus(l)	Western Wood-Pewee	F	F	F	U	F	F
Contopus virens(l)	Eastern Wood-Pewee	F	F	F	U	F	F
Contopus cinereus	Tropical Pewee					U	F
Empidonax flaviventris(l)	Yellow-bellied Flycatcher	F	F	R		F	F
Empidonax virescens(l)	Acadian Flycatcher	?	R			R	?
Empidonax alnorum(l)	Alder Flycatcher	U	U	U		U	U
Empidonax traillii(l)	Willow Flycatcher	U	U	U		U	U
Empidonax minimus(l)	Least Flycatcher			R		R	R
Empidonax flavescens	Yellowish Flycatcher		F	C	C	C	
Sayornis nigricans	Black Phoebe	F	R			F	F
Colonia colonus	Long-tailed Tyrant					?	U
Attila spadiceus	Bright-rumped Attila	F	F	F	F	F	F
Rhytipterna holerythra(e)	Rufous Mourner	U	R	U		C	F
Myiarchus tuberculifer	Dusky-capped Flycatcher	C	C	F		F	C
Myiarchus nuttingi	Nutting's Flycatcher	R	R				
Myiarchus tyrannulus	Brown-crested Flycatcher	F					
Pitangus sulphuratus	Great Kiskadee	F	F			?	C
Megarynchus pitangua	Boat-billed Flycatcher	C	C	U		U	C
Myiozetetes similis	Social Flycatcher	C	C	*		U	C
Myiozetetes granadensis	Gray-capped Flycatcher					?	F
Myiodynastes hemichrysus	Golden-bellied Flycatcher			F	F	F	
Myiodynastes maculatus(l)	Streaked Flycatcher	U					
Myiodynastes luteiventris(l)	Sulphur-bellied Flycatcher	C	C	C		F	F
Legatus leucophaius	Piratic Flycatcher	U				R	R
Tyrannus melancholicus	Tropical Kingbird	C	C			R	C
Tyrannus tyrannus(l)	Eastern Kingbird	U	U	U	R	U	F
Tyrannus forficatus(l)	Scissor-tailed Flycatcher	R					

Genera Incertae Sedis

Schiffornis turdinus(e)	Thursh-like Schiffornis					R	R
Pachyramphus versicolor(e)	Barred Becard			R	R		
Pachyramphus cinnamomeus	Cinnamon Becard					C	C
Pachyramphus albogriseus	Black-and-white Becard		?	R	R	R	
Pachyramphus aglaiae	Rose-throated Becard					*	
Tityra semifasciata	Masked Tityra	C	F	U		F	F
Tityra inquisitor	Black-crowned Tityra						U

Cotingidae (cotingas)

Cotinga amabilis	Lovely Cotinga					U	U
Cephalopterus glabricollis(e)	Bare-necked Umbrellabird			R	R	U	U
Procnias tricarunculata(e)	Three-wattled Bellbird	U	C	C	C	C	?

Pipridae (manakins)

Manacus candei	White-collared Manakin						U
Corapipo altera(e)	White-ruffed Manakin					C	C
Chiroxiphia linearis	Long-tailed Manakin	C	C				

Oxyruncidae (sharpbills)

Oxyruncus cristatus(e)	Sharpbill					U	

Vireonidae (Vireos)

Vireo flavifrons(l)	Yellow-throated Vireo	U	U	R		U	U
Vireo solitarius(l)	Blue-headed Vireo		R	R			

Scientific Name[a]	Common name	Life Zone[b]					
		Zone 1 Prmtn Moist	Zone 2 Prmtn Wet	Zone 3 L Mntn Wet	Zone 4 L Mntn Rain	Zone 5 Prmtn Rain	Zone 6 Wet, Prmtn T
Vireo leucophrys	Brown-capped Vireo		C	C			
Vireo philadelphicus(l)	Philadelphia Vireo	F	F	R		R	R
Vireo olivaceus(l)	Red-eyed Vireo	F	F	F		F	F
Vireo flavoviridis(l)	Yellow-green Vireo	F	U	R		R	U
Hylophilus ochraceiceps	Tawny-crowned Greenlet	F	F			C	C
Hylophilus decurtatus	Lesser Greenlet	C	C	F		C	C
Vireolanius pulchellus(e)	Green Shrike-Vireo					F	C
Cyclarhis gujanensis(e)	Rufous-browed Peppershrike	F	F	F			

Corvidae (jays)

Calocitta formosa	White-throated Magpie-Jay	F	R				
Cyanocorax morio	Brown Jay	C	C	C		R	C
Cyanolyca cucullata	Azure-hooded Jay		R	C	C	C	

Hirundinidae (swallows)

Progne subis(l)	Purple Martin			R	R		
Progne chalybea	Gray-breasted Martin	F	R	R		R	R
Tachycineta thalassina(l)	Violet-green Swallow			*		*	
Pygochelidon cyanoleuca	Blue-and-white Swallow	C	C	F	F	R	U
Stelgidopteryx serripennis(l)	Northern Rough-winged Swallow	F	F	R	R	R	F
Stelgidopteryx ruficollis(l)	Southern Rough-winged Swallow	U	U			R	F
Riparia riparia(l)	Bank Swallow	R	R	R	R	R	R
Petrochelidon pyrrhonota(l)	Cliff Swallow	R	R	R	R	R	R
Hirundo rustica(l)	Barn Swallow	C	U	R	R	U	F

Troglodytidae (wrens)

Campylorhynchus zonatus	Band-backed Wren					C	C
Thryothorus atrogularis	Black-throated Wren					U	F
Thryothorus nigricapillus	Bay Wren					F	C
Thryothorus thoracicus	Stripe-breasted Wren					C	C
Thryothorus rutilus	Rufous-breasted Wren	U	R				
Thryothorus rufalbus	Rufous-and-white Wren	F	F				
Thryothorus modestus	Plain Wren	C	C	*			
Troglodytes aedon	House Wren	C	C	C	U	F	C
Troglodytes ochraceus(e)	Ochraceous Wren			C	C	C	
Henicorhina leucosticta	White-breasted Wood-Wren		F			C	C
Henicorhina leucophrys	Gray-breasted Wood-Wren			C	C	C	
Microcerculus philomela	Nightingale Wren					F	F
Cyphorhinus phaeocephalus	Song Wren					F	F

Cinclidae (dippers)

Cinclus mexicanus	American Dipper					C	C

Sylviidae (gnatcatchers)

Microbates cinereiventris	Tawny-faced Gnatwren					C	C
Ramphocaenus melanurus	Long-billed Gnatwren					F	F

Turdidae (Thrushes)

Myadestes melanops(l)	Black-faced Solitaire		U	C	C	C	U
Catharus aurantiirostris	Orange-billed Nightingale-Thrush	C	C				

Scientific Name[a]	Common name	Zone 1 Prmtn Moist	Zone 2 Prmtn Wet	Zone 3 L Mntn Wet	Zone 4 L Mntn Rain	Zone 5 Prmtn Rain	Zone 6 Wet, Prmtn T
Catharus fuscater	Slaty-backed Nightingale-Thrush			C	C	C	
Catharus frantzii	Ruddy-capped Nightingale-Thrush			U	F	U	
Catharus mexicanus	Black-headed Nightingale-Thrush		C	U		C	C
Catharus minimus(l)	Gray-cheeked Thrush	?	R	R		R	?
Catharus ustulatus(l)	Swainson's Thrush	C	C	C	U	C	C
Hylocichla mustelina(l)	Wood Thrush	U	U	R		U	F
Turdus plebejus(e)	Mountain Robin	F	F	C	C	C	R
Turdus obsoletus(e)	Pale-vented Thrush					F	F
Turdus grayi	Clay-colored Robin	C	C	C		C	C
Turdus assimilis	White-throated Robin		F	C		R	F

Mimidae (mockingbirds and thrashers)

Dumetella carolinensis(l)	Gray Catbird					R	?

Bombycillidae (waxwings)

Bombycilla cedrorum(l)	Cedar Waxwing	?	R				

Ptilogonatidae (silky flycatchers)

Phainoptila melanoxantha	Black-and-yellow Silky-flycatcher				F		

Parulidae (wood warblers)

Vermivora pinus(l)	Blue-winged Warbler					U	R
Vermivora chrysoptera(l)	Golden-winged Warbler		F	F	U	C	C
Vermivora peregrina(l)	Tennessee Warbler	C	C	U		C	C
Parula pitiayumi	Tropical Parula			U		C	C
Dendroica petechia(l)	Yellow Warbler	U	R			R	R
Dendroica pensylvanica(l)	Chestnut-sided Warbler		*	*		C	C
Dendroica caerulescens(l)	Black-throated Blue Warbler		R	R			
Dendroica coronata(l)	Yellow-rumped Warbler	R	R	R	R	R	R
Dendroica virens(l)	Black-throated Green Warbler	U	C	C	U	C	R
Dendroica townsendi(l)	Townsend's Warbler		U	U			
Dendroica occidentalis(l)	Hermit Warbler		R	R			
Dendroica fusca(l)	Blackburnian Warbler	U	F	F	U	F	F
Dendroica discolor(l)	Prairie Warbler		R			R	R
Dendroica cerulea(l)	Cerulean Warbler		R	R		R	R
Mniotilta varia(l)	Black-and-white Warbler	F	F	F		F	F
Setophaga ruticilla(l)	American Redstart					R	R
Helmitheros vermivorus(l)	Worm-eating Warbler	F	C	R			
Seiurus aurocapillus(l)	Ovenbird	F	F	F			
Seiurus noveboracensis(l)	Northern Waterthrush	U	U	R	R	U	U
Seiurus motacilla(l)	Louisiana Waterthrush	U	R	R	R	U	U
Oporornis formosus(l)	Kentucky Warbler	U	F			F	F
Oporornis philadelphia(l)	Mourning Warbler	R	R	R		U	U
Oporornis tolmiei(l)	MacGillivray's Warbler		R				
Geothlypis trichas(l)	Common Yellowthroat					R	?
Geothlypis semiflava	Olive-crowned Yellowthroat					C	C
Geothlypis poliocephala	Gray-crowned Yellowthroat	C	C				C
Wilsonia pusilla(l)	Wilson's Warbler	C	C	C	U	C	C

Scientific Name[a]	Common name	Zone 1 Prmtn Moist	Zone 2 Prmtn Wet	Zone 3 L Mntn Wet	Zone 4 L Mntn Rain	Zone 5 Prmtn Rain	Zone 6 Wet, Prmtn T
Myioborus miniatus	Slate-throated Redstart	U	U	C		C	
Myioborus torquatus	Collared Redstart			*	C		
Basileuterus culicivorus	Golden-crowned Warbler	C	C	U		C	C
Basileuterus rufifrons	Rufous-capped Warbler	F	F				
Basileuterus tristriatus	Three-striped Warbler			C	C	C	
Phaeothlypis fulvicauda	Buff-rumped Warbler			*		F	F
Zeledonia coronata	Wrenthrush				C		

Coeribidae (bananaquit)

Coereba flaveola	Bananaquit	F	F	F		C	C

Thraupidae (tanagers)

Chlorospingus ophthalmicus	Common Bush-Tanager			C	C	C	U
Chlorospingus pileatus	Sooty-capped Bush-Tanager				F		
Chrysothlypis chrysomelaena(e)	Black-and-yellow Tanager					F	F
Chlorothraupis carmioli(e)	Olive Tanager					C	C
Lanio leucothorax	White-throated Shrike-Tanager					F	F
Habia rubica	Red-crowned Ant-Tanager	U					
Piranga flava(e)	Hepatic Tanager		F	F	F	F	F
Piranga rubra(l)	Summer Tanager	F	F	U		F	C
Piranga olivacea(l)	Scarlet Tanager	U	U	U		F	F
Piranga ludoviciana(l)	Western Tanager					R	
Piranga leucoptera	White-winged Tanager		R			?	
Ramphocelus sanguinolentus	Crimson-collared Tanager			*		C	C
Ramphocelus passerinii	Passerini's Tanager					C	C
Thraupis episcopus	Blue-gray Tanager	C	F	*		F	C
Thraupis palmarum	Palm Tanager	U	*			F	C
Bangsia arcaei(e)	Blue-and-gold Tanager					F	F
Euphonia affinis	Scrub Euphonia		*				
Euphonia luteicapilla	Yellow-crowned Euphonia	F	R	R		U	U
Euphonia hirundinacea	Yellow-throated Euphonia	C	C	U			
Euphonia elegantissima	Blue-hooded Euphonia		U	C			
Euphonia anneae(e)	Tawny-capped Euphonia					F	F
Chlorophonia callophrys(e)	Golden-browed Chlorophonia	C	C	C	C	C	
Tangara florida	Emerald Tanager					F	F
Tangara icterocephala(e)	Silver-throated Tanager		U	C	C	C	C
Tangara guttata	Speckled Tanager					R	U
Tangara gyrola(e)	Bay-headed Tanager					C	C
Tangara lavinia	Rufous-winged Tanager					R	R
Tangara larvata	Golden-hooded Tanager					U	F
Tangara dowii(e)	Spangle-cheeked Tanager		*	U	F	U	
Dacnis venusta(e)	Scarlet-thighed Dacnis	U	U	C	U	C	C
Chlorophanes spiza(e)	Green Honeycreeper					F	F
Cyanerpes lucidus	Shining Honeycreeper					*	
Cyanerpes cyaneus	Red-legged Honeycreeper	F	U	*			R

Emberizidae (emberizids)

Volatinia jacarina	Blue-black Grassquit	U					C
Sporophila aurita	Variable Seedeater	U	R			C	C
Oryzoborus funereus	Thick-billed Seedfinch					?	C
Amaurospiza concolor	Blue Seedeater	R	R			R	
Tiaris olivacea	Yellow-faced Grassquit	C	C	C	U	U	C
Haplospiza rustica	Slaty Finch			R	R		
Acanthidops bairdii(e)	Peg-billed Finch				R		

Scientific Name[a]	Common name	Life Zone[b]					
		Zone 1 Prmtn Moist	Zone 2 Prmtn Wet	Zone 3 L Mntn Wet	Zone 4 L Mntn Rain	Zone 5 Prmtn Rain	Zone 6 Wet, Prmtn T
Diglossa plumbea(e)	Slaty Flowerpiercer			R	F	F	
Lysurus crassirostris	Sooty-faced Finch			R	U	F	
Pselliophorus tibialis(e)	Yellow-thighed Finch				F		
Atlapetes albinucha	White-naped Brush-Finch		F	F	F	F	
Buarremon brunneinuchus	Chestnut-capped Brush-Finch		F	F	F	F	
Arremon aurantiirostris	Orange-billed Sparrow					F	F
Arremonops conirostris	Black-striped Sparrow					C	C
Melozone leucotis	White-eared Ground-Sparrow	C	C				
Aimophila ruficauda	Stripe-headed Sparrow	U	*				
Melospiza lincolnii(l)	Lincoln's Sparrow	?	R				
Zonotrichia capensis	Rufous-collared Sparrow	C	C	F	F	R	C
Cardinalidae (cardinals and saltators)							
Saltator coerulescens	Grayish Saltator	U	U				
Saltator maximus	Buff-throated Saltator	F	F			F	C
Saltator atriceps	Black-headed Saltator						F
Saltator grossus	Slate-colored Grosbeak					U	F
Caryothraustes poliogaster	Black-faced Grosbeak						R
Pheucticus tibialis(e)	Black-thighed Grosbeak			F	F	F	
Pheucticus ludovicianus(l)	Rose-breasted Grosbeak	F	U	R		F	F
Cyanocompsa cyanoides	Blue-black Grosbeak						U
Guiraca caerulea	Blue Grosbeak	U				R	R
Passerina cyanea(l)	Indigo Bunting	U	U			R	
Spiza americana(l)	Dickcissel	?	R			R	?
Icteridae (blackbirds)							
Sturnella magna	Eastern Meadowlark	F	F			*	
Quiscalus mexicanus	Great-tailed Grackle	F	F			*	
Molothrus aeneus	Bronzed Cowbird	F	F	R		R	F
Scaphidura oryzivora	Giant Cowbird	U				R	F
Icterus dominicensis	Black-cowled Oriole					?	?
Icterus spurius(l)	Orchard Oriole					R	R
Icterus galbula(l)	Baltimore Oriole	C	F	U		F	F
Amblycercus holosericeus	Yellow-billed Cacique		?			R	F
Cacicus uropygialis(e)	Scarlet-rumped Cacique					R	F
Psarocolius wagleri(e)	Chestnut-headed Oropendola	U	U	U		C	F
Psarocolius montezuma	Montezuma Oropendola	R	R			R	C

[a]Migratory status: (l) = long-distance migrant; (e) = elevational migrant (based on Stiles 1985).
[b]Status codes: R, rare; U, uncommon; F, fairly common; C, common; *, known to occur; ?, status uncertain.

Appendix 10

Mammals of Monteverde

Robert M. Timm
Richard K. LaVal

Scientific Name	Common Name[a]	Abundance[b]	Distribution[c]
Marsupialia	*Marsupials*		
Didelphidae	American opossums		
Caluromys derbianus	Woolly Opossum	Uncommon	1, 2, 3
	Zorro colorado		
Chironectes minimus	Water Opossum	Uncertain	1
	Zorro de agua		
Didelphis marsupialis	Common Opossum	Abundant	1, 2, 3, 4, 5, 6
	Zorro pelón or Zarigüeya		
Marmosa mexicana	Mexican Mouse Opossum	Common	2, 3, 5, 6
	Zorro ici or Zorricí		
Micoureus alstoni	Alston's Opossum	Uncommon	2, 3, 6
	Zorro ici or Zorricí		
Philander opossum	Gray Four-eyed Opossum	Uncommon	1, 2, 3, 5
	Zorricilla or Zorillo		
Insectivora	*Shrews*		
Soricidae	Shrews		
Cryptotis nigrescens	Blackish Small-eared Shrew	Common	2, 3, 4, 6
	Musaraña, Antitorinco, or Topo		
Cryptotis sp.[d]	Small-eared Shrew	Rare	4
	Musaraña		
Cryptotis sp.	Small-eared Shrew	Rare	3
	Musaraña		
Chiroptera[e]	*Bats*		
Emballonuridae[f]	Sac-winged bats		
Mormoopidae	Mustached bats		
Pteronotus gymnonotus	Big Naked-backed Bat	Rare	1, 2, 3, 4
Pteronotus parnellii	Parnell's Mustached Bat	Uncommon	1, 2, 3, 4, 6

Scientific Name	Common Names[a]	Abundance[b]	Distribution[c]
Phyllostomidae	Leaf-nosed bats		
Phyllostominae	Gleaning bats		
Lonchorhina aurita	Sword-nosed Bat	Uncommon	5, 6
Micronycteris hirsuta	Hairy Big-eared Bat	Rare	2
Micronycteris microtis[g]	Little Big-eared Bat	Uncommon	1, 2, 3, 4, 6
Micronycteris schmidtorum	Schmidt's Big-eared Bat	Uncertain	6
Micronycteris sylvestris	Tri-colored Big-eared Bat	Rare	2
Mimon bennettii/cozumelae	Big-eared Bat	Rare	2
Phylloderma stenops	Peters' Spear-nosed Bat	Rare	6
Phyllostomus discolor	Pale Spear-nosed Bat	Common	1, 2
Phyllostomus hastatus	Greater Spear-nosed Bat	Rare	6
Tonatia sp.	Round-eared Bat	Uncertain	6
Trachops cirrhosus	Fringe-lipped or Frog-eating Bat	Uncommon	1, 2, 3, 4, 6
Vampyrum spectrum	False Vampire Bat	Rare	2, 3, 4, 6
Glossophaginae	Nectar-feeding bats		
Anoura cultrata	Handley's Tailless Bat	Uncommon	2, 3, 4, 6
Anoura geoffroyi	Geoffroy's Tailless Bat	Common	1, 2, 3, 4, 5
Choeroniscus godmani	Godman's Long-nosed Bat	Uncommon	1, 2, 3, 4
Glossophaga commissarisi	Commissaris' Long-tongued Bat	Common	1, 2, 3, 4
Glossophaga soricina	Pallas' Long-tongued Bat	Common	1, 2, 3, 6
Hylonycteris underwoodi	Underwood's Long-tongued Bat	Common	2, 3, 4, 5
Lonchophyllinae	Nectar-feeding bats		
Lonchophylla robusta	Panama Long-tongued Bat	Rare	2, 3, 6
Carolliinae	Short-tailed bats		
Carollia brevicauda	Silky Short-tailed Bat	Common	1, 2, 3, 4, 5, 6
Carollia castanea	Allen's Short-tailed Bat	Uncommon	1 2 6
Carollia perspicillata	Short-tailed Fruit Bat	Rare	1, 2, 6
Stenoderminae	Fruit-eating bats		
Artibeus aztecus	Highland Fruit-eating Bat	Rare	2, 6
Artibeus jamaicensis	Jamaican Fruit Bat	Common	1, 2, 3, 4, 6
Artibeus intermedius	Davis' Fruit Bat	Uncommon	2
Artibeus lituratus	Big Fruit Bat	Uncommon	1, 2, 3, 4
Artibeus phaeotis	Pygmy Fruit-eating Bat	Uncommon	6
Artibeus toltecus	Lowland Fruit-eating Bat	Abundant	1, 2, 3, 4, 5, 6
Centurio senex	Wrinkle-faced Bat	Rare	1, 2, 3
Chiroderma sp.	Shaggy-haired Bat	Rare	6
Ectophylla alba	Caribbean White Bat	Rare	6
Enchisthenes hartii	Little Fruit-eating Bat	Uncommon	1, 2, 3, 4
Sturnira lilium	Yellow-shouldered Bat	Uncommon	1, 2
Sturnira ludovici	Anthony's Bat	Abundant	1, 2, 3, 4, 5, 6
Sturnira mordax	Talamancan Bat	Common	2, 3, 4, 5, 6
Vampyrodes caraccioli	Great Stripe-faced Bat	Rare	2
Vampyressa pusilla	Little Yellow-eared Bat	Rare	2, 3
Platyrrhinus vittatus	Greater Broad-nosed Bat	Common	1, 2, 3, 4, 5
Desmodontinae	Vampire bats		
Desmodus rotundus	Common Vampire Bat Vampiro	Uncommon	1, 2, 3, 5, 6
Diphylla ecaudata	Hairy-legged Vampire Bat Vampiro	Rare	2
Natalidae	Funnel-eared bats		
Natalus stramineus	Mexican Funnel-eared Bat	Uncertain	1
Thyropteridae	Disk-winged bats		
Thyroptera tricolor	Spix's Disk-winged Bat	Uncommon	2, 3, 4, 6
Vespertilionidae	Vespertilionid bats		
Antrozous dubiaquercus	Doubtful Oak Bat	Rare	2, 3
Eptesicus brasiliensis (= *andinus*)	Brazilian Brown Bat	Uncommon	2, 3, 4
Eptesicus fuscus	Big Brown Bat	Uncommon	2, 3, 4
Lasiurus blossevillii (= *borealis*)	Southern Red Bat	Rare	2, 4
Lasiurus castaneus	Tacarcuna Bat	Rare	4
Lasiurus ega	Southern Yellow Bat	Rare	2, 4
Myotis elegans	Elegant Myotis	Uncommon	6
Myotis keaysi	Hairy-legged Myotis	Abundant	2, 3, 4, 5
Myotis nigricans	Black Myotis	Common	1, 2, 3, 4
Myotis oxyotus	Montane Myotis	Rare	1, 2

Scientific Name	Common Names[a]	Abundance[b]	Distribution[c]
Myotis riparius	Riparian Myotis	Rare	1, 2
Molossidae	Free-tailed bats		
Eumops auripendulus	Shaw's Mastiff Bat	Uncertain	6
Molossus sinaloae	Sinaloan Mastiff Bat	Uncertain	1, 2
Tadarida brasiliensis	Brazilian Free-tailed Bat	Uncertain	2
Primates	*Primates*		
Cebidae	New-World monkeys		
Alouatta palliata	Mantled Howler Monkey	Common	1, 2, 3, 4, 5, 6
	Mono congo		
Ateles geoffroyi	Black-handed Spider Monkey	Rare	3, 4, 5, 6
	Mono colorado		
Cebus capucinus	White-faced Capuchin	Common	1, 2, 3, 4, 5
	Mono carablanca		
Xenarthra	*Edentates*		
Bradypodidae	Three-toed sloths		
Bradypus variegatus	Brown-throated Three-toed Sloth	Rare	1
	Perezoso de tres dedos		
Choloepidae	Two-toed sloths		
Choloepus hoffmanni	Hoffmann's Two-toed Sloth	Common	1, 2, 3, 4, 5, 6
	Perezoso de dos dedos		
Dasypodidae	Armadillos		
Cabassous centralis	Northern Naked-tailed Armadillo	Rare	2, 3, 4
	Cusuco zopilote		
Dasypus novemcinctus	Nine-banded Armadillo	Abundant	1, 2, 3, 4, 5, 6
	Cusuco		
Myrmecophagidae	Anteaters		
Cyclopes didactylus	Silky Anteater	Uncertain	2, 6
	Serafín de platanar or Tapacara		
Myrmecophaga tridactyla	Giant Anteater		
	Oso caballo or Hormiguero	Extirpated	
Tamandua mexicana	Northern Tamandua	Uncommon	1, 2, 3, 5, 6
	Oso hormiguero		
Lagomorpha	*Rabbits*		
Leporidae	Rabbits and hares		
Sylvilagus brasiliensis	Forest Rabbit	Rare	2, 3
	Conejo		
Sylvilagus floridanus	Cottontail Rabbit	Uncommon	1
	Conejo		
Rodentia	*Rodents*		
Geomyidae	Pocket gophers		
Orthogeomys cherriei	Cherrie's Pocket Gopher	Uncommon	1, 2, 3, 6
	Taltusa or Tartusa		
Sciuridae	Squirrels		
Microsciurus alfari	Alfaro's Pygmy Squirrel	Common	2, 3, 4, 5, 6
	Ardillita		
Sciurus granatensis[h]	Neotropical Red Squirrel	Common	1, 2, 3, 4, 5, 6
	Ardilla or Chisa negra		
Sciurus variegatoides	Variegated Squirrel	Abundant	1, 2, 3
	Ardilla or Chisa rosilla		
Heteromyidae	Pocket mice		
Heteromys desmarestianus	Desmarest's Spiny Pocket Mouse	Common	1, 2, 3, 4, 5, 6
	Rata		
Muridae	Long-tailed rats and mice		
Nyctomys sumichrasti	Sumichrast's Vesper Rat	Uncommon	1, 2
	Ratón		

Scientific Name	Common Names[a]	Abundance[b]	Distribution[c]
Oligoryzomys fulvescens	Pygmy Rice Mouse Ratón	Rare	2, 3
Oligoryzomys vegetus	Pygmy Rice Mouse Ratón	Rare	2, 4
Oryzomys albigularis	Tome's Rice Rat Ratón	Uncommon	3, 4
Oryzomys alfaroi	Alfaro's Rice Rat Ratón	Uncommon	2, 3
Oryzomys bolivaris (= *bombycinus*)	Long-whiskered Rice Rat Ratón	Rare	6
Ototylomys phyllotis	Big-eared Climbing Rat Ratón	Uncertain	1, 2
Peromyscus nudipes	Naked-footed Mouse Ratón	Abundant	1, 2, 3, 4, 5
Reithrodontomys creper	Chiriquí Harvest Mouse Ratón	Uncommon	4
Reithrodontomys gracilis	Slender Harvest Mouse Ratón	Common	1, 2, 3, 6
Reithrodontomys sp.[i]	Harvest Mouse Ratón	Rare	4
Rheomys raptor	Goldman's Water Mouse Ratón	Rare	2, 3, 4, 6
Scotinomys teguina	Alston's Brown Mouse Ratón	Uncommon	2, 3, 4, 6
Sigmodon hispidus	Hispid Cotton Rat Ratón	Rare	1, 2
Tylomys watsoni	Watson's Climbing Rat Rata azul	Common	2, 3, 4, 5, 6
Erethizontidae	Porcupines		
Coendou mexicanus	Prehensile-tailed Porcupine Puercoespín	Common	1, 2, 3, 4, 5, 6
Agoutidae	Pacas		
Agouti paca	Paca Tepezcuintle	Uncommon	1, 2, 3, 4, 5, 6
Dasyproctidae	Agoutis		
Dasyprocta punctata	Agouti Guatusa	Common	1, 2, 3, 4, 5, 6
Carnivora	*Carnivores*		
Canidae	Coyotes, foxes, and dogs		
Canis latrans	Coyote Coyote	Uncommon	1, 2
Urocyon cinereoargenteus	Gray Fox Tigrillo or Zorragris	Common	1, 2, 3, 5
Mustelidae	Skunks, weasels, and otters		
Conepatus semistriatus	Striped Hog-nosed Skunk Zorro hediondo	Common	1, 2, 3, 4, 6
Eira barbara	Tayra Tejón or Tolomuco	Common	1, 2, 3, 4, 5
Galictis vittata	Grison Grisón or Tejón	Rare	2, 3, 5, 6
Lutra longicaudis	Southern River Otter Perro de agua or Nutria	Rare	1, 2, 3, 4, 5, 6
Mustela frenata	Long-tailed Weasel Comadreja	Uncommon	1, 2, 3, 4, 5, 6
Procyonidae	Raccoons		
Bassaricyon gabbii	Olingo Martilla	Common	1, 2, 3, 5, 6
Nasua narica	White-nosed Coati Pizote	Abundant	1, 2, 3, 4, 5, 6
Potos flavus	Kinkajou Martilla or Mico de noche	Common	1, 2, 3, 4, 5, 6
Procyon lotor	Raccoon Mapachín	Common	1, 2, 3, 4, 5, 6

Scientific Name	Common Names[a]	Abundance[b]	Distribution[c]
Felidae[j]	Cats		
Felis concolor	Puma	Uncommon	1, 2, 3, 4, 5, 6
	Puma or León de montaña		
Felis pardalis	Ocelot	Uncommon	1, 2, 3, 4, 5, 6
	Manigordo or Ocelote		
Felis tigrina	Little Spotted Cat	Uncertain	1, 3, 4, 6
	Tigrillo or Gato tigre		
Felis wiedii	Margay	Uncommon	2, 3, 4, 5, 6
	Caucél		
Felis yaguarondi	Jaguarundi	Uncommon	1, 2, 3, 4, 5, 6
	Tcholomuco		
Panthera onca	Jaguar	Rare	3, 4, 5, 6
	Tigre		
Artiodactyla	*Deer and peccaries*		
Dicotylidae	Peccaries		
Tayassu pecari	White-lipped Peccary		
	Chancho de monte or Cariblanco	Extirpated	
Pecari tajacu	Collared Peccary	Common	3, 4, 5, 6
	Saíno or Zahino		
Cervidae	Deer		
Mazama americana	Brocket Deer	Uncommon	1, 3, 4, 5, 6
	Cabro or Corzo		
Odocoileus virginianus	White-tailed Deer	Uncommon	1, 2
	Venado cola blanca		
Perissodactyla	*Tapirs and horses*		
Tapiridae	Tapirs		
Tapirus bairdii	Baird's Tapir	Uncommon	3, 4, 5, 6
	Danta		
Species introduced into the area by humans[k]			
Mus musculus	House Mouse	Abundant	Commensal
	Ratón		
Rattus rattus	Black or Roof Rat	Abundant	Commensal
	Ratón		

[a]The common name(s) for each species is in English and Spanish. Spanish names are used within the Monteverde area. Because non-mammalogists cannot easily distinguish bats, there are few local common names in Spanish, other than "murciélago" or "vampiro."

[b] Abundance categories: Abundant = often observed and/or captured in appropriate habitats; Common = frequently observed in appropriate habitats; Uncommon = only occasionally observed in appropriate habitats; Rare = very few records for Monteverde; Extirpated = previously known from the area but no longer in the region due to overhunting and habitat destruction; Uncertain = of unknown abundance.

[c]Distribution numbers indicate Holdridge (1967) life zones (see Fig. 1.5).

[d]An undescribed species (Woodman 1992, Woodman and Timm 1993).

[e]Undoubtedly other species of molossids occur in the area, but have yet to be detected.

[f]This family is widespread in the tropical lowlands, and we suspect that several species will be found at the lower elevations in the area.

[g]The species referred to as *Micronycteris megalotis* in the literature was a composite of two valid species: *Micronycteris microtis*, which occurs from Mexico through Central America to northern South America, and *M. megalotis*, which occurs throughout much of the northern half of South America. All previous literature references to *M. megalotis* in Costa Rica should be attributed to *M. microtis*.

[h]Previous lists report the medium-sized squirrel from Monteverde as being *Sciurus deppei*. *S. granatensis* and *S. deppei* are similar in appearance and difficult to distinguish in the field. Both species are medium-sized brown squirrels, although *S. granatensis* is larger (total length for *S. deppei*, 343–387 mm; for *S. granatensis*, 382–440 mm). The distinguishing field characters are presence of a small white throat patch in *S. deppei*; the throat of *S. granatensis* is orange. The tail of *S. deppei* is narrower and darker than that of *S. granatensis*, and the tail hairs throughout the length of the tail in *S. deppei* are tipped with white, whereas the tail of *S. granatensis* is bushier and tipped with tan, orange, or reddish hairs.

[i]A new species being described by R. Timm.

[j]A variety of generic names for species of cats are in use, reflecting different opinions as to their systematic relationships. Wozencraft (1993) used *Puma concolor* for the Puma, *Leopardus pardalis* for the Ocelot, *Leopardus tigrinus* for the Little Spotted Cat, *Leopardus wiedii* for the Margay, and *Herpailurus yaguarondi* (frequently spelled *yagouaroundi*) for the Jaguarundi.

[k]These introduced Old-World rodents will cross forested tracts but are found in abundance only around human habitations and rarely occur in natural areas.

References

Literature Cited

American Ornithologists' Union. 1998. Check-list of North American birds (7th ed.). American Ornithologists' Union, Washington, D.C.

Campbell, J. A., and W. W. Lamar. 1989. The venomous reptiles of Latin America. Comstock, Ithaca, New York.

Croat, T. B. 1978. The flora of Barro Colorado Island. Stanford University Press, Palo Alto, California.

Cronquist, A. 1981. An integrated system of classification of flowering plants. Columbia University Press, New York.

Dinerstein, E. 1986. Reproductive ecology of fruit bats and the seasonality of fruit production in a Costa Rican cloud forest. Biotropica 18:307–318.

Donnelly, M. A. 1994. Amphibian diversity and natural history. Pages 199–209 in L. A. McDade, K. S. Bawa, H. A. Hespenheide, and G. S. Hartshorn, editors. La Selva: ecology and natural history of a neotropical rain forest. University of Chicago Press, Chicago.

Duellman, W. E. 1970. The hylid frogs of Middle America. Monographs Museum of Natural History University of Kansas No. 1. University of Kansas, Lawrence.

———. 1990. Herpetofaunas in Neotropical rainforests: comparative composition, history, and resource use. Pages 455–505 in A. H. Gentry, editor. Four neotropical rainforests. Yale University Press, New Haven, Connecticut.

Fogden, M. P. 1993. An annotated checklist of the birds of Monteverde and Peñas Blancas. Published by the author, Monteverde, Costa Rica.

Guyer, C. 1994. The reptile fauna: diversity and ecology. Pages 199–209 in L. A. McDade, K. S. Bawa, H. A. Hespenheide, and G. S. Hartshorn, editors. La Selva: ecology and natural history of a neotropical rain forest. University of Chicago Press, Chicago.

Haber, W. A. 1991. Lista provisional de las plantas de Monteverde, Costa Rica. Brenesia 34:63–120.

Haber, W. A., and K. S. Bawa. 1984. Evolution of dioecism in Saurauia (Dilleniaceae). Annals of the Missouri Botanical Garden 71:289–293.

Holdridge, L. R. 1967. Life zone ecology. Tropical Science Center, San José, Costa Rica.

Kress, W. J., and J. H. Beach. 1994. Flowering plants reproductive systems. Pages 161–182 in L. McDade, K. S. Bawa, H. A. Hespenheide, and G. S. Hartshorn, editors. La Selva: ecology and natural history of a neotropical rain forest. University of Chicago Press, Chicago.

Lynch, J. D. 1979. The amphibians of the lowland tropical forests. Pages 189–215 in W. E. Duellman, editor. The South American herpetofauna: its origin, evolution, and dispersal. Monographs Museum of Natural History University of Kansas No. 7. University of Kansas, Lawrence.

Mabberley, D. J. 1987. The plant-book. A portable dictionary of the higher plants. Cambridge University Press, Cambridge.

Myers, C. W., and A. S. Rand. 1969. Checklist of amphibians and reptiles of Barro Colorado Island, Panama, with comments on faunal change and sampling. Smithsonian Contributions to Zoology No. 10:1–11.

Peters, J. A., B. Orejas Miranda, R. Donoso Barros, and P. E. Vanzolini. 1986. Catalogue of the Neotropical Squamata. Smithsonian Institution Press, Washington, D.C.

Pounds, J. A., M. P. L. Fogden, J. M. Savage, and G. C. Gorman. 1997. Tests of null models for amphibian declines on a tropical mountain. Conservation Biology 11:1307–1322.

Savage, J. M. 1972. The Harlequin Frogs, genus *Atelopus*, of Costa Rica and western Panama. Herpetologica 28:77–94.

———. 1975. Systematics and distribution of the Mexican and Central American stream frogs related to *Eleutherodactylus rugulosus*. Copeia 1975: 254–306.

Savage, J. M., and W. R. Heyer. 1969. The tree frogs (family Hylidae) of Costa Rica: diagnosis and distribution. Revista de Biología Tropical 16:1–127.

Savage, J. M., and J. J. Talbot. 1978. The giant anoline lizards of Costa Rica and western Panama. Copeia 1978:480–492.

Savage, J. M., and J. Villa. 1986. Introduction to the herpetofauna of Costa Rica. Contributions to Herpetology No. 3:1–207.

Scott, N. J., J. M. Savage, and D. C. Robinson. 1983. Checklist of reptiles and amphibians. Pages 367–374 *in* D. H. Janzen, editor. Costa Rican natural history. University of Chicago Press, Chicago.

Standley, P. C. 1937. Flora of Costa Rica. Field Museum of Natural History, Botanical Series 18:1–1616.

Starrett, P. H., and J. M. Savage. 1973. The systematic status and distribution of Costa Rican glass frogs, genus *Centrolenella* (family Centrolenidae), with description of a new species. Bulletin of the Southern California Academy of Sciences 72:57–78.

Stiles, F. G. 1985. Conservation of forest birds in Costa Rica: problems and perspectives. Pages 141–168 *in* A. W. Diamond and T. E. Lovejoy, editors. Conservation of tropical forest birds. International Council for Bird Preservation, Cambridge.

Utley, J. 1983. A revision of the middle American thecophylloid Vrieseas (Bromeliaceae). Tulane Studies in Zoology and Botany 24:1–24.

Villa, J., L. D. Wilson, and J. D. Johnson. 1988. Middle American herpetology: a bibliographic checklist. University of Missouri Press, Columbia.

Wake, D. B. 1987. Adaptive radiation of salamanders in Middle American cloud forests. Annals of the Missouri Botanical Garden 74:242–264.

Wake, D. B., and J. F. Lynch. 1976. The distribution, ecology, and evolutionary history of plethodontid salamanders in tropical America. Science Bulletin of the Los Angeles County Museum of Natural History 25:1–65.

Woodman, N. 1992. Biogeographical and evolutionary relationships among Central American small-eared shrews of the genus *Cryptotis* (Mammalia: Insectivora: Soricidae). Ph.D. dissertation, University of Kansas, Lawrence.

Woodman, N., and R. M. Timm. 1993. Intraspecific and interspecific variation in the *Cryptotis nigrescens* species complex of small-eared shrews (Insectivora: Soricidae), with the description of a new species from Colombia. Fieldiana: Zoology (New Series) 74:1–30.

Woodson, R. E., and R. W. Schery. 1943–1980. Flora of Panama. Annals of the Missouri Botanical Garden, Vols. 30–67 (various numbers).

Wozencraft, W. C. 1993. Order Carnivora. Pages 279–348 *in* D. E. Wilson and D. M. Reeder, editors. Mammal species of the world: a taxonomic and geographic reference (2nd ed.) Smithsonian Institution Press, Washington, D.C.

Index

(Note: an *f* after a page locator indicates a figure; a *t* indicates a table.)

lupeol, 452
Lutra longicaudis (Southern River Otter), 233

MacArthur Foundation, 359
madero negro. *See Gilricidia sepium*
magnesium, 391
maize, 409
Malathion, 410
male-male competition
　among lek-mating birds, 189
　in frogs and toads, 163, 164
　in long-horned beetles, 114
mammals. *See also names of specific mammals*
　arboreal, 239–240
　change in abundance of, 232–234
　interactions with other taxa, 228, 229
　pollination by, 249–250
　reproductive ecology, 226–228
　research on, 235
　seed dispersal by, 257
　species diversity of, 223, 224–225
　species list of, 553–557
　systematics, 225–226
manganese, 391
Mantled Howler Monkey. *See Alouatta palliata*
manure management, 395, 396
Margarodidae, 105
Margay. *See Felis wiedii*
marketing, coffee, 401
Marmosa mexicana (Mexican Mouse Opposum), 229, 235
mate choice, in female birds, 189
maternal investment, of treehoppers, 104
mating behavior, of long-horned beetles, 114
mating systems, of Brown Jays, 212
maturation, in birds, 189
mayflies, 84
Meadow Treefrog. *See Hyla pseudopuma*
Megalopodinae, 115–116
Melastomataceae, 70
　pollination of, 249
　seed dispersal in, 256
Meliaceae, 49
Meliosma subcordata, 262
Meliponinae, 137–138
Membracidae, 103–104
Mendenhall, Hubert and Mildred, 356
metamorphosis, 106, 122
Mexican Mouse Opposum. *See Marmosa mexicana*
mice, 236
　aggression in, 238
　pollination by, 275–276
Miconia, 312
microbes, biomass of, 336
microbial infestation, of fruit, 211

microclimate, 33
　and invertebrate abundance, 337
microsatellites, 204
Microsciurus alfari (Alfaro's Pygmy Squirrel), 236
midges, 83, 429
migration
　altitudinal, 255, 361, 367
　　in birds, 183 and corridors, 439–442
　　in insects, 96, 130
　　in mammals, 229, 231
　　and seed dispersal, 263
　in birds, 183–184, 194
　corridors, 427
　in froghoppers, 410
　in insects, 438
　in lepidopterans, 118–119, 120
　seasonal in mammals, 231
milk quality, 397
mimicry, 121–122
　in hymenopterans, 126
　intersexual, 251, 279–281
　in long-horned beetles, 114
　in wasps, 130, 131–132
mineralization, 334
mineral supplements, 396, 400
mineral weathering, 27
Ministry of Agriculture and Ranching, 393, 410
Ministry of Education, 360
Ministry of Natural Resources, Energy, and Mines, 353
Ministry of the Environment and Energy, 353
Missouri Botanical Garden, 39
mist, 18
mistletoes, 81–82
　colonization of host trees, 265
　as food for birds, 200
　seed dispersal, 288–289
mites, 139
　nectar-feeding, 250
　in soil, 337
moisture availability, and frog habitats, 166
molecular techniques, 431
Molothrus aeneus (Bronzed Cowbird), 419
molt, in birds, 195
Monge, Juan José, 390t
monitoring systems, 203, 429, 431
monkeys, 233
Montane Anole. *See Norops altae*
Montanoa guatemalensis (Tubú), 366, 449
Monteverde
　maps of, 7f, 8f
　regions of, 5–9
　research in, 9, 11–13
　settlement of, 3–5, 10–11, 353–356
Monteverde 2020, 378–379
Monteverde Butterfly Garden, 355, 374, 382–383, 390t

Monteverde Cloud Forest Preserve, 351, 374, 439
　and economic growth, 376
　education, 360
　origins and development, 357–360
Monteverde Conservation League, 170, 198, 203, 351, 358, 361–367, 397, 430, 441, 448
　education by, 364–365
　origins and development, 362–364
Monteverde Flora Project, 39–40
Monteverde Institute, 373
　origins and development, 369–370
Monteverde Reserve Complex, 351, 367, 439
　map of, 6f
Monteverde salamander. *See Bolitoglossa subpalmata*
mortality. *See also* embryo mortality
　rates of trees, 319
　sources of in amphibians and reptiles, 159–161
mosquitoes, 122
　as fungi hosts, 84
moss, 78–79
　amphibians and reptiles associated with mats of, 168
　use in bird nests, 191
Moss, Martha, 372
moths, 118–122
　pollination by, 248
Mountain Lion. *See Felis concolor*
Mountain Robin. *See Turdus plebejus*
mushrooms, 61
Mussuranas, 161
Mustela frenata (Long-tailed weasel), nest predation by, 229
mutualism, 245, 273
　loss of, 421
Myadestes melanops (Black-faced Solitaire)
　diet breadth, 260
　habitat preferences of, 266
　migration in, 184, 263
　seed dispersal by, 263, 284, 285f
　seed passage rate, 262
mycorrhizae, 323, 338–339
Myrmecophaga tridactyla (Giant Anteater), 223, 224
myrmecophytes, 291–293
Myrsinaceae, pollination of, 249

Nadkarni plots, 90
Naked-footed Mouse. *See Peromyscus nudipes*
Nasua narica (White-nosed Coati), 233
　nest predation by, 229
national financial crisis, 393
National Geographic Society, 356
national park system, 352, 353
natural disturbances, 308–310
　and pollination, 253
　and regeneration, 313
natural history walks, 360